P9-DXI-157

Psychopharmacology
Drugs, the Brain, and Behavior
SECOND EDITION

Psychopharmacology

Drugs, the Brain, and Behavior

SECOND EDITION

Jerrold S. Meyer
University of Massachusetts

Linda F. Quenzer
University of Hartford

Chapter 17, *Environmental Neurotoxicants and Endocrine Disruptors*
by Susan A. Rice, Susan A. Rice and Associates, Inc.

Chapter 21, *Neurodegenerative Diseases*
by Jennifer R. Yates, Ohio Wesleyan University

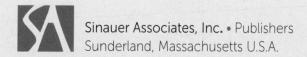

Sinauer Associates, Inc. • Publishers
Sunderland, Massachusetts U.S.A.

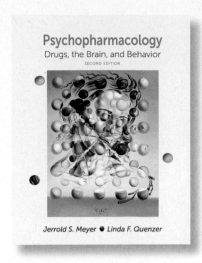

About the cover

Galatea of the Spheres (1952) by Salvador Dalí.
© Salvador Dalí, Fundació Gala-Salvador Dalí,
Artists Rights Society (ARS), New York, 2013.

Psychopharmacology: Drugs, the Brain, and Behavior, Second Edition
Copyright © 2013 by Sinauer Associates, Inc.
All rights reserved. This book may not be reproduced in whole or in part without
permission from the publisher.

For information, address
Sinauer Associates, P.O. Box 407, Sunderland, MA 01375-0407 U.S.A.
Fax: 413-549-1118
Email: publish@sinauer.com
Internet: www.sinauer.com

Library of Congress Cataloging-in-Publication Data

Meyer, Jerrold S., 1947-
 Psychopharmacology : drugs, the brain, and behavior / Jerrold S. Meyer, Linda F.
Quenzer. -- 2nd ed.
    p. ; cm.
 Includes bibliographical references and index.
 ISBN 978-0-87893-510-9
 I. Quenzer, Linda F. II. Title.
 [DNLM: 1. Psychotropic Drugs--pharmacokinetics. 2. Psychotropic Drugs--therapeutic
use. 3. Brain Chemistry--drug effects. 4. Mental Disorders--drug therapy. 5. Nervous
System--drug effects. 6. Psychopharmacology--methods. QV 77.2]

 615.7'88--dc23

                    2012047199

Printed in U.S.A.

5 4 3 2

To our students,
who challenge and inspire us

Brief Contents

Contents

3 Chemical Signaling by Neurotransmitters and Hormones   77

4 Methods of Research in Psychopharmacology   107

5 Catecholamines 143

6 Serotonin 167

7 Acetylcholine 185

8   Glutamate and GABA   201

9   Drug Abuse and Addiction   227

10   Alcohol   265

Psychopharmacology of Alcohol   266

Alcohol has a long history of use   266

What is an alcohol and where does it come from?   267

The pharmacokinetics of alcohol determines its bioavailability   268

Chronic alcohol use leads to both tolerance and physical dependence   270

Alcohol affects many organ systems   273

BOX 10.1   *The Role of Expectation in Alcohol-Enhanced Human Sexual Response   274*

BOX 10.2   *Gender Differences in Alcohol Effects   280*

Neurochemical Effects of Alcohol   283

Animal models are vital for alcohol research   283

Alcohol acts on multiple neurotransmitters   284

Alcoholism   291

Defining alcoholism and estimating its incidence have proved difficult   291

The causes of alcoholism are multimodal   293

Multiple treatment options provide hope for rehabilitation   297

11   The Opioids   305

Narcotic Analgesics   305

The opium poppy has a long history of use   306

Minor differences in molecular structure determine behavioral effects   307

Bioavailability predicts both physiological and behavioral effects   308

Opioids have their most important effects on the CNS and on the gastrointestinal tract   308

Opioid Receptors and Endogenous Neuropeptides   309

Receptor binding studies identified and localized opioid receptors   309

Four opioid receptor subtypes exist   310

Several families of naturally occurring opioid peptides bind to these receptors   312

BOX 11.1   *Opioid Modulation of Feeding   314*

Opioid receptor–mediated cellular changes are inhibitory   315

Opioids and Pain   317

The two components of pain have distinct features   318

Opioids inhibit pain transmission at spinal and supra-spinal levels   320

Other forms of pain control depend on opioids   321

Opioid Reinforcement, Tolerance, and Dependence   324

Animal testing shows significant reinforcing properties   324

Dopaminergic and nondopaminergic components contribute to opioid reinforcement   324

Long-term opioid use produces tolerance, sensitization, and dependence   325

Several brain areas contribute to the opioid abstinence syndrome   327

BOX 11.2   *What is OxyContin?   328*

Neurobiological adaptation and rebound constitute tolerance and withdrawal   329

Environmental cues have a role in tolerance, drug abuse, and relapse   330

Treatment Programs for Opioid Addiction   331

Detoxification is the first step in the therapeutic process   331

BOX 11.3   *Role of NMDA Receptors in Tolerance and Dependence   332*

Treatment goals and programs rely on pharmacological support and counseling   334

12   Psychomotor Stimulants: Cocaine and the Amphetamines   339

13   Nicotine and Caffeine   373

14 Marijuana and the Cannabinoids   401

15 Hallucinogens, PCP, and Ketamine   429

16 Inhalants, GHB, and Anabolic–Androgenic Steroids 451

17 Environmental Neurotoxicants and Endocrine Disruptors 477

18   Anxiety Disorders: Sedative–Hypnotic and Anxiolytic Drugs   509

19   Affective Disorders: Antidepressants and Mood Stabilizers   543

Preface

When we set out to write the First Edition of *Psychopharmacology: Drugs, the Brain, and Behavior*, we were struck by the recent, exciting developments in the field and the remarkable rate of progress elucidating the underlying neurobiological mechanisms of psychoactive drug action. Since publication of that edition, there has been no discernible slowdown in the progress of basic psychopharmacology research. Indeed, whole new research directions have arisen as psychopharmacologists have begun to apply emerging areas of biology such as epigenetics, to understanding how drugs affect neural and behavioral functioning. On the other hand, as you work your way through the book, it is worth considering that the numerous recent breakthroughs in what we might call "cellular psychopharmacology" have not yet led to comparable advances in developing new medications for devastating neuropsychiatric disorders such as major depression, schizophrenia, and addiction. Although the reasons for this disappointment are not fully known, it seems inevitable that at some point (hopefully soon!), we will see a surge in new drug treatments for these and other disorders that afflict so many in the population.

This Second Edition of the text is completely updated to incorporate new research findings, new methodological advances, and novel drugs of abuse like *Salvia*, "bath salts," and "Spice" that have emerged since publication of the First Edition. Most chapters have new opening vignettes and breakout boxes, and new photographs, drawings, and graphs have been added to bring attention both to updated material and to completely new topic areas for discussion. A dedicated website for the book (sites.sinauer.com/psychopharm2e) is now available that offers Web Boxes (advanced topics for interested readers), study resources such as flashcards, web links, and animations that visually illustrate key neurophysiological and neurochemical processes important for psychopharmacology. Two completely new chapters have been added to the book: Chapter 17 *Environmental Neurotoxicants and Endocrine Disruptors* covers environmental neurotoxins (e.g., insecticides and heavy metals) and endocrine disrupters (e.g., PCBs and bisphenol A) and Chapter 21 *Neurodegenerative Diseases* covers topics such as Alzheimer's disease and Parkinson's disease. The relevance of the neurodegenerative disease chapter should be obvious, as pharmaceutical agents are among the standard treatments for patients suffering from such disorders. A chapter on neurotoxins and endocrine disrupters is somewhat more unusual for a psychopharmacology text. However, the addition of such a chapter was deemed timely given the significant public concerns over exposure to various environmental pollutants (such as those covered in the chapter) and the fact that these agents have drug-like actions on the nervous and endocrine systems.

Importantly, in preparing the new edition of the book we have maintained our conviction that a deep understanding of the relationship between drugs and behavior requires basic knowledge of how the nervous system works and how different types of drugs interact with nervous system function (i.e., mechanisms of drug action). We have also continued to present the methods and findings from behavioral pharmacological studies using animal models alongside key studies from the human clinical research literature. Pharmacologists must depend on in vitro preparations and laboratory animal studies for determining mechanisms of drug action, for screening new compounds for potential therapeutic activity, and, of course, for basic toxicology and safety testing. In cases in which clinical trials have already been performed based on promising preclinical results, both sets of findings are presented. In other instances in which clinical trials had not yet been undertaken at the time of our writing, we have striven to point you towards new directions of drug development so that you can seek out the latest information using your own research efforts.

The Second Edition of *Psychopharmacology: Drugs, the Brain, and Behavior* retains the same four-section organization as the First Edition. Chapters 1 through 4 provide extensive foundation materials, including the basic principles of pharmacology, neurophysiology and neuroanatomy, cell signaling (primarily synaptic transmission), and current methods in behavioral and neuropharmacology. Chapters 5 through 8 describe key features of major neurotransmitter systems, including the catecholamines, serotonin, acetylcholine, glutamate and GABA. These are the neurotransmitter systems most often associated with psychoactive drug effects, and presentation of their neurochemistry, anatomy, and function lays the groundwork for the chapters that follow. Chapters 9 through 17 cover theories and mechanisms of drug addiction, all the major substances of abuse, and the effects of environmental neurotoxins and endocrine disrupters. Finally, Chapters 18 through 21 consider the neurobiology of neuropsychiatric and neurodegenerative disorders and the drugs used to treat these disorders. Among the neuropsychiatric disorders, special emphasis is placed on affective disorders such as major depression and bipolar disorder, various anxiety disorders, and schizophrenia. An outline at the beginning of every chapter presents the chapter's organization, which should be helpful to instructors for determining class reading assignments and to students for identifying the major topics covered in each chapter. New in this edition is the use of bulleted instead of paragraph-based interim summaries, which better highlights the key points made in each part of the chapter.

It has been our privilege in the First Edition of *Psychopharmacology: Drugs, the Brain, and Behavior* to introduce so many students to the study of drugs and behavior. With this new and updated edition, we hope to continue this tradition and perhaps inspire some of you to continue your studies in graduate school and join the thousands of researchers worldwide who are working to better understand and ultimately defeat illnesses like addiction, depression, schizophrenia, and Alzheimer's disease.

Acknowledgments

This book is the culmination of the efforts of many dedicated people who contributed their ideas and

hard work to the project. We'd like to thank and acknowledge the outstanding editorial team at Sinauer Associates: Sydney Carroll, Danna Niedzwiecki, and Chelsea Holabird, thank you all for your suggestions for improving the First Edition, your help and guidance throughout the process of writing and revising, and not least for your patience (textbook writing is a slow process when one is simultaneously teaching, conducting research, and meeting administrative responsibilities). You were unwavering in your vision to produce the best possible psychopharmacology textbook. David McIntyre did a superb job of seeking out just the right photographs for the book, as well as creating a few of his own when needed. We are indebted to other key staff members of Sinauer Associates who worked on this project, including Chris Small and Janice Holabird. We also wish to acknowledge the contributions of Graig Donini, the editor on the First Edition of the book, and Peter Farley, who first encouraged us to develop an undergraduate version of the "big book" and began working with us on that project. And we must acknowledge Precision Graphics for the beautiful job rendering the illustrations.

The following reviewers contributed many excellent suggestions for improving the book:

A. Michael Anch, Saint Louis University
Aileen M. Bailey, St. Mary's College of Maryland
Karen Brebner, St. Francis Xavier University
Wayne Briner, University of Nebraska at Kearney
Scott I. Cohn, Western State College of Colorado
Melloni Cook, University of Memphis
Asad Dalia, University of Cincinnati
Heather Dickinson-Anson, University of California, Irvine
S. Tiffany Donaldson, University of Massachusetts Boston
Perry Fuchs, University of Texas at Arlington
William S. Griesar, Washington State University
Josh Gulley, University of Illinois, Urbana-Champaign
Derek Hamilton, University of New Mexico
Eric Jackson, University of New Mexico
Heather Kimmel, Emory University
Daewoo Lee, Ohio University
Linda Lockwood, Metropolitan State College of Denver
Jill McGaughy, University of New Hampshire
Dennis K. Miller, University of Missouri, Columbia
Laurence J. Nolan, Wagner College, New York
Dr. Robert L. Patrick, Brown University
Franca Placenza, University of Toronto Scarborough
Joseph H. Porter, Virginia Commonwealth University
Adam Prus, Northern Michigan University
Fred Shaffer, Truman State University
Tim Schallert, University of Texas at Austin

Mark S. Schmidt, Columbus State University
Donald F. Slish, Plattsburgh State University
David Tam, University of North Texas
Sandy Venneman, University of Houston-Victoria
Gary L. Wenk, Ohio State University
Ilsun M. White, Morehead State University
Xiaojuan Xu, Grand Valley State University
Yueping Zhang, Lewis & Clark College

We are grateful to several readers of the First Edition, especially Scott Hooper at Ohio University, who alerted us to minor errors and material in need of clarification. Most of all, we are indebted to our spouses, Melinda Novak and Ray Rosati, who supported and encouraged us and who willingly sacrificed so much of our time together during this lengthy project. Linda gives special thanks to her husband Ray for providing extensive editorial advice during the final production period.

Media and Supplements to accompany *Psychopharmacology*, Second Edition

eBook

Psychopharmacology, Second Edition is available as an eBook, in several different formats. Please visit the Sinauer Associates website at www.sinauer.com for more information.

For the Student

Companion Website
(sites.sinauer.com/psychopharm2e)

New for the Second Edition, the *Psychopharmacology* Companion Website includes a variety of resources to help students learn and review the material presented in the textbook, and to expand the coverage of the textbook. The site includes the following:

- *Chapter Outlines & Summaries*: Detailed reviews of each chapter
- *Flashcards & Key Terms*: A great way for students to learn and review the key terminology introduced in each chapter
- *Animations*: Detailed, narrated animations of some of the key complex processes described in the textbook
- *Web Boxes:* Novel and cutting-edge topics for special discussion
- *Web Links*: A collection of suggested websites related to each chapter
- *Complete glossary*

For the Instructor

Instructor's Resource Library

Available to qualified adopters of the textbook, the *Psychopharmacology*, Second Edition Instructor's Resource Library provides instructors a range of resources to help them prepare their lectures and assess their students. The IRL includes the following:

- *Textbook Figures & Tables*: All of the figures (art and photos) and tables from the textbook are provided both as high-resolution and low-resolution JPEG images.
- *PowerPoint Presentations*: Two presentations are provided for each chapter of the textbook:
  - All figures and tables from the chapter, ready to insert into custom presentations
  - A complete lecture presentation that includes comprehensive lecture notes and selected figures
- *Test Bank* (see below for details)
- *Computerized Test Bank* (see below for details)

Test Bank

Included in the Instructor's Resource Library, the *Psychopharmacology*, Second Edition Test Bank includes 50 test questions per chapter, consisting of approximately 40 multiple-choice, and 10 short-answer. The questions have been designed to provide instructors with a good selection of factual and conceptual questions, at a range of difficulty levels. The test bank is provided as Microsoft Word files.

Computerized Test Bank

(Included in the Instructor's Resource Library)
In addition to the Microsoft Word version of the Test Bank, all questions are available in Wimba's Diploma test-creation software (software included). Diploma makes it easy to create quizzes and exams using any combination of publisher-provided questions and an instructor's own questions, and to print or publish exams for online use.

Course Management System Support

Using the Computerized Test Bank provided in the Instructor's Resource Library, instructors can easily create and export quizzes and exams (or the entire test bank) for integration into their course management system, such as Blackboard, WebCT, Desire2Learn, and Moodle.

Psychopharmacology
Drugs, the Brain, and Behavior
SECOND EDITION

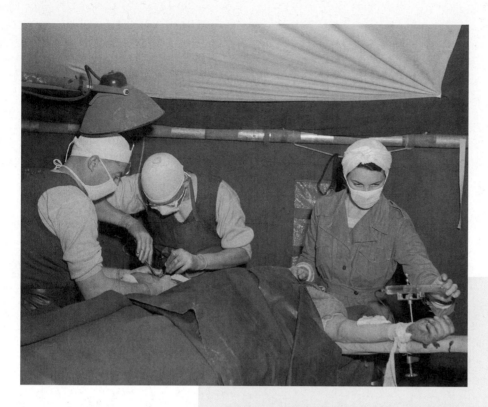

A mobile army surgical hospital (MASH unit) provides care for wounded soldiers near the frontlines of the battlefield during the allied invasion of Italy in World War II.

Principles of Pharmacology 1

THE ITALIAN CAMPAIGN OF WORLD WAR II involved the Allied invasion of Sicily and the Italian mainland during the period from 1943 to 1945. The ultimate victory left 60,000 Allied soldiers dead and 320,000 casualties. Among the casualties were American troops who were treated by a Harvard-based anesthesiologist named Henry Beecher. The prolonged intense bombardment by the Germans caused significant shortages of supplies and medications, including those given to relieve pain, such as morphine. Out of that desperate circumstance came a fascinating finding that has generated enormous research since that time. It seems that as supplies of morphine dwindled to nothing, Dr. Beecher's nursing assistant, in an effort to be compassionate, injected the soldiers with saline solution while reassuring them that they were getting the potent painkiller. To her total amazement, she observed that the inert injection dramatically reduced the soldiers' agony and prevented the drop in blood pressure that leads to life-threatening shock. This initial discovery prompted Beecher to return to Harvard after the war and empirically study the healing art of deception as it relates to improved patient care and modern drug testing. Beecher revolutionized how new medications were tested and initiated the use of a placebo group, whose outcome would be compared with that of the group receiving the medication to be tested. At last, there was an impartial way to determine whether the new drug was truly effective. Chapter 1 describes this placebo effect in greater detail.

Pharmacology: The Science of Drug Action

Pharmacology is the scientific study of the actions of drugs and their effects on a living organism. Until the beginning of the last century, pharmacologists studied drugs that were almost all naturally occurring substances. The importance of plants in the lives of ancient man is well documented. Writings from as early as 1500 BC describe plant-based medicines used in Egypt and in India. The Ebers Papyrus describes the preparation and use of more than 700 remedies for ailments as varied as crocodile bites, baldness, constipation, headache, and heart disease. Of course, many of these treatments included elements of magic and incantation, but there are also references to some modern drugs such as castor oil and opium. The Chinese also have a very long and extensive tradition in the use of herbal remedies that continues today. World Health Organization estimates suggest that in modern times, as many as 80% of the people in developing countries are totally dependent on herbs or plant-derived medicinals. And in 1999, in the United States, modern herbal medicines and drugs based on natural products represented half of the top 20 drugs on the market (Hollinger, 2008). Many Americans are enamored with herbal medications despite limited clinical support for their effectiveness because they believe these treatments are more "natural." Nevertheless, serious dangers have been associated with some of them. **Web Box 1.1** discusses the benefits and dangers of herbal remedies.

When placed in historical context, it can be seen that drug development in the United States is in its infancy. The rapid introduction of many new drugs by the pharmaceutical industry has forced the development of several specialized areas of pharmacology. Two of these areas are of particular interest to us. **Neuropharmacology** is concerned with drug-induced changes in the functioning of cells in the nervous system, and **psychopharmacology** emphasizes drug-induced changes in mood, thinking, and behavior. In combination, the goal of **neuropsychopharmacology** is to identify chemical substances that act on the nervous system to alter behavior that is disturbed because of injury, disease, or environmental factors. Additionally, neuropsychopharmacologists are interested in using chemical agents as probes to gain an understanding of the neurobiology of behavior.

When we speak of **drug action**, we are referring to the specific molecular changes produced by a drug when it binds to a particular target site or receptor. These molecular changes lead to more widespread alterations in physiological or psychological functions, which we consider **drug effects**. The site of drug action may be very different from the site of drug effect. For example, atropine is a drug used in ophthalmology to dilate the pupil of the eye before eye examinations. Atropine has a site of action (the eye muscles of the iris) that is close to the site of its ultimate effect (widening the pupil), so it is administered directly to the eye. In comparison, morphine applied to the eye itself has no effect. Yet when it is taken internally, the

drug's action on the brain leads to "pinpoint" pupils. Clearly, for morphine, the site of effect is far distant from the site of its initial action.

Keep in mind that because drugs act at a variety of target sites, they always have multiple effects. Some may be **therapeutic effects**, meaning that the drug–receptor interaction produces desired physical or behavioral changes. All other effects produced are referred to as **side effects**, and they vary in severity from mildly annoying to distressing and dangerous. For example, amphetamine-like drugs produce alertness and insomnia, increased heart rate, and decreased appetite. Drugs in this class reduce the occurrence of spontaneous sleep episodes characteristic of the disorder called *narcolepsy*, but they produce anorexia (loss of appetite) as the primary side effect. In contrast, the same drug may be used as a prescription diet control in weight-reduction programs. In such cases, insomnia and hyperactivity are frequently disturbing side effects. Thus therapeutic and side effects can change, depending on the desired outcome.

It is important to keep in mind that there are no "good" or "bad" drugs because all drugs are just chemicals. It is the way a drug is procured and used that determines its character. Society tends to think of good drugs as those purchased at a pharmacy and taken at the appropriate dosage for a particular medicinal purpose, and "bad" drugs as those acquired in an illicit fashion and taken recreationally to achieve a desired psychological state. Even with this, the differences are blurred, because many people consider alcohol to be "bad" even though it is purchased legally. Morphine and cocaine have legitimate medicinal uses, making them "good drugs" under some conditions, although they can, when misused, lead to dangerous consequences and addiction, making the same drugs "bad." Finally, many "good" prescription drugs are acquired illicitly or are misused by increasing the dose, prolonging use, or sharing the drug with other individuals, leading to "bad" outcomes. As you will read in later chapters, the ideas of Americans on appropriate drug use have changed dramatically over time (see the section on the history of the use of narcotics in Chapter 11 and cocaine in Chapter 12).

Many of the drug effects we have described so far have been **specific drug effects**, defined as those based on the physical and biochemical interactions of a drug with a target site in living tissue. In contrast, **nonspecific drug effects** are those that are based not on the chemical activity of a drug–receptor interaction, but on certain unique characteristics of the individual. It is clear that an individual's background (e.g., drug-taking experience), present mood, expectations of drug effect, perceptions of the drug-taking situation, attitude toward the person administering the drug, and other factors influence the outcome of drug use. Nonspecific drug effects help to explain why the same individual self-administering the same amount of ethyl alcohol may experience a sense of being lighthearted and gregarious on one occasion, and depressed and melancholy on another. The basis for such a phenomenon may well be the varied neurochemical states existing within the individual at different times, over which specific drug effects are superimposed.

One common example of nonspecific effects is the **placebo**. Many of you automatically think of a placebo as a "fake" pill. A placebo *is* in fact a pharmacologically inert compound administered to an individual; however, in many instances it has not only therapeutic effects, but side effects as well. Just as many of the symptoms of illness may have psychogenic or emotional origins, belief in a drug may produce real physiological effects despite the lack of chemical activity. These effects are not limited to the individual's subjective evaluation of relief, but include measurable physiological changes such as altered gastric acid secretion, blood vessel dilation, hormonal changes, and so forth.

In a classic study, two groups of patients with ulcers were given a placebo. In the first group, the medication was provided by a physician, who assured the patients that the drug would provide relief. The second group also received the placebo, but it was administered by a nurse, who described it as experimental in nature. In group 1, 70% of the patients found

significant relief, but in group 2, only 25% were helped by the "drug" (Levine, 1973).

In pharmacology, the placebo is essential in the design of experiments conducted to evaluate the effectiveness of new medications because it eliminates the influence of expectation on the part of the subject. This control group is identical to the experimental group in all ways, and subjects are unaware of the substitution of an inactive substance (e.g., sugar pill, saline injection) for the test medication. Comparison of the two groups provides information on the effectiveness of the drug beyond subject expectation.

The large contribution of nonspecific factors and the high and variable incidence of placebo responders make the **double-blind experiment** highly desirable. In these experiments, neither the patient nor the observer knows what treatment the patient has received. Such precautions ensure that the results of any given treatment will not be colored by overt or covert prejudices on the part of the patient or the observer. If you would like to read more about the use of placebos in both clinical research and therapeutics and the associated ethical dilemmas, refer to the articles by Brown (1998) and Louhiala (2009).

Throughout this chapter, we present examples that include both therapeutic and recreational drugs that affect mood and behavior. Since there are usually several names for the same substance, it may be helpful for you to understand how drugs are named (**Box 1.1**).

BOX 1.1 Pharmacology in Action

Naming Drugs

Drug names can be a confusing issue for many people because drugs that are sold commercially, by prescription or over the counter, usually have four or more different kinds of names. All drugs have a chemical name that is a complete chemical description suitable for synthesizing by an organic chemist. Chemical names are rather clumsy and are rarely used except in a laboratory setting. In contrast, generic names (also called nonproprietary names) are official names of drugs that are listed in the United States Pharmacopeia (USP). The generic name is a much shorter form of the chemical name but is still unique

to that drug. For example, one popular antianxiety drug has the chemical name 7-chloro-1,3-dihydro-1-methyl-5-phenyl-2H-1,4-benzodiazepin-2-one and the generic name diazepam. The brand name, or trade name, of that drug (Valium) specifies a particular manufacturer and a formulation. A brand name is trademarked and copyrighted by an individual company, which means that the company has an exclusive right to advertise and sell that drug.

Slang or street names of commonly abused drugs are another way to identify a particular chemical. Unfortunately, these names

change over time and vary with geographic location and particular groups of people. In addition, there is no way to know the chemical characteristics of the substance in question. Some terms are used in popular films or television and become more generally familiar, such as "crack" or "ice," but most disappear as quickly as they appeared. The National Institute on Drug Abuse has compiled a list of more than 150 street names for marijuana and more than 75 for cocaine, including coke, big C, nose candy, snow, mighty white, Foo-foo dust, Peruvian lady, dream, doing the line, and many others.

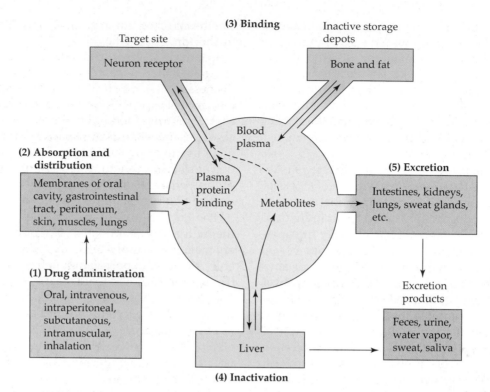

Figure 1.1 Pharmacokinetic factors that determine bioavailability of drugs From the site of administration (1), the drug moves through cell membranes to be absorbed into the blood (2), where it circulates to all cells in the body. Some of the drug molecules may bind to inactive sites such as plasma proteins or storage depots (3), and others to receptors in target tissue. Blood-borne drug molecules also enter the liver (4), where they may be transformed into metabolites and travel to the kidneys and other discharge sites for ultimate excretion (5) from the body.

Pharmacokinetic Factors Determining Drug Action

Although it is safe to assume that the chemical structure of a drug determines its action, it quickly becomes clear that additional factors are also powerful contributors. The dose of the drug administered is clearly important, but more important is the amount of drug in the blood that is free to bind at specific target sites (**bioavailability**) to elicit drug action. The following sections of this chapter describe in detail the dynamic factors that contribute to bioavailability. Collectively, these factors constitute the **pharmacokinetic** component of drug action; they are listed below and illustrated in **Figure 1.1**.

1. *Routes of administration*. How and where a drug is administered determines how quickly and how completely the drug is absorbed into the blood.

2. *Absorption and distribution*. Because a drug rarely acts where it initially contacts the body, it must pass through a variety of cell membranes and enter the blood plasma, which transports the drug to virtually all of the cells in the body.

3. *Binding*. Once in the blood plasma, some drug molecules move to tissues to bind to active target sites (receptors). While in the blood, a drug may also bind (**depot binding**) to plasma proteins or may be stored temporarily in bone or fat, where it is inactive.

4. *Inactivation*. Drug inactivation, or **biotransformation**, occurs primarily as a result of metabolic processes in the liver. The amount of drug in the body at any one time is dependent on the dynamic balance between absorption and inactivation. Therefore, inactivation influences both the intensity and the duration of drug effects.

5. *Excretion*. The liver metabolites are eliminated from the body with the urine or feces. Some drugs are excreted in an unaltered form by the kidneys.

Although these topics are discussed sequentially in the following pages, keep in mind that in the living organism, these factors are at work simultaneously. In addition to bioavailability, the drug effect experienced will also depend on how rapidly the drug reaches its target, the frequency and history of prior drug use (see the discussion on tolerance later in the chapter), and, finally, nonspecific factors that are characteristics of individuals and their environment.

Methods of drug administration influence the onset of drug action

The route of administration of a drug determines how much drug reaches its site of action and how quickly the drug effect occurs. There are two major categories of administration methods. **Enteral** methods of administration use the gastrointestinal (GI) tract (*enteron* is the Greek word for "gut"); agents administered by these methods are generally slow in onset and produce highly variable blood levels of drug. The most common enteral method of administration is oral, but rectal administration with the use of suppositories is another enteral route. All other routes of administration are **parenteral** and include those that do not use the alimentary canal, such as injection, pulmonary, and topical administration.

Oral administration (PO) is the most popular route for taking drugs because it is safe, self-administered, and economical, and it avoids the complications and discomfort of injection methods. Drugs that are taken orally come in the form of capsules, pills, tablets, or liquid, but to be effective, the drug must dissolve in stomach fluids and pass through the stomach wall to reach blood capillaries. In addition, the drug must be resistant to destruction by stomach acid and stomach enzymes that are important for normal digestion. Insulin is one drug that can be destroyed by digestive processes and for this reason, it cannot be administered orally.

Movement of the drug from the site of administration to the blood circulation is called **absorption**. Although some drugs are absorbed from the stomach, most drugs are not fully absorbed until they reach the small intestine. Many factors influence how quickly the stomach empties its contents into the small intestine, and hence determine the ultimate rate of absorption. For example, food in the stomach, particularly if it is fatty, slows the movement of the drug into the intestine, thereby delaying absorption into the blood. The amount of food consumed, the level of physical activity of the individual, and many other factors make it difficult to predict how quickly the drug will reach the intestine. In addition, many drugs undergo extensive first-pass metabolism. **First-pass metabolism** is an evolutionarily beneficial function because potentially harmful chemicals and toxins that are ingested pass via the portal vein to the liver, where they are chemically altered by a variety of enzymes before passing to the heart for circulation throughout the body (**Figure 1.2**). Unfortunately, some therapeutic

drugs taken orally may undergo extensive metabolism (more than 90%), reducing their bioavailability. Drugs that show extensive first-pass effects must be administered at higher doses or in an alternative manner, such as by injection. Because of these many factors, oral administration produces drug plasma levels that are more irregular and unpredictable and rise more slowly than those produced by other methods of administration.

Rectal administration requires the placement of a drug-filled suppository in the rectum, where the suppository coating gradually melts or dissolves, releasing the drug to be absorbed into the blood. Depending on the placement of the suppository, the drug may avoid some first-pass metabolism. Drug absorbed from the lower rectum into the hemorrhoidal vein bypasses the liver. However, deeper placement means that the drug is absorbed by veins that drain into the portal vein, going to the liver before the general circulation. Bioavailability of drugs administered in this way is difficult to predict because absorption is irregular. Although rectal administration is not used as commonly as oral administration, it is an effective route in infants, and in individuals who are vomiting, unconscious, or unable to take medication orally.

Intravenous (IV) injection is the most rapid and accurate method of drug administration in that a precise quantity of the agent is placed directly into the blood and passage through cell membranes such as the stomach wall is eliminated (see Figure 1.2). However, the quick onset of drug effect with IV injection is also a potential hazard. An overdose or a dangerous allergic reaction to the drug leaves little time for corrective measures, and the drug cannot be removed from the body as it can be removed from the stomach by stomach pumping.

For drug abusers, IV administration provides a more dramatic subjective drug experience than self-administration in other ways, because the drug reaches the brain almost instantly. Drug users report that intravenous injection of a cocaine solution usually produces an intense "rush" or "flash" of pure pleasure that lasts for approximately 10 minutes. This experience rarely occurs when cocaine is taken orally or is taken into the nostrils (snorting; see the discussion on topical administration). However, intravenous use of street drugs poses several special hazards. First, drugs that are impure or of unknown quality provide uncertain doses, and toxic reactions are common. Second, lack of sterile injection equipment and aseptic technique can lead to infections such as hepatitis, human immunodeficiency virus (HIV), and endocarditis (inflammation of the lining of the heart). Fortunately, many cities have implemented free needle programs,

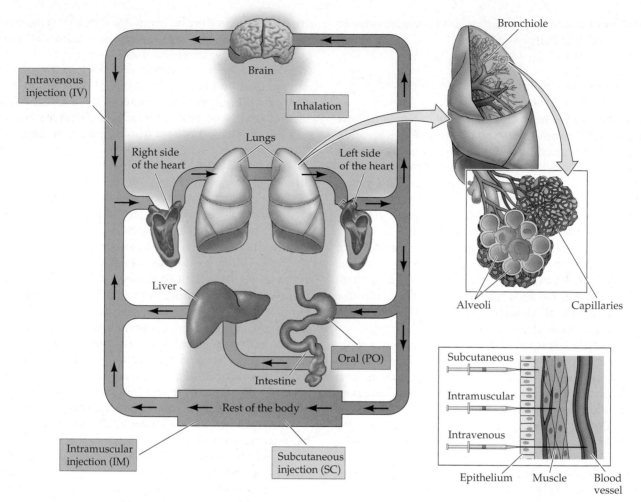

Figure 1.2 Routes of drug administration First-pass effect. Drugs administered orally are absorbed into the blood and must pass through the liver before reaching the general circulation. Some drug molecules may be destroyed in the liver before they can reach target tissues. The arrows indicate the direction of blood flow in the arteries (colored red) and veins (blue). (Inset) Pulmonary absorption through capillaries in the alveoli. Rapid absorption occurs after inhalation because the large surface area of the lungs and the rich capillary networks provide efficient exchange of gases to and from the blood. (Inset) Methods of administration by injection. The speed of absorption of drug molecules from administration sites depends on the amount of blood circulating to that area.

which significantly reduce the probability of cross-infection. Third, many drug abusers attempt to dissolve drugs that have insoluble filler materials, which, when injected, may become trapped in the small blood vessels in the lungs, leading to reduced respiratory capacity or death.

An alternative to the IV procedure is **intramuscular (IM)** injection, which provides the advantage of slower, more even absorption over a period of time. Drugs administered by this method are usually absorbed within 10 to 30 minutes. Absorption can be slowed down by combining the drug with a second drug that constricts blood vessels, because the rate of drug absorption is dependent on the rate of blood flow to the muscle (see Figure 1.2). To provide slower, sustained action, the drug may be injected as a suspension in vegetable oil. For example, IM injection

of medroxyprogesterone acetate (Depo-Provera) provides effective contraception for 3 to 6 months without the need to take daily pills. One disadvantage of IM administration is that in some cases, the injection solution can be highly irritating, causing significant muscle discomfort.

Intraperitoneal (IP) injection is rarely used with humans, but it is the most common route of administration for small laboratory animals. The drug is injected through the abdominal wall into the peritoneal cavity—the space that surrounds the abdominal organs. IP injection produces rapid effects, but not as rapid as those produced by IV injection. Variability in absorption occurs, depending on where (within the peritoneum) the drug is placed.

In **subcutaneous (SC)** administration, the drug is injected just below the skin (see Figure 1.2) and is absorbed at a rate that is dependent on blood flow to the site. Absorption is usually fairly slow and steady, but there can be considerable variability. Rubbing the skin to dilate blood vessels in the immediate area increases the rate of absorption. Injection of a drug in a nonaqueous solution (such as peanut oil) or implantation of a drug pellet or delivery device further slows the rate of absorption. Subcutaneous implantation of drug-containing pellets is most often used to administer hormones. Implanon and Nexplanon are two contraceptive implants now available in the United States. The hormones are contained in a single small rod about 40 mm (1.5 inches) long that is implanted through a small incision just under the skin of the upper arm. A woman is protected from pregnancy for a 3-year period unless the device is removed.

Inhalation of drugs, such as those used to treat asthma attacks, allows drugs to be absorbed into the blood by passing through the lungs. Absorption is very rapid because the area of the pulmonary absorbing surfaces is large and rich with capillaries (see Figure 1.2). The effect on the brain is very rapid because blood from the capillaries of the lungs travels only a short distance back to the heart before it is pumped quickly to the brain via the carotid artery, which carries oxygenated blood to the head and neck. The psychoactive effects of inhaled substances can occur within a matter of seconds.

Inhalation is the method preferred for self-administration in cases when oral absorption is too slow and much of the active drug is destroyed before it reaches the brain. Nicotine released from the tobacco of a cigarette by heat into the smoke produces a very rapid rise in blood level and rapid central nervous system (CNS) effects, which peak in a matter of minutes. Tetrahydrocannabinol (THC), an active ingredient of marijuana, and crack cocaine are also rapidly absorbed after smoking. In addition to the inherent dangers of the drugs themselves, disadvantages of inhalation include irritation of the nasal passages and damage to the lungs caused by small particles that may be included in the inhaled material.

Topical application of drugs to mucous membranes, such as the conjunctiva of the eye, the oral cavity, nasopharynx, vagina, colon, and urethra generally provides local drug effects. However, some topically administered drugs can be readily absorbed into the general circulation, leading to widespread effects. **Intranasal administration** is of special interest because it causes local effects such as relieving nasal congestion and treating allergies, but it can also have systemic effects, in which case the drug moves across a single epithelial cell layer into the bloodstream, avoiding first-pass liver metabolism. Even more important is the fact that intranasal administration

allows the blood–brain barrier to be bypassed, perhaps by achieving direct access to the fluid that surrounds the brain (cerebrospinal fluid [CSF]), and from there to extracellular fluid found in the intercellular spaces between neurons. Hence neuropeptides such as the hormone oxytocin can be administered by intranasal sprays to achieve significant concentrations in the brain. **Box 1.2** describes a study that evaluated the effects of intranasal oxytocin administration on social behavior in autistic adults.

Intranasal absorption can also be achieved without dissolving the drug. Direct application of finely powdered cocaine to the nasal mucosa by sniffing leads to rapid absorption, which produces profound effects on the CNS that peak in about 15 to 30 minutes. One side effect of "snorting" cocaine is the formation of perforations in the nasal septum, the cartilage that separates the two nostrils. This damage occurs because cocaine is a potent vasoconstrictor. Reducing blood flow deprives the underlying cartilage of oxygen, leading to necrosis. Additionally, contaminants in the cocaine act as chemical irritants, causing tissue inflammation. Cocaine addicts whose nasal mucosa has been damaged by chronic cocaine "snorting" may resort to application of the drug to the rectum, vagina, or penis.

Although the skin provides an effective barrier to the diffusion of water-soluble drugs, certain lipid-soluble substances (i.e., those that dissolve in fat) are capable of penetrating slowly. Accidental absorption of industrial and agricultural chemicals such as tetraethyl lead, organic phosphate insecticides, and carbon tetrachloride through the skin produces toxic effects on the nervous system and on other organ systems. Chapter 17 discusses some of these environmental toxins in greater detail. **Transdermal** (i.e., through the skin) drug administration with skin patches provides controlled and sustained delivery of drug at a preprogrammed rate. The method is convenient because the individual does not have to remember to take a pill, and it is painless without the need for injection. It also provides the advantage of avoiding the first-pass effect. In cases of mass vaccination campaigns, such as those undertaken during pandemics, transdermal delivery is much quicker than other methods, and it reduces the dangers of accidental needle sticks of health care workers and unsafe disposal of used needles. Patches consist of a polymer matrix embedded with the drug in high concentration. Transdermal delivery is now a common way to prevent motion sickness with scopolamine, reduce cigarette craving with nicotine patches, relieve angina pectoris with nitroglycerin, and provide hormones after menopause or for contraceptive purposes. The major disadvantage of transdermal delivery is that because skin is designed to prevent materials from entering the body,

BOX 1.2 Clinical Applications

Treating Autism with Intranasal Oxytocin

Oxytocin is a hormone manufactured in the hypothalamus and released by the pituitary that has numerous peripheral effects on reproductive events, including facilitating birth and lactation. In addition, it acts as a modulator of nerve cell function within the brain and is involved in regulation of emotion. In particular, oxytocin injected into the brain of rodents enhances monogamous pair bonding, maternal–infant attachment, and approach behavior including sexual activity. In fact, some have called it the "love" hormone. In animal studies the hormone is injected intracerebrally, but that is an unrealistic approach to human therapeutics. Instead, to test the central effects of oxytocin on human behavior, intranasal administration has been used to bypass the blood–brain barrier. In healthy human subjects, oxytocin increases trust in others, enhances positive social memories, enhances attachment security, modulates memory for facial identity, and increases time spent looking at the eyes of faces, which provides socially important cues such as the other individual's mental state. MacDonald and MacDonald (2010) summarize the prosocial effects of oxytocin and provide an evolutionary history of the hormone.

Individuals suffering from high-functioning autism have normal language and intellectual abilities but show significant impairment in social interactions. They have particular problems in understanding and responding to social cues,

so they have trouble interpreting other people's feelings and intentions. Some show no interest in other people at all; others do not understand how to form friendships despite their desire to do so, and their social interactions are severely limited. Their inability to make rapid intuitive judgments in social situations impairs their expression of appropriate human affiliative behavior and prevents experiencing empathy with the emotions of others.

Individuals with autism and related autism spectrum disorders have lower levels of plasma oxytocin because they do not show the typical developmental increases and have reduced capacity to synthesize the hormone. Additionally, the discovery that a certain genetic polymorphism for the oxytocin receptor is more prevalent in autistic individuals and is linked to lower empathy has suggested the oxytocin hypothesis of autism. Given the effects of the neuropeptide in rodents and in healthy humans, Andari and colleagues (2010) hypothesized that oxytocin would enhance social behaviors in adults with high-functioning autism. Because eye contact is a very basic component of social skills, their behavioral measures included recording eye movement as subjects (oxytocin-treated autistic adults, placebo-treated autistic adults, and healthy controls) performed a face perception task. They found that oxytocin-treated autistic individuals compared with placebo-treated autistic adults

showed far more visual scanning of faces, especially around the eye region.

The second measure involved decision making and emotional response during a computer-simulated ball tossing game. In this task, each of the three fictitious ball tossers responded differently to the subject's ball toss. One tossed more times to the subject ("Good reciprocal response"); the second rarely reciprocated the ball tossed to him by the subject ("Bad"); and the third reciprocated one-for-one ("Neutral"). Placebo-treated autistic adults did not discriminate among the conditions; that is, they showed no emotional response to the "individuals" they played with and tossed the ball equally to all three. In contrast, oxytocin treatment apparently improved the autistic individuals' skill in processing socially relevant cues because they tossed much more to the "Good" player and very little to the "Bad," as you would anticipate for healthy subjects. Rating scales completed after the ball toss game showed that subjects receiving oxytocin experienced positive emotions toward the "Good" player and negative affect toward the "Bad," again showing that they understood the social context of reciprocal social behavior. Although the study is a small one, it provides incentive to investigate further whether treatment with intranasal oxytocin may be a therapeutic option for addressing one of the core symptoms of high functioning autism—poor social functioning.

a limited number of drugs are able to penetrate. However, techniques are continuing to be developed to increase skin permeability through a variety of methods. For instance, hand-held ultrasound devices that send low-intensity sound energy waves through surrounding fluid in the tissue temporarily increase the size of the pores in the skin, allowing absorption of large molecules from a skin patch. Other "active" patch systems that help to move large molecules through the skin use inotophoresis, which involves applying a small electrical current to the reservoir or the patch. The electrical charge repels drug molecules with a similar charge and forces them through the skin at a predetermined rate. If the amount and duration of current are changed, drug delivery can be restricted to the skin for local effects or can be forced more deeply into the blood. This process is also capable of pulling molecules out through the skin for monitoring. Such monitoring might be used by diabetic individuals to more frequently evaluate levels of blood glucose. An additional approach uses mechanical disruption of the skin. Small arrays of microneedles about 1 micron in diameter and 100 microns long and coated with drug or vaccine are placed on the skin. The needles penetrate the superficial layer of the skin—the stratum corneum—where the drug is delivered without stimulating underlying pain receptors. This method provides the opportunity for painless vaccinations and drug injections that can be self-administered. These and other developing techniques have been described by Langer (2003) and Banga (2009).

Special injection methods must be used for some drugs that act on nerve cells, because a cellular barrier, the blood–brain barrier (discussed later in the chapter), prevents or slows passage of these drugs from the blood into neural tissue. For example, **epidural** injection is used when spinal anesthetics are administered directly into the cerebrospinal fluid surrounding the spinal cord of a mother during childbirth, bypassing the blood–brain barrier. In animal experiments, a microsyringe or a cannula enables precise drug injection into discrete areas of brain tissue (**intracranial**) or into the cerebrospinal fluid–filled chambers, the ventricles (**intracerebroventricular**). In this way, experimenters can study the electrophysiological, biochemical, or behavioral effects of drugs on particular nerve cell groups. This method is described in Chapter 4. Animal research has evolved into potentially important treatment methods for human conditions such as cerebral meningitis (inflammation of one of the protective membranes covering the brain). An **infusion pump** implanted under the skin of the scalp can be programmed to deliver a constant dose of antibiotic into the cerebral ventricles; this device permits treatment of brain infection, when antibiotics are normally prevented from passing the blood–brain barrier. These infusion pumps have important uses in delivering drugs systemically as well. With appropriate software, it is possible to provide pulsed administration of an agent that mimics the normal biological rhythm, for example, of hormones. An exciting development has been the addition of feedback regulation of these pumps, which includes a sensor element that monitors a substance such as blood glucose in a diabetic individual and responds with an appropriate infusion

of insulin delivered from an implantable pump that acts much like an artificial pancreas. The downside to these pumps is the risk of infection and frequent clogging, which reduces their usefulness in maintaining stable drug concentrations over prolonged periods.

Many disorders of the CNS are characterized by abnormal changes in gene activity, which alter the manufacture of an essential protein such as an enzyme or a receptor. **Gene therapy** refers to the application of deoxyribonucleic acid (DNA), which encodes a specific protein to a particular target site. DNA can be used to increase or block expression of the gene product to correct the clinical condition. One significant difficulty in the application of gene therapy involves creating the appropriate gene delivery system. Such a delivery system, which is called a *vector*, is needed to carry the gene into the nuclei of target cells to alter protein synthesis. Administering gene therapy is clearly more challenging when disorders of the CNS, rather than disorders of any other part of the body, are treated. Vectors are usually injected directly into the brain region targeted for modification. **Viral vectors** are frequently considered for this delivery system because of the special ability of a virus to bind to and enter cells and their nuclei, where they insert themselves into the chromosome to alter DNA. Because viruses vary in terms of binding, cell entry proteins, and other properties, a variety of viruses are being evaluated.

Lim and colleagues (2010) provide a review of viral vector delivery as an approach to treating diseases of the CNS. Human trials have been increasing in number, but much research remains to be done before the safety and usefulness of gene therapy are fully demonstrated. Concerns expressed by researchers include the following: that an immune response will be initiated by the introduction of foreign material, that the viral vector may recover its ability to cause disease once it is placed in the human cell, and that inserting the vector in the wrong place could induce tumor growth. Nevertheless, many animal studies are highly encouraging, and gene therapy is believed to have enormous potential for the treatment of debilitating disorders of the nervous system such as stroke-induced damage, spinal cord injury, chronic pain conditions, and neurodegenerative disorders such as Alzheimer's disease, Parkinson's disease, and Huntington's disease.

IMPACT ON BIOAVAILABILITY Because the route of administration significantly alters the rate of absorption, blood levels of the same dose of a drug administered by different routes vary significantly. **Figure 1.3** compares drug concentrations in blood over time for various routes of administration. Keep in mind that the peak level for each method reflects not only differences in absorption rate, but also the fact that

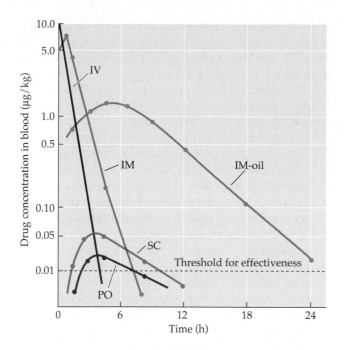

Figure 1.3 The time course of drug blood level depends on route of administration The blood level of the same amount of drug administered by different procedures to the same individual varies significantly. Intravenous (IV) produces an instantaneous peak when the drug is placed into the blood and a rapid decline. Intramuscular (IM) administration produces rapid absorption and rapid decline, although IM administration in oil (IM-oil) shows slower absorption and gradual decline. Slow absorption after subcutaneous (SC) administration means that some of the drug is metabolized before absorption is complete. For this reason, no sharp peak occurs, and overall blood levels are lower. Oral (PO) administration produces the lowest blood levels and a relatively short time over threshold for effectiveness in this instance. (After Levine, 1973.)

slow absorption provides the opportunity for liver metabolism to act on some of the drug molecules before absorption is complete. Advantages and disadvantages of selected methods of administration are summarized in **Table 1.1**.

Multiple factors modify drug absorption

Once the drug has been administered, it is absorbed from the site of administration into the blood to be circulated throughout the body and ultimately to the brain, which is the primary target site for **psychoactive drugs** (i.e., those drugs that have an effect on thinking, mood, and behavior). We have already shown that the rate of absorption is dependent on several factors. Clearly, the route of administration alters absorption because it determines the area of the absorbing surface, the number of cell layers between the site of administration and the blood, the amount of drug destroyed by metabolism or digestive processes, and the extent of binding to food or inert complexes. Absorption is also dependent on drug concentration, which is determined in part by individual differences in age, sex, and body size. Finally, absorption is dependent on the solubility and ionization of the drug.

TRANSPORT ACROSS MEMBRANES Perhaps the single most important factor in determining plasma drug levels is the rate of passage of the drug through the

TABLE 1.1 Advantages and Disadvantages of Selected Routes of Drug Administration		
Route of administration	Advantages	Disadvantages
Oral (PO)	Safe; self-administered; economical; no needle-related complications	Slow and highly variable absorption; subject to first-pass metabolism; less-predictable blood levels
Intravenous (IV)	Most rapid; most accurate blood concentration	Overdose danger; cannot be readily reversed; requires sterile needles and medical technique
Intramuscular (IM)	Slow and even absorption	Localized irritation at site of injection; needs sterile equipment
Subcutaneous (SC)	Slow and prolonged absorption	Variable absorption depending on blood flow
Inhalation	Large absorption surface; very rapid onset; no injection equipment needed	Irritation of nasal passages; inhaled small particles may damage lungs
Topical	Localized action and effects; easy to self-administer	May be absorbed into general circulation
Transdermal	Controlled and prolonged absorption	Local irritation; useful only for lipid-soluble drugs
Epidural	Bypasses blood–brain barrier; very rapid effect on CNS	Not reversible; needs trained anesthesiologist; possible nerve damage

(A)

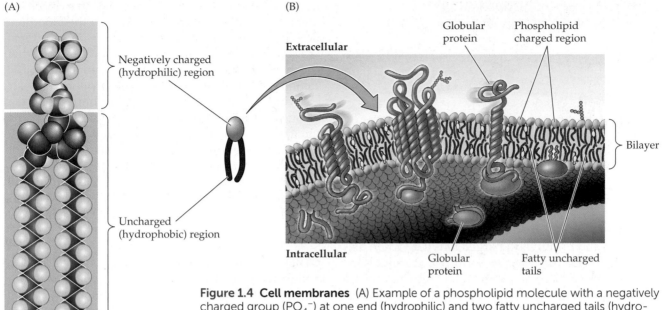

(B)

Figure 1.4 **Cell membranes** (A) Example of a phospholipid molecule with a negatively charged group (PO_4^-) at one end (hydrophilic) and two fatty uncharged tails (hydrophobic). (B) The arrangement of individual phospholipid molecules forms a bilayer, with negatively charged heads attracted to the water molecules of both intracellular and extracellular fluids. The fatty tails of the molecules are tucked within the two charged layers and have no contact with aqueous fluid. Embedded in the bilayer are protein molecules that serve as receptors or channels.

various cell layers (and their respective membranes) between the site of administration and the blood. To understand this process, we need to look more carefully at cell membranes.

Cell membranes are made up primarily of complex lipid (fat) molecules called **phospholipids**, which have a negatively charged region at one end and two uncharged lipid tails (**Figure 1.4A**). These molecules are arranged in a bilayer, with their phosphate ends forming two almost continuous sheets filled with fatty material (**Figure 1.4B**). This configuration occurs because the polar heads are attracted to the polar water molecules. Hence the charged heads are in contact with both the aqueous intracellular fluid and the aqueous extracellular fluid. Proteins that are found inserted into the phospholipid bilayer have functions that will be described later (see Chapter 3). The molecular characteristics of the cell membrane prevent most molecules from passing through unless they are soluble in fat.

LIPID-SOLUBLE DRUGS Drugs with high lipid solubility move through cell membranes by **passive diffusion**, leaving the water in the blood or stomach juices and entering the lipid layers of membranes. Movement across the membranes is always in a direction from higher to lower concentration. The larger the concentration difference on each side of the membrane (called the **concentration gradient**), the more rapid is

the diffusion. Lipid solubility increases the absorption of drug into the blood and determines how readily a drug will pass the lipid barriers to enter the brain. For example, the narcotic drug heroin is a simple modification of the parent compound morphine. Heroin, or diacetylmorphine, is more soluble in lipid than is morphine, and it penetrates into brain tissue more readily, thus having a quicker onset of action and more potent reinforcing properties.

One way to predict the relative rate of movement of a drug through cell membranes is to estimate its lipid solubility using its **partition coefficient**. To measure the coefficient, a drug first is mixed with water and then is combined with the same volume of oil or a lipid solvent such as chloroform. After settling, the oil and the water form two distinct layers, which are then separated, and the amount of drug found in each is compared. The ratio of the amount of drug dissolved in oil divided by its concentration in water is the oil/water partition coefficient. A higher concentration of drug in the oil compared with that in the water indicates greater lipid solubility and more rapid passage through cell membranes. The characteristic that determines oil/water solubility is the extent of ionization of the molecule.

IONIZED DRUGS Most drugs are not readily lipid soluble because they are weak acids or weak bases that can become ionized when dissolved in water. Just as

TABLE 1.2	pH of Body Fluids
Fluid	pH
Stomach fluid	1.0–3.0
Small intestine	5.0–6.6
Blood	7.35–7.45
Kidney urine	4.5–7.5
Saliva	6.2–7.2
Cerebrospinal fluid (CSF)	7.3–7.4

common table salt (NaCl) produces positively charged ions (Na$^+$) and negatively charged ions (Cl$^-$) when dissolved in water, many drugs form two charged (ionized) particles when placed in water. Although NaCl is a strong electrolyte, which causes it to almost entirely dissociate in water, most drugs are only partially ionized when dissolved in water. The extent of **ionization** depends on two factors: the relative acidity/alkalinity (pH) of the solution, and an intrinsic property of the molecule (pK$_a$).

Acidity or alkalinity is expressed as pH, which is described on a scale of 1 to 14, with 7 being neutral. Acidic solutions have a lower pH, and alkaline (basic) solutions have a pH greater than 7.0. Drugs are dissolved in body fluids that differ in pH (**Table 1.2**), and these differences play a role in drug ionization and movement from one body fluid compartment to another, for example, from the stomach to the bloodstream, or from the bloodstream into the kidney urine.

The second factor determining ionization is a characteristic of the drug molecule. The pK$_a$ of a drug represents the pH of the aqueous solution in which that drug would be 50% ionized and 50% non-ionized. In general, drugs that are weak acids ionize more readily in an alkaline environment and become less ionized in an acidic environment. The reverse is true of drugs that are weak bases. If we put the weak acid aspirin (acetylsalicylic acid) into stomach acid, it will remain primarily in a non-ionized form (**Figure 1.5**). The lack of electrical charge makes the drug more lipid-soluble and hence readily absorbed from the stomach to the blood. In the intestine, where the pH is around 5.0 to 6.0, ionization increases and absorption through that membrane is reduced compared with that of the stomach.

This raises the question of why aspirin molecules do not move from the stomach to the blood and back to the stomach again. In our example, aspirin in the acidic gastric fluid is primarily in non-ionized form and thus passes through the stomach wall into the blood.

In blood (pH 7.4), however, aspirin becomes more ionized; it is said to be "trapped" within the blood and does not return to the stomach. Meanwhile, the circulation moves the aspirin molecules away from their concentrated site at the stomach to maintain a concentration gradient that favors drug absorption.

Drugs that are highly charged in both acidic and basic environments are very poorly absorbed from the gastrointestinal tract and cannot be administered orally. This explains why South American hunters readily eat the flesh of game killed with curare-poisoned arrows. Curare is highly ionized in both the acidic stomach and the alkaline intestine, so the drug does not leave the digestive system to enter their blood.

OTHER FACTORS Factors other than ionization have a significant influence on absorption as well. For instance, the much larger surface area of the small intestine and the slower movement of material through the intestine, as compared with the stomach, provide a much greater opportunity for absorption of all drugs. Therefore, the rate at which the stomach empties into the intestine very often is the significant rate-limiting factor. For this reason, medication is often prescribed to be taken before meals and with sufficient fluid to move the drug through the stomach and into the intestine.

Since drug absorption is closely related to the concentration of the drug in body fluids (e.g., stomach), it should certainly be no surprise to you that the drug dosage required to achieve a desired effect is directly related to the size of the individual. In general, the larger the individual, the more diluted the drug will be in the larger fluid volume, and less drug will reach target sites within a given unit of time. The average dose of a drug is typically based on the response of individuals between the ages of 18 and 65 who weigh 150 pounds. However, for people who are very lean or obese, the average dose may be inappropriate because of variations in the ratio of fat to water in the body. For these individuals, body surface area, which reflects both size and weight, may serve as a better basis for determining drug dose. The sex of the individual also plays a part in determining plasma drug level because in the female, adipose tissue, relative to water, represents a larger proportion of the total body weight. Overall, the total fluid volume, which contains the drug, is relatively smaller in women than in men, producing a higher drug concentration at the target site in women. It should be obvious also that in the smaller fluid volume of a child, a standard dose of a drug will be more concentrated and therefore will produce a greater drug effect.

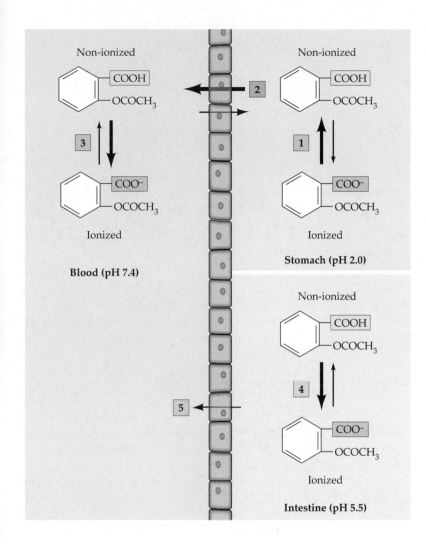

Figure 1.5 Effect of ionization on drug absorption On the right side of the cell barrier in stomach acid (pH 2.0), aspirin molecules tend to remain in the non-ionized form (1), which promotes the passage of the drug through the cell walls (2) to the blood. Once the intact aspirin molecules reach the blood (pH 7.4), they ionize (3) and are "trapped" in the blood to be circulated throughout the body. In the lower portion of the figure, when the aspirin has reached the intestine, it tends to dissociate to a greater extent (4) in the more basic pH. Its more ionized form reduces passage (5) through the cells to the blood, so absorption from the intestine is slower than from the stomach.

oxygen, glucose, and amino acids, and it carries away carbon dioxide and other waste products. Despite the vital role that blood circulation plays in cerebral function, many substances found in blood fluctuate significantly and would have disruptive effects on brain cell activity if materials were transferred freely between blood and brain (and the brain's associated cerebrospinal fluid).

Cerebrospinal fluid (**CSF**) is a clear, colorless liquid that fills the subarachnoid space that surrounds the entire bulk of the brain and spinal cord and also fills the hollow spaces (ventricles) and their interconnecting channels (aqueducts), as well as the centrally located cavity that runs longitudinally through the length of the spinal cord (central canal) (**Figure 1.6A**). CSF is manufactured by cells of the choroid plexus, which line the cerebral ventricles. In contrast to the wide fluctuations that occur in the blood plasma, the contents of the CSF remain quite stable. Many substances that diffuse out of the blood and affect other organs in the body do not seem to enter the CSF, nor do they affect brain tissue. This separation between brain capillaries and the brain/CSF constitutes what we call the blood–brain barrier. **Figure 1.6B** shows an enlargement of the relationship between the cerebral blood vessels and the CSF.

The principal component of the blood–brain barrier is the distinct morphology of brain capillaries. Figure 1.7 shows a comparison between typical capillaries found throughout the body (**Figure 1.7A**) and capillaries that serve the CNS (**Figure 1.7B**). Because the job of blood vessels is to deliver nutrients to cells while removing waste, the walls of typical capillaries are made up of endothelial cells that have both small gaps (**intercellular clefts**) and larger openings (**fenestrations**) through which molecules can pass. In addition,

Drug distribution is limited by selective barriers

Regardless of the route of administration, once the drug has entered the blood, it is carried throughout the body within 1 or 2 minutes and can have an action at any number of receptor sites. In general, those parts of the body in which blood flow is greatest will have the highest concentration of drug. Since blood capillaries have numerous pores, most drugs can move from blood and enter body tissues regardless of lipid solubility, unless they are bound to protein (see the discussion on depot binding later in this chapter). High concentrations of drugs will be found in the heart, brain, kidneys, and liver. Because the brain receives about 20% of the blood that leaves the heart, lipid-soluble drugs are readily distributed to brain tissue. However, the blood–brain barrier limits the movement of ionized molecules from the blood to the brain.

BLOOD–BRAIN BARRIER Blood plasma is supplied by a dense network of blood vessels that permeate the entire brain. This system supplies brain cells with

(A)

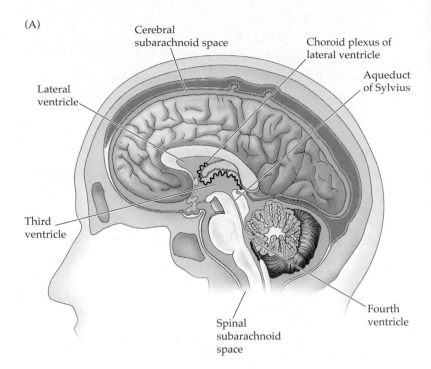

Figure 1.6 Distribution of cerebrospinal fluid (A) Cerebrospinal fluid (CSF; blue) is manufactured by the choroid plexus within the cerebral ventricles. In addition to filling the ventricles and their connecting aqueducts, CSF fills the space between the arachnoid membrane and the pia mater (sub-arachnoid space) to cushion the brain against trauma. (B) Enlarged diagram to show detail of CSF-filled subarachnoid space and its relationship to cerebral blood vessels. Note how the blood vessels penetrate the brain tissue.

(B)

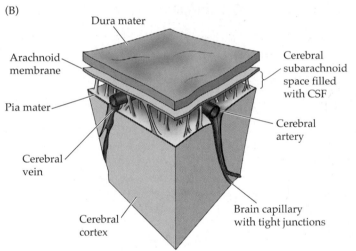

general capillaries have **pinocytotic vesicles** that envelop and transport larger molecules through the capillary wall. In contrast, in brain capillaries, the intercellular clefts are closed because adjoining edges of the endothelial cells are fused, forming **tight junctions**. Also, fenestrations are absent and pinocytotic vesicles are rare. Although lipid-soluble materials can pass through the walls of the blood vessels, most materials are moved from the blood of brain capillaries by special transporters. Surrounding brain capillaries are numerous glial feet—extensions of the glial cells called **astrocytes**. By filling in the extracellular space around capillaries, these astrocytic glial feet apparently help maintain the endothelial tight junctions. Also, it is likely that the close interface of astrocytes with both nerve cells and brain capillaries provides the astrocytes with a unique opportunity to modify neuron function.

Before we go on, we should emphasize that the blood–brain barrier is selectively permeable, not impermeable. Although the barrier does reduce diffusion of water-soluble (i.e., ionized) molecules, it does not impede lipid-soluble molecules.

Finally, the blood–brain barrier is not complete. Several brain areas are not isolated from materials in the blood. One of these is the **area postrema**, or CTZ (chemical trigger zone), which is located in the medulla of the brainstem. This area, the "vomiting center," causes vomiting when toxic substances are detected in the blood. The interaction between blood and brain is necessary to efficiently couple a toxic stimulus with the potentially lifesaving response. A second area is the **median eminence** of the hypothalamus. Capillary fenestrations in this brain region allow neurohormones manufactured by the hypothalamus to move into the blood traveling to the pituitary gland. These neurohormones, or releasing factors (e.g., growth hormone–releasing factor), regulate anterior pituitary hormone secretion. Chapter 3 discusses the hypothalamic factors more fully. A limited blood–brain barrier exists in other regions of the brain wherever a functional interaction (e.g., blood monitoring) is required between blood and neural tissue.

The limited permeability of the blood–brain barrier is important in psychopharmacology because we need to know which drugs remain non-ionized at plasma pH and readily enter the CNS, and which drugs only circulate throughout the rest of the body. Minor differences in drug molecules are responsible for the relative selectivity of drug action. For example, physostigmine readily crosses the blood–brain barrier and is useful for treating the intoxication caused by some agricultural pesticides. It does so by increasing the availability of the neurotransmitter acetylcholine. In contrast, the structurally related but highly ionized drug neostigmine is excluded from the brain and increases acetylcholine only peripherally. Its restriction by the blood–brain barrier means that neostigmine can be

(A) Typical capillary

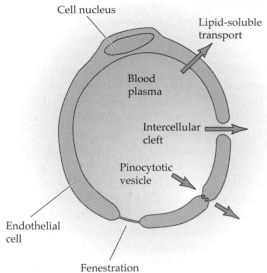

(B) Brain capillary

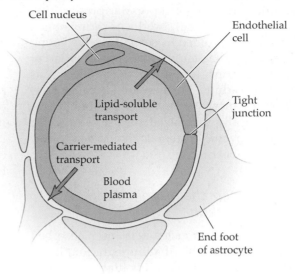

Figure 1.7 Cross section of typical capillaries and brain capillaries (A) Capillaries found throughout the body have characteristics that encourage movement of materials between the blood and surrounding cells. (B) Brain capillaries minimize movement of water-soluble molecules through the blood vessel wall because there are essentially no large or small clefts or pinocytotic sites. (After Oldendorf, 1975.)

used to treat the muscle disease myasthenia gravis without significant CNS side effects, but it would not be effective in treating pesticide-induced intoxication. As mentioned in an earlier section, because many drugs that are ionized do not pass through the blood–brain barrier, direct delivery of the drug into brain tissue by intracranial injection may be necessary.

PLACENTAL BARRIER A second barrier, unique to women, is found between the blood circulation of a pregnant mother and that of her fetus. The placenta, which connects the fetus with the mother's uterine wall, is the means by which nutrients obtained from the digestion of food, O_2, CO_2, fetal waste products, and drugs are exchanged. As is true for other cell membranes, lipid-soluble substances diffuse easily, and water-soluble substances pass less easily. The potential for transfer of drugs from mother to fetus has very important implications for the health and well-being of the developing child. Potentially damaging effects on the fetus can be divided into two categories: acute toxicity and teratogenic effects.

The fetus may experience acute toxicity in utero after exposure to the disproportionately high drug blood level of its mother. In addition, after birth, any drug remaining in the newborn's circulation is likely to have a dramatic and prolonged action because of slow and incomplete metabolism. It is well known that

opiates such as heroin readily reach the fetal circulation, and that newborn infants of heroin- or methadone-addicted mothers experience many of the signs of opiate withdrawal. Certain tranquilizers, gaseous anesthetics, alcohol, many barbiturates, and cocaine all readily pass into the fetal circulation to cause acute toxicity. In addition, alcohol, cocaine, and the carbon monoxide in cigarette smoke all deprive the fetus of oxygen. Such drugs pose special problems because they are readily accessible and are widely used.

Teratogens are agents that induce developmental abnormalities in the fetus. The effects of teratogens such as drugs (both therapeutic and illicit), exposure to X-rays, and some maternal infections (e.g., German measles) are dependent on the timing of exposure. The fetus is most susceptible to damaging effects during the first trimester of pregnancy, because it is during this period that many of the fetal organ systems are formed. Each organ system is maximally sensitive to damaging effects during its time of cell differentiation (**Table 1.3**). Many drugs can have damaging effects on the fetus despite minimal adverse effects in the

TABLE 1.3 Periods of Maximum Teratogenic Sensitivity for Several Organ Systems in the Human Fetus

Organ system	Days after fertilization
Brain	15–60
Eye	15–40
Genitalia	35–60
Heart	15–40
Limbs	25–35

mother. For example, the vitamin A–related substance isotretinoin, which is a popular prescription acne medication (Accutane), produces serious birth defects and must be avoided by sexually active young women. Experience has taught us that evaluation of drug safety must consider potential fetal effects, as well as effects on adults. Furthermore, because teratogenic effects are most severe during the time before pregnancy is typically recognized, the use of any drug known to be teratogenic in animals should be avoided by women of childbearing age.

Depot binding alters the magnitude and duration of drug action

We already know that after a drug has been absorbed into the blood from its site of administration, it circulates throughout the body. Thus high concentrations of drug may be found in all organs that are well supplied with blood. In addition to these reservoirs, drug binding occurs at inactive sites, where no measurable biological effect is initiated. Such sites, called **drug depots**, include plasma protein (e.g., albumin), muscle, and fat. Any drug molecules tied up in these depots cannot reach active sites, nor can they be metabolized by the liver. However, the drug binding is reversible, so the drug remains bound only until the blood level drops, causing it to unbind gradually and circulate in the plasma.

The binding of a drug to inactive sites (**depot binding**) has significant effects on the magnitude and duration of drug action. Some of these effects are summarized in **Table 1.4**. First, depot binding reduces the concentration of drug at its sites of action because only freely circulating (unbound) drug can pass across membranes. Onset of action of a drug that binds readily to depot sites may be delayed and its effects reduced because the number of drug molecules reaching the target tissue is dependent on its release from inactive sites. Individual differences in the amount of depot binding explain in part why some people are more sensitive than others to a particular drug.

Second, because binding to albumin, fat, and muscle is rather nonselective, many drugs with similar physiochemical characteristics compete with each other for these sites. Such competition may lead to much-higher-than-expected free drug blood level of the displaced drug, producing a drug overdose. For example, the antiseizure drug phenytoin is highly protein bound, but aspirin can displace some of the phenytoin molecules from the binding sites because aspirin binds more readily. When phenytoin is displaced from plasma protein by aspirin, the elevated drug level may be responsible for unexpected side effects or toxicity. Many psychoactive drugs, including the antidepressant fluoxetine (Prozac) and the tranquilizer diazepam (Valium), show extensive (more than 90% of the drug molecules) plasma protein binding and may contribute to drug interactions.

Third, bound drug molecules cannot be altered by liver enzymes because the drug is not free to leave the blood to enter liver cells for metabolism. For this reason, depot binding frequently prolongs the time that the drug remains in the body. This phenomenon explains why some drugs, such as THC, which is stored in fat and is only slowly released, can be detected in urine for many days after a single dose. Such slow release means that an individual could test positive for urinary THC (one active ingredient in marijuana) without experiencing cognitive effects at that time. The prolonged presence of drugs in body fat and inert depots makes preemployment and student drug testing possible.

Finally, depots may be responsible for terminating the action of a drug, as in the case of the rapid-acting CNS depressant thiopental. Thiopental, a barbiturate

TABLE 1.4 Effects of Drug Depot Binding on Therapeutic Outcome	
Depot-binding characteristics	Therapeutic outcome
Rapid binding to depots before reaching target tissue	Slower onset and reduced effects
Individual differences in amount of binding	Varying effects:
	High binding means less free drug, so some people seem to need higher doses
	Low binding means more free drug, so these individuals seem more sensitive
Competition among drugs for depot-binding sites	Higher-than-expected blood levels of the displaced drug, possibly causing greater side effects, even toxicity
Bound drug is not metabolized	Drug remains in the body for prolonged action
Binding to depots follows the rapid action at targets (redistribution)	Rapid termination of drug action

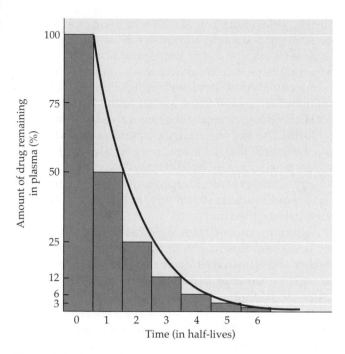

Figure 1.8 First-order kinetics of drug clearance Exponential elimination of drug from the blood occurs when clearance during a fixed time interval is always 50% of the drug remaining in blood. For example, the half-life of orally administered dextroamphetamine (Dexedrine) is approximately 10 hours. Therefore, 10 hours (1 half-life) after the peak plasma concentration has been reached, the drug concentration is reduced to about 50% of its initial value. After 20 and 30 hours (i.e., two and three half-lives) have elapsed, the concentration is reduced to 25% and 12.5%, respectively. After six half-lives, the drug is essentially eliminated, with 1.6% remaining. The curve representing the rate of clearance is steeper early on, when the rate is more rapid, and becomes more shallow as the rate of clearance decreases.

biotransformation (metabolism) of the drug and excretion of metabolites that have been formed. Drug clearance reduces blood levels and in large part determines the intensity and duration of drug effects. The easiest way to assess the rate of elimination consists of intravenously administering a drug to establish a peak plasma drug level, then collecting repeated blood samples. The decline in plasma drug concentration provides a direct measure of the clearance rate without complication by absorption kinetics.

DRUG CLEARANCE Drug clearance from the blood usually occurs exponentially and is referred to as **first-order kinetics**. Exponential elimination means that a constant *fraction* (50%) of free drug in the blood is removed during each time interval. The exponential function occurs because only a small fraction of clearance sites are occupied, so the rate is concentration dependent. Hence when blood levels are high, clearance occurs more rapidly, and as blood levels drop, the rate of clearance is reduced. The amount of time required for removal of 50% of the drug in blood is called the **half-life**, or $t_{1/2}$. **Figure 1.8** provides an example of half-life determination for the stimulant dextroamphetamine (Dexedrine), a drug used to treat attention deficit hyperactivity disorder. Although this drug is essentially eliminated after six half-lives (6 × 10 hours), many psychoactive drugs have half-lives of several days, so clearance may take weeks after even a single dose. A list of the half-lives of some common drugs is provided in **Table 1.5**.

Half-life is an important characteristic of a drug because it determines the time interval between doses. For example, because about 88% of the drug is

used for intravenous anesthesia, is highly lipid soluble; therefore, rapid onset of sedation is caused by entry of the drug into the brain. Deep sedation does not last very long because the blood level falls rapidly as a result of redistribution of the drug to other tissues, causing thiopental to move from the brain to the blood to maintain equilibrium. High levels of thiopental can be found in the brain 30 seconds after IV infusion. However, within 5 minutes, brain levels of the drug have dropped to threshold anesthetic concentrations. In this way, thiopental induces sleep almost instantaneously but is effective for only about 5 minutes, followed by rapid recovery.

Biotransformation and elimination of drugs contribute to bioavailability

Drugs are eliminated from the body through the combined action of several mechanisms, including

TABLE 1.5	Half-life of Some Common Drugs	
Drug	Trade/Street name	Half-life
Cocaine	Coke, big C, snow	0.5–1.5 hours
Morphine	Morphine	1.5–2 hours
Nicotine	Tobacco	2 hours
Methylphenidate	Ritalin	2.5–3.5 hours
THC	Marijuana	20–30 hours
Acetylsalicylic acid	Aspirin	3–4 hours
Ibuprofen	Advil	3–4 hours
Naproxen	Aleve	12 hours
Sertraline	Zoloft	2–3 days
Fluoxetine	Prozac	7–9 days

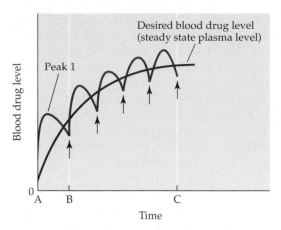

Figure 1.9 Achieving steady state plasma levels of drug
The scalloped line shows the pattern of accumulation during repeated administration of a drug. The arrows represent the times of administration. The shape of the scallop is dependent on both the rate of absorption and the rate of elimination. The smooth line represents drug accumulation in the blood during continuous intravenous infusion of the same drug.

eliminated in three half-lives, a drug given once a day should ideally have a half-life of 8 hours. A shorter half-life would mean that effective blood levels would not be maintained over 24 hours with once-a-day dosing, and this would diminish the effectiveness of the drug. Such a drug would require multiple administrations in one day or use of a sustained-release product. A half-life significantly longer than 8 hours would lead to drug accumulation because there will be drug remaining in the body when the next dose is taken. Drug accumulation increases the potential for side effects and toxicity.

The principal goal of any drug regimen is to maintain the plasma concentration of the drug at a constant desired level for a therapeutic period. However, the target therapeutic concentration is achieved only after multiple administrations. For instance, as **Figure 1.9** shows, a predictable fluctuation in blood level occurs over time as a result of the dynamic balance between absorption and clearance. After oral administration at time A, the plasma level of a drug gradually increases to its peak (peak 1) followed by a decrease because of drug biotransformation, elimination, or storage at inactive sites. If first-order kinetics is assumed, after one half-life (time B), the plasma drug level has fallen to one-half its peak value. Half-life determines the time needed to reach the **steady state plasma level**, which is the desired blood concentration of drug achieved when the absorption/distribution phase is equal to the metabolism/excretion phase. For any given daily dose of a drug, the steady state plasma level (Figure 1.9, time C) is approached after a period of time equal to five half-lives. For example, if we need

the blood level of drug X with a half-life of 4 hours to be 1000 mg, we might administer 500 mg at the outset. After 4 hours, the blood level would drop to 250 mg, at which time we could administer another 500 mg, raising the blood level to 750 mg. Four hours later, another 500 mg could be added to the current blood level of 375 mg, bringing the new value to 875 mg, and so forth. The amount of drug continues to rise until a maximum of 1000 mg is reached because more drug is given than is metabolized. However, as we reach the steady state level after approximately five half-lives, the amount administered approximates the amount metabolized (500 mg).

Although most drugs are cleared from the blood by first-order kinetics, under certain conditions some drugs are eliminated according to the zero-order model. **Zero-order kinetics** means that drug molecules are cleared at a constant rate regardless of drug concentration; this is graphically represented as a straight line (**Figure 1.10**). It happens when drug levels are high and routes of metabolism or elimination are saturated (i.e., more drug molecules are available than sites). A classic example of a drug that is eliminated by zero-order kinetics is high-dose ethyl alcohol. When two or more drinks of alcohol are consumed in a relatively short time, alcohol molecules saturate

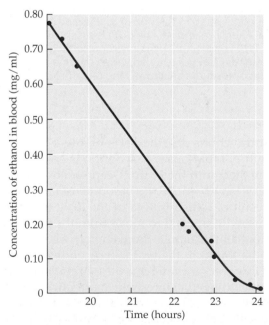

Figure 1.10 Zero-order rate of elimination The curve shows the decline of ethanol content in blood after intravenous administration of a large dose to laboratory animals. The x-axis represents the time beginning 19 hours after administration. Plotted data show the change from zero-order to first-order kinetics when low concentrations are reached between 23 and 24 hours after administration. (After Levine, 1973.)

TABLE 1.6   Varied Effects of Phase I and Phase II Metabolism

Active drug	Active metabolites and inactive metabolites[a]

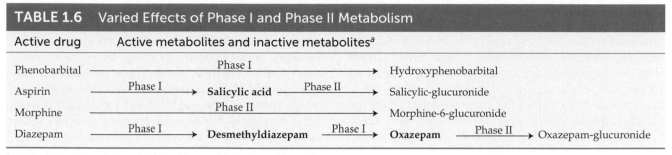

Phenobarbital — Phase I → Hydroxyphenobarbital

Aspirin — Phase I → **Salicylic acid** — Phase II → Salicylic-glucuronide

Morphine — Phase II → Morphine-6-glucuronide

Diazepam — Phase I → **Desmethyldiazepam** — Phase I → **Oxazepam** — Phase II → Oxazepam-glucuronide

[a]Bold terms indicate active metabolites.

the enzyme-binding sites (i.e., more alcohol molecules than enzyme-binding sites are present), and metabolism occurs at its maximum rate of approximately 10 to 15 ml/hour, or 1.0 ounce of 100-proof alcohol per hour regardless of concentration. The rate here is determined by the number of enzyme molecules. Any alcohol consumption that occurs after saturation of the enzyme will raise blood levels dramatically and will produce intoxication. Although zero-order biotransformation occurs at high levels of alcohol, the biotransformation rate shifts to first-order kinetics as blood levels are reduced (see Figure 1.10).

BIOTRANSFORMATION BY LIVER MICROSOMAL ENZYMES
Most drugs are chemically altered by the body before they are excreted. These chemical changes are catalyzed by enzymes and can occur in many tissues and organs, including the stomach, intestine, blood plasma, kidney, and brain. However, the greatest number of chemical changes, which we call *drug metabolism* or **biotransformation**, occur in the liver.

There are two major types of biotransformation. Type I biotransformations are sometimes called phase I because these reactions often occur before a second metabolic step. Phase I changes involve *nonsynthetic* modification of the drug molecule by oxidation, reduction, or hydrolysis. Oxidation is by far the most common reaction; it usually produces a metabolite that is less lipid soluble and less active, but it may produce a metabolite with equal or even greater activity than the parent drug. Type II, or phase II, modifications are *synthetic* reactions that require the combination (called *conjugation*) of the drug with some small molecule such as glucuronide, sulfate, or methyl groups. Glucuronide conjugation is particularly important for inactivating psychoactive drugs. These metabolic products are less lipid soluble because they are highly ionized and are almost always biologically inactive. In summary, the two phases of drug biotransformation ultimately produce one or more inactive metabolites, which are water soluble, so they can be excreted more readily than the parent drug. Metabolites formed in the liver are returned to the circulation

and are subsequently filtered out by the kidneys, or they may be excreted into bile and eliminated with the feces. Metabolites that are active return to the circulation and may have additional action on target tissues before they are further metabolized into inactive products. Obviously, drugs that are converted into active metabolites have a prolonged duration of action. **Table 1.6** shows several examples of the varied effects of phase I and phase II metabolism. The sedative drug phenobarbital is rapidly inactivated by phase I metabolism. In contrast, aspirin is converted at first to an active metabolite by phase I metabolism, but phase II action produces an inactive compound. Morphine does not undergo phase I metabolism but is inactivated by phase II reactions. Finally, diazepam (Valium), a long-lasting antianxiety drug, has several active metabolites before phase II inactivation.

The liver enzymes primarily responsible for metabolizing psychoactive drugs are located on the smooth endoplasmic reticulum, which is a network of tubules within the liver cell cytoplasm. These enzymes are often called **microsomal enzymes** because they exhibit particular characteristics on biochemical analysis. Microsomal enzymes lack strict specificity and can metabolize a wide variety of xenobiotics (i.e., chemicals that are foreign to the living organism), including toxins ingested with food, environmental pollutants, and carcinogens, as well as drugs. Among the most important liver microsomal enzymes is the **cytochrome P450 (CYP450)** enzyme family. Members of this class of enzyme, which number more than 50, are responsible for oxidizing most psychoactive drugs, including antidepressants, morphine, and amphetamines. Although they are primarily found in the liver, cytochrome enzymes are also located in the intestine, kidney, lungs, and nasal passages, where they alter foreign molecules. Enzymes are classified into families and subfamilies by their amino acid sequences, as well as by the gene encoding the protein, and they are designated by a number, a letter, and a number sequence. Among the cytochrome enzymes that are particularly important for psychotropic drug metabolism are CYP450 1A2, 3A4, and 2D6, and several in the 2C subfamily.

FACTORS INFLUENCING DRUG METABOLISM   The enzymes of the liver are of particular interest to psychopharmacologists because several factors significantly influence the rate of biotransformation. These factors alter the magnitude and duration of drug effects and are responsible for significant drug interactions. These drug interactions can either increase bioavailability, causing adverse effects, or reduce blood levels, which may reduce drug effectiveness. Additionally, variations in the rate of metabolism explain many of the individual differences seen in response to drugs. Factors that modify biotransformation capacity include the following: (1) enzyme induction; (2) enzyme inhibition; (3) drug competition; and (4) individual differences in age, gender, and genetics.

Many psychoactive drugs, when used repeatedly, cause an increase in a particular liver enzyme (called **enzyme induction**). Increased numbers of enzyme molecules not only cause the drugs to speed up their own rate of biotransformation two- to threefold, but they can also increase the rate of metabolism of all other drugs modified by the same enzyme. For example, repeated use of the antiseizure drug carbamazepine (Tegretol) increases the number of CYP450 3A4 enzyme molecules, leading to more rapid metabolism of carbamazepine and many other drugs, producing a lower blood level and a reduced biological effect. Among the drugs metabolized by the same enzyme are oral contraceptives. For this reason, if carbamazepine is prescribed to a woman who is taking oral contraceptives, the hormone dose must be increased or an alternative means of birth control used (Zajecka, 1993). When drug use is terminated, there is a gradual return to normal levels of metabolism.

Another common example is cigarette smoke, which increases CYP450 1A2 enzymes. People who are heavy smokers may need higher doses of drugs such as antidepressants and caffeine that are metabolized by the same enzyme. Such changes in drug metabolism and elimination explain in part why some drugs lose their effectiveness with repeated use—a phenomenon known as *tolerance* (see the discussion on tolerance later in the chapter); these changes also cause a reduced effect of other drugs (cross-tolerance). Clearly, drug-taking history can have a major impact on the effectiveness of the drugs that an individual currently takes.

In contrast to drug-induced induction of liver enzymes, some drugs directly inhibit the action of enzymes (**enzyme inhibition**); this reduces the metabolism of other drugs taken at the same time that are metabolized by the same enzyme. In such cases, one would experience a much more intense or prolonged drug effect and increased potential for toxicity. Monoamine oxidase inhibitors (MAOIs), used to treat depression, act in the brain by preventing the destruction of certain neurotransmitters by the enzyme monoamine oxidase (MAO). The same enzyme is found in the liver, where it normally metabolizes amines such as tyramine, which is found in red wine, beer, some cheeses, and other foods. When individuals who are taking these antidepressants eat foods rich in tyramine, dangerous high blood pressure and cardiac arrhythmias can occur, making normal foods potentially life threatening. Further detail on this side effect of MAOIs is provided in Chapter 19.

In addition, because MAOIs are not specific for MAO, they have the potential to cause adverse effects unrelated to MAO function. They inhibit several microsomal enzymes of the cytochrome P450 family, producing elevated blood levels of many drugs and potentially causing increased side effects or unexpected toxicity.

A second drug–food interaction involves the ingestion of grapefruit juice, which significantly inhibits the biotransformation of many drugs metabolized by CYP450 3A4, including numerous psychiatric medications. A single glass (5 ounces) of grapefruit juice elevates the blood levels of those drugs significantly by inhibiting their first-pass metabolism. The effect is caused by chemicals in grapefruit that are not found in oranges, such as bergamottin. Inhibition persists for 24 hours and dissipates gradually after several days, but it can be a hazard for those taking medications daily because it causes significant drug accumulation.

A second type of inhibition, based on **drug competition** for the enzyme, occurs for drugs that share a metabolic system. Because the number of enzyme molecules is limited, an elevated concentration of either drug reduces the metabolic rate of the second, causing potentially toxic levels. Cytochrome P450 metabolism of alcohol leads to higher-than-normal brain levels of other sedative–hypnotics, for example, barbiturates or Valium, when administered at the same time, producing a potentially dangerous drug interaction.

Finally, differences in drug metabolism due to genetic and environmental factors can explain why some individuals seem to be extremely sensitive to certain drugs, but others may need much higher doses than normal to achieve an effect. Over 40 years ago, the first **genetic polymorphisms** (genetic variations among individuals that produce multiple forms of a given protein) for drug-metabolizing enzymes were identified. Large variations, for instance, were found in the rate of acetylation of isoniazid, a drug used to treat tuberculosis and subsequently found to relieve depression. Acetylation is a conjugation reaction in which an acetyl group is attached to the drug. In an early experiment, blood levels of isoniazid were measured 6 hours after its oral administration

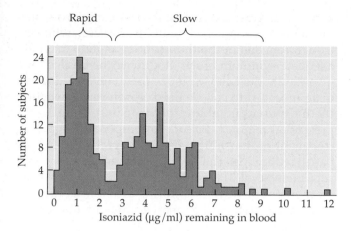

Figure 1.11 Two genetic populations for isoniazid metabolism Six hours after oral administration of isoniazid to 267 subjects, blood levels of the drug were measured. The bimodal frequency distribution shows that one sub-population of subjects consisted of rapid metabolizers who had an average of 1 µg/ml remaining in the blood. A second portion of the population included much slower metabolizers who had an average of 4 to 5 µg/ml of drug remaining. Note that several subjects had extremely slow metabolism, making them very likely to show toxic side effects, particularly if the drug were taken chronically. (After Evans, 1960.)

to 267 subjects. The bimodal distribution in **Figure 1.11** clearly shows that some individuals metabolized much of the drug during the 6 hours ("rapid inactivators"), but members of a second group ("slow inactivators") eliminated far less drug and thus are more likely to develop toxic side effects at normal doses. In addition to isoniazid, the metabolism of more than a dozen related drugs and chemicals is affected by these genetic variations. It is significant that 44% to 54% of American Caucasians and African Americans, 60% of Europeans, 10% of Asians, and only 5% of Eskimos are slow inactivators (Levine, 1973). Other enzymes also show wide genetic differences. For example, approximately 50% of certain Asian groups (Chinese, Japanese, and Koreans) have reduced capacity to metabolize acetaldehyde, which is an intermediary metabolic step in the breakdown of alcohol. The resulting elevation in acetaldehyde causes facial flushing, tachycardia, a drop in blood pressure, and sometimes nausea and vomiting. The reduced metabolic capacity is caused by a specific mutation in the gene for aldehyde dehydrogenase (Wall and Ehelers, 1995).

Along with variations in genes, other individual differences may influence metabolism. Significant changes in nutrition or in liver function, which accompany various diseases, lead to significantly higher drug blood levels and prolonged and exaggerated effects. Advanced age is often accompanied by a reduced ability to metabolize drugs, while children under the age of two also have insufficient metabolic capacity and are vulnerable to drug overdose. In addition, both the young and the elderly have reduced kidney function, so clearance of drugs for them is much slower. Gender differences in drug metabolism also exist. For example, the stomach enzymes that metabolize alcohol before it reaches the bloodstream are far less effective in women than in men. This means that for an identical dose, a woman will have a much higher concentration of alcohol reaching her blood to produce biological effects. If you would like to read more about some of the clinical concerns related to differences in drug metabolism, see Applegate (1999).

RENAL EXCRETION Although drugs can be excreted from the body in the breath, sweat, saliva, feces, or breast milk, the most important route of elimination is the urine. Therefore, the primary organ of elimination is the kidney. The kidneys are a pair of organs, each about the size of a fist. They are responsible for filtering materials out of the blood and excreting waste products. As filtered materials pass through the kidney tubules, necessary substances such as water, glucose, sodium, potassium, and chloride are reabsorbed into the blood.

Most drugs are readily filtered by the kidney unless they are bound to plasma proteins or are of large molecular size. However, because reabsorption of water from the tubules makes the drug concentration greater in the tubules than in the surrounding blood vessels, many drug molecules are reabsorbed back into the blood. Ionization of drugs reduces reabsorption because it makes the drugs less lipid soluble. Liver biotransformation of drugs into ionized (water-soluble) molecules traps the metabolites in the kidney tubules, so they can be excreted along with waste products in the urine.

Reabsorption from the tubules, similar to diffusion across other membranes (discussed earlier), is pH-dependent. When tubular urine is made more alkaline, weak acids are excreted more rapidly because they become more ionized and are not reabsorbed as well, that is, they are "trapped" in the tubular urine. If the urine is acidic, the weakly acidic drug will be less ionized and more easily reabsorbed; thus excretion will be less. The opposite is true for a weakly basic drug, which will be excreted more readily when tubular urine is acidic rather than basic. This principle of altering urinary pH is frequently used in the treatment of drug toxicity, when it is highly desirable to remove the offending drug from the body as quickly as possible. In the case of phenobarbital poisoning, for example, kidney excretion of this weakly acidic substance is greatly enhanced by alkalinization of the urine with sodium bicarbonate. This treatment leads to ionization and trapping of the drug within the tubules, from whence it is readily excreted. Acidifying the urine by administering intravenous ammonium chloride will increase the percentage of ionization of weakly basic drugs, which enhances their excretion. For example, acidifying the urine increases the rate of excretion of amphetamine and shortens the duration of a toxic overdose episode.

Therapeutic Drug Monitoring

For a drug to be clinically effective while producing minimal side effects, optimum blood levels and hence drug concentration at the target site must be maintained throughout the treatment period. Optimum blood levels are determined in clinical trials before Food and Drug Administration (FDA) approval. However, wide variation in rates of absorption, metabolism, and elimination among individuals because of differences in gender, age, genetic profile, disease state, and drug interactions can lead to significant differences in blood levels. Blood levels that are too low prevent desired clinical outcomes, and for individuals with higher-than-normal blood levels, unwanted side effects and toxicity may occur. In the future, pharmacogenetic screening of individuals (see the last section of this chapter) will allow personalized prescription of drug doses, but presently, the appropriate dosage of a drug is determined most often by the clinical response of a given individual. Under some conditions, such as for drugs with serious side effects, multiple blood samples are taken after drug administration to determine plasma levels of drug (**therapeutic drug monitoring**). Short-term blood sampling may be done to establish the optimum dosage for a patient taking a new medication. After each dosage correction by the physician, it may take some time to reach steady state (approximately five half-lives), so monitoring may continue for several days or weeks, until the optimum dosage has been determined. For drugs that must be taken over the life span, periodic monitoring may be performed regularly. Monitoring detects changes in pharmacokinetics due to aging, hormonal changes during pregnancy and menopause, stress, changes in medical condition, or addition of new medications. Many of the monitored psychotropic drugs such as antiepileptic drugs, including carbamazapine, some antidepressants, and drugs used as mood stabilizers such as lithium and valproic acid, are taken on a long-term basis.

Therapeutic drug monitoring is especially important for drugs that have a narrow therapeutic index (i.e., the dose needed for effectiveness is very similar to the dosage that causes serious side effects (see the section on pharmacodynamics). Because blood levels rise gradually to a peak and then fall to a trough just before the next administration (see Figure 1.9), drug monitoring can ensure that the peak remains below the blood level associated with toxic effects, while the trough remains in the therapeutic range to maintain adequate symptom relief. Modifying the dosage for a given individual can optimize treatment. In addition, drug monitoring can be used to determine whether the individual is taking the drug according to the prescribed regimen. Failure to comply with the drug treatment protocol often can be corrected by further patient education. The American Association for Clinical Chemistry (2011) provides additional information on therapeutic drug monitoring at www.labtestsonline.org/understanding/analytes/therapeutic_drug/glance.html.

Section Summary

- The effects of a drug are determined by (1) how much of the drug reaches its target sites, where it has biological action; and (2) how quickly the drug reaches those sites.

- Interacting pharmacokinetic factors that determine how much free drug is in the blood (bioavailability) include method of administration, rate of absorption and distribution, binding at inactive sites, biotransformation, and excretion.

- The route of administration determines both onset and duration of drug action.

- The method of administration influences absorption of the drug because it determines the area of the absorbing surface, the number of cell layers through which the drug must pass, and the extent of first-pass metabolism.

- Oral and rectal routes of administration are enteral because they involve the gastrointestinal tract; all other methods are called parenteral.

- Each method of administration provides distinct advantages and disadvantages involving rate of onset, blood level of drug achieved, duration of action, convenience, safety, and special uses.

- Absorption is dependent on method of administration, solubility and ionization of the drug, and individual differences in age, sex, and body size.

- Lipid-soluble drugs are not ionized and readily pass through fatty membranes at a rate dependent on the concentration gradient.

- Drugs that are weak acids tend to remain nonionized (lipid soluble) in acidic body fluids such as stomach juices; they are more readily absorbed there than in the more alkaline intestinal fluid. Drugs that are weak bases are more ionized in the acidic stomach fluid, so they are absorbed less readily there than from the more basic intestine, where ionization is reduced.

- Drug distribution is determined by the volume of blood flow to the tissue, but drug concentration in the CNS is limited by the blood–brain barrier that is formed by specialized brain capillaries that have few pores to allow drugs to leave the circulation. Only lipid-soluble drugs readily enter the brain.

- The placental barrier separates maternal circulation from fetal circulation, but it does not impede passage of most drug molecules.

- Drug molecules bound to inactive depots, including plasma proteins, muscle, and fat, cannot act at target sites, nor can they be metabolized, so the magnitude, onset, and duration of drug action are affected.

- Drug clearance from the blood usually occurs by first-order kinetics such that a constant fraction (50%) of the free drug is removed during each time interval. This interval is called the drug half-life. Some drugs are cleared according to zero-order kinetics, in which clearance occurs at a constant rate regardless of drug concentration.

- The steady state plasma level is the desired blood concentration of drug achieved when the absorption/distribution phase is equal to the metabolism/excretion phase. The steady state plasma level is approached after a period of time equal to five half-lives.

- Enzymatic drug metabolism or biotransformation occurs primarily in the liver and produces chemical changes in the drug molecule that make it inactive and more water soluble. The cytochrome P450 family of enzymes consists of the most important type of liver enzyme for transforming psychotropic drugs.

- Drug metabolism occurs in two steps. Phase I consists of oxidation, reduction, or hydrolysis and produces an ionized metabolite that may be inactive, equally active, or more active than the parent drug. Phase II metabolism involves conjugation of the drug with a simple molecule provided by the body, such as glucuronide or sulfate. Products of phase II metabolism are always inactive and are more water soluble.

- The kidney is most often responsible for filtration of metabolites from the blood before excretion in the urine. Alternatively, metabolites may be excreted into bile and eliminated with the feces.

- Factors that change the biotransformation rate may alter the magnitude and duration of drug effects, cause drug interactions, and explain variability in individual response to drugs. Chronic use of some drugs can induce (increase) the quantity of liver enzymes, thereby decreasing bioavailability. Drugs that inhibit liver enzymes increase the blood levels of a drug, enhancing its action. Competition among drugs for metabolism by the same enzyme increases blood levels of one or both drugs. Genetic differences and individual differences in age, sex, nutrition, and organ function may influence the rate of drug metabolism.

- Therapeutic drug monitoring involves taking multiple blood samples to directly measure plasma levels of drug after a drug has been administered. Monitoring is done to identify the optimum dosage for a patient to maximize therapeutic potential and minimize side effects. It is especially important for drugs with serious side effects, and when there are changes in an individual's pharmacokinetics due to aging, hormonal changes, stress, the addition of new medications, or other events.

Pharmacodynamics: Drug–Receptor Interactions

Pharmacodynamics is the study of the physiological and biochemical interaction of drug molecules with target tissue that is responsible for the ultimate effects of a drug. Drugs can be classified into a wide variety of categories (**Box 1.3**), but all the drugs that we are concerned with affect cell function in target tissue by acting on receptors. Knowing which receptors a drug acts on and where these receptors are located is crucial for understanding what actions and side effects will be produced.

Receptors, large protein molecules located on the surface of or within cells, are the initial sites of action of biologically active agents such as neurotransmitters, hormones, and drugs (all referred to as ligands). A **ligand** is defined as any molecule that binds to a receptor with some selectivity. Because most drugs do not readily pass into neurons, neuropharmacology most often is interested in receptors found on the outside of cells that relay information through the membrane to affect intracellular processes (**Figure 1.12A**). Which of the many possible intracellular changes occurs depends on whether the receptor is coupled with an ion channel to alter the membrane potential or with a G protein to produce longer lasting changes such as activation of an enzyme (see Chapter 3). The essential goal of neuropharmacology is to identify drugs that can act at neurotransmitter receptors to enhance or reduce normal functioning of the cell and bring about a clinically useful effect.

The second type of receptor is found within the target cell, either in the cytoplasm (e.g., glucocorticoids)

BOX 1.3   Pharmacology in Action

Drug Categories

As we learned earlier in this chapter, all drugs have multiple effects, which vary with dose and bioavailability, the nature of the receptors occupied, and the drug-taking history (e.g., tolerance) of the individual. For these reasons, drugs can be categorized in any of several classes, depending on the trait of interest. One might classify drugs according to chemical structure, medical use, legal status, neurochemical effects, abuse potential, behavioral effects, and many other categories. Amphetamine may be described as a CNS stimulant (based on increased brain activity and behavioral arousal), an anorectic used for diet control (medical use), a sympathomimetic (because it neurochemically mimics the effects of the sympathetic nervous system), or a Schedule III drug (a controlled substance based on the federal government's assessment of abuse potential). Because we are particularly interested in brain function and behavior, the classification used in this text emphasizes CNS action and behavioral effects.

CNS stimulants produce increased electrical activity in the brain and behavioral arousal, alertness, and a sense of well-being in the individual. Among drugs in this class are amphetamine, cocaine, and methylphenidate (Ritalin), as well as the methylxanthines, which include caffeine, theophylline, and theobromine. Nicotine may also be included here because of its activating effect on CNS neurons, although behaviorally for some individuals, the drug clearly has a calming effect. Classification is complicated by the fact that drug effects are dose dependent, and drugs occasionally produce dramatically different effects at different doses. Low and moderate doses of amphetamine, for example,

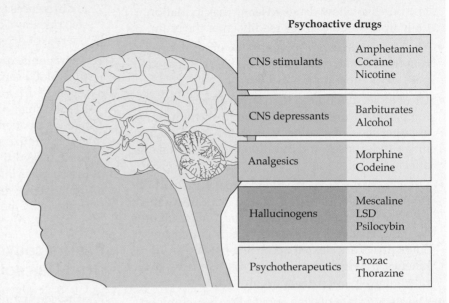

Psychoactive drugs

CNS stimulants	Amphetamine Cocaine Nicotine
CNS depressants	Barbiturates Alcohol
Analgesics	Morphine Codeine
Hallucinogens	Mescaline LSD Psilocybin
Psychotherapeutics	Prozac Thorazine

stimulate physical activity, but at high doses, locomotion may be reduced and replaced by meaningless stereotyped, repetitive acts that have clear psychotic characteristics.

CNS depressants include a variety of drugs that depress CNS function and behavior to cause a sense of relaxation and drowsiness. Some of the sedative–hypnotics are useful for these sedating qualities and in their ability to relieve anxiety or induce sleep. At high doses, more profound mental clouding occurs, along with loss of coordination, intoxication, and coma. Significant drugs in this group include the barbiturates (such as Seconal), the benzodiazepines (including Valium), and ethyl alcohol, all of which will be considered in later chapters. Some might include marijuana in this class because of its relaxing and depressant qualities at low doses, although at higher doses, hallucinogenic characteristics may occur prominently.

Analgesics are drugs that frequently have CNS-depressant qualities, although their principal effect

is to reduce the perception of pain. The most important drugs in this class are the narcotics. Narcotics, or opiates, such as morphine or codeine are derived from the opium poppy; the synthetic narcotics (sometimes called *opioids*) include heroin, meperidine (Demerol), methadone, and fentanyl. All opiate-like drugs produce relaxation and sleep, as well as analgesia. Under some circumstances, these drugs also produce a powerful sense of euphoria and a desire to continue drug administration. Non-narcotic analgesics, of course, also belong in this class but have little effect on behavior and do not produce relaxation or sleep. They include aspirin, acetaminophen (Tylenol), and ibuprofen (Motrin).

Hallucinogens, or mind-altering drugs, are often called "psychedelics" because their primary effect is to alter one's perceptions, leading to vivid visual illusions or distortions of objects and body image. As a group, these drugs produce a wide variety of effects on brain chemistry and neural activity. They

BOX 1.3 *(continued)*

include many naturally occurring substances such as mescaline and psilocybin. Certainly, LSD belongs in this class, as does MDMA (street name: "ecstasy"). The drug PCP (street name: "angel dust") and its analog ketamine (street name: "special K"), which is used as an animal sedative, might belong in the class of CNS depressants, but their ability to cause profound hallucinogenic experiences and their use as a model for psychotic behavior prompt their placement in this category.

Psychotherapeutic drugs as a classification is intended to suggest that some psychoactive drugs are used almost entirely to treat clinical disorders of mood or behavior:

antipsychotics, antidepressants, and mood stabilizers. These drugs have distinctly different mechanisms of action and are rarely used outside the therapeutic realm. Antipsychotics reduce symptoms of schizophrenia, including hallucinations and bizarre behavior. Examples include haloperidol (Haldol) and chlorpromazine (Thorazine). Antidepressants also belong in this classification; they are used to treat disorders of mood. Among the most familiar are amitriptyline (Elavil), sertraline (Zoloft), and fluoxetine (Prozac). Although drugs in this class do reverse the symptoms of clinical depression, they do not produce the effects of CNS stimulants nor do they produce euphoria. Finally,

mood stabilizers reduce the dramatic mood swings between mania and depression that characterize bipolar disorder. Lithium carbonate (Lithonate) is still most often prescribed, but valproate (Depakote) and carbamazepine (Tegretol) are increasingly popular. Each of these types of drugs will be described in subsequent chapters of this text.

Clearly, many of the drugs you may be interested in have not been mentioned: hormones such as the anabolic steroids and contraceptives, inhalants including household products and glues, and others. Many of these would require special categories for classification, but this text addresses some of those topics in Chapter 16.

---

or in the nucleus (e.g., sex steroid receptors). Most of the hormones that act on the brain to influence neural events use this type of receptor. Hormonal binding to intracellular receptors alters cell function by triggering changes in expression of genetic material within the nucleus, producing differences in protein synthesis (**Figure 1.12B**). Sex hormones act in this way to facilitate mating behavior and other activities related to reproduction, such as lactation. This mechanism is described more fully in Chapter 3.

Extracellular and intracellular receptors have several common features

Several characteristics are common among receptors in general. The ability to recognize specific molecular shapes is one very important characteristic. The usual analogy of a lock and key suggests that only a limited

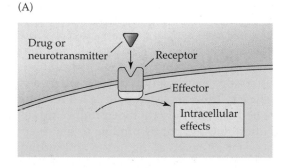

Figure 1.12 Two principal types of receptors (A) Most drugs and neurotransmitters remain outside the cell and bind to receptors on the exterior cell surface. When these receptors are activated, they initiate changes in an effector causing intracellular changes such as movement of ions or changes in enzyme activity. (B) Many hormones are capable of entering the cell before acting on an intracellular receptor that changes the expression of specific genes within the nucleus. The altered protein synthesis in turn leads to changes in cell function that may include altering gluconeogenesis, modulating the menstrual cycle, and others.

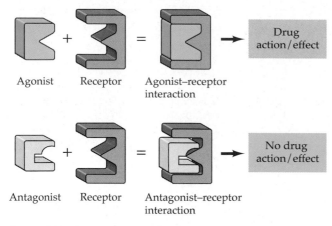

Agonist   Receptor   Agonist–receptor
                     interaction

Drug
action/effect

Antagonist   Receptor   Antagonist–receptor
                       interaction

No drug
action/effect

Figure 1.13 Agonist and antagonist interactions with receptors The agonist molecule has an excellent fit for the receptor (high affinity) and produces a significant biological response (high efficacy). The antagonist in this case fits less well and has very low efficacy. Note that if both the agonist and the antagonist are present simultaneously, they will compete to fit into the same receptor, producing a partial drug effect. (After Carroll, 1996.)

group of neurochemicals or drugs can bind to a particular receptor protein to initiate a cellular response. These neurochemicals are called **receptor agonists**. Molecules that have the best chemical "fit" (i.e., have the highest **affinity**) attach most readily to the receptor. However, just as one may put a key in a lock but may not be able to turn the key, so too a ligand may be recognized by a receptor, but it may not initiate a biological action. Such ligands are considered to have low **efficacy**. These molecules are called **receptor antagonists** because not only do they produce no cellular effect after binding, but by binding to the receptor, they prevent an "active" ligand from binding; hence they "block" the receptor (**Figure 1.13**). **Partial agonists** demonstrate efficacy that is less than that of full agonists, but more than that of an antagonist at a given receptor. Finally, when **inverse agonists** bind to a receptor, they initiate a biological action, but it is an action that is opposite to that produced by an agonist. Hence drugs can vary in efficacy along a continuum, ranging from full agonist action with maximal efficacy to partial agonist action to the inactive antagonist to partial inverse agonists with some inverse efficacy to full inverse agonists that show maximal inverse

efficacy (**Figure 1.14**). The importance of these distinctions will become apparent in later chapters as we discuss specific drug classes.

We should mention here that drugs can show agonist action in ways other than by activating a receptor. In this more general sense, drugs are agonists if they enhance synaptic function by increasing neurotransmitter synthesis or release, or by prolonging the action of the neurotransmitter within the synapse. Likewise, drugs that show antagonist action may do so by reducing neurotransmitter synthesis or release, or by terminating the action of the neurotransmitter more quickly. These actions will be described more fully in Chapter 3.

A second significant feature of receptors is that binding or attachment of the specific ligand is temporary. When the ligand dissociates (i.e., separates) from the receptor, it has opportunities to attach once again.

Third, ligands binding to the receptor produce a physical change in the three-dimensional shape of the protein, thus initiating a series of intracellular events that ultimately generate a biobehavioral effect. How much intracellular activity occurs depends on the number of interactions with the receptor and the ability of the ligand to alter the shape of the receptor, which reflects its efficacy.

Fourth, although we tend to think about receptors as a permanent characteristic of cells, these proteins in fact have a life cycle just as other cell proteins do. Not only is there a normal life span for receptors, but receptors are modified both in number (long-term regulation) and in sensitivity (more rapid regulation via second messengers). Long-term regulation, called **up-regulation** when receptor numbers increase, or **down-regulation** when receptors are reduced in number, reflects compensatory changes after prolonged absence of receptor agonists or chronic activation of the receptor, respectively. This phenomenon was initially observed in muscle, where it was found that if the nerve serving a particular muscle was cut (thereby eliminating release of the neurotransmitter from the nerve endings), a compensatory increase in neurotransmitter receptors occurred over the muscle surface. Recently, the same phenomenon has been found to occur in the CNS, not only when nerves are severed, but also when nerve activity is chronically reduced by drugs. For instance, chronic use of

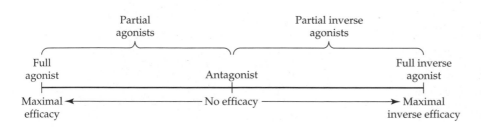

Partial
agonists

Partial inverse
agonists

Full
agonist

Antagonist

Full inverse
agonist

Maximal
efficacy

No efficacy

Maximal
inverse efficacy

Figure 1.14 Continuum of drug efficacy Independent of affinity, drugs can vary in efficacy along a continuum from full agonist action having maximum efficacy to antagonist action with no efficacy to full inverse agonist efficacy. Partial agonists and partial inverse agonists fall in between.

receptor antagonists leads to subsequent up-regulation of receptors. Likewise, drugs that activate a nerve pathway or that act as agonists at the receptor cause a reduction in receptor proteins if they are administered repeatedly. In each case, the change in receptor number requires 1 to 2 weeks of altered activity. Change in sensitivity due to second messenger–induced function is far more rapid. These changes will be discussed more fully in Chapter 3.

Finally, we have already learned that once drugs are absorbed, they are distributed throughout the body, where multiple sites of action (receptors) mediate different biobehavioral effects. However, the receptor proteins of a given drug may have different characteristics in different target tissues. These varied receptors, called **receptor subtypes**, will be discussed more extensively later in the book. The goal of neuropharmacology is to design drugs that bind with greater affinity to one receptor subtype so as to initiate a highly selective therapeutic effect, without acting on related receptor subtypes and producing side effects. For instance, **Figure 1.15** shows the three mildly stimulant drugs caffeine, theophylline, and theobromine, all of which belong to the xanthine class and have noticeably similar structures. However, subtle differences in structure are responsible for differences in the magnitude of biological effects, depending on which xanthine receptor subtypes they bind to most effectively. You can see in **Table 1.7** that caffeine is more effective at the xanthine receptor subtype in the CNS to produce alertness than

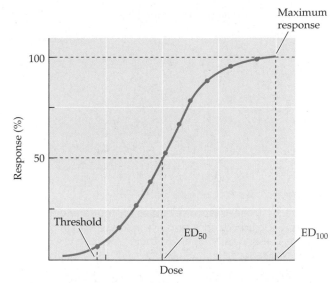

Figure 1.16 **Dose–response curve** The classic S-shape describes the gradual increase in biological response that occurs with increasing doses of a drug (drug–receptor activation). Threshold is the dose that produces the smallest measurable response. The dose at which the maximum response is achieved is the ED_{100} (100% effective dose), and the ED_{50} is the dose that effectively produces 50% of the maximum response.

are xanthines found in tea (theophylline) or cocoa (theobromine). In contrast, theophylline is the most active of the three in stimulating the heart and causing increased urine output (diuresis).

Dose–response curves describe receptor activity

One important method used to evaluate receptor activity is the **dose–response curve**, which describes the extent of biological or behavioral effect (response) produced by a given drug concentration (dose). A typical curve is shown in **Figure 1.16**. When plotted on a semilog scale, the curve takes on a classic S-shape. At

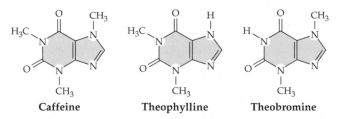

Figure 1.15 **Chemical structures** of the xanthines caffeine, theophylline, and theobromine.

TABLE 1.7 Relative Biological Activity[a] of Xanthines[b]			
Biological effects	Caffeine	Theophylline	Theobromine
CNS stimulation	1	2	3
Cardiac stimulation	3	1	2
Respiratory stimulation	1	2	3
Skeletal muscle stimulation	1	2	3
Diuresis	3	1	2

Source: Ritchie, 1975.

[a]Each drug acts more effectively on some xanthine receptor subtypes than others. 1 = most active; 3 = least active.

[b]Derivatives of xanthine are a group of alkaloids used as mild stimulants and bronchodilators.

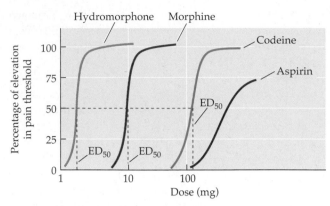

Figure 1.17 Dose–response curves for four analgesic agents Each curve represents the increase in pain threshold (the magnitude of painful stimulus required to elicit a withdrawal response) as a function of dose. ED_{50} doses for hydromorphone, morphine, and codeine help in comparisons of potency. The linear portions of the curves for the opiate analgesics are parallel, suggesting that they work through the same mechanism. Aspirin is not an opiate and relieves pain by a very different mechanism of action, so the shape of the curve is distinct. In addition, the maximum effectiveness of aspirin never reaches the level of the opiates. (After Levine, 1973.)

low doses, the drug-induced effect is slight because very few receptors are occupied. In fact, the threshold dose is the smallest dose that produces a measurable effect. As the dose of the drug is increased, more receptors are activated, and a greater biological response occurs. The ED_{50} (50% effective dose) is the dose that produces half the maximal effect, and maximum response occurs at a dose at which we assume the receptors are fully occupied[1] (we might call it the ED_{100}).

If we were to graph the effects of several pain-relieving drugs, we might find a relationship similar to the one shown in **Figure 1.17**. The first three curves show the dose–response characteristics for hydromorphone, morphine, and codeine—all drugs from the opiate analgesic class. For each drug, increasing the concentration produces greater analgesia (elevation in pain threshold) until the maximum response is achieved. The absolute amount of drug necessary to produce a specific effect indicates the **potency** of the drug. Differences in potency among these three drugs can be seen by comparing the ED_{50} across all of them. Hydromorphone requires approximately 2 mg, morphine needs 10 mg to achieve the same effect, and

codeine needs more than 100 mg. Therefore, morphine is more potent than codeine, and hydromorphone is more potent than either. The relative position of the curves on the *x*-axis indicates potency and reflects the affinity of each drug for the receptor that mediates the measured response. Although the three differ in affinity for the receptor, each reaches the same maximum on the *y*-axis, indicating that they have identical efficacy. The fact that the linear portions of the curves are parallel to one another indicates that they are working by the same mechanism. Although the concept of potency provides some means of comparison, its practical use is limited. As you can see, a lower-potency drug is frequently just as effective and requires only a somewhat higher dose. If the low-potency drug also produces fewer side effects or is less expensive, then it may in fact be the preferred drug. You might consider these issues the next time a drug advertisement makes claims for being the most potent of its kind available.

Figure 1.17 also shows the dose–response curve for aspirin. In contrast to the first three drugs, aspirin is not an opioid, and the distinctive shape of its dose–response curve indicates that although aspirin may relieve pain, it does not act on the same receptors, or work by the same mechanism. In addition, regardless of how much aspirin is administered, it never achieves the same efficacy as the opiates.

The therapeutic index calculates drug safety

Among the multiple responses to any drug, some are undesirable or even dangerous side effects that need to be evaluated carefully in a therapeutic situation. For example, **Figure 1.18** depicts three distinct pharmacological effects produced by drug A, which is prescribed to reduce anxiety. The blue curve shows the percent of individuals who experience reduced anxiety at various doses of the drug. The purple curve shows the percent of persons suffering respiratory depression (a toxic effect) from various doses of the same drug. By comparing the ED_{50} for relieving anxiety (i.e., the dose at which 50% of the population shows reduced anxiety) and the TD_{50} (50% toxic dose; the dose at which 50% of the population experiences a particular toxic effect) for respiratory depression, you can see that for most individuals, the toxic dose is much higher than the dose that produces the desired effect. An alternative interpretation is that at the dose needed to provide significant clinical relief for many patients (50%), almost none of the patients would be likely to experience respiratory depression. Therefore, pharmacologists would say that the drug has a relatively favorable **therapeutic index** ($TI = TD_{50}/ED_{50}$). In contrast, the dose of drug A that produces sedation and mental clouding (red curve) is not very

---

[1]This assumption is not warranted in all cases, however, as can be seen in those models of receptor pharmacology that describe "spare receptors." Readers interested in the complexities of receptor occupancy theory should refer to a standard textbook in pharmacology.

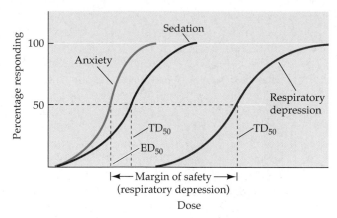

Figure 1.18 Comparison of ED$_{50}$ and TD$_{50}$ The therapeutic index (TI) is calculated by comparing the dose of drug required to produce a toxic effect in 50% of individuals (TD$_{50}$) with the dose that is effective for 50% (ED$_{50}$). Each drug may have several therapeutic indices based on its toxic effects or side effects of concern. Because the optimum condition is to have a drug that is effective at a low dose with no toxicity except at very high doses, the TI will be large for a safer drug. The figure shows a large margin of safety for an antianxiety drug that can produce respiratory depression.

different from the ED$_{50}$. This small difference means that the probability is high that a dose that is effective in reducing anxiety is likely to also produce significant mental clouding and sedation, which may represent serious side effects for many people who might use the drug.

Receptor antagonists compete with agonists for binding sites

We have already introduced the concept of receptor antagonists as those drugs that compete with agonists to bind to receptors but fail to initiate an intracellular effect, thereby reducing the effects of the agonists. These are called **competitive antagonists**. As the name implies, they can be displaced from those sites by an excess of the agonist, because an increased concentration of active drug can compete more effectively for the fixed number of receptors. A simple example will clarify. If we assume that the agonist and the antagonist have similar affinities for the receptor, then if both 100 molecules of drug and 100 molecules of antagonist were present at the receptor, the probability of an agonist acting on the receptor would be 1 to 1. If agonist molecules were increased to 1000, the odds of agonist binding rise to 10 to 1; at 1,000,000 agonist molecules, the odds favor agonist binding by 10,000 to 1. Certainly at this point, the presence of the antagonist is of no consequence for the biobehavioral effect as measured.

Figure 1.19A illustrates the effect of a competitive antagonist, naloxone, on the analgesic effect of morphine. The blue line shows a typical dose–response curve for the analgesic effect of morphine. When subjects were pretreated with naloxone, the dose–response curve shifted to the right (red line), demonstrating that for any given dose of morphine, naloxone-pretreated subjects showed less analgesia. The addition of naloxone diminished the potency of morphine. The figure also shows that the inhibitory action of naloxone was overcome by increasing the amount of morphine administered, that is, the same maximum effect (analgesia) was achieved, but more morphine was required. If you look at the chemical structures of the two drugs in Figure 11.3, you will see the striking similarity and will understand how the two drugs compete to be recognized by the same receptor protein.

(A)

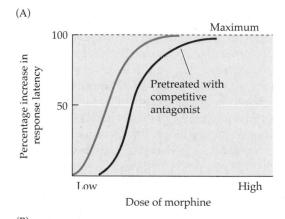

(B)

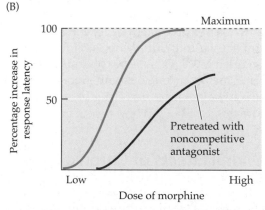

Figure 1.19 Drug antagonism (A) The effect of a competitive antagonist (naloxone) on the analgesic effect of morphine. The addition of a competitive antagonist essentially reduces the potency of the agonist, as is shown by the parallel shift of the dose–response curve to the right. (B) In contrast, adding a noncompetitive antagonist usually produces a distinct change in the shape of the dose–response curve, indicating that it does not act at the same receptor site. Also, regardless of the increase in morphine, the maximum efficacy is never reached.

We have emphasized receptor antagonism because, in combination with the concept of dose dependency, it is a vital tool in pharmacology. If we want to know whether a specific ligand–receptor interaction is responsible for a particular biological effect, the biological effect must be shown to occur in proportion to the amount of ligand present (dose) and, furthermore, the effect must be reduced in the presence of a competitive antagonist.

Of course, other types of antagonism can occur. **Noncompetitive antagonists** are drugs that reduce the effects of agonists in ways other than competing for the receptor. For example, a noncompetitive antagonist may impair agonist action by binding to a portion of the receptor other than the agonist binding site, by disturbing the cell membrane supporting the receptor, or by interfering with the intracellular processes that were initiated by the agonist–receptor association. **Figure 1.19B** illustrates the effect of a noncompetitive antagonist on the analgesic effect of morphine. In general, the shape of the dose–response curve will be distorted, and the same maximum effect is not likely to be reached.

Furthermore, although pharmacologists are concerned with molecular actions at the receptor, biobehavioral interactions can result in several different possible outcomes. **Physiological antagonism (Figure 1.20A)** involves two drugs that act in two distinct ways but interact in such a way that they reduce each other's effectiveness in the body. For example, one drug may act on receptors in the heart to increase heart rate, and the second may act on distinct receptors in the brainstem to slow heart rate. Clearly, two agents may have **additive effects** if the outcome equals the sum of the two individual effects (**Figure 1.20B**). Finally, **potentiation** refers to the situation in which the combination of two drugs produces effects that are greater than the sum of their individual effects (**Figure 1.20C**). Potentiation often involves issues of pharmacokinetics such as altered metabolic rate or competition for depot binding, which may elevate free drug blood levels in unexpected ways.

Biobehavioral Effects of Chronic Drug Use

Many prescription and over-the-counter drugs are taken on a regular basis for chronic medical or psychiatric conditions. These drugs are taken for periods of weeks, months, or even years. Recreational drugs are most often used repeatedly rather than on only a single occasion. When a drug is used on several occasions (i.e., chronically administered), changes in the magnitude of response to the drug frequently occur. Most often, the response diminishes with chronic use

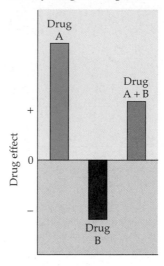

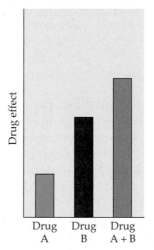 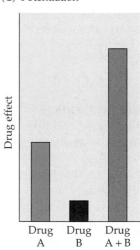

Figure 1.20 Possible results of the interaction of two drugs (A) Physiological antagonism results when two drugs produce opposite effects and reduce each other's effectiveness. (B) Additive effects are seen when the combined drug effect equals the sum of each drug alone. (C) Potentiation is said to occur when combined drug effects are greater than the sum of individual drug effects.

(tolerance), but occasionally, the effects are increased (sensitization). In some cases, selected effects of a particular drug decrease while others increase in magnitude, as is true for the stimulant drug amphetamine. It should be clear that an individual's drug-taking history has a significant influence on drug action.

Repeated drug exposure can cause tolerance

Drug **tolerance** is defined as a diminished response to drug administration after repeated exposure to that drug. In other words, tolerance has developed when

TABLE 1.8   Significant Characteristics of Tolerance
Reversible when drug use stops
Dependent on dose and frequency of drug use and drug-taking environment
May occur rapidly, after long periods of chronic use, or never
Not all effects of a drug show the same degree of tolerance
Several different mechanisms explain multiple forms of tolerance

increasingly larger doses of a given drug must be administered to obtain the same magnitude of biological effect that occurred with the original dose. Development of tolerance to one drug can diminish the effectiveness of a second drug. This phenomenon, called **cross-tolerance**, serves as the basis for a number of drug interactions. For example, the effective anticonvulsant dose of phenobarbital is significantly larger in a patient who has a history of chronic alcohol use than in a patient who has not developed tolerance to alcohol.

CHARACTERISTICS OF TOLERANCE   Although the appearance of tolerance varies, several general features are worth mentioning. These characteristics are summarized in **Table 1.8**. First, as is true for biological processes in general, tolerance is reversible; that is, it gradually diminishes if use of the drug is stopped. Additionally, the extent of tolerance that develops is dependent on the pattern of drug administration; that is, the dose and frequency of drug use, as well as the environment in which it occurs. Chronic heroin users may take as much as 1800 mg without ill effects,

despite the fact that the lethal range for a novice heroin user is 200 to 400 mg.

However, regardless of dose and frequency, some drugs induce tolerance relatively rapidly (LSD), while others require weeks of chronic use (barbiturates) or never cause significant tolerance (antipsychotics). In some cases, tolerance even develops during a single administration, as when an individual experiences significantly greater effects of alcohol as his blood level rises than he experiences several hours later, when his blood level has fallen to the same point. This form of tolerance is called **acute tolerance**.

It is important to be aware that not all biobehavioral effects of a particular drug demonstrate tolerance equally. For example, morphine-induced nausea and vomiting show rapid development of tolerance, but the constipating effects of the drug rarely diminish even after long-term use. Sometimes the uneven development of tolerance is beneficial, as when tolerance develops for the side effects of a drug but not for its therapeutic effects. At other times, the uneven development of tolerance poses a hazard, as when the desired effects of a drug diminish, requiring increased doses, but the lethal or toxic effects do not show tolerance. Chronic barbiturate use is one such example. As more drug is taken to achieve the desired effect, the dose gets increasingly close to the lethal dose that causes respiratory depression.

Finally, several types of tolerance may occur and have distinct mechanisms. Although some drugs never induce tolerance at all, others may cause several types of tolerance (refer to **Table 1.9** for examples). The three principal forms are metabolic tolerance, pharmacodynamic tolerance, and behavioral tolerance. A fourth type, called acute tolerance, has already been described earlier in this chapter.

TABLE 1.9 Types of Tolerance Exhibited by Selected Drugs[a]			
Drug or drug class	Metabolic tolerance	Pharmacodynamic tolerance	Behavioral tolerance
Barbiturates	+	+	+
Alcohol	+	+	+
Morphine	+	+	+
Amphetamine	−	+	+
Cocaine	−	+	+
Caffeine	−	+	?
Nicotine	−	+	?
LSD	−	+	−

[a]+ indicates the drug produces the type of tolerance indicated; − indicates that the drug does not produce the indicated type of tolerance; ? indicates evidence is mixed regarding whether the drug produces the indicated type of tolerance.

METABOLIC TOLERANCE (DRUG DISPOSITION TOLER-ANCE)   **Drug disposition tolerance**, or **metabolic tolerance**, occurs when repeated use of a drug reduces the amount of that drug that is available at the target tissue. The most common form of drug disposition tolerance occurs when drugs increase their own rate of metabolism. It is clear that many drugs are capable of liver microsomal enzyme induction (see the discussion on biotransformation earlier in this chapter), which results in increased metabolic capacity. A more efficient metabolism reduces the amount of drug available to target tissue and diminishes drug effects. All drugs metabolized by the induced enzyme family will likewise show a reduced effect (cross-tolerance). Drug disposition tolerance requires repeated administration over time for protein synthesis to build new enzyme proteins. Well-documented examples of inducers of liver enzymes such as cytochrome P450 include drugs from many classes, including the sedative phenobarbital, the antibiotic rifampicin, the antiseizure medication phenytoin, cigarette smoke, and anabolic steroids.

PHARMACODYNAMIC TOLERANCE   The most dramatic form of tolerance that develops to the central actions of certain drugs cannot be explained on the basis of altered metabolism or altered concentration of drug reaching the brain. **Pharmacodynamic tolerance** occurs when changes in nerve cell function compensate for continued presence of the drug. In an earlier section, we described the normal response to chronic receptor activation as receptor down-regulation. Once receptors have down-regulated, a given amount of drug will have fewer receptors to act on, and therefore will produce less of a biological effect. Compensatory up-regulation (increased receptor number) occurs in cases in which receptor activation is chronically reduced. Other cellular adjustments to chronic drug use will be described in later chapters that focus on individual agents such as ethanol, amphetamine, caffeine, and others.

BEHAVIORAL TOLERANCE   Although many instances of tolerance can be attributed to cell physiology and chemistry, a behavioral component involving learning and adaptation has been demonstrated by numerous investigators. **Behavioral tolerance** (sometimes called *context-specific tolerance*) is seen when tolerance occurs in the same environment in which the drug was administered, but tolerance is not apparent or is much reduced in a novel environment. Several types of learning (classical conditioning and operant conditioning) may play a part in the development of behavioral tolerance, as well as in the withdrawal syndrome characteristic of physical dependence (see Chapter 9).

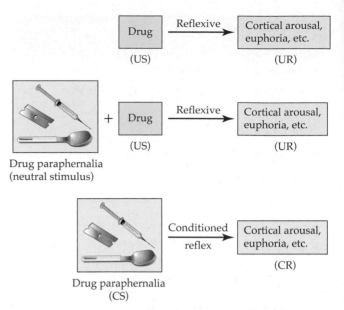

Figure 1.21 Classical conditioning of drug-related cues   Although drug-taking equipment and the immediate environment initially serve as a meaningless stimulus for the individual, their repeated pairing with the drug (unconditioned stimulus; US), which naturally elicits euphoria, arousal, or other desirable effects (unconditioned response; UR), gives the drug-taking equipment new meaning. Ultimately, the equipment and the environment alone (now a conditioned stimulus; CS) could elicit drug effects (conditioned response; CR) in the absence of the drug.

Pavlovian, or **classical conditioning** plays an important role in drug use and in tolerance. In the original experiments with Pavlov's dogs, the meaningless bell (neutral stimulus) was presented immediately before the meat (unconditioned stimulus) was presented, which elicited reflexive salivation (unconditioned response). After repeated pairings, the bell took on the characteristic of a conditioned stimulus, because when presented alone, it could elicit salivation—now a conditioned response. Since many psychoactive drugs elicit reflexive effects such as cortical arousal, elevated blood pressure, or euphoria, they can act as unconditioned stimuli, and the drug-taking procedure or stimuli in the environment may become conditioned stimuli that elicit a conditioned response even before the drug is administered (**Figure 1.21**). These results may explain why the various rituals and procedures of drug procurement and use may elicit reinforcing effects similar to those produced by the drug itself. An example of this phenomenon is the "needle freak," who by the act of injection alone derives significant morphine-like effects. Why the conditioned response is similar to the unconditioned response in some cases and different from (even opposite) the unconditioned response in other cases is not entirely clear. Nevertheless, both occurrences are well documented.

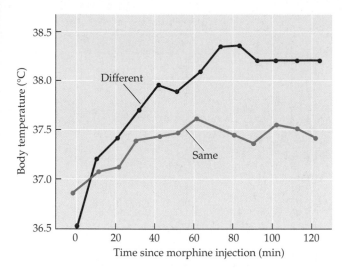

Figure 1.22 Tolerance to morphine-induced hyperthermia After an identical series of prior morphine injections (5 mg/kg SC for 10 days), rats were tested with a morphine injection, and changes in body temperature were measured for the next 2 hours. One group of rats was given morphine in the same environment in which they were previously treated ("Same"), and the second group was tested in a novel environment ("Different"). Animals treated in the same environment show much less hyperthermia; this indicates tolerance. (After Siegel, 1978.)

Siegel (1985) suggests that tolerance is due at least in part to the learning of an association between the effects of a given drug and the environmental cues that reliably precede the drug effects. For development of tolerance, the "anticipatory" response (conditioned response) must be compensatory in nature; that is, the environment associated with administration of the drug elicits physiological responses opposite to the effect of the drug. For instance, in animals repeatedly experiencing the hyperthermic effects of injected morphine, the injection procedure alone *in the same environment* leads to a compensatory drop in body temperature. **Figure 1.22** shows the results of a study of two groups of rats given an identical course of morphine injections (5 mg/kg SC for 10 days), which would normally produce evidence of tolerance to the hyperthermic effect. On test day, rats given morphine in the identical environment (the "Same" animals) showed the expected decrease in hyperthermia—an indication of tolerance. Animals given morphine in a novel environment (the "Different" animals) did not show the same extent of tolerance. The conclusion drawn is that classically conditioned environmental responses contribute to the development of tolerance to morphine. Some researchers believe that environmentally induced tolerance may explain why addicts who use their drug in a new environment or who alter their drug-taking routine may suddenly show much

greater response to the same dose of the drug they had used the day before. This phenomenon may explain at least some of the fatal drug overdoses that occur each year. Although environment is clearly significant in drug tolerance, keep in mind that neural changes that underlie learning or behavioral tolerance are subtle alterations in physiology that may be similar to pharmacodynamic tolerance.

The appearance of tolerance to a psychoactive drug is often manifested in a task in which **operant conditioning** plays some part. For example, Leblanc et al. (1976) showed that administration of alcohol (2.5 g/kg IP) to rats initially disrupted the performance of traversing a moving belt, but repeated administrations had less and less effect. The improved performance could be identified as a type of tolerance, but the apparent tolerance could be due to learning of a new skill (the ability to run a treadmill while under the influence of the drug), which we would expect to improve with practice. How do we know that the improvement is not due to changes in metabolic rate or to pharmacodynamic tolerance? The answer can be found by adding a second group of animals, which had the same number of alcohol treatments and the same number of practice sessions on the treadmill, but the drug was administered *after* each practice session. If tolerance in the first group was due to metabolic changes, the extent of tolerance in the two groups should have been identical, but in fact, the second group showed significantly less tolerance. The same type of tolerance is demonstrated by the alcoholic individual who learns to maneuver fairly efficiently while highly intoxicated to avoid detection, whereas a less experienced alcohol abuser with the same blood alcohol level may appear behaviorally to be highly intoxicated.

Vogel-Sprott developed these ideas further by suggesting that if tolerance were due to learning, then reinforcement of a compensatory response to the drug effect should be necessary for tolerance to develop. In a series of experiments, subjects given ethyl alcohol were monetarily rewarded when their motor skill task performance while intoxicated matched their scores while sober. Under these conditions, researchers measured rapid development of tolerance through repeated drinking sessions for subjects who were given feedback about their performance (i.e., how their score compared with their nonalcohol score) and monetary reward; they found minimal or no increase in tolerance to drinking sessions for subjects who were given no feedback about performance, and for whom reward was unrelated to sober performance (Vogel-Sprott, 1997). Hence, reinforcing the ability to resist the effects of alcohol on performance led to behavioral tolerance.

STATE-DEPENDENT LEARNING   State-dependent learning is a concept that is closely related to behavioral tolerance. Tasks learned in the presence of a psychoactive drug may subsequently be performed better in the drugged state than in the nondrugged state. Conversely, learning acquired in the nondrugged state may be more available in the nondrugged state. This phenomenon, which has been called state-dependent learning, illustrates the difficulty in transferring learned performance from a drugged to a nondrugged condition (**Figure 1.23**). An example of this is the alcoholic individual who during a binge hides his supply of liquor for later consumption but is unable to find it while he is sober (in the nondrugged state). Once he has returned to the alcoholic state, he can readily locate his cache.

One explanation for state dependency is that the drug effect may become part of the environmental "set," that is, it may assume the properties of a stimulus itself. A drugged subject learns to perform a particular task in relationship to all internal and external cues in the environment, including, it is argued, drug-induced cues. Thus in the absence of drug-induced cues, performance deteriorates in much the same way as if the test apparatus was altered. It has been shown in animal studies that the decrease in performance is very much related to the change in environmental cues, and that a particular drug state does provide readily discriminable stimuli (Overton, 1984). Further discussion of the cueing properties of drugs follows in Chapter 4.

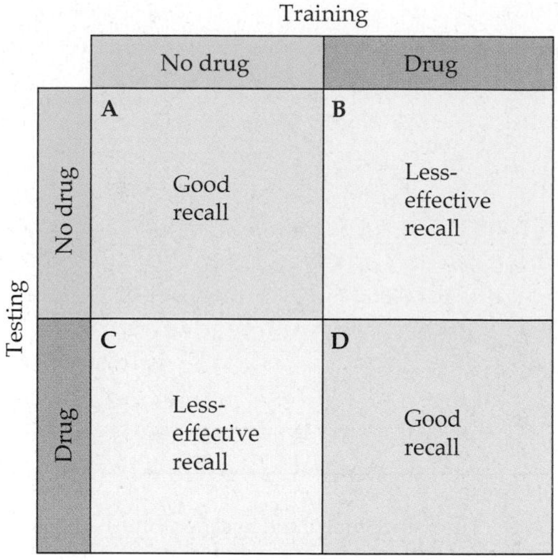

Chronic drug use can cause sensitization

Despite the fact that repeated drug administration produces tolerance for many drug effects, sensitization can occur for others. **Sensitization**, sometimes called *reverse tolerance*, is the enhancement of particular drug effects after repeated administration of the same dose of drug. For instance, prior administration of cocaine to animals significantly increases motor activity and stereotypy (continuous repetition of a simple action such as head bobbing) produced by subsequent stimulant administration. Chronic administration of higher doses of cocaine has been shown to produce an increased susceptibility to cocaine-induced catalepsy, in which the animal remains in abnormal or distorted postures for prolonged intervals, as well as hyperthermia and convulsions (Post and Weiss, 1988). Cocaine and amphetamine are examples of drugs that induce tolerance for some effects (euphoria) and sensitization for others.

As is true for tolerance, the development of sensitization is dose-dependent and the interval between treatments is important. Further, cross-sensitization with other psychomotor stimulants has been

Training

	No drug	Drug
No drug	**A** Good recall	**B** Less-effective recall
Drug	**C** Less-effective recall	**D** Good recall

Testing

Figure 1.23 Experimental design to test state-dependent learning Four different conditions show the difficulties involved in transferring learning from one drug state to another. Individuals trained without drug and tested without drug (A) show maximum performance that is not much different from the performance of those trained and tested under the influence of the drug (D). However, subjects asked to perform in a state different from the training condition (B and C) showed recall that was less efficient.

documented. Conditioning also plays a significant role in the appearance of sensitization. Pretreatment with the stimulant followed by testing in dissimilar environments yields significantly less sensitization than occurs in the identical environment. However, in contrast to drug tolerance, the augmentation of response to drug challenge tends to persist for long periods of abstinence, indicating that long-term physiological changes may occur as a result of stimulant administration. Further discussion of sensitization will be provided in Chapter 3. Young and Goudie (1995) is an excellent source for additional details on the role of classical and operant conditioning in the development of tolerance to behavioral effects of drugs.

Pharmacogenetics and Personalized Medicine in Psychiatry

Pharmacogenetics (sometimes called *pharmacogenomics*) is the study of the genetic basis for variability in drug response among individuals. Its goal is to identify genetic factors that confer susceptibility to specific side effects, or to predict good or poor therapeutic response. By referring to genetic information on each patient, it should be possible for the clinician to select the most appropriate drug for that individual—the ultimate in personalized medicine.

Variability in response to a given drug among individuals may be explained by heritability of pharmacokinetic or pharmacodynamic factors. Genetic variation in pharmacokinetic factors such as absorption, distribution, and elimination leads to differences in bioavailability after a fixed dose of drug, and to subsequent differences in biobehavioral effects. Of the pharmacokinetic factors, pharmacogenetic evaluation of the drug-metabolizing enzymes has been the most studied because variations in metabolic rate produce large differences in drug blood level among individuals and in subsequent clinical effects, as well as side effects. The many genetic polymorphisms (i.e., variations of a gene) of the cytochrome P450 enzyme family are of particular significance in neuropsychopharmacology because those enzymes are responsible for metabolizing most psychoactive drugs. Genetic knowledge of an individual's metabolic function can be used to adjust the dose of drug to achieve optimum blood level and subsequent optimum therapeutic response. Hence individuals with a genetic polymorphism associated with rapid metabolism by a given cytochrome P450 enzyme could be given a higher dose of drug to ensure therapeutic effectiveness. In contrast, for individuals who have an identified polymorphism for slow metabolism, a lower dose could be used to achieve effective blood levels while preventing toxic side effects. Knowing the inherited level of function of a drug-metabolizing enzyme is clearly useful in determining the correct dose of a drug for a given individual, but it is important to recall that multiple genetic factors, demographic factors such as gender, ethnicity, and age, environmental factors including diet, cigarette smoking, and concomitant use of multiple medications also contribute to the rate of drug metabolism (Arranz and Kapur, 2008). Hence genetic profile explains only a portion of the variance in drug blood levels and in clinical outcomes.

Genetic polymorphisms may also influence pharmacodynamic drug targets, that is, sites of action of the agent. These sites include receptors, transporters, and other membrane proteins, as well as downstream intracellular signaling cascades. Pharmacogenomic studies of drug response typically examine the association between drug effects and polymorphisms in genes suspected to have a role in the mechanism of action of that drug or in the pathophysiology of the disorder. Efforts are made to correlate the gene variant with the therapeutic or side effects of a given drug. One example involves antidepressants that target the reuptake transporter to increase the function of the neurotransmitter serotonin. Several studies have shown that individuals with the long variant of the gene for the serotonin transporter have a better response to treatment with particular drugs and are more likely to show remission (i.e., complete elimination of symptoms of depression) than individuals with the short allele, at least in Caucasian populations (Schosser and Kasper, 2009). Likewise, the short allele is associated with reduced efficacy of those antidepressants.

It is anticipated that routine genetic screening of patients will provide several advantages. Predicting how patients with distinct genetic profiles will respond to a particular medication before treatment begins would avoid the current costly and time-consuming method of trial and error to determine the best drug and the appropriate dose. Additionally, it is anticipated that genotyping will identify those individuals who are most susceptible to dangerous or debilitating side effects. Minimizing side effects should increase compliance with the drug regimen, and this would lead to fewer instances of relapse.

Despite encouraging basic biomedical research showing the potential of genomic screening, multiple challenges remain for the routine application of pharmacogenomics in clinical practice. One major challenge in the application of pharmacogenetics is that patients are not routinely genotyped, so a database of genetic information that can predict clinically meaningful treatment response outcomes remains to be built. Performing such studies for the database is difficult, expensive, and labor intensive because they require a large sample size for statistical validity and prolonged periods of monitoring therapeutic outcomes and side effects. Also, although several FDA-approved pharmacogenomics tests are commercially available, there are limited facilities to perform the analysis and interpret the huge amount of data. This makes genotyping relatively expensive at this point in time. It is anticipated that with increased use, the costs will diminish and genetic screening may become a routine procedure. However at present, only a few drugs are labeled with genomic information to guide clinical decisions and encourage routine genetic screening of patients.

Another challenge for pharmacogenetics involves the procedural difficulties involved in making the statistical cost-benefit analyses needed to show that genetic screening adds sufficient value in patient outcome to justify expenditures of the limited healthcare budget. Thus far, clinical use of genetic screening has been limited to selecting specialized drugs for unusual patients and regulating the dosage of drugs when the therapeutic index is narrow. However, screening may also be beneficial when it is difficult to predict which individuals will experience particularly dangerous adverse effects. It must be concluded that pharmacogenetics holds great promise for better psychiatric treatment, but further development will be needed if it is to reach its clinical potential.

Section Summary

- Drugs have biological effects because they interact with receptors on target tissues.

- Drugs or ligands that bind and are capable of changing the shape of the receptor protein and subsequently altering cell function are called agonists.

- Ligands that attach most readily are said to have high affinity for the receptor.

- Antagonists are capable of binding and may have high affinity while producing no physiological change, hence they have little or no efficacy. Antagonists "block" agonist activity by preventing agonists from binding to the receptor at the same moment.

- Inverse agonists bind to a receptor and initiate a biological action that is opposite that produced by an agonist.

- In general, binding of the specific ligand to a receptor is reversible.

- Receptor number changes to compensate for either prolonged stimulation (causing down-regulation) or absence of receptor stimulation (up-regulation of receptors).

- Dose–response curves show that with increasing doses, the effect increases in a linear fashion until the maximum effect is reached.

- The ED_{50} is the dose that produces a half-maximal (50%) effect. The more potent drug is one that has the lower ED_{50}.

- Comparison of the TD_{50} (50% toxic dose) with the ED_{50} for a single drug provides the therapeutic index (TI), which is a measurement of drug safety.

- Competitive receptor antagonists reduce the potency of an agonist; this is shown by a parallel shift of the dose–response curve to the right with no change in the maximum effect.

- Biobehavioral interactions of drugs can produce physiological antagonism, additive effects, or potentiation.

- Chronic drug use may lead to a reduction in biobehavioral effects called tolerance, but in some circumstances, drug effects increase with repeated use—a phenomenon called sensitization.

- Cross-tolerance may occur if repeated use of one drug reduces the effectiveness of a second drug.

- Tolerance is generally a reversible condition that depends on dose, frequency of use, and the drug-taking environment. Not all drugs induce tolerance, and not all effects of a given drug undergo tolerance to the same extent or at the same rate.

- Metabolic tolerance occurs when drugs increase the quantity of liver-metabolizing enzymes; this more rapidly reduces the effective blood level of the drug.

- Pharmacodynamic tolerance depends on adaptation of the nervous system to continued presence of the drug by increasing or decreasing receptor number or by producing other compensatory intracellular processes.

- Behavioral tolerance occurs when learning processes and environmental cues contribute to the reduction in drug effectiveness. Pavlovian conditioning and operant conditioning can contribute to the change in drug response.

- Sensitization is dependent on dose, intervals between treatments, and the drug-taking environment. Cross-sensitization with other drugs in the same class can occur. Unlike tolerance, sensitization is not readily reversible, and it persists for long periods of abstinence caused by long-term physiological changes to cells.

- Pharmacogenetics strives to identify genetic polymorphisms in individuals that predict good or poor therapeutic response to a specific drug or susceptibility to specific side effects. Genetic variation in pharmacokinetic factors such as rate of drug metabolism is responsible for determining drug blood level and subsequent biobehavioral effects. Genetic polymorphisms may influence the targets for drugs such as receptors and transporters.

Go to the COMPANION WEBSITE

sites.sinauer.com/psychopharm2e
for Web Boxes, animations, flashcards, and other study resources.

Recommended Readings

Arranz, M. J. and Kapur, S. (2008). Pharmacogenetics in psychiatry: Are we ready for widespread clinical use? *Schizophr. Bull.*, 34, 1130–1144.

Bausell, R. B. (2007). *Snake Oil Science*. New York: Oxford University Press.

Brown, W. A. (1998). The placebo effect. *Sci. Am.*, 278, 90–95.

Hollinger, M. A. (2008). *Introduction to Pharmacology* (3rd ed.). New York: CRC Press.

Langer, R. (2003). Where a pill won't reach. *Sci. Am.*, 288, 50–57.

Meyer, U. A. (1996). Overview of enzymes of drug metabolism. *J. Pharmacokinet. Biopharm.*, 24, 449–459.

Swerdlow, J. L. (2000). Nature's Rx. *Natl. Geogr. Mag.*, 197, 98–117.

Zivin, J. A. (2000). Understanding clinical trials. *Sci. Am.*, 282, 69–75.

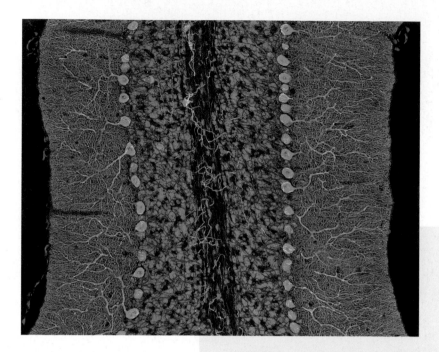

A fluorescent micrograph of a section of cerebellum displays several distinctive cell layers including flask-shaped Purkinje cells.

Structure and Function of the Nervous System 2

MICHELLE WAS A FIRST-SEMESTER SENIOR ENGLISH MAJOR when she first noticed that she was unusually fatigued and often felt dizzy and weak, barely able to lift her legs to climb stairs. She said it felt as though she were walking through oatmeal. As the semester wore on, Michelle found she had increasing trouble reading her assignments because of blurred vision and a sense that the words were moving on the page. Although these symptoms disappeared temporarily, they recurred with greater intensity just a few weeks later. When she realized she was almost too weak to walk and began slurring her speech, she made an appointment to see her hometown doctor. After a series of tests, Michelle's doctor told her she had multiple sclerosis (MS)—a progressive, degenerative autoimmune disease in which the immune system attacks the nerve cells in the brain and spinal cord, producing sensory and motor deficits. The doctor tried to reassure her. He said that MS is a disease that is characterized by remissions (absence of symptoms) and relapses, and that some people go years before experiencing another episode. During remission, many people lead perfectly normal lives. However, it is a disease that can be treated but not cured. Fortunately, there are disease-modifying drugs that reduce the relapse rate and subsequently slow the progression of MS. This chapter describes nervous system structure and function. By the end of the chapter, you should have a good idea of what causes MS, and why Michelle experienced the particular symptoms she did.

As we already know, psychopharmacology is the study of how drugs affect emotion, memory, thinking, and behavior. Drugs can produce these widespread effects because they modify the function of the human brain, most often by altering the chemical nature of the nervous system. To gain an understanding of drug action, we first need to know a bit about individual nerve cell structure and

Figure 2.1 Varied shapes of neurons
These drawings are from actual nerve cells stained by the Golgi technique. Neurons are drawn to different scales to show their varied structures.

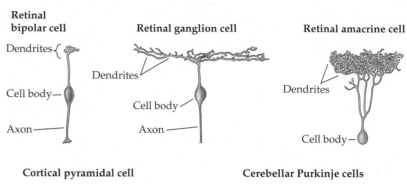

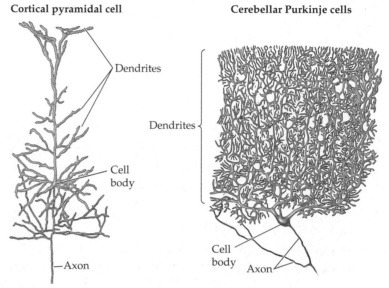

electrochemical function. Second, we need to have an essential understanding of how these individual cells form the complex circuits that represent the anatomical basis for behavior. We hope that for most readers, Chapter 2 will be a review of (1) the structure of nerve cells; (2) electrochemical properties of neurons; and (3) anatomy of the nervous system, as we put the individual neurons together into functional units. Chapter 3 follows up with greater detail on the chemical nature of nerve cell function.

Cells of the Nervous System

All tissues in the body are composed of cells, and the special characteristics of those cells determine the structure and function of the tissue or organ. Understanding how those cells became specialized (differentiated) is of tremendous importance to basic science as well as clinical research. **Box 2.1** describes embryonic stem cells and their potential in research and therapeutics. Embryonic stem cells destined to form the nervous system become two primary types of cells: nerve cells called **neurons** and supporting cells called **glial cells** that provide metabolic support, protection, and insulation for neurons (see the section on glial cells later in the chapter). The principal function of neurons is to transmit information in the form of electrical signaling over long distances. **Sensory neurons**, which are sensitive to environmental stimuli, convert physical stimuli in the world around us and in our internal environment into an electrical signal and transmit that information to circuits of **interneurons**, which are nerve cells within the brain and spinal cord. Interneurons form complex interacting neural circuits and are responsible for conscious sensations, recognition, memory, decision making, and cognition. In turn, **motor neurons** direct a biobehavioral response appropriate for the situation. Although these neurons have common features, their structural arrangements and sizes vary according to their specific functions. **Figure 2.1** provides some examples of the many possible shapes of neurons that were first described by the nineteenth-century

histological studies of the Spanish neuroanatomist Ramón y Cajal. For much of the twentieth century, neuroscientists relied on the same set of techniques developed by early neuroanatomists to describe and categorize the diversity of cell types in the nervous system.

Histological methods that prepare tissue for microscopic study involve preparing very thin slices of the brain after it has been perfused with a salt solution to remove the blood, and treating the tissue with fixative that kills potentially damaging microorganisms, stops enzymatic damage, and hardens normally soft tissue. After slicing, one of several types of stain is applied to make fine cellular details visible. The Golgi technique, developed in 1873 by the Italian scientist Camillo Golgi, stains only a few cells in their entirety for detailed visualization of individual neurons (see Figure 2.1); others selectively stain myelin to view bundles of axons. Still others selectively stain cell bodies or degenerating axons that identify damaged cells. After staining the tissue, slices are examined with light or electron microscopy. Although variations on this basic technique are still frequently used, from the late 1970s onward, remarkable new technologies (see Chapter 4) in cell biology and molecular biology provided investigators with many additional tools with

BOX 2.1   The Cutting Edge

Embryonic Stem Cells

Stem cells are undifferentiated (i.e., unspecialized) cells that have the ability to proliferate, that is, they replicate themselves over long periods of time by cell division. A second distinguishing feature is that although they are unspecialized, stem cells have the capacity to become any specific tissue or organ cell type, such as red blood cell, muscle, or neuron, each with its unique structure and functions. This is possible because all cells of the body have identical genetic material, but some genes are activated and others are silenced to produce a cell type with all the appropriate proteins to perform its specialized functions. Hence in a nerve cell, particular genes are silenced, and in a heart cell, other genes are silenced. Embryonic stem cells are derived primarily from a portion of very early-stage embryos that would normally become the three germ layers that ultimately develop into all the different tissues of the body. The cells are maintained in a laboratory cell culture dish and multiply, potentially yielding millions of embryonic stem cells (see figure). If after 6 months, the cells have not differentiated into specific tissue cells, they are considered pluripotent, having more than one potential outcome. Scientists attempt to control differentiation to a specific cell type by changing the chemicals in the culture dish, or by inserting specific genes into the cells to provide direction.

There are several potential benefits from stem cell research. First, in the laboratory, the differentiated cells can be used to develop model systems to improve our understanding of how an organism develops from a single cell. Knowing something about what genes and molecular controls direct normal differentiation may provide important clues as to the nature of disease-causing aberrations and the causes of cancer and birth

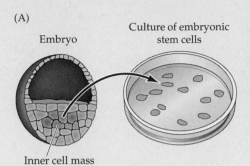

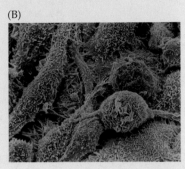

(A) Embryo — Inner cell mass — Culture of embryonic stem cells

Culture of embryonic stem cells (A) Embryonic stem cells are cultured from the inner cell mass of an early-stage embryo. (B) Scanning electron micrograph of cultured embryonic stem cells.

defects, both of which are due to abnormal cell differentiation and cell division. This understanding can lead to new strategies for treatment. Second, drug development can be more efficient if multiple cell lines are used to screen new drugs for potential toxic effects on various cell types from multiple organs. Such preliminary testing would also reduce harm to animals or humans. Third, the most publicized potential application of stem cell research is the use of stem cells for cell transplantation therapies for degenerative diseases or diseased organs. Promising results from initial research with stem cells involved animal models of Parkinson's disease, which showed that administered stem cells migrate to the damaged area of the brain and replace lost dopamine neurons, producing significant improvement in motor function. Others used the cells to replace lost oligodendroglial cells that provide myelin in a rat model of human demyelinating disease (Brüstle et al., 1999). Stem cells can also be directed to form specific classes of CNS neurons. For example, by providing appropriate inductive signals and transcription factors, stem cells can be directed to become motor neurons. These cells replicate in the spinal cord, extend axons, and form synapses with target muscle (Wichterle et al., 2002).

Successes with rat models have encouraged early trials in human patients. Efforts have been made to replace inactive pancreatic β-cells in individuals with type 1 diabetes to restore normal levels of insulin. Additional trials have been initiated to evaluate stem cell use in Parkinson's disease, amyotrophic lateral sclerosis (ALS), macular degeneration, and severe burns. The first trials to treat paraplegic patients after injury to the thoracic region of the spinal cord are under way. The list of neurodegenerative disorders that might someday be tackled by stem cell transplantation is long and includes Alzheimer's disease, amyotrophic lateral sclerosis, stroke, brain trauma and tumors, multiple sclerosis, Tay-Sachs disease, Duchenne muscular dystrophy, and many others. Evidence also suggests that there is reduced proliferation of brain stem cells in patients with schizophrenia, depression, and bipolar disorder, which may someday be corrected by stem cell transplantation. The potential for this type of treatment is enormous, but whether results in humans will resemble those of the animal research must still be determined. Among the hurdles remaining is the need to increase basic research into the cellular events that lead to differentiation

(Continued on next page)

BOX 2.1 *(continued)*

of pluripotent stem cells into the specific types of cells needed. In addition, steps may be needed to modify the stem cells to avoid immune rejection of the tissue. Finally, methods of delivery of the cells into the appropriate part of the body will need to be developed for each type of cell therapy. Clearly, treatment of brain disorders is particularly challenging.

A second approach to cell therapy is to use adult stem cells, which are found in many tissues, including brain, blood, skin, heart, and other organs. These cells normally function to repair the damaged tissue of the organ in which they reside and so are not pluripotent but are limited in differentiation to cell types within that organ. For instance, cardiac progenitor cells normally repair heart muscle, although at too slow a rate to help someone with significant damage, such as after a heart attack. There is some limited evidence for transdifferentiation of adult cells, which means that certain stem cell types can differentiate into cell types characteristic of tissues other than that of their origin. However, transdifferentiation is somewhat controversial among researchers and it is not clear whether it occurs in humans. Hence in general, adult stem cells are considered much more limited in their therapeutic potential than those derived from embryos. A second limitation with adult stem cells is that there are only a small number of stem cells

in each tissue so isolating them is difficult. Furthermore, once they are removed from the body, their ability to divide is limited, making it more difficult to make the large quantities needed for transplantation. The number of adult cells further decreases with age, and the older cells may have more DNA damage, which may explain their shorter life span compared with pluripotent stem cells. One potential advantage is that there may be less risk of immune rejection because the patient's own cells would be isolated, multiplied in cell culture, and then readministered to the same individual.

Psychopharmacology is particularly interested in neural stem cells that are found in only two brain areas: the subventricular zone that lines the lateral ventricles and the hippocampal dentate gyrus. These cells support neurogenesis—the birth of new nerve cells throughout the life span—but also differentiate into oligodendroglia and astrocytes. The importance of neurogenesis in the hippocampus has become an important focus of research into the mechanism of action of antidepressants—a topic that will be discussed further in Chapter 19.

In an effort to overcome the ethical and political hurdles imposed on embryonic stem cell research that have restricted government funding, scientists have developed *induced* pluripotent stem cells (IPS cells). IPS cells are

created by genetically reprogramming mature cells to develop the characteristics of the embryonic stem cell, essentially reversing the cell's differentiated fate. These cells have the cell markers of embryonic cells, reproduce in cell culture, and can develop into a wide variety of cells. Further, they avoid the controversial use of human embryos. IPS cells have been useful in drug development and testing and basic research, but they have not been used for transplantation. One advantage of these cells is that they would be a match to the cell donor, so they should not be rejected by the immune system. However, a significant downside is that genetic reprogramming requires the use of viral vectors to get the genetic material into the adult cells. Since the use of the retrovirus may produce cancers, alternative nonviral techniques must be developed. Furthermore, more careful evaluation and comparison of IPS cells with embryonic stem cells and adult stem cells are needed to promote understanding of how they differentiate, and to evaluate the potential for causing genetic errors or cancer. Unfortunately, some recent research suggests that IPS cells are less efficient at proliferation than embryonic stem cells, have higher rates of cell death, and prematurely lose their ability to divide (Feng et al., 2010). It is clear that much more research is needed before these cells will be useful therapeutically.

which to identify minute differences in the structural features of neurons, trace their multiple connections, and evaluate physiological responses.

Neurons have three major external features

Although neurons come in a variety of shapes and sizes and utilize various neurochemicals, they have several principal external features in common (**Figure 2.2**). These features include (1) the **soma**, or cell body, which contains the nucleus and other organelles that maintain cell metabolic function; (2) the **dendrites**, which are treelike projections from the soma that receive

information from other cells; and (3) the **axon**, the single tubular extension that conducts the electrical signal from the cell body to the terminal buttons on the axon terminals. Like all other cells, neurons are enclosed by a semipermeable membrane and are filled with a salty, gelatinous fluid—the **cytoplasm**. Neurons are also surrounded by salty fluid (**extracellular fluid**), from which they take oxygen, nutrients, and drugs, and into which they secrete metabolic waste products that ultimately reach the blood and then are filtered out by the kidneys (see Chapter 1). Like other cells, neurons have **mitochondria**, which are responsible for generating energy from glucose in the form of adenosine triphosphate

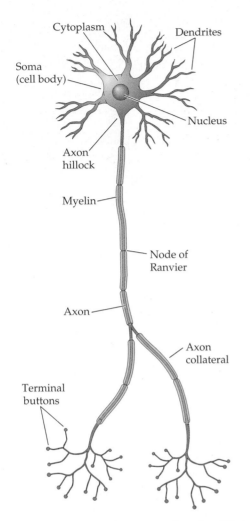

Figure 2.2 **Principal parts of neurons** Despite differences in size and shape, most neurons have numerous features in common.

(ATP). Mitochondria are found throughout the cell, but particularly where energy needs are great. Since neurons use large quantities of ATP, mitochondrial function is critical for survival, and ATP is synthesized continually to support neuron function. The assumption that the rate of synthesis of ATP reflects neuron activity is an underlying premise of several neurobiological techniques that give us the opportunity to visualize the functioning of brain cells (see Chapter 4 for a discussion of positron emission tomography [PET] and functional magnetic resonance imaging [fMRI]).

DENDRITES   The general pattern of neuron function involves the dendrites and soma receiving information from other cells across the gap between them, called the **synapse**. On the dendrites of a single neuron as well as on the soma there may be thousands of receptors, that respond to neurochemicals released by other neurons. Depending on the changes produced in the receiving cell, the overall effect may be either excitatory or inhibitory. Hence each neuron receives and integrates a vast amount of information from many cells; this function is called **convergence**. The integrated information in turn can be transmitted to a few neurons or to thousands of other neurons; this process is known as **divergence**. If we look a bit more carefully using higher magnification, we see that dendrites are usually covered with short **dendritic spines** (Figure 2.3) that dramatically increase the receiving surface area. The complex architecture of the dendritic tree reflects the complexity of synaptic connections with other neurons and determines brain function. Dendrites and their spines exhibit the special feature of being constantly modified and can change shape rapidly in response to changes in synaptic transmission (Fischer et al., 1998). Long-lasting changes in

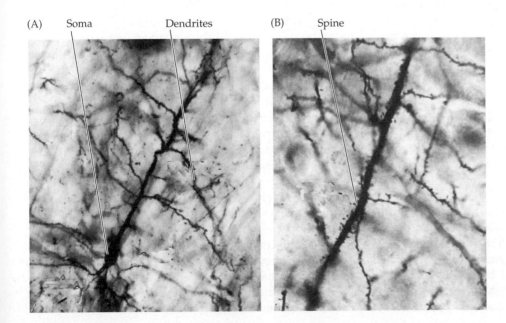

Figure 2.3 **Dendritic trees with spines** (A) A neuron with its dendrites is clearly apparent at 100× magnification. (B) Higher magnification (250×) shows multiple spines all along the dendrite. (From Jacobson, 1972.)

synaptic activity change the size and number as well as the shape of dendritic spines from thin to mushroom-shaped; this apparently serves as the basis for more efficient signaling. These changes occur throughout life and permit us to continue to learn new associations as we interact with our environment.

Evidence suggesting the importance of dendritic spines to learning comes from studies of human patients and animal models of mental impairment. Individuals with mental retardation have dendritic spines that are unusually small and immature-looking; this may result either from failure of maturation of small spines into larger spines or an inability to maintain spine structure. It is impossible to retain knowledge acquired during development without the large spines, and that failure manifests as intellectual deficiencies. In contrast, schizophrenic individuals experiencing a profound thought disorder have normally *sized* dendritic spines but reduced spine density, particularly in the prefrontal cortex. Although their intelligence is in the normal range, cognitive and negative symptoms of the disorder include poor working memory, lack of attention, poor episodic memory, and low motivation—all of which may be explained by poor connectivity between neurons. Further investigation into the cellular mechanisms of dendritic spine size and density may provide the means to visualize and modify spine dynamics and perhaps may lead to new ways to diagnose and treat brain disorders. For further details on dendritic spine dynamics, the reader is directed to a review by Kasai and colleagues (2010).

AXONS AND TERMINAL BUTTONS   The single long extension from the soma is the axon. Axons are tubular in structure and are filled with axoplasm (i.e., cytoplasm within the axon). Axons vary significantly in both length and diameter. Their function is to transmit the electrical signal (action potential) that is generated at the **axon hillock** down the length of the axon to the terminals. The axon hillock is that portion of the axon that is adjacent to the cell body.

Although there is usually only one axon for a given neuron, axons split or bifurcate into numerous branches called **axon collaterals**, providing the capacity to influence many more cells. At the ends of the axons are small enlargements called **terminal buttons**, which are located near the dendrites or somas of other cells. Terminal buttons are also called *boutons* or *axon terminals*. Terminal buttons contain small packets (**synaptic vesicles**) of neurochemicals (called **neurotransmitters**) that provide the capacity for chemical transmission of information across the synapse to adjacent cells or to the target organ. Neurons are frequently named according to the neurotransmitter that they synthesize and release. Hence cells that release dopamine are

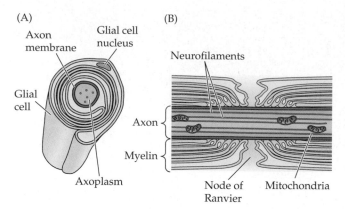

Figure 2.4 Myelin sheath (A) Cross section of an axon with multiple layers of glial cell wraps forming the myelin sheath. (B) Longitudinal drawing of a myelinated axon at a node of Ranvier.

dopaminergic neurons, those that release serotonin are serotonergic, and so forth.

Most axons are wrapped with a fatty insulating coating, called **myelin**, created by concentric layers of glial cells (**Figure 2.4A**). There are two types of glial cells that form the myelin sheath: Schwann cells, which myelinate peripheral nerves that serve muscles, organs, and glands; and oligodendroglia, which myelinate nerves within the brain and spinal cord. The myelin sheath provided by both types of glial cells is not continuous along the axon but has breaks in it where the axon is bare to the extracellular fluid. These bare spots, called **nodes of Ranvier (Figure 2.4B)**, are the sites at which the action potential is regenerated during conduction of the electrical signal along the length of the axon. The myelin sheath increases the speed of conduction along the axon; in fact, the thicker the myelin, the quicker the conduction. While a small number of neurons are unmyelinated and conduct slowly, others are thinly wrapped, and some rapidly conducting neurons may have a hundred or more wraps. Myelination also saves energy by reducing the effort required to restore the neuron to its resting state after transmission of the electrical signal. The best example of the importance of myelin to neuron function comes from the disease multiple sclerosis (MS), which was introduced in the opening vignette. The particular symptoms Michelle and any other person with MS experience depends on which neurons have lost their myelin sheath. MS is described more fully in Chapter 21.

SOMA   The cell body is responsible for the metabolic care of the neuron. Among its important functions is the synthesis of proteins that are needed throughout the cell for growth and maintenance. These proteins include such things as enzymes, receptors, and components

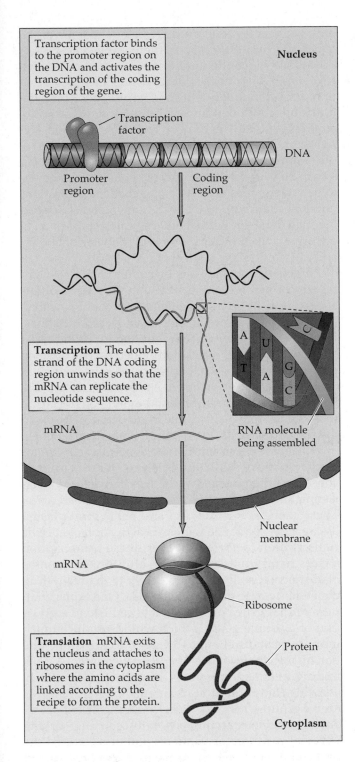

Transcription factor binds to the promoter region on the DNA and activates the transcription of the coding region of the gene.

Nucleus

Transcription factor

DNA

Promoter region

Coding region

Transcription The double strand of the DNA coding region unwinds so that the mRNA can replicate the nucleotide sequence.

mRNA

RNA molecule being assembled

Nuclear membrane

mRNA

Ribosome

Translation mRNA exits the nucleus and attaches to ribosomes in the cytoplasm where the amino acids are linked according to the recipe to form the protein.

Protein

Cytoplasm

Figure 2.5 Stages of protein synthesis Activation of a gene by a transcription factor initiates the formation of mRNA within the nucleus, followed by translation into a protein on the ribosomes in the cytoplasm.

the full genetic library of information, each cell type manufactures only those proteins needed for its specific function. Hence liver cells manufacture enzymes to metabolize toxins, and neurons manufacture enzymes needed to synthesize neurotransmitters and carry out functions necessary for neural transmission. In addition, which specific genes are activated is determined in part by our day-to-day experience. Neurobiologists are finding that experiences such as prolonged stress and chronic drug use may turn on or turn off the production of particular proteins by modifying transcription factors. **Transcription factors** are nuclear proteins that direct protein production. Transcription factors such as CREB bind to the **promoter region** of the gene adjacent to the coding region, modifying its rate of transcription.

Transcription occurs in the nucleus, where messenger RNA (mRNA) makes a complementary copy of the active gene. After moving from the nucleus to the cytoplasm, mRNA attaches to organelles called **ribosomes**, which decode the recipe and link the appropriate amino acids together to form the protein. This process is called **translation**. Some of the basic steps in protein synthesis are shown in **Figure 2.5**.

EPIGENETICS   We already said that environmental events can alter the rate of gene expression through induction of transcription factors. In addition, there are longer-lasting environmentally induced epigenetic modifications that determine which genes will be turned on or off and how much gene expression occurs. These changes may persist through the lifetime of the organism and may even be passed on to future generations if modifications are present in the germ cell line (i.e., eggs and sperm). These events occur despite the fact that the basic structure of the DNA is not altered. Instead, the simple covalent attachment of methyl groups (**DNA methylation**) to particular locations on a gene usually decreases expression of that gene. A second type of modification is **chromatin remodeling**. Chromatin is a complex of small spherical histone proteins around which the DNA wraps (**Figure 2.6A**). Environmentally induced acetylation, methylation, or phosphorylation of the lysine residues of histone tails can loosen the chromatin structure, allowing transcription factors to bind to the DNA and activate expression of the gene (**Figure 2.6B**). In other cases, chemical modification of the histone tails makes the chromatin more tightly packed, which represses gene expression by physically limiting the access of transcription factors (**Figure 2.6C**).

of the cell membrane. Within the nucleus are pairs of chromosomes that we inherited from our parents. **Chromosomes** are long strands of deoxyribonucleic acid (DNA), and **genes** are small portions of chromosomes that code for the manufacture of a specific protein molecule. Hence the **coding region** of a gene provides the "recipe" for a specific protein such as a receptor or an enzyme. Although every cell in the body contains

(A)

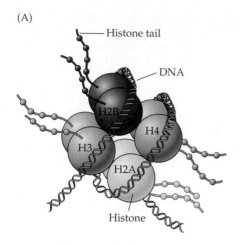

(B) **Active**

(C) **Inactive**

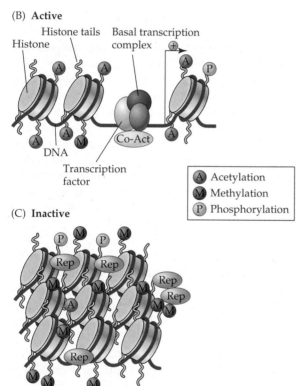

Figure 2.6 Epigenetic regulation of gene transcription
(A) Chromatin is a complex of DNA, histone proteins, and nonhistone proteins (not shown). (B) When histone tails are acetylated, charges open up the chromatin, creating an active state that allows transcription factors to bind to the promoter region of a gene to enhance transcription. (C) The inactive state of chromatin is caused by methylation of histone tails, which pulls the chromatin tighter and prevents the binding of transcription factors, reducing transcription of the gene. (After Tsankova et al., 2007.)

Epigenetic modification of gene expression has been understood since the 1970s because the phenomenon is central to cell differentiation in the developing fetus. Because all cells in the organism have identical DNA, they differentiate into organ-specific cells

only when epigenetic processes turn on some of the genes and turn off others in utero. However, pre- or postnatal epigenetic modification can also occur in response to environmental demands such as starvation or overabundance of food, stress, poor prenatal nutrition, childhood abuse and neglect, exposure to environmental toxins, and so forth. For example, significant overeating leads to weight gain but also produces epigenetic changes that cause the genes for obesity to be overexpressed and the genes for longevity to be underexpressed. These epigenetic modifications not only contribute to the weight gain and shortened life span of the individual but also can be passed on to offspring, which increases their probability of obesity and early mortality (Kaati et al., 2007).

Epigenetic mechanisms became a major focus of research when it became clear that epigenetic differences caused by environmental factors could potentially explain a lot of previously unanswered questions. For instance, it may explain why monozygotic twins who have identical genes do not necessarily develop the same disorders, such as schizophrenia or bipolar disorder, cancer, or diabetes. Apparently, despite the identical genes, environmental events have caused those genes to be expressed in different patterns in the two individuals. Epigenetic events may also help to explain the persistence of the drug-taking behavior characteristic of addiction (see Chapter 9). Drugs of abuse cause neuroadaptive changes that are very long-lasting and that persist, despite years of abstinence. These changes in structural and behavioral plasticity are associated with increased activation of specific transcription factors. However, these transcription factors return to baseline levels after several months of abstinence, so they are not likely to maintain drug dependence over prolonged periods. One explanation may be that drugs of abuse enhance histone acetylation of multiple genes, which would produce much more persistent changes in gene expression. The potential for clinical use of epigenetic manipulations in drug treatment programs is suggested by a study showing that inhibition of an enzyme that removes acetyl groups from histone, which increased acetylation in nucleus accumbens, reduced drug-seeking behavior in laboratory animals and also reduced the probability of relapse when the mice were re-exposed to cocaine (Malvaez et al., 2010).

Epigenetic research may also help us understand the link between early life events such as abuse or neglect and the increased occurrence of clinical depression (see Chapter 19) and anxiety disorders (see Chapter 18) later in life. These topics will be discussed more fully in later chapters on the clinical disorders. The ultimate goal for neuropharmacology is to develop drugs that can be used to manipulate epigenetic

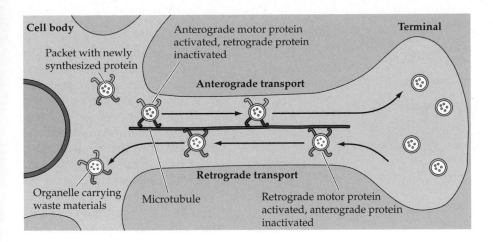

Figure 2.7 Axoplasmic transport
The movement of newly synthesized proteins from the soma to the axon terminals (anterograde) is powered along the micro-tubules by a motor protein called kinesin. Old proteins are carried from the terminals to the soma (retrograde) by the motor protein dynein.

factors, for example, to deacetylate histone or increase methylation of DNA to treat psychiatric disorders that have genetic components, such as autism, schizophrenia, depression, Alzheimer's disease, and others. In essence, the drug could be used to enhance gene expression that may have been suppressed by the disorder or turn off expression of genes that are associated with the development of symptoms.

AXOPLASMIC TRANSPORT Having said that proteins are synthesized within the soma and knowing that proteins are needed throughout the neuron, we must consider how these proteins are moved to the required destination. The process is called **axoplasmic transport**, and it depends on structures of the cytoskeleton. The **cytoskeleton**, as the name suggests, is a matrix composed of tubular structures, which include microtubules and neurofilaments that form a meshlike mass that provides shape for the cell. In addition, the microtubules, which run longitudinally down the axon, provide a stationary track along which small packets of newly synthesized protein are carried by specialized motor proteins (**Figure 2.7**). Movement of materials occurs in both directions. Newly synthesized proteins are packaged in the soma and transported in an anterograde direction toward the axon terminals. At the terminals, the contents are released, and retrograde axonal transport carries waste materials from the axon terminals back to the soma for recycling.

Characteristics of the cell membrane are critical for neuron function

One of the more important characteristics of neurons is the cell membrane. In Chapter 1 we learned that neuronal membranes are essentially a phospholipid bilayer that prevents most materials from freely passing (see Figure 1.4), unless they are lipid soluble. In addition to phospholipids, membranes have proteins inserted into the bilayer. Many of these proteins are **receptors**—large molecules that are the initial sites of action of neurotransmitters, hormones, and drugs. Details of these receptors and their functions are described in Chapter 3. Other important proteins associated with the membrane are enzymes that catalyze biochemical reactions in the cell. The third important group of proteins consists of ion channels and transporters. Because the membrane is not readily permeable to charged molecules, special devices are needed to move molecules such as amino acids, glucose, and metabolic products across the membrane. Movement of these materials is achieved by transporter proteins, which are described further in Chapter 3. In addition, charged particles (ions), such as potassium (K^+), sodium (Na^+), chloride (Cl^-), and calcium (Ca^{2+}), that are needed for neuron function can be moved through the membrane only via ion channels. These channels are protein molecules that penetrate through the cell membrane and have a water-filled pore through which ions can pass.

Ion channels have several important characteristics. First, they are relatively specific for a particular ion, although some allow more than one type of ion to pass through. Second, most channels are not normally open to allow free passage of the ions, but are in a closed configuration that can be opened momentarily by specific stimuli. These channels are referred to as **gated channels**. The two types of channels of immediate interest to us are **ligand-gated channels** and **voltage-gated channels**. Looking at **Figure 2.8A**, you can see that when a drug, hormone, or neurotransmitter binds to a receptor that recognizes the ligand, the channel protein changes shape and opens the gate, allowing flow of a specific ion to move either into or out of the cell. The direction in which an ion moves is determined by its relative concentration; it always travels from

(A)

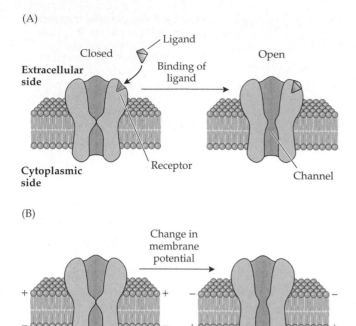

(B)

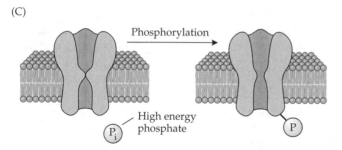

(C)

Glial cells provide vital support for neurons

Glial cells have a significant role in neuron function because they provide physical support to neurons, maintain the chemical environment of neurons, and provide immunological function. The four principal types include oligodendroglia, Schwann cells, astrocytes, and microglia. **Schwann cells** and **oligodendroglia**, described earlier, produce the myelin sheath on neuronal axons of the peripheral nervous system (PNS) and the central nervous system (CNS), respectively. Schwann cells and oligodendroglia differ in several ways in addition to their location in the nervous system. Schwann cells (**Figure 2.9A**) are dedicated to a single neuron, and these PNS axons, when damaged, are prompted to regenerate axons because of the Schwann cell response. First, the Schwann cells release growth factors, and second, they provide a pathway for regrowth of the axon toward the target tissue. Oligodendroglia, (**Figure 2.9B**) in contrast, send out multiple paddle-shaped "arms," which wrap many different axons to produce segments of the myelin sheath. In addition, they do not provide nerve growth factors when an axon is damaged, nor do they provide a path for growth.

Two other significant types of glial cells are the astrocytes and microglia. **Astrocytes** are large, star-shaped cells that have numerous extensions. They intertwine with neurons and provide structural support; in addition, they help to maintain the ionic

Figure 2.8 Ion channels (A) When a ligand (neurotransmitter, hormone, or drug) binds to a receptor on the channel, the ligand-gated channel protein changes shape and opens the gate, allowing passage of a specific ion. (B) A voltage-gated channel is opened when the electrical potential across the membrane near the channel is altered. (C) Modification of a channel by a second messenger, which produces intracellular phosphorylation (addition of a phosphate group) and regulates the state of the channel. (After Siegelbaum and Koester, 1991.)

high to low concentration. Hence, given an open gate, Na^+, Cl^-, and Ca^{2+} will move into the cell, while K^+ moves out (see later in this chapter). A second type of channel, which will be of importance later in this chapter, is the type that is opened by voltage differences across the membrane. These channels are opened not by ligands, but by the application of a small electrical charge to the membrane surrounding the channel (**Figure 2.8B**). Other channels are modified by second messengers (**Figure 2.8C**), but discussion of these will have to wait until Chapter 3. Regardless of the stimulus opening the channel, it opens only briefly and then closes again, limiting the total amount of ion flux.

TABLE 2.1	Functions of Glial Cells
Cell	**Function**
Astrocytes	Provide structural support
	Maintain ionic and chemical environment
	Store nutrients to provide energy for neurons
	Perform phagocytosis
Microglia	Perform phagocytosis
	Provide immune system function
Schwann cells	Form myelin sheath on a single axon in the PNS
	Release growth factors following neuron damage
	Provide a channel to guide axons to targets
Oligodendroglia	Form myelin sheath on multiple axons in the CNS
	Inhibit regrowth of axons following neuron damage

(A)

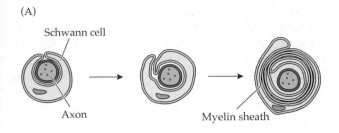

(B)

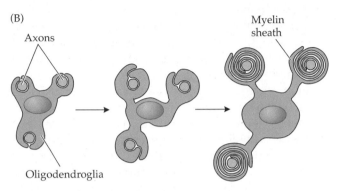

Figure 2.9 Glial cells forming myelin (A) Schwann cells in the PNS dedicate themselves to a single axon and wrap many times to form the myelin for one segment. (B) Each oligodendroglia in the CNS sends out multiple sheetlike arms that wrap around segments of multiple nearby axons to form the myelin sheath.

environment around neurons and modulate the chemical environment as well by taking up excess neurochemicals that might otherwise damage cells. Because astrocytes have a close relationship with both blood vessels and neurons, it is likely that they may aid the movement of necessary materials from the blood to nerve cells. **Microglia** are far smaller than astrocytes and act as scavengers that collect at sites of neuron damage to remove dying cells. In addition to this phagocytosis, microglia are the primary source of immune response in the CNS and are responsible for the inflammation reaction that occurs after brain damage. **Table 2.1** summarizes the functions of glial cells.

Section Summary

- Neurons are surrounded by a cell membrane and are filled with cytoplasm and the organelles needed for optimal functioning.
- Among the most important organelles are the mitochondria, which provide energy for the metabolic work of the cell.
- The principal external features of a neuron are the soma, treelike dendrites, and a single axon extending from the soma that carries the electrical signal all the way to the axon terminals.

- Axon terminals contain synaptic vesicles filled with neurotransmitter molecules that are released into the synapse between cells when the action potential arrives.
- The dendrites of a neuron are covered with minute spines that increase the receiving surface area of the cell. These spines are reduced in size in individuals with intellectual impairment and reduced in number in those with schizophrenia.
- Thousands of receptors that respond to neurotransmitters released by other neurons are found on the dendrites, dendritic spines, and soma of the cell.
- The axon hillock is located at the juncture of soma and axon and is responsible for summation (or integration) of the multiple signals required to generate an action potential.
- Conduction of the action potential along the axon is enhanced by the insulating property of the myelin created by nearby glial cells.
- The nucleus of the cell is located within the soma, and protein synthesis occurs there. Transcription of the genetic code for a specific protein by mRNA occurs within the nucleus, and translation of the "recipe," carried by the mRNA, occurs on the ribosomes in the cytoplasm. Ribosomes link together appropriate amino acids to create the protein.
- Changes in synaptic activity increase or decrease the production of particular proteins by activating transcription factors in the nucleus.
- Epigenetics is the study of how environmental demands such as diet, environmental toxins, stress, prenatal nutrition, and many others turn on or turn off the expression of specific genes. Although epigenetic markers do not modify DNA, they can last a lifetime and may be transmitted to future generations. Two common markers are DNA methylation and chromatin remodeling.
- Future drug development will target epigenetic factors to treat psychiatric disorders that have genetic components by turning on protective genes or turning off genes associated with symptom development.
- Newly manufactured proteins are packaged into vesicles in the soma and are moved by motor proteins that slide along the neuron's microtubules (part of the cytoskeleton) to the terminals (anterograde transport). Protein waste and cell debris are transported from the terminals back to the soma (retrograde transport) for recycling.
- The cell membrane is a phospholipid bilayer that prevents most materials from passing through, unless the material is lipid soluble. Special

transporters carry other essential materials, such as glucose, amino acids, and neurotransmitters into the cell. Ion channels allow ions such as Na^+, K^+, Cl^-, and Ca^{2+} to move across the membrane. Other proteins associated with the membrane include receptors and enzymes.

• Four types of glial cells are found in the nervous system. Schwann cells and oligodendroglia produce the myelin sheath on peripheral and central nervous system neurons, respectively. Astrocytes regulate the extracellular environment of the neurons and provide physical support and nutritional assistance. Microglia act as phagocytes to remove cellular debris and provide immune function.

Electrical Transmission within a Neuron

The transmission of information within a single neuron is an electrical process and depends on the semipermeable nature of the cell membrane. When the normal resting electrical charge of a neuron is disturbed sufficiently by incoming signals from other cells, a threshold is reached that initiates the electrical signal (action potential) that conveys the message along the entire length of the axon to the axon terminals. This section of the chapter looks at each of the stages: resting membrane potential, local potentials, threshold, and action potential.

Ion distribution is responsible for the cell's resting potential

All neurons have a difference in electrical charge inside the cell compared with outside the cell, called the **resting membrane potential**. This can be measured by placing an electrode on the exterior of the cell in the extracellular fluid, and a second, much finer microelectrode into the intracellular fluid inside the cell (**Figure 2.10**). The inside of the neuron is more negative than the outside, and a voltmeter would tell us that the difference is approximately –70 millivolts (mV), making the neuron **polarized** in its resting state.

Selective permeability of the membrane and uneven distribution of ions inside and outside the cell are responsible for the membrane potential. This means that when the cell is at rest, there are more negatively charged particles (ions) inside the cell and more positively charged ions outside the cell. **Figure 2.11** shows the relative concentration of different ions on either side of the membrane. Inside we find many large, negatively charged molecules, such as proteins and amino acids, which cannot leave the cell. Potassium is also in much higher concentration (perhaps 20 times higher) inside than out. In contrast, Na^+ and Cl^- are present in greater concentration outside the cell than inside.

Several forces are responsible for this ion distribution and membrane potential. The concentration gradient and electrostatic pressure for the K^+ ion are particularly important; K^+ moves more freely through the membrane than other ions because some of its channels are not gated at the resting potential. Recall that ions move through relatively specific channels and that most are gated, meaning that they are normally held closed until opened by a stimulus. Since the inside of the cell normally has numerous large, negatively charged materials that do not move through the membrane, the positively charged K^+ ion is pulled into the cell because it is attracted to the internal negative charge (**electrostatic pressure**) (see Figure 2.11). However, as the concentration of K^+ inside rises, K^+ responds to the concentration gradient by moving out of the cell. The concentration

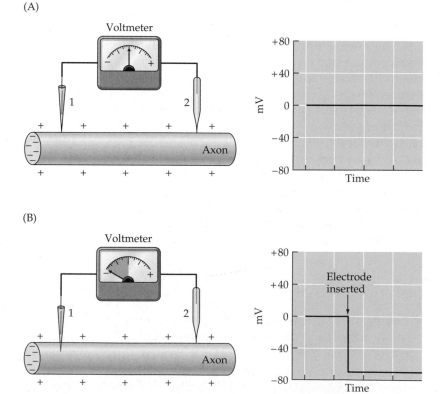

Figure 2.10 Membrane potential recording from a squid axon (A) When both electrodes are applied to the outside of the membrane, no difference in potential is recorded. (B) When the microelectrode is inserted into the axoplasm, a voltage difference between inside and outside is recorded. The graphs show the voltage change when one electrode penetrates the cell.

Units of concentration				
● Na⁺	● K⁺	● Cl⁻	○ Ca²⁺	● Protein

	Na^+	K^+	Cl^-	Ca^{2+}	Protein
Outside cell	440	20	560	10	few
Inside cell	50	400	40–150	0.0001	many

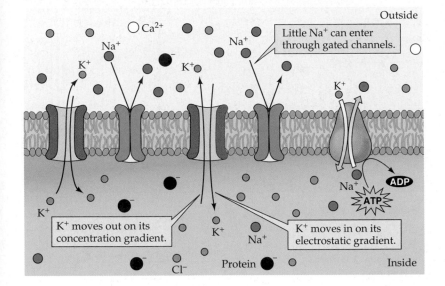

Figure 2.11 Distribution of ions inside and outside a neuron at resting potential Na^+ and Cl^- are more concentrated outside the cell and cannot move in freely through their gated channels. Some K^+ channels are not gated, allowing the concentration of the ion to force K^+ outward while electrostatically it is pulled in. At −70 mV, equilibrium between the two forces is reached. The Na^+–K^+ pump helps to maintain the ion distribution. It requires significant energy (ATP) to move ions against their concentration gradients.

gradient is a force that equalizes the amount or concentration of material across a biological barrier. When the two forces on K^+ (inward electrostatic force and outward concentration gradient) are balanced (called the **equilibrium potential for potassium**), the membrane potential is still more negative inside (−70 mV). In addition, because small amounts of Na^+ leak into the cell, an energy-dependent pump (the **Na⁺–K⁺ pump**) contributes to the resting potential by exchanging Na^+ for K^+ across the membrane. For every three ions of Na^+ pumped out, two K^+ ions are pumped in, keeping the inside of the cell negative.

In summary, all cells are polarized at rest, having a difference in charge across their membranes. The potential is due to the uneven distribution of ions across the membrane, which occurs because ions move through relatively specific channels that normally are not open. K^+ has greater ability to move freely through ungated channels. Although all cells are polarized, what makes neurons different is that rapid changes in the membrane potential provide the means for neurons to conduct information; this, in turn, influences hundreds of other cells in the nervous system. The rapid change in membrane potential that is propagated down the length of the axon is called the **action potential**. For a cell to generate an action potential, the membrane potential must be changed from resting (−70 mV) to the **threshold** for firing (−50 mV). At −50 mV, voltage-gated Na^+ channels open, generating a rapid change in membrane potential. Before we look

closely at the action potential, let's see what happens to a neuron to cause the membrane potential to change from resting to threshold.

Local potentials are small, transient changes in membrane potential

Although the membrane potential at rest is −70 mV, various types of stimuli that disturb the membrane can open ion channels momentarily, causing small, local changes in ion distribution and hence electrical potential differences called **local potentials**. To visualize the small changes in membrane potential, we attach our electrodes to an amplifier and to a computer that measures and records the changing voltage over time (**Figure 2.12**). For instance, applying a small, positive electrical current or momentarily opening gated Na^+ channels allows a relatively small number of Na^+ ions to enter the cell. These ions enter because Na^+ is more concentrated outside than inside, so the concentration gradient drives the ions in. The oscilloscope shows that positively charged ions make the inside of the cell slightly more positive in a small, localized area of the membrane, bringing the membrane potential a tiny bit closer to the threshold for firing. This change is called a local **depolarization** and is excitatory. Other stimuli may open Cl^- channels, which allow Cl^- into the cell because the ion's concentration is greater on the outside of the cell. The local increase in the negatively charged ion makes the cell

(A)

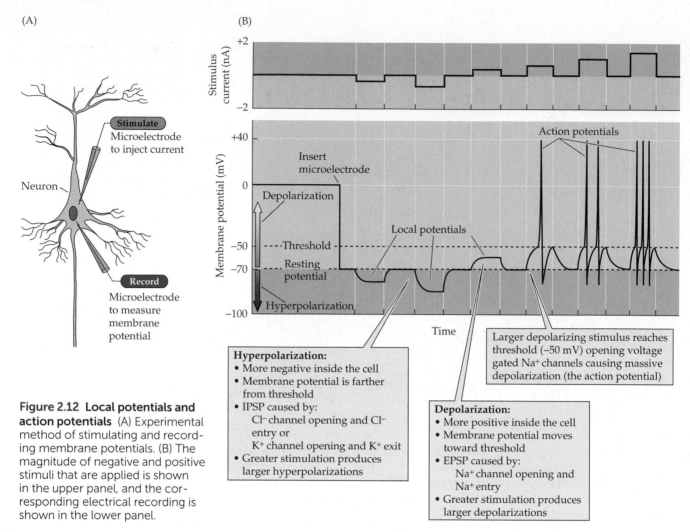

Figure 2.12 Local potentials and action potentials (A) Experimental method of stimulating and recording membrane potentials. (B) The magnitude of negative and positive stimuli that are applied is shown in the upper panel, and the corresponding electrical recording is shown in the lower panel.

slightly more negative inside and brings the resting potential farther away from threshold. This **hyperpolarization** of the membrane is inhibitory. Finally, if gated K⁺ channels are opened by a stimulus, K⁺ is driven outward locally on the basis of its concentration gradient. Because positively charged ions leave the cell, it becomes just slightly more negative inside, making the membrane potential farther from threshold and causing local hyperpolarization. These local potentials are of significance to psychopharmacology because when drugs or neurotransmitters bind to particular receptors in the nervous system, they may momentarily open specific ion channels (see Figure 2.8), causing an excitatory or inhibitory effect. Because neurotransmitters act on the postsynaptic membrane, the effects are called **excitatory postsynaptic potentials (EPSPs)** or **inhibitory postsynaptic potentials (IPSPs)**.

These local potentials (hyperpolarizations and depolarizations), generated on the dendrites and cell body, have several significant characteristics. First,

they are graded, meaning that the larger the stimulus, the greater is the magnitude of hyperpolarization or depolarization. As soon as the stimulus stops, the ion channels close and the membrane potential returns to resting levels. These local potentials decay rapidly as they passively travel along the cell membrane. Finally, local potentials show summation, sometimes called **integration**, meaning that several small depolarizations can add up to larger changes in membrane potential, as several hyperpolarizations can produce larger inhibitory changes. When hyperpolarizations and depolarizations occur at the same time, they cancel each other out. The receptor areas of a neuron involved in local potential generation receive information from thousands of synaptic connections from other neurons that at any given instant produce IPSPs or EPSPs (as well as other biochemical changes to be described in Chapter 3). Integration of EPSPs and IPSPs occurs in the axon hillock (**Figure 2.13**) and is responsible for generation of the action potential if the threshold for activation is reached.

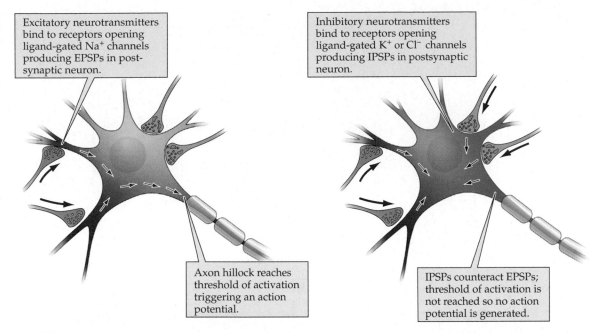

Excitatory neurotransmitters bind to receptors opening ligand-gated Na$^+$ channels producing EPSPs in post-synaptic neuron.

Inhibitory neurotransmitters bind to receptors opening ligand-gated K$^+$ or Cl$^-$ channels producing IPSPs in postsynaptic neuron.

Axon hillock reaches threshold of activation triggering an action potential.

IPSPs counteract EPSPs; threshold of activation is not reached so no action potential is generated.

Figure 2.13 Summation of local potentials Many inhibitory and excitatory synapses influence each neuron, causing local electrical potentials (IPSPs and EPSPs) as well as biochemical changes. At each instant in time, the electrical potentials summate and may reach the threshold for firing. Integration of electrical events occurs at the axon hillock, where the action potential is first generated. The action potential is then conducted along the axon to the axon terminals.

Sufficient depolarization at the axon hillock opens voltage-gated Na$^+$ channels, producing an action potential

The summation of local potentials at the axon hillock is responsible for generation of the action potential. The –50 mV membrane potential (threshold) is responsible for opening large numbers of Na$^+$ channels that are voltage gated, that is, the change in voltage across the membrane near these channels is responsible for opening them (**Figure 2.14**). Because Na$^+$ is much more concentrated outside the cell, its concentration gradient moves it inward; in addition, since the cell at threshold is still negative inside, Na$^+$ is driven in by the electrostatic gradient. These two forces move large numbers of Na$^+$ ions into the cell very quickly, causing the rapid change in membrane potential from –50 mV to +40 mV (called the *rising phase of the action potential*) before the Na$^+$ channels close and remain closed for a fixed period of time while they reset. The time during which the Na$^+$ channels are closed and cannot be opened, regardless of the amount of excitation, prevents the occurrence of another action potential and is called the **absolute refractory period**. The closing of Na$^+$ channels explains why the maximum number of action potentials that can occur is about 1200 impulses per second. The action potential is a rapid change in membrane potential that lasts only

about 1 millisecond. When the membrane potential approaches resting levels, the Na$^+$ channels are reset and ready to open.

Meanwhile, during the rising phase, the changing membrane potential due to Na$^+$ entry causes voltage-gated K$^+$ channels to open, and K$^+$ moves out of the cell. K$^+$ channels remain open after Na$^+$ channels have closed, causing the membrane potential to return to resting levels. The membrane potential actually overshoots the resting potential, so the membrane remains hyperpolarized for a short time until the excess K$^+$ diffuses away or is exchanged for Na$^+$ by the Na$^+$–K$^+$ pump. Because the membrane is more polarized than normal, it is more difficult to generate an action potential. The brief hyperpolarizing phase is called the **relative refractory period** because it takes more excitation to first reach resting potential and further depolarization to reach threshold. The relative refractory period explains why the intensity of stimulation determines rate of firing. Low levels of excitation cannot overcome the relative refractory period, but with increasing excitation, the neuron will fire again as soon as the absolute refractory period has ended.

If the threshold is reached, an action potential occurs (first at the hillock). Its size is unrelated to the amount of stimulation; hence it is considered all-or-none. Reaching the threshold will generate the action

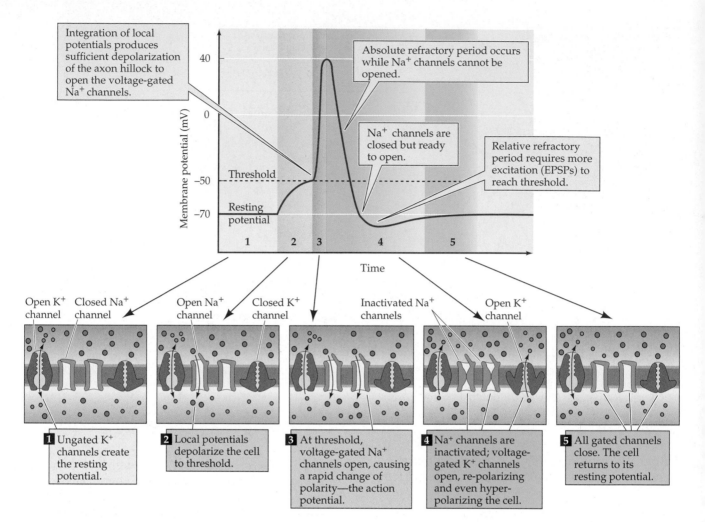

Integration of local potentials produces sufficient depolarization of the axon hillock to open the voltage-gated Na⁺ channels.

Absolute refractory period occurs while Na⁺ channels cannot be opened.

Na⁺ channels are closed but ready to open.

Relative refractory period requires more excitation (EPSPs) to reach threshold.

Membrane potential (mV)

40
0
−50   Threshold
−70   Resting potential

1   2   3   4   5

Time

Open K⁺ channel   Closed Na⁺ channel

Open Na⁺ channel   Closed K⁺ channel

Inactivated Na⁺ channels

Open K⁺ channel

1 Ungated K⁺ channels create the resting potential.

2 Local potentials depolarize the cell to threshold.

3 At threshold, voltage-gated Na⁺ channels open, causing a rapid change of polarity—the action potential.

4 Na⁺ channels are inactivated; voltage-gated K⁺ channels open, re-polarizing and even hyper-polarizing the cell.

5 All gated channels close. The cell returns to its resting potential.

Figure 2.14 Stages of the action potential Opening and closing of Na⁺ and K⁺ channels are responsible for the characteristic shape of the action potential.

potential, but more excitatory events (EPSPs) will not make it larger; fewer excitatory events will not generate an action potential at all. The action potential moves along the axon because positively charged Na⁺ ions spread passively to nearby regions of the axon, which changes the membrane potential to threshold and causes the opening of other voltage-gated Na⁺ channels (**Figure 2.15**). The regeneration process of the axon potential continues sequentially along the entire axon and does not decrease in size; hence it is called *nondecremental* (i.e., it does not decay). In myelinated axons, the speed of conduction is as much as 15 times quicker than in nonmyelinated axons because regeneration of the action potential occurs only at the nodes of Ranvier. This characteristic makes the conduction seem to jump along the axon, so it is called **saltatory conduction**. In addition, myelinated axons use less energy because the Na⁺–K⁺ pump, which uses large amounts of ATP, has to work only at the nodes rather

than all along the axon. Now that we understand normal neuron firing, it is time to look at **Web Box 2.1**, which describes abnormal firing during epileptic seizures.

Drugs and poisons alter axon conduction

As we will learn, most drugs act at synapses to modify chemical transmission. However, a few alter action potential conductance along the axon. Drugs that act as local anesthetics, such as procaine (Novocaine), lidocaine (Xylocaine), and benzocaine (Anesthesin), impair axonal conduction by blocking voltage-gated Na⁺ channels. It should be apparent that if voltage-gated Na⁺ channels cannot open, an action potential cannot occur, and transmission of the pain signal cannot reach the brain. Hence the individual is not aware of the damaging stimulus. Local anesthetics are injected into specific sites between the tissue damage and the CNS to prevent conduction, but saxitoxin is a poison that blocks voltage-gated Na⁺ channels throughout the nervous system because it is ingested. (Saxotoxin is found in shellfish exposed to the "red

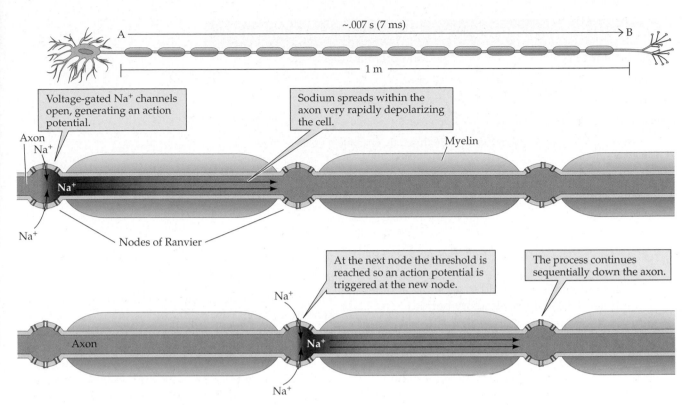

Figure 2.15 Conduction along myelinated axons The generation of the action potential at one node spreads depolarization along the axon, which in turn changes the membrane potential to threshold and opens voltage-gated Na⁺ channels at the next node of Ranvier.

tide" [caused by the organism *Gonyaulax*]). Oral ingestion circulates the toxin throughout the body and causes conduction failure and subsequent death due to suffocation.

Section Summary

- At rest, neurons have an electrical charge across the membrane of –70 mV (resting potential), with the inside being more negative than the outside.

- The resting potential results from the balance between two competing forces on K⁺ ions. Electrostatic pressure moves K⁺ inward because it is attracted by negatively charged molecules trapped inside the cell. The concentration gradient for K⁺ pushes ions out of the cell in an effort to distribute them evenly.

- The Na⁺–K⁺ pump also helps to maintain the negative membrane potential by exchanging three Na⁺ ions (moved out of the cell) for two K⁺ ions (taken in).

- Local potentials are small, short-lived changes in membrane potential found largely on the soma and dendrites after the opening of ligand-gated channels.

- Excitatory postsynaptic potentials (EPSPs) or depolarizations occur when ligand-gated Na⁺ channels open and allow Na⁺ to enter the cell on its concentration gradient, making it slightly more positive and bringing the membrane potential closer to the threshold for firing. Opening Cl⁻ channels allows Cl⁻ to enter on its concentration gradient, making the cell more negative and farther from the threshold, causing hyperpolarizations called inhibitory postsynaptic potentials (IPSPs). When ligand-gated K⁺ channels open, K⁺ exits on its concentration gradient, leaving the cell more negative inside and farther from the threshold producing an IPSP.

- The summation of all EPSPs and IPSPs occurring at any single moment in time occurs at the axon hillock. If the threshold (–50 mV) is reached, voltage-gated Na⁺ channels open, allowing large amounts of Na⁺ to enter the cell to produce the massive depolarization known as the action potential.

- At the peak of the action potential (+40 mV), voltage-gated Na⁺ channels close and cannot be opened until they reset at the resting potential, so no action potential can occur during this time (the absolute refractory period).

- As the cell becomes more positive inside, voltage-gated K⁺ channels open and K⁺ exits from the cell, bringing the membrane potential back toward

TABLE 2.2 Characteristics of Local Potentials and Action Potentials	
Local potentials	Action potentials
Graded	All-or-none
Decremental	Nondecremental
Spatial and temporal summation	Intensity of stimulus coded by rate of firing
Produced by opening of ligand-gated channels	Produced by opening of voltage-gated channels
Depolarization or hyperpolarization	Depolarization

resting levels. The overshoot by K$^+$ causes the cell to be more polarized than normal, so it is more difficult to reach the threshold to generate another action potential (relative refractory period).

- The action potential moves down the length of the axon by sequential opening of voltage-gated Na$^+$ channels.

- In myelinated axons, regeneration of the action potential occurs only at the nodes of Ranvier, producing a rapid, saltatory conduction that is more energy efficient because the Na$^+$–K$^+$ pump needs to exchange ions only at the nodes.

- The characteristics of local and action potentials are summarized in **Table 2.2**.

Organization of the Nervous System

Thus far we have described the structure of individual neurons and their ability to conduct electrical signals. Clearly, neurons never function individually but form interacting circuits referred to as *neural networks*. Such complexity allows us to make coordinated responses to changes in the environment. For example, as we perceive a potential danger, we suddenly become vigilant and more acutely aware of our surroundings. Meanwhile, internal organs prepare us for action by elevating heart rate, blood pressure, available energy sources, and so forth. Most of us will also calculate the probable outcome of fighting or running before taking a defensive or aggressive stance. Even simple responses require complex coordination of multiple nuclei in the brain and spinal cord. The following section describes the organization of neurons into brain regions that serve specific functions. This section provides only the highlights of functional neuroanatomy and emphasizes those brain structures that receive more attention in subsequent chapters. **Box 2.2** provides a quick review of the terms used to describe the location of structures in the nervous system.

The nervous system comprises the central and peripheral divisions

The nervous system includes the central nervous system, or CNS (the brain and spinal cord), and the peripheral nervous system, or PNS (all nerves outside the CNS) (**Figure 2.16A**). The PNS in turn can be further divided into the somatic system, which controls voluntary muscles with both spinal nerves and cranial nerves, and the autonomic nervous system, which consists of autonomic nerves and some cranial nerves that control the function of organs and glands. The autonomic nervous system has both sympathetic and parasympathetic divisions, which help the organism to respond to changing energy demands. **Figure 2.16B** provides an overall view of the divisions of the nervous system. We begin by looking more closely at the peripheral nervous system.

SOMATIC NERVOUS SYSTEM   Each spinal nerve consists of many neurons, some of which carry sensory information and others motor information; hence they are called *mixed nerves*. Within each mixed nerve, sensory information is carried from the surface of the body and from muscles into the dorsal horn of the spinal cord by neurons that have their cell bodies in the dorsal root ganglia (**Figure 2.17**). These signals going into the spinal cord are called **sensory afferents**. Mixed nerves also have motor neurons, which are cells beginning in the ventral horn of the spinal cord and ending on skeletal muscles. These are called **motor efferents** and are responsible for voluntary movements.

The 12 pairs of cranial nerves that project from the brain provide functions similar to those provided by the spinal nerves, except that they serve primarily the head and neck; hence they carry sensory information such as vision, touch, and taste into the brain and control muscle movement needed for things like chewing and laughing. They differ from the spinal nerves in that they are not all mixed nerves; several are dedicated to only sensory or only motor function. In addition,

(A)

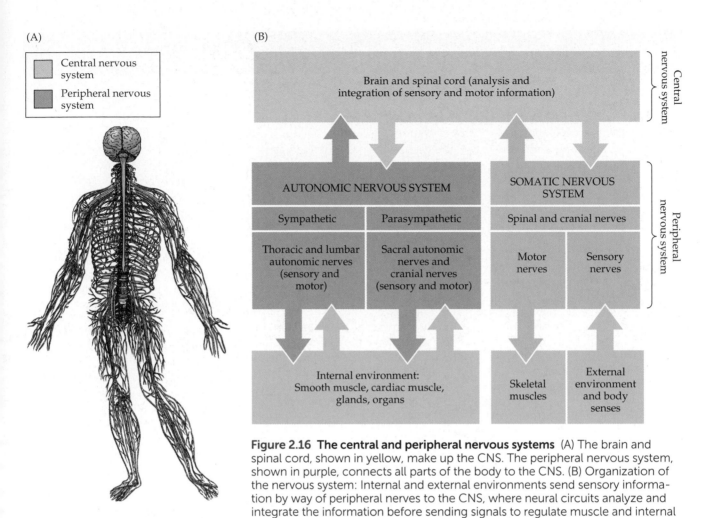

Central nervous system

Peripheral nervous system

(B)

Central nervous system

Brain and spinal cord (analysis and integration of sensory and motor information)

Peripheral nervous system

AUTONOMIC NERVOUS SYSTEM

Sympathetic

Thoracic and lumbar autonomic nerves (sensory and motor)

Parasympathetic

Sacral autonomic nerves and cranial nerves (sensory and motor)

SOMATIC NERVOUS SYSTEM

Spinal and cranial nerves

Motor nerves

Sensory nerves

Internal environment: Smooth muscle, cardiac muscle, glands, organs

Skeletal muscles

External environment and body senses

Figure 2.16 The central and peripheral nervous systems (A) The brain and spinal cord, shown in yellow, make up the CNS. The peripheral nervous system, shown in purple, connects all parts of the body to the CNS. (B) Organization of the nervous system: Internal and external environments send sensory information by way of peripheral nerves to the CNS, where neural circuits analyze and integrate the information before sending signals to regulate muscle and internal organ function.

several of the cranial nerves innervate glands and organs rather than skeletal muscles; this means that they are part of the autonomic nervous system (see the next section). The most unique cranial nerve is the vagus nerve (nerve X), because it communicates with numerous organs in the viscera, including the heart, lungs, and gastrointestinal tract. The vagus consists of both sensory and motor neurons.

AUTONOMIC NERVOUS SYSTEM   The autonomic nerves, collectively called the autonomic nervous system (ANS), regulate the internal environment by innervating smooth muscles such as the intestine and urinary bladder, cardiac muscle, and glands, including the adrenal and salivary glands. The purpose of the ANS is to control digestive processes, blood pressure, body temperature, and other

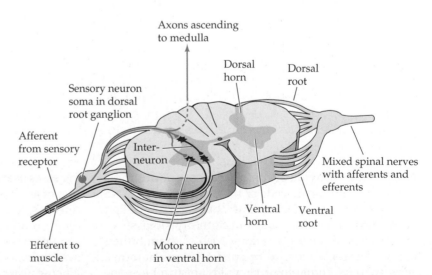

Axons ascending to medulla

Sensory neuron soma in dorsal root ganglion

Afferent from sensory receptor

Inter-neuron

Dorsal horn

Dorsal root

Mixed spinal nerves with afferents and efferents

Ventral horn

Ventral root

Efferent to muscle

Motor neuron in ventral horn

Figure 2.17 Spinal nerves of the peripheral nervous system Cross section of the spinal cord shows mixed spinal nerves with sensory afferents entering the dorsal horn and motor efferents leaving the ventral horn to innervate skeletal muscles. Note that the soma for the afferent neuron is in the dorsal root ganglion.

BOX 2.2   The Cutting Edge

Finding Your Way in the Nervous System

To discuss anatomical relationships, a systematic method to describe location in three dimensions is needed. The directions are based on the **neuraxis**, an imaginary line beginning at the base of the spinal cord and ending at the front of the brain. For most animals, the neuraxis is a straight line; however, because humans walk upright, the neuraxis bends, changing the relationship of the brain to the spinal cord (Figure A). For this reason, both the top of the head and the back of the body are called **dorsal**; **ventral** refers to the underside of the brain and the front surface of the body. To avoid confusion, sometimes the top of

the human brain is described as **superior** and the bottom as **inferior**. In addition, the head end of the nervous system is **anterior** or **rostral**, and the tail end is **posterior** or **caudal**. Finally, **medial** means "toward the center or midline of the body," and **lateral** means "toward the side." We can describe the location of any brain area using these three pairs of dimensional descriptors.

Much of our knowledge about the structure of the nervous system comes from examining two-dimensional slices (Figure B). The orientation of the slice (or **section**) is typically in any one of three different planes:

- **Horizontal** sections are slices parallel to the horizon.
- **Sagittal** sections are cut on the plane that bisects the nervous system into right and left halves. The **midsagittal** section is the slice that divides the brain into left and right symmetrical pieces.
- **Coronal** (or **frontal**) sections are cut parallel to the face.

Identifying specific structures in these different views takes a good deal of experience. However, computer-assisted evaluation allows us to visualize the brain of a living human in far greater detail than was previously possible.

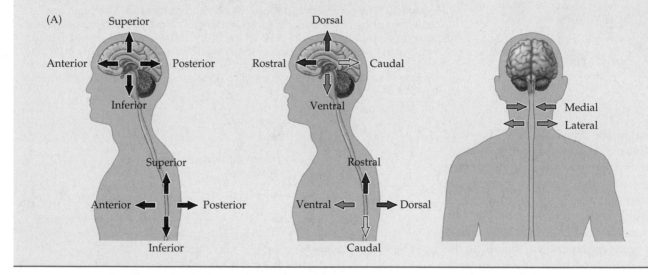

(A)

functions that provide or conserve energy appropriate to the environmental needs of the organism. The ANS is divided into two components, the sympathetic and parasympathetic divisions, and both divisions serve most organs of the body (**Figure 2.18**). Although their functions usually work in opposition to one another, control of our internal environment is not an all-or-none affair. Instead, activity of the **sympathetic** division predominates when energy expenditure is necessary, such as during times of stress, excitement, and exertion; hence its nickname is the "fight-or-flight" system. This system

increases heart rate and blood pressure, stimulates secretion of adrenaline, and increases blood flow to skeletal muscles, among other effects. The **parasympathetic** division predominates at times when energy reserves can be conserved and stored for later use; hence this system increases salivation, digestion, and storage of glucose and other nutrients; it also slows heart rate and decreases respiration.

In addition to contrasting functions, the two branches of the ANS have anatomical differences, including points of origin in the CNS. The cell bodies

BOX 2.2 *(continued)*

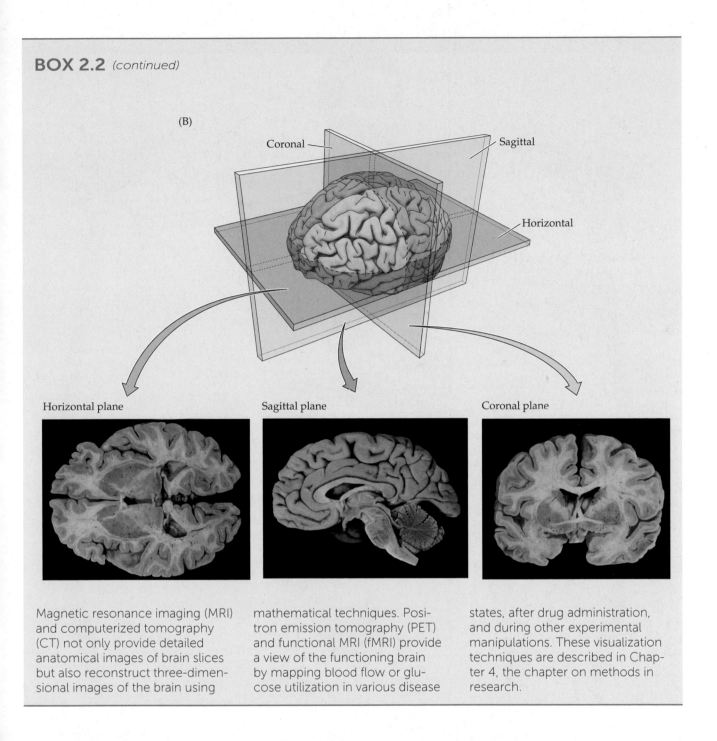

(B)

Coronal

Sagittal

Horizontal

Horizontal plane

Sagittal plane

Coronal plane

Magnetic resonance imaging (MRI) and computerized tomography (CT) not only provide detailed anatomical images of brain slices but also reconstruct three-dimensional images of the brain using mathematical techniques. Positron emission tomography (PET) and functional MRI (fMRI) provide a view of the functioning brain by mapping blood flow or glucose utilization in various disease states, after drug administration, and during other experimental manipulations. These visualization techniques are described in Chapter 4, the chapter on methods in research.

of the efferent sympathetic neurons are in the ventral horn of the spinal cord at the thoracic and lumbar regions (see Figure 2.18). Their axons project for a relatively short distance before they synapse with a cluster of cell bodies called *sympathetic ganglia*. Some of these ganglia are lined up very close to the spinal cord; others such as the celiac ganglion are located somewhat farther away. These preganglionic fibers release the neurotransmitter acetylcholine onto cell bodies in the ganglia. These postganglionic cells project their axons for a relatively long distance to the target tissues, where they release the neurotransmitter norepinephrine.

In contrast, the cell bodies of the efferent parasympathetic neurons are located either in the brain (cranial nerves III, VII, IX, and X) or in the ventral horn of the spinal cord at the sacral region. Preganglionic neurons travel long distances to synapse on cells in the parasympathetic ganglia that are not neatly lined up along the spinal cord but are close to individual target organs. The preganglionic fibers release acetylcholine, just as the sympathetic preganglionics do. However,

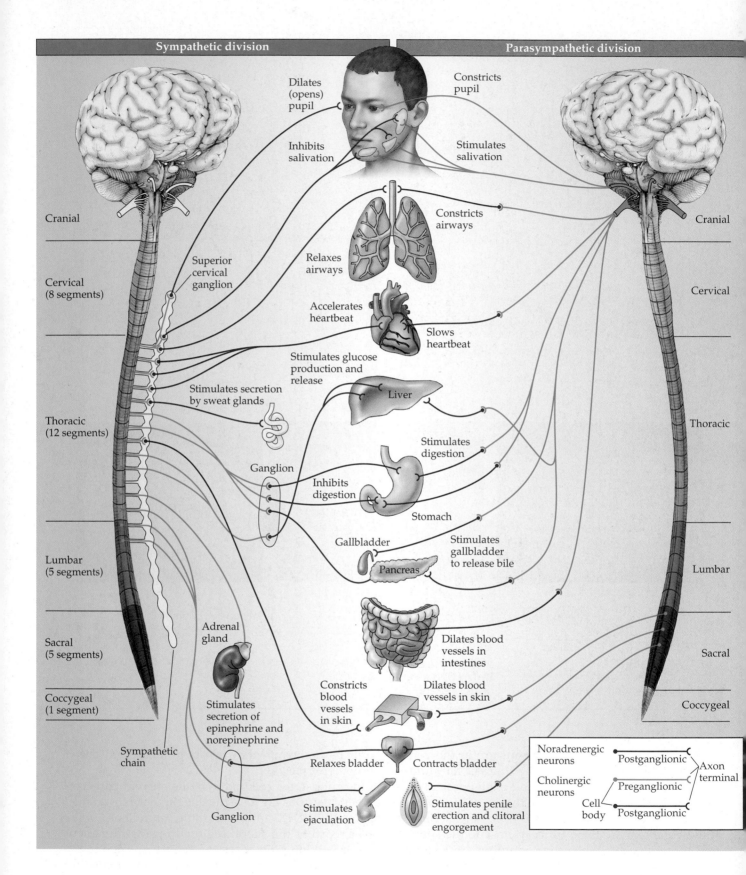

Sympathetic division

Parasympathetic division

Dilates (opens) pupil

Constricts pupil

Inhibits salivation

Stimulates salivation

Cranial

Cervical (8 segments)

Thoracic (12 segments)

Lumbar (5 segments)

Sacral (5 segments)

Coccygeal (1 segment)

Cranial

Cervical

Thoracic

Lumbar

Sacral

Coccygeal

Superior cervical ganglion

Constricts airways

Relaxes airways

Accelerates heartbeat

Slows heartbeat

Stimulates glucose production and release

Stimulates secretion by sweat glands

Liver

Stimulates digestion

Ganglion

Inhibits digestion

Stomach

Gallbladder

Pancreas

Stimulates gallbladder to release bile

Adrenal gland

Stimulates secretion of epinephrine and norepinephrine

Sympathetic chain

Dilates blood vessels in intestines

Constricts blood vessels in skin

Dilates blood vessels in skin

Relaxes bladder

Contracts bladder

Ganglion

Stimulates ejaculation

Stimulates penile erection and clitoral engorgement

Noradrenergic neurons — Postganglionic — Axon terminal

Cholinergic neurons — Preganglionic

Cell body — Postganglionic

◀ **Figure 2.18 Autonomic nervous system (ANS)** The internal organs, smooth muscles, and glands served by the ANS have both sympathetic and parasympathetic regulation. The two divisions have opposing effects on the organs; the sympathetic effects prepare the individual for action, and the parasympathetic effects serve to generate and store energy and reduce energy expenditure. Acetylcholine is the neurotransmitter released in all autonomic ganglia because preganglionic fibers are cholinergic neurons. At the target organs, the parasympathetic neurons release acetylcholine once again, while sympathetic neurons release norepinephrine (noradrenergic neurons). Their anatomical and neurotransmitter differences are described in the text and are summarized in Table 2.3.

parasympathetic postganglionic neurons, which are quite short, also release acetylcholine. Understanding the autonomic nervous system is especially important for psychopharmacologists because many psychotherapeutic drugs alter either norepinephrine or acetylcholine in the brain to relieve symptoms, but by altering those same neurotransmitters in the peripheral nerves, these drugs often produce annoying or dangerous side effects, such as elevated blood pressure, dry mouth, and urinary problems (all related to autonomic function). **Table 2.3** summarizes the differences between the two divisions of the ANS.

CNS functioning is dependent on structural features

The tough bone of the skull and vertebrae maintains the integrity of the delicate tissue of the brain and spinal cord. Three layers of tissue called **meninges** lie just within the bony covering and provide additional protection. The outermost layer, which is also the toughest, is the **dura mater**. The **arachnoid**, just below the dura, is a membrane with a weblike sublayer

(subarachnoid space) filled with cerebrospinal fluid (CSF). Finally, the **pia mater** is a thin layer of tissue that sits directly on the nervous tissue.

The CSF not only surrounds the brain and spinal cord but also fills the irregularly shaped cavities within the brain, called **cerebral ventricles**, and the channel that runs the length of the spinal cord, called the **central canal**. CSF is formed by the choroid plexus within the lateral ventricle of each hemisphere and flows to the third and fourth ventricles before moving into the subarachnoid space to bathe the exterior of the brain and spinal cord (see Figure 1.6A). CSF not only protects the brain but also helps in the exchange of nutrients and waste products between the brain and the blood. This exchange is possible because the capillaries found in the choroid plexus do not have the tight junctions typical of capillaries in the brain. These tight junctions constitute the blood–brain barrier, a vital mechanism for protecting the delicate chemical balance in the CNS. Return to Chapter 1 for a review of the blood–brain barrier.

The CNS has six distinct regions reflecting embryological development

The six anatomical divisions of the adult CNS are evident in the developing embryo. It is important to know about the development of the brain because exposure to harmful events, including therapeutic and illicit drugs, environmental toxins, and stress, will have different outcomes depending on the timing of the insult and the developmental event occurring at that time. You will read more about this in later chapters on clinical disorders and in the chapter on alcohol. The CNS starts out as a fluid-filled tube that soon develops three enlargements at one end that become the adult hindbrain, midbrain, and forebrain,

TABLE 2.3 Characteristics of the Sympathetic and Parasympathetic Divisions of the ANS

Sympathetic	Parasympathetic
Energy mobilization	Energy conservation and storage
Origin in thoracic and lumbar spinal cord	Origin in cranial nerves and sacral spinal cord
Relatively short preganglionic fibers; long postganglionics	Long preganglionic fibers ending near organs; short postganglionics
Releases acetylcholine in ganglia and norepinephrine at target	Releases acetylcholine at both ganglia and target

(A) Embryonic development of the human brain

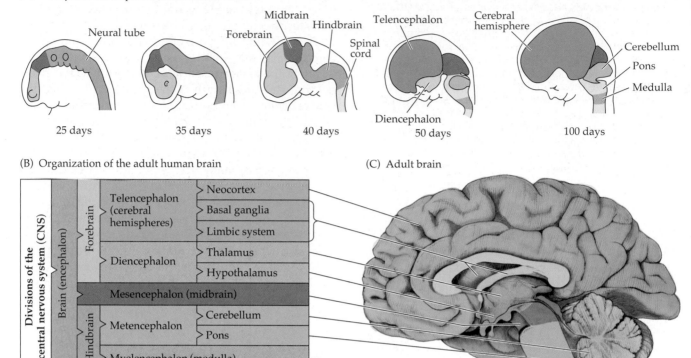

25 days   35 days   40 days   50 days   100 days

(B) Organization of the adult human brain   (C) Adult brain

Figure 2.19 Divisions of the central nervous system
(A) Beginning with the primitive neural tube in the human embryo, the CNS develops rapidly, and by day 50 of gestation, the six divisions of the adult CNS are apparent in the fetus. (B) The organization of the CNS (brain and spinal cord) is presented in the table and color coded to match the divisions shown in the adult brain (sagittal section) (C).

drugs, modify the interactions of these neurons. The principal divisions of the CNS are summarized in **Figure 2.19B,C**.

NEUROTROPHIC FACTORS Neurotrophic factors are proteins that act as neuron growth factors and influence not only neuron growth, but also cell differentiation and survival. Nervous system development and maintenance of synaptic connections over the life span are dependent on the presence of neurotrophic factors such as nerve growth factor (NGF), brain-derived neurotrophic factor (BDNF), neurotrophin-3, and neurotrophin-4/5. Although similar in structure and general function, neurotrophins show some specificity. For example, NGF, the first neurotrophic factor to be discovered, is synthesized and secreted by peripheral target organs and guides the development of axonal processes of nearby neurons to establish synaptic connections with the target organ. Additionally, the presence of neurotrophic factors determines which neuronal connections survive and which are unnecessary and are eliminated by cell death. Apparently, the large population of neurons competes for the limited amount of neurotrophic factor in the target tissue, and those that are not supported by access to neurotrophins die, while those that respond to NGF establish appropriate synaptic connections. This process ensures that the number of connections is appropriate for

while the remainder of the neural tube becomes the spinal cord (**Figure 2.19A**). The structural organization of these regions reflects the hierarchical nature of their functions. Each level has overlapping functions, so that higher levels partially replicate the functions of lower ones but provide increased behavioral complexity and refined nervous system control. The fluid-filled chamber itself becomes the ventricular system in the brain and the central canal in the spinal cord. Within 2 months of conception, further subdivisions occur: the hindbrain enlargement develops two swellings, as does the forebrain. These divisions, in ascending order, are the spinal cord, myelencephalon, metencephalon, mesencephalon, diencephalon, and telencephalon. Each region can be further subdivided into clusters of cell bodies, called **nuclei**, and their associated bundles of axons, called **tracts**. (In the PNS, they are called **ganglia** and **nerves**, respectively.) These interconnecting networks of cells will be the focus of much of the remainder of this book, because drugs that alter brain function, that is, psychotropic

(A)

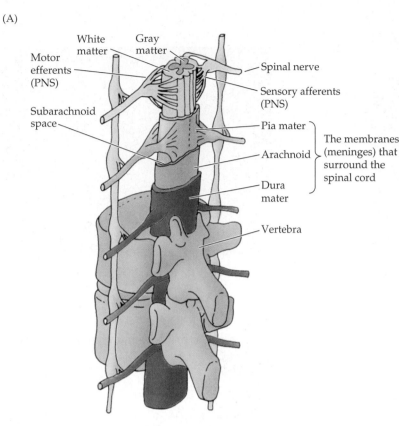

Figure 2.20 Spinal cord (A) A view of the spinal cord showing its relationship to the protective layers of meninges and the bony vertebra. Note the clearly defined gray matter and white matter in cross section. (B) Schematic diagram of the ascending sensory tracts shown in blue and the descending motor tracts in red.

(B)

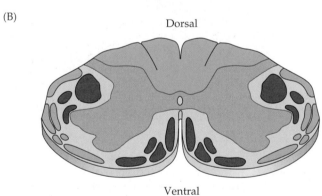

cases, neurotrophic factors are transported from the soma to the axon terminals, where their release modifies nearby cell bodies or nerve terminals of other neurons. For example, neurotrophins determine which of the cell dendrites grow and which retract, a process that influences synaptic activity and plasticity, quite independent of their role in cell survival. Research into the involvement of neurotrophic factors in mood disorders has suggested the neurotrophic hypothesis of depression and other psychiatric disorders. The importance of neurotrophic factors as potential therapeutic agents for neurodegenerative diseases such as Alzheimer's disease (see Chapter 21) and psychiatric disorders (see Chapter 19) will be discussed further in later chapters.

SPINAL CORD   The spinal cord is made up of gray and white matter. The former appears butterfly-shaped in cross section (**Figure 2.20A**) and is called *gray matter* because the large numbers of cell bodies in this region appear dark on histological examination. The cell bodies include cell groups that receive information from sensory afferent neurons entering the dorsal horn and cell bodies of motor neurons in the ventral horn that send efferents to skeletal muscles. The white matter surrounding the butterfly-shaped gray matter is made up of myelinated axons of ascending pathways that conduct sensory information to the brain as well as myelinated axons of descending pathways from higher centers to the motor neurons that initiate muscle contraction (**Figure 2.20B**).

As we move up the spinal cord and enter the skull, the spinal cord enlarges and becomes the **brainstem**. Examination of the ventral surface of the brain (**Figure 2.21A**) shows that the brainstem with its three principal parts—medulla, pons, and midbrain—is clearly visible. The brainstem contains the reticular formation, a large network of cells and interconnecting fibers that extends up the core of the brainstem for most of its length (described later in the section on the metencephalon). Additionally, the brainstem is the origin of numerous cranial nerves that receive sensory information from the skin and joints of the face, head, and

the target tissue. NGF guides the growth of sympathetic neurons and a subpopulation of sensory ganglion cells. A second neurotrophic factor, BDNF, in the periphery is released from skeletal muscles and guides motor neuron development and survival. Other neurotrophins aid the survival of other subsets of peripheral sensory neurons. It is also clear that glial Schwann cells, which myelinate neurons of the peripheral nervous system, release a growth factor when their axon is damaged. The growth factor in this case leads to regeneration of the damaged axon. In the CNS, neurotrophins like BDNF may be released by target neurons (rather than organs) to maintain appropriate synaptic connections, but in some cases, the neurotrophin acts on the same neuron that produces it for autoregulation. Additionally, in some

(A) Ventral view

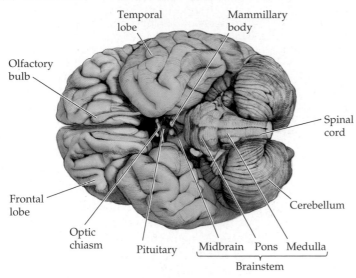

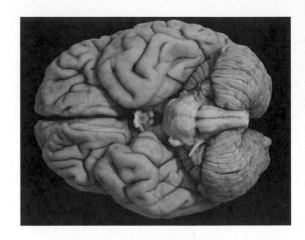

(B) Midsagittal view

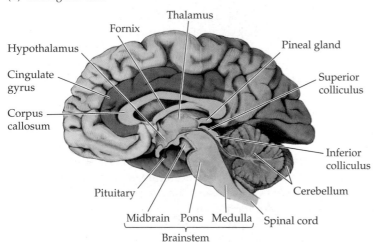

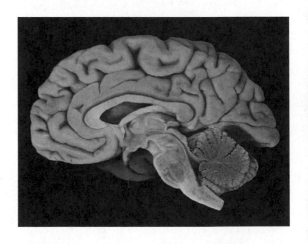

Figure 2.21 Two views of the human brain The drawings on the left in each panel label the structural features that are visible on the ventral external surface (A) and the midsagittal (midline) section (B). The right side of each panel shows the same view of a human postmortem brain specimen. (Courtesy of Mark Williams and Dale Purves, Duke University Medical Center.)

neck, as well as providing motor control to the muscles in that region. Finally, a significant volume of the brainstem is made up of ascending and descending axons coursing between the spinal cord and higher brain regions. The relationships of the structures of the brainstem are apparent in the midsagittal view (**Figure 2.21B**).

MYELENCEPHALON   The first major structure of the brainstem that we encounter is the myelencephalon, or medulla. Within the **medulla**, multiple cell groups regulate vital functions, including heart rate, digestion,

respiration, blood pressure, coughing, and vomiting. When an individual dies from a drug overdose, the cause is most often depression of the respiratory center in the medulla. Also located in the medulla is the **area postrema**, or the vomiting center, described in Chapter 1 as a cluster of cells with a reduced blood–brain barrier that initiates vomiting in response to toxins in the blood. Drugs in the opioid class such as morphine act on the area postrema and produce vomiting, a common unpleasant side effect of treatment for pain. The nuclei for cranial nerves XI and XII, which control the muscles of the neck and tongue, are also located in the medulla.

METENCEPHALON   Two large structures within the metencephalon are the pons and the cerebellum (see Figure 2.21). Within the central core of the pons and extending rostrally into the midbrain and caudally into the medulla is the **reticular formation**. The reticular formation is not really a structure but a collection of perhaps 100 small nuclei forming a network that plays an important role in arousal, attention, sleep, and muscle tone, as well as in some cardiac and respiratory reflexes. One nucleus, called the **locus coeruleus**, is of particular importance to psychopharmacology because it is a cluster of cell bodies that distribute their axons to many areas of the forebrain. These cells are the principal source of all neurons that use the neurotransmitter norepinephrine. When active, these cells cause arousal, increased vigilance, and attention. Drugs such as amphetamine enhance their function, causing sleeplessness and enhanced alertness.

Other cell groups within the pons that also belong to the reticular formation are the **dorsal** and **median raphe nuclei**. These two clusters of cells are the source of most of the neurons in the CNS that use serotonin as their neurotransmitter. Together, cell bodies in the dorsal and median raphe send axons releasing serotonin to virtually all forebrain areas and function in the regulation of diverse processes, including sleep, aggression and impulsiveness, neuroendocrine functions, and emotion. Because it has a generally inhibitory effect on CNS function, serotonin may maintain behaviors within specific limits. Drugs such as LSD (lysergic acid diethylamide) produce their dramatic hallucinogenic effects by inhibiting the inhibitory functions of the raphe nuclei (see Chapter 15).

The **cerebellum** is a large foliated structure on the dorsal surface of the brain that connects to the pons by several large bundles of axons called **cerebellar peduncles**. The cerebellum is a significant sensorimotor center and receives visual, auditory, and somatosensory input, as well as information about body position and balance, from the vestibular system. By coordinating sensory information with motor information received from the cerebral cortex, the cerebellum coordinates and smoothes out movements by timing and patterning skeletal muscle contractions. In addition, the cerebellum allows us to make corrective movements to maintain our balance and posture. Damage to the cerebellum produces poor coordination and jerky movements. Drugs such as alcohol at moderate doses inhibit the function of the cerebellum and cause slurred speech and staggering.

MESENCEPHALON   The midbrain has two divisions: the tectum and the tegmentum. The tectum, the dorsal-most structure, consists of the superior colliculi, which are part of the visual system, and the inferior colliculi, which are part of the auditory system (see Figure 2.21B). These nuclei are involved in reflexes such as the pupillary reflex to light, eye movement, and reactions to moving stimuli.

Within the **tegmentum** are several structures that are particularly important to psychopharmacologists. The first is the **periaqueductal gray (PAG)**, which surrounds the cerebral aqueduct that connects the third

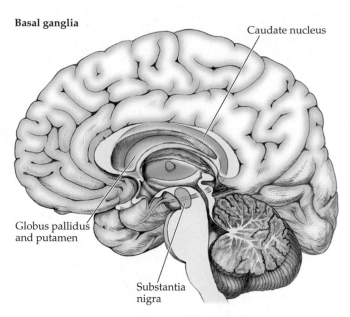

Basal ganglia

Caudate nucleus

Globus pallidus and putamen

Substantia nigra

Figure 2.22 The basal ganglia These four structures form neural pathways that utilize dopamine as their neurotransmitter. These neural circuits constitute a system for motor control.

and fourth ventricles. The PAG is one of the areas that are important for the modulation of pain. Local electrical stimulation of these cells produces analgesia but no change in the ability to detect temperature, touch, or pressure. The PAG is rich in opioid receptors, making it an important site for morphine-induced analgesia. Chapter 11 describes the importance of natural opioid neuropeptides and the PAG in pain regulation. The PAG is also important in sequencing species-specific actions, such as defensive rage and predation.

The **substantia nigra** is a cluster of cell bodies whose relatively long axons innervate the striatum, a component of the basal ganglia (**Figure 2.22**). These cells constitute one of several important neural pathways that utilize dopamine as their neurotransmitter. This pathway is called the nigrostriatal tract. (The names of neural pathways often combine the site of origin of the fibers with their termination site, hence *nigrostriatal*, meaning "substantia nigra to striatum.") This neural circuit is critical for the initiation and modulation of movement. Cell death in the substantia nigra is the cause of Parkinson's disease—a disorder characterized by tremor, rigidity, and inability to initiate movements. An adjacent cluster of dopaminergic cells in the midbrain is the **ventral tegmental area (VTA)**. Some of these cells project axons to the septum, olfactory tubercle, nucleus accumbens, amygdala, and other limbic structures in the forebrain (see the section on the telencephalon). Hence these cells form the mesolimbic tract (note that "meso" refers to

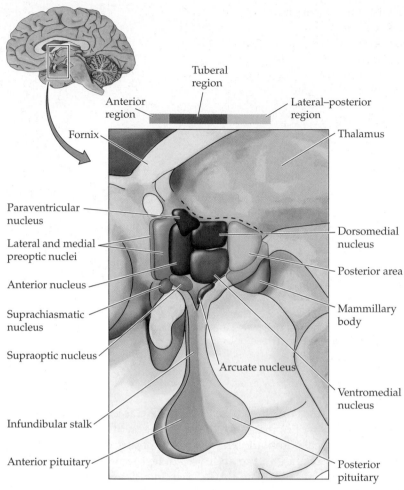

Figure 2.23 **Hypothalamus** The hypothalamus is a cluster of nuclei at the base of the forebrain that is often subdivided into three groups based on region: anterior, tuberal, and lateral–posterior. Each of the nuclei has its own complex pattern of neural connections and regulates one or several components of homeostatic function and motivated behavior.

direct its attention to selectively important sensory messages while diminishing the significance of others; hence the thalamus helps to regulate levels of awareness.

The second diencephalic structure, the **hypothalamus**, lies ventral to the thalamus at the base of the brain. Although it is much smaller than the thalamus, it is made up of many small nuclei that perform functions critical for survival (**Figure 2.23**). The hypothalamus receives a wide variety of information about the internal environment and, in coordination with closely related structures in the limbic system (see the section on the telencephalon), initiates various mechanisms important for limiting the variability of the body's internal states (i.e., they are responsible for homeostasis). Several nuclei are involved in maintaining body temperature and salt–water balance. Other nuclei modulate hunger, thirst, energy metabolism, reproductive behaviors, and emotional responses such as aggression. The hypothalamus directs behaviors for adjusting to these changing needs by controlling both the autonomic nervous system and the endocrine system and organizing behaviors in coordination with other brain areas. Axons from nuclei in the hypothalamus descend into the brainstem to the nuclei of the cranial nerves that provide parasympathetic control. Additionally, other axons descend farther into the spinal cord to influence sympathetic nervous system function. Other hypothalamic nuclei communicate with the contiguous pituitary gland by two methods: neural control of the posterior pituitary and hormonal control of the anterior pituitary. By regulating the endocrine hormones, the hypothalamus has widespread and prolonged effects on body physiology. Of particular significance to psychopharmacology is the role of the paraventricular nucleus in regulating the hormonal response to stress because stress has a major impact on our behavior and vulnerability to psychiatric disorders. **Box 2.3** describes the neuroendocrine response to stress and previews its significance for psychiatric ills and their treatment.

midbrain). Other cells in the VTA project to structures in the prefrontal cortex, cingulate cortex, and entorhinal areas and are considered the mesocortical tract. All three of these dopamine pathways are of significance in our discussions of Parkinson's disease (see Chapter 21), drug addiction (see Chapter 9), and schizophrenia (see Chapter 20).

DIENCEPHALON   The two major structures in the diencephalon are the thalamus and the hypothalamus. The **thalamus** is a cluster of nuclei that first process and then distribute sensory and motor information to the appropriate portion of the cerebral cortex. For example, the lateral geniculate nucleus of the thalamus receives visual information from the eyes before projecting it to the primary visual cortex. Most incoming signals are integrated and modified before they are sent on to the cortex. The functioning of the thalamus helps the cortex to

TELENCEPHALON   The cerebral hemispheres are the largest region of the brain and include the external cerebral cortex, the underlying white matter, and subcortical structures belonging to the basal ganglia and limbic system. The **basal ganglia** include the caudate, putamen,

BOX 2.3   Of Special Interest

Neuroendocrine Response to Stress

The principal neuroendocrine response to stress is often referred to as the HPA axis because it depends on the interaction of the hypothalamus (H), the pituitary (P) gland, and the adrenal (A) gland. HPA axis activation is one part of complex emotional responses orchestrated by the amygdala. In essence, stress causes the secretion of corticotropin releasing factor (CRF) by the paraventricular nucleus of the hypothalamus into the blood vessels ending in the anterior pituitary (see figure). The binding of CRF in that gland causes the release of adrenocorticotropic hormone (ACTH) into the general blood circulation. ACTH subsequently binds to the adrenal cortex to increase the secretion of cortisol and other glucocorticoids, all of which contribute to the mobilization of energy to cope with stress or exertion. Under optimum conditions, cortisol feeds back to the hypothalamus (and hippocampus) to shut down HPA activation and return cortisol levels to normal.

Although HPA activity is critical for survival and adaptation to the environment, overuse of this adaptive mechanism leads to damaging changes to the brain and body. Damaging effects of prolonged cortisol response include such events as lower inflammatory response causing slower wound healing and immune system suppression. Stress has also been linked to an exacerbation of autoimmune diseases such as multiple sclerosis, gastric problems, diabetes, elevated blood pressure, premature aging, and many other disorders. In addition, stress affects neuron structure and brain function.

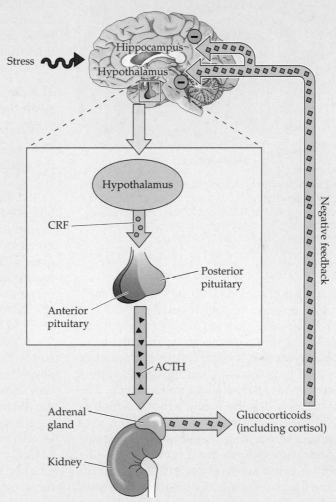

Several later chapters in this text will describe the relationship between stress and alcoholism, the damaging effect of stress on cells in the hippocampus and its relationship to clinical depression, and the impact of early life traumas that alter the set point of the HPA axis, making it overly responsive to stressors later in life. The differential activation of stress response circuitry in men and women will also be addressed in the chapter on anxiety disorders. In Chapter 20, you will learn how stress-induced epigenetic events may alter the expression of a gene that is linked to the cognitive deficits characteristic of schizophrenia. All of these issues point to the critical need to evaluate more thoroughly the significant interaction between psychiatric and systemic medical disorders with the hope for potential new approaches to prevent and treat disabling conditions.

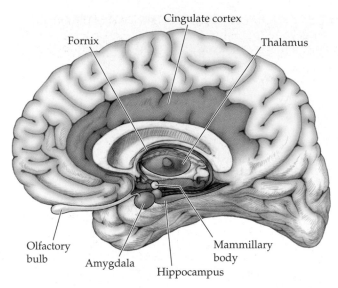

Cingulate cortex

Fornix

Thalamus

Olfactory bulb

Amygdala

Hippocampus

Mammillary body

Figure 2.24 Limbic system Multiple subcortical structures interconnect to form the limbic system, which is critical for learning, memory, and emotional responses. Rich connections of limbic areas with association areas of the cortex contribute to decision making and planning.

and globus pallidus, and, along with the substantia nigra in the midbrain, comprise a system for motor control (see Figure 2.22). Drugs administered to control symptoms of Parkinson's disease act on this group of structures.

The **limbic system** is a complex neural network that is involved in integrating emotional responses and regulating motivated behavior and learning. The limbic system includes the limbic cortex, which is located on the medial and interior surface of the cerebral hemispheres and is transitional between allocortex (phylogenetically older cortex) and neocortex (the more recently evolved six-layer cortex). A significant portion of the limbic cortex is the cingulate. Chapter 11 describes the importance of the anterior portion of the cingulate in mediating the emotional component of pain. Some of the significant subcortical limbic structures are the amygdala, nucleus accumbens, and hippocampus, which is connected to the mammillary bodies and the septal nuclei by the fornix, the major tract of the limbic system (**Figure 2.24**). The **hippocampus** is most closely associated with the establishment of new long-term memories and spatial memory and has been the focus of research into Alzheimer's disease and its treatment, as you will read in Chapter 7. Additionally, the vulnerability of the hippocampus to high levels of stress hormones suggests its involvement in clinical depression and antidepressant drug treatment (see Chapter 19). The **amygdala** plays a central role in coordinating the various components of emotional responses through its profuse connections with the

olfactory system, hypothalamus (which is sometimes included in the limbic system, even though it is a diencephalic structure), thalamus, hippocampus, striatum, and brainstem nuclei, as well as portions of the neocortex, such as the orbitofrontal cortex. The amygdala and associated limbic areas play a prominent role in our discussions of antidepressants, alcohol, and antianxiety drugs. Chapters that describe the reinforcing value of abused substances also focus on limbic structures, notably the **nucleus accumbens**.

The cerebral cortex is divided into four lobes, each having primary, secondary, and tertiary areas

The cerebral cortex is a layer of tissue that covers the cerebral hemispheres. In humans, the cortex (or "bark") is heavily convoluted and has deep grooves called **fissures**, smaller grooves called **sulci**, and bulges of tissue between called **gyri**. Thus the bulge of tissues immediately posterior to the central sulcus is the postcentral gyrus. The convolutions of the cortex greatly enlarge its surface area, to approximately 2.5 square feet. Only about one-third of the surface of the cortex is visible externally; the remaining two-thirds is hidden in the sulci and fissures. **Figure 2.25** shows some of the external features of the cerebral cortex. There may be as many as 50 to 100 billion cells in the cortex, arranged in six layers horizontal to the surface. Since these layers have large numbers of cell bodies, they appear gray; hence they are the gray matter of the cerebral cortex. Each layer can be identified by cell type, size, density, and arrangement. Beneath the six layers, the white matter of the cortex consists of millions of axons that connect one part of the cortex with another, or connect cortical cells to other brain structures. One of the largest of these pathways is the **corpus callosum** (see Figure 2.21B), which connects corresponding areas in the two hemispheres. In addition to the horizontal layers, the cortex has a vertical arrangement of cells that form slender vertical columns running through the entire thickness of the cortex. These vertically oriented cells and their synaptic connections apparently provide functional units for integration of information between various cortical regions.

The central sulcus and the lateral fissure (see Figure 2.25) visually divide the cortex into four distinct lobes in each hemisphere: the **parietal lobe**, **occipital lobe**, and **temporal lobe**, all of which are sensory in function, and the **frontal lobe**, which is responsible for movement and executive planning. Within each lobe is a small primary area, adjacent secondary cortex, and tertiary areas called association cortex. Within the occipital lobe is the primary visual

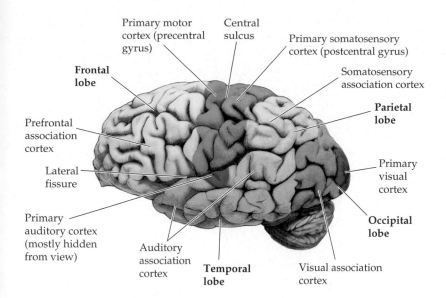

Figure 2.25 Lateral view of the exterior cerebral cortex The four lobes of the cerebral cortex are shown with distinct colors. Within each lobe is a primary area (darker in color) and secondary and tertiary association cortices. The caudal-most three lobes carry out sensory functions: vision (occipital), auditory (temporal), and somatosensory (parietal). The frontal lobe serves as the executive mechanism that plans and organizes behavior and initiates the appropriate sequence of actions.

cortex, which receives visual information from the thalamus that originated in the retina of the eye. The primary auditory cortex receives auditory information and is located in the temporal lobe; the primary somatosensory cortex, which receives information about body senses such as touch, temperature, and pain, is found in the parietal lobe just posterior to the central sulcus. Neither the gustatory cortex, which involves taste sensations, nor the primary olfactory area, which receives information regarding the sense of smell, is visible on the surface, but both lie within the folds of the cortex. The **primary cortex** of each lobe provides conscious awareness of sensory experience and the initial cortical processing of sensory qualities. Except for olfaction, all sensory information arrives in the appropriate primary cortex via projection neurons from the thalamus. In addition, except for olfaction, sensory information from the left side of the body goes to the right cerebral hemisphere first, and information from the right side goes to the left hemisphere. Visual information is somewhat different in that the left half of the visual field of each eye goes to the right occipital lobe and the right half of the visual field of each eye goes to the left occipital lobe.

Adjacent to each primary area is **secondary cortex**, which consists of neuronal circuits responsible for analyzing information transmitted from the primary area and providing recognition (or perception) of the stimulus. These areas are also the regions where memories are stored. Farther from the primary areas are association areas that lay down more-complex memories that involve multiple sensory systems such that our memories are not confined to a single sensory system but integrate multiple characteristics of the event. For example, many of us remember pieces of music from

the past that automatically evoke visual memories of the person we shared it with, or the time in our lives when it was popular. These **tertiary association areas** are often called the parietal–temporal–occipital association cortex because they represent the interface of the three sensory lobes and provide the higher-order perceptual functions needed for purposeful action.

Within the frontal lobe, the primary motor cortex mediates voluntary movements of the muscles of the limbs and trunk. Neurons originating in primary motor cortex directly, or in several steps, project to the spinal cord to act on spinal motor neurons that end on muscle fibers. As was true for the sensory systems, the motor neurons beginning in the frontal cortex are crossed, meaning that areas of the right primary motor cortex control movements of limbs on the left side of the body, and vice versa. Adjacent to the primary motor cortex is the secondary motor cortex, where memories for well-learned motor sequences are stored. Neurons in this area connect directly to the primary motor cortex to direct movement. The rest of the frontal lobe comprises the prefrontal cortex, which receives sensory information from the other cortices via the large bundles of white matter running below the gray matter. Emotional and motivational input is contributed to the prefrontal cortex by limbic and other subcortical structures. The prefrontal cortex is critical for making decisions, planning actions, and evaluating optional strategies. Impaired prefrontal function is characteristic of several psychiatric disorders, including borderline personality disorder, memory loss after traumatic brain injury, attention deficit hyperactivity disorder, and others. The significance of this brain region for the symptoms and treatment of schizophrenia is discussed in Chapter 20.

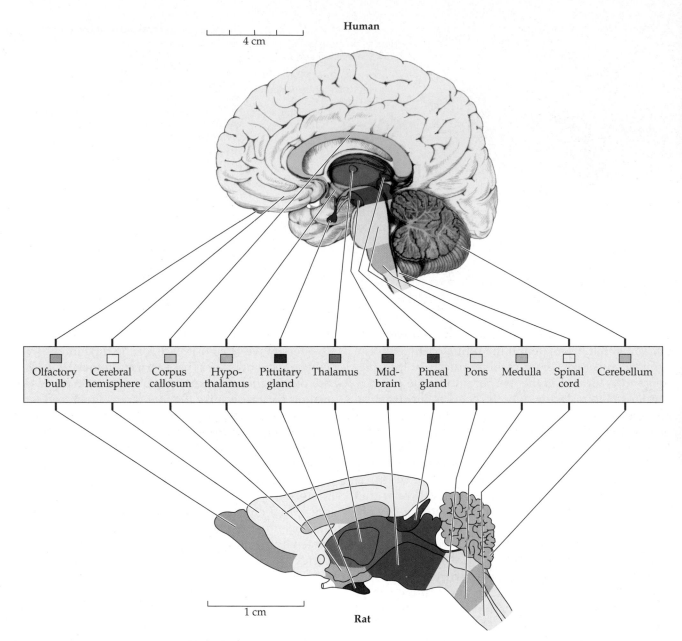

Figure 2.26 Comparison of human and rat brains Mid-sagittal views of the right hemispheres of human and rat brains show extensive similarities in brain structures and their relative topographic location. The brains differ in that the cerebral hemispheres are relatively much larger in the human brain, while the rat has a relatively larger midbrain and olfactory bulb. The rat brain has been enlarged about six times in linear dimensions relative to the human brain. (From Breedlove et al., 2010.)

Rat and human brains have many similarities and some differences

Since the rat is one of the most commonly used animals in neuroscience and psychopharmacological research, it may be helpful to compare the neuroanatomy of the rat brain with that of the human brain. Overall, evolutionary biology has shown great conservation of brain structures during the evolution of mammals. Having common ancestry, the basic mammalian brain plan is the model for the human brain.

In fact, looking farther back in the evolutionary tree, all vertebrates show a striking similarity. Despite differences in absolute and relative sizes of the whole brain, all mammalian brains have the same major subdivisions, which are topographically organized in relatively the same locations with similar neural connections among structures. **Figure 2.26** shows the striking correspondence of brain structures in the brains of rats and humans. Extensive similarities can also be found for individual nuclei, fiber tracts, and types of

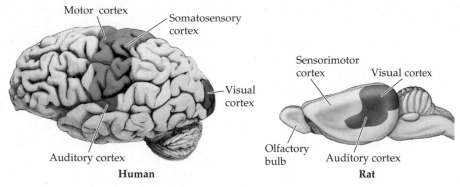

Figure 2.27 Lateral view of the left hemisphere of human and rat brains Note that the expanded human cortex does not involve the primary sensory or motor cortex (colored area). Human cortical expansion involves the secondary and tertiary association areas that are responsible for higher-order perception and cognition. (After Bear et al., 2007.)

cells, although human neurons are much larger than rat neurons and have more elaborate dendritic trees.

Despite the many similarities, there are also notable differences. What differs among mammals is the relative size of the brain regions, which likely reflects the environmental conditions encountered by each species and the importance of the function of that brain region for adaptation of the species. For example, the rat has relatively larger olfactory bulbs than humans, apparently because the very sensitive sense of smell in that species provided evolutionary advantages for survival for these nocturnal rodents. More striking is the difference in cerebral cortex. The paired cerebral hemispheres occupy a much greater proportion of the brain in the human than in the rat. The six-layered nature of the neocortex (the outermost layers of the cerebral hemispheres) is characteristic of all mammals, and it is the newest part of the cerebral cortex to evolve. In humans, the surface area of the neocortex is approximately 2322 cm^2 (2.5 ft^2), which explains why the surface must bend and fold to fit within the skull, producing the extensively convoluted surface. As much as two-thirds of the neocortex is not visible on the surface but is buried in the grooves. In contrast, the surface of the rat cerebral cortex is smooth and has no gyri or fissures (**Figure 2.27**). It is also clear from Figure 2.27 that the expanded surface area of the human cortex does not involve the primary sensory areas (colored pink, green, and orange), which are the first cortical areas to receive input from ascending sensory pathways, nor does it involve the primary motor cortex (colored blue). Instead, one can see enlargement of the secondary sensory association areas responsible for the complex sensory processing, perception, and function (such as speech) of which humans are capable. Additionally, tertiary association areas of the cortex

are greatly expanded, reflecting the human capacity for cognitive processing, reasoning, abstract thinking, and decision making.

Section Summary

- The central nervous system (CNS) includes the brain and the spinal cord. The remaining nerves of the body constitute the peripheral nervous system (PNS).

- The PNS is divided into the somatic nervous system, which includes spinal nerves that transmit sensory and motor information for skeletal muscles, and the autonomic nervous system, which serves smooth muscles, glands, and visceral organs.

- The autonomic nervous system has two divisions: the sympathetic, which serves to mobilize energy for times of "fight-or-flight"; and the parasympathetic, which reduces energy usage and stores reserves.

- The CNS is protected by a bony covering, three layers of meninges (dura, arachnoid, and pia), and cerebrospinal fluid.

- Neurotrophic factors are neuronal growth factors that guide the development of neurons, regulate dendritic growth and retraction, and aid in survival of neurons.

- The CNS can be divided into six regions containing multiple nuclei and their associated axons, which form interconnecting neural circuits: spinal cord, myelencephalon, metencephalon, mesencephalon, diencephalon, and telencephalon.

- The gray matter of the spinal cord constitutes cell bodies that receive sensory information and cell bodies of motor neurons that serve muscles. The white matter consists of tracts of myelinated axons that carry signals in the ascending direction to the brain and descending tracts for cortical control of the spinal cord.

- Continuous with the spinal cord is the myelencephalon or medulla, which contains nuclei that serve vital functions for survival, such as respiration, heart rate, and vomiting.

- The metencephalon includes two major structures. The cerebellum functions to maintain posture and balance and provides fine motor control and coordination. The pons contains several nuclei that represent the origins of most of the tracts utilizing the neurotransmitters norepinephrine (the locus coeruleus) and serotonin (the raphe nuclei).

- Beginning in the medulla, running through the pons, and extending into the midbrain is the reticular formation—a network of interconnected nuclei that control arousal, attention, and survival functions.

- The mesencephalon or midbrain contains nuclei that control sensory reflexes such as pupillary constriction. Other nuclei (substantia nigra and ventral tegmental area) are the cell bodies of neurons that form three major dopaminergic tracts. The periaqueductal gray organizes behaviors such as defensive rage and predation and serves as an important pain-modulating center.

- The diencephalon contains the thalamus, which relays information to the cerebral cortex, and the hypothalamus, which is important for maintaining homeostasis of physiological functions and for modulating motivated behaviors, including eating, aggression, reproduction, and so forth. The many nuclei that constitute the hypothalamus control both the autonomic nervous system and the endocrine system.

- The telencephalon includes both the cerebral cortex and multiple subcortical structures, including the basal ganglia and the limbic system. The basal ganglia modulate movement.

- The limbic system is made up of several brain structures with perfuse interconnections that modulate emotion, motivation, and learning. Some of the prominent limbic structures are the amygdala, hippocampus, nucleus accumbens, and limbic cortex.

- The six-layered cerebral cortex is organized into four lobes: the occipital, temporal, and parietal, which are the sensory lobes involved in perception and memories, and the frontal, which regulates motor movements and contains the "executive mechanism" for planning, evaluating, and making strategies.

- Although there are differences in absolute and relative size, rat and human brains have the same major subdivisions that are topographically organized in similar locations. Rat brains have relatively larger olfactory bulbs and midbrains. Human brains have expanded secondary and tertiary association areas of the cerebral cortex that serve higher-order sensory perception and cognitive functions.

Go to the **COMPANION WEBSITE**

sites.sinauer.com/psychopharm2e
for Web Boxes, animations, flashcards, and other study resources.

Recommended Readings

Breedlove, S. M. and Watson, N. V. (2013). *Biological Psychology* (7th ed.). Sunderland, MA: Sinauer.

Diamond, M. C., Scheibel, A. B., and Elson, L. M. (1985). *The Human Brain Coloring Book*. New York: HarperCollins.

Jiang, Y., Langley, B., Lubin, F. D., Renthal, W., Wood, M. A., Yasui, D. H., Kuman, A., Nestler, E. J., Akbarian, S., and Beckel-Mitchener, A. C. (2008). Epigenetics in the nervous system. *J. Neurosci.*, 28, 11753–11759.

Nicholls, J. G., Martin, A. R., Fuchs, P. A., Brown, D. A., Diamond, M. E., and Weisblat, D. A. (2012). *From Neuron to Brain* (5th ed.). Sunderland, MA: Sinauer.

Purves, D., Augustine, G. J., Fitzpatrick, D., Hall, W. C., LaMantia, A-S., and White, L. E. (2012). *Neuroscience* (5th ed.). Sunderland, MA: Sinauer.

Swerdlow, J. L. (1995). Quiet miracles of the brain. *Natl. Geogr. Mag.*, 187, 2–41.

Welker, W., Johnson, J. I., and Noe, A. Comparative mammalian brain collections. www.brainmuseum.org

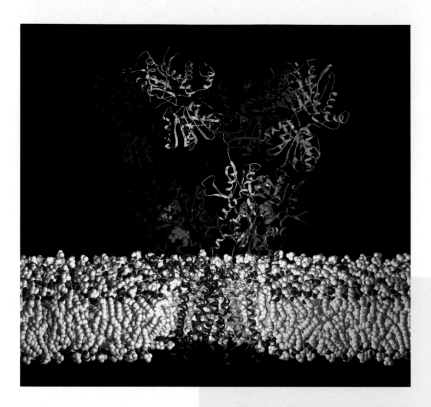

An AMPA receptor for glutamate is depicted in the cell membrane, each color representing one of the four protein subunits that comprise the receptor.

Chemical Signaling by Neurotransmitters and Hormones 3

IF YOU ARE READING THIS TEXTBOOK, you have probably taken one or more courses in psychology, biology, or neuroscience, in which you learned that the nerve cell (neuron) is the basic functional unit of the nervous system, and that information is usually transmitted from one nerve cell to another by the release of a chemical substance called a **neurotransmitter**. Of course, these basic facts seem so obvious to us now, but they were not always obvious and had to be acquired over years of painstaking observation and experimentation, along with some good old-fashioned luck. Indeed, the discovery of chemical neurotransmission is marked by two great controversies involving some of the greatest pioneers in the relatively young history of neuroscience. The first controversy centered around two different views of nervous system structure: (1) the neuron doctrine, which proposed that the nervous system is composed of individual cells that are not physically connected, and that information flow is unidirectional from one cell to another; and (2) the reticulum theory, which proposed instead that the nervous system consists of a series of vast continuous networks, in which all network elements are physically interconnected, and information can flow in any direction among these elements. The most distinguished proponents of these theories were two extraordinary late-nineteenth-century histologists—a reserved and humble Spaniard named Santiago Ramón y Cajal (sometimes considered the "father" of modern neuroscience), who strongly favored the neuron doctrine, and an outspoken and arrogant Italian named Camillo Golgi (discoverer of the remarkable silver staining method that bears his name), who was a fierce advocate of the reticulum theory and a bitter rival of Cajal. Despite working with what we now consider primitive tools, sometimes in a make-shift kitchen laboratory, and often in obscurity (particularly in the early stages of Cajal's career), the two scientists ultimately made such great contributions that they shared the 1906 Nobel Prize in Physiology or Medicine "in recognition of their work on the structure of the nervous system."[1]

By 1906, the neuron doctrine controversy was already resolved in the minds of most researchers, with Golgi still a notable exception. Yet a second great controversy was starting to brew concerning the mechanism by which these separate nerve cells communicate with each other. Some researchers, particularly neurophysiologists like John Eccles, argued that communication between axon terminals and dendrites occurred by means of electrical currents that cross the gap between sending and receiving cells. In contrast, the work of various pharmacologists suggested that information might instead be transmitted by release of a chemical substance. Confirmation of chemical transmission was first obtained in the autonomic nervous system, which was much more amenable than the brain to this type of research. One of the defining studies was a brilliant experiment performed by the German pharmacologist Otto Loewi in 1920. Loewi stimulated the vagus (parasympathetic) nerve of a frog heart, causing slowing of the heartbeat. He then immediately transferred the fluid that had been bathing the first heart to a second heart, from which the vagus nerve had been removed. Remarkably, the second heart slowed down as well, proving that a chemical substance had been released into the fluid due to the vagal stimulation. Loewi and the British pharmacologist Henry Dale, who had been investigating both the autonomic and neuromuscular systems, were co-recipients of the 1936 Nobel Prize in Physiology or Medicine for their respective contributions to the discovery of chemical neurotransmission. Still, it wasn't until the 1960s and later that researchers generally accepted this process as the primary basis for intercellular communication in the brain, not just in the peripheral nervous system.[2]

This historical summary has introduced you to one of the body's great systems of cellular communication—the system of synaptic transmission. Throughout the rest of this chapter, you will learn more about

synapses, neurotransmitters, and the mechanisms of neurotransmitter action. The final section is devoted to another important communication system, the endocrine system, which is responsible for the secretion of hormones into the bloodstream.

Chemical Signaling between Nerve Cells

The word **synapse** was coined in 1897 by the British physiologist Charles Sherrington. He derived the term from the Greek word *synapto*, which means "to clasp." Using only a light microscope, Sherrington could not see the actual point of communication between neurons, but physiological experiments had shown that transmission occurs in only one direction (from what we now call the **presynaptic cell** to the **postsynaptic cell**). The synapse was considered to be the specialized mechanism underlying this neuronal communication. Sherrington correctly inferred that sending (presynaptic) and receiving (postsynaptic) cells do not actually touch each other, as discussed above. Of course, the concept of chemical transmitter substances had barely been conceived, much less confirmed experimentally.

Our current knowledge of synaptic structure comes from the electron microscope, which gives us much greater magnification than the standard light microscope. The most common synapses in the brain are **axodendritic synapses**. In these synapses, an axon terminal from the presynaptic neuron communicates with a dendrite of the postsynaptic cell. An electron micrograph displaying this kind of synapse is shown in **Figure 3.1** (see also **Figure 3.2A**). The dendrites of

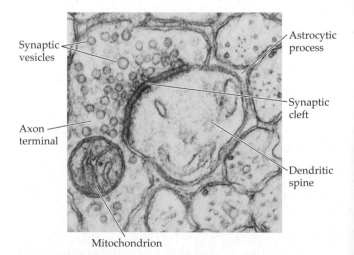

Figure 3.1 An electron micrograph of an axodendritic synapse illustrating the major features of a typical connection between an axon terminal of the presynaptic cell and a dendritic spine of the postsynaptic cell. (From Peters et al., 1991.)

---

[1]www.nobelprize.org/nobel_prizes/medicine/laureates/1906/

[2]Students interested in learning more about these controversies and discoveries are referred to three excellent sources: *Nerve Endings: The Discovery of the Synapse*, by Richard Rapport, which recounts the stories of Cajal and Golgi; *The War of the Soups and the Sparks: The Discovery of Neurotransmitters and the Dispute Over How Nerves Communicate*, by Eliot Valenstein, which gives the history of the discovery of chemical transmission; and Loewi's 1960 autobiographical sketch published in *Perspectives in Biology and Medicine*, in which he reminisces about his famous frog heart experiment and the nighttime dream that prompted it.

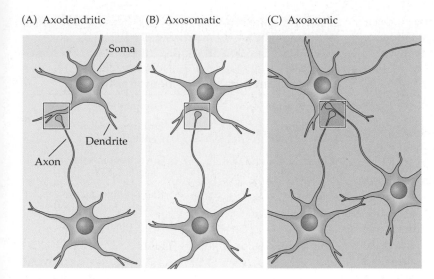

(A) Axodendritic   (B) Axosomatic   (C) Axoaxonic

Soma

Dendrite

Axon

Figure 3.2 The three types of synaptic connections between neurons

transmitter release from the terminal. This is called **presynaptic inhibition** of release. Enhanced release of transmitter, on the other hand, is called **presynaptic facilitation**.

In neuronal communication, the receiving cell may be another neuron, or it may be a muscle cell or a cell specialized to release a hormone or other secretory product. The connection point between a neuron and a muscle is called a **neuromuscular junction** instead of a synapse. A neuromuscular junction has many structural and functional similarities to a conventional synapse, and much has been learned about synaptic transmission by studying neuromuscular junctions.

some neurons have short spines along their length, which are reminiscent of thorns growing out from a rosebush. When spines are present, they are important locations for synapses to form; this is the case for the synapse shown in Figure 3.1. There is an exceedingly small (about 20 nm, which is 20×10^{-9} m) gap between presynaptic and postsynaptic cells that must be traversed by neurotransmitter molecules after their release. This gap is called the **synaptic cleft**. In the axon terminal, we can see many small saclike objects, termed **synaptic vesicles**, each of which is filled with several thousand molecules of a neurotransmitter. As we shall see, these vesicles are normally the source of transmitter release. The electron micrograph also shows a profile of a mitochondrion in the axon terminal. Mitochondria are the cellular organelles responsible for energy (adenosine triphosphate, or ATP) production. They are needed in large quantities in the terminals for various functions such as ion pumping and transmitter release. Finally, we see that the synapse is surrounded by processes (fibers) from astrocytes. In Chapter 8, we'll discuss an important role for these glial cells in regulating transmission by amino acid transmitters.

Other types of synapses are also present in the brain. For example, **axosomatic synapses** are synapses between a nerve terminal and a nerve cell body (**Figure 3.2B**). They function in a manner similar to axodendritic synapses. **Axoaxonic synapses** involve one axon synapsing on the terminal of another axon (**Figure 3.2C**). This unusual arrangement permits the presynaptic cell to alter neurotransmitter release from the postsynaptic cell directly at the terminals. For example, activity at an axoaxonic synapse may reduce

Neurotransmitter Synthesis, Release, and Inactivation

As has been mentioned, neurotransmitters are chemical substances released by neurons to communicate with other cells. Scientists first thought that only a few chemicals were involved in neurotransmission, but more than 100 chemicals have now been identified. As there are many thousands of chemicals present in any cell, how do we know whether a particular substance qualifies as a neurotransmitter? Verifying a chemical's status as a neurotransmitter can be a difficult process, but here are some of the important criteria:

- The presynaptic cell should contain the proposed substance along with a mechanism for manufacturing it.

- A mechanism for inactivating the substance should also be present.

- The substance should be released from the axon terminal upon stimulation of the neuron.

- Receptors for the proposed substance should be present on the postsynaptic cell. (Receptors are discussed in greater detail later in the chapter.)

- Direct application of the proposed substance or of an agonist drug that acts on its receptors should have the same effect on the postsynaptic cell as stimulating the presynaptic neuron (which presumably would release the substance from the axon terminals).

- Applying an antagonist drug that blocks the receptors should inhibit both the action of the applied substance and the effect of stimulating the presynaptic neuron.

Even if all criteria have not yet been met for a suspected neurotransmitter, there is often sufficient evidence to make a strong case for transmitter candidacy.

Neurotransmitters encompass several different kinds of chemical substances

Despite the great numbers of neurotransmitters, most of them conveniently fall into several chemical classes. The major types of transmitters and examples of each are shown in **Table 3.1**. A few neurotransmitters are categorized as **amino acids**.[3] Amino acids serve numerous functions: they are the individual building blocks of proteins, and they play other metabolic roles besides their role as neurotransmitters. In Chapter 8, we'll cover the two most important amino acid neurotransmitters, glutamate and γ-aminobutyric acid (GABA). Several other transmitters are **monoamines**, which are grouped together because each possesses a single (hence "mono") amine group. Monoamine transmitters are derived from amino acids through a series of biochemical reactions that include removal of the acidic part (–COOH) of the molecule. Consequently, we say that the original amino acid is a **precursor** because it precedes the amine in the biochemical pathway. In Chapters 5 and 6, we will discuss the best-characterized monoamine transmitters: dopamine (DA), norepinephrine (NE), and serotonin (5-HT). One important neurotransmitter that is neither an amino acid nor a monoamine is acetylcholine (ACh; see Chapter 7). Together with ACh, amino acid and monoamine neurotransmitters are sometimes called "classical" transmitters because they were generally discovered before the other categories.

Besides the classical transmitters, there are several other types of neurotransmitters. The largest group of "nonclassical" neurotransmitters are the **neuropeptides**, whose name simply means "peptides found in the nervous system." Peptides are small proteins, typically made up of 3 to 40 amino acids instead of the 100+ amino acids found in most proteins. Neuropharmacologists are very interested in the family of neuropeptides called *endorphins and enkephalins*, which stimulate the same opioid receptors that are activated by heroin and other abused opioid drugs (see Chapter 11). Other neuropeptides relevant to neuropsychiatric illness and drug treatment include the following: corticotropin-releasing factor (CRF), which is believed to play a role in anxiety and depression (see Chapters 18); brain-derived neurotrophic factor (BDNF), which has also been implicated in depression (see

TABLE 3.1 Major Categories of Neurotransmitters[a]

Classical neurotransmitters	Nonclassical neurotransmitters
Amino acids	**Neuropeptides**
Glutamate	Endorphins and enkephalins
γ-aminobutyric acid (GABA)	Corticotropin-releasing factor (CRF)
Glycine	Brain-derived neurotrophic factor (BDNF)
	Many others
Monoamines	**Lipids**
Dopamine (DA)	Anandamide
Norepinephrine (NE)	**Gases**
Serotonin (5-HT)	Nitric oxide (NO)
Acetylcholine	

[a]It should be noted that this is only a small sample of the more than 100 substances known or suspected to be neurotransmitters in the brain.

Chapter 19); orexin/hypocretin, which is involved in reward-seeking behavior and addiction, as well as in sleep and wakefulness; and vasopressin and oxytocin, two closely related substances that may help regulate social and affiliative behaviors. A few transmitters are considered **lipids**, which is the scientific term for fatty substances. For example, in Chapter 14, we discuss a substance called *anandamide*, a lipid made in the brain that acts like marijuana (or, more specifically, Δ^9-tetrahydrocannabinol [THC], which is the major active ingredient in marijuana). Finally, the most recently discovered and most intriguing group of neurotransmitters are the **gaseous transmitters**. Later in this chapter, we discuss nitric oxide, the best known of these unusual transmitters, and we will see that these substances break some of the normal rules followed by other transmitter molecules.

When scientists first discovered the existence of neurotransmitters, it was natural to assume that each neuron made and released only one transmitter substance,[4] suggesting a simple chemical coding of cells in the nervous system. Much research over the past 25

---

[3]Amino acids are so named because they contain both an amino group (–NH$_2$) and a carboxyl group (–COOH), the latter of which releases a hydrogen ion (H$^+$) and thus acts as an acid.

[4]This notion has sometimes been called "Dale's Law," although what Henry Dale actually proposed is subtly different: that if one branch of a cell's axon was found to release a particular chemical substance when stimulated, then all axonal branches of that cell would also release that substance (notice that this statement doesn't preclude the cell from releasing multiple substances from its various branches).

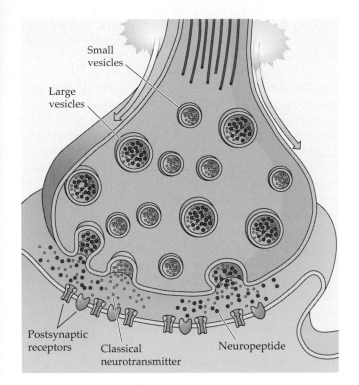

Figure 3.3 **Axon terminal of a neuron that synthesizes both a classical neurotransmitter and a neuropeptide** The small vesicles contain only the classical transmitter, whereas the large vesicles contain the neuropeptide and the classical neurotransmitter, which are stored and released together.

has two different types of synaptic vesicles: small vesicles, which contain only the classical transmitter, and large vesicles, which contain the neuropeptide along with the classical transmitter (**Figure 3.3**).

Classical transmitters and neuropeptides are synthesized by different mechanisms

How and where in the nerve cell are neurotransmitters manufactured? Except for the neuropeptides, transmitters are synthesized by enzymatic reactions that can occur anywhere in the cell. Typically, the enzymes required for producing a neurotransmitter are shipped out in large quantities to the axon terminals, so the terminals are an important site of transmitter synthesis. The neuropeptides are different, however. Their precursors are protein molecules, within which the peptides are embedded. The protein precursor for each type of peptide must be made in the cell body, which is the site of almost all protein synthesis in the neuron. The protein is then packaged into large vesicles, along with enzymes that will break down the precursor and liberate the neuropeptide (**Figure 3.4**). These vesicles are transported to the axon terminals, so that release occurs from the terminals, as with the classical transmitters. On the other hand, new neuropeptide molecules can be generated only in the cell body, not

years has shattered that initial assumption. We now know that many neurons make and release two, three, and occasionally even more, different transmitters. Some instances of transmitter coexistence within the same cell involve one or more neuropeptides, along with a classical transmitter. In such cases, the neuron

Figure 3.4 **Features of neurotransmission using neuropeptides** Neuropeptides are synthesized from larger precursor proteins, which are packaged into large vesicles by the Golgi apparatus. During transport from the cell body to the axon terminal, enzymes that have been packaged within the vesicles break down the precursor protein to liberate the neuropeptide. After it is released at the synapse and stimulates postsynaptic receptors, the neuropeptide is inactivated by degradative enzymes.

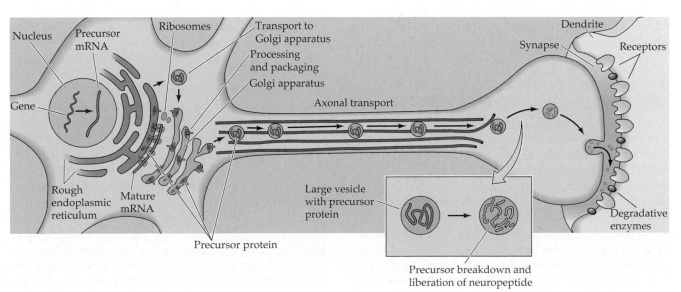

in the terminals. An important consequence of this difference is that replenishment of neuropeptides is slower than for small-molecule transmitters. When neurotransmitters are depleted by high levels of neuronal activity, small molecules can be resynthesized rapidly within the axon terminal. In contrast, neuropeptides cannot be replenished until large vesicles containing the peptide have been transported to the terminal from their site of origin within the cell body.

Neuromodulators are chemicals that don't act like typical neurotransmitters

Some investigators use the term **neuromodulators** to describe substances that don't act exactly like typical neurotransmitters. For example, a neuromodulator might not have a direct effect itself on the postsynaptic cell. Instead, it might alter the action of a standard neurotransmitter by enhancing, reducing, or prolonging the transmitter's effectiveness. Such effects may be seen when monoamine transmitters such as DA, NE, or 5-HT modulate the excitatory influence of another transmitter (e.g., glutamate) on the postsynaptic cell. Peptides that are co-released with a classical transmitter may also function as neuromodulators. Yet another common property of neuromodulators is diffusion away from the site of release to influence cells more distant from the releasing cell than is the case at a standard synapse. This phenomenon has been termed **volume transmission** to distinguish it from the tight cell-to-cell synaptic interactions that constitute **wiring transmission** (Fuxe et al., 2010). No matter which criteria you use, though, the dividing line between neurotransmitters and neuromodulators is vague. For example, a particular chemical like serotonin may sometimes act within the synapse, but in other circumstances, it may act at a distance from its site of release. Therefore, we will refrain from talking about neuromodulators and instead will use the term neuro-transmitter throughout the remainder of the book.

Neurotransmitter release involves the exocytosis and recycling of synaptic vesicles

As shown in **Figure 3.5**, synaptic transmission involves a number of processes that occur within the axon terminal and the postsynaptic cell. We will begin our discussion of these processes with a consideration of neurotransmitter release from the terminal. When a neuron fires an action potential, the depolarizing current sweeps down the length of the axon and enters all of the axon terminals. This wave of depolarization has a very important effect within the terminals: it opens large numbers of voltage-sensitive calcium (Ca^{2+}) channels, causing a rapid influx of Ca^{2+} ions

into the terminals. The resulting increase in Ca^{2+} concentration within the terminals is the direct trigger for neurotransmitter release.

EXOCYTOSIS   You already know that the neurotransmitter molecules destined to be released are stored within synaptic vesicles, yet these molecules must somehow make their way past the membrane of the axon terminal and into the synaptic cleft. This occurs through a remarkable process known as **exocytosis**. Exocytosis is a fusion of the vesicle membrane with the membrane of the axon terminal, which exposes the inside of the vesicle to the outside of the cell. In this way, the vesicle is opened, and its transmitter molecules are allowed to diffuse into the synaptic cleft. If you look back at the synapse shown in Figure 3.1, you can see that some vesicles are very close to the terminal membrane, whereas others are farther away. In fact, transmitter release doesn't occur just anywhere along the terminal, but only at specialized regions near the postsynaptic cell, which stain darkly on the electron micrograph. These release sites are called **active zones**. For exocytosis to take place, a vesicle must be transported to an active zone by a mechanism that isn't yet fully understood. There, the vesicle must "dock" at the active zone, much like a boat docking at a pier. This docking step is carried out by a cluster of proteins—some located in the vesicle membrane and others residing in the membrane of the axon terminal. Docking is followed by a step called priming, which readies the vesicle for exocytosis once it receives the Ca^{2+} signal. Indeed, Ca^{2+} channels that open in response to membrane depolarization are concentrated in active zones near the sites of vesicle docking, so the protein machinery is exposed to particularly high concentrations of Ca^{2+} when the channels open. One or more proteins that are sensitive to Ca^{2+} then cause the vesicle and terminal membranes to fuse, and this allows the vesicle to open and the transmitter to be released. This process is illustrated in **Figure 3.6**.

Discussion of the various proteins involved in vesicle docking and fusion is beyond the scope of this book, but it's nevertheless important to note that some of these proteins are targets for various drugs or naturally occurring toxins. For example, botulism poisoning results from a bacterial toxin (botulinum toxin) that blocks transmitter release at neuromuscular junctions, thus causing paralysis. Researchers have found that this blockade of release is due to enzymes within the toxin that attack some of the proteins that are required for the exocytosis process. This topic is covered in greater detail in Chapter 7, where we will also see how botulinum toxin has come to be used therapeutically in a wide range of neuromuscular disorders. Recent studies performed in the roundworm

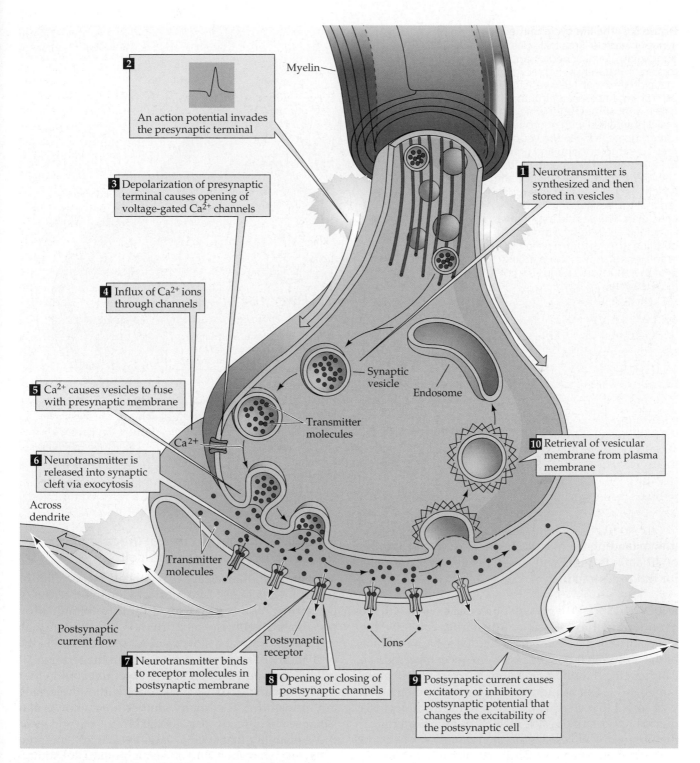

2 An action potential invades the presynaptic terminal

Myelin

1 Neurotransmitter is synthesized and then stored in vesicles

3 Depolarization of presynaptic terminal causes opening of voltage-gated Ca^{2+} channels

4 Influx of Ca^{2+} ions through channels

Synaptic vesicle

Endosome

5 Ca^{2+} causes vesicles to fuse with presynaptic membrane

Transmitter molecules

Ca^{2+}

10 Retrieval of vesicular membrane from plasma membrane

6 Neurotransmitter is released into synaptic cleft via exocytosis

Across dendrite

Transmitter molecules

Postsynaptic current flow

Postsynaptic receptor

Ions

7 Neurotransmitter binds to receptor molecules in postsynaptic membrane

8 Opening or closing of postsynaptic channels

9 Postsynaptic current causes excitatory or inhibitory postsynaptic potential that changes the excitability of the postsynaptic cell

Figure 3.5 Processes involved in neurotransmission at a typical synapse using a classical neurotransmitter

Caenorhabditis elegans[5] have shown that ethanol can acutely affect neurotransmitter release by acting on at least two different presynaptic proteins involved in the exocytosis process (Barclay et al., 2010). We don't yet know how important this mechanism is for

[5]*Caenorhabditis elegans*, or simply *C. elegans*, is a nematode that is an important model organism in many areas of biology, including pharmacology. Its usefulness derives from the discovery that every worm has exactly the same number and location of cells in its body (including just 302 neurons), and that genetic mutations are easily produced and screened in this species. The basic molecular pathway for programmed cell death in the brain and in other organs (see Chapter 8) was first worked out in *C. elegans*.

Figure 3.6 The life cycle of the synaptic vesicle Small vesicles containing classical neurotransmitters are constantly being recycled in the axon terminal. New vesicles bud off from membranous structures called endosomes, after which the vesicles are filled with neurotransmitter molecules. Mature vesicles then undergo docking and priming, followed by Ca^{2+}-dependent fusion with the axon terminal membrane, which permits release of the contents of the vesicles into the synaptic cleft. The vesicle membrane is rapidly retrieved by a process of budding from the terminal membrane, endocytosis, and merging with the endosomes, thus completing the cycle.

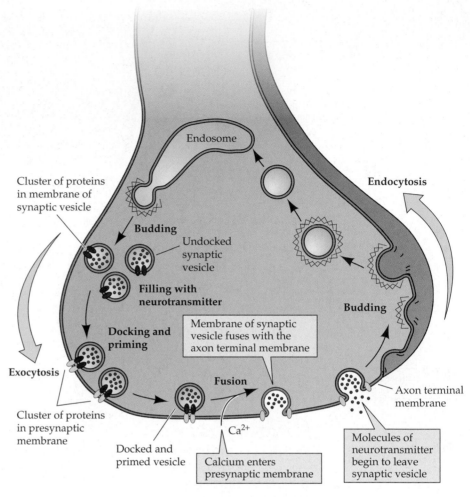

Endosome

Endocytosis

Cluster of proteins in membrane of synaptic vesicle

Budding

Undocked synaptic vesicle

Filling with neurotransmitter

Budding

Docking and priming

Membrane of synaptic vesicle fuses with the axon terminal membrane

Exocytosis

Fusion

Axon terminal membrane

Cluster of proteins in presynaptic membrane

Ca^{2+}

Docked and primed vesicle

Calcium enters presynaptic membrane

Molecules of neurotransmitter begin to leave synaptic vesicle

understanding the intoxicating or addictive properties of ethanol, but this will surely be an important topic for future research.

ENDOCYTOSIS   When a synaptic vesicle fuses with the axon terminal to release its transmitter contents, the vesicle membrane is temporarily added to the membrane of the terminal. If this process were never reversed, we can imagine that the terminal membrane would grow larger and larger as more and more vesicle membrane was added to it. In reality, a process called **endocytosis** quickly retrieves the vesicle membrane from the terminal membrane. New vesicles are then rapidly formed and are refilled with neurotransmitter molecules, so they can participate again in transmitter release. This continuous release and re-formation of vesicles is termed **vesicle recycling** (see Figure 3.6). It is worth noting that recycling only occurs with the small vesicles containing classical transmitters, not with the larger neuropeptide-containing vesicles. You'll recall that neuropeptide precursor proteins must be packaged into the large vesicles in the cell body; therefore, recycling of such vesicles cannot occur at the axon terminal.

Several mechanisms control the rate of neurotransmitter release by nerve cells

Neurotransmitter release is regulated by several different mechanisms. The most obvious is the rate of cell firing. When a neuron is rapidly firing action potentials, it will release much more transmitter than when it is firing at a slow rate. A second factor is the probability of transmitter release from the terminal. It might seem odd that an action potential could enter a terminal and open Ca^{2+} channels without releasing any transmitter. Yet many studies have shown that synapses in different parts of the brain vary widely in the probability that even a single vesicle will undergo exocytosis in response to an action potential. Estimated probabilities range from less than 0.1 (10%) to 0.9 (90%) or greater for different populations of synapses. We don't yet know why these probabilities can vary so much, but it is clearly an important factor in the regulation of neurotransmitter release.

A third factor in the rate of transmitter release is the presence of **autoreceptors** on axon terminals or cell bodies and dendrites (**Figure 3.7**). An autoreceptor on a particular neuron is a receptor for the same

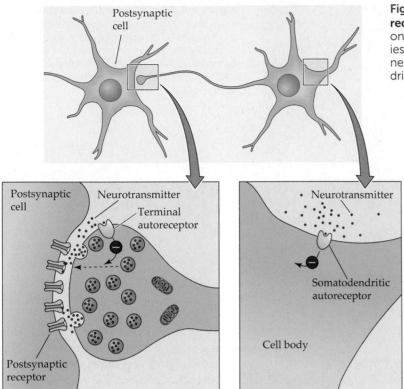

Figure 3.7 Terminal and somatodendritic auto-receptors Many neurons possess autoreceptors on their axon terminals and/or on their cell bodies and dendrites. Terminal autoreceptors inhibit neurotransmitter release, whereas somatodendritic autoreceptors reduce the rate of cell firing.

neurotransmitter released by that neuron (*auto* in this case means "self"). Neurons may possess two different types of autoreceptors: **terminal autoreceptors** and **somatodendritic autoreceptors**. Terminal autoreceptors are so named because they are located on axon terminals. When they are activated by the neurotransmitter, their main function is to inhibit further transmitter release. This function is particularly important when the cell is firing rapidly and high levels of neurotransmitter are present in the synaptic cleft. Think of the thermostat ("autoreceptor") in your house, which shuts off the furnace ("release mechanism") when the level of heat ("neurotransmitter") gets too high. Somatodendritic autoreceptors are also descriptively named, in that they are autoreceptors found on the cell body (soma) or on dendrites. When these autoreceptors are activated, they slow the rate of cell firing, which ultimately causes less neurotransmitter release because fewer action potentials reach the axon terminals to stimulate exocytosis.

Researchers can use drugs to stimulate or block specific autoreceptors, thereby influencing the release of a particular neurotransmitter for experimental purposes. For example, administration of a low dose of the drug apomorphine to rats or mice selectively activates the terminal autoreceptors for DA. This causes lessened DA release, an overall reduction in dopaminergic transmission, and reduced locomotor activity among animals. A different drug, whose name is abbreviated 8-OH-DPAT, activates the somatodendritic autoreceptors for 5-HT and powerfully inhibits the firing of serotonergic neurons. The behavioral effects of administration of 8-OH-DPAT include increased appetite and altered responses on several tasks used to assess anxiety.

Finally, you'll recall from our earlier discussion that in addition to autoreceptors, axon terminals may also have receptors for other transmitters released at axoaxonal synapses. Such receptors have come to be known as **heteroreceptors**, to distinguish them from autoreceptors. Heteroreceptors also differ from autoreceptors in that they may either enhance or reduce the amount of transmitter being released from the axon terminal.

Neurotransmitters are inactivated by reuptake and by enzymatic breakdown

Any mechanical or biological process that can be turned on must have a mechanism for termination (imagine the problem you would have with a car in which the ignition could not be turned off once the car had been started). Thus, it is necessary to terminate the synaptic signal produced by each instance of transmitter release, so the postsynaptic cell is free to respond to the next release. This termination is accomplished by

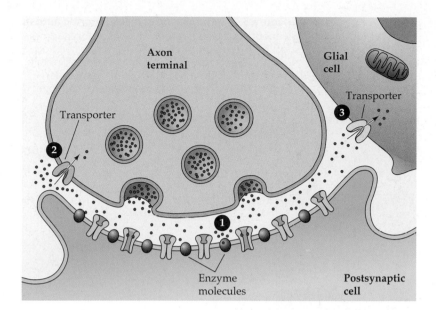

Figure 3.8 Neurotransmitter inactivation Neurotransmitter molecules can be inactivated by (1) enyzmatic breakdown; (2) reuptake by the axon terminal; or (3) uptake by nearby glial cells. Cellular uptake is mediated by specific membrane transporters for each neurotransmitter.

removing neurotransmitter molecules from the synaptic cleft. How is this done?

Several different processes responsible for neurotransmitter removal are shown in **Figure 3.8**. One mechanism is enzymatic breakdown within or near the synaptic cleft. This mechanism is very important for the classical neurotransmitter ACh, for the lipid and gaseous transmitters, and also for the neuropeptide transmitters. An alternative mechanism involves removal of the neurotransmitter from the synaptic cleft by a transport process that makes use of specialized proteins called **transporters** located on the cell membrane. This mechanism is important for amino acid transmitters like glutamate and GABA and also for monoamine transmitters such as DA, NE, and 5-HT. Transport out of the synaptic cleft is sometimes accomplished by the same cell that released the transmitter, in which case it is called **reuptake**. In other cases, the transmitter may be taken up either by the postsynaptic cell or by nearby glial cells (specifically astrocytes). Some important psychoactive drugs work by blocking neurotransmitter transporters. Cocaine, for example, blocks the transporters for DA, 5-HT, and NE. Many antidepressant drugs block the 5-HT transporter, the NE transporter, or both. Since these transporters are so important for clearing the neurotransmitter from the synaptic cleft, it follows that when the transporters are blocked, neurotransmitter molecules remain in the synaptic cleft for a longer time, and neurotransmission is enhanced at those synapses.

When neurotransmitter transporters are active, some transmitter molecules removed from the synaptic cleft are reused by being packaged into recycled vesicles. However, other transmitter molecules are broken down by enzymes present within the cell.

Thus, uptake and metabolic breakdown are not mutually exclusive processes. Many transmitter systems use both mechanisms. Finally, it is important to keep in mind the distinction between autoreceptors and transporters. Even though both may be present on axon terminals, they serve different functions. Terminal autoreceptors modulate transmitter release, but they don't transport the neurotransmitter. Transporters take up the transmitter from the synaptic cleft, but they are not autoreceptors.

Section Summary

- Synapses may occur on the dendrite (axodendritic), cell body (axosomatic), or axon (axoaxonic) of the postsynaptic cell.

- Most neurotransmitters fall into one of the following categories (with acetylcholine as a notable exception): amino acid transmitters, monoamine transmitters, lipid transmitters, neuropeptide transmitters, and gaseous transmitters.

- Neurons commonly synthesize and release two or more neurotransmitters, often from different categories.

- Classical neurotransmitters (amino acids, monoamines, and acetylcholine) are mainly synthesized in the nerve terminal and then are transported into synaptic vesicles; neuropeptides are synthesized and are packaged into vesicles in the cell body.

- Neurotransmitters are released from nerve terminals by a Ca^{2+}-dependent process called exocytosis.

- Neurotransmitter release is controlled by the rate of cell firing, the release probability at a specific synapse, and inhibitory terminal and somatodendritic autoreceptors.

- Depending on the neurotransmitter, termination of transmitter action is accomplished by the processes of uptake (including reuptake by the presynaptic cell) and/or enzymatic breakdown.

Neurotransmitter Receptors and Second-Messenger Systems

Chemical signaling by neurotransmitters requires the presence of molecules on the membrane of the postsynaptic cell called **receptors** that are sensitive to the neurotransmitter signal. As we shall see, there are several different mechanisms by which neurotransmitter receptors alter activity of the postsynaptic cell, some of which involve complex biochemical pathways known as **second-messenger systems**.

There are two major families of neurotransmitter receptors

In Chapter 1, you were introduced to the concept of a drug receptor. Many of the receptors for psychoactive drugs are actually receptors for various neurotransmitters. For this reason, it is very important to understand the characteristics of neurotransmitter receptors and how they function.

Virtually all neurotransmitter receptors are proteins, and in most cases, these proteins are located on the plasma membrane of the cell. As we saw earlier, the cell possessing the receptor may be a neuron, a muscle cell, or a secretory cell. The neurotransmitter molecule binds to a specific site on the receptor molecule, which activates the receptor and produces a biochemical alteration in the receiving cell that may affect its excitability. For example, postsynaptic receptors on neurons usually influence the likelihood that the cell will generate an action potential. The effect of receptor activation may be either excitatory (increasing the probability of an action potential) or inhibitory (decreasing the probability of an action potential), depending on what the receptor does to the cell (see following sections). Recall that if a particular drug mimics the action of the neurotransmitter in activating the receptor, we say that the drug is an agonist at that receptor (see Chapter 1). If a drug blocks or inhibits the ability of the neurotransmitter to activate the receptor, then the drug is called an antagonist.

Two key concepts are necessary for understanding neurotransmitter receptors. First, almost all neurotransmitters discovered so far have more than one kind of receptor. Different varieties of receptors for the same transmitter are called **receptor subtypes** for that transmitter. The existence of subtypes adds complexity to the study of receptors, making the task of pharmacologists (as well as students!) more difficult. But this complexity has a positive aspect: If you can design a drug that stimulates or blocks just the subtype that you're interested in, you may be able to treat a disease more effectively and with fewer side effects. This is one of the central ideas underlying modern drug design and the continuing search for new pharmaceutical agents.

The second key concept is that most neurotransmitter receptors fall into two broad categories: **ionotropic receptors** and **metabotropic receptors**. A particular transmitter may use only receptors that fit one or the other of these general categories, or its receptor subtypes may fall into both categories. As shown in **Table 3.2**, ionotropic and metabotropic receptors differ in both structure and function, so we will discuss them separately.

IONOTROPIC RECEPTORS Ionotropic receptors work very rapidly, so they play a critical role in fast neurotransmission within the nervous system. Each ionotropic receptor is made up of several proteins called **subunits**, which are assembled to form the complete receptor before insertion into the cell membrane. Four or five subunits are needed, depending on the overall structure of the receptor (**Figure 3.9A**). At the center of the receptor is a channel or pore through which ions can flow. The

TABLE 3.2 Comparison of Ionotropic and Metabotropic Receptors

Characteristics	Ionotropic receptors	Metabotropic receptors
Structure	4 or 5 subunits that are assembled and then inserted into the cell membrane	1 subunit
Mechanism of action	Contain an intrinsic ion channel that opens in response to neurotransmitter or drug binding	Activate G proteins in response to neurotransmitter or drug binding
Coupled to second messengers?	No	Yes
Speed of action	Fast	Slower

(A)

(B)

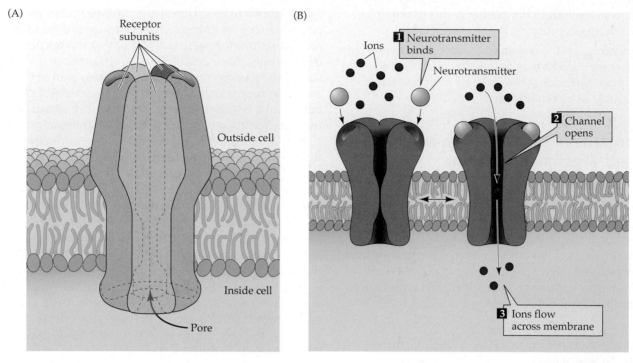

Receptor
subunits

Outside cell

Inside cell

Pore

Ions

1 Neurotransmitter
binds

Neurotransmitter

2 Channel
opens

3 Ions flow
across membrane

Figure 3.9 Structure and function of ionotropic receptors (A) Each receptor complex comprises either five (as shown) or four protein subunits that form a channel or a pore in the cell membrane. (B) Binding of the neurotransmitter to the receptor triggers channel opening and the flow of ions across the membrane.

receptor also possesses one or more binding sites for the neurotransmitter. In the resting state with no neurotransmitter present, the receptor channel is closed, and no ions are moving. When the neurotransmitter binds to the receptor and activates it, the channel immediately opens and ions flow across the cell membrane (**Figure 3.9B**). When the neurotransmitter molecule leaves (dissociates from) the receptor, the channel quickly closes. Because of these features, a common alternative name for ionotropic receptors is **ligand-gated channel receptors**.[6] Another feature of ionotropic receptors is that they can undergo a phenomenon called **desensitization**, in which the channel remains closed even though there may be ligand molecules bound to the receptor (the details of this process are beyond the scope of the chapter). Once this occurs, the channel must resensitize before it can be activated once again.

Some ionotropic receptor channels allow sodium (Na^+) ions to flow into the cell from the extracellular fluid. Because these ions are positively charged, the cell membrane is depolarized, thereby producing an

excitatory response of the postsynaptic cell. One of the best-known examples of this kind of excitatory ionotropic receptor is the nicotinic receptor for ACh, which we'll discuss further in Chapter 7. A second type of ionotropic receptor channel permits the flow of Ca^{2+} as well as Na^+ ions across the cell membrane. As we will see shortly, Ca^{2+} can act as a **second messenger** to trigger many biochemical processes in the postsynaptic cell. One important ionotropic receptor that functions in this way is the N-methyl-D-aspartate (NMDA) receptor for the neurotransmitter glutamate (see Chapter 8). Finally, a third type of receptor channel is selective for chloride (Cl^-) ions to flow into the cell. These ions are negatively charged, thus leading to hyperpolarization of the membrane and an inhibitory response of the postsynaptic cell. A good example of this kind of inhibitory ionotropic receptor is the $GABA_A$ receptor (see Chapter 8). From this discussion, you can see that the characteristics of the ion channel controlled by an ionotropic receptor are the key factor in determining whether that receptor excites the postsynaptic cell, inhibits the cell, or activates a second-messenger system.

METABOTROPIC RECEPTORS Metabotropic receptors act more slowly than ionotropic receptors. It takes longer for the postsynaptic cell to respond, but its response is somewhat more long-lasting than in the case of ionotropic receptors. Metabotropic receptors are composed of only a single protein subunit, which winds its way back and forth through the cell membrane seven times. Using the terminology of cell biology, we say that these receptors

---

[6]This terminology distinguishes such channels from voltage-gated channels, which are controlled by voltage across the cell membrane rather than by binding of a ligand such as a neurotransmitter or a drug.

inhibiting certain enzymes in the cell membrane (**Figure 3.11B**). These enzymes are sometimes called **effector enzymes** because they produce biochemical and physiological effects in the postsynaptic cell. Most of the effector enzymes controlled by G proteins are involved in either the synthesis or the breakdown of small molecules called *second messengers*. Second messengers were first discovered in the 1960s and later found to play an important role in the chemical communication processes of both neurotransmitters and hormones. In these processes, the neurotransmitter or hormone was considered to be the "first messenger," and the "second messenger" within the receiving cell (the postsynaptic cell, in the case of a neurotransmitter) then carried out the biochemical change signaled by the

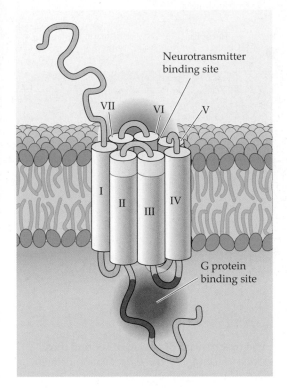

Figure 3.10 Structure of metabotropic receptors Each receptor comprises a single protein subunit with seven transmembrane domains (labeled here by Roman numerals).

have seven transmembrane domains; in fact, they are sometimes abbreviated 7-TM receptors (**Figure 3.10**). It is important to note that metabotropic receptors do not possess a channel or pore. How, then, do these receptors work?

Metabotropic receptors work by activating other proteins in the cell membrane called **G proteins**. Consequently, another name for this receptor family is **G protein–coupled receptors**. Many different kinds of G proteins have been identified, and how a metabotropic receptor influences the postsynaptic cell depends on which G protein(s) the receptor activates. However, all G proteins operate by two major mechanisms. One is by stimulating or inhibiting the opening of ion channels in the cell membrane (**Figure 3.11A**). Potassium (K^+) channels, for example, are stimulated by specific G proteins at many synapses. When these channels open, K^+ ions flow out of the cell, the membrane is hyperpolarized, and consequently the cell's firing is suppressed. This is a common mechanism of synaptic inhibition used by various receptors for ACh, DA, NE, 5-HT, and GABA, and some neuropeptides like the endorphins. Note that the K^+ channels controlled by G proteins are not the same as the voltage-gated K^+ channels that work together with voltage-gated Na^+ channels to produce action potentials.

The second mechanism by which metabotropic receptors and G proteins operate is by stimulating or

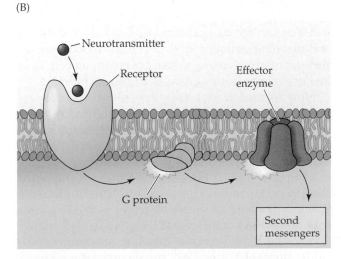

Figure 3.11 Functions of metabotropic receptors Metabotropic receptors activate G proteins in the membrane, which may either (A) alter the opening of a G protein–gated ion channel, or (B) stimulate an effector enzyme that either synthesizes or breaks down a second messenger.

first messenger. When everything is put together, this mechanism of metabotropic receptor function involves (1) activation of a G protein, followed by (2) stimulation or inhibition of an effector enzyme in the membrane of the postsynaptic cell, followed by (3) increased synthesis or breakdown of a second messenger, followed by (4) biochemical or physiological changes in the postsynaptic cell due to the altered levels of the second messenger (see Figure 3.11B). This sequence of events is an example of a biochemical "cascade."

Second messengers work by activating specific protein kinases within a cell

Second-messenger systems are too complex to be completely covered in this text. We will therefore highlight a few of the most important systems and how they alter cellular function. One of the key ways in which second messengers work is by activating enzymes called **protein kinases** (**Figure 3.12**). Kinases are enzymes that **phosphorylate** another molecule, that is, they catalyze the addition of one or more phosphate groups ($-PO_4^{2-}$) to the molecule. As the name suggests, a protein kinase phosphorylates a protein. The substrate protein might be an ion channel, an enzyme involved in neurotransmitter synthesis, a neurotransmitter receptor or transporter, a structural protein, or almost any other kind of protein. The phosphate groups added by the kinase then alter functioning of the protein in some way. For example, an ion channel might open, a neurotransmitter-synthesizing enzyme might be activated, a receptor might become more sensitive to the neurotransmitter, and so forth. Furthermore, kinases can phosphorylate proteins in the cell nucleus that turn on or turn off specific genes in that cell. You can see that protein kinases activated by second messengers are capable of producing widespread and profound changes in the postsynaptic cell, even including long-lasting changes in gene expression.

Now let us consider a few specific second messengers and their protein kinases. The first second messenger to be discovered was **cyclic adenosine monophosphate** (**cAMP**). Levels of cAMP are controlled by receptors for several different neurotransmitters, including DA, NE, 5-HT, and endorphins. Cyclic AMP stimulates a protein kinase called **protein kinase A** (**PKA**). A related second messenger is **cyclic guanosine monophosphate** (**cGMP**). One of the key regulators of cGMP is the novel gaseous messenger nitric oxide (**Box 3.1**). Cyclic GMP has its own kinase known as **protein kinase G** (**PKG**). A third second-messenger system is sometimes termed the **phosphoinositide second-messenger system**. This complex system, which works by breaking down a phospholipid in the cell membrane, actually liberates two second

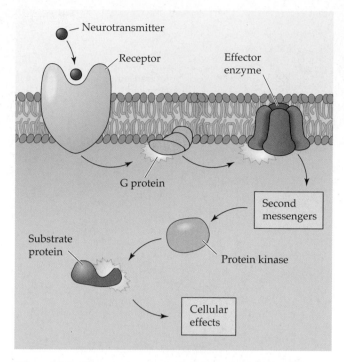

Figure 3.12 The mechanism of action of second messengers Second messengers work by activating protein kinases to cause phosphorylation of substrate proteins within the postsynaptic cell.

messengers: **diacylglycerol** (**DAG**) and **inositol trisphosphate** (**IP₃**). Working together, these messengers cause an elevation of the level of Ca^{2+} ions within the postsynaptic cell and activation of **protein kinase C** (**PKC**). The phosphoinositide system is controlled by receptors for several neurotransmitters, including ACh, NE, and 5-HT. Finally, Ca^{2+} itself is a second messenger. Calcium levels in the cell can be increased by various mechanisms, including the phosphoinositide second-messenger system, voltage-sensitive Ca^{2+} channels, and, as mentioned earlier, certain ionotropic receptors like the NMDA receptor. The protein kinase activated by Ca^{2+} requires the participation of an additional protein known as *calmodulin*. Hence, it is called **calcium/calmodulin kinase** (**CaMK**). Ca^{2+} also helps to activate PKC. **Table 3.3** summarizes these second-messenger systems and their associated protein kinases.

TABLE 3.3 Second-Messenger Systems and Protein Kinases

Second-messenger system	Associated protein kinase
Cyclic AMP (cAMP)	Protein kinase A (PKA)
Cyclic GMP (cGMP)	Protein kinase G (PKG)
Phosphoinositide	Protein kinase C (PKC)
Calcium (Ca^{2+})	Calcium/calmodulin kinase (CaMK)

BOX 3.1   The Cutting Edge

Just Say NO

A few neurotransmitters don't follow the rules outlined in this chapter. The most striking of these are two small molecules that are gases at room temperature: **nitric oxide (NO)** and **carbon monoxide (CO)**. Yes, there is good evidence that the potentially deadly CO found in automobile exhaust and poorly ventilated furnaces is actually a signaling molecule in the brain. But we know much more about the workings of NO, so that will be the main focus of this discussion.

Nitric oxide is produced from the amino acid arginine in a simple biochemical reaction catalyzed by the enzyme **nitric oxide synthase (NOS)**. There are several forms of NOS, one of which is found primarily in neurons and another that is present in endothelial cells (the cells that make up the walls of blood vessels). The enzyme NOS, and therefore NO formation, is stimulated by increases in Ca^{2+} within the cell. The physiological role of NO has often been investigated using drugs that block NO synthesis by inhibiting NOS. Two such drugs are 7-nitroindazole (7-NI) and N-nitro-L-arginine methyl ester (L-NAME). After its release, NO is eventually inactivated by chemically reacting with oxygen (O_2) to yield NO_2 or NO_3.

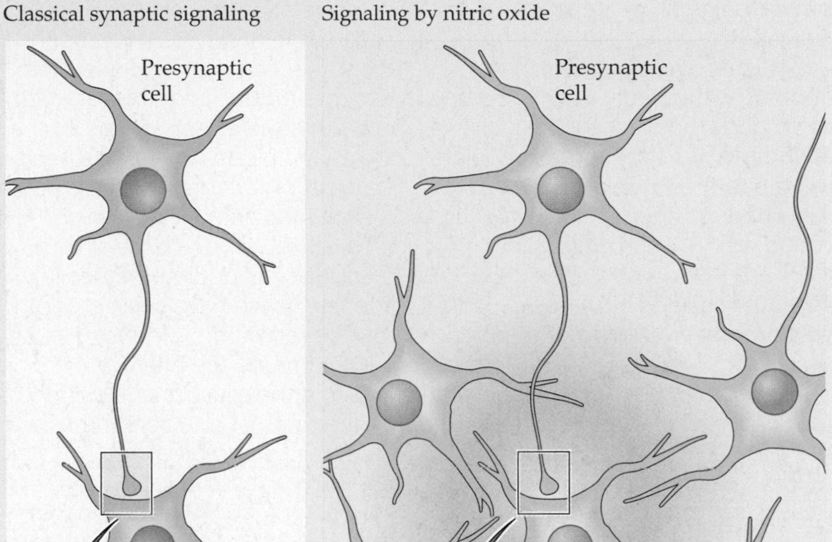

For several reasons, we say that NO breaks the normal rules for a neurotransmitter. First, as a gas, it readily passes through membranes. Thus it cannot be stored in synaptic vesicles, as can most transmitter substances. So nerve cells must make NO on demand when it is needed. Second, since NO is not present in vesicles, it is not released by exocytosis but simply diffuses out of the nerve cell through the cell membrane. Third, once it reaches the extracellular fluid, NO is not confined to the synapse but

Classical synaptic signaling

Presynaptic cell

Postsynaptic cell

Presynaptic cell

Neurotransmitter

Postsynaptic cell

Intracellular signal

Signaling by nitric oxide

Presynaptic cell

Presynaptic cell

Postsynaptic cell

Nitric oxide

may travel some distance until it reaches target cells. Finally, in many cases, NO is released by the postsynaptic rather than the presynaptic cell in the synapse. You'll recall that some neurotransmitter receptors can increase Ca^{2+} levels within the postsynaptic cell. This may occur either through an ionotropic receptor such as

the NMDA receptor or through a metabotropic receptor like certain of the receptors for ACh. If NOS is present and is activated by this rise in Ca^{2+}, then NO will be produced by the postsynaptic cell, pass through the cell membrane, and travel to neighboring cells. One of

(Continued on next page)

BOX 3.1 *(continued)*

the affected cells may even be the presynaptic cell, thus giving us an instance of neural transmission in reverse! Some of these features of NO signaling, and how they differ from the features of more typical synaptic signaling, are shown in the figure.

The discovery of NO came about unexpectedly from the study of smooth muscle cells that surround the walls of arteries, regulating the rate of arterial blood flow. A number of chemical substances, including the neurotransmitter ACh, were known to relax these smooth muscle cells, thus causing vasodilation (widening of the blood vessels) and increased blood flow. However, the mechanism by which this occurred was unclear until the early 1980s, when researchers showed that endothelial cells were necessary for the relaxant effects of ACh on the muscle. In addition, they showed that ACh stimulated the endothelial cells (by increasing intracellular Ca^{2+} levels) to produce a chemical factor that traveled to nearby muscle cells and caused them to relax. This chemical factor was subsequently shown to be NO. The discovery of NO and of its role in regulating cardiovascular function was recognized by the awarding of the 1998 Nobel Prize in Physiology or Medicine to the three key pioneers in these discoveries: Robert Furchgott, Louis Ignarro, and Ferid Murad.

One of the major mechanisms by which NO acts on its target cells involves activating an enzyme that synthesizes the second messenger cGMP. In smooth muscle, it is the rise in cGMP within the cells that leads to the relaxation response and resulting dilation of the arteries. Since the discovery of the relationship between NO and cGMP, this system has been the subject of many studies. One valuable outcome of this research concerns the effects of these agents on blood flow to the penis. An erection occurs when the penis is engorged with blood, which requires relaxation of the smooth muscles surrounding the penile arteries. As we have seen, smooth muscle relaxation is induced by cGMP. In turn, the amount of cGMP in the muscle cells depends on the rates of both its synthesis (due to NO) and breakdown. Cyclic GMP breakdown is catalyzed by the enzyme **cGMP phosphodiesterase**. Several different drugs have been developed that inhibit cGMP phosphodiesterase in the penis, thereby elevating cGMP levels and facilitating the erection. Such compounds, including sildenafil (Viagra), tadalafil (Cialis), and vardenafil (Levitra), have helped many men overcome problems with erectile dysfunction.

Of course, the development of erectile dysfunction medications is not the only reason why pharmacologists are interested in NO. This messenger substance has also been implicated in the behavioral changes that occur in animals following repeated treatment with abused drugs. When rats or mice are chronically administered opioid drugs such as morphine, they develop a characteristic tolerance to the analgesic effects of these compounds. Such tolerance is attenuated either by treatment with an NOS inhibitor such as 7-NI (Santamarata et al., 2005) or by a targeted genetic mutation that reduces expression of nNOS, the neuronal form of this enzyme (Heinzen and Pollack, 2004). Interestingly, studies by Itzhak and colleagues found that knocking out the nNOS gene also blunts the locomotor sensitizing effects of repeated cocaine or alcohol treatments in adult male mice, but not in adult females or in adolescent animals of either sex (Balda et al., 2008; Itzhak and Anderson, 2008; Balda et al., 2009). Thus, we can generally conclude that nNOS is a significant mediator of some of the neural and behavioral adaptations that occur after chronic administration of various abused drugs. The dependence of these adaptations on the presence of nNOS seems to be age- and sex-specific for reasons that aren't yet known. Despite these limitations, however, it is possible that medications designed to alter NO levels may eventually be developed to help treat drug addicts because of the hypothesized involvement of tolerance and sensitization in the development of drug dependence. In addition, NOS inhibitors may be used therapeutically to minimize the development of tolerance in patients taking opioids for relief of chronic pain.

Tyrosine kinase receptors mediate the effects of neurotrophic factors

There is one more family of receptors that you need to learn about: the **tyrosine kinase receptors**. These receptors mediate the action of **neurotrophic factors**, proteins that stimulate the survival and growth of neurons during early development and are also involved in neuronal signaling. Nerve growth factor (NGF) was the first neurotrophic factor to be discovered, but many others are now known, including BDNF, which was mentioned earlier, neurotrophin-3 (NT-3), and NT-4.

Three specific tyrosine kinase receptors are used by these neurotrophic factors: trkA (pronounced "track A") for NGF, trkB for BDNF and NT-4, and trkC for NT-3. The trk receptors are activated through the following mechanism. After the neurotrophic factor binds to its receptor, two of these complexes come together in the cell membrane, which is a process that is necessary for receptor activation (**Figure 3.13**). When the two trk receptors are activated, they phosphorylate each other on tyrosine residues[7] (hence the "tyrosine kinase receptor") located within the cytoplasmic

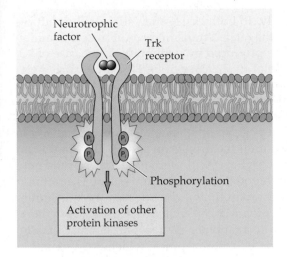

Figure 3.13 Activation of trk receptors Neurotrophic factors stimulate trk receptors by bringing two receptor molecules into close proximity in the cell membrane, which then leads to reciprocal phosphorylation of tyrosine residues and activation of other protein kinases.

region of each receptor. This process then triggers a complex sequence involving additional protein kinases, including some that differ from those described in the previous section. Tyrosine kinase receptors and the neurotrophic factors they serve generally participate more in regulation of long-term changes in gene expression and neuronal functioning than in rapid synaptic events that determine the rate of cell firing.

Pharmacology of Synaptic Transmission

Drugs can either enhance or interfere with virtually all aspects of synaptic transmission. Synaptic effects form the basis of almost all of the actions of psychoactive drugs, including drugs of abuse, as well as those prescribed for the treatment of serious mental disorders such as depression and schizophrenia. **Figure 3.14** illustrates the major ways in which such drugs can alter the neurotransmission process.

Drugs may either increase or decrease the rate of transmitter synthesis. If the drug is a chemical precursor to the transmitter, then the rate of transmitter formation may be increased. Two examples of this approach involve L-dihydroxyphenylalanine (L-DOPA), which is the precursor to DA, and 5-hydroxytryptophan (5-HTP), which is the precursor to 5-HT. Because patients suffering from

---

[7]Proteins are long chains of amino acids. When amino acids are strung together in the synthesis of a protein, each adjacent pair of amino acids loses a water molecule (an H from one amino acid and an OH from the other). What remain are called "amino acid residues." Each residue is named for the specific amino acid from which it was derived from, such as tyrosine in this case. Tyrosine kinases are differentiated from the kinases mentioned earlier (e.g., PKA), because those kinases phosphorylate proteins on residues of the amino acids serine and threonine instead of tyrosine. This difference, in turn, is important because it influences how phosphorylation affects the functioning of the target protein.

Figure 3.14 Summary of the mechanisms by which drugs can alter synaptic transmission NT = neurotransmitter; + denotes a mechanism that stimulates or facilitates transmission; − denotes a process that inhibits transmission.

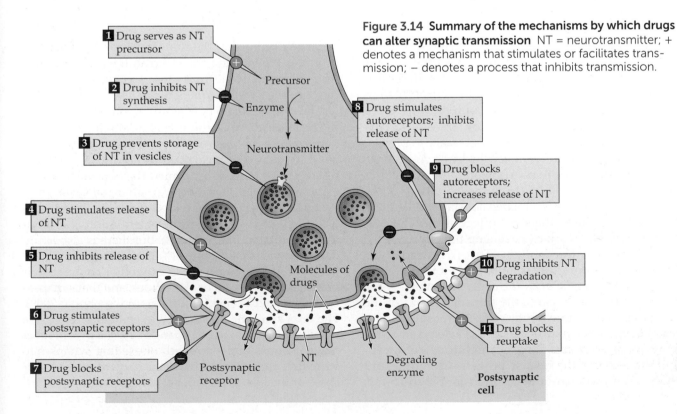

1 Drug serves as NT precursor

2 Drug inhibits NT synthesis

3 Drug prevents storage of NT in vesicles

4 Drug stimulates release of NT

5 Drug inhibits release of NT

6 Drug stimulates postsynaptic receptors

7 Drug blocks postsynaptic receptors

8 Drug stimulates autoreceptors; inhibits release of NT

9 Drug blocks autoreceptors; increases release of NT

10 Drug inhibits NT degradation

11 Drug blocks reuptake

Precursor

Enzyme

Neurotransmitter

Molecules of drugs

Postsynaptic receptor

NT

Degrading enzyme

Postsynaptic cell

Parkinson's disease are deficient in DA, the primary treatment for this neurological disorder is L-DOPA (see Chapter 5 for more information). Alternatively, a drug decreases levels of a neurotransmitter by inhibiting a key enzyme needed for transmitter synthesis. Alpha-methyl-para-tyrosine inhibits the enzyme tyrosine hydroxylase, which helps manufacture both DA and NE, whereas para-chlorophenylalanine inhibits the 5-HT–synthesizing enzyme tryptophan hydroxylase.

Besides administering a precursor substance, you can also enhance the action of a neurotransmitter by reducing its inactivation. This can be accomplished in two ways. First, levels of the transmitter can be increased by blocking the enzyme involved in its breakdown. Physostigmine blocks the enzyme acetylcholinesterase, which breaks down ACh, whereas phenelzine blocks monoamine oxidase (MAO), an enzyme that is important in the breakdown of DA, NE, and 5-HT. As we will see in Chapter 19, phenelzine and other MAO-inhibiting drugs are sometimes used to treat patients with depression. For neurotransmitters that use transporters for reuptake out of the synaptic cleft, a second way to reduce neurotransmitter inactivation is to block those transporters. This increases the amount and prolongs the presence of the transmitter in the synaptic cleft, thereby enhancing its effects on the postsynaptic cell. As described previously, cocaine blocks the transporters for DA, NE, and 5-HT, and drugs that more selectively prevent reuptake of 5-HT are commonly used as antidepressant medications (see Chapters 12 and 19).

Other drugs affect neurotransmitter storage or release. For example, reserpine blocks the storage of DA, NE, and 5-HT in synaptic vesicles. Reserpine treatment initially causes a burst of neurotransmitter release as the vesicles empty out, but this is followed by a period of extremely low transmitter levels, because storage in vesicles is necessary to prevent breakdown of transmitter molecules by enzymes present in the axon terminal. Amphetamine stimulates the release of DA and NE from the cytoplasm of the axon terminal, whereas a related substance called fenfluramine produces the same effect on 5-HT. These releasing agents work by reversing the effects of the neurotransmitter transporters. That is, instead of the transporters taking up transmitter molecules into the neuron from the synaptic cleft, they work in the reverse direction to carry the transmitter out of the neuron and into the synaptic cleft. As we saw earlier, some drugs alter neurotransmitter release in a different way, by stimulating or inhibiting autoreceptors that control the release process. Clonidine and 8-OH-DPAT stimulate autoreceptors for NE and 5-HT,

respectively. In both cases, such stimulation reduces release of the related transmitter. Autoreceptor inhibition can be produced by yohimbine in the case of NE and pindolol in the case of 5-HT. Not surprisingly, administration of these compounds increases transmitter release.

One final mechanism of action can be seen in drugs that act on postsynaptic receptors for a specific neurotransmitter. If the drug is an agonist for a particular receptor subtype, it will mimic the effect of the neurotransmitter on that receptor. If the drug is a receptor antagonist, it will inhibit the effect of the transmitter on the receptor. Many psychoactive drugs, both therapeutic and recreational, are receptor agonists. Examples include benzodiazepines, which are agonists at benzodiazepine receptors and are used clinically as sedative and antianxiety drugs (see Chapter 18); opioids like heroin and morphine, which are agonists at opioid receptors (see Chapter 11); nicotine, which is an agonist at the nicotinic receptor subtype for ACh (see Chapter 7); and THC, which is an agonist at cannabinoid receptors (see Chapter 14). Receptor antagonists are likewise important in pharmacology. Most drugs used to treat schizophrenic patients are antagonists at the D_2 receptor subtype for DA (see Chapter 20), but the widely ingested substance caffeine is an antagonist at receptors for the neurotransmitter adenosine (see Chapter 13).

Synaptic Plasticity

For many years after the first visualization of synapses in the 1950s using the electron microscope, most researchers believed that these structures were stable once they were formed. Since it was also thought (erroneously) that no new neurons could be generated in the mature brain, there was no obvious need for new synapses because existing ones presumably could be strengthened or weakened as needed. Subsequent research has, indeed, confirmed that various kinds of experiences (e.g., learning) can alter the strength of synaptic connections activated by those experiences (see discussion of long-term potentiation and long-term depression in Chapter 8). But there is also abundant evidence that even in adulthood, axons can grow new terminals, dendrites can expand or contract their branches and/or gain or lose spines, and that synapses can be created or lost (Holtmaat and Svoboda, 2009). The term **synaptic plasticity** was coined to reflect the whole variety of synaptic changes, ranging from functional changes in the strength of existing synapses to structural changes involving the growth of new synapses or the loss of previously existing ones.

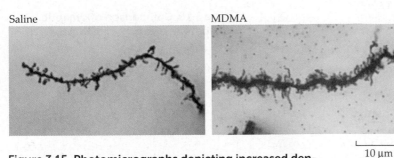

Saline   MDMA

10 μm

Figure 3.15 Photomicrographs depicting increased dendritic spine density in nucleus accumbens neurons from adult male rats treated repeatedly with MDMA. Animals were administered 5.0 mg/kg MDMA or saline vehicle twice daily, for 3 days in a row, followed by 4 days of no treatment. This dosing regimen was continued for 3 weeks, after which the animals remained drug free for another 4 weeks. Brains of the MDMA and control rats were stained using the Golgi-Cox method to visualize dendritic arbors and spines in several brain areas, including the nucleus accumbens core. Note the increased spine density and thickening in the photomicrograph obtained from an MDMA-treated animal compared to a saline-treated control. (From Ball et al., 2009.)

While the majority of research on synaptic plasticity has focused on synaptic changes due to sensory/environmental stimuli or learning and memory, there is growing recognition that psychoactive drugs can also trigger profound synaptic plasticity, especially under conditions of repeated drug exposure. One recent example can be seen in the results of Ball and coworkers (2009), who treated rats intermittently for 3 weeks with the stimulant drug 3,4-methylenedioxymethamphetamine (MDMA; also known as "ecstasy"). Four weeks after the last drug dose, investigators examined the density of dendritic spines in the nucleus accumbens, a brain area important for the behavior-activating effects of stimulants like MDMA. As illustrated in **Figure 3.15**, a large increase in spine density was noted among treated rats compared with controls, which received only injections of the saline vehicle. It is important to note that when other rats pretreated in the same way with MDMA or saline were tested for their behavioral responses to a later challenge dose of MDMA, the drug-pretreated animals showed a sensitized response to the challenge (see Chapter 1 for a discussion of sensitization). Given these findings, it is possible that the increased density of dendritic spines in the nucleus accumbens contributed to the behavioral sensitization observed in the MDMA-pretreated rats. Moreover, as we shall see later in Chapter 9, synaptic plasticity in this same brain area is thought to play a key role in the rewarding properties of many drugs of abuse.

Section Summary

- Most neurotransmitters make use of multiple receptor subtypes.
- Neurotransmitter receptors fall into two categories: ionotropic and metabotropic.
- Ionotropic receptors are composed of multiple subunits and form an intrinsic ion channel that is permeable either to cations such as Na^+ (and sometimes also Ca^{2+}) or to anions such as Cl^-. These receptors respectively mediate fast excitatory or fast inhibitory transmission.
- Metabotropic receptors are coupled to G proteins in the cell membrane and mediate slower transmission involving ion channel opening (e.g., inhibitory K^+ channels) or second-messenger synthesis or breakdown.
- Second messengers work by activating protein kinases that phosphorylate target proteins in the postsynaptic cell.
- Some important second-messenger systems and their respective kinases are the cAMP (protein kinase A), cGMP (protein kinase G), Ca^{2+}/calmodulin (calcium/calmodulin kinase), and phosphoinositide (protein kinase C) systems.
- Neurotrophic factors like NGF and BDNF work by activating tyrosine kinase receptors.
- Psychoactive drugs usually exert their subjective and behavioral effects by modifying synaptic transmission in one or more of the following ways: (1) increasing or decreasing transmitter synthesis; (2) reducing transmitter inactivation by inhibiting enzymatic breakdown or blocking reuptake; (3) stimulating transmitter release; and (4) acting as agonists or antagonists at transmitter receptors on the postsynaptic or presynaptic (i.e., autoreceptors) cell.
- Synaptic plasticity refers to functional and structural changes in synaptic connectivity. Such plasticity can be produced not only by sensory and experiential stimuli but also by psychoactive drugs.

Synaptic   **Endocrine**

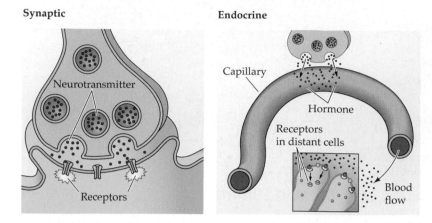

Figure 3.16 Comparison of synaptic and endocrine communication

The Endocrine System

As we have seen, neurotransmitters normally travel only a tiny distance before reaching their target at the other side of the synaptic cleft, or sometimes a little farther away. Another method of cellular communication, however, involves the release of chemical substances called **hormones** into the bloodstream. Hormones are secreted by specialized organs called **endocrine glands**. Upon reaching the circulation, hormones can travel long distances before reaching target cells anywhere in the body. To respond to a given hormone, a target cell must possess specific receptors for that hormone, just as a postsynaptic cell must to respond to a neurotransmitter. Moreover, sometimes the same substances (e.g., norepinephrine, epinephrine) are used both as neurotransmitters within the

brain and as hormones within the endocrine system. Thus, synaptic and endocrine communications are similar in many respects, although they differ in terms of the proximity of the cells involved and the anatomic features of the synapses described earlier (**Figure 3.16**).

Endocrine glands can secrete multiple hormones

As shown in **Figure 3.17**, numerous endocrine glands are located throughout the body. Some of these glands secrete more than one type of hormone. We'll now briefly describe each gland and its associated hormone(s), including the chemical classification and functions of that hormone.

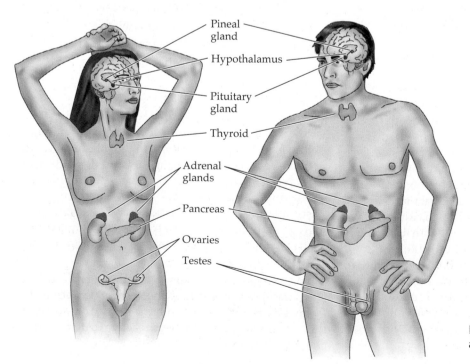

Figure 3.17 Major endocrine glands and their location in the body

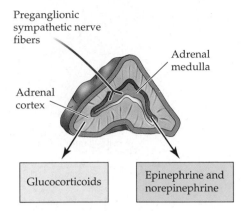

Figure 3.18 Structure of the adrenal gland, showing the outer cortex and the inner medulla

The **adrenal glands** lie over each kidney. The adrenals are actually two separate glands that have come together during embryonic development (**Figure 3.18**). The inner part of the gland, which is called the **adrenal medulla**, is derived from nervous system tissue. Like a sympathetic ganglion, it receives input from the preganglionic fibers of the sympathetic nervous system (see Chapter 2). Cells of the adrenal medulla, which are called **chromaffin cells**, secrete the hormones **epinephrine** (**EPI**) and **norepinephrine** (**NE**), both of which are monoamines. Physical or psychological stressors stimulate the release of EPI and NE as part of the classic "fight-or-flight" response. Once in the bloodstream, these hormones mobilize glucose (sugar) from the liver to provide immediate energy, and they also divert blood from the internal organs (e.g., the organs of digestion) to the muscles, in case physical action is needed. Some of their effects contribute to the physical sensations that we experience when we're highly aroused or stressed, such as a racing heart and cold, clammy hands.

The outer part of the adrenal gland, the **adrenal cortex**, secretes hormones called **glucocorticoids**. Which glucocorticoid is present depends on the species: humans and other primates make **cortisol** (sometimes called *hydrocortisone*), whereas rats and mice make **corticosterone**. Glucocorticoids belong to a class of molecules known as **steroids**, all of which are derived from the precursor cholesterol. One of the main functions of glucocorticoids is to maintain normal blood glucose levels while helping to store excess glucose for future use. These hormones are also secreted in increased amounts during stress and normally help us cope with stressful experiences. However, there is substantial evidence that chronic stress may lead to serious consequences—possibly even damage to certain parts of the brain—if high glucocorticoid levels persist for long periods of time (Heuser and Lammers, 2003).

Other glands that secrete steroid hormones are the **gonads**: the **ovaries** in females and the **testes** in males. The ovaries secrete female sex hormones called **estrogens** (such as **estradiol**) and **progestins** (mainly **progesterone**), whereas the testes secrete male sex hormones called **androgens** (such as **testosterone**). These hormones determine some of the physical differences between males and females (the so-called secondary sex characteristics) that occur after puberty. Testosterone also has two other important roles. During early development, this hormone acts within the brain to produce neural changes important for determining later gender-based differences in behavior. Later on, it plays a significant role in stimulating sexual motivation in males and even in females (both genders possess some quantity of each other's sex hormones).

Within the pancreas is an endocrine gland known as the **islets of Langerhans**. Cells within this tissue secrete two hormones: **insulin** and **glucagon**. Insulin release is stimulated by food intake and together with glucagon, it plays an important role in regulating glucose and other sources of metabolic energy. Lack of insulin gives rise to the serious disorder diabetes. Both insulin and glucagon are peptide hormones, similar to the neuropeptides discussed earlier but somewhat larger in size.

Residing in the throat is the **thyroid gland**, which secretes **thyroxine** (**T4**) and **triiodothyronine** (**T3**). These hormones are important for normal energy metabolism. Underactivity of the thyroid gland (hypothyroidism) causes feelings of weakness and lethargy (even mimicking some of the symptoms of clinical depression), whereas thyroid overactivity (hyperthyroidism) leads to excessive energy and nervousness. These two thyroid hormones are made from the amino acid tyrosine, which is the same precursor used to make DA, NE, and EPI (see Chapter 5).

The **pineal gland** is situated just over the brainstem and is covered over by the cerebral hemispheres. This gland secretes the hormone **melatonin**, which is synthesized using the neurotransmitter 5-HT as a precursor. Melatonin has been implicated in the control of various rhythmic functions, which differ depending on the species. In humans and in many other vertebrates, most melatonin secretion occurs during the night, which suggests a possible role in controlling sleep rhythms. Tablets that contain small amounts of melatonin can be purchased over the counter in drug stores and supermarkets, and for some people, these tablets induce drowsiness and faster sleep onset.

The **pituitary gland** is sometimes called the "master gland," because it secretes several hormones that control other glands. The pituitary is found just under the hypothalamus and is connected to that brain structure by a thin stalk. Like the adrenals, the pituitary

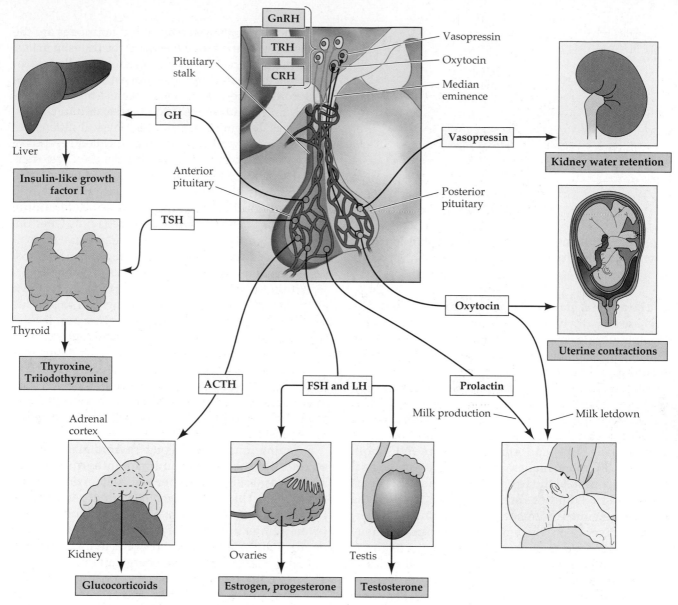

Figure 3.19 Organization of the hypothalamic–pituitary axis Note that the axon terminals of the hypothalamic-releasing hormone neurons are located near blood capillaries in the median eminence, whereas oxytocin and vasopressin neurons send their axons all the way into the posterior lobe of the pituitary gland. For the purpose of simplicity, not all hypothalamic-releasing hormones are shown. ACTH = adrenocorticotropic hormone; CRH = corticotropin-releasing hormone; FSH = follicle-stimulating hormone; GH = growth hormone; GnRH = gonadotropin-releasing hormone; LH = luteinizing hormone; TRH = thyrotropin-releasing hormone; TSH = thyroid-stimulating hormone.

actually comprises two separate glands with different hormones that serve distinct functions. The **anterior pituitary** secretes **thyroid-stimulating hormone (TSH**; also known as thyrotropin), **adrenocorticotropic hormone (ACTH)**, **follicle-stimulating hormone (FSH)**, **luteinizing hormone (LH)**, **growth hormone (GH)**, and **prolactin (PRL)**. TSH stimulates the thyroid gland, and ACTH promotes the synthesis and release of glucocorticoids from the adrenal cortex. FSH and LH together control the growth and functioning of the gonads, whereas LH also stimulates estrogen and androgen secretion by the ovaries and testes, respectively. GH stimulates the production of insulin-like growth factor I (IGF-I) from peripheral organs such as the liver; IGF-I is critical for skeletal growth during development. Lastly, PRL promotes milk production by the mammary glands.

The pituitary stalk connecting the hypothalamus with the pituitary gland contains blood vessels that carry special **hypothalamic-releasing hormones (Figure 3.19)**. These hormones are mainly neuropeptides manufactured by various groups of neurons in the hypothalamus. Instead of forming normal synapses, these neurons release peptides into blood capillaries in a region called the **median eminence**. Blood vessels then carry releasing hormones to the hormone-secreting cells of the anterior pituitary. For example, **thyrotropin-releasing hormone** (**TRH**) is a hypothalamic peptide that stimulates the release of TSH, **corticotropin-releasing hormone** (**CRH**) (alternatively called *corticotropin-releasing factor*, or CRF) stimulates ACTH release (corticotropin is another name for ACTH), and **gonadotropin-releasing hormone** (**GnRH**) stimulates both FSH and LH. We can see that the endocrine system sometimes functions through the interactions of several glands, with one gland controlling another until the final hormone is secreted. For example, stress does not directly cause increased glucocorticoid secretion from the adrenal cortex. Instead, stress leads to enhanced CRH release from the hypothalamus, which provokes ACTH release from the anterior pituitary; ACTH travels through the bloodstream to the adrenal glands, where it stimulates the secretion of glucocorticoids. Because of this complicated control system, it may take a few minutes before the level of glucocorticoids in our blood is significantly increased. Thus the endocrine system works much more slowly than chemical communication by neurotransmitters.

In addition to blood vessels that connect the hypothalamus to the anterior pituitary, the pituitary stalk contains the axons of specialized secretory neurons located in the hypothalamus. These axons reach the **posterior pituitary**, where, like the hypothalamic neurons mentioned earlier, they form endings on blood vessels instead of other cells. Secretory neurons synthesize and release the peptide hormones **vasopressin** and **oxytocin** from the posterior pituitary into the bloodstream. Vasopressin (also called *antidiuretic hormone*) acts on the kidneys to increase water retention (i.e., make the urine more concentrated). Alcohol

inhibits vasopressin secretion, which is one of the reasons why people urinate so frequently when they drink (it's not just the increased fluid consumption). Oxytocin is known mainly for two important physiological functions in female mammals: stimulation of uterine contractions during childbirth, and triggering of milk letdown from the breasts during lactation. In recent years, interesting findings from animal studies have suggested that both oxytocin and vasopressin may play an important role in pair-bonding, parenting, and other kinds of affiliative behavior (Lim and Young, 2006). These simple molecules may even play a role in normal and abnormal social behaviors in humans, although much more research needs to be done before such a role is fully understood (Bora et al., 2009).

Mechanisms of hormone action vary

As mentioned in Chapter 1, two broad types of receptors are used in cellular communication: extracellular (membrane) receptors and intracellular receptors. Earlier in the present chapter, we observed that most neurotransmitter receptors are located on the cell membrane. In contrast, hormones use various types of receptors, both extracellular and intracellular.

Peptide hormones function by means of membrane receptors (**Figure 3.20A**). Some of these are just like metabotropic neurotransmitter receptors, working through second-messenger systems. One example is the receptors for CRH, which stimulate formation of the second messenger cAMP. However, some hormones, such as insulin, use tyrosine kinase receptors that are similar to the trk receptors described earlier.

Steroid and thyroid hormones operate mostly through intracellular receptors (**Figure 3.20B**). These receptors are proteins just like the membrane receptors for neurotransmitters or peptide hormones, but they

(A)

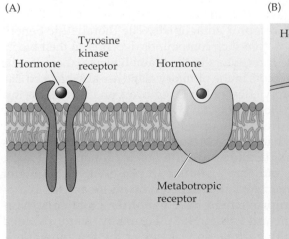

(B)

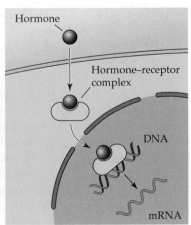

Figure 3.20 Hormonal signaling is mediated by a variety of extracellular (A) and intracellular (B) receptors.

are generally located within the cell nucleus, where they function as **transcription factors** to either turn on or turn off the expression of specific genes within the cell. Since gene expression determines which proteins are made by the cell, the ultimate effects of steroid and thyroid hormones are seen in the altered synthesis of particular proteins. This process takes much longer (many minutes to a few hours or longer) than the rapid effects typically produced by membrane receptors. On the other hand, changes in gene expression and protein synthesis are also longer-lasting, thus allowing an animal or person to keep responding to a hormone long after it is released. In addition to this classical, relatively slow action of steroid hormones, there is now good evidence that some of these hormones (e.g., glucocorticoids, estrogens) can exert rapid effects on neuronal excitability via membrane receptors (Micevych and Dominguez, 2009; Prager and Johnson, 2009).

Why is the endocrine system important to pharmacologists?

By this time, you may be wondering why pharmacologists are concerned about hormones and the endocrine system. Actually, there are a number of good reasons, four of which we'll briefly mention here:

1. Both therapeutic and abused drugs can alter the secretion of many hormones, causing physiological abnormalities. For example, chronic alcoholism can lead to reduced testosterone levels, testicular atrophy, and impotence in men. Alcoholic women may have menstrual disorders and at least temporarily may become infertile (see Chapter 10).

2. Hormones may alter subjective and behavioral responses to drugs. This is illustrated in the important role of female sex hormones as well as glucocorticoids in modulating sensitivity to drugs of abuse such as cocaine and amphetamine (**Box 3.2** and **Web Box 3.1**).

3. Hormones themselves sometimes have psychoactive properties like those of certain drugs. We mentioned earlier that melatonin has a sedative effect on many people. In addition, thyroid hormones are occasionally prescribed along with an antidepressant drug to enhance the therapeutic response.

4. The secretion of pituitary hormones and other hormones dependent on the pituitary is controlled by neurotransmitter systems in the brain. This fact sometimes enables us to use the endocrine system as a "window to the brain" that tells us whether a particular neurotransmitter system has been altered by disease (such as a psychiatric or neurological disorder), injury, or the effect of a psychoactive drug.

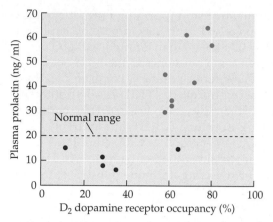

Figure 3.21 Relationship between estimated dopamine D_2 receptor occupancy and plasma prolactin concentrations in a group of schizophrenic patients Patients were treated for 4 weeks with 2, 6, or 12 mg daily of the antipsychotic drug raclopride At the end of the treatment period, D_2 receptor occupancy in the putamen was measured using positron emission tomography, and plasma prolactin concentrations were measured by radioimmunoassay in each patient. All three patients who received the lowest dose of raclopride and two of six patients who received the intermediate dose exhibited plasma prolactin levels within the normal range (red circles; the dashed line depicts the upper limit of this range) and, in almost all cases, showed a low percentage of estimated D_2 receptor occupancy. The remaining patients (blue circles) had >50% estimated D_2 receptor occupancy and correspondingly elevated prolactin levels. (After Nordstrom and Farde, 1998.)

Let's look at a more detailed example that relates to both the first and fourth reasons to study the interactions between psychoactive drugs and hormones. Secretion of the hormone prolactin is inhibited by the neurotransmitter DA acting on D_2 receptors expressed by the prolactin-synthesizing cells in the pituitary gland (see Chapter 5 for more information on the DA system). The DA that regulates this system under normal conditions comes from neurons located at the base of the hypothalamus. Several drugs that are used to treat psychiatric disorders, particularly schizophrenia, are D_2 receptor antagonists. The therapeutic benefit derived from such compounds depends on their blocking of D_2 receptors in the brain; however, because the D_2 receptors in the pituitary gland are also blocked, the inhibitory effect of DA is removed, and this results in a rise in blood prolactin levels.

Studies of this phenomenon have revealed that more than 50% of brain dopamine D_2 receptors must be occupied for prolactin levels to increase (**Figure 3.21**), and that a similar (if not greater) degree of receptor blockade seems to be necessary for symptom improvement in schizophrenic patients (Nordstrom and Farde, 1998). For many years, elevated circulating prolactin was one of the few biomarkers

BOX 3.2 Pharmacology in Action

Sex Hormones and Drug Abuse

Surveys have shown that use and abuse of illicit drugs are generally more common in men than in women. This gender difference can be seen, for example, in the results of the yearly National Survey of Drug Use and Health, which is carried out every year by the federal government's Substance Abuse and Mental Health Services Administration (Office of Applied Studies, 2009). Nevertheless, even though there are more male than female drug users, other findings suggest greater vulnerability of females to drug abuse. Such findings include a greater rate of escalation of drug use and greater difficulty quitting among women compared with men (Becker and Hu, 2008).

Gender differences in drug use and abuse are likely related to a variety of different factors, some cultural and others biological. Particularly relevant to this chapter is the potential role of sex hormones in drug sensitivity. We focus here on the effects of the female gonadal hormones estradiol and progesterone on responses to cocaine, as this has been a very active area of research for many years.

As discussed in the recent review by Evans and Foltin (2010), there are fewer cocaine-dependent women than men, and this is consistent with the overall gender difference in drug abuse previously mentioned. However, the authors also note that despite the difference in the sheer numbers of women and men who suffer from cocaine dependence, there is evidence that women who do take cocaine progress to dependence more rapidly than men and also relapse more quickly after treatment. Could this greater vulnerability in women be related to sex hormones? This issue has been addressed in various studies examining the subjective effects of cocaine administered in a laboratory setting to experienced cocaine

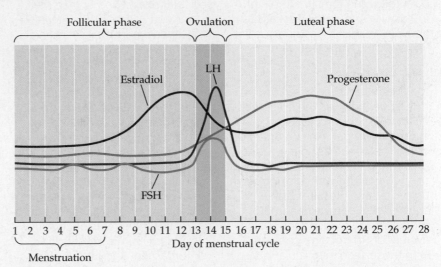

(A) Changes in circulating hormone levels during the menstrual cycle

users recruited for research purposes. The first and most basic question concerns whether men and women differ in the subjective effects produced by taking the drug. The answer is mainly no; women overall respond to cocaine in a similar manner to men (Evans and Foltin, 2010). However, when we say "overall," we mean that there is no gender difference when the stage of the menstrual cycle is not controlled in the experiment. Before going further, it is important to briefly discuss the stages of the menstrual cycle and the hormonal changes that occur at each stage.

The human menstrual cycle has a period of approximately 28 days that consists of two main stages: follicular and luteal. During the follicular stage, a single follicle containing an immature egg (oocyte) in the woman's ovary begins to mature in preparation for ovulation. As shown in Figure A, circulating progesterone levels are low during this phase, whereas estradiol levels are beginning to rise. Because of positive feedback on the pituitary gland, the high estradiol levels eventually trigger a surge of LH that acts on the follicle to trigger ovulation. After releasing the egg (ovum), the follicle changes into

a corpus luteum and begins to secrete large amounts of progesterone. If the egg is not fertilized, progesterone levels subsequently decline, menstruation occurs, and the cycle begins again.

Research on the effects of menstrual cyclicity, hormones, and cocaine sensitivity has focused on estradiol and progesterone rather than LH or FSH for two reasons. First, large changes in the levels of the two pituitary hormones LH and FSH are relatively short-lived, occurring primarily around the time of ovulation, whereas more sustained changes in estradiol and progesterone occur as a function of stage of the cycle. Second, LH and FSH have relatively little effect on the brain (in contrast to the gonads, of course), whereas estrogen and progestin receptors are present in significant numbers of neurons, and activation of those receptors alters neuronal activity. When Evans, Foltin, and coworkers tested the positive subjective effects of different doses of smoked cocaine (6, 12, or 25 mg) on women during either the midfollicular phase (6–10 days after the beginning of menstruation) or the midluteal phase (7–12

(Continued on next page)

BOX 3.2 *(continued)*

days following the LH surge), the intensity of the drug effect at 12- and 25-mg doses was significantly lower during the luteal compared to the follicular phase (Evans and Foltin, 2010; Figure B, left). Since a major difference between the two testing periods was the level of circulating progesterone, investigators subsequently determined the effect of artificially increasing progesterone during the follicular phase by treating women with this hormone before testing. Results clearly showed that administration of progesterone reduced the subjective effects of cocaine compared with those seen in follicular-phase women who received placebo instead (Figure B, right). Note two other interesting outcomes from this study. First, the same progesterone treatment given to men had no effect on their sensitivity to cocaine, indicating that the influence of the hormone was gender specific. Second, we can see that women in the follicular phase of their cycle (without exogenous progesterone treatment) responded to cocaine similarly to men, whereas women with elevated levels of progesterone responded less strongly than men. Indeed, other work by the same research team found a gender difference in cocaine sensitivity between luteal phase women and men (with the women being less sensitive), but not between

follicular phase women and men (Evans and Foltin, 2010). Interestingly, these menstrual cycle and hormonal effects were observed only when the women smoked the cocaine, not when they took the drug intranasally (i.e., by snorting).

We can safely conclude from these findings that high levels of progesterone reduce the positive subjective effects of smoked (but not intranasal) cocaine in women, but not in men. Other studies using female rats and monkeys have similarly shown that progesterone decreases the effects of cocaine in standard animal models of reinforcement and drug-seeking behavior (Carroll and Anker, 2010; Quinones-Jenab and Jenab, 2010). Although the mechanisms underlying these effects are not yet known, one intriguing possibility is related to the metabolism of progesterone to a substance called allopregnanolone. Allopregnanolone is found not only in the bloodstream but also in the brain. Its principal neuronal action is to enhance the activity of one type of receptor for the inhibitory neurotransmitter γ-aminobutyric acid (GABA), namely, the GABA$_A$ receptor (see Chapter 8 for additional information on the GABA system). Since stimulation of GABA$_A$ receptors decreases the firing of DA neurons involved in cocaine reinforcement, Quinones-Jenab and Jenab

(2010) have hypothesized that enhancement of GABA$_A$ receptor activity by allopregnanolone is part of the mechanism by which progesterone blunts the reinforcing effects of cocaine (and, by extension, the positive subjective effects in women). Most importantly, the discovery of progesterone's interactions with cocaine (and also with other drugs of abuse not discussed here because of space limitations) raises the possibility that progesterone, allopregnanolone, or similarly acting compounds could be developed as medications for the treatment of drug dependence. Future research along with clinical trials will determine whether such medications eventually pass the key tests of safety and effectiveness.

(B) Effects of the menstrual cycle and of progesterone administration on the subjective responses to smoked cocaine The positive subjective response to smoking 6, 12, or 25 mg of cocaine (measured as "Good Drug Effect") was significantly greater when women were tested during the follicular phase of their menstrual cycle than during the luteal phase (left). Administration of 150 mg progesterone orally to women during the follicular phase (when levels of this hormone are normally low) reduced the subjective response to cocaine but had no effect in men when compared with placebo treatment (right). (After Evans and Foltin, 2010.)

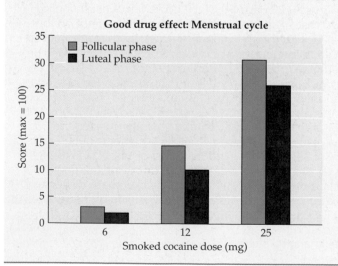

Good drug effect: Menstrual cycle

Legend:
- Follicular phase
- Luteal phase

Y-axis: Score (max = 100)
X-axis: Smoked cocaine dose (mg)

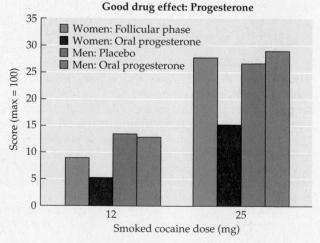

Good drug effect: Progesterone

Legend:
- Women: Follicular phase
- Women: Oral progesterone
- Men: Placebo
- Men: Oral progesterone

Y-axis: Score (max = 100)
X-axis: Smoked cocaine dose (mg)

available that could serve as an index of central D_2 receptor occupancy (Green and Brown, 1988). However, chronically high prolactin levels (termed *hyperprolactinemia*) can have adverse consequences, including menstrual abnormalities in women, as well as breast abnormalities, sexual dysfunction, and mood disturbances in both women and men (Madhusoodanan et al., 2010). Fortunately, newer antipsychotic drugs have been developed that are less likely to produce this potentially serious side effect (Hamner, 2002), and modern neuroimaging methods have supplanted measurement of plasma prolactin as the best way to assess drug binding to central D_2 receptors (see Chapter 20).

Section Summary

- Hormones are released into the bloodstream, where they may travel long distances before reaching target cells in the body. Despite important differences between synaptic and endocrine communications, the same substance is sometimes used as both a neurotransmitter and a hormone.

- The adrenal gland is composed of the inner medulla and the outer cortex, both of which are activated by stress. The chromaffin cells of the adrenal medulla secrete the hormones EPI and NE, whereas the adrenal cortex secretes glucocorticoid steroids such as cortisol and corticosterone.

- Other steroid hormones that are synthesized and released by the gonads include estrogens and progesterone from the ovaries in females, and androgens such as testosterone from the testes in males. These gonadal steroids are responsible for many of the secondary sex characteristics that appear after puberty; testosterone is additionally involved in sexual differentiation of the brain during early development, as well as in stimulation of sexual motivation later in life.

- The islets of Langerhans and the thyroid gland secrete hormones important in energy metabolism. Insulin and glucagon are released from separate populations of cells within the islets of Langerhans, and together these two peptide hormones regulate the disposition of glucose and other sources of metabolic energy. Lethargy and excessive energy are behavioral symptoms of hypothyroidism and hyperthyroidism, respectively, and are due to abnormally low or abnormally high levels of the two thyroid hormones, thyroxine and triiodothyronine.

- The pineal gland, which is situated just over the brainstem, synthesizes the hormone melatonin using 5-HT as a precursor. Melatonin has been implicated in the regulation of various types of rhythmic activity, including sleep.

- The pituitary gland is found just under the hypothalamus and is connected to it. The pituitary is divided into two separate glands, the anterior and posterior pituitary glands, which serve different functions.

- The anterior pituitary secretes TSH, ACTH, FSH, LH, GH, and PRL. TSH and ACTH stimulate the thyroid and adrenal glands (cortex), respectively, whereas FSH and LH together control the growth and functioning of the gonads. GH stimulates skeletal growth during development, and PRL plays an important role in promoting milk production during lactation.

- The hypothalamic-releasing hormones TRH, CRH, and GnRH are neuropeptides synthesized within the hypothalamus that trigger the release of TSH, ACTH, and the gonadotrophins FSH and LH. Because of this organizational structure, in which several glands must stimulate each other until the final hormone product is secreted, the endocrine system works much more slowly than chemical communication by neurotransmitters.

- The posterior pituitary secretes two small peptide hormones, vasopressin and oxytocin. Vasopressin enhances water retention by the kidneys, whereas oxytocin stimulates uterine contractions during childbirth and also triggers milk letdown from the breasts during lactation. These hormones may also promote affiliative behaviors in some species.

- The actions of hormones are mediated by several different kinds of receptors. Some are metabotropic receptors similar to those discussed for various neurotransmitters. Others are intracellular receptors that function as transcription factors that control gene expression, and still others are tyrosine kinase receptors.

- The endocrine system is important to pharmacologists for several reasons. These include the fact that (1) drugs can adversely alter endocrine function; (2) hormones may alter behavioral responses to drugs; (3) hormones themselves sometimes have psychoactive properties; and (4) the endocrine system can be used as a window to the brain to help us determine the functioning of a specific neurotransmitter system by measuring changes in hormone secretion under appropriate conditions.

Go to the **COMPANION WEBSITE**

sites.sinauer.com/psychopharm2e
for Web Boxes, animations, flashcards,
and other study resources.

Recommended Readings

Fuxe, K., Dahlström, A. B., Jonsson, G., Marcellino, D., Guescini, M., Dam, M., Manger, P., and Agnati, L. (2010). The discovery of central monoamine neurons gave volume transmission to the wired brain. *Prog. Neurobiol.*, 90, 82–100.

Greengard, P. (2001). The neurobiology of slow synaptic transmission. *Science*, 294, 1024–1030.

Langer, S. Z. (2008). Presynaptic autoreceptors regulating transmitter release. *Neurochem. Int.*, 52, 26–30.

Malenka, R. (Ed.). (2009). *Intercellular Communication in the Nervous System*. San Diego: Academic Press.

Nelson, R. J. (2011). *Behavioral Endocrinology*. Sunderland, MA: Sinauer.

Ryan, T. A. and Reuter, H. (2001). Measurements of vesicle recycling in central neurons. *News Physiol. Sci.*, 16, 10–14.

Walmsley, B., Alvarez, F. J., and Fyffe, R. E. W. (1998). Diversity of structure and function at mammalian central synapses. *Trends Neurosci.*, 21, 81–88.

This miniature CT scanner provides extraordinary detail of brain structure with minimal discomfort to animal subjects.

Methods of Research in Psychopharmacology 4

IN THE SUMMER OF 1982, when George Carillo and Juanita Lopez arrived at the Santa Clara Medical Center, they were almost totally paralyzed and unable to speak. After impressive investigative work, the chief neurologist J. William Langston found several young individuals with similar motor impairments: slow shuffling gate, tremors, blank facial expression, and constant drooling.[1] How could such young people show signs of advanced Parkinson's disease when it normally begins after age 50? It turns out that all of these young individuals were drug addicts who had taken the same synthetic opioid drug that had been accidentally contaminated during manufacturing with MPTP—a chemical that irreversibly and selectively attacks and destroys the dopamine neurons in the substantia nigra. Within only a few days of drug use, they showed the devastating symptoms that take years to develop in elderly patients with Parkinson's disease. Despite the potential health care crisis and massive efforts to publicize the danger to prevent additional cases, scientists became excited by the possibility of using MPTP to study Parkinson's disease. When it was discovered that MPTP could induce symptoms of Parkinson's in mice and non-human primates, a new animal model was created that finally provided a means of testing new drugs and treatments. Out of personal devastation came a bright ray of hope for millions of people around the globe.

---

[1]Readers interested in learning more about this story and a group of related cases are referred to *The Case of the Frozen Addicts*, by Langston and Palfreman (1995).

Research Methods for Evaluating the Brain and Behavior

The discovery of chemical transmission of information between nerve cells paved the way for the birth of neuropsychopharmacology. Since then, an explosion of research has been directed toward understanding the nature of brain function and the biology of what makes us human. With the variety and power of new analytic tools and techniques, we can look inside the brain to find answers to questions that touch individual lives. Even nonscientists can appreciate the advances in neuroscience research that bring us ever closer to understanding the essence of human behavior, as well as some of the most troubling problems of mankind: dementia, depression, autism, and neurodegenerative disorders.

The new tools provide the means to explore the brain to answer our questions, but it takes disciplined and creative scientific minds and teamwork to pose the right questions and to optimally use available tools. The scientific method, utilizing rigorous hypothesis testing under controlled conditions, is the only real method that we have to investigate how molecules responsible for nerve cell activity relate to complex human behaviors and thinking. Analysis spans the entire range from molecular genetics to cell function to integrated systems of neuronal networks, and finally to observable behavior. To understand the brain requires a convergence of efforts from multiple disciplines, which together form the basis of neuroscience: psychology, biochemistry, neuropharmacology, neuroanatomy, endocrinology, computer science, neuropsychology, and molecular biology. Ultimately, we acquire knowledge by integrating information derived by a wide variety of research techniques from all of these fields.

As you might expect, the list of techniques is very long and gets longer every day. Chapter 4 focuses on a few of the more common methods and helps you to understand the purpose of each method, as well as some of its potential weaknesses. Perhaps the most important goal of this chapter is to encourage you, when you read scientific papers, to critically evaluate the methods and controls used, because the conclusions we draw from experiments are only as good as the methodology used to collect the data.

In the first part of this chapter, we focus on behavioral pharmacology. Behavior, mood, and cognitive function represent the focus of neuropsychopharmacology, so it is of tremendous importance to understand and critically evaluate the techniques used to quantify behavioral changes. The second part of the chapter emphasizes techniques that look at the locations and functions of neurotransmitters and neurotransmitter receptors. The methods described are both **in vivo**, meaning observed in the living organism, and **in vitro**, which refers to measurements performed outside the living body (traditionally in a test tube). We also look at a variety of rather remarkable imaging techniques that permit us to visualize the activity of the living human brain. Because genetic engineering is an increasingly powerful tool, we will describe its use in psychopharmacology. Both the biochemical and behavioral techniques selected will be used in subsequent chapters. Although this chapter is artificially divided into sections, keep in mind that much of the most informative research in psychopharmacology utilizes techniques of neuroscience in combination with behavioral analysis. Feel free to return to this chapter to review a method when you encounter it later.

Techniques in Behavioral Pharmacology

Evaluating Animal Behavior

The techniques of behavioral pharmacology allow scientists to evaluate the relationship between an experimental manipulation such as a lesion or drug administration and changes in behavior. In a well-designed experiment, it is necessary to compare the behavior of the experimental treatment group with that of placebo control subjects. Neurobiological techniques such as selective lesioning and intracerebral drug administration, described in the second section of this chapter, tell us very little unless we have an objective measure of the behavioral consequences. Behavioral measures are crucial for (1) understanding the neurochemical basis of behavior, as well as drug-induced changes in that behavior; (2) developing animal models of psychiatric disorders; and (3) screening the large number of newly designed and synthesized drug molecules in preclinical pharmaceutical settings. Although this chapter is divided into two distinct sections, it is important to realize that much of the research in psychopharmacology integrates methods of neuroscience with behavioral procedures.

Animal testing needs to be valid and reliable to produce useful information

Animal studies clearly provide several advantages over studies using human subjects. The most obvious advantage is the use of rigorous controls. The living conditions (e.g., diet, exercise, room temperature, exposure to stress, day–night cycle) of animal

Figure 4.1 A poster used to counter the claims of animal rights activists increases public awareness about the benefits of animal research. (Courtesy of the Foundation for Biomedical Research.)

subjects can be regulated far more precisely than those of humans. In addition, the histories of animal subjects are well known, and the genetic backgrounds of a group of animals are very similar and well characterized. Finally, animals are the most appropriate subjects for the study of mechanisms of drug action because an understanding of the electophysiological and neurochemical bases of drug effects often requires invasive techniques that are obviously unethical with human subjects. Consider, for example, the valuable information gained from transgenically manipulated animals. In addition, drugs can be administered to animal subjects in ways not generally appropriate for humans, for example, over long periods of time to determine toxic effects or the potential for addiction. Finally, the brains and behaviors of non-human mammals and humans are similar enough to allow generalization across species. For example, lesions of the central nucleus of the amygdala of rats produce profound changes in the conditioned emotional response of these animals. Likewise, tumors, strokes, and surgical procedures that damage the human amygdaloid complex produce profound changes in fearfulness, anxiety, and emotional memory.

The impact of animal testing in biomedical research on the quality of human life (**Figure 4.1**) is discussed in a thought-provoking manner by Hollinger (2008), as

are its alternatives. The need for animal experimentation is best seen under conditions when research using human subjects is impossible, as when testing the effects of alcohol on fetal development. Ethical constraints prohibit researchers from administering varying doses of alcohol to groups of pregnant women to evaluate the effects on their newborns. Instead, data collected on alcohol consumption during pregnancy and the occurrence of fetal alcohol syndrome (FAS) suggest a relationship that tells us that the more alcohol a pregnant female consumes, the more likely it is that her infant will show signs of FAS. Although we know that infants of mothers who consume alcohol are more likely to show fetal abnormalities, the type of study described shows only a **correlational relationship**; we cannot assume that alcohol *causes* FAS because other factors may be responsible for both. For example, poverty, poor diet, or other drug use may lead to increased alcohol consumption *and* cause developmental defects in the fetus. Therefore, to learn more about how alcohol affects fetal development, we need to perform animal studies. Since animal testing remains an important part of new drug development and evaluation, strict animal care guidelines have been developed to ensure proper treatment of subjects. The animal-testing stage provides an important step between basic science and the treatment of human conditions.

The Health Extension Act of 1985 provided strict guidelines for the care of animals used in biomedical and behavioral research. The goals of that legislation include humane animal maintenance and experimentation that limits both the use of animals and animal distress. Each research institution must have an animal care committee that reviews each scientific protocol with three considerations in mind:

1. The research should be relevant to human or animal health, advancement of knowledge, or the good of society.

2. Alternative methods such as computer simulations that do not require animal subjects must be considered.

3. Procedures must avoid or minimize discomfort, distress, and pain.

Periodic inspection of living conditions ensures that they are appropriate for the species and contribute to health and comfort; size, temperature, lighting, cleanliness, access to food and water, sanitation, and medical care are ensured. Animal care and use committees have the authority to veto any studies that they feel do not meet all predetermined criteria. You can find a full copy of the guidelines prepared in 2011 at www.grants.nih.gov/grants/olaw/Guide-for-the-Care-and-Use-of-Laboratory-Animals.pdf.

Some animal tests used to evaluate drug effects on physiological measures such as blood pressure or body temperature closely resemble tests used for humans. These tests have high **face validity**. However, for many psychiatric disorders, the symptoms are described in typically human terms, such as feelings of guilt, delusions, altered mood, or disordered thinking. In these cases, a correlated, quantifiable measure in an animal is substituted for a more cognitive human behavior for testing purposes. When the correlation is strong, a drug that modifies rat behavior in a specific way can be expected to predictably alter a particular human behavior, even though the two behaviors may seem unrelated. For instance, if a new drug were to reduce apomorphine-induced hyperactivity in rats, tests on humans might show it to be effective in treating schizophrenia (see Chapter 20). Tests such as these have low face validity. However, if the drug effects observed in the laboratory test closely parallel or predict the clinical effect, the tests may be said to demonstrate **predictive validity**. **Construct validity** refers to the extent to which the animal measurement tool actually measures the characteristic being investigated. A test with high construct validity optimally would create the disease in the animal or would mimic the neural and behavioral features of the disorder. To be optimal, an animal behavioral test, in addition to having predictive validity, should also do the following:

1. Be *specific* for the class of drug being screened. For example, if antidepressants produce a consistent response in a behavioral test, we probably would not want to see analgesic drugs producing the same effect.
2. Be *sensitive* so that the doses used are in a normal therapeutic range and show a dose–response relationship.
3. Demonstrate the same *rank order of potency* (i.e., ranking drugs according to the dose that is effective) in the animal test as the order of potency of the therapeutic action of the drugs.

In addition, good behavioral measures have high **reliability**, meaning that the same results will be recorded each time the test is used (Treit, 1985). Valid and reliable animal tests are an important component of preclinical trials for new drug development. Unfortunately, many of the methods currently used in the laboratory have not predicted accurately clinical effects in humans. The development of new tasks for behavioral analysis is necessary to improve the transfer of results from animal testing to useful outcomes for patients (see the section on translational research at the end of this section).

A wide variety of behaviors are evaluated by psychopharmacologists

There are many behavioral tests used by psychopharmacologists, and they vary considerably in complexity, time needed to be carried out, and cost, as well as validity and reliability. In this next section, we will describe just a few of the available procedures, many of which will be referred to in subsequent chapters.

SIMPLE BEHAVIORAL OBSERVATION   Many simple observations of untrained behaviors require little or no instrumentation. Among the observations made are measures of tremors, ptosis (drooping eyelids), salivation, defecation, catalepsy, reflexes, response to tail pinch, and changes in eating or drinking. Animals demonstrating **catalepsy** are still and immobile and sometimes will remain in an unusual posture if positioned by the experimenter. The time it takes for the animal to return to normal posture gives an indication of the extent of catalepsy. The use of catalepsy as a test to identify antipsychotic drugs that produce motor side effects demonstrates the usefulness of screening tests that are not clearly related to human behavior (see Chapter 20).

MEASURES OF MOTOR ACTIVITY   These measures identify drugs that produce sleep, sedation, or loss of coordination and, in contrast, drugs that stimulate activity. Spontaneous activity can be measured in a variety of ways. One popular method counts the number of times infrared light beams (invisible to rodents) directed across a designated space are broken. Automated video tracking with computerized analysis is a second method. A third, less automated technique (**open field test**) involves placing the animal in a prescribed area that is divided into squares so the investigator can record the number of squares traversed in a unit of time. It is also possible to count the number of fecal droppings and to observe the amount of time an animal spends along the walls of the chamber rather than venturing toward the open space. High fecal counts and low activity seen primarily at the perimeter of the cage are common indicators of anxiety.

OPERANT CONDITIONING   Operant conditioning has also made contributions to the study of the effects of drugs on behavior. It is a highly sensitive method that can be used to evaluate a wide variety of behaviors including analgesia, anxiety, addiction potential, drug discrimination, as well as learning and memory. The underlying principle of operant conditioning is that consequences control behavior. An animal performs because it is reinforced for doing so. Animals learn to respond to obtain rewards and avoid punishment.

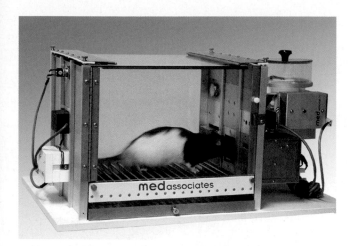

Figure 4.2 Rat in an operant chamber The rat can be trained to press the lever (response) to activate a food delivery mechanism (reinforcement). An animal can also learn to press the lever to terminate or postpone shocks that can be delivered through the grid floor. (Courtesy of Med Associates, Inc.)

Although it is possible to teach many types of operant responses, depending on the species of animal used, experiments are typically carried out in an operant chamber (Skinner box). An operant chamber is a soundproof box with a grid floor that can be electrified for shock delivery, a food or water dispenser for rewards, lights or loudspeaker for stimulus cue presentation, and levers that the animal can press (**Figure 4.2**). Computerized stimulus presentation and data collection provide the opportunity to measure the total number of responses per unit time. In addition, the technique records response rates and interresponse times, which provide a stable and sensitive measure of continuous behavior.

In a brief training session, the animal learns to press the lever to receive a food reinforcer. Once the behavior is established, the requirements for reinforcement can be altered according to a predetermined schedule (**schedule of reinforcement**). The rate and pattern of the animal's behavior are controlled by the schedule; this allows us to examine the effect of a drug on the pattern of behavior. For instance, on a fixed-ratio (FR) schedule, reinforcement is delivered after a fixed number of responses. Thus, an FR-3 schedule means that the animal must press the lever three times to receive one food pellet. Changing the fixed ratio from 3 to 20 or 45 will tell us how hard the animal is willing to work for the reinforcement. Interval schedules also are commonly used and are characterized by the availability of reinforcement after a certain amount of time has elapsed (rather than a particular number of bar presses). Thus, on an FI-2 schedule (fixed interval of

2 minutes), reinforcement follows the first response an animal makes after 2 minutes have passed since the last reinforcement. Responses made during the 2-minute interval are "wasted," that is, they elicit no reinforcement. This schedule produces a pattern of responding that includes a pause after each reinforcement and a gradual increase in the rate of responding as the interval ends. For a description of other variations in schedules and their use in drug testing, see Carlton (1983).

MEASURES OF ANALGESIA Analgesia is the reduction of perceived pain without loss of consciousness. Analgesia testing with human subjects is difficult because the response to experimentally induced pain is quite different from that to chronic or pathological pain, in which anxiety and anticipation of more pain influence the individual's response. Of course, we cannot know whether an animal "feels pain" in the same way that a human does, but we can measure the animal's avoidance of a noxious stimulus. One simple test is the **tail-flick test**, in which heat produced by a beam of light (the intensity of which is controlled by a rheostat) is focused on a portion of a rat's tail (**Figure 4.3**). The latency between onset of the stimulus and the animal's removal of its tail from the beam of light is assumed to be correlated with pain intensity.

A variation of the operant FR schedule utilizes negative reinforcement, which increases the probability of a response that terminates an aversive condition. This technique can be easily applied to **operant analgesia**

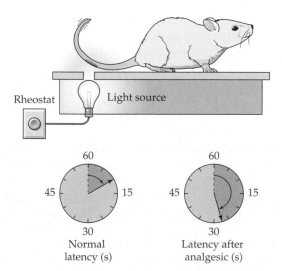

Figure 4.3 The tail-flick test of analgesia measures the response of the animal to a thermal stimulus. The quantitative measure made is the time between onset of the light beam, which provides heat, and movement of the tail. The clocks show that the response to the noxious stimulus is delayed after treatment with an analgesic that is known to reduce pain in humans. (After Hamilton and Timmons, 1990.)

Figure 4.4 The radial arm maze has a central start box (S) and a number of arms or alleys radiating from the center. Goal areas (G) containing food are at the end of each arm.

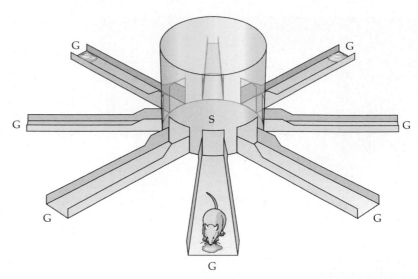

testing. First, the animal is trained to turn off an unpleasant foot shock by pressing the lever. In the test phase, the researcher administers increasing amounts of foot shock up to the point at which the animal responds by pressing the lever. The lowest shock intensity at which the animal first presses is considered the aversive threshold. Analgesic drugs would be expected to raise the threshold of electric shock. The method is very sensitive even to mild analgesics such as aspirin. However, an independent measure of sedation is necessary to distinguish between failure to respond due to analgesia and failure to respond due to behavioral depression.

TESTS OF LEARNING AND MEMORY   Objective measures of learning and memory, accompanied by careful interpretation of the results, are important whether you are using animal or human subjects. Keep in mind that these tests very often do not determine whether altered responses are due to drug-induced changes in attention or motivation, consolidation or retrieval of the memory, or other factors contributing to overall performance. Unless these other factors are considered, tests of learning are open to misinterpretation. Despite the challenges posed, finding new ways to manipulate the neurotransmitters involved in these functions will be central to developing drugs that are useful in treating memory deficits due to normal aging or neurological injuries or diseases such as Alzheimer's and other dementias. There are a wide variety of tests available that depend on the presentation of information (training stage) followed by a delay and then the opportunity for performance (test stage). Higher cognitive processes can be evaluated by creating situations in which reorganization of the information presented is necessary before the appropriate response can be made.

MAZES   Although the size and complexity of mazes can vary dramatically, what they have in common is a start box at the beginning of an alley with one (**T-maze**) or more (**multiple T-maze**) choice points that lead to the final goal box, which contains a small piece of food or another reward. A hungry rat is initially given an opportunity to explore the maze and find the food goal. On subsequent trials, learning is evaluated on the basis of the number of errors at choice points and/or the time taken to reach the goal box. Careful evaluation of results is needed because drug-induced changes in behavior may be due to a change in either learning or motivation (e.g., Does the drug make the animal more or less hungry? Sedated? Disoriented?). This task can also be used to evaluate working memory if the goal is alternated from side to side at each trial.

Spatial learning tasks help us investigate the role of specific brain areas and neurotransmitters, such as acetylcholine, in forming memories for the relative locations of objects in the environment. One special type of maze, the **radial arm maze**, is made up of multiple arms radiating away from a central choice point (**Figure 4.4**) with a small piece of food at the end of each arm. With very little experience, normal rats learn to forage efficiently by visiting each arm only once on a given day, indicating effective spatial memory for that particular episode. The task can be made more complex by blocking some arms on the initial trial before the animal is returned to the central choice point. The animal is expected to remember which arms have already been entered and move down only those that still contain food. For a normal rat, the task is not complex because it mimics the foraging behavior of animals in the wild, where they must remember where food has been found. But animals with selective lesions in the hippocampus (and other areas) as well as those injected with a cholinergic-blocking drug show significant impairment. Low doses of alcohol also interfere with spatial memory. Because the arms are identical, the animals must use cues in the environment to orient themselves in the maze, hence the need for spatial memory. The task is similar to our daily activity of driving home from work. Not only do we need to recognize each of the landmarks along our route, but we must learn the relative locations of these objects with respect to each other. As we move along our route, our perceptions of the objects and their relative locations to us tell us where we are and where we should be going.

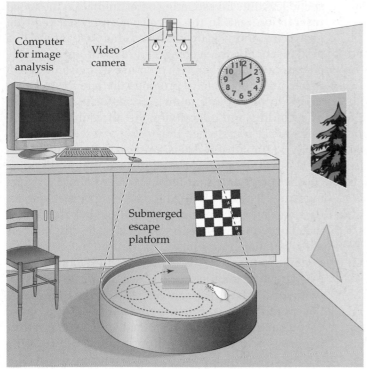

Figure 4.5 The Morris water maze is a circular pool filled with opaque water. The escape platform is approximately 1 cm below the water level. The rat's task is to locate the submerged, hidden platform by using visuospatial cues available in the room. A video camera is mounted above the pool and is connected to the video recorder and the computer link to trace the individual swim path. (After Kolb and Whishaw, 1989.)

Failure in this complex cognitive process is characteristic of patients with Alzheimer's disease who wander away and fail to find their way home.

A second test of spatial learning, the **Morris water maze**, uses a large, circular pool of water that has been made opaque by the addition of milk or a dye. Animals placed in the pool must swim until they find the escape platform that is hidden from view just below the surface of the water (**Figure 4.5**). The subject demonstrates that it has learned the spatial location of the submerged platform by navigating from different starting positions to the platform. Since there are no local cues to direct the escape behavior, successful escape requires that the subject learn the spatial position of the platform relative to landmarks outside the pool. When curtains surrounding the pool are drawn to block external visual cues, performance falls to chance levels, demonstrating the importance of visuospatial cues. As a laboratory technique, the water maze has several advantages. No extensive pretraining is required, and testing can be carried out over short periods of time. Escape from water motivates without the use of food or water deprivation or electric shock; this makes interpretation of drug studies easier, in that drug-induced changes in motivation are less likely. One disadvantage, however, is that water immersion may cause endocrine or other stress effects that can interact with the drugs administered.

DELAYED-RESPONSE TEST This design assesses the type of memory often impaired by damage to the prefrontal cortex in humans. It is similar to tasks included in the Wechsler Memory Scale, which is used to evaluate working memory deficits in humans. In this task (**Figure 4.6**), an animal watches the experimenter put a piece of food

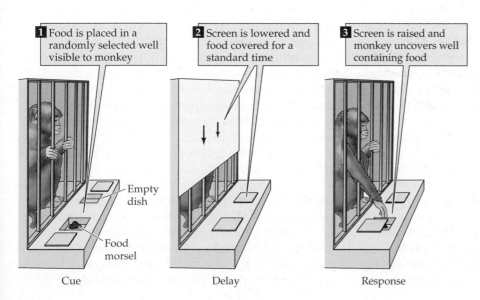

1 Food is placed in a randomly selected well visible to monkey

2 Screen is lowered and food covered for a standard time

3 Screen is raised and monkey uncovers well containing food

Empty dish

Food morsel

Cue   Delay   Response

Figure 4.6 The delayed-response task evaluates working memory by imposing a delay between stimulus presentation and testing. (After Goldman-Rakic, 1987.)

into one of the food boxes in front of it. The boxes are then closed, and a sliding screen is placed between the monkey and the boxes for a few seconds or minutes (the delay). At the end of the delay, the screen is removed and the animal has the opportunity to recall under which of the covers food is available.

Visual short-term memory can be tested by slightly modifying the procedure. At the beginning of the trial, an object or other stimulus is presented as the sample. After a short delay, during which the sample stimulus is removed, the animal is given a choice between two or more visual stimuli, one of which is the same as the sample. If the animal chooses the pattern that matches the sample, it is given a food reward; an incorrect response yields no reward. This task is a good example of the use of operant conditioning. To make the correct choice after the interval, the animal must "remember" the initial stimulus.

MEASURES OF ANXIETY   There are many biobehavioral measures available for identifying novel antianxiety compounds and for evaluating the neurochemical basis of anxiety. Cryan and Sweeney (2011) have reviewed the animal models and discuss their importance for drug discovery. Most anxiety models use induced fearfulness as an analogy to human anxiety. Some use unconditioned animal reactions such as a tendency to avoid brightly lit places or heights; others depend on traditional learning designs. The **light–dark crossing task** involves a two-compartment box with one side brightly lit (normally avoided by rodents) and the other side dark. Measures include the number of crossings between the bright and dark sections and the amount of time spent on each side, as well as total motor activity. Anxiety-reducing drugs produce a dose-dependent increase in the number of crossings and in overall activity while also increasing the amount of time spent in the light. Similar to the light–dark crossing task is the **open field exploration test**. In this test, the animal is allowed to freely explore the test chamber, which is a novel and unprotected environment that is usually brightly lit. Both the number and pattern of the animal's movements are monitored either manually or with an automated system. Rodents typically explore the periphery of the chamber while staying in contact with the walls. Antianxiety drugs increase the amount of time spent in the unprotected center of the box. The **elevated plus-maze** is a cross-shaped maze raised 50 cm off the floor that has two open arms (normally avoided because of aversion to heights) and two arms with enclosed sides. This quick and simple test shows a selective increase in open-arm exploration following treatment with antianxiety drugs and a reduction after treatment with caffeine and amphetamine—drugs considered to increase anxiety. In another naturalistic task, more fearful animals will

spend less time investigating other animals in the **social interaction test**. In the **novelty suppressed feeding paradigm**, animals are presented their usual food in a new, potentially threatening environment, or conversely are provided novel food in their usual environment. In either case, the novelty prolongs the latency to begin eating. In very young animals, anxiety can be evaluated by recording and quantifying the **ultrasonic vocalizations** of rat pups when they are separated from their mothers. Antianxiety drugs suppress such vocalizations.

The **water-lick suppression test** (**Vogel test**) is a **conflict procedure** that reliably screens anxiety-reducing drugs while requiring little training of the animals. Rats deprived of water quickly learn to lick the tip of a metal drinking spout for liquid. During testing, animals are given the opportunity to drink from the spout for a 3-minute session. However, after every 20 licks, the rats receive a mild tongue shock, which causes them to suppress responding. The conflict between the urge to lick the spout and the desire to avoid the shock is a classic paradigm for anxiety. Pretreatment with anxiety-reducing drugs prevents the lick suppression.

One classic method used to evaluate anxiety in animals is the **Geller-Seifter conflict test**. The animals are first trained to press a lever in the operant chamber for a standard (food or water) reinforcer. Once the behavior is established, the test sessions involve two stages. In the first, the animals press the lever for the reinforcer. After 10 or 15 minutes, a tone signals a change in the procedure: at this point lever pressing produces a reinforcer (approach) that is accompanied by a foot shock (avoidance), producing an approach–avoidance "conflict" for the subject. As you would expect, lever pressing is steady during the reinforced situation but is reduced and variable during the conflict procedure. Antianxiety drugs have no effect on the reinforced schedule but increase the lever pressing during the conflict procedure, indicating that punishing situations are less inhibiting than normal. The non-punished segment controls for any drug-induced change in motivation or motor function. If you make the assumption that overly anxious individuals are excessively concerned with the many possible bad results (punishment) of their actions, then the model has reasonable face validity. Naturally, one must be sure that the drugs being tested are not analgesics, which might also be expected to increase responding during the conflict session. Operant tests of this type have two major disadvantages: (1) they are much more time-consuming because of the training required, and (2) they are evaluating a behavior that is artificially contrived rather than naturally occurring. Nevertheless, they have been used as screening devices for many years and have proved to be quite sensitive and specific to anxiolytic drug effects.

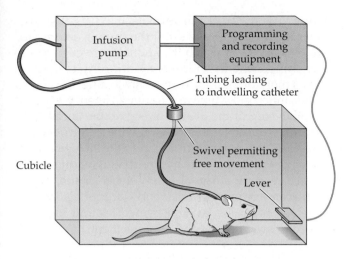

Figure 4.7 The drug self-administration method predicts abuse liability of psychoactive drugs. Pressing the lever according to a predetermined schedule of reinforcement triggers drug delivery into a vein or into discrete brain areas.

MEASURES OF FEAR Several common measures of fear involve classical conditioning. The **conditioned emotional response** depends on presentation of a signal (a light or tone) followed by an unavoidable electric shock to form a classically conditioned association. When the warning signal is presented during ongoing behavior, the behavior is suppressed (i.e., "freezing" occurs). Although this method has not always produced consistent results when used to screen antianxiety drugs, it has become an important tool in understanding the role of the amygdala and its neurochemistry in the conditioned fear response.

A second method is **fear-potentiated startle**, which refers to enhancement of the basic startle response when the stimulus is preceded by the presentation of a conditioned fear stimulus. For example, if a light has been previously paired with a foot shock, the presentation of that light normally increases the magnitude of the startle response to a novel stimulus, such as a loud clap.

METHODS OF ASSESSING DRUG REWARD AND REINFORCEMENT The simple FR schedule has been used very effectively in identifying drugs that have abuse potential, that is, drugs that are capable of inducing dependence. We assume that if an animal will press a lever to receive an injection of drug into the blood or into the brain, the drug must have reinforcing properties. The drug **self-administration method (Figure 4.7)** used with rodents is a very accurate indicator of abuse potential in humans. For instance, animals will readily self-administer morphine, cocaine, and amphetamine—drugs that we know are readily abused by humans. In contrast, drugs like aspirin, antidepressants, and antipsychotic drugs

are neither self-administered by animals nor abused by humans. **Table 4.1** lists some of the drugs that are reinforcing in the rhesus monkey. Compare this list with what you know about substances abused by humans.

Furthermore, we can ask the animal which of several drugs it prefers by placing two levers in the operant chamber and training the animal to press lever A for one drug and lever B for the alternative. If given free access to the levers, the animal's choice will be readily apparent. An additional question we can pose involves how much the animal really "likes" a particular drug. By varying the schedule of reinforcement from FR-10 to FR-40 or -65, we can tell how reinforcing the drug is by how hard the animal works for the injection. The point at which the effort required exceeds the reinforcing value is called the **breaking point**. The higher the breaking point, the greater is the reinforcement of the drug and, presumably, the greater is the abuse potential in humans. Drugs like cocaine sustain incredibly high rates of responding; animals will lever press for drug reinforcement until exhaustion.

A modification of the method allows the animal to self-administer a weak electrical current to discrete brain areas via an indwelling electrode (**electrical self-stimulation**). The underlying assumption is that certain brain areas constitute "reward" pathways. It is assumed that when the animal works to stimulate a particular cluster of neurons, the electrical activation causes the release of neurotransmitters from nerve terminals in the region, which, in turn, mediate a rewarding effect. The fact that pretreatment with certain drugs, such as morphine or heroin, increases responding for even low levels of electrical stimulation indicates that the drugs

TABLE 4.1 Drugs That Act as Reinforcers in the Rhesus Monkey	
Category	**Specific drug**
Central stimulants	Cocaine
	Amphetamine
	Methylphenidate (Ritalin)
	Nicotine
	Caffeine
Opioids	Morphine
	Methadone
	Codeine
CNS depressants	Pentobarbital
	Amobarbital
	Chlordiazepoxide (Librium)
	Ethyl alcohol

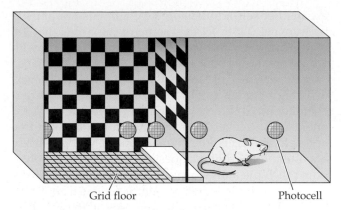

Figure 4.8 Place-conditioning apparatus The apparatus consists of two distinctly different compartments that vary in the pattern and texture of the floor and walls. Photocells monitor the animal's movement. Each compartment is repeatedly paired with either drug or saline injection. On the test day, the animal is allowed free access to both compartments, and the amount of time spent in each tells us whether the drug effect was rewarding or aversive. (After Stolerman, 1992.)

enhance the brain reward mechanism (Esposito et al., 1989). In combination with mapping techniques, this method provides an excellent understanding of the neural mechanisms of reward and the effects of psychoactive drugs on those pathways.

Although several popular measures used to evaluate the rewarding and reinforcing effects of drugs are operant techniques, a method called **conditioned place preference** relies on a classically conditioned association between drug effect and environment (**Figure 4.8**). During conditioning trials over several days, the animal is injected with either drug or saline and is consistently placed in one compartment or the other, so that

it associates the environment with the drug state. The rewarding or aversive effect of the drug is determined in a test session in which the animal is given access to both compartments and the amount of time spent in each is monitored. If the drug is rewarding, the animal spends much more time in the compartment associated with the drug. If the drug is aversive, the animal prefers the compartment associated with saline injection. Additionally, researchers may study the biological basis for the rewarding effects by pretreating animals with selected receptor antagonists or neurotoxins to modify the place preference. O'Brien and Gardner (2005) have reviewed many behavioral principles and methods related to drug reward and reinforcement.

DRUGS AS DISCRIMINATIVE STIMULI A discriminative stimulus is any stimulus that signals reinforcement for a subject in an operant task. For example, "light on" in the chamber may signal that reinforcement is available following pressing one of two available levers, while "light out" may signal that reinforcement is available only by pressing the other lever. An animal that learns to press one lever in the presence of "light on" and the opposite lever during the "light out" period can discriminate between the two conditions. Although discriminative stimuli are usually changes in the physical environment, internal cues after drug administration can also be discriminative (**Figure 4.9**). Thus on days when an animal receives an injection of a particular drug and experiences the internal cues associated with that drug state (like the "light on"), it can learn to press one lever for reinforcement. On days when the animal receives a saline injection and experiences different internal cues, it learns to press the alternative lever, as in the "light off" condition. The animal's response depends on its discriminating among internal cues produced by the drug.

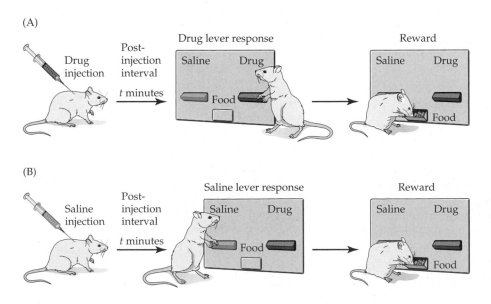

(A)

Drug injection — Post-injection interval — *t* minutes — Drug lever response — Saline Drug — Food — Reward — Saline Drug — Food

(B)

Saline injection — Post-injection interval — *t* minutes — Saline lever response — Saline Drug — Food — Reward — Saline Drug — Food

Figure 4.9 Drug discrimination testing (A) shows a rat being injected with a drug before being placed in an operant chamber. If it presses the right lever ("drug"), it receives a food reward. If it presses the left (saline) lever, no reinforcement occurs. (B) On days that the rat receives a saline injection before it is placed in the operant chamber, it receives food reinforcement if it presses the saline lever, and no reinforcement if it presses the drug lever. Discrimination of internal drug cues determines the animal's response.

By using this technique, we can find out how the animal experiences a drug cue. For example, if an animal has been trained to lever press on the left after receiving morphine, and on the right on days it was pretreated with saline, other opioids can be substituted for the internal cue and signal to the animal that reinforcement can be obtained by pressing the "morphine" lever. In this way, it has been shown that the opioid drugs heroin and methadone are experienced similarly to morphine (i.e., they show generalization to morphine). In contrast, drugs like amphetamine or marijuana, which apparently produce subjective effects very different from those of morphine, do not lead to pressing the "morphine" lever. In this way, novel drugs can be characterized according to how similar their internal cues are to those of the known drug. This can be useful in screening new therapeutic drugs by determining whether animals respond as they did when trained on a known effective agent. The same technique can be used to identify the neurochemical basis for a given drug cue. The drug cue can be challenged with increasing doses of a suspected neurotransmitter antagonist until the cue has lost its effect. Likewise, neurotransmitter agonists can be substituted to find which more closely resembles the trained drug cue. Drug discrimination testing is relatively easy to do and requires no surgical procedures. However, it is time consuming because of the extensive training time and the limitation of generalization testing to only once or twice a week (with continued retraining on the remaining days). The technique has high predictive validity, meaning that results from animal tests are usually quite similar to those from human testing in analogous experimental designs. Solinas and colleagues (2006) provide an excellent description of the basic methodology of drug discrimination, as well as an assessment of advantages and disadvantages. For an example of the utility of drug discrimination testing, read **Box 4.1.**

BOX 4.1   Pharmacology in Action

Using Drug Discrimination Testing

In a recent study of human subjects, researchers used drug discrimination testing to evaluate the role of the $GABA_B$ receptor subtype (you will learn more about GABA receptors in Chapter 8) in the discriminative-stimulus effects of Δ^9-tetrahydrocannabinol (THC), the active ingredient in marijuana (Lile et al., 2012). Subjects were evaluated for psychomotor performance with tests of balance, finger-to-nose coordination, and gait, as well as several cognitive tasks. Physiological assessments such as heart rate and body temperature were made, and self-report questionnaires of their subjective experience (Anxious, Forgetful, Stoned, and others) were used. The subjects were 18- to 30-year-old marijuana users from the community. The subjects learned to discriminate orally administered (30 mg) THC from placebo using computer-displayed circles labeled "Drug X" and "Not Drug X" on a fixed-interval, 1-second schedule for 60 seconds. Points accumulated on the correct selections were exchanged for money (28 cents per point up to a maximum of $50 per session). On average, it took 4.3 training sessions to achieve discrimination.

On the test day, administration of the $GABA_B$ agonist baclofen produced THC-appropriate responding, which suggests that baclofen was subjectively experienced, similarly to THC. Furthermore, when baclofen was given along with THC, drug-appropriate responding was enhanced, indicating that baclofen potentiated the effect of THC. Surprisingly, although baclofen alone produced THC responding, it did not produce subjective interoceptive effects according to the self-reporting. This difference suggests that drug discrimination testing was more sensitive in detecting internal cues than was self-reporting. Apparently the subjects were not aware of the internal cues that guided their behavior. However, the $GABA_B$ agonist did enhance self-reported subjective effects when administered along with THC. The fact that baclofen potentiated some of the physiological effects of THC suggests a role for the $GABA_B$ receptor in those effects. It also suggests that concomitant administration of low doses of the two drugs might be useful therapeutically because side effects of each of the drugs would be minimized. Baclofen is currently used to reduce the spasticity associated with multiple sclerosis, and THC (Dronabinol) is useful for reducing anorexia in patients with AIDS and for reducing nausea and vomiting in patients undergoing chemotherapy (see Box 14.1). Because baclofen can be substituted for THC, others have suggested the potential use of baclofen for reducing some of the signs of withdrawal from THC, which would encourage further abstinence. Clearly, this preliminary research is only the first step toward practical application.

BOX 4.2 Clinical Applications

Drug Testing for FDA Approval

All new drugs produced and sold in the United States by pharmaceutical companies must be approved by the Food and Drug Administration (FDA). For approval, they must be demonstrated to be both effective and safe. Design and testing of new drugs is a long, complex, and expensive procedure involving extensive evaluation in both laboratory and clinical settings. The approval process utilizes many of the methods we have discussed so far, in addition to extensive testing in humans (Zivin, 2000).

The figure shows a timeline of typical drug development beginning with preclinical trials, which include in vitro neuropharmacological methods, such as receptor binding, autoradiography, and so forth. In vivo animal studies provide important information about pharmacokinetics (absorption, distribution, and metabolism), effective dose range, and toxic and lethal doses. In addition, animal

behavioral models and animal models of neurological and psychiatric disorders provide a means to screen and evaluate potentially useful drugs. After preclinical testing, a drug that is considered safe is tested with humans in three distinct phases. In Phase 1, the drug is evaluated for toxicity and pharmacokinetic data in a small group of healthy human volunteers. In Phase 2, limited clinical testing is conducted to evaluate the effectiveness of the drug in treating a particular disease. Finally, the drug is tested again in large clinical trials (Phase 3) involving thousands of patients at multiple testing sites around the country. After the third phase has been completed, the FDA can evaluate the data collected on both effectiveness and safety. Finally, if the drug receives FDA approval, it can be marketed and sold. Once in general use, the drug may still be evaluated periodically and new warnings issued

to maximize safety by monitoring adverse reactions, dangerous drug interactions, and product defects.

Although arguments that new drugs are excessively expensive for the consumer are valid, it is important to understand that as few as 20% of new drugs that are tested reach final approval. This means that the remaining 80% are eliminated only after testing that is both time-consuming and expensive. If we look at the total cost in today's dollars for research and development of the average drug approved by the FDA, we see a startling increase over time. In 1975, the average cost was $100 million; twelve years later costs increased to $300 million. By 2005 the cost of the average drug was over four-fold greater at $1.3 billion, and in 2011 the figure rose further to an amazing $5.8 billion (Roy, 2012). This enormous increase in the cost of developing new drugs has been primarily

TRANSLATIONAL RESEARCH Despite the difficulties associated with developing animal models of human psychiatric conditions, it is an extremely important step in translational research. Translational research represents an effort to transform discoveries from basic neuroscience research into clinical applications for treating mental disorders—an important goal of psychopharmacology. Translational research is not a new concept, and a good deal of early research in psychopharmacology was directed toward the ultimate goal of developing more effective medications. However, more recently, there has been greater emphasis on improving the predictability of therapeutic effects based on animal research, because running lengthy and expensive human clinical trials (**Box 4.2**) on drugs that prove ineffective makes new drug development both slow and costly. This, in turn, makes medication more expensive and delays the opportunity for effective treatment. Since pharmaceutical companies have been criticized for emphasizing research

and development of highly profitable drugs rather than those that are most innovative and/or those that address unmet medical needs, the research contribution of biotechnology companies and universities has become increasingly important. In response to the need for additional cutting-edge therapeutics for significant psychiatric disorders, the National Institutes of Health (NIH) has begun a consortium of academic health centers to nurture *interdisciplinary* research teams, whose goal is to develop inventive research tools to stimulate the development of drugs for clinical use. It is estimated that up to 60 such research teams comprising molecular and psychopharmacological researchers, clinical investigators, and representatives of the pharmaceutical industry will be established in the very near future (www.commonfund.nih.gov/clinicalresearch/overviewtranslational.aspx). Open access websites will further enhance communication among researchers and will encourage information sharing.

BOX 4.2 *(continued)*

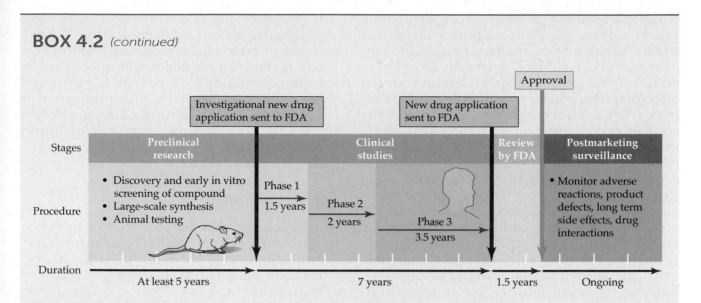

driven by the expenses associated with Phase III trials, which have gotten larger, more complex, and longer in duration. For these reasons, improvements in translational research that transfers results from animal testing and basic neuroscience to predictable clinical outcomes for patients are critical (see the text). If more drugs moved successfully through the 3 phases, the average development costs for drugs ultimately approved by the FDA would go down.

To protect its investment, a pharmaceutical company patents its drug so that no other company can sell it for a period of 20 years. The company develops a trade name (also called a proprietary name) and has exclusive rights to market that product. After 20 years, the drug becomes "generic," and other companies can manufacture and sell their own formulations of the drug after proving to the FDA that they are equivalent to the original, with similar bioavailability.

Once the patent has expired, the drug may acquire a variety of trade names, each developed by the individual manufacturer. For example, the newly patented antidepressant drug vilazodone is called Viibryd by its manufacturer. In contrast, because the patent on chlordiazepoxide has expired, the original manufacturer is still marketing Librium, but other pharmaceutical companies now produce chlordiazepoxide under the trade names Reposans, Sereen, and Mitran.

As is true for methods in neuropharmacology and molecular biology, animal testing and behavior analysis continue to undergo improvement and refinement. It has long been wondered whether the translation of animal data into useful human drug treatments was hindered because drug effects were frequently tested on an adaptive animal response to a specific challenge, which may produce effects quite different from the response in humans with existing pathology. For instance, is it likely that drugs that suppress the normal aggression of a resident rodent on an intruder in its territory will also be effective in reducing pathological aggression in humans? Such questions have led researchers to suggest that the best models for translation to human treatment are those that depend on creating abnormal behaviors or neurobiological changes that closely resemble some of the focal symptoms of the disorder (Miczek and de Wit, 2008). Certainly, as molecular research continues to identify genetic differences

associated with psychiatric disorders, additional animal models utilizing genetic mutations will be developed. For example, in one mouse model of the anxiety disorder obsessive-compulsive disorder (OCD), selective deletion of genes produces animals that as adults show OCD-like behaviors such as excessive grooming with severe hair loss analogous to the compulsive washing seen in some individuals with OCD, self-injurious behavior, and increased anxiety. Furthermore, these behaviors respond to treatment with the same serotonergic agonists that are effective for individuals treated for OCD. Additionally, the mice show abnormal corticostriatal connectivity—again, similar to human neuropathology (OCD will be described further in Chapter 18). These similarities suggest the value of this genetic model in studying the etiology of OCD and in screening potential therapeutic agents (Yang and Lu, 2011). Be sure to refer to the section on genetic engineering for a discussion of the limitations of gene mutations.

Selective brain lesioning can also be used to induce a pattern of behavior and neurochemical change that mimics significant components of psychiatric syndromes. In one model of schizophrenia developed in the early 1990s, neonatal mice are subjected to ventral hippocampal lesioning, which alters the developmental trajectory of the animals. Although their behaviors are normal early in life, at rodent pubescence, behaviors and physiological changes emerge that resemble multiple symptoms of schizophrenia. This model is appealing because schizophrenia is considered a neurodevelopmental disorder whose diagnostic symptoms most often begin in adolescence and early adulthood. Similar to schizophrenic patients, these lesioned rats show limbic dopamine dysregulation, hyperresponsiveness to stress and amphetamine injection, impaired functional development of the prefrontal cortex, and other abnormalities. This model is providing a template to study the impact of genetic, environmental, and pharmacological factors contributing to the pathophysiology of schizophrenia. The model was described in detail and evaluated in a recent review (Tseng et al., 2009), as well as in Chapter 20.

Another approach to improving translational research is to make the results from animal studies better predictors of therapeutic efficacy by developing parallel methodologies. To correct the situation, the National Institute of Mental Health (NIMH) has funded a series of conferences for interdisciplinary researchers focused on cognitive processes, because cognitive dysfunction, including deficits in attention, memory, and behavioral regulation, are central to many psychiatric disorders. Researchers first worked to identify the most important cognitive processes that should be tested and then developed testing methods for human subjects in parallel with animal models (Barch et al., 2009). Among the tasks that evaluate cognitive function that have been adapted for use with humans, non-human primates, and rodents is the **stop-signal task**. This is a commonly employed procedure used to measure impulsivity. Impulsivity or failure of behavioral inhibition is a significant component of disorders such as attention deficit hyperactivity disorder (ADHD), OCD, and substance abuse, among others. Impulsivity represents failure of an important cortical control mechanism that suppresses the execution of responses that are inappropriate in a changing environment, hence decreasing flexible behaviors. The stop-signal task requires the subject (human or otherwise) to rapidly press one button or lever when a square is displayed, and the other button or lever when any other shape appears. Periodically, a tone, which is the "stop" signal, is sounded following the visual presentation. The tone

indicates that the subject should withhold responding. This paradigm can be used to integrate neurochemical contributions to the task performance derived from rodent pharmacological studies with imaging results in humans performing the same tasks. It is anticipated that the synthesis of discoveries will translate into more effective treatments for enhancing behavioral inhibition. For a more complete discussion, refer to the paper by Eagle et al. (2008).

Section Summary

- Techniques in behavioral pharmacology provide a means of quantifying animal behavior for drug testing, developing models for psychiatric disorders, and evaluating the neurochemical basis of behavior.

- Advantages of animal testing include having a subject population with similar genetic background and history, maintaining highly controlled living environments, and being able to use invasive neurobiological techniques.

- Animal testing includes a wide range of measures that vary not only in validity and reliability, but also in complexity, time needed for completion, and cost.

- Some measures use simple quantitative observation of behaviors such as motor activity and response to noxious stimuli.

- Operant behaviors controlled by various schedules of reinforcement provide a sensitive measure of drug effects on patterns of behavior. Operant behaviors are also used in tests of addiction potential, anxiety, and analgesia.

- Other methods assess more complex behaviors such as learning and memory using a variety of techniques such as the classic T-maze, as well as mazes modified to target spatial learning: the radial arm maze and Morris water maze. The delayed-response task assesses working memory.

- Many measures of anxiety use unconditioned animal reactions such as the tendency to avoid brightly lit places (light–dark crossing task, open field test), heights (elevated plus-maze), electric shock (Vogel test), and novelty (novelty suppressed feeding).

- In the more complex operant conflict test, the animal presses a lever for food reward (nonconflict) until a tone signals that future lever pressing will deliver the reinforcer accompanied by foot shock (conflict). Antianxiety drugs increase bar pressing during the punished session.

- To assess fear a classically conditioned response is established by presenting a light or tone followed by an unavoidable foot shock. The light or tone becomes a cue associated with shock, and when presented alone, it produces physiological and behavioral responses of fearfulness. When the conditioned fear stimulus precedes a startle-producing stimulus, the startle is much greater.

- The operant self-administration technique in which animals lever press for drugs rather than food reward is an accurate predictor of abuse potential in humans. Varying the schedule of reinforcement indicates how reinforcing a given drug is, because when the effort of lever pressing exceeds the reinforcement value, the animals fail to press further (the "breaking point").

- In conditioned place preference, animals learn to associate a drug injection with one of two distinct compartments, and saline with the other. On test day, if the drug is rewarding, the animal spends more time in the environment associated with the drug. If aversive, the animal stays in the saline-associated environment.

- Drug effects act as discriminative stimuli in operant tasks, which means that the lever-pressing response of an animal depends on its recognizing internal cues produced by the drug. Novel drugs can be characterized by how similar their internal cues are to those of the known drug.

- Translational research is the interdisciplinary approach to improving the transfer of discoveries from molecular neuroscience, animal behavioral analysis, and clinical trials, with the goal of more quickly and inexpensively developing useful therapeutic drugs.

- To make animal research more predictive of therapeutic benefits in humans, animal models that create abnormal behaviors or neurobiological changes that closely resemble the focal symptoms of the disorder are needed. Genetic manipulations and brain lesions are two approaches for achieving this goal.

- Developing parallel tasks for humans, non-human primates, and rodents will allow integration of neurochemical data from rodent studies with findings of imaging studies in humans performing the same task.

Techniques in Neuropharmacology

Multiple Neurobiological Techniques for Assessing the CNS

Answering questions in psychopharmacology requires expertise not only in the techniques of behavioral analysis, but also in methods that allow us to examine the anatomy, physiology, and neurochemistry of the brain. The most productive research will utilize multiple approaches to the same problem.

Stereotaxic surgery is needed for accurate in vivo measures of brain function

The classic techniques of physiological psychology (lesioning, microinjection, and electrical recording) are equally important in understanding the actions of psychoactive drugs. Stereotaxic surgery is an essential technique in neuroscience that permits a researcher to implant one of several devices into the brain of an anesthetized animal with significant precision. The stereotaxic device itself (**Figure 4.10A**) essentially serves as a means of stabilizing the animal's head in a fixed orientation, so that the carrier portion can be moved precisely in three dimensions for placement of the tip of an electrode or a drug delivery tube in a predetermined brain site. Brain site coordinates are calculated using a brain atlas, which is a collection of frontal sections of brain of appropriate species, in which distances are measured from skull surface features (**Figure 4.10B**). Accuracy of placement is determined histologically after the experiment is complete. The halo bracket (**Figure 4.10C**) is the equivalent apparatus used in human neurosurgery; the target site is identified with the use of a computerized imaging technique such as magnetic resonance imaging (MRI) or computerized tomography (CT) (see the section on imaging techniques later in this chapter).

LESIONING AND MICROINJECTION   Experimental ablation, or **lesioning**, uses a stereotaxic device to position a delicate electrode, insulated along its length except for the exposed tip, deep within the brain. The tissue at the tip is destroyed when a very-high-frequency radio current is passed through the electrode to heat the cells. The rationale of the experiment is that a comparison of the animal's behavior before and after the lesion will tell us something about the function of that brain area.

Electrolytic lesions destroy all tissue at the tip of the electrode, including cell bodies, dendrites, and

(A)

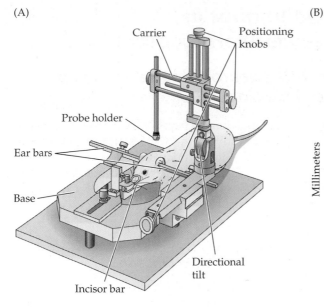

(B)

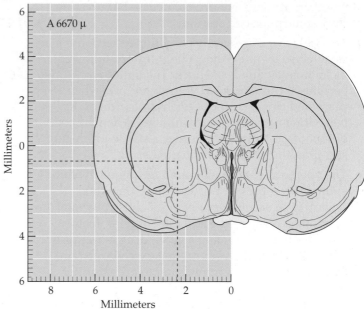

(C)

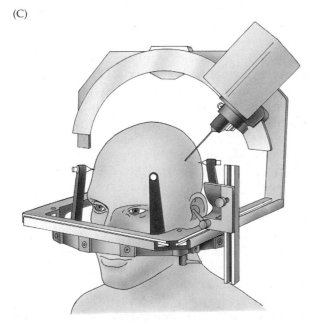

Figure 4.10 Stereotaxic surgery (A) A stereotaxic device used for precise placement of electrodes during brain surgery on animals. The base holds the anesthetized animal's head and neck in a stationary position. The carrier portion places the electrode or the cannula in a precise location based on the coordinates of the target area identified with the brain atlas (B). The precise target within the brain is defined by the intersection of 3 planes. The measurement (A 6670 μ) in the upper left corner indicates the anterior–posterior position of the brain slice. The lateral and dorsal–ventral dimensions can be read directly from the axes provided. (C) A similar apparatus is used for human brain surgery. The location of the procedure is determined by CT or MRI.

axons. Alternatively, a **neurotoxin** (a chemical that is damaging to nerve cells) can be injected via a cannula (a hollow tube inserted like an electrode) to destroy cells. Of course, the same type of cannula can be used to administer drugs or neurotransmitters that stimulate cells in the central nervous system (CNS) before behavior is evaluated (see the discussion of intracerebroventricular administration in Chapter 1). Chemical lesions have the advantage of being significantly more specific because neurotoxic chemicals, such as kainic acid or ibotenic acid, kill cell bodies in the vicinity of the cannula tip but spare the axons passing through the same area. In either case, this procedure can be used to identify the brain area responsible

for a drug-induced change in behavior. For instance, we might wonder which brain area is responsible for the reinforcing effects of a drug like amphetamine. Suppose that after lesioning the nucleus accumbens in the telencephalon, we find that rats no longer will self-administer amphetamine by pressing a lever in an operant chamber. We may want to conclude that the nucleus accumbens is responsible for reinforcement, but lesion studies must always be evaluated cautiously. Even when a lesion changes behavior, we still don't know what specific function that brain area served. In our example, further investigation would be needed to determine *how* the lesion interfered with self-administration. Does the nucleus accumbens modulate reinforcement? Or is it possible that the animal lost motor control or failed to remember the appropriate response? Furthermore, because of the small size of brain structures and their overlapping nature, behavioral change may be due to damage to adjacent brain regions or fibers passing through the region.

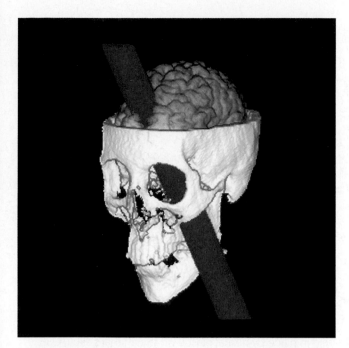

Figure 4.11 Computer reconstruction of the trajectory of the steel rod that penetrated Phineas Gage's skull during a nineteenth-century blasting accident. The massive damage to the frontal part of the brain and the behavioral deficits that he demonstrated after the accident stimulated thinking about the role of the frontal cortex in complex brain functions. Gage's skull is presently housed in the Warren Museum at Harvard Medical School. (After Damasio et al., 1994; courtesy of Hanna Damasio.)

The lesioning technique has always been a valuable tool for examining the relationship between brain structure and function in animals. In humans, of course, lesions cannot be produced intentionally, but accidents, trauma to the brain, strokes, and tumors ("accidents of nature") all provide a means to investigate the relationship between brain damage and function. Psychology students will certainly remember the story of Phineas Gage, whose skull and brain were penetrated by a long steel rod in a blasting accident (**Figure 4.11**). His case history has become famous as an example of profound behavioral changes following traumatic brain injury. Previously a mild-mannered man and a competent foreman of a work crew, after the accident Gage demonstrated childish behavior and an inability to organize his daily activities, displaying frequent uncontrolled outbursts and episodes of violence. However, several significant problems are involved in evaluating such case studies. First, although behavioral measures and neuropsychological testing after injury can identify deficits in function, it is rare that skills were evaluated before the injury. For this reason, it is difficult to know to what extent functioning changed as a result of the injury.

Second, until very recently, there was no way to know specifically where brain damage occurred. Scanning techniques like CT and MRI have greatly improved our ability to identify quite specifically the locus of damage. Third, "accidents of nature" produce unique damage to brain structures in each individual, so generalizations to a larger population are unwarranted.

Because neuropharmacologists are interested in neurochemical regulation of behavior, the lesioning techniques used are often specific for a neural pathway that uses a particular neurotransmitter. These **specific neurotoxins** most often are injected directly into the brain, where they are taken up by the normal reuptake mechanism of neurons. Once inside the cell, the toxin destroys the cell terminal. In this way, behavioral measures obtained before and after a neurotoxic lesion tell us about the role of the neurotransmitter in a particular behavior. For example, intracerebroventricular administration of 6-hydroxydopamine (6-OHDA) produces nerve terminal degeneration in both noradrenergic and dopaminergic cells and profound neurotransmitter depletion. More selective effects are achieved when the neurotoxin is injected directly into a target area. Earlier, we suggested that lesioning the nucleus accumbens reduced self-administration of amphetamine in rats. We might further test our understanding of the role of the nucleus accumbens in reinforcement by selectively destroying the large number of dopamine cell terminals in that area using the neurotoxin 6-OHDA before evaluating the drug-taking behavior.

MICRODIALYSIS   A different technique that uses stereotaxic surgery is **microdialysis**. Although researchers have been able to measure neurotransmitters released from brain slices in vitro for many years, microdialysis lets us measure neurotransmitters released in a specific brain region while the subject is actively engaged in behavior (**Figure 4.12A**).

The technique requires a specialized cannula made of fine, flexible tubing that is implanted stereotaxically (**Figure 4.12B**). The cannula is sealed along its length except at the tip, allowing investigators to collect material in extracellular fluid at nerve terminals at precise sites even deep within the brain. Artificial cerebrospinal fluid (CSF) is gently moved into the microdialysis cannula by a pump. The CSF in the cannula and in the extracellular fluid are identical except for the material to be collected. On the basis of the difference in concentration, the chemicals of interest move across the membrane from the synaptic space into the cannula. A second pump removes the CSF from the cannula into a series of tubes to be analyzed by high-performance liquid chromatography (HPLC) or another method.

(A)

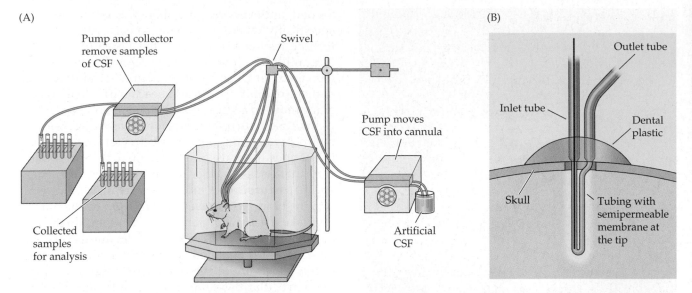

Figure 4.12 Collection of extracellular fluid with microdialysis (A) Microdialysis allows the collection of samples from deep within the brain in unanesthetized and freely moving animals under relatively normal conditions. The collected samples are identified and are measured by one of several analytic techniques, such as HPLC. (B) Typical

microdialysis probe, which uses flexible tubing that is sealed except at the tip, where it is semipermeable. It is held in place by dental plastic on the animal's skull. CSF, cerebrospinal fluid. (A after Philippu, 1984; B after Ungerstedt, 1984.)

A major improvement over older collection methods is that only tiny amounts of material need to be collected for accurate measurement. This improved accuracy is due to the development of highly sensitive analytic techniques (such as HPLC), which can be combined with microdialysis collection. HPLC, like other types of chromatography, serves two purposes. First, chromatography separates the sample into

component parts depending on characteristics of the sample, such as molecular size or ionic charge. Second, the concentration of the molecules of interest can be determined (**Figure 4.13**).

Microdialysis is important to neuropsychopharmacology because it can be used in several types of experiments that combine biochemical and behavioral analyses. For example, we might evaluate the

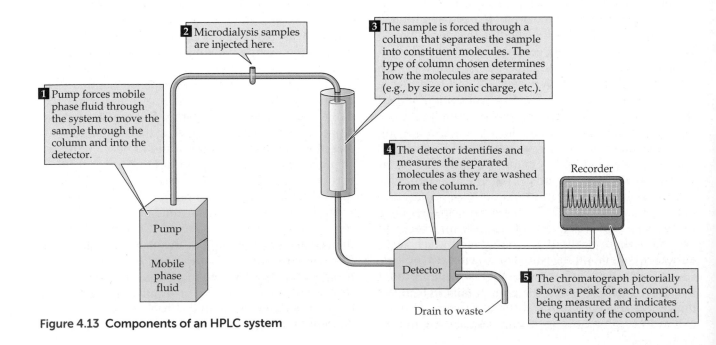

Figure 4.13 Components of an HPLC system

released neurochemicals during ongoing behaviors such as sleep and waking, feeding, or operant tasks to obtain a window into the functioning CNS. Second, we might investigate the effects of drugs on extracellular concentrations of neurotransmitters in selected brain areas. Since the sample can be collected from freely moving animals, correlated changes in behavior can be monitored simultaneously. Finally, the collection of extracellular materials at nerve terminals following discrete electrical or chemical stimulation of neural pathways is another valuable role.

A second method used to measure neurotransmitter release is **in vivo voltammetry**. Whereas microdialysis collects samples of extracellular fluid for subsequent analysis, in vivo voltammetry uses stereotaxically implanted microelectrodes to measure neurochemicals in the extracellular fluid of freely moving animals. In voltammetry, a very fine electrode is implanted, and a small electrical potential is applied. Changes in the flow of current at the electrode tip reflect changes in the concentration of electroactive substances such as neurotransmitters or their metabolites. A major advantage of this method is that because measurements are made continuously and require as little as 15 milliseconds to complete, researchers can evaluate neurotransmitter release as it is occurring in real time.

ELECTROPHYSIOLOGICAL STIMULATION AND RECORDING In a similar fashion, implanted **macroelectrodes** (**Figure 4.14A**) can be used to activate cells at the tip while the change in animal behavior during stimulation is evaluated. The minute amount of electrical current applied changes the membrane potential of those cells and generates action potentials. The action potentials in turn cause the release of neurotransmitter at the cell terminals to mimic normal synaptic transmission. Hence the electrical stimulation should produce biobehavioral effects that are similar to those seen upon injection of the natural neurotransmitter or neurotransmitter agonists into the brain. In addition, one would expect that stimulation of a given cell group should produce effects opposite those caused by a lesion at the same site. Macroelectrodes can also be used to record the summated electrical response of thousands of neurons in a specific brain region following drug treatment or other experimental manipulation in a freely moving animal. If we had found, for example, that lesioning the periaqueductal gray (PAG) in the midbrain prevented the pain-reducing effects of morphine, we might want to find out what effect activating those PAG neurons has. What we would find is that if electrodes implanted in the PAG are activated, the animal fails to respond to painful stimuli. Likewise, if pain-killing opioids like morphine or codeine are microinjected into that

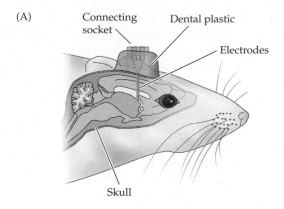

(A)

Connecting socket · Dental plastic · Electrodes · Skull

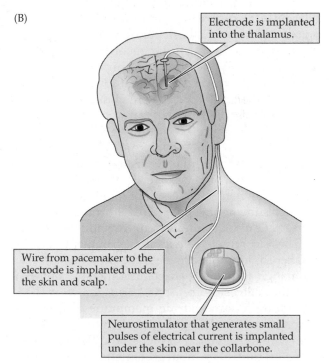

(B)

Electrode is implanted into the thalamus.

Wire from pacemaker to the electrode is implanted under the skin and scalp.

Neurostimulator that generates small pulses of electrical current is implanted under the skin near the collarbone.

Figure 4.14 Electrical brain stimulation and recording (A) Stereotaxically implanted electrodes held in place on the skull with dental plastic. After recovery, the animal can be plugged into a device that can electrically stimulate cells at the tip or monitor and record changes in electrical activity. (B) Diagram of the Tremor Control System, which consists of an insulated wire electrode surgically implanted deep in the brain. The electrode is connected to a pulse generator implanted under the skin near the collarbone. The generator is programmed to deliver the amount of electrical current needed to reduce the tremor on the opposite side of the body. Patients also can have individual control by passing a hand-held magnet over the skin above the pulse generator.

brain area via an indwelling cannula, the animal also demonstrates profound analgesia.

Many years of animal research into stereotaxic implantation of electrodes into the brain have translated into clinical benefits. **Figure 4.14B** shows the adaptation of the technique to humans being treated for Parkinson's disease. Small pulses of electrical current applied to the thalamus cause the cells to fire and release neurotransmitter, which reduces the tremor on the opposite side of the body.

An alternative to macroelectrode recording, which is a summation of electrical activity in a brain region, is single-unit recording, which uses **microelectrodes**. Stereotaxically implanting a fine-tipped electrode either into a single cell (**intracellular recording**) or into the extracellular fluid near a single cell (**extracellular recording**) monitors the response of individual cells under various conditions. Intracellular recording must involve an anesthetized animal, because the electrode must remain in a precise position to record the membrane potential of the cell. An advantage of extracellular single-cell recording is that it can be done in a mobile animal (**Figure 4.15**). The downside to extracellular recording is that the electrode records only the occurrence of action potentials in the nearby neuron and cannot monitor the change in the cell's membrane potential. Returning to our earlier example of morphine action, we find that the drug produces strong selective inhibition of neurons in the spinal cord, and this prevents the projection of pain information to higher brain centers, thereby contributing to the analgesic effect.

In addition to measuring membrane potentials of groups of cells and single cells, thanks to the Nobel Prize–winning research of Neher and Sakmann conducted in the 1970s, neuroscientists can study the function of *individual* ion channels, which collectively are responsible for the membrane potential. This technique, known as **patch clamp electrophysiology**, works best with individual cells in culture but can also be used on exposed cells in slices of brain. The method involves attaching a recording micropipette to a piece of cell membrane by suction. When the pipette is pulled away, a small membrane patch containing one or more ion channels remains attached. The subsequent electrical recording through the pipette represents in real time the channel opening, the flow of ions

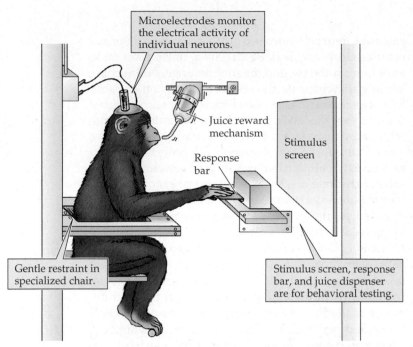

Figure 4.15 Extracellular microelectrode recording from single neurons in the brain of an awake, responding rhesus monkey. This experimental setup might be used to evaluate the effects of a previously administered drug on the animal's response to visual stimuli and on the electrical activity of a single cell.

(electrical current) during the brief period when it is open, and the channel closing.

Neurotransmitters, receptors, and other proteins can be quantified and visually located in the CNS

To both quantify and locate neurotransmitters and receptors in the CNS, several methods are required. To count or measure a particular molecule, a "soup" method is often used, in which a tissue sample is precisely dissected out and ground up, creating a homogenate before it is evaluated. Homogenates are used in any one of many possible neurochemical analyses, which are referred to as *assays*. In contrast, for localization, the landmarks of the tissue and the relationships of structures must be preserved, so the visualization method is done on an intact piece or slice of tissue. Hence, when we want to measure the number of receptors in a

TABLE 4.2 Methods Used to Quantify and Visualize Target Molecules in the Nervous System		
Target molecule	Tissue extract assay to quantify	Brain slice preparation to visualize
Receptor site	Radioligand binding	Receptor autoradiography
Receptors and other proteins	Radioimmunoassay (RIA)	Immunocytochemistry (ICC)
mRNA	Dot blot or Northern blot	In situ hybridization (ISH)

particular brain area, we are likely to use a radioligand binding assay in a tissue homogenate, but if we want to see where in the brain particular receptors are located (and measure them), we are more likely to use a slice preparation with autoradiography. **Table 4.2** summarizes the "soup" and "slice" techniques described in the following section of the chapter.

RADIOLIGAND BINDING   To study the number of receptors in a given brain region and their affinity for drugs, the **radioligand binding** method was developed. Once the brain region we are interested in is dissected out, it is ground up to make a homogenate. A ligand (usually a drug or chemical) that is radioactively labeled (now called the *radioligand*) is incubated with the tissue under conditions that optimize its binding. After a brief time, any radioligand that has not bound is removed, often by washing and filtering. The amount of radioligand bound to the tissue is then measured with a scintillation (or gamma) counter and reflects the number of receptors in the tissue.

Although the binding procedure is quite simple, interpretation of the results is more complex. How can we be sure that the radioligand is actually binding to the specific biological receptors of interest, rather than to other sites that represent artifacts of the procedure? Several criteria that must be met include (1) specificity; (2) saturability; (3) reversibility and high affinity; and (4) biological relevance. Specificity means that the ligand is binding only to the receptor we are concerned with in this tissue, and to nothing else. Of course, drugs often bind to several receptor subtypes, but they may also attach to other cell components that produce no biological effects. To measure the amount of a ligand that binds to the site that we are concerned with, we add very high concentrations of a nonradioactive competing ligand to some tubes to show that most of the radioactive binding is displaced. That which remains is likely to be nonspecifically bound to sites such as assay additives (e.g., albumin) or cellular sites (e.g., enzymes), which we are less interested in at the moment. Nonspecific binding is subtracted when the data are calculated for specific binding. When binding to specific subtypes of receptors is necessary, ligands must be designed to distinguish between receptor proteins.

Saturability means that there are a finite number of receptors in a given amount of tissue. By adding increasing amounts of radioligand to a fixed amount of tissue, one would expect to see gradual increases in binding until all sites are filled (**Figure 4.16A**). The point at which the binding curve plateaus represents maximum binding or B_{max}. Binding within the assay must also be reversible because a neurotransmitter in vivo will bind and release many times to initiate

repeated activation of the cellular action. This reversibility is demonstrated in binding assays because the radioactive ligand can be displaced by the same drug that is not radiolabeled (**Figure 4.16B**). If you compare the rate of dissociation with the rate of binding, you get an estimate of receptor affinity called the

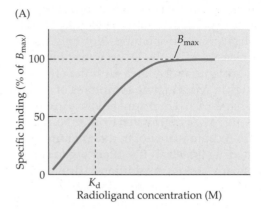

(A)

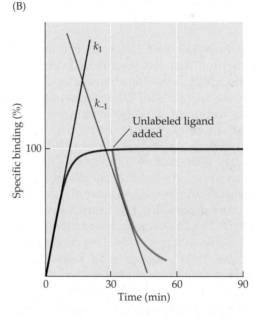

(B)

Figure 4.16 Radioligand binding to receptors (A) A hypothetical saturation curve shows that as radioligand concentration increases, specific binding to the receptor also increases until all sites are filled (B_{max}). The K_d is defined as the ligand concentration at which 50% of the receptors are occupied; it is an indication of receptor affinity and is called the dissociation constant. (B) Hypothetical association and dissociation curves. The red line represents the association of a radioligand with its receptors over time. The rate of association (k_1) is estimated by calculating the slope of the straight line that best fits the curvilinear data. After maximum binding has occurred (association and dissociation are in equilibrium), excess unlabeled ligand is added. The blue line represents the dissociation of the radioligand from its receptors in the presence of large amounts of unlabeled ligand. The slope of the straight line that best fits that portion of the curve provides an estimate of the rate of dissociation (k_{-1}).

dissociation constant or K_d. Clearly those ligands that bind readily and dissociate slowly have the highest affinity for the receptor. The unbinding (dissociation) of the ligand from the receptor must also be consistent with the reversal of physiological effects of the ligand.

Ideally, binding of chemically similar drugs should correlate with some measurable biochemical or behavioral effect. For example, the classic antipsychotic drugs all bind to a particular subtype of receptor (D_2) for the neurotransmitter dopamine. Not only do the drugs in this class bind to the D_2 receptor, but their affinity for the receptor correlates with the effectiveness of the drugs in reducing the symptoms of schizophrenia (see Chapter 20). Unfortunately, in vitro binding data does not always transfer to in vivo results because in vitro receptors are not in their natural environment. Also, drug effects in the intact organism are dependent on many factors in addition to drug–receptor interaction, for example, absorption and distribution. The use of in vivo receptor binding (see the next section) can help to account for absorption, distribution, and metabolism of the drug.

RECEPTOR AUTORADIOGRAPHY   Receptor binding is a classic tool in neuropharmacology that tells us about receptor number and affinity for a particular drug in a specific piece of brain tissue. When we want to visualize the distribution of receptors within the brain, we use receptor autoradiography. The process begins with standard radioligand binding as described previously, except that slide-mounted tissue slices rather than ground-up tissue are used. After the unbound radioactively labeled drug is washed away, the slices are processed by **autoradiography**. The slides are put into cassettes, a specialized autoradiographic film is placed on top of the slides so that it is in physical contact with the tissue sections, and the cassettes are stored in the dark to allow the radioactive material that is bound to receptors to act on the film. The particles that are constantly emitted from the radioactive material in the tissue expose the film and show not only the amount of radioligand bound but also its location. This method is especially good for studying the effects of brain lesions on receptor binding because each lesioned animal can be evaluated independently by comparing the lesioned and nonlesioned sides of the brain. This method might give us clues about how various psychoactive drugs produce their behavioral effects. For instance, mapping of the binding of cocaine in monkey brain shows a distinct pattern of localization and density in selected brain areas (**Figure 4.17**). With a clear understanding of anatomical distribution, we can begin to test specific hypotheses regarding the behavioral consequences of activating these receptors using microinjections of receptor-selective agonists and antagonists.

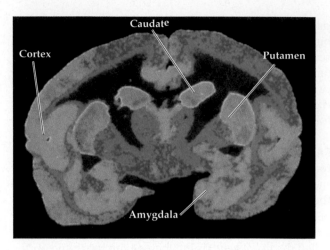

Figure 4.17 Autoradiogram of the distribution of cocaine binding in monkey brain The highest levels of cocaine binding are in areas colored yellow and orange. (Courtesy of Bertha Madras.)

IN VIVO RECEPTOR BINDING   The same autoradiographic processing can be done on brain slices of an animal that had previously been injected in vivo with a radiolabeled drug. The drug enters the general circulation, diffuses into the brain, and binds to receptors. Then the animal is killed, and the brain is sliced and processed by autoradiography. This technique shows the researcher where a particular drug or neurotransmitter binds in an intact animal. Unfortunately, results obtained with this technique are more difficult to interpret because of the complexities of bioavailability and distribution, diffusion through the blood–brain barrier, and metabolism of the drug. Nevertheless, its potential is tremendous because in vivo binding can be assessed in living human subjects using positron emission tomography (PET) (see the section on brain imaging) to map the pattern of drug–receptor binding and correlate it with clinical effects.

ASSAYS OF ENZYME ACTIVITY   Enzymes are proteins that act as biological catalysts to speed up reaction rates, but they are not used up in the process. We find many different enzymes in every cell, and each has a role in a relatively specific reaction. The enzymes that are particularly interesting to neuropharmacologists are those involved in the synthesis or metabolism of neurotransmitters, neuromodulators, and second messengers. In addition, neuropharmacologists are interested in identifying the conditions that regulate the rate of activity of the enzyme. For example, acute morphine treatment inhibits adenylyl cyclase activity. Adenylyl cyclase is the enzyme that synthesizes the second messenger cyclic adenosine monophosphate (cAMP). However, long-term exposure to morphine produces gradual but dramatic

(A)

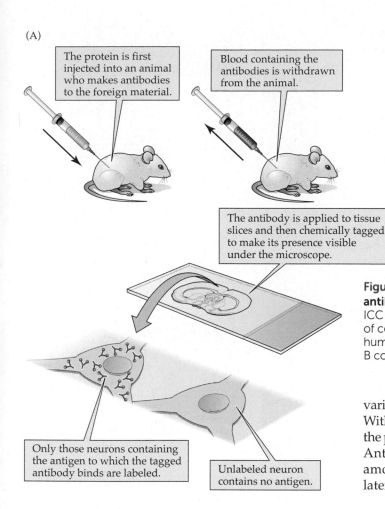

The protein is first injected into an animal who makes antibodies to the foreign material.

Blood containing the antibodies is withdrawn from the animal.

The antibody is applied to tissue slices and then chemically tagged to make its presence visible under the microscope.

Only those neurons containing the antigen to which the tagged antibody binds are labeled.

Unlabeled neuron contains no antigen.

(B)

Figure 4.18 Immunocytochemistry (ICC) uses tagged antibodies to locate molecules within cells (A) Steps in ICC localization. (B) Immunocytochemical identification of cells containing the neuropeptide hypocretin in the human lateral hypothalamus. (A after Bear et al., 2001; B courtesy of Jerome Siegel.)

up-regulation of the cAMP system, suggesting that the second-messenger system acts to compensate for the acute effect of opioid inhibition. It is perhaps one of the best studied biochemical models of opioid tolerance and is discussed further in Chapter 11.

Sometimes the mere presence of an enzyme within a cell cluster is important because it can be used to identify those cells that manufacture a specific neurotransmitter. The next section describes the use of antibodies and immunocytochemistry to locate enzymes in the brain.

ANTIBODY PRODUCTION Some of the newest methods for identifying and measuring receptors and other proteins are far more specific and sensitive than ever before because they use an antibody. An **antibody** is a protein produced by the white blood cells of the immune system to recognize, attack, and destroy a specific foreign substance (the antigen). Researchers use this immune response to create supplies of antibodies that bind to specific proteins (receptors, neuropeptides, or enzymes) they want to locate in the brain (**Figure 4.18A**). The first step is to create an antibody by injecting the antigen (e.g., the neuropeptide hypocretin) into a host animal and at

various times taking blood samples to collect antibodies. With the antibody prepared, we are ready to look for the peptide in tissue slices using immunocytochemistry. Antibodies can also be used to quantify very small amounts of material using radioimmunoassays (see later in this chapter).

IMMUNOCYTOCHEMISTRY For **immunocytochemistry (ICC)**, the brain is first fixed (hardened) using a preservative such as formaldehyde. Tissue slices are then cut and incubated with the antibody in solution. The antibody attaches to the antigen wherever cells that contain that antigen are present. In the final step, the antibody is tagged so that the antigen-containing cells can be visualized (see Figure 4.18A). This is usually accomplished by means of a chemical reaction that creates a colored precipitate within the cells or with the use of a fluorescent dye that glows when exposed to light of a particular wavelength. The researcher can then examine the tissue slices under a microscope to see which brain areas or neurons contain the antigen. This technique is limited only by the ability to raise antibodies. **Figure 4.18B** shows the visualization of cells that contain the neuropeptide hypocretin in the lateral hypothalamus of a healthy human subject. In patients with the sleep disorder narcolepsy, the number of hypocretin neurons is reduced by about 90% (Thannicakal et al., 2000). These results, along with animal experiments using neurotoxin lesioning and genetic modification, suggest that hypocretin in the hypothalamus may regulate the onset of sleep stages. ICC is similar to autoradiography in principle, but it is far more selective because the antibody

Figure 4.19 Radioimmunoassay (RIA) The steps in the RIA procedure that produce a typical standard curve. The curve in turn is used to calculate the amount of unknown antigen in a given sample.

(which recognizes only a very specific protein) is used, and it is much quicker because it does not require the development time of autoradiographic film.

RADIOIMMUNOASSAY Antibodies are also useful in quantifying physiologically important molecules in body fluids such as blood, saliva, or CSF, as well as in tissue extracts. **Radioimmunoassay (RIA)** is based on competitive binding of an antibody to its antigen (the molecule being measured). The use of antibodies makes the procedure highly specific for the molecule of interest and very sensitive (**Figure 4.19**).

RIA involves preparing a standard curve of known antigen concentrations against which unknown samples can be compared. The standard curve is created by first combining a preset amount of antibody with a known concentration of radioactively labeled antigen in all the assay tubes. At this point, all the tubes are identical, that is, all of the antibody would be reversibly attached to radioactive antigen. However, the experimenter then adds different, known concentrations of unlabeled antigen, which compete with the radioactively labeled antigen. The higher the concentration of unlabeled competitor antigen added, the lower the amount of radioactive antigen bound after the mixture has been incubated. Values are plotted as a standard curve and analyzed using appropriate computer software.

To determine how much of the antigen is present in any experimental sample, other test tubes are prepared in just the same way, except that samples containing unknown amounts of antigen are added, instead of the known antigen. By measuring the amount of radioactive antigen bound in the sample tubes compared with the standard curve, the amount of antigen in the sample can be calculated.

IN SITU HYBRIDIZATION   In situ hybridization (ISH) makes it possible to locate cells in tissue slices that are *manufacturing* a particular protein or peptide in much the same manner that ICC identifies cells *containing* a particular protein. ISH is particularly useful in neuropharmacology for detecting the specific messenger RNA (mRNA) molecules responsible for directing the manufacture of the wide variety of proteins essential to neuron function, such as enzymes, structural proteins, receptors, ion channels, and peptides. For example, **Figure 4.20A** shows the location of the mRNA for enkephalin, one of several opioid peptides in the adult rat brain (see

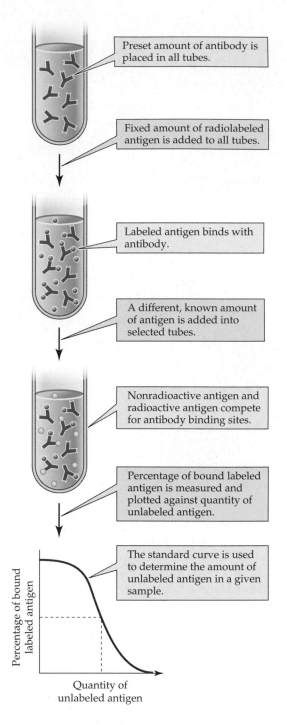

Preset amount of antibody is placed in all tubes.

Fixed amount of radiolabeled antigen is added to all tubes.

Labeled antigen binds with antibody.

A different, known amount of antigen is added into selected tubes.

Nonradioactive antigen and radioactive antigen compete for antibody binding sites.

Percentage of bound labeled antigen is measured and plotted against quantity of unlabeled antigen.

The standard curve is used to determine the amount of unlabeled antigen in a given sample.

Percentage of bound labeled antigen

Quantity of unlabeled antigen

Chapter 11). Because the method detects cells with a precise RNA sequence, it is exceptionally specific and extremely sensitive. Besides *locating* cells that contain specific mRNA, ISH is used to study *changes* in regional mRNA levels after experimental manipulations. The amount of mRNA provides an estimate of the rate of synthesis of the particular protein. This means that if chronic drug treatment caused a decrease in enkephalin mRNA, as shown in Figure 4.20A, we could conclude that the protein the mRNA codes for has been down-regulated, that is, less of that protein is being synthesized.

(A)

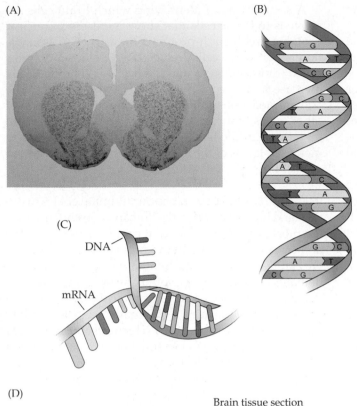

(C)

DNA

mRNA

(D)

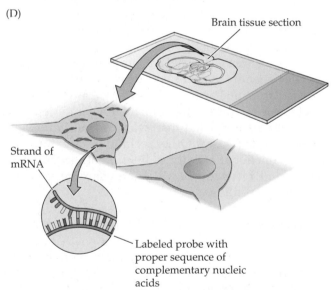

Brain tissue section

Strand of
mRNA

Labeled probe with
proper sequence of
complementary nucleic
acids

Figure 4.20 In situ hybridization (ISH) (A) Localization of enkephalin mRNA in a slice from rat brain. (B) Structure of a DNA molecule. The nucleotide bases always bind in a complementary fashion: thymine to adenine and guanine to cytosine. (C) A strand of mRNA has copied the code from a partially unraveled DNA molecule in the nucleus and will carry the genetic code to ribosomes in the cytoplasm, where the protein will be created. (D) In ISH, a labeled probe has been created with the correct sequence of complementary bases. When the strand of mRNA in the cell and the labeled probe hybridize, or bond to one another, the product labels the cell that contains the genetic code for the protein of interest. (A courtesy of Brian Sauer and Suzanne Pham.)

to the complementary base-pair sequences. After incubation, the tissue is washed and dehydrated before it is placed in contact with X-ray film or processed in other ways for visualization of cells containing the specific mRNA. This technique is extremely sensitive and can detect a very small number of cells that express a particular gene. If the researcher is interested only in measuring the amount of mRNA rather than visualizing its location, hybridization can be done using a tissue homogenate rather than a tissue slice. Two available methods of ISH that use homogenates are called Northern blot and dot blot.

DNA MICROARRAYS Microarrays, also called DNA chips or gene chips, provide the newest and most dramatic improvement in gene technology. Because the nervous system exhibits the greatest complexity of gene expression of all tissues, being able to examine all of the genes simultaneously can tell researchers which genes switch on and off together in response to a disease state, drug treatment, or environmental condition. One would assume that genes that increase or decrease their expression under the same condition probably work together to induce a cellular response. In addition, measuring the number of various RNAs in a sample tells us both the types and quantities of proteins present. A study by Mirnics and colleagues (2000) demonstrated the technical elegance of microarray by identifying multiple presynaptic proteins that are underexpressed in the frontal lobes of schizophrenic individuals. Their results provide a predictive and testable model of the disorder.

The method is similar to that described for ISH, but rather than measuring a single mRNA, microarrays consist of between 1000 and 20,000 distinct complementary DNA sequences on a single chip (a structural support) of approximately thumbnail size. Each spot is only about 50 to 150 μm in diameter. This makes it

As you may recall from Chapter 2, the double strands of DNA and the corresponding mRNA (**Figure 4.20B,C**) have unique base-pair sequences responsible for directing the synthesis of a particular protein with its unique amino acid sequence. ISH depends on the ability to create probes by labeling single-stranded fragments of RNA made up of base-pair sequences complementary to those of the mRNA of interest (**Figure 4.20D**). After the single strands have been prepared, they are labeled radioactively or with dyes. When the tissue slices or cells are exposed to the labeled probe, the probe attaches (binds, or hybridizes) possible to screen the expression of the entire genome of an organism in a single experiment on just a few chips. The tissue to be evaluated (e.g., the frontal lobe from a schizophrenic individual compared with a normal frontal lobe) is dissected, and the mRNAs are isolated and labeled, then hybridized to the large number of immobilized DNA molecules on the chip. A scanner automatically evaluates the extent of hybridization of each of the thousands of spots on the chip, and computer analysis is used to identify the patterns of gene activity. Several excellent reviews of the microarray procedure and its application in areas such as aging, neuropharmacology, and psychiatric disorders are available (Luo and Geschwind, 2001; Marcotte et al. 2001).

New tools are used for imaging the structure and function of the brain

Most conventional neurobiological techniques are designed to quantify or to localize significant substances in the nervous system. One of the greatest challenges in psychopharmacology has been to evaluate the functioning of the brain under various conditions, particularly in the living human being. Advances in technology not only make visualization of the CNS far more precise, but also provide the opportunity to visualize the functioning brain.

AUTORADIOGRAPHY OF DYNAMIC CELL PROCESSES   You are already familiar with the technique of autoradiography for mapping cell components such as neurotransmitter receptors that have been radioactively labeled. Another important application of autoradiography is the tracing of active processes in the brain such as cerebral blood flow, oxygen consumption, local glucose utilization, or local rates of cerebral protein synthesis. **2-Deoxyglucose autoradiography** is based on the assumption that when nerve cell firing increases, the metabolic rate, that is, the utilization of glucose and oxygen, also increases. By identifying cells that take up more glucose under experimental conditions such as drug treatment, we can tell which brain regions are most active. 2-Deoxyglucose (2-DG) is a modified form of the glucose molecule that is taken up by active nerve cells but is not processed in the same manner as glucose and remains trapped in the cell. If the 2-DG has been labeled in some way, the most active cells can be identified. The method involves injecting an animal with radioactive 2-DG before evaluating its behavior in a test situation. The experimenter then kills the animal, removes the brain, and slices it in preparation for autoradiography (as described earlier in this chapter). A similar (but nonlethal) technique can be performed with human subjects using PET, as described in the next section.

A second way of identifying which brain cells are active is to locate cells that show increases in nuclear proteins involved in protein synthesis. The assumption is that when cells are activated, selected proteins called transcription factors (such as **c-fos**) dramatically increase in concentration over 30 to 60 minutes. The c-fos protein subsequently activates the expression of other genes that regulate protein synthesis. c-Fos can be located in the brain using ICC to stain cells with increased levels of the fos protein and hence increased cell activity.

IMAGING TECHNIQUES   Since our ultimate goal is to understand how drugs affect the human brain and behavior, the most exciting advance in recent years has been the ability to visualize the living human brain. Although we can learn a lot by studying individuals with brain damage, until recently we could only guess at where the damage was located because the brain was not accessible until the individual died, often many years later. It was virtually impossible to know which specific brain area was responsible for the lost function. The human brain remained a bit of a "black box," and our understanding of the neural processes responsible for human thinking and behavior was advanced primarily through animal experiments. Because of recent advances in X-ray and computer technology, neuroscience now can not only safely visualize the detailed anatomy of the human brain but also identify the neural processes responsible for a particular mental activity. CT and MRI are techniques that create pictures of the human nervous system that show far greater detail than was previously possible with standard X-ray. Other techniques are designed to see functional activity in the human brain. These include PET, functional MRI, and computer-assisted electrical recording.

When standard X-rays are passed through the body, they are differentially absorbed depending on the density of the various tissues. Rays that are not absorbed strike a photographic plate, forming light and dark images. Unfortunately, the brain is made up of many overlapping parts that do not differ dramatically in their ability to absorb X-rays, so it is very difficult to distinguish the individual shapes of brain structures. **Computerized tomography** (**CT**) not only increases the resolution (sharpness of detail) of the image but also provides an image in three dimensions.

The individual undergoing a CT scan (sometimes called CAT scan, for computerized axial tomography) lies with his head placed in a cylindrical X-ray tube (**Figure 4.21A**). A series of narrow, parallel beams of radiation are aimed through the tissue and toward the X-ray detectors. The X-ray source is rotated around the head while the detectors move on the opposite side in parallel. At each point of rotation, the source

(A) Computerized tomography (CT)

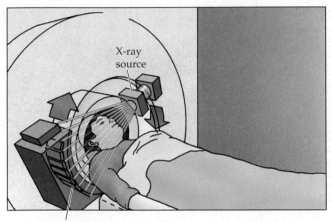

X-ray source

X-ray detector

(B)

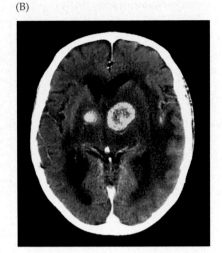

Figure 4.21 Computerized tomography (CT) (A) The cylindrical CT scanner rotates around the head, sending parallel X-ray beams through the tissue to be detected on the opposite side. A computerized image in the form of a brain slice is constructed from the data. (B) Horizontal CT scan showing a tumor (orange) at the level of the basal ganglia. Anterior is toward the top of the scan.

and detectors also move linearly. In this manner, they make a series of radiation transmission readings, which is calculated by a computer and visually displayed as a "slice" through the brain (**Figure 4.21B**). The slices can be reconstructed by the computer into three-dimensional images for a better understanding of brain structure.

Magnetic resonance imaging (**MRI**) further refines the ability to view the living brain by using computerized measurements of the distinct waves that different atoms emit when placed in a strong magnetic field and activated by radio-frequency waves. This method distinguishes different body tissues on the basis of their individual chemical composition. Because tissues contain different amounts of water, they can be distinguished by scanning the magnetic-induced resonance of hydrogen. The image provides exquisite detail and, as is true for CT, sequential slices can be reconstructed to provide three-dimensional images (**Figure 4.22**).

It did not take long for scientists to realize the power of their new tool, and they proceeded to use the computerized scanning technique to view the localization of radioactively labeled materials injected into a living human. **Positron emission tomography** (**PET**) does not create images of the brain but maps the distribution of a radioactively labeled substance that has been injected into an individual. To do this safely with human subjects, we must use radioisotopes that decay quickly rather than accumulate. Although radioactive isotopes used in many laboratory experiments

have relatively long half-lives, on the order of 1200 years for ^{3}H or 5700 years for ^{14}C, those used for PET have half-lives of 2 minutes (^{15}O), 20 minutes (^{11}C), or 110 minutes (^{18}F). Isotopes that decay and lose their radioactivity quickly (i.e., have a short half-life) emit positrons, which are like electrons except that they have a positive charge. When a positron expelled from the nucleus collides with an electron, both particles are annihilated and emit two gamma photons traveling in opposite directions. In a PET scanning device (**Figure 4.23A**), detectors surround the head to track these gamma photons and locate their origin. The

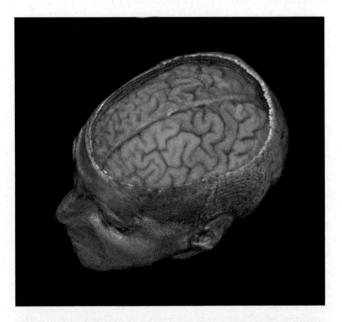

Figure 4.22 A three-dimensional image formed with MRI Computer technology provides the opportunity to create three-dimensional representations of the brain from sequential slices.

Figure 4.23 Positron emission tomography (PET) (A) A typical scanning device for PET. Notice the photodetectors that surround the head to track the gamma photons produced when a positron expelled from the nucleus collides with an electron. (B) PET scan image showing active brain areas by measuring regional cerebral blood flow under two conditions. The subject on the left, who was told to expect only mild discomfort from putting a hand into 47°C (116.6°F) water, showed less neuronal activity (correlated with less blood flow) in the anterior cingulate cortex than the subject on the right, who expected more pain. Highly active areas are colored orange, red, and white. Additional experiments might assess how certain drugs change the pattern of activation. (B from Rainville et al., 1997; courtesy of Pierre Rainville.)

(A) Positron emission tomography (PET)

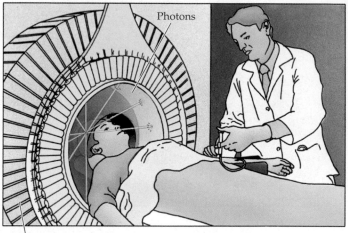

(B)

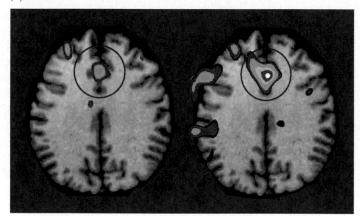

information is analyzed by computer and visualized as an image on the monitor.

PET is useful in neuropharmacology in several ways (Farde, 1996). First, a radioactively labeled drug or ligand can be administered, and the location of binding in brain tissue can be seen. The technique has been used successfully to localize neurotransmitter receptors and identify where drugs bind. Perhaps even more exciting is the use of PET to determine which parts of the brain are active during the performance of particular tasks or cognitive problem solving (**Figure 4.23B**). PET allows us to visualize brain activity, which is reflected in increases in glucose utilization, oxygen use, and blood flow, depending on which reagent has been labeled. Very much like autoradiography in living humans, PET can be used along with 2-DG to map brain areas that utilize increased glucose or demonstrate increased blood flow—both indicative of heightened neural activity.

Single-photon emission computerized tomography (SPECT) is very similar to PET imaging, but it is much simpler and less expensive because the radiolabeled probes do not have to be synthesized but are commercially available. When scanned, the radioactive compounds, either inhaled or injected, show the changes in regional blood flow. Although resolution is less accurate than with PET, SPECT data can be combined with CT or MRI scans to localize active areas more precisely than with SPECT alone.

Functional MRI (fMRI) has become the newest and perhaps the most powerful tool in the neuroscientist's arsenal for visualizing brain activity. To meet the increased metabolic demand of active neurons, the flow of blood carrying oxygen to these cells increases. Functional MRI can detect the increases in blood oxygenation caused by cell firing because oxygenated

hemoglobin (the molecule that carries oxygen in the blood and provides the red color) has a different magnetic resonance signal than oxygen-depleted hemoglobin. Functional MRI offers several advantages over PET. First, fMRI provides both anatomical and functional information for each subject, and the detail of the image is far superior. Second, because the individual does not have to be injected with radioactive material, the measures can be made repeatedly to show changes over time. For the same reason, the procedure is essentially risk free, except for the occasional case of claustrophobia caused by the scanner. Third, the process is so rapid that brain activity can be monitored in real time (i.e., as it is occurring). In combination with recording of electrical activity with electroencephalography (see the next section), fMRI can produce three-dimensional images that show neural activity in interconnecting networks of brain centers. Temporal sequencing of information processing becomes possible, so one can see the changing locations of brain

(A) Multichannel EEG recording

(B)

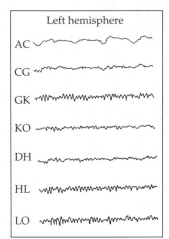

Figure 4.24 Electroencephalography (EEG) (A) In humans, changes in electrical activity of the brain are detected by recording electrodes that are attached to the surface of the individual's scalp. The electrodes record the activity of thousands of cells simultaneously. (B) Example of a typical electroencephalogram showing the differences in electrical potential between specific locations on the scalp.

activity during tasks and cognitive processes. For an excellent introduction to brain imaging and its relationship to cognitive processes, refer to Posner and Raichle (1994).

Pharmacological MRI (phMRI), a spin-off of fMRI, has developed into an important technique in drug development. Among its many uses, it provides the capability to investigate the mechanism of drug action by analyzing changes in brain function following drug administration. Second, it provides important information on the location of drug action within the CNS. Other important functions in early clinical studies include the ability to evaluate relationships between drug dose, drug plasma levels, brain receptor occupancy (using PET), and changes in brain function. Further, visualizing the time course of drug action can provide pharmacokinetic data. Finally, it has the potential to predict treatment response, avoiding weeks of treatment that often is needed to ultimately see a measurable clinical response. It could do this by screening patients' brain function profiles in response to the drug to determine if they will ultimately respond to that particular treatment. This use of phMRI would be an important tool in personalized medicine (see Chapter 1) by matching a given treatment to those individuals most likely to show beneficial results, and avoiding expensive and time-consuming treatment of a patient who will not have a good treatment outcome. This would be particularly important for high-risk, high-cost treatments, or those taking months to show clinical effectiveness.

ELECTROENCEPHALOGRAPHY (EEG) In addition to improved visualization techniques and methods of mapping metabolic function in the human brain, a third noninvasive method of investigating human brain activity is now used often in neuropharmacology: electrical recording with **electroencephalography (EEG)**. Electrodes are taped to the scalp in several locations (**Figure 4.24A**), and the electrical activity that is recorded reflects the sum of electrical events of populations of neurons. Multiple electrodes are used because a comparison of the signals from various locations can identify the origin of some waves. Although the method cannot identify specific cells that are active, it has been useful in studies of consciousness, sleep, and dreaming, as well as in studies of seizure activity. **Figure 4.24B** shows typical EEG records. Computer analysis of EEG signals can produce a color-coded map of brain electrical activity, which allows visualization of electrical response to changing stimuli. Brain electrical activity mapping (BEAM) is one of the available display systems. Because EEG can detect electrical events in real time, it is very useful for recording electrical changes that occur in response to momentary sensory stimulation; these changes are called **event-related potentials**, or sensory evoked potentials. Evaluation of electrical responses in various clinical populations has led to improved understanding of attention deficits and processing differences in individuals with schizophrenia, Huntington's disease, attention deficit hyperactivity disorder, and so forth.

Genetic engineering helps neuroscientists to ask and answer new questions

The excitement surrounding completion of the Human Genome Project, in which all human genetic material has been mapped, has permeated both the scientific and the popular press. Although the term *genetic engineering* evokes both excitement and some trepidation in most people, the technology has at the very least provided amazing opportunities for neuroscience. Genetic engineering involves procedures in which the DNA of the organism is altered (knockouts or knockins), or a foreign gene is added to the genetic material of the organism (transgenic). These procedures

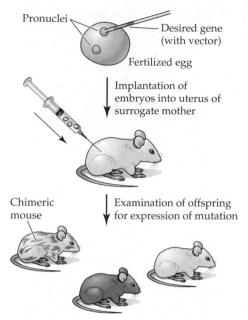

Pronuclei

Desired gene
(with vector)

Fertilized egg

Implantation of
embryos into uterus of
surrogate mother

Chimeric
mouse

Examination of offspring
for expression of mutation

Breeding of chimeric offspring to ultimately
produce homozygous transgenic mice

Figure 4.25 Illustration of genetic engineering Genetic
material is extracted from cells, injected into fertilized
eggs, and implanted in the uterus of a surrogate mother.
Offspring that are chimeric are mated with wild-type mice.
Any of their offspring that are heterozygous for the genetic
trait of interest are subsequently mated to produce some
homozygous mice of interest.

provide the opportunity to produce highly specific
mutations in the mouse genome to study subsequent
changes in brain function and behavior. **Figure 4.25**
shows the essential steps in genetic engineering.
Genes of interest are extracted or extracted and modified and then are injected into fertilized mouse eggs
taken from a pregnant mouse. After the injection procedure, the eggs are implanted in the uterus of a surrogate mother. Offspring are assessed for evidence of
the mutation. Chimeric mice, that is, those in which
the transgene is expressed in some cells and not in others, are subsequently mated with wild-type mice. The
offspring from these matings produce some heterozygous mice (i.e., those having one transgene and one
wild-type) that in turn will be mated to other heterozygous mice to ultimately produce some mice homozygous for the transgene. Because the gestation time
of the mouse is approximately 3 months, the entire
procedure takes about 9 to 12 months.

Creating **knockout mice** may represent the most
sophisticated of all lesioning techniques yet described.
With the ability to identify which piece of chromosomal DNA (i.e., the gene) is responsible for directing
the synthesis of a particular protein, neuroscience has
the opportunity to alter that gene, causing a change

in expression of the protein. In essence, we are producing an animal model that lacks a particular protein (e.g., enzyme, ion channel, receptor), so that we
can evaluate post-lesioning behavior. Comparing the
behavior and the drug response of altered mice with
those of unaltered animals will tell us about the function of the protein that has been deleted. We can also
use these animals to identify the importance of that
protein in specific drug effects.

In contrast to the knockout technique, to create
knockin mice, the inserted gene is modified so that it
produces a slightly different protein from that found
in wild-type mice. Often the protein manufactured
is different from that of normal mice by only a single
amino acid residue, allowing investigation of the relationship between protein structure and function. For
neuropharmacologists, the protein of interest is often a
receptor subtype or an enzyme that controls an important synthesizing or metabolizing process.

A second strategy involves the substitution of one
gene for another, producing **transgenic mice**. As we
learn more about the pathological genes responsible
for neuropsychiatric diseases such as Huntington's
and Alzheimer's diseases, it is possible to remove the
human genes and insert them into mice to produce
true animal models of the disorders. For an example,
see the work by Carter and coworkers (1999), which
measures motor deficits in mice transgenic for Huntington's disease (**Box 4.3**). With authentic animal
models, neuroscience will be able to identify the cellular processes responsible for a disorder and develop
appropriate treatments.

As is true for any revolutionary new technique,
caution in interpreting the results is warranted. First,
because behaviors are regulated not by single genes
but by multiple interacting genes, changing or eliminating only one alters only a small part of the overall
behavioral trait. Second, compensation by other genes
for the missing or overexpressed gene may mask
the functional effect of the mutation. Third, since the
altered gene function occurs in all tissues at all stages
of development, it is possible that changes in other
organs or in other brain areas are responsible for the
behavioral changes. Finally, because these animals
are developing organisms, environmental factors also
have a significant effect on the ultimate gene expression. Several articles provide greater detail on the
potential pitfalls of gene-targeting studies (Crawley,
1996; Gerlai, 1996; Lathe, 1996).

In addition to its use in creating "mutant" animals,
the genetic material can be inserted into cells (maintained in cell culture) that do not normally have a particular protein (e.g., receptor). The normal cell division
process produces large numbers of identically altered
cells, which we call **cloning**. These cells can then be

BOX 4.3 Pharmacology in Action

Transgenic Model of Huntington's Disease

Huntington's disease (HD) is characterized by progressive impairment in movement, such as slow, uncoordinated actions, involuntary jerking, and impaired gait, posture, and balance. Additionally, individuals develop cognitive dysfunction, which includes difficulty planning, lack of flexibility in thinking, poor impulse control, inability to focus attention, learning deficits, and others. Furthermore, there are marked mood and personality changes accompanied by a variety of psychiatric disorders. Further details of the symptoms of this disease, its progression, and approaches to treatment can be found in Chapter 21. This genetically transmitted disease strikes individuals when they are in their 30s and 40s and progresses over time. Individuals typically live 15 to 20 years after onset of symptoms, which means that their life span is significantly shortened. At

(A) Beam walking Mice were taught to walk across square or round elevated beams to reach an enclosed safety platform. The time to cross and the number of foot slips were recorded. Each data point represents the mean time to cross. (After Carter et al., 1999.)

present, although some symptoms can be treated initially, no treatment is available to modify the course of the disease. What is needed is a translational animal model of the disease that would lead to improved drug development.

Using a host of behavioral measures, Carter and colleagues (1999) characterized the progressive neurological symptoms in a model created by inserting the human Huntington's disease gene (R6/2) into mice. Because patients with HD show a variety of gradually worsening motoric deficits and progressive hypoactivity, a battery of tests measuring the motor function of the transgenic mice was started at 5 to 6 weeks of age and administered weekly for 10 weeks. Functioning of the transgenic mice was compared with that of wild-type control mice. To evaluate fine motor coordination and balance, the investigators used **beam walking**, which resembles a human gymnastic balance beam. They found no difference in performance between R6/2 transgenic mice and wild-type control mice at 5 to 6 weeks of age on either the raised square or the

round beam, although R6/2 mice were somewhat slower in performing the task (Figure A). However, by 8 to 9 weeks of age, the R6/2 mice took twelve times as long and made many more paw slips. At 13 to 14 weeks, many of the transgenic mice fell off the beam repeatedly. Motor coordination and balance were further evaluated on a **rotarod**—a horizontally oriented cylinder that is mechanically rotated at set speeds (Figure B). The researchers timed how long the mice remained on the rod (i.e., latency to fall). As you can see in Figure C, control mice readily maintained their balance and coordination for the maximum trial length at all speeds tested. In contrast, transgenic mice had difficulty at the highest speeds at 5 to 6 weeks, and by 13 to 14 weeks, they failed to maintain their coordination at any speed. When their **swimming performance** was examined at 5 to 6 weeks, R6/2 mice showed overall slowness, a tendency to float temporarily without making efforts to swim, and significant

(Continued on next page)

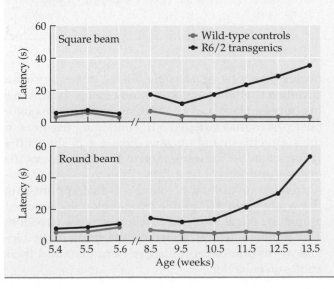

BOX 4.3 *(continued)*

(B) Rotarod

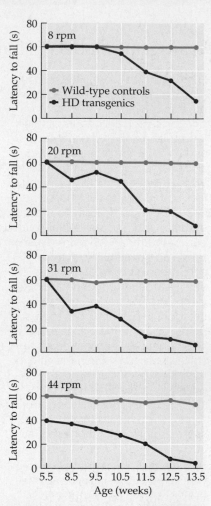

(C) Rotarod performance Data points represent the mean latency to fall (maximum trial length = 60 seconds) from the rotarod at various speeds of rotation. (After Carter et al., 1999.)

incoordination in swim movements that progressively worsened over time. Additionally, rather than the fluid, coordinated **gait** shown by healthy mice, transgenic mice showed staggering and weaving with uneven short strides, reminiscent of the patient with HD. In a final task, researchers examined the startle reflex to an intensely loud sound. Transgenic mice showed a decline in response only at the final time point. More important, the acoustic startle response is normally reduced when the intense stimulus is preceded by a small prepulse stimulus. Patients with HD characteristically show a deficit in that **prepulse inhibition of startle**. Likewise by 8 weeks, the transgenic mice showed significant deficits.

A variety of behavioral measures that reflect the symptoms of HD show clearly that R6/2 mice represent a valid model of the motoric deficits that gradually appear in patients with HD. Subsequent studies have shown other analogous characteristics, including the development of diabetes, deficits in spatial learning, shortened life span, and a host of pathological changes in the brain. You might be interested in reading more about these animals and some of the newer drugs tested on them that target progressive brain pathology and gene transcription. It is hoped that these drugs may become effective agents in preventing the progression of this devastating disease (Li et al., 2005).

used to screen new drugs using conventional pharmacological techniques for identifying agonists and antagonists.

A variation of gene modification uses short-term manipulations of genetic material by intraventricular injection of **antisense nucleotides** that bind to targeted mRNAs, delay their translation, and increase their degradation. Such treatment produces a reversible "mutant" animal, whose behavior or drug responsiveness can be evaluated. For instance, earlier research suggested that a decrease in the function of the neuropeptide called vasoactive intestinal peptide (VIP) in the hypothalamus (specifically, the suprachiasmatic

nucleus) may be responsible for the disturbances in circadian rhythm that occur during aging. To test this hypothesis, Harney et al. (1996) used antisense oligonucleotides that targeted VIP-containing neurons in the suprachiasmatic nucleus. **Figure 4.26** shows the reduction in VIP concentration in the suprachiasmatic nucleus at different times after antisense administration. What investigators found was that suppressing the synthesis of VIP in this brain region does indeed mimic the effect of age on cyclic hormone secretion. This technique is well suited for the study of the biological rhythm of reproductive hormones and their effects on behavior.

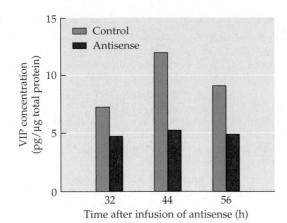

Figure 4.26 Effect of antisense on protein synthesis
Vasoactive intestinal peptide (VIP) concentrations in the suprachiasmatic nucleus of the hypothalamus are significantly reduced in animals treated with antisense oligonucleotides directed at VIP mRNA as compared with control animals. The decrease in VIP is apparent at each of the times measured. (After Harney et al., 1996.)

Behavioral and neuropharmacological methods complement one another

Bear in mind that under normal circumstances, several of these techniques are used in tandem to approach a problem in neuroscience from several directions (see **Web Box 4.1**). The power of these experimental tools is that when they are used together, a more reasonable picture emerges, and conflicting results can be incorporated into the larger picture. Only in this way can we uncover the neurobiological substrates of cognitive function and dysfunction. In every case, interpretation of these sophisticated approaches is subject to the same scrutiny required by the earliest lesion experiments. Remember, healthy skepticism is central to the scientific method.

Section Summary

- Using a stereotaxic device, lesioning destroys brain cells in selected areas with high-frequency radio current. More selective lesions are made by injecting an excitatory neurotoxin that destroys cell bodies in the region without damaging axons passing through, or by injecting a neurotoxin selective for a given neurotransmitter.

- Using a specialized cannula, microdialysis allows researchers to collect material from extracellular fluid from deep within the brain in a freely moving animal, so corresponding changes in behavior can be monitored simultaneously. The material is analyzed and quantified by high-pressure liquid

chromatography. In vivo voltammetry is a second way to measure the neurotransmitter released into the synapse.

- Macroelectrodes that are stereotaxically implanted are used to electrically stimulate deep brain regions while monitoring behavioral changes. They can also record electrical response following drug treatment or other experimental manipulation. Microelectrodes can record electrical activity from a single cell either inside the cell (intracellular) or near a single cell (extracellular).

- The function of individual ion channels is monitored with patch clamp electrophysiology.

- The radioligand binding method evaluates the number and affinity of specific receptor molecules in tissue homogenates. Verification of binding requires proof of selectivity, saturability, reversibility, high affinity, and biological relevance.

- To visualize the location of receptors in the brain, receptor autoradiography, both in vitro and in vivo, is used.

- The ability to make antibodies to proteins allows more precise cellular localization of receptors or other protein cell components such as enzymes with ICC. Antibodies are also used to very sensitively measure important molecules in body fluids or tissue extracts using radioimmunoassays that depend on competitive binding of an antibody to its antigen.

- ICC identifies cells that *contain* a given protein; the complementary technique ISH is used to locate cells in a tissue slice that are *manufacturing* a particular protein by detecting the corresponding mRNA. It can also determine changes in mRNA levels, which provide an estimate of the rate of synthesis of that protein. Although ISH measures a single mRNA, microarrays (or gene chips) screen up to 20,000 genes on a single support (chip). The entire genome can be screened in one experiment with the use of just a few chips.

- Although they use two distinct scanning technologies, CT and MRI create extremely detailed "slices" through the brain of living subjects that can also be displayed as a three-dimensional image. Their excellent detail of brain structure depends on computer analysis.

- PET maps the distribution of a radioactively labeled substance that has been injected into an individual. A labeled drug or ligand is administered to identify where drugs bind, and to localize neurotransmitter receptors. It can also allow visualization of regional brain activity during task performance, which is reflected in increased glucose utilization, oxygen use, and blood flow, depending on the reagent labeled. SPECT depends on similar technology at a lower cost but with less resolution.

- Functional MRI (fMRI) provides both anatomical and functional imaging of the human brain by allowing visualization of changes in regional blood oxygenation caused by cell firing. It monitors brain activity as it is occurring and, unlike PET, it requires no radioactivity. Pharmacological MRI utilizes fMRI to image brain function following drug administration, provides information on the location of drug action and pharmacokinetic data, and potentially can predict patient treatment response.

- EEG utilizes electrodes placed on the scalp of humans to measure the electrical activity of populations of neurons. Computer analysis of the data produces color-coded maps of brain activity in response to brief sensory stimulation.

- Deleting a specific gene in mice produces an animal model that lacks a particular protein (knockout) in order to evaluate post-lesion behavior and drug effects. Knockin mice have a gene inserted, so they produce a slightly different protein than is produced by wild-type mice. Transgenic mice are mice in which one gene is replaced by another.

- Antisense nucleotides that bind to targeted mRNAs produce a reversible mutant animal, whose behavior and drug response can be evaluated.

Go to the **COMPANION WEBSITE**

sites.sinauer.com/psychopharm2e
for Web Boxes, animations, flashcards, and other study resources.

Recommended readings

Buccafusco, J. (Ed.). (2009). *Methods of Behavior Analysis in Neuroscience* (2nd ed.). Frontiers in Neuroscience series. Boca Raton: CRC Press. Available online at: www.ncbi.nlm.nih.gov/books/NBK5228/

Buccafusco, J. J., Terry, A. V. Jr., Webster, S. J., Martin, D., Hohnadel, E. J., Bouchard, K. A., and Warner, S. E. (2008). The scopolamine-reversal paradigm in rats and monkeys: The importance of computer-assisted operant-conditioning memory tasks for screening drug candidates. *Psychopharmacology*, 199, 481–494.

Demeter, E., Sarter, M., and Lustig, C. (2008). Rats and humans paying attention: Cross-species task development for translational research. *Neuropsychology*, 22, 787–799.

Geyer, M. A. and Markou, A. (2002). The role of preclinical models in the development of psychotropic drugs. In K. David, D. Charney, J. T. Coyle, and C. Nemeroff (Eds.), *Neuropsychopharmacology: The Fifth Generation of Progress* (pp. 445–455). New York: Lippincott, Williams, and Wilkins. Available online at: www.acnp.org/publications/neuro5thgeneration.aspx

O'Brien, C. P. and Gardner, E. L. (2005). Critical assessment of how to study addiction and its treatment: Human and non-human animal models. *Pharmacol. Ther.*, 108, 18–58.

Porter, J. H. and Prus, A. J. (2009). Drug discrimination: 30 years of progress. *Psychopharmacology*, 203, 189–191.

Tecott, L. H. and Johnson, D. S. (2002). Gene targeting and transgenic technologies. In K. David, D. Charney, J. T. Coyle, and C. Nemeroff (Eds.), *Neuropsychopharmacology: The Fifth Generation of Progress* (pp. 241–251). New York: Lippincott, Williams, and Wilkins. Available online at: www.acnp.org/publications/neuro5thgeneration.aspx

Ward, R. D., Simpson, E. H., Kandel, E. R., and Balsam, P. D. (2011). Modeling motivational deficits in mouse models of schizophrenia: Behavior analysis as a guide for neuroscience. *Behav. Processes*, 87, 149–156.

Zhang, D. and Raichle, M. E. (2010). Disease and the brain's dark energy. *Nat. Rev. Neurol.*, 6, 15–28.

Students are increasingly turning to powerful stimulant drugs to stay awake and increase their concentration while studying.

Catecholamines 5

IF YOU ARE A COLLEGE STUDENT READING THIS CHAPTER, you probably have heard of so-called study drugs. Maybe you have taken them from time to time while pulling an all-nighter to finish up a term paper or study for final exams, but even if you haven't taken such drugs yourself, you probably know classmates who have. When the authors of this textbook were in college, we and most other members of our student generation relied just on caffeine in coffee or pills (e.g., NoDoz) to get us through these tough situations. However, in recent years, there has been a disturbing trend for more powerful stimulants such as amphetamine (Adderall) and methylphenidate (Ritalin) to be diverted from prescribed medical uses to nonprescribed uses such as staying awake to study. These drugs are often widely available on college campuses because of their use in the treatment of attention deficit hyperactivity disorder (ADHD). Students with ADHD who have legitimate prescriptions for Adderall or Ritalin may give away their pills to other students or sell them for a profit. Concerns about the nonmedical use of stimulants as study drugs are receiving growing attention not only in the scientific literature (Bogle and Smith, 2009; Garnier-Dykstra et al., 2012; Wilens et al., 2008) but also in the mass media (e.g., Cooper, 2011; D'Addario, 2010; Trudeau, 2009) and even in college newspapers (Battle, 2010; Hattoff, 2012).

In Chapter 12, we will present a detailed discussion of the mechanisms of action of amphetamine and methylphenidate, their application to the treatment of ADHD, and the risks associated with nonmedical use of these drugs. However, we have introduced the topic here because the therapeutic benefits, as well as the other effects of these compounds (e.g., increased arousal, reduced need for sleep), derive from their ability to produce massive increases in the synaptic levels of two neurotransmitters: **dopamine (DA)** and **norepinephrine (NE)**. These substances, along with the related compound **epinephrine (EPI)**,

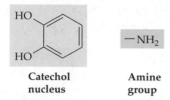

Figure 5.1 Structural features of catecholamines
A catechol nucleus and an amine group are found in all catecholamines.

make up a small but important group of neurotransmitters and hormones called **catecholamines**. The term catecholamine is derived from the fact that the members of this group all share two chemical similarities: a core structure of catechol and a nitrogen-containing group called an amine (**Figure 5.1**). The catecholamines, in turn, belong to a wider group of transmitters called either **monoamines** (transmitters that possess one amine group) or **biogenic amines** ("biogenic" refers to compounds made by living organisms). EPI and NE are sometimes called adrenaline and noradrenaline, respectively. It is important to note that the adjective forms for these substances are **adrenergic** and **noradrenergic**, although the term adrenergic is sometimes used broadly to refer to NE- as well as EPI-related features. The adjective form for DA is **dopaminergic**. Varying amounts of these substances are found within the central nervous system, the peripheral nervous system, and the inner part of the adrenal glands (adrenal medulla). The adrenal medulla secretes EPI and NE into the bloodstream, where they act as hormones. You will recall from Chapter 3 that stimulation of catecholamine secretion from the adrenal glands is a vital part of the physiological response to stress.

The main emphasis in this chapter is on DA and NE, as the neurotransmitter function of EPI is relatively minor. We begin by considering the basic neurochemistry of the catecholamines, including their synthesis, release, and inactivation. This will be followed by a discussion of the neural systems for DA and NE, including the anatomy of these systems, the receptors for DA and NE, and some of the drugs that act on these receptors.

Catecholamine Synthesis, Release, and Inactivation

The overall level of catecholamine neurotransmission depends on a complex interplay between neurotransmitter synthesis, release, and inactivation. Understanding each of these steps enables pharmacologists to design drugs that can modulate catecholamine activity, either for therapeutic or experimental purposes.

Tyrosine hydroxylase catalyzes the rate-limiting step in catecholamine synthesis

Classical transmitters (see Chapter 3) like the catecholamines are manufactured in one or more biochemical steps. These synthetic pathways offer neurons a mechanism for regulating the amount of transmitter available for release. At the same time, they offer us the opportunity to intervene with drugs that alter transmitter synthesis in specific ways. For example, we may administer a precursor that will be converted biochemically into a particular neurotransmitter. One application of this approach is seen in neurological disorders in which the neurons that make a certain transmitter have been damaged. Precursor therapy represents an attempt to boost transmitter synthesis and release in the remaining undamaged cells. Alternatively, we may give subjects a drug that blocks a step in the biochemical pathway, thereby causing a depletion of the transmitter synthesized by that pathway. Neurotransmitter depletion is not as widely used clinically, but nevertheless, it can be valuable in certain experimental settings.

The synthesis of catecholamine neurotransmitters occurs in several steps, as shown in **Figure 5.2**. The biochemical pathway begins with the amino acid **tyrosine**. Like other amino acids, tyrosine is obtained from dietary protein and is transported from the blood into the brain. Each of the steps in catecholamine formation depends on a specific enzyme that acts as a catalyst (an agent that increases the rate of a chemical reaction) for that step. Neurons that use DA as their transmitter contain only the first two enzymes, **tyrosine hydroxylase (TH)** and **aromatic amino acid decarboxylase (AADC)**, and thus the biochemical pathway stops at DA. In contrast, neurons that need to synthesize NE also possess the third enzyme, which is called **dopamine β-hydroxylase (DBH)**.[1]

The conversion of tyrosine to dihydroxyphenylalanine (DOPA) by TH occurs at a slower rate than subsequent reactions in the biochemical pathway. Consequently, TH is the **rate-limiting enzyme** in the pathway because it determines the overall rate of DA or NE formation. The activity of TH is regulated by a variety of factors, including how much DA or NE is present within the nerve terminal. High catecholamine levels tend to inhibit TH, thus serving as a negative feedback mechanism. Another important factor is

---

[1]It is worth noting some of the basics of how enzymes are named. Hydroxylases like TH and DBH add a hydroxyl group (–OH) to the molecule they're acting on. A decarboxylase like AADC removes a carboxyl group (–COOH) from the molecule. These reactions can be seen by following the biochemical pathway shown in Figure 5.2.

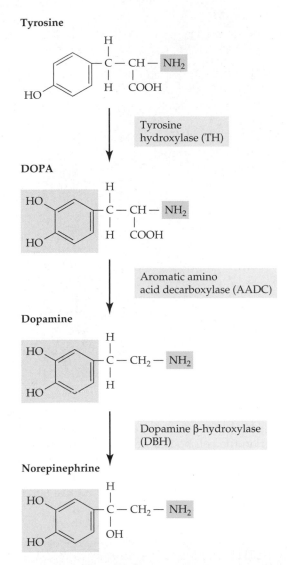

Figure 5.2 Multistep pathway of catecholamine synthesis Catecholamines are synthesized from the precursor amino acid tyrosine. Tyrosine hydroxylase and aromatic amino acid decarboxylase are found in all catecholaminergic neurons, whereas dopamine β-hydroxylase is present only in cells that use NE as their neurotransmitter.

the rate of cell firing because neuronal activity has a stimulatory effect on TH. These elegant mechanisms enable dopaminergic and noradrenergic neurons to carefully control their rate of neurotransmitter formation. When the levels are too high, TH is inhibited and catecholamine synthesis is slowed. But when the neurons are activated and firing at a high rate, such as during stress, TH is stimulated and catecholamine synthesis accelerates to keep up with the increased demand. Although the enzymes involved in synthesizing catecholamines (as well as other classical transmitters like acetylcholine and serotonin) can be found throughout the neurons using those transmitters, the rate of synthesis is greatest at the nerve endings near

the sites of transmitter release. As mentioned in Chapter 3, this is important for the refilling of recycling vesicles.

As would be expected from our earlier discussion, catecholamine formation can be increased by the administration of a biochemical precursor such as L-DOPA. Indeed, for many years, this compound has been the primary therapeutic agent used in the treatment of Parkinson's disease. Drugs that reduce catecholamine synthesis by inhibiting one of the synthetic enzymes are not as clinically important, but they have had widespread use in both animal and human research. The best example is a drug known as α-methyl-*para*-tyrosine (**AMPT**). This compound blocks TH, thereby preventing overall catecholamine synthesis and causing a general depletion of these neurotransmitters. In a group of psychiatric studies reviewed by Booij and colleagues (2003), AMPT treatment caused a return of depressive symptoms in many patients who had been successfully treated with antidepressant medication. These findings suggest that at least in patients that exhibited increased symptomatology, recovery was dependent on the maintenance of adequate catecholamine levels in the brain.

Catecholamines are stored in and released from synaptic vesicles

Once catecholamines have been synthesized, they are transported into synaptic vesicles for later release (**Figure 5.3**). Vesicular packaging is important not only because it provides a means of releasing a predetermined amount of neurotransmitter (usually several thousand molecules per vesicle), but also because it protects the neurotransmitter from degradation by enzymes within the nerve terminal (see the next section). A specific protein in the vesicle membrane is responsible for vesicular catecholamine uptake. This protein recognizes several different monoamine transmitters and therefore is called the **vesicular monoamine transporter** (**VMAT**). There are actually two related VMATs: VMAT1 is found in the adrenal medulla, whereas VMAT2 is present in the brain. Both of these vesicular transporters are blocked by an interesting drug called **reserpine**, which comes from the roots of the plant *Rauwolfia serpentina* (snake root). Blocking the vesicular transporter means that DA and NE are no longer protected from breakdown within the nerve terminal. As a result, both transmitters temporarily drop to very low levels in the brain. The behavioral consequence of this neurochemical effect is sedation in animals and depressive symptoms in humans. Many years ago, a study by the eminent Swedish pharmacologist Arvid Carlsson and his colleagues (Carlsson et al., 1957) showed that the sedative

Figure 5.3 Catecholaminergic neurons use a vesicular monoamine transporter protein (VMAT2) to transport neurotransmitter molecules from the cytoplasm of the cell to the interior of the synaptic vesicles. This transport system is blocked by reserpine, which causes a marked depletion of catecholamine levels resulting from a lack of protection of the transmitter from metabolizing enzymes located outside of the vesicles.

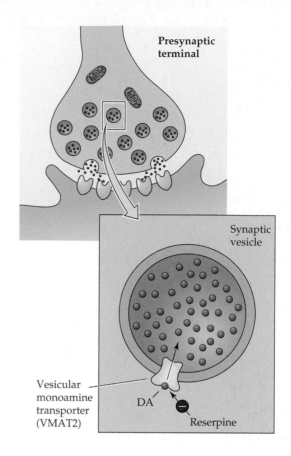

effects of reserpine could be reversed by restoration of catecholamines with DOPA, the immediate biochemical precursor of DA (**Figure 5.4**). Carlsson's work, which played a key role in the development of the catecholamine theory of depression (see Chapter 19), resulted in his being a co-recipient of the 2000 Nobel Prize in Physiology or Medicine.

Release of catecholamines normally occurs when a nerve impulse enters the terminal and triggers one or more vesicles to release their contents into the synaptic cleft through the process of exocytosis (see Chapter 3). Certain drugs, however, can cause a release of catecholamines independently of nerve cell firing. The most important of these compounds are the psychostimulants **amphetamine and methamphetamine**. In contrast to the behavioral sedation associated with reserpine-induced catecholamine depletion, catecholamine release leads to behavioral activation. In laboratory animals such as rats and mice, this activation may be shown by increased locomotor activity. At high doses, locomotor activation is replaced by **stereotyped behaviors** consisting of intense sniffing, repetitive head and limb movements, and licking and biting. Researchers believe that locomotion and stereotyped behaviors represent a continuum of behavioral activation that stems from increasing stimulation of DA receptors in the nucleus accumbens and striatum. In humans, amphetamine and methamphetamine produce increased alertness, heightened energy, euphoria, insomnia, and other behavioral effects (see Chapter 12).

Catecholamine release is inhibited by autoreceptors located on the cell bodies, terminals, and dendrites of dopaminergic and noradrenergic neurons. Terminal autoreceptors and other features of a typical dopaminergic neuron are illustrated in **Figure 5.5**. Recent

(A)

(B)

Figure 5.4 Role of catecholamine depletion in the behavioral depressant effects of reserpine (A) Rabbits injected with reserpine (5 mg/kg IV) showed extreme behavioral sedation that was reversed by subsequent treatment with DOPA (200 mg/kg IV) (B). (From Carlsson, 2001; photographs courtesy of Arvid Carlsson.)

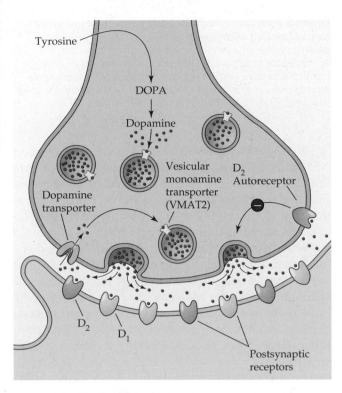

Figure 5.5 A typical dopaminergic neuron possesses autoreceptors on the membrane of its terminals. When these receptors are stimulated, they inhibit subsequent DA release by the cell.

varicosities in the lateral geniculate nucleus (part of the thalamus) of a 21-day-old rat (Latsari et al., 2004). One can readily see the numerous varicosities along each axon that release NE onto postsynaptic neurons in this brain area.

As will be discussed below, the DA and NE systems possess several different subtypes of receptors. Here we will just mention that the DA autoreceptor is of the D_2 receptor subtype, and the NE autoreceptor is of the α_2 subtype. For technical reasons, it has been extremely difficult to determine how important these autoreceptors are for the normal functioning of catecholamine neurons and in terms of their responses to various pharmacological agents. However, Bello and colleagues (2011) recently developed a powerful genetic method for deleting the D_2 receptor gene *just* from the DA neurons in mice, thus eliminating the DA autoreceptors but allowing normal expression of postsynaptic D_2 receptors (i.e., D_2 receptors in non-DA neurons). Results showed that the DA neurons from the mutant mice released more DA, that the mice mutants were more spontaneously active than controls (we will see later that DA plays a key role in regulating locomotor activity), and that the animals were more sensitive to the behavioral effects of

evidence indicates that at least in the case of DA, these autoreceptors inhibit neurotransmitter release by enhancing the opening of a specific type of voltage-gated K^+ channel in the nerve terminal (Martel et al., 2011). One possible mechanism for this effect would be shortening the duration of action potentials entering the terminal, thereby reducing Ca^{2+} influx and vesicle exocytosis. Consequently, if a dopaminergic cell fires several action potentials in a row, we can imagine that DA released by the first few impulses stimulates the terminal autoreceptors and reduces the amount of DA released by the later action potentials. On the other hand, the somatodendritic autoreceptors function in a different way. As mentioned in Chapter 3, these autoreceptors inhibit release indirectly by reducing the rate of firing of the cell.

Although the DA nerve terminal illustrated in Figure 5.5 looks like a typical axon bouton, it is worth noting that in many parts of the nervous system, both DA and NE axons form *en passant* ("in passing") synapses in which the fibers exhibit repeated swellings (termed **varicosities**) along their length that are filled with synaptic vesicles and that represent the sites of neurotransmitter release. The photomicrograph shown in **Figure 5.6** was produced using an antibody against DBH that allowed staining of the noradrenergic

Figure 5.6 Noradrenergic fibers innervating the lateral geniculate nucleus of a 21-day-old rat show varicosities along the length of each fiber. The tissue was stained using immunocytochemistry with an antibody to DBH, and noradrenergic fibers were visualized with dark-field microscopy, which reverses the light and dark areas of the image (i.e., darkly stained fibers appear light). (From Latsari et al., 2004.)

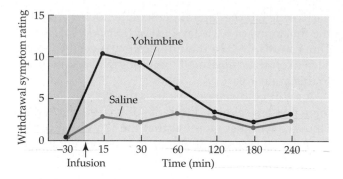

Figure 5.7 Noradrenergic activity contributes to symptoms of opioid withdrawal When opioid-dependent patients were infused intravenously either with the α_2-receptor antagonist yohimbine (0.4 mg/kg) or a saline control solution, yohimbine but not saline caused a rapid increase in experimenter-rated withdrawal symptoms over the next 60 minutes. (After Stine et al., 2002.)

cocaine (a drug that exerts many of its effects through the DA system; see Chapter 12 for more details). These findings confirm that D_2 autoreceptors are, indeed, functionally active under normal circumstances and also influence behavioral responses to dopaminergic agents.

Drugs that stimulate autoreceptors, like the neurotransmitter itself, inhibit catecholamine release. In contrast, autoreceptor antagonists tend to enhance the rate of release by preventing the normal inhibitory effect of the autoreceptors. We can see these effects illustrated dramatically in the case of the noradrenergic α_2-autoreceptor system. Withdrawal from opioid drugs such as heroin and morphine activates the noradrenergic system, which is one of the factors leading to withdrawal symptoms such as increased heart rate, elevated blood pressure, and diarrhea. For this reason, α_2-agonists such as **clonidine (Catapres)** are often used to treat the symptoms of opioid withdrawal because of their ability to stimulate the autoreceptors and inhibit noradrenergic cell firing. In contrast, experimental administration of the α_2-antagonist **yohimbine**, which blocks the autoreceptors and thus increases noradrenergic cell firing and NE release, was found to provoke withdrawal symptoms and drug craving in opioid-dependent patients (Stine et al., 2002) (**Figure 5.7**). Norepinephrine may also be involved in producing feelings of anxiety, especially in patients suffering from a mental illness called *panic disorder* (see Chapter 18). Consequently, yohimbine induces anxiety in such patients and may even trigger a panic attack (Charney et al., 1998). Such an effect obviously provides no therapeutic benefit, but it has yielded useful research information related to a possible role for NE in panic disorder and other anxiety-related disturbances.

Catecholamine inactivation occurs through the combination of reuptake and metabolism

Inactivation of catecholamines depends on the two different kinds of processes first mentioned in Chapter

3. The first process is reuptake. Much of the DA and NE that is released synaptically is taken up again into the nerve terminal by means of specific transporter proteins in the nerve cell membrane. That is, dopaminergic neurons contain a **DA transporter** (see Figure 5.5), whereas noradrenergic neurons contain a slightly different protein that is logically called the **NE transporter**. After the neurotransmitter molecules are returned to the terminal, some of them are repackaged into vesicles for re-release, and the remainder are broken down and eliminated. It is important to keep in mind that neurotransmitter transporters differ from the autoreceptors discussed earlier in terms of both structure and function.

The importance of reuptake for catecholamine functioning can be seen when the DA or NE transporter is missing. For example, mutant mice lacking a functional gene for the DA transporter do not show the typical behavioral activation in response to psychostimulants like cocaine or amphetamine, whereas genetic deletion of the NE transporter gene causes increased sensitivity to these same drugs (F. Xu et al., 2000). A role for the NE transporter in cardiovascular function was demonstrated by a case study of identical twins carrying a mutation of the NE transporter gene (Shannon et al., 2000). These patients exhibited abnormally high NE levels in the bloodstream, along with heart rate and blood pressure abnormalities. These findings are consistent with animal studies showing that transporter-mediated uptake plays a vital role in the normal regulation of catecholamine activity.

Since the transporters are necessary for the rapid removal of catecholamines from the synaptic cleft, transporter-blocking drugs enhance the synaptic transmission of DA or NE by increasing the amount of neurotransmitter in the synaptic cleft. This is an important mechanism of action of several kinds of psychoactive drugs, including the **tricyclic antidepressants**, which inhibit the reuptake of both NE and the non-catecholamine transmitter serotonin (5-HT) (see Chapter 19). There are also a few compounds in clinical use that more selectively inhibit NE uptake by blocking the NE transporter. These include **reboxetine (Edronax)**, which is an antidepressant drug, and **atomoxetine (Strattera)**, which is used in the treatment of ADHD. Finally, another important transporter-blocking drug is **cocaine**, which inhibits the reuptake of all three major monoamine transmitters: DA, NE, and 5-HT (see Chapter 12).

Although reuptake can quickly terminate the synaptic actions of catecholamines, there must also be processes of metabolic breakdown to prevent excessive neurotransmitter accumulation. The breakdown of catecholamines primarily involves two enzymes: **catechol-O-methyltransferase (COMT)** and **monoamine oxidase (MAO)**. There are two types of MAO: MAO-A and MAO-B. The relative importance of each one depends on the species, the brain area, and which neurotransmitter is being metabolized. The action of COMT and MAO, either individually or together, gives rise to several catecholamine **metabolites** (breakdown products). We mention only the most important ones here. In humans, DA has only one major metabolite, which is called **homovanillic acid (HVA)**. In contrast, NE breakdown gives rise to several important compounds, including **3-methoxy-4-hydroxy-phenylglycol (MHPG)** and **vanillymandelic acid (VMA)**. Metabolism of NE within the brain primarily leads to MHPG, whereas VMA is the more common metabolite in the peripheral nervous system. The brain metabolites HVA and MHPG make their way into the cerebrospinal fluid for subsequent clearance from the brain into the bloodstream and, along with VMA, are eventually excreted in the urine. Levels of these substances in the various fluid compartments (i.e., blood and urine for all three metabolites, and cerebrospinal fluid for HVA and MHPG) provide a rough indication of catecholaminergic activity in the nervous system. Such measurements have sometimes been used to help discern the possible involvement of these neurotransmitters in mental disorders such as depression and schizophrenia (see Chapters 19 and 20).

Not surprisingly, drugs that inhibit catecholamine-metabolizing enzymes lead to an accumulation of these transmitters. Historically, this has been most important in the case of **MAO inhibitors** such as **phenelzine (Nardil)** or **tranylcypromine (Parnate)**, both of which are nonselective MAO inhibitors (i.e., they block both MAO-A and MAO-B) that have long been used in the treatment of clinical depression (see Chapter 19 for additional discussion of the use of MAO inhibitors in depression). More recently, COMT inhibitors such as **entacapone (Comtan)** and **tolcapone (Tasmar)** are being used as supplemental therapies to enhance the effectiveness of L-DOPA in treating Parkinson's disease. This is done not so much to prevent the metabolism of DA but rather to block the metabolism of L-DOPA by COMT before the precursor reaches the brain.

Section Summary

- The major catecholamine transmitters in the brain are DA and NE.
- Catecholamines are synthesized in several steps from the amino acid tyrosine. The first, and also rate-limiting, step in this biochemical pathway is catalyzed by the enzyme TH.
- Once they have been synthesized, catecholamines are stored in synaptic vesicles for subsequent release.
- The process of release is controlled by inhibitory autoreceptors located on the cell body, dendrites, and terminals of catecholamine neurons. DA autoreceptors are of the D_2 subtype, whereas NE autoreceptors are of the α_2 subtype.
- Catecholamines are inactivated by reuptake from the synaptic cleft mediated by specific DA and NE transporters, and also by enzymatic degradation. MAO and COMT are two enzymes that are important in catecholamine metabolism.
- The major catecholamine metabolites are HVA for DA, and MHPG and VMA for NE.
- Certain drugs can modify catecholaminergic function by acting on the processes of synthesis, release, reuptake, or metabolism. Some of these compounds are used either clinically to treat various disorders or experimentally to study the DA or NE system.

Organization and Function of the Dopaminergic System

The dopaminergic system originates in several cell groups located primarily in the brainstem. Ascending fibers from these cells innervate a number of forebrain areas where they release DA onto five different receptor subtypes.

Two important dopaminergic cell groups are found in the midbrain

In the early 1960s, Swedish researchers first began to map the location of DA- and NE-containing nerve cells and fibers in the brain using the fluorescence method (Dahlström and Fuxe, 1964). They developed a classification system in which the catecholamine cell groups (clusters of neurons that stained for either DA or NE) were designated with the letter "A" plus a number from 1 to 16. According to this system, cell groups A1 to A7 are noradrenergic, whereas groups A8 to A16

Figure 5.8 The ascending DA system can be divided into three pathways The nigrostriatal pathway (A) originates in the substantia nigra (A9 cell cluster) and innervates the caudate–putamen (striatum). The mesolimbic pathway (B and C) originates in the VTA (A10 cell cluster) and innervates various limbic system structures such as the nucleus accumbens, hippocampus, lateral septum, and amygdala (not shown here). The mesocortical pathway (C) also originates in the VTA and innervates the cerebral cortex.

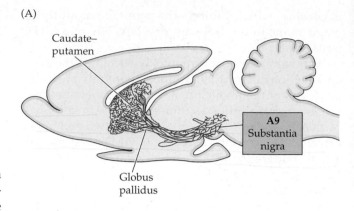

(A)

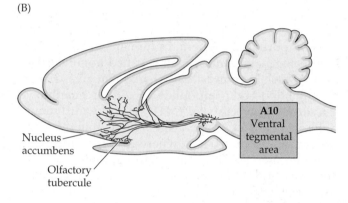

(B)

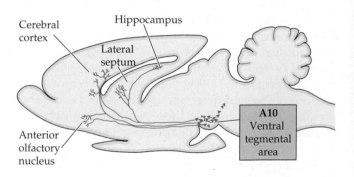

(C)

are dopaminergic. In this book, we will focus on only a few catecholaminergic cell groups that are of particular interest to psychopharmacologists. To identify the various systems arising from these cells, we will use both the Swedish classification system and standard anatomical names.

Several dense clusters of dopaminergic neuronal cell bodies are located near the base of the mesencephalon (midbrain). Particularly important is the A9 cell group, which is associated with a structure called the **substantia nigra**, and the A10 group, which is found in a nearby area called the **ventral tegmental area (VTA)**. Axons of dopaminergic neurons in the substantia nigra ascend to a forebrain structure known as the caudate–putamen or striatum. Nerve tracts in the central nervous system are often named by combining the site of origin of the fibers with their termination site. Hence, the pathway from the substantia nigra to the striatum is called the **nigrostriatal tract** (**Figure 5.8A**).

Two other important ascending dopaminergic systems arise from cells of the VTA. Some of the axons from these neurons travel to various structures of the limbic system, including the nucleus accumbens, septum, amygdala, and hippocampus. These diverse projections constitute the **mesolimbic dopamine pathway** ("meso" represents mesencephalon, which is the site of origin of the fibers; "limbic" stands for the termination of fibers in structures of the limbic system) (**Figure 5.8B**). Other DA-containing fibers from the VTA go to the cerebral cortex, particularly the prefrontal area. This group of fibers is termed the **mesocortical dopamine pathway** (**Figure 5.8C**). Together, the mesolimbic and mesocortical pathways are very important to psychopharmacologists because they have been implicated in the neural mechanisms underlying drug abuse (see Chapter 9) and also schizophrenia (see Chapter 20).

A few other sites of dopaminergic neurons can be mentioned briefly. For example, a small group of cells in the hypothalamus gives rise to the **tuberohypophyseal dopamine pathway**. This pathway is important in controlling the secretion of the hormone prolactin by the pituitary gland. There are also DA-containing neurons within sensory structures such as the olfactory bulbs and the retina.

Ascending dopamine pathways have been implicated in several important behavioral functions

One of the key functions of DA innervation of the striatum via the nigrostriatal tract is to facilitate voluntary movement. Loss of this function is illustrated dramatically in the case of Parkinson's disease, which involves a massive loss of DA neurons in the substantia nigra and consequent DA denervation of the striatum. Parkinson's disease is characterized by progressive motor dysfunction, typically beginning with tremors and advancing to postural disturbances, akinesia (lack of movement), and rigidity (see Chapter 21 for a more extensive discussion of this disorder). In experimental

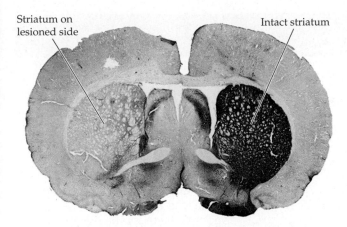

Striatum on lesioned side

Intact striatum

Figure 5.9 Damage to the nigrostriatal pathway on one side of the brain causes degeneration of dopaminergic fibers in the striatum on that side. This is shown in the photomicrograph of a tissue section through the brain of a rat that had received a unilateral 6-OHDA lesion of the medial forebrain bundle, which contains the axons of the nigrostriatal pathway. The section, which was stained using an antibody against tyrosine hydroxylase, depicts the loss of dopaminergic fibers and terminals in the striatum on the side of the lesion. (Photomicrograph courtesy of Michael Zigmond and Annie Cohen.)

animals, a range of symptoms, including those seen in Parkinson's disease, can be produced by administering **neurotoxins** that damage or destroy midbrain DA neurons and lesion their ascending pathways. Two such compounds are **6-hydroxydopamine (6-OHDA)** and **1-methyl-4-phenyl-1,2,3,6-tetrahydropyridine (MPTP)**. Although the two substances produce similar damage to the dopaminergic system with similar functional consequences, here we focus on the effects produced by 6-OHDA administration. The use of MPTP as a DA neurotoxin will be covered later in Chapter 21. To lesion the central dopaminergic system with 6-OHDA, one must inject the drug directly into the brain since it does not readily cross the blood–brain barrier. The toxin is taken up mainly by the catecholaminergic neurons (thus sparing neurons that use other neurotransmitters) because of its close structural similarity to DA. Once the toxin is inside, the nerve terminals are severely damaged, and sometimes the entire cell dies. Animals with bilateral 6-OHDA lesions of the ascending dopaminergic pathways show severe behavioral dysfunction. They exhibit sensory neglect (they pay little attention to stimuli in the environment), motivational deficits (they show little interest in eating food or drinking water), and motor impairment (like patients with Parkinson's disease, they have difficulty initiating voluntary movements). It is also possible to damage the nigrostriatal DA pathway on only one side of the brain, as illustrated in

Figure 5.9. In this case, the lesioned animals display a postural asymmetry characterized by leaning and turning toward the damaged side of the brain because of the dominance of the untreated side. The severe abnormalities seen following either bilateral or unilateral lesions of the DA system indicate how important this neurotransmitter is for many behavioral functions, not just for initiation of movement.

The profound motor disturbances associated with Parkinson's provide the most obvious and well-known evidence for the role of DA in movement regulation in humans. However, other important evidence comes from the discovery of genetic mutations that interfere with DA synthesis. These mutations and the clinical symptoms they produce are discussed in **Box 5.1.**

There are five main subtypes of dopamine receptors organized into D_1- and D_2-like families

In the previous chapter, we discussed the concept of receptor subtypes. The neurotransmitter DA uses five main subtypes, designated D_1 to D_5, all of which are metabotropic receptors. That is, they interact with G proteins and they function, in part, through second messengers. Various studies have shown that the D_1 and D_5 receptors are very similar to each other, whereas the D_2, D_3, and D_4 receptors represent a separate family. The D_1 and D_2 receptors were discovered first, and they are the most common subtypes in the brain. Both types of receptors are found in large numbers in the striatum and the nucleus accumbens, which are major termination sites of the nigrostriatal and meso-limbic DA pathways, respectively. Thus, D_2 receptors not only function as autoreceptors, as mentioned earlier, they also play an important role as normal post-synaptic receptors. Interestingly, these receptors are additionally found on cells in the pituitary gland that make the hormone prolactin. Activation of D_2 receptors by DA from the hypothalamus leads to inhibition of prolactin secretion, whereas the blockade of these receptors stimulates prolactin release. We will see in Chapter 20 that nearly all current antischizophrenic drugs are D_2 receptor antagonists—a characteristic that is believed to play a key role in the therapeutic efficacy of these compounds.

In the early stages of research on DA receptors, investigators discovered that D_1 and D_2 have opposite effects on the second-messenger substance cyclic adenosine monophosphate (cAMP) (Kebabian and Calne, 1979). More specifically, D_1 receptors stimulate the enzyme adenylyl cyclase, which is responsible for synthesizing cAMP (see Chapter 3). Consequently, the rate of cAMP formation is increased by stimulation of

BOX 5.1   Clinical Applications

Mutations that Affect Dopamine Synthesis

About 35 years ago, Segawa and colleagues (1976) reported a genetic disorder characterized by progressive dystonia (a type of movement disorder in which the patient experiences involuntary muscle contractions that may result in repetitive twisting movements, postural problems, tremors, and/or rigidity). Although there are many different types and causes of dystonia, in this instance the symptoms usually appear in childhood (around 6 to 8 years of age) and show diurnal (across the day) variation, with the least symptomatology upon awakening and worsening of symptom severity as the day goes on (Gordon, 2007; Segawa, 2010). Subsequent research showed that Segawa's disease is produced by mutations in the gene coding for the enzyme guanosine triphosphate cyclohydrolase 1 (GCH-1). GCH-1 plays an indirect but important role in DA synthesis because this enzyme catalyzes the first step in the formation of tetrahydrobiopterin, a necessary co-factor used by TH in converting tyrosine to DOPA (see Figure 5.2). Even with the mutated gene, patients with Segawa's disease usually have some GCH-1 activity and therefore can synthesize a certain amount of DA. However, levels of tetrahydrobiopterin (and therefore presumably DA as well) decline over the course of the day, which explains why symptoms are the least severe in the early morning but become more so as the day progresses. The key role of DA in this disorder is shown by the fact that symptoms are greatly improved if the patient is treated with L-DOPA. As is evident from Figure 5.2, this drug bypasses the TH step, thus allowing normal amounts of DA to be synthesized by the brain. As we will see later

in Chapter 21, L-DOPA is also the standard treatment for patients with Parkinson's disease.

What about mutations directly in the biochemical pathway shown in Figure 5.2? Although rare, such mutations occasionally do occur and when they do, the effects are more severe than in the case of GCH-1 mutations. For example, infants born with loss-of-function mutations of the TH gene begin to show movement disorders as early as the first several months of life (Kobayashi and Nagatsu, 2005; Wevers et al., 1999). Symptoms include hypokinesis (reduced movement) and either hypotonia (reduced muscle tone) or rigidity. Analysis of cerebrospinal fluid (CSF) shows very low levels of the DA metabolite HVA but normal levels of the serotonin metabolite 5-hydroxyindoleacetic acid (Wevers et al., 1999). Moreover, in one postmortem case study of a 19-year-old, who probably suffered from a TH mutation, biochemical analysis revealed approximately 90% decreases in TH activity and DA levels in the putamen (the part of the human striatum most important for movement regulation) compared with normal controls (Rajput et al., 1994). As in the case of Segawa's disease, treatment with L-DOPA (sometimes augmented with other drugs to enhance the production or inhibit the metabolism of the DA that is produced) is the most effective remedy for reducing symptoms.

Clinically significant mutations in the gene for AADC, which converts DOPA to DA, have also been reported in a small number of patients. It is no surprise that such patients develop severe motor problems similar to those seen in patients with TH mutations (Allen et al., 2009; Pons et al., 2004).

L-DOPA is not the typical therapy for patients with AADC deficiency because lack of that enzyme precludes synthesis of much DA from its precursor. Rather, patients are typically treated with DA receptor agonists (because the postsynaptic receptors are still present and functional) along with pyridoxine (vitamin B$_6$), which is converted by the body to pyridoxal phosphate, a necessary co-factor for AADC (Allen et al., 2009). The mechanism of the clinical benefit of pyridoxine is not fully understood, but one notion is that co-factor excess optimizes any residual enzyme activity that may be present in the patient.

Perceptive readers will have noted that a deficiency either in TH or AADC should result in decreased levels of NE, as well as DA, because noradrenergic neurons express both enzymes, and DA itself is the immediate precursor of NE. For this reason, one might question whether the motor abnormalities seen in patients with TH and AADC deficiency are related to DA or NE depletion. One way to resolve this question is to consider the effect of mutations leading to a deficiency in DBH, the enzyme responsible for converting DA to NE. As was discussed in Chapter 2 and again later in this chapter, NE is the postganglionic transmitter of the sympathetic nervous system and is also the precursor of EPI synthesis in the adrenal medulla. Interestingly, the major clinical symptoms of DBH deficiency are due to reduced NE levels in the sympathetic system, as well as to reduced circulating NE and EPI from the adrenals. Such symptoms include orthostatic hypotension (sudden drop in blood pressure when going from a sitting to a standing position), sexual

BOX 5.1 *(continued)*

dysfunction, ptosis (droopy eye-lids), and nasal congestion (Senard and Rouet, 2006). Patients are treated with L-threo-dihydroxyphe-nylserine (DOPS), a substance that can be converted to NE through a pathway that bypasses DBH. Note that the absence of severe motor abnormalities in DBH-deficient patients supports the contention that the presence of such abnor-malities in TH- and AADC-deficient individuals is due to lack of DA, not NE.

We have seen that a genetic deficiency in DA synthesis leads to significant motor problems

that begin during development (early infancy in the case of TH or AADC deficiency, childhood in the case of GCH-1 deficiency) and that can be treated successfully as long as DA neurotransmission can be adequately restored. It is worth noting that mutant mice that have been genetically engineered to completely lack TH activity inevitably die either in utero or rela-tively soon after birth if they are left untreated (Kobayashi and Nagatsu, 2005). Although this fact may seem discrepant with findings in human patients, it is possible that fetuses that carry the most severe

loss-of-function TH mutations also die before birth and are spontane-ously aborted without diagnosis, and that some human patients would not survive beyond infancy without L-DOPA treatment. We do not know whether the additional (e.g., motivational) symptoms of 6-OHDA lesions observed in ani-mal models would be present in TH-deficient human patients if they did not receive treatment. These interesting questions reveal some of the complexities that arise when human clinical research is com-pared with studies using animal models.

D_1 receptors. In contrast, D$_2$ receptor activation inhib-its adenylyl cyclase, thereby decreasing the rate of cAMP synthesis (**Figure 5.10**). These opposing effects can occur because the receptors activate two different G proteins: G_s in the case of D_1 receptors, and G_i in the case of D_2 receptors. Resulting changes in the level of cAMP within the postsynaptic cell alter the excitability of the cell (i.e., how readily it will fire nerve impulses) in complex ways that are beyond the scope of this dis-cussion. A second important mechanism of D$_2$ recep-tor function involves the regulation of membrane ion channels for potassium (K^+). In some cells, D_2 receptor stimulation activates a G protein that subsequently enhances K^+ channel opening. As we saw in Chapter 3, opening of such channels causes hyperpolarization of the cell membrane, thus decreasing the excitability and rate of firing of the cell.

Dopamine receptor agonists and antagonists affect locomotor activity and other behavioral functions

Many studies of DA pharmacology have used com-pounds that directly stimulate or block DA receptors. **Apomorphine** is a widely used agonist that stimu-lates both D_1 and D_2 receptors. At appropriate doses, apomorphine treatment causes behavioral activa-tion similar to that seen with classical stimulants like amphetamine and cocaine. There is also a new use for apomorphine—treating erectile dysfunction in men (marketed under the trade name Uprima). At present, the best-known remedy for this disorder is, of course, Viagra. You will recall that the mechanism of action of Viagra, which involves inhibiting the breakdown of

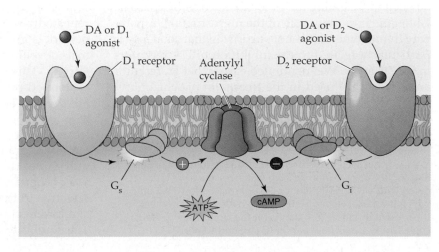

Figure 5.10 Signaling mechanisms of D$_1$ and D$_2$ receptors Activation of D_1 receptors stimulates the enzyme adeny-lyl cyclase and enhances DA synthesis, whereas activation of D_2 receptors inhib-its adenylyl cyclase and decreases DA synthesis. These effects are produced by the activation of different G proteins in the postsynaptic cell membrane, namely, G_s for the D_1 receptor and G_i for the D_2 receptor.

cyclic guanosine monophosphate (cGMP) in the penis, was discussed in Chapter 3. In contrast, apomorphine seems to increase penile blood flow (which is necessary for an erection) by acting through DA receptors in the brain. This effect of apomorphine has actually been known for some time, but clinical application for this purpose was previously thwarted by undesirable side effects (particularly nausea) and poor drug availability when taken orally. These problems have been overcome to some extent through the development of a lozenge that is taken sublingually (under the tongue), thereby bypassing the digestive system and delivering the drug directly into the bloodstream.

Psychopharmacologists also make use of drugs that are more selective for members of the D_1 or D_2 receptor family. Receptor-selective agonists and antagonists are extremely important in helping us understand which behaviors are under the control of a particular receptor subtype. The most commonly used agonist for D_1 receptors is a compound known as **SKF 38393**.[2] Administration of this compound to rats or mice elicits self-grooming behavior. **Quinpirole** is a drug that activates D_2 and D_3 receptors, and its effect is to increase locomotion and sniffing behavior. These responses are reminiscent of the effects of amphetamine or apomorphine, although quinpirole is not as powerful a stimulant as the former compounds.

The typical effect of administering a DA receptor antagonist is suppression of spontaneous exploratory and locomotor behavior. At higher doses, such drugs elicit a state known as **catalepsy**. Catalepsy refers to a lack of spontaneous movement, which is usually demonstrated experimentally by showing that the subject does not change position when placed in an awkward, presumably uncomfortable posture (**Figure 5.11**). Nevertheless, the subject is neither paralyzed nor asleep, and in fact it can be aroused to move by strong sensory stimuli such as being picked up by the experimenter. Catalepsy is usually associated with D_2 receptor blockers such as **haloperidol**, but it can also be elicited by giving a D_1 blocker such as **SCH 23390**. Given the important role of the nigrostriatal DA pathway in movement, it is not surprising that catalepsy is particularly related to the inhibition of DA receptors in the striatum. We mentioned earlier that D_2 receptor antagonists are used in the treatment of schizophrenia. The therapeutic benefit of these drugs is thought to derive from their blocking of DA receptors mainly

Figure 5.11 Catalepsy can be produced by DA receptor antagonists, particularly drugs that block D_2 receptors. Shown here is a 10-day-old rat pup that had received an SC injection of the D_2 antagonist haloperidol (1 mg/kg) 1 hour earlier. Pups treated in this manner often spent an entire 3-minute testing period immobile with their forepaws resting on the elevated bar, whereas control pups not given haloperidol got off the bar within a few seconds. (Photograph by Jerrold Meyer.)

in the limbic system. It should be clear from the present discussion, however, that the same drugs are also likely to produce inhibition of movement and other troublesome motor side effects because of simultaneous interference with dopaminergic transmission in the striatum. The various effects of DA receptor agonists and antagonists have given researchers a lot of useful information about the behavioral functions of DA. A newer approach is to manipulate the genes for individual components of the dopaminergic system and determine the behavioral consequences of such manipulations. Results from this approach are discussed in **Box 5.2**.

We conclude this section by considering the consequences of administering a D_2 receptor antagonist repeatedly rather than just once or twice. When haloperidol is given on a long-term basis to rats, the animals develop a syndrome called **behavioral supersensitivity**. This means that if the haloperidol treatment is stopped (to unblock the D_2 receptors) and subjects are then given a DA agonist like apomorphine, they respond more strongly than control subjects not pretreated with haloperidol. Since the experimental and control animals both received the same dose of apomorphine, this finding suggests that somehow the DA receptors in the experimental group are more sensitive to the same pharmacological stimulation. A similar effect occurs after DA depletion by 6-OHDA. The similarity between the effects of haloperidol and

---

[2]Many drugs used in research never receive common names like cocaine or reserpine. In such instances, the drug is designated with an abbreviation for the pharmaceutical company at which it was developed, along with an identifying number. In the present instance, SKF stands for the Smith Kline & French company, which is now part of GlaxoSmithKline.

BOX 5.2   The Cutting Edge

Using "Gene Knockout" Animals to Study the Dopaminergic System

Many researchers use techniques from molecular biology to investigate how neurotransmitter systems function and how they control various behaviors. One of the most powerful tools in this field of molecular pharmacology is the production of gene knockout mice. In these strains of mice, a particular gene of interest has been "knocked out" (i.e., rendered inactive) by special genetic procedures (see Chapter 4). Application of this technology has yielded important clues as to how the dopaminergic system regulates various behavioral functions.

One interesting approach taken by Richard Palmiter and colleagues at the University of Washington was to selectively knock out the gene for tyrosine hydroxylase (TH) in dopaminergic neurons (note that this is different from a general TH knockout mouse strain, in which the enzyme is completely absent in all catecholamine-producing cells). Although this approach required very skillful genetic manipulations, the investigators succeeded in creating mice that were virtually devoid of DA in the dopaminergic system but still possessed relatively normal amounts of NE. There is some similarity between these DA-deficient mice and genetically normal animals that have been given DA lesions with 6-OHDA, although one important difference is that the dopaminergic neurons themselves are undamaged in the genetic mutants. DA-deficient mice appear to behave and grow normally from birth until about 2 weeks of age, at which time they begin to show slower weight gain than wild-type (genetically normal) mice (Zhou and Palmiter, 1995). If untreated, they all die by 4 weeks of age. The DA-deficient mice can be saved by

daily injections of L-DOPA, which, as discussed earlier, bypasses the TH step (see Figure 5.2) in the biochemical pathway and therefore allows the neurons to make DA. But if L-DOPA treatment is suspended, the mice show a tremendous reduction in movement and seem to have no interest in eating food or drinking, despite the fact that they can physically grasp food and swallow liquids that are placed directly into their mouths. The decreased movement in these animals is reminiscent of Parkinson's disease and supports a critical role for DA in spontaneous locomotor activity. Dopamine also seems to be involved in the neural systems governing food and water intake, although the exact nature of this involvement is still not clear.

Other strains of mutant mice have been generated that lack either the DA transporter or one of the DA receptors. It turns out that each gene knockout produces a unique behavioral phenotype (which refers to the behavior of the mutant strain compared with that of normal animals). The most obvious characteristic of DA transporter knockout mice is that they are extremely hyperactive (Giros et al., 1996) (Figure A). This effect is understandable in light of the fact that without a transporter on their terminals, the dopaminergic neurons cannot remove DA from the synaptic cleft. Consequently, the postsynaptic DA receptors are exposed to excessive amounts of transmitter, and this has an activating effect on the animal's behavior.

Holmes and coworkers (2004) have reviewed the behavioral effects seen in various DA receptor knockout mice. Because of space limitations, we discuss here only a few of the results reported

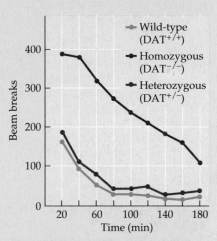

(A) Mutant mice lacking the dopamine transporter (DAT) (homozygous $DAT^{-/-}$) show increased locomotor activity when compared with genetically normal wild-type mice ($DAT^{+/+}$) or heterozygous mice ($DAT^{+/-}$) that carry one copy of the DAT gene. Mice were tested in a photocell apparatus, and the number of photobeam breaks was recorded every 20 minutes for a total of 3 hours. All groups showed a gradual habituation to the apparatus, as indicated by decreasing beam breaks, but the activity of the DAT knockout mice ($DAT^{-/-}$) was consistently higher than that of the other two groups. (After Giros et al., 1996.)

by the many studies in this area. D_1 receptor knockout mice, the first to be generated, are similar to DA-deficient mice in that they appear normal at birth. However, by the age of weaning, they begin to show reduced growth and may even die if their normally dry food isn't moistened to make it more palatable. In adulthood, these animals reportedly show complex behavioral abnormalities, including increased locomotor activity and reduced habituation in an open field, deficits in motor coordination in the rotarod test, and reduced self-grooming behavior (recall that D_1 receptor agonists given to wild-type rodents stimulate grooming

(Continued on next page)

BOX 5.2 *(continued)*

behavior). Dopamine, particularly acting through D_1 receptors, has been implicated in various cognitive processes, including attention and working memory. It is interesting to note, therefore, that D_1 receptor knockout mice also exhibit deficits in several kinds of cognitive tasks (Holmes et al., 2004). Contrasting results with respect to motor function are observed after disruption of the D_2 receptor gene. D_2 knockout mice show impairment in spontaneous movement, coordination, and postural control. Nevertheless, the degree of impairment seems to depend strongly on which genetic strain of mouse is used to create the mutation. This is partly because different strains already vary considerably in their behavior before any genes are knocked out (indeed, the same issue of background strain has arisen in the analysis of behavioral changes in D_1 receptor knockout mice). The necessity of having functional activity in at least one of the two main DA receptors is shown by the observation that double knockout of both D_1 and D_2 receptor genes leads to fatality during the second or third week of postnatal life (Kobayashi et al., 2004). This effect is due mainly to poor feeding behavior, as was seen in the DA-deficient mice of Palmiter's group. However, in this case, the animals cannot be rescued by treatment with L-DOPA since their neurochemical deficit lies in a lack of postsynaptic DA responsiveness rather than in a lack of presynaptic DA synthesis.

Other DA receptor knockout mice have also been generated and studied, although not as extensively as the D_1 and D_2 receptor knockouts. D_3 receptor knockout mice show complex behavioral changes that may be indicative of a reduced tendency to inhibit behavioral responses in

(B) Mutant mice lacking D_1 receptors are insensitive to the locomotor-stimulating effects of cocaine. Wild-type ($D_1^{+/+}$) and homozygous mutant mice ($D_1^{-/-}$) were injected twice daily for 7 consecutive days with either cocaine (20 mg/kg intraperitoneally) or a saline control solution. The animals were tested in a photocell apparatus for 30 minutes after each injection to record their locomotor activity. Cocaine greatly increased locomotor activity in the wild-type but not the mutant mice on all test days. (After M. Xu et al., 2000.)

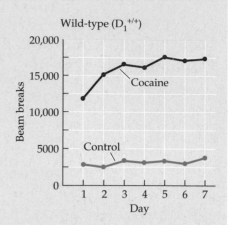

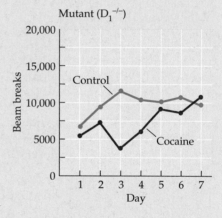

novel test situations (Holmes et al., 2004). Absence of either the D_4 or D_5 receptor has little apparent effect in standard behavioral tests; however, as discussed below, D_4 receptor knockout mice differ from wild-type animals in their responsiveness to several psychoactive drugs. Finally, beyond the behavioral disturbances seen in mice lacking certain DA receptors, physiological abnormalities have been observed in some cases. For example, because of the previously mentioned role of D_2 receptors in inhibiting prolactin secretion from the pituitary gland, mice that lack this receptor develop chronic hyperprolactinemia (elevated circulating prolactin levels). Moreover, DA is critically involved in the regulation of salt balance and blood pressure, in part through CNS mechanisms and in part through the action of DA receptors in the kidneys. As a consequence, knocking out *any* of the DA receptors leads to hypertension (high blood pressure) through one or another type of mechanism (Zeng et al., 2007).

Pharmacologists have naturally taken advantage of these mutant strains of mice to study how disruptions in various DA system genes affect reactions to different psychoactive drugs. Several studies have looked at behavioral responses to psychostimulant drugs such

as cocaine, amphetamine, and methamphetamine because DA is already known to play an important role in the effects of these compounds. DA transporter knockout mice and mice lacking either the D_1 or D_2 receptor show either reduced or in some cases no increase in locomotion after psychostimulant treatment (Holmes et al., 2004; M. Xu et al., 2000) (Figure B). Therefore, both the DA transporter on the presynaptic side and the D_1 receptor on the postsynaptic side play pivotal roles in the behavior-stimulating effects of cocaine and amphetamine (see Chapter 12). In contrast, mutant mice that lack the D_4 receptor are actually hypersensitive to the stimulating effects of cocaine and methamphetamine.

Other studies have examined behavioral responses to ethanol

BOX 5.2 *(continued)*

(alcohol) in various strains of DA receptor knockout mice. Ethanol can produce either locomotor stimulation or inhibition, depending on dose (low doses tend to be stimulatory, whereas higher doses are sedating) and other factors. The locomotor stimulatory effects of ethanol are enhanced in D_2 and D_4 receptor knockout mice, whereas ethanol-induced sedation is blunted in mice lacking the D_2 receptor (Holmes et al., 2004).

Voluntary ethanol consumption is also reduced in D_1 and D_2 knockout mice, suggesting that these two receptor subtypes play an important role in the rewarding effects of this substance.

These results show that by acting through different receptor subtypes, a single transmitter such as DA may influence many different behaviors and physiological functions and may also play a complicated role in the responses

to psychoactive drugs. In some cases, genetically engineered mice have largely confirmed theories that researchers had previously formulated using more traditional pharmacological approaches. In other cases, however, the use of such animals has provided new and exciting insights into the interactions between neurotransmitters, drugs, and behavior.

6-OHDA is because both treatments persistently reduce DA stimulation of D_2 receptors. Haloperidol accomplishes this by blocking the receptors, whereas 6-OHDA achieves the same result by causing a long-lasting depletion of DA. Various studies suggest that the supersensitivity associated with haloperidol or 6-OHDA treatment is related at least in part to an increase in the density of D_2 receptors on postsynaptic cells in the striatum. This phenomenon, which is called **receptor up-regulation**, is considered to be an adaptive response whereby the lack of normal neurotransmitter (in this case DA) input causes the neurons to increase their sensitivity by making more receptors.

Section Summary

- The dopaminergic neurons of greatest interest to neuropsychopharmacologists are found near the base of the midbrain in the substantia nigra (A9 cell group) and the VTA (A10 cell group).

- Neurons in the substantia nigra send their axons to the striatum, thus forming the nigrostriatal tract. This pathway plays an important role in the control of movement and is severely damaged in Parkinson's disease.

- Dopaminergic neurons in the VTA form two major dopaminergic systems: the mesolimbic system, which has terminations in several limbic system structures (e.g., nucleus accumbens, septum, amygdala, hippocampus), and the mesocortical system, which terminates in the cerebral cortex (particularly the prefrontal cortex). The mesolimbic and mesocortical DA systems have been implicated in mechanisms of drug abuse, as well as in schizophrenia.

- Researchers have identified five main DA receptor subtypes, designated D_1 to D_5, all of which are metabotropic receptors. These subtypes fall into two families, the first consisting of D_1 and D_5, and the second consisting of D_2, D_3, and D_4. The most common subtypes are D_1 and D_2, both of which are found in large numbers in the striatum and the nucleus accumbens. These subtypes can be differentiated partly on the basis that D_1 receptors stimulate adenylyl cyclase, thus increasing the rate of cAMP synthesis, whereas D_2 receptors decrease the rate of cAMP synthesis by inhibiting adenylyl cyclase. Activation of D_2 receptors can also enhance the opening of K^+ channels in the cell membrane, which hyperpolarizes the membrane and therefore reduces cell excitability.

- Some of the drugs that affect the dopaminergic system, including DA receptor agonists and antagonists, are presented in **Table 5.1**. In general, enhancement of dopaminergic function has an activating effect on behavior, whereas interference with DA causes suppression of normal behaviors ranging from temporary sedation and catalepsy to the profound deficits observed after treatment with a DA neurotoxin such as 6-OHDA.

- When D_2 receptor transmission is persistently impaired either by chronic antagonist administration or by denervation (e.g., 6-OHDA lesions), animals become supersensitive to treatment with a D_2 agonist. This response is mediated at least in part by up-regulation of D_2 receptors by postsynaptic neurons in areas such as the striatum.

TABLE 5.1 Drugs That Affect the Dopaminergic System	
Drug	**Action**
DOPA	Converted to DA in the brain
Phenelzine	Increases catecholamine levels by inhibiting MAO
α-Methyl-*para*-tyrosine (AMPT)	Depletes catecholamines by inhibiting tyrosine hydroxylase
Reserpine	Depletes catecholamines by inhibiting vesicular uptake
6-Hydroxydopamine (6-OHDA)	Damages or destroys catecholaminergic neurons
Amphetamine	Releases catecholamines
Cocaine and methylphenidate	Inhibit catecholamine reuptake
Apomorphine	Stimulates DA receptors generally (agonist)
SKF 38393	Stimulates D_1 receptors (agonist)
Quinpirole	Stimulates D_2 and D_3 receptors (agonist)
SCH 23390	Blocks D_1 receptors (antagonist)
Haloperidol	Blocks D_2 receptors (antagonist)

Organization and Function of the Noradrenergic System

The noradrenergic system has both a central and peripheral component. The cell bodies of the central noradrenergic system are found in the brainstem and their ascending fibers innervate a wide range of forebrain structures, whereas peripheral noradrenergic neurons are an important component of the sympathetic nervous system. NE released from these cells acts on adrenergic receptors located either in the central nervous system or in peripheral target organs.

Norepinephrine is an important transmitter in both the central and peripheral nervous systems

The NE-containing neurons within the brain are located in the parts of the brainstem called the *pons* and the *medulla*. Of particular interest is a structure known as the **locus coeruleus** (**LC**), a small area of the pons that contains a dense collection of noradrenergic neurons corresponding roughly to the A6 cell group (according to the numbering system described previously). At first glance, the LC might not

seem to be a very impressive structure; the rat LC contains a few more than 3000 nerve cells out of the millions of neurons present in the entire rat brain. Nevertheless, these cells send fibers into almost all areas of the forebrain, thereby providing nearly all of the NE in the cortex, limbic system, thalamus, and hypothalamus (**Figure 5.12**). The LC also provides noradrenergic input to the cerebellum and the spinal cord.

Norepinephrine also plays an important role in the peripheral nervous system. Many neurons that have their cell bodies in the ganglia of the sympathetic branch of the autonomic nervous system (see

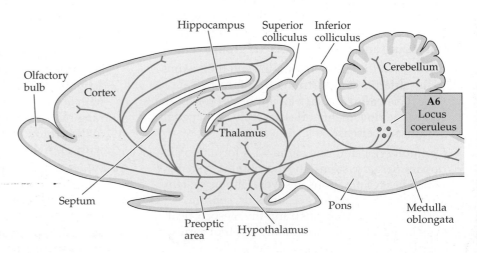

Figure 5.12 The locus coeruleus (LC) contains a dense cluster of noradenergic neurons designated the A6 cell group. These cells send their fibers to almost all regions of the forebrain, as well as to the cerebellum and spinal cord.

Chapter 2) use NE as their transmitter. These cells, which send out their fibers to various target organs throughout the body, are responsible for the autonomic actions of NE that are described later. We mentioned earlier in the chapter that NE (as well as EPI) functions as a hormone secreted by the adrenal glands directly into the bloodstream. In this way, NE can reach an organ such as the heart through two routes: it can be released from sympathetic noradrenergic neurons at synapse-like contacts with cardiac cells, and it can be released from the adrenal glands and travel to the heart through the circulatory system. On the other hand, blood-borne NE does not reach the brain, because it is effectively excluded by the blood–brain barrier.

Norepinephrine and epinephrine act through α- and β-adrenergic receptors

Receptors for NE and EPI are called *adrenergic receptors* (an alternate term is **adrenoceptors**). Like DA receptors, adrenergic receptors all belong to the general family of metabotropic receptors. However, they serve a broader role by having to mediate both neurotransmitter (mainly NE) and hormonal (mainly EPI) actions of the catecholamines.

Early studies by Ahlquist (1948, 1979) and other investigators suggested the existence of two adrenoceptor subtypes, which were designated alpha (α) and beta (β). Since the time of Ahlquist's pioneering research, many experiments have shown that the α- and β-adrenoceptors actually represent two families, each composed of several receptor subtypes. For present purposes, we will distinguish between α_1- and α_2-receptors, and also between β_1 and β_2. Postsynaptic adrenoceptors are found at high densities in many brain areas, including the cerebral cortex, thalamus, hypothalamus, and cerebellum, and various limbic system structures such as the hippocampus and amygdala. In addition, α_2-autoreceptors are located on noradrenergic nerve terminals and on the cell bodies of noradrenergic neurons in the LC and elsewhere. These autoreceptors cause an inhibition of noradrenergic cell firing and a reduction in NE release from the terminals.

Like DA D_1 receptors, both β_1- and β_2-adrenoceptors stimulate adenylyl cyclase and enhance the formation of cAMP. In contrast, α_2-receptors operate in a similar manner as D_2 receptors. That is, α_2-receptors reduce the rate of cAMP synthesis by inhibiting adenylyl cyclase, and they can also cause hyperpolarization of the cell membrane by increasing K^+ channel opening. Yet another kind of mechanism is used by receptors of the α_1 subtype. These receptors operate through the phosphoinositide second-messenger system, which, as we saw in Chapter 3, leads to an increased concentration of free calcium (Ca^{2+}) ions within the postsynaptic cell.

The central noradrenergic system plays a significant role in arousal, cognition, and the consolidation of emotional memories

Neurochemical, pharmacological, and electrophysiological studies in experimental animals indicate that the central noradrenergic system is involved in a large number of behavioral functions, only some of which can be discussed here because of space limitations. We have chosen to focus on the role of this system in arousal, cognition, and the consolidation of memories of emotional experiences. Later chapters will present evidence for involvement of NE in various psychiatric disorders, particularly mood and anxiety disorders.

A large body of literature has demonstrated that the firing of LC noradrenergic neurons and the activation of adrenergic receptors in the forebrain are important for both behavioral and electrophysiological (i.e., EEG) arousal[3] (Berridge, 2008). One of the earliest indications of this relationship comes from studies in the 1970s and 1980s showing that LC neurons fire more rapidly during waking than during sleep, and that changes in the firing of these cells come *before* the transition between these behavioral states. Later work by Berridge and colleagues implicated the noradrenergic pathways from the LC to the medial septal and medial preoptic areas in the wakefulness-promoting effects of NE. In one experiment, for example, researchers microinjected the α_1-receptor agonist **phenylephrine** and/or the general β-receptor agonist **isoproterenol** directly into the medial septal area of rats. The animals were then monitored to determine the amount of time they spent awake or asleep. As illustrated in **Figure 5.13**, each drug individually increased the amount of time spent awake, and at the low doses used in the study, the combination of treatments produced the strongest effect. These results show that both α_1- and β-receptors are involved in NE-mediated arousal and wakefulness.

Another brain area to which the LC projects is the prefrontal cortex (PFC), a cortical region that expresses α_1- and α_2-adrenoceptors, and that plays an important role in many cognitive functions such as attention and working memory. Activation of α_2-receptors in the PFC using selective agonists such as **clonidine**

---

[3]During states of drowsiness and slow-wave sleep, EEG measurements taken from the cortex show a predominant pattern of slow, high-voltage, synchronized waveforms. During a state of aroused wakefulness, the cortical EEG instead shows a predominance of fast, low-voltage, desynchronized waves.

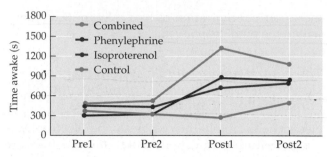

Figure 5.13 Rats showed increased time awake after administration of small amounts of either an α₁- or a β-adrenergic agonist directly into the medial septum. The α₁-agonist was phenylephrine (10×10^{-9} mol injected), and the β-agonist was isoproterenol (4×10^{-9} mol injected). Control injections were of the vehicle used to dissolve the active drugs. Behavioral state (asleep versus awake) was determined for two 30-minute intervals prior to drug administration (Pre1 and Pre2) as well as two 30-minute postdrug intervals (Post1 and Post2), the first of which began 15 minutes after treatment. Note that the greatest effect was obtained with the combined injection of both drugs. (After Berridge et al., 2003.)

or **guanfacine** has been shown to enhance working memory under a variety of conditions (e.g., in animals with NE depletion, aged animals that suffer from a natural reduction in catecholamine levels, and animals tested under particularly demanding task conditions) (Ramos and Arnsten, 2007). In contrast, activation of α₁-receptors in the PFC has a deleterious effect on cognitive functions that require this brain area. These differing effects raise the question of how an organism's own NE might regulate PFC functioning. We know from a large amount of research that stressful situations stimulate NE release in the PFC and impair performance on PFC-dependent tasks. It is interesting to note that NE has a lower affinity for α₁-receptors than for the specific subtype of α₂-receptor found in high levels in the PFC. Taking all of this information together, Ramos and Arnsten (2007) proposed that NE primarily facilitates PFC functioning and PFC-dependent cognitive tasks under normal (i.e., nonstressful) conditions mainly by activating α₂-adrenoceptors in this brain area. On the other hand, the heightened release of NE associated with stress would increase the amount of α₁-adrenoceptor activation, which presumably overrides the beneficial effects of the α₂-receptors and leads to cognitive impairment.

Finally, there is substantial evidence from animal studies that NE, EPI, and glucocorticoid hormones modulate the consolidation of emotional memories. One type of behavioral task often used to study the mechanisms of memory consolidation is the one-trial **passive avoidance learning** paradigm (sometimes also called *inhibitory avoidance learning*). This paradigm

uses a two-chamber apparatus with one side brightly lit and the other side dark. The two sides are separated by a partition with an opening in it to allow passage of the animal. For the training (learning) trial, a rat or a mouse is first placed in the brightly lit side, which it naturally finds aversive. However, when the animal spontaneously moves from the lit to the dark side, it is given a footshock on the dark side (**Figure 5.14A**). This single experience is sufficient to produce long-lasting avoidance of the dark side, which is typically measured on a test trial one or more days after the learning by determining the increased length of time (latency) that it takes for a trained animal to move from the lit to the dark side compared with unshocked controls. A major advantage of such a one-trial learning paradigm is that memory consolidation (i.e., transfer of information from short-term to long-term memory) for the task occurs entirely during the single period of time after the learning trial. Another feature of this paradigm is that the footshock induces a certain amount of fear and stress in the animals and thus can be considered a paradigm for emotional learning.

It is well established that the stress associated with one-trial passive avoidance learning leads to increased EPI and glucocorticoid secretion from the adrenal glands (see Chapter 3), as well as activation of central noradrenergic neurons and increased NE release within the brain. The first clue that these substances are involved in memory consolidation for this task came from the results of Gold and van Buskirk (1975), who used a weak footshock that produced relatively little fear-related memory in control rats as indicated by short latencies to enter the dark (shocked) side of the apparatus in the test trial. However, when EPI was injected subcutaneously into the animals immediately after the training trial or 10 minutes later (but not 30 or 120 minutes later), the latencies were significantly increased, suggesting increased memory consolidation. Later studies not only confirmed a role for EPI in modulating performance on the one-trial passive avoidance task, they additionally implicated NE, glucocorticoids, and other neurotransmitters/neuromodulators acting within the basolateral amygdala (a brain area known to be crucial for fear-related learning and memory) (McGaugh, 2004; McIntyre et al., 2003). A proposed model illustrating the relevant chemicals and neuroanatomical pathways is shown in **Figure 5.14B**. Note first that peripheral EPI does not cross the blood–brain barrier and therefore must influence the basolateral amygdala indirectly. Existing evidence suggests that EPI in the bloodstream stimulates β-adrenoceptors on sensory nerve endings of the vagus nerve, which then sends information to noradrenergic neurons in a brainstem structure known as

(A)

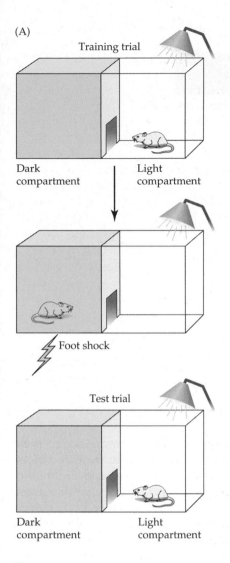

the nucleus of the solitary tract (NTS). In turn, these neurons and noradrenergic neurons of the LC project to the basolateral amygdala. NE released from both pathways further enhances memory consolidation of the passive avoidance learning primarily through activation of β-adrenoceptors and the cAMP second messenger system. Glucocorticoids from the adrenal cortex (which readily cross the blood–brain barrier) also positively modulate memory consolidation via glucocorticoid receptors (GRs) in both the basolateral amygdala and the NTS. Finally, Figure 5.14B points to an involvement of acetylcholine, γ-aminobutyric acid (GABA), and opioid peptides (e.g., endorphins, enkephalins) in the memory consolidation process; however, consideration of these other substances is beyond the scope of the present discussion.

Several medications work by stimulating or inhibiting peripheral adrenergic receptors

Adrenergic agonists or antagonists are frequently used in the treatment of nonpsychiatric medical conditions because of the widespread distribution and important functional role of adrenergic receptors in various peripheral organs (**Table 5.2**). For example, general adrenergic agonists that activate both α- and β-receptors have sometimes been used in the treatment of bronchial asthma. Stimulating the α-receptors causes constriction of the blood vessels in the bronchial lining, thus reducing congestion and edema (tissue swelling)

(B)

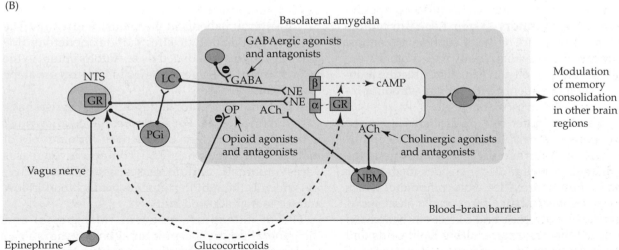

Figure 5.14 Modulation of emotional memories by NE, epinephrine, and glucocorticoid hormones (A) Emotional learning and memory in animals such as rats and mice are often studied using the one-trial passive avoidance learning paradigm illustrated here and described in the text. (B) Memory consolidation of passive avoidance learning is influenced by a variety of neurotransmitters and hormones, whose influences converge on the basolateral complex of the amygdala. ACh, acetylcholine; cAMP, cyclic adenosine monophosphate; GABA, γ-aminobutyric acid; GR, glucocorticoid receptor; LC, locus coeruleus; NBM, nucleus basalis magnocellularis; NE, norepinephrine; NTS, nucleus of the solitary tract; OP, endogenous opioid peptides; PGi, nucleus paragigantocellularis; α, α-adrenergic receptors; β, β-adrenergic receptors. (B after McIntyre et al., 2003.)

TABLE 5.2 Location and Physiological Actions of Peripheral α- and β-Adrenergic Receptors		
Location	Action	Receptor subtype
Heart	Increased rate and force of contraction	β
Blood vessels	Constriction	α
	Dilation	β
Smooth muscle of the trachea and bronchi	Relaxation	β
Uterine smooth muscle	Contraction	α
Bladder	Contraction	α
	Relaxation	β
Spleen	Contraction	α
	Relaxation	β
Iris	Pupil dilation	α
Adipose (fat) tissue	Increased fat breakdown and release	β

by restricting blood flow to the tissue. On the other hand, β-receptor stimulation leads to relaxation of the bronchial muscles, thereby providing a wider airway. Although general adrenergic agonists can be effective antiasthma medications, they also cause several adverse side effects. For this reason, asthma is more commonly treated with a selective $β_2$-adrenoceptor agonist such as **albuterol** (**Ventolin**). Such drugs are packaged in an inhaler that delivers the compound directly to the respiratory system. The β-receptors found in the airways are of the $β_2$ subtype, in contrast to the heart, which contains mainly $β_1$-receptors. Consequently, albuterol is effective in alleviating the bronchial congestion of patients with asthma without producing adverse cardiovascular effects.

Even over-the-counter cold medications are based on the properties of peripheral adrenergic receptors. Thus, the $α_1$-receptor agonist phenylephrine is the key ingredient in several decongestant medications available in most pharmacies. This compound, which may be taken either in tablet form or in a nasal spray, constricts the blood vessels and reduces inflamed and swollen nasal membranes resulting from colds and allergies. In the form of eye drops, it is also used to stimulate α-receptors of the iris to dilate the pupil during eye examinations or before surgery of the eyes.

Alpha$_2$-receptor agonists such as clonidine are commonly used in the treatment of hypertension (high blood pressure). The therapeutic benefit of these drugs is a result of their ability to inhibit activity of the sympathetic nervous system while stimulating the parasympathetic system. The consequence of these actions is to reduce the patient's heart rate and blood pressure. Unfortunately, sedation and feelings of sleepiness are common side effects of clonidine treatment. On the other hand, these effects and others have been exploited therapeutically with the development of **dexmedetomidine** (**Precedex**), an $α_2$-agonist with combined sedative, anxiolytic (antianxiety), and analgesic (pain-reducing) effects that is particularly useful for surgical patients in the intensive care unit. The sedative and anxiolytic effects of dexmedetomidine are believed to be mediated by $α_2$-autoreceptors in the LC, whereas the analgesic effect probably occurs at the level of the spinal cord.

Adrenergic receptor antagonists likewise have varied clinical uses. For example, the $α_2$-antagonist yohimbine helps in the treatment of certain types of male sexual impotence. This compound increases parasympathetic and decreases sympathetic activity, which is thought to stimulate penile blood inflow and/or to inhibit blood outflow.

The $α_1$-antagonist **prazosin** (**Minipress**) and the general β-adrenoceptor antagonist **propranolol** (**Inderal**) are both used clinically in the treatment of hypertension. Prazosin causes dilation of blood vessels by blocking the $α_1$-receptors responsible for constricting these vessels. In contrast, the main function of propranolol is to block the β-receptors in the heart, thereby reducing the heart's contractile force. The discovery that $β_1$ is the major adrenoceptor subtype in the heart has led to the introduction of $β_1$-selective antagonists such as **metoprolol** (**Lopressor**). These compounds exhibit fewer side effects than the more general β-antagonist propranolol. Beta-receptor antagonists like propranolol and metoprolol are also useful in the treatment of cardiac arrhythmia (irregular heartbeat) and angina pectoris (feelings of pain and constriction around the heart caused by deficient blood flow and oxygen delivery to the heart).

Finally, it should be mentioned that propranolol and other β-antagonists have also been applied to the treatment of generalized anxiety disorder, which is one of the most common types of anxiety disorder (see Chapter 18). Many patients with generalized anxiety disorder suffer from physical symptoms such as palpitations, flushing, and tachycardia (racing heart). Beta-blockers do not alleviate anxiety per se, but instead they may help the patient feel better by reducing some of these distressing physical symptoms of the disorder. A summary of compounds that affect the noradrenergic system centrally and/or peripherally is presented in **Table 5.3**.

Section Summary

- The most important cluster of noradrenergic neurons is the A6 cell group, which is located in a region known as the locus coeruleus. These neurons innervate almost all areas of the forebrain and mediate many of the important behavioral functions of NE.

- NE and EPI activate a group of metabotropic receptors called adrenoceptors. They are divided into two broad families, α and β, which are further subdivided into α_1, α_2, β_1, and β_2. Both β-receptor subtypes enhance the synthesis of cAMP, whereas α_2-receptors inhibit cAMP formation.

- Another mechanism of action of α_2-receptors involves hyperpolarization of the cell membrane by stimulating K^+ channel opening. In contrast, α_1-receptors increase the intracellular concentration of Ca^{2+} ions by means of the phosphoinositide second-messenger system.

- The noradrenergic system is involved in many behavioral functions, including arousal, cognition, and the consolidation of emotional memories (e.g., related to fear-inducing situations).

- The arousal- and wakefulness-promoting effects of NE are primarily mediated by pathways from the LC to the medial septal and medial preoptic areas.

- The cognitive-enhancing effects of NE are mediated by activation of α_2-adrenoceptors in the PFC.

- The memory consolidation effects of NE require activation of β-adrenoceptors in the basolateral amygdala, with additional involvement of peripheral EPI acting on the vagus nerve and adrenal

TABLE 5.3   Drugs That Affect the Noradrenergic System

Drug	Action
Phenelzine	Increases catecholamine levels by inhibiting MAO
α-Methyl-*para*-tyrosine (AMPT)	Depletes catecholamines by inhibiting tyrosine hydroxylase
Reserpine	Depletes catecholamines by inhibiting vesicular uptake
6-Hydroxydopamine (6-OHDA)	Damages or destroys catecholaminergic neurons
Amphetamine	Releases catecholamines
Cocaine and methylphenidate	Inhibit catecholamine reuptake
Nisoxetine	Selectively inhibits NE reuptake
Phenylephrine	Stimulates α_1-receptors (agonist)
Clonidine	Stimulates α_2-receptors (agonist)
Albuterol	Stimulates β-receptors (partially selective for β_2)
Prazosin	Blocks α_1-receptors (antagonist)
Yohimbine	Blocks α_2-receptors (antagonist)
Propranolol	Blocks β-receptors generally (antagonist)
Metoprolol	Blocks β_1-receptors (antagonist)

glucocorticoids acting on both the basolateral amygdala and NTS.

- Adrenergic agonists are used therapeutically for various physiological and psychological disorders. These include the α_1-agonist phenylephrine, which helps relieve nasal congestion; the α_2-agonist clonidine, which is used in the treatment of hypertension and drug withdrawal symptoms; and β_2-agonists such as albuterol, which is an important medication for relieving bronchial congestion in people suffering from asthma.

Go to the **COMPANION WEBSITE**

sites.sinauer.com/psychopharm2e
for Web Boxes, animations, flashcards, and other study resources.

Recommended Readings

Iversen, L., Iversen, S., Dunnett, S., and Bjorklund, A. (Eds.). (2009). *Dopamine Handbook*. New York: Oxford University Press.

Neve, K. A. (Ed.). (2009). *The Dopamine Receptors* (2nd ed.). Totowa, NJ: Humana Press.

Ordway, G. A., Schwartz, M. A., and Frazer, A. (2007). *Brain Norepinephrine: Neurobiology and Therapeutics*. Cambridge: Cambridge University Press.

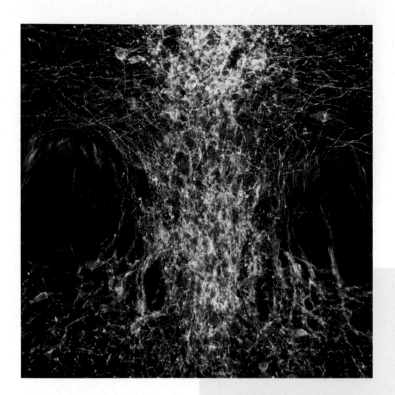

The serotonergic neurons of the dorsal raphe nucleus (shown here in pink) are located in the midbrain and send their axons to many forebrain areas.

Serotonin 6

THE PATIENT WAS A 34-YEAR-OLD MARRIED WOMAN who was brought to the hospital's emergency room by her husband at 3:00 in the morning. Half an hour earlier, he had found his wife lying on the floor of their home, and he immediately brought her to the hospital. Doctors in the emergency room noted symptoms of agitation, mental confusion and disorientation, sweating, and muscular rigidity. The patient also had a mild fever of 38.3°C (100.9°F) and exhibited rapid but shallow breathing. Over time, her neuromuscular symptoms worsened, and she spiked a fever of 42.3°C (108°F). Despite receiving extensive supportive care from hospital staff, the woman died of cardiopulmonary arrest 20 hours after she was admitted.

This real case report was published in 2005 by Sener and colleagues. What caused this unfortunate woman's demise? Her husband determined that his wife had intentionally consumed large amounts of two prescription medications, presumably for the purpose of committing suicide. The medications—paroxetine and moclobemide—act to boost levels of the neurotransmitter **serotonin** (paroxetine works by blocking reuptake of serotonin, whereas moclobemide slows the rate of serotonin metabolism by inhibiting monoamine oxidase A). Clinicians have known for some time that excessive doses of serotonergic agents, particularly in combination, as occurred in the present case, can lead to a dangerous and even life-threatening set of symptoms called the **serotonin syndrome**.

Although the serotonin syndrome is rare, this neurotransmitter (more technically known as **5-hydroxytryptamine**, or **5-HT**) has been featured in the popular culture as the culprit in just about every human malady or vice, including depression, anxiety, obesity, impulsive aggression and violence, and even drug addiction. Can a single neurotransmitter really have such far-reaching behavioral consequences?

The answer is not a simple one—5-HT probably does influence many different behavioral and physiological systems, yet the ability of this chemical to either destroy us (if imbalanced) or to cure all that ails us (if brought back into equilibrium) has unfortunately been oversold by a sensationalist media aided and abetted by a few publicity-seeking scientists. In this chapter, we will learn about the neurochemistry, pharmacology, and functional characteristics of this fascinating neurotransmitter.

Serotonin Synthesis, Release, and Inactivation

The level of serotonergic transmission depends on the relative contributions of synthesis, release, and inactivation of the transmitter.

Serotonin synthesis is regulated by enzymatic activity and precursor availability

Serotonin is synthesized from the amino acid **tryptophan**, which comes from protein in our diet. As shown in **Figure 6.1**, the biochemical pathway comprises two steps. The first step is catalyzed by the enzyme **tryptophan hydroxylase**, which converts tryptophan to **5-hydroxytryptophan (5-HTP)**. 5-HTP is then acted upon by **aromatic amino acid decarboxylase (AADC)** to form 5-HT. In 2003, researchers discovered that there are two forms of the tryptophan hydroxylase gene, designated *TPH1* and *TPH2*. *TPH2* is expressed by **serotonergic neurons** (neurons that use 5-HT as their neurotransmitter), whereas *TPH1* is expressed by certain types of non-neuronal cells, including 5-HT–secreting enterochromaffin cells located in the gut and melatonin-secreting cells in the pineal gland.

Many features of the 5-HT synthesis pathway are similar to those of the pathway described in the previous chapter involving the formation of dopamine (DA) from the amino acid tyrosine. Just as the initial step in the synthesis of DA (i.e., tyrosine to DOPA) is the rate-limiting step, the conversion of tryptophan to 5-HTP is rate-limiting in the 5-HT pathway. Furthermore, just as tyrosine hydroxylase is found only in neurons that synthesize catecholamines, tryptophan hydroxylase in the brain is similarly a specific marker for the serotonergic neurons. Another important point is that the second enzyme in the pathway, AADC, is the same for both catecholamines and 5-HT.

Synthesis of serotonin in the brain can be stimulated by giving animals a large dose of tryptophan, but administration of 5-HTP is even more effective because it is converted so rapidly and efficiently to

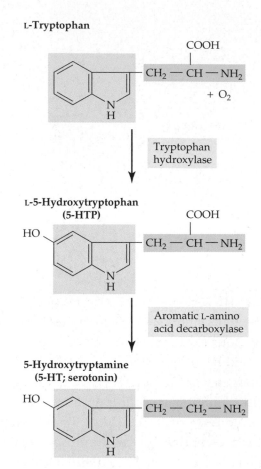

Figure 6.1 Synthesis of serotonin Serotonin (5-HT) is synthesized from the amino acid tryptophan in two steps catalyzed by the enzymes tryptophan hydroxylase and aromatic amino acid decarboxylase.

5-HT. There is also an interesting link between food intake and 5-HT synthesis that was first discovered many years ago by John Fernstrom and Richard Wurtman (1972). Imagine a group of rats that have been fasted overnight and then fed a protein-rich meal. The level of tryptophan in their blood goes up, and thus you probably would expect brain 5-HT to rise as well, since an injection of pure tryptophan produces such an effect. Surprisingly, however, Fernstrom and Wurtman found that consumption of a protein-rich meal did not cause increases in either tryptophan or 5-HT in the brain, even though tryptophan levels in the bloodstream were elevated. The researchers explained this result by showing that tryptophan competes with a group of other amino acids (called large neutral amino acids) for transport from the blood to the brain across the blood–brain barrier (**Figure 6.2**). Consequently, it's the *ratio* between the amount of tryptophan in the blood and the overall amount of its competitors that counts. Most proteins contain larger amounts of these

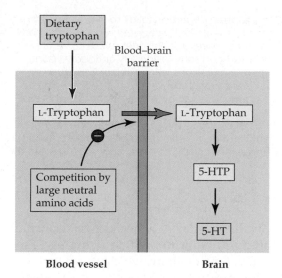

Blood–brain barrier

Dietary tryptophan

L-Tryptophan

Competition by large neutral amino acids

L-Tryptophan

5-HTP

5-HT

Blood vessel   **Brain**

Figure 6.2 Tryptophan entry into the brain and 5-HT synthesis are regulated by the relative availability of tryptophan versus large neutral amino acids that compete with it for transport across the blood–brain barrier. In rats, a high-protein, low-carbohydrate meal does not increase brain tryptophan levels or 5-HT synthesis rate, due to this competitive process. However, the ratio of circulating tryptophan to large neutral amino acids is elevated after a high-carbohydrate, low-protein meal, thereby enhancing entry of tryptophan into the brain and stimulating 5-HT synthesis.

competitor amino acids than tryptophan; thus when these proteins are consumed, the critical ratio either stays the same or even goes down.

Even more surprising was an additional finding of Fernstrom and Wurtman. When these researchers fed previously fasted rats a meal low in protein but high in carbohydrates, that experimental treatment led to increases in brain tryptophan and 5-HT levels. How could this be the case? You might already know that eating carbohydrates (starches and sugars) triggers release of the hormone **insulin** from the pancreas. One important function of this insulin response is to stimulate the uptake of glucose from the bloodstream into various tissues, where it can be metabolized for energy. But glucose is not the only substance acted on by insulin. This hormone also stimulates the uptake of most amino acids from the bloodstream; tryptophan, however, is relatively unaffected. Because of this difference, a low-protein, high-carbohydrate meal will increase the ratio of tryptophan to competing amino acids, allowing more tryptophan to cross the blood–brain barrier and more 5-HT to be made in the brain.

Do the dietary effects observed in rats also occur in humans eating typical meals? Wurtman and colleagues (2003) addressed this issue by measuring the plasma ratio of tryptophan to large neutral amino

acids in subjects eating either a high-carbohydrate, low-protein breakfast (consisting of waffles, maple syrup, orange juice, and coffee with sugar) or a high-protein, low-carbohydrate breakfast (consisting of turkey ham, Egg Beaters, cheese, grapefruit, and butter). As predicted, the high-carbohydrate, low-protein meal did increase the ratio of tryptophan to large neutral amino acids, whereas this ratio was decreased by the high-protein, low-carbohydrate meal. However, the average increase noted after the high-carbohydrate, low-protein meal was only about 14%, which may not have much effect on brain 5-HT levels.

Pharmacological depletion of 5-HT has been widely used to assess the role of this neurotransmitter in various behavioral functions. One method often used in rodent studies consists of administering the drug *para*-**chlorophenylalanine** (**PCPA**), which selectively blocks 5-HT synthesis by irreversibly inhibiting tryptophan hydroxylase. One or two high doses of PCPA can reduce brain 5-HT levels in rats by 80% to 90% for as long as 2 weeks, until the serotonergic neurons make new molecules of tryptophan hydroxylase that haven't been exposed to the inhibitor. Because PCPA can cause adverse side effects in humans, researchers have developed an alternative approach that has been particularly valuable for studying the role of 5-HT in mood and mood disorders. Based in part on the rat studies of Fernstrom and Wurtman, this method involves the administration of an amino acid "cocktail" containing a large quantity of amino acids except for tryptophan. This cocktail leads to temporary depletion of brain 5-HT for two reasons: (1) the surge of amino acids in the bloodstream stimulates protein synthesis by the liver, which reduces the level of plasma tryptophan to below its starting point; and (2) the large neutral amino acids in the cocktail inhibit entry of the remaining tryptophan into the brain. The 5-HT depletion produced by this method is not nearly as great or as long-lasting as that produced by PCPA. However, several studies have shown that giving the amino acid cocktail to previously depressed patients may cause a reappearance of depressive symptoms. In one case, 15 women who had suffered from repeated episodes of major depression but who were recovered at the time of the study were given either a tryptophan-free or tryptophan-containing amino acid mixture under double-blind conditions (Smith et al., 1997). Whereas the tryptophan-containing mixture had no effect on mood or depressive symptoms, the tryptophan-free mixture led to significant increases in depression ratings for 10 of the subjects, as well as an overall increase in self-reported feelings of sadness (**Figure 6.3**). Such findings implicate 5-HT in mood regulation and further suggest that in patients successfully treated with

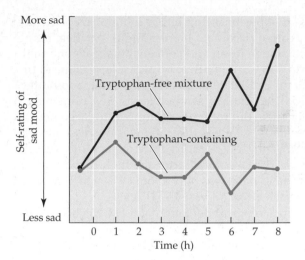

Figure 6.3 Rapid tryptophan depletion leads to symptom relapse in recovered depressed patients. Subjects were women who had a past history of recurrent depressive episodes, were currently in remission, and were not currently taking any antidepresssant medications. On separate occasions, each subject was given a mixture of amino acids either with or without tryptophan. The tryptophan-containing mixture had no effect on mood, whereas the tryptophan-free mixture elicited an increase in self-rated sadness. In two-thirds of subjects, tryptophan depletion further caused clinically significant depressive symptoms, as determined by the Hamilton Depression Rating Scale (not shown). (After Smith et al., 1997.)

antidepressant medications, symptom improvement may depend on continued activity of the serotonergic system (see also Chapter 19).

Similar processes regulate storage, release, and inactivation of serotonin and the catecholamines

Serotonin is transported into synaptic vesicles using the same vesicular transporter found in dopaminergic and noradrenergic neurons—VMAT2 (vesicular monoamine transporter). As with the catecholamines, storage of 5-HT in the vesicles plays a critical role in protecting the transmitter from enzymatic breakdown in the nerve terminal. Consequently, the VMAT blocker reserpine depletes serotonergic neurons of 5-HT, just as it depletes catecholamines in dopaminergic and noradrenergic cells.

Serotonergic autoreceptors control release of 5-HT in the same way as the DA and NE autoreceptors discussed in the previous chapter. Terminal autoreceptors directly inhibit 5-HT release, whereas other autoreceptors on the cell body and dendrites of the serotonergic neurons (somatodendritic autoreceptors) indirectly inhibit release by slowing the rate of firing of the neurons (**Figure 6.4**). Somatodendritic autoreceptors are of the 5-HT_{1A} subtype, whereas the terminal autoreceptors are either of the 5-HT_{1B} or 5-HT_{1D} subtype, depending on the species (see later discussion of 5-HT receptors).

Release of 5-HT can be directly stimulated by a family of drugs based on the

structure of amphetamine. These compounds include **para-chloroamphetamine**, which is mainly used experimentally; **fenfluramine**, which at one time was prescribed for appetite suppression in obese patients, and **3,4-methylenedioxymethamphetamine** (**MDMA**), which is a recreational and abused drug. Besides their acute behavioral effects, these drugs (particularly *para*-chloroamphetamine and MDMA) can exert toxic effects on the serotonergic system (**Box 6.1**).

When we examine the processes responsible for inactivation of 5-HT after its release, many similarities to the catecholamine systems become apparent. After 5-HT is released, it is rapidly removed from the synaptic cleft by a reuptake process. Analogously to

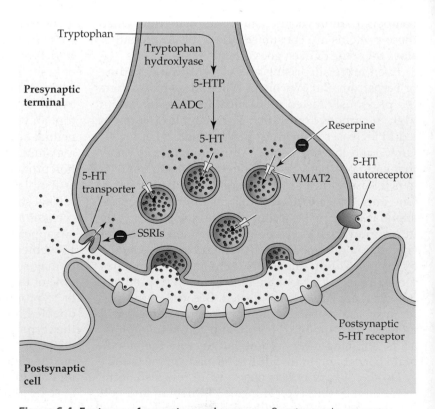

Figure 6.4 Features of a serotonergic neuron Serotonergic neurons express the vesicular monoamine transporter VMAT2, the 5-HT transporter (SERT), and 5-HT_{1B} or 5-HT_{1D} autoreceptors in their terminals.

BOX 6.1   History of Psychopharmacology

"Ecstasy"—Harmless Feel-Good Drug, Dangerous Neurotoxin, or Miracle Medication?

Over the years, pharmaceutical companies have synthesized many thousands of new compounds in the search for drugs that might be useful in the treatment of one or another medical disorder. Unfortunately, a vast majority of these compounds are discarded either because they do not produce a useful biological effect, or because they fail somewhere along the rigorous process of safety and efficacy testing (see Box 4.2). Of course, occasionally a drug is discovered that does produce an interesting set of biological actions that are ultimately exploited for therapeutic benefit, illicit recreational use, or sometimes both. The present discussion deals with one such compound—3,4-methylenedioxymethamphetamine (MDMA), which is known on the street by a variety of names including "ecstasy," "E," "X," "Adam," and "love drug." When someone purchases a pill that the seller says is ecstasy, it may or may not actually contain MDMA. For this reason, we will use the term MDMA when we are referring to the pure chemical compound (e.g., as might be used in a controlled animal study); however, we will use the term ecstasy when we are referring to the human clinical literature on this topic because of the uncertainty associated with the purchase and consumption of street drugs that contain variable and unknown amounts of MDMA.

The early history of the discovery of MDMA and the route by which it became a recreational drug have been thoroughly reviewed by Freudenmann et al. (2006), Pentney (2001), and Rosenbaum (2002). Chemically, MDMA is a close relative of amphetamine and methamphetamine, and it shares some but not all of their

biological and behavioral characteristics (e.g., neurochemically, all three compounds acutely release catecholamines and 5-HT from their respective nerve terminals, although MDMA has a more potent effect on 5-HT release than is seen with amphetamine or methamphetamine). MDMA was first synthesized by the Merck pharmaceutical company in Germany in 1912. Although many textbooks and other sources claim that MDMA was produced as part of a project to find new anorectic (appetite-suppressing) compounds, original documents demonstrate that Merck was, in fact, seeking new hemostatic agents (drugs that would help stop bleeding) (Freudenmann et al., 2006). Although Merck went so far as to patent MDMA in 1914 and did perform some later unpublished studies on the drug, the company never marketed it for any therapeutic use.

Hardman and colleagues reported the first study on the effects of MDMA on experimental animals in 1973. This work had actually been conducted 20 years earlier under a classified contract from the U.S. Army to investigate the mechanisms of action of mescaline and other potential hallucinogenic compounds with a similar chemical structure (later declassification of the results allowed them to finally be published). More important, the first information regarding the influence of MDMA on humans was published by Alexander Shulgin and David Nichols in 1978. Shulgin was an American chemist who, while working for the Dow Chemical company, had become interested in developing and characterizing new mind-altering drugs. He began the practice of taking the drugs himself and/or offering

them to close colleagues and friends (Benzenhöfer and Passie, 2010). After leaving Dow in 1966, Shulgin continued this work as a private researcher and consultant. In the Shulgin and Nichols 1978 article, which included a report on the effects of taking MDMA (75 to 150 mg orally, which is a common recreational dose even now), the authors stated that "the drug appears to evoke an easily controlled altered state of consciousness with emotional and sensual overtones. It can be compared in its effects to marijuana, to psilocybin devoid of the hallucinatory component, or to low levels of MDA (p. 77)." It is noteworthy that the authors mention MDA (3,4-methylenedioxyamphetamine), which, although studied before MDMA, was later discovered to be a biologically active metabolite of the latter compound.

Following this "rediscovery" of MDMA, events started to move rapidly in several different directions. MDA, which (as noted previously) produces similar psychological effects to those elicited by MDMA, had already been proposed as a potential adjunct to psychotherapy due to its purported ability to increase empathy between therapist and client (Naranjo et al., 1967). After experiencing the effects of MDMA himself, Shulgin apparently decided that this drug would be even better therapeutically than MDA. Consequently, in the 1970s, he began to distribute MDMA to many psychotherapists for use during their therapy sessions (although both the distribution and use of MDMA were performed quietly because of the uncertain legal status of this

(Continued on next page)

BOX 6.1 *(continued)*

compound) (Pentney, 2001). During this same period, MDMA was (perhaps inevitably) gradually beginning to make its way onto the street. By the early 1980s, "Adam" or "ecstasy," depending on where one lived, was growing in popularity. Use was particularly heavy in Dallas, Austin, and other parts of Texas. Therefore, it was no surprise when MDMA began to attract the attention of the Drug Enforcement Administration (DEA), an arm of the U.S. Justice Department that determines the legal status of drugs and prosecutes users of illegal substances. Several research laboratories had already been studying the short- and long-term effects of MDMA in laboratory animals such as rats and monkeys and had found alarming evidence for large depletions of 5-HT in the forebrains of animals given high doses of this compound. Moreover, if brain slices were stained with an anti-5-HT antibody to allow visualization of serotonergic axons in the forebrain, most of the staining disappeared within a week after high-dose MDMA exposure. In a particularly striking study by Hatzidimitriou and coworkers (1999) using squirrel monkeys, some of the animals exhibited a marked reduction in staining even 7 years after receiving drug treatment (see figure). The DEA held hearings concerning the status of MDMA in 1985, and, largely because of the testimony of the animal researchers, the Agency assigned the drug Schedule I status. As discussed further in Chapter 9, Schedule I is the most restrictive schedule and is reserved for substances that have no recognized medical use and high abuse potential (e.g., heroin).

In hindsight, we know that the scheduling of MDMA did not prevent its continued recreational use each year by thousands of young people, often at "raves" and other dances. These users presumably either don't care what happens to their brain's serotonergic system, or they don't believe that the drug is as dangerous as was argued in that original DEA hearing over 25

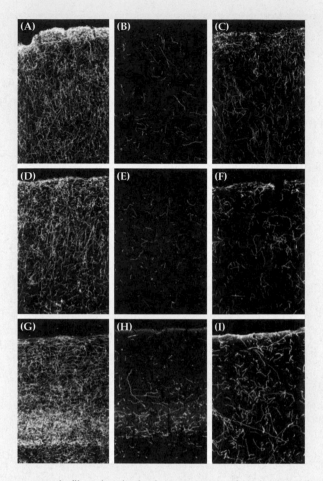

Reduced serotonergic fiber density in the neocortex of squirrel monkeys treated with MDMA Serotonergic axons were stained with an antibody against 5-HT and then visualized using dark-field microscopy (this makes the background appear dark and the stained fibers appear light). The panels show fiber staining in tissue sections from the frontal cortex, parietal cortex, and primary visual cortex, respectively, of a control monkey that had received only saline (A, D, and G), a monkey that had received subcutaneous injections of 5mg/kg MDMA twice daily for 4 days and was then killed 2 weeks later (B, E, and H), and a monkey that had received the same MDMA treatment but was killed 7 years later (C, F, and I). MDMA exposure produced a massive reduction of 5-HT–immunoreactive fibers in all three cortical areas at 2 weeks post-treatment, and noticeable deficits were still apparent even after 7 years of recovery. (From Hatzidimitriou et al., 1999.)

years ago. So who is right? Sufficient scientific evidence now indicates that frequent high doses of ecstasy are associated with significant neuropsychiatric impairment that may be related to serotonergic dysfunction (Karlsen et al., 2007); however, whether actual degeneration of serotonergic nerve fibers occurs, as opposed to biochemical abnormalities without anatomical damage, remains a point of controversy (Biezonski and Meyer, 2011). It is also unclear whether occasional low doses of MDMA produce any lasting behavioral or neurochemical impairment.

The final part of this historical survey of MDMA/ecstasy is perhaps the most fascinating. We mentioned earlier that in the 1970s and 1980s, MDMA was being administered in an unregulated way by many psychotherapists to their clients to assist in the therapeutic process. This practice mostly stopped once MDMA was given a Schedule I classification in 1985. However, around the year 2000, a private organization called the Multidisciplinary

BOX 6.1 *(continued)*

Association for Psychedelic Studies (MAPS) began to initiate the process of organizing, obtaining regulatory permissions, and raising funding for controlled studies into the use of low-dose MDMA treatment as an adjunct to psychotherapeutic treatment of patients with several different disorders, particularly severe posttraumatic stress disorder (PTSD). The first such study to be completed and published was a double-blind, placebo-controlled pilot study involving a group of women with chronic PTSD who had been resistant to previous attempts at treatment. Results showed significant improvement in the clinical response when MDMA was added to the standard psychotherapy procedure (Mithoefer et al., 2010). Clearly, more work needs to be done in this area, and these initial positive findings must be replicated by other research groups. Nevertheless, it is intriguing to consider that we may have now come full circle with a drug originally discovered in a program to develop new compounds for hemostasis and later found to be neurotoxic when used recreationally at high doses, but potentially beneficial for patients with severe treatment-resistant PTSD when given at low, controlled doses in a therapeutic setting.

DA and NE, this mechanism involves a protein on the nerve terminal known as the **5-HT transporter**, also known as **SERT** (see Figure 6.4). This protein turns out to be a key target of drug action. For example, the introduction of **fluoxetine** (better known as **Prozac**) in late 1987 spawned a whole new class of antidepressant drugs based on the idea of inhibiting 5-HT reuptake. These compounds are, therefore, called **selective serotonin reuptake inhibitors** (**SSRIs**) (see Chapter 19). Certain abused drugs such as cocaine and MDMA likewise interact with SERT, but they are not selective in their effects because they also influence the DA transporter. Mutant mice lacking a functional SERT exhibit an astonishing array of behavioral and physiological abnormalities that presumably arise as the result of chronic enhancement of serotonergic activity (since the neurotransmitter cannot be taken up after it is released) during the animal's lifetime (Murphy and Lesch, 2008; Murphy et al., 2008) (**Figure 6.5**). Some of the functions that can be ascribed to 5-HT on the basis of the phenotype of SERT knockout mice are discussed in the last part of this chapter.

You will recall that DA and NE are metabolized by two different enzymes—monoamine oxidase (MAO) and catechol-*O*-methyltransferase (COMT). Because 5-HT is not a catecholamine, it is not affected by COMT. However, its breakdown is catalyzed by MAO to yield the metabolite **5-hydroxyindoleacetic acid** (**5-HIAA**). The level of 5-HIAA in the brains of animals or in the cerebrospinal fluid of humans or animals is often used as a measure of the activity of serotonergic neurons. This practice is based on research showing that when these neurons fire more rapidly, they make more 5-HT, and a corresponding increase in the formation of 5-HIAA occurs.

Section Summary

- The neurotransmitter 5-HT is synthesized from the amino acid tryptophan in two biochemical reactions. The first and rate-limiting reaction is catalyzed by the enzyme tryptophan hydroxylase.

- Brain 5-HT synthesis is controlled, in part, by tryptophan availability. Thus, 5-HT synthesis is reduced by administration of an amino acid mixture lacking tryptophan, whereas synthesis is increased by consumption of a high-carbohydrate, low-protein meal (which increases the plasma ratio of tryptophan to other large neutral amino acids that compete for transport across the blood–brain barrier).

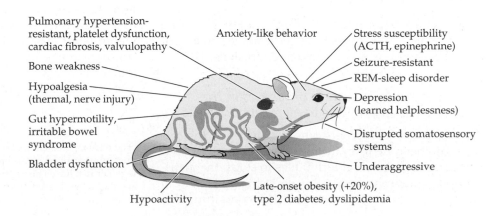

Figure 6.5 Behavioral and physiological phenotypes of SERT knockout mice Widespread SERT expression both in the brain (by serotonergic neurons and their axons and terminals) and in various peripheral tissues leads to dysfunction in many behavioral and physiological systems when normal 5-HT uptake is impaired by loss of this transporter. (After Murphy and Lesch, 2008.)

Pulmonary hypertension-resistant, platelet dysfunction, cardiac fibrosis, valvulopathy

Bone weakness

Hypoalgesia (thermal, nerve injury)

Gut hypermotility, irritable bowel syndrome

Bladder dysfunction

Hypoactivity

Anxiety-like behavior

Stress susceptibility (ACTH, epinephrine)

Seizure-resistant

REM-sleep disorder

Depression (learned helplessness)

Disrupted somatosensory systems

Underaggressive

Late-onset obesity (+20%), type 2 diabetes, dyslipidemia

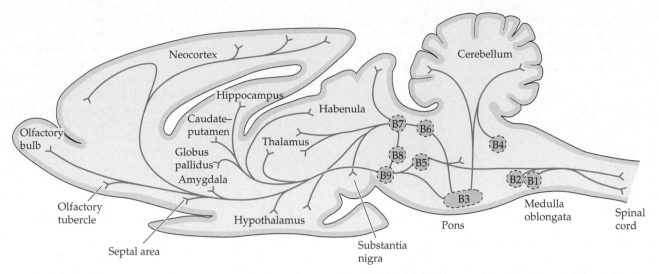

Figure 6.6 Anatomy of the serotonergic system The B7 cell group corresponds to the dorsal raphe, and the B8 cell group corresponds to the median raphe.

- VMAT2 is responsible for loading 5-HT into synaptic vesicles for subsequent release.
- Serotonin release is inhibited by autoreceptors located on the cell body, dendrites, and terminals of serotonergic neurons. The terminal autoreceptors are of either the 5-HT$_{1B}$ or 5-HT$_{1D}$ subtype, depending on the species, whereas the somatodendritic autoreceptors are of the 5-HT$_{1A}$ subtype.
- Several compounds have been identified that cause 5-HT release, one of which is MDMA. At high doses, this drug can produce serotonergic toxicity characterized by long-lasting depletion of 5-HT and other markers of serotonergic neurons.
- Serotonergic transmission is terminated by reuptake of 5-HT from the synaptic cleft. This process is mediated by the 5-HT transporter, which is an important target of several antidepressant drugs.
- Serotonin is ultimately metabolized by MAO to form the major breakdown product 5-HIAA.

Organization and Function of the Serotonergic System

There is a widespread distribution of 5-HT in the brain, which contributes to its participation in a variety of behavioral and physiological functions.

The serotonergic system originates in the brainstem and projects to all forebrain areas

The Swedish researchers who first mapped the catecholamine systems in the 1960s (see Chapter 5) used the same experimental techniques to study the distribution of neurons and pathways using 5-HT. But in this case, they designated the 5-HT–containing cell

groups with the letter "B" instead of "A," which they had used for the dopaminergic and noradrenergic cell groups. It turns out that almost all of the serotonergic neurons in the CNS are found along the midline of the brainstem (medulla, pons, and midbrain), loosely associated with a network of cell clusters called the **raphe nuclei**.[1] Of greatest interest to neuropharmacologists are the **dorsal raphe nucleus** and the **median raphe nucleus**, located in the area of the caudal midbrain and rostral pons. Together, these nuclei give rise to most of the serotonergic fibers in the forebrain. Virtually all forebrain regions receive serotonergic innervation, including the neocortex, striatum and nucleus accumbens, thalamus and hypothalamus, and limbic system structures such as the hippocampus, amygdala, and septal area (**Figure 6.6**).

There is a large family of serotonin receptors, most of which are metabotropic

One of the remarkable properties of 5-HT is the number of receptors that have evolved for this transmitter. At the present time, pharmacologists have identified at least fourteen 5-HT receptor subtypes. Among these is a group of five different 5-HT$_1$ receptors (designated 5-HT$_{1A}$, 5-HT$_{1B}$, 5-HT$_{1D}$, 5-HT$_{1E}$, and 5-HT$_{1F}$), along with a smaller group of three 5-HT$_2$ receptors (5-HT$_{2A}$, 5-HT$_{2B}$, and 5-HT$_{2C}$) and additional

---

[1]The term *raphe* is Greek for "seam" or "suture." In biology, the term is applied to structures that look as if they are joined together in a line. This is applicable to the raphe nuclei, which are aligned with each other along the rostral–caudal axis of the brainstem.

receptors designated 5-HT$_3$, 5-HT$_4$, 5-HT$_{5A}$, 5-HT$_{5B}$ (not expressed in humans), 5-HT$_6$, and 5-HT$_7$. All of these receptors are metabotropic, except for the 5-HT$_3$ receptor, which is an excitatory ionotropic receptor. The attentive reader will have noticed that there is no 5-HT$_{1C}$ subtype listed. One of the serotonergic receptors initially had that designation; however, this receptor was later determined to belong to the 5-HT$_2$ family by structural and functional criteria and therefore, it was renamed 5-HT$_{2C}$. The following discussion will focus largely on 5-HT$_{1A}$ and 5-HT$_{2A}$ receptors, which are the best-known receptor subtypes in terms of their cellular and behavioral effects. We will subsequently touch on two other subtypes that have successfully been targeted for therapeutic purposes.

5-HT$_{1A}$ RECEPTORS   5-HT$_{1A}$ receptors are found in many brain areas, but they are particularly concentrated in the hippocampus, the septal area, parts of the amygdala, and the dorsal raphe nucleus. In the forebrain, these receptors are located postsynaptically to 5-HT–containing nerve terminals. As mentioned earlier, 5-HT$_{1A}$ receptors additionally function as somatodendritic autoreceptors in the dorsal and median raphe nuclei. 5-HT$_{1A}$ receptors work through two major mechanisms. First, the receptors reduce cAMP synthesis by inhibiting adenylyl cyclase (**Figure 6.7A**). The second mechanism involves increased opening of K$^+$ channels and membrane hyperpolarization, which we have seen is a property shared by D$_2$ dopamine receptors and α$_2$-adrenergic receptors. You will recall that this hyperpolarization leads to a decrease in firing of either the postsynaptic cell (in the case of 5-HT$_{1A}$ receptors located postsynaptically) or the serotonergic neuron itself (in the case of the 5-HT$_{1A}$ autoreceptors).

Several drugs act as either full or partial agonists at 5-HT$_{1A}$ receptors, including **buspirone**, **ipsapirone**, and **8-hydroxy-2-(di-n-propylamino)tetralin (8-OH-DPAT)**. Some of the behavioral effects produced by administering a 5-HT$_{1A}$ agonist are described in the last part of this chapter. The most widely used 5-HT$_{1A}$ receptor antagonist is the experimental drug **WAY 100635**, which was originally developed by the Wyeth-Ayerst pharmaceutical company (hence the WAY designation). Administration of this compound in the absence of a 5-HT$_{1A}$ agonist has provided important information about the degree to which 5-HT$_{1A}$ receptors (either autoreceptors or postsynaptic receptors) are occupied by endogenous 5-HT under baseline conditions.

5-HT$_{2A}$ RECEPTORS   Large numbers of 5-HT$_{2A}$ receptors are present in the cerebral cortex. This receptor subtype is also found in the striatum, in the nucleus accumbens, and in a variety of other brain areas. Similar to α$_1$-adrenergic receptors, 5-HT$_{2A}$ receptors function mainly by activating the phosphoinositide second-messenger system (**Figure 6.7B**). You will recall that this system increases Ca^{2+} levels within the postsynaptic cell and also activates protein kinase C (PKC). Thus our discussion of different neurotransmitters and their receptor subtypes has included common mechanisms of transmitter action that occur over and over again. These mechanisms may involve a second messenger such as cAMP or Ca^{2+}, or some type of ion channel such as K$^+$ channels, which are opened by a wide variety of receptors. **1-(2,5-Dimethoxy-4-iodophenyl)-2-aminopropane (DOI)** is a 5-HT$_{2A}$ agonist that is widely used experimentally, whereas **ketanserin** and **ritanserin** are typical 5-HT$_{2A}$ antagonists.

(A)

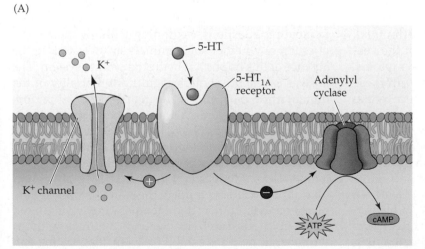

(B)

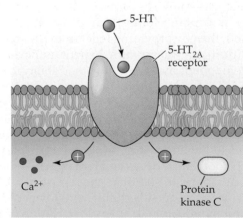

Figure 6.7 5-HT$_{1A}$ and 5-HT$_{2A}$ receptors operate through different signaling mechanisms   5-HT$_{1A}$ receptors inhibit cAMP production and activate K$^+$ channel opening (A), whereas 5-HT$_{2A}$ receptors increase intracellular Ca^{2+} levels and stimulate protein kinase C via the phosphoinositide second-messenger system (B). For purposes of simplification, the G proteins required for coupling the receptors to their signaling pathways are not shown.

Giving DOI or another 5-HT$_{2A}$ agonist to rats or mice leads to a characteristic "head-twitch" response (periodic, brief twitches of the head), which is a useful measure of 5-HT$_{2A}$ receptor stimulation in these species. More interesting is the fact that DOI and related drugs are **hallucinogenic** (hallucination-producing) in humans. Indeed, the hallucinogenic effects of **lysergic acid diethylamide (LSD)** are believed to stem from its ability to stimulate 5-HT$_{2A}$ receptors. LSD and other hallucinogens are discussed in greater detail in Chapter 15.

In recent years, blockade of 5-HT$_{2A}$ receptors has become a major topic of discussion and research with respect to the treatment of schizophrenia. As mentioned in the previous chapter, traditional antischizophrenic drugs that work by blocking D$_2$ dopamine receptors often produce serious movement-related side effects, some of which can resemble Parkinson's disease. Such side effects are much less severe, however, with later-generation drugs such as **clozapine (Clozaril)** and **risperidone (Risperdal)**. Both clozapine and risperidone block 5-HT$_{2A}$ receptors, in addition to exerting their effects on the dopamine system. This has led to the hypothesis that a combination of D$_2$ and 5-HT$_{2A}$ receptor antagonism leads to symptom improvement in schizophrenic patients while minimizing the side effects associated with previous antischizophrenic drugs that don't affect the 5-HT$_{2A}$ receptor (see Chapter 20).

OTHER RECEPTOR SUBTYPES   Widespread expression of other serotonergic receptor subtypes, both within the nervous system and in non-neural tissues, has led to the development of various medications that target these receptors. Two well-known examples pertain to the 5-HT$_{1B/1D}$ and 5-HT$_3$ subtypes. Abnormal dilation of blood vessels within the brain is one of the key factors contributing to migraine headaches. A class of 5-HT$_{1B/1D}$ agonists known as triptans (e.g., sumatriptan [Imitrex], zolmitriptan [Zomig]) causes constriction of the vessels, thereby providing relief from migraine symptoms. Additional therapeutic benefit associated with these compounds may come from their ability to reduce central 5-HT release by stimulating terminal serotonergic autoreceptors (Hamel, 2007). 5-HT$_3$ receptors are located on peripheral terminals of the vagus nerve, one function of which is to transmit sensory information from the viscera (including the gastrointestinal tract) to the brain. Cancer chemotherapy drugs and radiation treatment have both been found to stimulate the release of 5-HT in the gut, which subsequently stimulates the vagal 5-HT$_3$ receptors and induces (via the vagus) activation of the vomiting center in the brainstem. Consequently, 5-HT$_3$ antagonists such as ondansetron (Zofran) and granisetron (Kytril) are sometimes used to counteract the nausea and vomiting associated with cancer treatments.

Multiple approaches have identified several behavioral and physiological functions of serotonin

It is clear from numerous neurochemical and pharmacological studies in both animals and humans that the serotonergic system helps regulate many behavioral and physiological functions. In human clinical research, serotonergic function has been investigated using several different methodological approaches, including:

- Determining the association between levels of cerebrospinal fluid (CSF) 5-HIAA or postmortem regional brain 5-HT and 5-HIAA concentrations and behavioral traits or, in some cases, the occurrence of neuropsychiatric disorders

- Assessing behavioral, subjective, and physiological responses to pharmacological challenges with SSRIs or with receptor agonists or antagonists

- Identifying associations between psychiatric disorders and polymorphisms in the genes for SERT or for various serotonergic receptors

Some findings relating SERT polymorphisms with risk for major depression will be presented later, in the chapter on affective disorders (Chapter 19). With respect to CSF and brain concentrations of 5-HIAA and 5-HT, there are a number of interesting findings relating the serotonergic system to aggressive behavior, particularly impulsive aggression. These and other results linking 5-HT to aggression are discussed in **Box 6.2**.

Recent studies using powerful genetic methods have shed new light on the functions of the serotonergic system. Specifically, it is now possible to generate mutant mice that possess virtually no serotonergic neurons in their brain. Naturally, this procedure raises several fascinating questions, beginning with the most basic question of whether such animals survive at all in the absence of this important neurotransmitter system. The answer is yes, but there is significant mortality of the mutant mice, particularly during the neonatal period. Among surviving animals, researchers have thus far identified two major physiological deficits. First, mice lacking central serotonergic neurons have significant problems with thermoregulation (regulation of body temperature) (Hodges and Richerson, 2010). In particular, unlike wild-type mice, the mutants do not adequately maintain their body temperature when placed into a cold environment. Second, the mice without serotonergic neurons exhibit frequent, long-lasting episodes of apnea (cessation of breathing), especially when they are young. This is illustrated in **Figure 6.8**, which not only depicts a long apneic episode in a 4-day-old mutant mouse but also shows restoration of more

BOX 6.2   The Cutting Edge

Serotonin and Aggression

What is aggression, and how do we define and conceptualize aggressive behaviors? In the case of human aggression, the intent of the actor is important. Thus, a common definition of aggression in human studies is "behavior that is intended to cause physical or psychological harm or pain to the victim." Human aggression is often classified as either premeditated (instrumental) or impulsive (reactive) (Siever, 2008). Premeditated aggression is planned, rather than provoked by immediate frustration or threat. In contrast, impulsive aggression is a suddenly provoked behavior that occurs in response to conditions of frustration, threat, or stress. It is typically accompanied by feelings of anger and/or fear and by activation of the sympathetic nervous system.

Whereas studies of human aggression can benefit from self-reports of intentionality and emotional state, animal studies must operationalize the concept of aggression. This difference in approach has led to the development of several formal typologies of aggressive behavior. For example, Moyer (1968) proposed that aggression in animals could be categorized as predatory, inter-male, fear-induced, irritable, territorial, maternal, or instrumental aggression. A more recent review by Nelson and Chiavegatto (2001) lists a variety of different types of aggression that can be observed in animals under naturalistic and/or specific experimental conditions (see table).

The neural circuit underlying aggressive behavior in humans has been elucidated using a combination of approaches, including brain imaging studies and examination of behavioral changes in patients with lesions of various brain areas (produced by stroke, tumor, head trauma, or other forms of brain injury). These approaches have implicated a circuit that includes several key cortical areas (orbitofrontal cortex, temporal cortex, and cingulate cortex) and a group of subcortical limbic system structures (amygdala, hypothalamus, and hippocampus) (Siever, 2008). The neural circuit involved in aggression in rodents includes many of the same areas but also incorporates the bed nucleus of the stria terminalis (BNST; a brain area sometimes considered part of an "extended" amygdala) and the periaqueductal grey (Nelson and Trainor, 2007). In both cases, all of the brain areas mentioned receive substantial serotonergic innervation and express several different 5-HT receptor subtypes.

One basic approach to understanding the influence of 5-HT on aggressive behavior is to examine the global relationship between 5-HT activity and levels of aggression. This may be done naturalistically by correlating some measure of serotonergic function such as cerebrospinal fluid 5-HIAA concentrations with measures of aggression. Alternatively, investigators can use pharmacological methods to increase or decrease overall 5-HT levels and/or transmission

(Continued on next page)

Types of Aggression

Category of aggression	Function and/or experimental conditions
Predatory	Attack of a predator on a prey animal
Anti-predatory	Attack of a prey animal against its predator
Sex-related	Aggression that occurs in the context of a sexual interaction between two animals
Dominance	Aggression (usually between males) involved in the establishment or maintenance of rank within their group's dominance hierarchy
Maternal	Attack by a mother in the defense of her offspring
Territorial	Aggression that occurs in the context of defending one's territory; in the laboratory this is commonly modeled using the resident-intruder test in which a strange male is introduced into the home cage of a resident male
Defensive	Attack elicited by a fear-inducing stimulus
Irritable	Attack elicited by extreme frustration or stress; in the laboratory this may be modeled by the application of a brief electric shock

Source: Nelson and Chiavegatto, 2001.

BOX 6.2 *(continued)*

throughout the brain. For example, increasing extracellular 5-HT (thereby enhancing serotonergic transmission) can be achieved by systemic administration of an SSRI or (in the case of mice) by deletion of the *SERT* gene. In contrast, serotonergic transmission can be decreased by pharmacological inhibition of tryptophan hydroxylase (thus blocking 5-HT synthesis) or by administration of a 5-HT neurotoxin. Taken together, these studies have revealed that relatively high serotonergic levels/activity are associated with reduced aggressive behavior, whereas relatively low serotonergic levels/activity are associated with increased aggressive behavior (Carrillo et al., 2009; Ferrari et al., 2005; Holmes et al., 2002; Siever, 2008). It is important to note, nevertheless, that these findings vary, depending on such factors as the genetic background of the animal, the specific drug treatment regimen used, the type of aggression being studied, and other experimental parameters (Carrillo et al., 2009). Moreover, in some cases, heightened aggressive behavior is not a specific behavioral effect but rather is part of a

more general pattern of increased impulsivity on the part of the animals or humans.

More detailed information regarding the relationship between 5-HT and aggression has been obtained by focusing on the roles of specific 5-HT receptor subtypes. Rodent studies have directed a lot of attention to the 5-HT_{1A} and 5-HT_{1B} receptors. Agonists at either of these subtypes lead to a reduction in aggressive behavior, whereas mutant male mice lacking the 5-HT_{1B} receptor exhibit increased aggression (although this behavioral change may be related, at least in part, to enhanced impulsivity by the animals) (Nelson and Chiavegatto, 2001; Nelson and Trainor, 2007). Some researchers have pointed out that the ability of a 5-HT_{1B} agonist to reduce levels of aggression seems to be paradoxical because this receptor subtype functions as an inhibitory terminal autoreceptor, and therefore, activation of the receptor leads to decreased 5-HT release (which should theoretically stimulate aggressive behavior); however, 5-HT_{1B} receptors are also located on other neurotransmitter

terminals as inhibitory heteroreceptors (see Chapter 3); thus 5-HT_{1B} agonists could be suppressing aggressive behavior by acting through other neurotransmitter systems.

In human studies, there has been interest in members of the 5-HT_2 receptor family. For example, some evidence suggests that antipsychotic drugs that exert significant 5-HT_{2A} receptor antagonism help reduce violent behavior in schizophrenic patients with a highly aggressive behavior pattern. Given the findings of a combination of preclinical and clinical studies, Siever (2008) has proposed that impulsive aggression in humans is based on the balance of prefrontal cortical 5-HT_{2A} and 5-HT_{2C} activity, with high activity of 5-HT_{2A} receptors facilitating aggressiveness but high activity of 5-HT_{2C} receptors reducing aggressiveness. Ultimately, it would be of great benefit to society if compounds that selectively inhibit violent aggressive tendencies could be found, but thus far, the search for such compounds (sometimes referred to as *serenics*) has not been successful.

---

normal breathing after administration of the 5-HT_{2A} agonist DOI. These results implicate the lack of activation of 5-HT_{2A} receptors in the abnormal breathing patterns of animals lacking serotonergic neurons. Moreover, they support growing evidence that abnormalities in the serotonergic system may be involved in the etiology of sudden infant death syndrome (SIDS), a disorder that has been linked to breathing problems in the infant (Kinney et al., 2009). Such findings have thus far implicated 5-HT in two critical physiological systems, one involving thermoregulation and the other involving respiratory control. We look forward to future studies in which these same mutant mice are tested behaviorally in models of depression, anxiety, learning and memory, and addiction.

Pharmacological studies designed to investigate the functional role of 5-HT have used a variety of tools, ranging from serotonergic neurotoxins to drug

challenges with selective receptor agonists and antagonists (as noted previously for human research studies). Serotonergic neurotoxins include the previously mentioned compounds *para*-chloroamphetamine and MDMA. Another compound called **5,7-dihydroxytryptamine (5,7-DHT)** has also been widely used to produce serotonergic lesions in experimental animals, although one limitation of using 5,7-DHT is that it must be given directly into the brain because it doesn't cross the blood–brain barrier. 5,7-DHT causes massive damage to serotonergic axons and nerve terminals in the forebrain, yet cell bodies in the raphe nuclei are usually spared. Due to space limitations, we cannot review all of the behavioral effects produced by lesioning the serotonergic system; however, various studies have reported changes in hunger and eating behavior, anxiety, pain sensitivity, and learning and memory. The following paragraphs briefly describe

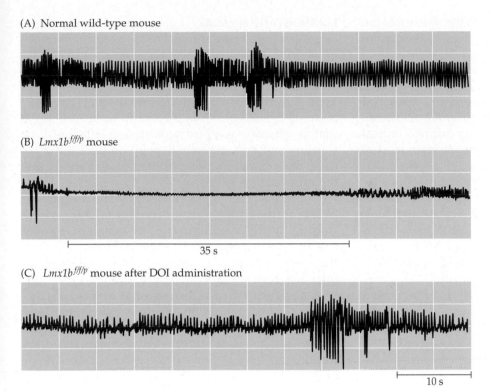

(A) Normal wild-type mouse

(B) *Lmx1b^{f/f/p}* mouse

|— 35 s —|

(C) *Lmx1b^{f/f/p}* mouse after DOI administration

|— 10 s —|

Figure 6.8 Apnea in a neonatal mutant mouse lacking central serotonergic neurons Top trace illustrates the normal breathing pattern of a 4-day-old wild-type mouse. The middle trace shows the breathing pattern of a mutant mouse of the same age that lacks central serotonergic neurons (the mutant genetic construct is denoted as *Lmx1b^{f/f/p}*). Note the 35-second period of apnea during which no breathing occurred. The bottom trace demonstrates that administration of the 5-HT$_{2A}$ agonist DOI to the mutant mice led to a more normal pattern of breathing as shown by the absence of apneic episodes. (After Hodges and Richerson, 2010.)

the involvement of specific receptor subtypes in these behavioral functions.

HUNGER AND EATING BEHAVIOR   Serotonin has long been known to influence hunger and eating behavior. Pharmacological studies have shown that 5-HT$_{1B}$ or 5-HT$_{2C}$ receptor agonists, as well as 5-HT$_6$ antagonists, produce **hypophagia** (reduced food intake) and weight loss in rodent models (Magalhães et al., 2010). Such findings have led to an interest in targeting these receptors in the development of new antiobesity compounds (Garfield and Heisler, 2009). In contrast, administration of a 5-HT$_{1A}$ receptor agonist leads to **hyperphagia** (excessive eating behavior). This effect appears to result from stimulation of somatodendritic 5-HT$_{1A}$ autoreceptors, thereby inhibiting the activity of serotonergic neurons and reducing 5-HT release in the forebrain.

ANXIETY   A large body of research has established a key role for 5-HT in the regulation of anxiety. As we shall see in Chapter 18, SSRIs are among the drugs used most commonly in the treatment of several kinds of anxiety disorders. One of the key receptor subtypes thought to be involved in the anxiolytic (antianxiety) effects of these compounds is the 5-HT$_{1A}$ receptor, and indeed the partial 5-HT$_{1A}$ agonist **buspirone** (trade name **BuSpar**) is sometimes prescribed as an antianxiety medication. Experimental animal studies have similarly linked the 5-HT$_{1A}$ receptor to the modulation of anxiety-like behaviors. Several strains of 5-HT$_{1A}$ knockout mice have

been generated, all of which show increased anxiety-like behavior in standard tests such as the elevated plus-maze or a similar test known as the elevated zero-maze (Akimova et al., 2009) (**Figure 6.9**). Interestingly, an elegant series of experiments by Gross and colleagues (2002) demonstrated that this behavioral phenotype of enhanced anxiety-like behavior occurs due to the lack of 5-HT$_{1A}$ receptors in forebrain areas during early post-

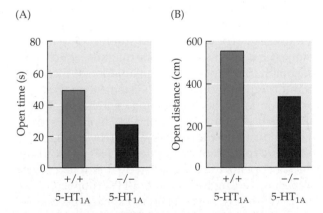

(A)

(B)

Figure 6.9 Genetic deletion of the 5-HT$_{1A}$ receptor increases anxiety-like behavior in the elevated zero-maze Wild-type (5-HT$_{1A}$^{+/+}) and 5-HT$_{1A}$ knockout (5-HT$_{1A}$^{-/-}) mice were tested in the elevated zero-maze, which is a circular apparatus with open and closed areas like the elevated plus-maze. Compared with wild-type mice, knockout animals showed increased anxiety, as indicated by less time spent (A) and less distance traveled (B) in open areas of the maze. (After Heisler et al., 1998.)

natal development and is not due to the absence of the receptor in the adult animals at the time of behavioral testing. Put another way, the presence or absence of this receptor subtype during development alters the neural circuitry regulating the baseline expression of anxiety-like behavior of the mice once they have reached adulthood. This finding raises the intriguing possibility that deficient 5-HT_{1A} receptor activity during a critical developmental period could give rise to later onset of anxiety disorders in humans.

5-HT_{2A} and 5-HT_{2C} receptors also regulate anxiety-like behaviors in rodent models. Administration of the $5\text{-HT}_{2A/2C}$ receptor agonist m-chlorophenylpiperazine (mCPP) increases anxiety-like behavior, whereas genetic deletion of either the 5-HT_{2A} or 5-HT_{2C} receptor has an anxiolytic effect in mice (Heisler et al., 2007; Weisstaub et al., 2006). With respect to the 5-HT_{2A} subtype, normal anxiety-like behavior could be reinstated by selective restoration of these receptors just in the cerebral cortex (Weisstaub et al., 2006). This finding suggests that 5-HT_{2A} receptor modulation of anxiety is mediated by receptors located in one or more neocortical areas, which may include the prefrontal cortex, as has been shown in other research (Etkin, 2009).

PAIN In addition to the use of serotonergic drugs in the treatment of migraine headaches, 5-HT has also been implicated in the processing of pain signals at the level of the spinal cord. Dorsal root sensory neurons carry pain information from peripheral sites such as the skin and synapse within the dorsal horn of the spinal cord. A descending pain modulatory system originates in the periaqueductal gray area of the caudal midbrain, synapses on the raphe nuclei of the rostral medulla (particularly the raphe magnus) and nearby parts of the medullary reticular formation, and then descends farther to the dorsal horn. Of particular interest here are the serotonergic neurons of the raphe magnus, which have been shown to influence the transmission of incoming pain information to ascending systems that carry this information to higher processing centers (see Figure 11.15). The best-known effect of 5-HT in this system is that it inhibits pain transmission, thereby producing a hypoalgesic (pain-reducing) effect. 5-HT–induced hypoalgesia appears to be mediated by multiple receptor subtypes, including 5-HT_{1B} and 5-HT_3 (Lopez-Garcia, 2006). Interestingly, however, under some experimental conditions, activation of spinal 5-HT_3 receptors can lead to hyperalgesia (pain enhancement) instead of hypoalgesia. Thus, 5-HT clearly plays a role in modulating pain transmission within the spinal cord; however, this role is complex and involves several receptor subtypes that together can produce either inhibitory or excitatory modulation.

LEARNING AND MEMORY Learning and memory processes can be powerfully influenced by the administration of various serotonergic receptor agonists and antagonists. Because space considerations do not permit us to consider all of the receptors that have been investigated in this regard, we will focus here on the 5-HT_{1A}, 5-HT_4, and 5-HT_6 subtypes. It is important to keep in mind that the effects of receptor agonists and antagonists on learning and memory may depend on the dose of the drug, the specific task being studied, and, in some cases, the species being tested.

One of the tasks used to investigate the role of 5-HT in learning and memory is **contextual fear conditioning**. In this paradigm, rats or mice are exposed to a novel environment (i.e., test chamber) in which they receive an electric footshock. When placed back into the chamber at a later time, these animals display a species-typical fear response of freezing (not moving), even though no additional shock has been applied. Hence, the animals have learned in a single trial to associate fear with the environmental context. Researchers have shown that systemic administration of the 5-HT_{1A} agonist 8-OH-DPAT before the training trial produces a dose-dependent reduction in freezing behavior when animals are tested 1 or 24 hours later (Ögren et al., 2008) (**Figure 6.10**). The same drug doses have no effect when given after the training. This led investigators to conclude that 5-HT_{1A} receptor activation produces a deficit in encoding (initial memory formation) but not in consolidation (transfer of information from short-term to long-term memory stores) of the fear association. The hippocampus, which is known to be necessary for contextual fear conditioning, has a high level of 5-HT_{1A} postsynaptic receptors. Additional studies showed that the memory-impairing effect of 8-OH-DPAT could be reproduced by direct infusion of the drug into the dorsal hippocampus. Moreover, this effect was blocked by prior infusion of the 5-HT_{1A} antagonist WAY 100635, thereby confirming the receptor selectivity of 8-OH-DPAT (Ögren et al., 2008). The reason why activation of hippocampal 5-HT_{1A} receptors leads to memory impairment is likely related to the previously mentioned action of this receptor to hyperpolarize, and thereby inhibit firing of, the postsynaptic cell. Other studies have indicated that impairment of learning and memory produced by various pharmacological manipulations can sometimes be reversed by blocking 5-HT_{1A} receptors. This raises the important possibility that 5-HT_{1A} antagonists could prove to be cognitive enhancers in humans with certain kinds of cognitive dysfunction (King et al., 2008).

5-HT_4 receptors are expressed most highly in the basal ganglia and the hippocampus. Somewhat lower

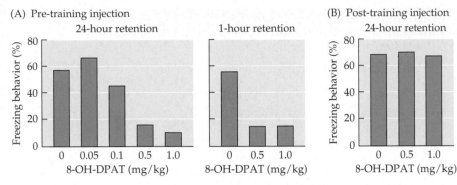

Figure 6.10 Pretraining stimulation of 5-HT$_{1A}$ receptors leads to dose-dependent impairment of one-trial contextual fear conditioning in mice. Mice were injected subcutaneously with 0.05 to 1.0 mg/kg of the 5-HT$_{1A}$ receptor agonist 8-OH-DPAT and then were given one trial in a contextual fear conditioning paradigm. (A) Higher doses of 8-OH-DPAT led to reduced freezing behavior when the mice were returned to the shock chamber either 1 hour or 24 hours later. (B) No effect was observed when the drug was administered after training, which was interpreted to mean that 5-HT$_{1A}$ activation impaired memory encoding but not memory consolidation in this emotional learning task. (After Ögren et al., 2008.)

levels of expression are found in the prefrontal cortex, septal area, and amygdala. In contrast to the 5-HT$_{1A}$ subtype, 5-HT$_4$ receptors depolarize the postsynaptic cell and therefore exert an excitatory effect. Studies in rodents and monkeys have demonstrated enhancement of learning and memory in an assortment of different tasks following administration of 5-HT$_4$ partial agonists such as RS67333 and RS17017 (King et al., 2008). Such enhancement may depend, in part, on facilitation of cholinergic transmission in the cortex and the hippocampus (see Chapter 7 for a discussion of the role of acetylcholine in cognitive function). Consequently, 5-HT$_4$ receptor agonists may have therapeutic potential for treating cognitive disorders that are known to involve cholinergic dysfunction, such as Alzheimer's disease.

Finally, the highest levels of 5-HT$_6$ receptors are found in the striatum, nucleus accumbens, and olfactory tubercles. Intermediate levels are present in the hippocampus, cortex, amygdala, and hypothalamus. 5-HT$_6$ receptor activation leads to stimulation of cAMP synthesis and, at least in some cells (e.g., cholinergic interneurons in the striatum), has been shown to increase cell excitability. As reviewed by Fone (2008), 5-HT$_6$ receptor antagonists facilitate the memory of platform location in rats trained on the Morris water maze task (see Chapter 4). Also, improved task acquisition and retention (memory) have been shown to result from administration of 5-HT$_6$ receptor antagonists to aged rats. Another memory task that revealed enhancement by 5-HT$_6$ antagonist treatment is the **novel object recognition** task. In this paradigm, animals are given several minutes to explore two objects in a testing arena. After this initial exploration phase, the animals are removed from the arena for a time (typically ranging from 15 minutes to 1 hour), during which one of the objects is replaced by a novel one. Animals are then returned to the testing arena, and the amount of time spent exploring familiar and novel objects is recorded. Due to an innate motivation to explore novelty, rodents will spend significantly more time exploring the novel compared with the familiar object if they still remember the familiar one. Several studies have demonstrated that administration of a 5-HT$_6$ antagonist improves performance on the novel object recognition task, apparently by enhancing memory consolidation (Fone, 2008). On the basis of these preclinical findings, several 5-HT$_6$ antagonists are currently under development for the treatment of cognitive deficits in Alzheimer's disease and schizophrenia (Liu and Robichaud, 2009).

Section Summary

- Most of the serotonergic neurons in the CNS are associated with the raphe nuclei of the brainstem. Together, the dorsal and median raphes send 5-HT–containing fibers to virtually all forebrain areas.
- At least 14 different 5-HT receptor subtypes have been identified. Some of these fall within groups, such as the 5-HT$_1$ family (5-HT$_{1A}$, 5-HT$_{1B}$, 5-HT$_{1D}$, 5-HT$_{1E}$, and 5-HT$_{1F}$) and a smaller group of three 5-HT$_2$ receptors (5-HT$_{2A}$, 5-HT$_{2B}$, and 5-HT$_{2C}$). The remaining 5-HT receptors are designated 5-HT$_3$, 5-HT$_4$, 5-HT$_{5A}$, 5-HT$_{5B}$, 5-HT$_6$, and 5-HT$_7$. All of the 5-HT receptors are metabotropic, except for the

TABLE 6.1	Drugs That Affect the Serotonergic System
Drug	**Action**
para-Chlorophenylalanine	Depletes 5-HT by inhibiting tryptophan hydroxylase
Reserpine	Depletes 5-HT by inhibiting vesicular uptake
para-Chloroamphetamine, fenfluramine, and MDMA	Release 5-HT from nerve terminals (MDMA and *para*-chloroamphetamine also have neurotoxic effects)
Fluoxetine, paroxetine	Inhibit 5-HT reuptake
5,7-Dihydroxytryptamine	5-HT neurotoxin
Buspirone, ipsapirone, and 8-OH-DPAT	Stimulate 5-HT_{1A} receptors (agonists)
WAY 100635	Blocks 5-HT_{1A} receptors (antagonist)
DOI	Stimulates 5-HT_{2A} receptors (agonist)
Ketanserin and ritanserin	Block 5-HT_{2A} receptors (antagonists)
Sumatriptan and zolmitriptan	Stimulate $5\text{-HT}_{1B/1D}$ receptors (agonists)
Ondansetron and granisetron	Block 5-HT_3 receptors (antagonists)

5-HT_3 receptor, which is an excitatory ionotropic receptor.

- Two of the best-characterized 5-HT receptor subtypes are the 5-HT_{1A} and 5-HT_{2A} receptors. High levels of 5-HT_{1A} receptors have been found in the hippocampus, the septum, parts of the amygdala, and the dorsal raphe nucleus. In the raphe nuclei, including the dorsal raphe, these receptors are mainly somatodendritic autoreceptors on the serotonergic neurons themselves. In other brain areas, 5-HT_{1A} receptors are found on postsynaptic neurons that receive serotonergic input. 5-HT_{1A} receptors function by inhibiting cAMP formation and by enhancing the opening of K^+ channels within the cell membrane. Among a variety of compounds that act on the 5-HT_{1A} receptor subtype are the agonist 8-OH-DPAT and the antagonist WAY 100635.

- 5-HT_{2A} receptors are present in the neocortex, striatum, and nucleus accumbens, as well as in other brain regions. This receptor subtype activates the phosphoinositide second-messenger system, which increases the amount of free Ca^{2+} within the cell and stimulates protein kinase C. When given to rodents, 5-HT_{2A} receptor agonists such as DOI trigger a head-twitch response. In humans, such drugs (which include LSD) produce hallucinations. Certain drugs used in the treatment of schizophrenia can block 5-HT_{2A} receptors, and some researchers hypothesize that such blockade may reduce certain harmful side effects usually associated with antischizophrenic medications.

- Other 5-HT receptor subtypes are currently targeted for specific medical conditions. Thus, $5\text{-HT}_{1B/1D}$ agonists such as sumatriptan and zolmitriptan are used for the treatment of migraine headaches, whereas 5-HT_3 antagonists such as ondansetron and granisetron offer relief from the nausea and vomiting that can be produced by cancer chemotherapy and radiation treatments.

- Mutant mice lacking central serotonergic neurons show deficits in thermoregulation, as well as frequent episodes of apnea, especially when they are young. The latter finding supports the theory that SIDS in humans may arise from abnormalities in the serotonergic system.

- Pharmacological approaches have elucidated a key role for various 5-HT receptors in the regulation of many other functions, including eating behavior (5-HT_{1B}, 5-HT_{2C}, and 5-HT_6), anxiety (5-HT_{1A}, 5-HT_{2A}, and 5-HT_{2C}), pain (5-HT_{1B} and 5-HT_3), and learning and memory (5-HT_{1A}, 5-HT_4, and 5-HT_6). Findings from this research have led to the discovery of novel compounds that may prove valuable in treating a variety of disorders involving these functions.

- **Table 6.1** lists some of the major drugs that influence serotonergic transmission, including various 5-HT receptor agonists and antagonists.

Go to the **COMPANION WEBSITE**

sites.sinauer.com/psychopharm2e
for Web Boxes, animations, flashcards, and other study resources.

Acetylcholine 7

IF YOU WERE A SCIENTIFIC RESEARCHER, how much discomfort would you be willing to endure as a subject in your own experiments? For example, would you be willing to take a drug that would cause complete paralysis, thus preventing you from breathing, while you might still be fully conscious and aware of the sensations of asphyxia? Remarkably, that is exactly what was done independently by two researchers, Frederick Prescott and Scott Smith, in the mid-1940s (Prescott et al., 1946; Smith et al., 1947). Both were experimenting with curare, a toxin present in the bark of several South American plants that was discovered centuries ago by native tribes, who used the substance to tip their poison arrows for hunting and fighting. According to Mann (2000), some tribes calibrated the potency of their curare-containing plant extracts based on the effects of the material on prey animals. For example, a highly potent preparation was called "one-tree" curare, because a monkey hit with an arrow containing this preparation only had time to leap to one nearby tree in its attempts to escape before it died.

Accounts of the effects of curare were first brought back to Europe by Sir Walter Raleigh at the end of the 16th century, but as late as the 1940s, some pharmacologists were still unsure as to whether curare caused unconsciousness and/or analgesia, in addition to paralysis. This was important information since curare was still occasionally being administered during medical (including surgical) procedures without the accompaniment of a known anesthetic agent. Answering this question was the primary rationale offered by Smith and colleagues when they published the account of his experience under curare alone. Prescott and coworkers focused instead on determining the optimal dose and method of administration as an adjunct (i.e., additional medication) to a regular anesthetic, but their paper also provides a graphic account of Prescott's reactions to receiving curare

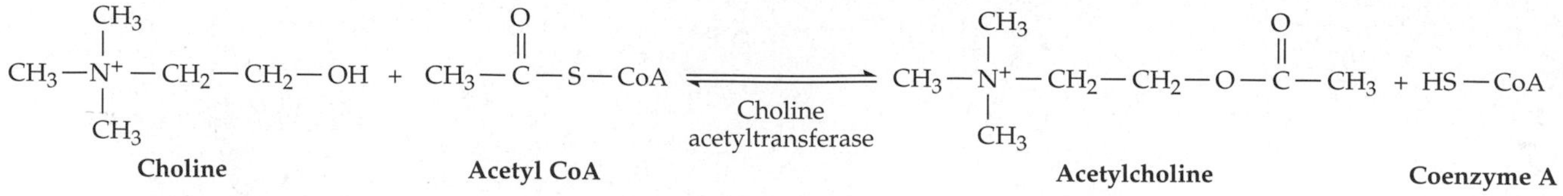

Figure 7.1 Synthesis of acetylcholine (ACh) by choline acetyltransferase

by itself. On the basis of self-reports given by both subjects after recovery from the drug, the results were conclusive—curare does NOT cause anesthesia. Indeed, both men were fully awake as their growing paralysis prevented them from breathing, and they began to become asphyxiated. Both teams provided artificial respiration to their subjects during the experiment; however, the method used by Prescott's group was less effective, which resulted in a subjective experience described in the paper as "terrifying."[1]

How does curare work to induce muscular paralysis? And why doesn't it alter conscious experience when given to an individual? As we shall see in this chapter, the toxic agent in curare blocks a particular kind of receptor for the neurotransmitter **acetylcholine** (**ACh**; adjective form, **cholinergic**). Acetylcholine is a particularly fascinating transmitter—a molecule that is life-sustaining in its function but that is also the target of some of the most deadly known toxins, both naturally occurring and man-made.

Acetylcholine Synthesis, Release, and Inactivation

Although ACh is synthesized by only a small number of neurons in the brain, this transmitter plays an important role in several important behavioral functions. The following sections examine the processes through which this vital transmitter is produced, released, and inactivated. Since both too much and too little ACh is dangerous or even deadly, we also take a look at the various agents that act to either increase or limit the level of ACh in the body.

Acetylcholine synthesis is catalyzed by the enzyme choline acetyltransferase

In contrast to the multiple steps required to synthesize the catecholamine transmitters, ACh is formed in a single step from two precursors: **choline** and **acetyl**

coenzyme A (**acetyl CoA**) (**Figure 7.1**). The choline comes mainly from fat in our diet (choline-containing lipids), although it is also produced in the liver. Acetyl CoA is generated within all cells by the metabolism of sugars and fats. The synthesis of ACh is catalyzed by the enzyme **choline acetyltransferase (ChAT)**, which does just what its name implies: it transfers the acetyl group ($-COCH_3$) from acetyl CoA to choline to form ACh. Choline acetyltransferase is present in the cytoplasm of the cell, and this enzyme is found only in neurons that use ACh as their transmitter. This specificity allows us to identify cholinergic neurons by staining for ChAT.

The rate of ACh synthesis is controlled by several factors, including the availability of its precursors inside the cell as well as the rate of cell firing. Thus cholinergic neurons make more ACh when more choline and/or acetyl CoA is available, and when the neurons are stimulated to fire at a higher rate. Although knowledge of these regulatory processes has helped researchers understand how the cholinergic system functions, it has not yet led to the development of useful pharmacological agents. For example, it has been difficult to find highly selective inhibitors of ChAT, and even if such drugs are eventually isolated, it is not clear that inhibiting ACh synthesis has any obvious clinical usefulness. At one time, it was thought that boosting brain ACh levels by administering large doses of choline might be beneficial for patients with Alzheimer's disease, since damage to the cholinergic system is one of the factors contributing to the cognitive deficits seen in that disorder. However, not only did choline treatment fail to produce symptom improvement, peripheral metabolism of this compound unfortunately caused the patients to give off a strong fishy odor!

Many different drugs and toxins can alter acetylcholine storage and release

The axon terminals of cholinergic neurons contain many small synaptic vesicles that store ACh for release when the nerve cell is active. It is estimated that a few thousand molecules of transmitter are present in each vesicle. Vesicles are loaded with ACh by a transport protein in the vesicle membrane called, appropriately,

[1]Readers interested in learning more about the history of curare, including how Prescott and Smith came to perform their bold experiments, are referred to an excellent account by Anderson (2010).

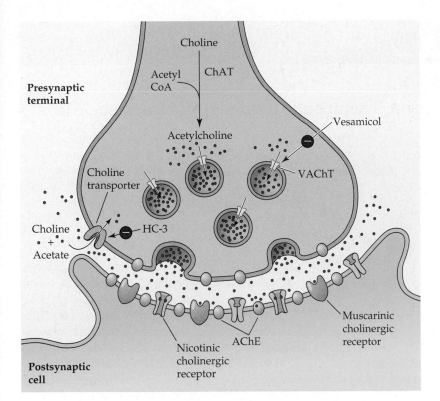

Figure 7.2 A cholinergic synapse illustrating the processes of ACh synthesis and metabolism, presynaptic choline uptake, and vesicular ACh uptake and release. Postsynaptic nicotinic and muscarinic ACh receptors are also shown.

The release of ACh is dramatically affected by various animal and bacterial toxins. For example, a toxin found in the venom of the black widow spider, *Latrodectus mactans*, leads to a massive release of ACh at synapses in the peripheral nervous system (PNS). Overactivity of the cholinergic system causes numerous symptoms, including muscle pain in the abdomen or chest, tremors, nausea and vomiting, salivation, and copious sweating. Ounce for ounce, black widow spider venom is 15 times more toxic than prairie rattlesnake venom, but a single spider bite is rarely fatal in healthy young adults because of the small amount of venom injected into the victim. In contrast to the effects of black widow spider venom, toxins that cause botulism poisoning potently inhibit ACh release. As described in **Box 7.1**, this inhibition of cholinergic activity can be deadly because of muscular paralysis.

the **vesicular ACh transporter** (**VAChT**) (**Figure 7.2**). This protein can be blocked by a drug called vesamicol. What effect would you expect vesamicol to have on cholinergic neurons? Would you predict any drug-induced change in the distribution of ACh between the cytoplasm and the synaptic vesicles within the cholinergic nerve terminals? Furthermore, if redistribution of ACh occurred, what effect would this have on ACh release by the cells? If you predicted that vesamicol treatment would decrease vesicular ACh but increase the level of ACh in the cytoplasm, you were correct. This is because vesamicol doesn't affect the rate of ACh synthesis; therefore, ACh molecules that normally would have been transported into the vesicles remain in the cytoplasm of the terminal. Moreover, because synaptic vesicles are the main source of ACh release when the cholinergic neurons fire, such release is reduced in the presence of vesamicol. We can imagine that the cholinergic vesicles are still present and are continuing to undergo exocytosis when the neurons are activated, but the amount of ACh available within the vesicles to be released is abnormally low.

Acetylcholinesterase is responsible for acetylcholine breakdown

Levels of ACh are carefully controlled by an enzyme called **acetylcholinesterase** (**AChE**), which breaks down the transmitter into choline and acetic acid (**Figure 7.3**). Within the cell, AChE is present at several strategic locations. One form of the enzyme is found inside the presynaptic cell, where it can metabolize excess ACh that may have been synthesized. Another form of AChE is present on the membrane of the postsynaptic cell to break down molecules of ACh after their release into the synaptic cleft. Finally, a unique type of AChE is found at neuromuscular junctions, which are specialized synapses between neurons and muscle cells where ACh is released by motor neurons

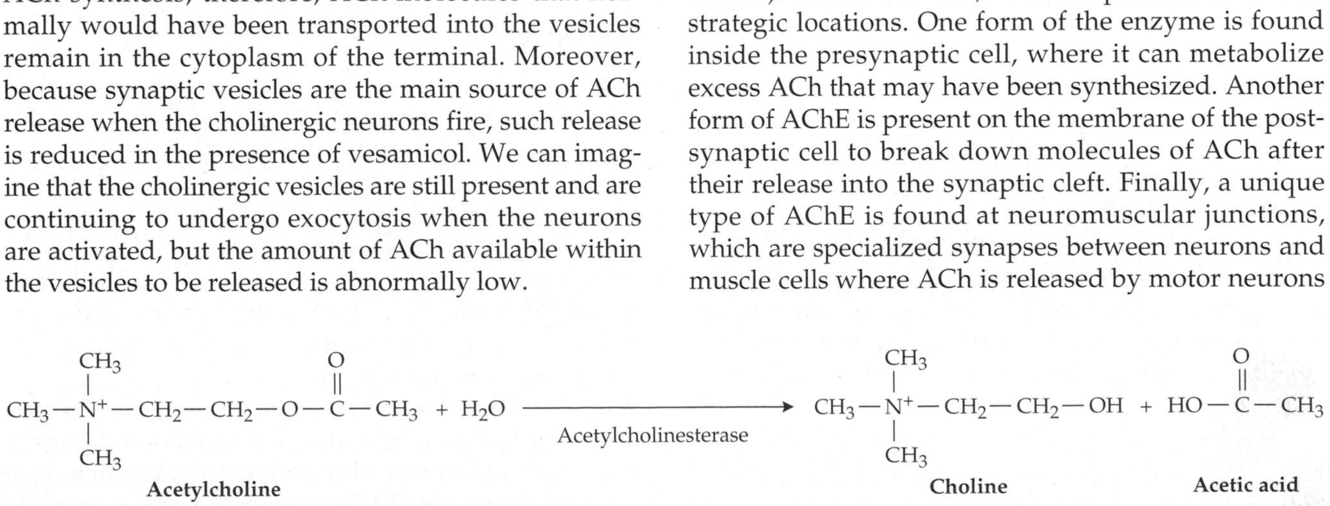

Figure 7.3 Breakdown of ACh by acetylcholinesterase

BOX 7.1   Pharmacology in Action

Botulinum Toxin—Deadly Poison, Therapeutic Remedy, and Cosmetic Aid

The bacterium *Clostridium botulinum*, which is responsible for botulism poisoning, produces what is perhaps the most potent toxin known to pharmacologists. The estimated lethal dose of botulinum toxin in humans is 0.3 μg; in other words, 1 gram (equivalent to the weight of three aspirin tablets) is enough to kill more than 3 million individuals. *Clostridium botulinum* does not grow in the presence of oxygen; however, it can thrive in an anaerobic (oxygen-free) environment such as a sealed food can that has not been properly heated to kill the bacteria.

Botulinum toxin actually consists of a mixture of seven related proteins known as botulinum toxins A through G. These proteins are taken up selectively by the cholinergic neurons that innervate our skeletal muscles. The toxin molecules interfere with the process of ACh release at neuromuscular junctions, thereby causing muscle weakness and even paralysis (see figure). Symptoms of botulism poisoning include blurred vision, difficulty speaking and swallowing, muscle weakness, and gastrointestinal distress. Most victims recover, although a small percentage die as the result of severe muscle paralysis and eventual asphyxiation.

Once the mechanism of action of botulinum toxin became known,

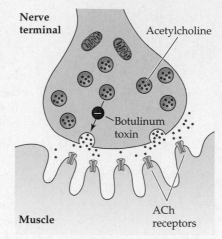

Mechanism of action of botulinum Botulinum toxin blocks ACh release at the neuromuscular junction by preventing fusion of synaptic vesicles with the nerve terminal membrane.

researchers began to consider that this substance, if used carefully and at very low doses, might be helpful in treating clinical disorders characterized by involuntary muscle contractions. After appropriate testing, in 1989 the U.S. Food and Drug Administration approved the use of purified botulinum toxin A for the treatment of strabismus (crossed eyes), blepharospasm (spasm of the eyelid), and hemifacial spasm (muscle spasms on just one side of the face). Since that time, this substance has been administered for a variety of other disorders, including

spastic cerebral palsy, dystonias (prolonged muscle contractions, sometimes seen as repeated jerking movements), and achalasia (failure of sphincter muscles to relax when appropriate).

Most remarkably, dermatologists have been using botulinum toxin (trade name, Botox) for cosmetic purposes in patients with excessive frown lines, worry lines, or crow's-feet around the eyes. Such "dynamic wrinkles," as they are called, result from chronic contraction of specific facial muscles. When injected locally into a particular muscle or surrounding area, Botox causes paralysis of that muscle as the result of blockade of ACh release from incoming motor nerve fibers. This leads to a reduction in the offending lines or wrinkles, although each treatment remains effective for only a few months, after which it must be repeated.

According to recent surveys, increasing numbers of people are turning to Botox treatments for purely cosmetic purposes. Depending on one's perspective, this trend might be considered either horrifying or liberating. Nevertheless, until true antiaging techniques are developed, it is safe to say that some folks will use whatever methods are available to appear younger than they really are.

---

to stimulate muscular contraction. Muscle cells actually secrete AChE into the space between themselves and the cholinergic nerve endings, and enzyme molecules become immobilized there by attaching to other proteins within the neuromuscular junction. This unique location helps the transmission process function very precisely at neuromuscular junctions. Immediately after a squirt of ACh causes a particular muscle

to contract, the transmitter is metabolized extremely rapidly so that the muscle can relax until the next command arrives to squirt out some more ACh and contract that muscle once again.

Once ACh has been broken down within the synaptic cleft, a significant portion of the liberated choline is taken back up into the cholinergic nerve terminal by a **choline transporter** in the membrane of the terminal

Normal neuromuscular
junction

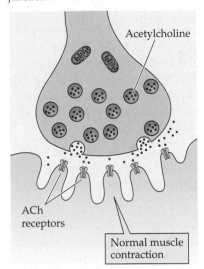

Neuromuscular junction in
myasthenia gravis

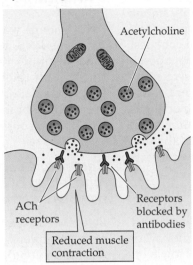

Figure 7.4 Myasthenia gravis, an auto-immune disorder In myasthenia gravis, antibodies interfere with cholinergic transmission at the neuromuscular junction by binding to and blocking the muscle ACh receptors.

(see Figure 7.2). If the choline transporter is blocked by means of the drug **hemicholinium-3 (HC-3)**, the rate of ACh production declines. Furthermore, mutant mice in which the choline transporter has been knocked out die within about 1 hour after birth (Ferguson et al., 2004). The cause of death in these animals is lack of normal breathing due to failure to sustain ACh synthesis and release at the neuromuscular junction. These findings tell us that utilization of recycled choline plays a critical role in maintaining ongoing ACh synthesis.

Drugs that block AChE prevent inactivation of ACh, thereby increasing the postsynaptic effects of the transmitter. One such drug is **physostigmine (Eserine)**, a compound isolated from Calabar beans (the seeds of a woody plant found in the Calabar region of Nigeria). Physostigmine crosses the blood–brain barrier and thus exerts effects on the central nervous system (CNS). Accidental poisoning leads to slurred speech, mental confusion, hallucinations, loss of reflexes, convulsions, and even coma and death. Nineteenth-century missionaries to West Africa discovered societies that used extracts of the Calabar bean to determine the guilt of accused prisoners (Davis, 1985). The defendant was considered innocent if he was fortunate enough to regurgitate the poison or, alternatively, if he could manage to walk 10 feet under the influence of the toxin (in which case vomiting was induced). Needless to say, however, most prisoners did neither and were consequently judged guilty and were permitted to die a horrible death.

Neostigmine (Prostigmin) and **pyridostigmine (Mestinon)** are synthetic analogs of physostigmine

that do not cross the blood–brain barrier. These drugs are beneficial in the treatment of a serious neuromuscular disorder called <u>myasthenia gravis</u>. Because ACh is released at neuromuscular junctions, the muscle cells obviously possess cholinergic receptors so that they can respond to the neurotransmitter.

For reasons that are not yet clear, patients with myasthenia gravis develop antibodies against their own muscle cholinergic receptors. Thus, myasthenia gravis is an example of an **autoimmune disorder**, a condition in which a part of the body is attacked by one's own immune system. In this case, the antibodies block muscle acetylcholine receptors and eventually cause these receptors to be broken down by the muscle cells (**Figure 7.4**). Loss of receptor function causes the patient's muscles to be less sensitive to ACh, which, in turn, leads to severe weakness and fatigue. By inhibiting AChE, neostigmine and pyridostigmine prolong the action of ACh at the neuromuscular junction, which causes increased stimulation of the remaining undamaged cholinergic receptors.

Physostigmine, neostigmine, and pyridostigmine are reversible AChE inhibitors, which means that ACh breakdown is restored after the drug dissociates from the enzyme. Certain other compounds, however, produce a nearly irreversible inhibition of AChE activity. Weaker versions of these chemicals are widely used as insecticides, since preventing ACh breakdown is just as harmful to ants and wasps as it is to humans. More-toxic varieties of irreversible AChE inhibitors have unfortunately been developed as "nerve gases" for use in chemical warfare. These agents go by names such as **Sarin** and **Soman**. They are designed to be dispersed as a vapor cloud or spray, which allows their entry into the body through skin contact or by inhalation. In either case, the drug quickly penetrates into the bloodstream and is distributed to all organs, including the brain. Symptoms of nerve gas poisoning, which include profuse sweating and salivation, vomiting, loss of bladder and bowel control, and convulsions, are due to rapid ACh accumulation and overstimulation of cholinergic synapses throughout both the CNS and the PNS. Death occurs through asphyxiation due to paralysis of the muscles of the diaphragm.

Sarin gas was used by terrorists in an infamous Tokyo subway attack in 1995. During the Persian Gulf War of 1990–1991, as well as the subsequent conquest of Iraq, Allied forces were very concerned about possible use of this agent by the Iraqi army. Consequently, tablets of pyridostigmine bromide (PB) were widely distributed to Allied troops for use as a nerve gas antidote. How can a reversible AChE inhibitor be an antidote against Sarin or Soman? It appears that the temporary interaction of PB with the enzyme protects AChE from permanent inactivation by the nerve gas. This protective effect, however, requires that the antidote be administered ahead of time—before exposure to the toxic agent. Therefore, soldiers were instructed to take three PB pills daily at times when they were thought to be at risk for nerve gas attack. However, some soldiers took the drug much more frequently, thus leading to heavy exposure. Review of scientific findings by the Research Advisory Committee on Gulf War Veterans' Illnesses (2008) led the committee to conclude that such exposure may have contributed significantly to the development of "Gulf War illness," a complex multisymptom disorder currently thought to afflict at least 25% of U.S. veterans who served in that combat theater.

Section Summary

- ACh is synthesized from choline and acetyl CoA in a single reaction catalyzed by the enzyme choline acetyltransferase. The rate of ACh synthesis is controlled by precursor availability and is increased by cell firing.

- ACh is loaded into synaptic vesicles by the specific vesicular transporter VAChT.

- A variety of animal and bacterial toxins influence the cholinergic system either by stimulating or inhibiting ACh release.

- Following its release into the synapse or neuromuscular junction, ACh is rapidly degraded by the enzyme AChE.

- Much of the choline liberated from ACh breakdown is taken back up into the cholinergic nerve terminal by a choline transporter that plays a critical role in maintaining ongoing ACh synthesis.

- Drugs that block AChE cause prolongation of ACh action at postsynaptic or muscular cholinergic receptors. Reversible AChE antagonists are used in the treatment of the neuromuscular disorder myasthenia gravis, whereas irreversible AChE inhibitors are the main ingredients of dreaded nerve gases.

Organization and Function of the Cholinergic System

Acetylcholine was first identified as a neurotransmitter in the PNS. We have already noted that ACh is the transmitter released at neuromuscular junctions throughout the body. This substance additionally plays a crucial role in both the sympathetic and parasympathetic branches of the autonomic nervous system, and, of course, within the CNS as well.

Cholinergic neurons play a key role in the functioning of both the peripheral and central nervous systems

Before we examine the function of cholinergic neurons, let's briefly review the organization of the autonomic nervous system. Both the sympathetic and parasympathetic branches consist of preganglionic neurons, which are cells located within the CNS that send their axons to the autonomic ganglia, as well as ganglionic neurons located within the ganglia that innervate various target organs throughout the body. The preganglionic neurons of both branches are cholinergic, as are the ganglionic neurons of the parasympathetic system (we saw in Chapter 5 that norepinephrine is the transmitter of the sympathetic ganglionic neurons). **Figure 7.5** illustrates the chemical coding of these cells and the synapses they make. Widespread involvement of ACh in both the neuromuscular and autonomic systems explains why drugs that interfere with this transmitter exert such powerful physiological effects and sometimes are highly toxic.

Parasympathetic branch

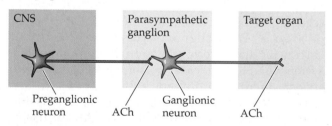

Sympathetic branch

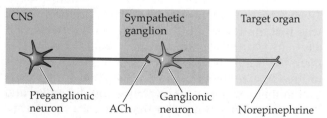

Figure 7.5 Cholinergic synapses in the parasympathetic and sympathetic branches of the autonomic nervous system

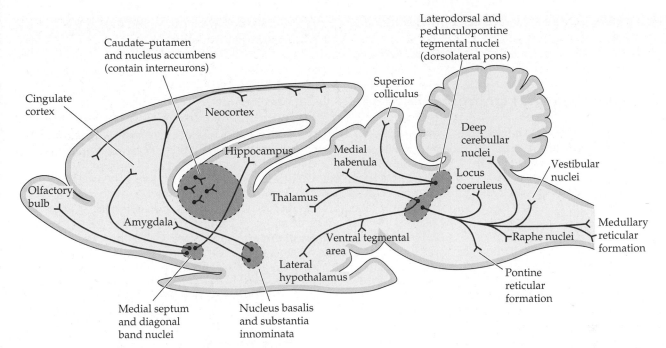

Figure 7.6 Anatomy of cholinergic pathways in the brain The cell bodies of cholinergic neurons are located primarily in the striatum, nucleus basalis, medial septum, diagonal band nuclei, substantia innominata, pedunculopontine tegmental nucleus, and dorsolateral tegmental nucleus. Note that the basal forebrain cholinergic cell groups send fibers to all areas of the cortex, as well as to limbic system structures such as the hippocampus and amygdala. Cell groups of the pedunculopontine tegmental and dorsolateral tegmental nuclei primarily innervate subcortical structures that do not receive input from the basal forebrain system, caudate–putamen, and nucleus accumbens.

Within the brain, the cell bodies of cholinergic neurons are clustered within just a few areas (**Figure 7.6**). Some of these nerve cells, such as the ones found within the striatum, are interneurons. In Chapter 5, we saw that dopaminergic input to the striatum plays a critical role in the regulation of movement. This regulation depends in part on the balance between ACh and dopamine (DA), that is, when DA is low, as in Parkinson's disease, the resulting neurotransmitter imbalance contributes to motor symptoms of the disorder. Consequently, anticholinergic drugs such as **orphenadrine (Norflex)**, **benztropine mesylate (Cogentin)**, and **trihexyphenidyl (Artane)** are sometimes prescribed instead of L-DOPA in the early stages of Parkinson's disease.

Other cholinergic neurons send their axons longer distances to innervate many different brain areas. For example, a diffuse collection of cholinergic nerve cells called the **basal forebrain cholinergic system (BFCS)** comprises neurons interspersed among several anatomical areas, including the nucleus basalis, substantia innominata, medial septal nucleus, and diagonal band nuclei. The BFCS is the origin of a dense cholinergic innervation of the cerebral cortex, as well as the hippocampus and other limbic system structures. As discussed in **Box 7.2**, this system plays a significant role in

cognitive function. Another set of important cholinergic cells is located in the dorsolateral pons within the **laterodorsal** and **pedunculopontine tegmental nuclei** (abbreviated **LDTg** and **PPTg**, respectively). One pathway from these cells projects to the midbrain DA cell groups (the LDTg to the ventral tegmental area and the PPTg to the substantia nigra), where it exerts a powerful excitatory influence on dopamine neuron firing, mediated, in part, by activation of postsynaptic nicotinic cholinergic receptors (Maskos, 2008). Indeed, these nicotinic receptors are intimately involved in the reinforcing effects of nicotine in experimental animals (see Chapter 13). Among the other pathways arising from the LDTg and the PPTg are excitatory projections to brainstem and thalamic areas that play important roles in behavioral arousal, sensory processing, and initiation of rapid-eye-movement sleep (Kobayashi and Isa, 2002; McCarley, 2007).

There are two acetylcholine receptor subtypes, nicotinic and muscarinic

Like dopamine (DA) and norepinephrine (NE), ACh has many different kinds of receptors. The story can be simplified a little by recognizing that the various cholinergic receptors belong to one of two families:

BOX 7.2   The Cutting Edge

Acetylcholine and Cognitive Function

Research over many years has led to the view that ACh plays an important role in cognitive functioning. The earliest evidence for this notion came from observations that the general antimuscarinic agents atropine and scopolamine can produce amnesic effects in humans. Indeed, during the first half of the twentieth century, it was common for obstetricians to administer morphine and scopolamine to women during labor. The resulting state, often called "twilight sleep," enabled patients to avoid both the pain and the memory of labor; however, the procedure unfortunately had adverse effects on the newborn infant and therefore is rarely used in modern obstetrics. Behavioral pharmacologists later began to administer scopolamine (or occasionally atropine instead) to experimental animals, particularly rats and mice, and found that these compounds produced deficits in the acquisition and maintenance of many different kinds of learning tasks. The initial interpretation of these findings was that the drugs interfered with memory consolidation, which is consistent with the reported amnesic effects of scopolamine in humans. Indeed, some authors have argued that ACh in the hippocampus plays an important role in the encoding of episodic memories (i.e., memories of experiences, events, and situations) (Hasselmo and Sarter, 2011). However, others have concluded that deficits in attention and sensory discrimination are the most selective consequences of blocking muscarinic receptors (Klinkenberg and Blokland, 2010).

Studies using muscarinic blockers yielded important information regarding the role of ACh in cognitive function. Nevertheless, such studies suffered from two significant limitations. First, they targeted only one of the major classes of cholinergic receptors, effectively ignoring the potential involvement of nicotinic receptors. Second, because the drugs were usually administered systemically, there was no way to determine *where* in the brain the critical cholinergic neurons and their projections were located.

Localization of the key cholinergic neurons ultimately resulted from the use of lesion studies. Researchers first found that gross destruction of tissue within the basal forebrain using electrolytic or radiofrequency lesions caused various kinds of deficits in learning and memory. This crude approach was later supplanted by the more sophisticated method of using excitotoxic lesions to kill only neuronal cell bodies while sparing fibers of passage (see Chapter 8). However, even with this technical advance there were still interpretive problems because the cholinergic neurons of the basal forebrain cholinergic system (BFCS) are intermingled with neurons using other neurotransmitters, all of which are killed by excitotoxic lesions. Fortunately, this problem was solved with the introduction of a selective cholinergic neurotoxin called **192 IgG–saporin**. This odd-sounding substance contains a monoclonal antibody, 192 IgG, which binds specifically to a cell surface protein expressed by basal forebrain cholinergic neurons. The other part of the molecule, saporin, is a cellular toxin obtained from the soapwort plant, *Saponaria officinalis*. When 192 IgG–saporin is injected into the region of the BFCS, cholinergic neurons take up the toxin because of binding of the antibody part of the molecule. As a result, those neurons are destroyed, while neighboring noncholinergic cells are spared.

Although some investigators have reported learning deficits in animals subjected to 192 IgG–saporin lesions of the BFCS (Wrenn and Wiley, 1998), the most consistent effects have been in studies focusing on attentional processes (Baxter, 2001). Furthermore, several studies suggest that a particularly important role for ACh is the facilitation of sensory cues by stimulating cholinergic receptors in the prefrontal cortex (Hasselmo and Sarter, 2011). Such a role is illustrated in the results of two studies shown in the figure. Figure A presents the results of a microdialysis experiment that found a substantial increase in ACh release in the frontoparietal cortex of animals performing a signal detection task requiring sustained attention (Sarter and Parikh, 2005). Note that this increased ACh release was much greater than the release that occurred in animals performing other tasks that don't impose the same attentional demands. Figure B illustrates the effects of basal forebrain 192 IgG–saporin lesions on performance of the same signal detection task. It is evident that the lesions produced highly significant reductions in the ability of the animals to detect the signal when it was presented (line graphs), whereas there was no effect on the percentage of correct rejections (i.e., responses on the lever associated with nonsignal presentation; bar graphs).

Over 30 years ago, Raymond Bartus and colleagues proposed that the cognitive decline that often occurs with aging is due, at least in part, to dysfunction of the BFCS (Bartus et al., 1982). This spurred tremendous interest in

BOX 7.2 (continued)

(A)

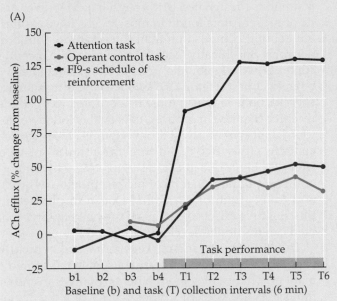

(B)

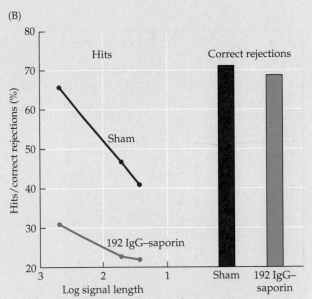

Cortical ACh is important for normal attentional processing (A) Rats were tested in a task of sustained attention while ACh release in the frontoparietal cortex was measured by microdialysis. For comparison, the animals were tested either in an operant control task similar to the attention task with respect to motivation and response requirements but without the same attentional demands, or with another nonattentional task utilizing a fixed-interval (FI) 9-second schedule of reinforcement. During the period of task performance, the attention task produced much greater cortical ACh release than the other two tasks, suggesting that the BFCS is activated by attentional processing.

(B) The effects of 192 IgG–saporin infusions into the BFCS on attention were determined by measuring the percentage of correct signal detections ("hits") when a weak signal was presented. Note that 192 IgG–saporin lesioned rats had significantly fewer hits than sham-lesioned controls at all signal strengths; this is interpreted as a deficit in attention. Both groups had approximately the same percentage of correct rejections on trials in which the signal was not presented. This result indicates that the lesions did not produce global cognitive or motor impairment in these animals. (After Sarter and Parikh, 2005.)

the BFCS, not only with respect to normal aging but also regarding a possible role in the age-related disorder, Alzheimer's disease. Indeed, the cholinergic hypothesis of Alzheimer's dementia subsequently led to the development of acetylcholinesterase inhibitors for treating this disorder (see Chapter 21). Although damage to the BFCS almost certainly contributes to the cognitive deficits seen in patients with Alzheimer's, it is only part of the problem, because widespread loss of other cells and synaptic connections throughout the cerebral cortex and hippocampus also occurs. Nevertheless, there is continued interest in developing novel cholinergic agents such as α4β2 or α7 nicotinic receptor agonists, which might prove helpful not only in Alzheimer's dementia but also in the cognitive deficits associated with schizophrenia and certain other neuropsychiatric disorders (Radek et al., 2010; Thomsen et al., 2010).

nicotinic receptors and **muscarinic receptors**. Nicotinic receptors were so named because they respond selectively to the agonist nicotine, an alkaloid found in the leaves of the tobacco plant.[2] The pharmacology of nicotine is discussed in Chapter 13. Muscarinic receptors are selectively stimulated by muscarine, another alkaloid, which was first isolated in 1869 from the fly agaric mushroom, *Amanita muscaria*.

NICOTINIC RECEPTORS Nicotinic receptors are highly concentrated on muscle cells at neuromuscular junctions, on ganglionic neurons of both the sympathetic and parasympathetic systems, and on certain neurons in the brain. They are ionotropic receptors, which, you will recall from Chapter 3, means that they possess an

[2]Alkaloids are nitrogen-containing compounds, usually bitter-tasting, that are often found in plants.

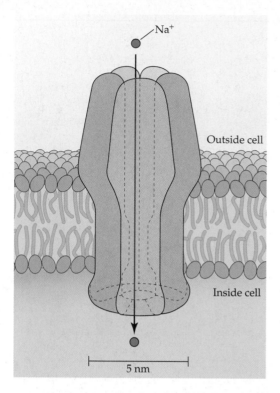

Figure 7.7 Structure of the nicotinic ACh receptor The receptor comprises five protein subunits that are arranged to form a central pore or channel that allows Na$^+$ (and to some extent Ca^{2+}) ions to flow into the cell when the receptor is activated.

ion channel as an integral part of the receptor complex (**Figure 7.7**). When ACh binds to a nicotinic receptor, the channel opens very rapidly, and sodium (Na$^+$) and calcium (Ca^{2+}) ions enter the neuron or muscle cell. This flow of ions causes depolarization of the cell membrane, thereby increasing the excitability of the cell. If the responding cell is a neuron, its likelihood of firing is increased. If it is a muscle cell, it responds by contracting. In this manner, nicotinic receptors mediate fast excitatory responses in both the CNS and the PNS. Another important function of nicotinic receptors within the brain is to enhance the release of neurotransmitters from nerve terminals. In this case, the nicotinic receptors are located presynaptically, right on the terminals. Thus, activation of nicotinic receptors by ACh can stimulate cell firing if the receptors are located postsynaptically on dendrites or cell bodies, or the receptors can stimulate neurotransmitter release without affecting the firing rate of the cell if they are located presynaptically on nerve endings.

The structure of the nicotinic receptor has been known for many years. Each receptor is a complex that contains five proteins (called **subunits**) that are assembled and then inserted into the cell membrane. These subunits are identified by the Greek letters α,

β, γ, δ, and ε. However, their complexity is increased by the existence of 10 different kinds of α subunits (designated α1 through α10) and 4 different kinds of β subunits (designated β1 through β4). Moreover, the nicotinic receptors found in muscle cells have a different subunit composition than the receptors found in neurons. Specifically, each muscle nicotinic receptor contains two α1 subunits, one β1, one γ, and either a δ or an ε subunit (**Figure 7.8**). Two ACh binding sites are present, both of which must be occupied to open the receptor channel. In contrast, neuronal nicotinic receptors do not contain any γ, δ, or ε subunits. Instead, each contains either two α and three β subunits or five α subunits. Figure 7.8 illustrates two particularly important types of neuronal nicotinic receptors—(α4)$_2$(β2)$_3$ and (α7)$_5$—both of which have been implicated in the cognitive effects of ACh and are current targets of medications under development (see Box 7.2).

In a living organism, receptors are typically exposed to neurotransmitters in a somewhat sporadic manner. That is, at some moments, many transmitter molecules are present in the vicinity of a particular receptor, whereas at other moments, few transmitter molecules are nearby, because the releasing neuron has slowed its firing or perhaps become completely silent for a brief time. On the other hand, we can perform pharmacological experiments (or we can ingest substances such as nicotine), causing receptors to be continuously exposed to high concentrations of an agonist drug for seconds or even longer intervals of minutes or hours. When nicotinic receptors are subjected to continuous agonist exposure, they become **desensitized**. Desensitization represents an altered state of the receptor in which the channel remains closed regardless of whether molecules of an agonist such as ACh or nicotine are bound to the receptor. After a short while, desensitized receptors spontaneously **resensitize** and then are capable of responding again to a nicotinic agonist.

Even if cells are continuously exposed to nicotinic stimulation, not all of the receptors are desensitized. Those that remain active produce a persistent depolarization of the cell membrane. If this continues for very long, a process called **depolarization block** occurs, in which the resting potential of the membrane is lost, and the cell cannot be excited until the agonist is removed and the membrane repolarized. A chemical relative of ACh called **succinylcholine** is a powerful muscle relaxant that is useful in certain surgical procedures in which anesthesia alone may not provide sufficient relaxation. Unlike ACh, succinylcholine is resistant to breakdown by AChE; thus it continuously stimulates the nicotinic receptors and induces a depolarization block of the muscle cells. It is important to note that one of the paralyzed muscles is

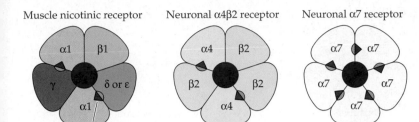

Figure 7.8 Three common types of nicotinic ACh receptors

ACh binding site

Figure 7.8 Three common types of nicotinic ACh receptors The muscle nicotinic receptor shown on the left is designated as $(\alpha1)_2(\beta1)(\gamma)(\delta/\varepsilon)$, which means that each receptor complex contains two α1 subunits, one β1 subunit, one γ subunit, and one δ or ε subunit . There is only one form of the γ, δ, and ε subunits, which is why no numbering is needed in those cases. Nicotinic receptors in neurons are more complex because of the variety of α and β subunit combinations that have been detected in these cells. For simplicity, we are depicting here just two important kinds of neuronal nicotinic receptors found in the brain: $(\alpha4)_2(\beta2)_3$ and $(\alpha7)_5$. Note that the muscle and the $(\alpha4)_2(\beta2)_3$ receptors have two ACh binding sites, whereas the $(\alpha7)_5$ receptor has five ACh binding sites. Whether two or five such sites are present, all must be occupied by ACh or another agonist such as nicotine for the receptor channel to open.

the diaphragm (the large muscle responsible for inflating and deflating the lungs), so the patient must be maintained on a ventilator until the succinylcholine is finally eliminated and the effect wears off.

Mecamylamine is an antagonist at neuronal nicotinic receptors that blocks these receptors both centrally and in autonomic ganglia. The ganglionic blocking effect has been exploited therapeutically with the use of mecamylamine (Inversine) as an antihypertensive agent. In contrast, D-tubocurarine is a well-known antagonist of muscle nicotinic receptors. This substance is the main active ingredient of curare, the paralytic agent discussed in the introduction to this chapter. D-Tubocurarine has relatively little effect on central cholinergic transmission not only because of its selectivity for muscle nicotinic receptors but also because it exhibits low penetrance across the blood–brain barrier.

MUSCARINIC RECEPTORS   As mentioned earlier, muscarinic receptors represent the other family of ACh receptors. Like the receptors for DA and NE, muscarinic receptors are all metabotropic. Five different types of muscarinic receptors (designated M_1 through M_5) have been identified, each with specific pharmacological characteristics and coded for by a different gene. Muscarinic receptors operate through several different second-messenger systems. Some activate the phosphoinositide second-messenger system, while others inhibit the formation of cyclic adenosine monophosphate

(cAMP). Another important mechanism of muscarinic receptor action is the stimulation of potassium (K^+) channel opening. As mentioned in previous chapters, this leads to hyperpolarization of the cell membrane and a reduction in cell firing.

Muscarinic receptors are widely distributed in the brain. Some areas containing high levels of muscarinic receptors are the neocortex, hippocampus, thalamus, striatum, and basal forebrain. Receptors in the neocortex and hippocampus play an important role in the cognitive effects of ACh described earlier in this chapter, whereas those in the striatum are involved in motor function. Researchers have investigated the functional roles of these receptors not only by using selective agonists and antagonists but also by generating knockout mice for each receptor. Results of these genetic studies are helping pharmacologists design medications targeted at a variety of neuropsychiatric and physiological disorders. Among the interesting findings are those pertaining to the M_5 muscarinic receptor, which is expressed in the brain primarily in the hippocampus, hypothalamus, and midbrain DA areas (i.e., the substantia nigra pars compacta and the ventral tegmental area, or VTA). We mentioned earlier that cholinergic neurons in the LDTg exert an excitatory effect on VTA dopamine neurons mediated by nicotinic receptors on the postsynaptic cells. As shown in **Figure 7.9A**, M_5 receptors on the DA cells also contribute significantly to this excitatory effect. Interestingly, these receptors appear to be involved in the rewarding and dependence-producing effects of abused drugs that are studied with the use of animal models. As reviewed by Wess and colleagues (2007), M_5 receptor knockout mice exhibit deficits in both morphine and cocaine reward using place-conditioning and/or drug self-administration procedures. **Figure 7.9B** shows that in the place-conditioning paradigm, morphine doses that produced a robust place preference in normal animals had no effect on knockout mice. Loss of M_5 receptor function also reduced withdrawal symptoms in mice that were made dependent on morphine, but it had no effect on morphine-induced analgesia (Basile et al., 2002). Although transgenic manipulation eliminated M_5 muscarinic receptors throughout the entire brain, it is likely that receptors located in the VTA play a key role in this modulation of drug reward and

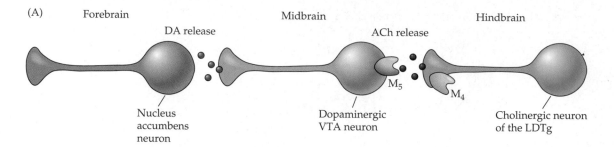

(A)   Forebrain   Midbrain   Hindbrain

DA release   ACh release

Nucleus   Dopaminergic   Cholinergic neuron
accumbens   VTA neuron   of the LDTg
neuron

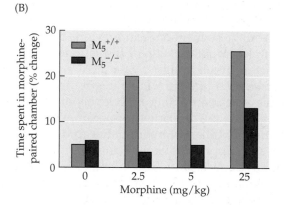

(B)

Figure 7.9 Role of M$_5$ muscarinic receptors in midbrain dopaminergic cell activity and in morphine reward
(A) ACh released by LDTg cholinergic neurons acts on M$_5$ muscarinic receptors expressed by VTA DA neurons to stimulate these cells and enhance dopamine release in the nucleus accumbens. M$_4$ receptors shown on the terminals of the cholinergic neurons are thought to be autoreceptors inhibiting ACh release from the terminals. (B) M$_5$ receptors likewise are implicated in the rewarding effects of morphine, as shown by a place-conditioning study comparing genetically normal mice (also known as wild-type; shown here as M$_5^{+/+}$) with M$_5$ knockout mice (mutant mice lacking the M$_5$ receptor; shown here as M$_5^{-/-}$). Morphine reward in the wild-type animals was demonstrated by increased time spent in the drug-paired chamber compared with controls given saline injections (0-mg/kg dose group). In the knockout animals, no rewarding effect of morphine was noted, except for a partial effect at the highest drug dose. (B after Basile et al., 2002.)

dependence through the known involvement of DA in these processes (see Chapter 9 for more information).

Outside of the brain, muscarinic receptors are found at high densities in the cardiac muscle of the heart, in the smooth muscle associated with many organs (e.g., bronchioles, stomach, intestines, bladder, urogenital organs), and in the insulin-secreting β-cells of the pancreas. These peripheral muscarinic receptors are activated by ACh released from postganglionic fibers of the parasympathetic nervous system. Stimulation of the parasympathetic system has two effects on the heart: a slowing of heart rate and a decrease in the strength of contraction, both of which are mediated by M$_2$ muscarinic receptors in cardiac muscle. In contrast, smooth muscle cells express M$_3$ receptors

and typically are excited by receptor activation, thus causing contraction of the muscle. Pancreatic β-cells receive their parasympathetic innervation through the vagus nerve, which exhibits increased activity at the beginning of a meal. The resulting release of ACh acts on β-cell M$_3$ receptors to stimulate insulin secretion, thus regulating blood glucose levels during and following food consumption (**Figure 7.10**). In one form of type 2 diabetes, the pancreas secretes insufficient amounts of insulin, which results in chronically elevated concentrations of glucose in the bloodstream. Recently, investigators have expressed interest in the possibility that muscarinic regulation of β-cell insulin release might be a future target of medications being developed to treat the insulin-insufficiency form of type 2 diabetes (Ruiz de Azua et al., 2011).

Finally, muscarinic receptors (mainly of the M$_3$ subtype) also mediate other secretory responses of the autonomic system such as salivation and lacrimation (tearing). Unfortunately, many of the drugs used to treat depression, schizophrenia, and other major psychiatric disorders produce serious side effects because of their blockade of peripheral muscarinic receptors. Patients particularly complain about the so-called **dry-mouth effect** (technically referred to as *xerostomia*), which reflects reduced production of saliva resulting from muscarinic antagonism. For some, the dry-mouth effect is severe enough to cause the patient to stop taking his or her medication. If the medication is continued, the chronic lack of salivation can lead to mouth sores, increased tooth decay, and difficulty in chewing and swallowing food. Later in the book, we will see that pharmaceutical companies have worked to develop newer medications that react less with muscarinic receptors and therefore do not produce the dry-mouth effect.

Several muscarinic receptor agonists occur in nature, including muscarine, from *Amanita muscaria*; **pilocarpine**, from the leaves of the South American shrub *Pilocarpus jaborandi*; and **arecoline**, which is found in the seeds of the betel nut palm *Areca catechu*. These substances are sometimes referred to as **parasympathomimetic agents**, because their ingestion mimics many of the effects of parasympathetic activation. Thus, poisoning due to accidental ingestion of

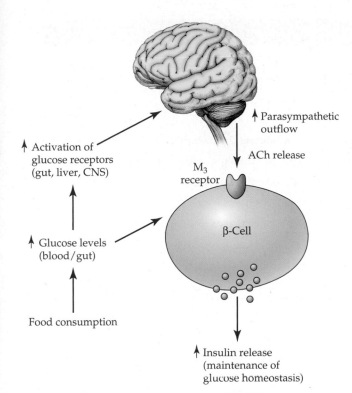

Figure 7.10 M₃ muscarinic receptors regulate insulin release by pancreatic β-cells Elevated levels of glucose caused by food consumption stimulate glucocoreceptors in the gut, liver, and CNS. This stimulation leads to enhanced release of ACh by the vagus nerve of the parasympathetic system and activation of M₃ receptors on the β-cells. Insulin produced by these cells assists in uptake and utilization of glucose by peripheral tissues such as the liver and skeletal muscles.

Amanita or any of the other plants leads to exaggerated parasympathetic responses, including lacrimation, salivation, sweating, pinpoint pupils related to constriction of the iris, severe abdominal pain, strong contractions of the smooth muscles of the viscera, and painful diarrhea. High doses can even cause cardiovascular collapse, convulsions, coma, and death.

Given the autonomic effects of muscarinic agonists, it is understandable that antagonists of these receptors would inhibit the actions of the parasympathetic system. Such compounds, therefore, are called **parasympatholytic agents**. The major naturally occurring muscarinic antagonists are **atropine** (also sometimes called hyoscamine) and the closely related drug **scopolamine** (hyoscine). These alkaloids are found in a group of plants that includes the deadly nightshade (*Atropa belladonna*) and henbane (*Hyoscyamus niger*) (**Figure 7.11**). Extracts of these plants are toxic when taken systemically—a fact that was exploited during the Middle Ages, when the deadly nightshade was used as a lethal agent to settle many political and family intrigues. On the other hand, a cosmetic use of the plant also evolved,

in which women instilled the juice of the berries into their eyes to cause pupillary dilation (by blocking the muscarinic receptors on the constrictor muscles of the iris). The effect was considered to make the user more attractive to men. Indeed, the name *Atropa belladonna* reflects these two facets of the plant, since *bella donna* means "beautiful woman" in Italian, whereas Atropos was a character in Greek mythology whose duty it was to cut the thread of life at the appropriate time.

Muscarinic antagonists have several current medical applications. Modern ophthalmologists use atropine just as women of the Middle Ages did, except in this case, they are dilating the patient's pupils to obtain a better view of the interior of the eye. Another use is in human and veterinary surgery, where the drug reduces secretions that could clog the patient's airways. Atropine is also occasionally needed to counteract the effects of poisoning with a cholinergic agonist. Scopolamine in therapeutic doses produces drowsiness, euphoria, amnesia, fatigue, and dreamless sleep. As mentioned in Box 7.2, this drug was historically used along with narcotics as a preanesthetic medication before surgery, or alone prior to childbirth to produce "twilight sleep," a condition characterized by drowsiness and amnesia for events that occur during the duration of drug use.

Despite their therapeutic uses, muscarinic antagonists can themselves be toxic when taken systemically at high doses. CNS effects of atropine poisoning include restlessness, irritability, disorientation, hallucinations, and delirium. Even higher doses can lead to CNS depression, coma, and eventually death by respiratory paralysis. As in the case of nicotinic drugs, these toxic effects point to the delicate balance of cholinergic activity in both the CNS and the PNS that is necessary for normal physiological functioning.

Figure 7.11 Deadly nightshade (*Atropa belladonna*) is a natural source of the muscarinic antagonist atropine.

TABLE 7.1   Drugs and Toxins That Affect the Cholinergic System

Drug	Action
Vesamicol	Depletes ACh by inhibiting vesicular uptake
Black widow spider venom	Stimulates ACh release
Botulinum toxin	Inhibits ACh release
Hemicholinium-3	Depletes ACh by inhibiting choline uptake by the nerve terminal
Physostigmine, neostigmine, and pyridostigmine	Increase ACh levels by inhibiting acetylcholinesterase reversibly
Sarin and Soman	Inhibit acetylcholinesterase irreversibly
Nicotine	Stimulates nicotinic receptors (agonist)
Succinylcholine	Nicotinic receptor agonist that causes depolarization block
Mecamylamine and D-tubocurarine	Block nicotinic receptors (antagonists)
Muscarine, pilocarpine, and arecoline	Stimulate muscarinic receptors (agonists)
Atropine and scopolamine	Block muscarinic receptors (antagonists)

Section Summary

- Acetylcholine is an important neurotransmitter in the PNS, where it is released by motor neurons innervating skeletal muscles, by preganglionic neurons of both the parasympathetic and sympathetic branches of the autonomic nervous system, and by ganglionic parasympathetic neurons.

- In the brain, cholinergic neurons include a group of interneurons within the striatum, a diffuse system of projection neurons that constitute the basal forebrain cholinergic system (BFCS), and a group of brainstem neurons in the laterodorsal and pedunculopontine tegmental (LDTg and PPTg) nuclei.

- The BFCS plays an important role in cognitive functioning, whereas the LDTg and the PPTg exert multiple roles, including stimulation of midbrain dopamine neurons, behavioral arousal, sensory processing, and initiation of rapid-eye-movement sleep.

- Cholinergic receptors are divided into two major families: nicotinic and muscarinic receptors.

- Nicotinic receptors are ionotropic receptors comprising five subunits. When the receptor channel opens, it produces a fast excitatory response resulting from an influx of Na^+ and Ca^{2+} ions across the cell membrane.

- Nicotinic receptors in neurons and muscles possess somewhat different subunits, and this leads to significant pharmacological differences between the two types of receptors.

- With continuous stimulation by an agonist, nicotinic receptors are subject to a phenomenon called desensitization, in which the channel will not open despite the presence of the agonist. These receptors also can lead to a process of depolarization block involving temporary loss of the cell's resting potential and an inability of the cell to generate action potentials.

- There are five kinds of muscarinic receptors, designated M_1 through M_5, all of which are metabotropic receptors. Muscarinic receptors function through several different signaling mechanisms, including activation of the phosphoinositide second-messenger system, inhibition of cAMP synthesis, and stimulation of K^+ channel opening.

- Muscarinic receptors are widely distributed in the brain, with particularly high densities in various forebrain structures.

- Muscarinic receptors are also found in targets of the parasympathetic system, including the heart, secretory glands, and smooth muscle found in many internal organs. Consequently, muscarinic agonists are called parasympathomimetic agents, whereas antagonists are considered parasympatholytic in their actions.

- Blockade of muscarinic receptors in the salivary glands leads to the dry-mouth effect, which is a serious side effect of many drugs used to treat various psychiatric disorders.

- **Table 7.1** presents some of the drugs that affect the cholinergic system, including nicotinic and muscarinic receptor agonists and antagonists.

Go to the **COMPANION WEBSITE**

sites.sinauer.com/psychopharm2e
for Web Boxes, animations, flashcards,
and other study resources.

Recommended Readings

Albuquerque, E. X., Pereira, E. F., Alkondon, M., and Rogers, S. W. (2009). Mammalian nicotinic acetylcholine receptors: From structure to function. *Physiol. Rev.*, 89, 73–120.

Benarroch, E. E. (2010). Acetylcholine in the cerebral cortex: Effects and clinical implications. *Neurology*, 75, 659–665.

Langmead, C. J., Watson, J., and Reavill, C. (2008). Muscarinic acetylcholine receptors as CNS drug targets. *Pharmacol. Ther.*, 117, 232–243.

The *Doogie* mouse is a genetically engineered strain that exhibits enhanced learning and memory.

Glutamate and GABA   8

IN 1966, DANIEL KEYES PUBLISHED A SCIENCE FICTION NOVEL entitled *Flowers for Algernon*, in which an experimental brain operation turns a mentally retarded young man into a genius. The book spawned an Oscar-winning movie adaptation called *Charly*, starring Cliff Robertson as the protagonist. Tragically, Charly's intellectual ascent was only temporary, and in any case, most people probably wouldn't want to endure brain surgery to increase their IQ. On the other hand, the possibility of a "smart pill" would be appealing to many. An informal survey conducted by Marilyn vos Savant (author of the "Ask Marilyn" column in the popular Sunday newspaper magazine *Parade*) found that if given a choice, a large majority of respondents would prefer raising their intelligence to improving their physical appearance. Likewise, most students would probably appreciate an easy way to improve their learning skills, perhaps enabling them to "ace" all their courses without too much difficulty.

Although no genius pills are yet in sight, researchers actually have been hard at work to find drugs that improve cognitive function. Some cognitive-enhancing compounds, which are called nootropics,[1] act on the cholinergic system (see Chapter 7). Others influence the amino acid neurotransmitter glutamate, which is the subject of the first part of the present chapter. The effects of nootropic drugs have thus far been relatively modest. However, there have been occasional advances that have received national attention. For example, a group of investigators headed by Joe Tsien at Princeton University made a big splash in September 1999, when they published an exciting paper showing that a genetic modification involving one of the receptors for glutamate (called the NMDA receptor) could enhance learning and

---

[1]The term *nootropic* comes from two Greek words: *noos*, which means "mind," and *tropein*, which means "toward."

long-term memory in mice (Tang et al., 1999). Tsien and colleagues called their genetically engineered mouse the *Doogie* mouse, after the former TV show *Doogie Howser, M.D.*, which featured a boy genius who became a doctor at a young age. More recently, a group of compounds called ampakines that target another glutamate receptor, the AMPA receptor, have also received substantial attention as potential cognitive enhancers. We will learn more about these developments and the role of glutamate in learning and memory later in this chapter. The second part of the chapter covers γ-aminobutyric acid (GABA), another important amino acid neurotransmitter.

Glutamate

Glutamate is the term we use for the ionized (i.e., electrically charged) form of the amino acid glutamic acid. Since most of the glutamic acid in our bodies is in this ionized state, we will refer to it as glutamate throughout the text. Like other common amino acids, glutamate is used by all of our cells to help make new proteins. But glutamate also has numerous other biochemical functions (e.g., in energy metabolism); this is reflected in the fact that it is the most abundant amino acid in the brain. Glutamate and **aspartate** (the name for the ionized form of aspartic acid) are the two principal members of a small family of **excitatory amino acid neurotransmitters**. These transmitters are so named because they cause a powerful excitatory response when applied to most neurons in the brain or spinal cord. We will focus on glutamate—a much more widely used excitatory amino acid transmitter that has been more intensively studied than aspartate.

Glutamate Synthesis, Release, and Inactivation

When a nerve cell synthesizes a molecule of dopamine (DA), acetylcholine (ACh), or serotonin (5-HT), it is almost always done for the purpose of neurotransmission. Moreover, in the brain, these substances are localized specifically within the cells that use them as transmitters. However, we must recognize that the situation is different for glutamate because of its roles in protein synthesis and general cellular metabolism. First, all neurons and glial cells contain significant amounts of glutamate, although neurons that use glutamate as a transmitter (called **glutamatergic neurons**) possess even greater concentrations than other cells in the brain. Second, glutamatergic neurons are thought to segregate the pool of glutamate that they use for transmission from the pool of glutamate used for other cellular functions.

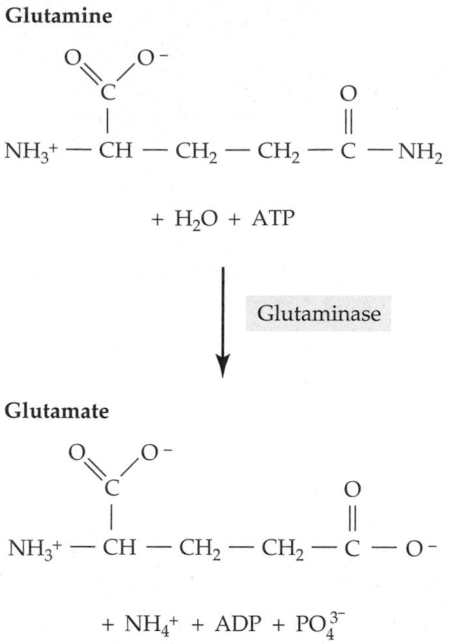

Figure 8.1 Glutamate is synthesized from glutamine by the enzyme glutaminase. This reaction requires energy provided by the breakdown of adenosine triphosphate (ATP) into adenosine diphosphate (ADP) and phosphate (PO_4^{3-}).

These facts complicate both our ability to determine which nerve cells actually are glutamatergic and our understanding of how these cells synthesize, release, and dispose of the transmitter-related glutamate. Nevertheless, researchers have accumulated considerable information, which we summarize in this section.

Neurons generate glutamate from the precursor glutamine

Glutamate can be synthesized by several different chemical reactions. Most molecules of glutamate are derived ultimately from the normal metabolic breakdown of the sugar glucose. The more immediate precursor for much of the transmitter-related glutamate is a related substance known as **glutamine**. Neurons can transform glutamine into glutamate using an enzyme called **glutaminase** (**Figure 8.1**). We will see in the next section that the role of glutamine in glutamate synthesis involves a fascinating metabolic partnership between glutamatergic neurons and neighboring glial cells, specifically astrocytes.

Glutamate packaging into vesicles and uptake after release are mediated by multiple transport systems

For a long time, no one knew how glutamate got into synaptic vesicles for the purpose of storage and release.

(A)

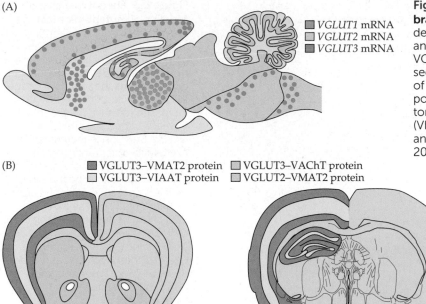

- ▨ *VGLUT1* mRNA
- ▢ *VGLUT2* mRNA
- ▦ *VGLUT3* mRNA

Figure 8.2 Distribution of VGLUTs in the rat brain (A) Sagittal section through the brain depicting anatomical areas (uniform colors) and cell clusters (dots) that express mRNA for VGLUT1, VGLUT2, or VGLUT3. (B) Coronal sections depicting regions of co-localization of VGLUT proteins with the vesicular transporters for acetylcholine (VAChT), the inhibitory neurotransmitters GABA and glycine (VIAAT), and the monoamine transmitters DA and 5-HT (VMAT2). (After El Mestikawy et al., 2011.)

(B)

- ▨ VGLUT3–VMAT2 protein
- ▢ VGLUT3–VIAAT protein
- ▢ VGLUT3–VAChT protein
- ▢ VGLUT2–VMAT2 protein

Then between the years 2000 and 2002, researchers discovered *three* distinct proteins that package glutamate into vesicles: **VGLUT1**, **VGLUT2**, and **VGLUT3** (**VGLUT** standing for **vesicular glutamate transporter**). These proteins serve as good markers for glutamatergic neurons because unlike glutamate itself, they are found only in cells that use glutamate as a neurotransmitter. Glutamatergic neurons generally possess either VGLUT1 or VGLUT2 (but usually not both), with VGLUT3 being less abundant than the other two transporters. As illustrated in **Figure 8.2A**, *VGLUT1* gene expression occurs primarily in the cortex and hippocampus, whereas *VGLUT2* gene expression is found mostly in subcortical structures (El Mestikawy et al., 2011). VGLUT2 knockout mice die immediately after birth, signifying the critical importance of glutamate signaling in VGLUT2-expressing neurons for life-sustaining functions (Wallén-Mackenzie et al., 2010). In contrast, VGLUT1 knockout mice survive birth but eventually begin to die during the third week of life, whereas mice lacking VGLUT3 are viable but are completely deaf (Seal et al., 2008). The reason for this unusual defect is that the inner hair cells of the cochlea use glutamate as their neurotransmitter, and the only vesicular transporter they express is VGLUT3. Consequently, when the inner hair cells from VGLUT3 knockout mice are stimulated by sound waves striking the eardrum, they have no glutamate in their vesicles to transmit the stimulus to the auditory nerve.

Remarkably, VGLUT3 and to a lesser extent VGLUT1 and VGLUT2 mRNA and protein are some-times co-expressed with markers of other classical neurotransmitters, implying that in neurons with such co-expression, glutamate is also stored and presumably is released as a co-transmitter. **Figure 8.2B** illustrates some important areas of co-expression of a vesicular glutamate transporter with the vesicular monoamine transporter 2 (VMAT2) in DA and 5-HT neurons (depending on the brain region), the vesicular acetylcholine transporter (VAChT) in cholinergic neurons, or the vesicular inhibitory amino acid transporter (VIAAT), which is expressed in both GABA and glycine neurons (see Part II of this chapter). After the discovery of these numerous examples of vesicular transporter co-expression, investigators began to ask important questions such as whether a glutamate and another transporter (e.g., VMAT2) are present on the same vesicles in the nerve terminal, or whether neurons exhibiting this kind of transporter co-expression segregate their vesicles into two different types (i.e., one type of vesicle that takes up and releases glutamate and a second type of vesicle that takes up and releases the other transmitter synthesized by that neuron). Evidence suggests that both types of situations can exist (El Mestikawy et al., 2011); however, more research is needed to identify the mechanism involved in vesicular segregation (when it occurs) and more importantly, the functional significance of glutamate as a co-transmitter with other classical transmitters such as DA, 5-HT, ACh, GABA, and glycine.

After glutamate molecules are released into the synaptic cleft, they are rapidly removed by other glutamate transporters located on cell membranes. Always

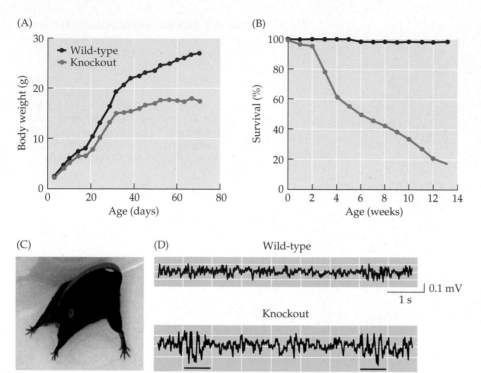

Figure 8.3 Phenotypic characteristics of mutant mice lacking EAAT2 (A) EAAT2 knockout mice exhibited a reduction in weight gain compared with genetically normal wild-type mice, particularly once they reached 30 days of age. (B) The knockout mice showed increased mortality beginning at 3 weeks of age. (C) and (D) Mice lacking EAAT2 had increased brain excitability that manifested as spontaneous behavioral seizures (note the abnormal posture in C, which is caused by epileptic activity in the brain) and seizure-like EEG changes (underlined traces in D) when given a subthreshold dose of the convulsant agent pentylenetetrazole. Note that at this drug dose, the wild-type mice showed no such EEG changes. (After Tanaka et al., 1997.)

keep in mind that the plasma membrane transporters that remove neurotransmitters from the synaptic cleft are distinct from the transporters on the vesicle membranes that are responsible for loading the vesicles in preparation for transmitter release. In the case of glutamate, five different plasma membrane transporters have been identified and have different cellular localizations. Because these transporters take up aspartate as well as glutamate, they are called **EAAT1** to **EAAT5** (**EAAT** standing for **excitatory amino acid transporter**). EAAT1 is expressed heavily in specialized glial cells of the cerebellum and is important for normal cerebellar function. EAAT2 is widely expressed in astrocytes throughout the brain and plays a critical role in taking up glutamate after its release. As we will see later, prolonged high levels of glutamate in the extracellular fluid are very dangerous, producing excessive neuronal excitation and even cell death. The importance of EAAT2 in glutamate clearance was shown by Tanaka and coworkers (1997), who found that knockout mice lacking EAAT2 (termed GLT-1 in their paper due to the use of a different terminology) developed spontaneous epileptic seizures, were more susceptible than wild-type mice to experimentally induced seizures and brain injury, and had a greatly shortened life span (**Figure 8.3**). Of the remaining transporters, EAAT3 is the main neuronal glutamate transporter throughout the brain, EAAT4 is expressed mainly by Purkinje cells in the cerebellum, and EAAT5 is present in several types of cells within the retina.

The importance of plasma membrane transporters in regulating extracellular glutamate levels raises the possibility that abnormal regulation of any of these transporters could produce pathological effects resulting in neurological disease. Such a causative role has not yet been established for any particular disease; however, evidence suggests that down-regulation of EAAT2 could play some role in the development of **amyotrophic lateral sclerosis** (**ALS**; also known as Lou Gehrig's disease), a neurological disorder involving degeneration of motor neurons in the spinal cord and cortex (Rattray and Bendotti, 2006) (see Chapter 21). These and other findings suggesting a possible role for glutamate transporters in various neuropathological conditions have led to an interest in developing drugs that might up-regulate or otherwise influence the activity of these transporters (Beart and O'Shea, 2007; Sheldon and Robinson, 2007).

Besides playing a key role in removing excess glutamate from the extracellular space, astrocyte transporters are also intimately involved in the metabolic partnership between neurons and astrocytes. After astrocytes have taken up glutamate by means of EAAT1 or EAAT2, they convert a major portion of it to glutamine by means of an enzyme called **glutamine synthetase**. Glutamine is then transported out of the astrocytes and picked up by neurons, where it can be converted back into glutamate by glutaminase, as described earlier. This interplay between glutamatergic neurons and neighboring astrocytes is illustrated

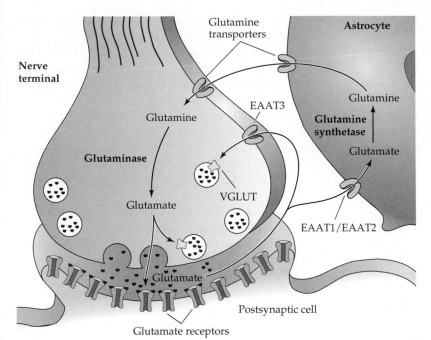

Glutamine transporters

Glutamine

Glutaminase

Glutamate

VGLUT

EAAT3

Nerve terminal

Glutamate

Astrocyte

Glutamine

Glutamine synthetase

Glutamate

EAAT1/EAAT2

Glutamate receptors

Postsynaptic cell

Figure 8.4 Cycling of glutamate and glutamine between glutamatergic neurons and astrocytes After neurons release glutamate, it can be transported back into the nerve terminal by EAAT3 or into nearby astrocytes by EAAT1 or EAAT2. Inside the astrocyte, glutamate is converted into glutamine by the enzyme glutamine synthetase. The glutamine can be later released by the astrocytes, taken up by neurons, and converted back into glutamate by the enzyme glutaminase.

in **Figure 8.4**. It is reasonable to wonder why such a complex system has evolved: Why don't the neurons themselves have the primary responsibility for glutamate reuptake, as we have seen previously for the catecholamine neurotransmitters and for serotonin? Although we aren't certain about the answer to this question, it's worth noting that glutamine does not produce neuronal excitation and therefore is not potentially dangerous, as glutamate is. Hence, glial cell production of glutamine may be the brain's way of storing glutamate in a form that is "safe" but still available for use once the glutamine has been transferred to the neurons and reconverted to glutamate.

Section Summary

- Glutamate and aspartate are amino acid neurotransmitters that have potent excitatory effects on neurons throughout the brain and spinal cord. Although glutamate is contained within all cells because of its multiple biochemical functions, glutamatergic neurons are thought to possess higher glutamate concentrations than other cells and to segregate their neurotransmitter pool of this amino acid.

- Many of the glutamate molecules that are released synaptically are synthesized from glutamine in a chemical reaction catalyzed by the enzyme glutaminase.

- Glutamate is packaged into vesicles by the vesicular transporters VGLUT1, VGLUT2, and VGLUT3.

In some neurons, these transporters are expressed with markers for other neurotransmitters such as 5-HT, DA, ACh, and GABA, indicating that glutamate is a co-transmitter in these cells.

- After they are released, glutamate molecules are removed from the extracellular fluid by five different excitatory amino acid transporters, designated EAAT1 to EAAT5. Uptake of glutamate into astrocytes by EAAT2 is especially important for glutamate clearance, as can be seen by the fact that mutant mice lacking this transporter exhibit seizures, neuronal cell death, and a shortened life span. Abnormalities in EAAT2 may also be present in certain neurological disorders, particularly ALS.

- Glutamate taken up by astrocytes is converted to glutamine by the enzyme glutamine synthetase.

- This glutamine subsequently can be transported from the astrocytes to the glutamatergic neurons, where it is transformed back into glutamate by the enzyme glutaminase and then reutilized. This constitutes an important metabolic interplay between glutamatergic nerve cells and their neighboring glial cells.

Organization and Function of the Glutamatergic System

Glutamate is considered to be the workhorse transmitter for fast excitatory signaling in the nervous system. Not only is it used in many excitatory neuronal pathways, but the most important receptors for glutamate are ionotropic receptors that produce fast postsynaptic responses (see the next section). We will not discuss a large number of glutamatergic pathways here but will simply mention several that have been extensively studied. We will also consider a few important functions of the glutamatergic system.

Glutamate is the neurotransmitter used in many excitatory pathways in the brain

In the cerebral cortex, glutamate is the main neurotransmitter used by the pyramidal neurons. These cells, which are named on the basis of their pyramid-like shape, are the major output neurons of the cortex. Their axons project to numerous subcortical structures, including the striatum, the thalamus, various limbic system structures, and regions of the brainstem. Glutamate is also used in the numerous parallel fibers of the cerebellar cortex and in several excitatory pathways within the hippocampus.

Because glutamate is found throughout the brain, it is more difficult to assign specific functional roles to this neurotransmitter than it is for some of the other transmitters covered previously. Glutamate is undoubtedly involved in many different behavioral and physiological functions under both normal and abnormal conditions. Among the most important are synaptic plasticity (i.e., changes in the strength of synaptic connections), learning and memory, cell death in some neurological disorders, and possibly also the development of various psychopathological disorders, including drug addiction and schizophrenia. Later in this chapter we will consider the role of glutamate in synaptic plasticity, learning and memory, and neuronal cell death. Current findings regarding the possible involvement of glutamate in drug addiction, schizophrenia, and other types of psychopathology will mainly be taken up in other chapters of this book (with the exception of a few examples presented in the section on metabotropic glutamate receptors).

Both ionotropic and metabotropic receptors mediate the synaptic effects of glutamate

Glutamate receptors are divided into two broad families: a group of ionotropic receptors for fast signaling and a group of slower metabotropic receptors that function by means of second-messenger systems. We will focus first on the ionotropic receptors, since they are most important for understanding the mechanisms of glutamate action in the brain. Note that glutamate receptors are also used by aspartate and possibly by other excitatory amino acid transmitters that may exist. Hence, these receptors are sometimes called excitatory amino acid receptors rather than simply glutamate receptors.

IONOTROPIC GLUTAMATE RECEPTORS   There are three subtypes of ionotropic glutamate receptors. Each is named for a relatively selective agonist for that receptor subtype. First is the **AMPA receptor**, which is named for the selective agonist AMPA (α-amino-3-hydroxy-5-methyl-4-isoxazole propionic acid), a synthetic (not naturally occurring) amino acid analog. Most fast excitatory responses to glutamate are mediated by stimulation of AMPA receptors. The second ionotropic receptor subtype is the **kainate receptor**, which is named for the selective agonist kainic acid. Even though kainic acid powerfully stimulates kainate receptors in the mammalian brain, this substance actually comes from a type of seaweed called *Digenea simplex*. The third ionotropic glutamate receptor is the **NMDA receptor**, the agonist of which is obviously NMDA (*N*-methyl-D-aspartate). Like AMPA, NMDA is a synthetic amino acid. Thus, we see that pharmacologists have had to take advantage of several unusual compounds (either man-made or plant-derived) to distinguish between the different ionotropic receptor subtypes, since glutamate itself obviously must activate all of these receptors.

Like the nicotinic receptors discussed in the previous chapter, ionotropic glutamate receptors depolarize the membrane of the postsynaptic cell, which leads to an excitatory response. For the AMPA and kainate receptors, this depolarizing effect is produced mainly by the flow of sodium (Na^+) ions into the cell through the receptor channel. In the case of NMDA receptors, the channel conducts not only Na^+ but also significant amounts of calcium (Ca^{2+}). Because Ca^{2+} can function as a second messenger within the postsynaptic cell (see Chapter 3), this is an interesting case in which an ionotropic receptor (the NMDA receptor) directly activates a second-messenger system (**Figure 8.5**).

Going back to the nicotinic receptor (see Figure 7.8), recall that the complete receptor contains five separate proteins (subunits) that come together to form the receptor channel. Ionotropic glutamate receptors are

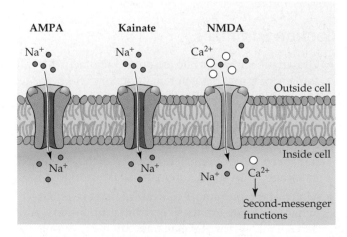

Figure 8.5 All ionotropic glutamate receptor channels conduct Na⁺ ions into the cell but NMDA receptor channels also conduct Ca²⁺ ions. Once inside the cell, Ca²⁺ can activate several important second-messenger functions.

similarly formed from multiple subunits, but in this case, there are four subunits comprising each receptor complex. It is interesting to note that each receptor subtype (AMPA, kainate, and NMDA) is composed of a different set of subunits; this explains why the three subtypes differ in their pharmacology. Not only does each subtype have its own selective agonist, but various receptor antagonists have also been developed that have helped us understand the behavioral and physiological functions of these receptors.

One widely used antagonist called **NBQX** (6-nitro-7-sulfamoyl-benzo(f)-quinoxaline-2,3-dione) can block both AMPA and kainate receptors, although it is somewhat more effective against the former subtype. This compound has no effect on NMDA receptors. Rats and mice treated with high doses of NBQX exhibit sedation, reduced locomotor activity and ataxia (impaired coordination in movement; an example in humans is staggering), poor performance in the rotarod task (another test of coordination), and protection against electrically or chemically induced seizures. These findings indicate a broad role for AMPA (and possibly also kainate) receptors in locomotor activity, coordination, and brain excitability (as shown by the seizure results).

NMDA receptors possess a number of characteristics not found in the other glutamate ionotropic receptors (**Figure 8.6**). First, as we've already mentioned, unlike AMPA and kainate receptor channels, the channels for NMDA receptors allow Ca^{2+} ions to flow into the postsynaptic cell, thus triggering Ca^{2+}-dependent second-messenger activities. Second, NMDA receptors are very unusual in that two different neurotransmitters are required to stimulate the receptor and open its ion channel. The first neurotransmitter, of course, is glutamate. But in addition to the binding site for glutamate on the NMDA receptor complex, there is also a binding site that recognizes the amino acid **glycine**. The importance of this is that if the glycine binding site isn't occupied at the same time as the glutamate binding site, the NMDA receptor channel remains closed. If that isn't complicated enough, it appears that another amino acid, **D-serine**, may be more important than glycine for interacting with the second binding site. In any case, either glycine or D-serine is considered to be a **co-agonist** with glutamate at the NMDA receptor, since one or the other of these substances is just as necessary as glutamate for receptor activation. However, because the co-agonist binding site is thought to be occupied under most conditions, the presence or absence of glutamate is the more important factor in determining channel opening.

There are two additional binding sites on the NMDA receptor that affect its function. One is a site within the receptor channel that binds magnesium

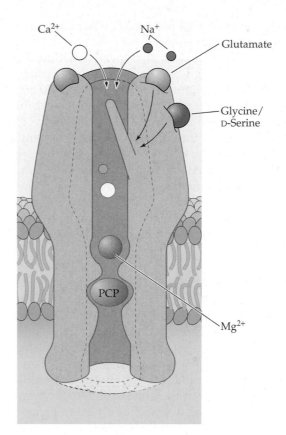

Figure 8.6 NMDA receptor properties The NMDA receptor is activated by simultaneous binding of glutamate and a co-agonist, either glycine or D-serine. The receptor channel can be blocked by Mg^{2+} ions under resting conditions and also by the presence of the abused drug phencyclidine (PCP).

(Mg^{2+}) ions. When the cell membrane is at the resting potential (typically –60 or –70 mV), Mg^{2+} ions are bound to this site relatively tightly. This causes the receptor channel to be blocked, even if glutamate and either glycine or D-serine are present to activate the receptor. However, if the membrane becomes depolarized, then the Mg^{2+} ions dissociate from the receptor and permit the channel to open if glutamate and either glycine or D-serine are present. Consider the implications of this property of NMDA receptors. How does the membrane become depolarized? The answer, of course, is that some other source of excitation (other than NMDA receptors) must have already activated the cell. This other source of excitation could have been glutamate acting through AMPA (or potentially kainate) receptors, or a different transmitter such as acetylcholine acting through nicotinic receptors. The point is that an NMDA receptor is a kind of biological "coincidence detector." That is, the channel only opens when two events occur close together in time: (1) glutamate is released onto the NMDA receptor, and

(2) the cell membrane is depolarized by stimulation of a different excitatory receptor.

The second site, which is also located within the receptor channel, recognizes the abused drugs **phencyclidine** (**PCP**) and **ketamine**, as well as **MK-801** (**dizocilpine**), a compound more commonly used for research purposes. When any of these drugs binds to the PCP site, it blocks the channel and thus prevents ion flow. Because these compounds do not interfere with the ability of glutamate to bind to its site on the receptor, they are noncompetitive rather than competitive antagonists of the NMDA receptor. As will be discussed further in Chapter 15, most of the behavioral effects of PCP and ketamine are due to NMDA receptor antagonism.

METABOTROPIC GLUTAMATE RECEPTORS   Besides the three ionotropic receptors, there are also eight different metabotropic glutamate receptors. They are designated **mGluR1** to **mGluR8**. Through their coupling to G proteins, some of these receptors inhibit cyclic adenosine monophosphate (cAMP) formation, whereas others activate the phosphoinositide second-messenger system. Finally, certain metabotropic glutamate receptors are located on nerve terminals, where they act as presynaptic autoreceptors to inhibit glutamate release. The novel amino acid L-AP4 (L-**2-amino-4-phosphonobutyrate**) is a selective agonist at these glutamate autoreceptors, thereby suppressing glutamatergic synaptic transmission.

Metabotropic glutamate receptors are widely distributed throughout the brain, and they participate in many normal functions, including locomotor activity, motor coordination, cognition, mood, and pain perception. Recognition of this involvement has led to increasing interest in the development of mGluR drugs for the treatment of numerous neuropsychiatric disorders such as depression, anxiety disorders, disorders characterized by cognitive deficits, and drug addiction (Krystal et al., 2010; Moussawi and Kalivas, 2010; O'Connor et al., 2010; Simonyi et al., 2010). Here we will briefly discuss some recent developments regarding the potential use of mGluR compounds in the treatment of schizophrenia. One emerging theory of schizophrenia suggests a role for abnormally high glutamate release in this disorder. Agonists at mGluR2 can inhibit glutamate release in experimental animals; this has led to testing of such compounds both in animal models of schizophrenia and more recently in schizophrenic patients (Krystal et al., 2010). **Figure 8.7** illustrates the dose-dependent inhibition of amphetamine-induced hyperactivity in rats (a classical animal test for antipsychotic efficacy) by the mGluR2/3 agonist LY404039 (Rorick-Kehn et al., 2007). Subsequent studies by the same research group established that this effect was due to activation of mGluR2, not mGluR3, receptors (Fell et al., 2008). In

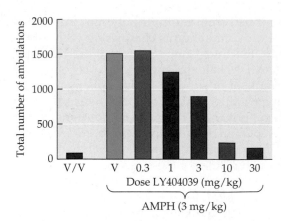

Figure 8.7   The mGluR2/3 agonist LY404039 dose dependently inhibits amphetamine-induced hyperlocomotion in male rats. Rats were challenged with 3 mg/kg of amphetamine (AMPH) injected subcutaneously (SC). The number of ambulations (movements within a test cage) was significantly increased in animals given amphetamine plus the LY404039 vehicle (V) compared with the control group, which was given both drug vehicles (V/V). LY404039 given orally (PO) led to a dose-dependent reduction in activity compared with that seen in amphetamine-challenged animals given the LY404039 vehicle. (After Rorick-Kehn et al., 2007.)

2007, Patil and coworkers reported encouraging data that LY2140023, a prodrug[2] of LY404039 with greater bioavailability in humans, significantly improved the symptoms of schizophrenic patients when compared with placebo treatment. Unfortunately, a subsequent clinical trial failed to obtain similar positive results with LY2140023 (Kinon et al., 2011). Although the latest findings do not rule out a possible role for mGluR2 agonists in the treatment of schizophrenia, more research in this area is clearly needed.

AMPA and NMDA receptors play a key role in learning and memory

Earlier, we mentioned that AMPA and NMDA receptors are two glutamate receptor subtypes that have been strongly implicated in the processes of learning and memory. It is vitally important to recognize that research in this area is not conducted merely for academic or theoretical reasons. On the contrary, so many neuropsychiatric disorders can result in cognitive impairment (including but not limited to neurodegenerative diseases like Alzheimer's disease, Parkinson's disease, and Huntington's disease, as well as schizophrenia, major depression, autism spectrum disorders, and attention deficit hyperactivity disorder) that

---

[2]A prodrug is a compound that is converted metabolically into the active agent after it is administered.

(A)

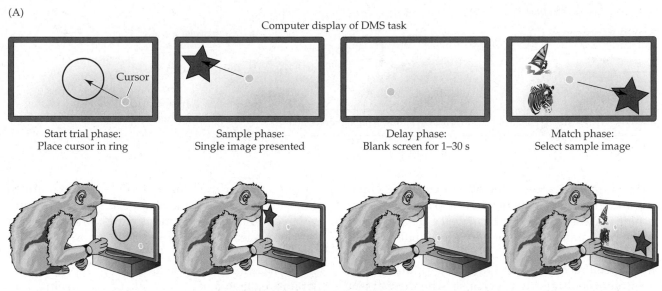

Computer display of DMS task

Start trial phase:
Place cursor in ring

Sample phase:
Single image presented

Delay phase:
Blank screen for 1–30 s

Match phase:
Select sample image

(B)

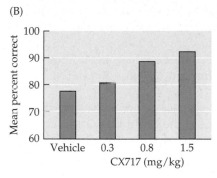

Figure 8.8 Ampakine-induced performance improvement on a delayed match-to-sample (DMS) memory task in monkeys (A) Each trial in the DMS task had four phases: (1) in the start trial phase, the monkey placed a hand-controlled cursor into a circular ring displayed on a computer screen; (2) in the sample phase, a single image of a clip-art object such as a red star was displayed on the screen, after which the monkey had to move the cursor into the image; (3) movement of the cursor into the sample image triggered a delay phase of 1 to 30 seconds, during which the screen was blank; (4) in the match phase, the sample image was displayed in a random location on the screen, along with one to five additional "nonmatch" images; to make the correct response, the monkey had to move the cursor into the sample image, after which it was rewarded with a sip of fruit juice. (B) The ampakine CX717 administered by IV injection produced a dose-dependent improvement in overall performance on the DMS task. (After Porrino et al., 2005.)

a major ongoing search is under way to identify new compounds that can improve cognitive function (i.e., cognitive enhancers; see Kantak and Hofmann, 2011).

One class of cognitive enhancers that has been studied extensively is the **ampakines**. As summarized by Arai and Kessler (2007), these compounds positively modulate AMPA receptor activity (i.e., they enhance the action of glutamate) but do not directly activate the receptor themselves. Although ampakines appear to act by several mechanisms, one mechanism involves reducing the rate of AMPA receptor desensitization. In Chapter 3, we introduced the idea that ionotropic receptors can undergo a process of desensitization in which the receptor channel closes even though a neurotransmitter or a drug agonist is still bound to the receptor. By reducing the rate of AMPA receptor desensitization, the receptor channel stays open longer, and glutamate can exert a more prolonged excitatory effect on the postsynaptic cell.

Ampakines have been demonstrated to enhance cognitive function in several kinds of animal models. One example is shown in **Figure 8.8A**, which

illustrates a memory task in monkeys called delayed match-to-sample. The figure shows that the monkey must remember a sample image displayed briefly on a computer screen for a variable length of time (the delay), after which the original image and two other images are presented, and the subject must select the originally displayed image. **Figure 8.8B** shows that the ampakine CX717 dose dependently improved the performance of the monkeys on this task (Porrino et al., 2005). Interestingly, subsequent studies by the same research team have begun to use brain imaging methods to determine how this compound might be working in the monkey brain to enhance cognitive function (Hampson et al., 2009). On a more discouraging note, the few clinical trials that have thus far been published on the use of ampakines to enhance cognition in human subjects have not yielded positive results. Nevertheless, these and other potential cognitive enhancers continue to be explored because of the importance of finding drugs that will be effective in reversing cognitive dysfunction in the various disorders mentioned earlier.

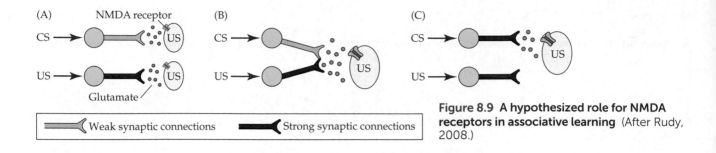

Figure 8.9 A hypothesized role for NMDA receptors in associative learning (After Rudy, 2008.)

The NMDA receptor is the other ionotropic glutamate receptor subtype believed to play a key role in learning and memory. It has been well established that release of glutamate from a nerve terminal coupled with strong activation of NMDA receptors in the postsynaptic cell receiving that glutamate input can lead to a strengthening of that synapse. The mechanism underlying this phenomenon, which is called **long-term potentiation** (**LTP**), will be described shortly. In the meantime, we will simply point out that one aspect of this mechanism involves the coincidence detection feature of the NMDA receptor mentioned earlier (i.e., the fact that the postsynaptic cell membrane must be depolarized simultaneously with occupation of agonist binding sites on the receptor). A possible link between this coincidence detection feature and learning can most readily be seen in the case of associative learning, which involves the pairing of two events, such as two different stimuli or a stimulus and a response. All psychology students have encountered a simple kind of associative learning called classical (Pavlovian) conditioning, as exemplified by Pavlov's original experiment with dogs. Like the opening of an NMDA receptor channel, classical conditioning is based on the close timing of two events: the pairing of a conditioned stimulus (the bell in Pavlov's experiment) with an unconditioned stimulus (the meat powder). Figure 8.9 depicts what is thought to be occurring at the synaptic level in this kind of simple associative learning. Neurons that receive input from the unconditioned stimulus (US) start out with strong connections to their postsynaptic partners, while neurons that receive input from the conditioned stimulus (CS) initially have weak connections with the US postsynaptic cells (**Figure 8.9A**). However, repeated pairings of the CS and the US (**Figure 8.9B**) theoretically strengthen the synaptic connections between the CS input neurons and the postsynaptic cells, because those latter cells (which express NMDA receptors) are being depolarized at the same time that the nerve terminals of the CS neurons are releasing glutamate. Finally, presentation of the CS alone elicits a strong response in the US postsynaptic cells (**Figure 8.9C**), which then can trigger the conditioned response.

Other, more direct lines of evidence have linked NMDA receptors with learning. First, several studies have found that treatment with NMDA receptor antagonists leads to impaired acquisition of various tasks, especially those involving spatial learning. This makes sense in light of the fact that the hippocampus, a brain area that is necessary for spatial learning, contains a high density of NMDA receptors. Second, as has been mentioned, NMDA receptors play a key role in LTP (**Box 8.1**). Many investigators believe that LTP could underlie various kinds of learning and memory, including but not limited to those mediated by the hippocampus.

The third line of evidence brings us back to the *Doogie* mouse mentioned at the beginning of this chapter. Unlike the knockout mice discussed in previous chapters, this strain of mouse was genetically engineered to *overexpress* one of the subunits of the NMDA receptor, namely the NR2B subunit (Tang et al., 1999). This resulted in more-efficient NMDA receptor functioning and possibly increased levels of the receptor in the transgenic animals. Compared with normal controls, the *Doogie* mice showed enhanced LTP. They also showed improved learning and memory on several tasks. For example, the *Doogie* mice demonstrated enhanced fear conditioning and faster extinction of the learned fear response compared with normal mice. These transgenic animals also performed better in the Morris water maze, which is a spatial navigation task (see Chapter 4). Finally, subjects were tested in a novel object recognition task, in which they were initially allowed to explore two objects for a period of 5 minutes. After an interval of 1 hour, 1 day, 3 days, or 1 week, a novel object was substituted for one of the two original (familiar) objects, and exploratory behavior was again tested. Because subjects tend to spend more time exploring unfamiliar objects, recall of the remaining original object would be demonstrated by less exploration of that stimulus. Researchers expected that if the original object was forgotten, subjects would spend approximately equal amounts of time exploring both objects in the recall test. The results indicated that both normal (wild-type) and *Doogie* mice had good recall at the 1-hour test because both groups explored

BOX 8.1 The Cutting Edge

Role of Glutamate Receptors in Long-Term Potentiation

Long-term potentiation (LTP) refers to a persistent (at least 1 hour) increase in synaptic strength produced by a burst of activity in the presynaptic neuron. This burst of firing is produced experimentally by a single brief train of electrical stimuli (e.g., 100 stimuli over a period of 1 second) that is sometimes called a **tetanic stimulus** (or simply a **tetanus**). The synaptic enhancement produced by the tetanus is measured by changes in the excitatory postsynaptic potential (EPSP) recorded in the postsynaptic cell. Two different forms of LTP have been discovered: **early LTP** (**E-LTP**), which lasts only a few hours at most, and **late LTP** (**L-LTP**), which can last for days or even months when produced in an animal instead of a brain slice (which is usually how E-LTP is studied). We will focus most of our discussion on E-LTP, which was discovered first and the conditions of which are required for L-LTP. At the end of our discussion, we will mention some of the additional conditions needed to produce L-LTP.

Although LTP occurs in many brain areas, it was first discovered in the hippocampus and has been studied most extensively in that structure. The hippocampus from a rat or a mouse is cut into slices around 200 μm (0.2 mm) thick. These slices are then placed in a dish where the neurons can be maintained in a healthy state for many hours while the investigator stimulates them and records their electrophysiological responses. The important cellular anatomy of a hippocampal slice is illustrated in Figure A. Without going into great detail, it is sufficient to know that all of the pathways shown in the diagram use glutamate as their transmitter, and that LTP occurs at all of the synaptic connections

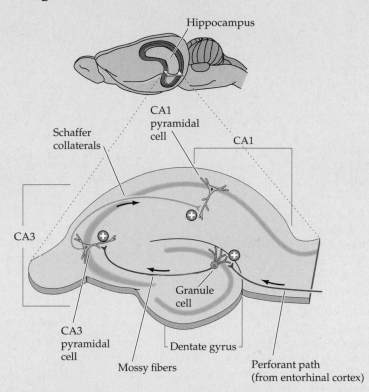

(A) Long-term potentiation of synaptic transmission can be studied in vitro using the hippocampal slice preparation.

depicted. However, the majority of LTP studies have focused on the pyramidal neurons of the CA1 region of the hippocampus, which receive excitatory glutamatergic inputs from CA3 neurons via the Schaffer collaterals.

Figure B depicts what happens to a typical synapse on a CA1 pyramidal neuron before, during, and after the tetanic stimulus. A test pulse (single electrical stimulation) of the presynaptic cell is used to assess the strength of the synaptic connection. The test pulse elicits the release of a small amount of glutamate from the presynaptic nerve endings. As shown in the left panel, this glutamate binds to both AMPA and NMDA receptors in the postsynaptic membrane.

A small EPSP is produced mainly by activation of the AMPA receptors. However, the NMDA receptor channels fail to open because the membrane is not depolarized sufficiently to release the Mg^{2+} block of those channels. As long as test pulses are separated in time, you can give many of these pulses and not see any enhancement of the EPSP. But look at what happens in response to a tetanic stimulus (middle panel). Much more glutamate is released, and this causes prolonged activation of the AMPA receptors and greater postsynaptic depolarization. This permits Mg^{2+} ions to dissociate from the NMDA receptor channels and Ca^{2+} ions

(Continued on next page)

BOX 8.1 (continued)

Single stimulus

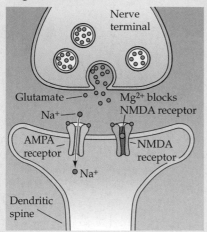

Tetanus

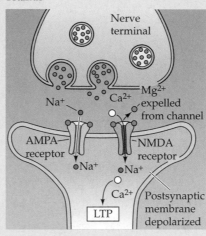

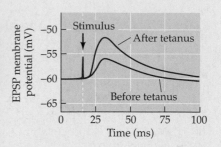

(B) Long-term potentiation is induced by a tetanic stimulation of the presynaptic input.

to enter the cell through these channels. Acting as a second messenger, these Ca^{2+} ions alter the functioning of the postsynaptic cell so that the same test pulse given before now produces an enhanced EPSP (right panel).

E-LTP can be divided into two phases: an **induction phase**, which takes place during and immediately after the tetanic stimulation, and an **expression phase**, which represents the enhanced synaptic strength measured at a later time. NMDA receptors play a critical role in the induction phase but not in the expression phase. We know this because application of an NMDA receptor antagonist to the hippocampal slice during the tetanus blocks induction, but the same drug applied during the test pulse does not prevent the enhanced EPSP. In contrast, AMPA receptors are necessary for LTP expression, since it is an AMPA receptor–mediated EPSP that is facilitated in LTP.

The biochemical mechanisms thought to underlie E-LTP are illustrated in Figure C. The influx of Ca^{2+} ions through the NMDA receptor channels activates several protein kinases, including one type of calcium/calmodulin protein kinase called CaMKII (see Chapter 3). There are two important

consequences of postsynaptic Ca^{2+} influx and kinase activation: (1) phosphorylation of existing AMPA receptors, which enhances

their sensitivity to glutamate, and (2) insertion of additional AMPA receptors into the postsynaptic membrane. This insertion is

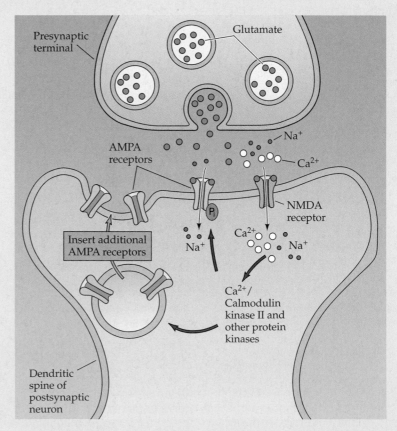

(C) The mechanism underlying LTP involves modification of AMPA receptors in the postsynaptic cell.

BOX 8.1 *(continued)*

actually a modulation of the normal process that we call **receptor trafficking**, in which neurotransmitter receptors (in this case, AMPA receptors) are continuously moved into and out of the postsynaptic membrane. Clearly, a process such as LTP that promotes increased receptor movement into the membrane will increase the strength of signaling at that synapse.

If we try to link LTP to learning and memory, a very significant limitation of E-LTP is that it lasts only a few hours at most. Yet we all know from experience that memories can last a lifetime. Therefore, we need a process that strengthens synaptic connections for a significantly longer period of time than E-LTP, which leads us to L-LTP. How is L-LTP produced, and how does it differ from E-LTP? First, we need much stronger presynaptic (tetanic) stimulation. For example, some L-LTP studies utilize four

bursts of electrical stimuli instead of the single stimulus burst required for E-LTP. Second, we know that L-LTP (unlike E-LTP) requires protein synthesis, since the administration of a protein synthesis inhibitor blocks L-LTP production. This is an important distinction because numerous animal studies have shown that memory consolidation (the formation of a long-term memory store) also requires protein synthesis (Wang and Morris, 2010). Finally, several additional biochemical mechanisms are triggered in the postsynaptic cell, the result of which is a stabilization of the extra AMPA receptors that have been added to the membrane. One pivotal candidate thought by some investigators to orchestrate this stabilization is a novel form of protein kinase C called **protein kinase Mzeta** (**PKMzeta**) (Sacktor, 2008). Investigators are continuing to study PKMzeta and how it may

be involved in memory consolidation for different kinds of behavioral tasks.

We have seen that glutamate and two of its receptor subtypes are intimately involved in an important form of synaptic plasticity called LTP. Learning and memory are generally thought to require synaptic changes in the brain. Could LTP be one of these kinds of changes? Recall that NMDA receptor blockade not only prevents LTP induction but also leads to deficits in certain learning tasks. Although researchers are still debating the issue, it's a reasonable bet that LTP (particularly L-LTP) will eventually be shown to underlie at least some kinds of learning and memory or other cognitive processes. If so, then neuropharmacologists might be able to develop drugs that improve these processes by enhancing LTP.

---

the novel stimulus to a much greater extent than the original stimulus at that time point (**Figure 8.10**). At the 1-day and 3-day tests, however, the controls showed little memory of the original stimulus (i.e., they explored both stimuli to about the same extent), whereas the transgenic mice continued to show a clear preference for the novel object. At the 1-week recall interval, neither group of mice remembered the original stimulus. Thus enhancement of NMDA receptor function produced significant improvement in long-term memory, although this improvement was gone by 1 week after the initial stimulus exposure.

Genetic manipulations often produce multiple behavioral and physiological effects, some of which may be undesirable. Indeed, that is what was later found for the *Doogie* mouse. NMDA receptors are involved in many functions besides learning and memory, one of which is pain perception. As a result, overexpression of the NR2B receptor subunit in the *Doogie* mouse caused the animals to have increased sensitivity to inflammation-related pain (Wei et al., 2001). Perhaps we should heed the tragic lesson of Charly in the book *Flowers for Algernon*, which showed that altering the brain may carry risks in addition to providing potential benefits.

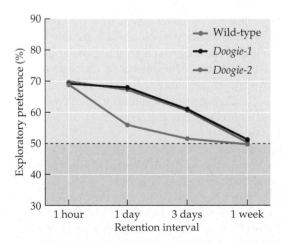

Figure 8.10 Enhanced memory shown by *Doogie* mice in the novel object recognition task The graph illustrates exploratory preference for the novel object measured as a percentage of the total exploration time spent exploring the novel object (a 50% score indicates equal exploration of novel and familiar objects). Note that *Doogie-1* and *Doogie-2* represent two different strains of transgenic mice, which behaved similarly on this task. (After Tang et al., 1999.)

(A)

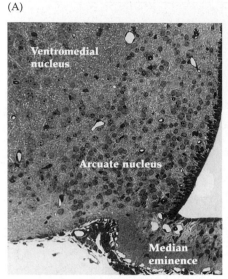

(B)

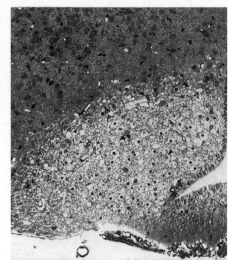

Figure 8.11 **Damage to the arcuate nucleus following adminis- tration of MSG** (A) The arcuate nucleus of the hypothalamus of an untreated 10-day-old mouse. (B) Damage to the arcuate nucleus is revealed by the loss of cell stain- ing in a littermate subject injected 6 hours earlier with MSG. (From Olney et al., 1971; courtesy of John Olney.)

High levels of glutamate can be toxic to nerve cells

Despite the vital role of glutamate in normal neural and behavioral functioning, this neurotransmitter sys- tem also has a dark side. More than 50 years ago, two researchers published a report showing retinal dam- age in mice following subcutaneous injection of the sodium salt of glutamic acid—monosodium glutamate (MSG) (Lucas and Newhouse, 1957). Furthermore, this toxic effect of glutamate was more severe in infant than in adult mice. Twelve years later, Olney (1969) presented the first evidence that MSG also produces brain damage in young mice. As shown in **Figure 8.11**, one of the injured areas was a part of the hypothala- mus known as the arcuate nucleus. The arcuate nucle- us plays an important role in controlling the endocrine system. Consequently, MSG-induced damage to this structure produced devastating effects as the animals matured, including stunted skeletal growth, extreme obesity, and reproductive abnormalities, particularly among female subjects.

Subsequent research showed that glutamate could lesion any brain area of adult animals when injected directly into that structure. This effect was shared by other excitatory amino acids, including kainate and NMDA, and the damage was shown to occur at post- synaptic sites but not at nerve terminals. These and other findings led to the **excitotoxicity hypothesis**, which proposed that the effects produced by exces- sive exposure to glutamate and related excitatory amino acids are caused by a prolonged depolarization of receptive neurons that in some way leads to their eventual damage or death. Administration of an excit- atory amino acid kills nerve cells but spares fibers of passage (i.e., axons from distant cells that are merely

passing through the lesioned area). Thus excitotoxic lesions are more selective than lesions produced by passing electrical current through the targeted area (called electrolytic lesions), since the latter method damages both cells and fibers of passage. For this reason, excitotoxic lesions have replaced electrolytic lesions in many research applications.

The mechanisms underlying amino acid excitoxic- ity have been studied primarily using cultured nerve cells. In such tissue culture models, neuronal cell death is most readily triggered by strong activation of NMDA receptors. Nevertheless, non-NMDA recep- tors (AMPA and/or kainate receptors) may contribute to the excitotoxic effects of glutamate, and under cer- tain conditions, these receptors can even mediate cell death themselves without NMDA receptor involve- ment. When both NMDA and non-NMDA recep- tors are subjected to prolonged stimulation by a high concentration of glutamate, a large percentage of the cells die within a few hours. The mode of cell death in this case is called **necrosis**, which is characterized by **lysis** (bursting) of the cell due to osmotic swelling and other injurious consequences of prolonged glutamate receptor activation. But a different pattern occurs if either the neurotransmitter concentration or the time of exposure is significantly reduced. In this case, the osmotic swelling is temporary, and the cells appear to return to a normal state. However, there may be a delayed response that emerges over succeeding hours and that is characterized by a gradual disintegration of the cells and their eventual death. This delayed excito- toxic reaction is highly dependent on NMDA recep- tor activation, since it can be elicited by the selective application of NMDA or blocked by the presence of an NMDA receptor antagonist such as MK-801.

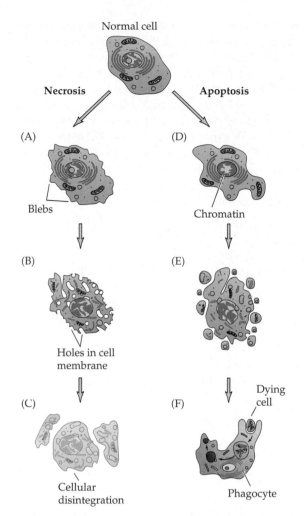

Normal cell

Necrosis   Apoptosis

(A)   (D)

Blebs   Chromatin

(B)   (E)

Holes in cell
membrane

(C)   (F)   Dying
                                                      cell

Cellular   Phagocyte
disintegration

Figure 8.12 Cell death by necrosis versus apoptosis During the initial stages of necrosis (A), the cell swells and the membrane forms protrusions called blebs. In the next stage (B), the membrane begins to break up and release the contents of the cell cytoplasm. Finally, the cell disintegrates completely (C). In apoptotic cell death, the cell also blebs (D), but instead of swelling, it shrinks. At the same time, the chromatin (genetic material) condenses within the cell nucleus. The cell then breaks up into smaller pieces (E) that are subsequently engulfed and digested by phagocytes (F).

In contrast to the necrotic reaction, which occurs relatively quickly, the later-appearing type of cell death is known as **apoptosis** (sometimes also called **programmed cell death**). Apoptosis involves a complex cascade of biochemical events that lead to disruption of the cell's nucleus, DNA breakup, and ultimately cell death. One of the differences between necrosis and apoptosis is that apoptotic cells do not lyse and spill their contents into the extracellular space. Instead, they are cleared away by other cells through a process called phagocytosis (**Figure 8.12**). A significant amount of apoptosis occurs normally during fetal brain development because the brain generates more cells than will be needed later on. However,

under the right conditions, it appears that excitotoxic treatments can also activate the cell death program, thereby leading to inappropriate and excessive loss of nerve cells.

Does excitotoxicity ever occur in humans? The answer appears to be yes. The best established example of excitotoxic brain damage in humans is the damage produced by ingesting large amounts of an excitatory amino acid called **domoic acid**. This toxin is made by several species of marine algae; is taken up and concentrated by certain shellfish, crabs, and fish; and is passed on to humans who eat the tainted food. Domoic acid poisoning first came to the attention of health officials in 1987, when more than 100 people in Prince Edward Island, Canada, were afflicted after consuming blue mussels contaminated with domoic acid. The victims developed various neurological symptoms such as headache, dizziness, muscle weakness, mental confusion, and, in some cases, permanent loss of short-term memory. Three people died. Since that time, unsafe levels of domoic acid in seafood have periodically been found off the West Coast of the United States and Canada. Fortunately, government officials have taken appropriate actions to minimize the danger to local residents. But because it is impossible to prevent all wildlife from being exposed to the toxin, many dolphins, sea lions, and seabirds have become ill and died from ingesting domoic acid. In fact, Alfred Hitchcock's film *The Birds* is now believed to be based on a 1961 incident in Santa Cruz County, California, in which domoic acid–poisoned seabirds began to crash into pedestrians, automobiles, and buildings (Bargu et al., 2012). In reality, the birds were not attacking the town, but rather had become weak and disoriented because of the effects of the toxin.

Excitotoxic brain damage is also believed to occur in people who experience brain **ischemia**, which is an interruption of blood flow to the brain, and in some cases of traumatic brain injury (Lau and Tymianski, 2010). Ischemia can result from either a stroke (focal ischemia, where the interruption is localized to the specific region of the stroke) or a heart attack (global ischemia, where blood flow to the entire brain is interrupted). One consequence of ischemia is a massive release of glutamate in the affected area, thereby leading to prolonged NMDA receptor activation. Many animal studies have found that treatment with an NMDA receptor antagonist successfully reduces the amount of ischemic cell loss, particularly in models of focal ischemia. Unfortunately, human clinical trials with the same drugs have thus far been largely disappointing. Compounds that appeared promising in preclinical studies failed to show therapeutic benefit in patients and sometimes led to severe side effects. Indeed, noncompetitive NMDA receptor antagonists that bind to the PCP site within the receptor channel can produce psychotic-like symptoms in people (see Chapter 15). Other studies have tested the effectiveness of antagonists at the glycine site on the NMDA receptor, AMPA or kainate receptor antagonists, drugs that inhibit glutamate release, and a variety of compounds that target downstream consequences of glutamate receptor activation (Lau and Tymianski, 2010). Like the NMDA receptor antagonists, many compounds that yielded promising results in preclinical (animal) studies have failed human clinical trials because of lack of efficacy, unacceptable side effects, or both. Consequently, the search continues for drugs that will help reduce the degree of damage produced by ischemic brain injury.

Section Summary

- Glutamate is believed to be the workhorse for fast excitatory signaling in the nervous system. There are numerous glutamatergic pathways in the brain, including the projections of the pyramidal neurons of the cerebral cortex, the parallel fibers of the cerebellar cortex, and several excitatory pathways within the hippocampus.

- AMPA, kainate, and NMDA receptors constitute the three subtypes of ionotropic glutamate receptors. Each is named for an agonist that is relatively selective for that subtype. All of these receptors permit Na^+ ions to cross the cell membrane, thereby producing membrane depolarization and an excitatory postsynaptic response. NMDA receptors also conduct Ca^{2+} ions and can trigger Ca^{2+}-dependent second-messenger actions within the postsynaptic cell.

- AMPA and kainate receptors possess different protein subunits that give them somewhat different electrophysiological and pharmacological properties. Behavioral functions of AMPA receptors have been revealed through the use of the antagonist NBQX. Administration of high doses of this compound to rodents leads to sedation, ataxia, deficient rotarod performance, and protection against seizures, indicating involvement of this receptor subtype in locomotor activity, coordination, and brain excitability.

- NMDA receptors are distinct from the AMPA and kainate receptor subtypes in several ways, in addition to the difference in ionic conductances. First, the opening of NMDA receptor channels requires a co-agonist in addition to glutamate. This co-agonist may be either glycine or D-serine. Second, NMDA receptors possess a binding site

for Mg^{2+} ions within the receptor channel. When the cell membrane is at the resting potential, this site is occupied and the channel is blocked even if the receptor has been activated by agonists. However, depolarization of the membrane reduces Mg^{2+} binding, thus allowing the channel to open. Consequently, for the NMDA receptor to function, some other synaptic input must excite the cell at the same time that glutamate and either glycine or D-serine bind to the receptor. Third, NMDA receptors also possess a channel binding site that recognizes PCP, ketamine, and MK-801. These compounds act as noncompetitive antagonists of the NMDA receptor.

- There are also eight different metabotropic receptors for glutamate, designated mGluR1 to mGluR8. These G protein–coupled receptors typically either inhibit cAMP formation or stimulate the phosphoinositide second-messenger system. Some metabotropic receptors, those that are sensitive to the selective agonist L-AP4, function as presynaptic autoreceptors to inhibit glutamate release. Compounds acting at various mGluRs are being tested for their possible usefulness in treating a variety of neuropsychiatric disorders, including schizophrenia.

- NMDA and AMPA receptors are believed to play an important role in learning and memory. NMDA receptor antagonists impair the acquisition of various learning tasks. Activation of this receptor is necessary for the induction of hippocampal LTP, a mechanism of synaptic strengthening. In contrast, LTP expression involves increased trafficking of AMPA receptors into the postsynaptic membrane. E-LTP may underlie certain types of learning acquisition, whereas L-LTP is emerging as a potential mechanism for memory consolidation. Evidence of a role for LTP in learning and memory comes from the mutant *Doogie* mouse, which exhibits overexpression of one of the NMDA receptor subunits, enhanced LTP, and improved performance on a fear conditioning task, the Morris water maze spatial learning task, and a novel object recognition task.

- Excessive exposure to glutamate and other excitatory amino acids can damage or even kill nerve cells through a process of depolarization-induced excitotoxicity. This process is usually mediated primarily by NMDA receptors, with some contribution from AMPA and/or kainate receptors. One type of excitotoxic cell death occurs via necrosis, which involves cellular swelling and eventual lysis. Alternatively, delayed cell death may occur via apoptosis, which involves disruption of the cell nucleus and breakdown of DNA.

- In humans, excitotoxic cell death can be caused by ingestion of food contaminated with the algal toxin domoic acid. Excitotoxicity is also thought to be a major contributory factor to the brain damage that occurs in focal ischemia (e.g., stroke) and traumatic brain injury. Various drugs targeting glutamate receptors or glutamate release have proved beneficial in treating animal models of focal ischemia, but human trials with such compounds thus far have been disappointing.

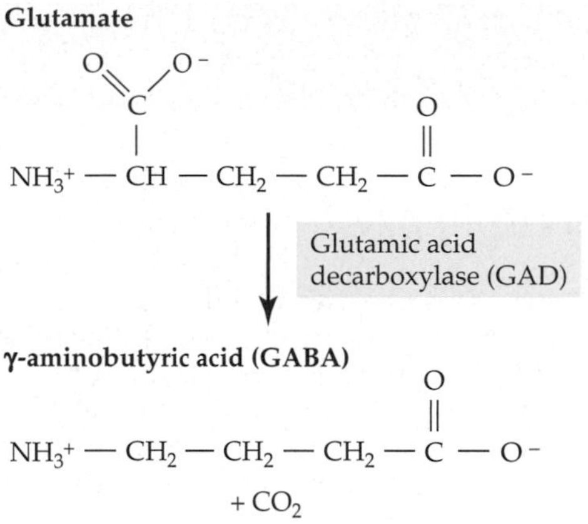

GABA

Earlier in this chapter we saw that glutamate and, to a lesser extent, aspartate play a dominant role in fast excitatory transmission in the central nervous system (CNS). Inhibitory transmission is equally important in behavioral control mechanisms. The significance of neural inhibition is evident from the fact that blocking the action of either of the two major inhibitory amino acid transmitters leads to convulsions and even death. These two transmitters are **GABA (γ-aminobutyric acid)** and glycine. The remainder of this chapter focuses primarily on GABA, which is the more important of the two transmitters in the brain.[3]

GABA Synthesis, Release, and Inactivation

Whereas the amino acids glutamate and aspartate participate widely in cellular metabolism, including protein synthesis, the only function of GABA is to serve as a neurotransmitter. Hence, it is manufactured only by GABAergic neurons. This section of the chapter will discuss the synthesis, release, and inactivation of GABA.

GABA is synthesized by the enzyme glutamic acid decarboxylase

GABA is synthesized from glutamate in a single biochemical step, which is catalyzed by the enzyme **glutamic acid decarboxylase (GAD)** (**Figure 8.13**). It is interesting to note that the principal inhibitory neurotransmitter in the brain, namely, GABA, is made from the principal excitatory transmitter, glutamate. GAD is localized specifically to GABAergic neurons;

Figure 8.13 GABA is synthesized from glutamate by the enzyme glutamic acid decarboxylase (GAD).

therefore, researchers can identify such neurons by staining for GAD.

Several drugs, including **allylglycine, thiosemicarbazide**, and **3-mercaptopropionic acid**, are known to block GABA synthesis. As noted earlier, a significant reduction in GABA synthesis leads to convulsions; this indicates the importance of this transmitter in regulating brain excitability. On the other hand, it also shows that GAD inhibitors are normally used to study GABAergic transmission only in vitro, not in vivo.

GABA packaging into vesicles and uptake after release are mediated by specific transporter proteins

Like the vesicular transporters that take up glutamate into synaptic vesicles, the **vesicular GABA transporter (VGAT)** was discovered fairly recently. Subsequent studies revealed an interesting and unexpected feature of this protein, namely, that it is also found in neurons that use glycine as a transmitter. Thus the same transporter is used to load GABA or glycine into synaptic vesicles. For this reason, this transporter is sometimes referred to as **VIAAT (vesicular inhibitory amino acid transporter)** instead of VGAT. This situation of transport of multiple neurotransmitters by the same protein is similar to the previously discussed example of VMAT, the vesicular monoamine transporter, which is responsible for vesicle filling of three different neurotransmitters: dopamine (DA), norepinephrine (NE), and serotonin (5-HT).

Following the synaptic release of GABA, it is removed from the cleft by three different transporters on the membranes of nerve cells and glia, designated **GAT-1, GAT-2**, and **GAT-3**. GAT-1 and GAT-2 seem to be expressed in both neurons and astrocytes, whereas GAT-3 is found in astrocytes only. GAT-1 has

---

[3]Although glycinergic neurons are present in the brain, their role has been studied more extensively in the spinal cord.

BOX 8.2   Clinical Applications

GABA and Epilepsy

The term epilepsy refers to a class of neurological disorders characterized by recurrent convulsive and nonconvulsive seizures. It is estimated that nearly 3 million Americans are affected by seizure disorders, and approximately 200,000 new cases are diagnosed each year (Epilepsy Foundation, 2011). The seriousness of this disorder can be seen in the fact that postmortem studies of patients with epilepsy have shown brain cell loss in vulnerable areas such as the hippocampus, and that an excitotoxic, NMDA receptor–mediated process may be involved in such loss. In the present discussion, we will focus on the possible role of GABA in the etiology and maintenance of seizure disorders.

One of the characteristic features of epilepsy is that during the **interictal period** (the period between seizures), principal neurons (i.e., pyramidal cells) in the cortex and certain subcortical structures exhibit periodic episodes of prolonged depolarization called a **paroxysmal depolarization shift** (PDS). During a PDS, the cell membrane is depolarized much longer than for a typical EPSP and as a result, the cell fires a burst of action potentials (Browne and Holme, 2008). This massive depolarization is followed by the second phase, which is a period of hyperpolarization that reflects

the activation of inhibitory mechanisms impinging on the cells. One of the processes thought to underlie the transition from interictal discharges to the generation of a full-blown seizure is a decrease in the hyperpolarizing phase, and thus a failure of inhibition. Given that GABA is one of the main transmitters involved in neuronal inhibition, it seems possible that GABAergic dysfunction might play a role in the epileptogenic process (Sperk et al., 2004; Treiman, 2001). A loss of GABA-mediated inhibition might also be important in the development of **status epilepticus**, a highly dangerous condition characterized either by a continuous seizure lasting longer than 30 minutes or by episodes of repeated seizures that recur so quickly that the patient has insufficient time to recover from one seizure before another one begins.

Although most cases of epilepsy have no known genetic cause, in some instances mutations have been discovered either in the GABAergic system or in other systems (e.g., voltage-gated ion channels) that can be causally linked to the seizure disorder. Epilepsy-related mutations in GABA$_A$ receptor subunits include γ2 (childhood absence epilepsy, infant myoclonic epilepsy, or generalized epilepsy with febrile seizures [GEFS]), α1 (juvenile myoclonic epilepsy [JME]),

and δ (GEFS or JME) (Armijo et al., 2005; Macdonald et al., 2004). Absence epilepsy is a disorder in which the patient exhibits absence (also called petit mal) seizures characterized by a brief loss of consciousness and staring into space without any muscular convulsions. Myoclonic epilepsy is a seizure disorder accompanied by muscle twitches (myoclonus) that may begin in infancy or childhood. Febrile seizures are childhood seizures triggered by high fever. Such seizures are not by themselves considered to be a form of epilepsy, but children who suffer from febrile seizures may subsequently develop an epileptic disorder. These associations between mutations in specific GABA$_A$ receptor subunits and various types of seizure disorders confirm that normal GABA$_A$ receptor functioning is required to prevent abnormal increases in brain excitability.

Even cases of epilepsy that do not involve mutations in the GABA$_A$ receptor may involve dysregulation of the GABAergic system. Much of the evidence for this notion comes from studies of epileptic tissue obtained surgically from patients who failed to respond to standard drug treatments. Surgical intervention occurs most commonly in cases of **temporal lobe sclerosis**, a condition in which uncontrolled neuronal activity in the temporal

received particular attention for two reasons. First, this transporter has been found at the nerve terminals of GABAergic neurons; therefore, it is likely to be important for GABA reuptake by these cells. Second, in contrast to GAT-2 and GAT-3, a selective inhibitor of GAT-1 is available for pharmacological study. Administration of this compound, **tiagabine**, elevates extracellular GABA levels and enhances GABAergic transmission in several brain areas, including the cortex

and the hippocampus. Given the fact that depleting GABA (e.g., by blocking GAD activity) causes seizures, we might predict that tiagabine protects against seizure onset. Indeed, tiagabine was licensed in 1997 under the trade name **Gabitril** for use as an adjunctive therapy (an additional treatment given along with more-standard antiepileptic drugs) in treatment-resistant patients with partial seizures (seizures involving only part of the brain). Tiagabine appears to be

BOX 8.2 *(continued)*

Neurotransmitter modulation of spontaneous neuronal activity in brain slices from patients with epilepsy. Patients with temporal lobe epilepsy who responded poorly to antiepileptic drug treatment underwent surgery for unilateral removal of the tissue responsible for seizure initiation. After this tissue had been sliced and maintained temporarily in vitro, electrical activity was recorded from the subiculum under baseline (Control) conditions and in response to (A) the GABA$_A$ receptor antagonist bicuculline (BIC) or (B) a combination of the glutamate NMDA receptor antagonist 2-amino-5-phosphonovalerate (APV) plus the non-NMDA antagonist NBQX. Both pharmacological treatments completely blocked spontaneous electrical discharges—an effect that was reversed when the drugs were washed out of the slice. (From Cohen et al., 2002.)

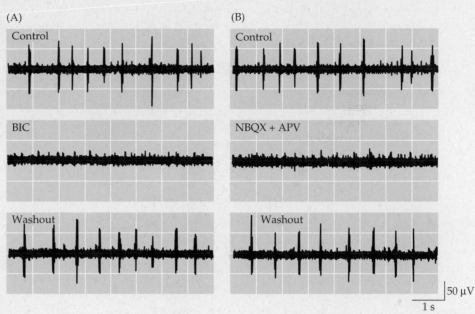

lobe leads to excitotoxic death of hippocampal neurons in the area of recurrent seizure generation. Although surgical removal of brain tissue is obviously of serious concern to the patient, researchers have utilized this opportunity to study human epileptic brain tissue to attempt to determine how it may be malfunctioning. One approach used in this research has been to perform electrical recordings of hippocampal slices obtained from patients. These recordings showed that pyramidal cells and interneurons from the subiculum (an area responsible for most of the output of the hippocampal formation) exhibited spontaneous activity similar to interictal discharges seen in EEGs from patients with epilepsy, and, most importantly, this activity was mediated not only by ionotropic glutamate receptors (as might be expected) but also by GABA$_A$ receptors (Cohen et al., 2002; Huberfeld et al., 2007) (see figure). Additional experiments demonstrated that the shift in GABA$_A$-mediated responses from inhibitory to excitatory was due to the fact that opening of the receptor channel resulted in Cl$^-$ *efflux* from the cell instead of the normal Cl$^-$ *influx* (thus causing membrane depolarization instead of hyperpolarization). Interestingly, it turns out that GABA$_A$ receptors behave this way during early brain development because of differences in the relative concentrations of Cl$^-$ ions inside versus outside the cells compared with those of the mature brain (i.e., during development, the Cl$^-$ ion concentration inside these neurons is much greater than it is later on). These findings suggest that one factor in this form of severe temporal lobe epilepsy may be the return of at least some hippocampal GABA$_A$ receptor–expressing neurons to an earlier developmental state, at least with respect to their regulation of Cl$^-$ ion distribution.

---

clinically beneficial in this role and it is being tested as a monotherapy (single treatment) for certain kinds of epilepsy. The critical role of GABA in regulating brain excitability and the ability of GABA-enhancing agents to help prevent seizures have led researchers to investigate whether abnormalities in the GABAergic system might be involved in at least some forms of epilepsy. This topic is taken up in **Box 8.2**.

Whereas the immediate inactivation of GABA in the synapse occurs through a combination of neuronal and astroglial uptake, there is also a cellular mechanism for metabolizing and recycling this neurotransmitter. GABA breakdown occurs through several steps, beginning with the enzyme **GABA aminotransferase (GABA-T)** and leading eventually to the final product, succinate. It is worth noting that a by-product

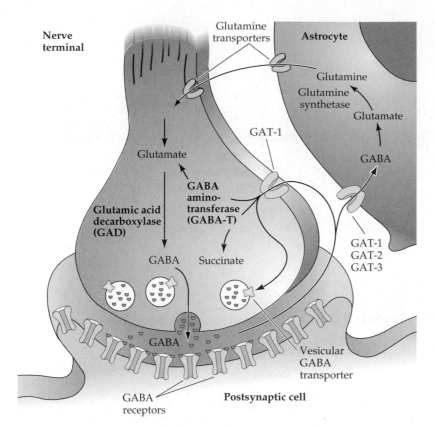

Nerve terminal

Glutamine transporters

Astrocyte

Glutamine

Glutamine synthetase

Glutamate

GAT-1

Glutamate

GABA amino-transferase (GABA-T)

GABA

Glutamic acid decarboxylase (GAD)

GABA   Succinate

GAT-1
GAT-2
GAT-3

GABA

Vesicular GABA transporter

GABA receptors

Postsynaptic cell

Figure 8.14 Cycling of GABA between glutamatergic neurons and astrocytes After neurons release GABA, it can be transported back into the nerve terminal by GAT-1 or transported into nearby astrocytes by GAT-2 or GAT-3. Inside the cell, GABA is metabolized to glutamate and succinate by GABA aminotransferase (GABA-T). In the case of astrocytes, the glutamate is converted into glutamine by the enzyme glutamine synthetase. The glutamine can later be released by the astrocytes, taken up by neurons, converted back into glutamate by the enzyme glutaminase, and finally used to resynthesize GABA.

of this metabolic pathway is the formation of one molecule of glutamate for every molecule of GABA that is broken down. GABA-T is found in both GABAergic neurons and astrocytes. Hence, within GABAergic neurons, some of the glutamate regenerated by the action of GABA-T could be used to synthesize more GABA. Moreover, some of the glutamate produced by GABA-T in astrocytes could be converted to glutamine by astrocytic glutamine synthetase, and the glutamine could subsequently be transported to the GABAergic neurons to be converted back to glutamate by the enzyme glutaminase (**Figure 8.14**). This shows that the metabolic interplay between neurons and glial cells discussed earlier for glutamate is equally important for GABA.

Vigabatrin is an irreversible inhibitor of GABA-T. By preventing GABA metabolism, administration of this drug leads to a buildup of GABA levels within the brain. By now, you should be able to predict correctly that vigabatrin has anticonvulsant effects in animals and humans. Like tiagabine, vigabatrin (trade name, **Sabril**) is being used clinically as either an adjunctive treatment or as the primary therapeutic agent for certain types of epilepsy, particularly infantile spasms (repeated generalized seizures in young infants). However, there are a number of recent reports that use of vigabatrin can lead to constriction of the visual field in both adults and children. Since there are

GABAergic interneurons in the retina, visual abnormalities could be related to drug effects on these cells. In light of these findings, physicians must consider the risk-to-benefit ratio when considering vigabatrin treatment of patients with epilepsy.

Section Summary

- GABA is the major inhibitory amino acid neurotransmitter in the brain. This transmitter is synthesized from glutamate in a single biochemical reaction catalyzed by GAD, an enzyme found only in GABAergic neurons.

- Because of the widespread inhibitory effects of GABA on neuronal excitability, treatment with drugs that inhibit GABA synthesis by blocking GAD leads to seizures.

- GABA is taken up into synaptic vesicles by the vesicular transporter VGAT (also known as VIAAT, because the same vesicular transporter is used by glycine).

- After release into the synaptic cleft, GABA is removed from the cleft by three different transporters designated GAT-1, GAT-2, and GAT-3. Astrocytes express all three of these transporters and therefore must play a significant role in GABA uptake. GAT-1 is also found in GABAergic neurons, and the GAT-1 inhibitor tiagabine (Gabitril) is used clinically in the treatment of some patients with epilepsy.

- In addition to uptake, the other process that regulates GABAergic transmission is GABA metabolism. The key enzyme in GABA breakdown is GABA-T, which is present in both GABAergic neurons and astrocytes. A by-product of the reaction catalyzed by GABA-T is glutamate, which is the precursor of GABA. Hence, GABA breakdown in neurons or in glial cells may involve a recycling process that assists in the formation of new GABA molecules.

- Vigabatrin (Sabril) is an irreversible inhibitor of GABA-T and thereby elevates GABA levels in the brain. Like tiagabine, vigabatrin has been licensed for the treatment of certain types of epilepsy. However, there are reports that repeated vigabatrin use can lead to visual system abnormalities in adults and children; therefore, caution should be exercised when this compound is administered to patients.

Organization and Function of the GABAergic System

Like glutamate, GABA is used by many populations of neurons in the brain. Here we discuss some features of the anatomy of the GABAergic system, subtypes of GABA receptors, and a few basic functions of GABAergic transmission.

Some GABAergic neurons are interneurons, while others are projection neurons

Fonnum (1987) has estimated that as many as 10% to 40% of the nerve terminals in the cerebral cortex, hippocampus, and substantia nigra use GABA as their neurotransmitter. Even the lower range of this estimate indicates that a lot of GABAergic transmission takes place, when you consider the dozens of different neurotransmitters that may be present within a specific brain region. In addition to the three structures just mentioned, other brain areas rich in GABA are the cerebellum, striatum, globus pallidus, and olfactory bulbs.

In some structures, such as the cortex and the hippocampus, GABA is found in large numbers of local interneurons. However, there are also GABAergic projection neurons that carry inhibitory information longer distances within the brain. For example, GABAergic neurons of the striatum project to the globus pallidus and the substantia nigra. When DA input to the striatum is damaged in Parkinson's disease, the result is abnormal firing of the striatal GABAergic neurons, which causes the motor abnormalities seen in this neurological disorder (see Chapter 21). GABA is also the transmitter used by Purkinje cells of the cerebellar cortex. These neurons, which project to the deep cerebellar nuclei and to the brainstem, have an important function in fine muscle control and coordination. This is illustrated in a rare disorder involving degeneration of cerebellar Purkinje cells. Patients with this disorder, which is known as Holmes cerebellar degeneration, show ataxia when walking, impaired fine hand movements, defective speech, and tremors.

The actions of GABA are mediated by ionotropic GABA$_A$ receptors and metabotropic GABA$_B$ receptors

Like glutamate, GABA makes use of both ionotropic and metabotropic receptors. However, only one type of each is used: the **GABA$_A$ receptor**, which is ionotropic, and the **GABA$_B$ receptor**, which is metabotropic. Our discussion will concentrate on the GABA$_A$ receptor because of its prominent role in GABAergic transmission and because it is a crucial target of many important psychoactive drugs.

STRUCTURE AND FUNCTION OF THE GABA$_A$ RECEPTOR

GABA$_A$ receptors are ion channels that permit Cl$^-$ ions to move across the cell membrane from outside to inside. This causes inhibition of the postsynaptic cell as the result of membrane hyperpolarization. More Cl$^-$ ions flow through open GABA$_A$ receptor channels when the membrane has previously been depolarized by excitatory synaptic inputs. In such cases, these receptors function to blunt depolarization and prevent the cell from firing an action potential.

Structurally, each GABA$_A$ receptor contains five subunits. Three or four different *kinds* of subunits may be found within a particular GABA$_A$ receptor complex. These different kinds of subunits are designated by the Greek letters α, β, γ, and δ. Most GABA$_A$ receptors are thought to contain two α subunits, two β subunits, and one γ subunit (**Figure 8.15**). There are multiple isoforms of all of these subunits (six different α's, three different β's, and three different γ's), the importance of which will become apparent when we discuss drugs that modulate GABA$_A$ receptor function. A small number of receptors contain a δ subunit instead of a γ subunit. Such receptors typically are found in combination with two α4 or α6 subunits (along with the normal two β subunits) and are localized outside the normal synaptic area (Belelli et al., 2009). These extrasynaptic receptors respond to low

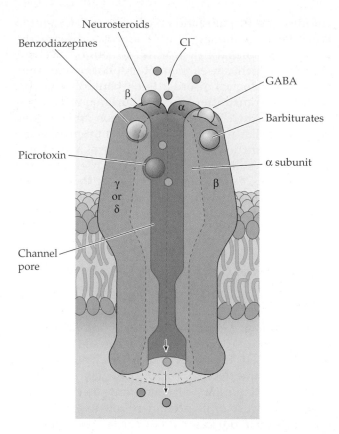

Neurosteroids
Benzodiazepines
Cl⁻
β
α
GABA
Barbiturates
Picrotoxin
α subunit
γ or δ
β
Channel pore

Figure 8.15 The GABA_A receptor consists of five subunits
that form a Cl⁻-conducting channel. In addition to the
GABA binding site on the receptor complex, there are additional modulatory sites for benzodiazepines, barbiturates,
neurosteroids, and picrotoxin. Note that the locations of
the various binding sites are depicted arbitrarily and are not
meant to imply the actual locations of these sites on the
receptor.

Figure 8.16 The fly agaric mushroom, *Amanita muscaria*

levels of GABA that have avoided immediate uptake
following release and have escaped from the synaptic
cleft. Their role is to exert a mild tonic (continuous)
hyperpolarizing and thus inhibitory effect on the cells
that express those receptors.

The classic agonist for the GABA_A receptor is a
drug called **muscimol**. This compound is found in the
mushroom *Amanita muscaria* (**Figure 8.16**), which was
mentioned in the last chapter as the original source
of the cholinergic agonist muscarine. In earlier times,
this mushroom apparently would be chopped up and
placed in a dish with milk to attract flies. Ingestion
of muscimol and the related compound ibotenic acid
would make the flies stuporous and easy to catch. The
common name for *A. muscaria* is therefore "fly agaric"
(*agaric* is an old term meaning "mushroom"). Rudgley (1999) discusses the custom of eating fly agaric, as
practiced by various Siberian peoples for hundreds of
years. The mushroom was prized for its stimulatory
and hallucinogenic qualities—effects that can also be

obtained by drinking urine from an intoxicated individual (not a very appealing idea to most Westerners!).[4] One of the interesting hallucinatory effects produced by the fly agaric is macroscopia, which refers
to the perception of objects as being larger than they
really are. When administered to humans at relatively high doses, pure muscimol causes an intoxication
characterized by hyperthermia (elevated body temperature), pupil dilation, elevation of mood, difficulties in concentration, anorexia (loss of appetite), ataxia,
catalepsy, and hallucinations. Many of these effects
are similar to those associated with more traditional
hallucinogenic drugs such as lysergic acid diethylamide (LSD; see Chapter 15).

Bicuculline is the best-known competitive antagonist for the GABA_A receptor. It blocks the binding of
GABA to the GABA_A receptor, and when taken systemically, it has a potent convulsant effect. **Pentylenetetrazol** (**Metrazol**) and **picrotoxin** are two other
convulsant drugs that inhibit GABA_A receptor function by acting at sites distinct from the binding site
of GABA itself. Pentylenetetrazol is a synthetic compound that once was used as convulsant therapy for
major depression. Although it is no longer used for
that purpose, it still has value for the induction of
experimental seizures in laboratory animals. Picrotoxin is obtained from the seeds of the East Indian shrub
Anamirta cocculus. Because neither pentylenetetrazol
nor picrotoxin blocks GABA from interacting with
the GABA_A receptor, these agents are noncompetitive
rather than competitive receptor antagonists.

[4]Fly agaric intoxication was apparently enjoyed not only by
Siberians but by their reindeer as well. Animals were observed
to eat the mushrooms of their own accord, and were also sometimes given urine to drink from a person who had previously
partaken.

For psychopharmacologists, the most remarkable property of the $GABA_A$ receptor is its sensitivity to certain CNS-depressant drugs that display an anxiolytic (antianxiety), sedative–hypnotic (sedating and sleep-inducing), and anticonvulsant profile. Among such drugs are the **benzodiazepines (BDZs)** and the **barbiturates**. There is overwhelming evidence that the principal mechanism of action of BDZs and barbiturates involves potentiating the effects of GABA on the $GABA_A$ receptor. **Ethanol** (drinking alcohol) is another CNS-depressant drug that has many of the same properties as BDZs and barbiturates. Although the actions of ethanol are complex, one of its major effects is likewise to enhance $GABA_A$ receptor activity. All of these positive modulators of the $GABA_A$ receptor can lead to dependence when used in excess, and this topic is discussed in subsequent chapters on sedative–hypnotic and anxiolytic drugs (see Chapter 18) and ethanol (see Chapter 10).

How do BDZs, barbiturates, and ethanol exert their influence on the $GABA_A$ receptor? The first two classes of drugs interact with sites on the receptor complex that are distinct from the GABA binding site. This concept is illustrated in Figure 8.15, which also shows the presence of a modulatory site for picrotoxin and related convulsant drugs. Details of the interaction of ethanol with the $GABA_A$ receptor are still being worked out. Although the pharmacology of BDZs is covered extensively in Chapter 18, it is worth noting here some of the key features of the interactions of BDZs with the $GABA_A$ receptor.

The recognition site for BDZs on the $GABA_A$ receptor complex is considered a bona fide BDZ receptor because these drugs bind directly to the site, and such binding is necessary for BDZs to exert their behavioral and physiological effects. When a BDZ such as **diazepam** (trade name **Valium**) binds to the BDZ receptor, the potency of GABA to open the receptor channel is increased. BDZs cannot activate the $GABA_A$ receptor by themselves; thus, they have no effect in the absence of GABA. However, it is important to recognize that not all $GABA_A$ receptors are sensitive to BDZs. Genetic engineering studies in mice have shown that BDZ binding and functional sensitivity to BDZs require the presence of a γ subunit (usually γ2), along with α1, α2, α3, or α5 subunits and any β subunit (Sieghart and Sperk, 2002). Most $GABA_A$ receptors in the brain have such a composition and thus are BDZ-sensitive, but receptors that contain α4 or α6 subunits will not be affected by administration of a BDZ.

Diazepam and related BDZs are agonists at the BDZ receptor on the $GABA_A$ receptor complex. Researchers have discovered certain compounds that modulate the $GABA_A$ receptor in a direction opposite that of a BDZ agonist. Such compounds have been termed **inverse agonists** at the BDZ receptor (see Chapter 1 for discussion of inverse agonists). If a BDZ agonist enhances the effectiveness of GABA on the receptor, then a BDZ inverse agonist reduces the effectiveness of GABA, although it doesn't actually block GABA in the way that a GABA receptor antagonist does. Like a BDZ agonist, an inverse agonist has no effect in the absence of GABA. The behavioral profile of a BDZ inverse agonist is the opposite of that of a BDZ agonist. Consequently, BDZ inverse agonists are anxiogenic (anxiety-producing), arousing, and proconvulsant (seizure-promoting) instead of anxiolytic, sedating, and anticonvulsant. Finally, let's think about what it means for the brain to have a receptor (e.g., the BDZ receptor) that responds to a class of synthetic drugs[5] rather than to one of the brain's own neurotransmitters. This last point is the subject of **Web Box 8.1**.

The $GABA_A$ receptor is additionally modulated by a family of substances known as **neurosteroids**. These substances are made from cholesterol and possess a steroid structure similar to that of the glucocorticoids and gonadal steroids (see Chapter 3). However, they are synthesized in the brain (hence the term *neurosteroid*), and they are thought to act as local signaling molecules rather than as hormones. Allopregnanolone, tetrahydrodeoxycorticosterone, and dehydroepiandrosterone (DHEA) are among the most extensively studied neurosteroids. Like BDZ agonists, most neurosteroids enhance $GABA_A$ receptor function and produce sedative–hypnotic and anxiolytic effects behaviorally. However, as depicted in Figure 8.15, neurosteroids seem to interact with the receptor at a site other than the BDZ binding site.

STRUCTURE AND FUNCTION OF THE $GABA_B$ RECEPTOR   As mentioned earlier, the other GABA receptor subtype is a metabotropic receptor termed $GABA_B$. Interestingly, unlike virtually all other known metabotropic receptors, the $GABA_B$ receptor requires two different subunits in order to assemble in the membrane and work properly (Bettler and Tiao, 2006). Like $GABA_A$ receptors, the $GABA_B$ receptor exerts an inhibitory effect on the postsynaptic cell. This effect is mediated by several mechanisms, including inhibition of cAMP formation and stimulation of K^+ channel opening. Drugs that function as agonists or antagonists at $GABA_A$ receptors have no effect on the $GABA_B$ receptor. However, $GABA_B$ receptors can be activated by a selective agonist called **baclofen (Lioresal)**, which has been used for many years as a muscle relaxant and an antispastic agent.

---

[5]BDZs were developed by pharmaceutical companies and do not occur naturally in the brain, except perhaps in very small quantities (and evidence for that is inconclusive).

Section Summary

- Many brain areas, including the cerebral cortex, hippocampus, substantia nigra, cerebellum, striatum, globus pallidus, and olfactory bulbs, are rich in GABA. GABAergic neurons may function as interneurons, as in the cortex and hippocampus, or they may function as projection neurons, as in pathways originating in the striatum and in the cerebellar Purkinje cells.

- There are two general GABA receptor subtypes: ionotropic $GABA_A$ receptors and metabotropic $GABA_B$ receptors. $GABA_A$ receptors conduct Cl^- ions into the postsynaptic cell, causing membrane hyperpolarization and an inhibitory effect on cell excitability.

- Each receptor is composed of five subunits, usually including two α subunits, two β's, and one γ, or two α's, one β, and two γ's. A small number of $GABA_A$ receptors contain a δ subunit instead of γ.

- Muscimol is a $GABA_A$ receptor agonist derived from the mushroom *Amanita muscaria* (fly agaric). Ingestion of this mushroom or of pure muscimol causes hallucinations (including macroscopia) and other behavioral and physiological effects similar to those associated with LSD.

- $GABA_A$ receptor antagonists include the competitive antagonist bicuculline and the noncompetitive inhibitors pentylenetetrazol (Metrazol) and picrotoxin, all of which are seizure-inducing.

- The effects of GABA on the $GABA_A$ receptor are enhanced by several kinds of CNS-depressant drugs, such as BDZs, barbiturates, and ethanol. With respect to their effects on behavior, these compounds display anxiolytic, sedative–hypnotic, and anticonvulsant properties.

- BDZs bind to a specific site on the $GABA_A$ receptor complex that is considered to be a BDZ receptor. Although BDZs amplify the effects of GABA, they have no effect on $GABA_A$ receptor function in the absence of the neurotransmitter. BDZ sensitivity requires the presence of a γ subunit (usually $\gamma2$), any β subunit, and an $\alpha1$, $\alpha2$, $\alpha3$, or $\alpha5$ subunit.

- Inverse agonists at the BDZ receptor also require the presence of GABA, but such compounds reduce instead of enhance the effectiveness of GABA in activating the $GABA_A$ receptor. BDZ inverse agonists produce behavioral effects opposite to those produced by BDZ agonists, namely, anxiety, arousal, and increased susceptibility to seizures.

- The metabotropic $GABA_B$ receptor is composed of two different subunits and functions by inhibiting cAMP formation and stimulating K^+ channel opening. These receptors are not influenced by drugs that act on the $GABA_A$ receptor, but they can be activated by the selective agonist baclofen (Lioresal)—a muscle relaxant and an antispastic agent.

Go to the **COMPANION WEBSITE**

sites.sinauer.com/psychopharm2e
for Web Boxes, animations, flashcards, and other study resources.

Recommended Readings

Bannerman, D. M., Rawlins, J. N., and Good, M. A. (2006). The drugs don't work—or do they? Pharmacological and transgenic studies of the contribution of NMDA and GluR-A-containing AMPA receptors to hippocampal-dependent memory. *Psychopharmacology*, 188, 552–566.

Mula, M. (2011). GABAergic drugs in the treatment of epilepsy: Modern or outmoded? *FutureMed. Chem.*, 3, 177–182.

Rudy, J. W. (2008). *The Neurobiology of Learning and Memory*. Sunderland, MA: Sinauer.

Sieghart, W. (2006). Structure, pharmacology, and function of $GABA_A$ receptor subtypes. *Adv. Pharmacol.*, 54, 231–263.

Tan, K. R., Rudolph, U., and Lüscher, C. (2011). Hooked on benzodiazepines: $GABA_A$ receptor subtypes and addiction. *Trends Neurosci.*, 188–197.

Traynelis, S. F., Wollmuth, L. P., McBain, C. J., Menniti, F. S., Vance, K. M., Ogden, K. K., Hansen, K. B., Yuan, H., Myers, S. J., and Dingledine, R. (2010). Glutamate receptor ion channels: Structure, regulation, and function. *Pharmacol. Rev.*, 62, 405–496.

Tuttolomondo, A., Di Sciacca, R., Di Raimondo, D., Arnao, V., Renda, C., Pinto, A., and Licata, G. (2009). Neuron protection as a therapeutic target in acute ischemic stroke. *Curr. Top. Med. Chem.*, 9, 1317–1334.

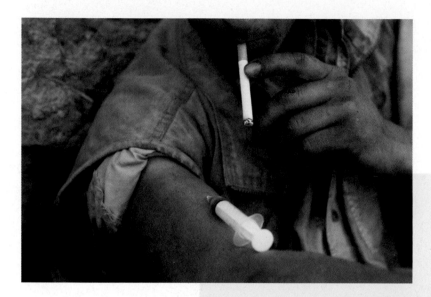

Two of the most addicting routes of drug administration are intravenous injection and inhalation or smoking.

Drug Abuse and Addiction 9

BOB HAD BEGUN DRINKING AT THE AGE OF 12, sneaking beers from his family's refrigerator. Thirty years later, when he and his wife Kathy sought counseling for their marital problems, alcohol had come to dominate much of Bob's life. According to his conversations with the counselor, his drinking had gotten "really bad" after his marriage and the birth of his children. Around that time, he began to feel trapped in an undesirable job because of the needed income. In addition, the demands of child care caused his wife to pay less attention to him than before, and their sexual relations became much less frequent. Bob's response to these problems was to increase his drinking. Upon returning home from work, he would have "a cocktail or two" before dinner. After a while, one or two cocktails became three, four, or even more. Furthermore, Bob didn't want to be bothered with the family's problems until he was "relaxed," meaning intoxicated. Unfortunately, the combination of his intoxication and feelings of guilt made him impatient and irritable when he was approached by family members. Eventually, Kathy and the children began to avoid him much of the time, leading their own lives and dealing with their problems without Bob's input.

Bob's situation at work was also deteriorating. At lunchtime, he frequently went out to a nearby bar for a sandwich and cocktails instead of joining his coworkers at the company cafeteria. He got away with this for a while, but finally his boss smelled liquor on his breath. Although he wasn't fired, his performance evaluations began to suffer and he received a stern warning that another incident of drinking during working hours would lead to disciplinary action.

By the time Bob and Kathy went to the counselor after 20 years of marriage, Bob's life was a mess. Despite attempts to control his habit, he was continuing to drink daily and had developed a powerful tolerance to alcohol. His marriage was in crisis. His job was in jeopardy.

(A)

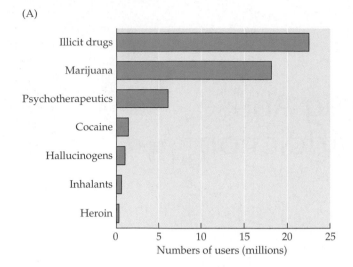

(B)

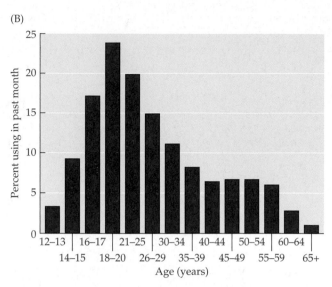

He was two years behind on his income tax returns and was in debt to the government for several thousand dollars. According to Kathy, their house was in danger of falling apart because of numerous repair projects that Bob had promised to carry out but had never done. Their son, who was a freshman in college, was failing half his courses. Their younger daughter "hated" Bob, and her main interactions with him were either to fight or to ridicule him.

The above is an actual case study presented by Joseph Nowinski (1996) in a discussion of 12-step recovery from drug addiction. It dramatically illustrates what we might call the "paradox" of addiction. That is, how can a person develop and maintain a pattern of behavior (in this case, repeated, heavy alcohol consumption) that is so obviously destructive to the individual's life? No one has a complete explanation for this paradox, but a variety of theories have been proposed. The aim of this chapter is to introduce you to several facets of this intriguing problem, including various psychosocial, genetic, and neurobiological factors thought to underlie the development and maintenance of an addicted state. We will describe the history and current prevalence of drug use in the United States, as well as the laws that determine which substances are legal and which are not. Finally, we will consider the important issue of whether drug addiction should be considered a disease.

Introduction to Drug Abuse and Addiction

The first part of this chapter considers the prevalence of psychoactive drug use in our society, the discovery and use of such drugs in earlier times, the history of drug laws in the United States, and the definition and characteristics of addiction.

Figure 9.1 Data on illicit drug use in the United States from the 2011 National Survey on Drug Use and Health. (A) shows the overall number of current drug users and the numbers of users of specific substances. (B) depicts the age distribution of illicit drug users.

Drugs of abuse are widely consumed in our society

Each year, the Substance Abuse and Mental Health Services Administration conducts a National Survey on Drug Use and Health, which estimates the prevalence and incidence of drug use among civilians 12 years of age and older. According to the 2011 survey, approximately 22.5 million Americans (8.7% of the population) were current users[1] of at least one illicit drug[2] at that time (**Figure 9.1A**). Sixty-four percent of illicit drug users used only marijuana, and another 16% used marijuana along with one or more other substances. **Figure 9.1B** demonstrates that illicit drug use is low in 12- to 13-year-olds, peaks between the ages of 18 and 20 years, and declines slowly thereafter. The 2011 survey additionally found that approximately 3.1 million individuals aged 12 or older used a substance other than alcohol or tobacco for the first time that year. Marijuana was most frequently mentioned as the first drug to be tried, followed by recreationally used prescription drugs such as pain relievers, and then inhalants (e.g., glue or solvents). Only a very small percentage (0.03%) of people surveyed

[1]In this survey, "current use" is defined as use of a drug during the past month.

[2]For purposes of the survey, illicit drugs include marijuana/hashish, cocaine (including crack), ecstasy (not shown on the graph), heroin, hallucinogens, and inhalants. Also shown are prescription psychotherapeutic agents (e.g., sedatives or stimulants) used recreationally instead of for medicinal purposes.

mentioned cocaine or heroin as the first illicit drug to be used.

It is no surprise that legal drugs such as tobacco and alcohol are consumed even more widely than illicit substances. The 2011 survey estimated that more than 68 million Americans were current tobacco users (mostly cigarette smokers), 133 million drank alcohol, and, of the latter, about 16 million were heavy drinkers (defined as consuming 5 or more drinks at one time on 5 or more days within a single month). How did we reach a state where psychoactive drug use and abuse are so prevalent?

Drug use in our society has increased and has become more heavily regulated over time

Psychoactive drugs have been a part of human culture since antiquity. However, the substances available to drug users and the prevalence of use have varied in different periods.

HISTORICAL TRENDS   Many psychoactive substances such as nicotine, caffeine, morphine, cocaine, and tetrahydrocannabinol are made by plants and were available to ancient peoples in their native forms. Likewise, alcohol is a naturally occurring product of sugar fermentation by yeast. In his 1989 book *Intoxication: Life in Pursuit of Artificial Paradise*, Ronald Siegel presents many anecdotal accounts of wild animals becoming intoxicated after eating drug-containing plants. He goes on to suggest that early societies may have come to identify the pharmacological properties of such plants after first observing the behaviors of these intoxicated animals. More historical information on individual abused drugs is provided in later chapters. Here, we will focus on the history of drug use and cultural attitudes in the United States over the past 200 years.

Compared with the wide variety of psychoactive drugs available (legally or illegally) to twenty-first-century Americans, the situation was quite different 200 years ago. Alcohol and caffeine were widely used, and although the modern cigarette had not yet been invented, tobacco chewing was becoming increasingly popular within a large segment of the male population. Opium, either alone or in the form of laudanum (opium extract in alcohol), was available for the purpose of pain relief. On the other hand, there was no cocaine, heroin, marijuana, 3,4-methylenedioxymethamphetamine (MDMA, or "ecstasy"), methamphetamine, barbiturates, lysergic acid diethylamide (LSD), or phencyclidine (PCP). There were also few drug control laws, especially none at the federal level.

As time went on, however, a number of events and cultural trends set us on the path to where we are today. First, the alcohol temperance movement started to gain strength. The founding of this movement, which promoted abstention from hard liquor in favor of moderate beer or wine consumption, is generally credited to a highly regarded Philadelphia physician named Benjamin Rush. Rush not only identified a number of adverse physiological consequences of excessive drinking, he also argued that such consumption impaired the drinker's moral faculty, leading to irresponsible and even criminal acts. Although the temperance movement reached its height in the failed twentieth-century attempt at complete alcohol prohibition (except for "medicinal" use), its aftermath still colors the attitudes of many people toward the problems of alcohol and drug abuse. In particular, the equating of drug use with criminal behavior can be seen in the "War on Drugs" that has pervaded our society for so many years.

Second, advances in chemistry during the nineteenth century made it possible to purify the primary active ingredient of opium, namely, morphine, and then later the active ingredient of coca, which of course is cocaine. This allowed the drugs to be taken in much more concentrated form, increasing their addictive potential. But since the route of administration is also important, an equally significant event was the development of the hypodermic syringe in 1858 (**Figure 9.2**), which permitted the purified substances to be injected directly into the bloodstream. One consequence of this marriage of purified drug and improved delivery vehicle was the widespread use of morphine to treat wounded and ill soldiers during the Civil War. Many developed an opiate addiction, which was called "soldier's disease" in the common parlance.

Third, the increasing availability of purified drugs combined with the lack of drug control laws led to growing use of these substances in many different forms. Cocaine was the major ingredient in a variety of tonics and patent medicines sold over-the-counter. The most notorious of these was *Vin Mariani*, which was made by the French chemist Angelo Mariani by

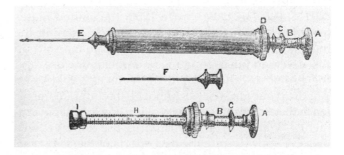

Figure 9.2 An early hypodermic syringe and needle used in the 1870s (From Morgan, 1981; original photograph from H. H. Kane, *The Hypodermic Injection of Morphia*, 1880, p. 21.)

soaking coca leaves in wine along with spices and other flavorings. Heroin was synthesized by Bayer Laboratories in 1874 and was first marketed 14 years later as a nonaddicting (!) substitute for codeine. If you've ever had a severe cough, the doctor probably prescribed a codeine-containing cough syrup. At the turn of the twentieth century, you could purchase heroin-containing cough syrup at any neighborhood pharmacy without a prescription (**Figure 9.3**). It does not surprise us now that the ready availability of these substances led many people to become dependent on them.

The last factor that we wish to mention here is the medicalization of drug addiction that occurred primarily in the second half of the twentieth century. The medicalization of addiction had two components: that addiction was now thought of as a disease and that drug addicts should be treated by the medical establishment. We can trace the origin of these views to the American Association for the Cure of Inebriates, an organization founded in 1870, which stated that inebriety (excessive drinking) was a disease and proposed that inebriates (alcoholics) be admitted to hospitals and sanitaria for help. However, this medical approach to alcoholism and drug abuse later faded and was not seriously revived until the early 1950s, when alcoholism was declared a disease first by the World Health Organization and subsequently by the American Medical Association. Alcoholics Anonymous (AA), which embraces many aspects of the disease model of alcoholism, was gaining prominence during this period. The disease model of drug addiction continues to be strongly promoted by the treatment community, by self-help groups such as AA and Narcotics Anonymous, and by much of the research establishment (including the National Institute on Drug Abuse, an agency of the National Institutes of Health). It is also the view most widely accepted by the lay public. On the other hand, this model has also been the subject of some criticism, as we shall see later in the chapter.

DRUGS AND THE LAW   Since 1980, the United States has witnessed the introduction of "crack" cocaine, the increased potency of heroin and marijuana sold on the street, an upsurge in methamphetamine use, and the rise of so-called club drugs such as MDMA and γ-hydroxybutyrate (GHB). Although these developments led to the establishment and continuation of our government's "War on Drugs," illicit drug use continues on a massive scale despite the best efforts of the drug warriors. At the federal level and in most states, the current political climate is strongly against any consideration of legalization or even decriminalization of any currently illegal drugs, including marijuana. Indeed, when Dr.

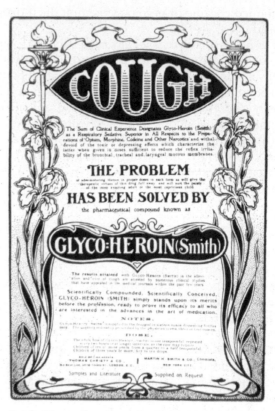

Figure 9.3   An early ad for heroin-containing cough syrup

Joycelyn Elders, President Bill Clinton's first Surgeon General, innocently mentioned in December 1993 that perhaps the issue of drug legalization should at least be openly discussed, it led to a tremendous public outcry and an immediate retraction by the Clinton administration. A year later, Dr. Elders was fired. Although she had made other controversial remarks before her dismissal, no one doubted that her first misstep was to bring up the notion of drug legalization.

Given the recent history of drug politics in the United States, it is easy to forget that things were not always this way. As discussed earlier, by the beginning of the twentieth century, there was widespread use of cocaine, opium, and heroin in over-the-counter or patent medicines. In the absence of any federal regulations governing the marketing, distribution, or purchase of these preparations, sales increased from $3.5 million in 1859 to $74 million in 1904 (Hollinger, 1995). Over time, however, the federal government became increasingly involved in controlling the commercialization of drugs (**Table 9.1**). This involvement began with an initial concern about the quality and purity of both medications and food, which led to the passage in 1906 of the Pure Food and Drug Act. The new law mandated the accurate labeling of patent medicines so that the consumer would be aware of the presence of alcohol, cocaine, opiates, or marijuana

TABLE 9.1   History of Federal Drug Legislation in the United States

Name of law	Year enacted	Purpose
Pure Food and Drug Act	1906	Regulated labeling of patent medicines and created the FDA
Harrison Act	1914	Regulated dispensing and use of opioid drugs and cocaine
Eighteenth Constitutional Amendment (Prohibition)	1920	Banned alcohol sales except for medicinal use (repealed in 1933)
Marijuana Tax Act	1937	Banned nonmedical use of cannabis (overturned by U.S. Supreme Court in 1969)
Controlled Substances Act	1970	Established the schedule of controlled substances and created the DEA

in such products. It also created the Food and Drug Administration (FDA), which is charged with assessing the potential hazards and benefits of new medications and with licensing their use. The Pure Food and Drug Act was clearly an educational approach to the drug problem, since the law did not make any of the above mentioned substances illegal to sell or use.

Around the same time that drug labeling and purity were under discussion, concern over the burgeoning problem of drug abuse and dependency was growing. For example, importation of opium grew rapidly between 1870 and 1900. Rightly or wrongly, opium smoking had become associated with Chinese laborers who had immigrated to the United States following the Civil War to work on the railroads. Meanwhile, China itself began a vigorous campaign against opium, viewing it as a symbol of Western imperialism.[3] These events culminated in the convening of the first International Opium Conference in 1911, where each participating country agreed to enact its own legislation restricting narcotic drug use except for legitimate medical purposes.

It took the United States several more years to pass its antinarcotic law, the Harrison Act of 1914. A major reason for the delay was lobbying by drug and patent medicine manufacturers who objected to the initial wording of the bill. The Act was designed to regulate the dispensing and use of opiates (opium and its derivatives such as morphine) and cocaine by means of the following provisions:

1. Use of these substances for nonmedical purposes was prohibited.
2. Pharmacists and physicians were required to register with the Treasury Department and to keep records of their inventory of narcotics.
3. Retail sellers of narcotics and practicing physicians had to pay a yearly $1 tax to the federal government.
4. Patent medicines containing small amounts of opium, morphine, heroin, or cocaine remained legal and could continue to be sold by mail order or in retail establishments.

Because of the third and fourth provisions, we can see that the principal aims of the Harrison Act were to control rather than abolish the use of opiates and cocaine and to link narcotic use with government revenue through taxation (it's worth noting that during the Prohibition era, the federal government finally managed to convict the notorious gangster Al Capone not on alcohol trafficking or murder, but rather on tax evasion!).

Many physicians had previously been providing maintenance doses of opiates or cocaine to patients who were addicted to these substances. However, because addiction was not considered a disease by government authorities at that time, one immediate effect of the Harrison Act was to cut addicts off from this source of drugs. The consequences are easily predicted. Addicts were forced to turn to street dealers and prices skyrocketed. According to Hollinger (1995), the cost of heroin increased from $6.50 per ounce to roughly $100 (a huge sum in the early 1900s). People who could not afford to pay these prices were forced into abstinence and withdrawal. One result of these events was the establishment of many municipal clinics to treat drug addicts. The clinic in New York City registered approximately 7700 patients between April

[3]In the eighteenth and nineteenth centuries, England profited enormously from Chinese purchase of opium obtained through the British colony in India. The Opium Wars of the mid-1800s at least partially revolved around the desire of Western powers to maintain this lucrative drug trade against China's wishes. Although the United States was not a participant in the wars, it benefited from favorable trade agreements negotiated after the conclusion of hostilities.

1919 and March 1920 (Morgan, 1981). Unfortunately, these clinics failed to solve the problem; most addicts went back to using street drugs soon after their treatment, and illegal drug sales continued to flourish.

The Harrison Act did not regulate the use of alcohol, which had nevertheless been a major social problem in the United States for many years. As a consequence of increasing support for the alcohol temperance movement mentioned previously, the Eighteenth Amendment to the Constitution went into effect in 1920. The new Prohibition law banned the dispensing of any beverage with alcohol content greater than 0.5% (1/10 the typical alcohol content of regular beer) except by physicians for medicinal purposes. Once again, the consequences were disastrous. Speakeasies (establishments where alcohol was sold illegally) sprang up everywhere, and the organized crime movement really took off during this period. The experiment in Prohibition finally ended in 1933.

Cannabis was another substance disregarded by the Harrison Act. The practice of marijuana smoking was initially associated with Mexican immigrants who entered the United States in the early 1900s. After World War I, public opposition to marijuana grew, and eventually numerous state laws were passed against its possession or sale. The federal government subsequently entered the picture with passage of the Marijuana Tax Act of 1937. This law was similar to the Harrison Act in banning nonmedical use of cannabis and levying a tax on importers, sellers, and dispensers of marijuana.

The Marijuana Tax Act was declared unconstitutional and was overturned by the U.S. Supreme Court in 1969. But in the very next year, the federal government passed a much broader law meant to apply to all potentially addictive substances. This was the Comprehensive Drug Abuse Prevention and Control Act (sometimes called the Controlled Substances Act [CSA]) of 1970. The CSA replaced or updated virtually all previous federal legislation concerning narcotic drugs and other substances thought to have abuse or addiction potential. Among other provisions, the CSA established five schedules of controlled substances, which are discussed later in this chapter. It also created the Drug Enforcement Agency (DEA), which was charged with enforcement of the CSA. Although this law has been revised several times since its inception, it remains the cornerstone of federal drug control legislation. Moreover, many states have adopted the Uniform Controlled Substances Act, a model drug control law patterned after the CSA.

Several conclusions have emerged from this brief survey of the history of federal drug laws. The first is that each time the federal government became more involved in drug regulation, the action resulted from increases in drug use and/or perceived societal dangers posed by such use. Those who wish to make drug laws more lenient must start by changing such antidrug perceptions. The second conclusion is that existing laws are not entirely consistent with available medical and scientific evidence. For example, we will see later that nicotine (obtained via tobacco) is more addictive than marijuana by all established criteria, yet tobacco smoking is legal, whereas marijuana smoking is not. A final conclusion is that legal mechanisms have only limited effectiveness in preventing drug use. This is most obvious in the events that occurred during Prohibition, as well as in the current widespread use of marijuana. We acknowledge that cocaine and heroin use would almost certainly be greater than it is now if those substances were legal. But millions of people have little trouble obtaining cocaine, heroin, or any other illicit drug they desire. Many would argue that a more important restraint on drug use is the individual's own concerns that a particular substance might harm her health, jeopardize other important goals or values, or put her at risk for becoming addicted to that substance.

Features of Drug Abuse and Addiction

Before proceeding further, try writing down your definition of drug addiction in one or two sentences. Were you easily able to come up with a satisfactory definition? If not, don't be concerned, because addiction is not a simple concept. This problem was highlighted by Burglass and Shaffer (1984) in the following (not entirely frivolous) description of addiction: "Certain individuals use certain substances in certain ways thought at certain times to be unacceptable by certain other individuals for reasons both certain and uncertain." The medical establishment has attempted to develop a broadly acceptable definition, yet experts continue to disagree about exactly what it means to be addicted to a drug (Walters and Gilbert, 2000).

Drug addiction is a chronic, relapsing behavioral disorder

Early views of drug addiction emphasized the importance of physical dependence. As you learned in Chapter 1, this means that abstinence from the drug leads to highly unpleasant withdrawal symptoms that motivate the individual to reinstate his drug use. It is true that some drugs of abuse, such as alcohol and opiates, can create strong physical dependence and severe withdrawal symptoms in dependent individuals. Certain other substances, however, produce relatively minor physical dependence. It may surprise you to learn that cocaine is one such substance, and that there was a time when cocaine was not considered to be addictive because of this lack of an opiate-like withdrawal syndrome.

Recent conceptions of addiction have focused more on other features of this phenomenon. First, there is an emphasis on behavior, specifically, the compulsive nature of drug seeking and drug use in the addict. The addict is often driven by a strong urge to take the drug, which is called drug **craving**. Second, addiction is thought of as a chronic, relapsing disorder. This means that individuals remain addicted for long periods of time, and that drug-free periods (**remissions**) are often followed by **relapses** in which drug use recurs despite negative consequences. This is the paradox of addiction mentioned earlier in the chapter. One widely cited definition of addiction that encompasses the first two of the three features just described is as follows: "a behavioral pattern of drug use, characterized by overwhelming involvement with the use of a drug (compulsive use), the securing of its supply, and a high tendency to relapse after withdrawal" (Goldstein, 1989).

The term *addiction* has strong negative emotional associations for most of us. Despite the fact that drug addicts live in all parts of the country and come from all walks of life, we usually think of them as urban and poor. Our mental images are those of an unwashed heroin user huddled in an alley "shooting up" with a dirty syringe, or an emaciated "crackhead" engulfed in a cloud of cocaine vapor in an inner-city crack house, or a wino staggering down the street begging for a little change to buy his next bottle. Although some drug addicts fit these images, many others do not. For this reason, and because of the conflicting definitions of addiction, the American Psychiatric Association stopped using the terms *addiction* and *addict* in its professional writings. This can be seen in the Association's *Diagnostic and Statistical Manual of Mental Disorders* (DSM) (American Psychiatric Association, 2000). The *DSM* represents an attempt to classify the entire range of psychiatric disorders, with objective criteria provided for the diagnosis of each disorder. Instead of using the term *drug addiction*, the *DSM* specifies a group of substance-related disorders, where *substance* refers to typical drugs of abuse as well as to some psychoactive medications that have abuse potential. At the time of this writing in late 2012, the fourth version of the *DSM* (i.e., *DSM-IV*) has been in use for many years and has been one of the mainstays of the research literature on addiction. Within the category of substance-related disorders, *DSM-IV* specifies two general disorders called **substance dependence** and **substance abuse**. Substance dependence, which is the more severe disorder, corresponds roughly to the notion of addiction. Substance

abuse is a less severe disorder that may or may not lead subsequently to substance dependence. Much of the addiction research that is cited in this textbook and in other sources makes use of the *DSM-IV* criteria for substance dependence in determining eligibility of subjects for inclusion in scientific studies (e.g., to investigate the neurobiological basis of addiction or to determine the therapeutic efficacy of novel treatments). However, the *DSM* has been under revision for a number of years, and the next volume, *DSM-5*, is expected to be released in May 2013. According to information posted online by the American Psychiatric Association, *DSM-5* has a new classification system for substance-related disorders. A general category called **substance use disorder** takes the place of both substance dependence and substance abuse in the *DSM-IV*. According to the proposed criteria, diagnosis of a substance use disorder requires that the individual has manifested a maladaptive pattern of substance use, over at least a 12-month period, that has led to significant impairment or distress by clinical standards. Moreover, at least two of eleven additional criteria must be met, these criteria including such features as craving for the substance; increasing use of the substance beyond the individual's original intent; unsuccessful attempts to control or stop using the substance; development of tolerance and/or withdrawal; failure to fulfill major obligations associated with the person's current role as breadwinner, parent, or student; continued use despite knowledge of social, interpersonal, or health problems caused by the substance; repeated use of the substance in hazardous situations such as driving a car; spending excessive time in obtaining and/or using the substance; and reduced amount of time spent in other activities because of substance use.[4]

You can see that there is no single criterion for substance use disorder. This reflects the fact that maladaptive drug use may result in many different adverse consequences, depending on which drug is being taken and on the amount and pattern of drug taking. Of course, someone with a long-standing, severe case of substance use disorder may meet virtually all of the listed criteria, not just a few. To reflect this fact, the new classification will have an important severity component. Specifically, individuals who meet only two or three of the specified criteria will be considered to have a moderately severe substance use disorder (similar to the substance abuse category in *DSM-IV*), whereas individuals who meet four or more criteria will be considered to have a severe disorder (similar to the substance dependence category in *DSM-IV*). Because the

[4]Source: www.psychiatry.org/File%20Library/Advocacy%20and%20Newsroom/Press%20Releases/2012%20Releases/12-43-DSM-5-BOT-Vote-News-Release--FINAL--3-.pdf

BOX 9.1   Of Special Interest

Should the Term "Addiction" Be Applied to Compulsive Behavioral Disorders That Don't Involve Substance Use?

The term *addiction* has traditionally been associated with harmful use of substances such as alcohol, cocaine, and heroin. But articles in the mainstream media now commonly use the same term when referring to behavioral problems that don't involve chemical substances. Examples include *gambling addiction*, *sex addiction*, *food addiction*, *Internet addiction*, and so forth. On what basis can we determine whether this is a legitimate use of *addiction*, or whether we should restrict the term to its original usage?

Researchers have identified at least eight domains of human behavior that, in some individuals, may exhibit similarities to addictive drug use. These domains are pathological gambling, eating disorders (including binge eating, anorexia nervosa, and bulimia), excessive Internet use, preoccupation with love, preoccupation with sex, excessive and compulsive exercising, workaholism, and compulsive shopping/spending. As stated by Grant and colleagues (2010), "the

essential feature of behavioral addictions is the failure to resist an impulse, drive, or temptation to perform an act that is harmful to the person or to others" (p. 234). Behavioral addictions are chronic and relapsing and interfere with other aspects of the individual's life. In all of these characteristics, behavioral addictions show close similarity with chemical addictions.

Although more research needs to be conducted, numerous studies have found parallels between behavioral and chemical addictions with respect to personality characteristics that contribute to vulnerability, comorbidity (i.e., individuals often suffer from multiple addictions), involvement of genetic factors, neural circuits involved in the addiction, and possible negative consequences for the addict (Frascella et al., 2010; Grant et al., 2010). Sussman and coworkers (2011) reviewed the literature on various behavioral and chemical addictions to ascertain known or likely similarities among these disorders. Nine areas of potential

negative consequences of each disorder were considered: roles (interference with the person's job or other major life roles), social relationships, legal issues (likelihood of committing criminal acts and/or facing legal problems), danger (likelihood of getting into dangerous situations), possibility of physical harm, possibility of financial loss, occurrence of emotional problems/trauma, development of tolerance or tolerance-like phenomena, and withdrawal or withdrawal-like symptoms upon abstinence. The results of the literature review, which are shown in the table, suggest that the strongest areas of similarity between chemical and behavioral addictions include impairment of social relationships, emotional problems, and the development of tolerance-like and withdrawal-like phenomena.

After reviewing the current literature on behavioral addictions, the *DSM-5* Substance-Related Disorders Work Group decided to include only pathological gambling in with the chemical addictions.

---

term *substance use disorder* is new and the old term *substance dependence* has been phased out, we will use the lay term *addiction* throughout this chapter to refer to maladaptive patterns of drug use that meet the criteria for severe substance use disorder or the definition given earlier by Goldstein. One exception to this policy is when a specific study is cited that recruited subjects using the *DSM-IV* criteria for substance dependence.

In addition to the general category of substance use disorder, the *DSM-5* (like its predecessor) will include specific diagnostic criteria for disorders related to alcohol, caffeine (which is not "addictive" in the usual sense but can still be misused with adverse health consequences), cannabis, hallucinogens, inhalants,

opiates, sedative–hypnotic drugs, stimulants, and tobacco. All of these substances are covered in detail in subsequent chapters of the book. It is important to note that mere use of any drug, whether alcohol, tobacco, marijuana, cocaine, or heroin, does not constitute a substance use disorder. As indicated in the *DSM*, the use must be *maladaptive*, which means that harm is occurring to the user. Someone who snorts cocaine occasionally may be doing something illegal and dangerous, in that there is potential for harm and for the subsequent development of a pattern of compulsive use. But if the *DSM* criteria for a substance use disorder are not met, we cannot claim that the person is an addict, or even that she is abusing the drug.

BOX 9.1 *(continued)*

Negative Consequences[a] of Chemical and Behavioral Addictions[b]

Area of conse-quence	Ciga-rettes	Alcohol	Illicit drugs	Eating	Gambling	Internet	Love	Sex	Exer-cise	Work	Shop-ping
Roles	+/–	+	+	+/–	+/–	+/–	+/–	+/–	–	–	–
Social	+	+	+	+	+	+	+	+	+	+	+
Legal	+/–	+	+	–	+/–	+/–	+/–	+/–	–	–	–
Danger	+/–	+	+	–	+/–	–	–	+/–	–	–	–
Physical	+	+	+	+	–	–	–	+/–	+	–	–
Financial	+/–	+	+	+/–	+	–	+/–	+/–	–	–	+
Emotional	+	+	+	+	+	+	+	+	+	+	+
Tolerance-like	+	+	+	+	+	+	+	+	+	+	+
Withdrawal-like	+	+	+	+	+	+	+	+	+	+	+

Source: Sussman et al., 2011.

[a]+, criterion is applicable; +/–, criterion might be applicable or is applicable some of the time; –, criterion is not applicable.

[b]Eating, eating disorders (especially binge eating); Gambling, pathological gambling; Internet, internet addiction; Love, love addiction; Sex, sex addiction; Exercise, exercise addiction; Work, workaholism; Shopping, shopping/spending addiction. Note that some of the proposed behavioral addictions, such as love addiction, have been studied much less than other addictions such as pathological gambling (see Sussman et al., 2011 for details). Consequently, some of the results shown in the table should be considered speculative until more data have been obtained.

This decision was based, at least in part, on the fact that this disorder has been studied most extensively among the behavioral addictions. Therefore, a sufficient knowledge base is available demonstrating the parallels between pathological gambling and chemical addictions (Wareham and Potenza, 2010). Nevertheless, there is growing information on other behavioral addictions such as sexual addiction (Garcia and Thibaut, 2010), food addiction (Avena et al., 2011), Internet addiction (Weinstein and Lejoyeux, 2010), and compulsive buying (Lejoyeux and Weinstein, 2010). Although these disorders will reside in other parts of the *DSM-5*, it is possible that additional research will lead to their inclusion with substance-related disorders in future editions of the *DSM*.

In recent years, we have seen growing discussion over whether the concept of addiction should be applied to other uncontrolled or compulsive behaviors such as binge eating, sexual preoccupation, pathological gambling, compulsive Internet use, and so forth. In fact, the Substance-Related Disorders Work Group, which developed the new classification system for the *DSM-5*, spent considerable time deliberating about whether to place these so-called "behavioral" addictions in the same general category as substance use disorders. In **Box 9.1**, we discuss the current status of behavioral addictions and the extent to which they show similarities to classical substance-based addictions.

There are two types of progression in drug use

Drug use can involve two different kinds of progression. In one type of progression characteristic of many young people, the individual starts out taking a legal substance such as alcohol or tobacco, later progresses to marijuana, and in a small percentage of cases moves on to cocaine, heroin, other illicit substances, or illegally obtained prescription drugs. One of the theories that attempts to account for this type of progression, namely, the **Gateway Theory**, is discussed in **Web Box 9.1**.

The second kind of progression pertains to changes in the amount, pattern, and consequences of drug use

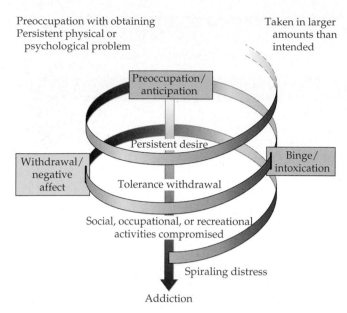

Preoccupation with obtaining
Persistent physical or
psychological problem

Taken in larger
amounts than
intended

Spiraling distress

Addiction

Figure 9.4 Cycles of pathological drug use that can lead to the development of addiction (After Koob and Zorrilla, 2010.)

as they affect the user's health and functioning. When an individual first experiments with an abused drug, he may or may not progress to regular, nonproblematic use or beyond. Despite the popular view that drugs like cocaine and heroin are instantly and automatically addictive, this is not the case. Indeed, one of the central unresolved questions in the addiction field is why some individuals eventually develop a pattern of compulsive drug use, whereas many others do not (Swendsen and Le Moal, 2011). **Figure 9.4** depicts a contemporary view of pathological drug use as a cyclical pattern that comprises three components: (1) periods of preoccupation with drugs and anticipation of upcoming use; (2) periods of drug intoxication that, in some cases, are associated with "bingeing" on the drug; and (3) periods following drug use that are characterized by withdrawal symptoms and negative affect (e.g., depressed mood or irritability). The figure includes some of the features of the cycle (e.g., taking drugs in larger amounts than intended and development of drug tolerance) that represent criteria for substance dependence in *DSM-IV* and/or substance use disorder in *DSM-5*. Over time, repeated cycles constitute a downward spiral that can ultimately result in addiction.

Interestingly, even after an individual becomes addicted to a drug, he may

show intermittent periods of reduced use or even abstinence. Such periods may be related to repeated attempts to stop drug use without help, or they may be associated with participation in a treatment program or incarceration in prison. **Figure 9.5** illustrates an example of this phenomenon taken from a longitudinal study of male opioid (heroin) addicts in San Antonio, Texas (Maddux and Desmond, 1981). The figure presents drug status data over periods ranging from 7 to 20 years for 10 representative subjects out of a total of nearly 250. Particularly striking is the diversity of patterns among the subjects. For example, subject 111 exhibited periods of either occasional or daily use interspersed with long intervals of abstinence. In contrast, subject 162 used daily for most of the 20-year period except when he was institutionalized in a hospital or prison. When considered across all 10 subjects, the numerous instances of abstinence followed by renewed drug use support the view mentioned earlier that addiction is a chronic, relapsing disorder.

For many people, the use of both alcohol and illicit drugs such as marijuana naturally declines once they reach adulthood and begin to take on the responsibilities associated with earning a living and having a family. This pattern is consistent with the data shown in Figure 9.1, as well as with data from longitudinal

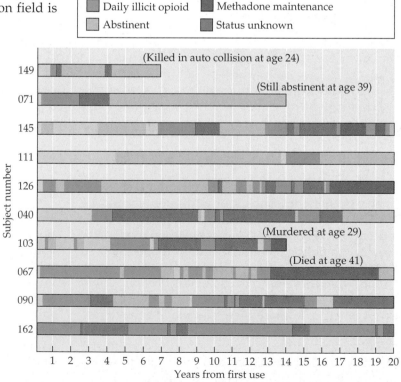

Figure 9.5 Patterns of opioid drug use over a 20-year period in ten heroin addicts (After Maddux and Desmond, 1981.)

TABLE 9.2   Schedule of Controlled Substances

Schedule	Description	Representative substances
I	Substances that have no accepted medical use in the U.S. and have a high abuse potential	Heroin, LSD, mescaline, marijuana, THC, MDMA
II	Substances that have a high abuse potential with severe psychic or physical dependence liability	Opium, morphine, codeine, meperidine (Demerol), cocaine, amphetamine, methylphenidate (Ritalin), pentobarbital, phencyclidine (PCP)
III	Substances that have an abuse potential less than those in Schedules I and II, including compounds containing limited quantities of certain narcotics and nonnarcotic drugs	Paregoric, barbiturates other than those listed in another schedule
IV	Substances that have an abuse potential less than those in Schedule III	Phenobarbital, chloral hydrate, diazepam (Valium), alprazolam (Xanax)
V	Substances that have an abuse potential less than those in Schedule IV, consisting of preparations containing limited amounts of certain narcotic drugs generally for antitussive (cough suppressant) and antidiarrheal purposes	

studies documenting a reduction in drug use beyond the period of adolescence (Chen and Kandel, 1995). Some writers have called this process "maturing out" of a drug-using lifestyle. Scattered reports indicate that maturing out may even occur for some addicts and not merely for heavy users; however, recovery from addiction is a complex process that cannot be accounted for by any single factor (Waldorf, 1983).

Which drugs are the most addictive?

Just as we all have mental images of drug addicts, we also have ideas about which drugs are the most addictive. Drugs thought to have high addictive potential are sometimes called "hard drugs." Aside from popular opinion, however, there are legal standards meant to classify drugs according to their addictive potential. The Controlled Substances Act of 1970 established a system by which most substances with abuse potential are classified into one of five different schedules. These schedules, along with representative drugs, are shown in **Table 9.2**. Schedule I substances are considered to have no medicinal value and thus can be obtained only for research use by registered investigators.[5] Items listed under Schedules II to V are available for medicinal purposes with a prescription from a medical professional such as a physician, dentist, or veterinarian. They can also be obtained for research use. Note that the **Schedule of Controlled Substances**

specifically excludes alcohol and tobacco, thus permitting these substances to be purchased and used legally without registration or prescription. The Schedule of Controlled Substances was formulated more than 40 years ago and was based not only on the scientific knowledge of that time but also partly on political considerations. Although it has been updated periodically since its inception, we may still ask whether this classification system accurately reflects our current understanding of various abused substances, or whether it continues to be too politicized. This issue is discussed in **Web Box 9.2**.

Section Summary

- High levels of drug use continue in our society despite significant governmental attempts to control such use.

- Although early ideas about addiction emphasized the role of physical dependence, recent conceptions have focused on the compulsive features of drug seeking and use (despite the potentially harmful consequences) and on the concept of drug addiction as a chronic, relapsing disorder characterized by repeated periods of remission followed by relapses.

- In *DSM-5*, maladaptive patterns of drug use are categorized by a disorder called substance use disorder. In its severe form, substance use disorder has characteristics that correspond closely to those usually associated with addiction.

- Young people often progress from legal substances like alcohol or tobacco to marijuana, and

[5]For all controlled substances, but particularly for Schedule I and II items, there are strict federal requirements for investigator registration, ordering, and recordkeeping. The substances must be maintained securely, as in a locked safe, with careful control over who has access to the drug supply.

some even go on to try cocaine, heroin, or illegally obtained prescription drugs. The gateway theory attempts to account for this progression, although other explanations have been offered to explain the same findings.

- A second kind of progression consists of cycles of pathological drug use consisting of three components: preoccupation–anticipation, binge–intoxication, and withdrawal–negative affect. Repeated cycles can cause spiraling distress in the user that eventually leads to addiction. Nevertheless, even addicts may show periods of abstinence interspersed among the intervals of regular drug consumption.

- The Schedule of Controlled Substances classifies potentially abused drugs into five categories, or schedules, on the basis of their degree of abuse potential and medicinal value. Alcohol and tobacco are not listed on the schedule, so they can be purchased for recreational use and without a prescription.

- Debate has arisen as to whether the Schedule of Controlled Substances is a reasonable classification system based on current scientific knowledge, or whether it has been driven too much by sociopolitical considerations.

Factors that Influence the Development and Maintenance of Drug Abuse and Addiction

Over the years, researchers have discovered a variety of different factors that contribute to the development and maintenance of drug abuse (defined here as maladaptive or harmful drug use that doesn't meet the full criteria for addiction) and addiction. In this section, we will discuss the most important of these factors, including how they are studied in animal models of addiction. Such models are critical for our ability to investigate the neurobiological underpinnings of addiction and to screen new pharmacological agents that might have therapeutic value in treating drug addicts. Later in the chapter, we will consider how different contributory factors are brought together in current theories of addiction.

The addiction potential of a substance is influenced by its route of administration

In Chapter 1, you learned about the various routes by which drugs can enter a person's body. Some routes of administration such as oral or transdermal result in relatively slow absorption of the drug and, therefore,

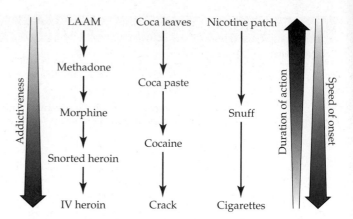

Figure 9.6 Relationship between route of administration and addiction potential of opiate drugs, cocaine, and nicotine. Opiates: LAAM (levo-alpha-acetyl-methadol) and methadone are orally administered treatments for opiate addiction, morphine taken orally has a more rapid onset and a shorter duration than methadone, and heroin may be taken by snorting, IV injection, or smoking (not shown) (see Chapter 11). Cocaine: coca leaves are chewed, coca paste is a crude extract of the leaves, powdered cocaine is often snorted, and crack cocaine is smoked (see Chapter 12). Nicotine: the nicotine patch is a transdermal delivery system used for smoking cessation, snuff is powdered tobacco leaves that are snorted, and cigarettes are smoked (see Chapter 13). (After Melichar et al., 2001.)

equally slow drug availability to the brain. In contrast, intravenous (IV) injection or inhalation/smoking yields rapid drug entry into the brain and a fast onset of drug action. Conversely, a fast onset is associated with a shorter duration of action. Researchers and addiction treatment providers have known for many years that the addiction potential of a substance is related to the route of administration, with routes that cause a fast onset of drug action having the greatest addiction potential. **Figure 9.6** illustrates this principle for opiate drugs, cocaine, and nicotine. Although we don't fully understand why IV injection and inhalation are associated with the greatest vulnerability to addiction, we do know that these routes produce the strongest euphoric effects (for a given dose) as a result of rapid drug delivery to the brain. It is also possible that repeated exposure of the brain to rapid as opposed to gradual drug delivery produces long-term neurobiological changes that are necessary for addiction to develop. A later section of this chapter discusses our current understanding of addiction neurobiology.

Most abused drugs exert rewarding and reinforcing effects

Most abused drugs act as **positive reinforcers**. This means that consuming the drug strengthens whatever preceding behavior was performed by the organism.

(A)

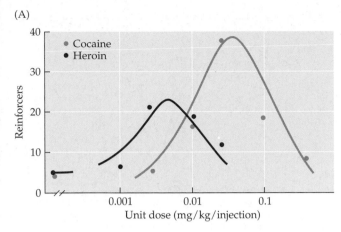

(B)

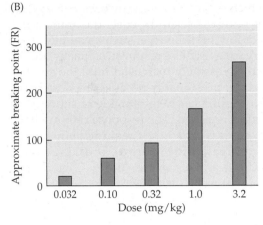

Figure 9.7 Features of intravenous drug self-administration by laboratory animals (A) Representative data for cocaine and heroin illustrate the typical inverted U-shaped curve relating dose per infusion to number of reinforcers (drug deliveries) obtained during a self-administration session. (B) Breaking point on a progressive-ratio schedule is an index of the reinforcing effectiveness of different doses of a drug. In this experiment, rats were trained to self-administer morphine on a continuous-reinforcement schedule, then were switched to a fixed-ratio (FR) schedule. The FR was increased daily (progressive-ratio schedule) until the breaking point was reached, as defined in this study by fewer than four drug injections in a day. The graph illustrates the estimated breaking points according to morphine dose per infusion. Within the dose range tested, it is clear that the drug's reinforcing properties rise dramatically as the dose is increased. (A after Bergman and Paronis, 2006; B after Weeks and Collins, 1987.)

Drug reward is a different but related concept that refers to the positive subjective experience (i.e., pleasure) associated with the drug. Examples include the euphoric feeling or "high" induced by a variety of drugs, and the feeling of relaxation induced by alcohol, marijuana, and sedative drugs such as barbiturates. Obviously the rewarding effects of a substance are likely to play an important role in its reinforcing properties, but other factors (e.g., increased alertness produced by stimulant drugs) may also play a role.

DRUG SELF-ADMINISTRATION Drug reinforcement is most often studied operationally by investigating an organism's propensity to self-administer the substance using procedures introduced in Chapter 4. As you will recall, an experimental animal such as a rat, mouse, or monkey is typically fitted with an IV catheter attached to a drug-filled syringe. When the animal performs an operant response such as pressing a lever or poking its nose into a hole in the wall of the apparatus, a pump is briefly activated that slightly depresses the plunger of the syringe and infuses a small dose of the drug directly into the animal's bloodstream. This is directly analogous to a drug addict giving himself an IV drug injection. The ability of animals to learn and maintain the lever-pressing/nose-poking response or of addicts to learn and maintain drug-seeking and drug-using behaviors means that the drug is acting as a reinforcer, just as food is a reinforcer for those who are hungry. Substances that are strong reinforcers in the IV self-administration paradigm virtually always have great abuse liability

in humans, particularly when taken intravenously or by smoking (the two routes of administration that produce the most rapid uptake of the drug by the brain). Classic examples of this kind are cocaine, heroin, and amphetamine or methamphetamine. In contrast, drugs that are not readily self-administered by animals, such as antidepressant or antipsychotic medications, are generally not addictive in humans.

One of the many factors that can be manipulated in the IV self-administration paradigm is the amount of drug (dose) given in each infusion. Studies on a variety of drugs have shown that when the drug is delivered using a simple schedule of reinforcement such as a fixed-ratio (FR) schedule (see Chapter 4), the typical dose–response function is an inverted U-shaped curve (**Figure 9.7A**). The ascending part of the curve is thought to reflect increasing reinforcing effectiveness of the drug over that range of doses. On the other hand, the descending limb is potentially attributable to multiple factors, including satiation to the drug, aversive reactions, or behaviorally disruptive side effects (e.g., extreme hyperactivity in the case of stimulant drugs, or sedation in the case of sedative–hypnotic agents). Because of the complications introduced by these factors, simple dose–response functions are not very useful for determining the reinforcing strength of one substance versus another. A better measure of the relative strength of drug reinforcement makes use of a **progressive-ratio** procedure. In this procedure, animals are initially trained to lever press on a continuous-reinforcement (CR) schedule, which means that each press is followed by drug delivery. In the second phase, the animals are switched to a low FR schedule, such as an FR-5 (one drug delivery for every five responses). Finally, the FR schedule is progressively increased until the animals stop responding, presumably because the dose being delivered is not sufficiently reinforcing to support the amount of effort required. The response ratio at which responding ceases is called the **breaking point** (sometimes termed **breakpoint** instead). Breaking points vary across drugs and also across doses. What do you think is the relationship between dose and breaking point? If you guessed that breaking point generally increases with higher doses, you were correct. This is illustrated in a study conducted by Weeks and Collins (1987) in which they compared the approximate breaking points for a range of morphine doses in rats. As the dose of morphine was increased, the breaking point also rose by a large amount (**Figure 9.7B**). Keep in mind, however, that if the dose of the drug being tested becomes too high, determination of the breaking point may be compromised by some of the same factors that can interfere with dose–response analyses.

Just as mere drug use by humans does not constitute a psychiatric disorder, self-administration of a drug by a rat, mouse, or monkey is not a model of addiction per se even though it demonstrates that the substance has positive reinforcing properties. To produce a more convincing model of addiction, researchers must implement procedures that result in additional features such as escalating self-administration and relapse to renewed drug-seeking behavior after a period of abstinence (Ahmed, 2012). Chapter 12 provides examples of procedures that lead to escalating cocaine self-administration by rats. Relapse is typically modeled in self-administration studies by stopping drug delivery (thus producing a forced abstinence that results in extinction of the operant response) and then exposing the animals to stimuli that are known to provoke renewed responding in an attempt to obtain the drug again. Three main types of stimuli are effective in this regard: (1) the experimenter delivering a small dose of the drug to the animal (known as **drug priming**), (2) subjecting the animal to stress, and (3) exposing the animal to environmental cues that were previously paired with drug delivery (prior to extinction). The general paradigm used in this type of research is illustrated in **Figure 9.8**.

The scientific literature on drug self-administration consists almost entirely of studies on experimental animals, yet this procedure is also applicable to humans. It is important to note, however, that study subjects are usually individuals who are already experienced users of the substance being investigated (Haney, 2009). In some cases, self-administration may be used to test the

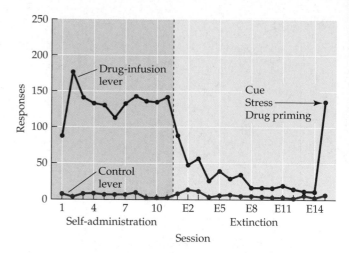

Figure 9.8 Representative data showing extinction and reinstatement of drug self-administration by drug-related cues, stress, or drug priming The graph depicts typical data from rats that were first stabilized on IV drug (e.g., cocaine) self-administration using an FR schedule of reinforcement. The red data points show the number of responses per session on a lever that is linked to drug delivery. Each drug infusion is accompanied by presentation of a cue, which is typically a light or a tone. The purple data points show the number of responses per session on a control lever that has no consequences when pressed. After 12 days of self-administration in this particular paradigm, the animals are switched to a 14-day extinction (E) phase in which pressing the drug lever no longer elicits either drug delivery or cue presentation. Note the rapid fall-off of responding during this phase. However, if the drug-paired cue is presented, if the animals are subjected to stress (e.g., foot shock), or if a priming dose of the drug is administered by the experimenter, the animals resume a high rate of responding on the drug lever despite the fact that the drug is still withheld (E14). This phenomenon, which is termed reinstatement, is considered to be an animal model of relapse to drug use after abstinence in drug addicts. (After Kalivas et al., 2006.)

effectiveness of current or prospective medications for individuals addicted to a particular drug. For example, **Figure 9.9** shows the results of a study in which heroin addicts were given the choice of an IV injection of heroin or money while receiving one of three doses of methadone maintenance treatment. It can be seen that subjects given a sufficiently large amount of methadone almost never chose the heroin because that dose of the methadone was effective in blocking the heroin-induced "high" (Comer et al., 2008).

The positive reinforcing effects of drugs undoubtedly play a significant role in addiction. Nevertheless, we may ask why the negative consequences of drug addiction (which can include such extreme effects as family breakup, loss of one's job and financial destitution, engaging in criminal activity to support drug purchases, damage to one's health, contracting needle-borne diseases such as AIDS or hepatitis, and even

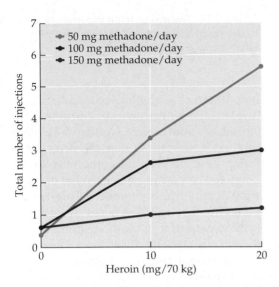

Figure 9.9 Choice of heroin infusions as a function of methadone maintenance dose Heroin addicts were stabilized on 50, 100, or 150 mg of methadone daily, after which they were tested for their choice of either an IV dose of heroin (0, 10, or 20 mg/70 kg) or a cash payment ranging from $2 to $38. The graph shows the number of heroin injections chosen as a function of heroin and methadone dose. (After Comer et al., 2008.)

that occur later in time. Even for humans, who have the ability to plan and to foresee the consequences of their actions in ways that animals cannot, this property of reinforcers has considerable influence over many behaviors, not just drug use. On the other hand, many individuals who take drugs once or even a few times stop their drug use before they develop a compulsive pattern and become addicted. This is true even for highly reinforcing drugs like cocaine and heroin. Thus, additional factors must contribute to the development of addiction in some drug users, but not in others.

PROCEDURES USED TO STUDY DRUG REWARD   Two different procedures are commonly used to study the rewarding properties of drugs (see Chapter 4). The first is a classical conditioning procedure called **place conditioning**. Animals (typically rats and mice) are trained in a two- or three-compartment apparatus in which one of the compartments is paired with the presence of a drug over several conditioning sessions. A test session is then conducted under drug-free conditions. If the drug produced a rewarding effect during training, the animal will spend more time in the drug-paired compartment than in a compartment that had been paired with a placebo. The second procedure makes use of **electrical self-stimulation** of the brain—a method in which the performance of an operant response causes the delivery of an electrical stimulus to a part of the brain's reward circuit (see later section for additional details on this circuit). Numerous studies have shown that the threshold for rewarding brain stimulation is reduced when animals have been treated acutely with various drugs of abuse (**Table 9.3**). Because a lower threshold indicates a more sensitive system, such results indicate that the underlying neural circuitry for drug reward overlaps with the circuitry for brain stimulation reward. On the other hand, withdrawal of animals from chronic treatment with these same substances causes an increased threshold for electrical self-stimulation. A similar phenomenon occurring in a drug-dependent

fatal overdose for some drugs) don't effectively counteract the positive reinforcement so that the individual stops using and remains abstinent. One possible answer concerns the temporal relationship between drug consumption and the positive or negative effects. Drug-induced euphoria occurs very quickly after consumption, particularly in the case of IV injection or inhalation (including smoking). In contrast, the negative consequences occur later in time and, in most cases, are linked to a long pattern of use rather than to a specific occasion of drug consumption. According to well-established principles of reinforcement, an event (euphoria) that occurs very soon after a response (drug consumption) exerts much greater control over that response than events (negative consequences)

TABLE 9.3	Drug Effects on Thresholds for Rewarding Brain Stimulation	
Drug class	Acute administration	Withdrawal from chronic treatment
Psychostimulants (cocaine, amphetamine)	↓	↑
Opiates (morphine, heroin)	↓	↑
Nicotine	↓	↑
Sedative–hypnotic drugs (ethanol)	↓	↑
THC	↓	↑

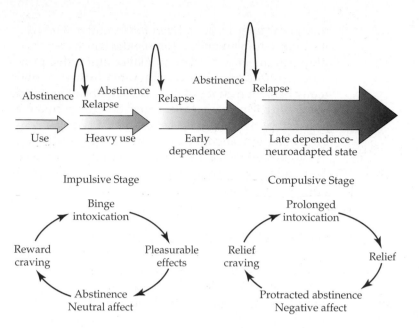

Figure 9.10 Transition from the impulsive to the compulsive phase of drug addiction (After Heilig and Koob, 2007.)

addict might contribute to the negative mood state and difficulty in experiencing pleasure (**anhedonia**) that are often reported during drug withdrawal.

DRUGS OF ABUSE CAN BE AVERSIVE RATHER THAN REWARDING Interestingly, drugs of abuse sometimes can be shown to exert aversive effects on animals or humans. For example, even though rats will self-administer nicotine under some conditions, they will also learn to press a lever to prevent experimenter-controlled infusions of the same drug. Considerable evidence suggests that a number of substances are reinforcing when under the animal's control but either are not as reinforcing or are even aversive when administered by the experimenter. For humans as well, drugs may produce aversive psychological or behavioral effects in addition to their rewarding effects. One example is the ability of cocaine to bring about feelings of anxiety that follow soon after the initial period of drug-induced euphoria. However, even though such aversive effects presumably inhibit the tendency toward future drug seeking and drug use, they may not be sufficient to outweigh the many factors promoting these behaviors.

circumstance.

Drug dependence leads to withdrawal symptoms when abstinence is attempted

Certain drugs of abuse such as alcohol and opiates (e.g., heroin or morphine) can lead to physical dependence when taken repeatedly. Some researchers have proposed that this process plays a key role in the establishment and maintenance of drug addiction. According to this idea, once an individual has become physically dependent as the result of repeated drug

use, attempts at abstinence lead to highly unpleasant withdrawal symptoms (also called an **abstinence syndrome**). This motivates the user to take the drug again (relapse) to alleviate the symptoms. In the language of learning theory, relief of withdrawal symptoms promotes drug-taking behavior through a process of negative reinforcement, thus leading ultimately to a continuous behavioral loop consisting of repeated abstinence attempts followed by relapses.[6]

Koob and Le Moal (2005) have proposed that in the development of addiction, drug-taking behavior progresses from an "impulsive" stage, in which the primary motivation for drug use is the substance's positive reinforcing effects, to a "compulsive" stage, in which the primary motivation is the negative reinforcement obtained by relief from drug withdrawal (**Figure 9.10**). The instigation of an aversive state (negative affect) of withdrawal that underlies such negative reinforcement is termed the "dark side" of addiction by Koob and Le Moal, and they further propose that this process is due to the gradual recruitment of an "anti-reward" system in the brain (depicted as a "neuroadapted state" in the figure). We will discuss this theory later in the section on addiction neurobiology.

One of the early proponents of an important role for physical dependence was Abraham Wikler, who studied and treated heroin addicts over a period of several decades. Because of lack of money or other factors, addicts do not have constant access to heroin. Over time, therefore, they are likely to undergo many episodes of withdrawal. Wikler argued that if these withdrawal reactions repeatedly occur in specific environments, such as the places where the addict either "hustles" for or takes the drug, the responses will become classically conditioned to the stimuli associated with those environments (Wikler, 1980). Consequently, even if an addict has been drug free for some length of time and is therefore no longer experiencing an acute abstinence syndrome, withdrawal symptoms can be triggered by exposure to the conditioned stimuli (**Figure 9.11**).

---

[6]Recall that negative reinforcement refers to the concept of reinforcement by removal of an undesirable stimulus (in this case, painful or distressing withdrawal symptoms).

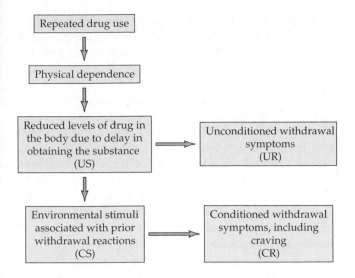

Figure 9.11 Development of conditioned drug withdrawal responses in dependent drug users CR, conditioned response; CS, conditioned stimulus; UR, unconditioned response; US, unconditioned stimulus.

As shown in the figure, drug craving is considered to be one of the crucial symptoms associated with conditioned withdrawal. Anna Rose Childress, Charles O'Brien, and their colleagues at the University of

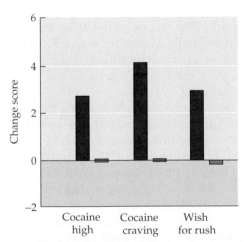

Figure 9.12 Subjective responses to a cocaine-related video were obtained from cocaine-dependent men and control subjects who had never taken cocaine. All subjects watched a 25-minute video depicting the acquisition and use of crack cocaine. Self-ratings of cocaine-related states were provided before and after the video, and change scores (after video minus before video) were determined. The cocaine-dependent group (red bars) showed significant increases in "cocaine high," "cocaine craving," and "wish for rush." For the control subjects, there was no change in "cocaine high" or "cocaine craving" and a small, statistically nonsignificant decrease in "wish for rush" (blue bars). (After Childress et al., 1999.)

Pennsylvania School of Medicine have been studying conditioned craving as well as other behavioral and physiological responses to drug-associated cues. For example, cocaine-dependent but not control subjects experienced a significant craving for cocaine, the desire for a cocaine-induced "rush" (see Chapter 12), and even the feeling of a "cocaine high" when watching a video that simulated a person obtaining, preparing, and then smoking crack cocaine (Childress et al., 1999) (**Figure 9.12**). Brain scans measuring regional cerebral blood flow during the video watching showed that these subjective responses were correlated with increased activation of the amygdala and the anterior cingulate cortex along with decreased activation of the basal ganglia. Thus, stimuli associated with the procurement and use of cocaine evoked craving and other drug-related responses as well as specific changes in brain activity. The conditioned nature of these responses is shown by the fact they occurred only in the cocaine-dependent subjects, not in control subjects who had not had any experience with this substance.

For drugs that produce significant physical and/or psychological dependence, such dependence undoubtedly is an important contributor to the maintenance of addiction because unpleasant withdrawal symptoms provide motivation to obtain and take the drug again. Nevertheless, the relative importance of this factor varies among different drugs. As mentioned earlier, some major drugs of abuse including cocaine do not produce strong physical dependence, although psychological dependence does occur in some users. In addition, drug-seeking behavior to obtain relief from withdrawal symptoms fails to explain relapse of addicts after they have gone through **drug detoxification** (elimination of the drug from one's system and passage through the abstinence syndrome). After the withdrawal symptoms have gone away, what still motivates an addict to take heroin again, for example? Research on addicts' self-reported reasons for returning to drug use as well as animal model studies such as depicted in Figure 9.8 suggest that many factors can contribute to relapse, including exposure to drug-related stimuli, stress, boredom, lack of other reinforcers, or simply a desire to "get high" again.

Discriminative stimulus effects contribute to drug-seeking behavior

Psychoactive drugs, including drugs of abuse, often produce powerful discriminative stimulus effects in animal studies (Ator and Griffiths, 2003). As summarized in Chapter 4, this means that drugs can produce internal states that can serve as cues controlling the

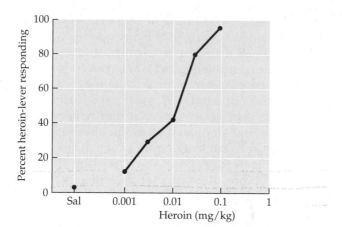

Figure 9.13 Dose-dependent discriminative stimulus effects of IV heroin in rhesus monkeys Monkeys were initially trained using a two-lever apparatus to discriminate IV heroin from saline vehicle (Sal) at a dose of either 0.03 or 0.1 mg/kg. Responses on the correct lever (heroin lever if the animals had received drug, saline lever if the animals had received saline) were reinforced with food. After acquisition of drug discrimination, the monkeys were tested on different doses of heroin to determine the dose necessary to elicit reliable responding on the heroin lever. Doses that elicited responding mainly on the saline lever presumably failed to produce a sufficient interoceptive cue to be detected by the animals. (After Platt et al., 2001.)

animal's behavior in a learning task. An example of drug discrimination is shown in **Figure 9.13**, which presents data showing the discrimination of different doses of IV heroin from saline vehicle in rhesus monkeys. Note that at the three lowest heroin doses, the animals mainly responded on the saline lever, indicating that those doses were not reliably discriminated from the vehicle. In contrast, 80% or more of the responses were made on the heroin lever at the two highest drug doses, demonstrating strong discrimination in that dose range. The discriminative stimulus effects of drugs in animals are considered to be analogous to the subjective effects that people experience when they take the same substances. Experienced users come to expect these subjective effects, and such expectations are thought to contribute to the persistence of drug-seeking and drug-using behaviors.

Addiction is a heritable disorder

Genetic variation is one of the likely sources of individual differences in vulnerability to addiction. Adoption and twin studies have yielded estimates of 0.3 to 0.8 for the **heritability** of substance use disorders (Urbanoski and Kelly, 2012). In the field of genetics, heritability is a mathematical term representing the estimated contribution of genetic variation within

a population to the total population variation for a particular trait (in this case, the trait is the presence or absence of a substance use disorder). Because the maximum heritability value is 1.0, it is clear that the remaining variability is due to environmental influences and gene x environment interactions.[7]

It is extremely important to recognize that there is no specific addiction gene, possession of which ensures that the individual will develop drug addiction. Rather, there appears to be a large number of genes that potentially influence susceptibility to addiction. Indeed, a literature review conducted several years ago by Li and colleagues (2008) found 1500 human genes that were identified in one or more studies as being addiction-related. Although many of these associations have not yet been replicated and thus may be spurious, there is reasonably strong evidence for a role for several genes in susceptibility to alcoholism or to tobacco addiction (Agrawal et al., 2012). Because alcohol and tobacco are legal substances, many more individuals are addicted to these substances than to cocaine or heroin for example, thereby providing large sample sizes for genetic analysis. For both alcoholism and tobacco addiction, the susceptibility genes include genes that code for enzymes involved in alcohol or nicotine metabolism. Receptors for dopamine (in the case of alcoholism) or acetylcholine (for nicotine) have also been implicated by genetic studies. When we say that a particular gene contributes to susceptibility to a substance use disorder, we mean that individuals who carry a specific **allele** (a particular form of a gene determined by differences in DNA sequence) of the gene are at increased risk of developing the disorder.

Broader analyses of genetic contributions to addiction have identified many potential susceptibility genes besides those mentioned above (Li et al., 2008; Uhl et al., 2008). Interestingly, the study by Li et al. found evidence for a common genetic involvement of five different molecular pathways across addictions to alcohol, nicotine, cocaine, and opiate drugs. Although it is beyond the scope of this chapter to discuss these pathways in detail, we note that one of them involves neurotransmitter–receptor interactions, another involves receptor signaling, and a third involves long-term potentiation (LTP; see Chapter 8).

---

[7]A gene x environment interaction occurs when a genetic contribution to a trait is only manifested in individuals who also experience a specific type of life event. For example, there might be evidence that a particular gene contributes to vulnerability for developing addiction in people who experience major stressful events in their life but not in people who don't have such experiences.

Psychosocial variables also contribute to addiction risk

It is important to consider individual differences in susceptibility to drug addiction not only at a biological level but also with respect to psychosocial variables (Kalant, 2009; Swendsen and Le Moal, 2011). We can categorize these variables as either increasing addiction risk or having a protective effect. Each category will be discussed in turn.

RISK FACTORS Many modulating factors can influence either the likelihood of someone becoming a drug addict or the probability that they will be able to achieve stable abstinence once addicted. For example, one survey relating sociodemographic variables to later development of a substance use disorder found increased risk to be associated with younger age, less education, nonwhite ethnicity, and lack of employment (Swendsen et al., 2009). The occurrence of stress and the ability of the person to cope with stress can also contribute to the risk for addiction. The life histories of drug addicts often show instances in which stressful events either promoted increased drug use or precipitated relapse from a previous period of abstinence. Numerous animal studies have confirmed that stress can increase the self-administration of abused drugs and can trigger renewed drug-taking behavior in models of relapse (Sinha, 2008; Stewart, 2000). For this reason, many treatment providers teach their clients new coping skills to deal with life stresses without relapsing.

Addicts and alcoholics are often diagnosed with an anxiety, mood, or personality disorder in addition to their drug problem (Swendsen and Le Moal, 2011). Such co-occurrences are called **comorbidity** in the medical literature. Some investigators have proposed that comorbid psychiatric disorders are causally related to addiction. For example, stressful life events could trigger anxiety and mood disorders such as depression, which in turn could lead to substance use in an attempt at self-medication. Indeed, this idea has sometimes been called the **self-medication hypothesis**. It predicts that individuals suffering from elevated anxiety should prefer alcohol and other sedative–anxiolytic drugs (**Figure 9.14**), whereas depressed individuals should seek out stimulant drugs such as cocaine or amphetamine. Also possible is a reverse direction of causality in which a substance use disorder gives rise to symptoms of anxiety and/or depressed mood. An alternative to these causal models is the hypothesis of **shared etiology**, which proposes that certain factors (genetic and/or environmental) contribute to an elevated risk of *both* addiction and other psychiatric disorders. Current evidence does not rule out any of these competing hypotheses.

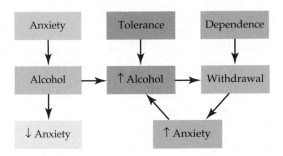

Figure 9.14 Self-medication hypothesis applied to the development of alcohol dependence Some people drink alcohol to alleviate anxiety. If anxiety is persistent and alcohol use continues, the onset of tolerance leads to increased alcohol consumption and potentially to the development of alcohol dependence. Attempts at abstinence now lead to withdrawal symptoms that include heightened anxiety, thereby provoking relapse to drinking. (After Lingford-Hughes et al., 2002.)

At the psychological level, there is an abundance of research on the relationship between personality variables and alcoholism or other types of drug addiction. Verheul and van den Brink (2000) proposed three different personality-related pathways to addiction: (1) behavioral disinhibition; (2) stress reduction; and (3) reward sensitivity. The behavioral disinihibition pathway hypothesizes that deviant behaviors such as substance abuse are linked to a trait cluster of impulsivity, antisociality, unconventionality, and aggressiveness, combined with low levels of constraint and harm avoidance. This pathway may be particularly relevant for drug abusers suffering from antisocial or borderline personality disorder. According to the stress reduction pathway, high scores on traits such as stress reactivity, anxiety, and neuroticism are indicative of heightened vulnerability to stressful life events. This pathway fits with the self-medication hypothesis mentioned above. The third pathway, termed reward sensitivity, relates drug abuse to the personality traits of sensation seeking, reward seeking, extraversion, and gregariousness. It suggests that individuals scoring high on these traits seek out drugs for their positive-reinforcing qualities.

Finally, familial and sociocultural influences can also influence the risk of developing a pattern of drug abuse or addiction. Familial factors have been studied most extensively in conjunction with the risk of alcoholism. For example, adult children of alcoholics are at increased risk for having alcohol or other substance abuse problems (Windle and Davies, 1999). In the case of alcohol itself, this may be related in part to modeling (imitation) of the parent's drinking behavior or to a heightened expectancy that drinking will lead to positive mood changes. Sociocultural studies have identified at least four different functions served by drug abuse (Thombs, 1999). The first involves social facilitation. Alcohol and other drugs are often consumed in a group setting, where the substance may enhance social bonds between participants. The second function is to remove the user from normal social roles and responsibilities, thereby allowing an escape from the burdens that may be associated with these responsibilities. Third, substance use may promote group solidarity within a particular ethnic group. A good example of this phenomenon is the association of Irish culture with heavy alcohol use and a high rate of alcoholism. Finally, substance abuse sometimes occurs within a "drug subculture" that embraces social rituals surrounding a particular subculture and rejects conventional social norms and lifestyles. Sociological studies have identified distinct subcultures for many different substances, including heroin, cocaine, alcohol, marijuana, methamphetamine, and PCP. This is not to say that all users of a particular substance participate in the rituals of a subculture, or that users necessarily limit themselves to just one substance. Nevertheless, one can find groups of individuals who share their common experiences with a specific drug of abuse, and who have a similar disdain for the "straight" lifestyle.

PROTECTIVE FACTORS   We can think about protective factors in drug addiction in two different ways. First, an absence of the various risk factors described in the previous section should be relatively protective with respect to drug abuse or addiction. Put another way, individuals who do not suffer from a preexisting personality or mood disorder, who do not exhibit the trait clusters mentioned earlier, who come from a stable family with no substance abuse, who do not belong to an ethnic group that promotes substance use, and who do not become involved in the social rituals surrounding drug use are at reduced risk for becoming addicted.

The second way that protective factors can operate is to help maintain a stable abstinence in previously drug-abusing or addicted individuals. Drug addicts who seek treatment tend to be the most heavily dependent and seriously affected individuals. Some will be able to overcome their dependence, but current research indicates that a majority will struggle with their drug problems for much of their remaining life. However, there is also ample evidence of alcoholics and drug addicts achieving long-term abstinence with little or no treatment (Bischof et al., 2001; Klingemann et al., 2009; Sobell et al., 2000). This has been termed **natural recovery** or spontaneous recovery. These individuals generally have less severe substance use problems than those seen by the treatment community. Even though this difference may be significant in facilitating spontaneous

recovery, very few recovered addicts report that they no longer have any desire for drugs. Therefore, it is important to know how the decision was made to stop drug use, and what experiences or actions may help protect these individuals from relapsing.

Recovered (i.e., stably abstinent) drug addicts and abusers recount many different tales of how they made and kept the decision to quit using drugs. It is often thought that the addict must hit "rock bottom" or go through an "existential crisis" before he'll be sufficiently motivated to stop using. Although this kind of experience is reported in some cases, many individuals find the means to abstain without reaching such a crisis situation. Spontaneous recovery from drug abuse or addiction may be triggered by a variety of major life changes. Some of these are positive changes such as marriage or having a spiritual/religious experience, whereas others are negative consequences of drug use such as health problems, financial problems, loss of one's job, social pressures, fear of imprisonment, or death of a drug-abusing friend. Once the decision has been made, the risk of relapse is reduced by such actions as moving to a new area, developing new social relationships with nonusers, obtaining employment, and engaging in substitute activities like physical exercise or meditation. The relative importance of different factors varies somewhat with different drugs of abuse. For example, health concerns are particularly important in motivating tobacco smokers to stop smoking, and, much more than other drug users, smokers cite simple willpower as a critical factor in maintaining abstinence (Walters, 2000).

In conclusion, achievement of stable abstinence either spontaneously or with the aid of treatment is greatly facilitated by certain behavioral changes that help protect the drug addict from relapse. Some of these changes involve avoidance of drug-associated cues (e.g., moving to a new location and shunning drug-using acquaintances), whereas other changes serve to provide substitutes for the former substance use, new sources of reinforcement, a new social support network, financial stability, and general structure to the individual's life.

The factors contributing to drug addiction can be combined into a biopsychosocial model

Figure 9.15 summarizes the effects of the factors discussed in this section on the development and maintenance of compulsive drug use (i.e., addiction). You can see that some of these factors promote the likelihood that addiction may occur, whereas others reduce this likelihood. A model that includes the full range of pharmacological, biological, and psychological/sociocultural factors that influence addiction risk

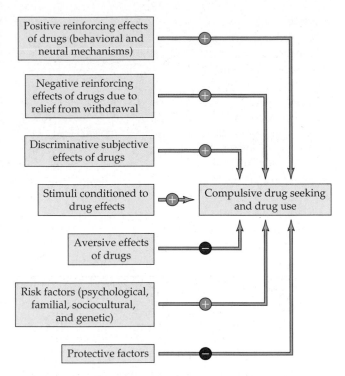

Figure 9.15 A biopsychosocial model of drug addiction (After Stolerman, 1992.)

can be called a **biopsychosocial model** of addiction. Although it is beyond the scope of this text to propose a detailed model of this kind, we believe that consideration of all such factors, crossing multiple levels of analysis, is necessary for achieving an adequate understanding of the addiction process.

Section Summary

- Several types of factors contribute to the development and maintenance of compulsive drug seeking and drug use.

- Most abused drugs produce positive reinforcing effects in humans and experimental animals, as shown by IV self-administration. The reinforcing efficacy of a drug can be investigated by means of a dose–response function (which typically yields an inverted U-shaped curve) or preferably by means of breaking point determination using a progressive-ratio schedule.

- In animals that have been trained to self-administer a drug by performing an operant response (e.g., a lever-press) and then have been extinguished on that response, renewed responding can be provoked by administering a priming dose of the drug, presenting a stimulus cue that was previously paired with drug delivery, or stressing the animal. This procedure is called reinstatement of

drug-seeking behavior and is considered to be an experimental model of relapse in an abstinent addict.

- The rewarding effects of drugs are studied using place-conditioning procedures, as well as the effects of drugs on the threshold for electrical self-stimulation of the brain. Acute administration of most abused drugs leads to a reduction in the self-stimulation threshold, whereas withdrawal from drug exposure in dependent animals leads to an increase in the threshold.

- Drugs also sometimes produce aversive effects, although these may not be sufficiently strong to outweigh other factors that promote compulsive drug use.

- Koob and Le Moal proposed that in the development of addiction, drug-taking behavior progresses from an impulsive stage (primary motivation for drug use is the positive reinforcing effect) to a compulsive stage (primary motivation is negative reinforcement from alleviation of unpleasant withdrawal symptoms). This shift is hypothesized to involve the recruitment of an anti-reward system in the brain.

- Through conditioning, environmental stimuli can elicit either drug-like or drug-opposite effects, both of which can motivate subsequent drug-seeking and drug-taking behavior.

- Psychoactive drugs, including drugs of abuse, can produce discriminative stimulus effects in animals that are thought to correspond to the subjective effects produced by these same compounds in human users. Experienced users come to expect these subjective effects, and such expectations are thought to contribute to the persistence of drug use.

- Addiction is a heritable disorder. There is no addiction gene per se; rather, specific alleles of many different genes are believed to contribute to the risk for development of addiction.

- Psychosocial variables may either increase addiction risk or have a protective effect. One risk factor is suffering from an anxiety, mood, or personality disorder. Some investigators have proposed a self-medication hypothesis that addicts are using drugs to treat the symptoms of a pre-existing psychiatric disorder. However, alternate hypotheses such as shared etiology have been put forth to explain the high comorbidity of such disorders with addiction.

- Personality variables such as impulsivity, antisociality, anxiety, high stress reactivity, sensation seeking, and extraversion have been associated with various pathways to drug addiction. The risk of becoming an addict is also affected by familial and

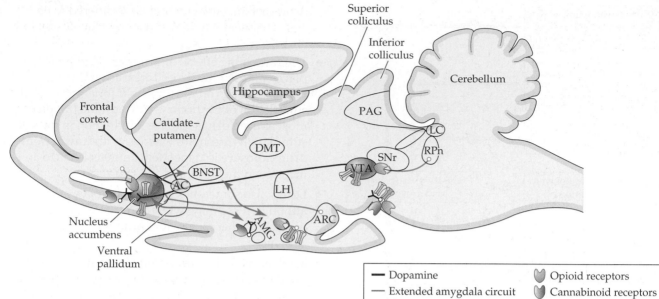

Figure 9.16 **The neural circuit responsible for the acute rewarding and reinforcing effects of abused drugs** Also shown are additional brain areas that provide points of reference for anatomical orientation. AC, anterior commissure; AMG, amygdala; ARC, arcuate nucleus of the hypothalamus; BNST, bed nucleus of the stria terminalis; DMT, dorsomedial nucleus of the thalamus; LC, locus coeruleus; LH, lateral hypothalamus; PAG, periaqueductal gray; RPn, reticular pontine nucleus; SNr, substantia nigra pars reticulata; VTA, ventral tegmental area. (After Koob and Volkow, 2010.)

sociocultural influences. For example, drugs may promote social facilitation, remove the user from normal social roles and responsibilities, promote solidarity within a particular ethnic group, or lead to association with a specific drug subculture.

- Finally, various protective factors can reduce the likelihood of an individual becoming addicted or can help prevent relapse in drug users attempting to maintain stable abstinence. These factors encompass the person's personality structure, social (including family) life, and environment. It seems possible for some substance abusers to achieve abstinence without formal treatment; however, heavily dependent individuals typically need the assistance of a structured treatment program.

- Combining the full range of pharmacological, biological, and psychological/sociocultural factors that influence addiction risk can be called a biopsychosocial model of addiction.

The Neurobiology of Drug Addiction

Research conducted over the past few decades has made tremendous progress in elucidating the neurobiological mechanisms that underlie the development of addiction. Much of this progress has been driven by technological advances in areas such as molecular pharmacology and neuroimaging. There is still much to learn; however, researchers are coming ever closer to understanding how drugs of abuse acutely alter brain function and, more importantly, how repeated exposure to these same substances can produce long-lasting changes in the brain that may lead to compulsive drug use, even in the presence of adverse consequences to the user (i.e., substance use disorder in

the *DSM-5*). We will first discuss the neurochemical mechanisms of drug reinforcement, including a particularly important role for dopamine (DA). Then we will summarize current information on the neuroadaptations produced by repeated drug exposure and how such changes in the brain are thought to underlie escalating drug use. In the third part of this section, we discuss the behavioral functions of the prefrontal cortex (PFC) and evidence for structural and functional abnormalities in this brain area in addiction. Finally, we address the question of whether addiction should be considered a disease.

Drug reward and reinforcement are mediated by a complex neuroanatomical and neurochemical circuit

Studies conducted primarily using rats and mice have allowed researchers to construct a **reward circuit** that mediates the acute rewarding and reinforcing effects (defined operationally as described previously) of most abused drugs. **Figure 9.16** depicts this circuit

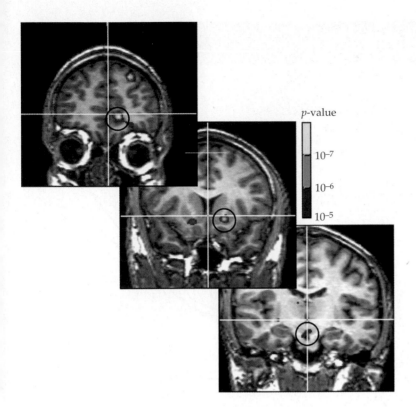

Figure 9.17 Activation of the human reward circuit by expectation of monetary rewards Subjects were given a task in which presentation of different visual cues signaled a low, medium, or high probability of either losing or winning a variable amount of money ($0.0, $1.00, or $5.00) on that trial. Regional brain activation was assessed on each trial type using functional magnetic resonance imaging (fMRI). The circled regions on the images presented here demonstrate that the medial prefrontal cortex (MPFC), nucleus accumbens (NAcc), and ventral tegmental area (VTA) all showed activation that was positively correlated with the expected value of the reward. The color scale is coded so that yellow represents the greatest degree of activation, followed by orange and then red. (From Haber and Knutson, 2010; original data from Knutson et al., 2005.)

superimposed on a sagittal section of a rodent brain. Anatomical pathways contained within this circuit include the mesolimbic and mesocortical DA pathways (shown in red) that originate in the ventral tegmental area (VTA) of the midbrain and terminate in the nucleus accumbens (NAcc), amygdala (AMG), and frontal cortex (FC). Other important connections are those within the extended amygdala system (shown in blue)—a collection of anatomically and functionally linked structures that includes the central nucleus of the amygdala, the shell of the NAcc, and the bed nucleus of the stria terminalis (BNST). Two additional pathways within the reward circuit are not shown in the figure for the purpose of clarity: the medial forebrain bundle (MFB), a collection of ascending and descending fibers that connects the VTA with areas

of the ventral forebrain including the NAcc, septal area, and olfactory tubercle; and an output pathway from the NAcc to the ventral pallidum (VP). It is important to note that neuroimaging studies have confirmed that the human brain possesses a reward circuit similar to that identified in animals, and that this circuit is activated by both drug and non-drug rewards (Haber and Knutson, 2010) (**Figure 9.17**).

The reward circuit can also be characterized neurochemically by considering the locations within the circuit that contain the specific molecular targets for each type of abused drug. For example, psychostimulants such as cocaine and amphetamine exert their rewarding effects by increasing transmission at the dopaminergic terminals in the NAcc (see Chapter 12). Opioid drugs (e.g., morphine and heroin) and endogenous opioid peptides (endorphins and enkephalins) activate the reward circuit by stimulating opioid receptors in the VTA, NAcc, and AMG (see Chapter 11). Opioid reward is mediated by a combination of DA-dependent (through increased DA release) and DA-independent mechanisms. Alcohol enhances the action of γ-aminobutyric acid (GABA) on $GABA_A$ receptors, and this enhances DA release in the NAcc and opioid peptide release in the VTA, NAcc, and AMG (see Chapter 10). Nicotine derived from tobacco activates the reward circuit by stimulating nicotinic cholinergic receptors in the VTA, NAcc, and AMG (see Chapter 13), whereas endogenous cannabinoids and $Δ^9$-tetrahydrocannabinol (THC) derived from marijuana are rewarding because of stimulation of cannabinoid receptors in the same brain areas (see Chapter 14). Both nicotine and THC enhance DA release in the NAcc through local mechanisms and/or by acting within the VTA.

The mesolimbic DA pathway from the VTA to the NAcc has been accorded a central role in drug reward and reinforcement. Animal studies have shown that virtually all drugs of abuse activate this pathway either by enhancing VTA cell firing or by increasing extracellular DA levels in the NAcc. Although there is widespread agreement that DA has an important role in the rewarding effects of both drugs and natural rewards like food, the exact nature of this role is still being debated (**Box 9.2**). Moreover, the dopaminergic system is *essential* for drug reward only for some substances (e.g., cocaine or amphetamine) and not for others (e.g., heroin or alcohol) (Koob and Volkow, 2010). It is important to note that the endogenous opioid and cannabinoid systems are also involved in the

BOX 9.2   The Cutting Edge

What Is the Role of Dopamine in Drug Reward?

There is strong agreement among addiction researchers that activation of dopaminergic transmission, particularly in the mesolimbic pathway, plays an important role in the rewarding and reinforcing effects of abused drugs. However, the nature of this role has been a point of debate for many years. In this box, we discuss several of the major theories regarding the relationship of DA to reward and summarize key experimental findings that either support or argue against each theory.

Components of Reward

"Reward" is not a unitary construct. Rather, it is composed of three broad components: emotion/affect, motivation, and learning/cognition (Berridge and Robinson, 2003). The emotional/affective component refers to subjective feelings of pleasure, which is the component that we think of most commonly when we use the term "reward." The motivational component of reward refers to the desire to obtain various types of incentives (e.g., food, water, shelter, a sexual partner, or drugs), the ability of sensory stimuli to acquire strong motivational properties (incentive salience), and the goal-directed actions aimed at obtaining incentives. The learning/cognitive component refers to the expectation (based on experience) that a particular action will lead to attainment of an incentive (reward expectancy) and strengthening of specific stimulus–response associations based on delivery of the incentive (reward learning). In theory, DA could be involved in any or all of these reward components, which helps explain why different theories have been proposed with respect to the role of this transmitter in reward.

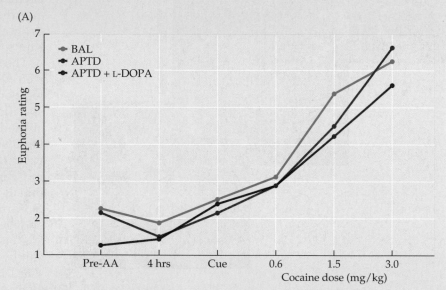

(A)

(A) No effect of catecholamine depletion on cocaine-induced euphoria Experienced cocaine users were divided into three groups on the basis of oral administration of an amino acid mixture that differed in composition: (1) group BAL received a balanced mixture that contained phenylalanine and tyrosine (catecholamine precursors) along with other standard dietary amino acids; (2) group APTD (acute phenylalanine-tyrosine depletion) received an amino acid mixture that was similar to BAL, except that it lacked phenylalanine and tyrosine; and (3) group APTD + DOPA received the same APTD amino acid mixture but was subsequently given two doses of L-DOPA before testing. The APTD manipulation is designed to deplete brain DA by reducing precursor availability, whereas the L-DOPA treatment was expected to reverse such depletion by bypassing the tyrosine hydroxylase step in the synthetic pathway (see Chapter 5). At the time points shown in the figure, the subjects were asked to rate their feelings of euphoria before administration of the amino acid mixture (pre-AA), 4 hours later, after presentation of cocaine-related paraphernalia (Cue), and then after intranasal self-administration (snorting) of increasing doses of cocaine. Although the drug produced a dose-dependent increase in feelings of euphoria, this response was unaffected by differences in the amino acid mixture. (After Leyton et al., 2005.)

Dopamine As the "Pleasure Transmitter"

The first proposed theory of DA's role in reward, and the theory that is most commonly seen in the lay press, is that release of DA in the NAcc produces feelings of pleasure by the organism. In the case of drugs, the corresponding feeling would be the euphoria or "high" experienced after taking the substance. One of the first investigators to associate DA with pleasure was the pharmacologist Roy Wise, who in his seminal 1980 paper stated, "The dopamine synapse qualifies as a reasonable candidate for the site in the brain where the *hedonic impact* [emphasis added] of the sensory message is first associated with the sense impressions of the external events which constitute natural rewards" (Wise, 1980, p. 94). Because of its alluring simplicity, this idea has continued to hold sway in the popular imagination. In short, DA makes you feel good! Unfortunately, there

BOX 9.2 *(continued)*

is considerable evidence arguing against this hypothesis. For example, Leyton et al. (2005) tested the subjective effects of intranasal cocaine in experienced users, some of whom had undergone prior depletion of catecholamines (including DA) before drug administration. Although catecholamine depletion blunted the subjects' craving for cocaine, it had no influence on cocaine-induced euphoria (Figure A). These and other findings both in humans and in experimental animals indicate that the hedonic aspects of naturally occurring and pharmacological rewards are relatively unaffected by dopaminergic manipulations (Berridge, 2007; Berridge et al., 2009). On the other hand, rodent studies have shown that facial responses to a sweet (rewarding) taste can be enhanced by local application of opioid drugs, cannabinoids, and benzodiazepines (but not by dopaminergic agents) at specific sites in the reward circuit, including areas within the NAcc and the ventral pallidum (Berridge and Kringelbach, 2008). These so-called affective "hot spots" may be key sites where synaptic transmission encodes the neural representation of pleasurable stimuli, and thus it is noteworthy that DA does not seem to be one of the neurotransmitters involved in such encoding. Although we don't yet know whether the same hot spots exist in the human brain, Berridge and Kringelbach (2008) point out that facial expressions seen in rats given the sweet stimulus (e.g., tongue protrusion) are similar in form to the expressions observed in human infants exposed to the same taste. This finding at least raises the possibility that similar neural mechanisms may be involved in these positive hedonic responses.

The evidence presented above argues against DA encoding the hedonic aspect of reward. Yet, recent findings in rodents using

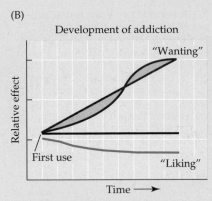

(B)

Development of addiction

(B) Sensitization of drug "wanting" but not drug "liking" is proposed to contribute to the development of addiction. The horizontal line represents the initial relative levels of "liking" and "wanting" during first use of the drug. (After Berridge et al., 2009.)

a relatively new and powerful experimental approach known as **optogenetics** seem to demand a re-evaluation of this view. Readers who are interested in learning more about optogenetic methods and their application to the study of DA and reward are directed to **Web Box 9.3**.

Dopamine As a Mediator of Incentive Salience

Berridge (2007) has hypothesized that DA is important for the *incentive salience* quality of rewards rather than for their hedonic properties. The concept of incentive salience is a key component of the **incentive sensitization** theory of addiction first proposed by Robinson and Berridge in 1993 and updated in subsequent reviews (e.g., Robinson and Berridge, 2000, 2008). A key feature of this theory is the distinction between drug *liking* (i.e., the euphoric feeling or "high") and drug *wanting* (i.e., craving). The psychological process leading to "wanting" is called incentive salience, because it is a process whereby certain stimuli (in this case, internal and external stimuli associated with drug use)

become extremely salient (attention-getting) and acquire incentive (attractive and desirable) properties. The incentive sensitization theory proposes that over the course of developing a drug addiction, the user experiences a marked increase in "wanting" the drug even though there is no change or even decrease in drug "liking" (Figure B). This disparity is thought to occur because different brain mechanisms are responsible for these two components of drug reward, and repeated drug use causes sensitization of the "wanting" system but no sensitization or even tolerance in the "liking" system. Berridge and Kringelbach (2008) argue that the "liking" system is focused on the restricted hedonic hot spots mentioned above, whereas the "wanting" system is a more widespread circuit that includes the mesolimbic DA pathway. Evidence of a relationship between DA and drug "wanting" comes from a variety of animal and human studies, including the previously mentioned cocaine study of Leyton and coworkers (2005), which found a reduction in cocaine craving ("wanting") after catecholamine depletion despite no effect on cocaine-induced euphoria ("liking").

Dopamine and Reward Prediction

Yet another hypothesis regarding the relationship between DA and reward has been proposed by Schultz (2010) largely on the basis of electrophysiological recording of the firing of midbrain DA neurons (substantia nigra and VTA) in awake monkeys under different behavioral conditions. As illustrated in Figure C, these cells showed a burst of activity in response to a novel sensory stimulus or an unsignaled (unexpected) reward such as a food treat. Interestingly, if the reward was paired in

(Continued on next page)

BOX 9.2 (continued)

(C)

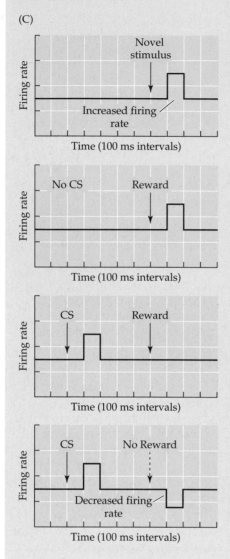

(C) Dopamine cell firing under various behavioral conditions Under baseline conditions, midbrain DA cells in monkeys fire intermittently at a low rate, as depicted by the straight horizontal lines. Brief (about 100 ms long) bursts of firing occur in response to novel stimuli (A), presentation of an unexpected reward (B), and presentation of a CS associated with reward (C). If an expected reward is withheld, DA cell firing is transiently suppressed (D).

a classical conditioning paradigm with a conditioned stimulus (CS) so that the CS reliably predicted the reward, DA cell firing came to be elicited by the CS rather than by the reward itself. Finally, if the conditioned monkeys were presented with the CS and then no reward followed, there was actually a depression in DA cell firing. According to Schultz, therefore, one of the key functions of DA neuronal firing is to signal the difference between prediction and actual occurrence of rewards (i.e., it encodes *reward-prediction error*). An unpredicted reward leads to increased firing, a predicted reward causes no change, and failure of a reward to occur after it is predicted leads to a brief depression in cellular activity. This reward-related role of DA seems to be linked to rapid and short-lived bursts of cell firing that cause large but transient increases in synaptic DA levels. Recent findings

additionally suggest that GABA neurons in the VTA interact with the DA neurons in their reward-prediction error function (Cohen et al., 2012). Other functions of DA that are disrupted in patients with Parkinson's disease (see Chapter 21) or in animals with neurotoxic lesions of the dopaminergic system (see Chapter 5) may be linked instead to the lower levels of synaptic DA produced by slow and steady firing of the neurons under baseline conditions (Schultz, 2007).

In conclusion, it seems likely that the role of DA in reward will continue to be debated for some time to come. Because there are multiple components of reward, DA may be involved in more than one aspect of this construct. Indeed, perhaps the role of DA in reward varies depending on the context. In such a global model, we could hypothesize that DA encodes hedonic state (i.e., pleasure) when the organism is engaged in consummatory behavior, DA mediates attribution of incentive salience when the organism is evaluating a variety of incentives in the environment, and DA functions as a reward-prediction error signal when the organism is awaiting an expected reward. Studies that evaluate multiple functions of this neurotransmitter are needed to test the validity of such a global hypothesis of dopaminergic function in reward.

---

rewarding effects of many abused drugs. Indeed, drug reward often can be blunted or even blocked by interfering with either of those systems (Solinas et al., 2008; Trigo et al., 2010).

Neuroadaptive responses to repeated drug exposure are thought to underlie the development of addiction

The rewarding effects of abused drugs clearly play an important role in the initial motivation to use these substances, and such effects presumably continue

to underlie subsequent controlled drug use in the casual or recreational user who has not developed a substance use disorder. However, most addiction researchers believe that other motivational processes come into play when repeated drug use culminates in a compulsive "need" for the drug, along with the other features of substance use disorder (i.e., addiction) noted in *DSM-IV* and *DSM-5*. There is good reason to believe that this motivational transition is caused by long-term changes in the brain that result from exposure to the drugs themselves. These **neuroadaptations** are manifested at multiple levels

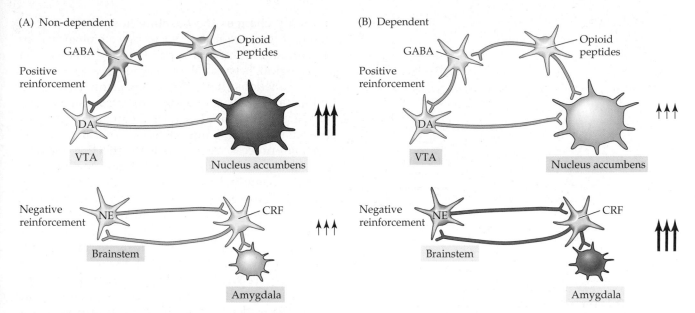

Figure 9.18 Neurochemical changes underlying the transition from positive to negative reinforcement in addiction (A) In a non-dependent individual, drug use is supported mainly by positive reinforcement mediated by the reward system (large arrows) and relatively little by the anti-reward system (small arrows). The part of the reward system involving dopamine (DA) and opioid peptides in the nucleus accumbens is illustrated. (B) In a dependent individual, the reward system has been down-regulated and the anti-reward system has been recruited. As a result, drug use is now supported mainly by negative reinforcement (alleviation of withdrawal symptoms). The part of the anti-reward system involving NE and CRF acting in the central amygdala is illustrated. VTA, ventral tegmental area. (After Koob, 2009.)

encompassing alterations in cellular structure, neural circuitry, neurotransmitter activity, and gene expression. Here we discuss some of the prominent neuro-adaptive changes that have been proposed to underlie the transition from recreational drug use to compulsive drug use in addiction.

RECRUITMENT OF THE ANTI-REWARD SYSTEM One of the major theories of addiction-related neuroadaptations was proposed by George Koob and Michel Le Moal (see reviews by Koob and Le Moal, 2008a, 2008b; Koob, 2009). These investigators suggest that two types of neuroadaptations occur in the transition to addiction. *Within-system* neuroadaptations take place within the reward circuit and constitute a progressive down-regulation of activity in this circuit. We can conceptualize this process as a type of tolerance such that the user experiences less and less pleasure from each episode of drug use. Indeed, addicts often report that they need to take drugs just to feel "normal" instead of feeling "high," as they did before becoming addicted. In contrast, *between-system* neuroadaptations involve the gradual recruitment of a

neural circuit that Koob and Le Moal call the **anti-reward system**. The neuroanatomical substrate of the anti-reward system is the previously mentioned extended amygdala, which includes the bed nucleus of the stria terminalis, the central nucleus of the amygdala, and part of the nucleus accumbens. However, the neurotransmitters involved in this system are very different from those that mediate reward. Instead, activation of the anti-reward system leads to increased release of norepinephrine (NE) and two neuropeptides, corticotropin-releasing factor (CRF) and dynorphin. This system has two major functions: it puts a limit or brake on reward (imagine a situation in which the hedonic effects of natural rewards like food and sex were unlimited), and it mediates some of the aversive effects of stress (e.g., increased anxiety). In a drug-dependent person or experimental animal, the anti-reward system is activated during drug withdrawal and plays a major role in the aversive effects of withdrawal and the negative reinforcement produced by renewed drug taking. **Figure 9.18** illustrates some of the key neurochemical components involved in drug reward before dependence (addiction) has occurred (i.e., dominance of positive reinforcement mediated by the reward system) compared with after dependence has taken place (i.e., dominance of negative reinforcement mediated by the anti-reward system). This model is particularly applicable to drugs that produce strong physical dependence, such as alcohol and opiates, although increased CRF in the central nucleus of the amygdala has also been implicated in animal models of cocaine and nicotine dependence (Koob and Le Moal, 2008a).

The opposing actions of the reward and anti-reward systems have been conceptualized by Koob and Le Moal as a modern updating of the classical **opponent-process model** of motivation proposed many years ago

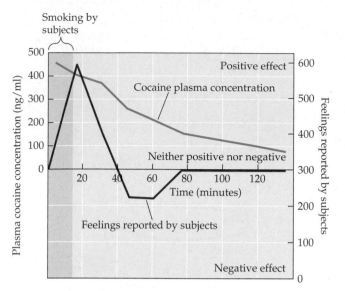

Figure 9.19 Euphoric followed by dysphoric feelings reported by subjects smoking cocaine paste Cocaine paste is a crude extract of coca leaves containing 30% to 90% cocaine base. The graph shows the time course of plasma cocaine concentrations and reported positive or negative mood from a representative subject who smoked cocaine paste (amount not reported) during the time shown in the figure. Note that even though cocaine was still present in the subject's system, the positive hedonic effect of the drug ended by 40 minutes and was replaced by a negative hedonic state (the "crash") characterized by feelings of fatigue, depression, anxiety, and cocaine craving that lasted the next 35 minutes. (After Van Dyke and Byck, 1982.)

by Solomon and Corbit (Solomon and Corbit, 1974; Solomon, 1977). The opponent-process model hypothesized that the neural mechanisms responsible for affect (mood and emotion) were organized such that any stimulus that provokes an initial strong affective reaction (e.g., a strong feeling of either pleasure or discomfort) automatically sets in motion an opposing affective response that is experienced after the initial stimulus ends. Think, for example, of the sequence of feelings produced by performing a dangerous physical activity such as skydiving for the first time: initial fear or anxiety followed by a pleasurable sense of relief after completion of the action. In the case of an abused drug, the primary affective response might be the "high," and the subsequent opposing response would be the dysphoric withdrawal reaction after the drug wears off (**Figure 9.19**). Solomon and Corbit (1974) further proposed that over time, repeated presentations of the stimulus altered the opponent process by strengthening its magnitude, reducing its latency to onset, and increasing its duration.

In applying the opponent-process model to addiction, Koob and Le Moal (2008a, 2008b) additionally hypothesized that a phenomenon called **allostasis**

gradually changes the baseline hedonic state (i.e., mood) of the drug user. Allostasis is a biological concept introduced by Sterling and Eyer (1988) in which a physiological, behavioral, or psychological variable (in this case, hedonic state) that is repeatedly challenged (in this case, by drug exposure) maintains stability by changing its set-point (its normal baseline level in the absence of the challenge). Figure 9.20 illustrates the opponent-process view of hedonic affective responses to a drug under different conditions, including an allostatic change in baseline hedonic state produced by repeated drug exposure. In a non-dependent organism, drug taking leads to an initial positive hedonic response (upward deflection of the line) that gradually wanes over time and is replaced by a negative (unpleasant) response (downward deflection) during drug withdrawal (**Figure 9.20A**). Finally, the organism returns to its baseline hedonic state. Once the organism has become dependent (addicted), the allostatic set-point has shifted downward (0') so that the baseline mood in the absence of the drug is negative (i.e., depressed mood, irritability, or anxiety is experienced) (**Figure 9.20B**). The positive hedonic response to the drug now barely crosses the neutral point (0), and thus the organism experiences only a small rewarding effect of the drug. Note the severe and protracted negative hedonic effect of drug withdrawal (strengthening of the opponent process), which produces powerful motivation to take the drug again. **Figure 9.20C** depicts drug-taking binges during withdrawal, during which the starting hedonic point (0'') is even lower, and the drug response only reaches neutrality (i.e., the addict takes the drug to feel "normal"). Finally, **Figure 9.20D** depicts relapse after prolonged abstinence from drug use. Because of long-lasting drug-induced neuroadaptations, the baseline mood remains low (0') but the positive hedonic response to the drug is actually strengthened. This hypothesized strengthening is based on the finding that in animals trained to self-administer a drug like cocaine, and then subjected to forced abstinence for a long time, re-exposure to the drug leads to a powerful enhancement of drug-seeking behavior.

ALTERED STRIATAL AND CORTICAL CIRCUITRY   In addition to recruitment of the anti-reward system, repeated drug exposure produces other changes in neural circuitry that contribute to the development of addiction. One such change is a transition from the NAcc (part of the ventral striatum) to the dorsal striatum (caudate-putamen) as a key control area for drug-taking behavior (Everitt et al., 2008). Because of strong evidence implicating the dorsal striatum in stimulus–response habit learning, this transition is proposed to play a significant role in the progression of drug taking from a reward-motivated behavior to a behavior that is automatic, habitual, and even

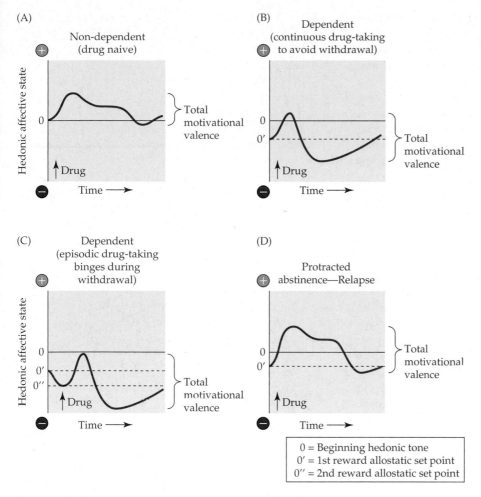

(A) Non-dependent (drug naive)

(B) Dependent (continuous drug-taking to avoid withdrawal)

(C) Dependent (episodic drug-taking binges during withdrawal)

(D) Protracted abstinence—Relapse

0 = Beginning hedonic tone
0' = 1st reward allostatic set point
0'' = 2nd reward allostatic set point

Figure 9.20 Hedonic responses to drug use during different stages of the addiction cycle (A) Drug use in a non-dependent individual produces a strong positive hedonic response (mood elevation) with a relatively weak opponent process (negative hedonic response) during withdrawal. (B) Development of a dependent (addicted) state leads to an allostatic reduction in hedonic set-point, a shorter positive hedonic response that reaches only a small elevation above neutrality, and a stronger and prolonged opponent process during withdrawal. (C) In a dependent individual undergoing episodic drug-taking binges to alleviate withdrawal, the allostatic set-point is even lower because of lingering withdrawal symptoms, and the positive hedonic response to the drug reaches only the original baseline of neutral hedonic tone. (D) After protracted abstinence, the hedonic set-point remains lower but the positive hedonic response is enhanced for reasons explained in the text. Note that the "total motivational valence," which represents the full range from positive to negative hedonic tone under each state and the motivational impulses driven by these changes, is expanded once the organism has become drug dependent. (After Koob and Le Moal, 2008a.)

compulsive. Related to this alteration in striatal function is a functional disruption of the glutamatergic pathway from the PFC to the NAcc. Experimental animal studies have shown that chronic treatment with cocaine or other abused drugs causes complex biochemical changes in glutamate homeostasis at the PFC–accumbens synapses (Kalivas, 2009). By interfering with normal transmission in this pathway, such changes impair the ability of the PFC to mediate response inhibition and impulse control. We don't yet know if the same glutamatergic dysregulation occurs in the development of addiction in human drug users. However, a later section of this chapter presents neuroimaging results that demonstrate impaired PFC function in drug addicts. Thus, it is possible that addiction involves abnormalities at the level of both the PFC and the synapses connecting this area with the NAcc.

GENETIC, EPIGENETIC, AND PROTEIN REGULATION Drugs of abuse exert powerful effects on the expression of many genes and, therefore, on the levels of the proteins encoded by those genes. A general conception of drug effects on gene/protein expression is shown in Figure 9.21. The pattern shown in **Figure 9.21A** represents changes in neural proteins that are rapidly increased (or decreased in some cases) by initial drug exposure, but exhibit tolerance to subsequent exposures. The pattern in **Figure 9.21B** is representative of other proteins that may accumulate with repeated drug exposures but then return to baseline either rapidly or more slowly during prolonged abstinence. Finally, the pattern shown in **Figure 9.21C** occurs for a small number of proteins that may accumulate and remain persistently elevated for a long time in the absence of further drug-taking behavior. It is reasonable to assume that proteins in category A help to mediate acute drug-induced behavioral and physiological responses that undergo tolerance when episodes of use occur frequently. Category B proteins could, over time, play a role in the transition from recreational use to addiction, and proteins in category C might be important for maintaining the "addicted" state in the sense of persistent vulnerability to relapse even after a long period of abstinence.

Here we will focus on the transitional proteins of category B, because category A proteins (which include many molecules involved in cell signaling and second messenger systems) by themselves cannot mediate the development of addiction, and some of the major category C proteins identified thus far are structural proteins necessary for long-lasting drug-induced synaptic changes (e.g., increased growth of dendritic spines in the NAcc). Within category B, one particular protein stands out, namely, a transcription factor called **ΔFosB**. As you learned in Chapter 2, transcription factors are proteins located in the cell nucleus that either stimulate or inhibit expression of a target gene (i.e., the rate of mRNA transcription from that gene) and accordingly up- or down-regulate levels of the protein encoded by the gene. ΔFosB is a member of the Fos family of transcription factors that are rapidly induced in areas such as the NAcc and the dorsal striatum after administration of many different drugs of abuse including cocaine, amphetamine, methamphetamine, alcohol, opiates, and cannabinoids. Whereas most Fos proteins show only a transient response to drug administration and tolerance during repeated drug use episodes (i.e., they belong to category A), ΔFosB gradually accumulates in certain cells including a subset of neurons within the NAcc (Nestler, 2008). This accumulation, which lasts for at least several weeks after the last drug administration, occurs because the protein has a very long half-life once it has been synthesized by the cell.

The behavioral relevance of ΔFosB accumulation has been investigated using mice that have been genetically engineered to overexpress this protein selectively in the same NAcc and dorsal striatum cells that normally show ΔFosB induction in response to drug administration. Compared with wild-type mice, ΔFosB-overexpressing animals show enhanced sensitivity to a variety of drug effects with the exception of morphine-induced analgesia (**Table 9.5**). Some of the proteins regulated by ΔFosB are involved in glutamate transmission and structural plasticity (e.g., increased

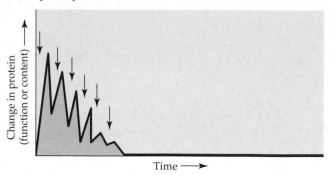

(A) Rapid response and tolerance

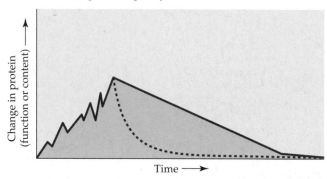

(B) Accumulating and temporary abstinence

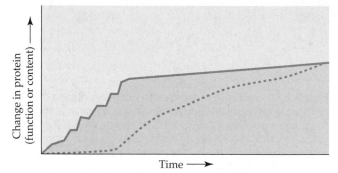

(C) Enduring in abstinence

Figure 9.21 Patterns of neuroadaptive protein expression with repeated drug exposure (A) Some proteins respond to drug administration (downward arrows) with an increase (or decrease; not shown) in expression, a rapid return to baseline levels, and tolerance to repeated episodes of use. (B) Proteins in this category accumulate with repeated drug use episodes and then return to baseline either slowly (solid line) or quickly (dashed line) during temporary abstinence before drug use recurs. (C) Proteins in this category show a persistent accumulation, usually following repeated drug use episodes (solid line) or alternatively during abstinence (dashed line). (After Kalivas and O'Brien, 2008.)

dendritic branching and dendritic spine density) within the NAcc (Nestler, 2008). Together with pharmacological results indicating enhanced drug reward and sensitization following ΔFosB overexpression, these findings support the idea that ΔFosB may play a significant role in the transition from controlled drug use to addiction.

TABLE 9.4 Behavioral Phenotype of Drug Responses in Mutant Mice[a] Compared with Wild-type Mice

Drug	Phenotype
Cocaine	Increased locomotor response to acute administration
	Increased locomotor sensitization to repeated administration
	Conditioned place preference at lower doses
	Acquisition of self-administration at lower doses
	Higher breaking-point of self-administration under a progressive ratio schedule
Morphine	Conditioned place preference at lower doses
	Increased development of physical dependence and withdrawal
	Decreased analgesia to initial exposure and more rapid tolerance
Alcohol	Increased anxiolytic (anxiety-reducing) responses

Source: Nestler, 2008.

[a]The mutant mice overexpress ΔFosB in the NAcc and dorsal striatum.

The behavioral effects produced by elevated ΔFosB are mediated by long-term changes in the synthesis of proteins whose genes are regulated by this transcription factor. What are the mechanisms by which this occurs? The answer seems to be that ΔFosB modulates gene (and ultimately protein) expression through epigenetic mechanisms (Nestler, 2008). As you learned in Chapter 2, epigenetics involves chromatin modifications that alter gene expression without changing the nucleotide sequence of the DNA strand. These modifications are of two types: methylation of the DNA at specific cytosines (the C in the genetic alphabet AGCT) in the promoter region of the gene, or various modifications of the histone proteins that form complexes around which the DNA double helix is wrapped. The best-studied type of histone modification is acetylation, or the attachment of acetyl groups to specific sites along the tail of the protein (see Figure 2.6). DNA methylation usually promotes compaction of the chromatin, thereby repressing gene expression, whereas histone acetylation facilitates gene expression by opening the chromatin and allowing the transcriptional machinery to bind to DNA (Wong et al., 2011). ΔFosB exerts both types of effects, thus up-regulating some proteins and down-regulating others. This remarkable specificity is illustrative of the way that drugs, working through transcription factors such as ΔFosB, can produce widespread and long-lasting neuroadaptive changes that underlie not only addiction but also the therapeutic actions of drugs used to treat psychiatric disorders such as major depression and schizophrenia (see Chapters 19 and 20).

The general notion of how epigenetic mechanisms might interact with other factors to promote and maintain the addicted state is shown in **Figure 9.22**.

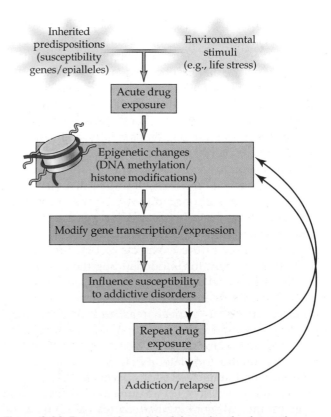

Figure 9.22 Proposed model of the role of epigenetic mechanisms in addiction Note: epialleles are inherited alleles of a gene that possess the same DNA sequence but differ epigenetically (e.g., one allele might be transcriptionally active, whereas another is silenced by prior DNA methylation). (After Wong et al., 2011.)

According to this model, inherited predispositions toward drug use and environmental stimuli such as stress promote initial drug-seeking behavior and drug use. Acute drug exposure, in turn, produces epigenetic changes in the expression of certain critical genes, and this subsequently facilitates repeated drug use, triggers additional epigenetic processes, and so forth, until the individual has become addicted (Wong et al., 2011). Although many studies with experimental animals suggest an important role for epigenetic mechanisms in the development of addiction (McQuown and Wood, 2010; Robison and Nestler, 2011), evidence in humans is much more limited thus far. Nevertheless, just as epigenetic therapies are being introduced to fight various cancers (Cherblanc et al., 2012), researchers have become hopeful that similar approaches might also prove therapeutically beneficial in the treatment of drug addiction.

Structural and functional abnormalities in the prefrontal cortex contribute to the symptoms of addiction

Brain imaging studies comparing addicted subjects with healthy controls have revealed both structural and functional abnormalities in the PFC in the addict group. Before describing these findings, it is useful to summarize some of the major behavioral functions of the PFC and the major subregions that are believed to mediate these functions. The PFC is best known for its role in **executive function**, which consists of higher-order cognitive abilities including planning, organization, problem solving, mental flexibility, and valuation of incentives. Damage either to the PFC or to certain parts of the circuitry that connects the PFC with the rest of the brain can cause major impairments in executive function. It is important to note, however, that the PFC contributes not only to executive function, but also to the regulation of emotional and motivational processes. All three of these aspects of PFC functioning could be important for understanding the psychological and behavioral differences between addicted and non-addicted individuals. The PFC has massive projections to various subcortical areas, and some researchers have proposed an organization of these projections into three main circuits: (1) a dorsolateral circuit that projects from the dorsolateral PFC (DLPFC) to the dorsolateral caudate nucleus and is particularly important for executive function; (2) a ventromedial circuit that connects the anterior cingulate cortex (ACC) with the NAcc and is involved in drive and motivation; and (3) an orbitofrontal circuit that projects from the orbitofrontal cortex (OFC) to the ventromedial caudate and has been associated with behavioral inhibition and impulse control (Alvarez and Emory, 2006).

Imaging studies using structural magnetic resonance imaging (MRI; see Chapter 4) have shown reduced gray matter volume in many different populations of drug addicts (i.e., people addicted to alcohol, cocaine, methamphetamine, heroin, or nicotine) (Goldstein and Volkow, 2011). Volume reductions have been reported in the DLPFC, ACC, and OFC, and in some cases the extent of the difference compared with healthy control subjects was related to the severity and/or longevity of drug use. Moreover, some studies have found significant gray matter reductions even after long-term abstinence. We do not yet know whether abnormalities in brain structure *precede* addiction and contribute to its development, whether such abnormalities are *caused* by repeated drug exposure, or whether both relationships might occur to some degree.

Functional abnormalities in the PFC have been investigated using either functional MRI (fMRI), which measures regional blood flow, or positron emission tomography (PET) imaging with radiolabeled fluorodeoxyglucose, which measures regional glucose uptake and metabolism (see Chapter 4). Although these two approaches measure different physiological parameters, both serve as indices of regional neural activity. Functional imaging has again revealed deficits in the DLPFC, ACC, and OFC in people who are chronic abusers or are addicted to several different substances, including alcohol, cocaine, and methamphetamine (Volkow et al., 2009, 2012). Some PET imaging studies have also demonstrated that in addiction, DA D_2 receptor binding in the striatum is significantly correlated with regional PFC glucose metabolism (i.e., low striatal D_2 receptor levels are associated with low PFC neural activity). An example of the relationship between striatal D_2 receptor binding and OFC glucose metabolism in cocaine and methamphetamine addicts is presented in **Figure 9.23**. Decreased striatal D_2 receptor binding has been found not only in subjects addicted to one of the above mentioned substances but also in heroin and nicotine addicts, and such decreases can persist for months after discontinuation of drug use (Volkow et al., 2009).

The striatum has connections back to the cerebral cortex (including the PFC), thus creating a cortical–striatal loop. Actually, several such loops exist, each mediating a different type of function (e.g., motor control, stimulus–response habit learning, emotional regulation). Input from midbrain DA neurons (mainly those in the substantia nigra pars compacta) act on striatal D_1 and D_2 receptors to modulate striatal outflow and, therefore, activity in these cortical–striatal loops. Thus, reduced striatal D_2 receptor levels might be responsible for some of the functional deficits observed in the PFC that, at least in part, underlie the lack of impulse control and planning, poor emotional

(A)

DA D$_2$ receptors

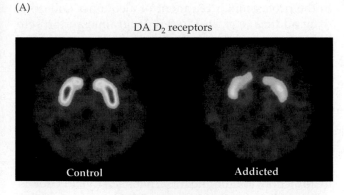

Brain glucose metabolism

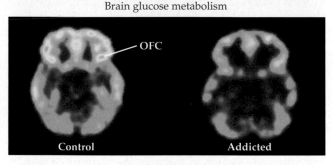

(B)

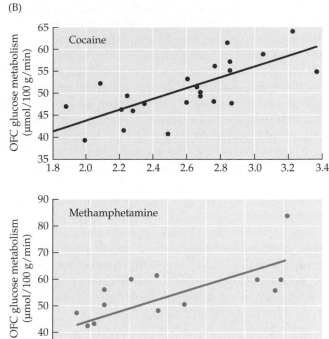

Figure 9.23 Relationship between striatal D$_2$ receptor binding and OFC glucose metabolism in cocaine and methamphetamine addicts. Subjects who were addicted either to cocaine or to methamphetamine were given PET scans to determine D$_2$ receptor binding in the striatum and glucose metabolism in the OFC. (A) Representative scans of striatal D$_2$ binding (top) and regional brain glucose metabolism (bottom) in healthy control and cocaine-addicted subjects. (B) Significant positive correlation between D$_2$ binding and OFC glucose metabolism in both cocaine and methamphetamine addicts. (After Volkow et al., 2011.)

regulation, and abnormal salience attribution (i.e., increased drug salience) seen in drug addicts (Volkow et al., 2009, 2011, 2012). Volkow and colleagues have proposed an **impaired response inhibition and salience attribution (iRISA)** model to describe the role of the PFC in the transition from a healthy state to one of addiction (Goldstein and Volkow, 2011). According to this model, deficits in PFC function (which either may precede or may be a consequence of chronic drug use) produce a syndrome characterized by impaired ability to inhibit maladaptive or harmful behaviors (e.g., drug use, risky sexual behavior, gambling) and dysregulated salience attribution such that normal reinforcers have reduced salience, whereas abused drugs and drug-related cues (environmental stimuli paired with drug use) have acquired greatly increased salience. **Figure 9.24** depicts PFC functioning according to the iRISA model during three different states: (A) a healthy state, (B) a state of withdrawal and drug craving, and (C) a state of intoxication and drug bingeing (Goldstein and Volkow, 2011). The

authors have subdivided the PFC into a dorsal component, which is involved principally in "cold" cognitive functions characteristic of executive functions, and a ventral component, which principally mediates "hot" functions related to emotional regulation.

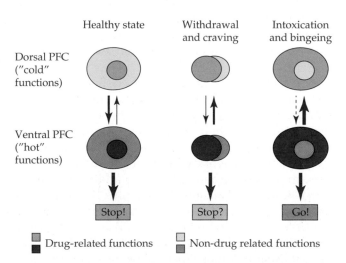

Figure 9.24 The iRISA model of PFC involvement in addiction The figure depicts the relative involvement of "cold" (higher cognitive) functions of the dorsal PFC and of "hot" (emotionally related) functions of the ventral PFC in the ability to control the motivation to seek out and use drugs (shown by the Stop and Go signals). See the text for additional details. (After Goldstein and Volkow, 2011.)

Furthermore, drug-related functions (e.g., incentive salience/drug wanting, drug-seeking behaviors) are shown in dark shades, whereas non-drug-related functions are shown in lighter shades. In the healthy state, non-drug-related functions dominate drug-related functions, the dorsal PFC exerts adequate inhibitory control over the ventral PFC, and drug-taking behavior can be controlled as shown by the "Stop!" During drug withdrawal and craving, drug-related functions have begun to overtake those unrelated to drugs, and the ability of the dorsal PFC to exert behavioral control is diminished. These changes lead to a conflict over drug-taking behavior and increased vulnerability to resumption of drug seeking and use ("Stop?"). Finally, during repeated drug bingeing and intoxication, the "hot" drug-related functions of the ventral PFC act to suppress the "cold" non-drug-related activity of the dorsal PFC and cause the addict to engage overwhelmingly in attending to, seeking out, and taking drugs without restraint ("Go!").

Is addiction a disease?

It is likely that all of the neurobiological mechanisms described in the previous sections play a significant role in drug abuse and addiction. The reward system mediates the acute rewarding and reinforcing effects of abused drugs, which are particularly relevant for the initial stages of drug use and abuse. Several types of drug-induced neuroadaptations underlie the transition from controlled to uncontrolled drug use in addiction. Deficits in the PFC, a key behavioral control area of the brain, also contribute to the development and maintenance of the addicted state. But having all of this information does not, in itself, provide a simple answer to an important question, namely, *whether addiction is a disease.*

The most widely accepted model of addiction in our society is the **disease model**. Not only has this view been popularized in the mass media, but addicts themselves and their treatment providers usually ascribe to this model. The disease model of addiction arose from early work with alcoholics and was only later applied to cocaine and opioid addiction (Meyer, 1996). Benjamin Rush, the Philadelphia physician who founded the alcohol temperance movement, was also the first to consider alcoholism a disease. This view was later expanded and promoted by E. M. Jellinek in his influential book, *The Disease Concept of Alcoholism* (Jellinek, 1960). For many years now, alcoholism has been formally considered a disease by medical organizations such as the World Health Organization and the American Medical Association. Indeed, the disease model is sometimes called a **medical model**. Not surprisingly, it is the leading model used both

in the professional treatment of alcoholics and other drug addicts (e.g., in 12-step programs) and in self-help groups such as Alcoholics Anonymous (AA) and Narcotics Anonymous. It should be noted that the disease model is not an alternative to the various neurobiological models, or even the more inclusive biopsychosocial model presented above. Rather, it is a way of thinking about the fundamental nature of addiction and the best approach to treating it.

The current disease model of addiction is based largely on evidence of dysregulation of brain function in addiction, and on the idea that such dysfunction is, at least partly, caused by repeated drug exposure (i.e., the neuroadaptations described above). This notion was presented forcefully in an article entitled, "Addiction Is a Brain Disease, and It Matters," by Alan Leshner, former Director of the National Institute on Drug Abuse. Leshner said, "That addiction is tied to changes in brain structure and function is what makes it, fundamentally, a brain disease. A metaphorical switch in the brain seems to be thrown as a result of prolonged drug use. Initially, drug use is a voluntary behavior, but when the switch is thrown, the individual moves into the state of addiction, characterized by compulsive drug seeking and use" (Leshner, 1997; p. 46).

The disease model has had a tremendously valuable impact on society's reaction toward drug abuse and addiction. For a long time, excessive drug use and addiction were seen primarily as signs of personal and moral weakness. Indeed, this earlier view has sometimes been termed a **moral model** of addiction. Initial development of the disease model sought to remove the social stigma of addiction (after all, no one *blames* you for coming down with a disease) and to involve the medical profession in helping addicts deal with their problem through treatment programs. It is important to note, though, that our society is still ambivalent about disease versus moral conceptions of drug use. Although you can get treatment for alcohol or tobacco abuse without fear of prosecution because these substances are legal, abuse of heroin, cocaine, or marijuana often leads to a jail sentence instead of medical help.

A second key benefit of the disease model involves reducing the sense of guilt experienced by the recovering addict. For example, there may be strong feelings of remorse for past problems caused by the person's drug use. If such problems are viewed as stemming from a disease, then the therapeutic process may benefit. As one alcoholic put it, "Calling it [alcoholism] a disease allows us to put the guilt aside so that we can do the work that we need to do" (Thombs, 1999, p. 71). In addition, even for a highly motivated individual in an intensive treatment program, there is a great likelihood that one or more lapses (brief instances of drug use) will occur before long-term abstinence is attained. The danger is that the resulting feelings of guilt and diminished self-worth will engender a sense of hopelessness that leads to a complete loss of control and full-blown relapse back into compulsive use. Belief that such lapses are the consequence of a disease process instead of a moral failing is thought to help the individual resist these destructive feelings, although it obviously does not guarantee a successful treatment outcome.

Despite its wide acceptance, however, the disease model of addiction has been criticized by some writers, both within and outside of the research community. To understand these criticisms, we must first consider what a disease is. According to one medical dictionary, a disease is "a pathological condition of the body that presents a group of clinical signs and symptoms and laboratory findings peculiar to it and that sets the condition apart as an abnormal entity differing from other normal or pathological body states" (Thomas, 1993). Let's see how this definition applies to a classical infectious disease such as bacterial pneumonia. The patient arrives at the doctor's office complaining of severe cough, shortness of breath, pain in the chest, chills, and a high fever. These clinical signs and symptoms are the initial indicators of a possible diagnosis. The doctor suspects bacterial pneumonia and orders a chest X-ray and a sputum culture. The X-ray shows inflammation of the lungs, and the culture comes back positive for *Pneumococcus*, one of the bacterial strains that cause pneumonia. These laboratory findings confirm a diagnosis of pneumococcal pneumonia and call for the patient to be placed on an appropriate antibiotic (which the doctor has probably already started on the basis of her preliminary findings).

Do the same principles apply to addiction? Imagine a second patient arriving at the doctor's office with the following symptoms: he has had at least six or seven drinks of liquor almost every day for the past 8 years; he often has cravings for alcohol; he doesn't become drunk even after four or five drinks; if he doesn't drink any alcohol for a day or two, he becomes extremely irritable, anxious, and unable to sleep; he has tried to stop drinking numerous times without success; he recently lost his job because of repeated tardiness and absence from work; and he has been arrested twice for driving under the influence of alcohol. These are very clear signs and symptoms of alcoholism. Can the doctor now perform some laboratory tests to confirm the diagnosis? She might test his liver function and determine that he suffers from cirrhosis (a serious liver condition that occurs in some chronic alcoholics), but cirrhosis is a *consequence* of alcoholism, not a cause. In fact, there are no laboratory tests

that can identify the etiology (cause) of an addictive process in the same way that a sputum culture can identify the source of someone's pneumonia or a tissue biopsy can identify the source of another person's cancer. Addiction can be diagnosed *only* through the clinical signs and symptoms.

One criticism of the disease model of addiction emphasizes this difference between addiction and most other recognized disease conditions (for example, see Schaler, 2000). However, a key counterargument is that *all* psychiatric disorders, not just addiction, must be diagnosed by means of the patient's mental and behavioral symptoms. Just as there are no blood tests or brain scans that can identify someone who is suffering from addiction (or, using *DSM-5* terminology, severe substance use disorder), there are no laboratory tests that enable a psychiatrist to determine whether a patient has schizophrenia, major depression, or obsessive–compulsive disorder. Therefore, the lack of such a test for addiction cannot be used to disqualify it as a disease unless we are willing to similarly disqualify all other psychiatric disorders. The fact that we presently have no anatomical, biochemical, or neurological tests to identify drug-addicted individuals does not conflict with the evidence mentioned earlier for long-term neuroadaptive effects of chronic drug exposure. First of all, we do not yet know whether the same neural changes underlie all drug addictions. Researchers have long believed that what we call schizophrenia is actually a number of diseases that have been grouped together because of a core symptom cluster. The same could be true of addiction. Second, it is likely that complex *patterns* of neural abnormalities are responsible for psychiatric illnesses such as addiction. If so, it will be difficult to find any one or two differences between drug-addicted and non-drug-addicted people that are sufficiently reliable to serve as diagnostic indicators.

Finally, the disease model is criticized by theoreticians and practitioners who use behavioral approaches to understanding and treating substance abuse and addiction. While not excluding genetic and neurochemical factors, such approaches emphasize the role of learning and other cognitive processes in both the development and treatment of substance abuse problems (Heyman, 2009; Rotgers, 1996). Accordingly, addiction is viewed not as a disease, but as a behavior pattern that comes about as the result of interaction between many factors, including the person's environment (e.g., the availability of drugs and peer pressure to use them), behavioral modeling of drug use by others, the positive-reinforcing effects of abused drugs, the reinforcing consequences of avoiding or eliminating drug withdrawal, and conditioning to drug-related stimuli.

In summary, the disease model of addiction can be defended, but only with the caveats that currently apply to other psychiatric disorders. Ultimately, it may not make much difference to researchers whether addiction is considered a disease or not, as long as the full range of contributory factors is acknowledged. As we mentioned earlier, however, the disease model continues to play a central role in addiction treatment. As George Vaillant states in his landmark study of alcoholism, "In our attempts to *understand* and to *study* alcoholism, it behooves us to employ the models of the social scientist and of the learning theorist [we would also include the models of the neuroscientist]. But in order to *treat* alcoholics effectively, we need to invoke the model of the medical practitioner" (Vaillant, 1995, p. 22).

Section Summary

- A reward circuit mediates the acute rewarding and reinforcing effects of most abused drugs. One of the key components of this circuit is the DA pathway from the VTA to the NAcc. Virtually all drugs of abuse activate this pathway, either by enhancing VTA cell firing or by increasing extracellular DA levels in the NAcc.

- Researchers have proposed several different roles for DA in reward. One popular belief is that DA in the NAcc mediates feelings of pleasure. Other proposed roles include attribution of incentive salience in the incentive sensitization theory of addiction and encoding of reward-prediction error. In Robinson and Berridge's incentive sensitization theory, drug "wanting" increases over time, whereas drug "liking" either remains unchanged or decreases in intensity.

- The endogenous opioid and cannabinoid systems have also been implicated in drug reward.

- The transition from controlled, recreational drug use to addiction is related to neuroadaptations produced by repeated drug exposure.

- One such neuroadaptation involves recruitment of an anti-reward system that is centered around the extended amygdala and is activated during stress and drug withdrawal. Neurochemically, activation of the anti-reward system results in increased release of NE, CRF, and dynorphin.

- The opposing actions of the reward system and the anti-reward system have been conceptualized by Koob and Le Moal in an opponent-process model of addiction. According to this model, early drug use is motivated primarily by positive-reinforcing effects (reward circuit), whereas later drug use (after addiction has taken place) is motivated primarily by negative reinforcement produced by alleviation of aversive withdrawal symptoms (anti-reward system). The opponent-process model further hypothesizes the development of an allostatic reduction in baseline hedonic tone (mood) that persists even after long-term abstinence from drugs.

- Other neuroadaptations are related to a transition in the control of drug-taking behavior from the NAcc (ventral striatum) to the caudate-putamen (dorsal striatum), as well as alterations in glutamate homeostasis at the synapses connecting the PFC with the NAcc.

- Drugs of abuse produce both transient and longer-lasting changes in gene and protein expression. The transcription factor ΔFosB can be induced in the NAcc for relatively long periods by a variety of abused drugs, and this factor acts through epigenetic mechanisms to regulate other genes that may contribute to the transition from recreational drug use to addiction.

- Drug addicts show reduced gray matter volume and neural activity in major subareas of the PFC, including the DLPFC, ACC, and OFC. Decreased neural activity (specifically, glucose metabolism) is correlated with decreased D_2 receptor binding in the striatum, which has also been observed in drug addicts. Volkow and colleagues have proposed the iRISA model, which emphasizes a role for abnormal PFC functioning in addiction.

- The most influential model of addiction in our society is the disease or medical model, which is based on brain dysfunction brought about by repeated drug exposure. Despite some criticism of this view, the disease model has played an important role in helping people deal with guilt associated with their addiction and also in promoting social acceptance of medical treatment for drug addicts.

Go to the **COMPANION WEBSITE**

sites.sinauer.com/psychopharm2e
for Web Boxes, animations, flashcards,
and other study resources.

Recommended Readings

Erickson, C. K. (2007). *The Science of Addiction: From Neurobiology to Treatment*. New York: Norton.

Kuhar, M. (2011). *The Addicted Brain: Why We Abuse Drugs, Alcohol, and Nicotine*. Upper Saddle River, NJ: FT Press.

Lingford-Hughes, A., Watson, B., Kalk, N., and Reid, A. (2010). Neuropharmacology of addiction and how it informs treatment. *Br. Med. Bull.*, 96, 93–110.

Drinking games can produce danger-ously high blood levels of alcohol.

Alcohol 10

IMAGINE YOURSELF AT A FRIDAY NIGHT RAGER just getting under way. Students are mingling and dancing to pop music while someone taps a keg behind the bar. When we look around an hour later, some changes have occurred. Guys from the soccer team are chanting the time as one of their number performs a keg stand. In the middle of the dance floor, an upperclassman grinds with a freshman girl, their hands all over each other. Many other students dance wildly, their glazed eyes indicating that the fun they are having probably will not be remembered in the morning. A group of Asians come in, and most grab beers, but unlike most students, several decline, knowing how sick the alcohol will make them within minutes. Nobody notices the girl passed out in the chair in the corner; much more attention is focused on the two guys yelling and shoving each other next to the Beirut table.

Alcohol, an amazing beverage, used by people all over the world for thousands of years, is responsible, we assume, for all the effects we see here: loss of coordination and judgment, enhanced sexuality, memory loss and stupor, increased hostility and aggression, and, for some, the potential for unpleasant side effects. Can such a simple molecule chemically produce all these diverse effects by acting on specific neurotransmitters, or might the setting, the mood of the participants, and their expectations be major contributors?

Psychopharmacology of Alcohol

Alcohol, after caffeine, is the most commonly used psychoactive drug in America and is certainly the drug that is most abused. Despite the fact that alcohol has dramatic effects on mood, behavior, and thinking, and that its chronic use is damaging to the individual, the individual's family, and society, most people accept its use. In fact, many people do not consider alcohol to be a drug. How many people do you know who shun taking over-the-counter (OTC) or prescription medicines because they don't want to take "drugs" but will have a beer at a party or a cocktail before dinner? How many parents of high school students have you heard say that they are relieved that their child was caught only drinking alcohol illegally, not using "real" drugs? How many books and magazine articles have been titled "Drugs and Alcohol," as though alcohol was not included in the drug category? The popularity of alcohol use means that almost everyone has an idea about its effects. Some of these ideas are based on fact, but frequently people's beliefs about alcohol are misconceptions based on myth and "common" wisdom. Our job is to present the empirical evidence that describes not only the acute effects of the drug and its mechanism of action in the brain but also some of its long-term effects on other organ systems.

Figure 10.1 Engraving of Gin Lane by artist William Hogarth (1697–1764), depicting the popular opinion that the "lower classes" drank gin and got drunk.

Alcohol has a long history of use

Alcohol use in America began with the very first immigrants, but its history is really very much longer than that. Perhaps as early as 8000 BC, mead was brewed from fermented honey, producing the first alcoholic beverage. Archeological evidence shows that around 3700 BC, the Egyptians prepared the first very hearty beer, called *hek*, which might have been thick enough to stand up a spoon, and wine may have first come from Babylonia in 1700 BC. Later still, the popularity of alcohol among the Romans may have contributed to the decline of the Empire. Certainly many historians believe that the civilization was doomed by the corruption of society, alcohol intemperance, and moral decay, but the mental instability of the Roman nobility is an additional factor. Some members of the noble class exhibited signs of confusion and dementia, which may have been due to lead poisoning caused by alcohol prepared with a flavor enhancer that had a high lead content. *Aqua vitae* (meaning "the water of life" in Latin) represents the first distilled conversion of wine into brandy during the Middle Ages in Italy. Production of gin by the Dutch is frequently credited with the start of serious alcohol abuse in Europe. Not only was gin far more potent than wine and very inexpensive to buy, but it was introduced during a time

of social upheaval. Gin turned out to be a common method of dealing with the poor living conditions and social instability caused by the newly created urban societies following the feudal period. Gin consumption became associated with the lower class, while the more respectable middle class drank beer (**Figure 10.1**).

Colonial Americans brought their habit of heavy drinking from Europe, and alcohol had a large part in their daily lives. The American tavern was not just a place for food and drink and overnight accommodation, it was also the focal point in each town for conducting business and local politics, and for mail delivery. The Continental Army supplied each soldier with a daily ration of rum, and employers and farmers supplied their workers with liquor on the job. Students, then as now, had reputations for hard drinking, and Harvard University operated its own brewery. At some point, the celebrations at graduation ceremonies became so wild and unrestrained that the administration developed strict rules of behavior. American drinking of alcohol remained at a high level until the 1830s, when the temperance movement began a campaign to educate society about the dangers of long-term alcohol consumption. Although their initial goal was to reduce rather than prevent alcohol consumption, later offshoots of the group used social and religious arguments to convince Americans that alcohol itself was the source of evil in the world and was directly responsible for broken families, poverty, social disorder, and crime. Some of these same arguments are currently being used to regulate the use of other drugs in our society, such as marijuana, heroin, and cocaine.

In 1917, Congress passed a law that in 1920 became the Eighteenth Amendment to the American Constitution; it prohibited the "manufacture, sale, transportation, and importation" of liquor. Despite its intent, the period of Prohibition increased illegal manufacturing that often produced highly toxic forms of alcohol, increased consumption of distilled spirits rather than beer because they were easier to hide and store, and made drinking in illegal speakeasies a fad. Medicinal "tonics" containing up to 75% alcohol became increasingly popular. Worst of all, Prohibition increased the activity of organized crime mobs that were heavily involved in the sale and distribution of alcohol. By 1933, most Americans realized that the experiment was a failure, and the Eighteenth Amendment was repealed by Congress during the presidency of Franklin D. Roosevelt. (For a brief history of alcohol use in America, see Goode, 1993.) Today, the use of alcohol is restricted by age and circumstance (e.g., prohibited when operating a motor vehicle) and is regulated to some extent by an increased tax on the cost of consumption (the "sin tax").

What is an alcohol and where does it come from?

Alcohols come in many forms, and although they have similarities in structure, they have very different uses. Ethyl alcohol is the alcohol with which we are most familiar because it is used as a beverage. Ethyl alcohol has only two carbon atoms, a complement of hydrogens, plus the –OH (hydroxyl group) characteristic of all alcohols (**Figure 10.2**). Methyl alcohol, or wood alcohol, has an even simpler chemical structure but is highly toxic if consumed, because the liver metabolites of methyl alcohol include formic acid and formaldehyde. Drinking wood alcohol causes blindness, coma, and death. It is commonly used as a fuel, an antifreeze, and an industrial solvent. Isopropyl alcohol has a small molecular side chain that changes its characteristics and makes it most useful as rubbing alcohol or as a disinfectant. It is also dangerous to consume.

Ethyl alcohol (or ethanol) is the form we focus on in this chapter. It is produced by fermentation—a process that occurs naturally whenever microscopic yeast cells in the air fall on a product containing sugar, such as honey, fruit, sugar cane, or grains like rye, corn, and others. The material that provides the sugar determines the type of alcoholic beverage, for example, grapes

Figure 10.2 Chemical structures of three commonly used forms of alcohol

(wine), rice (sake), or grains (beer). Yeast converts each sugar molecule into two molecules of alcohol and two molecules of carbon dioxide. This fermentation process is entirely natural and explains why alcohol has been discovered in cultures all over the world. The fermentation process continues until the concentration of alcohol is about 15%, at which point the yeast dies. Most wines have alcohol content in this range. To achieve higher alcohol concentrations, distillation is necessary. Distillation requires heating the fermented mixture to the point where the alcohol boils off in steam (since it has a lower boiling point than water), leaving some of the water behind. The alcohol vapor passes through a series of cooling tubes (called a still) and condenses to be collected as "hard liquor," or distilled spirits, such as whiskey, brandy, rum, tequila, and so forth. The alcohol concentration of these beverages varies from 40% to 50%. A second way to increase alcohol concentrations to above 15% is to add additional alcohol; this procedure is used to make fortified wines such as sherry. Flavoring and sugar may also be added to produce liqueurs such as crème de menthe (mint), amaretto (almond), and ouzo (anise). Regardless of the form, alcohol is high in calories, which means that it provides heat or energy when it is metabolized. However, no nutritional value is associated with those calories because alcohol provides no proteins, vitamins, or minerals that are necessary components of a normal diet. For this reason, individuals who chronically consume large quantities of alcohol in lieu of food frequently suffer from inadequate nutrition, leading to health problems and brain damage.

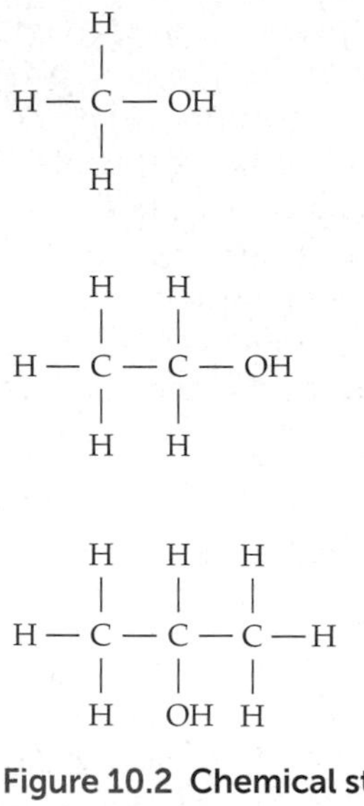

Although it would make the most sense to describe alcohol content as a percentage, if you look at a bottle of distilled spirits, you are more likely to see alcohol content described according to "proof." This convention is based on an old British army custom of testing an alcoholic product by pouring it on gunpowder and attempting to light it. If the alcohol content is 50%, the gunpowder burns, but if the alcohol is less concentrated, the remaining water content prevents the burning. Hence, the burning of the sample was 100% "proof" that it was at least 50% alcohol. The proof number now corresponds to twice the percent of alcohol concentration.

The pharmacokinetics of alcohol determines its bioavailability

To evaluate the effects of alcohol in the central nervous system (CNS), we need to know how much alcohol is freely available to enter the brain from the blood (i.e., its bioavailability). Ethyl alcohol is a unique drug in several respects. Although alcohol is a small, simple molecule that cannot be ionized, it nevertheless readily mixes with water and is not high in lipid solubility. Despite these characteristics, it is easily absorbed from the gastrointestinal (GI) tract and diffuses throughout the body, readily entering most tissues, including the brain. The rates of absorption, distribution, and clearance of alcohol are modified by many factors, all of which contribute to the highly variable blood levels that occur after ingestion of a fixed amount of the drug. For this reason, behavioral effects are described on the basis of **blood alcohol concentration** (**BAC**) rather than the amount ingested. In general, it takes a BAC of 0.04% (i.e., 40 mg of alcohol per 100 ml of blood) to produce measurable behavioral effects. Keep in mind that one "drink" may take the form of one 12-ounce can of beer, one 5-ounce glass of wine, a cocktail with 1.5 ounces of spirits, or a 12-ounce wine cooler, but each will raise your blood level by the equivalent amount (**Figure 10.3**).

ABSORPTION AND DISTRIBUTION   Since oral administration is about the only way the drug is used recreationally, absorption will necessarily occur from the GI tract: about 10% from the stomach and 90% from the small intestine. The small molecules move across membrane barriers by passive diffusion from the higher concentration on one side (the GI tract) to the lower concentration on the other (blood). Of course, this means that the more alcohol you drink in a short period of time or the more alcohol you drink in an undiluted form (i.e., more concentrated), the more rapid will be the movement from stomach and intestine to blood, producing a higher blood level (**Figure 10.4A**). The presence of food in the stomach slows absorption because it delays movement into the small intestine through the pyloric sphincter, a muscle that regulates the movement of material from stomach to intestine (**Figure 10.4B**). Milk seems to be particularly effective in delaying absorption. In contrast, carbonated alcoholic beverages such as champagne are absorbed more rapidly because carbonation speeds the movement of materials from the stomach into the intestine.

Gender differences also exist in the absorption of alcohol from the stomach because certain enzymes (particularly alcohol dehydrogenase) that are present in gastric fluid are about 60% more active in men than in women, leaving a higher concentration of alcohol that will be absorbed more rapidly in women (Freeza et al., 1990). Further, taking aspirin generally inhibits gastric alcohol dehydrogenase, but to a greater extent in women than in men. Because women have lower levels of alcohol dehydrogenase to begin with, aspirin use before drinking may essentially eliminate any gastric metabolism of alcohol in women (Roine et al., 1990). Ulcer medications (such as Tagamet or Zantac) also impair gastric metabolism, increasing alcohol concentrations and hence increasing absorption.

Figure 10.3 Alcohol content A comparison of alcohol content of various beverages shows an equivalent amount despite differences in volume. To calculate the amount of alcohol in a given beverage, multiply the number of ounces in the container by the percent alcohol content by volume. Note that the alcohol content of beer varies from 3% to well over 10% for some microbrews.

	Wine	Beer	Hard liquor	Wine cooler
Volume (ounces)	5	12	1.5	12
×				
Percent alcohol by volume	12	5	40	5
Ethyl alcohol per serving (ounces)	0.60	0.60	0.60	0.60

(A) Different oral doses

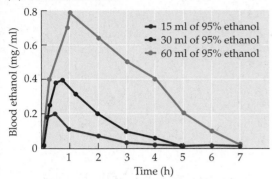

(B) Full or empty stomach

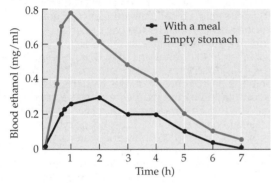

Figure 10.4 Blood levels of alcohol after oral administration (A) Larger oral doses of alcohol produce higher concentrations in the stomach, and this causes faster absorption and higher peak blood levels. (B) The presence of food in the stomach slows absorption of alcohol and prevents the sharp peak in blood level.

Once alcohol is in the blood, it circulates throughout the body. It readily moves by passive diffusion from the higher concentration in the blood to all tissues and fluid compartments. Body size and gender play a part in the distribution of alcohol and in the magnitude of its effect. The same amount of alcohol, say one beer, is much more concentrated in the average woman than in the average man because her fluid volume is much smaller as a result of her size, and because women have a higher fat-to-water ratio.

METABOLISM Of the alcohol that reaches the general circulation, approximately 95% is metabolized by the liver before it is excreted as carbon dioxide and water in the urine. The remaining 5% is excreted by the lungs and can be measured in one's breath by using a Breathalyzer, which provides law enforcement officials a means to calculate alcohol levels. Alcohol metabolism is different from that of most other drugs in that the rate of oxidation is constant over time and does not occur more quickly when the drug is more concentrated in the blood. The rate of metabolism is quite variable from one person to another, but the average rate is approxi-

mately 1 to 1.5 ounces or 12 to 18 ml of 80-proof alcohol per hour. Because the metabolic rate is constant for an individual, if the rate of consumption is faster than the rate of metabolism, alcohol accumulates in the body, and the individual becomes intoxicated.

Several enzyme systems in the liver are capable of oxidizing alcohol. The most important is **alcohol dehydrogenase**, which we already know is also found in the stomach and reduces the amount of available alcohol for absorption—a good example of the first-pass effect (see Chapter 1). Alcohol dehydrogenase converts alcohol to acetaldehyde, a potentially toxic intermediate, which normally is rapidly modified further by **acetaldehyde dehydrogenase** (**ALDH**) to form acetic acid. Further oxidation yields carbon dioxide, water, and energy (**Figure 10.5A**). ALDH exists in several genetically determined forms with varying activities. About 10% of Asian individuals (e.g., Japanese, Korean, Chinese) have genes that code only for an inactive form of the enzyme (**Figure 10.5B**). For these individuals, drinking even small amounts of alcohol produces very high levels of acetaldehyde, causing intense flushing, nausea and vomiting, tachycardia, headache, sweating, dizziness, and confusion. Because these individuals almost always totally abstain from using alcohol, they are at no risk for alcoholism. Another 40% of the Asian population has genes that code for both the active and inactive enzyme. These heterozygous individuals exhibit a more intense response to alcohol but not necessarily an unpleasant one. They are partially protected from alcohol dependence and have less vulnerability, making the *ALDH* gene a marker for low risk of alcoholism.

The second class of liver enzymes that convert alcohol to acetaldehyde are those that belong to the **cytochrome P450** family. The enzyme of importance within this family is CYP 2E1, which is sometimes called the **microsomal ethanol oxidizing system** (**MEOS**). These enzymes metabolize many drugs in addition to alcohol. When alcohol is consumed along with these other drugs, they must compete for the same enzyme molecules; therefore, alcohol consumption may lead to high and potentially dangerous levels of the other drugs. Be sure to look for warnings on both prescription and OTC medications before consuming alcohol with any other drug. In contrast to the acute effect, when alcohol is consumed on a regular basis these liver enzymes *increase* in number, which increases the rate of metabolism of alcohol as well as any other drugs normally metabolized by these enzymes. The process, called **induction** of liver enzymes, serves as the basis for metabolic tolerance, which is described in the next section. Finally, prolonged heavy use of alcohol causes liver damage that significantly impairs metabolism of alcohol and many other drugs.

(A)

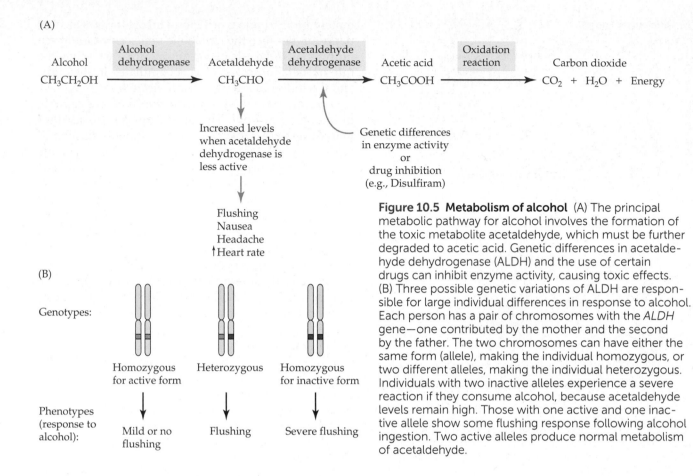

Figure 10.5 Metabolism of alcohol (A) The principal metabolic pathway for alcohol involves the formation of the toxic metabolite acetaldehyde, which must be further degraded to acetic acid. Genetic differences in acetaldehyde dehydrogenase (ALDH) and the use of certain drugs can inhibit enzyme activity, causing toxic effects. (B) Three possible genetic variations of ALDH are responsible for large individual differences in response to alcohol. Each person has a pair of chromosomes with the *ALDH* gene—one contributed by the mother and the second by the father. The two chromosomes can have either the same form (allele), making the individual homozygous, or two different alleles, making the individual heterozygous. Individuals with two inactive alleles experience a severe reaction if they consume alcohol, because acetaldehyde levels remain high. Those with one active and one inactive allele show some flushing response following alcohol ingestion. Two active alleles produce normal metabolism of acetaldehyde.

Given the pharmacokinetic factors just described, you know that the amount of alcohol in the blood depends on how much an individual has consumed and on rates of absorption and metabolism. **Table 10.1** provides a rough estimate of BAC that is based on the number of drinks consumed in 1 hour and the body weight of the individual, assuming the metabolism of approximately 1 ounce per hour.

Chronic alcohol use leads to both tolerance and physical dependence

Several types of tolerance for the biobehavioral effects of alcohol occur with repeated consumption. Prolonged use can also lead to physical dependence and cross-dependence with other sedative–hypnotic drugs such as the benzodiazepines.

TOLERANCE   The effects of alcohol are significantly reduced when the drug is administered repeatedly; hence, **tolerance** occurs. There is also **cross-tolerance** with a variety of other drugs in the sedative–hypnotic class, including the barbiturates and the benzodiazepines. Each of the four mechanisms that we described in Chapter 1 contributes to alcohol tolerance.

1. **Acute tolerance** occurs within a single exposure to alcohol. Several of the subjective and behavioral drug effects are greater while the blood level of alcohol is increasing and are less while the blood level is falling even if the BAC is the same at both times (**Figure 10.6A**). LeBlanc and colleagues (1975) found that alcohol-induced incoordination in rats was 50% less while blood levels were falling as measured by the amount of time off a mini-treadmill during a single exposure to alcohol. More problematic is the finding that interoceptive cues that determine the subjective evaluation of intoxication undergo acute tolerance, particularly in binge drinkers,[1] although in some studies, social drinkers also reported feeling less intoxicated by alcohol on the declining limb of the blood alcohol curve compared with the ascending limb. Failure to accurately predict their blood alcohol levels and the amount of impairment they will experience leads individuals to risk driving while legally intoxicated. Unfortunately, although binge drinkers perceive that they are less intoxicated on the

---

[1]Binge drinking is generally defined as 5 or more drinks for men and 4 or more drinks for women on a single 2-hour occasion.

TABLE 10.1 Estimated BAC and Impairment for Men and Women According to Body Weight[a]

Drinks	Approximate Blood Alcohol Concentration[b] (Men)							
	Body weight (pounds)							
	100	120	140	160	180	200	220	240
0	0.00	0.00	0.00	0.00	0.00	0.00	0.00	0.00
1	0.04	0.03	0.03	0.02	0.02	0.02	0.02	0.02
2	0.08	0.06	0.05	0.05	0.04	0.04	0.03	0.03
3	0.11	0.09	0.08	0.07	0.06	0.06	0.05	0.05
4	0.15	0.12	0.11	0.09	0.08	0.08	0.07	0.06
5	0.19	0.16	0.13	0.12	0.11	0.09	0.09	0.08
6	0.23	0.19	0.16	0.14	0.13	0.11	0.10	0.09
7	0.26	0.22	0.19	0.16	0.15	0.13	0.12	0.11
8	0.30	0.25	0.21	0.19	0.17	0.15	0.14	0.13
9	0.34	0.28	0.24	0.21	0.19	0.17	0.15	0.14
10	0.38	0.31	0.27	0.23	0.21	0.19	0.17	0.16

Drinks	Approximate Blood Alcohol Concentration (Women)							
	Body weight (pounds)							
	90	100	120	140	160	180	200	220
0	0.00	0.00	0.00	0.00	0.00	0.00	0.00	0.00
1	0.05	0.05	0.04	0.03	0.03	0.03	0.02	0.02
2	0.10	0.09	0.08	0.07	0.06	0.05	0.05	0.04
3	0.15	0.14	0.11	0.10	0.09	0.08	0.07	0.06
4	0.20	0.18	0.15	0.13	0.11	0.10	0.09	0.08
5	0.25	0.23	0.19	0.16	0.14	0.13	0.11	0.10
6	0.30	0.27	0.23	0.19	0.17	0.15	0.14	0.12
7	0.35	0.32	0.27	0.23	0.20	0.18	0.16	0.14
8	0.40	0.36	0.30	0.26	0.23	0.20	0.18	0.17
9	0.45	0.41	0.34	0.29	0.26	0.23	0.20	0.19
10	0.51	0.45	0.38	0.32	0.28	0.25	0.23	0.21

Source: Pennsylvania Liquor Control Board, 1995.

[a]Note: Your body can get rid of one drink per hour.

[b]0.2–0.04 = Impairment begins; 0.05–0.07 = Impaired driving; 0.08 and greater = Legal intoxication

descending limb of the blood alcohol curve and are more willing to drive an automobile at that time, their driving performance as measured on a simulated driving test was significantly worse than on the ascending limb. Deterioration of driving skills may be due to fatigue or to the fact that these individuals fail to compensate for their intoxication, which they fail to recognize (Marczinski and Fillmore, 2009). This differential development of acute tolerance for various effects of alcohol may explain why binge drinkers are responsible for about 80% of the alcohol-impaired driving incidents each year. Why acute tolerance occurs is not entirely clear, but some rapid adaptation of neuronal membranes is one possibility.

2. Chronic alcohol use significantly increases the P450 liver microsomal enzymes that metabolize the drug. More rapid metabolism means that

(A) Acute tolerance

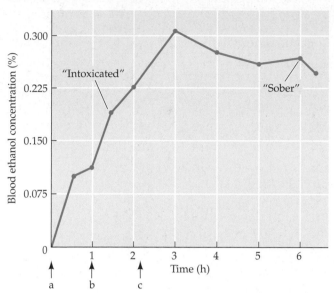

(B) Metabolic tolerance

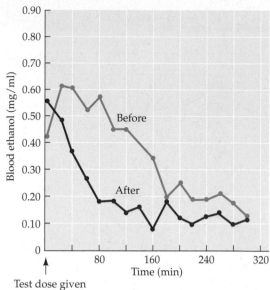

Test dose given

Figure 10.6 Tolerance to alcohol (A) After three doses of alcohol (a, b, c), signs of intoxication (such as incoordination in the balance beam test) appeared during the rising phase of blood alcohol levels at about 0.20%. However, as blood alcohol was declining, the human subject became "sober" at a higher concentration (about 0.265%), showing that acute tolerance had occurred. In this case sober does not mean unimpaired in skills other than the balance beam test. Note that the high blood levels for intoxication reflect the fact that the subject was a chronically heavy user of alcohol. (B) Blood alcohol levels were calculated at 20-minute intervals after a test dose was given at time zero. The blue line represents blood levels before a 7-day period of drinking; the red line shows blood levels in the same person after 7 days of drinking (3.2 grams of ethanol per kilogram of body weight per day in individual doses). Tolerance after repeated alcohol consumption is shown by the more rapid decrease in blood alcohol. (A after Mirsky et al., 1941; B after Goldstein et al., 1974.)

blood levels of the drug will be reduced (**Figure 10.6B**), producing diminished effects (**metabolic tolerance**).

3. Neurons also adapt to the continued presence of alcohol by making compensatory changes in cell function. The mechanism of this **pharmacodynamic tolerance** is described in later sections dealing with specific neurotransmitters.

4. Finally, there is also clear evidence of **behavioral tolerance**. Rats, like humans, seem to be able to learn to adjust their behaviors when allowed to practice while under the influence of alcohol (Wenger et al., 1981). Although initially unsuccessful, rats readily learned to run on a treadmill by trial and error despite administration of alcohol. Other rats given the same amount of drug each day *after* their treadmill session showed only minimal improvement when tested on the treadmill under the influence of alcohol. This small amount of improvement may have been due to metabolic tolerance.

Classical conditioning may also contribute to behavioral tolerance. In animal experiments, alcohol initially reduces body temperature, but when the drug is administered repeatedly in the same environment, a compensatory increase in body temperature occurs, and this reduces the initial hypothermia (low body temperature). If these animals are given saline instead of alcohol in this environment, they show *only* the compensatory mechanism and their body temperature rises (hyperthermia). The importance of environment is further demonstrated by evidence that in a novel environment, tolerance is significantly less because no conditioned hyperthermia is present (Le et al., 1979).

PHYSICAL DEPENDENCE We know that prolonged use of alcohol produces **physical dependence** because a significant withdrawal syndrome occurs when drinking is terminated. As you already know, the intensity and duration of withdrawal (i.e., abstinence) signs are dependent on the amount and duration of drug taking (**Figure 10.7**). In addition, alcohol shows **cross-dependence** with other drugs in the sedative–hypnotic class, including barbiturates and benzodiazepines. A quick review of Chapter 1 will remind you that withdrawal signs can be eliminated by taking the drug again or by taking any drug in the same class that shows cross-dependence.

Some investigators suggest that the "**hangover**" that occurs after even a single bout of heavy drinking

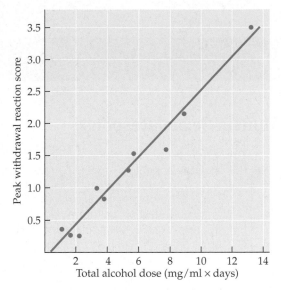

Figure 10.7 Relationship between alcohol dose and withdrawal severity A linear relationship exists between the total alcohol dose (amount of alcohol consumed multiplied by number of days of alcohol exposure) and the maximum withdrawal response at abstinence in mice. Withdrawal response was calculated on the basis of standard physiological and behavioral measures. (After Goldstein, 1972.)

may in fact be evidence of withdrawal, although others consider it a sign of acute toxicity. Possible explanations for hangover symptoms include residual acetaldehyde in the body; alcohol-induced gastric irritation; rebound drop in blood sugar; excess fluid loss the previous night; and perhaps toxic effects from congeners, which are small quantities of by-products from fermentation and distillation that may accumulate after heavy drinking. The classic symptoms of hangover are recognized by many social drinkers who on occasion consume an excess of alcohol. Among the usual signs are nausea and perhaps vomiting, headache, intense thirst and dry mouth that feels a bit like cotton balls, fatigue, and general malaise.

Withdrawal from repeated heavy drinking over months or years produces an intense abstinence syndrome that develops within a few hours after drinking stops and may continue over 2 to 4 days, depending on the dose previously consumed. Generally, symptoms include tremor (the "shakes") and intense anxiety, high blood pressure and rapid heart rate, excessive sweating, rapid breathing, and nausea and vomiting. A small percentage of alcoholics undergoing withdrawal demonstrate more-severe effects called **delirium tremens**, or **DTs**. Signs of DTs include irritability, headaches, agitation, and confusion. In addition, convulsions; vivid and frightening hallucinations that include snakes, rats, or insects crawling on their bodies; total disorientation; and delirium may occur. Withdrawal signs such as unstable blood pressure, depression and anxiety including panic attacks, and

sleep disturbances may last for several weeks. Because the most extreme symptoms are potentially life-threatening, detoxification of an alcoholic individual (see the section on alcoholism later in the chapter) should always be done under medical supervision. The signs of withdrawal are characteristically a "rebound" phenomenon and represents a hyperexcitable state of the nervous system after the prolonged depressant effects of alcohol. The neuroadaptive mechanisms responsible are described more completely later in this chapter.

Alcohol affects many organ systems

Alcohol, like all drugs, produces dose-dependent effects that are also dependent on the duration of drug taking. Because it is so readily absorbed and widely distributed, alcohol has effects on most organ systems of the body. As you read this section, keep in mind that no evidence suggests that light to moderate consumption of alcohol is harmful, and it may even have some minor beneficial effects. However, the transition from moderate to heavy drinking that leads to the chronic intoxication associated with alcoholism is a part of the same dose–response curve, and the precise point at which alcohol becomes damaging is not clear for a particular individual.

A second thing to keep in mind is that the environment and expectations have a great influence on many of the behavioral effects of alcohol. A host of well-controlled studies clearly show that a subject's *belief* that alcohol will produce relaxation, sexual desire, or aggression may have a far greater effect on the individual's behavior than the pharmacological effects of the drug, at least at low to moderate doses. Pronounced behavioral effects occur under placebo conditions when the individual believes that he has ingested alcohol. Refer to **Box 10.1**. As you might expect, the environment plays less of a role in the effects of alcohol as the dose increases.

CNS EFFECTS As is true for all drugs in the sedative–hypnotic class, at the lowest doses an individual feels relaxed and less anxious. In a quiet setting she may feel somewhat sleepy, but in a social setting where sensory stimulation is increased, the relaxed state is demonstrated by reduced social inhibition, which may make the individual more gregarious, talkative, and friendly or inappropriately outspoken. Self-perception and judgment are somewhat impaired, and one may feel more confident than reality proves true. Reduced judgment and overconfidence may increase risk-taking behaviors and may make sexual encounters more likely. Of additional concern is the effect of alcohol-induced loss of judgment on the initiation of unsafe sex practices that may lead to increased risk for AIDS and other sexually

BOX 10.1   Pharmacology in Action

The Role of Expectation in Alcohol-Enhanced Human Sexual Response

One problem in evaluating the effects of alcohol on behavior is that individuals have expectations about how alcohol will affect them. It is frequently believed (in our culture) that alcohol will increase sociability, reduce anxiety and tension, increase aggression, and enhance sexual responses. However, many of the effects of alcohol, especially at low doses, are due more to the individual's expectation of effect than to the drug's pharmacological effect (Marlatt and Rohsenow, 1980).

As you probably recall, experiments measuring drug effects have at least two groups of subjects: a drug treatment group and a placebo (nondrug) group, who generally assume they are also receiving the drug. Since both groups expect to receive the drug, any difference in their scores reflects the effect of the drug alone. However, because both groups believe they are getting the drug, there is no direct measure of the extent of **expectancy**. A further elaboration of the research design that more specifically tests the role that expectation plays is a four-block or 2 × 2 design (see figure). In this design, half the subjects are *told* that they will get alcohol and half are *told* that they will get placebo. Half of each of the two groups will actually get alcohol. Thus, two groups get what they are expecting, and two groups are deceived and receive the opposite treatment.

To be effective, these experiments must completely deceive the subjects; this includes providing the alcohol in a way that it cannot be detected, such as combining vodka and tonic and at relatively low doses. In addition, subjects must be deceived about the purpose of the experiment, for instance, by being told that they

are involved in a taste test of different vodkas or different tonic waters.

Results from experiments using the 2 × 2 design support the hypothesis that when subjects think they have received alcohol, their behavior reflects their *expectations* of the drug effect. For example, in one study, college students watched erotic videos showing heterosexual and homosexual activities. The low dose of alcohol administered (0.04%) did not have an effect on physiological arousal as measured by penile tumescence, but an expectancy effect occurred. The group *expecting* to receive alcohol showed more physical and subjective arousal than the group that did not expect to receive alcohol, regardless of whether they actually received alcohol or not (Wilson and Lawson, 1976). This seems to be a case in which a drinker's beliefs about the effects of a drug become a self-fulfilling prophecy, and actions match expectations.

Another way to isolate pharmacological effects from expectations is to look at cross-cultural studies. Those of us who drink alcohol or observe others drinking may believe that alcohol induces our amorous nature, makes us more sexually appealing, and enhances our basic sexuality. But does it really? The observations of the anthropologists MacAndrew and Edgerton (1969) say something quite different. They found, for example, that the Camba of Bolivia are a people with strong, almost puritanical taboos regarding sexual activities. When intoxicated, they become extremely gregarious and outgoing, maintaining festivities long into the night. However, regardless of the revelry, they never fail to maintain strict sexual limits. The Tarhumara of Mexico also strictly limit sexual encounters under normal conditions. However, when they are drunk, mate swapping becomes the norm and is not considered inappropriate. For the Lepcha of Sikkim, sex is the primary recreation beginning at age 10 or 11 and continuing through old age. Adultery is expected and generates no ill will. Sex is an open topic for conversation and humor. During harvest festival time, large amounts of homemade liquor are consumed, and the Lepchas' casual sexual customs become wildly promiscuous to enhance the harvest. With adult encouragement, even 4- and 5-year-olds imitate copulation with each other. Nevertheless, their very strict guidelines regarding incest taboos are never broken even when Lepchas are quite drunk.

How can we explain experiences so different from our own? Does alcohol have a predetermined biological effect on sexual activity? Or does it induce disinhibition only within the context and limits of a given culture? How do *our* cultural expectations influence the effects of the drug?

(A)

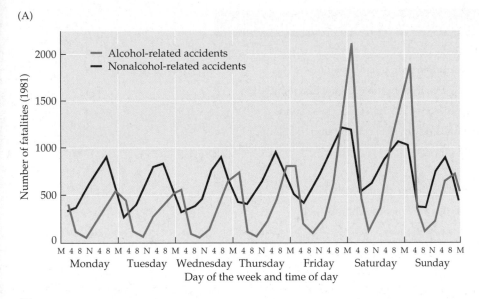

(B)

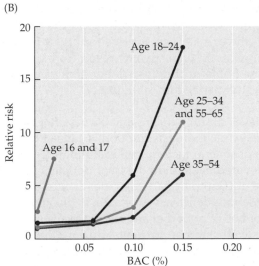

Figure 10.8 Relationship between alcohol use and traffic accidents
(A) The number of fatal auto accidents varies by day of the week, time of day, and alcohol involvement. Note that alcohol-related fatalities peak on Friday and Saturday nights after midnight, and that on other days, accidents involving alcohol also occur most frequently late at night. Nonalcohol-related fatalities appear to be greatest during rush hours on weekdays and just before midnight on weekends. (B) The relationship between BAC and relative risk for auto accidents is affected by several factors, including age of the driver and years of driving experience. Note that, in general, alcohol has a less detrimental effect on driving as drivers get older, but the 55-to-65-year age group is similar to the 25-to-34-year age group, which may indicate an interaction with age-related decreases in reaction time. The rapid rise in the number of accidents at BAC over 0.10% has prompted all states to reduce the definition of legal intoxication from 0.10% to 0.08%. M, midnight; N, noon. (A after NIAAA, 1983; B after OECD, 1978.)

transmitted diseases. In a large representative sample of 12,069 young men and women, a significant relationship between alcohol use and sexual risk taking was found even after controls were applied for age, education, and family income (Parker et al., 1994). Because the relationship between alcohol use and unsafe sex is correlational, no clear cause-and-effect relationship can be assumed, and other factors such as rebellion against societal expectations may be responsible for both.

Acute effects of alcohol on memory vary with dose and task difficulty (Jung, 2001). At low doses, memory deficits are based more on expectation than on the quantity of alcohol actually consumed. Further, under high-stress conditions, alcohol may enhance performance by minimizing the damaging effects of anxiety. However, high doses of alcohol rapidly consumed may produce total amnesia for events that occur during intoxication, despite the fact that the individual

is behaving quite normally. This amnesia is called a **blackout**, and it is a common occurrence for alcoholics but also occurs in about 25% of social drinkers (Campbell and Hodgins, 1993).

Reduced coordination leads to slurred speech, impaired fine-motor skills, and delayed reaction time. Reductions in reaction times for multiple stimuli, along with reductions in attention, increased sedation and drowsiness, and impaired judgment and emotional control, contribute to the increased probability of being involved in automobile accidents. Alcohol is involved in about half of all highway deaths, and there is a distinct temporal pattern of high-risk alcohol-related deaths (**Figure 10.8A**). In addition, a clear statistical relationship between BAC and the relative risk for an accident has been reported. At a BAC lower than 0.05%, the chances of having an accident are about the same as for nondrinking drivers,

TABLE 10.2   Blood Alcohol Concentration and Effects on Behavior

BAC	Effects on behavior
0.02–0.03	Minimal effects; slight relaxation; mild mood elevation
0.05–0.06	Decreased alertness; relaxed inhibitions; mildly impaired judgment
0.08–0.10	Loss of motor coordination; slower reaction times; less caution
0.14–0.16	Major impairment of mental and physical control; slurred speech; exaggerated emotions; blurred vision; serious loss of judgment; large increases in reaction time
0.20–0.25	Staggering; inability to walk or dress without help; tears or rage with little provocation; mental confusion; double vision
0.30	Conscious but in a stupor; unaware of surroundings
0.45	Coma; lethal for 50% of the population

but between 0.05% and 0.10%, the curve rises steeply to seven times the nondrinking rate. It is this large increase that has prompted all states to change their blood level for legal intoxication from 0.10% to 0.08%. Beyond 0.10%, risk increases dramatically by 20 to 50 times. However, the relationship is complex, and BAC interacts with both age and driving experience (**Figure 10.8B**). Use Table 10.1 to estimate the amount of alcohol that you must consume in 1 hour to reach the BAC that increases risk.

In addition to involvement in automobile fatalities, alcohol use is associated with homicide, rape, and other violent activities, although the direct pharmacological effect of alcohol is less clear. **Web Box 10.1** looks at this relationship. Aggression and many of the other effects of alcohol on behavior are highly dependent on the environment, the user's mental set, and her expectations.

With increasing doses, mild sedation deepens and produces sleep. Alcohol suppresses rapid-eye-movement (REM) episodes (periods when the most dreaming occurs), and withdrawal after repeated use produces a rebound in REM sleep that may interfere with normal sleep patterns and produce nightmares. Higher doses produce unconsciousness and death. The blood alcohol level that is lethal in 50% of the population is in the range of 0.45%, which is only about five or six times the blood level (0.08%) that produces intoxication. Fortunately, most people do not reach a lethal blood level because at around 0.15%, vomiting may occur, and a BAC of 0.35% usually causes unconsciousness, thereby preventing further drinking. However, if alcohol is consumed very rapidly, as might occur in binge drinking, lethal blood levels may be reached before the individual passes out.

The usual symptoms of **alcohol poisoning** include unconsciousness; vomiting; slow and irregular breathing; and skin that is cold, clammy, and pale bluish in color. Death from acute alcohol ingestion is caused by depression of the respiratory control center in the brainstem. Once the respiratory mechanism is depressed, the drinker can survive for about 5 minutes, although brain damage may result from oxygen deprivation. Some of the dose-dependent effects of alcohol are summarized in **Table 10.2**.

BRAIN DAMAGE   Brain damage that occurs after many years of heavy alcohol consumption is caused by the interaction of several factors, including high levels of alcohol, elevated acetaldehyde, liver deficiency, and inadequate nutrition. In particular, heavy alcohol use produces a serious deficiency in vitamin B_1 (thiamine) as the result of both a poor diet and failure to absorb that vitamin, as well as other nutrients, during digestion. Because thiamine is critical for brain glucose metabolism, its deficit causes cell death. One result is **Wernicke–Korsakoff syndrome**, which in its first stage is characterized by confusion and disorientation, as well as tremors, poor coordination, and ataxia. In later stages, the patient shows a significant memory disorder. Although the patient remembers the remote past, he remembers almost nothing of what goes on around him. He may read the same page over and over, repeatedly ask the same questions, or tell the same story. Although the syndrome is progressive, treatment with massive doses of vitamin B_1 can stop the degenerative process (if alcohol use stops), although it cannot reverse it. Wernicke–Korsakoff syndrome is characterized by bilateral cell loss in the medial thalamus and the mammillary bodies of the hypothalamus. Although nutritional deficits are not the sole cause of the disorder, the importance of thiamine to the degenerative process is evident in animal studies. Feeding animals a thiamine-deficient diet or treating them with a thiamine antagonist produces lesions in the same brain areas and also impairs learning and memory (Langlais and Savage, 1995). Selective brain

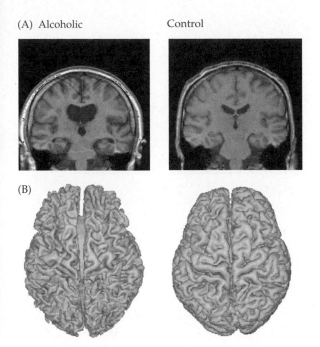

(A) Alcoholic   Control

(B)

Figure 10.9 Alcohol-induced brain damage (A) Brain images of an alcoholic male subject and a nonalcoholic male. Note the extreme difference in ventricle size, indicating tissue shrinkage in the brain of the alcoholic. (B) Exterior views of the brains (from above). In the alcoholic, the gyri are more narrow, and the sulci and fissure between the hemispheres are very enlarged, showing significant loss of tissue volume. (A from Pfefferbaum and Sullivan, 2004; B from Sullivan, 2000.)

lesions like those of Wernicke–Korsakoff syndrome are found in other individuals with severe nutritional deficiencies associated with gastrointestinal diseases, anorexia nervosa, or starvation.

Although thiamine deficiency causes the selective damage described in the previous paragraph, other brain areas frequently show cell loss that seems to be unrelated to diet. The enlarged ventricles in the brains of alcoholics attest to the extensive shrinkage of brain tissue (**Figure 10.9A**). Exterior views of alcoholic brains compared with controls show smaller brain mass (**Figure 10.9B**). Frontal lobes are most affected, and this may be responsible for the personality changes, including apathy, disinhibition, and diminished executive functioning (ability to formulate strategies and make decisions) seen in alcoholics. Tissue shrinkage that occurs in medial temporal lobe structures, including the hippocampus and cholinergic cells in the basal forebrain, contributes to memory disturbances. Symptoms that implicate the hippocampus and the basal forebrain include failure to remember recent events and failure to form new memories. Cerebellar cell loss is correlated with ataxia and incoordination, particularly of the lower limbs. These brain changes

are probably caused by multiple mechanisms, but glutamate-induced hyperexcitability of neurons during abstinence (see the section on neurotransmitters later in the chapter) may play a central role (Fadda and Rossetti, 1998).

EFFECTS ON OTHER ORGAN SYSTEMS   Alcohol has many effects on the body outside the CNS, including the:

- Cardiovascular system
- Renal–urinary system
- Reproductive system
- Gastrointestinal system
- Liver

One well-known cardiovascular effect of alcohol is the dilation of peripheral blood vessels, which brings them closer to the surface of the skin and makes an individual look flushed and feel warm. Of course, vasodilation means that heat is actually being lost from the body rather than being retained. Although the myth of the Saint Bernard dog rescuing stranded skiers with a keg of brandy around his neck is widespread, in reality, drinking alcohol when you are truly cold produces an even more serious drop in body temperature. Heavy drinkers who fall asleep outside in cold climates risk death from hypothermia. Within the brain, vasodilation may improve cognitive function in older adults. At the end of a 6-year period, researchers found that people 55 years and older who consumed one to three drinks a day were less than half as likely to have developed dementia linked to poor oxygen supply to the brain as those people who did not drink at all.

In addition to aiding circulation, a low to moderate daily dose of alcohol (e.g., fewer than three drinks) may reduce the risk of heart disease, because it increases the amount of "good" cholesterol in the blood while reducing the "bad" (Gaziano and Hennekens, 1995) and seems to reduce the incidence of blood clots and stroke. However, these beneficial effects are counteracted when consumption is greater. Alcoholism is associated with a higher-than-expected incidence of high blood pressure, stroke, and inflammation and enlargement of the heart muscle, which may be alcohol-induced or due to malnutrition and vitamin deficiency.

The action of alcohol on the renal–urinary system produces larger volumes of urine that is far more dilute than normal. The loss of fluids is caused by reduced secretion of antidiuretic hormone. Although this is not normally a matter of concern, alcohol consumption should be avoided by individuals involved in strenuous athletic activities for which fluids need to be maintained. Further, athletes should not try to rehydrate with any beverage that contains alcohol.

The effect of alcohol on reproductive function is complex. Alcohol is widely believed to enhance sexual arousal and lower inhibitions. However, Box 10.1 shows that expectation plays a large part in the effects of alcohol on sexual response. Furthermore, we need to distinguish between psychological arousal and physiological response. In one study, male college students consumed alcohol to achieve a BAC of 0%, 0.025%, 0.050%, or 0.075% while watching an erotic film (George and Norris, 1991). A plethysmograph was attached around the penis to measure degree of erection (both rate of tumescence and maximum achieved) during the film viewing. **Figure 10.10A** shows that low doses of alcohol enhanced arousal to a small extent, but higher blood levels reduced the male sexual response. Parallel studies with college women measured sexual arousal by assessing vaginal blood pressure or orgasmic latency. Physiological measures of sexual arousal decreased with increasing alcohol levels (**Figure 10.10B**); however, reported subjective arousal was increased. Although laboratory evaluations of sexual response are necessarily artificial, and ethical restraint prohibits testing higher levels of alcohol, research in general supports the inverse nature of physiological and subjective arousal with low to moderate alcohol use.

When alcohol use is heavy and chronic, males may become impotent and may show atrophy of the testicles, reduced sperm production, and shrinkage of the prostate and seminal vesicles. Alcoholic women often experience disrupted ovarian function and show a higher-than-normal incidence of menstrual disorders.

Alcohol alters gastrointestinal tract function in several ways. It increases salivation and secretion of gastric juices, which may explain its ability to increase appetite and aid digestion, although higher concentrations irritate the stomach lining, and chronic use produces inflammation of the stomach (gastritis), as well as of the esophagus. Heavy alcohol use causes diarrhea, inhibits utilization of proteins, and reduces absorption and metabolism of vitamins and minerals.

Among the most damaging effects of heavy chronic alcohol consumption is liver dysfunction. Three distinct disorders may develop. The first is **fatty liver**, which involves the accumulation of triglycerides inside liver cells. The liver normally takes up and metabolizes fatty acids as part of the digestive process; however, when alcohol is present, it is metabolized first, leaving the fat for storage. The condition produces no warning symptoms but is reversible, so if drinking stops, the liver begins to use the stored fat and returns to normal. However, some individuals who have abused alcohol for many years develop a serious and potentially lethal condition called

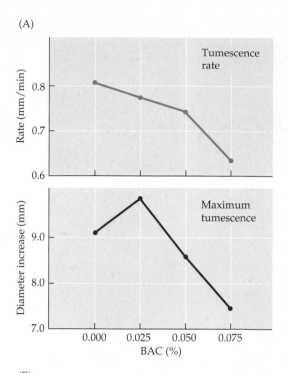

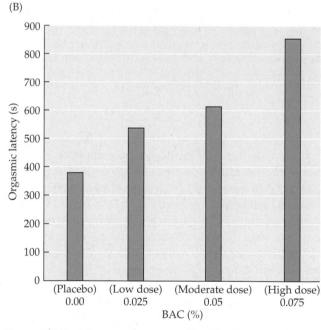

Figure 10.10 Effects of alcohol on sexual response (A) Changes in male sexual response occur after varying amounts of alcohol. With increasing concentrations of blood alcohol, both the rate of penile tumescence and the maximum size achieved decreased. (B) In women, increasing blood alcohol levels were directly proportional to orgasmic latency. (A after Farkas and Rosen, 1976; B after Blume, 1991.)

alcoholic hepatitis. Liver cell damage apparently is caused by accumulation of high levels of acetaldehyde (a metabolite of alcohol formed in the liver). Symptoms include inflammation of the liver, fever,

Figure 10.11 The effects of chronic alcohol use on the liver Portions of a healthy liver (left), a fatty liver (center), and a cirrhotic liver (right).

yellowing of the skin (jaundice), and pain. The death of liver cells stimulates the formation of scar tissue, which is characteristic of **alcoholic cirrhosis**. As scar tissue develops, blood vessels carrying oxygen are cut off, leading to further cell death. **Figure 10.11** compares pieces of normal liver, fatty liver, and cirrhotic liver from an alcoholic individual. Cirrhotic livers are usually firm or hard to the touch and develop nodules of tissue that give them a pebbly appearance. As cirrhosis continues, liver function decreases proportionately. Consumption of large quantities of alcohol over a prolonged period is necessary for the development of cirrhosis, and even among heavy drinkers, only 10% to 20% are likely to develop the disease. However, the incidence of alcoholic cirrhosis has increased over the past 10 years, and it is most common in men between 40 and 60 years of age. Although the liver damage is irreversible, cessation of drinking slows the rate of damage. For severe liver damage, the most effective treatment is liver transplant surgery. Although the damaging effects of alcohol are found in both men and women, there are significant gender differences (**Box 10.2**).

EFFECTS ON THE UNBORN Because alcohol readily passes through the placental barrier, the alcohol that a pregnant female consumes is delivered almost immediately to her fetus, who reaches the same BAC. The damaging developmental effects of prenatal alcohol exposure lead to **fetal alcohol syndrome** (**FAS**). One of the greatest tragedies of FAS is that it occurs at all. Fetal alcohol exposure is the most common cause of mental retardation in the United States and could be prevented. Although the damaging effects of alcohol on an adult generally take decades of heavy drinking, the developing embryo is

far more susceptible. The major and minor birth defects that constitute FAS present a challenge to families, social services, and the educational system. The cost for serving those individuals with only the most severe symptoms is more than $321 million a year in the United States, and billions more might be spent on special care for the less impaired (Williams et al., 1994).

Diagnostic signs and symptoms include the following:

1. *Mental retardation and other developmental delays.* The average IQ for an individual with FAS is 68. Such an individual generally attains an average reading level of a fourth grader and the average math skills of second grade. The development of typical motor milestones is delayed, and evidence of poor coordination, slow response times, and language disabilities is common.

2. *Low birthweight (below the 10th percentile).* In addition, infants fail to thrive, exhibiting poor catch-up growth.

3. *Neurological problems.* Some infants are born with high alcohol levels and experience withdrawal from the drug, which includes tremors and seizures starting within 6 to 12 hours of birth and lasting as long as a week. Abnormal electroencephalogram recordings persist, and the infant shows a high degree of irritability and hypersensitivity to sound. These infants show poor sucking reflexes, hyperactivity, attentional deficits, and poor sleep patterns.

4. *Distinctive craniofacial malformations.* These include a small head, small wide-set eyes with drooping eyelids, a short upturned nose, a thin upper lip, and flattening of the vertical groove between the nose and upper lip (**Figure 10.12A**). The infants may also show low-set and nonparallel ears, malformations of the ear that produce hearing deficits, cleft palate, and reduced growth of the lower jaw.

5. *Other physical abnormalities.* Cardiac defects such as a hole between the chambers or deformed blood vessels in the heart, failure of kidney development, undescended testes, and skeletal abnormalities in fingers and toes are common.

How sure are we that alcohol itself is teratogenic (i.e., causes birth defects)? After all, women who use high doses of alcohol often have poor nutrition, smoke cigarettes or use other drugs, have poor health overall, and receive poor prenatal care. These issues have been well controlled in animal research that can regulate the amount of alcohol, the pattern of consumption, the timing of alcohol use during the pregnancy, and the diet of the mother. Early conclusions and subsequent research agree that prenatal alcohol does

BOX 10.2 Of Special Interest

Gender Differences in Alcohol Effects

Research into the effects of alcohol has traditionally focused on males because it is generally assumed that drinking and drinking problems are far more prevalent among men. Although males are more likely to be heavy drinkers and binge drinkers, annual National Household Surveys have shown that both sexes start drinking at younger ages, and that the number of females who drink excessively is increasing. Hence more research is needed in the area of gender-specific differences in the effects of alcohol on the brain and body, as well as family dynamics and the potential for alcohol-induced damage in the offspring of a female drinker.

Although the prevalence of alcoholism is higher in men (20%) than in women (5% to 6%), there is general agreement among researchers that both alcohol-induced organ damage and related medical issues are more severe in women and develop more quickly (reviewed by Ceylan-Isik et al., 2010; Mancinelli et al., 2009). Female alcoholics have a significantly higher death rate than male alcoholics. This vulnerability is due to metabolic, genetic, physiological, neurobiological, and hormonal factors. We have already mentioned that less efficient gastric metabolism by alcohol dehydrogenase and the smaller fluid volume in women causes more rapidly rising and higher blood levels for equivalent doses. Since BAC predicts the effects of alcohol, women experience more acute effects, including increased memory impairment, greater probability of experiencing blackouts, and increased motor impairment. Pharmacokinetic differences determine the time course of alcohol levels and the degree of organ exposure, which increase a woman's risk and speed up the occurrence of potential liver damage, circulatory disorders, breast cancer, fertility impairment, and a range of reproductive problems. Estrogen may also speed up liver damage because of its role in inflammatory processes, and the use of oral contraceptives may contribute still further. Females are also more sensitive to acetaldehyde-induced depression of cardiac contraction, which may be the basis for the higher rates of cardiomyopathy reported in alcoholic women.

Alcohol-induced brain damage and reduced brain volume in women take fewer years of heavy drinking than in men. Imaging studies have shown greater reductions in both gray and white matter in women alcoholics, accompanied by expected impairments in cognitive and psychomotor function. Reduced volume of the hippocampus has been reported in alcohol-abusing adolescents compared with others of the same age, but girls are apparently more vulnerable than boys to alcohol-induced shrinkage. Thiamine deficiency is greater in alcoholic women, and this may explain some of the increased risk for dementia and Wernicke–Korsakoff syndrome. Low thiamine in combination with exposure to toxins in the environment is predictive of greater teratogenic effects in pregnancy. In general, ingested lead is rapidly excreted, but under higher exposure, thiamine acts as a regulator of lead levels. Alcohol-induced thiamine reduction permits an accumulation of lead in the alcoholic female in bone, hair, and liver, where impaired mitochondrial function and decreasing cellular energy reserves (adenosine triphosphate [ATP]) occur. Additionally, the lead has a synergistic effect with alcohol on the developing fetus, producing greater neurobehavioral impairment in offspring and more impaired postnatal development.

It is of significant interest that the effects of alcohol use on neurotransmitter systems vary with gender. For instance, one recent study examined gender differences in DA release in response to alcohol consumption among social drinkers (Urban et al., 2010). PET imaging following ethanol ingestion showed significant release of DA in the nucleus accumbens, to a greater extent for males than for females. Additionally, among male but not female subjects, there was a positive correlation between their subjective evaluation of alcohol-induced activation and the amount of DA released; this may contribute to differences in early reinforcing effects that lead to compulsive use. Of further importance was the inverse relationship found between the frequency of the maximum number of drinks consumed per 24 hours according to self-reported drinking and DA release, once again only in men. This relationship indicates that heavier drinking individuals (i.e., those consuming more in 24 hours), who have a greater potential for addiction, release less DA. It is possible that reduced DA release may parallel the transition from a social drinker to a stronger habit. Differences in DA release among men and women may provide a neurobiological mechanism to explain the increased vulnerability to alcoholism in men. Many other sex-specific differences in DA signaling in various brain regions have been reported, including

BOX 10.2 *(continued)*

larger numbers of DA cells in the female mesocortical tract and sex-specific specializations in DA receptor localization and number of D_2 receptors. The mechanism responsible for gender differences and its significance for reward and addiction are not clear at this time, although gonadal steroid hormone modulation is a distinct possibility. Ceylan-Isik and colleagues (2010) review gender differences in the effects of alcohol on DA, as well as on GABA and glutamate.

---

induce both physical defects and behavioral deficits in animals that closely resemble those seen in humans. Single large doses of alcohol given to pregnant mice produced abnormalities in the developing fetuses (**Figure 10.12B**), including eye damage, smaller brains, and facial deformities similar to those seen in human babies with FAS. The amount of alcohol responsible was equivalent to that consumed when a woman drinks a quart of whiskey over 24 hours.

Blood alcohol level is important in estimating the risk and severity of teratogenic effects, but the pattern of alcohol use that contributes to the peak maternal blood alcohol level is equally important. In one rodent study, 12 equally spaced doses of alcohol that produced maternal blood levels up to 0.12% did not affect fetal brain growth. In contrast, the same total amount of alcohol given in condensed fashion raised maternal blood levels to a range between 0.20% and 0.35% and caused a significant decrease in brain weight (Randall et al., 1990). Although this blood level is quite high, it is consistent with blood levels seen after binge drinking in humans.

Animal research is well supported by many studies with humans showing that heavy maternal drinking, particularly of the binge type, is associated with significant behavioral and emotional problems, as well as cognitive deficits, in offspring. However, the effects of low to moderate alcohol consumption on fetal development are somewhat less clear. Although multiple studies have shown deficits in attention, aggressive behavior, and learning difficulties after moderate prenatal alcohol exposure, others have reported no measurable adverse outcomes following low to moderate amounts. Oddly, in a limited number of studies, researchers reported a J-shaped relationship between amount of maternal alcohol consumed and scores on measures of hyperactivity, emotional difficulties, and conduct problems (Kelly et al., 2009). This means that children whose mothers were light drinkers (not more than 1 to 2 drinks per week or per occasion) showed

(A)

Figure 10.12 Fetal alcohol syndrome (A) Distinctive craniofacial malformations in a child with FAS. (B) Fetal abnormalities in mice exposed to alcohol in utero. (B from Sulik et al., 1981.)

(B) Normal

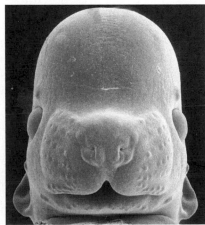

Exposed to alcohol

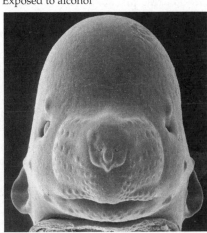

fewer problems than those whose mothers were totally abstinent. Why light drinking seemed to be beneficial is unclear. As expected, children of heavy drinking mothers showed significantly more problems than those of the abstainers.

The discrepancies among studies are troubling because evidence suggesting that low levels of alcohol are relatively safe could encourage women to drink during pregnancy and if erroneous could lead to less optimal fetal outcomes. On the other hand, if small amounts of alcohol are safe to consume, women who drank lightly early in their pregnancy (when many are unaware of their status) would experience less guilt, anxiety, and stress over unintentionally harming their child. Unfortunately, correlational epidemiological studies such as these are plagued with methodological difficulties because in this retrospective research, women may inaccurately recall the quantity, timing, frequency, and pattern of alcohol use, all of which are critical factors determining fetal outcome. Some may under-report their consumption because of social pressure against drinking during pregnancy. In addition, many other variables such as the psychological health of the mother, maternal medical issues and other drugs being used, socioeconomic differences, level of stress experienced, adequacy of maternal nutrition, genetics, and parenting styles are likely to modulate the effects of prenatal alcohol and behavioral outcomes in the child. Others have suggested that the differences among studies may reflect the particular cognitive test used and its sensitivity or the manner in which behavioral outcomes are evaluated. Additionally, sociocultural differences, including the type of liquor consumed and whether it is part of a meal, may make results less generalizable across cultures (Todorow et al., 2010). Although controversy is likely to continue in the future, given that the threshold for adverse effects is unknown and that how it might vary from individual to individual is equally unclear, the safest option at this time is abstinence during pregnancy.

In addition to the amount and pattern of alcohol ingestion, the developmental stage of the fetus when exposed to alcohol is critical in determining the specific effects. Organ systems are most vulnerable to damage during the period of most rapid development. Alcohol ingestion at the time of conception significantly increases the risk of teratogenic effects, and within the first 3 weeks, the fetus may not survive. Alcohol use during the fourth to ninth weeks—a time when many women are unaware of their pregnancy—produces the most severe formative damage and severe mental retardation. Alcohol use later in pregnancy causes slowed growth. Since the brain is one of the first organ systems to begin to develop but

is the last to be complete, alcohol use at any point in the pregnancy can have damaging effects on the CNS. Obviously, if drinking is constant throughout fetal development, the effects will be much greater than if drinking is stopped mid-pregnancy.

Although the damaging effects of fetal alcohol exposure are clear, its precise mechanism is less certain. It has been suggested that acetaldehyde may be the toxic agent; other possible mechanisms include decreased blood flow in the uterine artery, reduced oxygen availability, and placental dysfunction, which reduces the transport of vital amino acids, glucose, folate, and zinc. Hormone-like substances called prostaglandins are suspected of mediating teratogenic effects because inhibitors of prostaglandins, such as aspirin, reduce alcohol-induced birth defects in animals. Additional research showed that ethanol acting on both glutamate and γ-aminobutyric acid (GABA) neurons may trigger significant cell death (apoptosis) in the developing brain (Ikonomidou et al., 2000).

Section Summary

- The small non-ionized alcohol molecule is absorbed from the GI tract by passive diffusion—a process slowed by food in the stomach. Absorption in women is faster because reduced gastric metabolism and smaller body size increase the concentration.

- 95% of alcohol is metabolized by the liver at a constant rate of 1 to 1.5 ounces per hour; 5% is excreted by the lungs.

- Alcohol dehydrogenase converts alcohol to the toxic product acetaldehyde. Further metabolism produces carbon dioxide, water, and energy.

- The cytochrome P450 enzyme CYP 2E1 metabolizes alcohol, as well as other drugs. Consuming them together may lead to dangerous blood levels because they compete for the limited amount of enzyme.

- Acute tolerance occurs within a single drinking episode and may lead to dangerous driving when binge drinkers perceive that they are less intoxicated on the descending limb of the blood alcohol curve.

- Chronic alcohol use increases cytochrome P450 enzymes (enzyme induction) so metabolism is more rapid, causing metabolic tolerance to the effects of alcohol and cross-tolerance to other drugs metabolized by the same enzyme.

- Continued presence of alcohol produces compensatory changes in neuron function (pharmacodynamic tolerance).

- Practicing an operant task under the influence of alcohol leads to improved performance (behavioral tolerance of the operant type). Repeated alcohol administration in the same environment leads to the development of a compensatory response that occurs only in that environment (behavioral tolerance of the classical conditioning type).

- Alcohol produces physical dependence and cross-dependence with other sedative–hypnotic drugs.

- Withdrawal after chronic heavy use lasts for days and includes tremor, anxiety, high blood pressure and heart rate, sweating, rapid breathing, and nausea and vomiting. Severe withdrawal effects called delirium tremens include hallucinations, convulsions, disorientation, and intense anxiety.

- Behavioral effects of alcohol are directly related to BAC, but at low doses, the environment and expectations of effects are significant.

- Dose-dependent effects on the CNS include relaxation, reduced anxiety, intoxication, impaired judgment, impaired memory, and sleep. Higher doses produce coma and death as the result of respiratory depression.

- Heavy long-term alcohol use causes a vitamin B_1 deficiency leading to cell death in the medial thalamus and mammillary bodies causing Wernicke–Korsakoff syndrome: tremors, ataxia, and poor memory consolidation. Multiple brain regions may be damaged by glutamate-induced excitotoxicity.

- Beneficial alcohol-induced cardiovascular effects include vasodilation, elevation of good cholesterol, and lowering of bad cholesterol. Alcoholism increases the risk of high blood pressure, stroke, and heart enlargement.

- Alcohol has a diuretic effect, increases sexual arousal while decreasing performance, increases appetite, and aids digestion by increasing gastric secretions.

- Liver damage associated with alcoholism includes fatty liver, alcoholic hepatitis, and alcoholic cirrhosis.

- Prenatal exposure to alcohol may produce FAS, which is characterized by mental retardation and other developmental delays, low birthweight, neurological problems, head and facial malformations, and other physical abnormalities.

- Effects of prenatal exposure are dependent on blood alcohol level, pattern of alcohol use, fetal developmental stage at time of exposure, maternal nutrition, genetics, and comorbid drug use.

- Studies of FAS in humans show significant behavioral and cognitive problems after high maternal drinking, particularly of the binge type. Because retrospective correlational studies have many methodological problems, the effects of low to moderate alcohol use are less clear, with reports of deficits, no effect, or even beneficial effects.

Neurochemical Effects of Alcohol

The neurochemical effects of alcohol have proved more difficult to examine than those of some other drugs. One important reason is the chemical nature of the alcohol molecule, which not only provides the means for easy penetration into the brain but, more importantly, influences the phospholipid bilayer of neurons. The latter action has a widespread impact on many normal cell functions and also modifies the actions of many neurotransmitter systems. In addition, the initial effects of alcohol must be separated from the neuronal changes that occur after long-term drug use. For these and other reasons, research using animal experimentation is particularly important.

Animal models are vital for alcohol research

Animal models are particularly important in alcohol studies for several reasons. First, because research animals are maintained in controlled and healthful environments, some of the common human correlates of heavy alcohol use are eliminated: poor nutrition, liver damage, associated psychiatric disorders, and use of multiple drugs. Second, animal models allow us to use methods that are not appropriate for human subjects. For example, studies using controlled chronic alcohol consumption can tell us about the long-term damaging effects on body functions and behavior and can model the effects of alcohol withdrawal. The effects of prenatal alcohol can be evaluated independently of issues such as maternal nutrition and substance abuse. Also, invasive procedures can be used to manipulate and measure the neurobiological correlates of intoxication, reinforcement, and behavioral effects of alcohol.

Third, genetic manipulations are possible (reviewed by Crabbe et al., 2010). When large numbers of animals (usually mice or rats) are screened, a few will be found to voluntarily drink large quantities of alcohol rather than water, while most drink little of the ethanol solution. Two populations of animals can be developed by selectively breeding the heaviest drinkers and the abstainers over several generations (**Figure 10.13**). Strains of alcohol-preferring or nonpreferring animals may model human alcohol consumption and abuse and can be used to study behavioral, biochemical, and genetic differences. Animals can be bred for numerous

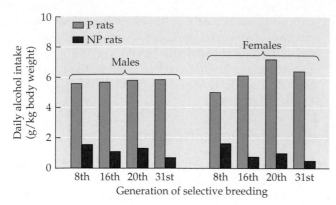

Figure 10.13 Average daily alcohol consumption for selected generations of rats bred for alcohol-preferring (P) and alcohol-nonpreferring (NP) behavior. Males and females show similar alcohol consumption. (After Stewart and Li, 1997.)

alcohol-related characteristics including sensitivity to alcohol, intensity of withdrawal, and so forth. A second type of study uses genetically altered animals that fail to express a particular protein. These knockout animals are used to evaluate the role of one particular protein, for example, a specific receptor, in the effects of ethanol. Fourth, animal models serve as screening tools for evaluating treatment strategies. Several excellent reviews of animal models of various components of alcoholism, including adolescent onset, motivation, abstinence, and relapse, are available for further study (Ripley and Stephens, 2011; Camarini et al., 2010).

The operant self-administration model used to evaluate the reinforcing effects of various drugs is described in Chapter 4. Although the paradigm is an important way to evaluate positive reinforcement and potential substance abuse, self-administration procedures are more difficult with alcohol than with other drugs of abuse because most animals will not spontaneously consume enough alcohol to produce intoxication. However, one of several "training" methods can be used to get animals to self-administer alcohol. With the first, all dry food is presented once a day during the drinking session. Initially, water is available, but gradually increasing amounts of alcohol are added over a number of sessions. Finally, food presentation occurs at a different time, but the animals continue to consume the alcohol. Alternatively, after operant training to lever-press for a sucrose solution, the sucrose is gradually reduced in concentration and alcohol is gradually substituted until the animals are self-administering high levels of alcohol.

It is important to realize that since animals do not naturally develop alcoholism or even alcohol abuse, no direct animal model of the complex human condition with its drinking pattern and quantity of consumption, development of compulsion to drink, and escalation of drinking despite aversive events is possible. The best efforts can model only specific components of alcoholism (i.e., biomarkers that contribute to the disorder). For example, chronically feeding rodents an alcohol diet and subjecting them to repeated episodes of withdrawal leads to impaired fear conditioning and poor cognitive processing. Similar impairments were subsequently noted in alcoholic individuals who had experienced repeated detoxification. These cognitive impairments were further found to be associated with withdrawal-induced loss of gray matter in the ventromedial prefrontal cortex (vmPFC). These types of models represent efforts to improve translational research and to move discoveries from animal research more quickly into clinical applications (see Chapter 4). These and other animal models are described by Ripley and Stephens (2011).

Alcohol acts on multiple neurotransmitters

Because alcohol is such a simple molecule, it readily crosses cell membranes, including the blood–brain barrier, and can be detected in the brain within minutes after consumption. Alcohol has both specific and nonspecific actions. *Nonspecific actions* depend on its ability to move into membranes, changing the fluid character of the lipids that make up the membrane (**Figure 10.14**). As you might expect, the protein molecules that are embedded in that membrane are likely to function differently when their "environment" changes so dramatically and becomes less rigid. In contrast, at low to moderate doses, alcohol seems to interact with specific sites on particular proteins, and these *specific actions* are probably responsible for most of the acute effects of ethanol at intoxicating doses. Alcohol not only influences several ligand-gated channels but also directly alters second-messenger systems. For example, ethanol stimulates the G protein (G_s) that activates the cyclic adenosine monophosphate (cAMP) second-messenger system (Figure 10.14, step 7). The ability to identify specific sites of ethanol action ultimately will lead to discovery of new drugs that will compete with ethanol to prevent particular undesirable effects.

This section describes the acute effects of alcohol on several neurotransmitters, suggesting possible connections between the transmitter action and specific effects of alcohol. In addition, it examines the neuroadaptations that occur with repeated alcohol use as they link to tolerance and dependence. Throughout this discussion, keep in mind that no neurotransmitter system works in isolation; changes in each one certainly modify other neurotransmitters in an interdependent fashion.

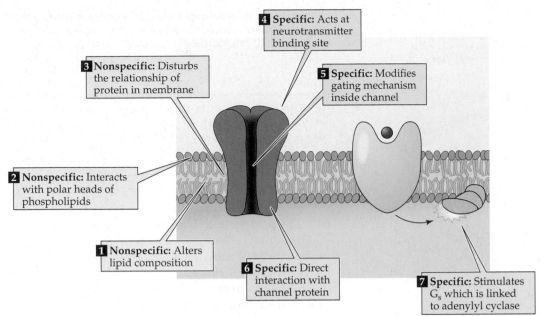

4 **Specific:** Acts at neurotransmitter binding site

5 **Specific:** Modifies gating mechanism inside channel

3 **Nonspecific:** Disturbs the relationship of protein in membrane

2 **Nonspecific:** Interacts with polar heads of phospholipids

1 **Nonspecific:** Alters lipid composition

6 **Specific:** Direct interaction with channel protein

7 **Specific:** Stimulates G_s which is linked to adenylyl cyclase

Figure 10.14 Effects of alcohol on neuronal membranes Alcohol acts at both specific and nonspecific sites, including membrane phospholipids, ligand-gated channels, and second-messenger systems.

GLUTAMATE As you may recall from Chapter 8, glutamate is a major excitatory neurotransmitter in the nervous system and has receptors on many cells in the CNS. Of the several subtypes of glutamate receptor, alcohol has its greatest effect on the NMDA (*N*-methyl-D-aspartate) receptor, which is a ligand-gated channel that allows positively charged ions (Ca^{2+} and Na^+) to enter and cause localized depolarization. Glutamate action at NMDA receptors mediates associative learning (see Chapter 8) and also has a role in the damaging effects of excessive glutamate activity (excitotoxicity), as in the case of prolonged seizures or after stroke. Let's look at the role of NMDA receptors in several effects of alcohol: (1) memory loss associated with intoxication; (2) rebound hyperexcitability associated with the abstinence syndrome after long-term use; and (3) NMDA-mediated excitotoxicity associated with alcoholic brain damage.

Alcohol acutely inhibits glutamate neurotransmission by reducing the effectiveness of glutamate at the NMDA receptor. These effects occur at concentrations as low as 0.03%, blood levels normally achieved by social drinkers. Alcohol, like other glutamate antagonists, impairs learning and memory, as has been shown in studies of long-term potentiation (LTP) and conditioning (Fadda and Rossetti, 1998). In addition, alcohol significantly reduces glutamate release in many brain areas, including the hippocampus, as measured by microdialysis. Reduced glutamate release in the hippocampus is correlated with deficits in spatial memory. The combination of temporary inhibition of NMDA receptors by alcohol and reduced glutamate release may produce the amnesia that occurs for events that take place during intoxication (i.e., the blackouts so typical of heavy drinking) (Diamond and Gordon, 1997).

In the adult brain, repeated use of alcohol leads to a neuroadaptive *increase* in the number of NMDA receptors (up-regulation) in response to reduced glutamate activity. The number of NMDA receptors in both the cerebral cortex and hippocampus is elevated in human alcoholics, as well as in animal models of chronic alcohol exposure. In addition, in dependent rats, glutamate release, normally inhibited by alcohol, is dramatically increased at about 10 hours after withdrawal of alcohol. The time course (**Figure 10.15**) of CNS hyperexcitability and the seizures that are typical of the alcohol abstinence syndrome matches the pattern of increased glutamate release during withdrawal. Further, there is a strong positive correlation between the magnitude of glutamate output during withdrawal and the intensity of abstinence signs. This means that the increased glutamate acting on up-regulated NMDA receptors may be one neurochemical correlate of alcohol withdrawal. Additionally, the elevated glutamate activity during withdrawal causes excessive calcium influx, which contributes to cell death. Frequently experienced withdrawal may be responsible for some of the irreversible brain damage described earlier.

Additionally, studies with rats show that maternal BACs as low as 0.04% during the last trimester of pregnancy can impair NMDA receptors and decrease glutamate release in the newborn. Unlike in the mature brain, inhibition of glutamate systems

(A)

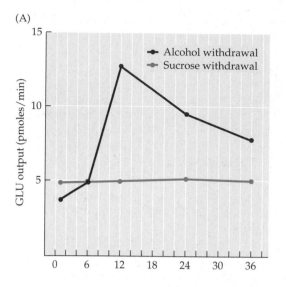

(B)

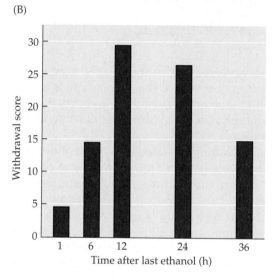

Figure 10.15 **Relationship between alcohol withdrawal and glutamate release** Withdrawal from chronic alcohol in dependent rats increases glutamate (GLU) release in the striatum (A) and behavioral rebound withdrawal hyperexcitability (B). The time course of the two withdrawal-related events is very similar. Experimental animals received intragastric delivery of ethanol at intoxicating concentrations (2–5 g/kg) every 6 hours for 6 consecutive days. Control animals received an equally caloric sucrose solution. On day 7, ethanol administration was terminated, and behavioral testing of abstinence signs and simultaneous microdialysis collection began. (After Fadda and Rossetti, 1998.)

it is not surprising to find that alcohol also modulates GABA function, both directly via GABA_A receptors and indirectly by stimulating GABA release.

What kind of biochemical and electrophysiological evidence suggests that alcohol increases GABA-induced Cl⁻ flux and hyperpolarization? First, picrotoxin (which blocks the Cl⁻ channel) and bicuculline (which competes with GABA for its receptor) antagonize both the hyperpolarization and some of the behavioral effects of alcohol. This suggests that both Cl⁻ conductance and GABA binding to the receptor are necessary for the effects of alcohol to occur. Second, manipulations that increase GABA (e.g., inhibiting its degradation) also increase alcohol-induced behavioral effects. Likewise, reducing GABA function with antagonists reduces signs of ethanol intoxication and its antianxiety effects (Grobin et al., 1998). Third, lines of mice bred for their sensitivity to some of the behavioral effects of alcohol show a relationship between the ability of ethanol to increase GABA-induced Cl⁻ entry and the intensity of their response to alcohol. Greater incoordination and loss of righting reflex in vivo corresponded to greater alcohol-induced Cl⁻ influx into the animals' brain preparations in vitro (Mihic and Harris, 1997).

Just as benzodiazepines modulate some GABA_A receptors and not others, depending on the isoform of subunits of the receptor that are present (see Chapter 8), so too alcohol acts on some GABA_A receptors and not others. For instance, male knockout mice lacking GABA_A receptors that have an α1 or β2 subunit show less loss of the righting reflex after alcohol administration, indicating that those receptors mediate the sedative–hypnotic effects of alcohol. Furthermore, some receptors respond to the low doses of alcohol achieved by social drinking, and others modulate GABA function only at the high concentrations associated with greater intoxication. GABA_A receptors that are highly sensitive to alcohol contain a δ subunit (instead of the more usual γ), along with α4 or α6 subunits and are located *extrasynaptically*. Although most GABA_A receptors located synaptically respond transiently to

in the fetus may disrupt normal brain development, resulting in *reduced* NMDA receptors in the adult. It is reasonable to suspect that a reduction in NMDA receptors is related to subtle impairments in learning and memory in children born to alcoholic mothers, but further investigation is required.

GABA   GABA (γ-aminobutyric acid) is a major inhibitory amino acid neurotransmitter described in Chapter 8. It binds to the GABA_A receptor complex and opens the chloride (Cl⁻) channel, allowing Cl⁻ to enter the cell to hyperpolarize the membrane. Many classic sedative–hypnotic drugs (see Chapter 18) such as the benzodiazepines (e.g., Valium) and the barbiturates (e.g., phenobarbital) are known to enhance the effects of GABA at the GABA_A receptor by binding to their modulatory sites on the receptor complex. Since the drugs in this class and alcohol produce many of the same actions and show both cross-tolerance and cross-dependence,

GABA released into the synapse, extrasynaptic receptors respond in a more persistent fashion to GABA that remains in the extracellular space to produce tonic inhibition. Because they are more sensitive to the effects of alcohol, these extrasynaptic receptors are more likely to have a role in the behavioral and subjective effects produced by low or moderate amounts of drinking.

Additionally, evidence from several studies suggests that extrasynaptic GABA receptors have a role in the reinforcing effects of oral ethanol and in that way may contribute to the development of alcohol abuse (Nie et al., 2011; Rewal et al., 2012). Using a gene silencing technique in adult rodents, researchers produced rats that had fewer δ and α4 subunit-containing $GABA_A$ receptors. These animals showed a lower preference for alcohol, consumed less alcohol, and bar pressed less for access to oral alcohol. Furthermore, this effect was specific for alcohol and did not alter the animals' response to other reinforcers (sucrose solution), nor did it interfere with bar-pressing motor performance. It is significant that reducing receptors specifically in the shell of the nucleus accumbens but not in the core region altered alcohol intake because the shell has long been associated with self-administration not only of alcohol but of other drugs of abuse (see the next section on dopamine). Additional evidence from knockout, knockin, and pharmacological studies is needed to clarify which receptor subtypes in which cellular and anatomical locations respond to high and low concentrations of alcohol to produce various ethanol-related responses.

In contrast to the acute GABA-enhancing effects of alcohol, repeated exposure to ethanol *reduces* $GABA_A$-mediated Cl^- flux. Also, chronic alcohol makes animals more sensitive to seizure-inducing doses of the GABA antagonist bicuculline. We might expect this result, since it should take less of the antagonist to reduce GABA function because it has already been down-regulated by chronic alcohol. This neuroadaptive mechanism apparently compensates for the initial GABA-enhancing effect of alcohol and may contribute to the appearance of tolerance and some of the signs of withdrawal such as hyperexcitability, seizures, and tremors because of reduced GABA-mediated inhibition. Benzodiazepines also lose their GABA-enhancing effects at the receptor in mice treated chronically with ethanol, and this may serve as a mechanism for cross-tolerance with other sedative–hypnotic drugs.

It seems appropriate to once again mention that neuronal excitability is caused by a balance between excitation and inhibition. Since GABAergic neurons frequently have glutamate receptors and GABA frequently modulates glutamate release, the compensatory changes in each of the neurotransmitter systems may reflect an interaction of the two (Fadda and Rossetti, 1998).

DOPAMINE Evidence from biochemical, electrophysiological, and behavioral studies suggests that the dopaminergic mesolimbic system plays a significant role in the reinforcement and motivational mechanisms underlying behaviors that are vital to survival (see Chapter 5). The pathway begins in the ventral tegmental area (VTA) of the midbrain and courses rostrally to innervate various limbic structures, including the nucleus accumbens (NAcc) and the central nucleus of the amygdala (**Figure 10.16**). The NAcc is particularly important because part of it (the shell) belongs to a network of structures called the extended amygdala, which is involved in integrating emotion with hormonal responses and sympathetic nervous system activity. The core of the NAcc is associated with the striatum, which modulates movement. Afferents to and efferents from the NAcc provide a means for combining motivational status, emotional content, and motor responses (DiChiara, 1997). The role of the NAcc in substance abuse seems to consist of supplying the primary reinforcing qualities that lead to repeated drug use and the incentive or motivation for the drug, which helps to explain why alcohol is so addictive for some people.

Increased dopaminergic transmission in the mesolimbic pathway occurs in response to administration of most drugs of abuse, including alcohol. In rats, alcohol consumption at intoxicating concentrations increases the firing rate of dopaminergic neurons in the VTA and subsequently elevates the amount of dopamine (DA) released in the NAcc, as measured by microdialysis, although the release is greater in genetically selected alcohol-preferring rats than in nonpreferring animals. Rats in operant chambers self-

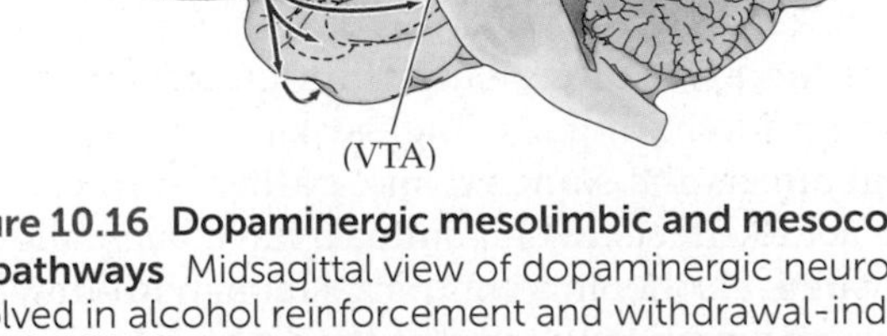

Figure 10.16 Dopaminergic mesolimbic and mesocortical pathways Midsagittal view of dopaminergic neurons involved in alcohol reinforcement and withdrawal-induced dysphoria. The ventral tegmental area (VTA) is the origin of neurons that innervate the nucleus accumbens, amygdala, hippocampus (mesolimbic), and the cortex (mesocortical).

(A)

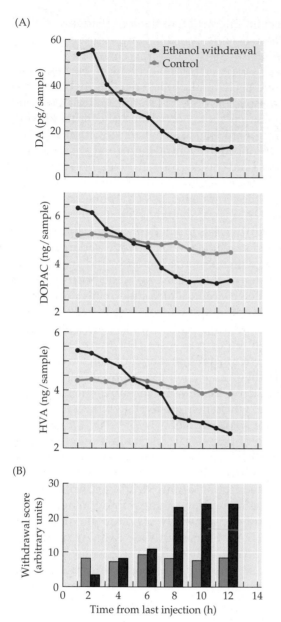

(B)

Figure 10.17 Dopamine turnover and alcohol withdrawal (A) Microdialysis collection of DA and its major metabolites, DOPAC and HVA, in the NAcc of rats at varying times after ethanol withdrawal shows significant reduction in DA turnover compared with control. (B) shows the development of abstinence signs in the same animals. Note the similarity in time course of biochemical measures and the occurrence of behavioral signs. The alcohol group received intoxicating doses of alcohol every 6 hours for 6 days before withdrawal. Control animals received sucrose of caloric value equal to the alcohol. The microdialysis collection of extracellular fluid and the behavioral measures of abstinence occurred at various times over the 12-hour period following ethanol withdrawal. Withdrawal scores were a composite of separate measures of tremor, vocalization on handling, bracing posture, rigidity, and others. (After Diana et al., 1993.)

administer ethanol directly into the VTA, which presumably activates those neurons (probably by inhibiting inhibitory cells). Microinjection of dopamine receptor antagonists into the NAcc reduces (but does not abolish) the self-administration of ethanol in rats, as you would expect because alcohol-induced DA release is ineffective when postsynaptic receptors are blocked.

Because alcohol consumption clearly increases mesolimbic cell firing, we might ask how alcohol withdrawal affects the same reward pathway. In contrast to the acute effects, when animals have been allowed to consume alcohol in a chronic fashion, withdrawal of the drug dramatically reduces the firing rate of mesolimbic neurons and decreases DA release in the NAcc (Diana et al., 1993). **Figure 10.17** shows the decrease in

synaptic DA in the NAcc, as well as the reduction in the DA metabolites 3,4-dihydroxyphenylacetic acid (DOPAC) and homovanillic acid (HVA), as measured by microdialysis at various times after the last injection of ethanol. This decrease began at approximately 5 hours after the last alcohol administration and reached a maximum at around 10 to 12 hours. The same animals showed behavioral signs of withdrawal that began at 8 to 10 hours and continued throughout the testing period. One might conclude that the behavioral signs, the reduced DA outflow, and the reduced mesolimbic cell firing, all of which were reversed by a single administration of alcohol, may represent the neurobiological correlate of the dysphoria associated with the alcohol withdrawal syndrome.

The reduction in mesolimbic DA is also reflected in a rebound depression of reinforcement mechanisms, as is shown by elevation of the threshold for intracranial stimulation. Elevated thresholds mean that more electrical current is needed to activate the reinforcing pathway (i.e., reinforcement is less rewarding than it was during the initial alcohol use). **Figure 10.18** shows that elevation of thresholds reached a maximum 6 to 8 hours after abrupt withdrawal and disappeared by 72 hours. This down-regulation of the neuronal system that mediates reward may be the neuroadaptive mechanism that is responsible for the negative emotional signs (dysphoria and depression) characteristic of withdrawal from many abused substances, including psychostimulants and opioids, as well as alcohol (Schulteis et al., 1995).

Although release of DA within the NAcc may be instrumental in ethanol-induced reinforcement, alcohol may increase mesolimbic firing indirectly secondary to its modulation of other neurotransmitter actions in the VTA, such as that produced by GABA, acetylcholine, serotonin, or endorphins. Despite the apparent importance of the dopaminergic neurons, almost total destruction of the mesolimbic terminals with 6-hydroxydopamine (6-OHDA) does not abolish self-administration of alcohol, suggesting that other

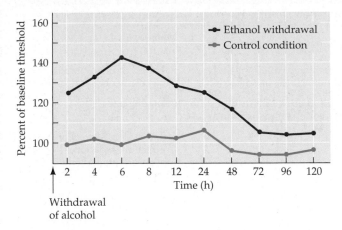

Figure 10.18 Rebound depression of reinforcement during withdrawal After alcohol withdrawal from dependent rats, a time-dependent increase in the current thresholds for electrical brain stimulation occurs, with maximum effect at 6 to 8 hours. The increase in threshold indicates that the animals need more stimulation to achieve reinforcement. Note that the x-axis is not a linear scale. (After Schulteis et al., 1995.)

dopamine-independent mechanisms contribute to ethanol reinforcement. One such mechanism may be the opioid peptide transmitters.

OPIOID SYSTEMS A family of neuropeptides (called endorphins) that have opiate-like effects modulate pain, mood, feeding, reinforcement, and response to stress, among other things (see Chapter 11). Opioids also contribute to the reinforcing effects of alcohol. Support for this statement comes from three types of studies (Froehlich, 1997). First, alcohol enhances endogenous opioid activity in both rodents and humans. Acute administration of alcohol increases endogenous opioid (endorphin and enkephalin) release from brain slices and the pituitary gland in vitro and also increases blood levels of opioids in humans in vivo. Opioids are released into the blood from the pituitary gland. Acute alcohol administration also increases gene expression of both endorphin and enkephalin in selected brain areas of rats, which would increase the amount of peptides available. In contrast, chronic alcohol administration reduces gene expression, making less of the peptides available for release. In human subjects, chronic alcohol use leads to reduced brain levels of endorphin. Since the release of DA in mesolimbic neurons is regulated by opioid cells in both the VTA and NAcc, alcohol-induced opioid release may produce reinforcement by modulating dopamine (Herz, 1997). Reduced opioid levels may contribute to the dysphoria that accompanies chronic alcohol use and withdrawal.

Second, if alcohol-induced enhancement of opioid systems is at least partially responsible for

reinforcement, then blocking opioid receptors should reduce alcohol consumption. Opioid receptor antagonists like naloxone and naltrexone, which compete for the endogenous opioid receptors, do significantly reduce alcohol self-administration in animals. Antagonists that act on specific subtypes (μ and δ) of opioid receptors (see Chapter 11) also reduce operant self-administration. Several clinical trials of opioid antagonists in alcoholic patients found reduced alcohol consumption, relapse, and craving, as well as a reported decrease in the subjective "high." (Further discussion can be found in the section on treatment of alcoholism later in this chapter.) Finally, μ-opioid receptor knockout mice fail to self-administer ethanol and in some experimental conditions show an aversion to the drug (Roberts et al., 2000).

Third, if opioids have a role in reinforcement, then perhaps we should expect to see a difference in the opioid systems of genetic strains of animals that show greater or lesser preference for alcohol. In rat strains that have been genetically bred for alcohol preference, endogenous opioid systems are generally more responsive to the effects of alcohol. For example, alcohol-preferring rats, when compared with alcohol-nonpreferring rats, released significantly more β-endorphin from the hypothalamus when infused with alcohol in vitro and showed enhanced β-endorphin gene expression in the pituitary. Additionally, alcohol-preferring rats have higher baseline levels of μ-opioid receptors in selected limbic areas, including the shell of the NAcc and the amygdala.

In addition to having a role in reinforcement, evidence suggests that opioids play a part in alcohol craving. In alcoholic individuals, positron emission tomography (PET) imaging was used to determine the number of μ-opioid receptors in the NAcc and in other brain areas associated with reinforcement and craving following several weeks of abstinence. Abstinence increased the μ-receptors found in these individuals, and the number of receptors was positively correlated with scores on the Obsessive-Compulsive Drinking Scale, indicating that as μ-opioid receptor numbers increased, craving scores also increased (Heinz et al., 2005). A similar correlation of receptor number in the frontal cortex with craving scores suggested to researchers that activation of opioid receptors may impair executive control, leading to an increased probability of relapse. These results may explain individual differences among alcoholics in their ability to abstain from alcohol use.

OTHER NEUROTRANSMITTERS Table 10.3 summarizes some of the cellular effects of alcohol and their contribution to behavior. Both animal and human studies implicate many more interacting neurotransmitter

TABLE 10.3   Role of Selected Neurotransmitters in Cellular and Behavioral Effects of Alcohol

Neurotransmitter	Acute cellular effects	Chronic cellular effects	Behavioral effects
Glutamate	Receptor antagonism and reduces release	——	Memory loss
	——	Up-regulation of receptors and rebound increase in release	Rebound hyperexcitability of the abstinence syndrome
	——	Extreme hyperexcitability and massive Ca^{2+} influx (rebound)	Brain damage
GABA	Acutely enhances GABA-induced Cl^- influx to hyperpolarize	——	Sedative effects: anxiety reduction, sedation, incoordination, memory impairment
	——	Neuroadaptive decrease in GABA function without change in receptor number	Tolerance and signs of hyper-excitability during with-drawal (seizures, tremors)
Dopamine	Acute increase in transmission in mesolimbic tract	——	Reinforcement
	——	Chronic effects show reduced firing rate, release, metabolism	Negative affect as a sign of withdrawal
Opioids	Acute increase in endog-enous opioid synthesis and release	——	Reinforcement
	——	Neuroadaptive decrease in endorphin levels	Dysphoria

systems in the action of alcohol than we have had the space to discuss. The effects of acute and chronic alcohol administration on these receptors are responsible for the changes in cell signaling, both rapid ionotropic and slower metabotropic actions. Second messengers such as cAMP and their cascade of effects within the cell may be responsible for more long-term changes in cell function, including altered gene expression. Further discussion of the neurochemical effects is beyond the scope of this chapter, but details can be found in several reviews (Sprow and Thiele, 2012).

Section Summary

- Ethanol has specific actions on multiple neu-rotransmitter systems but also has nonspecific actions that change the fluid nature of membrane phospholipids.

- Animal models in alcohol research do the follow-ing: (1) control for poor nutrition, liver damage, comorbid drug use, and psychiatric disorders associated with human alcoholic individuals; (2) permit the use of techniques inappropriate in humans; (3) allow genetic manipulations; and (4) provide means for investigators to evaluate treat-ment strategies.

- Alcohol acutely inhibits glutamate neurotransmis-sion by reducing the effects of glutamate at the NMDA receptor and reducing glutamate release.

- Modulation of glutamate by alcohol has a role in ethanol-induced memory impairment, rebound hyperexcitability during withdrawal, NMDA-mediated excitotoxicity causing brain damage, and the mental retardation associated with FAS.

- Chronic ethanol up-regulates NMDA receptors in humans and animal models and increases glutamate release, providing an explanation for the hyperexcitability and seizures seen at abrupt withdrawal.

- Alcohol enhances GABA-induced chloride entry and hyperpolarization by modulating $GABA_A$ receptors and stimulating GABA release.

- The effect of alcohol on synaptic $GABA_A$ receptors requires high concentrations that are associated with high levels of intoxication. Extrasynaptic $GABA_A$ receptors having δ and α_4 or α_6 subunits are extremely sensitive to the low concentrations of GABA that remain in the extracellular space, making them more likely to be mediators of low to moderate amounts of drinking.

- Extrasynaptic $GABA_A$ receptors in the shell region of the nucleus accumbens seem to mediate some of the reinforcing effects of alcohol.

- Chronic ethanol leads to down-regulation of $GABA_A$ receptors, making the organism more sen-sitive to seizure-inducing agents.

- Ethanol activates dopaminergic cells in the VTA, causing the release of DA in the NAcc to provide the positive reinforcement that leads to repeated drug taking.

- In physically dependent rodents, withdrawal of alcohol reduces the firing rate of mesolimbic neurons, decreases DA release in the NAcc, and causes rebound depression of reinforcement mechanisms as shown by an elevation in the threshold for intracranial self-stimulation.

- Acute alcohol increases opioid release and increases gene expression of opioid peptides. Chronic alcohol reduces gene expression and lowers levels of peptides.

- Blocking opioid receptors with naloxone reduces alcohol self-administration. Mu opioid receptor knockout mice fail to self-administer ethanol. High levels of μ-opioid receptors correlate with scores on craving.

- Alcohol-preferring rats release more opioids in response to ethanol and show enhanced opioid peptide gene expression.

- Ethanol modulates the function of many additional neurotransmitters to alter ionotropic and metabotropic signaling.

Alcoholism

Alcoholism is a serious and complex phenomenon that consists of psychological, neurobiological, genetic, and sociocultural factors, making it both difficult to define and treat. Regardless of the specific definition, alcoholism damages the health and well-being of the individual and those around him. Financial costs of alcoholism are huge and include medical treatment of alcohol-induced disease, loss associated with accidents on the road and at work, lost productivity, criminal justice costs, and financial disruption that accompanies the breakdown of families (**Table 10.4**). Many volumes have been written about alcohol use and alcoholism from various points of view—some emotionally evocative, others based on theoretical models or empirical research. The final section of this chapter presents a brief synopsis of some of the research findings.

Defining alcoholism and estimating its incidence have proved difficult

Chapter 9 describes substance use disorder and identifies some of the criteria used by professionals to diagnose the condition. In addition, the chapter provides multiple theoretical models of substance abuse and provides a critique of each. In this section, we look specifically at **alcoholism**, a form of substance abuse

that has been historically difficult to define because the drug is legal and is used by most individuals in a way that does not harm themselves or others. For the layman, a person with an "alcohol problem" may be anyone who drinks more than he or she does. However, it is difficult to objectively define inappropriate amounts of alcohol because the frequency and pattern of use are as significant as the total amount consumed. For example, consuming five alcoholic drinks over 1 week's time does not have the same physical and social consequences as consuming five drinks in a row, which is the usual definition of **binge drinking**. An alcoholic does not necessarily have to start each day with a drink, nor does he necessarily drink all day long, but he may drink very heavily periodically. Instead of emphasizing quantity, the diagnosis of alcoholism depends on identifying a cluster of behavioral, cognitive, and physical characteristics. For the clinician, the essential features of alcoholism are compulsive alcohol seeking and use despite damaging health and social consequences. Unfortunately, because other groups and government agencies use different criteria, there is still a great deal of variability in how professionals use the terms *addiction, misuse, abuse, dependency,* and *problem drinking*.

Many modern definitions are based on the work of Jellinek (1960), who made an early distinction between "chronic alcoholism," which includes the physical and behavioral consequences of long-term alcohol use, and "alcohol addiction," which is characterized by craving and lack of control. In addition, Jellinek was

TABLE 10.4 Estimated Costs of Excessive Drinking by Type of Cost[a]

Cost category	Total cost
Specialty care for alcohol abuse treatment	$10,668
Hospitalization attributed to alcohol-related illness	$5,156
Medical care for fetal alcohol syndrome	$2,538
Special education for fetal alcohol syndrome	$369
Decreased productivity at work	$74,102
Lost productivity due to absenteeism	$4,237
Lost productivity due to incarceration	$6,329
Lost productivity due to premature death	$65,062
Motor vehicle crashes	$13,718

Source: Bouchery et al., 2011.

[a]Costs are in millions of dollars for the year 2006 in the United States.

The typical alcoholic American

There's no such thing as typical. We have all kinds.
10 million Americans are alcoholic.
It's our number one drug problem.

Figure 10.19 A wide variety of individuals are alcoholics
(Courtesy of the National Library of Medicine.)

responsible for developing the disease model of addiction to replace the earlier moral model, which emphasized lack of willpower and personal weakness. His concept meant that alcoholism would be treated medically and nonjudgmentally, as is true for any other disease. This model suggests that once the addiction is formed, the individual no longer has control over his drug-taking behavior. Although most treatment in the United States is based on this medical model, it does have many critics.

Disparities in the definition of alcoholism have led to equally large differences in estimated incidence. Although you may think of an alcoholic as a poor, aging, homeless individual living on the street, in reality there is no such thing as a typical alcoholic (**Figure 10.19**). Although many homeless individuals do suffer from a variety of psychiatric disorders and abuse both illicit drugs and alcohol at high rates, only 5% of alcoholics fit that category. Based on the U.S. Government's annual survey of drug use, the rates of alcohol use in the United States have remained relatively steady

for the last 10 years. The most commonly accepted statistic is that approximately 10% of Americans have some problem with alcohol use, and as many as 10.5 million adults are dependent on alcohol. Significant gender differences are seen in alcohol use and abuse for all age groups. The 2011 National Household Survey of Drug Abuse found that more men (91.2%) than women (83.7%) consumed alcohol to some extent over their lifetime. Among drinkers age 18 and older, heavy drinking, defined as five or more drinks on the same occasion on each of 5 days in the past month, was reported in 10.2% of males and 3.4% of females. Binge alcohol use during the past month was also higher in men (32.5%) than women (16.7%). Although the percentage of men declined on most drinking measures during their 30s, women had higher rates on some drinking indices between the ages of 30 and 40. However, by age 60, indicators of problem drinking fell into the single digits for both genders (Substance Abuse and Mental Health Services Administration, 2011). Although problem drinking drops significantly in the elderly, problems associated with drinking can be more serious because of drug interactions and medical complications.

A closer focus on the drinking patterns of college students might be appropriate, since there has been a great deal of public concern regarding student accidents and fatalities where alcohol was involved. Several large-scale studies are available to guide you in further research (Hingson and Zha, 2009; Hingson et al., 2009; White et al., 2011). A variety of U.S. Government surveys have estimated that 44.7% of 18- to 24-year-old college students engaged in binge drinking at least once in the last month. That behavior has lead to a variety of serious outcomes for many. An estimated 15% of full-time 4-year college students suffered alcohol-related injury and 12% were assaulted by another drinking student. Furthermore, alcohol overdose deaths increased a dramatic three-fold between 1998 and 2005. Each year more than 5000 deaths in that age group have been attributed to alcohol use. Although this group reported a significant number of alcohol-related problems (**Table 10.5**), only 1% believed that they had a drinking problem.

Significant variation in estimates of alcohol-induced problems occurred across campuses, and these differences were reflected in the impact of binge drinking on the welfare of other students. Students who were not heavy drinkers on campuses that had the highest rates of heavy drinkers reported significantly more

TABLE 10.5 Percentage of Binge Drinkers Reporting Alcohol-Related Problems Since the Beginning of the School Year by Gender[a]

Alcohol-related problem	Percentage[b] Women	Men
General disorientation		
Have a hangover	81%	82%
Do something you later regret	48%	50%
Forget what you did	38%	41%
Sexual activity		
Engage in unplanned sex	26%	33%
Not use protection before sex	15%	16%
Violence		
Argue with friends	29%	32%
Damage property	6%	24%
Disciplinary action		
Have trouble with campus/local police	4%	10%
Personal injury		
Get injured	14%	17%
Get medical treatment for overdose	<1%	1%
School performance		
Miss a class	42%	45%
Get behind in schoolwork	31%	34%

Source: Wechsler et al., 1995a.

[a]Women binge drinkers report having four or more drinks in a row at least once during the past 2 weeks. Men binge drinkers report having five or more drinks in a row.

[b]Percentage of binge drinkers who report that, since the beginning of the school year, their drinking has caused them to experience each problem one or more times.

negative experiences associated with other students' drinking, including vandalism, violence, theft, and unwanted sexual advances. Jung (2001) provides a detailed discussion of student drug use with a strong research emphasis.

The causes of alcoholism are multimodal

No specific cause of alcoholism has been identified, but a variety of factors contribute to the vulnerability of any given individual. It is quite clear that multiple factors stem from three essential areas: (1) neurobiological; (2) psychological; and (3) sociocultural (**Figure 10.20**). Although we are forced to discuss them in a linear fashion, keep in mind that complex interactions

exist among the areas. Because the literature is extensive, this section will provide an overview and suggest methods for future research.

PSYCHOLOGICAL FACTORS Although no alcoholic personality has ever been defined, one vulnerability factor for alcoholism is the response to stress. Both animal and human studies show an interaction between both acute and chronic stress and initiation of alcohol use, maintenance of drug consumption, and relapse after withdrawal (Brady and Sonne, 1999). Some have used the term *symptomatic* drinking to describe the reinforcing effects of alcohol when stress and tension are relieved. The individual who no longer drinks on a social occasion but drinks each day after work to relieve tension represents an example of symptomatic drinking. However, although alcohol has been found to reduce anxiety in some cases, the relationship between stress and alcohol use is complex and depends on multiple variables, including the nature and timing of the stressor. For example, acute stress is often found to reduce alcohol consumption while chronic stress increases it. Animal studies show that the effects of stress on voluntary alcohol consumption depend on the nature of the stressor applied (e.g., restraint, forced swimming, social isolation), its acute or chronic nature, and whether the animal can predict the onset of the stress and/or control the stressful event. Furthermore, a circular association is seen because although alcohol can be shown to relieve stress under some conditions, alcohol also increases the function of brain and endocrine stress systems, making alcohol itself an additional stressor that may lead to further alcohol use

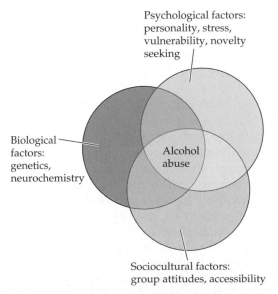

Figure 10.20 Three-factor vulnerability model Biological, psychological, and sociocultural influences contribute to the development of alcohol abuse.

(see Box 2.4 for an introduction to the neuroendocrine stress response of the hypothalamic–pituitary–adrenal [HPA] axis). Numerous rodent studies have shown that acute alcohol administration elevates levels of the stress hormones corticotropin-releasing factor (CRF), adrenocorticotropic hormone (ACTH), and glucocorticoids (e.g., cortisol). Furthermore, withdrawal of alcohol after several weeks of chronic administration produces more anxious behavior in rodents in the elevated plus-maze following restraint stress compared with controls. The fact that the anxious behavior could be reduced by blocking CRF receptors demonstrates that CRF mediates the anxiety. Additionally, during withdrawal, CRF expression was greater in brain areas regulating anxiety, including the bed nucleus of the stria terminalis and the central nucleus of the amygdala (see Chapter 18 for a discussion of the neural substrates of anxiety), and the behavioral stress response was enhanced. Likewise, in humans, alcohol withdrawal increases anxiety as well as alcohol consumption. More important, it appears that although postwithdrawal anxiety subsides within a few weeks, sensitization to stressors and increased reactivity persists for long periods. The fact that stressors frequently lead to further alcohol consumption suggests the potential usefulness of CRF receptor antagonists in preventing relapse.

Alcohol abuse has been found to be associated with high levels of lifetime anxiety. Consistent with the findings of rodent studies, stress early in life is a significant environmental risk factor for alcohol abuse in the adult, just as it predicts adult depression (see Chapter 19) and anxiety disorders (see Chapter 18). Although epidemiological studies consistently find high comorbidity (i.e., when two conditions coexist) between psychiatric disorders and substance abuse, it is interesting to note that anxiety disorders usually precede the development of drug use, while mood disorders are more likely to develop subsequent to drug use.

Another significant risk factor for alcoholism is family history, which is associated with greater cortisol response following psychosocial stress compared with individuals without a family history of alcoholism. Furthermore, alcohol has a greater suppressing effect on the stress responses in those with a family history. Since HPA reactivity to stressors shows significant heritability, researchers are working to identify gene polymorphisms that are involved in the differences, with the hope of developing targeted drug treatment plans for selected individuals. The fact that gene polymorphisms of the CRF_1 receptor are associated with risky drinking behavior suggests a potential screening method for identifying future problem behaviors and perhaps indicates the optimal treatment approach for these individuals should such behaviors develop.

Differences in individuals' stress response systems and in their perception and appraisal of stress may help to explain some of the differential vulnerability to alcohol abuse. These and other pivotal studies are summarized in an excellent review (Clarke and Schumann, 2009).

In an earlier section, we mentioned that alcohol increases DA transmission in the mesolimbic tract, thereby mediating reinforcement. It is significant that cortisol seems to sensitize the reward pathway, which means that alcohol-induced increases in the HPA axis function and subsequent elevations in cortisol make drug reinforcement more rewarding. Rodent studies showed that glucocorticoids enhance mesolimbic DA and increase drug-seeking behaviors. A striking relationship exists: even among individuals without substance abuse problems, those who secreted more cortisol in response to stress also released more mesolimbic DA and experienced greater subjective effects of psychostimulants. It is suspected that this relationship may cause some individuals to increase consumption beyond casual use. In contrast, as was mentioned in the section on dopamine, withdrawal reduces the mesolimbic neuron firing rate, which dampens the reward function, leading to a negative affective state that acts as a chronic internal stressor. Hence, although mild stress enhances DA-mediated reward, chronic stress further reduces the reward pathway function and increases craving—a state that would make relapse to alcohol consumption more likely (Uhart and Wand, 2009).

Novelty seeking by individuals may also increase the risk for using alcohol and other drugs of abuse. Bardo and colleagues (1996) reviewed extensive literature to show that exposure to novel events activates the dopaminergic mesolimbic pathway in a manner similar to that seen with most abused substances. Individual differences in the need for novelty and drug-seeking behavior are under genetic control and may explain why some individuals experiment with drugs initially and why some more readily become compulsive users. Differences in the need for stimulation have been applied to drug and alcohol prevention programs that use fast-paced, physiologically arousing, and unconventional message delivery to appeal to the target audience.

It is significant that the personality dimensions of high novelty seeking and low harm avoidance as assessed by teacher ratings as early as 6 years of age readily predicted early onset of substance use (i.e., smoking cigarettes, getting intoxicated, and using other drugs) in boys. This type of indicator of potential problems is important because it may be possible to initiate preventive measures as early as first grade and reduce the probability of substance use in the pre-teen and adolescent years. Numerous analyses of national surveys show that the younger individuals are when they first begin to drink (less than 13 years old), the greater is the probability that they may develop alcohol dependence later in life. This association occurs even for low levels of alcohol consumption but is exaggerated by binge drinking. Additionally, early drinking predicts other risky behaviors, including driving after drinking, riding with drinking drivers, becoming involved in physical fights, carrying weapons, and unintentionally injuring another person (Hingson and Zha, 2009). Impulse control problems such as compulsive gambling and antisocial behaviors are also predicted by early adolescent drinking. In replicating and expanding on earlier studies, Nees and colleagues (2012) found that behavior (risk taking and aversion for delayed reward), neural response in the brain reward circuitry in response to large versus small rewards, and personality (extraversion, impulsivity, sensation seeking, and novelty seeking) interacted and were predictive of early alcohol use and subsequent alcohol addiction, although personality traits represented the strongest predictor. Since genetics contributes to these phenotypic characteristics, future research may be directed toward evaluating genetic factors in early adolescent drinking models.

NEUROBIOLOGICAL FACTORS   One significant neurobiological factor in alcoholism is genetic vulnerability. Close relatives of alcoholics have a three to seven times greater risk for alcoholism than the general population. Both twin and adoption studies show that genetics is correlated with vulnerability, particularly for the more severe type of alcoholism. In adoption studies, the risk of alcoholism is higher in children of alcoholics even when they are adopted into nonalcoholic families. Alcoholism concordance rates are higher in monozygotic (54%) than in dizygotic (28%) twins, demonstrating the influence of genes but leaving significant variability to be explained by other factors. Overall, genetics explains 50% to 60% of the variance of risk for dependence in both men and women, although the percentage may be higher for some types of alcoholism than others. The heritability of alcohol abuse is less, at about 38%.

To help with genetic analysis, researchers try to establish subgroups of alcoholics on the basis of various characteristics such as severity, occurrence of withdrawal, gender, and so forth. Cloninger (1987) proposed a popular categorization called type I and type II alcoholics (**Table 10.6**). Type I alcoholics generally begin drinking later in life and experience guilt and fear about their alcoholism. These individuals rarely have trouble with the law or display antisocial activities. Many drink to escape stress or unpleasant situations in their environment. Most female alcoholics are type I, although many men also fit this description.

TABLE 10.6 Cloninger's Alcoholic Subtypes

Characteristics	Type I	Type II
Age of onset (years)	After 25	Before 25
Gender	Male and female	Male
Extent of genetic influence	Moderate	High
Environmental influence	High	Low
Alcohol used as escape	High	Low
Alcohol used to feel good	Low	High
Novelty-seeking personality	Low	High
Inability to control drinking	Infrequent	Frequent
Guilt and fear about alcohol	Frequent	Infrequent
Aggressive/antisocial action	Infrequent	Frequent
Inability to stop alcohol use	Infrequent	Frequent

Type II alcoholics are almost always male and display thrill-seeking, antisocial, and perhaps criminal activities. They have lower cerebrospinal fluid levels of the serotonin (5-HT) metabolite 5-hydroxyindoleacetic acid (5-HIAA)—a result that matches the human and animal literature regarding impulsivity and suicide. Type II alcoholics have greater genetic vulnerability and begin drinking at an early age.

To find genetic patterns in human alcoholics, several methods may be used. One method, called **linkage studies**, examines the inheritance pattern of genes using DNA analysis and the occurrence of alcoholism in many members of a large number of families. Researchers look for easily identified genetic markers and determine which are most closely related to alcohol-associated behaviors. One such evaluation of a Native American population identified two potential genes for alcoholism. One was located on chromosome 11p close to the genes for the D_4 dopamine receptor and tyrosine hydroxylase, an enzyme needed for DA and NE synthesis. The second was on chromosome 4p near the gene for the $GABA_A$ receptor complex (Enoch and Goldman, 1999).

The **case-control method** compares the genes of unrelated, affected and unaffected individuals to see whether members of the affected population have more of a particular form (allele) of genetic material. The gene does not necessarily have to be directly

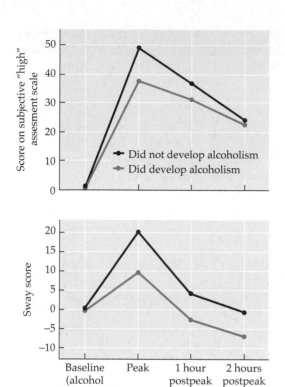

Figure 10.21 Low sensitivity to alcohol is a risk factor for alcoholism Subjective assessment of "high" and sway scores following a moderate dose (0.75 ml/kg) of alcohol in men who later developed alcohol dependence and in those who did not. Those vulnerable to alcoholism showed significantly less response to the same dose at peak blood level (1 hour) and 1 and 2 hours after the peak. (After Schuckit, 1994.)

associated with the disorder but may be a marker associated with a characteristic that increases the risk of developing alcoholism. For example, specific genes control the manufacture of aldehyde dehydrogenase (ALDH), the enzyme that converts the toxic metabolite acetaldehyde to acetic acid. Since individuals with the gene for the inactive form of the enzyme experience unpleasant effects when drinking alcohol, they have essentially no risk for alcoholism.

An additional risk factor that is genetically influenced (although no specific gene has been identified) is low sensitivity to alcohol. Alcoholics frequently report that early in their drinking, they experienced very little effect of alcohol unless they consumed large quantities. Schuckit (2000) measured subjective intoxication, "sway score" when balanced on a straight line, and hormonal response to alcohol in young sons of alcoholics compared with controls. The men who later developed alcoholism showed a reduced response to moderate levels of alcohol for each of the measures (**Figure 10.21**). More important, Schuckit found that the low response rate increased the risk for alcoholism

fourfold *regardless of family history* when the men were evaluated 8 years later.

Other case-control studies have looked for variants in genes involved in neurotransmitter metabolism, such as receptor subtypes, synthesizing enzymes, and reuptake transporters. For example, a genetic variant of the 5-HT transporter is associated with anxiety and with low sensitivity to alcohol, and this makes affected individuals more vulnerable to developing alcoholism.

Identifying an alcoholism gene in humans has not been very successful because the disorder is complex and highly variable among individuals. Many researchers doubt that there is a gene specific to alcoholism and believe that the condition may share genes with other "compulsive" behaviors such as gambling, eating disorders, and substance abuse.

Rodent models are extremely important in evaluation of the genetic contribution to isolated drinking behaviors. Researchers use selectively bred lines of animals that differ with respect to alcohol-related behaviors such as withdrawal sensitivity, alcohol consumption, and alcohol-induced hypothermia to search for clusters of genes that are linked to several alcohol behaviors. A second technique uses gene knockout animals, in which a particular gene is selectively deleted, before evaluating animal behaviors. For example, 5-HT$_{1B}$ receptor knockout mice self-administer twice as much alcohol but show less intoxication and less evidence of tolerance. They also self-administer cocaine more readily. When the dopamine D$_4$ receptor is knocked out, animals become supersensitive to alcohol, as well as to cocaine and amphetamine.

SOCIOCULTURAL FACTORS Social and cultural factors mold changing attitudes about drinking, as well as the definition of problem drinking. Group attitudes also determine how much alcohol is available in a particular environment, for example, by controlling hours of sale, public consumption, and advertising. The examination of cultural influences on drinking was pioneered by Bales (1946), who suggested that cultures of those who abstain from alcohol use or restrict it for religious purposes have the lowest alcoholism rates. In contrast, societies that engage in social drinking in public settings and in which drinking is condoned for personal reasons such as tension reduction have higher alcoholism rates. The importance of cultural influence is well demonstrated by the low alcoholism rate among Muslims and Mormons—two groups with religious prohibitions on alcohol use. A low rate of alcoholism is also seen in Jewish populations, who use alcohol in a religious ceremonial way among family and do not condone intoxication.

Levin (1989) contrasted attitudes in two Catholic countries, Italy and France, both of which produce and consume large quantities of alcohol. France has one of the highest alcoholism rates in the world, while Italy has only one-fifth the incidence seen in France. Among the differences of potential significance is that the French do not disapprove of drunkenness and consider refusal of alcohol as impolite. They drink both wine and hard liquor, drink with meals and in other contexts, and consume alcohol in the family setting and outside of it. The Italian culture disapproves of drunkenness and accepts abstinence. Alcohol consumption among Italians primarily consists of wine taken with meals within the family. Further discussion of cultural influences on vulnerability to alcoholism can be found in several sources, including McNeece and DiNitto (1998). An excellent pictorial article by Boyd Gibbons (1992) in *National Geographic* describes many cultural differences in alcohol use and abuse.

The most obvious conclusion that can be drawn from our discussion of etiology is that multiple factors contribute to alcoholism. The neurochemical effects of alcohol and genetic predisposition to heavy drinking; the personality, cognitive structure, and expectations of the individual; and social, cultural, and economic variables all affect the use of alcohol and vulnerability to alcohol dependence.

Multiple treatment options provide hope for rehabilitation

An increasing number of treatment programs for alcoholism have developed over the past few years, giving alcoholics increased hope for recovery. One of the major hurdles in treating an alcoholic is getting the individual into a treatment program. **Denial** of a problem with alcohol is a significant characteristic of alcoholics, who often fail to recognize that alcohol is the source of their problems and not the cure for them. Denial by the alcoholic is often aided by family members and friends who repair the damage caused by the drinker and make excuses for his behavior. These people are called **enablers**, since they enable the alcoholic to function without getting treatment. The alcoholic frequently needs to be coerced into treatment by spouses threatening separation and loss of children, employers threatening loss of employment, and the legal system (arrests and jail time).

The first step in treatment is **detoxification** because withdrawal symptoms are strong motivators and can be physiologically dangerous. Under medical care, detoxification involves substituting a benzodiazepine such as chlordiazepoxide (Librium) or diazepam (Valium). These drugs prevent alcohol withdrawal, including seizures and DTs. The long-acting nature of the drugs stabilizes the individual, and as the dose is gradually reduced, withdrawal symptoms are minimized. It should be mentioned that some symptoms of withdrawal increase in magnitude with successive withdrawals. This is true for seizure activity, and repeated episodes of withdrawal-induced seizures may be responsible for some of the long-term deficits in cognitive processing and emotional regulation that in turn may lead to less control over drinking.

PSYCHOSOCIAL REHABILITATION After detoxification, **psychosocial rehabilitation** programs help the alcoholic to prevent relapse through abstinence or to reduce the amount of alcohol consumed if relapse occurs (Fuller and Hiller-Sturmhofel, 1999). Several programs are available, but we provide here only a cursory survey of a few of them. The three basic types include individual and group therapy to provide emotional support and address psychological and social problems associated with dependence, residential alcohol-free treatment settings, and self-help groups such as Alcoholics Anonymous (AA). All of these methods reduce alcohol use among patients, although the relapse rate is extremely high. Approximately 40% to 70% resume drinking after one year (Finney et al., 1996).

AA is perhaps the best known of the self-help treatment programs and is the most frequently recommended. It is an organization in which all members are alcoholics because an underlying assumption is that only a peer group is able to understand alcoholics and help them accept their disorder and admit their powerlessness over it. The emphasis of the group is a spiritual one in which the individual relies on a "higher power" to help him remain sober. The self-help group provides peer support, role modeling, practical problem-solving advice, and a social support network. **Web Box 10.2** provides the 12 steps in the program and describes some of the benefits and drawbacks of AA.

The Community Reinforcement Approach (CRA) is one of the top-ranked treatment methods (Wolfe and Meyers, 1999). CRA assumes that environmental contingencies (rewards and punishers) are powerful in encouraging drinking behavior but, that they can be modified to become powerful reinforcers of nondrinking as well. If a nondrinking lifestyle is more appealing than a drinking one, the alcoholic will no longer turn to the drug. CRA focuses on problems (e.g., job loss, marital issues) as perceived *by the alcoholic individual* and helps the alcoholic set her own goals, enhances her motivation to achieve these goals, and teaches the skills needed to create the positive lifestyle she desires.

PHARMACOTHERAPEUTIC APPROACHES **Pharmacotherapeutic treatment** for alcoholism includes two basic strategies: making alcohol ingestion unpleasant and reducing its reinforcing qualities (Garbutt et al., 1999;

Swift, 1999). The drug **disulfiram** (Antabuse) inhibits ALDH, the enzyme that converts acetaldehyde to acetic acid in the normal metabolism of alcohol. An individual who drinks as little as a quarter of an ounce of alcohol within a week of taking disulfiram experiences a sharp rise in blood acetaldehyde accompanied by facial flushing, tachycardia, pounding in the chest, drop in blood pressure, nausea, vomiting, and other symptoms. This method is clearly aimed at making ingestion of alcohol unpleasant. Patients must be cautious about unknowingly consuming alcohol in beverages, foods, over-the-counter medications like cough syrup, or mouthwash. Because disulfiram can cause hepatitis, frequent liver function tests must be done. For obvious reasons, compliance with the drug-taking regimen is quite low, with sometimes as many as half of the subjects dropping out of the study. Disulfiram clearly does not treat alcoholism or reduce craving but may act as a motivational aid for those who are very determined to avoid alcohol. Unfortunately, rigorous double-blind studies show little difference in rates of abstinence between men on disulfiram and controls, although some studies show an increase in the duration of abstinence before relapse.

Preclinical animal studies described earlier (in the section on opioid systems) showed that μ-opioid agonists increase alcohol consumption and μ-antagonists decrease self-administration, presumably because they compete for the endogenous opioid receptors. In human alcoholics, **naltrexone**, which is an opioid receptor antagonist, reduces alcohol consumption and craving and improves abstinence rates, according to several double-blind studies (**Figure 10.22**), although it seems to be less promising in longer studies. It is assumed that naltrexone reduces the positive feelings and the subjective "high" of alcohol by blocking the effects of alcohol-induced endorphin release. Social drinkers report more negative effects and greater sedation from a moderate amount of alcohol when taking naltrexone. Increased abstinence rates in humans during naltrexone treatment show parallels with rodent studies in which naltrexone reduced the reinstatement of alcohol consumption triggered by priming injections of ethanol or ethanol-associated cues. Although clinical studies show significant effects, the effect size is small because only a fraction of individuals show meaningful benefit. Some of the variability in response may be due to genetics since evidence demonstrates that subjects with a family history of alcoholism respond better to naltrexone treatment than people with no family history. Furthermore a μ-receptor polymorphism that leads to reduced receptor expression predicts greater success for alcohol abstinence with naltrexone therapy. It is possible that naltrexone is more effective for those with a gene variant because they have a different type of alcoholism and may, for

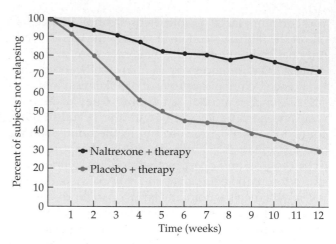

Figure 10.22 Effectiveness of naltrexone in alcoholism treatment Naltrexone along with coping skills therapy is more effective in preventing relapse than placebo and therapy over a 12-week period. At 12 weeks, relapse rates were approximately 65% for the placebo group compared with 30% for the naltrexone treatment group. (After O'Brien, 1994.)

example, differ in their reinforcement mechanisms (see Ripley and Stephens, 2011). Hence targeting the opioid receptor seems to produce substantial benefit for some individuals and limited benefit for others, which indicates the potential value of pharmacogenetic screening for individualizing treatment approaches (see Heilig et al., 2010). As is often the case in alcoholism rehabilitation, the effectiveness of naltrexone is most pronounced when accompanied by counseling aimed at enhancing individual coping skills and relapse prevention.

Several laboratory studies demonstrated the potential use of κ-opioid receptor antagonists in alcoholism treatment by demonstrating effects of selective opioid receptor subtype antagonism. In one such study, researchers showed that following a month of alcohol exposure, dependent animals and their nondependent controls were allowed to self-administer alcohol 6 hours after their last alcohol exposure (considered acute withdrawal). As expected, alcohol-dependent rodents self-administered more alcohol than did nondependent animals. Both the μ-receptor antagonist naltrexone and the dual κ/μ-opioid antagonist **nalmefene** were effective in reducing lever pressing for alcohol in a dose-dependent manner in both dependent and nondependent animals. However, nalmefene, because of its ability to antagonize κ-opioid receptors as well as μ-receptors, was more effective than naltrexone in reducing consumption among dependent animals. The third opioid antagonist tested, **nor-binaltorphimine**, which is a selective κ-opioid antagonist, reduced self-administration only in dependent animals. These results suggest that the μ-opioid receptor mediates acute reinforcing effects as shown by the ability to reduce alcohol self-administration with μ-antagonists. The fact that antagonists at κ-receptors reduced the withdrawal-induced increase in consumption of only dependent animals suggests that κ-receptors have a role in the development of alcohol dependence and withdrawal-induced alcohol consumption. This conclusion is supported by evidence that shows κ-opioid receptor up-regulation during chronic alcohol administration. It is suggested that this up-regulation may be responsible for an anhedonic state (i.e., the inability to experience pleasure) that develops during the formation of physical dependence and leads to dysphoria when drug cessation occurs. This dysphoria produces a withdrawal-induced increase in alcohol consumption (Walker and Koob, 2008). Studies such as these imply that blocking μ-receptor–induced reinforcement and κ-receptor–induced anhedonia may improve abstinence rates in alcoholic individuals for whom both events may lead to relapse. Whether these intriguing findings predict potential benefits in alcoholism treatment remains to be seen.

Acamprosate is one of the newer agents available for the treatment of alcoholism. Several large, well-controlled studies have shown that acamprosate increases nondrinking days by 30% to 50% and approximately doubles the rate of abstinence, even though most patients ultimately return to drinking. The drug is safe and produces few side effects except for diarrhea. Acamprosate acts as a partial antagonist at the glutamate NMDA receptor and significantly blocks the glutamate increase that occurs during alcohol withdrawal in rats (**Figure 10.23**), which may explain its therapeutic effects. Acamprosate has a chemical structure similar to that of GABA and returns basal GABA levels to normal in alcohol-dependent rats. Its ability to modify the functions of both GABA and glutamate in the nucleus accumbens may serve as the ultimate basis for its efficacy in preventing relapse.

Other available drugs have been tested in fewer well-controlled trials, but they have generally shown disappointing results despite encouraging findings with animal testing. Serotonergic agents such as the antidepressant fluoxetine, whose effectiveness is predicted by animal studies, have not consistently been effective in humans, although results are often complicated by the presence of depression or anxiety disorders. The dopamine antagonist tiapride, sold only in Europe, reduces the symptoms of alcohol withdrawal and increases abstinence. However, in at least one clinical trial, compliance was an issue, and only about half of subjects completed 1 month of treatment (Shaw

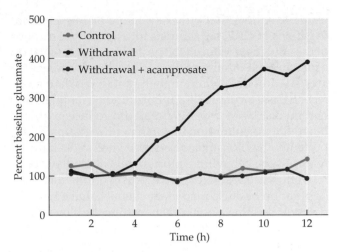

Figure 10.23 Acamprosate prevents withdrawal-induced glutamate release The red line shows the rebound release of glutamate (measured by microdialysis) that occurs in the nucleus accumbens when alcohol is withdrawn from dependent rats. Alcohol-dependent animals who are withdrawn from alcohol but receive acamprosate (purple line) are no different in glutamate release from non-alcohol-treated controls. (After Dahchour and DeWitte, 2000.)

et al., 1994). Likewise, although cannabinoid receptor antagonists reduce alcohol self-administration in numerous animal models, double-blind, placebo-controlled clinical trials report little efficacy in reducing alcohol consumption or relapse rates among alcoholics. Such failures of basic research to translate to effective clinical treatment may be due to several factors, including poor clinical research designs, inability to identify subpopulations of individuals that may benefit from treatment, and animal models that poorly predict efficacy in humans (see Ripley and Stephens, 2011). It is hoped that collaborative efforts in translational research, as described in Chapter 4, will produce more effective therapies in the future.

PROMISING NEW DIRECTIONS IN TREATMENT In an earlier section, we described the complex reciprocal interaction between stress and alcohol consumption and the importance of stress in leading to relapse in the abstinent alcoholic. Since both animal and human studies show that repeated episodes of intoxication and withdrawal lead to increased CRF_1 receptors in the amygdala, sensitization of the reactivity to stressors, and significantly elevated rates of alcohol consumption, it is reasonable to consider pharmacological interventions to minimize this stress response. One approach is to block the CRF_1 receptors that mediate both the hypothalamic-regulated neuroendocrine response and the extrahypothalamic CRF_1 receptors that modulate the behavioral response to stress. Several animal studies have shown that either systemic or intracerebral injections of **CRF$_1$ antagonists** into the central nucleus of the amygdala reduced the postwithdrawal escalation of alcohol self-administration to baseline consumption levels. Additionally, although the antagonist had no effect on basal alcohol self-administration in animals that had no history of dependence, it did reduce excessive binge-like consumption in nondependent animals. Importantly, the CRF$_1$ antagonists prevented stress-induced relapse-type behavior. Unfortunately, there have been few efforts to test CRF$_1$ antagonists on the alcoholic population because medicinal chemists have had difficulty in creating agents that penetrate the blood–brain barrier and achieve the high receptor occupancy needed for efficacy as determined by animal research.

An alternative target for modulating stress is the neuropeptide substance P and its neurokinin 1 receptor (NK1R). These receptors are densely located in the hypothalamus and the amygdala, and intracerebral injection of substance P into those areas produces anxiety in animal tests. Blocking the receptor or genetically deleting it reduces anxious behaviors. More to the point, NK1R knockout mice showed reduced alcohol consumption in a free-choice situation—a result that also occurred following administration of the NK1R antagonist L-703,606. In an animal model of relapse in which several cycles of alcohol exposure followed by deprivation caused increased alcohol intake in control animals, the increase in alcohol consumption was absent in NK1R knockout mice. An initial clinical study using 50 recently detoxified anxious alcoholic patients showed that the NK1R antagonist LY686017 significantly reduced craving and improved scores on a measure of general well-being. When subjects were exposed to both stress- and alcohol-related cues, LY686017 reduced craving along with the associated rise in the stress hormone cortisol. With the same subjects, researchers used functional magnetic resonance imaging (fMRI) to image regional brain activity in response to pictures that had either a negative or positive affect. Placebo-treated alcoholics showed enhanced neural activity to negative images in brain regions associated with emotional processing and reduced activity to positive stimuli compared with control individuals. The NK1R antagonist attenuated both of those neural responses. Hence subjects treated with the antagonist had less activation in the insula, a brain region associated with craving and addictive behaviors, in response to negative stimuli than was seen in the placebo-treated alcoholic subjects. In response to positive visual images, NK1R-treated alcoholics showed elevated response in the nucleus accumbens and the anterior cingulate cortex compared with the placebo-treated alcoholics. These changes represent a normalization of the brain response to emotional stimuli and may be a neural correlate of the enhanced clinical rating of well-being (reviewed by Heilig et al., 2010).

COMBINED PHARMACOTHERAPY AND TALK THERAPY The National Institute of Alcohol Abuse and Alcoholism (NIAAA) initiated a multisite, controlled clinical trial of treatments for alcohol dependence utilizing almost 1400 alcohol-dependent subjects (Anton et al., 2006). The focus of this research was to evaluate the efficacy of pharmacotherapy, behavioral treatment, and a combination on a number of alcohol-use parameters. The research, called Combining Medications and Behavioral Interventions (COMBINE), aimed to enhance treatment outcomes (www.cscc.unc.edu/COMBINE/). Investigators used four treatments singly and in combination: naltrexone, acamprosate, medical management, and combined behavioral intervention (CBI). Medical management was designed to be used in a normal medical setting by medical doctors and nurses to increase medication adherence and provide support for abstinence, while CBI was used in specialized alcohol treatment programs and provided more intense individual psychotherapy. A wide variety of physiological and behavioral outcomes were evaluated at multiple time points during the 16-week active phase of treatment, as well as during the posttreatment phase, but the principal measures included percent days of abstinence and time to the first heavy drinking. Results showed that the most effective treatments were medical management with either naltrexone or CBI, which led to 79% days of abstinence. The interaction of naltrexone and the behavioral intervention was particularly important because naltrexone with medical management also prolonged the time to the first heavy drinking. Oddly, in contrast to the findings of earlier studies, acamprosate had no effect either alone or in combination with either naltrexone or behavioral intervention. The authors suggest that the difference may be due to the fact that subjects from earlier successful acamprosate trials were inpatients who had a significantly longer period of abstinence before the trial began. The importance of these findings for treatment options is that pharmacotherapy with naltrexone and medical management can be provided by family doctors in readily available health care settings, and treatment does not depend on specialized treatment programs that are not always accessible to the alcohol-dependent population. It was interesting to see that during longer follow-up, CBI began to show significant benefit over medical management that was not evident in the initial clinical trial, although all treatments showed a diminishing outcome over time. It is likely that alcohol dependence should be treated much like other chronic conditions such as diabetes and hypertension with regular monitoring over time and rapid intervention with follow-up treatments as needed. Such monitoring and follow-up treatment should reduce the amount of health care needed to treat alcohol-related disease and associated costs in the long run.

Section Summary

- Alcoholism involves compulsive alcohol seeking and use despite damaging health and social consequences. Frequency and pattern of drinking are as important as the quantity consumed.

- Approximately 10% of Americans have an alcohol use problem. There are significant gender differences in alcohol use, binge drinking, and heavy drinking.

- Neurobiological, psychological, and sociocultural factors contribute to the vulnerability of a given individual to alcoholism.

- Stress reduces or increases alcohol consumption under different conditions. Alcohol increases the activity of the brain stress systems and neuroendocrine stress systems that may lead to further alcohol use. Sensitization to stressors persists long after withdrawal.

- Early life stress is a risk factor for adult alcohol abuse. Family history is a risk factor and is associated with a greater stress response and greater alcohol-induced suppression of the response.

- Cortisol sensitizes the DA mesolimbic pathway, which makes drug reinforcement more rewarding.

- Early (before age 13) drinking, impulse control problems, high novelty seeking, low harm avoidance, and aversion to delayed gratification predict future substance abuse.

- Genetics explains 50% to 60% of the variance of risk for alcohol dependence.

- Genes for the inactive form of acetaldehyde dehydrogenase, the enzyme that converts the toxic metabolite acetaldehyde, predict low risk for alcoholism because alcohol has unpleasant effects.

- Gene polymorphisms for the 5-HT reuptake transporter, the 5-HT$_{1B}$ receptor, and the D$_4$ receptor associated with anxiety or low sensitivity to alcohol increase vulnerability to alcohol abuse.

- Social and cultural factors determine attitudes about drinking and how much alcohol is available. Cultures that restrict use of alcohol have lower rates of alcoholism.

- Detoxification under medical supervision is the first step in treatment and is followed by benzodiazepine substitution to prevent withdrawal and gradual dose reduction.

- Psychosocial rehabilitation includes individual and group therapies, residential treatment settings, and self-help groups.

- Disufiram inhibits the enzyme that converts acetaldehyde to alcohol so that alcohol consumption causes very unpleasant effects such as nausea and vomiting.

- Naltrexone is an opioid receptor antagonist that reduces consumption and craving in some alcoholic individuals, perhaps by reducing the positive feeling caused by alcohol. Those with a family history of alcoholism and those with a μ-receptor polymorphism associated with reduced receptor expression respond better.

- Targeting the opioid κ-receptor with an antagonist reduced self-administration only in dependent animals, suggesting that the κ-receptor may have a role in the anhedonic states associated with physical dependence. Blocking μ- and κ-receptors with a dual antagonist like nalmefene may improve abstinence rates in humans.

- Acamprosate reduces the relapse rate. It reduces the glutamate increase that occurs at withdrawal and returns basal GABA levels to normal in the nucleus accumbens.

- Promising rodent studies targeting the stress response with CRF$_1$ antagonists suggest that they may be effective in reducing withdrawal-induced increase in consumption, as well as stress-induced relapse behavior.

- Animal studies suggest that blocking the NK1R for substance P reduces anxiety, alcohol consumption, and relapse behavior after withdrawal. In alcoholic patients, the antagonist reduced craving when patients were exposed to stress- and alcohol-related cues. The drug also normalized the brain response to emotional stimuli.

- The COMBINE study showed the most effect treatment for alcohol dependence is medical management along with either naltrexone or combined behavioral intervention. Since medical management with naltrexone can be provided by family doctors without special training, it provides more accessible health care.

Go to the **COMPANION WEBSITE**

sites.sinauer.com/psychopharm2e
for Web Boxes, animations, flashcards, and other study resources.

Recommended Readings

Becker, H. C., Lopez, M. F., and Doremus-Fitzwater, T. L. (2011). Effects of stress on alcohol drinking: A review of animal studies. *Psychopharmacology*, 218, 131–156.

Brickley, S. G. and Mody, I. (2012). Extrasynaptic GABA(A) receptors: Their function in the CNS and implications for disease. *Neuron*, 73, 23–34.

Gibbons, B. (1992). The legal drug. *Natl. Geogr. Mag.*, 181 (no. 2), 3–35.

Hingson, R. W., Zha, W., and Weitzman, E. R. (2009). Magnitude of and trends in alcohol-related mortality and morbidity among U.S. college students ages 18–24, 1998–2005. *J. Stud. Alcohol Drugs Suppl.*, 16, 12–20.

Hutchison, K. E. (2008). Alcohol dependence: Neuroimaging and the development of translational phenotypes. *Alcoholism Clin. Exp. Res.*, 32, 1111–1112.

Jung, J. (2001). *Psychology of Alcohol and Other Drugs: A Research Perspective*. London: Sage.

Knapp, C. (1996) *Drinking: A Love Story*. New York: Dell.

Koob, G. F. (2009). New dimensions in human laboratory models of addiction. *Addict. Biol.*, 14, 1–8.

Spanagel, R. (2009). Alcoholism: A systems approach from molecular physiology to addictive behavior. *Physiol. Rev.*, 89, 649–705.

Vallee, B. L. (1998). Alcohol in the Western world. *Sci. Am.*, June, 80–85.

Weiss, R. D. and Kueppenbender, K. D. (2006). Combining psychosocial treatment with pharmacotherapy for alcohol dependence. *J. Clin. Psychopharmacol.*, 26 (Suppl. 1), S37–42.

An Afghan farmer prepares opium poppy bulbs for harvest by scoring them with razors while in the field.

The Opioids 11

MOMENTS AFTER THE ARRIVAL OF THE AMBULANCE, a patient was rolled in on a stretcher to receive almost instant care by the emergency room staff. The patient was about 24 years old, Caucasian, and unconscious. Cardiac monitor leads were placed on his chest, and oxygen was immediately provided. His pulse was weak and his blood pressure extremely low. Heart rate and respiration rate were also depressed. The neurological exam revealed extreme pinpoint pupils, failure to respond to pain, and no response to verbal instructions. Although he was rather thin, his appearance was otherwise unremarkable except that one rolled-up shirt sleeve exposed needle track marks indicating intravenous (IV) drug use. The triad of coma, pinpoint pupils, and depressed respiration is a strong indicator of opioid poisoning, and physical evidence of IV drug use further confirms the diagnosis.

To any bystander, death seemed imminent. Nevertheless, 0.8 mg of IV naloxone (Narcan) was ordered immediately. Within a minute or two, respiratory rate had returned to normal, and soon after, the young man was alert enough to respond to a few questions. Although capable of walking out of the emergency room, our patient was convinced to remain overnight for further observation since the half-life of naloxone is somewhat shorter than that of heroin, and he might need a second naloxone infusion. How does a drug like heroin produce these potentially fatal effects? And what kind of miracle cure could reverse the condition so quickly? Chapter 11 tells you more about heroin and the other opioid drugs, as well as the specific opioid receptor antagonist naloxone.

Narcotic Analgesics

The opioid drugs all belong to the class known as **narcotic analgesics**. These drugs reduce pain without producing unconsciousness, but do produce a sense of relaxation and sleep, and at high doses, coma and death. As a class, they are the very best painkillers known to man. In addition to inducing analgesia, opioids have a variety of side effects and also produce a sense of well-being and euphoria that may lead to increased use of the drugs. Continued use leads to tolerance and sometimes physical dependence. In contrast to analgesics, **anesthetics** reduce all sensations by depressing the central nervous system (CNS) and produce unconsciousness.

The opium poppy has a long history of use

Opium is an extract of the poppy plant and is the source of a family of drugs known as the *opiates* or sometimes *opioids*.[1] Opium is prepared by drying and powdering the milky juice taken from the seed capsules of the opium poppy, *Papaver somniferum* (meaning "the poppy that causes sleep") just before ripening (**Figure 11.1**). When the capsules are sliced open, the juice leaks out and thickens into a red-brown syrupy material. In its crude state, it is very dark in color and forms small balls, called "black tar." Cultivation of the opium poppy has been successful in the temperate zones as far north as England and Denmark, but the majority of the world's supply comes from Southeast Asia, India, China, Iran, Turkey, and southeastern Europe. The plant grows to about 3 or 4 feet in height and has large flowers in white, pink, red, or purple. This variety is the only poppy that has significant psychoactive effects.

The opiates have been used both as medicine and for recreational purposes for several thousand years. As early as 1500 BC, the Egyptians described opiates' preparation and medicinal value. Archeological evidence from Cyprus dated as early as 1200 BC includes ceramic opium pipes and vases with poppy capsules for decoration. By the second century AD, the famous Greek physician Galen prescribed opium for a wide variety of medical problems, including headache, deafness, asthma, coughs, shortness of breath, colic, and leprosy, among others. But the Greek author Homer, in *The Odyssey*, refers to the drug's recreational properties when he describes the plant as eliciting a feeling of warmth and well-being followed by sleep. More modern use began in Europe, when news of the "miracle cure" was brought back by the religious crusaders from the Near East. Eating or smoking opium was accepted in Islamic countries such as Arabia, Turkey, and Iran, where it replaced the consumption of alcohol, which was prohibited. By 1680, an opium-based medicinal drink was introduced by

Figure 11.1 Preparing opium The unripe opium poppy capsule has been sliced and the crude opium is dripping from the incision.

the father of clinical medicine, the English physician Thomas Sydenham. His recipe for the drink called *laudanum* (meaning "something to be praised") included "2 ounces of strained opium, 1 ounce of saffron, and a dram of cinnamon and cloves dissolved in 1 pint of Canary wine." Drinking laudanum-laced wine was the accepted form of opium use in both Victorian England and America, especially among women, who considered it far more respectable than "common" alcohol use. Laudanum was also a common ingredient of many popular remedies for a wide variety of problems, including teething pain and restlessness in infants, muscle aches and pains, and alcoholism. Right up to the turn of the twentieth century, opium-containing products with names such as "A Pennyworth of Peace," "Mrs. Winslow's Soothing Syrup," and "White Star Secret Liquor Cure" could be ordered through the Sears, Roebuck and Co. catalog for about $4 a pint (**Figure 11.2**).

In nineteenth-century America, neither the federal government nor individual states chose to control the availability and advertising of drugs such as opium and cocaine. There was clearly no significant concern about safety, long-term health issues, or dependence. Finally, in 1914, the Harrison Narcotics Act was passed, which required physicians to report their prescriptions for opioids. Only in the 1920s did the Supreme Court broadly interpret the Harrison Act to limit prescriptions to *medical* use, making it illegal to provide opioids for addicted individuals or recreational use.

---

[1]*Opiate* refers specifically to substances derived directly from the opium poppy. *Opioid* is a broader term that includes opiates, synthetic substances, and endogenous peptides that bind to opioid receptors.

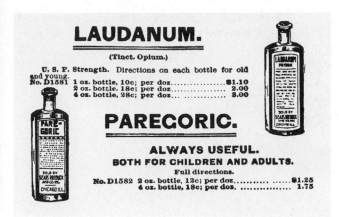

Figure 11.2 Mail order advertisement for opium preparations to treat pain and cough (laudanum) and diarrhea (paregoric) from the 1897 Sears, Roebuck and Co. catalog.

Minor differences in molecular structure determine behavioral effects

The principal active ingredient in opium was called *morphine*, after the Roman god of dreams, Morpheus, and it was first isolated in the early 1800s by a German chemist, Friedrich Wilhelm Sertürner. His extraction of morphine crystals from the milky juice of the poppy seed capsules is considered a milestone in the history of pharmacology because it was the first time the active ingredient of any medicinal plant was isolated. Having the extract enabled physicians to prescribe the painkiller in known dosages. In addition to morphine, opium contains other active ingredients, including codeine, thebaine, narcotine, and others. Although morphine was isolated from opium in the early 1800s, the structure of morphine was not identified until 1925 (**Figure 11.3**). The naturally occurring opiate codeine is identical in structure to morphine except for the substitution of a methoxy ($-OCH_3$) for a hydroxyl ($-OH$) group. This small molecular difference produces a drug that has less analgesic effect and fewer side effects than morphine but is still a potent cough suppressant. It was exciting for pharmacologists to discover that simple modifications of the morphine molecule produce great variations in potency, duration of action, and oral effectiveness. In many cases, these differences are due to differences in pharmacokinetics rather than to intrinsic activity. For example, heroin was manufactured by adding two acetyl groups onto the morphine molecule. This drug was developed by the Bayer Company to be more effective in relieving pain without the danger of addiction. Today we know that the pharmacological effects of morphine and heroin are essentially identical because heroin is converted to morphine in the brain. Heroin is, however, two to four times more potent when injected and is faster acting because the

change in the molecule makes the drug more lipid soluble and allows it to get into the brain much more quickly to act on receptors there. When taken orally, morphine and heroin are approximately equal in potency. The very rapid action of heroin is apparently also responsible for the dramatic euphoric effects achieved with that drug.

Some of the modifications to morphine's molecular structure produce **partial agonists**, which are drugs that bind readily to (i.e., have a high affinity for) the receptors but produce less biological effect (i.e., low efficacy). Therefore, when administered alone, they produce partial opioid effects, but when given along with an opioid that has higher effectiveness, they compete for the receptor and subsequently reduce the action of the more effective drug.

Other chemical modifications of the morphine molecule produce **pure antagonists** such as naloxone and nalorphine. These are drugs that have structures similar to those of the opiates but produce no pharmacological activity of their own (i.e., no efficacy). The receptor antagonists can prevent or reverse the effect of administered opioids because of their ability to occupy opioid receptor sites. As you saw in the opening paragraphs of this chapter, intravenously administered naloxone can revive an unconscious individual in a matter of seconds; it can reverse all of the opioid effects and save the lives of those brought to the emergency room after opioid overdose. Specific receptor antagonists are also important for understanding the mechanism of action of opioid

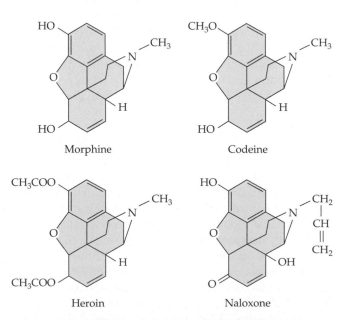

Figure 11.3 Molecular structure of morphine, codeine, heroin, and naloxone highlighting the similarities in structure. The minor differences contribute to effectiveness and side effects.

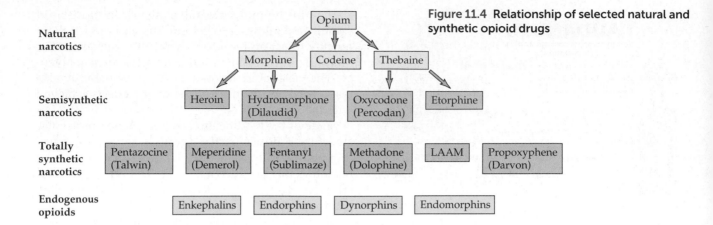

Figure 11.4 **Relationship of selected natural and synthetic opioid drugs**

analgesics. As you will learn a bit later, the four principal types of opioid receptors (μ, δ, κ and NOP-R) mediate different opioid actions.

The prototypic partial agonist is pentazocine (Talwin), but others in this category are nalbuphine (Nubain) and buprenorphine (Buprenex). Although as analgesics they are much less potent than morphine, they do not cause significant respiratory depression or constipation, and they have a reduced risk for dependence. While some narcotic drugs are natural derivatives, others are considered semisynthetic because they require chemical modifications of the natural opiates. For instance, hydromorphone (Dilaudid) and heroin are modifications of the morphine molecule; others are entirely synthetic and may have quite distinct structures (e.g., propoxyphene [Darvon], meperidine [Demerol]). Thebain, another constituent of opium, is chemically converted into several opioid compounds, including oxycodone, oxymorphone, buprenorphine, and etorphine. The relationship of the major opiates and some of their derivatives, as well as some of the synthetic opioids, is shown in **Figure 11.4**.

Bioavailability predicts both physiological and behavioral effects

When morphine is administered for medical purposes, it is usually injected intramuscularly or given orally. Oral administration is convenient but produces more variable blood levels for the reasons discussed in Chapter 1. Recreational users often smoke opium for its rapid absorption from the lungs, although "snorting" heroin also leads to rapid absorption through the nasal mucosa. In addition, subcutaneous administration ("skin popping") may precede the more dangerous "mainlining" (intravenous injection).

Although morphine has pronounced psychoactive effects, only a small fraction of the drug is capable of crossing the blood–brain barrier to act on opioid

receptors in the brain. Opioid distribution is fairly uniform in the rest of the body, and the drugs easily pass the placental barrier, exposing the unborn child to high levels. The newborn of an opioid-addicted mother suffers withdrawal symptoms within several hours after birth, which may have severe consequences for the infant, especially if the child is weak from inadequate prenatal nutrition. However, infants are readily stabilized with low doses of opioids to prevent abstinence signs, and the dose is gradually reduced. Following metabolism in the liver, most of the opioid metabolites are excreted in the urine within 24 hours.

Opioids have their most important effects on the CNS and on the gastrointestinal tract

The multiple effects of morphine and other opioids on the CNS are dose-related and are also related to the rate of absorption. At low to moderate doses (5 to 10 mg), pain is relieved, respiration is somewhat depressed, and pupils are constricted. The principal subjective effects are drowsiness, decreased sensitivity to the environment, and impaired ability to concentrate, followed by a dreamy sleep. Because opioids have actions in the limbic system, some researchers suggest that the drugs relieve "psychological pain," including anxiety, feelings of inadequacy, and hostility, which may lead to increased drug use. Morphine also suppresses the cough reflex in a dose-dependent manner and has actions on the hypothalamus that lead to decreased appetite, drop in body temperature, reduced sex drive, and a variety of hormonal changes. Each of these effects can be associated with opioid receptors in particular areas of the CNS.

At slightly higher doses, particularly if the drug is administered intravenously or inhaled, the individual experiences an abnormal state of elation or euphoria, which is referred to as the "kick," "bang," or "rush" and is compared with a "whole-body orgasm." Nonaddicts describe it as a sudden flush of warmth located in the pit of the stomach. To achieve the maximum euphoria, very rapid penetration into the brain is needed. Although it is experienced as intense pleasure, the "rush" is not the principal basis for abuse but acts as a powerful reinforcer that encourages repeated drug use.

It is also important to know that the euphoric effect does not always accompany IV administration. For many individuals being medically treated, the drug may produce dysphoria, consisting of restlessness and anxiety. In addition, the nausea and vomiting that may accompany low doses of morphine is increased with higher doses. It is directly related to morphine's effect on the chemical trigger zone (the area postrema) in the brainstem that elicits vomiting. Although clearly unpleasant for most individuals, for the addict, the nausea may become a "good sick" because it is closely associated with the drug-induced euphoria by classical conditioning.

At the highest doses, the opioids' sedative effects become stronger and may lead to unconsciousness. Body temperature and blood pressure fall. Pupils are now quite constricted and represent a clinical sign of opioid overdose in a comatose patient. Respiration is dangerously impaired because of morphine's action on the brainstem's respiratory center, which normally responds to high blood CO_2 levels by triggering increased respiration. Respiratory failure is the ultimate cause of death in overdose.

Apart from the CNS, the effects of morphine are greatest on the gastrointestinal tract. Opium was used for relief of diarrhea and dysentery even before it was used for analgesia. It remains one of the most important lifesaving drugs because of its ability to cause constipation and stop the life-threatening fluid loss associated with diarrhea that accompanies many bacterial and parasitic illnesses especially prevalent in developing countries. More modern treatment utilizes modified opioid molecules such as loperimide, which has been designed so that it cannot cross the blood–brain barrier. The major advantage is that it effectively slows gastrointestinal function but does not have any effect on the CNS. Unfortunately, when opioids are used for pain management, constipation is a common and disturbing side effect that does not diminish even after prolonged use.

Opioid Receptors and Endogenous Neuropeptides

The opioid drugs produce biobehavioral effects by binding to specific neuronal receptors. Since minor modifications of the morphine molecule produce

significant changes in effect, analyses of the molecular structure of the drugs provide sufficient information to hypothesize definite structural features of the opioid receptor. Further, naloxone's blocking effects can be overcome by increasing concentrations of morphine, which demonstrates competition for the receptor. Not long after opioid receptors were identified, the natural neuropeptide ligands that act at the receptors were characterized.

Receptor binding studies identified and localized opioid receptors

Although the existence of opioid receptors was evident, the initial attempts to label and locate these receptors in brain tissue using standard radioligand binding methods (see Chapter 4) proved to be a difficult task. Ultimately, the opioid receptor was labeled (Pert and Snyder, 1973) by making several technical refinements in the assay and separation procedure, as well as by having access to newer radioactive ligands that had a greater amount of radioactivity per drug molecule. The receptors that they identified met the criteria described in Chapter 4. First, **Figure 11.5A** shows the classic binding curve, demonstrating that as the amount of radioactive opioid (in this case, the antagonist naloxone) is increased, binding also increases and gradually tapers off until the receptors are fully occupied. The leveling off of the binding curve at B_{max} shows that a finite number of receptors exist in a given amount of tissue. This saturation would not occur if the radioligand happened to be "sticky" and attached randomly to many cellular materials. Second, looking at the concentrations used in the assay makes it clear that the binding sites have a high affinity for the opioids. Third, the binding was shown to be reversible, with a time course that matches the loss of physiological effectiveness. Fourth, the concentrations needed in the binding assay are meaningfully related to the concentration of agonist needed to elicit a biological response.

But how do we know that these sites are responsible for the opioids' pharmacological activity? Snyder (1977) calculated binding affinity by measuring the ability of a number of nonradioactive opioids to compete with radioactive naloxone for the receptors. They found that the relative potency of various opioids in the competition experiments closely paralleled their relative potencies in pharmacological effects on the intestine (**Figure 11.5B**). In this case, the pharmacological effect measured is the ability of opioids to inhibit electrically induced contraction of the ileum (the lowest portion of the small intestine). This inhibition occurs because opioids inhibit the release of neurotransmitter from stimulated nerves. Although many more-sophisticated methods are possible, opioid

(A)

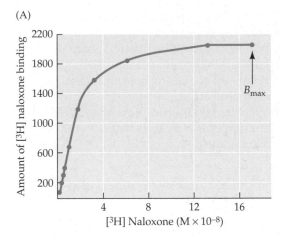

(B)

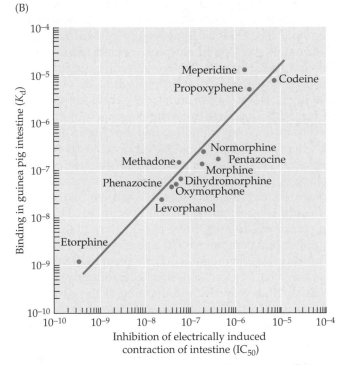

Figure 11.5 Opioid receptor binding (A) Binding of [³H] naloxone to rat brain shows the saturation of opioid receptors. As the concentration of the opioid ligand (naloxone) increases, binding to the receptors increases steadily until the receptors are filled at B_{max}. (B) There is a strong positive correlation between the concentration of opioid drugs needed to inhibit electrically induced contraction of the intestine (IC_{50}) and the concentration needed to bind to opioid receptors in the same tissue. The results show clearly that drugs that bind readily at low concentrations of ligand (e.g., etorphine) also are effective in inhibiting the intestinal contraction at low doses. Drugs that bind less well (e.g., codeine) also require higher concentrations to inhibit the contraction.

action on the ileum is considered a classic bioassay and is described in **Web Box 11.1**.

Once the receptors were labeled and characterized, autoradiography could be used to locate the receptors

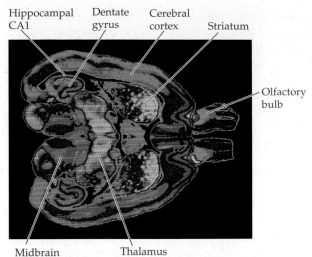

Figure 11.6 The distribution of opioid receptors in rat brain is shown in this autoradiogram. Higher densities, seen as warmer colors, occur in the striatum, medial thalamus, locus coeruleus, periaqueductal gray, and raphe nuclei. (Courtesy of Miles Herkenham, NIMH.)

in the brain. **Figure 11.6** shows a color-enhanced distribution of opioid receptors in rat brain.

Four opioid receptor subtypes exist

Although the classic dose–response curves used by Martin and colleagues (1976) suggested that several subtypes of opioid receptors exist, researchers needed to develop highly *selective* radioactive ligands to directly label the subtypes. Selectivity means that a given molecule readily binds to one receptor subtype and has relatively low binding affinity for the others (Simon, 1991). The three classical subtypes have been called μ (mu), δ (delta), and κ (kappa). A more recent addition to the opioid receptor family is the nociceptin/orphanin FQ receptor (NOP-R). Based on genetic criteria, the NOP-R and classical opioid receptors belong to the same family. The same is true for the opioid peptides and the ligand for the NOP-R, nociceptin/orphanin FQ (see the following section). However, despite their familial relationship, opioids do not bind to NOP-R, nor does nociceptin/orphanin FQ bind to opioid receptors. The four opioid receptor subtypes have distinct distributions in the brain and spinal cord, which suggests that they mediate a wide variety of effects.

The **μ-receptor** is the receptor that has a high affinity for morphine and related opioid drugs. The location of the μ-receptors has been mapped by autoradiography in several species (Mansour and Watson, 1993), including human brain postmortem (Quirion and Pilapil, 1991). Other researchers have performed

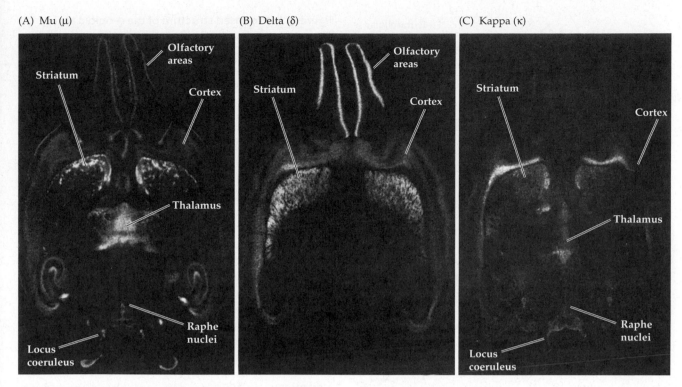

(A) Mu (μ) (B) Delta (δ) (C) Kappa (κ)

Figure 11.7 Autoradiograms of opioid receptor subtype binding in rat brain Notice the distinct locations of (A) μ-, (B) δ-, and (C) κ-receptors. (From Mansour et al., 1988.)

in vivo mapping using positron emission tomography (PET) imaging (Mayberg and Frost, 1990). The results consistently show a wide distribution of μ-receptors in both the brain and the spinal cord. The brain areas rich in μ-receptors (e.g., the medial thalamus, periaqueductal gray, median raphe, and clusters within the spinal cord) support their role in morphine-induced analgesia. Other high-density areas suggest a role in feeding and positive reinforcement (nucleus accumbens), cardiovascular and respiratory depression, cough control, nausea and vomiting (brainstem), and sensorimotor integration (thalamus, striatum) (Mansour and Watson, 1993; Carvey, 1998). **Figure 11.7A** is an autoradiogram of μ-receptor binding in the rat CNS.

The **δ-receptors** have a distribution similar to that of μ-receptors (**Figure 11.7B**) but are more restricted. They are predominantly found in forebrain structures such as the neocortex, striatum, olfactory areas, substantia nigra, and nucleus accumbens. Many of these sites are consistent with a possible role for δ-receptors in modulating olfaction, motor integration, reinforcement, and cognitive function. Delta receptors in areas overlapping μ-receptors suggest modulation of both spinal and supraspinal analgesia.

The **κ-receptors** (**Figure 11.7C**) have a very distinct distribution compared with the μ- and δ-receptors.

The κ-receptor was initially identified by high-affinity binding to ketocyclazocine, which is an opioid analog that produces hallucinations and dysphoria. This receptor is also found in the striatum and amygdala but additionally has a unique distribution in the hypothalamus and pituitary. These receptors may participate in the regulation of pain perception, gut motility, and dysphoria but also modulate water balance, feeding, temperature control, and neuroendocrine function.

The **NOP-R** are widely distributed in the CNS and the peripheral nervous system. They are found in high concentration in the cerebral cortex, limbic areas including the amygdala, hippocampus, and hypothalamus, as well as periaqueductal gray, thalamus, brainstem nuclei including the raphe nuclei, and spinal cord. The receptor localization suggests a role in analgesia, feeding, learning, motor function, and neuroendocrine regulation.

Once the genetic material for each of the four receptor types was isolated, it was inserted into cells (a process called **transfection**) maintained in culture to produce large numbers of identical cells (cloning). The **receptor cloning** and molecular sequencing of the opioid receptor subtypes provided several key pieces of information:

1. For each of the receptors, we now know the specific nucleic acid sequence making up the DNA that directs the synthesis of each receptor protein.

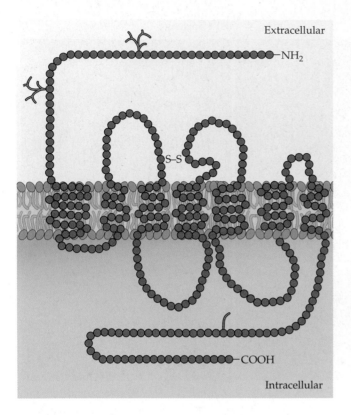

Extracellular

Intracellular

Figure 11.8 Proposed structure of the δ-opioid receptor Each circle represents an identified amino acid. The seven regions spanning the cell membrane are typical for receptors that are coupled to G proteins.

2. Using the nucleic acid sequence, the amino acids of the protein can be identified and compared with other families of receptor proteins.

3. The transfected cells can be used to study the intracellular changes induced by receptor agonists.

4. By radioactively labeling the genetic material, in situ hybridization makes it possible to visualize those cells in the brain that synthesize the receptor protein and more precisely localize the receptors themselves. (See Chapter 4 for a review of the techniques of molecular biology.)

Although the first opioid receptor to be successfully cloned was the δ-receptor (Evans et al., 1992; Kieffer et al., 1992), cloning of the others was soon to follow. Each of the four receptors has between 370 and 400 amino acids, and they bind with the ligands specific to each. All four of the protein receptors have a structure similar to the family of receptors that are linked to G proteins, which suggests that they mediate metabotropic (rather than ionotropic) responses. The structure of the δ-receptor, with the classic seven transmembrane portions, is shown in **Figure 11.8**.

Several families of naturally occurring opioid peptides bind to these receptors

Once the receptors were identified, researchers were quick to ask why the nervous system would have

receptors for the derivatives of the opium poppy. It seemed more reasonable to hypothesize that an endogenous neurochemical must exist to act on opioid receptors. Since the distribution of the receptors failed to match the regional distribution of any known neurotransmitter, it was assumed that a novel neurochemical would be identified. A second rationale for searching for an endogenous opioid involved the analgesia produced by electrically stimulating specific areas of the CNS such as the periaqueductal gray. In many animal studies as well as human clinical trials, the analgesic effect could be partially antagonized by the opioid receptor antagonist naloxone, which suggested that opioids were involved. It is clear to us now that electrical stimulation causes the release of a natural ligand that acts on those opioid receptors.

DISCOVERY   In 1974 two different laboratories identified a peptide in brain extracts and other tissues that mimicked opioid activity (electrophysiologically and in a mouse vas deferens bioassay) and could also bind to opioid receptors (Terenius and Wahlstrom, 1974; Hughes, 1975). They named the first peptide *enkephalin*, meaning "in the brain." Soon a number of peptides were found to have these properties and were called endogenous opioids, or **endorphins** (from *endo*, signifying "endogenous," and *-orphin*, from "morphine"). The great similarity in structure among the peptides led researchers to conclude that there were several larger peptides, called propeptides (or precursor peptides), that are broken into smaller active opioids. Any confusion was resolved when molecular biologists found that there are four large propeptides and each is coded for by a separate gene. These large peptides are called **prodynorphin** (254 amino acids), **pro-opiomelanocortin** or **POMC** (267 amino acids), **proenkephalin** (267 amino acids), and **pronociceptin/orphanin FQ** (180 amino acids). Each of the large peptides manufactured in the soma must be processed by enzymes (called proteases) that are packaged in the Golgi apparatus along with the peptide. These enzymes are responsible for chopping or cleaving the propeptide into individual peptide products that are stored in vesicles and are further processed as they are transported down the axon to be released at the synapse. Each of the large propeptides produces a number of biologically active opioid and non-opioid peptides (**Figure 11.9**). Some years later, Zadina and colleagues (1999) described a group of peptides with a distinct structure and distribution in the CNS. These

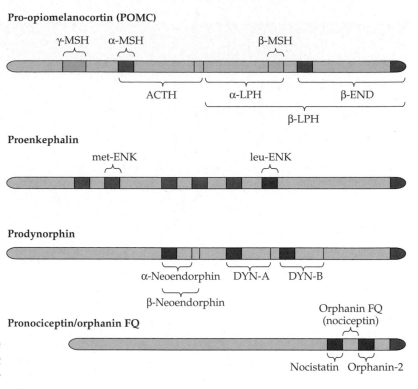

Figure 11.9 The four opioid propeptides and some of their possible products
POMC is cleaved into β-endorphin (β-END) and a number of other peptides, including γ- and α-melanocyte-stimulating hormone (MSH), adrenocorticotropic hormone (ACTH), and several forms of lipotropin (LPH). Proenkephalin cleavage produces several copies of met- and leu-enkephalin. Prodynorphin contains several endorphins (α- and β-neoendorphin) as well as dyn-orphin A and B. Pronociceptin/orphanin FQ cleavage produces one copy each of orphanin FQ, orphanin-2, and nocistatin. Note that the tiny enkephalin peptides are frequently found within the larger peptide fragments.

peptides, called **endomorphins**, bind quite selectively to the μ-receptor and are as potent as morphine in relieving pain. Thus far, their propeptide has not been identified.

LOCALIZATION Mapping of the pathways utilizing the endogenous opioids was achieved by in situ hybridization to visualize propeptide mRNA, and immunohistochemistry was used to localize the propeptide itself (see Chapter 4). These propeptides are found in the brain, spinal cord, and peripheral autonomic nervous system, concentrated in areas related to pain modulation and mood. In addition, POMC is found in particularly high concentration in the pituitary gland, which releases a variety of hormones in response to hypothalamic releasing factors. The hypothalamus releases corticotropin-releasing factor (CRF) in response to stress, which in turn increases adrenocorticotropic hormone (ACTH) release from the pituitary and ultimately glucocorticoids from the adrenal cortex (**Figure 11.10**). CRF also causes a rapid increase in POMC mRNA and subsequent increases in release of β-endorphin from the pituitary. Since a variety of stressors, such as painful foot shock,

Figure 11.10 Hypothalamic control of ACTH and β-endorphin release The hypothalamus releases CRF, which causes the anterior pituitary to secrete ACTH, which in turn acts on the adrenal gland to prepare the individual to deal with stress. CRF also influences β-endorphin synthesis and release from the pituitary in response to stress. Notice in the previous figure that ACTH and β-endorphin come from the same propeptide, POMC.

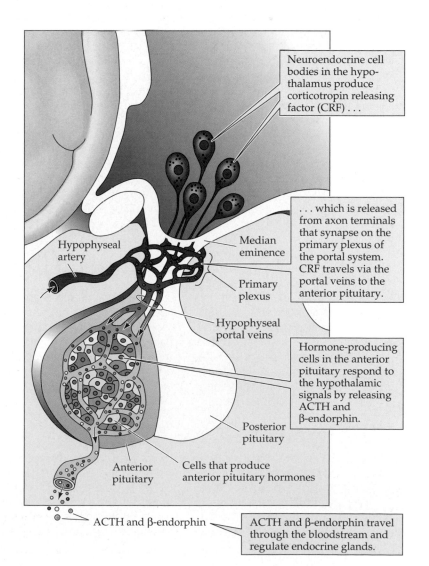

Neuroendocrine cell bodies in the hypothalamus produce corticotropin releasing factor (CRF) . . .

. . . which is released from axon terminals that synapse on the primary plexus of the portal system. CRF travels via the portal veins to the anterior pituitary.

Hormone-producing cells in the anterior pituitary respond to the hypothalamic signals by releasing ACTH and β-endorphin.

ACTH and β-endorphin travel through the bloodstream and regulate endocrine glands.

BOX 11.1   Of Special Interest

Opioid Modulation of Feeding

Among the many effects of opioids is their role in food consumption and taste preferences. Barbano and Cador (2007) and Peciña and Smith (2010) provide current reviews of the literature. In particular, opioids modulate the pleasure or palatability associated with food-related stimuli. Naloxone significantly reduces food consumption in either food-deprived or non-deprived subjects, as well as eating induced by stress, metabolic needs, or stimulation of brain sites that elicit feeding. The hypothesis that opioids specifically regulate the palatability or at least the reward value of highly palatable food has received considerable support. You learned in the chapter on drug abuse (Chapter 9) that the rewarding aspects of abused substances leading to compulsive use involve both hedonic factors ("liking") and incentive motivation ("wanting"). It is of considerable interest that those two factors also contribute to food reward, and opioid systems have been strongly implicated in both phenomena. One question that remains is whether compulsive overeating resembles drug abuse in other significant ways.

Endogenous opioid signaling and μ-receptor signaling in particular seem to modify the preference or liking of some foods over others in humans and other species. Opioid antagonists reduce consumption of a highly palatable food (such as chocolate cookies) and reinstate consumption of standard rat food pellets, while systemic morphine administration increases chocolate cookie consumption without increasing standard food consumption. Experiments show that morphine increases fat consumption in fat-preferring rats and carbohydrate consumption in carbohydrate-preferring rats. Although opioids seem to modulate palatability, some evidence suggests that the degree of palatability may depend on the ability of particular foods to enhance endogenous opioid activity. For example, by increasing the sucrose concentration, the inhibitory effect of naloxone on consumption of that solution is reduced. This may occur because the higher concentration of sucrose dose dependently increases the endogenous opioids, making them harder to inhibit with the antagonist. Further support comes from the finding that ingestion of a sweet solution or fat produces opioid-like analgesia and also potentiates the analgesic effects of morphine. Hence these and other studies indicate that sucrose and other palatable foods increase endogenous opioids.

In addition to modulating the "liking" of sweet or fatty foods, opioids modify the motivation or incentive toward those substances, as shown in experiments where μ-agonists increase the willingness of rats to lever press for palatable food reinforcement. In a similar manner, the μ-opioid agonists make food stimuli and cues associated with food more motivationally relevant, hence harder to resist. Additionally, opioid antagonists reduce the motivation for sweet or fatty food, as shown by reduced running performance for food reward.

Limbic brain regions appear to be the locus of opioid receptor–mediated effects on food palatability. The microinjection of morphine and selected opioid agonists into the nucleus accumbens elicits increased consumption, particularly of palatable foods. Since the dopaminergic mesolimbic neurons terminating in the nucleus accumbens are considered to be involved in central reward mechanisms, a link has been established between opioids, feeding, and reward mechanisms. Although much attention has been paid to the nucleus accumbens, it has become clear recently that liking and wanting are linked together via a network of interconnected brain regions in the limbic forebrain that use opioid neurotransmission.

The evidence supporting a role for opioid modulation of both the hedonic characteristic of feeding and the motivation for palatable foods has suggested that drugs targeting opioid systems may represent an approach to the treatment of obesity, a condition that is becoming increasingly worrisome because of its link to diabetes and heart disease. Studies with rodents show that naloxone reduces food consumption to a greater extent in genetically obese animals than in normal-weight littermates. In a similar manner, animals that have become obese by eating a palatable high-calorie diet respond to naloxone treatment by eating less. It is of interest that selective μ-antagonists reduce body weight as well as fat content in sedentary, obese mice, but not in lean mice. Furthermore, the same antagonists increase wheel running in obese but not in lean mice. In humans, preference for sucrose and fat is increased by the opioid agonist butorphanol and reduced after naloxone administration. In other studies, the antagonist naltrexone reduced the perceived pleasantness of a variety of desirable foods. Nevertheless, in the clinic, treatment for overeating with the antagonist naltrexone has produced mixed results. Some success has been reported for binge eating, but long-term eating compulsions have been more resistant to treatment. Clearly, compulsive eating and obesity is a complex phenomenon that involves genetics, personality factors, lifestyle choices, and social-economic issues as well as reinforcement, so it is possible that only a subset of obese individuals may be helped by opioid antagonism.

restraint, and swim stress, increase both CRF mRNA and POMC mRNA, it is likely that this opioid provides a physiological link between pain and stress regulation (Young, 1993). Overall, the widespread locations of the peptides strongly implicate them in many functions, including pain suppression, reward, motor coordination, endocrine function, feeding, body temperature and water regulation, and response to stress. **Box 11.1** describes some of the effects of opioids on feeding.

While some of the neurons containing the opioid propeptides have long projections, many more are small cells that form local circuits. Many of the peptides are co-localized with other neurotransmitters in the same neuron, including acetylcholine, GABA (γ-aminobutyric acid), serotonin, catecholamines, and other peptides. When peptides coexist with other neurotransmitters, they are likely to have a neuromodulatory role, that is, they modify the function of the neurotransmitter or produce changes in ion conductance and membrane potential.

Although we have four peptide families plus the endomorphins and three principal receptor subtypes, the peptides are not selective for a receptor type but show only a relative preference. The natural ligands for the δ-receptors are thought to be those derived from proenkephalin (enkephalins), and products from prodynorphin (dynorphin) are likely the natural κ-receptor agonists. The endomorphins bind preferentially to the μ-receptors, while POMC peptides (endorphins) bind readily to both μ- and δ-receptors. Since the NOP-R does not bind to opioids, it remained an "orphan" until two groups of researchers isolated a distinct peptide that one group called nociceptin because in contrast to opioids, it *lowers* pain threshold and the other group called orphanin FQ; hence it is now called nociceptin/

orphanin FQ (N/OFQ). Pronociceptin/orphanin FQ and its peptides deserve a bit more discussion because although they are similar to the opioids, there are significant differences. The prohormone is widely distributed throughout the brain and spinal cord, with especially high concentrations in limbic regions. Although distribution of its peptides is different from that of the classical opioid peptides, in other instances they are found to be co-localized with the opioids. Significant evidence suggests that there is *reciprocal* modulation of N/OFQ neurons and the classical opioids. Additionally, it is clear that although N/OFQ in some cases has similar effects as the opioid peptides, in other cases it may cause effects opposite to those caused by the opioids. For example, although it is an analgesic at the spinal cord level, in supraspinal regions it is pronociceptive and has anti-opioid properties, including suppressing opioid-mediated analgesia. Other effects include impairing motor performance, suppressing spatial learning, inducing feeding, and regulating stress-induced release of pituitary hormones. The peptide has many other functions and some that remain undiscovered. **Table 11.1** summarizes receptor subtype location, function, and preference for endogenous opioids.

Opioid receptor–mediated cellular changes are inhibitory

You are already aware that each of the four opioid receptor types is linked to G proteins. You may recall from Chapter 3 that there are multiple forms of G proteins that have two principal actions. Some G proteins directly stimulate or inhibit the opening of ion channels (see Figure 3.11A), and others stimulate or inhibit enzymes to alter second-messenger production (see

TABLE 11.1 Location, Function, and Endogenous Ligand for Opioid Receptor Subtypes

Receptor subtype	Endogenous ligand (prohormone source)	Location (most dense)	Functions
μ	Endomorphins (unknown), endorphins (POMC)	Thalamus, periaqueductal gray, raphe nuclei, spinal cord, striatum, brain stem, nucleus accumbens, amygdala, hippocampus	Analgesia, reinforcement, feeding, cardiovascular and respiratory depression, antitussive, vomiting, sensorimotor integration
δ	Enkephalin (proenkephalin), endorphins (POMC)	Neocortex, striatum, olfactory areas, substantia nigra, nucleus accumbens, spinal cord	Analgesia, reinforcement, cognitive function, olfaction, motor integration
κ	Dynorphins (prodynorphin)	Pituitary, hypothalamus, amygdala, striatum, nucleus accumbens	Neuroendocrine function, water balance, feeding, temperature control, dysphoria, analgesia
NOP-R	Nociceptin/orphanin FQ (pronociceptin/orphanin FQ)	Cortex, amygdala, hypothalamus, hippocampus, periaqueductal gray, thalamus, substantia nigra, brain stem, spinal cord	Spinal analgesia, supraspinal pronociception, feeding, learning, motor function, neuroendocrine function

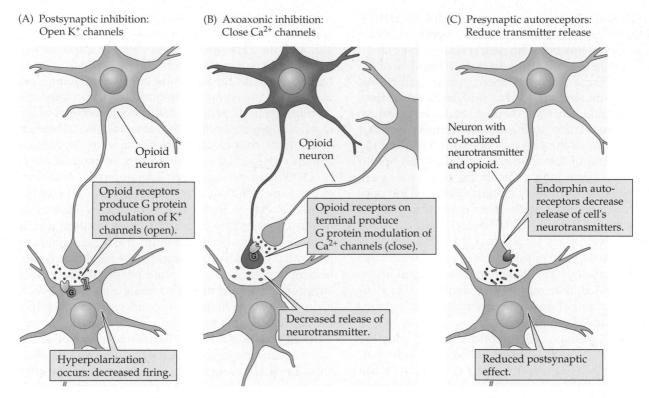

(A) Postsynaptic inhibition: Open K⁺ channels

Opioid neuron

Opioid receptors produce G protein modulation of K⁺ channels (open).

Hyperpolarization occurs: decreased firing.

(B) Axoaxonic inhibition: Close Ca²⁺ channels

Opioid neuron

Opioid receptors on terminal produce G protein modulation of Ca²⁺ channels (close).

Decreased release of neurotransmitter.

(C) Presynaptic autoreceptors: Reduce transmitter release

Neuron with co-localized neurotransmitter and opioid.

Endorphin auto-receptors decrease release of cell's neurotransmitters.

Reduced postsynaptic effect.

Figure 11.11 Inhibitory actions of endogenous opioids
Opioids inhibit nerve activity in several ways. (A) Opioids bind to receptors that activate a G protein that opens K⁺ channels to hyperpolarize the postsynaptic cells, thereby reducing the rate of firing. (B) Opioid receptors on nerve terminals (axoaxonic) activate G proteins that close Ca²⁺ channels, reducing the release of the neurotransmitter. (C) Presynaptic autoreceptors activate G proteins and reduce the release of a co-localized neurotransmitter. The mechanism may involve closing Ca²⁺ channels or opening K⁺ channels that hyperpolarize the presynaptic cell.

Figure 3.11B). Opioids and N/OFQ work by both of those mechanisms to open potassium (K⁺) channels, close calcium (Ca²⁺) channels, and inhibit adenylyl cyclase activity. The overall effects of the neuropeptides on nerve cell function include the reduction of membrane excitability and subsequent slowing of cell firing and inhibition of neurotransmitter release.

The neuropeptides reduce synaptic transmission in three principal ways: (1) by postsynaptic inhibition; (2) through axoaxonic inhibition; and (3) via presynaptic autoreceptors. First, opioid- and N/OFQ receptor–G protein activation opens K⁺ channels, which increases K⁺ conductance. Potassium exits the cell, forced by its concentration gradient, causing hyperpolarization. When the receptors are on the soma or dendrites of neurons, the hyperpolarization decreases the cell's firing rate (**Figure 11.11A**).

Second, opioids and N/OFQ also produce an inhibitory effect by closing voltage-gated Ca²⁺ channels. In this case (**Figure 11.11B**), receptors on the presynaptic terminal activate G proteins, which in turn close the Ca²⁺ channels. Reducing the amount of Ca²⁺ entering during an action potential proportionately decreases the amount of neurotransmitter released. For example, opioid-induced inhibition of norepinephrine and dopamine release has been found in many brain areas. As expected, this effect is prevented by the receptor antagonist naloxone. Note that naloxone does not antagonize N/OFQ because N/OFQ does not bind to opioid receptors. The inhibition of glutamate and substance P release in the spinal cord is of particular significance because those neurotransmitters are released from the afferent sensory neurons that transmit pain signals from the periphery into the CNS (see the section on opioids and pain).

Third, opioid autoreceptors also produce inhibitory effects. Somatodendritic autoreceptors hyperpolarize cells in the locus coeruleus by enhancing K⁺ conductance and subsequently reducing cell firing (not shown in figure). Elsewhere, presynaptic autoreceptors reduce the release of co-localized neurotransmitters (**Figure 11.11C**). In summary, neuropeptide effects on both K⁺ and Ca²⁺ channels produce inhibitory effects and reduce neurotransmitter release. These actions in the appropriate circuitry are ultimately responsible for the analgesic effects (DiChiara and North, 1992).

All four types of opioid receptor are also coupled to inhibitory G proteins (called G_i) that inhibit adenylyl cyclase, which normally synthesizes the second messenger cyclic adenosine monophosphate (cAMP). The reduced cAMP and subsequent decreased function of cAMP-dependent protein kinase may in part be responsible for opioid-induced ion channel changes; however, the immediate effects of the inhibition on cell function are not entirely clear. Nevertheless, the cAMP cascade has been implicated in chronic effects of opioids, including drug tolerance, dependence, and withdrawal. These topics are discussed in later sections.

Section Summary

- Opiates are derived from the opium poppy. Others are semisynthetic or totally synthetic narcotics.

- Minor differences in molecular structure determine whether the drugs are full agonists, partial agonists, or pure antagonists.

- Opioids relieve pain and produce drowsiness and sleep. Euphoria or dysphoria may occur. They cause pinpoint pupils, vomiting, suppression of the cough reflex, drop in body temperature, reduced appetite, constipation, and a variety of hormonal effects. Respiratory and cardiac depression may also occur at higher doses.

- Repeated use produces tolerance to many but not all of the drugs' effects, as well as physical dependence.

- Opioids bind to four opioid receptors (μ, δ, κ and NOP-R), which are widely and unevenly distributed in the central and peripheral nervous systems. Each of the receptors has been isolated and cloned and found to be coupled to G proteins that induce metabotropic effects. The principal cellular activities include actions on ion channels (open K^+, close Ca^{2+}), which are responsible for cell hyperpolarization and inhibition of neurotransmitter release, and inhibition of adenylyl cyclase.

- Endogenous ligands for the opioid receptors are small peptides that are cleaved from larger propeptides manufactured in the soma. Molecular biology has shown four distinct propeptides (prodynorphin, POMC, proenkephalin, and pronociceptin/orphanin FQ), which produce a variety of opioid and non-opioid fragments. The propeptide for a fourth endogenous peptide endomorphin is not known.

- Endogenous opioids inhibit synaptic transmission by postsynaptic inhibition, axoaxonic inhibition, and via presynaptic autoreceptors.

- The locations of these peptides in the brain, spinal cord, and pituitary implicate them in regulating pain, reward, stress response, water balance, feeding, body temperature, and endocrine function. Nociceptin/orphanin FQ acts at cellular and molecular levels much the same way as opioids, but often produces different and opposing effects. See Table 11.1 for location, function, and endogenous ligand for opioid receptor subtypes.

Opioids and Pain

Although we all feel that we intuitively understand what pain is like, it is really far more complex than is generally believed. Since opioids are therapeutically best known as analgesics, a further discussion of pain and its neural circuitry is needed.

Pain is distinct from other sensory systems in that it can be caused by a variety of stimuli detected by several types of nociceptors (detectors of noxious stimuli). The nociceptors are networks of free nerve endings that are sensitive to intense pressure, extreme temperature including heat and cold, electrical impulses, cuts, chemical irritants, and inflammation. Pain varies not only in intensity but also in quality and may be described as "pricking," "stabbing," "burning," "aching," and so forth. Its perception is also highly subjective, and no single stimulus will be described as painful by all individuals nor perhaps even by the same individual under different circumstances. Pain is modified by a number of factors, including strong emotion, environmental stimuli like stress, hypnosis, acupuncture, and opioid drugs.

Although we can get subjective reports of pain, quantification is difficult, particularly when analgesic drugs are tested. In the laboratory, when methods such as the application of sudden pressure, pinpricks, or stabs are used to induce pain, most analgesic drugs show ineffective or inconsistent analgesic effects. The failure of these drugs to show a significant reduction in pain is probably a result of the low emotional impact of those types of pain. More consistent results are obtained with the analgesics through the use of techniques that produce slowly developing or sustained pain. One technique used with human subjects is to stop blood flow to an exercising muscle with a tourniquet. With this method, the pain is slow in onset and is directly related to amount of exercise. Cutaneous pain in humans can be produced by the intradermal injection of various chemicals. A reliable method to test this kind of pain uses cantharidin to induce a blister, from which the outer layer of epidermis is removed to expose the blister base, on which small quantities of various agents can be applied for testing.

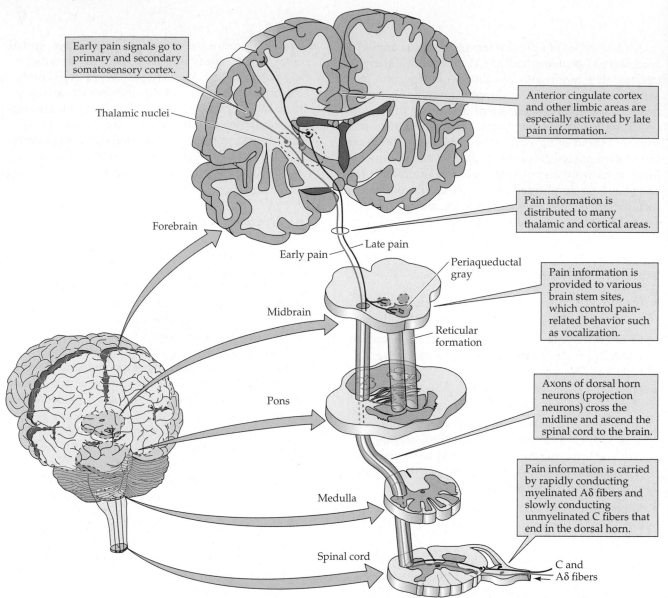

Early pain signals go to primary and secondary somatosensory cortex.

Thalamic nuclei

Anterior cingulate cortex and other limbic areas are especially activated by late pain information.

Pain information is distributed to many thalamic and cortical areas.

Forebrain

Early pain — Late pain

Periaqueductal gray

Pain information is provided to various brain stem sites, which control pain-related behavior such as vocalization.

Midbrain

Reticular formation

Pons

Axons of dorsal horn neurons (projection neurons) cross the midline and ascend the spinal cord to the brain.

Medulla

Pain information is carried by rapidly conducting myelinated Aδ fibers and slowly conducting unmyelinated C fibers that end in the dorsal horn.

Spinal cord

C and Aδ fibers

Techniques that have been designed to produce more-intense or more-persistent pain are infrequently used because finding subjects willing to participate in such experiments is difficult. Animal testing is overall more reliable, yielding conditions that are comparable to pathological pain in humans. This may be because the human subject in the experimental setting realizes that the pain stimulus poses no real threat, whereas for the animal subject, all pain is potentially serious. Animal tests are described in Chapter 4.

The two components of pain have distinct features

Pain is often described as having several components. "First," or early, pain represents the immediate sensory component and signals the onset of a noxious stimulus and its precise location to cause immediate withdrawal and escape from the damaging stimulus.

Figure 11.12 Ascending pain pathways Sensory neurons (Aδ and C fibers) activated by noxious stimuli enter the dorsal horn of the spinal cord. Dorsal horn neurons travel up the spinal cord on the contralateral side and ultimately reach various nuclei in the thalamus. Neurons transmitting "fast" (first pain) end first in the primary somatosensory cortex for well-localized sensory discrimination, before the information is transferred to the secondary somatosensory cortex, where pain recognition occurs. The slower-conducting neurons transmit information (second pain) to a variety of limbic areas, including the anterior cingulate cortex, which is important for the emotional or suffering aspect of pain.

"Second," or late, pain has a strong emotional component, that is, the unpleasantness of the sensation. Adaptation occurs more slowly to the secondary component, so it attracts our attention in prolonged fashion to motivate behaviors that limit further damage and aid recovery. Late pain is less localized and is often accompanied by autonomic responses such as sweating, fall in blood pressure, or nausea. The separation of these 2 components can be clearly seen in the patient who after receiving morphine for persistent pain, describes the pain as intense as before treatment but much less aversive.

These distinct components of pain are in part explained by the types of neuron that carry the signal. Fibers called Aδ are larger in diameter and are myelinated, so they conduct action potentials more rapidly than the thin and unmyelinated C fibers. The difference in speed explains why when you smash your finger in the car door, you first experience a sharp pain that is well localized but brief, followed by a dull aching that is a prolonged reminder of the damage your body has experienced. These neurons have their cell bodies in the dorsal root ganglia and terminate in the gray matter of the dorsal horn of the spinal cord, ending on projection neurons that transmit pain signals to higher brain centers (**Figure 11.12**).

A second distinction between the two components of pain is their route and final destination in the brain. Early pain is transmitted from the spinal cord via the spinothalamic tract to the posteroventrolateral (PVL) nucleus of the thalamus before going directly to the

primary and then secondary somatosensory cortex. The primary somatosensory cortex provides sensory discrimination of pain, while the secondary cortex is involved in the recognition of pain and memory of past pain. Late pain also goes to the thalamus, but in addition gives off collaterals to a variety of limbic structures such as the hypothalamus and amygdala, as well as the anterior cingulate cortex. The anterior cingulate has a role in pain affect, attention, and motor responses (Rainville, 2002).

For the first time, researchers have been able to demonstrate the temporal relationship between pain-evoked cortical activation and reported pain in human subjects. Ploner and colleagues (2002) subjected individuals to brief painful laser stimuli and continuously monitored the subjects' subjective pain rating while simultaneously recording faint magnetic fields on the surface of the skull using magnetoencephalography (MEG). Although MEG is somewhat inaccurate in precisely locating brain activity, it is excellent at showing the neural changes over very small units of time (from 1 millisecond to another). In this way, Ploner could trace a wave of brain activity from its origin to sequential brain areas during processing (**Figure 11.13A**).

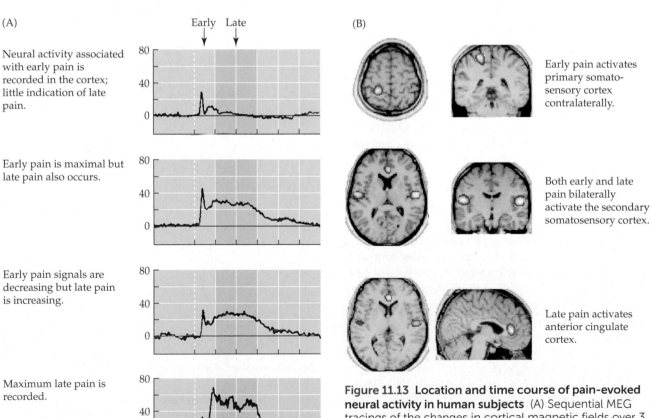

Figure 11.13 Location and time course of pain-evoked neural activity in human subjects (A) Sequential MEG tracings of the changes in cortical magnetic fields over 3 seconds following the initiation of the painful stimulus. (B) Brain areas that are active at corresponding points in time are shown as light-shaded areas that have been superimposed on magnetic resonance images. (From Ploner et al., 2002.)

When the cortical activation was superimposed on magnetic resonance images (**Figure 11.13B**), they showed that first pain (pain recognition), identified by subjects' ratings, was temporally related to activation of the primary somatosensory cortex, whereas second pain (identified by subjects' ratings of unpleasantness) was strongly associated with anterior cingulate activation. Both types of pain were associated with neural activity in the secondary somatosensory cortex.

Opioids inhibit pain transmission at spinal and supraspinal levels

By binding to opioid receptors, morphine and other opioid drugs mimic the inhibitory action of the endogenous opioids at many stages of pain transmission within the spinal cord and brain. To simplify, we can say that opioids regulate pain in three ways:

1. Within the spinal cord by small inhibitory interneurons;

2. By two significant descending pathways originating in the periaqueductal gray (PAG); and

3. At many higher brain sites, which explains opioid effects on emotional and hormonal aspects of the pain response.

As you know, information about pain, either from the surface or deep within the body cavity, is carried by neurons from the body into the spinal cord. Some of these primary afferent neurons end directly on projection neurons that transmit pain signals to higher brain centers (e.g., first to the thalamus and then to the somatosensory cortex) (**Figure 11.14A**). Others end on small excitatory interneurons (i.e., short neurons within the spinal cord) that in turn synapse onto the projection neurons (**Figure 11.14B**).

Opioids reduce the transmission of pain signals at the spinal cord in two ways. First, small inhibitory **spinal interneurons** release endorphins that inhibit the activation of the spinal projection neurons (**Figure 11.14C**). Morphine can act directly on those same opioid receptors to inhibit the transmission of the pain signal to higher brain centers that normally allow us to become aware of the sensory experience. Second, endorphins regulate several modulatory pathways that descend from the brain to inhibit spinal cord pain transmission either by directly inhibiting the projection neuron (A) or the excitatory interneuron (B), or by exciting the inhibitory opioid neuron (C). These **descending modulatory pathways** (**Figure 11.15**) begin in the midbrain and modify the pain information carried by spinal cord neurons.

The most important descending pathways begin in the PAG. The PAG is a brain area rich in endogenous opioid peptides and high concentrations of opioid

receptors, particularly μ and κ. Local electrical stimulation of the PAG produces analgesia but no change in the ability to detect temperature, touch, or pressure. Treatment of chronic pain in human patients with electrical stimulation of the PAG is frequently successful, although tolerance occurs with repeated use, and cross-tolerance (see Chapter 1) with injected morphine also occurs. This phenomenon suggests that electrical stimulation releases a morphine-like substance onto the same postsynaptic receptor sites occupied by exogenous morphine. Partial blockade of stimulation-induced analgesia with the specific opioid antagonist naloxone further supports that idea.

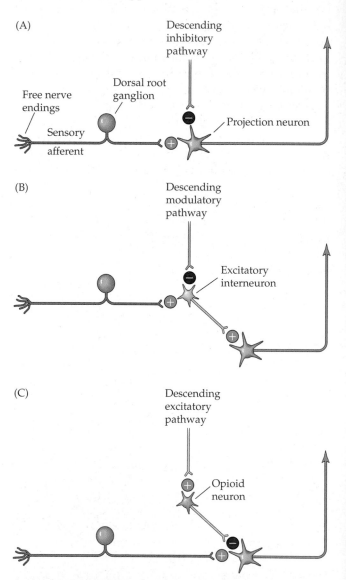

Figure 11.14 Pain transmission in the spinal cord is modified by descending modulatory neurons via (A) inhibition of the projection neuron; (B) inhibition of an excitatory interneuron; and (C) excitation of an inhibitory opioid interneuron. Opioid drugs can influence the activity of the descending pathways and can act directly on opioid receptors in the spinal cord.

The neurons beginning in the PAG end on cells in the medulla, including the serotonergic cell bodies of the nucleus of the raphe. Microinjection of opioids into the raphe produces significant analgesia. The serotonergic neurons descend into the spinal cord to inhibit cell firing there and in that way reduce pain transmission. Similarly, other cells originating in the PAG terminate in the brainstem in an area close to the locus coeruleus, an important cluster of noradrenergic cell bodies that also send axons to the spinal cord to modulate pain conduction. In both cases, these descending pathways are activated when opioids inhibit an inhibitory GABA "brake." Furthermore, neurotoxic lesions of the descending serotonergic and noradrenergic cells prevent systemic morphine-induced analgesia. Therefore, there are at least two major pathways that descend to the spinal cord to inhibit the projection of pain information to higher brain centers. However, the inhibitory action is direct in some cases, while at other times the inhibition occurs by acting on small spinal interneurons (as seen in Figure 11.15).

In summary, opioids modulate pain directly in the spinal cord and by regulating the descending pain inhibitory pathways ending in the spinal cord. In addition, significant opioid action occurs in other **supraspinal** (above the spinal cord) locations, including higher sensory areas and limbic structures, as well as the hypothalamus and the medial thalamus. A high concentration of endogenous opioids and the presence of opioid receptors suggest that these areas may be responsible for the emotional component of pain, as well as for autonomic and neuroendocrine responses. In one PET study, the endogenous activation of the μ-opioid system was evaluated during sustained pain. Zubieta and colleagues (2001) found a significant negative correlation between μ-opioid activity (measured as displacement of [^{11}C]carfentanil from μ-receptors) in the nucleus accumbens, amygdala, and thalamus and reported *sensory* pain scores (**Figure 11.16**). That is, the greater the μ-opioid activation, the lower was the individual's sensory pain score. The PAG also showed increased μ-receptor displacement, although it was not significant. When the scores on the *affective* component of pain were evaluated, increased μ-opioid activity was found in the bilateral anterior cingulate cortex, thalamus, and nucleus accumbens. These results indicate that endogenous μ-opioids modulate both the sensory and emotional components of pain and that morphine and other opioids likewise act at these sites. The existence of multiple circuits carrying

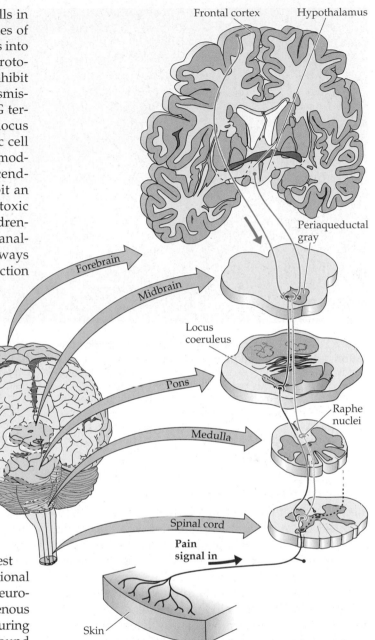

Figure 11.15 Descending pain modulation pathways Neurons from the periaqueductal gray descend to the brainstem nucleus of the raphe and the locus coeruleus. Serotonergic and adrenergic neurons, respectively, descend to the spinal cord to modulate the transmission of the pain signal at that level.

pain information demonstrates the redundancy and diffuse nature of pain transmission, which reflects its tremendous evolutionary significance for survival.

Other forms of pain control depend on opioids

ACUPUNCTURE The discovery of the endogenous opioids led to a dramatic increase in research into the

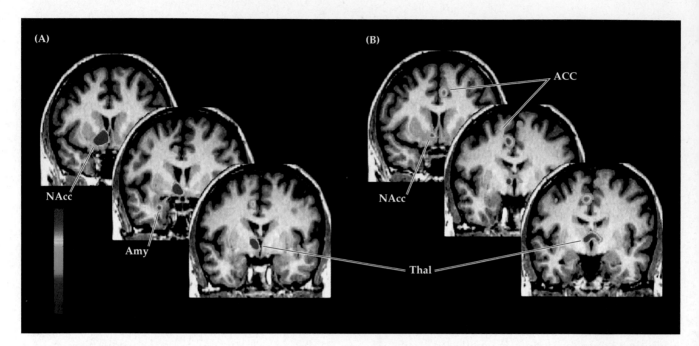

Figure 11.16 PET scans showing endogenous opioid activation during sustained pain In subjects injected with [¹¹C] carfentanil, endogenous opioid action is shown by the ability of the endogenous opioid to displace the radiolabeled μ-receptor ligand from the receptors. Pain was induced by continuous infusion of hypertonic saline in the masseter muscle and was compared with a control condition of isotonic saline infusion. (A) Activation of the μ-opioid system in the nucleus accumbens (NAcc), amygdala (Amy), and anterior thalamus (Thal) after the subjects were exposed to the prolonged noxious stimulus. These increases were negatively correlated with the subjects' *sensory* scores of pain. (B) μ-Opioid activity in the bilateral anterior cingulate cortex (ACC) and anterior thalamus and unilaterally in the NAcc. These increases were negatively correlated with pain *affect* scores. Therefore, the greater the μ-opioid activation in these areas, the lower was the emotional component of pain. (Courtesy of Dr. Jon-Kar Zubieta.)

mechanisms of the ancient Chinese method for pain relief called *acupuncture*. Acupuncture involves inserting a metallic needle into the skin to reach deep structures, such as muscles and tendons. Rhythmic movement of the needle or application of mild electrical current reduces pain perception. Beginning in the late 1950s, scientific studies using modern technology were initiated in China to determine the physiological basis of acupuncture-induced analgesia. Although naloxone was shown to reduce acupuncture-induced analgesia in human dentally evoked pain, it became clear that its antagonistic effect depended on the characteristics of the acupuncture treatment, which may be mediated by distinct opioid peptides. For instance, a look at electrically induced analgesia shows that the κ-receptor antagonist MR 2266 blocked 100-Hz electroacupuncture-induced analgesia, but not that induced by 2 Hz. In contrast the δ-opioid antagonist ICI 174864 blocked 2-Hz electroacupuncture-induced analgesia, but not that induced by 100 Hz. Further support for the selectivity comes from the finding that 2-Hz acupuncture develops cross-tolerance with δ- but not κ-agonists, while 100-Hz acupuncture shows cross-tolerance to κ-agonists but not δ-agonists. More direct measurements demonstrated that

2-Hz electroacupuncture caused significant elevations in the proenkephalin peptide, whose cleavage products would be expected to act at δ-receptors and 100 Hz raised CSF levels of dynorphin, which acts most robustly on κ-receptors (Han, 2004).

Because acupuncture releases endogenous opioids that you now realize have widespread effects in the brain and the gastrointestinal system, it is likely that it will be used effectively to treat other medical problems beyond pain (Cabýoglu et al., 2006). Electroacupuncture has been found to enhance the immune response and reduce gastric acid secretion. Since it activates the satiety center in the hypothalamus, it is potentially useful in treating obesity. Interestingly it has also been tested as a means to reduce the unpleasant signs of morphine withdrawal (see later in this chapter).

DUAL INHIBITION OF PEPTIDASES A different physiological approach to achieving antinociception involves enhancing the effects of endogenous enkephalin by inhibiting the two peptidase enzymes that degrade it (Noble and Roques, 2007). Microdialysis studies in rats showed that the dual inhibitors such as RB-101, RB-120,

RB-3007, and others increase the extracellular levels of enkephalin in vivo in numerous brain regions. These drugs are good examples of prodrugs because their lipophilic nature allows rapid passage of the blood–brain barrier into the brain, where a bond between the two inhibitors is biologically broken, making them active. Although inhibiting either one of the two peptidases produces only weak analgesic effects, inhibiting both produces far more robust dose-dependent effects in the hot plate, tail flick, and other animal tests of analgesia. The relatively long-lasting antinociceptive effects following intraperitoneal (IP), IV, or oral (PO) administration are blocked by naloxone. The importance of enkephalin to the pharmacological action of the dual inhibitors is further demonstrated by the lack of analgesic effect in mutant mice lacking proenkephalin. Which opioid receptor is involved is somewhat unclear because the analgesic effect is mediated by μ-receptors or both μ- and δ-receptors, depending on the nature of the pain (thermal, chemical, mechanical, or inflammatory) used in animal testing. The mechanism of action has clinical significance because it may explain a synergistic effect of a dual inhibitor and morphine. Research shows that a subanalgesic dose of RB-101 significantly potentiates a subanalgesic dose of morphine. Being able to use low doses of the two drugs for pain control would prevent the unwanted side effects caused by high doses of either one. One possible explanation for the synergism is that low doses of morphine increase the release of enkephalins that is further enhanced by the peptidase inhibition.

Of further importance is that because completely inhibiting the peptidases with high doses of dual inhibitors never achieves the maximum analgesic effect of morphine, it is assumed that endogenous enkephalin does not saturate opioid receptors and overstimulate them. This may be part of the reason that the dual inhibitors avoid some of the major disadvantages of morphine treatment. At doses that produce significant analgesia, the dual inhibitors do not depress either the rate or volume of respiration and induce only a partial tolerance to the analgesic effect. Furthermore, following chronic administration, naloxone administration fails to induce a morphine-like withdrawal syndrome, hence the risk of physical dependence is minimal. Low abuse potential is suggested by studies showing that animals rarely develop conditioned place preference or altered intracranial electrical self-stimulation behavior (see Chapter 4). Additionally, animals do not distinguish the dual inhibitors from saline in drug discrimination tests; nor do morphine-trained animals generalize to the dual inhibitors, which indicates that their interoceptive cues are different. These characteristics make the dual inhibitors tempting targets for future clinical trials once toxicology and safety studies have been completed.

GENE THERAPY On the basis of strong preclinical evidence using a variety of rodent models of pain, a small clinical trial of gene therapy in patients with intractable pain from terminal cancer was undertaken (Fink et al., 2011). This study used the cold sore virus HSV to act as the gene transfer vector because this virus is taken up from the skin by sensory nerve endings and transported along their axons to the nuclei in the cell bodies located in the corresponding dorsal root ganglia. The virus was modified so it could not replicate and was engineered to contain the gene coding for human proenkephalin. The newly synthesized proenkephalin would be expected to be packaged in vesicles, spliced into multiple enkephalin peptides, and ultimately released by the sensory nerve terminals in the dorsal horn of the spinal cord to inhibit pain signal conduction (see Figures 11.12 and 11.14). Earlier studies of the technique using laboratory animals showed significant analgesic effects that were blocked by pretreatment with naloxone, demonstrating the importance of opioid receptors. Additionally, the analgesic effect was additive with morphine and shifted the dose–response curve for morphine to the left, which indicates that less morphine was needed to achieve the same level of analgesia. Of potential importance is that the vector-mediated analgesia occurred in animals that were tolerant to the effects of morphine, quite possibly because the analgesic effect was mediated by δ-opioid receptors, while the morphine-induced analgesia depends primarily on μ-opioid receptors.

This clinical trial included only 10 subjects, all of whom had moderate to severe pain that was not eliminated by at least 200 mg of morphine. After receiving 10 injections in a single session into the skin where pain was localized, they were evaluated seven times over a 28-day follow-up and monthly thereafter for 4 months. Although there were reports of mild and transient side effects such as elevation of body temperature, no serious adverse effects were reported throughout the period of evaluation. Despite the small number of subjects and the lack of a placebo group, the researchers found an apparent dose response. The lowest dose produced no pain relief, while the higher doses reduced pain to 50% of pretreatment levels initially and continued to reduce pain to 20% over several weeks. These encouraging results are being expanded into a larger Phase II randomized, double-blind, placebo-controlled trial using similar patient populations.

Section Summary

- Nociceptors are free nerve endings that are sensitive to a variety of pain stimuli.
- Pain has two components. First, pain is the immediate sensory component carried by myelinated

Aδ-neurons and transmitted via the spinothalamic tract to the PVL nucleus of the thalamus before projecting to primary, then secondary somatosensory cortex. Second, pain is the emotional component carried by C fibers and transmitted to the thalamus with collaterals to limbic areas, including the anterior cingulate.

- Opioids (both endogenous and exogenous) act at spinal and supraspinal levels to relieve pain. Endorphin neurons in the spinal cord decrease the conduction of pain signals from the spinal cord to higher brain centers. Descending neurons from the periaqueductal gray activate pathways from the locus coeruleus (noradrenergic) and nucleus of the raphe (serotonergic) that impede pain signals in the spinal cord. Opioid receptors in the neocortex and limbic regions modulate the emotional component of pain to relieve the sense of suffering.

- Analgesic effects of electroacupuncture depend on opioids. 100-Hz acupuncture is blocked by κ-receptor antagonists, shows cross-tolerance to κ-agonists, and increases CSF levels of dynorphin. 2-Hz acupuncture is antagonized by δ-receptor blockers, shows cross-tolerance to δ-agonists, and elevates proenkephalin.

- Analgesia can be produced by drugs that inhibit both of the enkephalin degrading enzymes. Elevating endogenous enkephalin has fewer side effects than morphine: less respiratory depression, partial tolerance, and low abuse potential.

- A gene therapy clinical trial showed that the gene coding for proenkephalin carried by an HSV viral vector reduced pain in patients with cancer with minimal side effects.

Opioid Reinforcement, Tolerance, and Dependence

Although the opioids are the best pain-reducing drugs presently available, their use continues to be problematic because of the potential for abuse. The drugs in this class are highly reinforcing, and despite strict legal controls, they sometimes wind up in the hands of individuals who abuse these substances. Furthermore, chronic use leads to tolerance and ultimately to physical dependence.

Animal testing shows significant reinforcing properties

Experimental techniques used to demonstrate the reinforcement value of opioids are described in Chapter 4. Intracerebral electrical self-stimulation allows subjects to press a lever to self-administer a weak electrical current to certain brain areas that constitute central reward pathways. When the animal presses the lever, electrical activation causes release of neurotransmitters from the nerve terminals in the region, which in turn mediate a rewarding effect. The fact that morphine and other opioids lower the electrical current threshold for self-stimulation indicates that the drugs enhance the brain reward mechanism.

When the drug self-administration technique is used, one striking finding is that the reinforcement value and the pattern of opioid use in animals are quite similar to those seen in humans. Self-injection gradually increases over time until the animals self-administer a stable and apparently optimal amount of drug. The ability of animals to maintain a stable blood level is demonstrated by pretreatment with morphine, codeine, or meperidine, which subsequently reduces IV self-administration of morphine. In contrast, when some receptors are blocked with naloxone, the self-administration rate increases and matches that seen during morphine abstinence. It is evident from these studies that the animals learn to regulate with some accuracy the amount of morphine that they require. Dose–response curves can be used to compare the relative potencies of opioid drug reinforcement (Woods et al., 1993).

The endogenous opioid β-endorphin is also self-administered, which strongly suggests that it mediates opioid reinforcement. Beta-endorphin self-administration is blocked by either μ- or δ-receptor antagonists. Thus, both types of receptor are involved in reward processes. In contrast, κ-agonists fail to produce self-injection and may induce aversive states, leading to avoidance behavior (Shippenberg, 1993).

Dopaminergic and nondopaminergic components contribute to opioid reinforcement

Two important methods are used to identify the neurobiology of opioid reinforcement. In one, self-administration of opioid ligands microinjected into discrete brain areas is evaluated. In the second, selective lesions are used to identify the brain areas and neurotransmitter pathways that eliminate opioid-induced reinforcement.

Microinjection studies from many laboratories demonstrate the contribution of the dopaminergic mesolimbic pathway to opioid reinforcement. This pathway originates in the ventral tegmental area (VTA) of the midbrain and projects to limbic areas, including the nucleus accumbens (NAcc). Return to Figure 5.8 to review the important dopamine (DA) pathways in the brain. Self-administration of morphine or endogenous peptides occurs when the microcannula is implanted near the dopamine cell bodies within the

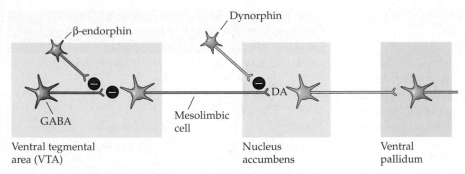

Figure 11.17 Model of the effects of opioids on meso-limbic dopaminergic cells The β-endorphin cell has an inhibitory effect on the normally inhibitory GABAergic cell, allowing the firing rate of the mesolimbic dopaminergic cells to increase and the cells to release more dopamine in the nucleus accumbens. In contrast, the axoaxonic dynorphin cell inhibits the release of dopamine from the mesolimbic cell by preventing calcium entry.

VTA. Intra-VTA microinjection of morphine or selective μ-agonists also produces conditioned place preference and reduces the threshold for intracranial electrical self-stimulation. Each of these results argues for a direct action of opioids on central reward mechanisms served by the mesolimbic pathway.

But what exactly happens to the cells in the VTA in the presence of opioids? First, both systemic opioids and opioids microinjected into the VTA increase dopaminergic cell firing, which subsequently increases the release of dopamine within the NAcc. Intraventricular β-endorphin produces similar enhancements of neuronal firing. In contrast, κ-agonists produce the opposite effects on mesolimbic neurons and reduce dopaminergic neuronal activity and subsequent DA turnover (release and metabolism). Since microinjected κ-agonists produce conditioned place *aversions*, it seems possible that the mesolimbic dopamine system may mediate aversive effects of opioids, as well as their reinforcing properties (Shippenberg et al., 1991).

A model of the opposing effects of opioid neurons on mesolimbic dopaminergic cells is shown in **Figure 11.17**. Beta-endorphin and opioid drugs seem to increase VTA cell firing by inhibiting the inhibitory GABA cells found in the VTA. They can decrease the release of GABA by opening K⁺ channels or reducing Ca²⁺ influx on GABA terminals. This inhibition of inhibitory neurons leads to increased firing and greater DA release in the NAcc. The endogenous peptide dynorphin, which acts on κ-receptors on the terminals of the DA neurons, can reduce the release of DA by similar mechanisms causing dysphoria.

How sure are we that mesolimbic DA is really important? DA receptor antagonists block the reinforcing effects of opioids when evaluated by each of the three behavioral measures. However, inducing lesions of dopaminergic neurons with the neurotoxin 6-hydroxydopamine (6-OHDA) reduces (but does *not* abolish) the reinforcement value. The fact that heroin self-administration is only *partially* reduced rather than eliminated by the lesion certainly suggests that other brain areas and other neurotransmitters in addition to DA are also involved. Although these studies clearly support earlier results showing that increased mesolimbic firing is a common link in the actions of many self-administered drugs, including ethanol, nicotine, and psychostimulants (see Chapter 9), opioids do not have to release mesolimbic DA to be reinforcing (Gerrits and Vanree, 1996).

Further, the mesolimbic pathway may be more specifically involved in the salience (or significance) of events to an individual. What we mean is that the dopaminergic cell firing may tell an organism when some event is important or meaningful, regardless of whether it is appetitive (positive) or aversive (negative). We would therefore have incentive (or motivation) to approach (in the case of a reinforcer) or avoid (in the case of a noxious event) a particular significant stimulus. This idea has been developed in the "incentive–sensitization" hypothesis of addiction (see the next section).

Long-term opioid use produces tolerance, sensitization, and dependence

You have just read about the acutely rewarding effects of opioids, which increase the likelihood that the drug will be used again. Chronic use subsequently leads to neuroadaptive changes in the nervous system, which are responsible for tolerance, sensitization, and dependence.

Tolerance (see Chapter 1) refers to the diminishing effects of a drug with repeated use, and it occurs for all of the opioids, including the endorphins. Although tolerance to the opioids develops quite rapidly, tolerance does not occur for all of the pharmacological effects to the same extent or at the same rate. For example, tolerance to the analgesic effect occurs relatively rapidly, but the constipating effects and the pinpoint pupils persist even after prolonged opioid use.

Cross-tolerance among the opioids also exists. For this reason, when tolerance develops to one opioid drug, other chemically related drugs also show a reduced effectiveness. For instance, following chronic heroin use, treatment with codeine will elicit a smaller-than-normal response even if the individual has never used codeine before. Since we now know that at least four types of opioid receptors exist, we might wonder whether the receptor subtype plays a role in cross-tolerance. Indeed, it seems that selective agonists for the μ-receptor reduce the effectiveness of other μ-receptor agonists, but only minimally reduce κ-agonist activity. Likewise, repeated exposure to κ-agonists diminishes the effects of other κ-agonists but not μ-agonists.

As is true for many drugs, several mechanisms are responsible for the development of tolerance to the opioids. An increased rate of metabolism with repeated use (metabolic tolerance) is responsible for some small portion of opioid tolerance. Classical conditioning processes also contribute to this phenomenon. However, most tolerance is based on changes in nerve cells that compensate for the presence of chronic opioids (pharmacodynamic tolerance). The cell mechanisms are discussed in more detail in the section on neurobiological adaptation and rebound.

Under some circumstances, repeated exposure to opioids produces **sensitization**. Sensitization refers to the increase in drug effects that occurs with repeated administration. Robinson and Berridge (2001) propose that in the case of substance abuse, the motivation (incentive) to approach, better called *craving* or desire for the drug, undergoes sensitization. Meanwhile, the neural mechanism responsible for the high, or liking of the drug, remains unchanged or decreases as tolerance develops over repeated administration. Both the decrease in liking and the increase in craving lead to further drug taking and may explain the intense compulsion to use a drug that no longer produces pleasurable effects.

The third consequence of chronic opioid use is the occurrence of **physical dependence** (see Chapter 9), which is a neuroadaptive state that occurs in response to the long-term occupation of opioid receptors. Beause the adaptive mechanism produces effects that oppose those of the opioid, when the drug is no longer present, cell function not only returns to normal but overshoots basal levels. The effects of drug withdrawal are *rebound* in nature and are demonstrated by the occurrence of a pattern of physical disturbances called the **withdrawal** or **abstinence syndrome**. Since opioids in general depress CNS function, we consider opioid withdrawal to be rebound hyperactivity (**Table 11.2**). You already know that opioid effects are

TABLE 11.2 Acute Effects of Opioids and Rebound Withdrawal Symptoms	
Acute action	Withdrawal sign
Analgesia	Pain and irritability
Respiratory depression	Panting and yawning
Euphoria	Dysphoria and depression
Relaxation and sleep	Restlessness and insomnia
Tranquilization	Fearfulness and hostility
Decreased blood pressure	Increased blood pressure
Constipation	Diarrhea
Pupil constriction	Pupil dilation
Hypothermia	Hyperthermia
Drying of secretions	Tearing, runny nose
Reduced sex drive	Spontaneous ejaculation
Flushed and warm skin	Chilliness and "gooseflesh"

due to drug action at various receptors in a variety of locations in the CNS and elsewhere in the body, so it should not be a surprise to learn that the abstinence signs reflect a loss of inhibitory opioid action at all of those same receptors as blood levels of the drug gradually decline. Withdrawal can also be produced by administering an opioid antagonist that competes with the drug molecules for the receptors and thus functionally mimics the termination of drug use. Note, however, that the withdrawal following antagonist administration is far more severe than that following drug cessation because the opioid receptors are more rapidly deprived of opioid.

Opioid withdrawal is not considered life-threatening, but the symptoms are extremely unpleasant and include pain and dysphoria, restlessness, and fearfulness, as well as several symptoms that are flu-like in nature. How severe the symptoms are and how long they last depend on a number of factors: the particular drug used, as well as the dose, frequency, and duration of drug use and the health and personality of the addict. To give an example, morphine withdrawal symptoms generally peak 36 to 48 hours after the last administration and disappear within 7 to 10 days. In contrast, methadone, which has a more gradual onset of action and is longer lasting, has a withdrawal syndrome that does not abruptly peak but increases to a gradual maximum after several days and decreases gradually over several weeks. Abstinence for the very long-acting opioid buprenorphine is even more prolonged, but as is true for all of the longer-lasting opioids, the withdrawal signs are milder (**Figure 11.18**). From this, you should conclude that the longer the

(A)

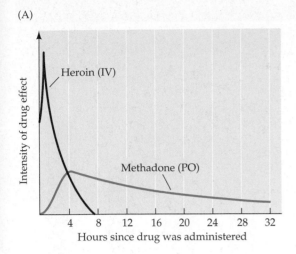

(B)

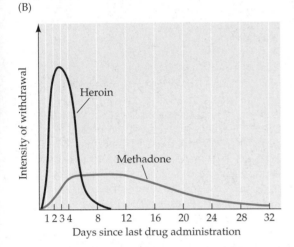

Figure 11.18 Relationship between acute effects and withdrawal (A) Time course showing the intensity and duration of the acute effects of IV heroin and oral methadone, and (B) the corresponding intensity and duration of withdrawal after chronic drug treatment.

duration of action of the opioid, the more prolonged is the abstinence syndrome but the lower the intensity of the syndrome. At the point when abstinence signs end, the user is considered to be **detoxified**.

Readministering the opioid any time during withdrawal will dramatically eliminate all the symptoms. In addition, administering any other opioid drug will stop or reduce the withdrawal symptoms because these agents show **cross-dependence**. This characteristic plays an important part in drug abuse treatment and is discussed further later in the chapter.

It may be surprising to learn that although physical dependence commonly occurs following chronic opioid use, it does not necessarily lead to abuse or addiction. Patients treated with opioids for protracted pain (e.g., postsurgical or cancer-related pain) show both tolerance and physical dependence, although withdrawal

signs can be minimized by gradually reducing the dose when pain relief is no longer needed. However, it is relatively rare to have a patient with chronic pain show addictive behaviors, such as craving and compulsive drug seeking. Physicians' unfounded fears of such addiction have prevented many individuals from receiving the relief from severe pain that they require. Failure to use adequate painkilling treatment produces much more suffering and subsequently much slower healing than is warranted. Transdermal patches and patient-controlled drug delivery systems are drug administration techniques that provide more humane control of pain and more effective recovery. Although effective relief from pain is vital to patients to enhance the quality of life, when opioids are diverted to illicit use, serious societal problems occur. **Box 11.2** describes the recent epidemic of abuse of oxycontin.

Several brain areas contribute to the opioid abstinence syndrome

The signs of withdrawal represent the rebound hyperactivity in many different systems, including the gastrointestinal tract, the autonomic nervous system, and many sites within the brain and spinal cord. To identify which of the many brain areas are involved in the appearance of the particular signs of abstinence, an animal model is used. Pellets of opioid drugs are implanted under the skin so that the subcutaneous administration produces significant blood levels of drug over a week or longer. After the animals have become physically dependent, selective intracerebral injection of an opioid antagonist produces distinctive and easily quantifiable signs of withdrawal. Withdrawal signs in rodents include jumping, rearing, "wet-dog" shakes, and increased locomotor behavior. Intracerebral injection of opioid antagonists into specific brain areas can help to identify which sites produce particular signs of abstinence. On the basis of these measures, no single brain area has been found to precipitate the entire withdrawal syndrome, but the locus coeruleus and the PAG are particularly sensitive to the antagonist in terms of precipitating withdrawal. As you will see in the next section, the locus coeruleus has become a neurochemical model for dependence.

In Chapter 9, you learned that the NAcc is a limbic structure that is particularly important for the reinforcement value of many abused substances. For this reason, it is somewhat surprising that microinjection of opioid antagonists into this area is not very effective in eliciting bodily signs of withdrawal in a dependent animal. However, Koob and coworkers (1992) have suggested that the NAcc may be important in the aversive stimulus effects or motivational aspect of opioid withdrawal. This conclusion was based on a series of experiments

BOX 11.2   Of Special Interest

What is OxyContin?

OxyContin has gotten a lot of attention in the news media, but what exactly is it? Oxycodone (Percodan, OxyContin) is a semisynthetic opioid that works in a manner similar to morphine. The short-acting drug Percodan is used to treat acute pain, while the long-acting time-release version OxyContin is used for cancer or musculoskeletal pain that is chronic and moderate to severe. These drugs have never been found to be better than morphine, which remains the gold standard for pain relief. Nor are they free from morphine-like side effects and the danger of addiction or fatal respiratory depression, especially when combined with CNS depressants such as alcohol.

OxyContin became a popular street drug because it produces a heroin-like euphoria when crushed to eliminate the time-release mechanism. It is then snorted, ingested, or dissolved and injected. It became a problem because it is less expensive than heroin and is relatively easy to access with fake or tampered prescriptions, with theft from pharmacies or family members, or via the Internet from other countries. There are unfortunate stories of the drug being purchased in small amounts from those with prescriptions who need the money to pay for their medication or to supplement their Social Security income. Occasionally, unconscionable physicians and pharmacists are found running OxyContin "pill mills" that increase the availability of the drug to those without medical need. "Doctor shopping" (visiting multiple doctors with complaints of pain) became highly visible when the radio commentator Rush Limbaugh admitted his addiction to the drug. The abuse problem may have been further magnified by hysterical media coverage that vilified an effective pain-relieving drug,

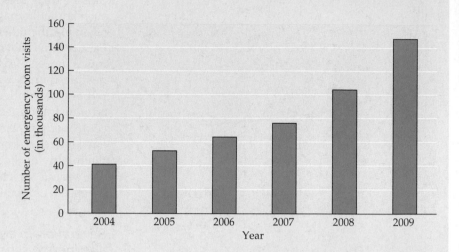

perhaps making the drug more popular. However, the coverage may have also pushed the authorities to deal with the problem. Even the Black Box warning on the package insert may have inadvertently encouraged users to take the drug in unintended ways by warning that crushing the pills would cause a rapid release. The fact that Oxy-Contin readily dissolves in water encourages the injection of the drug, which increases the subjective effects but also increases the dangers of overdose and medical problems associated with needle use.

The initial warning of the increase in OxyContin abuse came from Maine but rapidly expanded down the East Coast, hitting rural Appalachia and the Ohio Valley particularly hard. The spread of OxyContin use was paralleled by a dramatic increase in arrests for theft in those areas. As OxyContin abuse spread further, some officials have called it a national epidemic. Unfortunately, as the number of prescriptions increased, so did the number of unintended fatalities. In fact, the number of emergency room visits nationwide due to OxyContin rose dramatically from 2004 to 2010 (www. samhsa.gov/data) (see figure). Furthermore, data from the National

Vital Statistics System Mortality File from 1999 through 2006 show that fatal poisonings from opioid analgesics more than tripled from 4,000 to 13,800 deaths involving a higher percentage of non-Hispanic white males between 35 and 54 years of age than other groups (Warner et al., 2009). Jayawant and Balkrishnan (2005) describe the issues contributing to OxyContin abuse and the efforts by state and Federal government agencies, physicians' groups, and manufacturers to formulate a solution to the problem. In addition to professional education, the creation of a national pharmacy database to identify abusers, and tamper-resistant prescription pads, manufacturers have developed several opioid formulations to discourage abuse. One (Remoxy) is a slow-release oxycodone that is surrounded by a hard gelatin capsule that prevents tampering or the removal of the drug with a needle. The second (Acurox with niacin) is an immediate-release oxycodone that also contains niacin that produces flushing and other unpleasant effects if the drug is taken in higher than prescribed doses. It comes as a gel to prevent use by inhalation.

(A)

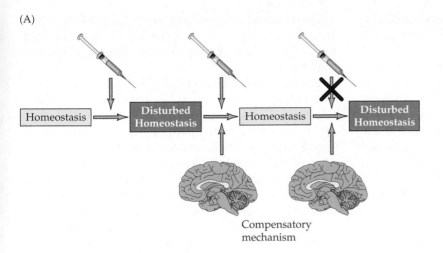

Compensatory
mechanism

Figure 11.19 Model of tolerance and withdrawal (A) Himmelsbach's theoretical model suggests that the nervous system adapts to the disturbing presence of a drug, so tolerance develops; but if the drug is suddenly withdrawn, the adaptive mechanism continues to function, causing a rebound in physiological effects (withdrawal). (B) Morphine acutely inhibits the synthesis of cAMP, but the effect becomes less as tolerance develops and neural adaptation occurs. If morphine is suddenly withdrawn, a far larger than normal amount of cAMP is produced, suggesting that the adaptive mechanism is still operating. With time, the cells once again adapt, now to the absence of the drug.

(B)

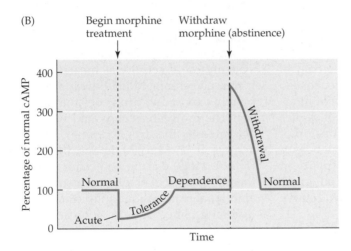

in which opioid-dependent rats experienced naloxone-precipitated withdrawal in a novel environment. Under such conditions, the animals develop a place aversion for the novel location and remain in an adjacent compartment (see Figure 4.8). Koob and colleagues were interested in finding out which brain area, when microinjected with antagonist, is responsible for the place aversion. They found that the areas most sensitive to low doses of antagonist are the NAcc, followed by the amygdala and the PAG. In conclusion, the brain areas implicated in the physiological response to opioid withdrawal are the PAG and the locus coeruleus, which may also mediate withdrawal-induced anxiety, while the NAcc is likely responsible for the aversive qualities of withdrawal, as well as some of the positive-reinforcing values of opioid use.

Neurobiological adaptation and rebound constitute tolerance and withdrawal

The classic hypothesis of opioid tolerance and dependence was first developed by Himmelsbach (1943) and is shown in **Figure 11.19A**. He suggested that

acute administration of morphine disrupts the organism's homeostasis, but repeated administration of the drug initiates an adaptive mechanism that compensates for the original effects and returns the organism to the normal homeostasis. At this point, tolerance to the drug would have occurred, since the same dose of morphine no longer produces the original disturbance. When morphine administration is abruptly stopped, the drug's effects on the body are terminated, but the adaptive mechanism remains active and overcompensates. The subsequent disruption of homeostasis is the withdrawal syndrome.

Although the Himmelsbach model was entirely theoretical, in the mid-1970s a physiological correlate was described by Sharma and coworkers (1975). They used cells with opioid receptors and maintained them in cell culture. They found that the acute administration of morphine caused an inhibition of adenylyl cyclase, the enzyme that manufactures cAMP (**Figure 11.19B**). Himmelsbach would call this stage "disturbed homeostasis." However, when the cells were kept in the morphine solution for 2 days, they showed tolerance to the drug's inhibitory effect. That is, after 2 days, they had levels of cAMP equal to control cells that had not been exposed to morphine. Apparently, the adaptive mechanism proposed by Himmelsbach became effective. When the opioid was abruptly removed from the cell culture solution or naloxone was added, the concentration of cAMP rose significantly above control levels because the adaptive mechanism was still operating, although the drug's inhibitory effect was gone. This rebound in cAMP levels corresponds with the withdrawal phenomenon and clearly represents disturbed homeostasis again. Other parts of the cAMP system such as cAMP-dependent protein kinase A (PKA) and phosphorylated neuronal proteins are also up-regulated by the chronic use of opioids.

The relationship of cAMP to neural activity and the withdrawal syndrome is suggested by the parallel time course of changes in those three factors. Nestler and coworkers (1994) examined the electrophysiological effects of morphine on cells in the locus coeruleus. The acute effect of opioids acting at μ-receptors consists of hyperpolarization and reduced rate of firing. Repeated exposure to opioids produced a gradual increase in firing rates of locus coeruleus cells as tolerance developed. Administration of an opioid antagonist after chronic opioid treatment induced a significant rise in firing rate to levels well above pretreatment levels, reflecting a rebound withdrawal that gradually returned to normal. A similar time course occurred for the overshoot of cAMP synthesis, the up-regulation of PKA and protein phosphorylation, and their return to control levels. Behavioral manifestations of abstinence also declined over the same 72-hour period. It is of interest that in subsequent research, Punch and colleagues (1997) showed that intra-locus coeruleus infusion of a PKA inhibitor attenuated several prominent behavioral signs of morphine withdrawal in dependent animals. Conversely activating PKA produced quasi-withdrawal symptoms in nondependent drug-naive animals.

Environmental cues have a role in tolerance, drug abuse, and relapse

We have already alluded to the idea that environmental factors can be classically conditioned to parts of the drug experience (see the section on behavioral tolerance in Chapter 1). Conditioning theory has also been applied to the development of tolerance to opioids. Siegel and Ramos (2002) and Tiffany et al. (1992) propose that narcotic tolerance is in part the result of the learning of an association between the effects of the drug and the environmental cues that reliably precede the drug effects. Several experiments have shown that after repeated drug administration in a particular environment, the animal begins to show anticipatory physiological responses when it is in that same situation. Thus it is argued that tolerance to the analgesic effects of morphine results because environmental cues regularly paired with drug administration begin to elicit the compensatory response of hyperalgesia, which diminishes the analgesic effect of the drug. Some have suggested this mechanism as the basis for some of the drug overdose fatalities among addicts. One would have to assume that an addict who has developed significant tolerance to his drug of choice

in his standard environment might find that his tolerance is much less if he uses the drug in a novel situation. His usual dose may then be enough to produce overdose.

Environmental factors can also clearly have a role in portions of the drug experience. For example, if euphoria is associated with certain stimuli such as the camaraderie of the drug-using subculture, drug acquisition activities, or drug injection rituals, those aspects of the environment will act as secondary reinforcers, strengthening the drug-taking behavior. What this means is that many components of drug-taking behavior become so closely associated with the drug-induced euphoria and sense of well-being that they are in themselves reinforcing. This association can be used to explain the unusual behavior of the "needle freak" who can inject any substance and achieve some measure of the "high" associated with drug taking. Childress et al. (1999) reported changes in limbic system neural activity as measured by PET scans of increased cerebral blood flow in drug users who were merely exposed to drug cues that increase their craving. The brain areas activated were similar to those activated by the drug (cocaine). Increased metabolic activity in the amygdala and the anterior cingulate (**Figure 11.20**) during cue-induced craving suggests the importance of emotional memory (amygdala) and emotional expectation (anterior cingulate) to the conditioning. Since these regions are both connected to the nucleus accumbens and are activated during drug exposure, it is reasonable to suggest that they help the individual learn the signals that are linked to rewarding events. When these cues, acting as secondary reinforcers, are present, they may act as **primers** that promote drug taking because they remind the individual of how the drug feels. Cue-induced craving and its neural mechanism have become an important focus of research because they are most closely associated with the compulsive drug-seeking behavior that characterizes drug abuse.

Abstinence symptoms can likewise be classically conditioned. Detoxified rats showed an increase in withdrawal "wet-dog" shakes when returned to a physically distinctive cage where they had undergone morphine withdrawal several months earlier (Wikler, 1973).

Objective (respiration rate, skin temperature, heart rate) and subjective elements of narcotic withdrawal symptoms can be experimentally conditioned to environmental stimuli in humans as well (Childress et al., 1986). The high rate of relapse among detoxified addicts may be due to the conditioned abstinence syndrome in the old environment. O'Brien (1993) and others have presented reports of addicts who describe withdrawal symptoms when they visit areas of prior

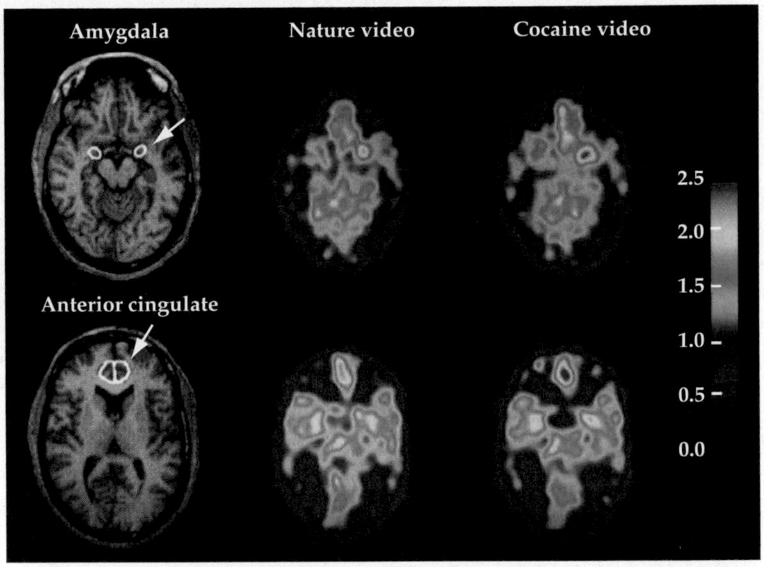

Figure 11.20 PET scans of cerebral blood flow in a cocaine addict while exposed to a non-drug-related video (nature) and during a cocaine-related video containing many cues. Areas with the greatest activity are shown in red. Activity in the amygdala and anterior cingulate is significantly increased during the cocaine video. (From Childress et al., 1999.)

drug use even years after the withdrawal syndrome has ended. These findings have convinced many researchers that learning is a critical factor in opioid addiction (**Box 11.3**). Under what circumstance individuals develop drug-enhancing associations or drug-opposing responses is not clear, but the mesolimbic DA pathway may be involved in both (Self and Nestler, 1995).

Treatment Programs for Opioid Addiction

Treating opioid addiction requires understanding the multiple contributors to the problem. Treatment clearly depends on more than eliminating the drug from the body (detoxification), since the relapse rate for detoxified addicts is very high. Ultimately, a host of behavioral and social factors must be identified and altered for a successful outcome.

Most drug treatment programs utilize a biopsychosocial model as the basis for therapy. Models in this category take into account the multidimensional nature of chronic drug use:

1. The physiological effects of the drug on nervous system functioning, as when the opioids activate the mesolimbic reward pathway;

2. The psychological status of the individual and her unique neurochemical makeup and history of drug use; and

3. The environmental factors that provide salient cues for drug taking and powerful secondary reinforcement.

Detoxification is the first step in the therapeutic process

Detoxification, or the elimination of the abused drug from the body, can be assisted or unassisted. Unassisted detoxification is often referred to as going "cold turkey," and many addicts experience withdrawal symptoms on a fairly regular basis because they have difficulty securing more drug. Alternatively,

detoxification may be assisted by the administration of a long-acting opioid drug, such as **methadone**, which reduces the symptoms to a comfortable level. The dose of methadone is gradually reduced over a 5- to 7-day period until it can be terminated with only mild symptoms. Sometimes the α_2-adrenergic agonist **clonidine** is used in this stage. Clonidine acts on noradrenergic autoreceptors to reduce norepinephrine activity. Since the noradrenergic neurons in the locus coeruleus are inhibited by opioids and the cells increase firing during withdrawal (see Nestler et al., 1994, described earlier), clonidine-induced inhibition of firing reverses this hyperexcitable state. The drug seems to relieve the chills, tearing, yawning, stomach cramps, sweating, and muscle aches that are associated with the activity of the locus coeruleus, but does not reduce the remaining withdrawal symptoms nor the subjective discomfort and craving (Gold, 1989; O'Brien, 1993). Unfortunately, clonidine itself has side effects including insomnia, dry mouth, sedation, joint pain, and dizziness. For these reasons, it is not very popular with addicts, who much prefer detoxification with an opioid.

An ultra-rapid detoxification that is completed in a few hours or over several days requires that withdrawal be initiated with opioid antagonists while the addict is treated with clonidine, a benzodiazepine, or general anesthesia. This method is considered by many to be extreme because it does not produce improved abstinence rates and is associated with potentially life-threatening events.

Rather than pharmacological intervention to prevent withdrawal, it is possible to use electroacupuncture (EA) instead. Using morphine-dependent rats, Wang and colleagues (2011) showed that 30 minutes

BOX 11.3   The Cutting Edge

Role of NMDA Receptors in Tolerance and Dependence

Despite the many centuries of effective treatment with opioid drugs, it has never been possible to separate effectiveness from the development of tolerance and dependence. The goal with opioid therapeutics has always been to keep the dose as low as possible to provide needed relief from pain and avoid the increasing side effects that occur as the dose is increased. Unfortunately, tolerance to the analgesic effect makes it necessary to raise the dose, while some of the most troubling side effects, such as constipation, do not decrease and therefore become an increasing problem. Also, although the withdrawal syndrome can be minimized by gradually tapering the dose of the drug, the risk of abstinence signs is something most clinicians would ideally avoid. Inturrisi (1997), Trujillo (2000), and others have suggested that if we could better understand the neural basis for opioid tolerance and dependence, we might administer non-opioid drugs that prevent these phenomena, along with opioids, without diminishing the analgesia.

Tolerance and physical dependence are reversible changes in behavior based on experience and neuroadaptation to the presence of the drug and hence represent the plasticity of the nervous system. Earlier, we described the contribution of learning processes such as drug–environment associations to tolerance and other components of drug taking. Since the neurotransmitter glutamate and its NMDA (*N*-methyl-D-aspartate) receptor are critical for associative learning and memory (see Chapter 8), researchers have begun to evaluate the role of that system in substance abuse. The earliest evidence supporting a role

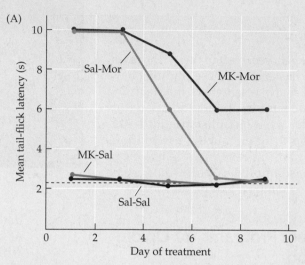

(A) Tolerance is reduced by MK-801. Each day for 9 days, four groups of rats were injected with a different combination of saline (Sal), MK-801 (MK), and morphine (Mor). Analgesia was tested with the tail-flick test on alternate days after treatment. Animals receiving only saline or saline + MK were not different from untreated animals (dashed line). Morphine (Sal-Mor) initially increased latency showing analgesia, but tolerance developed by day 7. In contrast, the MK-Mor group showed the same initial analgesia and much less tolerance over 9 days.

for glutamate in opioid tolerance and dependence used pretreatment with the noncompetitive NMDA antagonist dizocilpine (MK-801), along with chronic morphine. MK-801 reduced the development of tolerance to the analgesic effects of chronic morphine (9 days of treatment), as measured with the rat tail-flick test, but did not change the acute analgesic effects. The drug does not have analgesic effects itself (Figure A). Dizocilpine additionally interfered with the development of physical dependence to morphine, as demonstrated by naloxone-precipitated withdrawal after chronic treatment. It is important to realize that although the NMDA antagonist prevented the *acquisition* of tolerance and physical dependence, it did not reverse their *expression* if the antagonist was given after they had developed. This means that

the glutamate antagonist prevented the neural plasticity and learning component of tolerance and dependence. Other research also suggests NMDA receptor involvement in sensitization (reverse tolerance). The MK-801 treatment also prevents the plasticity changes when given chronically along with other drugs, including amphetamine, cocaine, nicotine, alcohol, benzodiazepines, barbiturates, and cannabinoids. It would appear that glutamate, acting at NMDA receptors that increase intracellular calcium, may have a common role in experience-induced changes for many drugs (Trujillo, 2000).

A good pharmacology student might now be wondering whether the NMDA receptor blockade with MK-801 is unique or whether other NMDA receptor antagonists would act similarly. As you see in the table, all the drugs that block

BOX 11.3 *(continued)*

NMDA receptors at several distinct sites (noncompetitive, competitive, or the glycine site) prevent morphine tolerance and, in those cases where tested, also block morphine dependence.

Thus far we have looked only at behavioral measures. Does NMDA antagonism also prevent opioid-induced neuronal changes after repeated administration? Mao and colleagues (1995) found that MK-801 prevented tolerance to the analgesic effects and in addition prevented the increase in protein kinase C (PKC) in the dorsal horn of the spinal cord that normally accompanies chronic opioid use. Increased opioid-induced PKC activation may phosphorylate the NMDA receptor, making it easier to be activated and thereby contributing to tolerance. Figure B will remind you that increased NMDA receptor action increases calcium entry, which in turn stimulates nitric oxide (NO) synthase, the enzyme needed to make nitric oxide, which may contribute to the development of tolerance. Evidence presented in the table suggests that, indeed, NO synthase inhibitors are also effective in reducing morphine tolerance and dependence. To test this model further, many more experiments are called for, but administering an NMDA antagonist along with morphine when treating chronic pain has great potential benefit for patients and may in addition provide a new direction for opioid addiction programs.

Drugs That Prevent Morphine Tolerance and/or Reduce Dependence in Rodents		
Drug type	Tolerance (analgesia)[a]	Dependence (withdrawal)
NMDA receptor antagonists		
Noncompetitive site:		
MK-801	+	+
Dextromethorphan	+	+
Dextrorphan	+	NT
Ketamine	+	NT
Phencyclidine	+	NT
d-methadone	+	NT
Competitive site:		
LY274614	+	+
NPC17742	+	NT
Glycine site:		
ACPC	+	NT
ACEA-1328	+	NT
Nitric oxide synthase inhibitors		
NOArg	+	+
NAME	+	+
7NI	NT	+

Source: Inturrisi, 1997.

[a] +, significantly reduced; NT, not tested.

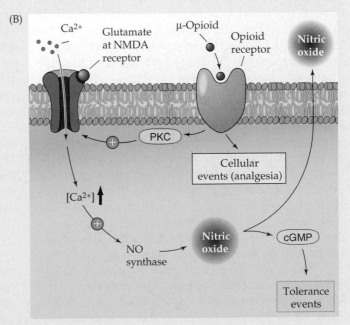

(B) Opioids acting at their receptor site produce cell changes causing analgesia. In addition, they activate protein kinase C (PKC), which phosphorylates the cation channel normally opened by glutamate, enhancing channel function. That action and its subsequent effects on NO synthesis may be responsible for tolerance. MK-801 prevents the increase in PKC and thereby prevents tolerance effects. Interrupting the intracellular pathway by preventing NO synthesis is apparently an additional site where the development of tolerance can be reduced.

of 100-Hz EA delivered 12 hours after the last morphine administration significantly reduced the classic signs of rodent withdrawal. They found an apparent "dose-dependent" effect in that a single EA treatment had a small effect, two sessions 11 hours apart had a significant effect, and four administrations had still greater effects on 4 out of 5 withdrawal signs measured. Perhaps even more interesting was the finding that EA restored the low levels of prodynorphin mRNA to normal in the spinal cord, hypothalamus, and PAG, which suggests that withdrawal is suppressed by increasing dynorphin synthesis. EA has been used in China to treat both opioid withdrawal and relapse for a number of years, but more recently, more controlled studies with animals and human addicts have been conducted. Cui et al. (2008) review that evidence.

Treatment goals and programs rely on pharmacological support and counseling

Treatment for heroin addiction offers several options and may be selected on the basis of availability in a given location, cost, or personal preference. Most programs begin with detoxification before starting intensive treatment on either an inpatient or an outpatient basis. Prolonged periods of follow-up care and supplementary services are advantageous in preventing relapse.

METHADONE MAINTENANCE   The most commonly used treatment method for heroin addiction is the **methadone maintenance program**. Originally developed by Dole and Nyswander (1965), the program involves the long-term substitution of one opioid drug for another. The rationale for the program is that by having his craving relieved, the addict is able to redirect his energy away from the activities needed to secure the drug toward more productive behaviors such as education or job training. The Center for Disease Control has a descriptive website about the methadone maintenance program that includes significant references and web links for further information (www.cdc.gov/idu/facts/methadonefin.pdf).

A large number of studies over many years have shown that when compared with any other treatment method, methadone maintenance was the most effective in reducing heroin and other illicit drug use. The percentage of patients who remain abstinent for 1 to 3 years after withdrawal of methadone has been reported to be as high as 80% among those who continue in the program for the recommended duration, while among those who drop out, the abstinence rate falls to 12%. One 6-year follow-up study found that 40% of former methadone patients were abstinent from opioids and free of other drug problems (Simpson et al., 1982). In addition, those addicts involved in the program showed significantly lower rates of criminal activity, HIV infection, and mortality, while showing greater involvement in becoming self-supporting (Bertschy, 1995). Prolonged involvement with the program is expected, and in many cases methadone is used in a chronic fashion, just as one would treat a diabetic with insulin. Alternatively, the individual may be gradually weaned from the drug support, but in these cases relapse rates are higher.

Among the hazards of methadone maintenance is the significant risk for accidental overdosing of the addict at the start of the treatment. Overdosing is a common event because it is difficult to determine the precise level of the addict's tolerance, making it difficult to choose the appropriate starting dose. Because methadone has such a long half-life, blood levels gradually increase for up to 5 days at the same dose (see steady state plasma levels in Chapter 1). Hence an initial ineffective dose can become toxic. Careful monitoring of the patient and dose adjustments must occur daily during the first 2 weeks and less frequently thereafter.

Methadone was chosen for use in opioid drug treatment programs for several reasons. First, cross-dependence with morphine or heroin means that it can prevent the more severe withdrawal associated with the abused drug. Second, the cross-tolerance that develops to repeated methadone use means that the normal euphoric effects of heroin are reduced or prevented. If an addict uses the illicit drug but gets little or no "rush," continued drug use should be less likely. Unfortunately, the tolerance can be overcome by high (and expensive) doses of heroin. In addition, methadone itself can produce a "rush" of euphoria if it is injected intravenously, which can lead to illegal diversion and trafficking of the drug. For this reason, most programs require *supervised* daily administration of *oral* methadone. The oral administration of methadone is a third important factor in the popularity of methadone maintenance because although little or no euphoria occurs with oral administration, the drug is fully effective in relieving craving for opioids. Craving is believed to be an important motive for relapse. In addition, oral administration reduces the use of the needle by the addict and the ritual surrounding its use. It also eliminates the danger of disease due to unsterile injection techniques. The spread of infectious diseases such as hepatitis and HIV is also reduced by eliminating the need to share contaminated needles.

Fourth, methadone is relatively long-acting, which produces a more constant blood level of drug such that the individual experiences fewer extremes of drug effect. A more even blood level produces a more stable daily experience and also normalizes body functions such as hormone secretion. Methadone is needed only once a day to prevent methadone withdrawal for 24 to 36 hours. The time course of drug action means daily contact and interaction with clinical staff who can provide behavioral therapy, group and family counseling, and support in education or job training. In addition, medical care can be provided. Of particular significance are the prenatal care for pregnant addicts and treatment of diseases, such as HIV, hepatitis, and syphilis, that are common among addicted pregnant females. Additionally, nutritional status is much improved, which leads to increased birth weight of infants born to mothers enrolled in the methadone program. However, since methadone passes the placental barrier like other opioids, the infant at delivery will sometimes show withdrawal signs, including tremors, twitching, seizures, vomiting, diarrhea, and poor feeding. These symptoms are treated by low doses of opioids, which are then tapered down until no drug is needed.

Fifth, methadone is considered medically safe even with long-term use and does not interfere with daily activities. Unfortunately, some side effects do not diminish with repeated use, so constipation, excessive sweating, reduced sex drive, and sexual dysfunction may persist during treatment for some individuals. It is noteworthy that long-term use of any opioid drug has few damaging effects on organ systems. The greatest dangers stem from poor living conditions, including inadequate diet, lack of medical care, and homelessness; dangerous and unlawful behaviors required to secure the drugs; and potentially fatal side effects of using contaminated needles or impure sources of drug. A description of clinical treatment guidelines can be found at www.cpso.on.ca/policies/guidelines/default.aspx?id=1984.

BUPRENORPHINE MAINTENANCE   Another opioid **buprenorphine** (Buprenex) is an opioid partial agonist and is used in the same manner as methadone. Because it has a high affinity but low efficacy at the μ-opioid receptor, as well as antagonist activity at the κ-receptor, it has weaker opioid effects and is less likely to result in overdose. It produces similar treatment results but has a longer duration of action and so produces more stable physiological effects and an extremely mild withdrawal syndrome. The neonatal abstinence syndrome is also extremely mild, although the developmental consequences of prenatal buprenorphine have not been fully determined in humans. However in rats, pre- and postnatal exposure to buprenorphine produced dose-dependent effects on several proteins needed for myelin formation, smaller-diameter myelinated axons, and reduced thickness of the myelin in the corpus callosum (Sanchez et al, 2008). Further studies should be conducted to determine the safety of the drug in treatment programs for addicted pregnant opioid addicts.

The longer duration of action also means less frequent administration (one to three times a week), which significantly reduces the costs of the program and gives an extra measure of freedom to the addict who needs daily clinic visits for methadone. Fewer clinic visits also tends to improve the relationship with members of the surrounding community, who often object to high rates of addict visits to their neighborhood. Buprenorphine is the only opioid substitute that can be prescribed in a physician's office that is not part of a federally regulated opioid treatment program. It is hoped that greater use of this drug will reduce costs and make more treatment facilities available.

In addition, because buprenorphine does not produce more than a mild euphoria when taken as directed, the addict can get a supply of the drug rather than just a single dose. To further reduce its potential for IV use, buprenorphine is available in a sublingual formulation (Suboxone) that also contains the antagonist naloxone. When taken sublingually, the buprenorphine is absorbed but the naloxone is not. If the tablet is crushed and injected intravenously in an effort to experience the euphoria, the naloxone blocks buprenorphine's effects. However, Suboxone can still be abused if crushed and snorted. Unfortunately, there has been an increase in law enforcement seizures of the drug that has been diverted to individuals without a prescription, and emergency department visits related to nonmedical use of buprenorphine more than tripled from 2006 to 2009 (**Figure 11.21**). Although buprenorphine is less likely to lead to overdose than methadone, in combination with CNS depressants, it can lead to respiratory depression and death.

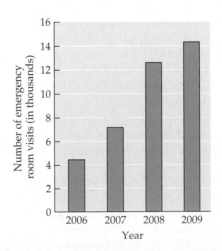

Figure 11.21 Estimated number of U.S. emergency department visits related to the nonmedical use of buprenorphine from 2006 to 2009. These visits include those in which buprenorphine was either the direct cause or a contributing factor. (After Center for Substance Abuse Research, 2011.)

USE OF NARCOTIC ANTAGONISTS   We have already described the utility of naloxone in reversing the effects of opioid toxicity. Antagonists also represent a component of some drug abuse treatment programs. After detoxification, antagonist treatment will block the effects of any self-administered opioid. Naltrexone (Trexan) is the most commonly used because it has a longer duration of action than naloxone and is effective when taken orally. It also has fewer side effects than cyclazocine, which may produce irritability, delusions, hallucinations, and motor incoordination. Nalmefene (Revex) is a newer pure opioid antagonist and is similar to naltrexone but more potent and longer-lasting.

This method is effective for addicts who are highly motivated, have strong family support, and are involved in careers (e.g., addicted medical personnel). Reliable patients have taken naltrexone for 5 to 10 years without relapse to drug-taking behavior and with minimal adverse effects on appetite, sexual behavior, or endocrine function (O'Brien, 1993). Unfortunately, this method appeals to only about 10% of the addicted population because a great deal of motivation is needed to voluntarily substitute an antagonist for a drug with highly reinforcing properties. Since craving for the drug is not eliminated, most less-motivated addicts stop antagonist treatment and return to drug use. Only about 27% of addicts in these treatment programs complete a 12-week preliminary session (Osborn et al., 1986).

VACCINES FOR ADDICTION TREATMENT   The rationale for using vaccines for the treatment of addiction is that abused substances must enter the brain to exert their behavioral effects. A vaccine would produce antibodies in the individual that would bind to the drug molecules in the blood circulation and prevent entry into the brain. Although it is not feasible to vaccinate the general population against every abused drug, vaccines might be useful in treating existing addiction to specific drugs. One such vaccine for opioids recognizes heroin and its active metabolites, 6-acetylmorphine and morphine (Stowe et al., 2011). This vaccine prevents the self-administration and analgesic effects of heroin in rats. Clinical trials with humans still need to be conducted.

COUNSELING SERVICES   Most often, addicts benefit from a **multidimensional approach** that includes a combination of detoxification, pharmacological support, and group or individual counseling. Counseling frequently is used to help addicts identify the environmental cues that trigger relapse for the individual. Having identified his "triggers," the addict must then design a behavioral response to those cues to prevent relapse. Furthermore, job training, educational counseling, and family therapy may be useful. Based on a model program for alcohol abuse treatment, Narcotics Anonymous is another option for motivated drug abusers to achieve drug abstinence.

Section Summary

- Animal studies show that opioids have reinforcing effects in self-administration paradigms, in conditioned place preference, and in reducing the threshold for electrical self-stimulation of the brain.

- Opioid drugs inhibit inhibitory GABA cells, increasing mesolimbic cell firing and DA release in the NAcc. Both dopaminergic and nondopaminergic mechanisms are necessary for the reinforcing effects.

- Opioid drugs demonstrate tolerance to many of the drug effects and cross-tolerance with other drugs in the same class, as well as with endogenous opioids.

- Prolonged use produces physical dependence, which is characterized by a classic rebound withdrawal syndrome that includes many flu-like symptoms, insomnia, depression, and irritability. Cross-dependence means that any drug in the opioid family can abruptly stop withdrawal symptoms.

- A model of the physiological mechanism for tolerance and dependence is the compensatory response of cells in the locus coeruleus to the acute inhibition of adenylyl cyclase.

- Classical conditioning of environmental cues associated with components of drug use is important in the development of tolerance and in maintaining the drug habit. Conditioned craving is significant in producing relapse in the detoxified addict.

- Detoxification is the first step in drug abuse treatment.

- Opioid abuse treatment programs include the substitution of one opioid, such as methadone or buprenorphine, for the abused drug. These substitutes, when given orally, produce no euphoria but eliminate craving for heroin and reduce exposure to HIV and hepatitis. The long-acting opioids stabilize the physiological effects and encourage contact with support staff. Methadone has a mild withdrawal. There are few damaging effects on organs with prolonged use.

- Compared with methadone, buprenorphine is longer acting, has a milder withdrawal and neonatal withdrawal, and can be prescribed in a physician's office. When combined with naloxone, abuse potential is reduced.

- Opioid antagonists are effective in blocking the opioid receptors so that self-administered narcotics have no effect.

- In rats, heroin vaccine binds to drug molecules which prevents entry to the CNS and reduces self-administration of opioids.

- The most successful treatment approaches are multidimensional ones.

Go to the **COMPANION WEBSITE**

sites.sinauer.com/psychopharm2e
for Web Boxes, animations, flashcards, and other study resources.

Recommended Readings

Gosnell, B. A. and Levine, A. S. (2009). Reward systems and food intake: Role of opioids. *Int. J. Obes. (Lond).*, 33 (Suppl. 2), S54–S58.

Gruber, S. A., Silveri, M. M., and Yurgelun-Todd, D. A. (2007). Neuropsychological consequences of opioid use. *Neuropsychol. Rev.*, 17, 299–315.

Javelot, H., Messaoudi, M., Garnier, S., and Rougeot, C. (2010). Human opiorphin is a naturally occurring antidepressant acting selectively on enkephalin-dependent delta-opioid pathways. *J. Physiol. Pharmacol.*, 61, 355–362.

Musto, D. F. (1991). Opium, cocaine, and marijuana in American history. *Sci. Am.*, 265, 40–47.

Lobmaier, P., Gossop, M., Waal, H., and Bramness, J. (2010). The pharmacological treatment of opioid addiction—A clinical perspective. *Eur. J. Clin. Pharmacol.*, 66, 537–545.

Wager, T. D., Scott, D. J., and Zubieta, J. K. (2007). Placebo effects on human mu-opioid activity during pain. *Proc. Natl. Acad. Sci.*, 104, 11056–11061.

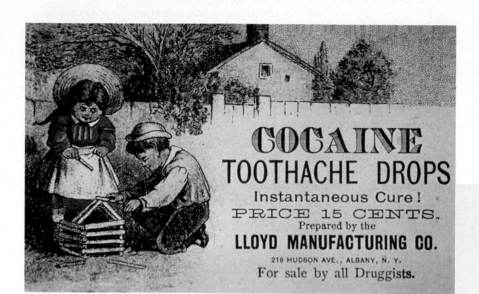

Because of its local anesthetic activity, cocaine was once an ingredient in over-the-counter medications for toothache.

Psychomotor Stimulants: Cocaine and the Amphetamines

12

"THE PSYCHIC EFFECT ... CONSISTS OF EXHILARATION AND LASTING EUPHORIA, which does not differ in any way from the normal euphoria of a healthy person.... One senses an increase of self-control and feels more vigorous and more capable of work.... Long-lasting, intensive mental or physical work can be performed without fatigue; it is as though the need for food and sleep, which otherwise makes itself felt peremptorily at certain times of the day, were completely banished.... Opinion is unanimous that the euphoria ... is not followed by any feeling of lassitude or other state of depression."

Any substance having the marvelous properties just described should be a boon to humankind. What is this miracle drug, then? The answer, unfortunately, is cocaine, and the nearly rapturous description quoted above comes from the writings of Sigmund Freud (*Über Coca*; reprinted in Byck, 1974, pp. 60–62).

Cocaine, amphetamine, and related compounds belong to a class of drugs called **psychomotor stimulants**. This term refers to the marked sensorimotor activation that occurs in response to drug administration. Indeed, psychomotor stimulants are characterized by their ability to increase alertness, heighten arousal, and cause behavioral excitement. This chapter considers the behavioral and physiological effects of these stimulants, their mechanisms of action, and their potential for producing abuse and dependence. Chapter 13 covers nicotine and caffeine, two less potent but more widely used stimulants.

Figure 12.1 Map of principal coca-growing regions of South America (Courtesy of Rosemary Mosher and Michael Steinberg.)

Figure 12.2 Coca chewing is still practiced by some Bolivian miners to help them work long hours in the mines. The miner on the right is chewing coca, while his partner consumes a snack.

Cocaine

Background and History

Cocaine is an alkaloid found in the leaves of the shrub *Erythroxylon coca*. The coca shrub is native to South America and is primarily cultivated in the northern and central Andes Mountains extending from Colombia into Peru and Bolivia (**Figure 12.1**). The inhabitants of these regions consume cocaine by chewing the leaves—a practice thought to have begun at least 2000 and perhaps as many as 5000 years ago, according to archeological evidence. Because cocaine is a weak base, coca chewers also include some lime or ash to make the pH of the saliva more alkaline (**Figure 12.2**). This decreases ionization of the cocaine and promotes absorption across the mucous membranes of the oral cavity.

Coca chewing was an important feature of ceremonial or religious occasions in the Incan civilization, and use of the drug was ordinarily restricted to the ruling classes up to the time of the Spanish conquest. After the fall of the Incan empire, coca chewing became more widespread and commonplace, and there are even reports that coca was used as a medium of exchange. Over time, many Spanish missionaries and churchmen argued that coca chewing was idolatrous and interfered with conversion of the natives to Catholicism. The practice was consequently discouraged and even banned in some areas. The Spaniards soon discovered, however, that without the stimulating and hunger-reducing effects of coca, Incan workers lacked the endurance necessary to work long hours in the mines and fields at high altitudes and with little food. Thus coca cultivation and chewing were restored with the blessing of the Spanish rulers and the church.

Although coca leaves were brought back to Europe, coca chewing never caught on, possibly owing to degradation of the active ingredient during the long sea voyage. But travelers to the New World had occasion to sample the leaf, and several came back with glowing reports of its beneficial effects. By the late 1850s, German chemists had isolated pure cocaine and had characterized it chemically. Over the next 30 years, cocaine became tremendously popular as many notable scientists and physicians lauded its properties. A chemist named Angelo Mariani concocted an infamous mixture of cocaine and wine (*Vin Mariani*), and the Italian neurologist Paolo Mantegazza wrote, "I would rather have a life span of ten years with coca than one of 1,000,000 centuries without coca" (Petersen, 1977). The most famous cocaine user of all, though, was Sigmund Freud. In 1885, Freud published the monograph *Über Coca* ("On Coca"), which extolled the drug's virtues and recommended its use in the treatment of alcoholism, morphine addiction, depression, digestive disorders, and a variety of other ailments. Freud also performed the first recorded psychopharmacological experiments on cocaine and published the results in a paper entitled "Contribution to the Knowledge of the Effect of Cocaine." In his last written comments about cocaine in 1887, Freud acknowledged its dangers when used to treat morphine addiction, although he continued to maintain that the drug was nonaddictive under other circumstances.[1] Others, however, were more perceptive. The harshest critic was the German psychiatrist A. Erlenmeyer, who labeled cocaine the "third scourge of the human race," after alcohol and opium.

Despite the warning signs emanating from Europe, cocaine's popularity grew in the United States during the late nineteenth and early twentieth centuries. By 1885, Parke Davis & Co. pharmaceuticals was manufacturing 15 different forms of cocaine and coca, including cigarettes, cheroots (a type of cigar), and inhalants. One year later, a pharmacist from Georgia named John Pemberton introduced a new beverage, "Coca-Cola," which contained cocaine from coca leaves and caffeine from cola nuts.[2] Coca-Cola and similar concoctions were marketed as suitable alternatives to alcoholic drinks because of the growing strength of the alcohol temperance movement at that time (**Figure 12.3**). Cocaine-containing tooth drops were even given to infants to relieve the discomfort of teething (the local anesthetic effects of cocaine are discussed further in the section on mechanisms of action). Not surprisingly, widespread cocaine abuse began to appear across the United States until President Taft declared cocaine to be "public enemy number one" in 1910. Congress then passed the 1914 Harrison Narcotic Act prohibiting the inclusion of cocaine (as well as opium) in over-the-counter medicines and specifying other restrictions on its import and sale (see Chapter 9). Subsequent state and federal laws, of course, placed even tighter regulations on cocaine distribution and use.

From the 1920s to the 1960s, cocaine use continued primarily among a relatively small group of avant-garde artists, musicians, and other performers. Beginning in the 1970s, however, two successive waves of increasing cocaine use were seen in the United States. The first involved an escalation of cocaine use by snorting or intravenous (IV) injection, whereas the

Figure 12.3 Coca-Cola ad from 1906

most recent epidemic of cocaine use has been driven by the smoking of "crack" cocaine.

According to estimates derived from the 2011 National Survey on Drug Use and Health (Substance Abuse and Mental Health Services Administration, 2012), approximately 1.4 million people aged 12 or older (0.5% of the population) were current users of cocaine at the time of the survey. By "current user," we mean that the individual had used cocaine at least once during the previous month. Of these current users, approximately 821,000 people met criteria for abuse of or dependence on cocaine. During 2011, more than 650,000 people aged 12 or older used cocaine for the first time. On the basis of past experience, we know that some of those individuals will subsequently begin to abuse and in some cases will become dependent on the drug, whereas others will not. Although we know some of the psychosocial and environmental characteristics that contribute to differences between those groups, it would be of great value to know more about the genetic and molecular determinants that may also contribute to vulnerability to cocaine abuse and dependence.

---

[1]In fairness to Freud, it should be noted that he normally took cocaine orally—a route of administration with less abuse potential than IV injection, smoking, or even snorting.

[2]Although cocaine itself was removed from the product in 1903, Coca-Cola continues to contain a non-narcotic extract from the coca leaf that is regularly prepared by a chemical company in the United States (Goldstein et al., 2009).

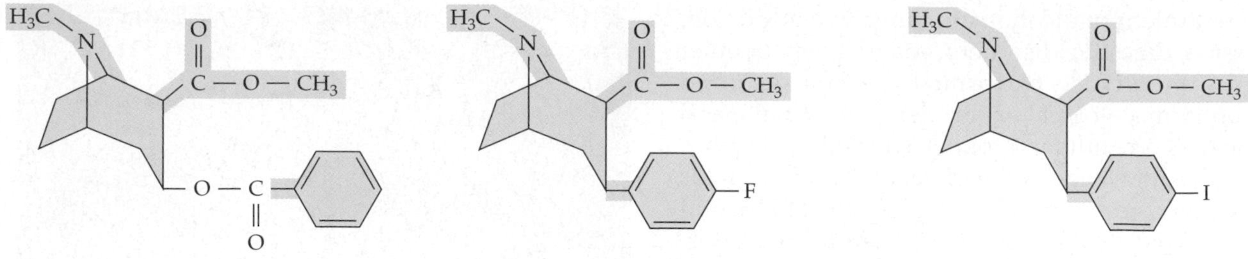

Cocaine

WIN 35,428 (CFT)

RTI-55 (β-CIT)

Figure 12.4 Chemical structures of cocaine, WIN 35,428, and RTI-55

Basic Pharmacology of Cocaine

Figure 12.4 presents the chemical structure of alkaloidal cocaine, which is its naturally occurring form. The molecule contains two rings: the six-carbon phenyl ring shown on the right and the unusual nitrogen (N)-containing ring shown on the left. Both are necessary for the drug's biological activity. Other features of the molecule have been manipulated with interesting results. For example, Figure 12.4 also depicts the structures of two synthetic cocainelike drugs: WIN 35,428 (also known as CFT) and RTI-55 (also called β-CIT). Notice that both compounds lack the ester (–O–CO–) linkage between the rings, and both possess a halogen (fluorine [F] or iodine [I]) atom on the phenyl ring. WIN 35,428 and RTI-55 are more potent than cocaine, and if available on the street, they presumably would be highly addictive. Fortunately, they are used only experimentally, primarily for in vitro studies on brain tissue.

Coca leaves contain between 0.6% and 1.8% cocaine. Initial extraction of the leaves results in a coca paste containing about 80% cocaine. The alkaloid is then converted to hydrochloride (HCl) salt and is crystallized. Cocaine HCl is readily water soluble and thus can be taken orally (as in *Vin Mariani*), intranasally (snorting), or by IV injection. One disadvantage of cocaine HCl is its vulnerability to heat-induced breakdown, thereby preventing it from being smoked. However, the hydrochloride salt can be transformed back into cocaine freebase by two different methods. The method developed first was to dissolve cocaine HCl in water, add an alkaline solution such as ammonia, and then extract the resulting cocaine base with an organic solvent, typically ether. The term **freebasing** refers to smoking cocaine that was obtained in this manner. However, because ether is highly flammable and explosive, a certain danger is involved not only in this method of preparing cocaine freebase but even in smoking it, since an ether residue may still be present if one is not careful. In the early 1980s, it was discovered that cocaine base could be made more safely by mixing dissolved cocaine HCl with baking soda, heating the mixture, and then drying it. Chunks of the dried, hardened mixture are known on the street as **crack** (so named because of the popping sounds produced when the chunks are heated), or "rock" cocaine. Such chunks are generally sold inexpensively in small amounts sufficient for only one or two doses (**Figure 12.5**). The cocaine that ends up in a user's bloodstream is the same substance regardless of whether its initial form was the hydrochloride salt or the freebase. However, the heat involved in smoking crack apparently produces unique chemical products that can be detected in the urine and potentially used to verify crack use.

Different routes of consumption yield somewhat different patterns and levels of plasma cocaine. Extremely rapid absorption occurs with both IV

Figure 12.5 Crystals of crack cocaine

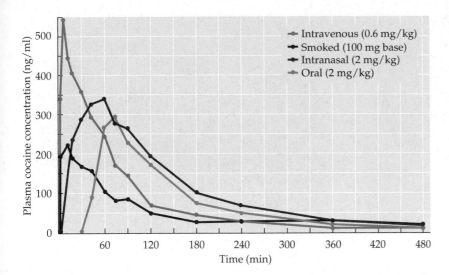

Figure 12.6 Time course of plasma cocaine concentrations following different routes of administration. Each curve shows the mean for ten human subjects. For cocaine freebase smoking, subjects were allowed only one to three puffs of the vapor from 100 mg of drug heated in a flask. The peak plasma concentrations produced under these conditions probably underestimate the levels occurring from recreational use. (After Jones, 1990.)

injection and smoking. Hence, typical single doses taken by these routes yield rather high concentrations of circulating cocaine, and even higher values can be attained with multiple doses that mimic the pattern of a cocaine "binge" (see the section on cocaine abuse later in the chapter). Absorption is somewhat slower following oral administration or snorting; consequently, these routes yield lower cocaine levels. **Figure 12.6** compares the time course of plasma cocaine concentrations as a function of route of administration. It is interesting to note that a few hours of coca leaf chewing delivers enough drug to mimic the plasma concentrations produced by a modest dose taken either orally or intranasally.

Although researchers normally measure blood levels of drugs in a peripheral vein such as the antecubital vein located in the arm, even more important for a psychoactive drug is the level present in the brain. Cocaine is sufficiently lipophilic (fat soluble) that it passes readily through the blood–brain barrier (see Chapter 1). This property particularly comes into play when cocaine is smoked, because it results in exposure of the brain to a very large surge in drug levels not reflected in peripheral venous concentrations. Rapid entry into the brain is believed to be an important factor in the strong addictive properties of crack cocaine.

Once absorbed into the circulation, cocaine is rapidly broken down by enzymes found in the bloodstream and the liver. It is also rapidly eliminated, with a half-life ranging from about 0.5 to 1.5 hours. For this reason, the subjective high produced by a single IV or smoked dose of cocaine may last only about 30 minutes. However, the breakdown products of cocaine persist in the body for a longer period of time. For example, in a heavy cocaine user, the major metabolite **benzoylecgonine** can be detected in the urine for several days following the last dose.

Alcohol or other depressant drugs are sometimes taken along with cocaine to "take the edge off" the extreme arousal produced by cocaine alone. By studying the combined effects of cocaine and alcohol, researchers have discovered an unexpected and potentially important interaction between these two compounds. When taken together, cocaine and alcohol (ethanol) produce a unique metabolite called **cocaethylene**. This substance not only has biological activity similar to that of cocaine itself, but it has a longer half-life. As we shall see later, cocaine can exert toxic effects on the heart and other organs. Such toxicity may be exacerbated in individuals consuming large amounts of cocaine and alcohol together.

Mechanisms of Cocaine Action

Cocaine is a complex drug because it interacts with several neurotransmitter systems. Most of the behavioral and physiological actions of cocaine can be explained by its ability to block the reuptake of three monoamine neurotransmitters: the two catecholamines dopamine (DA) and norepinephrine (NE), and also serotonin (5-HT). In earlier chapters, we learned that these transmitters are cleared from the synaptic cleft by membrane proteins called *transporters*. Cocaine binds to these transporters and inhibits their function. As shown for the DA transporter in **Figure 12.7**, such inhibition leads to increased neurotransmitter levels in the synaptic cleft and a corresponding increase in transmission at the affected synapses. Depending on the route of administration, this effect can occur very rapidly. Indeed, Yorgason et al. (2011) recently reported that intravenously administered cocaine in rats begins to block DA uptake within 5 seconds, with peak inhibition occurring approximately 30 seconds post-injection.

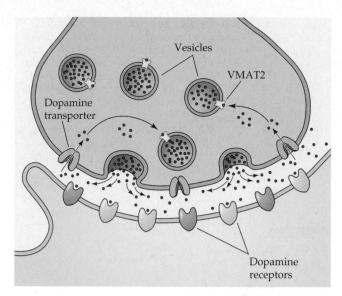
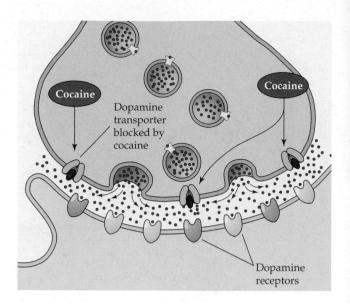

Figure 12.7 Mechanisms of cocaine action Cocaine increases synaptic DA levels by binding to the plasma membrane DA transporter and blocking reuptake of the neurotransmitter. A similar process occurs at serotonergic and noradrenergic synapses because of cocaine's inhibition of 5-HT and NE reuptake.

Cocaine does not affect all monoamine transporters equally. Based on in vitro studies using rat brain tissue, cocaine binds most strongly (with highest affinity) to the 5-HT transporter, followed by the DA transporter, and then the NE transporter (Ritz et al., 1990). On the other hand, later in this chapter we will see that blockade of DA reuptake appears to be most important for cocaine's stimulating, reinforcing, and addictive properties. Indeed, many drugs used in the treatment of depression block the 5-HT and/or the NE transporter (see Chapter 19). Yet these agents do not have the strong arousing effect produced by cocaine in nondepressed individuals, nor do they have any abuse potential. Nevertheless, 5-HT and NE must also be taken into account, as alterations in the DA system do not explain all of cocaine's effects.

At relatively high concentrations, cocaine additionally inhibits voltage-gated sodium (Na^+) channels in nerve cell axons. As these channels are necessary for neurons to generate action potentials, this action of cocaine causes a block of nerve conduction. Thus, when cocaine is applied locally to a tissue, it acts as a local anesthetic by preventing transmission of nerve signals along sensory nerves. Indeed, two synthetic local anesthetics that are widely used in medical and dental practice, procaine (Novocain) and lidocaine (Xylocaine), were developed from the structure of cocaine.

Section Summary

- Cocaine is an alkaloid derived from the leaves of the shrub *Erythroxylon coca*, which is indigenous to the northern and central Andes Mountains of South America.

- Although the peoples of that region have been chewing coca leaves for perhaps 5000 years, cocaine use did not become popular in Western cultures until after the pure compound was isolated in the late 1850s. Freud was one of many notable cocaine users in nineteenth-century Europe.

- In the United States, cocaine was a constituent of numerous popular beverages and over-the-counter pharmaceutical products in the late nineteenth and early twentieth centuries until its nonprescription use was banned by the Harrison Narcotic Act of 1914. Cocaine then went "underground" until the 1970s, at which time the first of two waves of increased cocaine use began in this country.

- Recent household survey data indicate that about 1.4 million people in the United States are current users of cocaine, although not all of these individuals are dependent on the drug.

- Cocaine HCl is water soluble and therefore can be taken orally, intranasally, or by IV injection. On the other hand, cocaine base (including crack cocaine) is the chemical form most suitable for smoking.

- The most rapid absorption and distribution of cocaine occur following IV injection and smoking, which may account for the highly addictive properties of these routes of consumption.

- One of the main cocaine metabolites is benzoylecgonine, whereas a compound called cocaethylene is also formed when alcohol is ingested along with cocaine.

- At typical doses, cocaine acts mainly to block synaptic uptake of DA, 5-HT, and NE by binding to their respective membrane transporters. This enhances transmission at monoaminergic synapses by increasing the synaptic concentrations of each transmitter.

- At higher concentrations, cocaine also blocks voltage-gated Na$^+$ channels, which leads to a local anesthetic effect.

Acute Behavioral and Physiological Effects of Cocaine

Cocaine is used and abused for the "high" and the "rush" produced by the drug. The pleasurable feelings associated with the "high" serve as a reinforcer, causing many users to use the drug repeatedly. In this section, we will discuss the behavioral and physiological effects of cocaine, and the neurochemical mechanisms underlying these effects.

Cocaine stimulates mood and behavior

Typical aspects of the cocaine "high" are feelings of exhilaration and euphoria, a sense of well-being, enhanced alertness, heightened energy and diminished fatigue, and great self-confidence. Taken by IV injection or by smoking, cocaine also produces a brief "rush," described by some users as involving a sense of great pleasure and power and by others as being like an intense orgasm. At low and moderate doses, cocaine often increases sociability and talkativeness. There are also reports of heightened sexual interest and performance under cocaine's influence, although the drug's legendary ability to enhance sexual prowess is highly exaggerated. Cocaine can apparently also increase aggressive behavior, which suggests that some of the street violence associated with cocaine might be attributable to a direct effect of the drug.

The major behavioral and subjective effects of cocaine and other psychostimulants are summarized in **Table 12.1**. Effects listed in the "mild to moderate" category are generally produced by single, low to moderate doses of cocaine either in naive subjects or in users who have not yet progressed to heavy, chronic patterns of drug intake. "Severe" effects are most likely to be seen with high-dose use, particularly in individuals with long-standing patterns of chronic intake. It is easy to see that many of the positive characteristics of cocaine that may contribute to its powerful reinforcing properties become negative or aversive with escalation of dose and duration. Some of these aversive effects (e.g., irritability) are present in most high-dose users, whereas others mainly occur in cases of cocaine-induced psychosis (e.g., incoherence or delusions; see the discussion on health consequences later in the chapter).

Cocaine and other psychomotor stimulants also cause profound behavioral activation in rats, mice, and other animals used in psychopharmacological studies. At low doses, such activation takes the form of increased locomotion, rearing, and mild sniffing behavior. As the dose is increased, these behaviors are replaced by **focused stereotypies** (repetitive, seemingly aimless behaviors performed in a relatively invariant manner) confined to a small area of the cage floor. Psychostimulant stereotypies vary according to species and other factors. In rats and mice, one observes intense sniffing, continuous head and limb movements, and licking and biting. Humans using large

TABLE 12.1 Mild to Moderate versus Severe Behavioral and Subjective Effects of Cocaine and Other Psychostimulants in Humans[a]

Mild to moderate effects	Severe effects
Mood amplification; both euphoria and dysphoria	Irritability, hostility, anxiety, fear, withdrawal
Heightened energy	Extreme energy or exhaustion
Sleep disturbance, insomnia	Total insomnia
Motor excitement, restlessness	Compulsive motor stereotypies
Talkativeness, pressure of speech	Rambling, incoherent speech
Hyperactive ideation	Disjointed flight of ideas
Increased sexual interest	Decreased sexual interest
Anger, verbal aggression	Possible extreme violence
Mild to moderate anorexia	Total anorexia
Inflated self-esteem	Delusions of grandiosity

Source: Post and Contel, 1983.

[a]The actual effects observed show individual variability and depend on the dose, route of administration, pattern and duration of use, and environmental context.

amounts of cocaine occasionally also exhibit motor stereotypies such as repetitive picking and scratching.

All species tested thus far readily learn to self-administer cocaine intravenously. Marilyn Carroll and colleagues (1990) were also able to train monkeys to smoke cocaine freebase, a procedure that has led to a number of follow-up studies on the mechanisms underlying self-administration via this route (e.g., Campbell et al., 1999). Furthermore, unlimited access to cocaine can lead to heavy self-administration, gradual debilitation of the animals, and a high rate of mortality. These findings underscore the drug's powerful reinforcing properties in animals and its high abuse potential in humans. On the other hand, it is important to recognize that such compulsivity is not observed under all circumstances. When cocaine is pitted against an alternative reinforcer under controlled laboratory conditions, preference for the drug in both monkeys and humans depends on the relative magnitude of each reinforcer (**Box 12.1**).

Animals can also learn to discriminate cocaine from vehicle treatment. Subjects initially trained on cocaine readily generalize to amphetamine, indicating a fundamental similarity in the cue properties of these two drugs. In contrast, there is much less generalization to caffeine, which is a weaker stimulant and which exerts its behavioral effects by a different mechanism than cocaine or amphetamine (see Chapter 13).

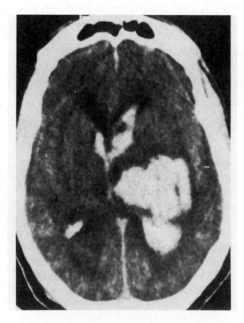

Figure 12.8 Computerized tomographic (CT) scan of a thalamic hemorrhage in a crack cocaine smoker The patient was a 45-year-old man who had smoked an unknown amount of crack and was found unconscious several hours later. The hemorrhage can be seen as the large, irregularly shaped white area on the middle to lower right side of the scan. (From Jacobs et al., 1989.)

Cocaine's physiological effects are mediated by the sympathetic nervous system

Cocaine is considered a **sympathomimetic** drug, which means that it produces symptoms of sympathetic nervous system activation. The physiological consequences of acute cocaine administration include increased heart rate, vasoconstriction (narrowing of blood vessels) and hypertension (increased blood pressure), and hyperthermia (elevated body temperature). At low doses, these physiological changes are usually not harmful to the individual. High doses of cocaine, however, can be toxic or even fatal. Some of the potential adverse consequences of heavy cocaine use are seizures, heart failure, stroke, and intracranial hemorrhage (Treadwell and Robinson, 2007) (**Figure 12.8**). A recent study in mice showed that even in the absence of an actual hemorrhage, the vasoconstrictive effects of cocaine can significantly interrupt blood flow to the brain, and that this phenomenon is exacerbated with repeated drug dosing (Ren et al., 2012).

Dopamine is important for many effects of cocaine and other psychostimulants

Several neurotransmitters, including 5-HT (Müller and Huston, 2006) and NE (Sofuoglu and Sewell, 2009), contribute to the behavioral responses of animals to cocaine, amphetamine, and related psychostimulant drugs. However, there is overwhelming evidence that DA plays the most important role in mediating these responses (Zhu and Reith, 2008). Of special relevance are the dopaminergic projections from the midbrain (substantia nigra and ventral tegmental area) to the striatum and nucleus accumbens, which were first described in Chapter 5.

Table 12.2 summarizes the results of numerous microinjection and lesion studies concerning the involvement of these DA systems in the behavioral effects of psychostimulants. For example, psychostimulants elicit a locomotor response when microinjected directly into the nucleus accumbens. Injection into the striatum instead leads to a pattern of stereotyped behavior. Another approach has been to lesion DA nerve terminals in either the accumbens or the striatum using the catecholamine neurotoxin 6-hydroxy-dopamine (6-OHDA). Such lesions cause a profound reduction of both DA and its transporter in the affected area, thereby preventing activation of dopaminergic transmission by psychostimulants. 6-OHDA lesions of the nucleus accumbens blunt psychostimulant-induced locomotion, whereas similar lesions of the striatum antagonize the stereotypies associated with higher drug doses.

BOX 12.1   The Cutting Edge

Is a Sweetened Water Solution More Reinforcing than Cocaine?

In a later section of this chapter, we will point out that only about 10% to 15% of people who start using cocaine by the intranasal route (i.e., snorting) eventually become dependent on the drug. Thus, merely trying cocaine or even using it recreationally for some period of time does not lead to dependence in the majority of users. Nevertheless, once dependence has been established, it seems very difficult for most individuals to "kick" their habit based on the high rates of relapse of subjects who have participated in various cocaine treatment programs. Later we will also describe evidence for procedures that lead to compulsive types of cocaine-taking behavior in experimental animals such as rats. However, it is interesting to note that such studies (i.e., of transition from mere cocaine self-administration to compulsive cocaine-taking behavior) are almost always conducted under conditions in which no alternative reinforcements are available to the animals. How does cocaine fare as a reinforcer when other reinforcers are available to choose from?

Perhaps the first study to address this question was reported in 1978 by Aigner and Balster. These experimenters used a complex experimental procedure with rhesus monkeys in which the animals performed a lever pressing response for either an IV cocaine infusion or a small amount of food. Both reinforcers were available around the clock, although each trial (i.e., behavior resulting in the delivery of a reinforcer) was separated from the next trial by a 15-minute intertrial interval. The animals were given no food other than what they earned by choosing the food lever over the cocaine lever. The results clearly showed

that most of the responses were made on the cocaine lever, such that the monkeys lost up to 10% of their body weight over the 8-day study.

The findings of Aigner and Balster seemed to indicate that cocaine was a supremely powerful reinforcer, so much so that animals would deprive themselves of needed food to obtain the drug. However, after the early period of self-administration studies, researchers began to move away from paradigms in which drugs such as cocaine were available for 24 hours a day in favor of paradigms utilizing limited periods of drug access. When a few studies began to be performed using such limited access periods, the evidence indicated that other reinforcers such as food or even a sweetened water solution were sometimes chosen by animals in preference to IV cocaine. This was the first sign that cocaine may not be as powerfully reinforcing as first thought (and as still asserted often in the popular media).

If that was the end of the story, we might not have chosen it for the topic of this box. However, this topic has recently been revisited in a powerful set of studies from the laboratory of Serge Ahmed (Lenoir et al., 2007; Cantin et al., 2010) in an attempt to better quantify the relative reinforcing potencies of cocaine versus a sweetened water solution. Here we will focus on the more recent of the two papers, which was designed to pit a saccharin-flavored solution against cocaine under a variety of experimental conditions. Interestingly, when a breaking point procedure was used with the two reinforcers, the average breaking point for cocaine was consistently higher than the average breaking point

for the saccharin solution. Thus, if the investigators had relied solely on this common measure of reinforcement strength, they would have concluded that cocaine was a more powerful reinforcer than the saccharin solution. However, a completely different story emerged when the two reinforcers were available concurrently. In that case, 24 of 29 rats (about 83%) tested responded more strongly on the saccharin lever than the cocaine lever, thus demonstrating a preference for the sweet solution over cocaine. The mean data over 6 choice days are depicted in Figure A, which shows that the saccharin preference was evident on the first choice day and then increased over the next few days.

Additional experiments were performed to support the validity of the apparent preference for the saccharin solution. In one of these experiments, which lasted a total of 6 months, a separate group of rats was trained to respond on alternate days for cocaine or saccharin for 59 days on a fixed-ratio schedule, followed by 40 alternating days of responding on a progressive ratio schedule, and then 52 days on which a choice was allowed between cocaine or the sweetened solution. Over this period of time, the rats self-administered an average of almost 1300 IV doses of cocaine (yielding an average cumulative dose of over 900 mg/kg), indicating that there was a substantial opportunity for the cocaine exposure to alter brain chemistry to cause an increased motivation to take the drug. Yet, when the animals were subsequently tested for responding during extinction when neither saccharin nor cocaine was available, there was greater

(Continued on next page)

BOX 12.1 *(continued)*

(A)

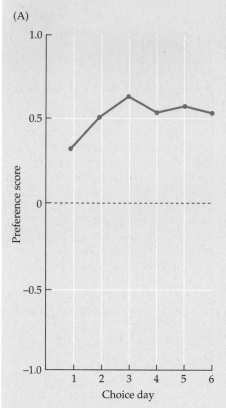

(A) Rats choose saccharin-sweetened water over intravenous cocaine Rats were trained to lever press either for water containing 0.2% saccharin or for IV cocaine (0.25 mg/infusion) on a fixed-ratio 1 schedule. After initial training, the animals were tested in a choice procedure during which both reinforcers were made available by pressing different levers. The data illustrate the relative preference for one reinforcer over the other, with positive values representing a preference for the sweetened water and negative values representing a preference for IV cocaine. The dashed line at 0.0 represents no preference, whereas 1.0 or −1.0 represents a complete preference for sweetened water or cocaine, respectively. The positive scores over the 6 test days show that the sweetened water was generally preferred over cocaine, although the drug was chosen on some trials because the mean scores did not reach 1.0 on any test day. (After Cantin et al., 2010.)

responding on the saccharin lever, indicating stronger seeking of the sweet solution reward than the cocaine reward. The authors conclude from these findings and other results not mentioned here that the majority of laboratory rats find a sweetened water solution to be more rewarding than cocaine, and they argue that such results conform to the clinical reports indicating that only a minority of people who use cocaine become dependent on it (Cantin et al., 2010; Ahmed, 2010). The results of these animal studies also fit with the proposed idea in the addiction field that a major risk factor for developing drug dependence and for relapsing during attempts at abstinence is a lack of other significant reinforcers in the person's life. However, it is important to mention an important caveat regarding the results reported by Ahmed's research group. Despite the fact that in some of their experiments rats had substantial exposure to cocaine through long periods of self-administration, and that the amount of past cocaine use had only a small effect on the relative preference of the animals, the investigators did not use any of the procedures discussed later in the chapter that have been found to elicit compulsive cocaine-taking behavior in rats. It would be interesting and informative to see whether the relative preference for cocaine versus a saccharin solution would remain the same if the rats were trained using the procedures that elicit cocaine-taking behaviors more indicative of compulsivity than mere self-administration of the drug.

Finally, we need to ask the question about whether a similar kind of choice situation has been tested in human cocaine users. The answer is yes, and the results depend on the type of subject (e.g., occasional cocaine user versus cocaine-dependent subject), the dose and route of cocaine administration, and the value of the alternative reinforcer (Haney, 2008). For

(B) Preference of regular cocaine users for cocaine versus money as a function of drug dose. In this study, active users of crack cocaine were given 5 trials involving the choice either to smoke a dose of cocaine base (0, 12, 25, or 50 mg) or to receive a $5.00 voucher for merchandise redeemable at a local retail store or supermarket. When the cocaine dose was 0, there were virtually no choices for the drug, but when the dose was 25 or 50 mg, cocaine was chosen on almost all the trials.
(C) The same subjects rated the subjective "high" produced by each drug dose using a visual analog scale (the subject placed a mark along a 100-mm line indicating the intensity of response from no response at all at the 0-mm point to the highest possible response at the 100-mm point). (After Collins et al., 2003.)

(B) Cocaine choice

(C) Ratings of "I feel high"

BOX 12.1 *(continued)*

example, an early study of occasional cocaine users by Higgins et al. (1994) found that these subjects would typically choose a mere $2 reward over snorting as much as 100 mg of cocaine HCl. In contrast, when regular crack cocaine smokers were given a choice between a merchandise voucher worth $5 and being allowed to smoke a given amount of cocaine base (which the subjects had briefly sampled to determine the effect of each dose), there was a clear relationship between dose and cocaine choice such that the two highest doses of 25 mg and 50 mg led to nearly complete choice of the cocaine over the money (Collins et al., 2003) (Figure B). Not coincidentally, these same doses also led to the most intense ratings of cocaine "high" by the subjects (Figure C). These findings suggest that the apparent low value of cocaine in rats, even after many sessions of self-administration, does not necessarily correspond to a low value of cocaine in humans who are regularly consuming highly addictive forms of cocaine such as crack.

The mesolimbic DA pathway to the nucleus accumbens also plays a key role in the reinforcing effects of cocaine and amphetamine in animals. Thus 6-OHDA lesions of the accumbens reduce the reinforcing properties of systemically administered cocaine or amphetamine. Moreover, rats will self-administer amphetamine directly into the nucleus accumbens (Hoebel et al., 1983). They will also self-administer cocaine into this area, but not as robustly as in the case of nomifensine, a more selective DA reuptake inhibitor (Carlezon et al., 1995). Although various explanations have been offered regarding why amphetamine is more effective than cocaine when microinjected into the nucleus accumbens, none of these explanations has been put to a rigorous experimental test.

More recently, the neurochemical mechanisms of cocaine action have been studied using genetic knockout mice. We saw in Chapter 5 that mutant mice lacking the DA transporter (DAT) fail to show hyperactivity following psychostimulant treatment. Most investigators expected that the rewarding effects of psychostimulants would similarly be lost in the absence of DAT. Although initial studies suggested that the rewarding and reinforcing effects of cocaine were still present in DAT knockout mice (Rocha et al., 1998; Sora et al., 1998), these findings were disputed in later studies. For example, Thomsen and coworkers (2009) ingeniously engineered a mutant DAT that was still functional for DA (i.e., was able to take up DA from the extracellular fluid) but was insensitive to cocaine. When these researchers tested mice homozygous for this mutant DAT on their responsiveness to IV cocaine, they found that the mice failed to self-administer the drug (above the levels of saline self-administration), in contrast to heterozygous mutants and wild-type mice (**Figure 12.9**).

Nucleus accumbens DA has also been implicated in cocaine reward using paradigms that test for **drug-seeking behavior** as a model of relapse in previously abstinent individuals. Such paradigms typically train animals to self-administer cocaine intravenously and then extinguish the operant response (e.g., pressing a

TABLE 12.2 Dopaminergic Projections to the Striatum and Nucleus Accumbens: Role in Psychostimulant-Induced Behaviors in Animals

Experimental manipulation	Brain area	Behavioral effect
Psychostimulant microinjection	Nucleus accumbens	Increased locomotor behavior
Psychostimulant microinjection	Striatum	Increased stereotyped behaviors
6-OHDA lesion	Nucleus accumbens	Decreased locomotor response following systemic administration of a low-dose psychostimulant
6-OHDA lesion	Striatum	Decreased stereotyped behaviors following systemic administration of a high-dose psychostimulant
6-OHDA lesion	Nucleus accumbens	Decreased reinforcing effectiveness of systemically administered psychostimulants
Amphetamine microinjection	Nucleus accumbens	Reinforcing to the animal
Cocaine microinjection	Nucleus accumbens	Reinforcing to the animal

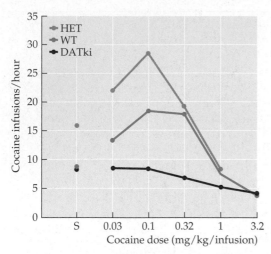

Figure 12.9 Lack of cocaine self-administration in mutant mice expressing a cocaine-insensitive DAT Mice were genetically engineered with a DAT "knockin" gene that produced a protein that transported DA across the cell membrane but was not blocked by cocaine. The graph shows the number of drug infusions per hour in wild-type (WT), homozygous DAT knockin (DATki), and heterozygous knockin (HET) mice. Note that the WT and HET groups showed significant dose-dependent cocaine self-administration that was abolished in the DATki group. The S data show the number of infusions obtained by each group when saline was substituted for cocaine. (After Thomsen et al., 2009.)

lever) by substituting saline for cocaine over a number of trials. Many studies have shown that following extinction, one can provoke a reinstatement of responding (i.e., drug seeking) by administering a single priming dose of cocaine to the animals through the IV catheter, despite the fact that the resumption of responding continues to result in the delivery of the saline vehicle instead of the drug. More relevant to the present discussion, two separate studies demonstrated that a reinstatement of cocaine-seeking behavior in previously extinguished rats could be stimulated by microinjection of either a D_1 or a D_2 DA receptor agonist directly into the nucleus accumbens (Bachtell et al., 2005; Schmidt et al., 2006). If these findings can be applied to human cocaine users, they suggest that DA acting within the nucleus accumbens may play an important role in the urge to take cocaine in dependent users who are attempting to maintain abstinence from their drug use.

Brain imaging has revealed the neural mechanisms of psychostimulant action in human subjects

Given the critical role of DA in the rewarding and reinforcing effects of psychostimulants, are the

mood-altering properties of these compounds in human users dependent on the same neurochemical system? Since researchers have not discovered any human subjects with genetic deletions of DAT, other experimental approaches are needed to address this question. One of the most exciting approaches has been to use brain imaging techniques such as positron emission tomography (PET) (see Chapter 4). For example, a research team headed by Nora Volkow, the current director of the National Institute on Drug Abuse, has used PET imaging to estimate DAT occupancy by behaviorally active doses of either cocaine or methylphenidate. Methylphenidate, a stimulant that is commonly used to treat attention deficit hyperactivity disorder (ADHD), also binds to DAT and blocks DA reuptake (ADHD is discussed further in Box 12.2, later in this chapter). This compound is preferred over cocaine for some studies because as a medication, it can be administered ethically to non-drug-abusing subjects, whereas cocaine cannot.

The studies of Volkow and colleagues (1999a) indicate that once a certain minimum level of DAT occupancy (about 40% to 60%) is attained following either cocaine or methylphenidate administration, the subject *may* experience a drug-induced "high." However, the intensity of the "high" and even the likelihood that a "high" will occur depend not only on the amount of DAT occupancy but also on at least two other factors. One factor is the rate at which transporter occupancy occurs after the drug has been taken. Thus routes of administration like smoking or IV injection that lead to quick drug entry into the brain and rapid DAT occupancy are more likely to produce an intense "high" than oral or intranasal administration, which are associated with delayed drug entry into the brain and slower DAT occupancy (Volkow et al., 1998, 2000). Although we don't yet know how the rate of DA reuptake blockade influences the subjective effects of psychostimulants, this information does help us understand why smoking and IV injection of psychostimulants have greater addiction potential than other routes of administration.

A second factor influencing the psychostimulant "high" is believed to be the baseline level of DA activity in the mesolimbic pathway. Volkow's group found that even with IV administration of cocaine or methylphenidate, some subjects failed to experience a "high," even with 60% or greater DAT occupancy, as indicated by PET imaging (Volkow et al., 1997, 1999b). However, when a different imaging procedure was used to assess the effects of IV methylphenidate on the occupancy of D_2 receptors by DA (not by the drug), there was a high correlation between this measure and the subjective "high" (Volkow et al., 1999c). What does this result mean? Imagine two subjects, A and

B. Because of individual differences in dopaminergic system activity, subject A starts with a relatively low level of baseline DA release, whereas subject B starts with a relatively high level of release. Both subjects are now given sufficient methylphenidate or cocaine to produce 60% DAT occupancy. Even with equivalent amounts of reuptake blockade, the effect of this blockade on stimulating postsynaptic DA receptors will be greater in subject B than in subject A because of the higher initial concentration of DA molecules in the synaptic cleft (**Figure 12.10**).

Several DA receptor subtypes mediate the functional effects of psychostimulants

Given that the functional effects of psychostimulants are dependent primarily on inhibition of DA uptake and the resulting increase in synaptic DA levels, it is necessary to consider which postsynaptic DA receptor subtypes mediate these effects. You will recall from Chapter 5 that there are five DA receptor subtypes: D_1 to D_5. D_1 and D_5 constitute the D_1-like family, whereas the D_2-like family comprises the D_2, D_3, and D_4 receptors. Numerous pharmacological studies have shown that relatively nonselective antagonists at either the D_1-like or the D_2-like family of receptors can reduce both the behaviorally activating and reinforcing effects of psychostimulants (Gold et al., 1989; Bergman et al., 1990; Fibiger et al., 1992). The obvious limitation of these studies is their inability to distinguish which member(s) of each receptor family are critical for the response being measured.

Fortunately, some progress in this area has come from the use of genetic knockouts lacking a particular DA receptor. With respect to the locomotor-stimulating effects of cocaine, the knockout studies have shown that D_1 receptors are absolutely required for such effects (Xu et al., 1994), whereas D_2 receptors are not (Chausmer et al., 2002). Likewise, mice lacking D_2 receptors were reported to self-administer cocaine, although with some differences in dose–response function compared with wild-type mice (Caine et al., 2002). In contrast, D_1 receptor knockout mice do not self-administer cocaine, which suggests a critical role for this receptor subtype in cocaine reinforcement (Caine et al., 2007).

Other intriguing results have come from pharmacological studies involving D_3 receptors, which are present in mesolimbic DA areas such as the nucleus accumbens. Recall from Chapter 9 that the rewarding effects of abused drugs like cocaine can be assessed by their ability to reduce the threshold for electrical self-stimulation of the brain. As shown in **Figure 12.11**, the D_3 receptor antagonist SB-277011-A completely blocked this effect of cocaine (Vorel et al., 2002). A more recent study found that YQA14, a novel D_3 receptor antagonist with greater selectivity than SB-277011-A, dose dependently inhibited cocaine self-administration in both rats and mice (Song et al., 2012). Together, these and other findings indicate an

(A) Low baseline DA release

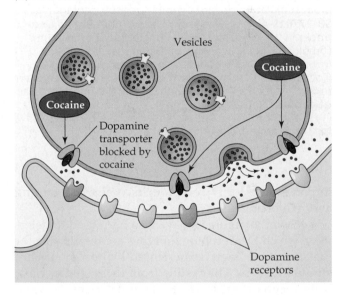

(B) High baseline DA release

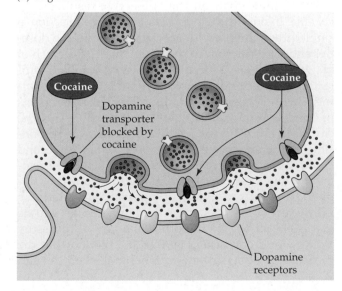

Figure 12.10 Hypothesized role of baseline DA release in the reinforcing effects of psychostimulants If the baseline level of release is low (A), then partial inhibition of DA reuptake by cocaine or methylphenidate has relatively little effect on postsynaptic DA receptor activation or behavior. However, if baseline DA release is high (B), then the same reuptake inhibition produces much greater receptor activation and more intense behavioral and subjective effects.

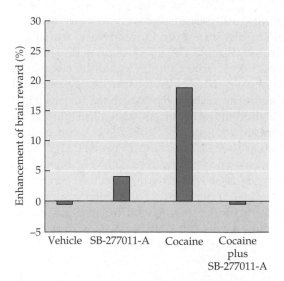

Figure 12.11 Prevention of cocaine's enhancement of brain stimulation reward by the D₃ receptor antagonist SB-277011-A Rats were implanted with stimulating electrodes in the medial forebrain bundle, and the minimum stimulus frequency capable of eliciting self-stimulation (reward threshold) was determined for each animal. Cocaine (2 mg/kg intraperitoneally) reliably enhanced brain reward by decreasing the reward threshold. This effect was completely blocked by SB-277011-A at a dose (3 mg/kg intraperitoneally) that had no significant effect by itself on the reward threshold. (After Vorel et al., 2002.)

important role for D_3 receptors in cocaine's rewarding and reinforcing effects.

Receptor antagonists have also been used to determine which DA receptor subtypes are responsible for the subjective "high" experienced by human psychostimulant users. The results from these studies have been inconsistent thus far. Two different research groups determined the influence of ecopipam, a D_1-like antagonist, on the subjective responses to cocaine. In one study involving IV cocaine injection, a single pretreatment with ecopipam produced a dose-dependent reduction in the drug "high" (Romach et al., 1999), whereas in another study in which subjects smoked cocaine base, several days of pretreatment with ecopipam actually increased self-reports of "high" (Haney et al., 2001). It is possible that the chronic administration of the antagonist was responsible for the unexpected effects observed in the second study. Other investigators found that acute pretreatment with either pimozide (D_2-like antagonist) or fluphenazine (mixed D_1/D_2 antagonist) had relatively little effect on amphetamine euphoria (Brauer and de Wit, 1995, 1997). On the other hand, two studies by Volkow and coworkers (1999, 2002) found that the pleasurable effects of methylphenidate were related

to low D_2 receptor availability in the striatum prior to drug administration. Considering these findings together, it appears that the role of specific DA receptor subtypes in the mood-elevating effects of psychostimulants still remains to be determined.

Section Summary

- Cocaine exerts powerful effects on mood and behavior. The cocaine "high" is characterized by feelings of exhilaration, euphoria, well-being, heightened energy, and enhanced self-confidence. Smoked or intravenously injected cocaine also causes a "rush" in the user.

- At high doses and/or with prolonged use, cocaine can give rise to a number of negative effects such as irritability, anxiety, exhaustion, total insomnia, and even psychotic symptomatology.

- In animal studies, cocaine elicits locomotor stimulation and, at higher doses, stereotyped behaviors.

- Cocaine can function as a discriminative stimulus, and it exhibits powerful reinforcing effects in standard self-administration paradigms.

- Physiologically, cocaine produces sympathomimetic effects such as increased heart rate, vasoconstriction, hypertension, and hyperthermia. High doses can be toxic or even fatal as the result of seizures, heart failure, stroke, or intracranial hemorrhage.

- Most of the subjective and behavioral effects of cocaine have been attributed to DAT inhibition and the resulting activation of dopaminergic transmission, particularly in the nucleus accumbens and striatum.

- Using different testing paradigms, D_1, D_2, and D_3 DA receptors have all been shown to play various roles in mediating the behavioral and possibly also the subjective effects of cocaine exposure.

Cocaine Abuse and the Effects of Chronic Cocaine Exposure

Most individuals who try cocaine do not progress to a pattern of abuse or dependence. Those who develop cocaine dependence experience tolerance and/or sensitization, and many adverse health effects including brain abnormalities and cognitive deficits. Treatments for cocaine dependence have yielded mixed results, with pharmacotherapies being especially disappointing thus far.

Experimental cocaine use may escalate over time to a pattern of cocaine abuse and dependence

Cocaine users give many different reasons for their initial decision to use the drug. Some of these reasons are to satisfy their curiosity; to facilitate social interactions; to relieve feelings of depression, anxiety, or guilt; to have fun and celebrate; or simply to get "high." Cocaine users typically describe early experimentation with both legal (e.g., alcohol) and illegal drugs, often beginning by 13 or 14 years of age. Early use of other substances may therefore be an important risk factor for the initiation of cocaine use.

People usually begin taking cocaine via the intranasal route, that is, by snorting it. As mentioned above, initial cocaine use most frequently does not lead to subsequent abuse or dependence. There are various reasons why the majority of people who try cocaine either do not continue their use, or if they do, they do not subsequently undergo a transition to cocaine abuse or dependence. Some individuals report a strong anxiety response as their initial reaction to cocaine and are thereby dissuaded from further experimentation. Other factors may likewise mitigate against the development of a long-term abuse pattern, including unavailability of the drug, the cost of maintaining a steady supply, the social and legal consequences of illicit drug use, and the very real fear of losing control over one's drug-taking behavior. These factors often lead to a termination of cocaine use, although there are some intranasal users who maintain long-term periodic and controlled cocaine consumption.

Surveys performed by the National Institute on Drug Abuse suggest that approximately 10% to 15% of initial intranasal users eventually become cocaine abusers. A smaller percentage, namely, 5% to 6%, already meet criteria for cocaine dependence within 24 months after their first use (O'Brien and Anthony, 2005). The details of this transition process certainly vary for different individuals, yet a few factors have been identified that may generally be important. The stimulating, euphoric, and confidence-enhancing effects described earlier provide a powerful reinforcing effect during the early stages of cocaine use. Furthermore, these aspects of cocaine reinforcement may be augmented by social responses from friends and acquaintances who respond positively to the user's newfound energy and enthusiasm. Over time, cocaine use escalates as the individual discovers that higher doses produce a more powerful euphoric effect. Even more importantly, the user may switch from intranasal administration to crack smoking, freebasing, or IV injection. For many, this is a significant event in their drug history because of the greater abuse potential of these latter routes of administration. Moreover, some individuals develop a pattern of **cocaine binges**, which are episodic bouts of repeated use lasting from hours to days with little or no sleep. During these periods, nothing is important to the user except maintaining the "high," and all available supplies of cocaine are consumed in this pursuit. A 3-day freebasing binge may involve the consumption of as much as 150 g of cocaine, which is an enormous amount. More than 25 years ago, Gawin and Kleber (1986, 1988) reported the presence of an abstinence syndrome that they observed following a cocaine binge. They proposed that this abstinence syndrome occurred in three phases, which they called *crash*, *withdrawal*, and *extinction*. During the crash, the user feels exhausted and suffers from a depressed mood. Later, during the withdrawal phase, some of the important symptoms include anhedonia (inability to experience normal pleasures), anergia (a lack of energy), anxiety, and a growing craving for cocaine that increases the risk of relapse. Symptoms subside during the extinction phase.

Other factors may also contribute to the transition from recreational cocaine use to abuse and dependence, to the maintenance of excessive cocaine use, and/or to relapse in individuals who are attempting to achieve abstinence from the drug. As described in Chapter 9 for drug addiction generally, such factors may include comorbidity with other psychiatric disorders, such as depression, anxiety disorders, or personality disorders, stress, exposure to environmental stimuli previously associated with cocaine use, or cocaine priming (i.e., exposure to a small amount of the drug that elicits craving for more) (Bossert et al., 2005; Crombag et al., 2008; Mahoney et al., 2007; Schottenfeld et al., 1993). Interestingly, animal studies indicate that cocaine craving and relapse to cocaine use actually increase over time (although not permanently) following withdrawal from drug use (Lu et al., 2004). This phenomenon, which has been termed **incubation** of cocaine craving, is consistent with the high rate of relapse in cocaine-dependent individuals, even those enrolled in treatment programs (see later in this chapter). Moreover, subjects diagnosed as cocaine-dependent show abnormal prefrontal cortical functioning that is manifested as deficits in inhibitory control and in monitoring and evaluating the consequences of their behavior (Garavan and Hesster, 2007). While these cognitive deficits may, in some cases, precede rather than be a consequence of their drug use, neuroimaging studies in monkeys have demonstrated that repeated cocaine exposure leads to increased effects on the prefrontal cortex compared with the effects observed at the initial dosing (Beveridge et al.,

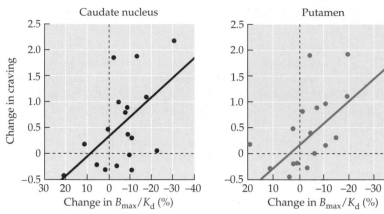

Figure 12.12 Relationship between striatal DA release and craving elicited by exposure to cocaine-related visual stimuli. Cocaine-addicted subjects were exposed to a video of cocaine-related cues including purchase, preparation, and smoking of the drug while undergoing PET scanning of striatal DA release measured by DA displacement of radiolabeled raclopride from D_2 receptors. The y-axis of the graph plots changes in subjective cocaine craving from before to the end of the video. The x-axis plots changes in DA release measured by alterations in raclopride binding. Significant positive correlations were found for both the caudate nucleus and the putamen, indicating that cue-induced cocaine craving is associated with heightened striatal DA release. (After Volkow et al., 2006.)

2008). These findings imply that at least some of the cognitive problems present in cocaine-dependent individuals may be traced to their history of drug use.

Neuroimaging studies have provided us with information on the neurobiology of cocaine craving in regular users of the drug. Several such studies using PET imaging have found that DA release is increased in the dorsal striatum (i.e., caudate and putamen) when cocaine users (diagnosed as having cocaine dependence in some of the cited studies) are presented with cocaine-related stimuli such as videotapes of subjects smoking cocaine (Volkow et al., 2006, 2008; Wong et al., 2006). These studies take advantage of the fact that raclopride, a drug that binds to D_2 receptors, can be displaced from the receptor by DA released from the dopaminergic nerve terminals. Consequently, reductions in raclopride binding as measured by PET imaging are interpreted as increased local DA release. The data shown in **Figure 12.12** illustrate the significant correlation between the craving elicited by the cocaine cues in one study and this measure of DA release in the caudate and putamen (Volkow et al., 2006). An increase in extracellular striatal DA by itself, as produced by oral methylphenidate administration, did not elicit cocaine craving unless cocaine cues were also presented (Volkow et al., 2008). This result suggests that brain areas that are responsive to emotional stimuli and that project to the midbrain DA neurons (e.g., excitatory glutamate inputs from the prefrontal cortex and/or the amygdala) may be involved in eliciting

this cue-related increase in striatal DA release. Finally, we should mention that research using functional magnetic resonance imaging (fMRI), which measures regional neural activity independently of specific neurotransmitters, has implicated many additional brain areas besides the striatum in the process of cocaine craving (e.g., Risinger et al., 2005). Thus, we can conclude that the midbrain–striatal DA pathway is part of a larger circuit that is activated when cocaine users experience craving for the drug.

Animal models can simulate the transition from recreational to compulsive cocaine use

Voluntary drug self-administration by an operant behavior such as a lever press or a nose poke has been a central approach in the quest to develop animal models of cocaine dependence. However, just as some people take cocaine recreationally even for long periods of time, yet do not develop a pattern of abuse or dependence, we cannot assume that mere self-administration by a rat or a mouse is equivalent to dependence on the drug. As discussed by Roberts and colleagues (2007), some of the aspects of cocaine dependence that have been modeled by animal researchers include (1) an escalation of drug intake by self-administering animals, (2) relapse to cocaine-seeking behavior after a period of abstinence, (3) cocaine-seeking behavior despite aversive consequences, and (4) increased breaking point when working to self-administer the drug on a progressive ratio schedule. Because of space limitations, we will present just a few examples of this type of research.

The first example comes from two seminal papers by Ahmed[3] and coworkers (Ahmed and Koob, 1998; Ahmed et al., 2002) in which they compared rats given a relatively short (1 hour per session) period of access to the cocaine self-administration procedure with animals given a long (6 hours per session) period of access. The first thing that they discovered was that the long-access (LgA) rats gradually escalated their daily cocaine intake, in contrast to the stable daily intake of the short-access (ShA) animals (**Figure 12.13A**). This dose escalation could be seen even when the first hour of cocaine intake in the LgA rats was compared with

---

[3]This is the same Serge Ahmed whose later work on cocaine versus sweetened water reward is highlighted in Box 12.1.

(A) Total intake

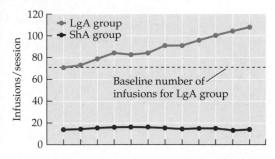

(B) First hour intake

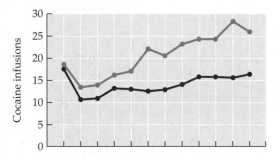

(C) Reward thresholds

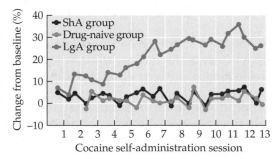

Cocaine self-administration session

Figure 12.13 Escalation of drug intake and increased reward thresholds in rats given long access to IV cocaine (A) Rats were initially trained to lever-press for IV cocaine infusions, after which the animals were divided into two groups: a short-access group (ShA) that had access to cocaine for 1-hour sessions, and a long-access group (LgA) that had access to cocaine for 6-hour sessions. Session 1 shown here is the first day of each experimental condition. The ShA rats maintained a low and stable intake across all 12 sessions. The LgA rats self-administered much more cocaine than the ShA animals even on session 1 because of the longer period of drug availability (6 hours versus 1 hour). Importantly, cocaine self-administration began to escalate in the LgA rats within a few sessions and continued to rise through the 12 sessions of the experiment. (B) Using the same escalation paradigm, LgA rats were shown to increase their cocaine-taking behavior even during the first hour of self-administration compared with the ShA group. (C) Thresholds for electrical self-stimulation of the brain were increased during the period of escalating cocaine intake in the LgA rats. Note that there was no change in the mean stimulation threshold for the ShA rats, which was similar to stimulation threshold measured in a drug-naive group. (A after Ahmed and Koob, 1998; B,C after Ahmed et al., 2002.)

A second example chosen for presentation is from an equally significant series of studies conducted by Deroche-Gamonet and colleagues (2004). They allowed their rats to self-administer cocaine over approximately 3 months, which is much longer than the typical study in this area. During this time period, they repeatedly tested their animals for the following aspects of cocaine dependence: (1) persistence of cocaine-seeking behavior during periods when the rats were given a cue that the drug was not available; (2) continued cocaine self-administration despite aversive consequences (electrical foot shock delivered at the same time as the drug infusion); (3) enhanced motivation for cocaine as indicated by an increase in the breaking point on a progressive ratio schedule; and (4) vulnerability to relapse based on a reinstatement procedure using a priming dose of cocaine following 5 days of abstinence from the drug. Importantly, because the investigators found a wide range of differences among the rats on these measures, they used the results from the reinstatement procedure to divide the animals into two groups: the top 40% with the highest amount of responding on the reinstatement test (HRein), and the lowest 40% in terms of responding on this test (LRein). All of the results were subsequently analyzed and presented as comparisons between these two subgroups. As presented in Figure 12.14, as the number of days of cocaine self-administration progressed, the HRein rats but not the LRein rats showed a sharp rise in number of responses (in this case, nose pokes) during the signaled no-drug period (**Figure 12.14A**), an increase in the number of cocaine infusions taken despite concurrent foot shock (**Figure 12.14B**), a significantly higher breaking point for cocaine self-administration (**Figure 12.14C**), and of course substantially greater responding

the single hour of intake allowed in the ShA rats (**Figure 12.13B**). To determine the neurobiological mechanism underlying this increase in cocaine self-administration, the researchers determined the thresholds for electrical self-stimulation of brain with electrodes implanted in the lateral hypothalamus. These measurements were taken both 3 hours and around 17 to 22 hours following the end of each self-administration session. The data show a clear elevation in the amount of current required to obtain electrical self-stimulation in the LgA rats compared with ShA animals or naive (drug-free) controls, indicating a dysfunction in the brain's reward circuit (**Figure 12.13C**). Together, the data reveal that longer periods of access to cocaine can lead to an escalation of intake that, in turn, down-regulates the reward circuit. This presumably makes the cocaine less rewarding and thus supports further increases in drug consumption, which parallels some of the reported findings (i.e., reduced cocaine-induced euphoria accompanied by increased use) in the clinical drug literature (Small et al., 2009).

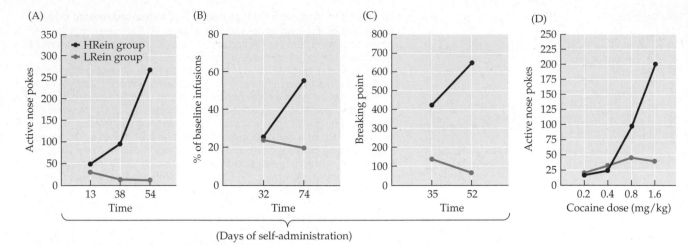

Figure 12.14 Emergence of addictive-like behaviors in a subgroup of rats self-administering cocaine over a long time period Rats self-administered IV cocaine by making a nose-poke response. The animals were divided into two groups: high cocaine reinstatement (HRein) and low reinstatement (LRein) based on the number of nose pokes when a priming dose of cocaine signaled renewed availability of the drug following a 5-day withdrawal period. The results show that the HRein group compared with the LRein group increased their cocaine-seeking behavior during periods of no drug availability (A), obtained a greater number of cocaine infusions when electric shock was paired with drug delivery (data expressed as % of baseline number of infusions) (B), showed a higher breaking point on a progressive ratio schedule (C), and showed a higher response rate in the reinstatement paradigm at the highest dose of cocaine (D). (After Deroche-Gamonet et al., 2004.)

for the higher doses of cocaine during the reinstatement test (**Figure 12.14D**). Based on these and other findings not shown, the researchers concluded that addiction results from a combination of prolonged exposure to the drug, which can be seen from the fact that changes in behavior occurred only after many self-administration sessions, and factors that lead to differential vulnerability among individuals, which accounts for the fact that only the HRein group showed these behavioral changes.

A third, more recent example comes from two studies by Belin and coworkers (2008, 2011). In the two studies together, researchers examined the potential role of three different traits in predicting the transition from mere self-administration of cocaine to compulsive use: (1) locomotor activity in response to a novel (inescapable) environment (one type of an animal model of novelty- or sensation-seeking in humans); (2) preference for a novel environment in a free-choice situation (an alternate animal model of novelty- or sensation-seeking behavior); and (3) impulsivity measured using a five-choice serial reaction-time visual attention task (a task that measures several behavioral parameters, including impulsive responding by the subject). Although the two studies had different aims, the results indicated a role for both sensation seeking (using the free-choice task; Belin et al., 2011) and impulsivity (Belin et al., 2008) in the development of compulsive cocaine-taking behavior in rats. These findings provide new support for the hypothesis that these two personality traits play a significant role in determining whether an individual who uses cocaine goes on to develop a pattern of cocaine abuse or dependence.

The point of this section is to emphasize that the development of valid animal models of drug abuse and dependence requires that researchers pay close attention to the range of clinical symptoms considered to be representative of the drug-dependent state and to determine the best experimental paradigms for reproducing those symptoms. The examples presented earlier show that progress in this area has been made with respect to cocaine abuse and dependence. Nevertheless, as we discuss later in the section on treatments for cocaine dependence, progress in developing new medications, which relies heavily on the results of animal model research, has been very disappointing thus far. Consequently, there is a critical need for continued exploration of novel models that will yield better predictability so that success of a newly developed medication in our animal models will translate to equivalent success when the medication is brought to human clinical trials.

Chronic psychostimulant exposure can give rise to tolerance or sensitization

As with many drugs, chronic exposure to psychostimulants can lead to reduced responsiveness, or tolerance. Yet the reverse effect, namely, sensitization, is also

(A)

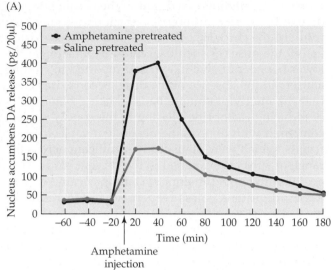

(B)

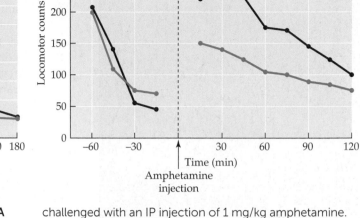

Figure 12.15 Amphetamine microinjection into the VTA causes sensitization to the behavioral and neurochemical effects of a subsequent systemic amphetamine challenge. Rats received three microinjections of either 2.5 μg/side D-amphetamine (red) or saline (blue) into the VTA over a 6-day period. Two weeks later, the animals were challenged with an IP injection of 1 mg/kg amphetamine. The amphetamine-pretreated rats exhibited greater DA release in the nucleus accumbens (A) and greater locomotor activity (B) than the saline-pretreated group. (After Vezina, 2004.)

often seen with psychostimulants. One of the amazing aspects of sensitization is that just a few exposures to cocaine or amphetamine can produce an increased responsiveness that lasts for weeks, months, or even up to at least a year (Paulson et al., 1991). Although this kind of long-lasting sensitization has usually been studied in experimental animals, a laboratory study by Boileau and colleagues (2006) demonstrated sensitized behavioral and neurochemical responses to amphetamine at 1 year after a mere four doses of the drug given orally to human subjects over a 2-week period.

How can psychostimulants produce both tolerance and sensitization? Various studies have shown that which kind of change you observe depends on the pattern of drug exposure, the response that's being measured, and the time interval that has elapsed since the last dose. For example, continuous cocaine infusion into rats causes tolerance to the drug's locomotor-stimulating effect (Inada et al., 1992), whereas once-daily cocaine injections lead to behavioral sensitization, as shown by enhanced stereotyped behaviors (Post and Contel, 1983). Sensitization can be divided into two phases: **induction**, which means the process by which sensitization is established, and **expression**, which refers to the process by which the sensitized response is manifested. During the period between these two phases (i.e., after the last drug dose has been administered), sensitization can actually increase in strength as the result of ongoing neurochemical changes in the brain.

In human cocaine users, evidence for both tolerance and sensitization has been observed, depending on what is being measured (Narendran and Martinez, 2008; Small et al., 2009). Importantly, researchers have generally reported that cocaine's euphoric effects tend to show tolerance over time, which would contribute to increased drug-taking behavior in an attempt to recapture the level of pleasure experienced during earlier episodes of use.

The neural mechanisms underlying both psychostimulant tolerance and sensitization have been studied extensively in animal models and to a lesser extent in humans using brain imaging methods. Animal studies have shown that the DA activity in the ventral tegmental area (VTA) plays an important role in locomotor sensitization to psychostimulants. This can be seen in **Figure 12.15**, in which animals given amphetamine pretreatment directly into the VTA show greatly heightened release of DA in the nucleus accumbens and an increased locomotor response when challenged later with a systemic injection of amphetamine (Vezina, 2004). However, the VTA is not the only brain region important for sensitization, as there is also evidence for alterations in the medial prefrontal cortex (which sends a glutamatergic projection to the VTA and nucleus accumbens) that contribute to cocaine sensitization (Steketee, 2005).

In contrast to the enhanced DA release that accompanies psychostimulant sensitization, PET imaging of cocaine-dependent individuals has indicated reduced

Placebo   MP

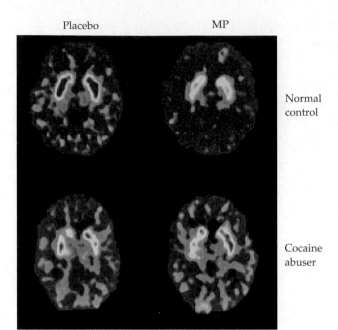

Normal control

Cocaine abuser

Figure 12.16 PET images showing striatal binding of radiolabeled raclopride in a cocaine abuser and a normal control subject after receiving either a placebo treatment or 0.5 mg/kg methylphenidate (MP) IV. Compared with the control, the cocaine-abusing subject had lower baseline raclopride binding (Placebo) and showed little reduction in binding following MP administration (compare the Placebo versus MP image for each subject). Highest levels of binding are shown in red. (From Volkow et al., 1997.)

DA activity in the striatum in response to a drug challenge (Narendran and Martinez, 2008). One experimental approach in this literature has been to label striatal DA receptors with the drug raclopride, which binds to the receptors sufficiently weakly that it can be displaced by the subject's endogenous DA (see the discussion of the experimental results presented earlier in Figure 12.12). Subjects are then challenged with methylphenidate, which increases extracellular (including synaptic) DA by blocking DA reuptake. If the DA neurons are releasing a large amount of DA, then the methylphenidate challenge will lead to a large decrease in radiolabeled raclopride binding because of competition from the DA that could not be taken up by the dopaminergic nerve terminals. On the other hand, if the amount of DA release is relatively low, then there will be a lower effect of the methylphenidate challenge on raclopride binding to the D_2 receptors. **Figure 12.16** from a study by Volkow and colleagues (1997) presents PET images from a typical healthy control subject compared with those from a representative cocaine-dependent subject under both baseline conditions (Placebo) and following the methylphenidate challenge (MP). Two things are evident from these images. First, the baseline level of

D_2 receptor binding is reduced in the cocaine-dependent subject. This difference, which either may be a result of the chronic cocaine use or may have existed before the onset of such use, could be a factor in the lower (i.e., depressive-like) mood reported in cocaine abusers in the absence of the drug. Second, it is clear that the methylphenidate had a much greater effect of reducing raclopride binding in the control subject compared with the cocaine-dependent subject. These results, which were statistically significant across the range of subjects examined in the present study, suggest that the dopaminergic system in cocaine-dependent individuals is less responsive to DA reuptake blockade (as would be produced by cocaine itself if given instead of methylphenidate), which is likely to contribute to the behavioral tolerance to cocaine that was mentioned earlier.

Repeated or high-dose cocaine use can produce serious health consequences

Cocaine use, especially at high doses, can have many adverse physiological and behavioral consequences. As we saw earlier, a single dose of cocaine may trigger a stroke or a seizure. But even without such drastic consequences, regular cocaine use has been associated with deleterious effects on brain structure and function. Various types of neuroimaging methods have shown that individuals who are abusing or are dependent on cocaine have abnormalities in both gray and white matter in the cerebral cortex and decreased volume of some cortical regions as well as the striatum (Barrós-Loscertales et al., 2011; Franklin et al., 2002; Lim et al., 2008). Other studies have compared neuropsychological test performance of abstinent cocaine-abusing subjects with that of control subjects. Overall, the results indicate that cocaine abuse is associated with significant impairment in many different cognitive functions, including verbal memory, attention, and motor function (Toomey et al., 2003; Browndyke et al., 2004). These cognitive deficits are likely to be related to some combination of the structural abnormalities just discussed, neurotransmitter-related (e.g., DA) dysfunction, or deficits in regional blood flow or glucose utilization.

Other organs or organ systems such as the heart, lungs, gastrointestinal system, and kidneys can also be adversely affected by cocaine. Complications associated with the heart range from chest pains to cardiac arrhythmias (irregular heart rate), cardiac myopathy (damaged heart muscle), and even myocardial infarction (heart attack). Frequent snorting of cocaine can lead to perforation of the nasal septum (the tissue that separates the two sides of the nose). Finally, ingestion of cocaine by a pregnant woman has variable effects on the unborn child. Many offspring seem to escape without obvious harm; others may show attention deficits or other behavioral or cognitive abnormalities; and in a small number of cases, the fetus is killed prior to birth (Ackerman et al., 2010; Bandstra et al., 2010).

Behaviorally, high-dose cocaine use can lead to panic attacks or the development of a temporary paranoid psychosis with delusions and hallucinations. One particularly frightening type of hallucination is called "cocaine bugs," which refers to the sensation of tiny creatures crawling over the user's skin. More than 100 years ago, some of Freud's colleagues were already seeing patients with these kinds of psychotic reactions. Cocaine psychosis occurs more frequently with repeated use, which is consistent with a growing sensitization to the drug.

Pharmacological, behavioral, and psychosocial methods are used to treat cocaine abuse and dependence

High rates of cocaine abuse and dependence in our society have spurred a great deal of interest in developing effective therapies for cocaine users. We will describe pharmacotherapeutic approaches, the idea of a cocaine vaccine, and programs that rely on behavioral and psychosocial methods.

PHARMACOTHERAPIES A large variety of compounds targeting several different neurotransmitters have been tested as potential medications to help cocaine users stop their current use and then to help maintain abstinence. All of the drugs to be mentioned below have demonstrated effectiveness in animal (usually rodent) models of cocaine-seeking behavior and/or cocaine relapse, and most have been tested at least minimally in human clinical trials. As we will discuss, some compounds seem more promising at the present moment than others on the basis of recent clinical testing. However, before continuing, we wish to emphasize that at the time of this writing, despite an enormous amount of effort devoted to the development of cocaine medications, there is not a single clinically licensed medication for this purpose. There are many reasons for this lack of success, but the main ones concern lack of therapeutic efficacy when the compound was tested in larger double-blind clinical trials, unacceptable side effects, or a combination of both.

For many years, the National Institute on Drug Abuse has been the main driving force in the effort to identify medications for cocaine dependence. At least some of this effort has been directed toward reducing cocaine's euphoric effects and/or the craving that ensues during cocaine withdrawal. Because of the well-known role of DA in cocaine reinforcement in animal models and its presumed involvement in

human cocaine addiction, much attention has been directed to various dopaminergic drugs, including receptor agonists, antagonists, and uptake inhibitors, that might compete with cocaine for access to the DA transporter (Platt et al., 2002). Most of these compounds have ultimately failed testing somewhere along the line, but there is current interest in several agents, including aripiprazole (a second-generation antipsychotic drug that is a partial agonist at both D_2 and $5-HT_{1A}$ receptors), methylphenidate, D_3 receptor antagonists, and atypical DA transporter inhibitors based on the structure of benztropine (Heidbreder and Newman, 2010; Karila et al., 2008; Tanda et al., 2009). Other drugs being studied as potential cocaine medications target neurotransmitters other than DA, including 5-HT, glutamate, and GABA (Kampman, 2010; Karila et al., 2008; Uys and LaLumiere, 2008).

Two very different compounds have recently attracted significant attention as potential therapeutic medications for cocaine dependence. One is modafinil, a stimulant that is currently approved for the treatment of narcolepsy and obstructive sleep apnea (Martínez-Raga et al., 2008). This compound has a complex mode of action, with various effects on the DA, NE, glutamate, and GABA systems. A number of human laboratory and clinical trials have shown promising results with modafinil, although the trials have generally been of relatively short duration (no longer than 12 weeks, which is common in clinical testing until a drug reaches phase III clinical trials). One recent example is a double-blind placebo-controlled study by Anderson and coworkers (2009), who found that in conjunction with once-weekly standardized cognitive-behavioral therapy (see next section on behavioral and psychosocial therapies), daily modafinil administration significantly reduced cocaine use among cocaine-dependent subjects who were not also diagnosed with alcohol dependence.

The other compound gaining attention is an old drug, namely, disulfiram, which for years has been marketed as Antabuse for the treatment of alcohol dependence (see Chapter 10). A high percentage of heavy cocaine users also abuse alcohol, which, in part, may be due to the production of the bioactive metabolite cocaethylene. The discovery that disulfiram might help cocaine-dependent patients occurred serendipitously when Antabuse was administered to patients with dual cocaine and alcohol dependence, and the drug was found to curb not only alcohol use but also cocaine consumption (Gaval-Cruz and Weinshenker, 2009). Subsequent studies have shown that disulfiram is also therapeutically efficacious in cocaine-dependent subjects who are not alcohol abusers. The mechanism underlying this effect is still under investigation, but several possibilities have been proposed. In addition to inhibiting the enzyme aldehyde dehydrogenase (the basis for disulfiram's antialcohol efficacy), this compound inhibits dopamine β-hydroxylase (DBH), the enzyme that synthesizes NE from DA, and it inhibits esterases that are involved in the breakdown of cocaine. Gaval-Cruz and Weinshenker (2009) argue that DBH inhibition is likely to be the most important mechanism underlying disulfiram's anticocaine activity, possibly by modulating cocaine reward and/or aversiveness or by reducing relapse in abstinent users.

COCAINE VACCINE   Through a much different approach, researchers have shown that vaccines against cocaine can be developed. The resulting antibodies may simply bind cocaine molecules, or alternatively, they may have catalytic activity that actually breaks down cocaine in the bloodstream. Both methods cause less cocaine to get into the brain, and both have been shown to reduce (or even completely block) cocaine self-administration and reinstatement in animals. Cocaine-binding antibodies (but not catalytic antibodies) have been tested in several clinical trials. Thus far, the results are mixed, as some subjects who developed relatively high antibody titers in their bloodstream did show reduced cocaine use, but many other subjects showed a poorer response to the vaccination and continued a high level of cocaine use (Kinsey et al., 2010). The development of anticocaine vaccines continues to be an active area of research with the hope that this approach will eventually prove effective in reducing cocaine dependence.

BEHAVIORAL AND PSYCHOSOCIAL THERAPIES   It should be apparent that researchers have not yet discovered any compound that is broadly effective in treating cocaine abusers. Although this situation could change with the development of newer medications, it is necessary to consider the potential role of behavioral and social therapies in dealing with this problem. While pharmacotherapy may aid in patient stabilization (e.g., by reducing craving or other abstinence symptoms), equally important are counseling and support structures that enable the patient to learn new coping responses, avoid triggers for relapse, and function effectively in a drug-free lifestyle.

There are a variety of different treatment programs for cocaine-dependent individuals (Penberthy et al., 2010). Many are conducted on an outpatient basis, although the most severe cases usually receive the greatest benefit from hospitalization and either short- or long-term inpatient treatment. **Psychosocial treatment programs** involve individual, group, or family counseling designed to educate the user, promote behavioral change, and alleviate some of the problems caused by cocaine abuse. Cognitive-behavioral therapies are aimed at restructuring cognitive (thought) processes and training the user either to

avoid high-risk situations that might cause relapse or to employ appropriate coping mechanisms to manage such situations when they occur. This approach is sometimes called **relapse prevention therapy**. Also available are 12-step programs such as Narcotics Anonymous or Cocaine Anonymous. The general approach of all 12-step programs is based on that of Alcoholics Anonymous, which is described in Chapter 10.

One of the most interesting approaches to treating cocaine users was developed by Stephen Higgins and coworkers at the University of Vermont (Higgins et al., 1991). This **contingency management program** is a behavioral treatment approach based on the premise that drug taking is an operant response that persists mainly as a result of the reinforcing properties of the drug. Hence altering reinforcement contingencies to reduce drug-associated reinforcement and to increase the availability of nondrug reinforcers should help promote abstinence and the adoption of a drug-free lifestyle. As part of this program, each negative urine test of the client is reinforced with a voucher. These vouchers cannot be redeemed for money per se, to avoid patients accumulating funds for drug purchases; however, they can be exchanged for retail items available locally. Another aspect of this program involves a community reinforcement approach (Hunt and Azrin, 1973), which is designed to enhance the patient's social (including family) relationships, recreational activities, and job opportunities. Not only are contingency management programs more effective than standard behavioral therapies in reducing cocaine use, such programs can be made even more successful by combining the program with appropriate medication. This is illustrated in **Figure 12.17**, which shows the effectiveness of the selective serotonin reuptake inhibitor citalopram versus placebo in reducing cocaine use (assessed by the probability of cocaine-positive urine tests) in cocaine-dependent subjects also receiving a combination of contingency management and cognitive-behavioral therapy (Moeller et al., 2007).

Years of research and clinical testing have demonstrated the difficulty of finding effective medications to treat cocaine dependence. Contingency management programs have shown some success, but they are labor-intensive and costly, particularly when paired with community reinforcement methods. Readers should also take note of the fact in the early stages of testing, clinical trials typically last only 12 weeks, and it is usually unknown whether reductions in cocaine usage continue after termination of the treatment. Nevertheless, the impact of cocaine abuse and dependence on society both economically and in terms of human suffering warrants the continued search for better treatment approaches.

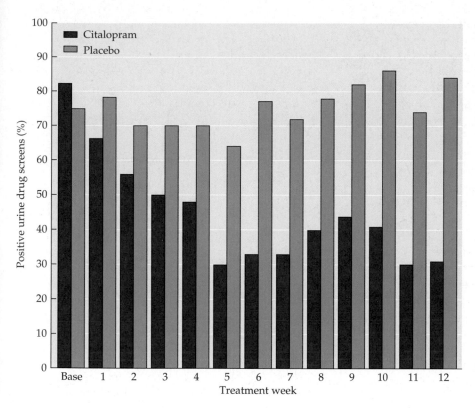

Figure 12.17 Abstinence from cocaine use over time in cocaine-dependent subjects treated with citalopram or placebo Treatment-seeking cocaine-dependent individuals received either 20 mg citalopram or placebo daily for 12 weeks in a double-blind study. All subjects additionally received cognitive-behavioral therapy and contingency management (awarding of vouchers for submitting twice-weekly drug-free urine samples). The graph illustrates the probability of cocaine-positive urine samples for subjects in each group over the course of the study. (After Moeller et al., 2007.)

Section Summary

- Early use of other substances seems to be an important risk factor for the initiation of cocaine use.

- Some users quickly stop taking cocaine for various reasons, some maintain controlled use for long periods, and still others progress to a pattern of uncontrolled use (i.e., abuse). Such a progression may come about through dose escalation and/or switching from intranasal use to smoking or IV injection—routes of administration with greater abuse potential.

- Cocaine abuse may be manifested by daily or near-daily use or by a pattern of bingeing. Many individuals who abuse cocaine also suffer from other psychiatric disorders.

- Cocaine craving and relapse to cocaine use increase over time following withdrawal, which has been called incubation of cocaine craving.

- Neuroimaging studies have found that cocaine-dependent subjects show abnormal prefrontal cortical functioning, and that cocaine-related cues elicit DA release in the dorsal striatum.

- Animal models of cocaine dependence include such features as escalation of drug intake, relapse to cocaine seeking after a period of abstinence, cocaine-seeking behavior despite aversive

consequences, and increased motivation to take cocaine as shown by an elevated breaking point on a progressive ratio schedule.

- Animal models have supported the hypothesis that both sensation seeking and impulsivity are traits that contribute to the development of compulsive cocaine use.

- Chronic exposure to cocaine or other psychostimulants can lead to tolerance and/or sensitization. Changes in drug responsiveness depend on the pattern of drug exposure, the outcome measure, and the time since the last dose.

- Animal studies have implicated increased dopaminergic activity in the VTA and increased nucleus accumbens DA release as being important for locomotor sensitization to psychostimulants.

- In contrast, human cocaine-dependent subjects show reduced DA release in the striatum compared with control subjects. However, this is consistent with evidence for tolerance to the drug's euphoric effects over time, thus leading to increased drug-taking behavior by these individuals.

- The adverse effects of repeated or high-dose cocaine use include stroke or seizure, abnormalities in both gray and white matter in the cortex, cardiovascular problems including heart attack, damage to other organ systems, and possible abnormalities in the development of offspring exposed prenatally to cocaine. High-dose cocaine use can also lead to panic attacks or the onset of a paranoid psychotic reaction.

- Finally, much effort in the area of treating cocaine abuse has been focused on the development of medications that might reduce craving and promote abstinence among users. Some of these medications act on the DA system (e.g., DA receptors or the DA transporter), whereas others that are being tested target the 5-HT, glutamate, and GABA systems. Two current drugs of interest for the treatment of cocaine dependence are modafinil and disulfiram. Anticocaine vaccines are also under experimental and clinical development.

- Current behavioral and psychosocial treatments include various types of counseling, cognitive-behavioral therapies aimed at relapse prevention, 12-step programs like Narcotics Anonymous and Cocaine Anonymous, and contingency management programs based on a combination of vouchers and a community reinforcement approach. Over time, these and other novel methods, along with new pharmacotherapies, may help reverse the devastating effects of cocaine on our society.

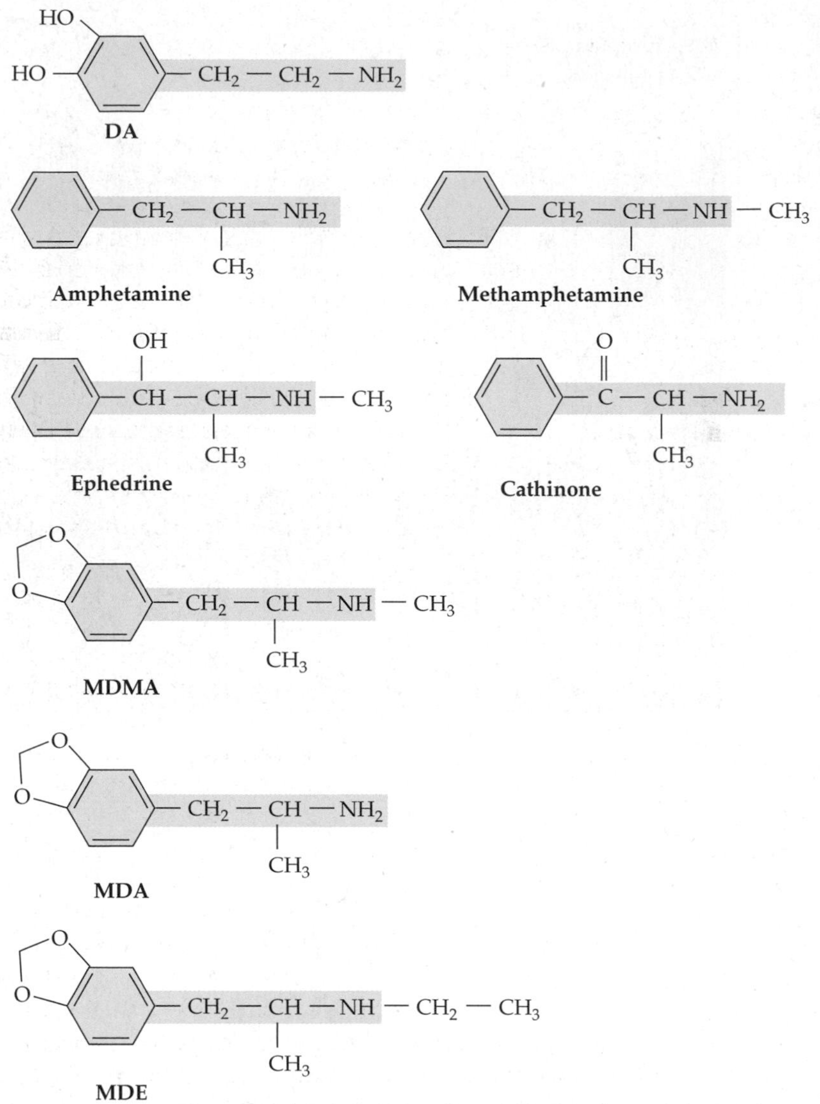

Figure 12.18 Amphetamine and related psychostimulants resemble the neurotransmitter DA in their chemical structure. This accounts for their potent effects on the dopaminergic system.

The Amphetamines

Background and History

Amphetamine is the parent compound of a family of synthetic psychostimulants. It is available in two chemical forms, L-amphetamine (trade name Benzedrine) and D-amphetamine (also called dextroamphetamine; trade name Dexedrine). Other members of this family are methamphetamine, 3,4-methylenedioxymethamphetamine (MDMA), 3,4-methylenedioxyamphetamine (MDA), and 3,4-methylenedioxy-N-ethylamphetamine (MDE). As can be seen in **Figure 12.18**, these compounds are structurally related to the neurotransmitter DA.

Figure 12.18 also shows two naturally occurring plant compounds that are similar in structure to amphetamine. One of these is cathinone, which is the

primary active ingredient in khat (alternately spelled qat) (*Catha edulis*), an evergreen shrub native to East Africa and the Arabian peninsula (**Figure 12.19**). A second amphetamine-like compound is ephedrine, which comes from the herb *Ephedra vulgaris*. Chinese physicians have used *Ephedra* (known to them as ma huang) for more than 5000 years as an herbal remedy. Like other amphetamine-like substances, ephedrine reduces appetite, and it also provides a subjective feeling of heightened energy. For these reasons, a number of companies began to market ephedra-containing dietary supplements as weight loss products sold in health food stores. These supplements became so popular that in 1999, the General Accounting Office estimated that Americans were consuming about 2

Figure 12.19 Khat for sale in an Ethiopian marketplace

billion doses of ephedra-containing products each year! Unfortunately, ephedrine sharply elevates blood pressure and exerts other sympathomimetic effects as well. These effects can increase the risk of heart attack or stroke, particularly with large drug doses or in vulnerable individuals. Because of the many reports of adverse reactions (including several deaths) associated with the use of ephedra, the U.S. Food and Drug Administration (FDA) became increasingly concerned about this substance. Then in February of 2003, national headlines were made when a young Baltimore Orioles pitcher named Steve Bechler collapsed and died during spring training in Florida. Struggling to control his weight, Bechler had been taking high doses of a popular ephedra-containing supplement, and the Broward County coroner ruled that ephedra was a likely contributory factor in the pitcher's death. As a consequence of this and other reported adverse reactions, the FDA officially banned the sale of ephedra-containing dietary supplements in 2004.

Interestingly, ephedra played a key role in the development of amphetamine. In the 1920s, purified ephedrine was found to be a valuable anti-asthmatic

agent because of its powerful bronchodilator (widening of the airways) action.[4] However, the medical profession soon became concerned that demand for ephedrine might exceed its supply and therefore began to search for an appropriate synthetic substitute. That substitute turned out to be amphetamine, which had first been synthesized in 1887 by Edeleano. The Smith, Kline & French pharmaceutical company introduced an amphetamine-containing inhaler in 1932. The inhaler, which contained 250 mg of Benzedrine in a cotton plug, proved to be effective in temporarily relieving nasal or bronchial congestion. Unfortunately, however, some individuals began to overuse these inhalers, particularly since many varieties could be purchased without a prescription. Other people learned to open the container, remove the amphetamine-containing plug, and chew the cotton, swallow it, or extract it to recover the drug for the purpose of injection. Amphetamine in tablet form was first marketed in 1935 as a treatment for a sleep disorder called **narcolepsy** (see the discussion on therapeutic uses of the drug). By the 1940s, amphetamine had become so widely embraced by the medical profession that one author documented 39 supposed clinical uses for the drug. In addition, many American military personnel were given amphetamine to forestall sleep and maintain a heightened level of alertness during prolonged periods on duty.

After World War II, the United States experienced a surge in the street use of amphetamine. During the 1950s and 1960s, students were casually using amphetamines in the same way that caffeine is presently taken to remain awake during pre-exam all-nighters. The peak of amphetamine use in the United States occurred during the early 1970s, when the legal production of amphetamine exceeded 10 billion (!) tablets, and at least one survey estimated that approximately 25% of young men had used stimulant drugs (mainly amphetamine or related compounds) on one or more occasions. Since that time, cocaine has generally supplanted amphetamine as the major abused psychostimulant. One exception to this trend has been a current upsurge in methamphetamine use in certain parts of the country.

In the following discussion, amphetamine and methamphetamine are presented together because of their similar neurochemical and behavioral effects. We will also consider recent developments in the recreational use and abuse of mephedrone and related

---

[4]Some decongestants still contain pseudoephedrine as their active ingredient, but availability of these drugs (i.e., having to obtain them from the pharmacist instead of their sitting on the shelf) is closely regulated since pseudoephedrine is used illegally to synthesize methamphetamine for street use.

compounds that are chemically related to cathinone. MDMA will not be covered here, as it was already discussed in Chapter 6 on serotonin.

Basic Pharmacology of the Amphetamines

Amphetamine is typically taken either orally or by IV or subcutaneous injection (the latter is sometimes called "skin popping"). Street names for amphetamine include "uppers," "bennies," "dexies," "black beauties," and "diet pills." Because absorption from the gastrointestinal tract is relatively slow, it may take up to 30 minutes for behavioral effects to be experienced after a typical oral dose of 5 to 15 mg. In contrast, IV injection provides a much more rapid and intense "high" than oral consumption and has much greater abuse potential.

Methamphetamine is more potent than amphetamine in its effects on the central nervous system and is therefore favored by substance abusers when it is available. Typical street names for methamphetamine are "meth," "speed," "crank," "zip," and "go." The drug can be taken orally, snorted, injected intravenously, or smoked. Smoking methamphetamine can be accomplished either by using a glass pipe or by heating the compound on a piece of aluminum foil (a practice sometimes called "chasing the dragon"). In the late 1970s, methamphetamine for recreational use was primarily being manufactured by various motorcycle gangs on the West Coast, and the practice of hiding the drug in motorcycle crankcases is what led to the street name "crank." Subsequently, methamphetamine hydrochloride in a crystalline form particularly suitable for smoking (called "ice" or "crystal" on the street) began showing up in Hawaii in the 1980s. This material has since spread to many parts of the country, particularly the West, South, and Midwest. Because "ice" is inexpensive to make and is highly addictive, it poses a serious risk for society's attempts to control and reduce the incidence of stimulant abuse (Gonzales et al., 2010; Maxwell and Rutkowski, 2008).

Some amphetamine or methamphetamine users (called "speed freaks") go on binges, or "runs," of repeated IV injections to experience recurrent highs. During a run, the drug is typically injected approximately every 2 hours for a period as long as 3 to 6 days or more. Little sleep or eating occurs during a run. The user finally becomes exhausted, ends the run, and goes to sleep for many hours. Barbiturates or other depressant drugs are sometimes used either to "take the edge off" during a run or to assist in sleeping following the run. Yet another approach is to moderate

the extreme stimulatory effect of IV amphetamine or methamphetamine by combining it with heroin to yield a so-called "speedball."

Amphetamine and methamphetamine are metabolized by the liver, although at a slow rate. Metabolites, as well as some unmetabolized drug molecules, are mainly excreted in the urine. The elimination half-life of amphetamine ranges from 7 to more than 30 hours depending on the pH of the urine. Methamphetamine has a similar half-life of approximately 10 hours. Because of these long half-lives, users obtain a much longer-lasting "high" from a single dose of amphetamine or methamphetamine than they can get from a dose of cocaine.

Mechanisms of Amphetamine and Methamphetamine Action

Amphetamine and methamphetamine are indirect agonists of the catecholaminergic systems. Unlike cocaine, which only blocks catecholamine reuptake, amphetamine and methamphetamine also release catecholamines from nerve terminals. At very high doses, these compounds can even inhibit catecholamine metabolism by monoamine oxidase.

Studies on the mechanism of catecholamine release by amphetamine have particularly focused on DA. The results of this research suggest that two related drug actions are involved. One action is to cause DA

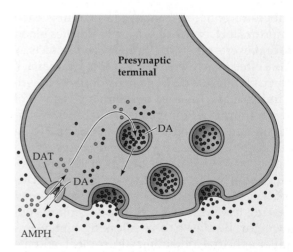

Figure 12.20 Mechanisms of amphetamine-stimulated DA release Amphetamine (AMPH) molecules enter DA nerve terminals in part through uptake by DAT. Once inside the terminal, the drug provokes DA release from the synaptic vesicles into the cytoplasm. In addition, DAT functions in a reverse direction to release DA from the cytoplasm into the extracellular fluid. The combined effect of these processes is a massive increase in synaptic DA levels.

molecules to be released from inside the vesicles into the cytoplasm of the nerve terminal. These DA molecules are subsequently transported outside of the terminal by a reversal of the DAT (**Figure 12.20**). The result is a massive increase in synaptic DA concentrations and an associated stimulation of dopaminergic transmission. Recent studies have shown that amphetamine-mediated reversal of DAT function is facilitated by an activation of protein kinase C and calcium/calmodulin kinase II, resulting in phosphorylation of the transporter (Robertson et al., 2009).

In animals, amphetamine- or methamphetamine-stimulated DA release has been demonstrated by using techniques such as in vivo microdialysis. Brain imaging studies have likewise provided evidence for DA release in humans following amphetamine administration either orally or by IV injection (Cárdenas et al., 2004; Drevets et al., 2001). It is important to recognize that the NE-releasing effects of amphetamines occur not only in the brain but also in the sympathetic nervous system. Consequently, these compounds exert potent sympathomimetic actions similar to those seen with cocaine.

Behavioral and Neural Effects of Amphetamines

Like cocaine, amphetamine causes heightened alertness, increased confidence, feelings of exhilaration, reduced fatigue, and a generalized sense of well-being in human users. A number of other effects have also been observed, including improved performance on simple, repetitive psychomotor tasks; a delay in sleep onset; and a reduction in sleep time, particularly with respect to REM (rapid-eye-movement) sleep. Indeed, amphetamine permits sustained physical effort without rest or sleep, which accounts for its distribution to military personnel during World War II, as well as its occasional use by truck drivers and other workers desirous of foregoing sleep for extended periods. The drug can also enhance athletic performance and is therefore one of the many banned substances in athletic competitions. In rodents and other animals, amphetamine elicits behavioral activation (locomotor stimulation and stereotypy) similar to that seen with cocaine. It is also highly reinforcing, as shown by numerous studies involving drug self-administration or place conditioning.

Amphetamine and methamphetamine have therapeutic applications but are also subject to abuse and dependence when used recreationally. Heavy use of these compounds can lead to psychotic reactions, neurotoxicity, and other adverse consequences.

Amphetamine and methamphetamine have therapeutic uses

As mentioned earlier, one medical use for amphetamine is in the treatment of narcolepsy; however, this drug is more recently being replaced by other stimulants such as modafinil (Didato and Nobili, 2009). Narcolepsy typically involves recurring and irresistible attacks of sleepiness during the daytime hours, often along with other symptoms, including cataplexy (sudden and transient loss of muscle tone that can be severe enough to cause bodily collapse, often brought about by strong emotional stimuli), hypnagogic hallucinations (vivid sensations that occur at the onset of sleep, upon awakening, or sometimes during a cataplectic attack), and sleep paralysis (muscle paralysis that persists after waking from a rapid-eye-movement sleep episode). Narcolepsy is caused by loss (perhaps autoimmune related) of hypothalamic neurons that secrete the neuropeptide hypocretin (also called orexin). Amphetamine and particularly methylphenidate are even more widely used in treating children with ADHD. This disorder is discussed further in **Box 12.2**.

Earlier in the chapter, Table 12.1 mentioned that cocaine has an anorexic effect (i.e., production of weight loss). Suppression of appetite and weight reduction are common to all psychostimulants, including not only cocaine but also amphetamine and methamphetamine. For many years, methamphetamine tablets (trade name Desoxyn) have been available as an antiobesity treatment. One of the mechanisms thought to underlie the appetite-suppressing effect of psychostimulants is the induction of an interesting neuropeptide called CART (cocaine- and amphetamine-regulated transcript) (Murphy, 2005). Needless to say, because of methamphetamine's high abuse potential, this treatment is now only rarely used to treat obese patients who have failed to respond to more conventional therapeutic approaches.

High doses or chronic use of amphetamines can cause a variety of adverse effects

Illicit use and abuse of amphetamines is a significant worldwide problem. The 2012 World Drug Report of the United Nations Office on Drugs and Crime reveals that 19 *metric tons* of amphetamine and 31 *metric tons* of methamphetamine were seized by authorities worldwide during 2010 (UNODC, 2012). Clandestine laboratories engaged in amphetamine production were found in dozens of countries. Additional data indicate that 14 million to 52.5 million people worldwide

BOX 12.2   Clinical Applications

Psychostimulants and ADHD

The most important clinical use for psychostimulants is in the treatment of a developmental disorder known as attention deficit hyperactivity disorder (ADHD). Children with ADHD exhibit extreme degrees of inattentiveness, impulsivity, and hyperkinesis (excessive motor activity). They have a very short attention span and impulsively turn their attention to almost anything in the environment. The *Diagnostic and Statistical Manual of Mental Disorders* identifies three different subtypes of ADHD: a predominantly inattentive subtype, a predominantly hyperactive–impulsive subtype, and a combined subtype. In severe cases of the hyperactive–impulsive or combined subtype, there may be destructiveness, stealing, lying, fire setting, and sexual "acting out." The child is frequently unruly in the classroom and disruptive of family interactions within the home.

ADHD is more prevalent in males than in females, but with differences in manifestation. Boys are more likely to exhibit hyperactivity and impulsivity, whereas girls are more likely to exhibit inattention (Rucklidge, 2010). Moreover, these sex differences tend to persist into adulthood. In general, adult ADHD patients show signs of distractibility, impulsivity, restlessness, hyperemotionality, and problems both at work and in interpersonal relationships. Moreover, such individuals are at heightened risk for developing conduct disorder, antisocial personality disorder, and/or substance abuse problems.

The relevance of psychostimulants for the treatment of ADHD is that low doses of these drugs produce a calming effect in more than half of affected children. This phenomenon was first reported by Bradley in 1937 and has since been observed in many other studies. Now many different stimulant medications are available for the treatment of ADHD that differ not only in the active ingredient but also in the length of action (short-acting, intermediate-acting, and long-acting). The active ingredient in most of these medications is D-amphetamine (e.g., Dexedrine), mixed amphetamine salts (e.g., Adderall), lisdexamfetamine (Vyvanse, which is a prodrug for D-amphetamine), or methylphenidate (e.g., Ritalin) (Kaplan and Newcorn, 2011). The major benefit of intermediate- and long-acting preparations is that a single dose given in the early morning will continue to benefit the child throughout the day without the need for additional dosing. A recently developed methylphenidate skin patch (Daytrana) serves the same function as the long-acting oral medications and is particularly useful for children who may have difficulty or may be unwilling to swallow pills. A major advance in ADHD treatment occurred in 2002 with the introduction of atomoxetine (Strattera), the first nonstimulant medication for ADHD. Atomoxetine is a selective norepinephrine transporter inhibitor, which is thought to work by enhancing the action of NE on adrenergic α_{2A} receptors in the prefrontal cortex (PFC) (see below). More recently, an extended-release formulation of guanfacine (Intuniv), which is a selective α_{2A} receptor agonist, has also been approved for the treatment of ADHD. Intuniv may be used alone or in combination with a stimulant to achieve maximum reduction in symptomatology. It is important to note that although many children are treated with drugs alone, concomitant psychotherapy and parental counseling are often required for best results. Moreover, there is recent evidence supporting the efficacy of cognitive-behavioral therapy, either with or without medication, in treating adults with ADHD (Knouse and Safren, 2010).

Certain safety concerns have been raised regarding the long-term use of stimulants to treat ADHD. One of the first concerns is the possibility that these compounds may result in reduced growth. Large-scale studies looking at average effects have found either small or no effects of long-term stimulant use on growth, although the possibility remains that some individual children could be adversely affected in this manner (Kaplan and Newcorn, 2011). Second, because of their sympathomimetic effects, stimulants cause small but measurable increases in heart rate and blood pressure. These compounds should, therefore, be avoided by any children or adults who have preexisting cardiovascular disease or are at increased risk of developing cardiovascular problems. Similarly, there is some concern (although not without controversy) that stimulants may exacerbate the occurrence of tics in patients with tic disorders. Clinicians concerned about this possibility have the option of prescribing atomoxetine or guanfacine for those patients. Finally, there is the issue of abuse potential of psychostimulants. When taken orally at standard therapeutic doses, methylphenidate or amphetamines usually do not produce feelings of euphoria because of their relatively slow uptake from the gastrointestinal tract. However, a "high" can occur when pills are crushed and are taken either intranasally (snorted) or by IV injection. Indeed, controlled laboratory studies have shown that the euphoric

BOX 12.2 *(continued)*

(A)

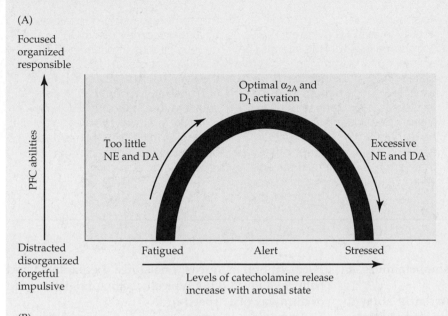

(B)

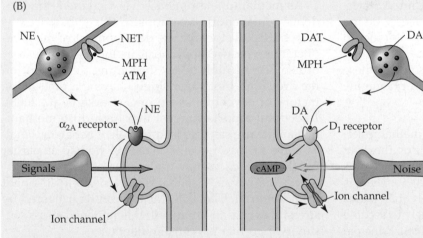

Hypothesized role of prefrontal cortical α_{2A} and D_1 receptors in cognitive performance and the treatment of ADHD (A) Activation of α_{2A} and D_1 receptors in the PFC is thought to depend on the organism's state of arousal. A moderate level of arousal leads to intermediate levels of receptor activation that are optimal for PFC functioning, whereas either too little or too much activation has detrimental effects on PFC functioning and cognitive performance. (B) Methylphenidate (MPH) administration increases extracellular NE and DA levels in the PFC by blocking the NE and DA transporters (NET and DAT), respectively, whereas atomoxetine (ATM) is a selective NET inhibitor. Electrophysiological recordings from rhesus monkeys suggest that α_{2A} receptor activation enhances noradrenergic signaling, and D_1 receptor activation reduces "noise" via a cAMP-dependent effect on ion channel opening. Thus, both effects enhance the signal-to-noise ratio at PFC pyramidal neurons, although by different mechanisms. (A after Arnsten, 2009; B after Gamo et al., 2010.)

response to IV methylphenidate is similar to that obtained from IV cocaine (Wang et al., 1997). Thus, both methylphenidate and the

various amphetamine formulations have significant abuse potential. Parents of medicated ADHD children need to be vigilant for signs

of either abuse by the child or distribution of the medication to siblings or friends for recreational use. No other significant adverse consequences have consistently been identified in humans undergoing long-term psychostimulant treatment for ADHD. On the other hand, animal model studies examining both behavioral and neurochemical effects of psychostimulants given repeatedly during the relevant developmental periods remind us that these compounds can exert powerful and widespread effects on the brain (Bock et al., 2010), and therefore, they should not be administered unless there has been a thorough evaluation of the child so that the risk/benefit ratio of drug treatment has been properly considered.

The PFC, particularly the right PFC, plays a critical role in "executive functions." These functions include cognitive flexibility, planning, inhibition of inappropriate responses, and selecting and attending to relevant sensory input while rejecting irrelevant input. Individuals with ADHD exhibit many of the same symptoms as people with damage to the right PFC, and brain imaging studies have found abnormalities of the right PFC in ADHD patients (Arnsten, 2009). The pyramidal (i.e., output) neurons of the PFC are innervated by both the noradrenergic and dopaminergic systems. The key receptors involved are α_{2A} in the case of NE and D_1 in the case of DA. Experimental animal studies have suggested that the role of NE activation of α_{2A} receptors is to enhance the strength of relevant sensory input to the PFC (i.e., increase the "signal"), whereas the role of DA activation of D_1 receptors is to weaken irrelevant sensory input (i.e., decrease the "noise") (Arnsten, 2007). These effects work together to increase

(Continued on next page)

BOX 12.2 *(continued)*

the signal-to-noise ratio of sensory input to the PFC, thus helping the individual attend to the appropriate stimuli. Bringing this information to bear on the issue of ADHD, Arnsten and colleagues have argued (1) that PFC functioning is an inverted U-shaped function of the activity of both catecholaminergic systems, and (2) that a critical mode of action of both stimulants and nonstimulants (i.e., atomoxetine and guanfacine) is

to enhance catecholaminergic activity in the PFC (Arnsten, 2009; Gamo et al., 2010) (see figure). The ability of psychostimulants to stimulate release of catecholamines, especially DA (amphetamines), or to block catecholamine uptake (methylphenidate) has led many researchers to postulate that DA activity in the PFC and/or other brain areas is deficient in patients with ADHD. This theory has been supported not only by the work of

Arnsten's research group but also by at least some brain imaging and genetic studies of patients with ADHD (Genro et al., 2010). Nevertheless, such studies have not yet conclusively proven the DA deficiency hypothesis of ADHD, and indeed there may well be multiple etiologies for ADHD, as has been postulated for other common neuropsychiatric disorders.

---

between the ages of 15 and 64 used amphetamines at least once during 2010.

Because methamphetamine is currently abused more heavily than amphetamine in the United States, this section of the chapter will focus primarily on the adverse behavioral, physiological, and neurobiological effects of chronic methamphetamine abuse. Nevertheless, it is important to note that at least some of these same effects can occur in cases of heavy amphetamine rather than methamphetamine use.

DEPENDENCE AND WITHDRAWAL   Chronic methamphetamine use commonly leads to dependence on the drug and a withdrawal syndrome when the individual undergoes abstinence (Cruickshank and Dyer, 2009). There is some evidence that females are more likely than males to use methamphetamine and are more likely to become dependent on the drug (Dluzen and Liu, 2008). Principal symptoms of methamphetamine withdrawal include depressed mood, increased anxiety, sleep disturbances, cognitive deficits, and craving for the drug. Users may also experience agitated behavior, reduced energy, and increased appetite. Withdrawal symptoms may take up to several weeks to subside, during which time the user is at particularly high risk for relapse.

PSYCHOTIC REACTIONS   More than 30 years ago, several research groups first described in some high-dose amphetamine users a psychotic reaction consisting of visual and/or auditory hallucinations, behavioral disorganization, and the development of a paranoid state with delusions of persecution. Users may experience the same hallucination of a parasitic skin infestation described earlier for cocaine. These reactions to amphetamine usually do not occur upon first exposure to the drug, but only after a chronic abuse pattern has developed.

Furthermore, in at least one study, the paranoia and hallucinations did not typically begin until the second or third day of a "speed run."

As methamphetamine use has increased, the incidence of psychotic reactions to this substance has grown. Risk factors for the development of methamphetamine-induced psychosis include a long history of use, use of high doses, becoming dependent on the drug, and (not surprisingly) having a preexisting history of psychotic symptoms (Darke et al., 2008). Anecdotal reports suggest that high-dose methamphetamine use can also lead to violent behavior. Finally, some methamphetamine users who had an earlier psychotic reaction may undergo spontaneous recurrences known as "flashbacks," even while abstinent from the drug. These flashbacks can be triggered by stressful events and may reflect heightened stress sensitivity in former psychostimulant users.

NEUROTOXICITY   There is a special danger to methamphetamine users that is due to the neurotoxic properties of this substance. Investigators have known for many years that administration of multiple doses of methamphetamine to animals causes long-lasting reductions in the levels of DA, tyrosine hydroxylase (the key enzyme in DA synthesis), and DAT in the striatum. These changes are indicative of damage to DA axons and terminals, which has been confirmed by histological experiments showing the presence of degenerating fibers. Methamphetamine also produces damage to serotonergic fibers in several parts of the brain, including the neocortex, hippocampus, and striatum. Although the detailed mechanisms underlying methamphetamine neurotoxicity are beyond the scope of this book, investigators have identified a number of likely candidates, including oxidative stress (cellular stress due to increased produc-

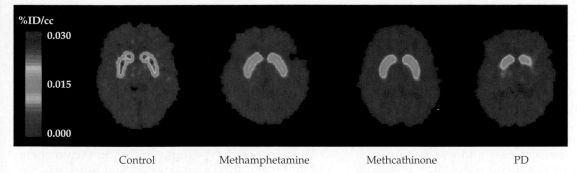

%ID/cc

0.030

0.015

0.000

Control   Methamphetamine   Methcathinone   PD

Figure 12.21 PET images of reduced striatal DAT binding associated with psychostimulant abuse Brain images were taken of a control subject, a subject who had previously abused methamphetamine, one who had abused methcathinone (a derivative of cathinone), and a patient suffering from Parkinson's disease (PD). The drug-using subjects were abstinent at the time of testing. DA transporter sites were labeled with the radiolabeled cocaine analog [^{11}C]WIN-35,428. The decreased DA transporter binding in the drug users suggests that damage may have occurred to the dopaminergic innervation of the striatum. Such damage is known to occur in PD, as can be seen in the drastically reduced binding in the PD patient. (From McCann et al., 1998.)

tion of oxygen-containing free radicals), excitotoxicity, neuroinflammation, and mitochondrial dysfunction (Cadet and Krasnova, 2009; Yamamoto et al., 2010).

Brain imaging as well as postmortem studies suggests that at least some human methamphetamine users may suffer from some of the same neurotoxic effects as methamphetamine-treated experimental animals. Such studies have shown loss of striatal DAT, decreased levels of striatal DA and metabolites, and reduced cortical 5-HT transporter binding in chronic methamphetamine users compared with control subjects (Cadet and Krasnova, 2009). **Figure 12.21** presents brain images illustrating the reduction in striatal DAT binding not only with chronic methamphetamine and methcathinone use but also in a Parkinson's disease patient, where the dopaminergic innervation of the striatum is known to be severely compromised. At this point, we can't be certain that the reduced DA transporter density in methamphetamine users is a sign of DA neurotoxicity, although such an interpretation is consistent with the animal studies. The loss of striatal DA could potentially predispose heavy users to an early onset of Parkinson's disease; however, results from Moszczynska and coworkers (2004) suggest that the motor component of the striatum is not affected severely enough in methamphetamine users to cause parkinsonian symptoms. On the other hand, both the dopaminergic and serotonergic deficits observed with chronic methamphetamine use are likely contributors to the range of cognitive deficits that have been described in these individuals (Ersche and Sahakian, 2007).

GENERAL PHYSICAL HEALTH In addition to the neurotoxic and cognitive effects just mentioned, heavy methamphetamine use has been associated with a variety of adverse health outcomes. Methamphetamine use has been associated with cardiovascular problems including elevated heart and blood pressure, atherosclerosis, and myocardial infarction, increased risk of stroke, and an increased mortality rate (Darke et al., 2008; Marshall and Werb, 2010). There is also anecdotal evidence for premature aging among chronic methamphetamine users. This can be seen from a website called Faces of Meth (www.facesofmeth.us/main.htm), which was developed by the Sheriff's Office of Multnomah County in Oregon, and which posts "mug shots" of the same people taken at different times during the course of their drug use (and arrest). Two of these photographs are shown in **Figure 12.22**, which illustrates the physical toll inflicted on heavy methamphetamine users over the course of just a few years. It is hoped that the message of these pictures will deter at least some people from becoming trapped in the scourge of methamphetamine use.

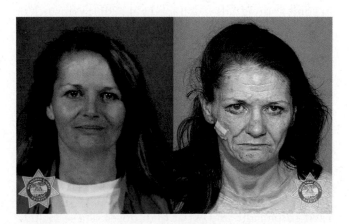

Figure 12.22 An example of the physical deterioration produced by chronic methamphetamine use

Mephedrone and related drugs are gaining popularity as substitutes for other amphetamine-like compounds

At the beginning of the section on amphetamines, we briefly mentioned and showed the structure of cathinone, a naturally occurring psychostimulant found in the khat plant of eastern Africa and Arabia. In recent years, there has been a surge in Europe and in the United States in the synthesis and use of 4-methylmethcathinone, a cathinone derivative also known as **mephedrone**. During this period, mephedrone and other stimulants were legally sold, particularly over the Internet, under the collective term "legal highs" (Vardakou et al., 2011). To further avoid the possibility of government prosecution, these compounds were typically called "bath salts," "plant food," or similar terms, with the website explicitly stating that the materials for sale were "not for human consumption." Of course, no one, including both buyers and government authorities, was being fooled by this ruse. Mephedrone and related compounds were finally banned by the U.S. Drug Enforcement Administration (DEA) in September, 2011, and even earlier by Britain, where the "legal high" problem has been particularly severe. In the remainder of this section, we will discuss the pharmacology and toxicology of mephedrone, while keeping in mind that despite the new regulations, both mephedrone itself and related designer drugs remain available on the Internet and through other means of distribution to individuals seeking to obtain these compounds.

Mephedrone is most commonly taken by snorting. Less common routes of administration include oral, intramuscular or IV injection, and rectal. Acute effects of the drug include euphoria and increased energy, as would be expected from a psychostimulant. Regular use of mephedrone may produce tolerance and symptoms of dependence and withdrawal in some individuals (Schifano et al., 2011; Winstock et al., 2010, 2011). Mephedrone inhibits both 5-HT and DA uptake by synaptosomes in vitro (Martinez-Clemente et al., 2011), and in animals it markedly increases extracellular levels of both neurotransmitters in the nucleus accumbens (Kehr et al., 2011). Consequently, mephedrone's neurochemical profile shares at least some similarity to that of other amphetamine-like compounds, including amphetamine itself, methamphetamine, and MDMA.

Although mephedrone is commonly thought of as safe by users, a number of reports describe effects that are indicative of mephedrone toxicity when used chronically and/or at high doses. These include sympathomimetic toxicity (excessive and prolonged sympathetic nervous system activity), agitation, seizures, and even death (Maskell et al., 2011; Wood et al., 2010, 2011). Recent animal studies suggest that high doses of mephedrone may result in serotonergic neurotoxicity similar to that observed with MDMA (see Chapter 6) (Hadlock et al., 2011). The brain image of a methcathinone user shown in Figure 12.21 also raises the possibility of dopaminergic neurotoxicity due to abuse of this class of compounds.

Thus, mephedrone exhibits the typical neurochemical and behavioral characteristics of other psychostimulants. Reports of dependence, withdrawal, and toxic reactions to this drug indicate that it poses the same risks as other compounds within this category. Unfortunately, although recent legal restrictions on mephedrone may curtail its availability to some extent, there is already evidence that illicit drug manufacturers are switching to other compounds that are not yet illegal and thus can once again be marketed as legal highs (Brandt et al., 2011).

Section Summary

- Amphetamine and methamphetamine are synthetic psychomotor stimulants that are closely related structurally to two similarly acting plant compounds, cathinone and ephedrine.

- Amphetamine was first introduced in the United States in 1932 in the form of a nasal inhaler. People soon realized that they could achieve powerful stimulatory and euphoric effects by consuming the drug orally or by injecting it. The incidence of amphetamine use and abuse grew until a peak was attained in the 1970s. Since that time, the drug has been largely supplanted by cocaine, except for a recent upsurge in methamphetamine use in certain parts of the country.

- Amphetamine is typically taken orally or by IV or subcutaneous injection. Crystalline methamphetamine, which is more potent than amphetamine, can also be taken by snorting or smoking. Some amphetamine or methamphetamine users take the drug repeatedly in binges called speed runs. Both drugs are metabolized slowly by the liver, thus causing a longer duration of action than cocaine.

- Amphetamine and methamphetamine are indirect catecholamine agonists. They stimulate release of DA and NE from nerve terminals and block the reuptake of these neurotransmitters. At high doses, there is also an inhibition of the catecholamine-degrading enzyme monoamine oxidase. Central DA release has been demonstrated in both animals and humans. Amphetamine and methamphetamine also have sympathomimetic effects that are due to their effects on NE in the sympathetic nervous system.

- Acute administration of amphetamine to humans leads to a well-known constellation of behavioral reactions, including increased arousal, reduced fatigue, and feelings of exhilaration. Sleep is delayed, and performance of simple, repetitive tasks is improved.

- Therapeutically, amphetamine is used in the treatment of narcolepsy. Both amphetamine and another stimulant, methylphenidate, are widely prescribed for children suffering from attention deficit hyperactivity disorder (ADHD). At relatively low doses, these stimulants produce calming and attention-enhancing effects that differ from the typical responses seen in adults taking higher drug doses.

- In experimental animals, amphetamine acts much like cocaine. It elicits dose-dependent stimulation of locomotion and stereotyped behaviors, and it is highly reinforcing in self- administration and place-conditioning paradigms.

- Heavy use of amphetamine or particularly methamphetamine can result in a number of adverse consequences, including the development of dependence, psychotic reactions that closely resemble paranoid schizophrenia, neurotoxicity of the DA system, and even signs of premature aging.

- There has been a recent surge in the use of the synthetic cathinone derivative mephedrone. Mephedrone exhibits most of the neurochemical and behavioral profiles of other amphetamine-like stimulants. It may also have the potential for neurotoxicity, although more research needs to be performed to confirm this idea.

Go to the **COMPANION WEBSITE**

sites.sinauer.com/psychopharm2e
for Web Boxes, animations, flashcards, and other study resources.

Recommended Readings

Iversen, L. (2008). *Speed, Ecstasy, Ritalin: The Science of Amphetamines*. New York: Oxford University Press.

Karch, S. B. (2006). *A Brief History of Cocaine, Second Edition*. Boca Raton: CRC Press.

Kosten, T. R., Newton, T. F., De La Garza, R. II, and Haile, C. N. (Eds.). (2012). *Cocaine and Methamphetamine Dependence: Advances in Treatment*. Washington, D.C.: American Psychiatric Publishing.

Rasmussen, N. (2008). *On Speed: The Many Lives of Amphetamine*. New York: New York University Press.

Columbus brought many gifts back from his visit to the New World, including leaves of the tobacco plant.

Nicotine and Caffeine 13

AS IS TAUGHT TO ALL AMERICAN SCHOOLCHILDREN, Christopher Columbus discovered the New World on October 12, 1492, having landed on an island in the Bahamas that he promptly named San Salvador. What is less widely taught is that a few days later, having sailed to a few other Bahamian islands in the meantime, Columbus wrote in his journal that his ship encountered a lone man in a canoe carrying with him "a piece of bread as big as his fist, a calabash [bottle-shaped gourd] of water, a piece of red earth, powdered and kneaded, and a few dried leaves which must be something of importance to these people, because they brought me some in San Salvador" (Burns, 2007; p. 15). Columbus later sailed to Cuba (thinking it was China) and sent two men, Rodrigo de Xerez and Luis de Torres, ashore to find the Chinese emperor and request a meeting with Columbus. What de Xerez and de Torres actually found was described later in an historical account by Bartoleme de las Casas as follows: "The two Christians [Xerez and Torres] met many men and women who were carrying glowing coal in their hands, as well as good-smelling herbs. They were dried plants, like small muskets made of paper that children play with during the Easter festivities. They set one end on fire and inhaled and drank the smoke on the other. It is said that in this way they become sleepy and drunk, but also that they got rid of their tiredness. The people called these small muskets *tobacco*" (Burns, 2007; pp. 16–17).

Thus did Europeans first encounter the smoking of tobacco, since this plant was native to the Americas but unknown in Europe. Although it does not appear that Columbus was particularly impressed with this smoking behavior, de Xerez had tried it and enjoyed it enough to bring some tobacco back to his hometown in Spain. He is accordingly considered to be the first Westerner to take

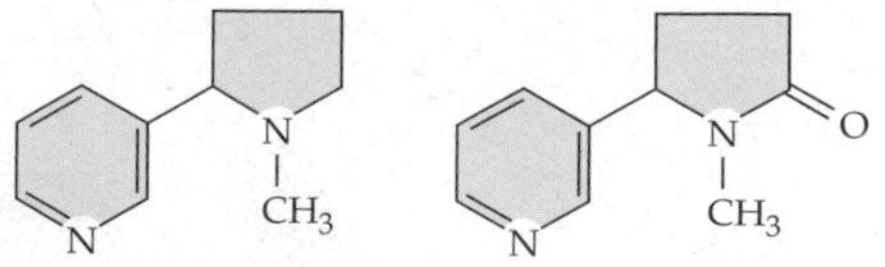

Nicotine   **Cotinine**

Figure 13.1 **Chemical structure of nicotine and the principal metabolite cotinine**

Figure 13.2 **Leaves of the *Nicotiana tabacum* plant** from which tobacco is derived

up the smoking habit (Burns, 2007). Unfortunately, the sight of tobacco smoke emanating from his nose and mouth so frightened the townspeople that they reported de Xerez to the Spanish Inquisition, which promptly sent him to prison. Over time, however, smoking became more acceptable and began to spread throughout Europe.

Nicotine, the psychoactive ingredient in tobacco, is the third most widely consumed recreational drug in the world after caffeine and alcohol. Every day, millions of men and women around the world consume this drug, usually by smoking tobacco in cigarettes, cigars, or pipes. What is the lure of nicotine? Why do so many people smoke, despite the known dangers of lung cancer and other respiratory diseases? The first part of this chapter will address these and other questions about nicotine and tobacco smoking. The second part of the chapter is concerned with the properties and mechanisms of action of caffeine, the other widely used and legal stimulant drug.

Nicotine

Background and History

Nicotine is an alkaloid found in tobacco leaves (**Figure 13.1**). There are two major species of tobacco plant: a large-leaf form and a small-leaf form. The large-leaf variety (*Nicotiana tabacum*), which is the principal source of modern-day tobacco, originated in South America, where it was domesticated by native peoples more than 5000 years ago (**Figure 13.2**). The small-leaf variety (*Nicotiana rustica*) is native to eastern North America and the islands of the West Indies. This is the species of tobacco plant encountered during Columbus's expedition to the New World in 1492. An early proponent was Jean Nicot de Villemain, the French ambassador to Portugal who was instrumental in introducing tobacco to his native country from Portugal. Indeed, the botanical name of the more popular tobacco plant, *Nicotiana tabacum*, is derived from both

Nicot's surname and *tabaco*, the term for "tobacco" in both Spanish and Portuguese.

In Britain, tobacco was initially scarce and thus costly. Early pipes, called "fairy pipes" in England and "elfin pipes" in Scotland, were extremely small to conserve the dried leaves. But the popularity of smoking grew so rapidly that by the early 1600s, it is estimated that there were thousands of shops in London alone where tobacco could be purchased. At first, most tobacco use took place through pipe smoking, cigar smoking, and chewing, but this was later supplanted to a large extent by the snorting of finely powdered tobacco leaves (snuff).

In 1610, England attempted to commercialize tobacco growing in the Virginia colony using the native *Nicotiana rustica*. However, this venture failed because the *rustica* species had a disagreeable flavor to Europeans compared with *N. tabacum*, which had been a Spanish monopoly up to that time. Luckily for the British, John Rolfe, the local leader of this effort, managed to obtain some *N. tabacum*, which grew just as well in Virginia as it had for thousands of years in South America. Thus was the American tobacco industry born.

Cigarettes began to be used in Europe in the midnineteenth century, and their popularity in the United States exploded over the next 30 years. This change was fostered by two separate developments: new methods of curing tobacco leaves that improved their flavor, and the invention of the cigarette machine. When cigarettes were rolled manually, a skilled worker could make about 2500 to 3000 cigarettes per day, which may seem like a large number. In 1884, however, a cigarette machine was built that could make 120,000 cigarettes in one day, and modern-day machines can produce 4000 to 8000 per minute!

Basic Pharmacology of Nicotine and Its Relationship to Smoking

When nicotine was first isolated in 1828 by Posselt and Reimann, it was found to constitute about 5% of the weight of dry tobacco leaves. However, this relatively minor fraction imbues tobacco with many physiological and psychological effects when the leaves are smoked, chewed, or snorted and the nicotine is absorbed into the human bloodstream. Without nicotine, it is quite likely that tobacco would be regarded as a useless weed.

The typical cigarette contains between 6 and 11 mg of nicotine, although no more than 1 to 3 mg actually reaches the bloodstream of the smoker. The amount of available nicotine depends mainly on features of the smoker's behavior such as the number of puffs and the length of each puff. Nicotine in the tobacco is vaporized by the 800°C temperature at the burning tip of the cigarette. It enters the smoker's lungs mainly on tiny particles called **tar**, a complex mixture of hydrocarbons of which some are known to be carcinogenic. Tar is an important contributor to the taste and smell of cigarette smoke, and along with nicotine, these sensory qualities contribute significantly to the reinforcing effects of smoking. Once the smoke has been inhaled, the nicotine readily passes through the absorbent surface of the lungs, whose total area has been estimated as about equal to the surface of a tennis court. Nicotine is absorbed to a lesser extent through the membranes of the mouth and nostrils when tobacco is chewed or snorted as snuff.

A typical smoker takes about 10 total puffs on a cigarette at intervals of approximately 30 to 60 seconds. Researchers have shown that each puff delivers a small burst of nicotine to the brain. If the person smokes 1½ packs (30 cigarettes) per day, 10 puffs per cigarette yields 300 separate "hits" of nicotine each day. The nicotine first reaches the brain in about 7 seconds, which is approximately twice as fast as when the drug is administered intravenously. Thus smoking a cigarette is the quickest and most efficient method of delivering nicotine to the brain, where the drug produces its reinforcing effects (see the section on behavioral and physiological effects later in the chapter). Reinforcement of a conditioned response is generally strongest when there is a short time interval between performing the response (e.g., pressing a lever for food or smoking a cigarette for nicotine) and obtaining the reinforcer. Consequently, the rapid transit of

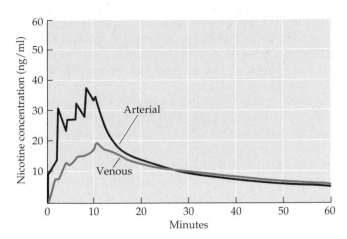

Figure 13.3 Time course of mean plasma concentrations of nicotine in arterial and venous blood obtained from six male smokers, each of whom smoked his usual brand of cigarettes for 10 minutes. Arterial nicotine concentrations rose more rapidly and reached a greater peak than the concentrations found in venous blood. (After Gourlay and Benowitz, 1997.)

nicotine to the brain is thought to powerfully reinforce smoking behavior. Moreover, the rapidly repeated, puff-by-puff drug delivery that occurs during smoking permits the user unmatched control over both the pattern of intake and the dose.

Blood levels of nicotine following smoking were initially measured in venous blood, which is the easiest and safest to obtain.[1] However, the brain (as well as any other organ) is actually exposed to the higher levels of nicotine present in arterial blood. Consequently, investigators have begun to measure the amounts of nicotine in the arterial circulation to obtain a better index of how much of the drug is reaching the brain. **Figure 13.3** illustrates the average time course of arterial and venous nicotine concentrations in a group of six subjects who each smoked for 10 minutes at a rate of 1 puff per minute. Note that arterial nicotine rises more rapidly and reaches a much greater peak than the concentration in venous blood. Within a few minutes, however, the arterial concentration falls to the same level as the venous concentration. From this point on, there is no more net uptake of nicotine from the bloodstream into tissues, at least until the next cigarette is smoked.

About 70% to 80% of nicotine in the body is transformed into the principal metabolite, **cotinine**, (see Figure 13.1) by a specific liver enzyme known as **cytochrome P450 2A6 (CYP2A6)**. Cotinine and other

---

[1]When blood is drawn from your arm for standard blood tests, it is normally taken from the antecubital vein and thus represents venous blood.

nicotine metabolites such as nicotine-N-oxide, nor-nicotine, and norcotinine are excreted mainly in the urine. Because of genetic variation, some individuals have low CYP2A6 activity and thus reduced nicotine metabolism. These individuals are less likely to become smokers and if they are tobacco dependent, they smoke fewer cigarettes than people who have normal levels of CYP2A6 (Tyndale and Sellers, 2001). Therefore, it appears that slow breakdown of nicotine exerts a somewhat protective effect against cigarette smoking. Wassanaar and coworkers (2011) recently reported that both normal levels of CYP2A6 activity and variation in a gene cluster that codes for subunits of the nicotinic cholinergic receptor (which plays a key role in nicotine reward; see the next section on nicotine mechanisms of action) contribute to smoking frequency, nicotine dependence, and the risk for developing lung cancer.

Although the elimination half-life of nicotine varies among individuals (presumably related at least partially to differences in the level of CYP2A6), it is typically around 2 hours. This requires that the user smoke repeatedly over the day to avoid withdrawal symptoms due to falling blood nicotine levels. Such withdrawal symptoms are discussed later in the chapter. Frequent smoking leads to ever increasing peak levels of nicotine across the day, since each dose builds on the residual nicotine left over from that day's previous cigarettes. However, this does not cause greater and greater effects, because of tolerance that has also developed over the same time period. Mild nicotine withdrawal emerges during the overnight period while the smoker is sleeping, yet at the same time the nicotine tolerance built up over the previous day partially dissipates. Because of these two processes, the individual awakens the next morning with a strong craving for a cigarette but also may experience the strongest or best response that she will have all day.

Mechanisms of Action

Nicotine works mainly by activating **nicotinic cholinergic receptors (nAChRs)**, one of the two basic subtypes of acetylcholine (ACh) receptor (see Chapter 7). You will recall that nAChRs are ionotropic receptors comprising five separate protein subunits, and that these subunits are somewhat different when we compare neuronal nicotinic receptors with those found on muscle cells. Neuronal receptors containing two α4 or α3 subunits along with three β subunits are much more sensitive to nicotine than those composed of five α7 subunits (Albuquerque et al., 2009). High-affinity nAChRs are found in many parts of the brain, including the cerebral cortex, thalamus, striatum,

hippocampus, and monoamine-containing nuclei such as the substantia nigra, ventral tegmental area (VTA), locus coeruleus, and raphe nuclei. Peripherally, such receptors are found in the ganglia of the autonomic (parasympathetic and sympathetic) nervous system.

High doses of nicotine lead to a persistent activation of nicotinic receptors and a continuous depolarization of the postsynaptic cell. As we saw in Chapter 7, this causes a depolarization block, and the cell cannot fire again until the nicotine is removed. In this way, a high dose of nicotine exerts a biphasic effect that begins with stimulation of nicotinic cholinergic functions but then turns to a nicotinic receptor blockade. This biphasic action accounts for the features of nicotine poisoning discussed later.

Section Summary

- Nicotine is an alkaloid found in tobacco leaves. Tobacco plants are native to North and South America, and these plants were domesticated several thousand years ago by Native Americans.

- When tobacco was first brought back to Europe from the New World, use of this substance was primarily by means of pipe smoking, cigar smoking, and chewing. Snorting finely powdered tobacco leaves (snuff) later became popular.

- Cigarettes were first introduced in the mid-nineteenth century, and cigarette smoking subsequently increased as the result of improved methods of curing the tobacco leaves, as well as the advent of modern cigarette manufacturing machines.

- A typical cigarette contains 6 to 11 mg of nicotine, of which only about 1 to 3 mg actually reaches the smoker's bloodstream. Nicotine is vaporized by the high temperature at the tip of the burning cigarette and enters the smoker's lungs on tiny particles called tar.

- Once in the lungs, the nicotine is readily absorbed into the blood and quickly reaches the brain. The rapid delivery of a small burst of nicotine to the brain following each puff on the cigarette is believed to be a powerful reinforcer of smoking behavior. Arterial rather than venous levels of nicotine are considered to be the best indicator of the amount of nicotine being delivered to the brain.

- Nicotine is metabolized primarily to cotinine by the liver enzyme CYP2A6. The cotinine and other nicotine metabolites are then excreted mainly in the urine. People who metabolize nicotine inefficiently because of a genetically determined low CYP2A6 activity seem to be less vulnerable to cigarette smoking than efficient metabolizers.

- The elimination half-life of nicotine is typically around 2 hours. Nicotine clearance from the body is an important reason why most smokers smoke throughout the day. Tolerance to at least some of nicotine's effects occurs during this period, but during sleep this tolerance partially dissipates and the smoker awakens in a state of mild withdrawal.

- The principal mechanism of nicotine action is to stimulate nicotinic cholinergic receptors in the brain and the autonomic nervous system. In particular, there are high-affinity nAChRs that most commonly are composed of two α4 or α3 subunits, along with three β2 subunits.

- The opening of nAChR channels permits Na^+ to flow across the cell membrane, thereby causing membrane depolarization and a fast excitatory response. High doses of nicotine can cause persistent activation of nicotinic receptors, leading to a temporary depolarization block of the postsynaptic cell.

Behavioral and Physiological Effects

If one wishes to determine the pharmacological effects of nicotine itself, separated from the complex behavioral aspects of smoking, it is necessary to give subjects the pure drug. This is routinely accomplished through the use of nicotine injections, nicotine patches, or nicotine-containing gum. Nevertheless, many early studies suffer from a significant methodological problem due to the use of current smokers, who are required to refrain from smoking for a specified period of time, typically ranging from 8 to 24 hours. Because nicotine abstinence produces withdrawal symptoms in dependent individuals, it is often difficult to determine whether nicotine-induced changes represent true differences from "normal," or simply reversal of withdrawal symptoms. Fortunately, researchers subsequently began to study subjects who had never smoked, thereby permitting us to compare the findings of those studies with the results from abstinent smokers.

Nicotine elicits different mood changes in smokers compared with nonsmokers

With respect to mood states, nicotine is usually found to increase calmness and relaxation in abstinent smokers. This fits well with numerous self-reports of smokers indicating that smoking a cigarette has a relaxing, tension-reducing effect. However, it seems likely that these mood changes are related at least partly to relief from nicotine withdrawal symptoms, because

nicotine administration to nonsmokers tends to elicit feelings of heightened tension or arousal, along with lightheadedness, dizziness, and even nausea (Kalman, 2002). If you either smoke now or have ever smoked in the past, you may recall having experienced some of these same effects when you tried your first cigarette.

Not all the mood-altering effects of smoking are related to nicotine intake. Perkins and coworkers (2010) recently examined the influence of smoking either nicotine-containing or denicotinized cigarettes on negative affect induced by several different mood-induction procedures, namely, (1) overnight abstinence from tobacco, (2) performance on a difficult computer task, (3) viewing of highly arousing negative mood slides, and (4) preparation of a speech for public presentation. The investigators found that smoking strongly reduced negative affect in the abstinence condition, with additional but smaller effects seen in the computer challenge and negative mood slide conditions. Interestingly, there was little difference between nicotine-containing and denicotinized cigarettes in any of these conditions (**Figure 13.4**). These findings suggest that in addition to nicotine, conditioned stimuli associated with smoking play a significant role in the calming effects of this behavior in regular smokers.

Nicotine enhances cognitive function

We saw in Chapter 7 that ACh plays an important role in certain aspects of cognitive functioning. Although this is mediated in large part by the muscarinic cholinergic receptors, nicotinic receptors could also be involved. On the basis of this hypothesis, a number of studies have examined the effects of nicotine on cognitive function.

Abstinent smokers given nicotine show enhanced performance on many kinds of cognitive and motor tasks, particularly those involving attentional demands. However, as in the case of mood effects, much of this enhancement appears to be due to alleviation of withdrawal-related deficits (Sherwood, 1993). On the other hand, a recent meta-analysis[2] by Heishman and coworkers (2010 of a wide variety of studies) supported the conclusion that nicotine has a positive influence on cognitive and motor functioning even in nonsmokers. This analysis found statistically significant effects of nicotine on fine motor performance, and on accuracy and response latency in certain types of attentional and memory tasks. One example comes from a study by

---

[2]Meta-analysis is a statistical tool that enables investigators to combine the results of many studies concerning the same experimental treatment, thereby increasing statistical power and determining with greater confidence whether the effect of the treatment in question is statistically reliable.

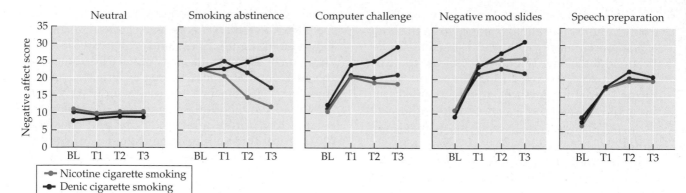

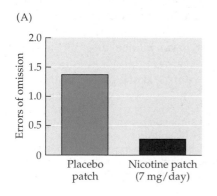

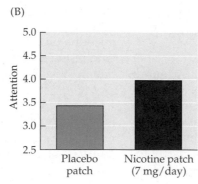

Figure 13.4 Influence of mood-induction procedure and smoking condition on negative affect The subjects were regular adult smokers (10 cigarettes or more per day) tested at four time points on the negative affect scale of the Diener and Emmons Mood Form: baseline (BL), before mood induction; T1, after 5 minutes of the mood induction procedure and before cigarette smoking; T2, after four cigarette puffs and 3 more minutes of mood induction; and T3, after another 10 minutes of mood induction during which ad lib smoking was allowed in the smoking groups. The Smoking Abstinence mood-induction procedure involved overnight abstinence (more than 12 hours) from smoking. The three cigarette conditions included smoking a standardized nicotine-containing cigarette, smoking a denicotinized (Denic) cigarette, and no smoking at all during the session. The No Smoking group showed significantly greater negative affect than either smoking group at T3 in the abstinence, computer challenge, and negative mood slide conditions. (After Perkins et al., 2010.)

Levin and colleagues (1998) that investigated the effects of nicotine administered transdermally (i.e., using a nicotine patch) to nonsmokers on accuracy in a continuous performance test of attention. In this test, subjects were instructed to respond as rapidly as possible by pressing a specific key on a computer keyboard when a target stimulus (the letter "X") was briefly displayed on a computer monitor, but to withhold their response when any other letter was displayed. Nicotine treatment led to a significant decrease in errors of omission (failing to respond to the target stimulus; **Figure 13.5A**) and to an increase in a measure of composite attention (**Figure 13.5B**), although the treatment did not significantly alter the number of errors of commission (responding to a nontarget stimulus). Even some everyday attentional tasks like searching a map may receive a subtle benefit from nicotine (Rusted et al., 2000). On the basis of evidence for nicotine-related cognitive enhancement, there has been considerable interest in the possible use of nicotinic receptor agonists in the treatment of Alzheimer's disease (see Chapter 21). Moreover, high smoking rates have been associated with certain other neuropsychiatric disorders such as schizophrenia that are characterized by significant cognitive dysfunction. Some researchers have hypothesized that smokers suffering from such disorders may be using nicotine in an attempt to self-medicate their cognitive deficits (Evans and Drobes, 2008).

Animal studies have also been useful in determining the cognitive effects of nicotine, since such studies obviously do not suffer from the problem of using subjects who are smokers. Rats given nicotine show improvement on a variety of different tasks, including tasks requiring sustained attention as well as working memory (Newhouse et al., 2004). Some examples can be found in studies using the 5-choice serial reaction time task (5-CSRTT) of attention (Bari et al., 2008). A typical 5-CSRTT apparatus consists of an operant chamber equipped with a food pellet dispenser, a food magazine where the pellets can be obtained, and a curved

Figure 13.5 Continuous nicotine administration to nonsmokers enhances performance on a continuous performance task of attention. The same subjects were tested under two conditions: a low-dose (7 mg/day) nicotine patch applied approximately 3 hours before attention testing, and a placebo patch applied instead of the nicotine patch. The nicotine patch reduced the number of errors of omission (A) and increased overall subject performance assessed using a composite attention score (B). (After Levin et al., 1998.)

Figure 13.6 Diagram of the type of apparatus used in the 5-choice serial reaction time task (After Bari et al., 2008.)

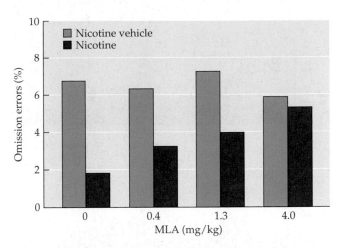

Figure 13.7 The α7 subunit-containing nicotinic receptor antagonist methyllycaconitine (MLA) dose-dependently blocks nicotine enhancement of attention in a 5-choice serial reaction time task. Nicotine (0.1 mg/kg SC) enhanced attentional performance, measured as percent omission errors, in animals given the MLA vehicle (0 mg/kg). Increasing doses of MLA progressively blunted the nicotine effect until it was no long present at the 4 mg/kg dose. (After Hahn et al., 2011.)

front containing five apertures, each of which can be illuminated with a signal light (**Figure 13.6**). During training and testing, one of the signal lights is illuminated for a brief period such as 500 milliseconds. The rat must sustain its attention sufficiently to detect the stimulus, which it signifies by poking its nose into the correct aperture. This permits the animal to receive a reinforcement (food pellet) in the food magazine. Computer software enables researchers to obtain data on variables such as accuracy (percentage of trials with a correct response), errors of omission (failure to respond to the signal, suggesting a lapse in attention), premature responses (responding before the signal was displayed), and response latency (time to respond after the signal was presented). Studies with the 5-CSRTT have found evidence for improved performance with either acute or chronic nicotine administration, but poorer performance during withdrawal from chronic nicotine (Semenova et al., 2007; Stolerman et al., 2000).

This same task was recently used to assess the role of nicotinic receptors differing in subunit composition in attention performance. The investigators determined whether the drug dihydro-β-erythroidine (DHβE), which blocks nicotinic receptors containing α4, α3, or α2 subunits, along with β2 or β4 subunits, or the drug methyllycaconitine (MLA), which blocks α7-containing nicotinic receptors (see Chapter 7), could antagonize the attention-promoting effects of nicotine. The results indicated that MLA dose-dependently blocked the influence of nicotine on omission errors (**Figure 13.7**), whereas DHβE had no effect on this outcome measure (Hahn et al., 2011). These findings suggest that nicotinic receptors containing α7 subunits play an important role in the ability of nicotine to enhance attentional function. Consistent with a role for this class of nicotinic receptors in cognition, another recent study reported that administration

of an α7 partial agonist AZD0328 to mice led to improved performance in the novel object recognition test of memory (Sydserff et al., 2009). Accordingly, drugs of this type are currently under consideration as potential cognitive enhancers in neuropsychiatric diseases such as schizophrenia and attention deficit hyperactivity disorder (ADHD).

Nicotine's reinforcing effects are mediated by activation of the mesolimbic dopamine system

Within a certain dose range, cigarette smokers will self-administer pure nicotine by intravenous (IV) injection (Harvey et al., 2004). This shows that nicotine by itself is reinforcing at the right dose (the drug is actually aversive at higher doses because of various side effects). On the other hand, it is clear that the reinforcement provided by smoking is much more complex than simply the delivery of nicotine to the individual. In a later section, we will discuss the relative contributions of nicotine versus other aspects of smoking in the reinforcing properties of this behavior.

Nicotine self-administration has also been investigated in laboratory animals. Although nicotine is not sought after as avidly as cocaine, amphetamine, or opioid drugs, nicotine self-administration has been demonstrated in rats, mice, dogs, and nonhuman primates (Tuesta et al., 2011). As in the case of cocaine and amphetamine, the mesolimbic dopamine (DA) pathway from the VTA to the nucleus accumbens

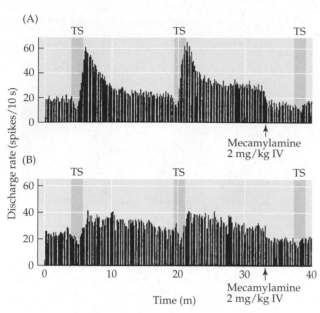

Figure 13.8 Activation of midbrain DA neuron by tobacco smoke Rats were connected to an artificial respirator through which tobacco smoke (TS) could be delivered. Smoke containing approximately 100 μg of nicotine was inhaled several times for 2 minutes during each trial (shaded area). Firing rates of a representative neuron in the VTA (A) and another neuron in the substantia nigra (B) are shown by the amplitude of the rate histogram. Tobacco smoke caused a substantial increase in VTA neuronal firing that returned to baseline within a few minutes. A smaller but still noticeable effect also occurred for cells in the substantia nigra. Note that prior IV infusion of the selective nicotinic receptor antagonist mecamylamine (lower right-hand part of each graph) completely blocked the effects of tobacco smoke on dopaminergic neuron firing, demonstrating that these effects are mediated by nicotinic cholinergic receptors. (From Fà et al., 2000.)

subunits in the activation of DA neurons and the elicitation of behavioral reinforcement (Changeux, 2010). Such studies have shown that IV self-administration of nicotine was lost in mice lacking the α4, α6, or β2 subunit, but was restored when the missing subunit was reexpressed specifically in the VTA. Indeed, there is evidence that VTA nicotinic receptors containing α6 and β2 subunits play a particularly important role in the addictive properties of nicotine (Brunzell, 2012). Nicotinic receptors are also found in the NAcc, where they contribute to nicotine reinforcement by modulating DA release from the mesolimbic nerve terminals (Exley et al., 2011). Finally, recent studies have shown that α5-containing nicotinic receptors in the medial habenula (a structure located in the posterior dorsal thalamus) reduce nicotine self-administration, particularly at higher doses (Fowler et al., 2011). Thus, it appears that nicotine's reinforcing effects depend on a complex interplay between different nicotinic receptor subtypes, some of which promote such effects and others that mediate a suppressant action.

Tobacco smoke contains compounds other than nicotine that inhibit both monoamine oxidase (MAO) A and B in the brain, as well as in several peripheral organs that express one or both of these enzymes (Lewis et al., 2007). **Figure 13.9** shows positron emission tomography (PET) scans demonstrating MAO-B inhibition in various organs of a smoker compared with a nonsmoker. Because MAO is important in the breakdown of DA, it is plausible that MAO inhibition might contribute to the reinforcing effects of smoking. Self-administration studies in rodents support this hypothesis, although the data are not yet clear as to

(NAcc) plays a key role in nicotine's reinforcing effects. High-affinity nicotinic receptors located in the VTA stimulate the firing of dopaminergic neurons, which causes increased DA release in the NAcc. Nicotine-induced activation of DA neurons has usually been investigated using injection of the drug; however, a group of Italian researchers found the same phenomenon when rats inhaled cigarette smoke (Fà et al., 2000) **(Figure 13.8)**. The importance of accumbens DA for nicotine reinforcement was demonstrated by Corrigall and coworkers (1992), who showed that lesioning the dopaminergic innervation of this area with 6-hydroxydopamine (6-OHDA) significantly attenuated nicotine self-administration.

Nicotine self-administration studies using knockout mice with a genetic deletion of specific nicotinic receptor subunits have provided key information regarding the involvement of these

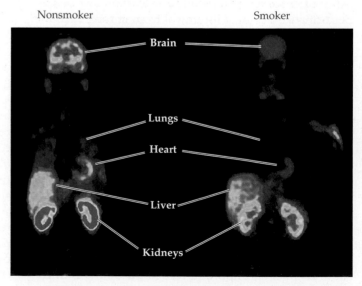

Figure 13.9 Whole-body PET scans illustrating reduced MAO-B activity in various organs of a smoker compared with a nonsmoker. (From Fowler et al., 2003.)

which MAO isoform is most important for such reinforcement (Kapelewski et al., 2011).

Nicotine produces a wide range of physiological effects

We mentioned earlier that nicotinic receptors are abundantly expressed in autonomic ganglia. Consequently, nicotine can activate elements of both the sympathetic and parasympathetic systems to cause a wide spectrum of physiological manifestations. For example, smoking a cigarette stimulates the adrenal glands to release epinephrine (adrenaline) and norepinephrine (noradrenaline). These hormones, along with direct nicotine-induced activation of sympathetic ganglia, lead to symptoms of physiological arousal such as tachycardia (increased heart rate) and elevated blood pressure. This mild physiological arousal is thought to contribute to the reinforcing features of smoking. On the other hand, the same effects could increase the smoker's risk for cardiovascular disease and cerebrovascular accidents (strokes), particularly if the smoker has high blood pressure to begin with.

The action of nicotine on parasympathetic ganglia increases hydrochloric acid secretion in the stomach, which exacerbates or contributes to the formation of stomach ulcers. There is also increased muscle contraction in the bowel, which sometimes leads to chronic diarrhea that is especially harmful to individuals vulnerable to colitis, a chronic irritability of the colon. Together, these autonomic nervous system effects contribute to the deleterious consequences of heavy and prolonged use of tobacco products (see the section on smoking-related illness).

One consequence that many cigarette smokers find desirable is the constraining effect of nicotine on body weight. Adult cigarette smokers weigh an average of 8 to 11 pounds less than gender- and age-matched nonsmokers, and quitting smoking usually results in weight gain (Audrain-McGovern and Benowitz, 2011). This effect of nicotine has been attributed to an increase in metabolic rate combined with appetite suppression. Nevertheless, no one would recommend smoking for weight control because the terrible health consequences of smoking far outweigh the modest benefit derived from losing a little weight.

Nicotine is a toxic substance that can be fatal at high doses

Nicotine is quite toxic; as little as 60 mg can be fatal to an adult. If you do the math based on the nicotine content of a typical cigarette, you will see that a single pack contains several lethal doses of the drug. Of course, cigarettes are only smoked one at a time, and most of the nicotine is not taken in because of burning of the tobacco and loss of sidestream smoke (smoke not inhaled by the smoker). Cases of nicotine poisoning sometimes occur through accidental swallowing of tobacco (usually by children), although nicotine exposure by this route is less toxic than would be expected due to slow absorption of the drug from the stomach, first-pass metabolism in the liver, and possible regurgitation of the tobacco remaining in the stomach due to nicotine activation of the chemical trigger zone (vomiting center) in the medulla. Toxic effects may also result from absorption of excessive nicotine through the skin when field workers are harvesting wet tobacco leaves or from exposure to pure nicotine used in certain insecticides. Indeed, the first reported case of nicotine poisoning was that of a florist who accidentally came into contact with a nicotine-containing insecticide that he had spilled onto a chair (Faulkner, 1933). Nicotine toxicity to insects is believed to have been an important driving force in the evolution of nicotine synthesis by tobacco plants (see **Web Box 13.1**).

The symptoms of nicotine poisoning include nausea, excessive salivation, abdominal pain, vomiting, diarrhea, cold sweat, headache, dizziness, disturbed hearing and vision, mental confusion, and marked weakness. This is quickly followed by fainting and prostration; falling blood pressure; difficulty in breathing; weakening of the pulse, which becomes rapid and irregular; and collapse. Left untreated, a fatal dose ends with convulsions followed shortly by respiratory failure due to depolarization block of the muscles of breathing. The treatment of nicotine poisoning involves inducing vomiting if the poison has been swallowed, placing adsorptive charcoal in the stomach, giving artificial respiration, and treating for shock.

Chronic exposure to nicotine induces tolerance and dependence

Repeated exposure to nicotine leads to a complex pattern of tolerance and, in some instances, sensitization. It is useful to distinguish between acute and chronic nicotine tolerance. For example, acute tolerance can be studied by pretreating subjects (e.g., by injection or by nasal spray) with either nicotine or vehicle, and then testing their responses to a subsequent nicotine challenge. In both smokers and nonsmokers, many behavioral and physiological responses are attenuated by nicotine pretreatment, indicating the occurrence of tolerance. In much the same way, cigarette smokers undergo a significant degree of nicotine tolerance during the course of the day. Acute tolerance is short-lived; after an overnight period of abstinence, smokers

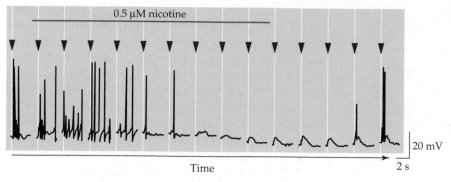

0.5 µM nicotine

Time

20 mV

2 s

Figure 13.10 Desensitization of midbrain DA neurons to continuous nicotine exposure DA neurons in the VTA were studied in rat midbrain tissue slices. Nicotinic receptor–mediated action potentials (upward traces) were induced in these neurons by periodic application of ACh (arrowheads). However, when nicotine was added to the fluid bathing the slice (horizontal bar), the action potentials gradually ceased as a result of desensitization of the receptors. When the nicotine was removed (far right), the receptors resensitized, as shown by the reappearance of action potentials following ACh application. (After Pidoplichko et al., 1997.)

awaken the next morning more sensitive to nicotine than at the end of the previous day. This neurobiological mechanism helps explain why smokers often report that the first cigarette of the day is the most pleasurable one.

Acute tolerance is related to a desensitization (i.e., temporary inactivation) of central nicotinic receptors, including those that mediate nicotine reinforcement (**Figure 13.10**). The nicotine from even a single cigarette is able to induce some degree of receptor desensitization. However, the properties of desensitization, including the concentration of nicotine required for desensitization, latencies to desensitize and to recover, and the proportion of receptors that are inactivated vary significantly with subunit composition. Receptors composed of both α and β subunits (e.g., α4β2) are desensitized at lower nicotine concentrations than α7-containing receptors, because the former have a higher affinity for nicotine (Picciotto et al., 2008). On the other hand, α4β2 nicotinic receptors recover more rapidly than α7 receptors, which may permit the high-affinity receptors to at least partially regain their sensitivity by the time the next cigarette is smoked. For this reason, some investigators theorize that individuals who smoke frequently over the course of a day undergo numerous cycles of nicotinic receptor activation, desensitization, and resensitization.

Long-term exposure to nicotine causes chronic tolerance. This chronic tolerance is superimposed on the acute within-a-day tolerance, and of course it is

present only in smokers and others who use tobacco frequently. An early clue to the existence of chronic nicotine tolerance was the observation that nicotine-related toxicity occurred much more frequently among tobacco harvesters who didn't smoke than among those who were smokers (Gehlbach et al., 1974). Laboratory studies have similarly found that many effects of nicotine administration are attenuated in smokers compared with nonsmokers. For example, a study by Foulds and coworkers (1997) showed that subcutaneous injection of a high dose of nicotine elicited an aversive reaction consisting of at least some symptoms of mild nicotine toxicity (nausea, dizziness, sweating, headache, palpitations, stomachache, or clammy hands) in nonsmokers, but no such reaction in smokers. This not only demonstrates the presence of chronic nicotine tolerance in smokers, but it also raises the possibility that tolerance to these aversive effects must occur before individuals can fully experience nicotine's reinforcing effects.

Interestingly, chronic exposure to nicotine elicits a compensatory response manifested by an up-regulation of high-affinity nicotinic receptor expression in many parts of the brain. In humans, this effect has been demonstrated using both neuroimaging and postmortem binding studies. For example, **Figure 13.11** shows a large increase in high-affinity nicotinic receptor binding in layer VI of the prefrontal cortex of a smoker compared with a nonsmoker (Perry et al., 1999). In rats, as few as four doses of nicotine spread across 2 days led to a significant increase in high-affinity nicotinic receptor binding in the hippocampus (Abreu-Villaça et al., 2003). On the other hand, other animal studies found no effect of chronic nicotine treatment on receptor subunit mRNA levels. Instead, nicotinic receptor up-regulation is thought to involve several posttranslational mechanisms (i.e., mechanisms that alter the processing of the protein subunits themselves) (Govind et al., 2009).

Nicotine tolerance and dependence have been demonstrated in laboratory animals by giving them continuous exposure to the drug (note that nicotine dependence in smokers is discussed in a later section). This is usually accomplished by implanting a small device known as an **osmotic minipump** under the skin of the animal. The minipump is filled with a nicotine solution and slowly infuses the solution subcutaneously at a constant rate for a set period such as 1 or 2 weeks. Some withdrawal symptoms (abstinence syndrome)

(A) Nonsmoker

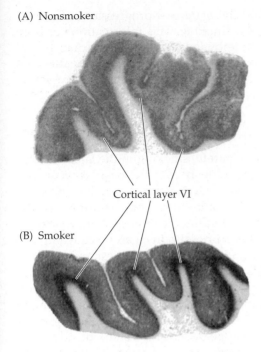

Cortical layer VI

(B) Smoker

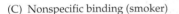

(C) Nonspecific binding (smoker)

Figure 13.11 Up-regulation of nicotinic receptor binding in the prefrontal cortex of smokers Postmortem slices of prefrontal cortex were incubated with radiolabeled epibatidine, a compound that binds to high-affinity nicotinic binding sites. (A) and (B) show total binding in a nonsmoker and a smoker, respectively, illustrating the particularly large amount of receptor up-regulation in cortical layer VI. (C) shows nonspecific epibatidine binding (i.e., binding to tissue elements other than nicotinic receptors), which was very low. (From Perry et al., 1999.)

(as indicated by the threshold for intracranial electrical self-stimulation) is also significantly reduced during nicotine withdrawal (Epping-Jordan et al., 1998)—an effect seen during withdrawal from other abused drugs as well. A decreased ability to experience rewarding stimuli might also be present during tobacco withdrawal in smokers and might contribute to the well-known difficulty in stopping smoking. Current evidence suggests that the nicotine abstinence syndrome is mediated by a combination of reduced DA activity in the NAcc and increased corticotropin-releasing factor (CRF) activity in the central nucleus of the amygdala (Bruijnzeel et al., 2012; Greider et al., 2010; Zhang et al., 2012).

Section Summary

- The mood-altering effects of nicotine depend on whether the subject is an abstinent smoker or a nonsmoker. In temporarily abstinent smokers, administration of pure nicotine usually increases calmness and relaxation. This effect is due, in part, to relief from nicotine withdrawal symptoms, because nicotine given to nonsmokers more often elicits feelings of tension, arousal, lightheadedness or dizziness, and sometimes nausea.

- Administration of nicotine to abstinent smokers also leads to enhanced performance on various cognitive tasks, particularly those involving attentional demands. In this case, however, some nicotine-related functional enhancement has also been reported for nonsmokers. Thus nicotine may produce certain positive effects in addition to its ability to alleviate withdrawal-related deficits.

- Animal studies have found that nicotine improves performance on tasks requiring sustained attention and working memory. Some results suggest that the attention-enhancing effects of nicotine are dependent primarily on α7-containing receptors.

- Within a certain dose range, pure nicotine is reinforcing to both humans and experimental animals. The reinforcing properties of nicotine are believed to involve activation of high-affinity receptors located in the VTA that stimulate the firing of DA neurons and increase DA release in the NAcc. This hypothesis is supported by the finding that nicotinic receptors in the VTA containing α4 and/or α6 in combination with β2 subunits are necessary for nicotine self-administration. In contrast, α5-containing nicotinic receptors in the medial habenula reduce the reinforcing properties of nicotine, particularly at high drug doses.

can be observed when the nicotine clears the animal's system when the pump either runs out of solution or is removed by the experimenter. However, a stronger reaction can be triggered by administering a nicotinic receptor antagonist such as **mecamylamine**, thereby blocking the action of any residual nicotine still present in the animal. In rats, typical nicotine withdrawal symptoms include gasps, shakes or tremors, teeth chatter, ptosis (drooping eyelids), reduced locomotor activity, and increased startle reactivity (Helton et al., 1993; Hildebrand et al., 1997). Brain reward function

- Nicotine additionally produces a variety of peripheral physiological effects. These include release of epinephrine and norepinephrine from the adrenal glands, tachycardia, and elevated blood pressure, all of which contribute to the arousing effects of the drug. Nicotine also increases hydrochloric acid secretion in the stomach and muscle contraction in the bowel, both of which can adversely affect the gastrointestinal tract. Finally, nicotine modestly increases metabolic rate and suppresses appetite, which accounts for why smokers typically gain weight after quitting.

- Nicotine is a toxic substance that can cause potentially dangerous symptoms such as nausea, salivation, abdominal pain, vomiting and diarrhea, confusion, and weakness. If a sufficient dose has been ingested, death may occur from respiratory failure. Treatment involves an attempt to remove the nicotine from the victim's stomach (if the nicotine has been swallowed), administration of artificial respiration, and dealing with drug-induced shock.

- Repeated exposure to nicotine can lead to tolerance and, in some cases, sensitization. Single doses of nicotine cause a rapid but transient form of acute tolerance that depends on desensitization of nicotinic receptors. Long-term nicotine exposure is associated with chronic tolerance, as a consequence of which smokers do not exhibit the adverse reactions to high doses of nicotine that are observed in nonsmokers. Smokers show an up-regulation of nicotinic receptor levels in many brain areas, seemingly as a compensatory response to the chronic receptor desensitization associated with repeated nicotine exposure.

- When rats are made dependent on nicotine by giving them continuous exposure to the drug, withdrawal symptoms can be observed if the dependent animals are administered a nicotinic receptor antagonist such as mecamylamine. This withdrawal syndrome has been related to reduced DA release in the NAcc and increased CRF activity in the central nucleus of the amygdala.

Cigarette Smoking

Useful information about the causes and consequences of smoking has been obtained by documenting changes in the prevalence of smoking over time and by identifying the characteristics of smokers and the pattern of progression from occasional to regular smoking. This information has been combined with knowledge about the mechanisms of nicotine action and data on the serious health consequences of smoking to develop smoking cessation programs.

How many people smoke, and who are they?

The amount of cigarette smoking in the United States has varied tremendously over the past 100 years. As illustrated in **Figure 13.12**, yearly per capita cigarette consumption was quite low at the beginning of the twentieth century but then rose steeply until the mid-1950s. There was a brief dip in cigarette consumption following publication of the first studies linking smoking with lung cancer, but consumption rose again with the marketing of filtered cigarettes. The decline in cigarette consumption since the 1960s coincides with the Surgeon General's reports on the health consequences of smoking, the appearance of antismoking ads, large increases in cigarette taxes, and general disapproval of smoking in many parts of society.

Figure 13.13 from the 2011 National Survey on Drug Use and Health shows that the national trend in the direction of reduced cigarette smoking has continued in recent years. Nevertheless, an estimated 56.8 million people aged 12 or older (representing 22% of the population) were current cigarette smokers at the time of the survey (Substance Abuse and Mental Health Services Administration, 2012). Cigarette smoking was more prevalent in men than women, in non-college graduates compared with college graduates, and in

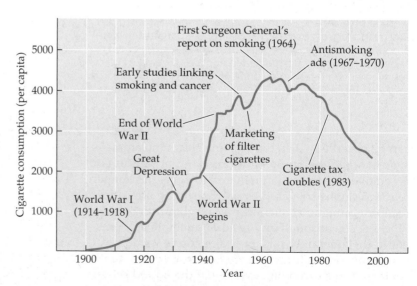

Figure 13.12 Yearly per capita cigarette consumption in the United States from 1900 to 1998 for individuals 18 years of age or older (After Smith and Fiore, 1999.)

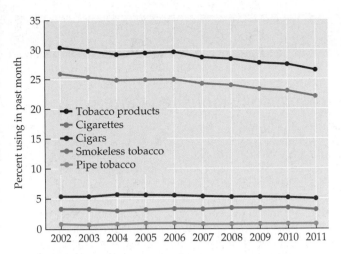

Figure 13.13 Past month tobacco use among persons aged 12 or older from 2002 to 2011 (After Substance Abuse and Mental Health Services Administration, 2012.)

unemployed compared with employed individuals. Across different racial and ethnic groups, the highest rate of smoking was reported by American Indians and Alaskan Natives, followed by whites, blacks, Hispanics, and then Asians.

In addition to the gender difference in smoking prevalence, there is emerging evidence that women tend to differ from men in the characteristics of their smoking behavior and in the determinants of smoking. Women typically smoke fewer cigarettes per day than men, they may prefer cigarettes with less nicotine, and they generally don't inhale as deeply. Some studies have also found that women are more influenced than men by the nonnicotine aspects of smoking (e.g., sensory or social factors) compared with reinforcement from nicotine, and women find it more difficult to quit smoking, even when given nicotine replacement therapy (Perkins et al., 1999). We don't yet understand the reasons for these significant gender differences.

Cigarette smokers progress through a series of stages in their smoking behavior

Most smokers pick up the habit during adolescence. Looked at another way, early smoking greatly increases the chances that one will smoke as an adult. For this reason, teenage smoking has received a lot of attention from researchers as well as from policy makers interested in reducing the prevalence of this behavior in our society. There are many theories about why teenagers take up smoking. Some of the hypothesized reasons include establishing feelings of independence and maturity (by defying parental wishes or societal norms), improving self-image and enhancing social

acceptance (assuming that one's friends are already smokers), counteracting stress and/or boredom, and simple curiosity. Moreover, young people tend to emphasize the positive elements of smoking while disregarding or denying the negative aspects, including the health consequences.

Early adolescent experimentation with cigarettes can lead to a variety of outcomes. Many individuals never develop any kind of smoking habit, whereas a small percentage become "chippers," smokers who maintain a pattern of regular smoking of a few cigarettes a day without showing the typical signs of dependence (Shiffman and Paty, 2006). Finally, there are individuals who develop an established pattern of smoking characterized by compulsive use, cravings for tobacco, and difficulty stopping this behavior. A considerable amount of research has focused on such questions as: what are the stages traversed in the development of the smoking habit? How rapidly do adolescents become "hooked" on smoking? And what is the role of nicotine dependence in adolescent smoking? **Box 13.1** discusses the current views on these and related questions.

Why do smokers smoke?

Researchers have identified multiple factors that contribute to the development and maintenance of a smoking habit. Nicotine is one obvious factor, but other influences are also important as discussed below.

SMOKING AND STRESS Smokers routinely report that smoking causes relaxation, alleviation of stress, and increased ability to concentrate. Consequently, some researchers have hypothesized that smoking (presumably through the delivery of nicotine) provides two specific advantages to the smoker: greater mood control (specifically with respect to stress reduction) and enhancement of concentration. This has been termed the **nicotine resource model**. An alternative model, sometimes called the **deprivation reversal model**, suggests that the positive effects of smoking actually represent the alleviation of irritability, stress, and poor concentration experienced by smokers between cigarettes. This model, therefore, proposes that having a smoking habit increases overall stress, which then must be countered by repeated smoking.

Researchers have debated these two ideas for many years and there are still proponents of both. However, studies by the British psychologist Andrew Parrott as well as other researchers argue strongly for the idea of deprivation reversal (Parrott, 2006). It seems that the short-term "relaxing" effect of smoking merely brings the smoker to the same state as a typical nonsmoker,

BOX 13.1   The Cutting Edge

What Is the Progression from First Cigarette to an Established Pattern of Smoking?

Nicotine is a highly addictive drug. Indeed, recent results from the National Epidemiologic Survey on Alcohol and Related Conditions found that over 67% of nicotine users eventually became dependent, whereas the percentages for alcohol, cocaine, and cannabis were only 22.7%, 20.9%, and 8.9%, respectively (Lopez-Quintero et al., 2011). Most cigarette smokers have their first contact with cigarettes during late childhood or adolescence. For our society to reduce the prevalence of smoking, we need to understand the consequences of this early exposure to cigarettes and nicotine, including the steps that occur during the progression from initial exposure to frequent smoking, and how early in their smoking habit young smokers develop nicotine dependence.

There is a consensus among researchers that smokers go through several different stages from initial experimentation with cigarettes to a regular smoking habit. However, there is less agreement as to the exact definition and features of each stage. After reviewing a number of studies on this topic, Mayhew and colleagues (2000) proposed the staging system shown in the table. Interestingly, adolescents' self-perceptions do not always fit well with the stages suggested by researchers such as Mayhew and her group. For example, a Canadian survey study by Leatherman and McDonald (2006) found that about 50% of adolescents who met the Mayhew et al. (2000) criteria for "regular smoker" did not even consider themselves to be smokers when given a yes-no choice of whether they were a smoker or not. Such findings underscore the importance of developing adolescent smoking taxonomies that correspond better to smokers' self-perceptions.

Besides possible questions about the exact stages presented in the table, there are at least two additional limitations of this taxonomy. First, Mayhew et al. (2000) propose that only established smokers (i.e., daily or near-daily smokers) are nicotine-dependent. Given the different methods for assessing dependence, many adolescents who smoke less frequently still exhibit significant signs of dependence (Colby et al., 2000; also see below). Second, merely designating a system of stages of smoking behavior doesn't tell us about the various trajectories that may occur as individuals move from a nonsmoking status to a dependent smoker. Again, different studies have proposed a variety of terms to describe the observed trajectories of acquiring nicotine dependence; however, researchers commonly find variations on the following four classes: (1) no dependence (individual exhibits no symptoms of dependence over the course of the study); (2) early onset and continued maintenance of dependence; (3) early onset of dependence but later remission; and (4) late onset of dependence. In a recent longitudinal study of Chicago public school children in grades 6 to 10, 47% of the children were in class 1, 21% were in class 2, 18% were in class 3, and 14% were in class 4 (Hu et al., 2008). A different study that categorized smoking trajectories over a 24-month period in secondary school students from Montreal, Canada reported four kinds of trajectories: low-intensity nonprogressing smokers (72% of the subjects), slow escalators (11%), moderate escalators (11%), and rapid escalators (6%) (Karp et al., 2005). These two studies used nicotine dependence criteria from the *Diagnostic and Statistical Manual of Mental Disorders*

Proposed Stages in the Development of a Smoking Habit

Stage	Definition
1a. Nonsmoking—precontemplation	Nonsmoker and doesn't intend to start smoking
1b. Nonsmoking—contemplation or preparation	Nonsmoker but is thinking about starting
2. Initiation or tried	Has smoked a few cigarettes only
3. Experimentation	Smokes occasionally/experimentally; not yet committed to smoking
4. Regular smoker	Smokes on a regular basis (for example, on weekends or at parties), but not too frequently and not daily
5. Established smoker	Smokes daily or almost daily, sometimes heavily; nicotine-dependent

Source: Mayhew et al., 2000.

BOX 13.1 *(continued)*

(*DSM-IV*) and the *International Classification of Diseases* (*ICD-10*), respectively.

Over 10 years ago, Joseph DiFranza and colleagues at the University of Massachusetts Medical School began to question the use of the standard *DSM-IV* or *ICD-10* criteria for defining nicotine dependence in adolescent smokers. These researchers reasoned first that these criteria had been developed from studies of adult smokers, and perhaps they didn't apply fully to younger individuals. Second, it seemed possible that relatively few experiences with smoking might set some adolescents on a trajectory that subsequently led to a pattern of regular smoking. To test these ideas, DiFranza and coworkers developed the Hooked on Nicotine Checklist (HONC) shown in the figure. The investigators then used this instrument to conduct a longitudinal survey (which they termed the Development and Assessment of Nicotine Dependence in Youths, or DANDY study) of almost 700 seventh-grade students in central Massachusetts. By roughly the end of the first year of the study, 39% of the subjects had puffed on a cigarette at least once, and 15% had progressed to smoking at least once a month (DiFranza et al., 2000). Importantly, more than half of the monthly smokers reported experiencing one or more symptoms on the HONC despite the fact that these individuals were still far from smoking on a daily basis. A follow-up of the same subjects 30 months after the beginning of the study found that HONC scores correlated highly with variables such as frequency of smoking and maximum amount of tobacco

---

The Hooked on Nicotine Checklist

1. Have you ever tried to quit but couldn't?

2. Do you smoke *now* because it is really hard to quit?

3. Have you ever left like you were addicted to tobacco?

4. Do you ever have strong cravings to smoke?

5. Have you ever felt like you really needed a cigarette?

6. Is it hard to keep from smoking in places where you are not supposed to, like school?

When you tried to stop smoking... (or, when you haven't used tobacco for a while...)

7. did you find it hard to concentrate because you couldn't smoke?

8. did you feel more irritable because you couldn't smoke?

9. did you feel a strong need or urge to smoke?

10. did you feel nervous, restless, or anxious because you couldn't smoke?

Source: DiFranza et al., 2002a.

---

smoked, and reporting of at least one symptom strongly predicted continued smoking through the end of the study (DiFranza et al., 2002a, 2002b). Furthermore, the median frequency of smoking at the time of the first symptom experience was two cigarettes smoked on 1 day per week. These findings prompted the authors to propose that "loss of autonomy" over tobacco use, meaning a diminution of the individual's ability to control his or her smoking behavior, signifies the onset of nicotine dependence. In addition, such loss of autonomy can occur early in the person's smoking history after relatively few smoking experiences (see also DiFranza et al., 2007; Scragg et al., 2008; Savageau et al., 2009; Doubeni et al., 2010).

It is important to note that the loss of autonomy hypothesis based on results from the HONC has been criticized by some investigators such as Dar and Frenk (2010). These authors had many

objections to this hypothesis, arguing for example that a positive response to just one item on the HONC is an inadequate criterion for determining that someone is nicotine dependent. However, DiFranza (2010) subsequently offered strong counterarguments to the criticisms made by Dar and Frenk. In conclusion, although there are legitimate reasons for researchers to disagree about the definition of nicotine dependence in adolescent smokers and the impact of a few cigarettes on the later development of such dependence, there is little doubt that the work of DiFranza and colleagues has played a major role in demonstrating that urges to smoke and difficulty quitting occur in a significant proportion of young cigarette smokers. These findings have important public health implications for the promotion of school-age programs aimed at reducing adolescent experimentation with cigarettes.

---

rather than producing a higher level of relaxation. In the long term, being a smoker is associated with increased stress and depressed mood, and quitting smoking generally ameliorates these effects.

THE ROLE OF NICOTINE IN SMOKING   Delivery of nicotine is obviously one of the key factors in smoking. As mentioned earlier, nicotine is intravenously self-administered by animals as well as by humans under the appropriate

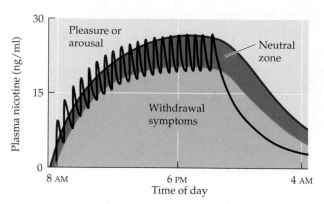

Figure 13.14 The daily smoking cycle and nicotine-induced mood changes Plasma nicotine is low in the morning as a result of overnight abstinence from smoking. Each cigarette over the course of the day leads to a spike followed by a decline in nicotine levels. The purple area in the figure depicts the zone of neutral affect (mood) between the pleasure and arousal produced by elevated nicotine levels (i.e., levels above the neutral zone) and the withdrawal symptoms produced by declining levels in a dependent smoker (i.e., levels below the neutral zone). Note that nicotine-induced positive effects diminish with repeated smoking episodes as a result of rapid tolerance to the drug's action, whereas withdrawal symptoms may become more pronounced. The nicotinic receptors resensitize significantly during overnight abstinence, allowing the cycle to repeat itself each day. (After Benowitz, 2010.)

conditions. Over a 24-hour period, a regular smoker undergoes repeated elevations and drops in plasma nicotine as shown in **Figure 13.14**. However, whereas cigarettes early in the day (beginning particularly with the first cigarette, which is smoked after the overnight period of abstinence) may elevate mood above the baseline level, later in the day even the peaks in plasma nicotine may not be sufficient to do more than merely maintain a neutral mood (by avoiding withdrawal symptoms) because of the nicotinic receptor desensitization discussed previously (Benowitz, 2010). Overnight abstinence permits the receptors to resensitize and the cycle to begin again the following day.

Other evidence for an involvement of nicotine comes from smoking behavior itself. Cigarettes devoid of nicotine (e.g., lettuce-based cigarettes) have never been commercially successful. Furthermore, it is well established that smoking intensity is increased when smokers of regular cigarettes switch to a brand that is low in nicotine and tar. This change in smoking behavior increases nicotine yields well beyond those specified by the Federal Trade Commission (FTC), which are based on standardized smoking by a machine.

Finally, withdrawal from regular tobacco use leads to significant abstinence symptoms that are thought to result primarily from removal of nicotine from the person's system. For habitual smokers who meet the

criteria for nicotine dependence, even a brief abstinence of a few hours leads to craving and a growing urge to smoke. These feelings correlate with a drop in nicotine levels in the individual's bloodstream. The much longer abstinence that occurs when people try to quit smoking leads to a more complex abstinence syndrome characterized not only by tobacco craving but also by irritability, impatience, restlessness, anxiety, insomnia, difficulty concentrating, and hunger and weight gain (Paolini and De Biasi, 2011). **Figure 13.15** presents the results from one study that examined the time course of withdrawal symptoms as well as the ability of nicotine gum to prevent such symptoms (Hughes et al., 1991). We can see that the abstinence syndrome was still present at 1 week postcessation, but except for hunger and weight gain, the average levels of most symptoms were at or near baseline at 4 weeks. These group data suggest that the abstinence syndrome from tobacco is relatively short-lasting. Nevertheless, the investigators found that about 20% to 25% of the subjects still reported significant symptoms at the 4-week time point. Nicotine gum clearly prevented almost all of the withdrawal symptoms except for hunger and weight gain, supporting the conclusion that most of these symptoms are due to nicotine dependence. Not shown in this figure, however, is the fact that even with the nicotine gum, more than two-thirds of the subjects were back smoking at a 6-month follow-up test despite lacking the typical withdrawal symptoms. These and other experimental results indicate that the nicotine abstinence syndrome is not the only reason that most regular smokers find it so difficult to quit their habit.

As mentioned earlier, chippers are long-term smokers who smoke regularly but smoke only a few cigarettes each day and do not become dependent. For example, Perkins and coworkers (2001) studied a cohort of nondependent smokers who had smoked an average of just 3.4 cigarettes per day for approximately 14 years. Interestingly, chippers develop tolerance to nicotine despite their limited exposure (Perkins et al., 2001). The finding that nicotine dependence and tolerance can be separated from each together suggests that they are produced by different physiological processes. It would be very useful to understand why some individuals can avoid nicotine dependence and maintain low levels of smoking, but unfortunately we don't yet know what characteristics differentiate chippers from more typical smokers.

THE ROLE OF OTHER FACTORS IN SMOKING Even though most of us think "nicotine" when we think about smoking, it cannot be the only factor responsible for maintaining this behavior. Indeed, given that many of the nicotinic receptors responsible for stimulating DA release in the NAcc are thought to be desensitized for most of

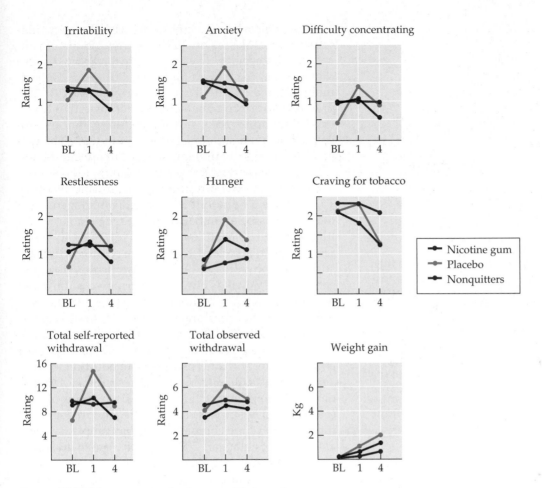

Figure 13.15 Time course of tobacco withdrawal symptoms and the effects of nicotine replacement therapy Regular smokers who wanted to quit smoking were randomly assigned to either a nicotine gum or a placebo gum group. Symptom ratings were obtained before the beginning of treatment (baseline, BL) and then again 1 and 4 weeks later. The figure illustrates data for those subjects who were abstinent at the 4-week test point compared with those who failed to quit during the study. (After Hughes et al., 1991.)

the day in regular smokers, why do such individuals continue to smoke throughout the day with relatively little direct nicotine reinforcement? One reason, of course, is because they are nicotine-dependent and want to avoid nicotine withdrawal symptoms. However, there is also strong evidence that sensory stimuli associated with the act of smoking, such as the taste and smell of inhaling cigarette smoke, become conditioned to the reinforcing effects of nicotine and are thus able to function as secondary reinforcers themselves (Rose, 2006). Indeed, formerly secret internal documents obtained from major cigarette manufacturers reveal that these companies know about the importance of the sensory qualities of tobacco smoke and manipulate these qualities to enhance smoker satisfaction (Carpenter et al., 2007).

One example of the power of nonnicotine elements of smoking comes from a laboratory study of (nonabstinent) experienced smokers who preferred puffing on a denicotinized cigarette over receiving an IV nicotine infusion that mimicked the rise in arterial nicotine concentrations produced by cigarette smoke (Rose, 2006) **(Figure 13.16)**. To understand how the sensory stimuli of smoking become conditioned to nicotine reinforcement, recall that each puff on a standard cigarette delivers a small burst of nicotine to the brain. Assuming 30 cigarettes per day (1½ packs) and 10 puffs per cigarette, a 10-year smoker has had over 1 million "learning trials" in which a mouthful of cigarette smoke was paired with one of those bursts of nicotine. Consider further that in a nonsmoker who has not developed such an association, the sensory qualities of cigarette smoke are harsh and unpleasant. For these reasons, it is likely that the sensory aspects of smoking help maintain this behavior under conditions where direct nicotine reinforcement is minimal because of receptor desensitization.

Additional factors such as the knowledge of upcoming opportunities to smoke contribute to the maintenance of the smoking habit. In support of this idea, Dar and coworkers (2010) recently reported that

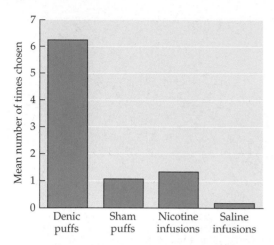

Figure 13.16 Components of tobacco smoke other than nicotine contribute to smoking behavior Regular smokers were given a choice of four alternatives: (1) puffing on a denicotinized (Denic) cigarette; (2) sham-puffing (puffing on a regular cigarette equipped with a filter that prevented smoke from reaching the subject; this condition controlled for the sensory-motor phenomena associated with puffing behavior); (3) IV infusions of nicotine in which each dose was equivalent to the amount of drug present in one puff of the subject's habitual brand of cigarettes; and (4) infusions of saline vehicle. The graph shows the responses for each choice over a 10-minute test period. (After Rose, 2006.)

the craving to smoke among flight attendants was more closely related to the time remaining in the flight than to the length of abstinence from nicotine (i.e., the overall length of the flight). Taken together with other findings, including those discussed above regarding the sensory features of smoking, it is clear that smoking is a complex behavior governed by multiple factors, both psychological and pharmacological.

Smoking is a major cause of illness and premature death

In 2010, the Surgeon General of the U.S. Department of Health and Human Services issued a comprehensive expert report on how tobacco smoke causes disease and premature death. The report noted that approximately one-half of all individuals who begin smoking during adolescence and continue with a long-term smoking habit die prematurely as a result of their exposure to tobacco. Government statistics show that cigarette smoking is the major preventable cause of death among Americans, with more than 430,000 people dying each year from tobacco-related causes (U.S. Department of Health and Human Services, 2010). The combination of medical costs and productivity losses associated with smoking-related illnesses is estimated to exceed $193 billion a year (Adhikari et al., 2008).

Cigarette smoking increases the risk for many life-threatening illnesses, including several kinds of cancer, cardiovascular disease, and respiratory disease (Forey et al., 2011; Shah and Cole, 2010; U.S. Department of Health and Human Services, 2010). The organs that can be adversely affected by either direct or secondhand smoke and the resulting cancers and chronic diseases are depicted in **Figure 13.17**. The deleterious effects of smoking stem from a combination of factors, including tar, carbon monoxide gas that is produced by the burning of tobacco, and nicotine. Tar contains a number of identified carcinogens, and the strong association between cigarette smoking and lung cancer has been known for well over 40 years. Smoking can also lead to other respiratory diseases such as emphysema and chronic bronchitis (together sometimes known as **chronic obstructive pulmonary disease**, or **COPD**). Although there is less public recognition of the relationship between smoking and cardiovascular disease, this relationship is actually quite strong. Smokers are at increased risk for heart attack, stroke, and atherosclerosis. In addition to these adverse effects of smoking on the respiratory and cardiovascular systems, evidence has been accumulating that long-term smokers suffer a decline in cognitive function over time compared with nonsmokers (Swan and Lessov-Schlaggar, 2007). Finally, pregnant smokers in particular should try to stop or at least cut back on their smoking habit. Smoking during pregnancy is the leading cause of low birthweight, which delays the infant's development and puts her at risk for other complications.

Behavioral and pharmacological strategies are used to treat tobacco dependence

Surveys indicate that 70% to 75% of current smokers in the United States would like to quit smoking, and about 40% to 45% of daily smokers actually attempt to quit each year. However, addiction to nicotine is so powerful that the success rate is very low. As was the case for one of the authors (JM) many years ago, the smoking habit can be overcome, but the process is difficult and usually requires multiple attempts to quit.

We will consider a variety of behavioral and pharmacological approaches for treating tobacco dependence. It is important to recognize that the success rate of any treatment approach is influenced by numerous variables, such as the duration of smoking behavior and the number of cigarettes smoked daily, the intensity of the abstinence syndrome, the motivation to quit, whether or not the smoker lives and/or works in a smoking environment, and so on. Furthermore, even if a given therapeutic program claims a high success

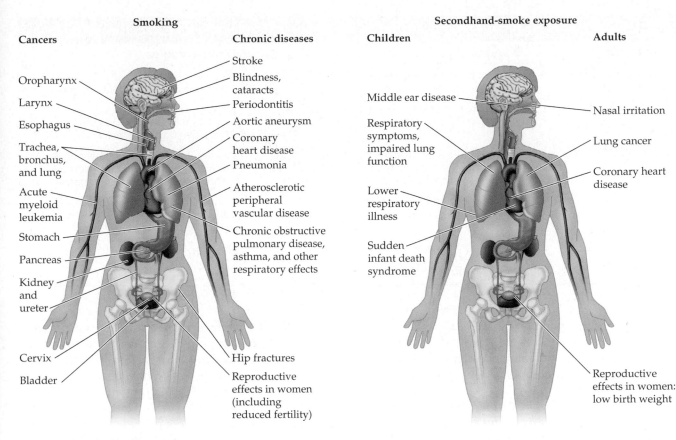

Smoking

Cancers

Oropharynx
Larynx
Esophagus
Trachea, bronchus, and lung
Acute myeloid leukemia
Stomach
Pancreas
Kidney and ureter
Cervix
Bladder

Chronic diseases

Stroke
Blindness, cataracts
Periodontitis
Aortic aneurysm
Coronary heart disease
Pneumonia
Atherosclerotic peripheral vascular disease
Chronic obstructive pulmonary disease, asthma, and other respiratory effects
Hip fractures
Reproductive effects in women (including reduced fertility)

Secondhand-smoke exposure

Children

Middle ear disease
Respiratory symptoms, impaired lung function
Lower respiratory illness
Sudden infant death syndrome

Adults

Nasal irritation
Lung cancer
Coronary heart disease
Reproductive effects in women: low birth weight

Figure 13.17 Adverse health effects of smoking and exposure to secondhand smoke (After U.S. Department of Health and Human Services, 2010.)

rate for its clients, such claims are meaningless unless there is careful follow-up for months and years to ascertain long-term abstinence.

BEHAVIORAL INTERVENTIONS   A number of strategies are directed toward discouraging young people from beginning tobacco use or giving it up if it is already habitually used. For example, various state and federal agencies sponsor antismoking appeals in the media, and the Surgeon General's office has mandated health warnings on cigarette packages for many years. Another approach is the levying of high taxes on tobacco products. This may not prevent people from starting to use these products, but it does reduce the amount of use.

Many smokers attempt to quit by using various self-help programs involving books or manuals. Although such programs are generally inexpensive, they don't appear to offer much benefit to the smoker. A bit more successful are individual or group counseling programs provided by health professionals, particularly those that provide social support and/or training in coping skills to their clients.

PHARMACOLOGICAL INTERVENTIONS   The most common pharmacological intervention for smoking cessation is **nicotine replacement**. This approach is based on several premises: (1) that the difficulty associated with smoking cessation is significantly related to nicotine withdrawal symptoms; (2) that blocking (or at least reducing) these symptoms by maintaining a certain circulating level of nicotine can assist in terminating smoking; and (3) that there are safer ways for individuals to obtain nicotine than by smoking.

Nicotine replacement was first accomplished by formulating a special nicotine-containing chewing gum (nicotine polacrilex), which has the advantage that nicotine can be absorbed by the buccal mucosa (mucous membranes lining the mouth) rather than the gastrointestinal tract, where absorption is minimal and there is substantial first-pass metabolism in the liver. Nicotine gum was approved as a pharmacotherapeutic aid in the treatment of cigarette dependence in 1984 under the trade name Nicorette. This was later followed by the transdermal nicotine patch (Nicoderm, Habitrol, Nicotrol), nicotine nasal spray (Nicotrol NS), nicotine inhaler (Nicotrol Inhaler), and nicotine lozenges (Commit Lozenges). The nasal spray and inhaler require a doctor's prescription, whereas nicotine gum, patches, and lozenges can be obtained over-the-counter (OTC). Making at least some nicotine medications available OTC

TABLE 13.1   Advantages and Disadvantages of Different Kinds of Nicotine Replacement Therapy

Treatment	Advantages	Disadvantages
Nicotine polacrilex (gum)	Easy to use; flexible dosing; OTC availability; rapid nicotine delivery	Frequent dosing needed; side effects such as jaw pain or mouth soreness
Nicotine lozenge	Easy to use; flexible dosing; OTC availability; rapid nicotine delivery	Frequent dosing needed; side effects such as heartburn or indigestion if lozenges consumed too rapidly
Transdermal nicotine patch	Easy to use; OTC availability; morning craving reduced with overnight use; few side effects except for possible skin irritation	Less flexible dosing and slower delivery of nicotine than with other treatments; overnight use may cause insomnia
Nicotine nasal spray	Flexible dosing; fastest nicotine delivery and reduction of cravings	Frequent dosing needed; initial side effects such as nose and eye irritation, sneezing, and coughing
Nicotine inhaler	Flexible dosing; use mimics the hand-to-mouth feature of smoking; few side effects except for mild throat irritation and coughing	Frequent dosing needed

was a significant advance in the battle against smoking, because some smokers are reluctant or unable financially to enter a formal treatment program yet may still be willing to try something they can obtain at a drug store without a prescription.

With all these choices available, which kind of nicotine replacement therapy should a smoker choose? **Table 13.1** lists some of the advantages and disadvantages of each nicotine delivery vehicle. Two additional points should be noted with respect to nicotine replacement therapy. First, combination treatments such as nicotine gum plus the patch or the nicotine inhaler plus the patch may be more effective than either treatment alone in helping some smokers quit their habit (George and O'Malley, 2004). Second, properly controlled studies examining the effectiveness of OTC nicotine replacement without additional supportive therapy reveal a relatively low success rate (Hughes et al., 2011). Consequently, smokers who desire to quit are advised to seek behavioral or psychosocial (supportive) therapy along with nicotine replacement to have the best chance to succeed.

Although nicotine replacement therapy continues to be refined and improved, two other pharmacological approaches have proven valuable in helping people quit smoking (Polosa and Benowitz, 2011). The first is bupropion (sustained-release formulation marketed as Zyban), a compound that was initially developed as an antidepressant. The efficacy of bupropion as a smoking cessation medication was discovered serendipitously when researchers noticed that depressed patients who were smokers and were given this compound for their depression reported reduced cigarette cravings and were able to quit smoking without additional therapeutic intervention. The antismoking properties of bupropion are thought to be related to its

actions as a DA uptake inhibitor and a weak antagonist at nicotinic cholinergic receptors. Somewhat more recently, a second drug, varenicline (Chantix), was introduced as a smoking cessation medication. Varenicline acts as a partial agonist at high-affinity $\alpha4\beta2$ nicotinic receptors that are expressed in the VTA, as well as in other brain areas. This partial agonism elicits a moderate amount of receptor activation, in contrast to the full receptor agonism produced by cigarette-derived nicotine. The resulting effect is a reduction of nicotine cravings and of adverse withdrawal reactions in the abstinent smoker.

Finally, you may recall that in the last chapter, we discussed efforts by researchers to develop a vaccine against cocaine. Similar work targeting nicotine is currently being conducted by several pharmaceutical companies, including Cytos AG, Celtic Pharma, and Nabi Biopharmaceuticals (Escobar-Chávez et al., 2011). Although preclinical animal studies yielded promising results for the vaccines produced by these firms, Phase II human clinical trials have thus far been disappointing in their lack of demonstrable efficacy. Thus, at the present time, the future of nicotine vaccines as useful smoking cessation treatments is uncertain.

Section Summary

- There are more than 56 million smokers in this country, according to the 2011 National Household Survey on Drug Use and Health. There are fewer female than male smokers, and women differ from men in their smoking habits. Smokers typically begin during adolescence, and many different reasons have been given for teenage smoking.

- Individuals go through several stages on the way from nonsmoking through occasional smoking and then eventually to established smoking. Several different kinds of trajectories have been reported for subjects progressing through these stages. On the basis of results from a questionnaire called the Hooked on Nicotine Checklist, DiFranza and coworkers have proposed that adolescents can lose autonomy over smoking after relatively few smoking experiences, and that such loss of autonomy is indicative of nicotine dependence and predicts a significant risk of developing a regular smoking habit later on.

- Because smokers commonly report that smoking causes relaxation, a reduction in stress, and increased concentration, some researchers have proposed a nicotine resource model hypothesizing that the nicotine obtained through smoking has the beneficial effects of increasing mood control (in relation to stress reduction) and enhancing concentration. However, accumulated evidence favors an alternative model, the deprivation reversal model, which argues that the positive effects experienced when smoking actually constitute the alleviation of withdrawal effects such as irritability, anxiety, and poor concentration.

- Nicotine dependence is one of the factors that maintains continued cigarette smoking. Repeated cigarette smoking during the day leads to nicotinic receptor desensitization, which is partially reversed by overnight abstinence. Dependent individuals who attempt to quit smoking experience a complex abstinence syndrome characterized by irritability, anxiety, insomnia, and of course tobacco craving.

- Chippers are long-term smokers who smoke a few cigarettes daily on a regular basis but do not become dependent. However, chippers do develop nicotine tolerance, which suggests that tolerance and dependence are produced by different physiological mechanisms.

- Although withdrawal symptoms undoubtedly play an important role in maintaining the smoking habit in dependent smokers, other factors also contribute to this habit, including the taste and smell of cigarette smoke.

- Chronic use of tobacco results in many adverse health consequences, including cancer, cardiovascular disease, and respiratory diseases such as emphysema and bronchitis. The deleterious effects of inhaling cigarette smoke have been related not only to nicotine but also to tar and carbon monoxide gas that is produced by the burning of tobacco.

- Many different treatment strategies have been developed to assist smokers in quitting. These include behavioral and pharmacological interventions. Nicotine replacement for the alleviation of withdrawal symptoms can be accomplished by means of nicotine gum, lozenges, patches, nasal spray, or inhaler. Two drugs are also available that help reduce cigarette cravings: the antidepressant bupropion (Zyban) and the partial nicotinic receptor agonist varenicline (Chantix). Finally, a nicotine vaccine that reduces nicotine availability to the brain has been under development for a number of years; however, clinical testing has not yet demonstrated significant therapeutic efficacy of this approach. Because breaking the smoking habit is almost always a difficult proposition, it is much better never to become dependent in the first place.

Caffeine

Background

If you are like most people living in Western societies, you probably had at least one cup of coffee (or perhaps tea) this morning, possibly followed by additional cups as the day progressed. Whether you like the taste of coffee (which is bitter when taken black) or not, you are probably consuming it at least partly for its pharmacological properties as a stimulant. This, of course, brings us to the subject of caffeine, the principal psychoactive ingredient in coffee.

The major source of caffeine is coffee beans, which are the seeds of the plant *Coffea arabica*. Tea leaves contain significant amounts of both caffeine and a related compound called *theophylline* (which is Greek for "divine leaf") (**Figure 13.18**). Caffeine is one of the most widely used drugs in the world. In the United States, for example, it is estimated that 80% to 90% of adults regularly drink caffeinated beverages. The typical caffeine content of various foodstuffs and OTC drugs is shown in **Table 13.2**. Taking these various sources together, the average adult caffeine intake in

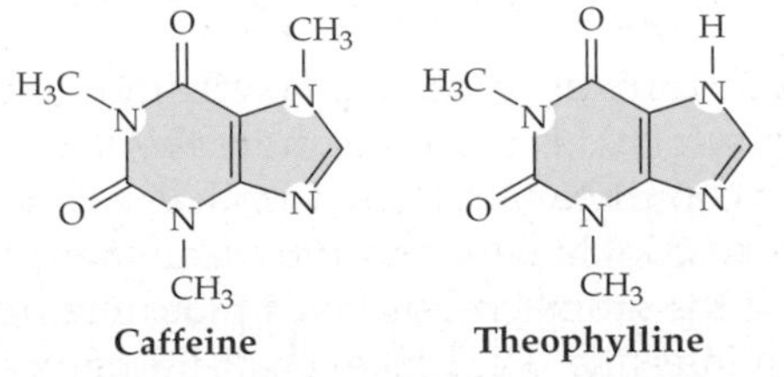

Caffeine   **Theophylline**

Figure 13.18 Chemical structures of caffeine and theophylline

TABLE 13.2 Typical Caffeine Content of Common Food Items and Drugs

Source	Caffeine content[a]
Beverages and foods	
Instant coffee	60 (12–169)/8-oz. cup
Brewed coffee	80 (40–110)/8-oz. cup
Short black coffee or espresso	107 (25–214)/standard serving
Starbucks Breakfast Blend coffee	415 (300–564)/Venti size
Iced coffee (commercial brands)	30–200/16-oz. bottle
Tea	27 (9-51)/8-oz. cup
Iced tea (commercial brands)	20–40/20-oz. bottle
Hot chocolate	5–10/8-oz. cup
Coca-Cola	49/12-oz. can
Dark chocolate	10–15/60-g serving
Sports gels and bars	
PowerBar caffeinated sports gel	25/40-g sachet
Carboshotz caffeinated sports gel	80/50-g sachet
PowerBar Acticaf Performance bar	50/65-g bar
Drugs	
No-Doz	200/tablet
Extra Strength Excedrin	65/tablet

Source: Burke, 2008.

[a]Typical value and range in mg per serving.

the United States has been estimated at 200 to 400 mg per day. As discussed later in the chapter, individuals who are compulsive coffee drinkers or who consume large amounts of caffeine-containing "energy drinks" can greatly exceed this dose. Children may also ingest considerable amounts of caffeine through consumption of caffeinated soft drinks and chocolate.

Basic Pharmacology of Caffeine

Caffeine is normally consumed orally through the beverages in which it is present. Under this condition, it is virtually completely absorbed from the gastrointestinal tract within 30 to 60 minutes. Caffeine absorption begins in the stomach but takes place mainly within the small intestine. The plasma half-life of caffeine varies substantially from one person to another, but the average value is about 4 hours. Consequently, people who drink coffee repeatedly over the course of a day experience gradually rising plasma caffeine concentrations. Most of this caffeine is then cleared from the circulation during sleep. The rate of plasma clearance is stimulated by smoking and is reduced when smoking is terminated. The resulting increase in plasma caffeine levels could contribute to cigarette withdrawal symptoms in heavy coffee drinkers, particularly since caffeine is anxiogenic (anxiety-provoking) at high doses (see the next section).

Caffeine is converted to a variety of metabolites by the liver. These metabolites account for almost all caffeine excretion, as only 1% to 2% of an administered dose is excreted unchanged. In humans, approximately 95% of caffeine metabolites are eliminated through the urine, 2% to 5% through the feces, and the remainder through other bodily fluids such as saliva.

Behavioral and Physiological Effects

Caffeine is best known for its ability to increase arousal; however, it can also enhance cognitive function and athletic performance when taken at appropriate doses. Regular use of caffeine can produce tolerance and dependence, and excessive ingestion poses significant health risks. Nevertheless, caffeine also has a few therapeutic uses that are mentioned below.

Acute subjective and behavioral effects of caffeine depend on dose and prior exposure

In laboratory animals such as rats and mice, caffeine has biphasic effects related to dose. At low doses, it has stimulant effects as shown by increased locomotor activity. At high doses, this effect is reversed and animals actually show reduced activity. This interesting dose–response function has been related to the neurochemical actions of caffeine, as discussed later in this chapter.

People ingest caffeine mostly for its stimulating and fatigue-reducing effects, as can be attested to by any student needing to "pull an all-nighter" before a big exam. The arousing effects of caffeine can disrupt sleep, particularly when the drug is consumed shortly before going to bed. On the other hand, caffeine can help reverse feelings of sleepiness when someone has been sleep deprived, and it has even been shown to improve driving performance when the driver is fatigued (Heatherley, 2011; Roehrs and Roth, 2008). At high doses of caffeine, humans do not show behavioral depression like rodents but rather experience feelings of tension and anxiety. Interestingly, patients suffering from panic disorder appear to be hypersensitive to caffeine's anxiogenic effects and may even suffer

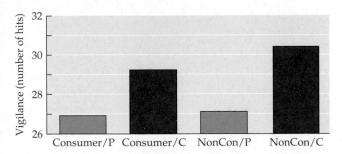

Figure 13.19 Effects of caffeine on attention Caffeine (C; 2 mg/kg) or a placebo (P) was administered to regular caffeine consumers who had undergone overnight withdrawal (Consumer) or to nonconsumers (NonCon) of caffeine. The same subjects were tested under both drug conditions on separate days. The figure shows performance on a vigilance task of sustained attention measured as the number of correct detections (hits) of a digit signal on a computer screen. Caffeine positively affected performance in both subject groups compared with placebo treatment. (After Smith et al., 2006.)

panic attacks in response to caffeine administration (Vilarim et al., 2011).

Caffeine does more than just increase our arousal. In controlled laboratory studies, humans receiving low or intermediate doses of caffeine report a variety of positive subjective effects, including feelings of well-being, enhanced energy or vigor, increased alertness and ability to concentrate, self-confidence, increased work motivation, and enhanced sociability (Glade, 2010). Caffeine is particularly effective in improving concentration in fatigued subjects and in the elderly (Nehlig, 2010). Many of the early studies demonstrating caffeine's enhancement of performance on cognitive tasks were conducted on regular caffeine users after some period of abstinence (usually either a few hours or overnight).

Because chronic caffeine consumption can lead to dependence and abstinence-related withdrawal symptoms (see later in this chapter), some investigators have proposed that cognitive enhancement may be due to alleviation of withdrawal symptoms rather than improvement over baseline levels (Rogers and Dernoncourt, 1998). However, more recent findings argue against this interpretation (Nehlig, 2010). For example, **Figure 13.19** presents some of the results from a study examining the influence of a single 2 mg/kg dose of caffeine on a variety of cognitive measures in both chronic caffeine consumers (tested after overnight abstinence) and nonconsumers (Smith et al., 2006). Note that on a measure of performance on a vigilance (i.e., sustained attention) task, there was no difference between the two groups (caffeine consumers and nonconsumers) when administered a placebo

instead of caffeine. This finding suggests a lack of performance decrement due to caffeine withdrawal. More importantly, both groups benefitted significantly from the caffeine treatment, supporting the interpretation that an appropriate dose of caffeine can increase attentiveness over baseline levels.

Caffeine consumption can enhance sports performance

The influence of caffeine on athletic performance has been a topic of research for many years. Most studies have examined the acute effects of moderate doses of caffeine (typically 3 to 6 mg/kg, which corresponds to about 200 to 400 mg for a 70-kg subject) administered before and sometimes also during performance of the sport (Burke, 2008). This research has demonstrated small but statistically significant benefits of caffeine both in endurance sports (e.g., distance running, cycling, swimming, rowing, cross-country skiing) and in short-term high-intensity activities (e.g., sprint running, sprint swimming, weight lifting) (Astorino and Roberson, 2010; Ganio et al., 2009). Variability of results within and across studies suggests that some individuals benefit more than others from caffeine, although the reason for such variability is not yet known. Tarnopolsky (2008) has proposed that several mechanisms may underlie the ergogenic (performance-enhancing) effects of caffeine, including increased force of muscle contraction, enhanced arousal and alertness as discussed earlier, and reduced pain perception.

Regular caffeine use leads to tolerance and dependence

What happens when people are chronically exposed to caffeine through regular coffee, tea, or soda consumption? For many years, it was believed that tolerance to the stimulating action of caffeine did not occur. However, there are now several studies showing that tolerance does develop to at least some of caffeine's subjective effects as well as its ability to disrupt sleep (Griffiths and Mumford, 1995). This may, for example, enable a heavy coffee drinker to consume caffeine shortly before bedtime and still fall asleep, whereas a late-night cup of coffee is likely to cause insomnia in someone who normally consumes little caffeine. Chronic caffeine use also produces tolerance to the cardiovascular and respiratory effects of the drug (see next section).

Perhaps those of you who are regular caffeine users have occasionally been forced to miss your morning cup of coffee or tea. It is likely that you experienced at least a few psychological and/or physical symptoms, including headache and lethargy or fatigue. If so, then you are dependent on caffeine. Don't worry though, as this is a very common type of drug dependence and is harmless except in a small percentage of individuals who have extremely high levels of caffeine intake. Controlled studies have demonstrated a range of caffeine withdrawal symptoms, including headache, drowsiness, fatigue, impaired concentration and psychomotor performance, and, in some cases, mild anxiety or depression. An intense craving for coffee may also be experienced. Symptoms of caffeine withdrawal can occur in individuals who are consuming as little as 100 mg/day, which is the equivalent of one 6-ounce cup of regular coffee or three cans of caffeinated soft drink (Juliano and Griffiths, 2004). If caffeine is withheld for a prolonged period of time, the abstinence syndrome lasts for a few days but then dissipates (**Figure 13.20**). It is important to note that despite the ability of caffeine to produce physical dependence, this compound does not meet the overall criteria necessary to be considered an addictive drug (Satel, 2006).

Researchers believe that relief from withdrawal is a major factor in chronic coffee drinking, particularly with regard to the first cup in the morning. This hypothesis is supported by controlled studies showing that physical dependence plays an important role in the reinforcing effects of caffeine and the choice to consume caffeinated beverages (Garrett and Griffiths, 1998). Caffeine withdrawal symptoms can be severe enough to cause occupational and/or social dysfunction in heavy users who have severe physical dependence on the drug. There is even evidence that some schoolchildren become dependent on caffeine as the result of heavy intake of cola and other caffeine-containing beverages or food. Indeed, frequent headaches have been reported in children and adolescents who were consuming at least 1.5 liters of cola drinks (containing about 200 mg of caffeine) per day (Hering-Hanit and Gadoth, 2003). In almost all cases, the headaches completely disappeared following gradual cessation of caffeine consumption.

Caffeine and caffeine-like drugs pose health risks but also exert therapeutic benefits

Acute caffeine administration leads to several effects on peripheral physiology, including increased blood pressure and respiration rate, enhanced water excretion (diuresis), and stimulation of catecholamine release from the adrenal medulla (Dews, 1982). These effects are most evident in people who are not regular caffeine consumers, indicating the production of tolerance under conditions of chronic caffeine intake.

Not surprisingly, the greatest health risks are associated with high levels of caffeine consumption. Chronic ingestion of excessive amounts of caffeine

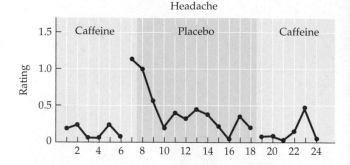

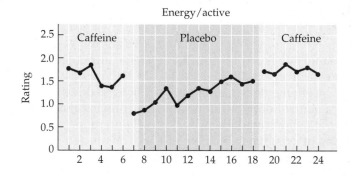

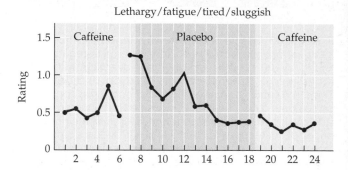

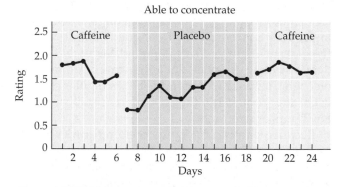

Figure 13.20 Time course of caffeine withdrawal in regular users During the first phase of the study (left panel in each graph), subjects were maintained on 100 mg of caffeine daily in capsule form while abstaining from all dietary sources of caffeine. During the second phase (middle panel), placebo capsules were substituted for caffeine without the knowledge of the subjects. In the third phase (right panel), caffeine administration was reinstated. Caffeine withdrawal symptoms rapidly appeared during abstinence; however, the symptoms gradually disappeared over the course of several days. (After Griffiths et al., 1990.)

(typically 1000 mg or more per day) can lead to a syndrome called **caffeinism**, which is characterized by restlessness, nervousness, insomnia, and physiological

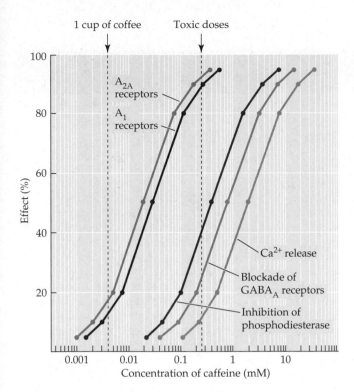

Figure 13.21 Concentration–response curves for caffeine's effects on various neurochemical processes Partial blockade of adenosine A_1 and A_{2A} receptors occurs at caffeine concentrations produced by typical doses such as those present in one or a few cups of coffee. In contrast, other effects of caffeine require concentrations in the toxic range. (After Daly and Fredholm, 1998.)

disorders such as Alzheimer's disease and Parkinson's disease (Daly, 2007).

Mechanisms of Action

Although the mechanism by which caffeine exerts its stimulant effects is not yet completely understood, substantial progress has been made over the past 25 to 30 years. It is clear that caffeine does not directly influence catecholamine systems in the manner of the psychomotor stimulants amphetamine and cocaine. How else might it work? When the biochemistry of the second messenger cyclic adenosine monophosphate (cAMP) was first being studied, investigators discovered that caffeine and theophylline are inhibitors of cAMP phosphodiesterase, the enzyme that breaks down cAMP. This led to the theory that the behavioral activation produced by caffeine or theophylline was caused by a buildup of brain cAMP concentrations. Subsequent research, however, demonstrated that such activation can occur at brain concentrations that are insufficient to inhibit phosphodiesterase. In addition, phosphodiesterase inhibitors that differ in their chemical structure from caffeine or theophylline are actually behavioral depressants rather than stimulants. These findings cast serious doubt on the relevance of this phosphodiesterase inhibition for the stimulant properties of caffeine and theophylline.

Subsequent research identified several other cellular actions of caffeine. These include blockade of $GABA_A$ receptors, stimulation of Ca^{2+} release within cells, and blockade of A_1 and A_{2A} receptors for a substance called **adenosine**. **Figure 13.21** illustrates idealized concentration–response functions for the various cellular effects of caffeine. We can see that at the levels of caffeine associated with one or a few cups of coffee, only the adenosine receptor blockade would come into play. The other effects require much higher doses, even into the toxic range associated with caffeinism.

There is now overwhelming evidence that blockade of adenosine receptors underlies caffeine-induced behavioral stimulation. To understand this mechanism, therefore, we need to say something about adenosine and its role in the nervous system. In biology and biochemistry classes, students learn about the role of adenosine as a constituent of the vital

disturbances including tachycardia (increased heart rate) and gastrointestinal upset. Because of the similar symptomatology, caffeinism is sometimes difficult to distinguish from a primary anxiety disorder. There is even a recent case study of a man who developed a psychotic reaction involving delusions and paranoia as a consequence of drinking more than a gallon of coffee every day (Hedges et al., 2009). Although we don't have reliable data on the prevalence of caffeinism in the United States, the popularity of coffee and caffeine-containing energy drinks (**Box 13.2**) suggests that this disorder may be more widespread than previously recognized. The factors underlying the development and maintenance of caffeinism have not yet been identified. However, one possibility is that individuals suffering from this disorder experience particularly strong withdrawal symptoms and craving when they attempt to curtail their usage.

Although caffeine is not usually regarded as a medicinal agent, it does have several therapeutic uses. First, caffeine has mild analgesic effects, and it can also potentiate the analgesic properties of aspirin and acetaminophen (Shapiro, 2008). For this reason, caffeine is a constituent of several OTC analgesic agents including Anacin and Excedrin. Probably the most important clinical use of caffeine is in the treatment of newborn infants suffering from apneic episodes (periodic cessation of breathing) (Sale, 2010). Premature infants whose respiratory system has not yet matured are particularly vulnerable to this disorder, and caffeine can be lifesaving in these babies by regularizing their breathing. Finally, caffeine as well as novel compounds that exert caffeine-like biochemical actions (see the next section) are currently under consideration for the treatment of asthma, type 2 diabetes, and some neurodegenerative

BOX 13.2   Of Special Interest

Do Caffeine-Containing Energy Drinks Pose a Risk to Your Health?

Energy drinks constitute the fastest growing segment of the beverage market. According to a 2012 press release from Zenith International, a consultant to the food and drink industry, global energy drink sales reached $37 billion in 2011. Worldwide consumption of energy drinks rose from 3.3 billion liters (equivalent to over 871 million gallons) in 2007 to 4.8 billion liters (over 1.2 billion gallons) in 2011. Of this total, 36% of energy drink consumption was reported in North America, 22% in the Asian Pacific region, 17% in Western Europe, and the remainder in other parts of the world. Zenith International predicts that the global market for energy drinks will rise by another 35% by 2016. Currently, the leading brands of energy drinks worldwide are Red Bull, Monster, and Burn, while 5-Hour Energy is the leading brand of energy shots.

Energy drinks are canned or bottled beverages claimed to boost energy and alertness, alleviate fatigue, assist recovery from lack of sleep, and improve athletic endurance and performance (Reissig et al., 2009). These drinks contain caffeine in varying amounts (listed either as caffeine itself or as guarana, a caffeine-containing plant extract), sugar (except for "diet" drinks), and often other ingredients such as the amino acid taurine, ginseng, sodium, and vitamins. Caffeine content of energy drinks varies widely, from 80 mg (similar to a standard cup of brewed coffee) in Red Bull to 400 mg (equivalent to 5 cups of coffee) in a single 5-ml serving of Fixx energy shot. A survey of college students at a state university in the Central Atlantic Region of the United States found that energy drinks were most often consumed in the following situations: insufficient sleep, a general desire for increased energy, needing to study or to work on a major

project, driving a car for a long period, partying (in which case the energy drink was consumed with alcohol), and recovering from a hangover (Malinauskas et al., 2007). The majority of energy drink consumers surveyed used these beverages from 1 to 4 days per month, but approximately 5% to 10% used energy drinks more than 10 days per month.

Do energy drinks work as advertised? Controlled studies either with a commercially available drink such as Red Bull or with prepared mixtures that duplicate typical energy drink constituents do indicate that these beverages can improve performance on measures of subjective alertness, concentration, memory, reaction time, and physical endurance (Alford et al., 2001; Scholey and Kennedy, 2004; Smit et al., 2004). Although some investigators have argued that the positive effects of energy drinks are simply due to reversal of caffeine deprivation (Smit et al., 2004), research described elsewhere in this chapter on the performance-enhancing effects of pure caffeine administration suggests that the caffeine content of energy drinks (or in some cases, caffeine in combination with other drink ingredients) may be capable of significantly improving performance beyond that of mere deprivation reversal.

Despite these positive findings, consumers should be aware that overconsumption of energy drinks can pose serious health risks. In 2010, there were 460 calls to U.S. regional poison control centers regarding possible poisoning from energy drinks (Bronstein et al., 2011). Some of these cases involved infants and children, although others involved adolescents and adults. Of these cases, 146 individuals suffered sufficiently severe symptoms that they were treated in a health care facility. Among the reported

effects of energy drink overdosing are agitation, tremors, seizures, damage to the liver and kidneys, gastrointestinal distress, respiratory problems, and cardiovascular abnormalities such as cardiac arrhythmia, tachycardia, and even heart failure (Gunja and Brown, 2012; Seifert et al., 2011). A small number of fatalities have also been reported, typically as the result of cardiac arrest (see, for example, Cannon et al., 2001; Rottlaender et al., 2012).

An additional concern has been raised concerning the combination of alcohol with an energy drink. A few energy drinks already contain alcohol, whereas in other cases, people consume energy drinks with alcohol-containing beverages at social events. The aim of such a combination may be to use the stimulant properties of the energy drink to counteract the debilitating effects of alcohol intoxication. Unfortunately, research has shown that even though subjects may feel less intoxicated after energy drink consumption, alcohol-related impairment of psychomotor performance is still present (i.e., the phenomenon of the "wide-awake drunk") (Verster et al., 2012).

In conclusion, the recent rapid growth of energy drink sales has caught the attention of researchers and policy makers alike. The studies reviewed above indicate that overconsumption of these beverages as well as use with alcohol can pose significant health risks. Children and adolescents are at particular risk for adverse reactions to energy drinks. This has led to increasing calls for more education about such risks and, in some countries, outright restrictions on the sale of energy drinks to minors (Committee on Nutrition and the Council on Sports Medicine and Fitness, 2011; Oddy and O'Sullivan, 2010).

energy-containing compound adenosine triphosphate (ATP) and as one of the nucleosides in RNA. However, adenosine in the brain also seems to serve a neurotransmitter-like function. It can be released into the brain extracellular fluid, where it acts on several different types of specific adenosine receptors in nerve cell membranes. Four different adenosine receptor subtypes have been identified: A_1, A_{2A}, A_{2B}, and A_3. Of these subtypes, the A_1 and A_{2A} receptors are responsible for mediating most of adenosine's effects in the brain and therefore are the major adenosine receptor targets of caffeine (Ribeiro and Sebastião, 2010).

Caffeine antagonism of adenosine receptors has been extensively studied with respect to the drug's arousing (sleep-inhibiting) and locomotor stimulating actions. Studies on cats have shown that extracellular adenosine levels in the basal forebrain are significantly elevated during prolonged wakefulness, and adenosine has been proposed as a key neurotransmitter/neuromodulator in the production of sleep (Ribeiro and Sebastião, 2010). The ability of caffeine to promote arousal and inhibit sleep was initially linked to antagonism of the adenosine A_1 receptor; however, studies on A_{2A} knockout mice have indicated that these receptors also play a key role in caffeine-mediated arousal (Chen et al., 2010). The behaviorally activating (psychostimulant-like) properties of caffeine are also dependent on antagonism of both A_1 and A_{2A} receptors, particularly in the striatum, where adenosine interacts with DA to modulate locomotor activity (Ferré, 2008).

Section Summary

- Caffeine is contained in a number of foods, especially coffee and tea. When consumed orally, it is readily absorbed from the gastrointestinal tract and is gradually metabolized and excreted with a typical half-life of approximately 4 hours.

- In rodents, caffeine has locomotor stimulant effects at low doses but actually reduces activity at high doses.

- Humans generally experience heightened arousal, reduced fatigue, and reduced sleep in response to normal amounts of caffeine. Higher doses can lead to feelings of tension and anxiety.

- Laboratory studies have demonstrated enhanced psychomotor performance following caffeine administration that, in general, is not simply due to an alleviation of caffeine withdrawal. When used by athletes, caffeine also enhances performance in both endurance sports and short-term high-intensity activities.

- Regular caffeine use leads to tolerance and physical dependence. Symptoms of caffeine withdrawal include headache, drowsiness, fatigue, impaired concentration, and reduced psychomotor performance.

- Caffeine produces various physiological effects, such as increased blood pressure and respiration rate, diuresis, and increased catecholamine release. Chronic excessive caffeine use, called caffeinism, is characterized by nervousness, insomnia, tachycardia, and gastrointestinal upset. There are additional health concerns over the growing use of caffeine-containing energy drinks.

- Caffeine has several clinical uses, including pain relief and the treatment of newborn infants with apnea.

- Although caffeine has a number of biochemical effects on the brain, its psychological and behavioral properties are mediated primarily by its ability to block A_1 and A_{2A} adenosine receptors. There is growing evidence from animal studies that adenosine is a sleep- or drowsiness-inducing factor released after a period of waking, which explains why caffeine use in humans causes increased alertness and suppression of sleep.

Go to the **COMPANION WEBSITE**

sites.sinauer.com/psychopharm2e
for Web Boxes, animations, flashcards, and other study resources.

Recommended Readings

DeBiasi, M. D. and Dani, J. A. (2011). Reward, addiction, withdrawal to nicotine. *Annu. Rev. Neurosci.*, 34, 105–130.

DiFranza, J. R., Wellman, R. J., Mermelstein, R., Pbert, L., Klein, J. D., Sargent, J. D., Ahluwalia, J. S., Lando, H. A., Ossip, D. J., Wilson, K. M., Balk, S. J., Hipple, B., Tanski, S. E., Prokhorov, A. V., Best, D., and Winikoff, J. P. (2011). The natural history and diagnosis of nicotine addiction. *Curr. Pediatr. Rev.*, 7, 88–96.

Gately, I. (2003). *Tobacco: A Cultural History of How an Exotic Plant Seduced Civilization.* New York: Grove Press.

Lorist, M. M. and Tops, M. (2003). Caffeine, fatigue, and cognition. *Brain Cogn.*, 53, 82–94.

Lovato, C., Watts, A., and Stead, L. F. (2011). Impact of tobacco advertising and promotion on increasing adolescent smoking behaviours. *Cochrane Database Syst. Rev.*, 10, CD003439.

Weinberg, B. A. and Bealer, B. K. (2002). *The World of Caffeine: The Science and Culture of the World's Most Popular Drug.* New York: Routledge.

State initiatives such as the 2012 Oregon Cannabis Tax Act are aimed at decriminalizing or even legalizing the possession and use of small amounts of cannabis, especially for medical purposes.

Marijuana and the Cannabinoids 14

YOU HAVE ALMOST CERTAINLY HEARD THE TERM "DRUG CZAR," which actually refers to the Director of the Office of National Drug Control Policy. At the time of this writing, our drug czar is Richard Gil Kerlikowske, who was selected by President Barack Obama to replace the former director, John P. Walters. If you thought that the existence of a drug czar and the current "War on Drugs" are relatively recent phenomena, you would be wrong by more than 80 years. The first federal official who might have been called a drug czar by our generation was Harry J. Anslinger, a man who was appointed in 1930 to be the first Commissioner of Narcotics in the Bureau of Narcotics of the United States Treasury Department.

We mention Harry Anslinger here because in the 1930s, he spearheaded a public relations campaign to portray marijuana as a social menace capable of destroying the youth of America. In congressional hearings that preceded passage of the 1937 Marijuana Tax Act, the first federal legislation passed to control marijuana sales, Anslinger testified as follows: "Those who are habitually accustomed to use of the drug [marijuana] are said to develop a delirious rage after its administration, during which they are temporarily, at least, irresponsible and liable to commit violent crimes. The prolonged use of this narcotic is said to produce mental deterioration. It apparently releases inhibitions of an antisocial nature which dwell within the individual" (Schaffer Library of Drug Policy). At the same time, Anslinger's Bureau of Narcotics was feeding information to the popular media about the evils of marijuana use. This stream of propaganda resulted in magazine articles with titles such as "Marihuana: Assassin of Youth" (*American Magazine*) and "Sex Crazing Drug Menace" (*Physical Culture*), as well as antimarijuana movies such as *Reefer Madness* (**Figure 14.1**) that are now regarded as cult classics.

Figure 14.1 **Poster advertising the 1936 film** *Reefer Madness*

for neuropharmacologists, cannabis plants contain 70 unique compounds that are collectively known as **cannabinoids**, as well as more than 400 other identified compounds (ElSohly and Slade, 2005). The psychoactive properties of some of these compounds, particularly a substance called Δ^9-**tetrahydrocannabinol** (**THC**), account for the use of cannabis as a drug. Although cannabinoids can be found to some extent in all parts of the plant, they are concentrated in a sticky yellowish resin that is secreted in particularly large amounts by the flowering tops of female plants.

Cannabis can be obtained in a number of different forms for the purpose of consumption. The most familiar to us is marijuana, which is derived from the Mexican word *maraguanquo*, meaning "an intoxicating plant." Marijuana refers to a crude mixture of dried and crumbled leaves, small stems, and flowering tops. Although marijuana can be consumed orally, as in cookies or brownies, it is usually smoked in rolled cigarettes known as "joints," in various kinds of pipes, or in hollowed-out cigars called "blunts." Marijuana potency (in terms of THC content) varies widely, depending on the genetic strain of the plant, as well as its growing conditions. One method of significantly increasing potency is to prevent pollination and hence seed production by the female plants. Marijuana produced by this method is called **sinsemilla** (meaning "without seeds").

Another type of cannabis derivative is **hashish**, which also may be smoked or eaten (**Figure 14.3**). Hashish potency greatly depends on how it has been prepared. In the Middle and Far East, for example, hashish generally refers to a relatively pure resin preparation with a very high cannabinoid content. Alternatively, the term may be used to describe solvent

Few people still believe the lurid stories spread so widely during the antimarijuana campaign of the 1930s. And yet marijuana remains a highly controversial subject in our society—castigated by many as a gateway to the so-called hard drugs (see Chapter 9), but praised by others as an unappreciated medical marvel. Where does the truth lie? In this chapter, we will attempt to separate the myths of marijuana from the scientific reality of this ancient drug.

Background and History of Marijuana

Marijuana (alternate spelling: marihuana) is produced from the flowering hemp, a weedlike plant given the botanical name of *Cannabis sativa* by Linnaeus in 1753 (**Figure 14.2**). Historically, hemp has served an important function in many cultures as a major source of fiber for making rope, cloth, and even paper. At times, its seeds have been used for their oil content and as bird feed. More importantly

Figure 14.2 **Cannabis plants**

Figure 14.3 The potent form of cannabis called hashish

extracts of leaves or resin that are more variable in their potency. A particularly powerful type of hash-ish is called **hash oil**. This is an alcoholic extract that has been reduced to an oily, viscous liquid ranging in color from amber to black. A single drop of hash oil may be placed on a standard tobacco cigarette and smoked, or a drop may be added to a marijuana ciga-rette to effectively double the dose.

Cannabis is believed to have originated in central Asia, probably in China. There is archeological evi-dence for the use of hemp fibers 8000 years ago (**Fig-ure 14.4**). Medical and religious use of cannabis can be traced back to ancient China, India, and the Middle East (Russo, 2007). From there, the substance spread to the Arab world, where the consumption of hashish became commonplace. Indeed, hashish is frequently mentioned in the Arabian folk stories that constitute *The Thousand and One Nights*. However, Western inter-est in this substance did not begin until the early to mid-nineteenth century, when some of Napoleon's soldiers reportedly brought hashish from Egypt back with them to France. Around the same time, a French

physician named Jacques-Joseph Moreau encoun-tered the intoxicating effects of hashish in the course of several trips to the Middle East. After returning to Paris, Moreau helped found a notorious association of French writers and artists known as *Le Club des Has-chischins* ("club of the hashish eaters"), which includ-ed such notables as Victor Hugo, Alexandre Dumas, Théophile Gautier, and Charles Baudelaire.

The history of cannabis in the United States dates back to the colonial era, when hemp was an important agricultural commodity. No less than George Wash-ington himself was a hemp farmer, which is ironic in view of the patriotic fervor associated with the con-temporary "War on Drugs." Yet domestic hemp grow-ers of the seventeenth and eighteenth centuries appar-ently had little awareness of the plant's intoxicating properties. Rather, historians believe that the social practice of consuming cannabis (mainly marijuana smoking) was brought into the United States in the early 1900s by Mexican immigrants crossing the Mexi-can–American border, and by Caribbean seamen and West Indian immigrants entering the country by way of New Orleans and other ports on the Gulf of Mexico.

Marijuana use rapidly spread outward from these points of origin. As a consequence of the antimarijua-na campaign described earlier, the federal government passed the Marijuana Tax Act in 1937. This legislation instituted a national registration and taxation system aimed at discouraging all use of cannabis for commer-cial, recreational, and medical purposes. Although the Marijuana Tax Act was overturned as unconstitution-al by the U.S. Supreme Court in 1969, marijuana and other forms of cannabis remain tightly regulated by state laws and by the federal Controlled Substances Act of 1970.

Basic Pharmacology of Marijuana

Modern cannabinoid pharmacology began in 1964, when two Israeli researchers named Gaoni and

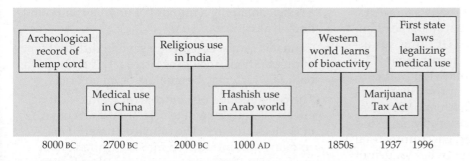

Figure 14.4 An 8000-year time line of cannabis use around the world
(After Childers and Breivogel, 1998.)

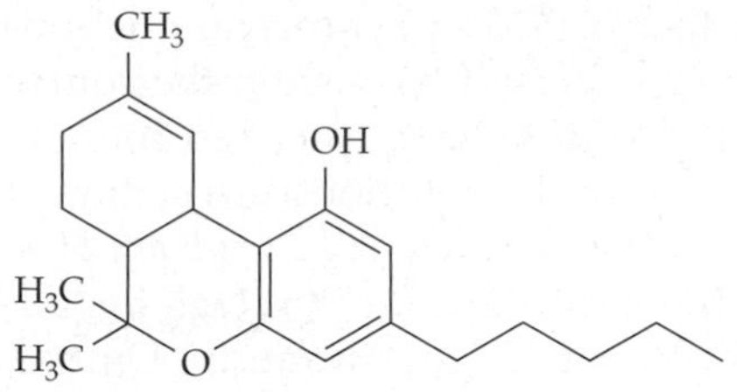

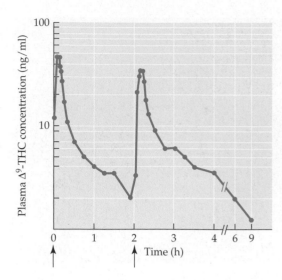

Figure 14.5 Chemical structure of Δ^9-tetrahydro-cannabinol (THC)

Mechoulam identified THC as the major active ingredient of *C. sativa* (**Figure 14.5**). Among the many other cannabinoids present are cannabinol and cannabidiol, but these compounds are not thought to contribute to the psychoactive properties of cannabis. Later on, we will discuss the brain's own chemicals that mimic the effects of THC, and we will also consider the development of selective cannabinoid antagonists that have contributed significantly to research in this area.

A typical hand-rolled marijuana cigarette ("joint") consists of around 0.5 to 1 gram of cannabis. If the THC content is 4% (although it can be even higher depending on the strain and growing conditions), then a 1-gram joint contains 40 mg of active ingredient that is available to the smoker. As in the case of nicotine in tobacco leaves (see Chapter 13), burning of the marijuana causes the THC to vaporize and to enter the smoker's lungs in small particles. But because of a variety of factors, only about 20% to 30% of the original THC content is absorbed in the lungs. In practice, the amount of THC absorbed is affected not only by the initial amount of plant material used and the potency of this material but also by the pattern of smoking. The effective dose and latency to onset of effects of smoked marijuana are influenced by puff volume, puff frequency, inhalation depth, and breath-hold duration (Gorelick and Heishman, 2006).

THC is readily absorbed through the lungs, resulting in rapidly rising levels in the blood plasma of the smoker (**Figure 14.6**). After peak levels are reached, plasma THC concentrations begin to decline as a result of a combination of metabolism in the liver and accumulation of the drug in the body's fat stores. In contrast, oral consumption of marijuana leads to prolonged but poor absorption of THC, thus resulting in low and variable plasma concentrations. The reduced bioavailability of THC following oral consumption compared with smoking probably results from both degradation in the stomach and first-pass hepatic metabolism, that is, once orally ingested THC has been absorbed from the gastrointestinal tract, it must pass through the liver, where much of it is metabolized before it can enter the general circulation. THC is converted into several metabolites,

Figure 14.6 Mean time course of plasma THC concentrations in subjects who smoked a marijuana cigarette containing approximately 9 mg of THC at the two time points indicated by the arrows. (After Agurell et al., 1986.)

notably 11-hydroxy-THC and 11-nor-carboxy-THC (THC-COOH). These substances as well as various minor metabolites are excreted primarily in the feces (about two-thirds of the administered dose) and the urine (about one-third of the administered dose). Even though THC levels in the bloodstream decline fairly rapidly after one smokes marijuana, complete elimination from the body is much slower because of persistence of the drug in fat tissue. Consequently, the elimination rate, or half-life ($t_{1/2}$), of THC is generally estimated at around 20 to 30 hours. Furthermore, the gradual movement of THC and fat-soluble metabolites back out of fat stores means that sensitive urine screening tests for THC-COOH can detect the presence of this metabolite more than 2 weeks following a single marijuana use.

Section Summary

- *Cannabis sativa*, the flowering hemp plant, exudes a resin containing a number of unique compounds known as cannabinoids.

- Cannabis can be obtained in several different types of preparations, including marijuana and hashish, both of which may be smoked or taken orally.

- The consumption of cannabis for its intoxicating effects is thought to date back thousands of years in Eastern cultures. The practice of marijuana smoking was introduced into the United States in the early 1900s by Mexican and West Indian immigrants.

- The most important naturally occurring cannabinoid is Δ^9-tetrahydrocannabinol (THC).

- Inhaled THC is rapidly absorbed from the lungs into the circulation, where it is almost completely bound to plasma proteins. Oral THC consumption yields slower absorption and a lower plasma peak than occurs following smoking.

- THC is extensively metabolized in the liver, and the metabolites are excreted mainly in the feces and urine. Following a single dose of THC, total clearance of the drug and its metabolites may take days because of sequestration of these compounds in fat tissue.

Mechanisms of Action

For many years, researchers interested in how THC and other cannabinoids work in the brain were hampered by the lack of an identified cellular receptor for these compounds. Subsequent discovery of cannabinoid receptors permitted the synthesis of selective cannabinoid agonists and antagonists, as well as elucidation of the endogenous cannabinoid system.

Cannabinoid effects are mediated by cannabinoid receptors

Pharmacological characterization of a central nervous system (CNS) **cannabinoid receptor** was announced in 1988 by a group of researchers that included William Devane and Allyn Howlett at St. Louis University, and Lawrence Melvin and M. Ross Johnson at the Pfizer pharmaceutical company (Devane et al., 1988).[1] This initial characterization was quickly followed by other studies showing significant expression of cannabinoid receptors in many brain areas such as the basal ganglia (including the striatum, globus pallidus, entopeduncular nucleus, and substantia nigra pars reticularis), cerebellum, hippocampus, and cerebral cortex (**Figure 14.7**). As discussed later, localization of cannabinoid receptors in these areas is consistent with the recognized behavioral effects of these compounds on locomotor activity, coordination, and memory.

Around the same time that the St. Louis University and Pfizer researchers were first characterizing the cannabinoid receptor pharmacologically, another group of scientists at the National Institute of Mental Health (NIMH) including Lisa Matsuda and Tom Bonner cloned a novel gene from rat cerebral cortex

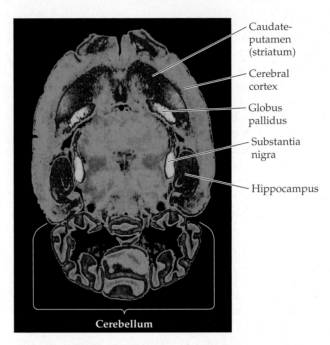

Figure 14.7 Autoradiogram of a horizontal section through a rat brain showing the distribution of CB_1 cannabinoid receptors. Color coding of receptor density: yellow > orange > red > blue. (Courtesy of Miles Herkenham, National Institute of Mental Health.)

Labels: Caudate-putamen (striatum); Cerebral cortex; Globus pallidus; Substantia nigra; Hippocampus; Cerebellum

that coded for a membrane protein with the characteristics of a G protein–coupled receptor. Further studies revealed that these investigators, who were working on an unrelated problem, had actually cloned the gene for the rat brain cannabinoid receptor (Matsuda et al., 1990). This is a good example of an approach that is sometimes called *reverse pharmacology*, namely, the cloning of a novel receptor gene, the identity of which must then be determined by more classical pharmacological methods. The CNS cannabinoid receptor is currently designated CB_1. An additional cannabinoid receptor, CB_2, was discovered later, first in the immune system and then in other tissues such as bone, adipose (fat) cells, and the gastrointestinal tract (Atwood and Mackie, 2010). CB_2 receptors are also expressed by microglia (the brain's immune cells), especially when those cells have been activated by neuroinflammatory or neurodegenerative events occurring in the brain. Recent evidence further suggests that CB_2 receptors may be expressed by neurons in some areas of the brain (Atwood and Mackie, 2010).

Cannabinoid receptors belong to the large family of metabotropic receptors, and they exert their cellular effects primarily through coupling to the G proteins G_i and G_o. The most important of these effects involve inhibition of cyclic adenosine monophosphate (cAMP) formation, inhibition of voltage-sensitive Ca^{2+} channels, and activation of K^+ channel opening (Howlett,

---

[1]Readers interested in more information on the history of the discovery and characterization of cannabinoid receptors are referred to the excellent review by Mackie (2007).

2005). Cannabinoid receptors can also influence gene expression through a complex system of protein kinases known as the mitogen-activated protein kinase (MAPK) system. Electron microscopy in conjunction with antibodies against the CB_1 receptor have been used to determine the location of these receptors within the synapse. In most instances, CB_1 receptors have been shown to exist on the axon terminal instead of the postsynaptic cell. By activating these presynaptic receptors, cannabinoids can inhibit the release of many different neurotransmitters including acetylcholine, dopamine, norepinephrine, serotonin, glutamate, and GABA (γ-aminobutyric acid) (Iversen, 2003).

Pharmacological studies reveal the functional roles of cannabinoid receptors

Various synthetic cannabinoid agonists and antagonists have been developed for both research and potentially also therapeutic use. These compounds include CP-55,940 and WIN 55,212-2, which are full agonists at both CB_1 and CB_2 receptors (Svíženská et al., 2008). Interestingly, THC has been shown to be a partial rather than a full CB_1 and CB_2 receptor agonist since this substance produces lower peak receptor-mediated effects than the above mentioned synthetic agonists. The first selective CB_1 antagonist was **SR 141716A** (also known as **rimonabant**), which was developed by the French pharmaceutical firm Sanofi Recherche. Besides its obvious value in determining CB_1-dependent effects of cannabinoids in animal model systems, rimonabant is easily administered to human subjects because it is orally active.

Administration of THC to mice leads to a classical "tetrad" of effects consisting of (1) reduced locomotor activity, (2) hypothermia (a decrease in core body temperature), (3) catalepsy as indicated by immobility in the ring test (a test that measures the animal's behavior after it is placed on a horizontal wire ring), and (4) hypoalgesia (reduced pain sensitivity) measured using the hot-plate or tail-flick test. These effects are mediated primarily by CB_1 receptors because they are largely absent in CB_1 knockout mice and they can be duplicated in wild-type animals by administration of a selective CB_1 receptor agonist (Pertwee, 2008; Valverde et al., 2005). CB_1 receptors also play an important role in the reward system, as shown by the reinforcing effects of CB_1 agonists in both animals and humans. This topic is discussed in greater detail later in the chapter.

We shall also see later that cannabinoids adversely affect human cognitive function, which has led to considerable interest in the effects of these compounds on learning and memory in laboratory animals. The results of this work indicate that cannabinoids disrupt

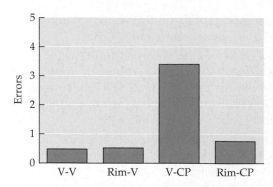

Figure 14.8 Hippocampal CB_1 receptors are responsible for memory impairment in the radial arm maze produced by cannabinoid agonist administration. Rats were trained to a high degree of performance on an 8-arm radial arm maze (see Chapter 4). After training was completed, intraperitoneal injection of CP-55,940 (0.05 mg/kg) along with a vehicle microinjection into the hippocampus (V-CP) produced a significant number of errors on the task compared with the control group (V-V), indicating an impairment in working memory. This effect was completely blocked by microinjection of rimonabant (0.06 µg) into the dorsal hippocampus (Rim-CP), whereas rimonabant by itself had no effect on maze performance (Rim-V). (After Wise et al., 2009.)

memory in several different kinds of learning tasks, including the radial arm maze, the Morris water maze, and the delayed non-match-to-position task (Riedel and Davies, 2005). Memory consolidation in the passive avoidance task may also be adversely influenced by cannabinoid administration. A recent study by Wise and coworkers (2009) found that either systemic administration or microinjection of THC or the synthetic cannabinoid agonist CP-55,940 directly into the dorsal hippocampus produced significant memory deficits in the radial arm maze. Moreover, these effects could be completely blocked by intrahippocampal infusion of rimonabant (**Figure 14.8**). Other studies have shown that cannabinoid administration inhibits the induction of long-term potentiation (LTP) in the hippocampal CA1 area (Riedel and Davies, 2005). Taken together, these findings support the hypothesis that CB_1 receptor activation in the hippocampus underlies the spatial learning deficits seen in animals given THC or other cannabinoids.

CB_2 agonist effects can be observed using the immune system as an example. In this case, such drugs inhibit the release of cytokines (immune cell signaling molecules such as interleukins and interferons) and can also either stimulate or inhibit the migration of immune cells toward the site of an inflammatory reaction (Miller and Stella, 2008). The involvement of CB_2 receptors in other functions is discussed below, as well as in Box 14.1, which deals with the potential therapeutic uses of cannabinoid-type drugs.

Endocannabinoids are cannabinoid receptor agonists synthesized by the body

The discovery and characterization of cannabinoid receptors finally enabled pharmacologists to study the cellular mechanisms by which marijuana produces its behavioral effects. Yet why should our brain possess receptors for substances made by a plant? This situation is reminiscent of the quandary faced by opiate researchers when opioid receptors were first identified as mediating the actions of morphine, which comes from a poppy plant (see Chapter 11). Accordingly, the same assumption was made that there must be an endogenous neurotransmitter-like substance that acts on the newly discovered receptors. Within a few years, a group headed by Raphael Mechoulam, the same Israeli scientist involved in the discovery of THC almost 30 years earlier, announced that they had isolated a substance with cannabinoid-like activity from pig brain (Devane et al., 1992). Chemical analysis revealed the substance to be a lipid with a structure related to that of arachidonic acid. The formal chemical name of this substance is **arachidonoyl ethanolamide** (**AEA**), but the researchers gave it the additional name **anandamide**, from the Indian Sanskrit word *ananda*, meaning "bringer of inner bliss and tranquility" (Felder and Glass, 1998, p. 186). Later studies demonstrated the existence of other arachidonic acid derivatives such as **2-arachidonoylglycerol** (**2-AG**) that also bind to and activate CB_1 receptors (**Figure 14.9**). Together, these substances came to be known as **endocannabinoids**, meaning endogenous cannabinoids. However, subsequent studies showed that 2-AG is present in the brain at much higher levels than anandamide, and it also exerts greater efficacy than anandamide on cannabinoid receptors (Sugiura, 2009). This combined with other evidence strongly suggests that 2-AG, not anandamide, is the principal endocannabinoid for both CB_1 and CB_2 receptors.

The endocannabinoids are generated from inositol phospholipids in the membrane that contain the fatty acid arachidonic acid within their structure. Unlike the classical neurotransmitters, however, endocannabinoids are too lipid soluble to be stored in vesicles since they would just pass right through the vesicle membrane. Consequently, current evidence indicates that these substances are made and released when needed. One mechanism for triggering endocannabinoid release is a rise in intracellular Ca^{2+} levels, which follows from the fact that some of the enzymes involved in the generation of these compounds are Ca^{2+} sensitive.

After being released, endocannabinoids are removed from the extracellular fluid by an uptake mechanism that is still under debate. Most of the

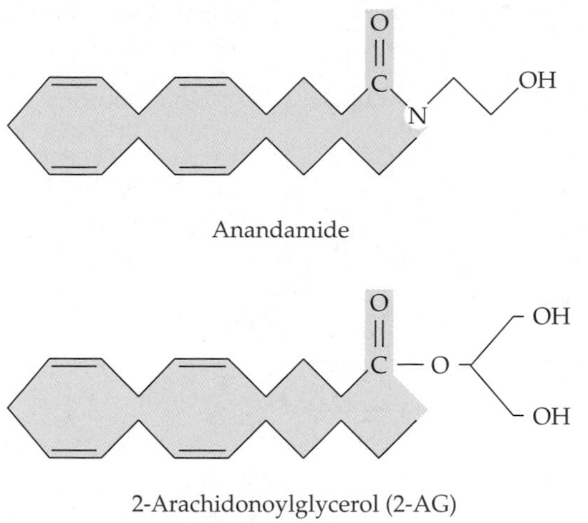

Figure 14.9 Chemical structures of the endocannabinoids anandamide and 2-arachidonoylglycerol (2-AG)

research on endocannabinoid uptake has come from studies on anandamide. On the basis of these studies, three potential uptake mechanisms have been proposed by different investigators: (1) uptake by means of a protein carrier in the cell membrane, (2) uptake by simple passive diffusion across the cell membrane, and (3) uptake by means of anandamide binding to a membrane protein followed by endocytosis of the anandamide–protein complex (Yates and Barker, 2009). It is clear that proof for a protein-mediated uptake mechanism will ultimately require cloning of the relevant gene and characterization of the gene product as a true carrier protein for anandamide (and possibly also 2-AG).

Once inside the cell, the endocannabinoids can be metabolized by several different enzymes. For anandamide, the best known enzyme involved in its degradation is called **fatty acid amide hydrolase** (**FAAH**). In contrast, 2-AG is thought to be broken down primarily by a different enzyme known as **monoacylglycerol lipase** (**MAGL**) (Ueda et al., 2010). Indeed, a recent study by Chanda and colleagues (2010) showed that mutant mice lacking MAGL exhibited a huge increase in brain 2-AG concentrations, and these mice also developed a desensitization of central CB_1 receptors. The latter effect is further evidence for a key role for 2-AG in activating CB_1 receptors within the brain.

On the basis of the discovery that many cannabinoid receptors are localized presynaptically, we might suspect that endocannabinoids are often released from postsynaptic cells to act on nearby nerve terminals. When a signaling molecule carries information in the opposite direction from normal (i.e., postsynaptic to presynaptic), it is called a **retrograde messenger**. One such retrograde messenger discussed in Chapter 3 is the gas nitric oxide. There is now overwhelming

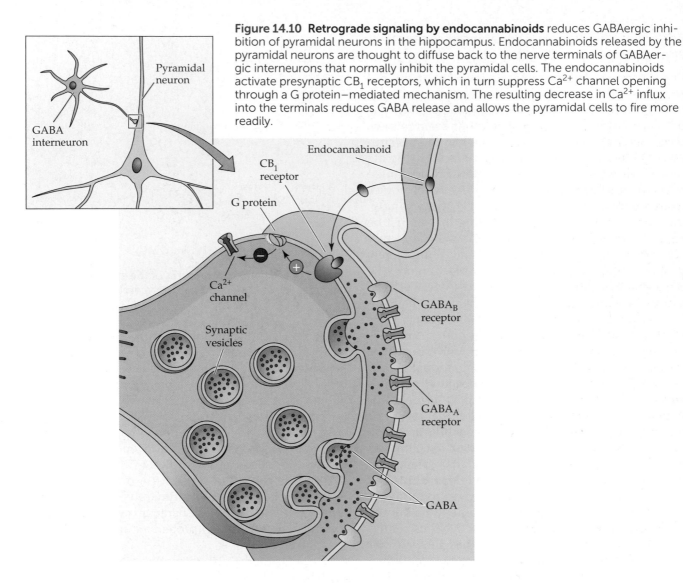

Figure 14.10 Retrograde signaling by endocannabinoids reduces GABAergic inhibition of pyramidal neurons in the hippocampus. Endocannabinoids released by the pyramidal neurons are thought to diffuse back to the nerve terminals of GABAergic interneurons that normally inhibit the pyramidal cells. The endocannabinoids activate presynaptic CB₁ receptors, which in turn suppress Ca²⁺ channel opening through a G protein–mediated mechanism. The resulting decrease in Ca²⁺ influx into the terminals reduces GABA release and allows the pyramidal cells to fire more readily.

evidence that endocannabinoids are also retrograde messengers at specific synapses in a number of brain regions, such as the hippocampus and the cerebellum (Piomelli, 2003; Wilson and Nicoll, 2002). These substances are synthesized and released in response to depolarization of the postsynaptic cell due to the influx of Ca²⁺ through voltage-gated Ca²⁺ channels. Following their release, the endocannabinoids cross the synaptic cleft, activate CB₁ receptors on the nerve terminal, and inhibit Ca²⁺-mediated neurotransmitter release from the terminal (Sugiura, 2009). In the hippocampus, for example, the endocannabinoids are generated by the pyramidal neurons, which are the principal output neurons of the hippocampus. The endocannabinoids diffuse to the nearby terminals of GABAergic interneurons that normally suppress the firing of the pyramidal cells. The resulting inhibition of GABA release temporarily permits the pyramidal cells to fire more rapidly (**Figure 14.10**). Other

examples of retrograde signaling by endocannabinoids have also been discovered, including cases in which stimulation of endocannabinoid synthesis and release cause presynaptic long-term depression (LTD) of neurotransmission (Chevaleyre et al., 2006). These findings are consistent with the widespread distribution of cannabinoid receptors in the brain.

The discovery of anandamide and 2-AG has raised interesting questions about whether this signaling system might be involved in the normal regulation of the same behavioral and physiological functions influenced by exogenous cannabinoids such as THC. This question has been addressed in two different ways: (1) by examining the effects of administering the CB₁ receptor antagonist rimonabant in the absence of an exogenous cannabinoid agonist (thus blocking the effects of the endogenous cannabinoids), and (2) by studying the phenotypic characteristics of CB₁ and CB₂ knockout mice. A few examples will be given from this large literature to illustrate some of the key functions of the central endocannabinoid system.

A number of studies have demonstrated that genetically normal animals given rimonabant as well as both CB_1 and CB_2 knockout mice exhibit **hyperalgesia** (increased pain sensitivity) to several different types of pain stimuli. These findings clearly demonstrate a role for endocannabinoids acting on both cannabinoid receptor subtypes in the modulation of pain perception (Buckley, 2008; Calignano et al., 1998; Valverde et al., 2005). The potential use of cannabinoid drugs in the treatment of pain disorders as well as many other medical conditions is discussed in **Box 14.1**.

Endocannabinoids have additionally been shown to play a significant role in hunger and eating behavior. CB_1 receptor antagonists reliably reduce food consumption in both experimental animals and human subjects, and more detailed studies suggest that endocannabinoids enhance both the incentive motivational properties of food and food-mediated reward (Kirkham, 2009). Recent work by DiPatrizio and coworkers (2011) further showed that endocannabinoids in the gut provide a signal that controls dietary intake of fat. Because of the early success of CB_1 antagonism in reducing food intake, rimonabant (under the trade name Accomplia) was approved and released by Sanofi-Aventis in the European Union in June 2006 as an anti-obesity agent. Unfortunately, reporting of adverse psychiatric side effects by some users resulted in voluntary suspension of marketing of Accomplia by the company in December 2008, followed shortly by withdrawal of approval of the medication by the European Medicines Agency. Nevertheless, targeting the cannabinoid system for the treatment of obesity has continued to be of interest to researchers and pharmaceutical companies (Lee et al., 2009). For example, Cluny et al. (2010) recently showed that AM6545, a CB_1 antagonist with limited penetration across the blood–brain barrier, significantly reduced food consumption and body weight in both rats and mice with a behavioral profile suggesting a lack of CNS-mediated aversive effects (**Figure 14.11**). Thus, future clinical testing may yet reveal that peripherally acting cannabinoid antagonists can successfully treat obesity without the side effects that compromised earlier attempts to use rimonabant in this capacity.

Potential endocannabinoid involvement in learning and memory has been investigated by comparing the performance of CB_1 knockout mice with that of their wild-type counterparts and by examining the influence of rimonabant treatment on normal animals (Marco et al., 2011; Zanettini et al., 2011). Although the literature shows some inconsistencies, a number of studies suggest that endocannabinoids play a greater role in the *extinction* of learned responses than in

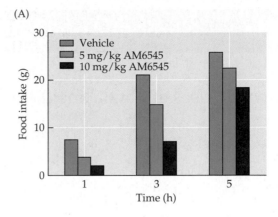

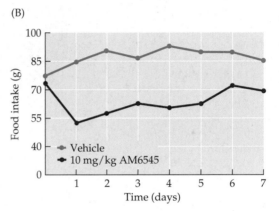

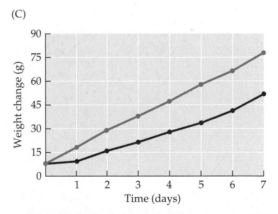

Figure 14.11 Food intake and body weight gain are reduced in rats treated with a peripherally restricted cannabinoid receptor antagonist. (A) Acute treatment with AM6545 produced a dose-dependent suppression of food intake 3 but not 5 hours after drug administration. (B) Daily treatment with AM6545 for a week suppressed food intake strongly during the first several days, after which the effect became more modest. (C) Over the same time period as in B, the drug-treated rats showed a slower weight gain than the vehicle control group. Other data not shown here indicated a lack of aversive effects of AM6545 dosing. (After Cluny et al., 2010.)

response acquisition. This phenomenon has been particularly well demonstrated in the case of extinction of auditory fear conditioning of rats and mice. This task

BOX 14.1 Clinical Applications

Therapeutic Uses of Cannabinoids

Medicinal use of cannabis in various cultures can be traced back for many hundreds, perhaps thousands, of years. During the late-nineteenth and early-twentieth centuries, crude cannabis extracts were accepted pharmaceuticals in Europe and the United States. Indeed, six different types of cannabis preparations were listed in an early edition of *The Merck Index* (1896) of pharmaceutical compounds. However, the medicinal use of cannabis gradually declined, in part because the available preparations tended to be unstable and had inconsistent potency.

Interest in the possible therapeutic benefits of cannabinoids was later revived following the discovery of THC and the subsequent manufacture and testing of various synthetic compounds. At present, both **dronabinol**, a synthetic form of THC sold under the trade name Marinol, and the THC analog **nabilone** (trade name Cesamet) are prescribed in oral form for the treatment of nausea and emesis (vomiting) in cancer chemotherapy patients who are not helped by other antiemetics. Dronabinol is also approved for use as an appetite stimulant in AIDS patients suffering from anorexia–cachexia (wasting syndrome). Patients contemplating use of these drugs should be aware that they can produce various side effects such as sedation, dizziness, confusion, dry mouth, and mild euphoria. Alternatively, dysphoria may occur in people unfamiliar with the effects of smoked marijuana. Fortunately, such side effects tend to be greatest when the drug is first taken and generally diminish within a few days or weeks.

Nabiximols (trade name Sativex) is a cannabis extract containing THC and cannabidiol (a

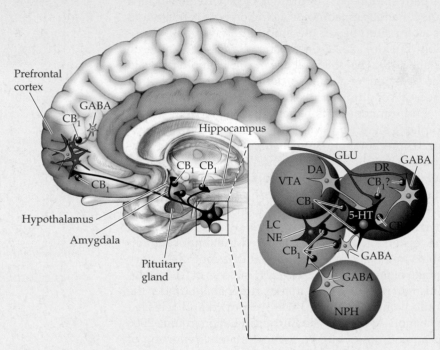

CB₁ receptors are widely expressed in the neural circuitry of the human brain that regulates mood. DR, dorsal raphe nucleus; LC, locus coeruleus; 5-HT, serotonin; NE, norepinephrine; NPH, nucleus prepositus hypoglossi; VTA, ventral tegmental area. (After Hill et al., 2009.)

cannabinoid that exerts biological effects independent of either CB_1 or CB_2 receptors) that is taken as an oral spray. This medication is currently licensed in a number of countries (not including the United States) for the treatment of neuropathic pain and spasticity in multiple sclerosis patients. At the time of this writing, nabiximols was undergoing Phase III clinical trials in the United States for the treatment of neuropathic pain in cancer patients. A number of years ago, Jamaican researchers also prepared eye drops from cannabis extracts (trade name Canasol) for the purpose of reducing ocular pressure in glaucoma patients. However, Canasol apparently was never licensed by the FDA for legal marketing in the United States.

New knowledge regarding the anatomy and functioning of the endocannabinoid system as well as the need for effective medications for numerous clinical disorders has led to an upsurge in research on cannabinoid medications. Novel cannabinoid drugs that do not cross the blood–brain barrier or that work as modulators instead of cannabinoid receptor antagonists or as inverse agonists are under development not only for the treatment of obesity (as noted earlier in the text) but also for irritable bowel syndrome and other disorders of the gastrointestinal system (Schicho and Storr, 2011). Other areas of medicine in which cannabinoid-based compounds might prove useful include pain (Sagar et al., 2009), cancer (Grimaldi and

BOX 14.1 (continued)

Capasso, 2011), neurodegenerative diseases (Scotter et al., 2010), and psychiatric disorders (Hill et al., 2009; Roser et al., 2010). For example, Piscitelli and Di Marzo (2012) provide an instructive example of how various features of endocannabinoid biochemistry, particularly reuptake and metabolism, are potential targets of medication development for the treatment of pain. With respect to psychiatric disorders, it is noteworthy that CB_1 receptors are located in many parts of the neural circuitry that control mood (see figure). Thus, compounds targeting the central endocannabinoid system might be useful as novel medications for patients suffering from major depression or other mood disorders.

Lastly, we come to the issue of medical marijuana, meaning the use of smoked marijuana as a medication. As reviewed by Cohen (2009a, 2009b), the notion of medical marijuana has been dominated much more by political considerations than by scientific evidence. Indeed, a number of states currently permit legal use of medical marijuana when approved by a physician, despite the fact that the DEA still classifies cannabis as a Schedule I substance. This puts the states in question (and residents of those states who use marijuana medicinally) in direct conflict with federal regulations. Most of the support for medical marijuana comes from anecdotal reports from patients that smoking

cannabis gives them greater symptom relief than is obtained from oral cannabinoid preparations such as dronabinol or nabilone. There have been a few clinical studies, such as those reviewed by Rog (2010), regarding the use of marijuana versus oral cannabinoid medications for alleviation of multiple sclerosis symptoms, but the results were equivocal. Given the potential for adverse health effects and abuse potential of smoked marijuana, most researchers currently favor the development of cannabinoid-based medications that avoid these negative consequences (Seely et al., 2011). This is an especially important consideration when the proposed medication will be taken on a daily basis over a long time.

involves the pairing of an auditory stimulus such as a tone with a foot shock as illustrated in **Figure 14.12A**. As a result, the tone becomes a conditioned fear stimulus that elicits freezing behavior (i.e., no movement except for breathing), which is the species-typical response to a fearful situation in rats and mice, and which is known to depend on a neural circuit involving the amygdala. A number of studies have shown that the endocannabinoid system is not required for acquisition of auditory fear conditioning. However, Marsicano and coworkers (2002) demonstrated that unlike mice possessing functional CB_1 receptors, CB_1 knockout mice do not show normal extinction of the freezing response when the tone alone without additional foot shock pairing is presented over a series of several days (**Figure 14.12B**). These investigators performed a number of additional experiments to determine the potential mechanism underlying this effect. One of their findings was that both anandamide and 2-AG levels were greatly increased in the basolateral amygdala complex immediately following the tone presentation on the first extinction day, but not under various control conditions (**Figure 14.12C**). No change in endocannabinoid levels was observed in the medial prefrontal cortex—another brain area implicated in the extinction of learned aversive responses. These and other findings not shown suggest that endocannabinoids released during extinction and acting on CB_1 receptors in the basolateral amygdala alter synaptic

plasticity in a manner that enables the animals to learn that the tone is no longer dangerous. Indeed, on the basis of the results from a number of fear extinction studies, Moreira and Wotjak (2009) hypothesized that the endocannabinoid system is involved in the alleviation of fear, thereby functioning to prevent fear responses from becoming too pervasive.

Recent findings have extended this rodent work on fear extinction to humans. Researchers have discovered a single nucleotide polymorphism (SNP) in the *FAAH* gene (C385A) that changes the amino acid proline at position 129 of the FAAH protein to a threonine. This amino acid substitution leads to a reduction in enzymatic activity, thereby increasing endogenous anandamide levels. Gunduz-Cinar and colleagues (2012) compared people who had at least one copy of the A allele (i.e., with an AA or AC genotype) with individuals homozygous for the C allele (CC genotype) on a fear habituation test in which the subjects were repeatedly exposed to threatening faces during a functional magnetic resonance imaging (fMRI) session. The results showed that the amygdala responses to these faces habituated much more rapidly in the subjects carrying at least one copy of the low-expressing A allele than in the homozygous CC subjects. Such findings are consistent with the hypothesis that increased anandamide levels due to reduced FAAH activity enhance the ability to turn off neural and behavioral responses to threatening stimuli.

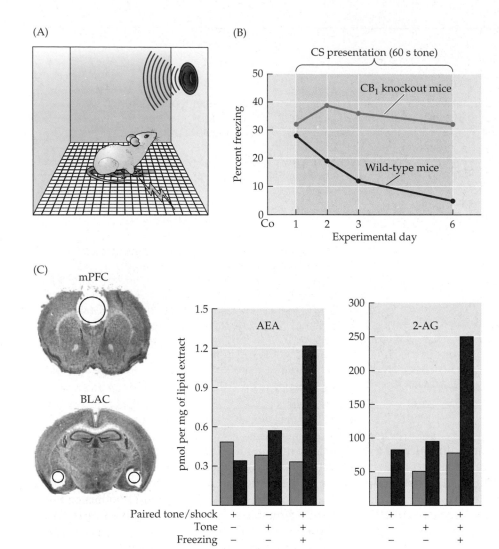

(A)

(B)

CS presentation (60 s tone)

CB₁ knockout mice

Wild-type mice

Percent freezing

Experimental day

(C)

mPFC

BLAC

AEA

2-AG

pmol per mg of lipid extract

Paired tone/shock	+	−	+		+	−	+
Tone	−	+	+		−	+	+
Freezing	−	−	+		−	−	+

Figure 14.12 Role of the endocannabinoid system in extinction of auditory fear conditioning (A) In auditory fear conditioning, a sound such as a tone is paired with a foot shock, thereby inducing a fear response (e.g., freezing behavior in rodents) to subsequent presentation of the tone. (B) Wild-type mice and CB₁ knockout mice were subjected to one trial of auditory fear conditioning (Co), after which they underwent four trials of tone only (CS) presentation 1, 2, 3, and 6 days later. The wild-type mice showed normal extinction of their fear response (shown by a reduced percent of time spent freezing) over days, whereas the mice lacking CB₁ receptors continued to exhibit the same fear response. (C) Levels of the endocannabinoids anandamide (AEA) and 2-arachidonoylglycerol (2-AG) were measured under different experimental conditions in the basolateral amygdala complex (BLAC) and medial prefrontal cortex (mPFC), two brain areas believed to play a role in the extinction of aversive memories. The histological sections show the areas punched out for the neurochemical measurements. The graphs show that both endocannabinoids were elevated in the BLAC (red bars) but not in the mPFC (blue bars) of mice that were subjected to initial auditory fear conditioning (paired tone/shock) and which subsequently froze when presented with the tone by itself (third sets of bars). These increases were not observed in control groups that either had initial tone/shock pairing but were not exposed to the tone CS during testing (first sets of bars) or were exposed to the tone CS without prior tone/shock pairing (second sets of bars). (B,C after Marsicano et al., 2002.)

Section Summary

- Two cannabinoid receptors, CB₁ and CB₂, have been identified and their genes cloned.

- The CB₁ receptor is the principal cannabinoid receptor in the brain, where it is expressed at a high density in the basal ganglia, cerebellum, hippocampus, and cerebral cortex.

- The CB₂ receptor was first identified in the immune system, but it is also found in a number of other tissues including the brain, where it is mainly localized in microglial cells.

- Cannabinoid receptors belong to the G protein–coupled receptor superfamily. Receptor activation can inhibit cAMP formation, inhibit voltage-sensitive Ca²⁺ channels, and activate K⁺ channels.

- CB_1 receptors are typically located on axon terminals, where they act to inhibit the release of many different neurotransmitters.

- Agonists at the CB_1 receptor include the synthetic full agonists CP-55,940 and WIN 55,212-2, and the partial agonist THC. The first selective CB_1 antagonist was SR 141716A, also known as rimonabant.

- THC administration to mice causes a classical tetrad of CB_1 receptor–mediated effects that consist of reduced locomotor activity, hypothermia, catalepsy, and hypoalgesia. CB_1 agonists also impair learning and memory consolidation in several different kinds of tasks.

- CB_2 receptor activation in the immune system causes cytokine release and changes in immune cell migration toward an inflammatory site.

- The brain synthesizes several substances, called endocannabinoids, that are neurotransmitter-like agonists at cannabinoid receptors. Anandamide was the first endocannabinoid to be discovered, but a potentially more important endocannabinoid is 2-AG.

- Endocannabinoids are generated on demand from arachidonic acid–containing membrane lipids by a Ca^{2+}-dependent mechanism and are released from the cell by a process that does not involve synaptic vesicles. They are removed from the extracellular space by an uptake process that has yet to be fully defined.

- Anandamide and 2-AG are degraded primarily by FAAH and MAGL, respectively.

- Endocannabinoids function as retrograde messengers since they are synthesized and released from postsynaptic cells and act on nearby nerve terminals to inhibit neurotransmitter release by inhibiting the opening of voltage-gated Ca^{2+} channels.

- Studies using rimonabant administration to genetically normal animals or mutant mice lacking functional CB_1 receptors have demonstrated that the endocannabinoid system plays a role in pain sensitivity, hunger and eating behavior, and learning and memory. This system seems to be particularly important in the extinction of learned fear responses.

- There are accepted therapeutic uses for orally administered dronabinol (synthetic THC) and the THC analog nabilone in treating nausea and vomiting in cancer chemotherapy patients, as well as the wasting syndrome in AIDS sufferers. In addition, the endocannabinoid system is being actively studied as a target in the treatment of many kinds of disorders, including obesity, pain

disorders, cognitive dysfunction, drug addiction, and psychosis.

Acute Behavioral and Physiological Effects of Cannabinoids

Cannabinoid use produces a range of behavioral and physiological effects that vary depending on the dose, the frequency of use, the characteristics of the user, and the setting in which use occurs.

Cannabis consumption produces a dose-dependent state of intoxication

The earliest recorded clinical studies on the intoxicating properties of cannabis were performed by Moreau, the French physician mentioned earlier who introduced hashish to nineteenth-century Parisian literary society. Moreau, who is sometimes called the "father of psychopharmacology," became interested in the possible relationship between hashish intoxication and the characteristics of mental illness. Consequently, he and his students meticulously recorded their subjective experiences after consuming varying amounts of hashish. Because of the potency of their preparation, these individuals reported profound personality changes and perceptual distortions, even frank hallucinations.[2] Hallucinogenic responses have also been reported either following a high dose of pure THC administered to subjects in a research setting, or as an occasional side effect of ingesting a synthetic cannabinoid for medicinal purposes (Koukkou and Lehmann, 1976; Timpone et al., 1997).

The lower cannabis doses associated with smoking one or two marijuana cigarettes produce a somewhat more modest reaction, although many of the same *kinds* of effects are found across the dose–response curve. As summarized in Iversen (2000), the subjective and behavioral effects commonly associated with marijuana use can be separated into four stages: the "buzz," the "high," the stage of being "stoned," and finally the "come-down." The "buzz" is a brief period of initial responding during which the user may feel lightheaded or even slightly dizzy. Tingling sensations in the extremities and other parts of the body are commonly experienced. The marijuana "high" is characterized by feelings of euphoria and exhilaration, as well as a sense of disinhibition that is often manifested as increased laughter. If the user has taken a sufficiently

---

[2]Moreau's work culminated in a book entitled *Du Hachich et de l'aliénation mentale* (*Hashish and Mental Alienation*), major excerpts of which can be found in Nahas (1975).

large amount of marijuana, his level of intoxication progresses to the stage of being "stoned." In this stage, the user usually feels calm, relaxed, perhaps even in a dreamlike state. Indeed, relaxation is the most common effect reported by cannabis users in self-report studies involving open-ended questions (Green et al., 2003). Sensory reactions experienced by users in the stage of being stoned include floating sensations, enhanced visual and auditory perception, visual illusions, and a tremendous slowing of time passage. Sociability can undergo different types of changes, in that the user may experience either an increased desire to be with others or a desire to be alone. The "comedown" stage is the gradual cessation of these effects, which varies in length depending on the THC dose and the individual's rate of THC metabolism.

Marijuana and other forms of cannabis also produce several physiological responses. There is increased blood flow to the skin, which leads to sensations of warmth or flushing. Heart rate is stimulated, which may be experienced by the user as a pounding pulse. Finally, marijuana increases hunger (the infamous "munchies"), an effect that is more than just street lore but has actually been documented in controlled laboratory studies of both humans (Foltin et al., 1988) and rats (Williams et al., 1998; also see Kirkham, 2009). Indeed, appetite stimulation is one of the recognized therapeutic uses for cannabinoids (see Box 14.1).

Not surprisingly, the marijuana "high" and its other subjective and physiological effects are dose dependent, in that the concentration of THC in a smoked marijuana cigarette has a direct relationship to the intensity of these effects (Cooper and Haney, 2008). Moreover, these effects are at least partially mediated by CB_1 receptors. Huestis and colleagues (2001, 2007) found that self-reported ratings of intoxication following the smoking of a single marijuana cigarette were significantly although not completely inhibited by prior treatment with rimonabant (**Figure 14.13**). Similar results were found for the heart rate–elevating effects of the drug. Either a higher dose of the antagonist is needed to fully block the effects of marijuana or some other mechanism in addition to CB_1 receptor activation (e.g., activation of central CB_2 receptors) is involved in producing these effects.

Smoking marijuana can also transiently evoke psychotic symptoms such as depersonalization (feeling separated from the self), derealization (feeling that the external world is unreal), agitation, and even paranoia (Sewell et al., 2009). Adverse reactions are most likely to occur in first-time users, although regular users may also experience these effects if they consume an unusually high dose. Flashbacks, which are widely known to occur in LSD users, have occasionally been reported for marijuana as well (Iversen, 2000).

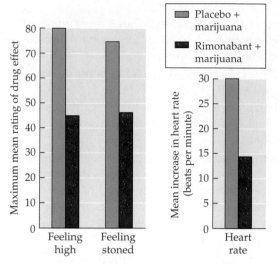

Figure 14.13 Reduction in the subjective and physiological effects of smoked marijuana by pretreatment with the CB_1 cannabinoid receptor antagonist rimonabant. Subjects received 90 mg of rimonabant or a placebo orally, after which they smoked either an active (2.64% THC content) or a placebo marijuana cigarette. Self-reported subjective effects and heart rate were measured over the next 65 minutes. The data shown represent the maximum mean effects of the active marijuana cigarette in the presence or absence of the receptor antagonist. (After Huestis et al., 2001.)

Although some authors have suggested the existence of a specific cannabis-induced psychosis, that concept remains questionable.

As with most psychoactive drugs, the psychological effects of marijuana vary greatly as a function not only of dose but also of the setting, the individual's past exposure to the drug, and his mental set, which refers to the expectation of what effects the drug will produce. The influence of expectancy was demonstrated by Kirk and coworkers (1998), who gave subjects capsules containing either THC or a placebo. The subjects were instructed beforehand that the capsules would contain placebo or one of several types of psychoactive compounds, but only for the "informed" group were cannabinoids included in the list of possible drugs. When asked to rate their responses to the substance they had consumed, the "informed" group gave higher ratings than the "uninformed" group in the categories of "like" drug and "want more drug." The expectation of consuming cannabinoids not only enhanced the pleasurable effects of actual cannabinoid administration, it also elicited a more positive reaction when the subjects were given placebo instead.

Plasma THC levels peak much more rapidly following intravenous (IV) THC injection or marijuana smoking than after oral ingestion (**Figure 14.14**). Consequently, users reach the peak "high" sooner with the first two routes of administration. Nevertheless, users

(A) Injection 5 mg

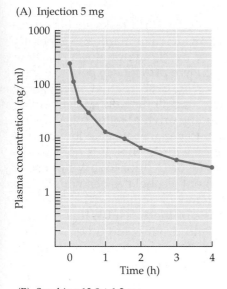

(B) Smoking 13.0 ± 1.2 mg

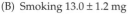

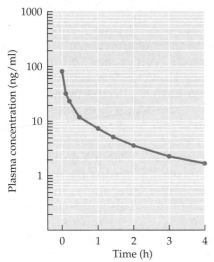

(C) Oral 20 mg

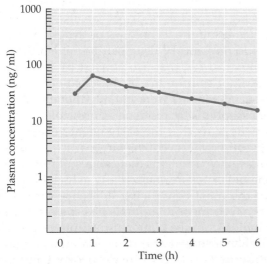

Figure 14.14 Time course of plasma THC concentrations as a function of route of THC administration. (After Agurell et al., 1986.)

who are smoking marijuana do not reach this peak until some time after the cigarette has been finished. This delay means that the maximum level of intoxication occurs when plasma THC concentrations are already declining, suggesting that the brain and plasma THC concentrations are not yet equilibrated at the time when the plasma level is peaking. Another possible factor is the contribution of active THC metabolites (whose peak does not coincide with that of THC itself) to the psychoactive properties of marijuana.

Marijuana use can lead to deficits in cognition and psychomotor performance

Clinical accounts of marijuana intoxication have often noted deficits in thought processes and in verbal behavior. These may include illogical or disordered thinking, fragmented speech, and difficulty in remaining focused on a given topic of conversation. The early descriptive work later gave rise to quantitative experimental assessments of marijuana's effects on learning, memory, and other cognitive processes. Marijuana or THC administration does not appear to impair subjects' ability to recall simple, "real-world" information. On the other hand, drug-induced performance decrements have been noted for a variety of verbal, spatial, time estimation, and reaction time tasks. With respect to memory, cannabinoids appear to interfere with all aspects of memory processing, namely, encoding, consolidation, and retrieval (Ranganathan and D'Souza, 2006), and some researchers have argued that adolescents are more vulnerable than adults to the influence of these substances on cognitive function (Schweinsburg et al., 2008). One example of THC's effects on memory can be seen in a study by Valerie Curran and colleagues at University College of London. These investigators demonstrated dose-dependent deficits in two different verbal memory tasks at 2 and 6 hours following oral THC administration to infrequent cannabis users (Curran et al., 2002) (**Figure 14.15**). It is interesting to note that significant prior marijuana usage may reduce the adverse cognitive effects of acute marijuana exposure, which has led to the hypothesis that behavioral ("cognitive") tolerance develops in heavy marijuana smokers (Hart et al., 2001).

Although memory and other cognitive functions are impaired shortly after smoking marijuana, most people do not smoke marijuana while they're at work or in class, or at other times when a high level of functioning is required. If marijuana is used only during recreational times (e.g., evenings and weekends), and if drug-related cognitive deficits do not outlast the period of use, then one could argue that such deficits are harmless. On the other hand, is it possible that heavy recreational use over a long period

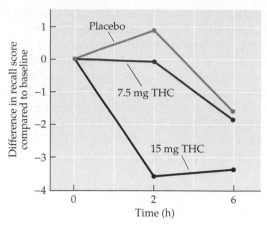

Figure 14.15 Oral THC produces a dose-dependent impairment in explicit memory Subjects were tested on a variety of cognitive tasks either before or after oral consumption of 7.5 mg or 15 mg THC (dronabinol) or a placebo. Each subject was tested under all three conditions using a double-blind crossover design. Explicit memory, which involves the recall of specific information or events, was examined using a prose recall task in which the subjects listened to a short passage of prose and were then tested on their ability to remember details of the story 45 minutes later. Testing occurred 1 hour before drug or placebo administration (0 time point = baseline) and again at 2 and 6 hours after treatment. The results shown in the figure represent the differences in recall scores at the 2- and 6-hour time points compared with baseline. The high dose of THC led to a significant decrement in prose recall at 2 hours, which corresponds to the approximate time of peak plasma drug levels following oral administration. The lower dose of THC did not differ significantly from the placebo condition. (After Curran et al., 2002.)

of time somehow compromises brain function such that cognitive problems persist even after drug use is stopped? The question of residual cognitive deficits from marijuana use is a controversial one, but a recent review by Crean and coworkers (2011) summarizes the current state of the field. Heavy cannabis use for a long period of time may lead to impaired executive functioning for at least 2 to 3 weeks following cessation of use. The affected functions include attention, the ability to concentrate, and inhibitory control. The adverse effects of cannabinoids on memory processes seem to have recovered by this time. Less information is available on truly long-term effects of prior cannabis use, ranging from 3 weeks to a few years. However, some of the data suggest that heavy, long-time users may continue to show impairment in decision making, planning, and concept formation.

In addition to its deleterious effects on cognitive/executive functioning, marijuana can negatively influence psychomotor performance. This has been demonstrated not only under controlled laboratory

conditions but also in real-world tasks such as driving an automobile. Low doses of marijuana generally produce relatively few psychomotor effects, particularly in subjects who have previous experience with the substance. However, even regular users show impaired psychomotor functioning under demanding task conditions (including driving) following a moderate or high dose of marijuana, or when a low dose of marijuana is combined with alcohol. It is not surprising, then, that recent (shortly prior to driving) use of cannabis with or without alcohol has been implicated as a risk factor in automobile accidents (Ramaekers et al., 2004). On the basis of these results, it is prudent for individuals to avoid driving and other activities requiring operation of heavy machinery for a significant period after smoking marijuana.

Cannabinoids are reinforcing to both humans and animals

Cannabinoids are obviously reinforcing to users who smoke marijuana recreationally or who consume cannabis by other means. However, cannabinoid reinforcement in humans has also been studied under controlled laboratory conditions. For example, Chait and Zacny (1992) found that regular marijuana users could discriminate THC-containing marijuana cigarettes from placebo cigarettes containing no THC, and that all subjects preferred the marijuana with THC when given a choice. In the same study, pure THC taken orally in capsule form was also preferred over a placebo. Chait and Burke (1994) subsequently related marijuana preference to THC content, as users reliably selected marijuana with a 1.95% THC content over marijuana containing only 0.63% THC.

As we have seen in earlier chapters, the rewarding and reinforcing properties of drugs can also be studied in animals using the techniques of drug-induced place conditioning and IV drug self-administration. Although most drugs that are abused by humans are rewarding or reinforcing in these experimental paradigms, cannabinoids were initially thought to be among the exceptions to this general principle. However, it now appears that the early negative studies were compromised by several factors, particularly the presence of aversive reactions that can result from initial cannabinoid exposure, particularly at high doses.

Perhaps the most convincing evidence for cannabinoid reinforcement in animals has come from a series of studies from the National Institute on Drug Abuse that demonstrated reliable self-administration of THC by squirrel monkeys (reviewed by Panlilio et al., 2010). The key factor in these experiments was the use of low drug doses that are within the range of

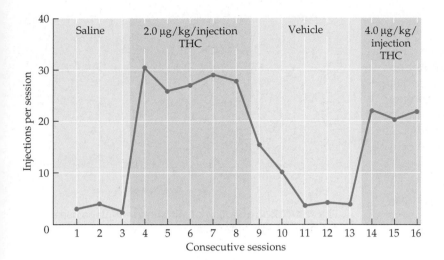

Figure 14.16 Acquisition of THC self-administration by squirrel monkeys Monkeys were initially trained in drug self-administration on a fixed-ratio (FR) 10 schedule using cocaine as the reinforcer (not shown). They were then switched to saline, which led to a nearly complete elimination of lever-pressing behavior. When THC (2.0 µg/kg/injection) was substituted for saline, lever pressing immediately increased to an amount sufficient to deliver approximately 30 drug injections per 1-hour session. Substitution with the vehicle again reduced operant responding until the active drug was made available once again. (After Tanda et al., 2000.)

estimated human THC intake from a single puff on a typical marijuana cigarette (**Figure 14.16**). Lever pressing for THC was completely blocked by pretreatment with rimonabant, indicating that the reinforcing effect was dependent on CB_1 receptor activation. These same investigators showed that THC can induce drug-seeking behavior (a model of relapse in human drug users) in monkeys (Justinová et al., 2008), and that the endocannabinoid 2-AG is also self-administered (and thus reinforcing) in the squirrel monkey model (Justinová et al., 2011). Other studies have also found that THC can produce a conditioned place preference in mice (Valjent and Maldonado, 2000), and that rats and mice will self-administer low doses of the synthetic CB_1 receptor agonist WIN 55,212-2 (Fattore et al., 2001; Martellotta et al., 1998). It is interesting to note that in the place-conditioning study, the rewarding properties of THC could be demonstrated only in mice that had been precxposed once to the drug in their home cage. This was interpreted by the authors to mean that first exposure to THC involves aversive responses that mask its rewarding effects. Preexposure outside of the experimental apparatus presumably reduces the occurrence of these responses when the THC is subsequently administered during the conditioning trials.

Once cannabinoids were shown to be reinforcing under appropriate conditions, researchers began to investigate the mechanisms underlying the reinforcing effects. One factor in cannabinoid reinforcement may be activation of the mesolimbic dopamine (DA) system, as cannabinoids have been found to stimulate the firing of DA neurons in the ventral tegmental area (VTA), and to enhance DA release in the nucleus accumbens. More surprisingly, there is substantial evidence for close interactions between the cannabinoid and opioid systems that play a critical role in cannabinoid reward and reinforcement. Various studies

have found that opioid agonists enhance cannabinoid self-administration, whereas opioid antagonists exert the opposite effect (Cooper and Haney, 2009). Nevertheless, we must be cautious in extrapolating the results to human users, as a similar opioid modulation of cannabinoid reward (as determined by self-report) has not been reliably demonstrated in human studies.

This section has focused on the rewarding and reinforcing properties of cannabinoids themselves. However, in recent years, a number of studies have examined the effects of either genetic deletion of CB_1 receptors or administration of rimonabant on responses to *other* drugs of abuse. The results of these studies suggest that the endocannabinoid system may play a significant role in the processes of reinforcement, dependence, and/or relapse for a number of other drugs, including ethanol (Colombo et al., 2005), opioids (Fattore et al., 2005; Robledo et al., 2008), nicotine (Castañé et al., 2005; Maldonado and Berrendero, 2010), and psychostimulants such as cocaine (Arnold, 2005; Wiskerke et al., 2008). Most previous findings have indicated that "cross-talk" between the endocannabinoid system and the neurochemical systems associated with other drugs of abuse involves the action of CB_1 receptors. However, a recent study by Xi and coworkers (2011) surprisingly found that systemic administration or microinjection into the nucleus accumbens of JWH133, a selective CB_2 receptor agonist, dose-dependently inhibited various effects of cocaine in mice, including cocaine-induced hyperactivity and cocaine self-administration. The effects of JWH133 could be blocked either by pretreatment with a CB_2 receptor antagonist or by administration to CB_2 receptor knockout mice instead of wild-type animals. Thus, future treatment approaches for drug dependence based on manipulating the endocannabinoid system might conceivably target either or both of the CB_1 and CB_2 receptors.

Section Summary

- The subjective characteristics of cannabis intoxication include feelings of euphoria, disinhibition, relaxation, altered sensations, and increased appetite. The euphoric effects produced by smoking marijuana appear to be mediated at least partly by CB_1 receptors. Psychopathological reactions can occur, particularly at high doses, or in the case of inexperienced users.

- Cannabis adversely affects memory, psychomotor performance, and other cognitive functions. The strongest effects occur during and for several hours after consumption. However, there is evidence for residual deficits that may last several weeks or possibly even longer.

- Although early studies failed to demonstrate cannabinoid reward or reinforcement in laboratory animals, more recent work has shown that THC can support self-administration and drug-seeking behavior in squirrel monkeys. Other cannabinoids, including the major endocannabinoid 2-AG and the synthetic CB_1 agonist WIN 55,212-2, are also self-administered by animals.

- Cannabinoid reinforcement has been shown to depend on the CB_1 receptor and may also involve dopamine, since cannabinoids stimulate the firing of DA neurons in the VTA and enhance DA release in the nucleus accumbens.

Cannabis Abuse and the Effects of Chronic Cannabis Exposure

According to Copeland and Swift (2009), about 4% of adults worldwide use cannabis in some form, with the greatest prevalence in North America, Australia, and New Zealand. Indeed, marijuana is the most widely used illicit drug in the United States. According to the 2011 National Survey on Drug Use and Health, more than 18 million Americans aged 12 or older were current marijuana users at the time of the survey (Substance Abuse and Mental Health Services Administration, 2012). This represented an increase from an estimated 14.4 million users in 2007, suggesting that government efforts to dissuade young people from trying marijuana have not been particularly successful.

Initial marijuana use typically occurs in adolescence and peaks during young adulthood. If an individual has not yet tried marijuana by his or her mid-twenties, he or she is unlikely to begin at a later age. This is shown in **Figure 14.17**, which is derived from a longitudinal study of 976 subjects drawn from upstate

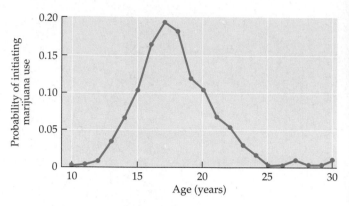

Figure 14.17 Probability of initiating marijuana use as a function of age (After Brooks et al., 1999.)

New York. In this cohort, the peak age for initiating marijuana use was 17, although a few children began as early 10 or 11 years of age. It is also the case that the prevalence of illicit drug use (including marijuana) declines with age. In the 2011 National Survey, for example, the percentage of responders who were current users of at least one illicit drug (typically marijuana) was 23.8% at 18 to 20 years of age, 11.1% at 30 to 34 years of age, and only 1.0% at 65 years or older.

Several factors seem to influence the likelihood of early marijuana use, including lax parental monitoring and early behavioral problems. For example, a recent study by Falls and colleagues (2011) found a significant association between early conduct problems and early initiation of marijuana use (i.e., before 15 years of age) in a large sample of college students. In addition, most adolescents have prior experience with alcohol and/or cigarettes before trying marijuana. For this reason, alcohol and tobacco have been hypothesized as "gateway" drugs to marijuana use, although not all findings are consistent with this hypothesis (e.g., see van Leeuwen et al., 2011). Some evidence also exists that marijuana, in turn, may serve as a gateway to other illicit drugs (e.g., cocaine) or to prescribed psychoactive drugs such as sedatives (Mayet et al., 2012). However, it is difficult to determine whether marijuana actually facilitates the progression to "hard drugs," or whether certain users are already predisposed to seek out these more dangerous substances because of some combination of personality traits, life circumstances, and other factors independent of their exposure to marijuana (see **Web Box 9.1**).

A further issue to consider is the progression from initial to regular (i.e., daily or near daily) marijuana use. Risk factors in the development of heavy marijuana use by adolescents include emotional problems in the family, heavy drug use in the household and/or by peers, dislike of school and poor school performance, and an early age of first use of marijuana (Gruber and

Pope, 2002). On the other hand, rates of marijuana use tend to be lower among adolescents from stable families with close parental supervision, as well as those who have strong career aspirations or assume adult responsibilities such as marriage and parenthood. Another important factor may be the degree to which the young person experiences positive reactions to his or her early use of cannabis. Researchers in New Zealand examined the relationship between the subjective responses to early cannabis use at 14 to 16 years of age and the likelihood of becoming cannabis-dependent by the age of 21, according to criteria of the *Diagnostic and Statistical Manual of Mental Illness* (*DSM-IV*) (Fergusson et al., 2003b). Individuals who reported more positive responses (i.e., feeling happy, feeling relaxed, laughing a lot, doing silly things, or getting very "high") to their early experience with cannabis were at greater risk of later dependence than those who reported fewer of these positive reactions. Finally, there is recent work by Brook and coworkers (2011) examining much longer-term trajectories of marijuana use frequency in a cohort of subjects from upstate New York over a period from 14 to approximately 37 years of age. The investigators identified five different patterns that they called (1) non-users or experimenters, (2) occasional users, (3) quitters or decreasers, (4) chronic users, and (5) increasing users (**Figure 14.18**). Programs aimed at reducing marijuana use and the development of dependence clearly need to identify and specifically target the factors that influence the usage patterns of the latter two groups.

Tolerance and dependence can develop from chronic cannabinoid exposure

For many drugs of abuse, regular heavy use leads to powerful tolerance as well as to physical and/or psychological dependence. Is this also the case for marijuana? We will first consider studies of cannabinoid tolerance in humans and animals.

TOLERANCE   The human literature on cannabis tolerance is somewhat variable. There are some reports that the "high" produced by a given dose of THC is similar in heavy or frequent marijuana users compared with light or infrequent users (Kirk and de Wit, 1999; Lindgren et al., 1981), suggesting an absence of tolerance to this effect. However, controlled laboratory studies involving 4 consecutive days of high doses of either smoked marijuana or oral THC provided evidence of tolerance to several (although not all) self-reported cannabinoid effects, including drug "high" and "good drug effect" (Haney et al., 1999, 1999b).

Studies in laboratory animals have been even more consistent, showing that animals exposed repeatedly

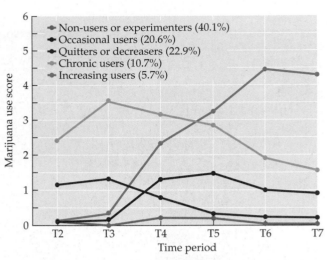

Figure 14.18 Trajectories of marijuana use from the adolescent period to approximately age 37   Subjects were recruited in 1975 at a mean age of 6.3 years (T1). Follow-up assessments of marijuana use were conducted in 1983 (T2; mean age, 14.1 years), 1985–1986 (T3; mean age, 16.3 years), 1992 (T4; mean age, 22.3 years), 1997 (T5; mean age, 27.0 years), 2002 (T6; mean age, 31.9 years), and 2005–2006 (T7; mean age, 36.6 years). Marijuana use scores were as follows: 0 = none; 1 = no more than a few times a year; 2 = once a month; 3 = several times a month; 4 = once a week; 5 = several times a week; and 6 = daily. (After Brook et al., 2011.)

to THC and other CB_1 agonists develop a profound tolerance to the behavioral and physiological effects of these compounds (González et al., 2005; Panagis et al., 2008). The rate of tolerance development depends on a variety of factors, including the species, choice of cannabinoid and dosing regimen, and which effect is being studied. Cannabinoid tolerance appears to be largely pharmacodynamic in nature, involving a combination of desensitization and down-regulation of CB_1 receptors. For example, Breivogel and coworkers (1999) found that rats given daily THC injections (10 mg/kg) over a 3-week period showed gradual reductions both in regional CB_1 receptor density and in cannabinoid agonist-mediated receptor activation (**Figure 14.19**). In some brain areas, the cannabinoid receptors were almost entirely desensitized following 3 weeks of THC exposure.

Interestingly, the results of a recent brain imaging study demonstrated a significant decrease in cortical but not subcortical CB_1 receptor binding in regular marijuana smokers (Hirvonen et al., 2012). The magnitude of the reduction was correlated with the number of years of smoking, and the effect was reversible by 4 weeks of continuous abstinence from cannabis. These findings provide a neurochemical basis for cannabinoid tolerance in humans (at least with respect to those drug effects that are cortically mediated) and

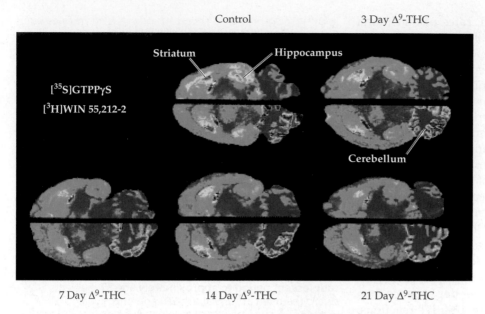

Control   3 Day Δ⁹-THC

[³⁵S]GTPPγS
[³H]WIN 55,212-2

Striatum   Hippocampus

Cerebellum

7 Day Δ⁹-THC   14 Day Δ⁹-THC   21 Day Δ⁹-THC

Figure 14.19 Desensitization of cannabinoid receptors produced by chronic THC exposure Rats were treated daily with 10 mg/kg THC or vehicle for 3 to 21 days, after which their brains were obtained and horizontal sections were prepared for autoradiography. Some sections were incubated with the synthetic cannabinoid agonist [³H] WIN 55,212-2 to determine the density of cannabinoid receptors in different brain areas. Other sections were incubated with [³⁵S]GTPγS in the presence of unlabeled WIN 55,212-2. This procedure allows the measurement of receptor-mediated G protein activation in each area. The autoradiograms show that chronic THC administration led to progressive reductions in both receptor density (lower sections) and receptor-mediated G protein activation (upper sections) throughout the brain. (Images courtesy of Steven Childers.)

may also have relevance for the production of cannabis dependence and withdrawal symptoms.

DEPENDENCE AND WITHDRAWAL On the basis of a number of epidemiological studies, it has been estimated that approximately 10% of individuals who have ever used cannabis will eventually become dependent (Copeland and Smith, 2009). Not surprisingly, the risk of dependence is related to drug use patterns. Thus, people who progress to daily use have a 50% probability of become dependent. The 2011 National Survey estimated that 4.2 million individuals in the United States were abusing or dependent on marijuana at the time of the survey (Substance Abuse and Mental Health Services Administration, 2012).

Cannabinoid withdrawal symptoms were first reported in laboratory studies in the 1970s. Later research began to recognize the existence of cannabis dependence in some marijuana users. Such dependence is manifested as a difficulty in stopping one's use, a craving for marijuana, and unpleasant withdrawal symptoms that are triggered by abstinence. Controlled studies of abstinence in long-term heavy marijuana users have reported a number of withdrawal symptoms, including irritability, increased

anxiety, depressed mood, sleep disturbances, heightened aggressiveness, and decreased appetite (Cooper and Haney, 2008, 2009). These withdrawal symptoms resemble those seen with several other drugs of abuse, most notably nicotine. Overall symptomatology is greatest during the first 1 to 2 weeks of withdrawal (**Figure 14.20**), but some symptoms may persist for a month or longer. Moreover, recent research has shown that exposure to marijuana-related cues can elicit increased craving in cannabis-dependent individuals (Lundahl and Johanson, 2011). Cannabinoid withdrawal can be alleviated by providing either smoked marijuana or oral THC, demonstrating a key role for this compound in both the development of dependence and the manifestation of withdrawal symptoms.

Early experimental studies in which animals were administered THC chronically and then were examined after the treatment was stopped found few if any signs of withdrawal. Although these results may seem to be at odds with reports of an abstinence syndrome in humans, researchers recognized that the absence of withdrawal symptoms might have been due to the long elimination half-life of THC, which causes the cannabinoid receptors to remain partially occupied for a significant time even after termination

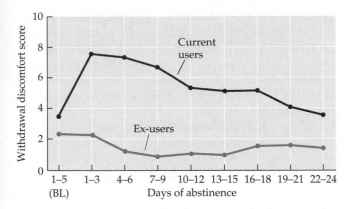

Figure 14.20 Time course of overall withdrawal discomfort in heavy marijuana users undergoing abstinence
Current marijuana users were compared with ex-users on a battery of 15 possible self-reported withdrawal symptoms over a 5-day baseline period (BL) during which marijuana use was permitted and then during a 45-day period of abstinence. Data shown represent the mean composite withdrawal scores (up to a possible maximum of 36) during baseline and the first 24 days of abstinence. (After Budney et al., 2003.)

of drug treatment. Once the CB$_1$ receptor antagonist rimonabant was developed, it could be used to test for dependence and withdrawal, since administration of the antagonist would abruptly block the receptors despite the continued presence of THC in the animal. This approach, which is called **precipitated withdrawal**, enabled researchers to demonstrate an abstinence syndrome characterized by tremors, wet-dog shakes, increased grooming behaviors (facial rubbing, licking, and scratching), ataxia, and hunched posture (González et al., 2005; Panagis et al., 2008). As expected, no withdrawal symptoms were observed in CB$_1$ knockout mice given chronic THC and then challenged with rimonabant. Although the precipitated withdrawal studies have convincingly shown that chronic treatment with THC or a synthetic cannabinoid can produce physical dependence in animals, there has been some criticism that these studies used very high cannabinoid doses compared with typical human recreational use patterns. Nevertheless, the reports of human abstinence symptoms confirm that dependence and withdrawal occur under naturalistic conditions, thereby supporting at least the basic conclusions drawn from the animal research.

The neurochemical mechanisms underlying the marijuana abstinence syndrome are not yet fully understood. Some of the important findings (using the precipitated withdrawal paradigm) include decreased DA cell firing in the VTA and reduced DA release in the nucleus accumbens, increased corticotropin-releasing factor (CRF) release in the central nucleus of the amygdala, increased secretion of stress hormones such as corticosterone, and various changes in the endocannabinoid system (González et al., 2005; Panagis et al., 2008). Together, these alterations could contribute to the mood reduction, irritability, and stress experienced by dependent cannabis users during periods of abstinence. Moreover, at least some of the same responses have been reported to occur during withdrawal from cocaine, alcohol, and opiates, thereby linking cannabinoids with substances generally considered to have greater abuse potential.

TREATMENT OF CANNABIS DEPENDENCE   Although most cannabis users do not become dependent and do not seek treatment, those who do develop cannabis dependence report many problems (besides craving and withdrawal symptoms) that adversely influence their functioning, including social problems, financial difficulties, and poor general satisfaction with life (Budney et al., 2007; Copeland and Swift, 2009). Some, although not all, such individuals eventually seek professional treatment for their problems.

Dependent marijuana users seeking treatment are typically entered into an outpatient program that may involve cognitive-behavioral therapy, relapse prevention training, and/or motivational enhancement therapy.[3] These approaches can also be combined with an incentive program in which participants who submit cannabinoid-negative urine samples earn vouchers redeemable for various goods and services. Although these different treatment programs have all met with some success, patients are highly vulnerable to relapse even after an initial period of abstinence (Kadden et al., 2007) (**Figure 14.21**). Thus, marijuana appears to be similar to other drugs of abuse with regard to the difficulty in achieving long-term treatment success in dependent individuals.

The idea of pharmacotherapy for cannabis dependence has not received a large amount of attention, but a few small-scale studies have used this approach to attempt to alleviate withdrawal symptoms. Medications tested to date include the antidepressants nefazodone and buspirone, the norepinephrine uptake inhibitor atomoxetine, the mood stabilizers divalproex and lithium carbonate (used to treat bipolar disorder), oral THC, and a combination of THC with the α_2-adrenergic agonist lofexidine (Budney et al., 2007; Copeland and Swift, 2009). Of these, the best success has been reported for THC, which suppresses cannabinoid withdrawal symptoms in a dose-dependent manner, and the combination of THC and lofexidine.

---

[3]Motivational enhancement therapy is a type of psychotherapy that seeks to elicit a desire for behavioral change on the part of the patient.

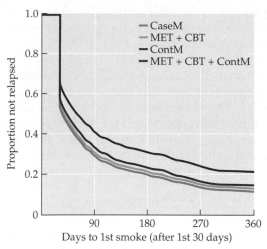

Figure 14.21 **Time course of relapse to first marijuana use after the first 30 days of treatment** Subjects meeting *DSM-IV* criteria for cannabis dependence were enrolled in one of four different treatment conditions. CaseM was a case management approach that focused on general life issues (e.g., occupational or educational goals) but did not incorporate any specific therapeutic intervention besides verbal praise for abstinence. This condition served as an active control condition. The MET + CBT condition combined motivational enhancement with cognitive-behavioral therapy and focused on learning techniques for coping with high-risk situations likely to cause relapse. The ContM (contingency management) condition provided reinforcement (i.e., vouchers that could be redeemed for items and services in the community) for submitting drug-free urine samples. The MET + CBT + ContM condition was a combination of the latter two therapeutic interventions and was predicted to yield the greatest benefit. The graph shows that by 1 year, about 80% of the subjects overall had relapsed. However, the ContM group exhibited a somewhat lower rate of relapse than the other treatment groups, especially the CaseM control group. (After Kadden et al., 2007.)

Because chronic marijuana use leads to cognitive impairments, Sofuoglu and colleagues (2010) recently suggested that cognitive enhancers such as those acting on the cholinergic system should be considered as potentially playing a useful role in mitigating such impairments.

Chronic cannabis use may lead to adverse behavioral and health effects

It is not unusual for dedicated cannabis users to consume the drug on a regular, even daily, basis for many years. Concern naturally has arisen over whether such lengthy periods of chronic drug exposure might lead to adverse psychological, neuropsychiatric, or physiological effects. Evidence for such effects is discussed in this final section of the chapter.

EDUCATIONAL PERFORMANCE Survey studies indicate that the amount of cannabis use by young people is inversely related to educational performance. That is, greater use is associated with poorer grades, more negative attitudes about school, and increased absenteeism (Lynskey and Hall, 2000). Furthermore, prospective longitudinal studies suggest that regular cannabis use beginning relatively early in life is a significant risk factor for poor performance in school and even dropping out (Brook et al., 2008; Townsend et al., 2007).

At the present time, we do not know whether there is a causal relationship between amount of cannabis use and educational achievement. Even if there is, the direction of causation would still need to be established. Does early cannabis use cause a lack of success in school, or does a lack of success early in one's academic career cause an increase in cannabis use? One hypothesis is that heavy cannabis use leads to persistent cognitive deficits, thereby impairing school performance (Jacobus et al., 2009). It is possible that students who use cannabis heavily over a long period of time could perform poorly in school because of the cognitive impairment. Recent findings of Meier and colleagues (2012) support this hypothesis. These researchers conducted a prospective study of cognitive function in approximately 1000 people in New Zealand, who were recruited into the study at 3 years of age and were subjected to neuropsychological testing at 13 (before the onset of cannabis use) and again at 38 years of age. The amount of cannabis use and the appearance of symptoms of cannabis dependence were significantly associated with neuropsychological impairment (including lower IQ) at 38 years, even after controlling for level of education. These are among the first data to suggest a causal relationship between long-term cannabis use and cognitive deficits. Despite these findings, it is important to consider alternate hypotheses, including the notion that the social context surrounding heavy cannabis use at a relatively early age promotes the rejection of mainstream social values such as educational achievement in favor of a more unconventional lifestyle (Fergusson et al., 2003a; Lynskey et al., 2003). This hypothesis attempts to account for poor school performance in heavy users without postulating a direct effect of cannabis on their performance.

Another possibility involves drug-related motivational changes that would have a negative impact on performance in the classroom. Indeed, research going back more than 30 years has found evidence for apathy, aimlessness, loss of achievement motivation, lack of long-range planning, and decreased productivity in chronic marijuana users. Together, these symptoms have been termed the **amotivational syndrome**

(Lynskey and Hall, 2000). We cannot rule out the possibility that some users experience a loss of drive and achievement motivation as a result of chronic, heavy exposure to cannabis. However, one could argue just as plausibly that such personality characteristics are a cause, rather than a consequence, of adopting a marijuana-centered lifestyle.

NEUROPSYCHIATRIC EFFECTS In recent years, various imaging methods have begun to examine the potential influence of chronic marijuana use on the brain. A recent review of structural magnetic resonance imaging (MRI) studies on long-term cannabis users found some evidence of alterations in temporal lobe structures such as the hippocampus, although the findings across studies were inconsistent (Lorenzetti et al., 2010). Research using other imaging techniques such as functional MRI and proton magnetic resonance spectroscopy (which measures regional concentrations of several different neurochemicals) has found abnormalities in several other structures, including the anterior cingulate cortex, a brain area rich in CB_1 receptors that plays an important role in emotional processing and behavioral inhibition (Gruber et al., 2009; Prescot et al., 2011). Thus, imaging methods suggest that chronic marijuana use is associated with several different kinds of abnormalities in the brain.

Over the past 15 years, several large-scale epidemiologic studies have found a significant relationship between early heavy marijuana smoking and increased risk for the later development of psychotic disorders such as schizophrenia. This has become an important new area of research that is discussed in greater detail in **Box 14.2**.

HEALTH EFFECTS In considering the potential health consequences of cannabis use, there is both good and bad news. The good news is that there is no published report of anyone dying as a result of cannabis overdose. This means that the use of this substance has a margin of safety that is lacking with many other substances of abuse such as heroin, cocaine, and sedative–hypnotic drugs. The bad news is that the lack of fatal overdosing does not mean that cannabis use, particularly in large amounts or for long periods of time, is without risk.

Because cannabis is almost always consumed by smoking, the possibility of lung damage is one obvious area of concern. Although marijuana joints and tobacco cigarettes contain different psychoactive ingredients (cannabinoids versus nicotine), the smoke they produce has the same kinds of irritants and carcinogens. Tar from cannabis smoke actually contains higher concentrations of certain carcinogens known as benzanthracenes and benzpyrenes. Even so, one might think that marijuana smoking is not harmful because

users typically smoke only one or a few joints a day, compared with the one or more packs of cigarettes smoked by regular tobacco users. Unfortunately, it appears that the amounts of tar and carbon monoxide taken in *per cigarette* are much greater for marijuana joints than for tobacco cigarettes (Wu et al., 1988). It is not surprising, therefore, that regular marijuana smoking is associated with various respiratory symptoms, including chronic cough, increased phlegm production, wheezing, and even bronchitis in some cases (Howden and Naughton, 2011; Tetrault et al., 2007). Furthermore, microscopic examination of bronchial biopsy specimens from marijuana users has revealed several kinds of cellular abnormalities, some of which are considered precancerous (Tashkin et al., 2002). Researchers have not yet established a relationship between long-term marijuana smoking and lung cancer (Mehra et al., 2006). Nevertheless, heavy use has definite risks for the respiratory system, and future studies may show that development of lung cancer is one such risk.

Evidence has also been accumulating that cannabinoids influence the immune system. Both CB_1 and particularly CB_2 receptors are expressed by various immune cells, and activation of these receptors generally suppresses immune function (Tanasescu and Constantinescu, 2010). Importantly, THC has been found to impair an organism's resistance to bacterial and viral infections under controlled experimental conditions (Cabral and Pettit, 1998). We don't yet know, however, whether marijuana use leads to an increased incidence of infectious disease under real-life conditions.

Another system susceptible to interference by cannabis use is the reproductive system. It is now clear that that the endocannabinoid system plays an important role in both the male and female reproductive systems (Bari et al., 2011; Sun and Dey, 2012), raising the possibility that marijuana smoking could have an adverse influence on reproduction. In support of this possibility, animal studies have consistently shown that THC suppresses the release of luteinizing hormone (LH), an important reproductive hormone secreted by the pituitary gland, in both males and females (Maccarone and Wenger, 2005). Other animal work has demonstrated pregnancy failure, retarded embryonic development, and even fetal death associated with THC administration, although similar findings have not yet been reported in controlled human studies. However, regular marijuana smoking by men has been shown to reduce testosterone levels, sperm counts, and possibly sperm motility (Rossato et al., 2008). Thus, marijuana seemingly has the potential to produce reproductive abnormalities, but more

BOX 14.2 The Cutting Edge

Is There a Relationship between Early Heavy Marijuana Smoking and Later Risk for Developing Psychosis?

Earlier in this chapter, we saw that heavy marijuana smoking causes short-term cognitive deficits, but any effects that persist after stopping seem to be modest. Similarly, immediate psychotic-like responses to cannabis are usually transient in nature. But what if young people knew that heavy marijuana use significantly increased their risk for developing a psychotic disorder such as schizophrenia later in life?

This important issue has now been addressed by a number of longitudinal cohort studies that tested whether there is a relationship between early marijuana smoking and a later onset of psychosis (Moore et al., 2007; Murray et al., 2007; Sewell et al., 2009). These studies were conducted in a number of different locations worldwide, including Germany, the Netherlands, the United Kingdom, Sweden, New Zealand, and the United States. The figure summarizes the findings from six studies according to the odds ratio of developing psychotic symptoms in heavy cannabis users compared with non-using control subjects. All studies found an increased odds ratio (increased risk) in the cannabis users, with this increase being statistically significant in five of the six since the 95% confidence

intervals (depicted as the error bars) do not reach an odds ratio of 1 (represented by the controls) in those studies. Also shown in the figure is that a meta-analysis performed on the studies taken together found an overall odds ratio of approximately 2. This is interpreted to mean that heavy (e.g., daily) marijuana use, which typically occurs during the adolescent to young adult period of life, is related to a doubling of the risk of later developing psychotic symptoms (including in some cases a full-blown schizophrenia). Recent studies conducted in the Netherlands have additionally suggested that a younger age of onset of cannabis use is related to a younger age of appearance of psychosis-related symptoms (Dragt et al., 2010, 2012).

Although many investigators are convinced that these studies conclusively demonstrate a relationship between early marijuana smoking and increased risk for later psychosis, others have questioned the methodology used in at least some of the research (McLaren et al., 2010; Minozzi et al., 2010). Furthermore, even if we accept that such a relationship is real, there are several possible interpretations of the results. For example, Sewell and colleagues suggest three possible models to account for the findings of these cohort studies: (1) an **association model**, in which individuals who are already vulnerable to developing psychosis have an increased likelihood of using cannabis when they're young; (2) a **causal model**, in which cannabis use (especially heavy use)

Increased probability of developing psychosis in heavy cannabis users The graph illustrates the odds ratio (the probability compared with a reference group) of developing any psychotic disorder in six separate epidemiological studies relating cannabis use to later psychosis. The criterion for heaviest cannabis use is specified for each study in parentheses. The blue squares and accompanying lines represent the odds ratio for that study along with the 95% confidence interval (CI; a 95% probability that the real odds ratio lies within the specified range). The open diamond shows the overall odds ratio from the six studies taken together and shows that heavy cannabis use is related to an increased risk of subsequently developing a psychotic disorder. CHDS, Christchurch Health and Development Study (New Zealand); ECA, Epidemiological Catchment Area (U.S.A.); EDSP, Early Developmental Stages of Psychopathology (Germany); NEMESIS, Netherlands Mental Health Survey and Incidence Study (Netherlands); NPMS, National Psychiatric Morbidity Survey (United Kingdom). (After Moore et al., 2007.)

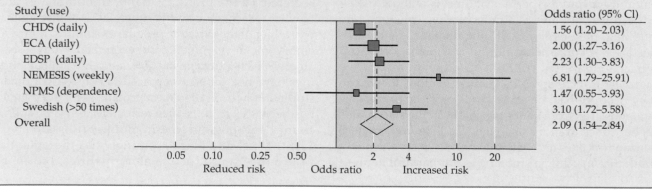

Study (use)	Odds ratio (95% CI)
CHDS (daily)	1.56 (1.20–2.03)
ECA (daily)	2.00 (1.27–3.16)
EDSP (daily)	2.23 (1.30–3.83)
NEMESIS (weekly)	6.81 (1.79–25.91)
NPMS (dependence)	1.47 (0.55–3.93)
Swedish (>50 times)	3.10 (1.72–5.58)
Overall	2.09 (1.54–2.84)

BOX 14.2 *(continued)*

predisposes individuals to develop psychosis later in life, and (3) an **indicator-variable model**, in which one or more other factors lead jointly to cannabis use and psychosis proneness. Current data do not permit us to choose one model over another, although it is worth noting that some investigators have proposed plausible biological mechanisms whereby heavy cannabis exposure during adolescence might perturb the brain in ways that could predispose the person to developing psychotic symptomatology (e.g., Murray et al., 2007). But even if we adopt some version of a causal model, it seems likely that significant cannabis use is a component factor that interacts with other factors (including genetics and the early environment) to increase the risk of later psychosis development. Thus, this relationship is a strong reason (besides the adverse health consequences discussed elsewhere in this section) for young people to abstain from using cannabis, or at least to minimize such use.

research is needed to confirm and extend the existing findings.

A number of studies have been performed on the offspring of women who smoked marijuana during pregnancy. These studies found few negative effects of these offspring at birth or at early ages. On the other hand, cognitive deficits, poor school achievement, and increased risk for tobacco and/or marijuana use later in life have all been associated with prenatal marijuana exposure (Minnes and Singer, 2011). Such findings highlight the importance of educating women about the dangers of continuing to smoke marijuana during pregnancy, as well as the development of treatment programs to serve marijuana-dependent women who become pregnant.

Finally, Aryana and Williams (2007) have briefly reviewed evidence that marijuana use may be associated with cardiovascular problems, even including myocardial infarction (heart attack) in some patients. This is a relatively poorly studied area that clearly needs more work for these ideas to be substantiated.

ADVERSE EFFECTS OF ABUSED DESIGNER CANNABINOIDS Beginning in 2004, advertisements began to appear on the Internet for new herbal preparations containing synthetic designer cannabinoids that were legal at the time. These substances were typically sold under the names "K2" or "Spice." Indeed, many of these preparations were found to contain potent CB_1 agonists when they were tested by forensic laboratories, and thus smoking the plant material would provide a powerful marijuana-like "high" (Seely et al., 2011). Moreover, these products were reported to produce a number of adverse physiological and psychological effects in users, and they could be expected to exhibit significant dependence potential if used repeatedly. In response to these concerns, in 2011 the U.S. Drug Enforcement Agency (DEA) placed the synthetic cannabinoids previously identified in K2 or Spice under Schedule I, which bans their recreational use. Nevertheless, at the time of this writing, there are still numerous ads on the Internet for herbal products using the same names, and it is unclear whether any such products continue to contain illegal synthetic cannabinoids.

Section Summary

- Marijuana is the most heavily used illicit drug in the United States.

- Early behavioral (e.g., conduct) problems have been associated with an increased likelihood of early marijuana use.

- Initial exposure to marijuana usually occurs during adolescence, after the individual has already had experience with alcohol and/or cigarettes. Some investigators have hypothesized that alcohol and tobacco are "gateway" drugs to marijuana, which then serves as a potential gateway to other illicit drugs. However, it is difficult to determine whether marijuana actually facilitates the progression to these more dangerous substances.

- Other factors such as family issues, poor school performance, and a strong positive response to early marijuana experience are risk factors for the transition to regular use and possibly dependence.

- Controlled laboratory studies have demonstrated tolerance to repeated THC exposure in both humans and experimental animals. Such tolerance is related to a desensitization and down-regulation of central CB_1 receptors.

- Heavy (e.g., daily) marijuana users are at significant risk for developing dependence on the drug and for undergoing withdrawal symptoms upon becoming abstinent. Withdrawal symptoms include heightened irritability, anxiety, aggressiveness, depressed mood state, sleep disturbances, reduced appetite, and craving for marijuana.

- Chronic THC exposure in laboratory rodents also causes the development of dependence that can be demonstrated using the procedure of precipitated withdrawal with rimonabant. Neurochemical studies of cannabinoid-dependent animals undergoing withdrawal have found reduced DA cell firing, increased CRF release, and endocannabinoid system changes that could contribute to some of the symptoms of cannabis withdrawal in human users.

- Individuals who have developed cannabis dependence report a number of life problems, which leads some of these individuals to seek treatment.

- Some success has been achieved with various kinds of psychotherapeutic interventions, and additional improvement in outcome has been reported by adding a voucher-based incentive program to the standard treatment approach. Nevertheless, most dependent individuals find it difficult to maintain long-term abstinence.

- Pharmacotherapeutic approaches to the treatment of cannabis dependence are now being investigated. Oral THC has been shown to reduce withdrawal symptoms in heavy marijuana users, but this approach has not yet been incorporated into any established treatment programs.

- Concerns have been raised over possible adverse consequences of chronic cannabis consumption. There is a negative association between the amount of cannabis use by young people and their educational performance, although it is not yet known whether this association is causal. It is possible that heavy cannabis use can produce persistent cognitive deficits and/or an amotivational syndrome characterized by apathy, loss of achievement motivation, and decreased productivity. Alternatively, early cannabis use may be linked to the adoption of an unconventional lifestyle that devalues educational striving and achievement.

- Neuroimaging studies of heavy cannabis users have reported structural and biochemical changes in certain brain regions (including the hippocampus and anterior cingulate cortex). Epidemiologic studies have found a positive relationship between early heavy cannabis use and later risk for developing psychosis.

- Health consequences of heavy marijuana smoking include respiratory problems, possible suppression of immune function, interference with the reproductive system in both men and women, and adverse effects on offspring development (when used by pregnant women).

- Synthetic designer cannabinoids marketed as "K2" or "Spice" began to be sold over the Internet in 2004. Because of the dependence potential of these substances, as well as reports of adverse effects, the DEA designated these cannabinoids as Schedule I in 2011.

Go to the **COMPANION WEBSITE**

sites.sinauer.com/psychopharm2e
for Web Boxes, animations, flashcards, and other study resources.

Recommended Readings

Earleywine, M. (2005). *Understanding Marijuana: A New Look at the Scientific Evidence.* New York: Oxford University Press.

Iverson, L. L. (2000). *The Science of Marijuana.* New York: Oxford University Press.

Kano, M., Ohno-Shosaku, T., Hashimotodani, Y., Uchigashima, M., and Watanabe, M. (2009). Endocannabinoid-mediated control of synaptic transmission. *Physiol. Rev.,* 309–380.

"Blotters" decorated with fanciful images are commonly used to disseminate LSD.

Hallucinogens, PCP, and Ketamine 15

"IT'S SAFE TO SAY THAT THIS IS THE STRONGEST EXPERIENCE I've had in my life. The setting of that experience could have been better, since I had a 30 minute window to trip on before going back to a meeting at work. I sat on a comfortable couch, and then an experienced friend of mine told me he would take the pipe after I smoked the *Salvia*; by this point I was a little skeptical about it having so much effect on my consciousness. By the time I took the second hit I felt completely paralyzed, and then saw my friend laughing and taking the pipe; after that I started falling and never really stopped for the whole trip.

Intense feeling of death or self dissociation was present during the whole trip and was the predominant 'theme,' not in a sad way, but in a self-reflexive, philosophical kind of way. First I felt continuously falling into nothingness, then the whole universe started to spin, ripping me apart by layers with every turn. I started to feel desperate to hold on to something, but couldn't, not even to reality. At this point the thought that I had to be leaving in a couple of minutes started to bother me, and I could see myself going back and forth between the 'Salvia' dimension and the 'real' dimension. Walking back to my meeting, I still felt my body dissolving with its surroundings, and had this great feeling of peace of mind, while still putting together the pieces of my trip and what it meant to me, helping me to recognize parts of me that I have never seen before."

The above is a self-reported account of someone's first experience with the hallucinogenic plant *Salvia divinorum*.[1] As we will see in the first section of this chapter, hallucinogenic substances like *Salvia*, LSD, and others have powerful effects on perceptual and conscious processes. Where do these substances come from, and how do they produce their effects? We will also cover PCP and ketamine—two other drugs also known for their mind-altering properties but that act through a different neurochemical mechanism than typical hallucinogens.

Hallucinogenic Drugs

Some substances are valued primarily for the unusual perceptual and cognitive distortions they produce. Users may find such distortions novel, stimulating, or even spiritually uplifting. Among the substances categorized in this way are **lysergic acid diethylamide (LSD)**, **mescaline**, **psilocybin**, **dimethyltryptamine (DMT)**, **5-methoxy-dimethyltryptamine (5-MeO-DMT)**, and **salvinorin A** (the main psychoactive ingredient of *Salvia*). Over the years, many different names have been given to this drug class, including **psychotomimetic** (psychosis-mimicking), **psychedelic** (mind-opening), and **hallucinogenic** (hallucination-producing). The term *psychotomimetic* is now rarely used in this context because most researchers no longer consider these compounds to be useful models of psychosis. Of the two remaining alternatives, the term *psychedelic* is often preferred by recreational users and by those who take such drugs in a quest for spiritual or mystical experiences. The modern pharmacological literature, however, strongly favors the term *hallucinogenic*, and we will follow that practice here. Specifically, we will define hallucinogens as substances whose primary effect is to cause perceptual and cognitive distortions without producing a state of toxic delirium.

Mescaline

Many hallucinogenic drugs either are synthesized by plants or are based on plant-derived compounds. Mescaline, for example, is found in several species of cactus, such as the **peyote cactus** (*Lophophor williamsii*) (**Figure 15.1**). When the crown (top part) of this small spineless cactus is cut off and dried, it is known as a **mescal button** or **peyote button**. These buttons can

Figure 15.1 Peyote cactus (Photo courtesy of Gerhard Köhres.)

be chewed raw or cooked and then eaten to obtain their psychoactive effects. Alternatively, the mescaline can be extracted from the cactus and consumed as a relatively pure powder. The peyote cactus is native to the southwestern United States and northern parts of Mexico, and archeological evidence suggests that inhabitants of these regions used peyote for at least a few thousand years before invasion by the Spanish. Indeed, a radiocarbon dating of mescaline-containing peyote buttons from Mexico found them to be 5700 years old (Bruhn et al., 2002). Peyote was used by Native Americans for religious and healing rituals, and such rituals continue to take place under the auspices of the Native American Church of the United States and Canada, which was founded in 1918.

Pure mescaline was first isolated from peyote in 1896 by Arthur Heffter and was synthesized in 1919 by Ernst Spath. However, the drug did not enter mainstream American culture until the famous novelist Aldous Huxley tried mescaline in 1953 and subsequently described his experience in a book entitled *The Doors of Perception*. Publication of this book and its sequel, *Heaven and Hell*, were among the seminal events that spawned a major rise in hallucinogenic drug use in the United States in the 1960s. At present, however, mescaline is not as readily available as various other hallucinogens because of the relatively high cost of synthesis and the lack of a large market for the drug.

Psilocybin

Numerous species of mushrooms manufacture alkaloids with hallucinogenic properties. These fungi, which are sometimes called "magic mushrooms" or

---

[1]The passage was taken from the site The Salvia Dream. Available at: www.the-salvia-dream.com/acquainted-to-death.html, accessed 4/22/12.

Figure 15.2 *Psilocybe* mushrooms

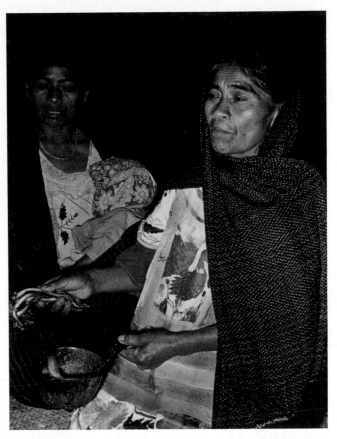

Figure 15.3 **María Sabina engaged in the mushroom eating ritual**

simply "shrooms," include members of the genera *Conocybe, Copelandia, Panaeolus, Psilocybe,* and *Stropharia,* which are found in many places around the world (**Figure 15.2**). Depending on the species, users take 1 to 5 g of dried mushrooms to obtain the desired effects. The dried material may be eaten raw, boiled in water to make tea, or cooked with other foods to cover its bitter flavor. The major ingredients of these mushrooms are psilocybin and the related compound **psilocin**. After ingestion, the psilocybin is enzymatically converted to psilocin, which is the actual psychoactive agent. A different species of mushroom, *Amanita muscaria* (fly agaric), produces a state of delirium that also includes hallucinations, but its primary active agents are muscimol and ibotenic acid.

The use of hallucinogenic mushrooms probably goes back at least as far historically as peyote use. There are two spectacular rock cave paintings in Algeria, dated at least to 3500 BC, depicting people holding mushrooms in their hands and dancing. The more famous of the two paintings shows a single man (possibly a shaman[2]) with a beelike head and mushrooms sprouting from his entire body. In Mexico and Central America, the Aztec and Mayan civilizations developed religious rituals around the eating of psilocybin-containing mushrooms.

After defeating the Aztecs, the Spaniards soon learned of their use of hallucinogenic mushrooms, which they called *teonanácatl,* meaning "flesh of the gods." The conquerors brutally suppressed mushroom eating along with other aspects of the Aztec religion, but they were unable to completely wipe it out. Nevertheless, the existence of hallucinogenic mushrooms in the New World was largely ignored until 1938, when

Richard Schultes of the Harvard Botanical Museum traveled to Oaxaca, Mexico, and collected specimens of several different types of mushrooms being used in sacred rituals by the Mazatec people of that region. The publication of Schultes' findings ultimately led Gordon Wasson, a wealthy investment banker and amateur mycologist (someone who studies fungi), to visit Oaxaca in 1953 and again in 1955. During the second visit, Wasson and a photographer friend became the first known Westerners to participate in a Native American mushroom eating ritual, which was led by a Mazatec curandera, or shaman, named María Sabina (**Figure 15.3**). In a 1957 *Life* magazine article entitled "Seeking the Magic Mushroom,"[3] Wasson describes his reaction as follows:

> We lay down on the mat that had been spread for us, but no one had any wish to sleep except the children, to whom mushrooms are not served. We were never more wide awake, and the visions came whether our eyes were opened or closed. They emerged from the center of the field of vision, opening up as they came, now rushing, now slowly, at the pace that our will chose. They were in

[2]In ancient cultures, shamans were people thought to possess special abilities to contact the spirit world.

vivid color, always harmonious. They began with art motifs…. Then they evolved into palaces with courts, arcades, gardens… Then I saw a mythological beast drawing a regal chariot. Later it was as though the walls of our house had dissolved, and my spirit had flown forth, and I was suspended in mid-air viewing landscapes of mountains, with camel caravans advancing slowly across the slopes, the mountains rising tier above tier to the very heavens…. For the first time the word ecstasy took on real meaning. For the first time it did not mean someone else's state of mind. (Wasson, 1957, pp. 102, 103, 109.)

Among those who read Wasson's account was Timothy Leary, a young clinical psychologist pursuing a mainstream academic career. But after gaining a lectureship at Harvard in late 1959, Leary began to have reservations about his chosen career path. Then while vacationing in Mexico the following summer, Leary ate a handful of "magic mushrooms" and underwent the same kind of transformative experience reported by Huxley several years earlier with mescaline. Leary returned to work, where he founded the Harvard Psychedelic Drug Research Program. In his own words, the purpose of this program was "to teach individuals how to self-administer psychoactive drugs in order to free their psyches without reliance upon doctors or institutions" (Leary, 1984, p. 35). Over the next few years, Leary and his colleague Richard Alpert (later known as Ram Dass) gave psilocybin to many graduate students and faculty members, as well as to notable artists, writers, and musicians. He also began experimenting with LSD, having taken the drug for the first time in 1962. Leary and Alpert's work became increasingly controversial, and they were dismissed from Harvard in 1963, but they continued their activities privately and went on to become leaders of the psychedelic movement.

Dimethyltryptamine and 5-Methoxy-Dimethyltryptamine

DMT and 5-MeO-DMT are found in a number of plants that are indigenous to South America. Native tribes in Brazil, Colombia, Peru, and Venezuela make hallucinogenic snuffs from plants containing these compounds. From the Amazonian rain forest also comes a strong reddish-brown drink called *ayahuasca*, which is a Quechua Indian word meaning "vine of the soul." This potent hallucinogenic brew requires

at least two different kinds of plants, typically stalks from the *Banisteriopsis caapi* vine as well as leaves from *Psychotria viridis* and/or *Diplopteris cabrerena*. *Psychotria* and *Diplopteris* provide DMT, whereas the vines contribute several alkaloids called β-carbolines, which are known to inhibit the enzyme monoamine oxidase (MAO). It is interesting to note that DMT is usually devoid of psychoactivity when taken orally, but this is not the case when people drink ayahuasca. Some researchers have hypothesized that the β-carbolines block DMT breakdown by peripheral MAO, thereby permitting the substance to reach the brain and exert its hallucinogenic effects. Recreational users in this country occasionally brew their own homemade version of ayahuasca, but more typically DMT is sold in powdered form and is taken by smoking.

In recent years, two orally active synthetic DMT analogs have been gaining in popularity. These are α-methyltryptamine (AMT) and 5-methoxy-diisopropyltryptamine. The latter compound is known on the street as "Foxy Methoxy," or simply "Foxy." Foxy is typically taken orally in tablet form, although the pills can also be crushed and then either snorted or smoked.

LSD

Unlike mescaline, psilocybin, and DMT, LSD is a synthetic compound, although its structure is based on a family of fungal alkaloids. The famous story about the synthesis of LSD and the discovery of its astonishing psychoactive potency is presented in **Box 15.1**. Once LSD was made available to psychiatrists and medical researchers in the late 1940s and early 1950s, the drug began to be intensively studied. Indeed, there were only six published papers on LSD before 1951, but from 1951 to 1962 more than 1000 LSD-related articles appeared in the scientific literature (U.S. Department of Health, Education, and Welfare, 1968). During this period, researchers were first beginning to appreciate that nerve cells in the brain communicate with each other chemically by means of neurotransmitters like serotonin (5-HT). When LSD was reported to alter serotonergic activity (see the section below on the pharmacology of hallucinogenic drugs), the finding generated tremendous excitement about the possibility of understanding human mental activity and behavior at a chemical and physiological level.

Some researchers approached LSD as a psychotomimetic drug that would help reveal the biochemical underpinnings of schizophrenia. However, the LSD model proved to be inadequate in a number of ways, and it subsequently gave way to a PCP/ketamine model that is discussed later in this chapter.

---

[3]The title of this article is generally considered to be the first use of the term "magic mushroom."

BOX 15.1   History of Psychopharmacology

The Discovery of LSD

LSD was first synthesized in 1938 by Albert Hofmann, a chemist working for the Sandoz pharmaceutical company in Switzerland. Sandoz was interested in alkaloids obtained from **ergot**, a substance produced by the parasitic fungus *Claviceps purpurea*, which can infest rye and wheat (see figure). Ergot is an extremely toxic material, and consumption of ergot-contaminated grain can cause a serious illness known as **ergotism**.

Although no outbreak of ergotism has occurred in recent years, the disease was quite common in the Middle Ages and is thought to have caused the death of as many as 40,000 people in the year 944. Nevertheless, ergot came to have medicinal value because it produces powerful contractions of the uterus that can help trigger labor and reduce postbirth uterine hemorrhage.

Hofmann began to combine **lysergic acid**, which is the core structure in all ergot alkaloids, with other compounds to see what would emerge. The twenty-fifth different substance synthesized in the course of this research was D-lysergic acid diethylamide, which Hofmann abbreviated LSD-25 (from the German name *Lyserg-Säure-Diäthylamid*). Hofmann's purpose in making this compound was to generate a new circulatory and respiratory stimulant (such drugs are sometimes called **analeptics**). This expectation was based on the structural similarity of LSD to nicotinic acid diethylamide, a known analeptic drug. However, LSD failed to show any analeptic activity, so the compound was temporarily abandoned.

Five years later, Hofmann decided to reexamine LSD, thinking that it might have useful pharmacological properties not recognized during initial testing. In the final stages of synthesizing a new batch of the compound, he was overcome by a series of strange sensations that

Fungus

prevented him from continuing in the lab. The following famous passage is taken from Hofmann's report to Sandoz, which describes the world's first LSD "trip":

Last Friday, April 16, 1943, I was forced to interrupt my work in the laboratory in the middle of the afternoon and proceed home, being affected by a remarkable restlessness, combined with a slight dizziness. At home I lay down and sank into a not unpleasant intoxicated-like condition, characterized by an extremely stimulated imagination. In a dreamlike state, with eyes closed (I found the daylight to be unpleasantly glaring), I perceived an uninterrupted stream of fantastic pictures, extraordinary shapes with intense, kaleidoscopic play of colors. After some two hours this condition faded away. (Hofmann, 1979, p. 58.)

Hofmann suspected that this amazing experience had come from accidentally ingesting a small amount of the newly synthesized LSD. Therefore, the following Monday, he carefully measured out a minute amount of the drug, 250 micrograms (1/4000 of a gram),

dissolved it in a small volume of water, and drank it. Hofmann soon underwent an even more intense experience than before. He somehow managed to ride his bicycle home with the help of a lab assistant (that day came to be known as "Bicycle Day"), and his hallucinations took a threatening form that later passed, leaving him the next day with a profound sense of well-being and a temporarily heightened perceptual awareness.

Hofmann's colleagues at Sandoz initially did not believe that LSD could be as potent as he claimed, but when they took minute quantities themselves, they were able to confirm Hofmann's result. Sandoz first marketed LSD in 1947 under the name Delysid for the purpose of helping neurotic patients uncover repressed thoughts and feelings. The company also suggested that psychiatrists self-administer the drug in order to better understand the perceptual distortions and hallucinations suffered by patients with schizophrenia.

Albert Hofmann continued to write and lecture about the positive effects of LSD and other hallucinogens, even after retiring from Sandoz in 1971. He passed away in 2008 at the age of 102.

Others believed that LSD could be a valuable tool in psychotherapy or psychoanalysis. One way of using LSD was in **psycholytic therapy**, which was mainly practiced in continental Europe. This therapeutic method was based on the concept of drug-induced "psycholysis," meaning psychic loosening or opening. It involved giving LSD in low but gradually increasing doses to promote the release of repressed memories and to enhance communication with the analyst. British, Canadian, and American psychiatrists, on the other hand, tended to prefer **psychedelic therapy**, in which the patient was typically given a single high dose of LSD with the hope of gaining insight into his or her problems through a drug-induced spiritual experience. During the 1950s and 1960s, a number of studies were performed using this technique to treat alcoholic patients (Dyck, 2005). Unfortunately, these studies were marred by poor experimental control and inconsistent findings, leading to cessation of this work by the early 1970s.

Interestingly, at the same time that LSD was being investigated as a possible aid to psychotherapy, it was also being considered by the U.S. government as a potential psychological weapon. In the early 1950s, the Central Intelligence Agency (CIA) began a top secret program called MK-ULTRA that was designed to investigate the possible use of LSD as a mind control agent (Lee and Shlain, 1992). In one particularly disgraceful part of this program, CIA operatives administered LSD to unsuspecting members of the public in order to observe their behavioral reactions. According to Lee and Shlain (1992), Fidel Castro and then Egyptian president Gamal Abdel Nasser were among the foreign leaders targeted for LSD "attacks," although it appears that no such attacks were actually carried out before the program was eventually disbanded.

LSD's popularity exploded with the hippie culture of the 1960s. As part of their nonconformist, anti-Establishment attitudes, hippies openly sought mind expansion through the use of psychedelic drugs, especially LSD. However, the inevitable backlash soon occurred amid growing anecdotal accounts as well as scientific reports of LSD-related problems. A 1965 federal law greatly restricted new research on LSD, and soon thereafter Sandoz stopped distributing LSD for research purposes and recalled all of the existing drug that had previously been supplied to investigators. After a long period of inactivity, however, clinical research on LSD has begun to make a slow comeback. An organization called MAPS (Multidisciplinary Association for Psychedelic Studies) has been promoting new research on the potential psychotherapeutic applications of hallucinogens (see the MAPS website at www.maps.org). Nevertheless, given the general cultural and governmental attitudes toward LSD and other hallucinogenic drugs, it seems unlikely that these compounds will enter mainstream psychiatric practice any time soon.

Recreational use of LSD was banned nationwide in 1967. Of course, LSD didn't disappear, it merely went underground. Indeed, in recent years, hallucinogenic drug use has increased as a new generation of young people has rediscovered these substances. LSD is active orally, and that is the standard mode of administration. As we read in Box 15.1, the drug is so potent that a single dose in crystalline form is barely visible to the naked eye. Consequently, larger amounts of LSD representing many doses are usually dissolved in water, and then droplets containing single-dose units are applied to a sheet of paper (a "blotter") and dried. The paper is subsequently divided into individual squares, often decorated with fanciful designs and sold as single-dose "tabs" to be swallowed by the user (see chapter opening photograph).

Salvinorin A

Salvia divinorum is a member of the mint family native to Oaxaca, the same region of Mexico mentioned earlier with respect to hallucinogenic mushrooms (**Figure 15.4**). Indeed, the plant's psychoactive properties were first reported by Albert Hofmann, the discoverer of LSD, and Gordon Wasson, of "magic mushroom" fame. Like psilocybin-containing mushrooms, *Salvia* was historically used in religious rituals by Mazatec shamans and then later attained the status of a recreational substance in Western countries such as the United States. At the time of this writing, the Drug Enforcement Agency (DEA) considers *Salvia* to be a "drug of concern" that, although not yet listed in the DEA's Schedule of Controlled Substances, may soon be placed in the Schedule I category along with other hallucinogens. This situation does not necessarily make *Salvia* legal in the United States, as 25 states have already enacted legislation prohibiting the sale and use of this substance (www.sagewisdom.org/legalstatus.html; accessed 12/20/12).

An unusual compound called salvinorin A is the principal psychoactive ingredient in *Salvia* (Cunningham et al., 2011). Recreational users may chew fresh *Salvia* leaves, smoke dried and crushed leaves, or consume a concentrated salvinorin A–containing extract either through sublingual and buccal absorption of a liquid preparation or by smoking a dried extract. Chewing *Salvia* leaves or placing a liquid extract under the tongue or into the cheek permits absorption of the compound through the oral mucosa. Few, if any, psychoactive effects are produced by swallowing *Salvia*, because the salvinorin A is inactivated in the

Figure 15.4 *Salvia divinorum*

gastrointestinal tract. On the other hand, the drug is quickly and effectively absorbed through the lungs when smoked, thereby yielding the most rapid and intense hallucinogenic experience.

There are several published studies of the subjective effects produced by *Salvia* use. In general, the substance produces vivid hallucinations, out-of-body experiences, and other feelings resembling but not identical to those produced by other hallucinogens (see the chapter's opening vignette). In an early study by Siebert (1994), the following themes were most commonly reported by users:

- Becoming objects (yellow plaid French fries, fresh paint, a drawer, a pant leg, a Ferris wheel, etc.)
- Visions of various two-dimensional surfaces, films, and membranes
- Revisiting places from the past, especially childhood
- Loss of the body and/or identity
- Various sensations of motion, or being pulled or twisted by forces of some kind
- Uncontrollable hysterical laughter
- Overlapping realities; the perception that one is in several locations at once (Siebert, 1994, p. 55)

Subsequent studies have reported that the subjective effects of *Salvia* have at least some similarity to the effects of LSD (González et al., 2006), DMT and psilocybin (Johnson et al., 2011), marijuana (Albertson and Grubbs, 2009), or the dissociative anesthetic ketamine (Dalgarno, 2007) (see later section on phencyclidine and ketamine).

Pharmacology of Hallucinogenic Drugs

The chemical structures of hallucinogenic drugs, their potency and time course of action, and the psychological and physiological responses to hallucinogen administration are well-characterized. Researchers have also obtained considerable information about the mechanisms of action of these substances, although the story is not yet complete.

Different hallucinogenic drugs vary in potency and in their time course of action

One way of comparing the potency of various hallucinogenic drugs is to consider the typical doses taken by recreational users. Common dose ranges for LSD, psilocybin, mescaline, DMT, and salvinorin A are presented in **Table 15.1**. You can see that these compounds vary widely in their potency, ranging from LSD as the most potent to mescaline as the least potent. All of the hallucinogens that are taken orally have a fairly similar time course of action. Depending on the dose and when the user last ate, the psychedelic effects of these substances generally begin within 30 to 90 minutes following ingestion. An LSD or mescaline "trip" typically lasts for 6 to 12 hours or even longer, whereas the effects of psilocybin-containing mushrooms may dissipate a bit sooner. In contrast, the time course of smoked DMT and *Salvia* presents a very different picture. The effects of those substances are felt within seconds, reach a peak over the next few minutes, and are over within an hour.

Hallucinogens produce a complex set of psychological and physiological responses

We have already given a description of some of the subjective experiences reported by users of hallucinogenic mushrooms as well as *Salvia*. In this section, we will focus on the psychological and physiological

TABLE 15.1	Route of Administration and Potency of Various Hallucinogenic Drugs	
Drug	Usual route of administration	Typical dose range
LSD	Oral	50–100 µg (0.05–0.10 mg)
Psilocybin	Oral	10–20 mg
Mescaline	Oral	200–500 mg
DMT	Smoking	20–50 mg
Salvinorin A	Smoking	200–1000 µg (0.2–1.0 mg)

Figure 15.5 Dose-dependent subjective effects of psilocybin using the Altered States of Consciousness rating scale Sub-dimensions of three of the five primary dimensions are shown: oceanic boundless-ness (orange), ego-disintegration anxiety (purple), and visionary restructuralization (blue). The numbers from 10 to 70 represent increasing intensity of each drug effect. (After Vollenweider and Kometer, 2010.)

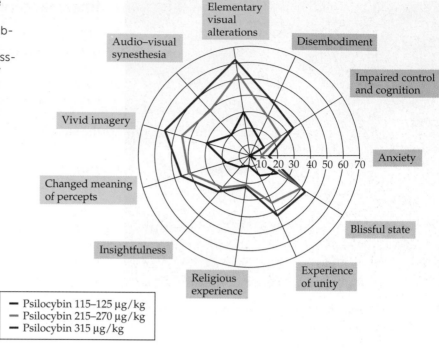

— Psilocybin 115–125 µg/kg
— Psilocybin 215–270 µg/kg
— Psilocybin 315 µg/kg

responses associated with the ingestion of LSD and psilocybin, two prototypical hallucinogens. As we noted earlier, other hallucinogens may have slightly different response profiles, but the core effects are similar across drugs. The state of intoxication produced by LSD and other hallucinogens is usually called a "trip," presumably because the user is taking a mental journey to a place different than his normal conscious awareness. The LSD trip can be divided into four phases: (1) onset; (2) plateau; (3) peak; and (4) "come-down." Trip onset occurs about 30 minutes to an hour after one takes LSD. Visual effects begin to occur, with intensification of colors and the appearance of geometric patterns or strange objects that can be seen with one's eyes closed. The next 2 hours of the trip represent the plateau phase. The subjective sense of time begins to slow and the visual effects become more intense during this period. The peak phase generally begins after about 3 hours and lasts for another 2 or 3 hours. During this phase, the user feels as if he's in another world in which time has been suspended. He sees a continuous stream of bizarre, distorted images that may be either beautiful or menacing. The user may experience **synesthesia**, a crossing-over of sensations in which, for example, colors are "heard" and sounds are "felt." The peak is followed by the "come-down," a phase lasting 2 hours or longer, depending on the dose. Most of the drug effects are gone by the end of the come-down, although the user may still not feel completely normal until the

following day. In addition to the sensory–perceptual effects just described, hallucinogenic drugs produce a wide variety of other psychological changes. These include feelings of depersonalization, emotional shifts to a euphoric or to an anxious and fearful state, and disruption of logical thought.

A hallucinogenic trip as a whole may be experienced either as mystical and spiritually enlightening (a "good trip") or as disturbing and frightening (a "bad trip"). Whether the user has a good or a bad trip depends in part on the dose; the individual's personality, expectations, and previous drug experiences; and the physical and social setting. But even in the best of circumstances, one cannot predict in advance the outcome of an LSD trip.

Scientific studies investigating the influence of hallucinogens on mental state often rely on psychometric instruments developed to quantify the effects of these compounds: the **Altered States of Consciousness (ASC) rating scale**, which was introduced by Dittrich (1998), or the **Hallucinogen Rating Scale** (Strassman et al., 1994). The following five primary dimensions make up the ASC scale: oceanic boundlessness, ego-disintegration anxiety, visionary restructuralization, reduced vigilance, and auditory alterations (Dittrich, 1998; Vollenweider and Kometer, 2010). Oceanic boundlessness refers to derealization and loss of ego boundaries (i.e., feeling one with the world), which corresponds closely to the positive mystical experiences often reported by users of hallucinogenic drugs. In contrast, the ego-disintegration anxiety dimension includes drug-induced thought disorder as well as negative emotional responses to the loss of ego boundaries. Dittrich (1998) likened this dimension to the experience of a "bad trip" on the part of the user. Visionary restructuralization refers to distortions of visual perception, including visual illusions, hallucinations, and visual synesthesias. The last two dimensions, reduced vigilance and auditory alterations (including auditory hallucinations), do not occur with all hallucinogenic drugs and are considered less important items in the ASC scale.

The five primary dimensions of the ASC rating scale can be further divided into subdimensions to provide more detailed information on drug-induced reactions. **Figure 15.5** shows the influence of increasing doses of psilocybin on subdimensions of the primary oceanic boundlessness, ego-disintegration anxiety, and visionary restructuralization dimensions. It should be noted that while the strongest responses are seen on elements of the visionary restructuralization dimension, all dimensions are represented, especially at higher drug doses (Vollenweider and Kometer, 2010).

Besides their psychological effects, hallucinogens also give rise to various physiological responses. In the case of LSD, these responses reflect activation of the sympathetic nervous system and include pupil dilation and small increases in heart rate, blood pressure, and body temperature. LSD use can also lead to dizziness, nausea, and vomiting, although such reactions are more likely to occur after consumption of peyote or psilocybin-containing mushrooms.

Most hallucinogenic drugs share a common indoleamine or phenethylamine structure

Most hallucinogenic drugs have either a serotonin-like or a catecholamine-like structure. The serotonin-like, or **indoleamine**, hallucinogens include LSD, psilocybin, psilocin, DMT, 5-MeO-DMT, and the synthetic tryptamines mentioned earlier. When the 5-HT molecule is oriented in the proper manner, it is easy to see how its basic structure is incorporated into the structures of these hallucinogenic compounds (**Figure 15.6**). Important studies in the early 1950s by John Gaddum in Scotland and by Edward Wooley and David Shaw in the United States led these investigators to conclude that LSD works by antagonizing the action of 5-HT in the brain. We shall see in the next section that LSD can be understood more as an agonist than as an antagonist in the serotonergic system. Nevertheless, the linking of 5-HT with such a powerful psychoactive drug as LSD brought this recently discovered neurotransmitter into the forefront of behavioral and psychiatric

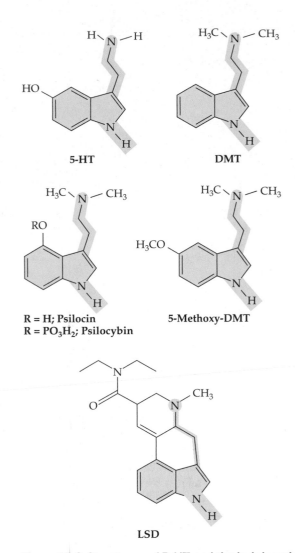

Figure 15.6 Structures of 5-HT and the indoleamine hallucinogens The core indoleamine structure in each compound is highlighted.

research—a place that it continues to hold to the present day.

Of the hallucinogens covered in this chapter, the only one that is catecholamine-like is mescaline. As shown in **Figure 15.7**, mescaline has structural similarities to the neurotransmitter norepinephrine (NE) as well as to the psychostimulant amphetamine. Indeed, amphetamine can produce hallucinogenic effects with prolonged administration of high doses, and several amphetamine analogs such as 2,5-dimethoxy-4-methylamphetamine (DOM, also known as "STP") and 3,4,5-trimethoxyamphetamine (TMA) possess even greater hallucinogenic properties. Together with mescaline, these NE- and amphetamine-related compounds are known as **phenethylamine** hallucinogens.

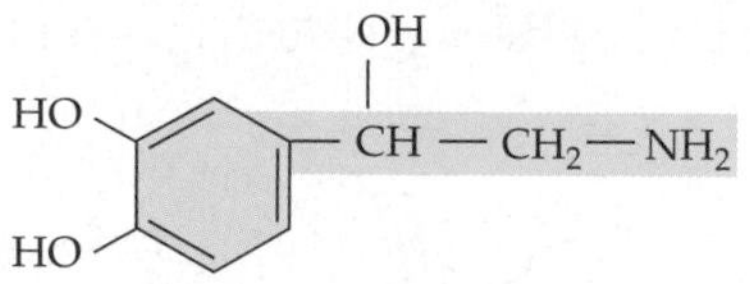

Figure 15.7 Structures of NE and the phenethylamine hallucinogens The core phenethylamine structure in each compound is highlighted.

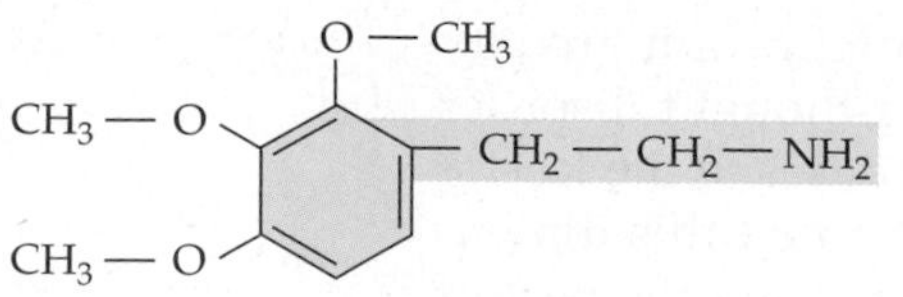

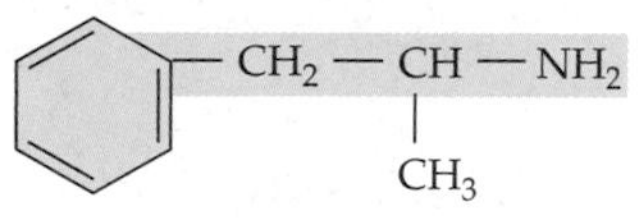

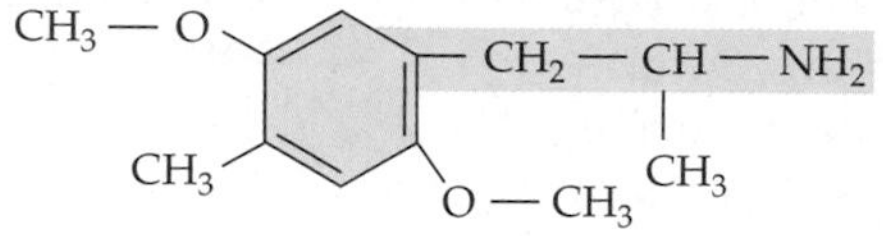

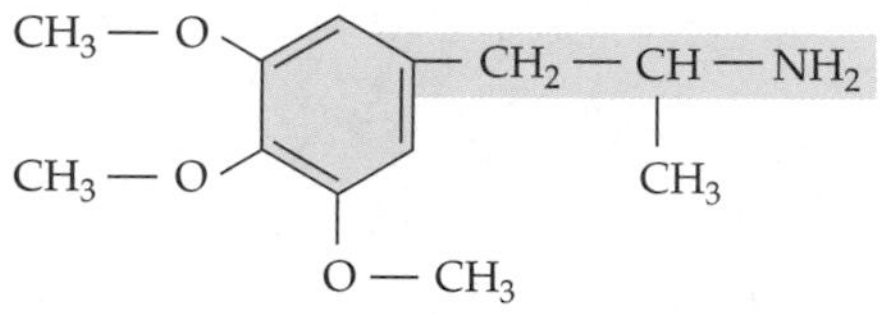

The most unusual hallucinogen structurally is salvinorin A. **Figure 15.8** presents the structure of this compound, which chemically is known as a neoclerodane diterpene. Also shown is a related drug called ketocyclazocine, which has a similar mechanism of action as salvinorin A and can also induce hallucinations.[4] The shared mechanism of action of these compounds is discussed in a later section.

Indoleamine and phenethylamine hallucinogens are 5-HT$_{2A}$ receptor agonists

Although we still don't completely understand how hallucinogens produce their dramatic perceptual and cognitive effects, some progress has been made. Over time it has become clear that the serotonergic system is intimately involved in this process, at least in the case of the indoleamine and phenethylamine hallucinogens. Beginning our exploration of hallucinogenic action with LSD, we can immediately see that this is a very complicated substance with respect to its potential effects on the serotonergic system. LSD binds with relatively high affinity to at least eight different serotonergic receptor subtypes: 5-HT$_{1A}$, 5-HT$_{1B}$, 5-HT$_{1D}$, 5-HT$_{2A}$, 5-HT$_{2C}$, 5-HT$_{5A}$, 5-HT$_6$, and 5-HT$_7$ (Nichols, 2004). In determining which of these receptor interactions might be responsible for producing hallucinogenic activity, it is useful to compare the receptor binding properties of indoleamine hallucinogens such as LSD with those of the phenylethylamine

hallucinogens. As shown in **Table 15.2**, such a comparison reveals that the only known common sites of interaction for both classes of compounds are the 5-HT$_{2A}$ and 5-HT$_{2C}$ receptor subtypes, raising the possibility that one or both of these receptor subtypes may play a central role in the subjective and behavioral effects of hallucinogenic drugs (Aghajanian and Marek, 1999).

Mechanisms of hallucinogenic activity have been studied not only using human subjects but also using behavioral tests in laboratory animals, such as the drug-induced head twitch response and drug discrimination tests (see Chapter 4), which are believed to parallel hallucinogenic-like effects in humans (Appel et al., 2004; Canal and Morgan, 2012; Fantegrossi et al., 2008). In the animal models, several different serotonergic receptor subtypes (including but not limited to 5-HT$_{2A}$ and 5-HT$_{2C}$ receptors) and even dopamine (DA) receptors contribute to the behavioral effects of various indoleamine and phenethylamine compounds (Halberstadt and Geyer, 2011). On the other hand, there is a general consensus that 5-HT$_{2A}$ receptor

TABLE 15.2 Known Interactions of LSD and Phenethylamine Hallucinogens with Specific 5-HT Receptor Subtypes[a]

Receptor subtype	LSD	Phenethylamines
5-HT$_1$ family	+	−
5-HT$_{2A}$	+	+
5-HT$_{2C}$	+	+
5-HT$_3$	−	−
5-HT$_4$	−	?
5-HT$_{5A}$	+	−
5-HT$_6$	+	?
5-HT$_7$	+	−

Source: Aghajanian and Marek, 1999.

[a]+, significant affinity for that receptor subtype; −, low affinity for that subtype; ?, no currently available data.

[4]Although ketocyclazocine is hallucinogenic, it also produces extreme dysphoria when administered and, therefore, is not used recreationally.

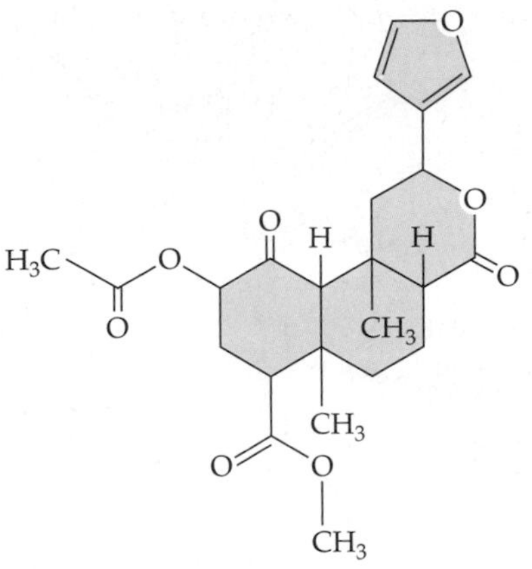

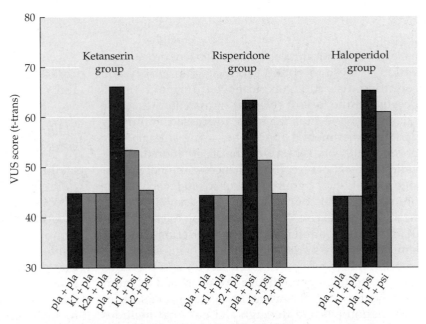

Figure 15.8 Structures of salvinorin A and ketocyclazocine

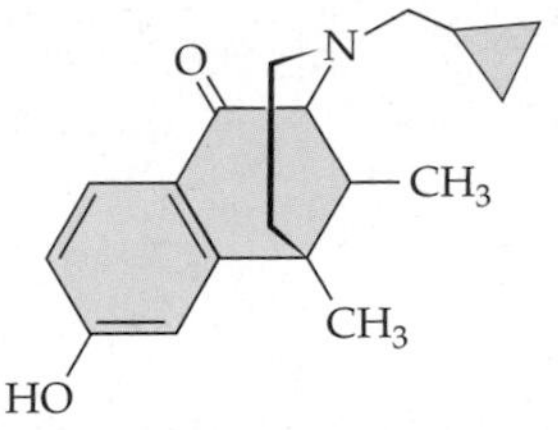

Salvinorin A

Ketocyclazocine

activation is the critical mechanism of action of these compounds in the genesis of hallucinatory experiences in humans (Halberstadt and Nichols, 2010). For example, a study by Vollenweider and colleagues (1998) found that psilocybin-induced visual illusions and hallucinations were dose-dependently blocked by ketanserin and risperidone, both of which are 5-HT$_{2A}$ receptor antagonists. Because risperidone also blocks DA D$_2$ receptors, it is important to note that haloperidol, an antagonist at D$_2$ but not 5-HT$_{2A}$ receptors, completely failed to prevent the hallucinogenic effects of psilocybin (**Figure 15.9**). 5-HT$_{2A}$ receptors in the cortex are believed to be particularly important in the action of indoleamine and phenethylamine hallucinogens. In accordance with that view, a recent neuroimaging study found that the intensity of subjective effects of psilocybin was significantly correlated with drug occupancy of 5-HT$_{2A}$ receptors in the prefrontal cortex and anterior cingulate cortex (Quednow et al., 2010).

Salvinorin A is a κ-opioid receptor agonist

When salvinorin A was discovered to be the primary psychoactive agent in *Salvia divinorum*, researchers discovered that its pharmacology was unlike that of the indoleamine and phenethylamine hallucinogens. In particular, salvinorin A has little effect on 5-HT$_{2A}$ or any other 5-HT receptors. Instead, this compound, along with the previously mentioned ketocyclazocine, is a potent agonist

at the κ-opioid receptor (Cunningham et al., 2011). Beyond the ability to activate this subtype of opioid receptor, little is known about how salvinorin A elicits hallucinogenic and mystical experiences.

The neural mechanisms underlying hallucinogenesis are not yet fully understood

In a previous section, we learned about the necessary role of 5-HT$_{2A}$ receptors in mediating the subjective effects of indoleamine and phenethylamine hallucinogens. Although the above-mentioned studies have helped identify *which* 5-HT receptor is most important for hallucinogenic drug effects, they do not tell

Figure 15.9 Blockade of psilocybin-induced visual illusions and hallucinations by 5-HT$_{2A}$ receptor antagonists Subjects received 0.25 mg/kg of oral psilocybin (psi) or placebo (pla), and then 80 minutes later they completed the Altered States of Consciousness (ASC) rating scale. The subjects were also pretreated with placebo, oral ketanserin (k1 = 20 mg, k2 = 40 mg), oral risperidone (r1 = 0.5 mg, r2 = 1.0 mg), or IV haloperidol (h1 = 0.021 mg/kg). The data shown are for the VUS (visionary restructuralization) subscale, which assesses hallucinatory phenomena, visual illusions, and other perceptual changes. In all cases, psilocybin increased VUS scores compared with placebo (pla + psi versus pla + pla). These increases were dose-dependently blocked by ketanserin (k1 + psi and k2 + psi versus pla + psi) and by risperidone (r1 + psi and r2 + psi versus pla + psi), but not by haloperidol (h1 + psi versus pla + psi). (After Vollenweider et al., 1998.)

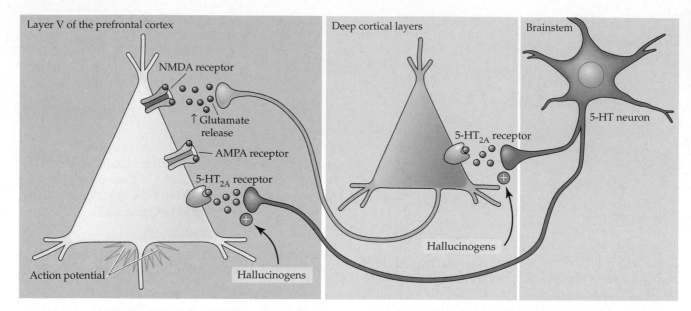

Figure 15.10 Proposed mechanism of action of indoleamine and phenethylamine hallucinogens Activation of $5\text{-}HT_{2A}$ receptors is believed to be necessary for the hallucinogenic effects of indoleamine and phenethylamine hallucinogens. Among the neurons affected by these drugs are pyramidal cells in cortical layer V that are directly stimulated as the result of activation of $5\text{-}HT_{2A}$ receptors on the cells themselves and are secondarily stimulated by glutamate released from other $5\text{-}HT_{2A}$ receptor–bearing pyramidal cells in the deep cortical layers that project to layer V. According to the model shown here, such activation disrupts the normal functioning of glutamatergic networks within the prefrontal cortex. (After Vollenweider and Kometer, 2010.)

us *where* the critical receptors are located, or *how* activation of these receptors produces the sensory and cognitive distortions experienced during a "trip." Because of the lack of relevant human studies, these questions have thus far been addressed mainly by various experimental approaches using animals. One prominent theory is based on the observation that activation of $5\text{-}HT_{2A}$ receptors enhances glutamate-mediated excitation of pyramidal neurons in layer V of the prefrontal cortex. Some investigators have hypothesized that this excess glutamate is being released from thalamocortical afferents, thereby interfering with thalamic filtering of sensory information being sent to the cortex (Aghajanian and Marek, 2000). Based on this notion, hallucinogenic drugs are proposed to interfere with the normal "gating," or screening, of sensory information passing through a circuit that includes the prefrontal cortex, thalamus, and striatum (Vollenweider and Geyer, 2001). The consequences of such interference would be overload at the cortical level, thereby accounting not only for the perceptual distortions associated with hallucinogenic drug use but also for simultaneous disturbances in cognition that are usually considered to be psychotic-like. Alternatively, $5\text{-}HT_{2A}$ receptor activation by hallucinogens may be disrupting the normal activity of excitatory glutamatergic networks within the prefrontal cortex (Béïque et al., 2007) (**Figure 15.10**). Regardless of the exact mechanism, increased excitation of prefrontal cortical pyramidal neurons appears to be a critical feature of hallucinogenic activity.

Hallucinogenic drug use leads to adverse effects in some users

Hallucinogens lack the high degree of abuse potential seen with most other recreational drugs such as opoids, psychostimulants, cannabis, alcohol, and nicotine. They do not produce physical withdrawal symptoms after chronic use, and they are not effective reinforcers in animal tests such as the self-administration paradigm. However, a hallucinogen dependence syndrome has been identified in a small number of users, particularly in individuals with early exposure to such compounds (Stone et al., 2006, 2007). Most hallucinogenic drugs, with the possible exceptions of DMT and salvinorin A, also produce rapid tolerance with repeated use. Early studies involving LSD administration to human subjects found that over a 4-day period of daily dosing, nearly complete tolerance was observed by the fourth day (Nichols, 1997). One likely mechanism underlying this tolerance is a down-regulation of $5\text{-}HT_{2A}$ receptors, which has been demonstrated in rats given several daily doses of LSD or psilocybin (Buckholtz et al., 1990). Surprisingly, mescaline administration did not result in $5\text{-}HT_{2A}$

Figure 15.11 LSD users sometimes experience acute panic or anxiety reactions to the drug (a "bad trip").

receptor down-regulation, despite the fact that this compound can produce behavioral tolerance similar to the indoleamine hallucinogens. Therefore, there may be multiple mechanisms that can give rise to hallucinogenic drug tolerance.

Despite the relative lack of addictive potential, hallucinogens can still cause serious problems for some users. As mentioned earlier, the user may have a "bad trip" in which he or she experiences an acute anxiety or panic reaction in response to the drug's effects (**Figure 15.11**). Although we don't understand the exact cause of these reactions, they are probably related to an interaction between the drug, the individual's emotional state going into the trip, and the external environment. In most cases, friends will talk the person through the ordeal. However, if this is unsuccessful, then it may be necessary to take the person to the hospital emergency room for treatment. The incidence of bad trips is not known, but existing data from older clinical studies of LSD administration suggest that they are rare when users are prescreened for emotional stability and the environmental conditions are carefully controlled.

Another potential complication of hallucinogen use is the occurrence of **flashbacks**. This term is defined in the *Diagnostic and Statistical Manual of Mental Disorders (DSM-IV)* as "the reexperiencing, following cessation of use of a hallucinogen, of one or more of the perceptual symptoms that were experienced while intoxicated with the hallucinogen" (American Psychiatric Association, 1994, p. 234). When flashbacks occur a long time after prior drug use and are sufficiently intense to cause major disturbance or impairment,

then the individual is considered to be suffering from hallucinogen persisting perception disorder (HPPD). A review of the literature on flashbacks and HPPD led to the conclusion that although some LSD users do suffer from HPPD, the prevalence of this disorder may not be very high considering the relatively few documented cases of HPPD in relation to the large number of people who have taken LSD over the years (Halpern and Pope, 2003). The neural mechanisms responsible for flashbacks have not yet been studied, although it is interesting to note that the use of other psychoactive drugs such as marijuana seems to trigger flashbacks in some cases.

The most severe adverse reaction to LSD or other hallucinogens is a psychotic reaction. At one time, opponents of these substances argued that development of psychosis was a major risk factor in their use. It now seems likely that prolonged psychotic episodes following hallucinogen use typically involve individuals who had already been diagnosed with a psychotic disorder such as schizophrenia or who had manifested pre-psychotic symptoms before taking the drug. However, exceptions do occasionally occur, as in the case of an 18-year-old German woman who smoked a marijuana cigarette that without her knowledge had been spiked with *Salvia* leaves and leaf extract (Paulzen and Gründer, 2008). Although the woman was an experienced cannabis user, she had never before taken *Salvia*. Soon after smoking the "joint," the woman was admitted to the psychiatric emergency service of a nearby hospital suffering from severe agitation, disorientation, disorganized behavior, and hallucinations. She subsequently began to exhibit self-mutilation and then developed life-threatening somatic symptoms that required admission to the intensive care unit. Her psychotic and somatic symptoms continued for a long period of time but she eventually improved and was discharged from the hospital in stable condition. This case study reminds us that hallucinogens are powerful drugs that have the capability of inducing a toxic psychosis under certain circumstances.

Section Summary

- Hallucinogens are substances that cause perceptual and cognitive distortions in the absence of delirium. Many hallucinogens such as mescaline, psilocybin, DMT, 5-MeO-DMT, and salvinorin A are plant compounds that were used for hundreds or thousands of years in spiritual or religious ceremonies before their discovery by Western culture. In contrast, LSD is a synthetic drug, although it is based on a series of alkaloids found in ergot fungus.

• Recognition of the powerful mind-altering properties of hallucinogenic drugs led to both clinical and recreational use beginning in the late 1950s and early 1960s. Some psychiatrists gave patients LSD in the course of psycholytic or psychedelic therapy. LSD became readily available on the street despite a federal ban on recreational use in 1967.

• Most hallucinogenic drugs are orally active, with a slow onset of action and a long time course of action. Two exceptions are DMT and *Salvia*, which are usually smoked, thereby leading to rapid drug effects and a much shorter duration of action. Of the commonly used hallucinogens, LSD is the most potent and mescaline is the least potent, based on the range of doses taken by users.

• An LSD "trip" can be divided into four phases: onset, plateau, peak, and "come-down." During the trip, the user experiences vivid visual hallucinations, a slowing of the subjective sense of time, feelings of depersonalization, strong emotional reactions, and a disruption of logical thought. Research on hallucinogens has made use of the Altered States of Consciousness rating scale, which consists of the following five dimensions: oceanic boundlessness, ego-disintegration anxiety, visionary restructuralization, reduced vigilance, and auditory alterations.

• Most hallucinogenic drugs are classified chemically as either indoleamines or phenethylamines. The indoleamines are related structurally to 5-HT, whereas the phenethylamines instead share a common structure with NE. Both classes of drugs are 5-HT$_{2A}$ receptor agonists. In contrast, salvinorin A, the active compound in *Salvia divinorum*, is a κ-opioid receptor agonist.

• The specific brain areas and mechanisms responsible for the production of hallucinogenic drug effects are not yet fully understood. However, recent research has implicated combined 5-HT$_{2A}$ and glutamate activation of pyramidal neurons in the prefrontal cortex, at least in the case of the indoleamine and phenethylamine hallucinogens.

• Hallucinogens are not dependence forming or addictive for most users, although tolerance can occur with repeated use and a hallucinogen dependence syndrome has been identified in a small percentage of cases. Use of hallucinogens can also lead

to other adverse effects such as "bad trips" and flashbacks. People who suffer from severe flashbacks long after discontinuing hallucinogenic drug use are diagnosed as having hallucinogen persisting perception disorder. At the present time, little is known about the causes or treatment of HPPD.

PCP and Ketamine

Background and History

This section of the chapter deals with two closely related compounds: **phencyclidine** and **ketamine**. Phencyclidine is usually abbreviated **PCP**, which comes from the drug's full chemical name, 1-(1-phenylcyclohexyl)piperidine (**Figure 15.12**). PCP (trade name Sernyl) was first tested in the mid-1950s by Parke, Davis and Company as a potential anesthetic agent. However, early studies revealed that the drug produced an unusual kind of anesthesia. Although subjects given PCP showed no responsiveness to nociceptive (painful) stimuli, they were not in the typical state of relaxed unconsciousness seen with traditional anesthetics like barbiturates. Instead, the subjects exhibited a trance-like or catatonic-like state characterized by a vacant facial expression, fixed and staring eyes, and maintenance of muscle tone. Indeed, it was not unusual for individuals to develop either rigidity or waxy flexibility—motor symptoms often observed in catatonic schizophrenic individuals.

PCP was initially thought to be clinically promising because it did not produce the respiratory depression associated with barbiturate anesthesia and thus possessed a high therapeutic index (see Chapter 1). However, early enthusiasm was soon tempered by reports of problematic reactions in many patients. In a few cases, this took the form of marked agitation rather than quieting during the drug-induced state. In other instances, PCP induced postoperative reactions ranging from blurred vision, dizziness, and mild disorientation to much more serious reactions involving hallucinations, severe agitation, and even violence.

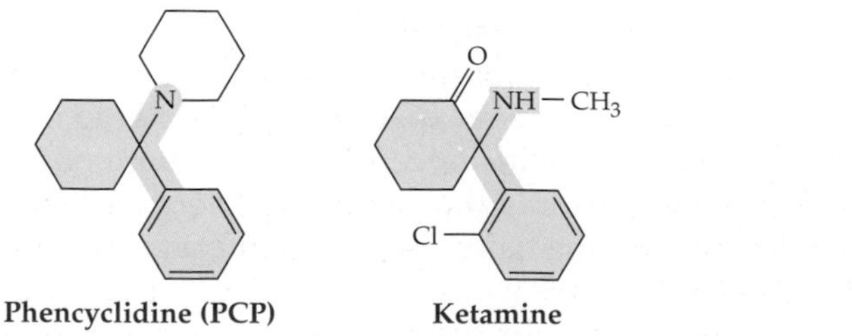

Phencyclidine (PCP)   **Ketamine**

Figure 15.12 Chemical structures of PCP and ketamine

These problems caused the clinical use of PCP to be terminated in 1965.

Of course, the abandonment of PCP as a medication did not prevent it from coming into illicit use. In 1967, PCP found its way onto the streets of several cities including San Francisco, where it was dubbed the "PeaCe Pill" by the drug culture protesting the Vietnam War. By the mid-1970s, PCP use and abuse under new street names such as "angel dust" and "hog" had become much more widespread across the country. Yet the popularity of this drug never rivaled that of marijuana or even cocaine or heroin, and the incidence of PCP use subsequently declined to a rather low level.

Ketamine came into being as a safer alternative to PCP. Even before PCP was withdrawn, Parke, Davis had begun to screen related compounds in the hope of finding one that would be less toxic in its behavioral effects. One such compound, designated CI-581, was synthesized in 1962 and was first tested in humans 2 years later. CI-581, later renamed ketamine, was less potent and shorter acting than PCP. Ketamine was soon found to be a valuable anesthetic for certain medical procedures, particularly in children, and it is also widely used by veterinarians as a general sedating and immobilizing agent. It is currently marketed legally as a prescription medication under the trade names Ketalar, Ketaset, and Vetalar. Despite its lower potency, ketamine can still cause adverse emergence reactions in human patients similar to those seen with PCP. Fortunately, the frequency of such reactions is low in infants and children—the groups for which ketamine is most commonly used.

Pharmacology of PCP and Ketamine

Although PCP and ketamine can be considered anesthetic agents, the subjective experience produced by these compounds is unlike that produced by more typical anesthetic drugs. In the sections below, we discuss the characteristics of PCP- and ketamine-induced dissociation, the mechanism of action of these compounds, PCP and ketamine abuse and dependence, and both current and possible future therapeutic applications of ketamine.

PCP and ketamine produce a state of dissociation

PCP is generally obtained in powdered or pill form, and the drug can be ingested by virtually any common route. It can be taken orally, administered intranasally (i.e., snorted), or injected intravenously or intramuscularly. Many PCP users apply the drug to tobacco,

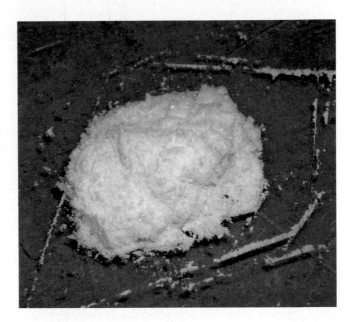

Figure 15.13 Ketamine crystals

marijuana, or parsley cigarettes for purposes of smoking. Illicitly used ketamine typically comes from the diversion or theft of medical- or veterinary-grade material. Ketamine is marketed commercially as an injectable liquid, but street sellers commonly evaporate the liquid to yield a powder that is either snorted directly or compressed into pill form (**Figure 15.13**). It is sold on the street under such names as "K," "special K," or "cat Valium." Users who don't wish to become too intoxicated often snort small lines or piles of ketamine called "bumps." However, initial snorting of ketamine can escalate over time to intramuscular or even intravenous (IV) injection of the liquid solution as the user becomes tolerant to the drug or seeks a more powerful effect.

The first studies on the subjective effects of PCP were conducted in the late 1950s and early 1960s. When given a subanesthetic dose of PCP, subjects reported feeling detached from their body, sensations of vertigo or of floating, numbness, and sometimes a dreamlike state. They also experienced a variety of affective reactions including drowsiness and apathy, loneliness, negativism or hostility toward the experimenters, or, alternatively, euphoria and inebriation toward them. Finally, all of the treated subjects exhibited a marked cognitive disorganization manifested by difficulty in maintaining concentration or focus, deficiencies in abstract thinking, and halting speech. These effects of PCP, which have been compared with the symptoms of schizophrenia, presumably account for the waning of the drug's popularity and its current low incidence of use. In fact, Edward Domino and Elliott Luby, two of the early researchers studying the influence of PCP on human subjects, recently noted, "It was astounding to us that phencyclidine [initially] became a major drug of abuse. Few of our volunteer subjects were ever willing to take the drug a second time" (Domino and Luby, 2012).

Domino and colleagues at the University of Michigan also published the first study on the pharmacological effects of ketamine in 1965. Low doses of ketamine yielded reactions similar to those mentioned in the previous paragraph for low-dose PCP administration. However, when subjects received doses in the anesthetic range (at least 1 mg/kg intravenously), the investigators observed a remarkable phenomenon. The subjects appeared to lose all mental contact with their environment for up to 10 minutes or longer, despite the fact that their eyes remained open and they retained significant muscle tone. When Domino described to his wife how the ketamine-treated subjects seemed to be disconnected from their environment, she proposed the term **dissociative anesthesia** to describe this unique state of detachment (E. F. Domino, personal communication). This term was subsequently applied to both ketamine and PCP.

More recent studies have documented the subjective experiences reported by ketamine users while in the dissociated state (**Table 15.3**). As noted in the table, the individual may feel separated from his body, perhaps floating above and looking down at himself. Some have described this as a "near-death" experience (Jansen, 2000, 2001), even though the person is not actually dying. This state of being, which is called the "K-hole," can be either spiritually uplifting or terrifying. As one user put it, "A K-hole can be anything from going to hell and meeting Satan to going to heaven and meeting God" (quote from *Time Out*, 2000, p. 20).

PCP and ketamine are noncompetitive antagonists of NMDA receptors

The principal molecular target for both PCP and ketamine is the NMDA (*N*-methyl-D-aspartate) receptor. To review briefly, the NMDA receptor is an important ionotropic receptor for the excitatory amino acid neurotransmitter glutamate. PCP and ketamine are both noncompetitive antagonists at the NMDA receptor complex, that is, they block the receptor at a site different from the site at which glutamate or NMDA binds. In fact, as we saw in Chapter 8, the PCP/ketamine binding site is found inside of the receptor's ion channel (see Figure 8.6). NMDA receptors are widely distributed in the brain and play a key role in glutamate signaling. The cerebral cortex and hippocampus contain significant numbers of NMDA receptors, and blockade of the receptors in these areas presumably

TABLE 15.3 Subjective Experiences Reported by Ketamine Users

Sensations of light coming through the body and/or of colorful visions

Complete loss of time sense

Bizarre distortions of body shape or size

Altered perception of body consistency (e.g., feeling as though one is made of a strange material such as rubber, plastic, or wood)

Sensations of floating or hovering weightlessly in space

Feelings of leaving one's body

Sudden insights into the mysteries of existence or of the self

Experiences of being "at one" with the universe

Visions of spiritual or supernatural beings

Source: Dalgarno and Shewan, 1996.

contributes to the cognitive deficits produced by PCP and ketamine. Another potential mechanism of PCP and ketamine action is increased *presynaptic* glutamate release (and therefore overactive glutamate transmission via non-NMDA receptors) within the cortex, which is a secondary consequence of NMDA receptor antagonism (Deakin et al., 2008; Gunduz-Bruce, 2009). Consistent with this hypothesis, a recent brain imaging study using proton magnetic resonance spectroscopy[5] found a significant increase in glutamate levels in the anterior cingulate cortex after a single IV infusion of ketamine (Stone et al., 2012). Moreover, this increase was significantly correlated with the positive psychotic symptoms induced by the drug treatment.

PCP and ketamine have significant abuse potential

Both PCP and ketamine are highly reinforcing in several different species of animals, as shown by drug self-administration. Indeed, both compounds are subject to abuse and dependence, although the prevalence of ketamine use and abuse is currently much greater than that of PCP.

REINFORCING EFFECTS Many PCP and, to a lesser extent, ketamine self-administration studies have been conducted using rhesus monkeys. Interestingly, early

[5]Magnetic resonance spectroscopy (MRS) is an imaging method that uses equipment similar to that used for magnetic resonance imaging (MRI), but instead of yielding information on brain structure or regional activation, it measures the levels of various brain chemicals.

studies on monkeys that self-administered high doses of PCP found that the animals took in sufficient quantities of the drug to be intoxicated almost continuously (Balster and Woolverton, 1980, 1981). Under the influence of PCP, the subjects could not support themselves on four legs, but instead were typically found near the response lever either in an awkward sitting position or lying on the cage floor. The ability to elicit self-intoxication in animals is not unique to PCP but has also been observed with cocaine, amphetamine, opioids, and in some cases alcohol.

PCP and ketamine activate midbrain DA cell firing and stimulate DA release, particularly in the prefrontal cortex. This enhancement of dopaminergic neurotransmission could contribute to PCP's and ketamine's reinforcing effects. On the other hand, rats will also self-administer PCP directly into the nucleus accumbens, and this local reinforcing effect appears to be DA-independent (Carlezon and Wise, 1996). Thus it seems likely that there are both dopaminergic and nondopaminergic mechanisms underlying PCP and ketamine reinforcement.

The pleasurable effects of IV ketamine were studied in healthy volunteers without prior exposure to this compound (Morgan et al., 2004). As illustrated in **Figure 15.14**, the investigators found dose-dependent increases in drug liking and in the desire for more drug, confirming that ketamine is rewarding not only in laboratory animals but also in humans.

USE AND ABUSE   As mentioned earlier, PCP is not widely used compared with many other substances of abuse. For example, the 2011 National Survey on Drug Use and Health found that about 48,000 people aged 12 or older used PCP for the first time that year, which contrasts with the 2.6 million people who tried marijuana for the first time (Substance Abuse and Mental Health Services Administration, 2012). Individuals who do use PCP have found some novel (and dangerous) drug combinations, including a combination variously referred to as "fry," "wet," or "illy," in which tobacco or marijuana cigarettes are dipped in a liquid containing PCP and embalming fluid (!) and then smoked (Peters Jr. et al., 2008).

In contrast to PCP, the use of ketamine has been growing because of the drug's popularity within the dance scene (Wolff and Winstock, 2006). Although ketamine has only recently come to the attention of the popular media, illicit use and abuse of this substance actually date back many years. Some abusers were, and continue to be, medical or veterinary practitioners who have easy access to ketamine in the course of their work. Ketamine was also favored by some intellectuals as a mind-expanding drug in the tradition of LSD. Two of the most famous ketamine users were Marcia Moore, a well-known astrologer and author in

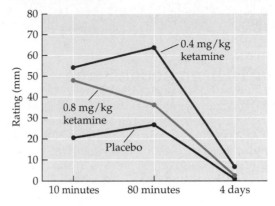

(A) Desire for drug

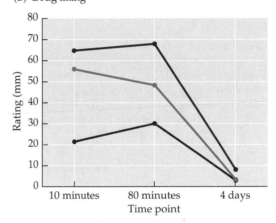

(B) Drug liking

Figure 15.14 IV ketamine administration produces dose-dependent rewarding effects in human subjects Subjects who had never used ketamine before were given an IV infusion of placebo or 0.4 or 0.8 mg/kg ketamine over a period of 80 minutes. At the 10- and 80-minute time points, as well as 4 days later (follow-up), the subjects were tested for their subjective responses to the drug using a visual analog scale (see Box 12.1, Figure B caption for a description of this method). Both doses produced increased desire for the drug (A) and increased drug liking (B) compared with placebo. (After Morgan et al., 2004.)

the 1970s, and Dr. John Lilly, a physician and researcher known for his groundbreaking studies on interspecies communication (e.g., with dolphins) and on the psychological effects of sensory isolation. Both Moore and Lilly became heavily dependent on ketamine, and both developed psychotic reactions as a result.[6]

Development of ketamine tolerance and dependence can be seen not only in the extreme cases of

---

[6]In Moore's case, the consequences were especially tragic when she left her home on a cold wintry night in 1979, climbed a tree, gave herself a ketamine injection, and froze to death while in a state of drug intoxication.

BOX 15.2   Pharmacology in Action

Getting High on Cough Syrup

One of the most annoying features of a bad cold is the persistent cough that it may bring on. That is why **antitussives**, medications that suppress the cough reflex, are big sellers in pharmacies across the country. The active ingredient in most of these over-the-counter products is an opioid-like compound called **dextromethorphan**. For example, dextromethorphan is the antitussive agent in Robitussin-DM cough syrup as well as in Coricidin HBP Cough & Cold tablets. Unlike codeine, an opioid agonist typically found in prescription cough medications, dextromethorphan does not directly stimulate opioid receptors. Instead, it is known to be a noncompetitive NMDA receptor antagonist, much like PCP and ketamine.

Cough medications based on dextromethorphan have been on the market for many years. The first one was Romilar, a dextromethorphan-containing tablet that was introduced in the 1960s. Romilar was meant to be a replacement for codeine-containing medications, since the latter were already being abused. However, it did not take long before users discovered the psychoactive properties of Romilar and began abusing it as well. The drug was eventually withdrawn from the market and was later replaced with a codeine-containing, prescription-only version. Pharmaceutical companies subsequently decided to put dextromethorphan into a cough syrup, presumably to discourage recreational use by requiring the ingestion of large amounts of the syrup to obtain a psychoactive effect. However, this has not prevented users, typically adolescents or young adults, from continuing to experiment with this substance. Indeed, data from the National Poison Data System show that the prevalence of dextromethorphan abuse more than doubled from 2000 to 2010 (Wilson et al., 2011).

Dextromethorphan is typically taken orally in the form of cough syrup or tablet. On the street, it goes by names like "DXM," "DM," or "Robo." The standard dose of dextromethorphan for cough suppression is 20 mg (found in 0.33 ounces of cough syrup), but recreational users take single doses that are 8 to 50 times higher (Banken and Foster, 2008). This requires drinking anywhere from a quarter of a typical 8-ounce bottle of cough syrup to as much as two whole bottles. There are even reports of heavy users ingesting three or four bottles in one day. Drinking this much cough syrup usually causes nausea and vomiting as a result of the effects of guaifenesin, an expectorant (agent that facilitates expulsion of phlegm from the throat or airways) found in most cough syrups. Some users have tried to avoid this unpleasant side effect by taking large amounts of dextromethorphan-containing Coricidin tablets. However, this is a very dangerous, even potentially fatal, practice because of the presence of chlorpheniramine in these tablets. Chorpheniramine is an antihistamine/anticholinergic agent that not only produces serious reactions by itself at high doses but also intensifies the effects of dextromethorphan by inhibiting its metabolism by the liver. Given the limitations associated with dextromethorphan use via standard cough medications, enterprising users have discovered methods for extracting the substance from cough syrup (Hendrickson and Cloutier, 2007). As a result, dextromethorphan has become available on the street or via the Internet in repackaged pills or capsules for oral administration, and even in powdered form for intranasal use (snorting). Indeed, tablets sold as "Ecstasy" occasionally contain dextromethorphan instead of the expected MDMA.

Users report that the subjective effects of dextromethorphan occur as a series of four dose-related "plateaus" (Romanelli and Smith, 2009). Low doses (1.5 to 2.5 mg/kg, which, for a 70-kg user, corresponds to approximately 2 ounces of cough syrup containing 120 mg of dextromethorphan) produce the first plateau, during which the user feels a mild euphoria and intoxication and may also experience slight perceptual effects. The second plateau is the most commonly sought after and requires a dose of 2.5 to 7.5 mg/kg, which consists of 2.8 to 8.5 ounces of cough syrup containing about 175 to 525 mg dextromethorphan. At this stage, the user suffers from impaired balance, experiences visual hallucinations when he closes his eyes, and is significantly more intoxicated than at the first plateau. The third plateau occurs at doses ranging from 7.5 to 15 mg/kg and yields more intense hallucinations, cognitive impairment, and partial dissociation. At the fourth plateau, produced by more than 15 mg/kg of dextromethorphan, the user becomes severely ataxic, experiences complete personality dissociation, and may become delusional. These effects resemble those produced by increasing doses of PCP or ketamine.

Sufficient doses of dextromethorphan produce not only visual hallucinations but other subjective changes typically seen with hallucinogenic drugs such as psilocybin and LSD. Reissig and coworkers (2012) recently investigated the subjective effects of oral

BOX 15.2 *(continued)*

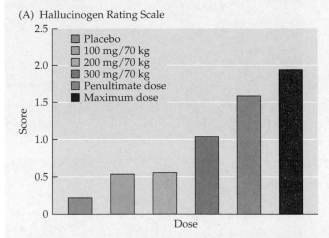

(A) Hallucinogen Rating Scale

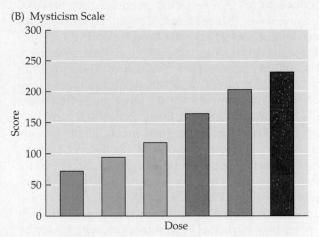

(B) Mysticism Scale

High doses of dextromethorphan produce subjective effects similar to those observed with classical hallucinogens Subjects who were experienced users of hallucinogenic drugs (including dextromethorphan in some cases) were given varying oral doses of dextromethorphan or placebo under relaxing conditions that facilitated the possibility of experiencing hallucinogenic drug–like effects. The highest possible drug dose was 800 mg/70 kg body weight, but not all subjects achieved that dose because of adverse effects in some cases. The graphs show scores on the Hallucinogen Rating Scale (perception scale), which reflects hallucinations, illusions, and synesthesias (A), and on a Mysticism Scale that has been used to assess both natural and drug-induced mystical experiences (B). The maximum and penultimate doses are the highest and next-to-highest doses tolerated by each subject. (After Reissig et al., 2012.)

dextromethorphan using several questionnaires, including the standard Hallucinogen Rating Scale as well as a Mysticism Scale to assess the intensity of drug-induced mystical experiences. The results showed that dextromethorphan dose-dependently produced a range of subjective effects similar to those reported following the use of classical hallucinogens. The figure illustrates two such effects, namely, increases in perceptual distortions (illusions and hallucinations) and in overall mystical experience.

Some users report positive experiences with dextromethorphan, but others have serious negative reactions. Acute toxicity can occur not only in users who take extremely high doses of dextromethorphan but also in a small percentage of individuals who are genetically deficient in their

metabolism of the drug (Schwartz, 2005). Extreme dextromethorphan intoxication has been linked to psychotic reactions, violent behavior, and even death (Amaladoss and O'Brien, 2011; Logan et al., 2009; Logan et al., 2012; Miller, 2005).

In summary, dextromethorphan is a powerful substance with psychoactive properties similar to the other drugs discussed in this chapter. It has substantial

abuse potential and can produce severe adverse reactions in users who are poor metabolizers of the compound and/or who take extremely high doses. Although dextromethorphan is not currently included in the Schedule of Controlled Substances, the DEA has listed it as a drug of concern, and it could be added to the Schedule at some future time.

Marcia Moore and John Lilly but also in the self-reports of other heavy users. Accounts of dose escalation and compulsive use are presented by Karl Jansen, a British psychiatrist who has investigated ketamine use for many years (Jansen, 2001; Jansen and Darracot-Cankovic, 2001). Interestingly, many of the ketamine-dependent subjects studied by Jansen are described as being highly intelligent, even PhD students. One straight-A PhD candidate said that overcoming his ketamine problem was "harder than heroin" (Jansen, 2001, p. 167).

Dextromethorphan, a common ingredient in over-the-counter cough and cold medications, is another noncompetitive NMDA receptor antagonist with abuse potential. This compound is discussed in **Box 15.2**.

PCP or ketamine exposure can cause a variety of adverse consequences

Chronic use of ketamine or PCP can produce many different negative effects. Some ketamine users develop distressing urological symptoms including bladder pain and incontinence (Wood et al., 2011). Furthermore, deficits in memory and other cognitive functions have been reported in chronic recreational ketamine users (Morgan and Curran, 2006). Some of these deficits seem to persist even following a significant reduction in drug consumption. Ketamine users also exhibited much greater delusional thinking than non-users (Morgan et al., 2009), although it is impossible to know from this study whether such abnormal ideation was caused by or preceded ketamine exposure. The neurobiological mechanisms underlying these psychological effects are not yet known, although brain imaging studies have found evidence for both gray and white matter abnormalities in chronic ketamine users (Liao et al., 2010, 2011). There is also a report of increased D_1 dopamine receptor binding in the prefrontal cortex of ketamine users, which may be a result of decreased presynaptic dopaminergic transmission in this brain area (Narendran et al., 2005).

Experimental animal studies have demonstrated additional effects of repeated PCP or ketamine exposure on the brain. Adolescent cynomolgus monkeys given 1 mg/kg ketamine intravenously every day for 6 months displayed a significant reduction in tyrosine hydroxylase immunoreactivity (used as a marker of DA axons and terminals) in the prefrontal cortex (Yu et al., 2012). This finding is consistent with the results of Narendran and coworkers (2005) in human ketamine users. The same ketamine-treated monkeys also showed substantial regional changes in neural activity compared with control animals when subjected to functional magnetic resonance imaging (fMRI). Other studies have demonstrated that repeated PCP administration leads to decreased NMDA receptor binding in mice (Newell et al., 2007), as well as a reduced number of asymmetrical spine synapses (usually considered to be excitatory glutamatergic synapses) in the prefrontal cortex in both rats (Elsworth et al., 2011b) and monkeys (Elsworth et al., 2011a). Even more striking, repeated administration of high doses of ketamine provokes apoptotic cell death in the developing brain of both rats and monkeys (Green and Coté, 2009) (**Figure 15.15**). Although lower doses do not produce such effects, researchers have nonetheless raised concerns about these findings given that ketamine is a recommended anesthetic agent for pediatric procedures that involve significant pain and/or require immobilization of the patient (Krauss and Green, 2000). A number of other anesthetics that work by enhancing $GABA_A$ receptor activity can also induce apoptosis when given to experimental animals during early development (Hays and Deshpande, 2011). Because of a lack of direct histological evidence, there is currently no way to know whether routine anesthetic administration

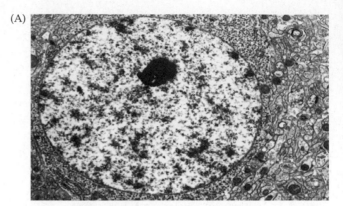

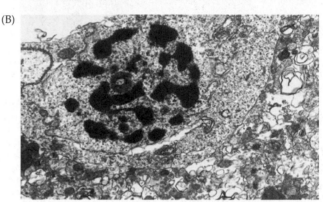

Figure 15.15 Electron micrographs depicting ketamine-induced neurodegeneration in the frontal cortex of an infant rat Seven-day-old rats were given 5, 10, or 20 mg/kg ketamine subcutaneously once, three times, or six times at 2-hour intervals. Animals were killed at 6 hours after the last injection, and their brains were prepared for histological examination using electron microscopy. The micrographs show normal neuronal morphology in the frontal cortex of a saline vehicle control rat (A) but fragmentation of the cell nucleus indicative of apoptotic cell death in the same brain area of a rat given six 20 mg/kg doses of ketamine (B). Lower doses or fewer treatments did not produce this neurodegenerative effect. (From Zou et al., 2009.)

during development in humans leads to apoptotic cell death in the brain. Some preliminary findings suggest that exposure to general anesthesia in infancy or early childhood, particularly on multiple occasions, may be associated with later cognitive deficits (Wilder, 2010). However, various confounding factors make this research difficult to interpret, and further studies are needed to clarify whether young humans are at risk when they undergo procedures that require general anesthesia.

Novel therapeutic applications have been proposed for ketamine

We have seen that ketamine is an approved anesthetic for veterinary use as well as for some procedures in human infants and children. Recent research suggests that this drug may have additional therapeutic applications in the treatment of major depression and in pain relief. Practitioners have known for many years that selective serotonin reuptake inhibitors (SSRIs), the first-line drugs prescribed for patients with major depression, require several weeks of administration before significant therapeutic benefit occurs (see Chapter 19). This so-called "therapeutic lag" is of significant concern not only because of the continued suffering of the patient, but also because a depressed patient who is suicidal could take her life before her mood improves. For reasons that are not yet understood, a single IV dose of ketamine has been demonstrated to produce rapid, although temporary, symptom improvement in clinically depressed subjects (Machado-Vieira et al., 2009; Murrough, 2012). Further clinical trials are under way to determine whether ketamine or a similar NMDA receptor antagonist could be developed as an approved treatment for major depression. Ketamine is also being tested for use as a non-opioid analgesic agent for a variety of chronic pain conditions (Cohen et al., 2011; Noppers et al., 2010; Prommer, 2012) and for postoperative analgesia (Laskowski et al., 2011). Because tolerance to repeated opiate drug treatment is partially mediated by the NMDA receptor, an additional benefit of ketamine administration is the ability to reverse opioid tolerance. Although these novel applications of ketamine are intriguing, caution is warranted because of the abuse potential of this compound and its propensity to induce psychotomimetic effects at higher doses.

Section Summary

- PCP and ketamine belong to the class of drugs known as dissociative anesthetics.

- PCP was withdrawn from clinical use because of its prominent adverse side effects, but ketamine, which is less potent than PCP, has significant applications in both human and veterinary medicine.

- The acute effects of PCP and ketamine include sensory distortions and altered body image, cognitive disorganization, and various affective changes. High doses of ketamine give rise to a state called the "K-hole," in which the user feels separated from his body, perhaps in the manner of a near-death experience.

- PCP and ketamine bind to a site within the NMDA receptor channel, thereby acting as noncompetitive receptor antagonists. A secondary consequence of NMDA receptor blockade is increased presynaptic glutamate release, which may contribute to the behavioral and subjective effects of PCP and ketamine.

- Both PCP and ketamine are reinforcing to animals, as indicated by drug self-administration. These reinforcing effects may be mediated by both dopaminergic and nondopaminergic mechanisms. Ketamine also produces pleasurable effects in human subjects.

- Although illicit use of ketamine has occurred for many years, the popularity of this compound is on the rise. Heavy ketamine users show dose escalation and compulsive use, which indicate the development of tolerance and dependence on the drug.

- Dextromethorphan is an opioid-like compound found in cough medications that also acts as a noncompetitive NMDA receptor antagonist. This drug has significant abuse potential because of its ability to produce subjective effects like those of both dissociative anesthetics and classical hallucinogens.

- Chronic ketamine or PCP exposure leads to a variety of adverse effects including urological symptoms, cognitive deficits, gray and white matter abnormalities, altered dopaminergic function, and a reduced number of asymmetrical spine synapses in the prefrontal cortex. Repeated high ketamine doses also cause apoptotic cell death in the developing brain of laboratory animals, which raises concern for the use of this compound as a pediatric anesthetic agent.

- Recent studies suggest that ketamine may have novel therapeutic applications in the treatment of major depression and for pain relief.

Go to the **COMPANION WEBSITE**

sites.sinauer.com/psychopharm2e
for Web Boxes, animations, flashcards,
and other study resources.

Recommended Readings

Hofmann, A. (1979). How LSD originated. *J. Psychoactive Drugs*, 11, 53–60.

Jansen, K. L. R. (2001). *Ketamine: Dreams and Realities*. Sarasota, FL: Multidisciplinary Association for Psychedelic Studies.

Schultes, R. E., Hofmann, A., and Rätsch, C. (2001). *Plants of the Gods: Their Sacred, Healing, and Hallucinogenic Powers*. Rochester, VT: Healing Arts Press.

Sinner, B. and Graf, B. M. (2008). Ketamine. *Handb. Exp. Pharmacol.*, 182, 313–333.

Ulrich, R. F. and Patten, B. M. (1991). The rise, decline, and fall of LSD. *Perspect. Biol. Med.*, 34, 561–578.

Young people are particularly attracted to inhalants because of their low cost and easy availability and the rapid "high" they produce.

Inhalants, GHB, and Anabolic–Androgenic Steroids 16

HAVE YOU EVER HEARD THE WORD "RESISTOLEROS"? If you have, it was probably used in reference to a Bay Area punk rock band that goes by that name. But there is another, more disturbing, use of the word. In many parts of Latin America, resistoleros are street children who are habitual glue sniffers. Their name comes from Resistol, which is a contact cement and shoemaker's glue that is widely sold in Latin American countries and is favored by many young glue sniffers. According to the International Assembly of the National Council for the Social Studies (2004), millions of homeless Latin American children are sniffing glues such as Resistol. Glue sniffing gives the children a temporary "high" and a numbness that helps them cope with their precarious existence, but it can also cause many long-term health problems including damage to the brain and other vital organs.

Glues belong to a broader class of abused substances known as **inhalants**. Most inhalants are perfectly legal, can easily be purchased at retail stores by people of any age, and are readily accessible in the home by anyone who can reach into a medicine cabinet or a kitchen drawer, or who can walk down the stairs to the basement or open the door to the garage. Moreover, in recent years these substances have been responsible for the abrupt death of a number of children and teenagers in many countries, including the United States. Indeed, the parents of children who have died from abusing inhalants invariably say that they never knew how dangerous these substances could be.

The first part of this chapter discusses where inhalants come from, how they affect behavioral and neural functioning, and what health risks they pose. Later sections of the chapter cover γ-hydroxybutyrate (GHB) and anabolic–androgenic steroids. Although inhalants, GHB, and steroids differ in their mechanisms of action, they share the fact that they are all relative newcomers to the drug abuse scene compared with many other substances such as alcohol, cannabis, tobacco, opioids, and the plant-derived hallucinogens.

Inhalants

Background

Inhalants represent a novel and diverse group of abused substances. They are also unusual in that users are typically children and adolescents.

Inhalants comprise a range of substances including volatile solvents, aerosols, and gases

Abused inhalants often come from everyday household items. These substances have the following characteristics:

1. They are either volatile (easily vaporized) liquids or gases at room temperature.
2. They are used by inhaling fumes from a rag saturated with the substance ("huffing"),[1] sniffing fumes from a container of the substance ("sniffing" or "snorting"), inhaling fumes of the substance inside a plastic or paper bag ("bagging"), inhaling the substance from a balloon, or spraying an aerosol of the substance directly into one's nose or mouth (e.g., "glading" from a can of air freshener or "dusting" from a dust removal spray can).
3. They do not belong to another defined class of abused substances (e.g., nicotine, tetrahydrocannabinol [THC], or cocaine, all of which can be inhaled through smoking).

Most inhalants can be categorized as volatile solvents, aerosols, or gases. **Volatile solvents** are chemicals that are liquid at room temperature but give off fumes that can be inhaled. Solvents are found in numerous household and industrial products, including adhesives, correction fluids, ink used in felt-tip marking pens, paint thinners and paint removers, dry-cleaning fluids, gasoline, and industrial degreasing agents. **Aerosols** are sprays that contain various solvents and propellants. Examples are hair sprays, deodorant sprays, spray paints, vegetable oil sprays used in cooking, and sprays used for household cleaning. The third category, **gases**, includes several gases found in domestic or commercial products, as well as anesthetic agents used in human and veterinary medicine. Sources of gaseous inhalants include whipped cream dispensers (which contain nitrous oxide, also known as "laughing gas"), propane tanks, butane lighters, and appliances that contain refrigerants such as refrigerators, freezers, and air conditioners. **Table 16.1** lists some abused inhalants that fall within these three classes.

A fourth group of inhalants, called **nitrites**, is often placed in a separate category apart from the solvents, aerosols, and gases. Whereas most inhalants are taken to obtain a euphoric effect, or "high," nitrites are typically used to heighten sexual arousal and pleasure. Furthermore, unlike other inhalants, which are thought to act directly on nerve cells, nitrites produce their subjective effects primarily by dilating blood vessels and causing muscle relaxation. Members of this group include amyl nitrite ("poppers"), butyl nitrite, and cyclohexyl nitrite. In the remainder of this section, we will focus on the first three classes of inhalants.

These substances are particularly favored by children and adolescents

Survey results indicate that more than 22 million Americans 12 years of age or older have used inhalants at least once in their lifetime (Howard et al., 2011). Inhalants are most commonly used by children and adolescents, with first use typically occurring between the ages of 12 and 16 (Nonnemaker et al., 2011). Indeed, it is not uncommon for inhalants to be the first substances tried by children, even sooner than alcohol, tobacco, or marijuana. Solvents and aerosols in particular can be obtained legally and inexpensively (in fact, there are almost certainly plenty of them at home already in the kitchen, basement, or garage), and it may be difficult for parents and teachers to detect the use of inhalants if the child is careful. This is not to say that adults don't use inhalants, because obviously some do. Nevertheless, this class of substances is unusual in its special attractiveness to young people.

Behavioral and Neural Effects

The sections below will discuss the subjective effects of inhalants, their mechanism of action, and their propensity for abuse and dependence.

Many inhalant effects are similar to alcohol intoxication

The acute effects of volatile and gaseous inhalants are often compared with those seen with alcohol intoxication. The user initially experiences euphoria,

---

[1]Although the term *huffing* has the specific meaning given here, it is often used more generally to denote the breathing in of an inhalant.

TABLE 16.1 Some Commonly Abused Inhalants

Compound	Principal uses
Acetone	Nail polish remover, adhesives, general solvent
Aliphatic and aromatic hydrocarbons	Gasoline, white spirits
Bromochlorodifluoromethane (BCF)	Fire extinguishers
n-Butane	Cigarette lighters, bottled fuel gas
Butanone (methyl ethyl ketone, MEK)	Adhesives, general solvent
Carbon tetrachloride	Grain fumigant, laboratory solvent
Chlorodifluoromethane (Halon or Freon 22)	Aerosol propellant
Chloroform	Laboratory solvent
Dichlorodifluoromethane (Halon 122 or Freon 12)	Aerosol propellant, refrigerant
Dichlorotetrafluoroethane (Halon 242 or Freon 114)	Aerosol propellant
Diethyl ether	Laboratory solvent
Enflurane	Anesthetic
Ethyl acetate	Adhesives
Halothane	Anesthetic
n-Hexane	General solvent
Isoflurane	Anesthetic
Methyl isobutyl ketone (MIBK)	General solvent
Nitrous oxide	Anesthetic, whipped cream dispensers
Propane	Bottled fuel gas
Tetrachloroethylene (perchloroethylene)	Dry-cleaning and degreasing agent
Toluene	Adhesives, acrylic paints, paint stripper
Trichloroethane (methylchloroform)	Dry-cleaning and degreasing agent, correction fluid
Trichloroethylene	Dry-cleaning and degreasing agent, chewing gum remover
Trichlorofluoromethane (Halon or Freon 11)	Aerosol propellant, refrigerant
Xylene	Woodwork adhesives, histology clearing agent

Source: Dinwiddie, 1994.

The pattern of inhalant effects varies not only with dose but also with frequency of use. Garland and Howard (2010) found that low-frequency inhalant users mainly reported positive effects of use (e.g., euphoria), whereas high-frequency users reported a mixture of positive and aversive effects (e.g., depressed mood, irritability, or suicidal thoughts). Some inhalant users experience delusional ideas, including the delusion that one can fly. In a study by Evans and Raistrick (1987), users who thought they could fly actually jumped out of windows or trees, leading to at least one broken bone and various minor injuries, but fortunately no fatalities.

Chronic inhalant use can lead to tolerance and dependence

Although most individuals who try inhalants discontinue their use relatively quickly, some escalate their usage and subsequently develop tolerance and dependence on these substances (Perron et al., 2009a). As with other abused substances, tolerant inhalant users need to take higher doses to obtain the expected euphoric effect. There is also growing evidence for an inhalant withdrawal syndrome, with symptoms such as nausea, fatigue, irritability, anxiety, sleep disturbances, and intense craving (Perron et al., 2009b, 2011). Not surprisingly, withdrawal symptoms are most commonly experienced by users who meet the criteria for inhalant dependence.

Little, if any, information has been published on the availability and efficacy of specific treatment programs for inhalant abuse and dependence. Treatment providers typically employ standard approaches used with other abused substances, such as 12-step programs, cognitive-behavioral therapy, and motivational enhancement. Remarkably, an exhaustive review conducted a few years ago found *no* published

stimulation, and disinhibition, which are followed by drowsiness and lightheadedness. Heavier exposure causes stronger depressant effects, characterized by slurred speech, poor coordination, ataxia, and lethargy. Sensory distortions, even hallucinations, may occur. Indeed, a recent study of Mexican teenagers found that some users took inhalants specifically for the resulting illusions and hallucinations (Cruz and Domínguez, 2011). Very high doses can lead to anesthesia, loss of consciousness, and coma.

randomized controlled trials of inhalant treatment outcomes (Konghom et al., 2010). This is clearly an area in need of study.

Rewarding and reinforcing effects have been demonstrated in animals

There are relatively few studies of inhalant reward and reinforcement using animal models, partly because of the difficulty of controlling airborne delivery of these substances by investigators who wish to model the typical route of human exposure. Nonetheless, procedures have been developed that demonstrate the ability of toluene vapors to support place conditioning in rats and mice (Funada et al., 2002; Lee et al., 2006). In the study by Funada and colleagues, place conditioning was conducted using an airtight inhalation shuttlebox in which the two compartments of the apparatus differed in the sensory cues they presented to the animals. Mice were given 10 conditioning sessions over 5 days, 1 session each day in the toluene-containing compartment, and an additional session in the compartment that contained only air. As shown in **Figure 16.1**, exposure to 700 parts per million (ppm) or more of toluene led to a significant preference for the toluene-associated side of the apparatus. Toluene and another solvent trichloroethane were also shown to be intravenously self-administered by mice (Blokhina et al., 2004).

The neural mechanisms underlying inhalant reward and reinforcement are likewise not well understood. In previous chapters, we saw that dopamine (DA) plays a role in the reinforcing properties of many abused drugs. Two studies found that toluene activated dopaminergic neurons in the ventral tegmental area (VTA) either when the solvent was inhaled by rats (Riegel and French, 2002) or when it was directly applied to the VTA in vitro (Riegel et al., 2007). Although such findings raise the possibility that DA is involved in inhalant reward and reinforcement, it will be important to test this hypothesis by determining whether DA receptor antagonists can block the effects of toluene in self-administration or place-conditioning paradigms.

Inhalants are central nervous system (CNS) depressants

Because of their more recent arrival on the scene, less is known about the mechanism of action of inhalants than of other abused substances. Furthermore, all inhalants may not work the same way because of their chemical diversity. Nevertheless, our understanding of these substances is increasing, and several important findings have been reported.

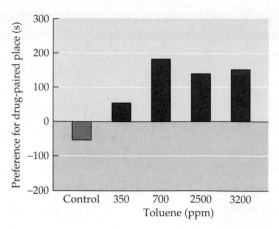

Figure 16.1 Rewarding effects of toluene in mice as shown by conditioned place preference. Mice were given two training sessions per day for 5 days. Each session lasted 20 minutes and involved pairing one compartment of an airtight chamber with toluene vapor and the other compartment, which differed from the first compartment in its sensory characteristics, with air. Toluene concentrations ranged from 350 to 3200 parts per million (ppm) as shown. On the test day, no toluene was administered and the mice were allowed to move freely between the two compartments. Toluene concentrations of at least 700 ppm resulted in a significant preference for the toluene-paired side as indicated by the amount of time spent on that side. Control mice not given any toluene showed no significant preference for either side. (After Funada et al., 2002.)

With respect to pharmacokinetics, inhalants are rapidly absorbed from the lungs into the bloodstream and quickly enter the brain because of their high lipid solubility. Madina Gerasimov and colleagues at the Brookhaven National Laboratory used positron emission tomography (PET) to investigate the localization of [^{11}C]toluene that had been administered to baboons (Gerasimov et al., 2002). The radiolabeled toluene reached all parts of the brain, but its distribution was not uniform (**Figure 16.2**). Quantitative measurements of the striatum, frontal cortex, thalamus, cerebellum, and white matter showed particularly high uptake in the striatum, thalamus, and deep cerebellar nuclei. These findings indicate that localization of inhalants within the brain needs to be taken into account by researchers who are trying to understand how these substances affect brain function and behavior.

The CNS-depressant actions of inhalants can best be explained by their effects on various ionotropic receptors. A number of studies have found that toluene, at least some other volatile solvents, and anesthetic agents enhance the function of inhibitory GABA$_A$ receptors and inhibit the activity of excitatory N-methyl-D-aspartate (NMDA) glutamate and nicotinic cholinergic receptors (Bowen et al., 2006). Several voltage-gated ion channels are also influenced by inhalants. A similar profile of ionotropic receptor effects has been

(A)   (B)

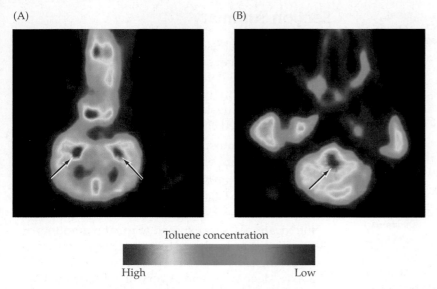

Toluene concentration

High   Low

Figure 16.2 PET images of brain uptake and distribution of radiolabeled toluene in a baboon The animal was injected intravenously with [¹¹C]toluene and then was imaged 2 minutes later. The arrows show toluene being concentrated in the striatum (A) and in the deep cerebellar nuclei (B). (After Gerasimov et al., 2002; images courtesy of Madina Gerasimov.)

MRI scans of chronic inhalant abusers with those of individuals who abused various other drugs such as cocaine, marijuana, alcohol, amphetamines, or opioids. The results indicated many more subcortical abnormalities in the inhalant-abusing group (Rosenberg et

demonstrated for other depressant drugs, particularly ethanol. Thus, it appears that inhalants reduce CNS excitability and cause behavioral impairment in much the same way that alcohol does.

Health risks associated with inhalant abuse

The health risks of inhalant use are significant. Even a single use can be fatal through several possible mechanisms such as cardiac arrhythmia (loss of normal heart rhythm). This outcome has been termed **sudden sniffing death syndrome** (Bowen, 2011; Phatak and Walterscheid, 2012). Although most users don't experience this syndrome, repeated inhalant use can damage not only the heart but also the liver, kidneys, lungs, and bone (**Figure 16.3**).

Of special concern to neuropharmacologists is the brain's vulnerability to inhalant toxicity. The brain tends to concentrate inhalants because of its high lipid content (especially white matter) and the tendency of these substances to readily dissolve in lipids. Consequently, chronic inhalant abuse has been associated with white matter degeneration, cerebellar dysfunction, and damage to both the cranial and peripheral nerves (Takagi et al., 2011; Williams et al., 2007). Several magnetic resonance imaging (MRI) studies have shown white-matter abnormalities indicative of damage to the myelin sheaths surrounding nerve cell axons in many brain areas. One such study compared

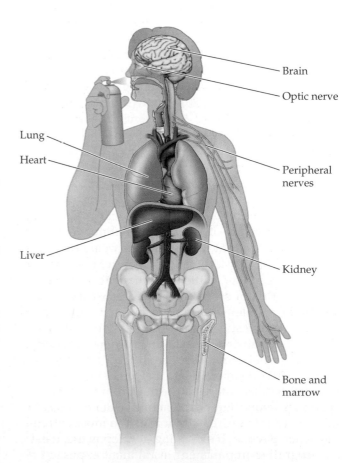

Figure 16.3 Organs and tissues damaged by repeated inhalant use (After Howard et al., 2011.)

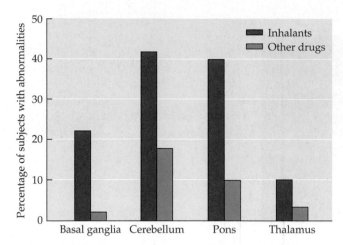

Figure 16.4 Subcortical structural abnormalities in inhalant abusers compared with abusers of other drugs. Chronic abusers of either inhalants (mainly toluene-containing solvents) or other drugs were given brain scans using MRI. A much greater percentage of the inhalant abusers than the other drug abusers showed structural abnormalities in various subcortical areas. (After Rosenberg et al., 2002.)

al., 2002) **(Figure 16.4)**. Moreover, several reports have described deficient performance by inhalant abusers on various neuropsychological tests, suggesting that the adverse effects of chronic inhalant exposure on the brain result in cognitive impairment (Lubman et al., 2008; Williams et al., 2007). Some recovery of function may occur after prolonged abstinence from inhalants (Dingwall and Cairney, 2011); however, more research is needed to determine the extent of recovery and how this process is related to the preceding pattern of inhalant exposure.

Lastly, it is important to note that significant fetal exposure to inhalants has been documented in cases where the mother either was an inhalant abuser or was exposed to inhalants occupationally. Offspring of such women are often born prematurely and with reduced birthweight. In the most extreme cases, the infant exhibits physical malformations of the head and face that are similar to the abnormalities seen in newborn offspring of some alcoholic women (see Chapter 10). In parallel with the concept of a fetal alcohol syndrome, investigators in the inhalant field have coined the term **fetal solvent syndrome** to describe the craniofacial anomalies seen in the affected infants (Bowen, 2011; Hannigan and Bowen, 2010). It is well established that infants suffering from fetal alcohol syndrome show significant cognitive deficits, including severe mental retardation in the most extreme cases. Some research indicating developmental delays and cognitive impairment in inhalant-exposed offspring has been published, but long-term outcome studies are still lacking at the time of this writing.

Section Summary

- Inhalants are abused substances that are often obtained from everyday household items. These substances are volatile liquids or gases at room temperature; are used by sniffing, inhaling, or spraying the substance; and do not belong to another defined class of abused drugs.

- Inhalants are most commonly used by children and adolescents, and they are often the first substance of abuse tried by a child.

- Low doses of volatile and gaseous inhalants produce effects resembling those seen with alcohol intoxication. Users exposed to greater amounts of these substances show stronger depressant effects, including slurred speech, poor coordination, ataxia, sleepiness, and at very high doses, loss of consciousness and even coma. Sensory distortions, including hallucinations, may also occur.

- Repeated inhalant use can lead to tolerance, dependence, and an abstinence syndrome when drug use is stopped. Withdrawal symptoms include nausea, fatigue, irritability, anxiety, sleep disturbances, and craving.

- Inhalants are reinforcing to humans because of their euphoric effects, and animal studies have also begun to establish the rewarding and reinforcing properties of these substances under controlled laboratory conditions. Increased firing of DA neurons in the VTA may play a role in inhalant reward and reinforcement.

- Inhalants are rapidly absorbed from the lungs and quickly enter the brain from the bloodstream because of their high lipid solubility. Distribution within the brain does not appear to be uniform, and this may influence the behavioral effects of these substances.

- The depressant effects of inhalants, particularly toluene (which is the best studied inhalant), can generally be attributed to enhancement of inhibitory $GABA_A$ receptor activity, as well as to inhibition of excitatory NMDA and nicotinic receptors.

- Inhalants present serious health risks including damage to the liver, kidneys, lungs, bone, and brain. Solvent abusers show cognitive impairment that may be related to the injurious effects of inhalants on the brain, such as white-matter abnormalities seen on MRI scans.

- Inhalant use can additionally lead to a rare disorder called sudden sniffing death syndrome, which in some cases results from an inhalant-induced cardiac arrhythmia. Moreover, some offspring exposed to inhalants in utero reportedly suffer from fetal solvent syndrome, which involves craniofacial abnormalities and possibly also cognitive deficits. These effects resemble those seen in individuals diagnosed with fetal alcohol syndrome.

Gamma-Hydroxybutyrate

Background

The second part of this chapter concerns **γ-hydroxybutyrate** (**GHB**), a simple chemical with a complicated history. As can be seen in **Figure 16.5A**, GHB is closely related structurally to the important inhibitory neurotransmitter GABA. In fact, GHB is actually produced in the brain in small amounts as a by-product of GABA metabolism (**Figure 16.5B**) and is thought to function as a novel neurotransmitter/neuromodulator (Castelli et al., 2008). A rare genetic disorder leads to overproduction of GHB as well as to a characteristic cluster of symptoms that may be related to excess levels of this substance (see **Web Box 16.1**). GHB can be taken up into GABAergic vesicles by the vesicular inhibitory amino acid transporter (VIAAT; see Chapter 8) (Muller et al., 2002), which raises the possibility that some GHB could be co-released with GABA when the neuron fires and vesicular exocytosis occurs at the nerve terminal.

The pharmacologic properties of exogenous GHB were first reported in 1960 by a French team headed by Henri Laborit, the same scientist who discovered the antipsychotic drug chlorpromazine. Laborit was looking for a GABA analog that would cross the blood–brain barrier more efficiently than GABA and thus might have therapeutic potential as a CNS-depressant compound. Although early studies did confirm the ability of GHB to produce sedation and even anesthesia in laboratory animals and humans, it later fell into disfavor as an anesthetic and is currently used for other therapeutic purposes (see later in this chapter).

In the United States, little attention was paid to GHB until the 1980s, when it began to be marketed by health food stores as a nutritional supplement for bodybuilders. Despite a lack of supporting evidence, GHB was claimed by manufacturers to reduce body fat and enhance muscle mass through its ability to stimulate growth hormone secretion by the pituitary gland. As time went on, the Food and Drug Administration (FDA) began to receive a number of reports of GHB-related illness, and in 1990 the FDA declared the drug to be unsafe and banned over-the-counter sales.

Despite the FDA ban, GHB use continued to grow, largely as the result of an upsurge in recreational use under various street names such as "liquid X," "liquid E," "Georgia home boy," "grievous bodily harm," "cherry meth," "organic quaalude," and "nature's quaalude." Some stores, as well as many Internet sites, sold GHB-containing formulations with commercial names like Remforce, Revivarant, Renewtrient, Blue Nitro, and SomatoPro. In addition, restrictions on GHB sales were circumvented by the introduction of kits for synthesizing the compound at home from the chemical precursor γ-butyrolactone (GBL)

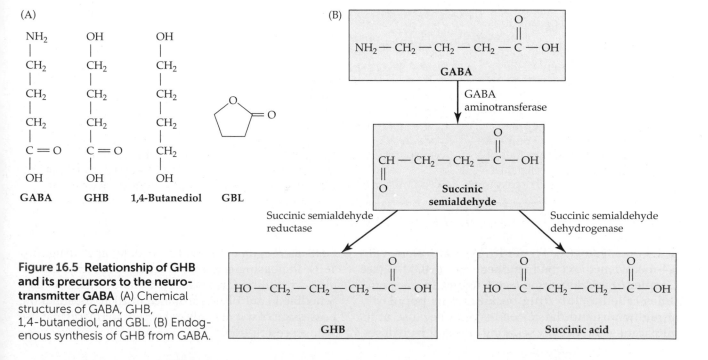

Figure 16.5 Relationship of GHB and its precursors to the neurotransmitter GABA (A) Chemical structures of GABA, GHB, 1,4-butanediol, and GBL. (B) Endogenous synthesis of GHB from GABA.

BOX 16.1   Of Special Interest

"Date Rape" Drugs

Men have long used alcohol to reduce women's sexual inhibitions, thereby making them more willing sexual partners. If the alcohol consumption has been sufficient to render the woman incapacitated, she is vulnerable to sexual assault including rape. Most drug-related sexual assaults are of this kind. However, in recent years, an insidious phenomenon has emerged in which a sedating drug is put clandestinely in a woman's drink so that she isn't even aware that anything is amiss until she wakes up hours later in the man's bed. Drugs are sometimes used in this way on a date, hence the term "date rape" drugs. However, there have also been instances in which a woman was sexually assaulted by a total stranger after being given one of these substances. For this reason, researchers in this area prefer to use the term "drug-facilitated sexual assault."

A number of different drugs have been used to assist in a sexual assault (see Schwartz et al., 2000), but besides alcohol, we will focus here on two compounds: GHB and a benzodiazepine called flunitrazepam (trade name Rohypnol). As we have seen, GHB is a CNS-depressant agent that can induce unconsciousness in sufficiently high doses. It is colorless and odorless, which facilitates its surreptitious use by the perpetrator (although the sodium salt of GHB has a distinctive salty flavor that could be detected unless the

The drink-testing coaster from Drink Safe

woman's beverage is already strongly flavored by fruit juice, for example). Its depressant effects add to those produced by alcohol, thereby increasing the likelihood that the victim will lapse into an unconscious state. Rohypnol is a powerful sleep-inducing agent that is used medicinally in Europe and Mexico but is not currently approved for sale in the United States. Nevertheless, it is readily available illicitly under street names like "roofies," "rophies," or "roche" (the drug is manufactured by the Hoffmann-La Roche pharmaceutical company). Besides inducing sleep, Rohypnol may also cause anterograde amnesia, which means a lack of memory for

events that occur while the recipient is under the influence of the drug. This can make it more difficult for prosecutors to prove a rape charge when Rohypnol is involved.

It is impossible to know how frequently drugs are used to perpetrate a sexual assault, partly because many assaulted women do not come forward for personal reasons, and partly because some of these compounds (e.g., GHB) are metabolized and cleared from the body relatively quickly. The incidence of GHB-facilitated sexual assaults appears to vary by country. Studies performed in the United States found the presence of GHB in about 3% to 4% of *all* reported

or 1,4-butanediol (see Figure 16.5A). GHB, along with 3,4-methylenedioxymethamphetamine (MDMA) (see Chapter 6) and ketamine (see Chapter 15), is sometimes called a **club drug** because of its popularity at nightclubs and dances or "raves." Because of its intoxicating and heavily sedating effects at high doses,

GHB also began to be used as a "date rape" drug (**Box 16.1**). Increasing concerns over the problems associated with illicit GHB use led to its designation as a Schedule I controlled substance in 2000, thus making possession of the drug illegal except for medicinal use with a prescription.

BOX 16.1 *(continued)*

sexual assault cases (Németh et al., 2010), whereas studies conducted specifically on *drug-facilitated* sexual assaults in the United Kingdom (U.K.) and in Paris found GHB in 8% of Parisian cases but in less than 1% of cases in the U.K. (Olszewski, 2009). In the U.K. as elsewhere, alcohol is implicated much more strongly than illicit drugs in the perpetration of sexual assaults.

The private sector has taken several steps to improve the detectability of potential date rape drugs by women. For example, Hoffmann-La Roche replaced its old Rohypnol formulation, which was colorless when dissolved in an alcoholic beverage, with a new tablet that turns blue when dissolved. Another commercial approach to preventing drug-facilitated sexual assault is the marketing of inexpensive devices to test one's drink for the

presence of certain illicit drugs. For example, a firm called Drink Safe Technologies offers both coasters and test strips designed to detect both GHB and ketamine, which has also been used as a date rape drug. The kits do not test for flunitrazepam (Rohypnol), although Drink Safe Technologies has stated that they omitted this test because the current incidence of flunitrazepam-related date rapes is low compared with the incidence of date rapes in which the victim is drugged with GHB or ketamine. As shown in the figure, each Drink Safe coaster contains two pairs of test circles located at the bottom corners of the card. If the coaster is being distributed by a bar or club, it may also include some type of advertisement or logo that has been selected by the proprietor of the establishment. The woman is instructed to place

a drop or two of her drink on one of the pairs of test circles and wait for about 1 minute. A positive test is indicated by either circle turning a darker blue color, which is interpreted as a drug-contaminated drink. It is important to note that the use of the Drink Safe coaster is not recommended for highly acidic beverages such as drinks containing large amounts of fruit juice. There are other limitations as well. The color change could be masked by the drink itself (e.g., red wine), or the bar or club could be so dark that confirming a modest color change would be difficult. Therefore, even though test coasters may help prevent some sexual assaults, women should remain alert for potential adulteration of their drinks even when such coasters are available and seem to indicate that everything is normal.

Behavioral and Neural Effects

The sections below will discuss the subjective and behavioral effects of GHB and its proposed mechanisms of action.

GHB produces behavioral sedation, intoxication, and learning deficits

Pure GHB is a solid powdery material; however, it is usually sold as a solution in water. GHB-containing solutions are clear, odorless, and almost tasteless. Such solutions are often packaged in small bottles similar to those used to package shampoo in hotel rooms (**Figure 16.6**). Typical recreational doses range from 1 to 3 g (approximately 14 to 42 mg/kg for a 70-kg adult), although some regular users may take as much as 4 or 5 g (about 57 to 71 mg/kg) at a time.

When a GHB-containing solution is drunk, the drug is rapidly absorbed from the gastrointestinal tract, enters the bloodstream, and crosses the blood–brain barrier without difficulty. The ensuing psychological and physiological effects are strongly dose related. Low doses of GHB produce an alcohol-like experience. Users report mild euphoria, relaxation,

and social disinhibition beginning approximately 15 minutes following drug ingestion (Abanades et al., 2006; Miotto et al., 2001). Higher doses of GHB can cause lethargy, ataxia, slurring of speech, dizziness, nausea, and vomiting. Memory impairment has also been reported following a high dose of GHB (Carter et al., 2006). Finally, overdosing on this compound is very dangerous, since respiration is depressed and the user may become unconscious or even comatose (Dyer, 1991). Alternatively, the individual may exhibit signs of seizure activity. Overdosing can readily occur if the user takes multiple doses over a short period of time, if there is a greater than expected concentration of GHB in the bottle, or if the

Figure 16.6 A bottle containing GHB

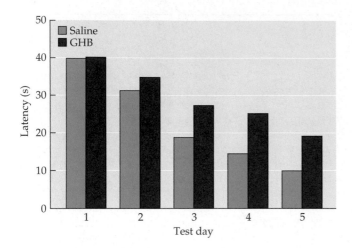

Figure 16.7 GHB impairs spatial navigation learning in adolescent female rats Female rats were trained in the Morris water maze for 5 days beginning at 30 days of age. The graph shows the latency to find the hidden platform in animals given either GHB (100 mg/kg IP) or saline vehicle 30 minutes before training each day. Beginning on day 3, the drug-treated group took longer than the controls to find the platform. This impairment was not observed in adult rats treated in the same way, indicating greater vulnerability to GHB-induced learning impairment during adolescence. (After Sircar et al., 2010.)

drug is taken in combination with alcohol or another sedative–hypnotic drug.

In laboratory animals, acute GHB administration causes sedation, reduced locomotor activity, and decreased anxiety in certain tests such as the elevated plus-maze. At higher doses, animals show signs of catalepsy. Some of these behavioral effects, particularly hypolocomotion and catalepsy, are thought to be due to GHB-induced inhibition of DA release. Other studies found impaired spatial learning in rats repeatedly given moderate doses of GHB (Pedraza et al., 2009; Sircar et al., 2010) (**Figure 16.7**). Such impairment may be related to neurotoxic effects of the drug treatment on the hippocampus, including reduced NMDA receptor expression and neuronal cell loss (Pedraza et al., 2009; Sircar et al., 2011).

Electroencephalographic (EEG) recordings have revealed the presence of a paradoxical CNS excitation at high doses of GHB that some investigators have likened to absence (petit mal) seizures in humans, and that may be related to the occasional reports of seizure activity in human overdose cases (Binienda et al., 2011). Absence seizures involve a temporary loss of consciousness and cessation of activity without the whole-body convulsions seen in a grand mal seizure.

Evidence for GHB reinforcement in animal studies has been inconsistent

As mentioned in the previous section, users report experiencing a euphoric effect when taking GHB. On the other hand, animal studies have yielded mixed results with respect to GHB as a reinforcer. Experiments with rats and mice using either self-administration or place-conditioning paradigms have generally supported the idea that GHB has rewarding and reinforcing properties (Itzhak and Ali, 2002; Nicholson and Balster, 2001). A recent study additionally showed that GHB can induce a conditioned place preference

when microinjected directly into the VTA (Watson et al., 2010). However, investigations of GHB IV self-administration by monkeys indicated at best only weak reinforcing properties (Nicholson and Balster, 2001). Although these overall findings are not easily reconciled, they do suggest that GHB reward and reinforcement can occur under the right conditions of dose, species, and experimental methodology. However, such effects are clearly not as robust as those seen with many other major drugs of abuse such as cocaine, opioids, and ethanol.

Effects of GHB are mediated by multiple mechanisms

Historically there has been much confusion regarding the mechanism of action of GHB. Fortunately, recent findings have begun to clarify the situation, although some uncertainties remain. First, it's important that we differentiate between potential sites of action of endogenous versus exogenous GHB. If GHB does function as a signaling agent in the brain, the receptors that mediate such signaling must have a high affinity for GHB because the endogenous levels of this compound are so low. Radioligand binding studies have, indeed, revealed the existence of sites in the rat brain that bind both GHB and the selective GHB antagonist NCS-382 with high affinity (Crunelli et al., 2006; Ticku and Mehta, 2008); however, the nature of these sites continues to be controversial. A proposed GHB-specific receptor was initially cloned from rat brain (Andriamampandry et al., 2003); this was followed several years later by the isolation of two clones from human brain tissue that were proposed to code for GHB receptor isoforms (Andriamampandry et al., 2007). These putative GHB receptors have the functional properties of metabotropic receptors, and they are heterogeneously distributed within the brain. In contrast, recent work by Absalom and coworkers (2012) showed that GHB can act as a high-affinity partial agonist at $GABA_A$ receptor subtypes containing α4, β (particularly β1), and δ subunits. At the present time, it is not known whether the previously mentioned high-affinity GHB binding sites consist of this

(A)

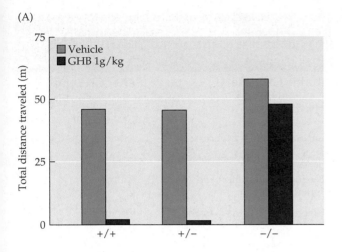

(B)

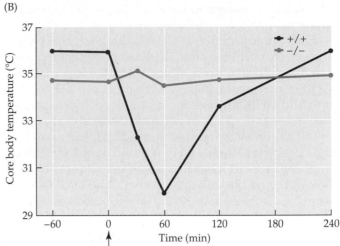

Figure 16.8 Loss of responses to exogenous GHB in mutant mice lacking functional GABA$_B$ receptors GHB (1 g/kg) was administered orally to wild-type mice (+/+), mice that were homozygous for a null mutation of the GABA$_{B1}$ receptor subunit, which is necessary for the formation of functional GABA$_B$ receptors (–/–) (see Chapter 8), and in one experiment, heterozygous GABA$_{B1}$ knockouts (+/–). The wild-type mice but not the homozygous mutants showed (A) a strong sedative effect of GHB as indicated by distance traveled in a locomotor activity cage, and (B) a transient reduction in core body temperature after dosing (shown by the arrow at time 0). (After Kaupmann et al., 2003.)

family of GABA$_A$ receptors, the cloned GHB-specific receptors, or a combination of the two. It is interesting to note, however, that GABA$_A$ receptors containing α4, β, and δ subunits are located at extrasynaptic sites and exert a tonic inhibition of the neurons in which they're expressed (see Chapter 8). Thus, it is possible that GHB acts along with GABA to activate these extrasynaptic GABA$_A$ receptors.

Exogenous administration of GHB, as occurs in human recreational or therapeutic use and in experimental animal studies, considerably elevates brain GHB concentrations. This increase permits an additional mechanism to come into play, namely, the activation of GABA$_B$ receptors (Crunelli et al., 2006). GHB is a weak agonist at GABA$_B$ receptors and, therefore, at high tissue concentrations it could activate these receptors directly. Alternatively, GHB-induced activation of GABA$_B$ receptors could be mediated by conversion of the drug to GABA within the brain. These two possibilities have not yet been resolved. The importance of GABA$_B$ receptor activation in the effects of exogenously administered GHB was shown by the fact that mutant mice lacking functional GABA$_B$ receptors retain high-affinity GHB binding sites but lack the behavioral and physiological responses to GHB treatment (e.g., reduced locomotor activity, hypothermia,

and induction of delta waves in the EEG) that are observed in wild-type control mice (Kaupmann et al., 2003) (**Figure 16.8**). Moreover, most of the effects of GHB administration are blocked by GABA$_B$ antagonists but not by the GHB receptor antagonist NCS-382 (Carter et al., 2009a; Castelli et al., 2004). However, experimental animals can be trained to discriminate GHB from the GABA$_B$ agonist baclofen, which is consistent with the notion that non-GABA$_B$ receptors like those discussed above may contribute to some of the effects of GHB.

Medical and Recreational Uses of GHB

Although GHB is discussed in the popular press primarily with regard to its recreational use and abuse, this compound also has recognized medical uses.

GHB is used therapeutically for the treatment of narcolepsy and alcoholism

In 2002, the sodium salt of GHB (also known as sodium oxybate; trade name Xyrem) was approved by the FDA for treating an unusual disorder called **narcolepsy**. Narcolepsy is characterized by disrupted nighttime sleep, excessive daytime sleepiness, and attacks of cataplexy (Nishino, 2007). Cataplexy is a sudden loss of muscle control that is typically triggered by a strong emotional reaction such as laughing or becoming angry or frustrated. A cataplexy episode may be minor, consisting of a few seconds of muscle weakness resulting in symptoms such as head dropping, knee buckling, or slurred speech. Alternatively, the patient may experience complete paralysis of the antigravity muscles that can last for several minutes. Recent research indicates that most narcoleptic patients suffer from a deficiency in hypocretin (also called orexin), a hypothalamic neuropeptide that is important for regulating sleep and wakefulness.

Early clinical studies of GHB in the 1960s and 1970s showed that bedtime administration of this compound promoted normal sleep, which led to the first trials of GHB in narcoleptic patients (Wedin et al., 2006). Not only did GHB improve nighttime sleep, but daytime sleepiness and attacks of cataplexy were also reduced over time in drug-treated subjects. Unfortunately, the rise in recreational GHB use and abuse, evidence implicating GHB in some cases of sexual assault (see Box 16.1), and the subsequent scheduling of GHB as a controlled substance in 1990 all contributed to a delay in the clinical development and FDA approval of sodium oxybate for the treatment of narcolepsy. Nevertheless, eventual introduction of this pharmacotherapy has led to significant symptom reduction in narcoleptic patients (Boscolo-Berto et al., 2012; Robinson and Keating, 2007).

Given the abuse potential of GHB, it was important to address the possible diversion of sodium oxybate for recreational instead of therapeutic use. Consequently, when the medicinal formulation was introduced to the U.S. market, it was accompanied by a unique national risk management program called the Xyrem Success Program, designed to minimize diversion and misuse of Xyrem. This program involves such factors as single-source manufacture (Jazz Pharmaceuticals), distribution through a central pharmacy, education of physicians and patients on appropriate use of the medication, and patient and physician registries. Thus far, the results have shown a low incidence of Xyrem diversion and abuse since the medication was introduced, indicating that the Xyrem Success Program has been quite successful in achieving its aims (Carter et al., 2009b).

Under the trade name Alcover, sodium oxybate is also approved in Italy and Austria as a pharmacotherapeutic treatment for alcoholism. Clinical studies have indicated that the drug is particularly useful in dealing with alcohol withdrawal symptoms and in helping prevent relapses (Caputo et al., 2009; Leoni et al., 2010). Some of these studies suggest that sodium oxybate compares favorably in therapeutic efficacy with the pharmacotherapies currently licensed in the United States, namely, disulfiram, naltrexone, and acamprosate (see Chapter 10 for more information on these medications). On the other hand, some investigators have argued that there is greater risk of misuse of sodium oxybate by alcoholic patients compared to individuals with narcolepsy (Sewell and Petrakis, 2011). Thus, if this compound is eventually accepted for the treatment of alcoholism in this country, it will probably be used under carefully controlled conditions (e.g., in inpatient settings).

TABLE 16.2 Commonly Reported Experiences during and after Recreational GHB Use

During GHB use	After GHB use
Euphoria	Sluggishness and exhaustion
Enhanced sexual experience	Amnesia
Increased feelings of well being	Confusion
Feelings of relaxation and tranquility	Anxiety
Heightened sensory perception	Insomnia
Disinhibition	Weakness
Loss of consciousness	Agitation

Source: Miotto et al., 2001.

GHB has significant abuse potential when used recreationally

Miotto and coworkers (2001) surveyed 42 regular GHB users in the Los Angeles area about their experiences while under the influence of GHB and the effects that occurred after drug use. As shown in **Table 16.2**, GHB users reported a sense of euphoria and well being, heightened sexuality and sensory perception, and feelings of relaxation and disinhibition during the period of drug intoxication. Loss of consciousness, which is a sign of GHB overdose, sometimes also occurred. In contrast to the (mostly) subjectively positive aspects of GHB intoxication, the period of drug "come-down" seemed to be rather unpleasant. Users commonly reported sluggishness, mental confusion and amnesia, weakness, and increased arousal, as indicated by feelings of anxiety and agitation and difficulty sleeping during the period following GHB consumption.

Numerous risks have been associated with recreational GHB use. The intoxicated state produced by this compound is similar to alcohol intoxication (i.e., drunkenness), and indeed GHB has been implicated in some instances of "driving under the influence" (Andresen et al., 2011). Excessive consumption (overdose) of GHB can cause an acute toxic reaction that includes unconsciousness or even coma, respiratory depression, bradycardia (slowed heart rate), and hypotension (Drasbek et al., 2006; Wood et al., 2011). Concurrent use of alcohol results in an additive response that is extremely dangerous. Most people who experience a GHB overdose recover without obvious adverse consequences (Munir et al., 2008); however, fatalities have been reported, mostly as the result of cardiorespiratory arrest (Zvosec et al., 2011).

Repeated GHB exposure can lead to the development of tolerance. For example, daily treatment of

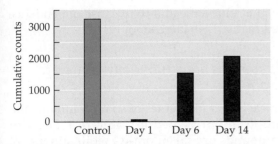

Figure 16.9 Tolerance to the locomotor-suppressant effects of GHB in mice Mice were given 200 mg/kg GHB IP for 14 days. Locomotor activity in a photobeam apparatus was measured for 2 hours following drug administration on days 1, 6, and 14 of treatment. The figure illustrates the number of beam breaks recorded from 30 to 60 minutes posttreatment on each of these days. Compared with control mice administered saline, the GHB-treated animals showed a nearly complete cessation of locomotor activity on day 1, whereas a partial return of activity was observed on subsequent test days. (After Itzhak and Ali, 2002.)

mice with 200 mg/kg GHB produced tolerance to the activity-suppressing effects of the drug (Itzhak and Ali, 2002) (**Figure 16.9**). Chronic GHB use by humans can elicit not only tolerance but also a syndrome of dependence and withdrawal when abstinence is attempted. Indeed, some dependent users engage in binges characterized by GHB consumption every 2 to 4 hours around-the-clock. Symptoms of GHB withdrawal include anxiety, agitation, tremor, tachycardia (increased heart rate), insomnia, confusion, and, in extreme cases, hallucinations and a state of delirium (Miotto et al., 2001; Wood et al., 2011). At the present time, little is known about the potential long-term effects of chronic GHB use. Nevertheless, it is clear that GHB is a dangerous drug with significant potential for abuse and dependence and the ability to produce toxic life-threatening effects when consumed in excessive amounts.

Section Summary

- GHB is an analog of the inhibitory neurotransmitter GABA. It is synthesized in the brain in small amounts and is thought to function as a neurotransmitter/neuromodulator that may be co-released with GABA at some synapses.

- GHB was developed pharmacologically as a CNS-depressant compound. It was later marketed in the United States as a bodybuilding supplement until over-the-counter sales were banned in 1990. Nevertheless, illicit GHB continues to be used recreationally and occasionally as a date rape drug at clubs.

- GHB is usually taken orally in the form of an aqueous solution. Low doses produce alcohol-like effects including mild euphoria, relaxation, and social disinhibition. Higher doses are associated with stronger sedating effects, as well as dizziness, nausea, vomiting, and memory impairment. Severe overdosing with GHB causes severe respiratory depression, unconsciousness, and even coma.

- Animals treated with GHB exhibit sedation, reduced locomotor activity, decreased anxiety behavior, and catalepsy at high doses. Impaired spatial learning has also been reported, which may be related to neurotoxic effects on the hippocampus.

- High doses of GHB can lead to EEG excitation resembling absence (petit mal) seizures in humans.

- The literature on GHB reinforcement is inconsistent; however, there is evidence that the drug has rewarding and reinforcing properties under the right experimental conditions.

- The functional effects of GHB are mediated by multiple mechanisms. The low levels of endogenous GHB are believed to act on putative high-affinity GBH-specific receptors and possibly also on $GABA_A$ receptors containing $\alpha4$, β, and δ subunits. High levels of exogenously administered GHB are additionally capable of activating $GABA_B$ receptors, which mediate many of the behavioral and physiological effects observed in GHB-treated animals.

- The sodium salt of GHB (also called sodium oxybate; trade name Xyrem), is approved in the United States for the treatment of the sleep disorder narcolepsy. This treatment improves nighttime sleep and reduces the incidence of daytime sleepiness and attacks of catalepsy. Under the trade name Alcover, sodium oxybate is approved in Italy and Austria for the treatment of alcoholism.

- Recreational GHB users reportedly experience euphoria, heightened sexuality, and feelings of relaxation during drug intoxication. In several respects, GHB intoxication resembles the state of alcohol intoxication, including impairment of psychomotor function and even loss of consciousness with overdose. The "come-down" following GHB use is characterized by sluggishness, mental confusion and amnesia, weakness, and increased arousal.

- Repeated GHB use can lead to tolerance, dependence, and withdrawal. Consumption patterns may escalate to dosing every 2 to 4 hours around-the-clock. Typical withdrawal symptoms include insomnia, anxiety, and tremors, although use of extremely high doses can apparently cause a psychotic reaction involving hallucinations, delirium, and extreme agitation.

Anabolic–Androgenic Steroids

In recent years, we have been inundated with numerous reports of formerly revered sports heroes being found guilty of taking various performance-enhancing substances (sometimes also called **doping agents**). Use of specific foods or drugs to enhance performance dates back at least to the ancient Greek and Roman athletes, who consumed a variety of natural substances thought to provide increased energy, strength, and endurance (Conti, 2010). Although many doping agents are currently available, especially to a world-class athlete, one particularly important category of performance enhancers is a group of compounds called **anabolic–androgenic steroids**. These are defined as steroid hormones that increase muscle mass (the anabolic part) and also have masculinizing, or testosterone-like, properties (the androgenic part).[2] On the street, these substances are usually just called anabolic steroids, but there are no members of the group that aren't also androgenic. Nevertheless, it is more convenient to use the shorthand term *anabolic steroids*, and that is the term that we will use in the remainder of this chapter.

Why are anabolic steroids being brought up in a chapter on substances of abuse? There is significant evidence that these hormones are abused by some users, and some researchers have theorized that anabolic steroids can produce an addiction-like dependence. Before we discuss these ideas, however, we will present basic information on these substances and how they entered the realm of bodybuilding and athletic competition.

Background and History

Compared with other substances of abuse, anabolic steroids have a unique structure and mechanism of action.

However, they share the ability to cause dependence when used regularly in large amounts.

Anabolic steroids are structurally related to testosterone

The chemical and trade names of some common anabolic steroids are presented in **Table 16.3**. Some of these compounds are taken orally, while others are injected intramuscularly. The latter are formulated for depot injection and maintain their potency for periods ranging from several days to 3 weeks, depending on the steroid. As shown in **Figure 16.10**, these compounds are all structurally related to testosterone, the principal androgen synthesized by the testes. However, because it is the anabolic rather than androgenic effects that are desired by most users, the chemical modifications that differentiate various synthetic steroids from testosterone are aimed at selectively enhancing their anabolic potency. Because the oral steroids are potentially vulnerable to first-pass metabolism in the liver, these compounds are chemically designed to minimize this problem and thus retain adequate bioavailability.

Anabolic steroids were developed to help build muscle mass and enhance athletic performance

American athletes knew little about these compounds before the 1954 World Weightlifting Championships

TABLE 16.3 Some Common Anabolic Steroids

Generic name	Trade name	Route of administration
Methandrostenolone	Dianabol	Oral
Testosterone undecanoate	Andriol	Oral
Oxandrolone	Oxandrin	Oral
Oxymetholone	Anadrol	Oral
Stanozolol	Winstrol	Oral or injection
Testosterone cypionate	Depot-Testosterone	Injection
Testosterone enanthate	Primotetson	Injection
Testerone propionate	Testoprop	Injection
Nandrolone phenylpropionate	Durabolin	Injection
Nandrolone decanoate	Deca-Durabolin	Injection
Methenolone acetate	Primobolan	Injection
Methenolone enanthate	Primobolan Depot	Injection
Trenbolone enanthate	None	Injection

---

[2]One of the first recorded uses of anabolic steroids was that of the 6th-century BC Olympian wrestler Milo of Croton, who ate a diet that included bull testicles in order to maintain his award winning performance (Conti, 2010).

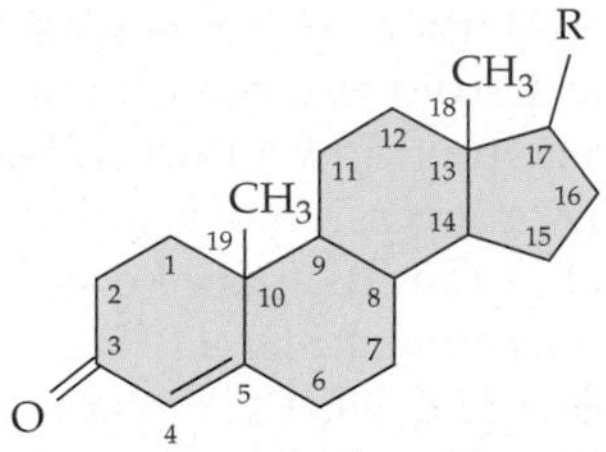

Core structure of
testosterone-related steroids

Compound	R
Testosterone	— OH
Testosterone enanthate	— O — CO(CH$_2$)$_5$CH$_3$
Testosterone undecanoate	— O — CO(CH$_2$)$_9$CH$_3$
Testosterone cypionate	— O — COCH$_2$CH$_2$ — (cyclopentyl ring) 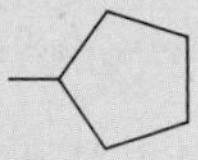
Nandrolone decanoate	— O — CO(CH$_2$)$_8$CH$_3$ (no methyl group at position 19)
Nandrolone phenproprionate	— O — CO(CH$_2$)$_2$ 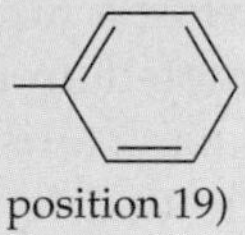 — (phenyl ring) (no methyl group at position 19)

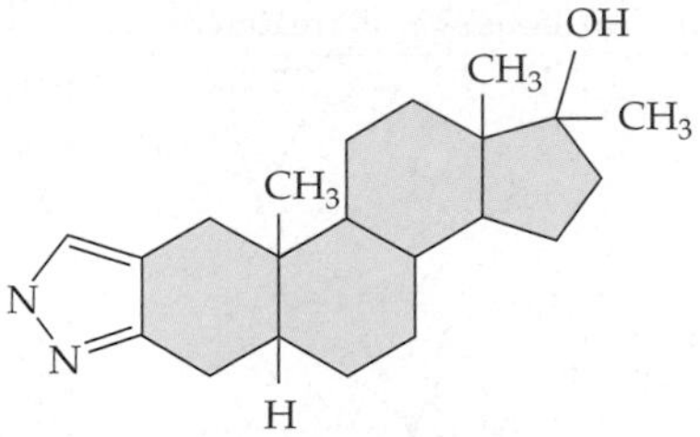

Stanozolol

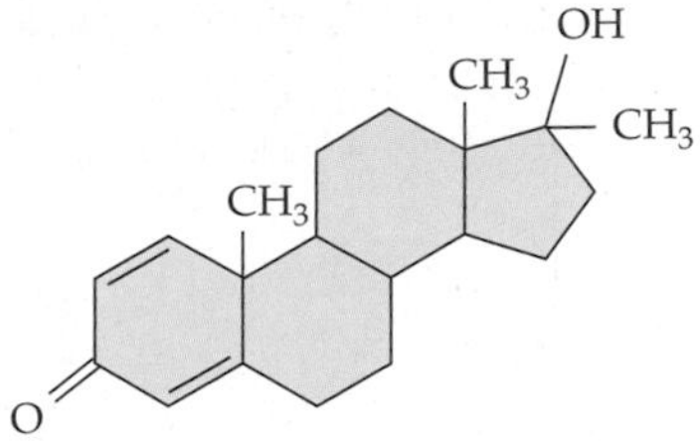

Methandrostenolone

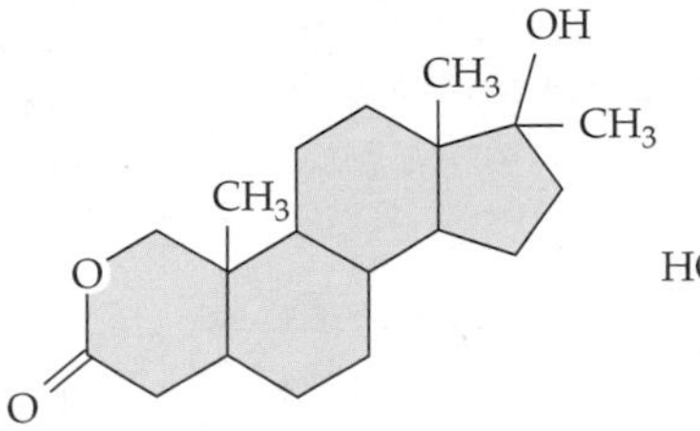

Oxandrolone

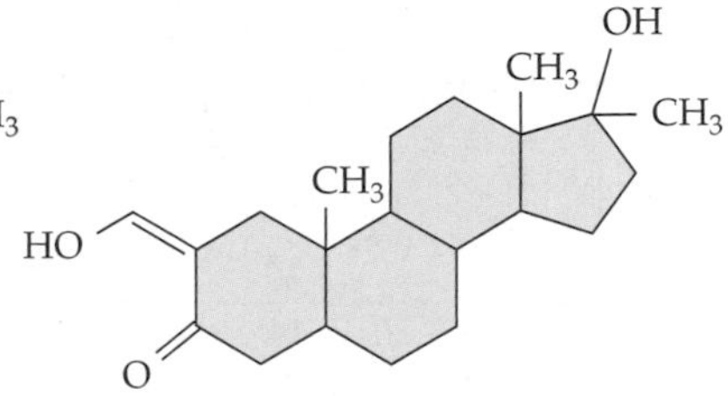

Oxymetholone

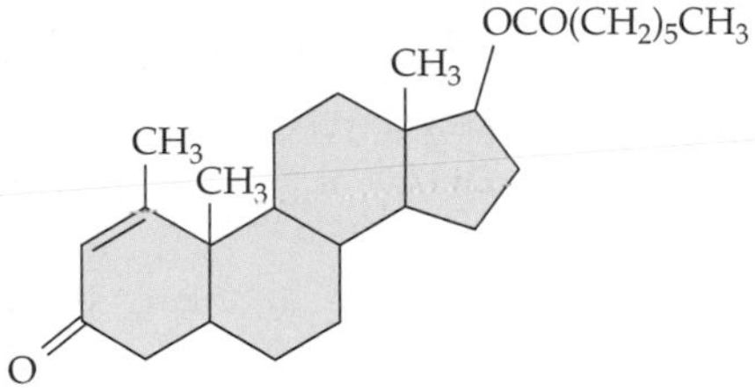

Methenolone enanthate

Figure 16.10 Chemical structures of some commonly abused anabolic steroids

held in Vienna, Austria. Until 1953, American weight-lifters had routinely beaten the Soviet team, but the Soviets outscored the Americans in that year and again in 1954. During the Vienna competition, the U.S. and Soviet Union team physicians reportedly went out in the evening for entertainment, and after a few drinks, the physician for the Soviet Union squad confided that some of his men were using testosterone. Dr. John Ziegler, who was the American physician, went back home and began to experiment with testosterone, but he didn't like the strong androgenic side effects. Ziegler expressed to the giant pharmaceutical company Ciba the need for a more anabolic, less androgenic compound. Within a few years, Ciba introduced Dianabol, an orally active compound with enhanced anabolic properties. When Dianabol was administered to elite weightlifters at the famous York Barbell Club in Pennsylvania, the drug produced spectacular results. Once the news got out, many similar compounds quickly followed, and strength athletes began to view steroids as the only way to reach the highest level of achievement. According to

a 1969 article in the magazine *Track and Field News* entitled "Steroids: Breakfast of Champions," these substances were readily available to athletes either from physicians who were willing to write the necessary prescription or even from some pharmacists who dispensed steroids without requiring a prescription (Hendershott, 1969). The "win at all costs" mentality of elite athletes can be seen in the results of a 1995 *Sports Illustrated* poll of almost 200 individuals who either had competed in the Olympics or were aspiring Olympians. When offered a scenario that the use of a banned performance-enhancing substance would (without fear of being caught) guarantee victory in every competition for the next 5 years but would subsequently result in death due to side effects, more than 50% of the respondents said that they would take the substance (Bamberger and Yaeger, 1997). Ziegler later recognized the monster that he had helped create, and by the time of his death in 1984, he profoundly regretted that part of his life.

Besides the Soviet Union, the German Democratic Republic (GDR, or East Germany) began secretly giving

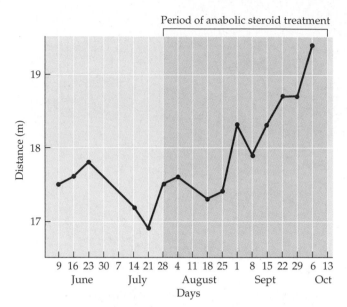

Figure 16.11 Performance enhancement of a former East German female shot-putter as a result of anabolic steroid treatment. Shot-put distance increased markedly over the 11-week period during which the athlete was given anabolic steroids. (After Franke and Beredonk, 1997.)

anabolic steroids to its elite athletes in the 1960s (Franke and Beredonk, 1997). The most commonly used compound in the GDR was chlordehydromethyltestosterone, known as Oral-Turinabol. The East Germans had especially great success with their female athletes, who won many Olympic and world championships with the aid of anabolic steroids. **Figure 16.11** illustrates the improved performance of a female shot-putter over an 11-week period of Oral-Turinabol treatment. Unfortunately, as we will see later, these competitors paid a high price for their achievements because of the powerful side effects of anabolic steroids in women.

Widespread public awareness of anabolic steroid use by elite athletes can be traced to the revelation that Ben Johnson, a Canadian sprinter and world record setter in the 100-meter dash at the 1988 Seoul Olympic Games, had been taking the banned steroid stanozolol during his training. Johnson was stripped of his Olympic gold medal and was suspended from athletic competition. More recently, a San Francisco–area enterprise called the Bay Area Laboratory Cooperative (BALCO) was reported to have provided anabolic steroids to a number of famous athletes, most notably Barry Bonds, who is the Major League Baseball career leader in home runs per season and total home runs. Both the public and sports journalists have responded strongly to allegations of steroid use, as reflected in the 2013 balloting for the Baseball Hall of Fame in which no suspected steroid user, including Bonds, Roger Clemens, and Sammy Sosa, was elected to the Hall.

By the mid-1980s, there were increasing reports of rampant anabolic steroid use not only in professional sports but also reaching down into colleges and even high schools. This progression was aided by the publication of practical guides to anabolic steroid use, such as Duchaine's *Underground Steroid Handbook* and Phillips' *Anabolic Reference Guide* (Kanayama et al., 2010a). In response, the U.S. Congress held a series of hearings between 1988 and 1990 that culminated in the Anabolic Control Act of 1991. This legislation classified 27 specific anabolic steroid preparations as Schedule III controlled substances, thus making their use illegal without a medical prescription. In addition, these substances are banned by many amateur and professional sports organizations, including the National Collegiate Athletic Association, the International Olympic Committee, the National Football League, the National Basketball Association, and Major League Baseball.

Anabolic steroids are currently taken by many adolescent and adult men

Despite legal restrictions governing the availability of anabolic steroids for nonmedical purposes, these compounds continue to be used and abused because of their availability from various websites without a prescription. For a number of years, the popular media have promoted an image of muscularity as one of the defining characteristics of masculinity, and this image has contributed to the expansion of anabolic steroid use beyond the traditional groups of strength athletes and bodybuilders. Indeed, a recent web-based survey of male anabolic steroid users found that improving one's physical appearance was rated just as important as increasing one's strength as a motivation for such use (Ip et al., 2011). Studies on the prevalence of anabolic steroid use have yielded an overall estimate that at least 3% of young men in Western countries have taken one or more of these substances at some time in their lives, including 1 to 3 million men in the United States (Kanayama et al., 2010b; Sjöqvist et al., 2008). As the use of anabolic steroids may begin in high school or even earlier, programs such as ATLAS (Adolescent Training and Learning to Avoid Steroids) have been developed to educate young people about the dangers of steroids and to deter their use (Mulcahey et al., 2010).

Anabolic steroids are taken in specific patterns and combinations

Anabolic steroids are taken in a variety of doses, patterns, and combinations (Mottram and George, 2000). Endurance athletes (e.g., marathon runners) and sprinters tend to take relatively low doses of steroids, whereas bodybuilders and strength athletes like

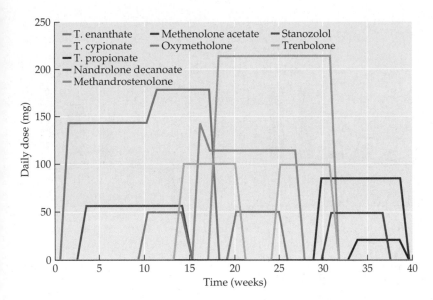

Figure 16.12 Typical dosing patterns of different anabolic steroids Each line depicts time-related increases and decreases in use of a particular steroid, sometimes in combination with another steroid. Together, these dosing regimens are illustrative of cycling, pyramiding, and stacking. (After Oberlander and Henderson, 2012.)

weightlifters may take up to 100 times the therapeutic doses of these hormones. Anabolic steroids are often used in patterns called **cycling**. Cycles are typically 6 to 12 weeks in duration, with periods of abstinence between successive cycles. Athletes use cycling for the following reasons:

1. To minimize the development of tolerance to the drug
2. To reduce the occurrence of adverse side effects
3. To maximize performance at an athletic competition
4. To avoid detection of a banned substance

Cycling is sometimes combined with **pyramiding**, in which the steroid dose is gradually increased until the midpoint of the cycle, and then is gradually decreased as the cycle is completed. Pyramiding is thought to reduce possible withdrawal effects resulting from sudden termination of steroid use. Another common feature of steroid use is **stacking**, which refers to the simultaneous use of two or more anabolic steroids. Stacking is often done by combining a short-acting oral steroid with a long-acting injectable preparation. **Figure 16.12** illustrates some typical patterns of concomitant steroid use demonstrating the phenomena of cycling, pyramiding, and stacking. It is important to note that many of the reasons offered for using anabolic steroids in these patterns are based on anecdotal information rather than on controlled scientific studies.

Finally, anabolic steroid users frequently engage in **polypharmacy**, in which additional substances are taken to augment the performance-enhancing properties of the steroids, to attempt to mask their presence in the individual's system, and/or to minimize some of the undesirable side effects that are discussed later on. The World Anti-Doping Agency (WADA) maintains a

record of positive doping results from accredited testing laboratories around the world. The 2010 WADA report reveals that more than 60% of positive doping tests that year were for anabolic agents (mainly steroids); 10.4% for stimulants such as amphetamine, methylphenidate, or cocaine; 9.6% for cannabinoids; 7.1% for masking agents including diuretics; 4.2% for glucocorticoids (taken for their anti-inflammatory and analgesic effects); 3.8% for β2-adrenergic receptor agonists; and the remainder for other substances (WADA, 2011) (**Figure 16.13**). These findings confirm that doping by elite athletes involves the use of a variety of other banned drugs in addition to anabolic steroids.

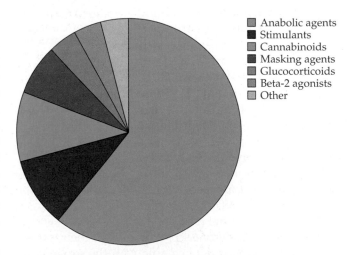

Figure 16.13 World Anti-Doping Agency analytical findings for banned substances The graph shows the relative percentage of banned substances detected in positive doping tests conducted by accredited laboratories in 2010. More than 60% of these tests included one or more anabolic agents, mainly steroids. (After World Anti-Doping Agency, 2011.)

Pharmacology of Anabolic Steroids

Anabolic steroids are unlike other abused substances discussed in this book because of their powerful action on muscle. However, they are similar to other abused substances in their ability to produce adverse health effects and dependence in some users.

Research is beginning to unravel the mechanism of action of anabolic steroids on muscle

Although users had long touted the beneficial effects of anabolic steroids on muscle mass and strength, many researchers remained unconvinced by these anecdotal reports because properly controlled scientific studies were lacking and arguments could be made that placebo effects, increased training motivation, or other confounding factors might be responsible for the enhanced performance of anabolic steroid users. However, a series of studies by Bhasin and colleagues showed that giving high doses of testosterone to healthy young men leads to muscle fiber hypertrophy (increased size), increased muscle mass, and enhanced strength (Bhasin et al., 1996, 2001; Sinha-Hikim et al., 2002). Some of the results from one of these studies are presented in Figure 16.14 (Bhasin et al., 2001). The subjects were given weekly injections of testosterone enanthate at different doses for a period of 20 weeks. They also received another drug at the same time to suppress endogenous testosterone secretion, so that their testosterone levels would depend solely on the exogenous treatment. The lowest doses (25 and 50 mg per week) produced subnormal circulating testosterone concentrations, the 125-mg dose produced concentrations in the normal range, and the 600-mg dose produced testosterone levels that were at least 4 times the average pretreatment concentration. As shown in **Figure**

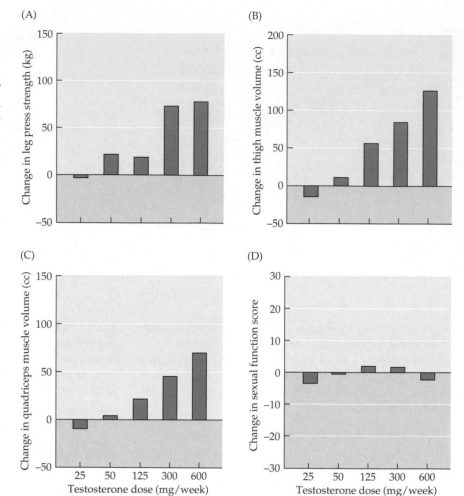

Figure 16.14 Increased muscle strength and volume following chronic testosterone administration to men. The subjects were healthy men, 18 to 35 years of age, who had prior weightlifting experience but who had not previously taken anabolic steroids. All subjects were given monthly treatments with a long-acting drug to suppress their endogenous testosterone synthesis. Matched groups were also administered weekly intramuscular injections of testosterone enanthate for 20 weeks at doses ranging from 25 to 600 mg per injection. A comparison of circulating testosterone levels at the beginning of the study (baseline) with levels present at the 16-week time point showed that the 25- and 50-mg doses produced testosterone concentrations significantly below baseline, the 125-mg dose produced concentrations similar to baseline, and the 300- and 600-mg doses produced testosterone levels that were approximately two to four times baseline, respectively (data not shown). Leg press strength (A), thigh muscle volume (B), quadriceps muscle volume (C), and sexual function as determined by sexual activity and desire (D) were assessed at baseline and at the end of the 20-week dosing period. Muscle strength and volume were enhanced by increasing doses of testosterone, whereas sexual function remained relatively constant regardless of dose. (After Bhasin et al., 2001.)

16.14A–C, anabolic steroid administration caused dose-dependent increases in muscle volume and strength. In contrast, sexual function was unchanged (**Figure 16.14D**), indicating that this aspect of androgen action is not influenced by testosterone level within the dose range used and over the time period of testing. The findings of Bhasin's group are very important because they were obtained under carefully controlled

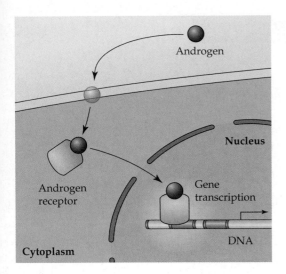

Figure 16.15 Mechanism of action of androgens in gene transcription Androgens enter target cells by diffusing across the cell membrane. After the hormone binds to androgen receptors in the cell cytoplasm, the hormone–receptor complex translocates to the cell nucleus, where it alters the transcription of specific genes.

conditions. However, it is worth noting that even greater effects may be obtained by users taking still higher doses of steroids and combining the treatment with intensive strength training.

Determining the mechanisms underlying the strength-enhancing effects of anabolic steroids has also proven challenging; however, researchers have begun to reach consensus as to the relevant processes. Anabolic steroids all have androgenic action, which means that they are agonists at the **androgen receptor**. These receptors are present in many different tissues, including skeletal muscle. In the inactive state, androgen receptors are located in the cytoplasm of the cell (**Figure 16.15**). Androgen molecules diffuse across the cell membrane and bind to the receptor, thereby activating it. The activated hormone–receptor complex then translocates into the cell nucleus, where it regulates the transcription of specific genes, depending on the cell type. The result in this case is to increase overall muscle protein synthesis with a particular influence on proteins needed for muscle growth.

Anabolic steroids exert several additional effects that contribute to muscle growth, two of which will be mentioned here. One important effect is to increase the proliferation of so-called satellite cells that are necessary for the formation of new myotubes (developing muscle fibers). A second effect is to promote the differentiation of local stem cells into muscle cells while inhibiting an alternate differentiation pathway into adipose (fat) cells (Kadi, 2008; Lippi et al., 2011). The discovery of these mechanisms has given researchers

considerable insight into how the use of anabolic steroids can enhance muscle growth, increase strength, and improve athletic performance.

Many adverse side effects are associated with anabolic steroid use

Table 16.4 presents some of the potential adverse side effects of anabolic steroid use. We will first discuss side effects that involve the user's physical condition, after which we will consider behavioral and psychological effects. Abnormalities in heart structure and function, high blood pressure, and reduced high-density lipoprotein (HDL) cholesterol have been reported in some anabolic steroid users (Angell et al., 2012; Turillazzi et al., 2011). Nascimento and Medei (2011) suggest that these cardiotoxic effects increase the risk of sudden cardiac death in steroid users. Liver toxicity, which is particularly associated with oral steroid use, ranges from mild effects such as elevated liver enzymes in the bloodstream to more serious but rarer complications including peliosis hepatis and liver tumors (Neri et al., 2011). The kidneys play an important role in the clearance of anabolic steroid metabolites. As with liver toxicity, steroid-associated renal toxicity typically manifests in a mild, unsymptomatic form characterized by elevations in creatinine and blood urea nitrogen (BUN) levels in the bloodstream (Turillazzi et al., 2011). On the other hand, excessive steroid use has been linked to severe impairment in renal function. Skin and hair problems are common in anabolic steroids users, with a particularly high risk of outbreaks of acne (Melnik et al., 2007) (**Figure 16.16A**). Steroid use can adversely influence reproductive function (all the way up to infertility in men; de Souza and Hallak, 2011) as well as secondary sex characteristics in both men and women. For example, **Figure 16.16B** illustrates the masculinizing effects of these compounds in women, which are irreversible. Young people who are still growing also need to be concerned about the possible stunting effects of anabolic steroids produced by premature closure of the epiphyses.[3] Which side effects occur depends on a number of factors, including the age and sex of the user, the type of steroid used (especially oral versus injectable), the dose, and the pattern and duration of use. Regardless, the long list of potential adverse health effects, some of which can be quite serious, certainly provides adequate warning to anyone who is contemplating the use of these substances.

---

[3]These are the end regions of long bones, which retain the capacity to further lengthen the bone. Once the epiphyses are "closed," the individual stops growing.

TABLE 16.4	Potential Health Consequences of Anabolic Steroid Use
Category	**Effects**
Cardiovascular effects	Left ventricular hypertrophy
	Abnormal cardiac structure and electrical activity
	Hypertension (high blood pressure)
	Decreased HDL cholesterol (the "good" kind of cholesterol)
Effects on the liver (particularly from oral steroid use)	Jaundice
	Peliosis hepatis (blood-filled cysts in the liver)
	Tumors
Effects on the kidneys	Elevated serum creatinine and blood urea nitrogen (BUN) levels
	Impaired renal function
Effects on the skin and hair	Oily skin and scalp
	Severe acne
	Male pattern baldness
Growth effects	Growth stunting in adolescents due to premature epiphyseal closure
Behavioral effects	Increased libido (sex drive)
	Mood changes (depression and mania)
	Increased anxiety, irritability, and aggressiveness
	Muscle dysmorphia
	Dependence
Specific effects on men	Testicular shrinkage
	Reduced sperm counts and possible infertility
	Prostate enlargement
	Gynecomastia (breast development)
Specific effects on women	Menstrual abnormalities
	Deepening of the voice
	Excessive hair growth, especially on the face
	Enlargement of the clitoris
	Decreased breast size

Chronic use of anabolic steroids has also been associated with a variety of psychological and behavioral effects. We will focus here on abnormalities in mood (ranging from mania to depression), body image, and anxiety/irritability and aggressiveness. The relationship between anabolic steroids and psychological and behavioral variables has been investigated using prospective studies (controlled administration of steroids or placebo to subject groups), naturalistic studies (investigation of steroid users compared with control subjects), and individual case reports. Naturalistic studies and case reports suffer from the limitation that differences observed between steroid users and non-users may have preceded the onset of use. Keeping this limitation in mind, current findings from the anabolic steroid literature suggest that a relatively small subset of vulnerable individuals does experience psychological and behavioral abnormalities following repeated exposure to high doses of these compounds. In such vulnerable individuals, heavy steroid use can

(A)

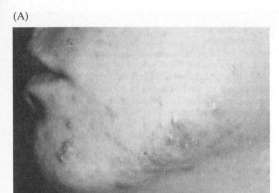

(B)

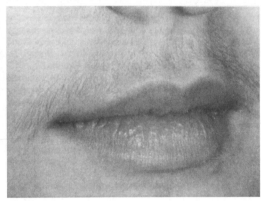

Figure 16.16 Facial acne and facial hair growth in anabolic steroid users Anabolic steroids can cause severe acne in users (A) and can also stimulate the growth of facial hair in women (B). (Photographs courtesy of Dr. Michael Scott.)

lead to extreme mood changes typically consisting of mania (abnormally elevated or irritable mood, racing thoughts, grandiosity, and sometimes including psychotic delusions) or hypomania (less intense manic symptoms with no psychosis) during periods of active use that contrast with depressive episodes during steroid withdrawal (Kanayama et al., 2008; Trenton and Currier, 2005). In severe cases, depressed mood has included suicidal ideation and behavior. Anabolic steroids have also been associated with an unusual male body image disorder called **muscle dysmorphia** (Rohman, 2009). This disorder, which has also been called "reverse anorexia," is characterized by a false perception that the sufferer is weak and small, constant checking of bodily appearance in mirrored surfaces, concealing one's body shape by means of loose-fitting and baggy clothing, and a preoccupation with working out and using steroids to enhance muscle growth. Finally, anabolic steroid use has long been associated with increased anxiety/irritability and

aggressiveness, leading, in the most extreme cases, to violent outbursts known on the street as "'roid rage." The relationship between steroids and aggressiveness is discussed in **Box 16.2**.

Regular anabolic steroid use causes dependence in some individuals

By the late 1980s and early 1990s, reports began to appear suggesting that some anabolic steroid users meet *DSM* (*Diagnostic and Statistical Manual of Mental Disorders*) criteria for dependence on these substances. Case studies and self reports by bodybuilders and athletes provide some insight into the nature of steroid dependence. One such case is that of Lyle Alzado, a three-time All-Pro NFL defensive end who played for 15 seasons with the Denver Broncos, Cleveland Browns, and Los Angeles Raiders before coming down with brain cancer and dying in 1992 at the age of 43. In a 1991 interview with *Sports Illustrated*, Alzado admitted taking steroids beginning in his college days and continuing throughout his NFL career and beyond. At the height of his steroid use, he would cycle 10 to 12 weeks on steroids and then go off the drugs for only 2 to 3 weeks before starting again. In his own words, "It was addicting, mentally addicting. I just didn't feel strong unless I was taking something." Alzado also described the aggressiveness produced by his steroid use. "I became very violent on the field. Off it, too. I did things only crazy people do. Once in 1979 in Denver, a guy side-swiped my car, and I chased him up and down hills through the neighborhoods. I did that a lot. I'd chase a guy, pull him out of his car, beat the hell out of him" (Alzado, 1991).

Kanayama and coworkers (2009) recently summarized the results of five field studies that assessed the prevalence of *DSM* dependence criteria in 426 anabolic steroid users. When these studies are taken together, the percentages of users exhibiting specific criteria were as follows: tolerance, 20.7%; withdrawal, 44.6%; taking the substance in larger amounts than intended, 27.9%; unable to cut down or control use of the substance, 12.0%; significant amount of time spent on substance-related activity, 28.6%; other activities reduced in favor of substance use, 17.8%; and continued substance use despite recognition of use-related problems, 24.9%. Most important, 33.8% of the users studied met three or more of the above criteria, indicating that they were classified as being dependent on anabolic steroids.

There are both similarities and differences in the characteristics of anabolic steroid dependence compared with the characteristics of dependence on typical drugs of abuse. One major similarity is the

BOX 16.2   Of Special Interest

Anabolic Steroids and "'Roid Rage"

You may have heard the term "roid rage" used to describe a sudden eruption of intense anger or violent behavior by someone taking anabolic steroids. Case reports have documented instances in which violent outbursts appear to be linked to heavy steroid use. But before we discuss such extreme examples of violent behavior, it's important to consider information about the general relationship between anabolic steroids and irritability and aggression. Several (although not all) studies comparing steroid users with non-users found evidence for increased agitation, irritability, feelings of aggression, aggressive behavior (including both verbal and nonverbal), and violence in the user group (Trenton and Currier, 2005). One particularly interesting study by Pagonis and coworkers (2006a) found large increases in hostility, phobic anxiety, paranoid ideation, and psychoticism (measured by means of the Symptom Checklist-90 [SCL-90]) following a cycle of steroid use compared with pre-cycle levels in a group of amateur and recreational athletes and bodybuilders. These changes were most marked in a subgroup characterized as heavy (ab)users, thereby demonstrating a dose dependency of the mood-altering effects of anabolic steroids.

The same research group additionally reported on two pairs of male monozygotic twins, of which one member of each twin pair was a steroid user. The SCL-90 again revealed noteworthy differences between users and non-users, with consistently higher hostility and paranoid ideation scores in the users (Pagonis et al., 2006b). The mechanism by which anabolic steroids increase irritability and

aggression in humans is not yet understood; however, studies on experimental animals such as rats and Syrian hamsters have demonstrated the ability of these hormones to elicit aggressive behavior and have provided much information on the underlying mechanisms in such animal models (Melloni Jr. and Ricci, 2010; Oberlander and Henderson, 2012).

Despite the ability of anabolic steroids to increase hostility and aggressive tendencies, outbursts of violent behavior are much less common. Nonetheless, data on over 6000 survey respondents from the National Longitudinal Study of Adolescent Health found a statistically significant association between steroid use and violent behaviors such as physical fighting (Beaver et al., 2008). Of course, a mere association doesn't demonstrate causation, as it is possible that individuals with a propensity to engage in violence also tend to be attracted to anabolic steroids to enhance their strength and physical appearance. Individual case studies may help in this regard, particularly if information is available to compare the person's behavior prior to the onset of steroid use with his behavior afterward. One extreme case of this kind is described in Katz and Pope (1990). Mr. X, as he is referred to, was a 23-year-old male who had been bodybuilding for 5 years. While in high school and prior to beginning his use of steroids, Mr. X drank alcohol socially and occasionally snorted cocaine with friends. He had no history of psychiatric illness, nor was he known to have ever committed a violent act. Indeed, his father was a minister, and Mr. X himself had been an active member of the church's youth ministry.

He was described by friends as a considerate, religious person. At the age of 21, Mr. X began the first of two cycles of anabolic steroid use in order to improve his competitive standing as a bodybuilder. During this time, he started to experience severe mood swings, including noticeable increases in irritability and argumentativeness. Quoting Katz and Pope,

On more than one occasion he tore chunks of aluminum out of cans with his teeth to intimidate bystanders. He also ripped telephones out of the wall on impulse. At this time, he met DSM-III-R criteria for a manic episode with decreased desire and need for sleep, explosive temper, extremely reckless behaviors with a high potential for dangerous and undesirable consequences, continued irritability, and grandiosity that reached delusional proportions. While out one weekend evening with some friends during the second course of anabolic steroids, the group stopped at a small market. While in the parking lot, Mr. X, without known or observed provocation, suddenly wrapped his arms around the telephone booth, tore it from its base, and threw it across the lot. The group left immediately and soon thereafter saw a hitchhiker on the road. Mr. X told the driver to stop. After the hitchhiker, a stranger to all present, entered the vehicle, Mr. X instructed the driver to drive to a remote spot in the woods. Once there, without instigation, Mr. X beat the victim repeatedly, tied him between two poles, smashed a wooden board over his back,

---

BOX 16.2 *(continued)*

and kicked him. The hitch-hiker was found dead the next morning (p. 220).

Mr. X was arrested, convicted, and incarcerated for his crime. Once off steroids, however, he reverted to his previous personality traits. In prison he was described as quiet, modest, and accommodating.

Indeed, he was astonished at the acts he had committed that fateful evening.

While case reports such as this do not prove a causal effect of anabolic steroids on violent behavior, they raise the possibility that such an effect may occasionally occur. On the other hand, this kind

of extreme "roid rage" is a rare event even among heavy users. We may speculate that some individuals are particularly susceptible to steroid-induced aggressiveness, and that steroid users who engage in violent acts (such as Mr. X) are among the susceptible group.

---

occurrence of withdrawal symptoms when substance use is discontinued. In the case of anabolic steroids, withdrawal symptoms can include fatigue, depressed mood, insomnia, restlessness, anorexia, decreased libido, dissatisfaction with body image, and a desire for more steroids (Brower et al., 1990, 1991). Important differences include the lack of an immediate steroid-induced euphoria or other intoxicating effect, relatively little impairment in the performance of daily activities, and less frequent occurrence of tolerance compared with many other abused substances (Kanayama et al., 2009). Moreover, even heavy steroid users rarely seek treatment for their problem, and specific treatment protocols for steroid dependence have yet to be developed and tested empirically (Brower, 2009; Kanayama et al., 2010a).

Information on the potential abuse liability of testosterone has also been obtained from self-administration and place-conditioning studies in rats, mice, and hamsters (Wood, 2008). For example, Wood and coworkers (2004) reported that hamsters would self-administer testosterone both intravenously and into the cerebral ventricles. The demonstration of testosterone reinforcement by the intracerebroventricular route is important in showing that this effect is mediated by the hormone's influence on the brain, not by its peripheral anabolic actions. On the other hand, the data also indicate that testosterone is not as strongly reinforcing as highly addictive drugs like cocaine, methamphetamine, or heroin, which is consistent with the lack of a rapid euphoric effect experienced by human anabolic steroid users.

Relatively little is known about the mechanisms underlying anabolic steroid reinforcement. However, there is evidence that this phenomenon probably is *not* mediated by the classical intracellular androgen receptors described earlier. For example, when different steroids were tested in self-administration or place-conditioning studies, their effects in these behavioral

models were not closely related to their affinity for the androgen receptor. More important, steroid self-administration still occurs in rats and mice carrying genetic mutations that greatly decrease androgen receptor functioning (Kohtz and Frye, 2012; Sato et al., 2008) (**Figure 16.17**). It is possible that some kind of membrane androgen receptor mediates these hormonal effects in models of self-administration and place conditioning; however, much additional research is required before this hypothesis can be confirmed.

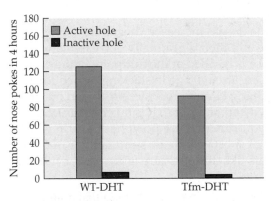

Figure 16.17 Intracerebroventricular self-administration of dihydrotestosterone in wild-type rats and rats carrying the testicular feminization (Tfm) mutation. Rats were trained to perform a nose-poke response for intracerebroventricular infusion of 1 μg of dihydrotestosterone (DHT) per every 5 responses (FR5 schedule of reinforcement). One hole for nose poking was active (associated with steroid delivery) and the other was inactive (responses in that hole had no consequence for the animal). Two groups were studied: wild-type (WT) rats and rats carrying the Tfm mutation, which codes for a nonfunctional androgen receptor. Although the Tfm rats responded somewhat less than the WT animals, both groups clearly acquired DHT self-administration (many more responses to the active compared with the inactive hole), indicating a positive reinforcing effect of the hormone in the absence of classical androgen receptors. (After Sato et al., 2008.)

Section Summary

- Anabolic–androgenic steroids are hormones that increase muscle mass and strength and also produce masculinizing effects in the user. These substances either contain the naturally occurring male sex hormone testosterone or are similar to testosterone in their chemical structure. Some anabolic steroids are taken orally, others by intramuscular injection.

- Anabolic steroids were initially developed for their muscle-building and performance-enhancing effects, but some current users take these substances mainly to attain a more muscular physical appearance. The Soviet Union was the first country in which steroids were administered to athletic competitors; however, the practice quickly spread to other countries. When the use and abuse of these substances became more widespread and numerous adverse side effects began to emerge, steroids were classified as Schedule III controlled substances in the United States. They were also banned by a variety of national and international athletic organizations.

- Anabolic steroids are usually taken in specific patterns and combinations. In the case of cycling, the steroid is taken in alternating on and off periods. Cycling can be combined with pyramiding, in which the dose is increased during the early part of the cycle and then is gradually decreased after the peak dose is reached at the midpoint of the cycle. Some users also engage in stacking, which refers to combining two or more steroids (often one that is injected and another that is taken orally). Steroid users frequently practice polypharmacy, in which additional substances (e.g., stimulants or masking agents like diuretics) are taken along with the steroid.

- Controlled studies have confirmed that anabolic steroids such as testosterone dose-dependently enhance muscle fiber size, muscle mass, and strength. These effects are mediated by intracellular androgen receptors and involve increased protein synthesis, proliferation of satellite cells that can form new myotubes, and differentiation of local stem cells into muscle cells.

- There are a number of adverse side effects of anabolic steroids. Chronic steroid users may exhibit cardiovascular problems such as abnormalities in heart structure and function, high blood pressure, and reduced circulating HDL. Other physiological side effects may include renal toxicity, skin and hair problems (e.g., severe acne), abnormal development of secondary sex characteristics, disruption of fertility, liver toxicity (particularly with oral steroid use), and risk of stunted growth in young users. Women are vulnerable to significant masculinizing effects of anabolic steroid use.

- Anabolic steroids have also been associated with a variety of psychological side effects. Mood shifts may range from depression to mania. Some individuals suffer from an unusual male body image disorder known as muscle dysmorphia. Case reports as well as controlled and naturalistic studies have also linked anabolic steroids with heightened irritability and aggressiveness manifesting, in the most extreme cases, as severe aggressive outbursts colloquially known as "'roid rage."

- A certain percentage of steroid users develop a characteristic pattern of dependence and withdrawal related to these substances. Intravenous and intracerebroventricular steroid self-administration has been demonstrated in laboratory animals, although steroids are not as strongly reinforcing as classical addictive drugs like cocaine or heroin. The mechanisms underlying steroid reinforcement are still being studied; however, recent research suggests that this phenomenon does not depend on the classical intracellular androgen receptor.

Go to the **COMPANION WEBSITE**

sites.sinauer.com/psychopharm2e
for Web Boxes, animations, flashcards, and other study resources.

Recommended Readings

Brower, K. J. (2002). Anabolic steroid abuse and dependence. *Curr. Psychiatry Rep.*, 4, 377–387.

Cooper, C. (2012). *Run, Swim, Throw, Cheat: The Science Behind Drugs in Sport*. Oxford: Oxford University Press.

National Institute on Drug Abuse. (2012). *Inhalant Abuse (Research Report Series)*. Available online at: www.drugabuse.gov/publications/research-reports/inhalant-abuse.

Nicholson, K. L. and Balster, R. L. (2001). GHB: A new and novel drug of abuse. *Drug Alcohol Depend.*, 63, 1–22.

A miner heats a ball of gold and mercury until only the gold remains. The process releases mercury vapor, which has devastating health consequences.

Environmental Neurotoxicants and Endocrine Disruptors 17

A SUN-DARKENED, WIZENED-LOOKING OLD MAN, supported by a distraught young man, erratically walked and stumbled into the emergency room (ER) of a small, semi-rural hospital. The old man's clothes and heavy boots were well worn and covered in dirt. As he got closer to the desk, the admitting clerk could see his drowsy eyes staring off into the distance. The young man nervously explained that he had found his grandfather wandering around in the hills after he did not come home as expected. The grandson said that his grandfather was not speaking coherently, and he did not seem to know where he was. Upon further questioning, it was determined that the high price of gold had prompted the old man to start reworking his gold mining claim about 6 months ago, after years of inactivity.

When the doctor examined the man, he saw an intention tremor, an inability to perform rapid alternating movements (adiadochokinesis, a clinical manifestation of cerebellar dysfunction), and mild rigidity. Hypertension and tachycardia also were present. The old man could not contribute to his medical history, but his grandson said that his grandfather had shaking hands for several months and recently had complained of headaches, fatigue, and a "pins and needles" feeling in his arms and legs.

When asked to explain what his grandfather did at the mine and if he had been exposed to anything, the young man said that his grandfather first mined the rock containing gold and then ground it up and mixed it with a silvery liquid until it formed a small ball (**Figure 17.1**). Then he heated the ball in a pan over a camp stove until just the gold was left. When asked where and how often this process was performed, the young man replied that when the weather was warm, the task was done outside almost every day, but since the weather was cold, his grandfather had moved the operation into the old mine shack.

Figure 17.1 Amalgamation Often the gold is so small that it is not easily seen or removed by panning methods—a lot can just float away. Mercury captures the gold in an amalgam. Gold miners crush rock that contains gold; extract as much rock by washing it away, or if the gold is in mud, just wash away the mud and let the gold settle out or float in the water; combine the remains (gold dust or bits) with mercury to form a ball (combined mercury and gold), as shown in the figure; and then burn off the mercury leaving the gold behind.

The ER doctor ordered standard blood and urine tests and urinary heavy metals. The urine sample revealed 748 μg mercury/l (normal range, 1 to 8 μg/l). The patient was given chelation therapy[1] with dimercaprol and gradually recovered from most effects over the next 6 months.

This chapter will explore the neurotoxic aspects of selected environmental toxicants and endocrine disruptors, including persistent and semi-persistent organic pollutants, insecticides, and toxic metals.

Neurotoxicity

Neurotoxicity is the adverse change in the structure or function of the central or peripheral nervous system. A **neurotoxicant**[2] is an element or compound that elicits this adverse effect by direct or indirect action on one or more components of the adult nervous system or the developing nervous system in utero or during childhood. Indirect actions include effects mediated via other systems that are necessary for the development or maintenance of nervous system function.

Neurotoxic effects may be transient or permanent and may manifest either immediately following exposure or at some later time, even years after exposure.

Individual neurotoxicants are found in many different chemical and product classes.

The mechanisms of neurotoxicity are far ranging but can be generalized into several broad classes: oxidative stress, cell death (necrosis or apoptosis; see Chapter 8), disruption of signaling pathways, disruption of homeostatic mechanisms, interference in neurotransmission, interference with synthesis or metabolism of key cellular components and macromolecules, and disruption of the endocrine system. Additionally, for the developing nervous system, mechanisms may include disruption of morphogenic signals (i.e., signals that regulate the structural development of the brain); interference with the morphogenic roles of hormones, neurotransmitters, and their receptors; and inappropriate stimulation of neuronal differentiation or apoptosis by various mechanisms. A diagram of brain development and the vulnerability of developmental processes is shown in **Figure 17.2**.

Exposures to environmental neurotoxicants and endocrine disruptors occur via air, water, soil, and food. Although these agents may exert toxicity in other organ systems, the nervous system is different because it is incompletely developed in children and neurogenesis is lacking in adults except for a few restricted brain areas; that is, in adults, destroyed neurons are not replaced, and their absence potentially affects multiple functions and numerous interconnections between cells of the nervous system and those of other organs.

The risk for neurotoxicity, as for any form of toxicity, is related to the intensity, frequency, and duration of exposure to the neurotoxic agent. Risk is also influenced by the physical and chemical (**physicochemical**) properties of the agent, the route of exposure,

---

[1]Chelation therapy is the administration of chelating agents. In the case of metals, it is the use of specific agents that will bind the metal at two or more sites (chelate) so that the metal will no longer react with biological molecules and will be eliminated from the body.

[2]The term *neurotoxin* is sometimes used in place of neurotoxicant; however, *neurotoxin* is generally reserved for those toxic substances produced by a living organism, such as botulinum toxin (botulism).

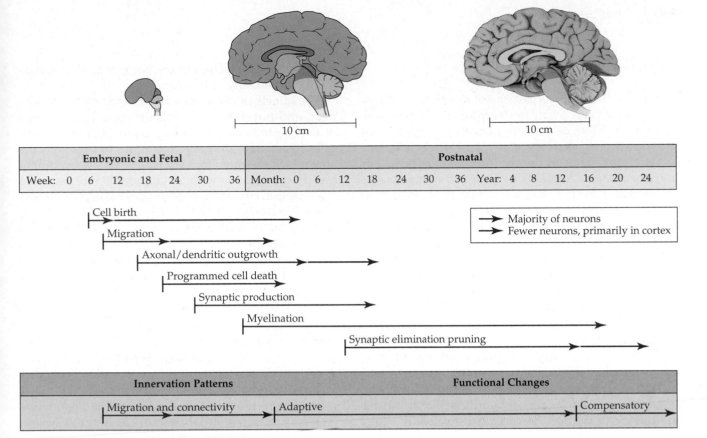

Embryonic and Fetal							Postnatal												
Week:	0	6	12	18	24	30	36	Month: 0	6	12	18	24	30	36	Year: 4	8	12	16	20	24

Cell birth
Migration
Axonal/dendritic outgrowth
Programmed cell death
Synaptic production
Myelination
Synaptic elimination pruning

→ Majority of neurons
→ Fewer neurons, primarily in cortex

Innervation Patterns	Functional Changes
Migration and connectivity → Adaptive	Compensatory

Figure 17.2 The development of the brain is shown from the embryonic and fetal stages on the left, progressing to 24 years of age on the right. The developmental processes and their duration are depicted in the center. Each process has its unique vulnerabilities to environmental insult. The bottom panel indicates that early alterations in normal processes can have lasting effects on neural connectivity and patterning, but later insults may be more adaptive or compensatory in nature. (After Andersen, 2003.)

the concentration achieved at the target site, and the inherent toxicity of the agent itself.

The young and the elderly are two potentially vulnerable populations with respect to the effects of neurotoxicants. For the young, the central nervous system (CNS) develops over an extended period postnatally, and any neurotoxic insult can induce morphological, functional, and behavioral changes that may persist throughout life. For the elderly, the natural aging process results in loss of nervous system plasticity and compensatory capacity.

Assessment of neurotoxicity in humans is based on clinical observations following exposure and the results of epidemiological studies specifically designed to investigate the association of exposure and neurotoxicity endpoints. Neuropsychological and behavioral testing performed in humans includes cognitive testing batteries, psychiatric and symptom questionnaires, behavioral and neurophysiological tests, and neuroimaging (e.g., magnetic resonance imaging [MRI], positron emission tomography [PET], and single-photon emission computed tomography [SPECT];

see Chapter 4). Additionally, blood and urine can be evaluated for neurochemicals, hormones, metabolites, and other biomarkers of interest.

Animal studies can raise questions of risk, help identify mechanisms of action, and explore the relationship of defined exposures (i.e., dose, route, and duration) to neurological endpoints. Several agencies throughout the world have developed guidelines for evaluating the potential neurotoxicity of agents in animal studies. The guidelines by the U.S. Environmental Protection Agency (EPA, 1998), as an example, give five categories of neurotoxicity evaluation:

1. Structural or neuropathological (e.g., morphological endpoints, **neurite** outgrowth, myelination of peripheral and central nerves, integrity of the blood–brain barrier)

2. Neurophysiological (e.g., axonal transport, electrophysiological indices, calcium homeostasis, hormone concentrations)

3. Neurochemical

4. Behavioral/neurological[3]

5. Developmental

Any identified adverse changes could then be investigated by appropriate means.

---

[3]The functional observational battery (FOB) is the primary means of screening and comprises a number of aspects of behavior and neurological functions to identify specific deficits in sensory and motor function.

Endocrine Disruptors

Endocrine disruption is just one of many mechanisms of action that can result in neurotoxicity. **Endocrine disruptors (EDs)**, as the name implies, interfere with the endocrine system and may cause adverse effects in development or in the reproductive, nervous, or immune system. An ED is a natural or synthetic substance that directly or indirectly interrupts the action of the endocrine system by altering the synthesis, metabolism, regulation, or transport of one or more hormones; altering the release of hormone from an endocrine gland; or altering the normal hormonal response at the level of the hormone receptor.

The first evidence for the adverse effects of what would later be described as an ED was published in 1971, when Herbst et al. (1971) reported that daughters born to women treated with diethylstilbestrol (DES) during pregnancy were diagnosed with uncommon vaginal adenocarcinomas during their teens and early 20s. DES is a synthetic nonsteroid with potent estrogenic properties that was administered during pregnancy to reduce the risk of complications and miscarriages. The effects and mechanisms of DES-induced endocrine disruption subsequently were investigated and confirmed in animal models. Since that time, there has been a growing awareness of the potential endocrine disrupting effects of environmental agents at low levels of exposure. In 2001, an expert panel for the U.S. National Toxicology Program (NTP) reported that there was sufficient evidence to support the endocrine disruption effects of DES, genistein (an isoflavone derived from soy inhibits thyroid hormone metabolism), methoxychlor (an insecticide that has estrogenic activity), and nonylphenol (an industrial chemical identified in drinking water supplies that has estrogenic activity) at low dose exposures (NTP, 2001). None of the recognized effects was directly related to the nervous system, and the only potential indirect effect was on brain sexual dimorphism by genistein and nonylphenol.

Endocrine disruptors can interfere at any level of the endocrine system, causing perturbations in normal function and homeostasis. For instance, EDs may mimic a natural hormone and bind to cellular receptors in the membrane, cytosol, or nucleus (see Chapter 3). As a mimic (or agonist), the ED can elicit the same response as the natural hormone, although the response may be different in magnitude. EDs can also act as antagonists and bind to a receptor without eliciting a response and prevent the binding of the endogenous hormone. Alternatively, EDs can bind and elicit a nontypical response. EDs also can have effects that are not dependent on hormone receptor binding. EDs can directly or indirectly interfere with normal hormone synthesis, metabolism, uptake, or release, thus affecting the availability of hormone.

The effects of hormones and EDs are dose dependent, and physiological concentrations can produce different effects than are produced by high or systemically toxic concentrations. Examples of dose-specific effects include signaling via a single steroid receptor at low doses versus signaling via multiple receptors due to nonselectivity at high doses, up-regulation at low doses versus receptor down-regulation at high doses, and high-dose cytotoxicity (toxicity to cells). The sensitivity of different organ systems to ED effects also can be related to differences in tissue receptor distribution and tissue specificity of endocrine-transcriptional elements.

As awareness of the effects of endocrine disruption grew, it was evident that endocrine disruption could also be responsible for perturbations in the nervous system resulting in neurological and neurobehavioral deficits. This chapter will focus on ED effects that potentially impact the nervous system.

The connection between the nervous and endocrine systems is complex and manifold. The nervous system is intimately involved in the actions of the endocrine system and vice versa, so much so that the term *neuroendocrine system* has been assigned to the interactions of the nervous and endocrine systems. As was previously mentioned in Chapter 3, the endocrine system consists of the following glands: pineal, hypothalamus, pituitary, thyroid, parathyroids, thymus, adrenals, pancreas, and ovaries in females, and testes in males. All endocrine glands act by secretion of a hormone into the bloodstream. That hormone then regulates some body system, which may be close in proximity or at some distance from the secreting gland.

One often thinks of hormones as steroids, but hormones also include amines (amino acid derivatives), polypeptides, and glycoproteins (proteins that contain one or more sugar molecules as part of their structure). Neurons can synthesize and release polypeptides that act as hormones and affect release of other hormones or hormone actions at target organs. An example is gonadotropin-releasing hormone (GnRH) a decapeptide from the basal hypothalamus that stimulates gonadotropin release from the anterior pituitary gland. If the synthesis or release of this hormone is altered, then downstream effects related to ovarian and testicular steroidogenesis (steroid hormone synthesis) and gametogenesis (formation of the gametes, namely, eggs and sperm) are also affected. Just as important as the hormones are the receptors for those hormones found throughout the body, including the CNS, where neurons of the noradrenergic, serotonergic, and dopaminergic systems express steroid hormone receptors.

(A)

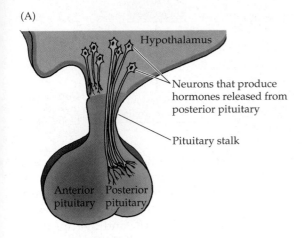

(B)

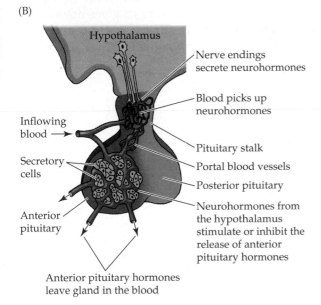

Figure 17.3 Neuroendocrine interactions at the hypothalamus and posterior and anterior pituitary (A) Neurons in the hypothalamus produce oxytocin and vasopressin. Action potentials travel down the axons to the axon terminals in the posterior pituitary where the hormones are released. (B) Neurohormones, known as releasing factors or hormones, are produced by and released from the hypothalamus. Hypothalamic hormones such as thyrotropin-releasing hormone (TRH), gonadotropin-releasing hormone (GnRH), growth hormone-releasing hormone (GHRH), and corticotrophin-releasing hormone (CRH), cause their corresponding hormones that are produced in the anterior lobe of the pituitary (throid-stimulating hormone [TSH], follicle-stimulating hormone [FSH], lutenizing hormone [LH], prolactin [PRL], growth hormone [GH], and adrenocorticotropic hormone [ACTH]) to be released into the circulation. (From Purves et al., 1998.)

A majority of studies published on potential EDs are related to the hypothalamic–pituitary–gonadal (HPG) axis and the hypothalamic–pituitary–thyroid (HPT) axis. The brief discussion here is limited to these two systems, but the principles of interaction apply for other components of the neuroendocrine system.

Hypothalamic–Pituitary–Gonadal (HPG) System

The hypothalamus controls reproductive function through complex interactions with the anterior pituitary. Endocrine disruptors can interfere with function in the adult and alter normal reproductive function. EDs can also have long-lasting effects on the developing organism. The regions of the hypothalamus that control the reproductive neuroendocrine systems undergo development during specific periods. That development is controlled in large part through exposure to endogenous estrogen and androgen hormones. Exogenous hormones may perturb steroidal actions by binding to steroid receptors, changing steroid metabolism, or altering normal sexual dimorphism. Disruption of normal brain sexual differentiation may affect both reproductive physiology and behavior later in life. For example, developmental exposures have been shown to affect mate preference behavior in rats that is passed on to subsequent generations through epigenetic modification of specific genes (Crews et al., 2007).

Hypothalamic–Pituitary–Thyroid (HPT) System

As mentioned previously, hormones released from the hypothalamus interact with the anterior pituitary. Thyrotropin-releasing hormone (TRH) is released from the hypothalamus and interacts in the anterior pituitary, where it causes release of thyrotropin, also known as thyroid-stimulating hormone (TSH). TSH,

The central neuroendocrine system is primarily responsible for the neural modulation of endocrine function near the brain, and it consists of interaction of the nervous and endocrine systems at the level of the hypothalamus and the posterior and anterior pituitary, as shown in **Figure 17.3**. Neural–endocrine interactions outside the area of the brain are often referred to as the diffuse neuroendocrine system. The central and diffuse neuroendocrine systems control diverse functions such as reproduction, metabolic energy balance, osmoregulation, and other homeostatic processes.

The neuroendocrine actions of EDs also may occur via non-hormonally mediated mechanisms. Numerous neurotransmitter systems such as dopamine (DA), norepinephrine (NE), serotonin (5-HT), glutamate, and others are sensitive to endocrine disruption via many mechanisms. The effects in these systems help to explain how EDs can negatively influence cognition, learning, memory, and other nonreproductive behaviors.

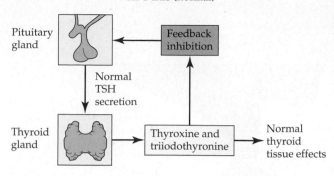

Figure 17.4 The normal release of TSH from the anterior pituitary and subsequent release of TH and its negative feedback. (After Baxter and Webb, 2009.)

as shown in **Figure 17.4**, stimulates the release of thyroid hormones (THs) (thyroxine [T4] and triiodothyronine [T3]). Under normal circumstances, the accumulation of TH will trigger a negative feedback response at the level of the anterior pituitary and inhibit TRH release and thus the downstream release of TH.

A complex neural circuitry in the hypothalamus regulates energy and metabolic homeostasis. Changes in thyroid gland function or interference with TH distribution or action may produce effects on

development, metabolism, or adult physiology. The function of the thyroid can be impacted directly or indirectly at different points of TH synthesis, release, transport, metabolism, and clearance. In addition, alterations in uptake of iodide (I^-) and disruption of the sodium/iodide co-transporter (NIS)[4] can affect thyroid hormone levels. **Figure 17.5** gives one an idea of the complexity of the HPT system and the multiple points at which an environmental neurotoxicant may interfere with normal TH synthesis.

[4]This cotransporter is also known as the Na^+/I^- symporter (NIS). NIS is a transmembranal protein that transports I^- along with Na^+ into follicular cells of the thyroid gland. I^- uptake is the first step in TH synthesis (Dohan et al., 2003).

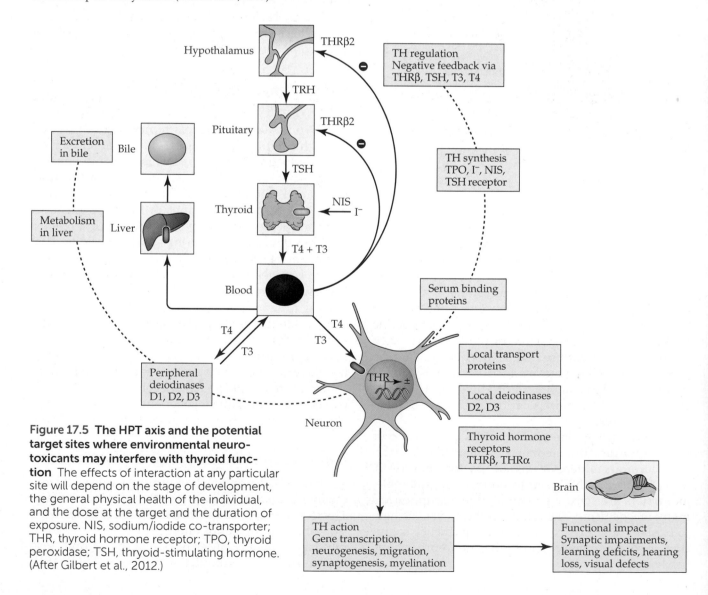

Figure 17.5 The HPT axis and the potential target sites where environmental neurotoxicants may interfere with thyroid function The effects of interaction at any particular site will depend on the stage of development, the general physical health of the individual, and the dose at the target and the duration of exposure. NIS, sodium/iodide co-transporter; THR, thyroid hormone receptor; TPO, thyroid peroxidase; TSH, thyroid-stimulating hormone. (After Gilbert et al., 2012.)

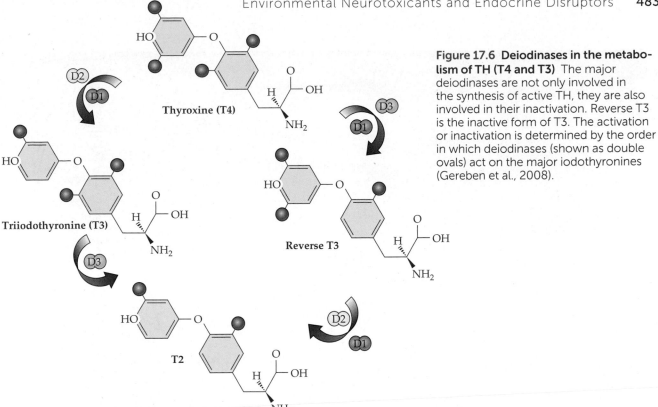

Figure 17.6 Deiodinases in the metabolism of TH (T4 and T3) The major deiodinases are not only involved in the synthesis of active TH, they are also involved in their inactivation. Reverse T3 is the inactive form of T3. The activation or inactivation is determined by the order in which deiodinases (shown as double ovals) act on the major iodothyronines (Gereben et al., 2008).

Once TH is secreted into the blood, its availability to cells can be affected by accessibility of specific carriers or binding proteins in the blood and by cell-specific transporters that control TH uptake into various tissues and cells. Inside the cell, T4 is converted to T3 by **deiodinases** (enzymes that remove iodine), which is an important step in TH action. There are several deiodinases present in tissues as shown in **Figure 17.6**. A number of environmental chemicals are known to affect deiodinase activity and produce symptoms and hormone levels that are not entirely consistent with hypothyroidism. In these cases, mechanistic studies are required to identify the etiology.

TH is known to play an essential role in normal brain development, and experimental hypothyroidism is associated with numerous neuroanatomical and behavioral effects, including deficits in learning and habituation, changes in anxiety, and hyperactivity in rats (Negishi et al., 2005; Zoeller and Crofton, 2005).

Figure 17.7 shows how TH mimetics might induce hyperthyroidism in some tissues while inducing hypothyroidism in others. The results are dependent on the distribution of tissues that can and cannot efficiently take up the TH mimetic.

The interested reader is invited to examine *The Endocrine Society's Scientific Statement*, which reviews studies of EDs and their mechanisms of action (Diamanti-Kandarakis et al., 2009) and two recent reviews published by Parent et al. (2011) and Vandenberg et al. (2012).

Section Summary

- Neurotoxicity is the adverse change in the structure or function of the nervous system.

- A neurotoxicant is an element or compound (agent) that elicits neurotoxicity via direct or indirect actions on the mature or developing nervous system.

HPT axis + TH mimetic

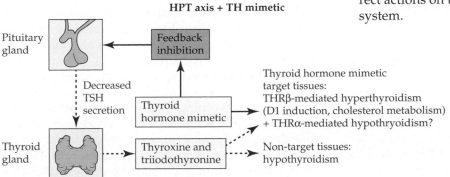

Figure 17.7 The influence of thyroid hormone (TH) mimetics on normal TH function potentially results in hyperthyroid-like effects in some tissues (target tissues) while producing hypothyroid-like effects in other tissues (non-target tissues). D1, deiodinase 1; THR, thyroid hormone receptor; TSH, thyroid-stimulating hormone. (After Baxter and Webb, 2009.)

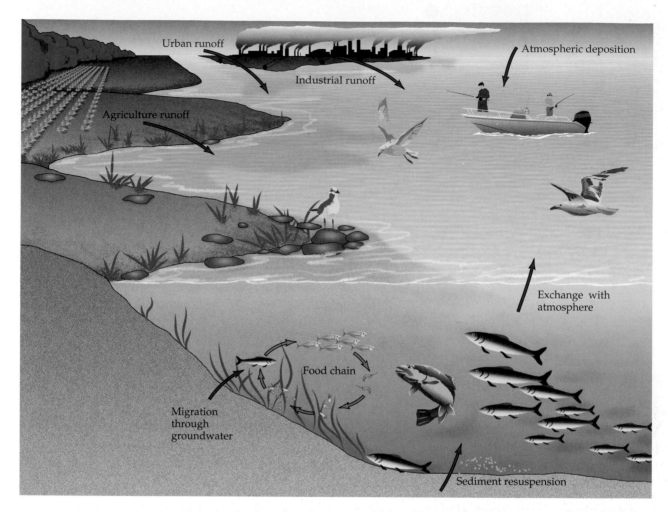

Figure 17.8 The distribution and accumulation of POPs in the environment and the food chain POPs enter the environment through atmospheric deposition and various types of runoff. Additionally, POPs deposited on land can reach surface waters by migrating through groundwater. Once in surface waters, the chemicals move up the food chain and become more concentrated by accumulating in the tissue of living organisms.

- Neurotoxicity is dependent on the agent, the exposure (dose, frequency, and duration), the route of exposure, the concentration at the target site, and the status of the nervous system (e.g., developing, mature, senescent).

- The mechanisms of neurotoxicity are numerous, including cell death, disruption of signaling pathways, and endocrine disruption, to name a few.

Persistent and Semi-Persistent Organic Pollutants

Persistent organic pollutants (POPs) are synthetic organic compounds that are resistant to environmental degradation through chemical, biological, and photolytic processes. The POPs are ubiquitous and persistent because of their physicochemical properties, which include low water solubility, high lipid solubility, semi-volatility, and relatively high molecular masses. POPs with molecular masses lower than 236 g/mole are less persistent in the environment (Ritter

et al., 1995). These pollutants are of concern because their persistence and lipid solubility result in **bioaccumulation** in fatty tissues and **bioconcentration** up the food chain. **Figure 17.8** depicts how POPs move in the environment, bioconcentrate in the aquatic food chain, and ultimately end up being consumed by humans and animals that eat fish or the animals that feed on fish. In addition to the aquatic cycles, animals bioaccumulate POPs by feeding on contaminated plants.

In May 1995, the United Nations Environment Programme Governing Council began investigating 12 priority POPs known as the "dirty dozen": aldrin, chlordane, DDT, dieldrin, endrin, heptachlor, hexachlorobenzene, mirex, polychlorinated biphenyls (PCBs), polychlorinated dibenzo-ρ-dioxins (PCDDs), polychlorinated dibenzofurans (PCDFs), and toxaphene (WHO, 2010). The list has been informally enlarged to include other organic pollutants, sometimes referred to as **semi-persistent organic pollutants (semi-POPs)**, such as bisphenol A (BPA), polycyclic aromatic hydrocarbons (PAHs), phthalates, and polybrominated diphenyl ethers (PBDEs), to name a few.

In the following sections, PCBs are discussed as an example of POPs, and PBDEs and BPA as examples of semi-POPs.

Polychlorinated Biphenyls (PCBs)

Polychlorinated biphenyls (**PCBs**) are synthetic chlorinated aromatic compounds that were used in industrial and consumer products such as dielectrical fluids in capacitors and transformers, hydraulic fluids, and lubricating oils, and in plasticizers. Although PCB production was banned in the late 1970s, they persist as environmental contaminants worldwide. There are 209 PCB **congeners** (chemicals synthesized by the same synthetic chemical reactions and procedures) containing from 1 to 10 chlorines (although technically not polychlorinated, the monochlorinated compounds are usually included in the discussion of PCBs) with corresponding molecular weights of 188.7 to 498.7 g/mole. The general structure of PCBs is shown in **Figure 17.9**.

The general population is exposed to PCBs primarily through ingestion of contaminated foods (e.g., fish, meat, dairy products). The fetus is exposed via placental transfer, and the infant via breast milk. Measurable levels of PCBs are found in the serum of a majority of the U.S. population (CDC, 2009, 2012a). Although individual congeners are present at low concentrations in human tissue, it is not unusual to be exposed simultaneously to a number of congeners with similar physicochemical properties because they migrate and bioaccumulate in similar manners. The longest half-lives for PCBs in humans are estimated to be 10 to 15 years (Ritter et al., 2011). Reports of longer half-lives have been attributed to ongoing exposure and weight gain (increased adipose tissue stores) with age.

There are two distinct categories of PCBs, referred to as *coplanar* and *non-coplanar* congeners. Coplanar molecules have a fairly rigid structure that potentially allows them to bind at the aryl hydrocarbon receptor (AhR)[5] and gives them a different toxicity profile than the non-coplanar congeners that do not bind at the AhR. As could be expected, classes of congeners with a similar mechanism of action are likely to act additively to produce effects. Although some studies have addressed specific PCB congeners, as opposed to mixtures, understanding the neurotoxicity of PCBs is hampered by the fact that many congeners have not been studied, and their potency as neurotoxicants is unknown. Overall, evidence for neurotoxicity of the PCBs is growing. No regulatory guidance for PCBs based on neurotoxicity, however, has been established by the EPA. Goodman et al. (2011) suggest that insufficient evidence from epidemiological studies, due to a lack of comparability across studies, make it impossible to establish a strong assessment based on a weight of evidence approach.

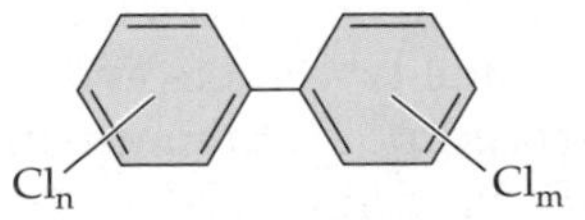

Neurotoxicity in adults

No reports of acute poisoning solely with PCBs have been identified. A variety of symptoms such as chloracne (an acne-like condition produced by some halogenated compounds), hyperkeratosis (abnormal thickening of the skin), goiter, pigmentation, abnormal nails, hearing loss, eye disorders, and jaundice are attributed to chronic PCB poisoning; however, there are no reports of PCB poisoning in the absence of other potential contaminants. In 1968 and 1979, there were mass poisonings via PCB-contaminated rice oil in Japan and Taiwan, respectively (Guo et al., 1999; Masuda, 2003). Clinical signs of toxicity were observed in thousands of people. Neurological studies performed in a subset of the Taiwan victims revealed electrophysiological sensory and motor neuropathies at 2 and 4 years post-exposure (Chia and Chu, 1985). In both the Japan and Taiwan incidents, the PCBs were co-contaminated with PCDDs and PCDFs, so it is impossible to know the contributions of these toxic compounds to the observed effects (WHO, 2010).

A more recent study of adults exposed chronically to PCBs via consumption of fish from the Great Lakes showed impaired memory and learning, but no effects on executive functioning (e.g., cognitive flexibility [or set shifting], response inhibition, working memory, attention, planning) and visuospatial function (Schantz et al., 2001). Other contaminants identified

Figure 17.9 General structure of PCBs The subscripts "m" and "n" refer to the number of chlorines attached to the phenyl rings.

---

[5]The AhR is a member of a family of transcription factors. The endogenous biomolecule that binds to this receptor is unknown. The receptor, however, is known to bind a variety of cyclical (ring-containing) exogenous molecules, some of which are naturally occurring, and others of which are generated by human activity (e.g., synthetic compounds like PCBs or compounds produced by combustion of fossil fuels).

from blood samples (i.e., lead, mercury, and dichloro-diphenyldichloroethylene [DDE]) were not associated with impairments. The authors were careful to state that their "study suggests … that PCB exposure during adulthood may be associated with impairments in certain aspects of memory and learning," and "it would be prudent to interpret the findings with caution until they have been replicated in an independent exposure cohort."

Neurotoxicity in children and the developing nervous system

The poisonings in Japan and Taiwan also raised awareness about the developmental toxicity of PCBs because the individuals most affected were children who had been exposed in utero. These children exhibited delayed cognitive development and behavioral problems, in addition to growth retardation (Guo et al., 2004). Further attention was drawn to this issue by studies of Jacobson and colleagues in the 1980s and 1990s that examined children from infancy to late childhood who had been exposed prenatally to PCBs through maternal fish consumption. They reported associations between higher PCB exposures and decrements in behavioral endpoints, such as decreased activity and hypotonic motor reflexes, and IQ. Voluminous research has been performed on PCB exposures and neurobehavioral endpoints; however, the findings have not been as consistent as one would hope. Several reviews have been written on one or more aspects of neuropsychological function following prenatal PCB exposure, and the interested reader is referred to those articles for additional information (Boucher et al., 2009; Schantz et al., 2003; Stewart et al., 2012). The following discussion gives a summary of the overall findings and controversies.

In an effort to identify a profile of cognitive effects from prenatal PCB exposure, Boucher et al. (2009) reviewed studies of nine prospective longitudinal birth cohorts from Canada, the Faroe Islands, Germany, Japan, the Netherlands, and the United States that examined prenatal PCB exposure and aspects of cognition in children. They identified the most consistently reported effect as impaired executive functioning. The authors also identified negative effects on processing speed, verbal abilities, and visual recognition memory in most of the studies. These effects appeared to be independent of sensory and motor functions.

Inconsistent results among epidemiological studies of PCBs and IQ have been interpreted by some as suggesting that, at most, a case could be made for subtle effects at low-level exposure. Stewart et al. (2012) hypothesized that confounding due to the presence

of non-PCB organochlorines such as DDE, hexachlorobenzene (HCB), and Mirex;[6] differences in maternal age, environmental factors, and parental IQ (leading to type I statistical error); and the presence of potential suppressor variables (leading to type II errors) could explain the lack of association between PCB exposure and IQ decrements in some studies. Their examination of the effects of confounding supported their hypothesis that IQ decreased but had been obscured. Additional studies with appropriate controls will be needed to lay the question to rest.

Studies of PCBs also are complicated by contaminants such as PCDDs and PCDFs. Measurement of PCDDs and PCDFs in epidemiologic studies has been rare because of analytical difficulties. In the Dutch PCB/PCDD study, however, lactational exposure to dioxin (a PCDD) was not associated with child cognitive abilities at 42 months of age (Patandin et al., 1999), suggesting that any observed effects were attributable to PCBs. Similarly, a German birth cohort study of PCDDs and PCDFs did not find an association with mental and psychomotor developmental indexes at 12 and 24 months of age (Wilhelm et al., 2008).

Developmental animal studies are supportive of the neurotoxic effects of PCBs. These studies have shown behavioral deficits across many different tests of executive function, including cognitive flexibility, working memory, and inhibitory control (Sable and Schantz, 2006). Animal PCB studies also have shown that altered motor behavior was associated with changes in cerebellar function and anatomy.

More recently, the question has been raised as to whether PCB exposure could be linked to the increased prevalence of attention deficit hyperactivity disorder (ADHD) (Eubig et al., 2010), although no human studies have directly assessed the association of ADHD with PCB exposure. Aspects of both executive functioning and attention are impaired in ADHD and with PCB exposure, which suggests a possible association. ADHD is a highly heritable disorder, however, and until human studies appropriately examine this confounder, the causal association of PCB exposure and ADHD is only speculation (Brondum, 2011).

Mechanisms of action

The mechanisms for the neurotoxic effects of PCBs are neither well known nor uniform across the 209 congeners. From the animal studies that have been conducted on individual congeners and congener mixes, the effects observed point to mechanisms related to

---

[6]Cohorts from the Great Lakes (Michigan and New York) showed the association of IQ with quartiles of PCBs and quartiles of HCB, both of which were similar in predicting IQ.

ED for some and to direct toxic action for others, while still other congeners and mixtures point to both mechanisms of action. Effects are seen with direct estrogenic or antiandrogenic activity, interaction at the AhR, interference with one or more aspects of thyroid function, and interference with neurotransmitter effects.

In rats, PCB congeners can affect the HPT axis in several ways, including causing a reduction in circulating levels of T4 or inhibiting the TSH response to thyrotropin-releasing hormone. From the available evidence, it appears that PCBs may exert different actions on thyroid function, depending on many factors.

PCBs also cause cell death, although mechanisms vary between congeners. Coplanar PCBs act through the AhR to induce cell death, while non-coplanar PCBs act through alteration of intracellular secondary messengers, alteration of cell membranes, or inhibition of DA synthesis.

Other potential mechanisms of action are interference in calcium homeostasis (affecting many calcium-dependent systems, including neurotransmitter release); inhibition of the DA transporter (responsible for reuptake of DA into the neuron) and the vesicular monoamine transporter (VMAT2) (responsible for packaging cytosolic DA into vesicles for later release); oxidative stress and production of reactive oxygen species (ROS); and alteration in long-term potentiation (LTP) (controlled by intracellular second messengers).

Polybrominated Diphenyl Ethers (PBDEs)

Polybrominated diphenyl ethers (**PBDEs**) are organobromine compounds that are used as flame retardants in products such as plastics, polyurethane foams, and electronics. PBDEs resemble PCBs in molecular structure and also have 209 possible congeners, containing from 1 to 10 bromines (although technically not polybrominated, the monobrominated compounds are usually included in the discussion on PBDEs) with corresponding molecular weights of 249.1 to 959.2 g/mole. See the structure of PBDEs in **Figure 17.10** and note the similarity to the PCBs.

PBDEs were commercially marketed as one of three mixtures: pentabrominated BDE (pentaBDE), octabrominated BDE (octaBDE), and decabrominated BDE (decaBDE) (ATDSR, 2004). PentaBDE, which was primarily used in North America, and octaBDE have been banned in the European Union (EU) and in several states in the United States. In 2004, the production of pentaBDE and octaBDE in the United States ceased voluntarily. Globally, decaBDE is the most widely used PBDE and is still produced in the United States and Europe. It must be remembered that all PBDE

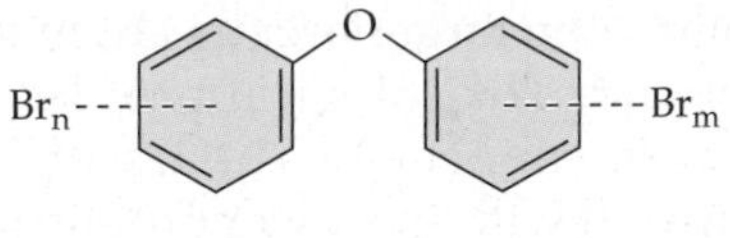

Figure 17.10 General structure of PBDEs The subscripts "m" and "n" refer to the number of bromines attached to the phenyl rings.

products are mixtures of congeners, not just a single congener.

Similar to PCBs, the PDBEs are lipophilic and bioaccumulate in the food chain (ATDSR, 2004). PBDEs have been detected in the air, sediments, soil, house dust, some foods, and many animal species. The general population is exposed to PBDEs primarily through diet and house dust. PBDEs have been detected in human tissues, blood, and breast milk. Five congeners of the tetra-, penta-, and hexaBDEs (congeners BDE-47, -99, -100, -153, -154) usually account for 90% of the total body burden (ATDSR, 2004; McDonald, 2005). Concentrations of PBDEs (primarily lower brominated congeners) are particularly high in breast milk (ATSDR, 2004). Estimated exposure of an infant through breast milk is about 0.3 µg/kg-day, with a range up to 4.1 µg/kg-day (Jones-Otazo et al., 2005). These levels are within the current **reference doses** (**RfDs**; estimates of the daily oral exposure of humans, including sensitive subgroups, which are not likely to cause harmful effects over a lifetime of exposure) of most PBDEs as set by the EPA (2008a-d).

Extremely high PBDE levels in humans also have been reported: maternal and fetal blood plasma concentrations as high as 580 and 460 ηg/g lipid, respectively (ATDSR, 2004), and a toddler with plasma levels of 418 ηg/g lipid (651 ηg/g if including BDE-209) (Costa and Giordano, 2007). These levels are nearly ten-fold that reported for the general U.S. population (Sjodin et al., 2008).

In rodents, the total body half-lives of all PBDEs are in the order of several days to several months; decaBDE is cleared most rapidly, with a half-life of less than 24 hours (ATDSR, 2004). The half-lives in humans are estimated to be several years for the lower brominated congeners, and days to months for the octa- to decaBDEs.

Neurotoxicity in adults

No reports were identified regarding PBDE neurotoxicity in adults. In contrast to the large database on PBDE body burden, there is almost no information on possible adverse health effects in humans from PBDE exposure. In rodents, PBDEs have low acute toxicity with oral LD_{50}s (lethal dose in 50% of animals) in animals greater than 5 g/kg (ATSDR, 2004). With chronic exposure, the target organs are liver, kidney, and thyroid gland. Toxicological profiles appear to be similar among congeners. The lesser potency of decaBDE compared with the lower brominated congeners appears to be related to differences in lipophilicity and bioaccumulation.

Neurotoxicity in children and the developing nervous system

Similar to adults, there is essentially no information on the neurotoxic effects of PBDEs in infants or children with acute or chronic exposure. There has been concern, however, regarding potential developmental neurotoxicity of PBDEs in humans (Costa and Giodano, 2007; McDonald, 2005). This concern arises from the following:

- PBDEs are known to cross the placenta and have been detected in fetal blood and liver.
- Developmental neurotoxicity has been reported following prenatal and early postnatal exposure of rodents to one or more PDBE congeners.
- Neurochemical changes are observed following developmental exposure of rodents to PBDEs.
- PBDEs affect TH homeostasis.
- PBDEs are excreted in milk.
- Infants and toddlers have the highest body burden of PBDEs because of exposure via maternal milk and house dust.
- Levels of PBDEs causing developmental neurotoxicity in animals are similar to those found in highly exposed infants and toddlers.
- Young animals have higher tissue concentrations than adults and may have a reduced ability to excrete PBDEs.

The daily intake of PBDEs for breast-fed infants, estimated at 20.6 ηg/kg-day in Taiwan, was correlated with lower birth weight and length, lower head and chest circumference, and decreased body mass index (Chao et al., 2007). Much higher infant PBDE exposure levels, however, have been estimated for Canada and the United States at 280 ηg/kg-day and 306 ηg/kg-day, respectively (Jones-Otazo et al., 2005; Schecter et al., 2006), which raises the question as to possibly greater effects in these populations.

Two epidemiological studies have shown significant effects following PDBE prenatal exposure. A longitudinal cohort study in New York of prenatal exposure to several PBDE congeners assessed neurodevelopmental effects at 12 to 48 months of age (Herbstman et al., 2010). Children with the highest exposure levels of three congeners (BDE-47, -99, and -100) scored

TABLE 17.1 EPA-Derived Chronic Oral RfDs for Single PBDE Congeners[a]

Congener	Number of chlorines	RfD[b]
BDE-47	4	100
BDE-99	5	100
BDE-153	6	200
BDE-10	10	7000

Source: EPA, 2008a–d.
[a]Based on developmental neurotoxicity in animals.
[b]Expressed in ηg/kg-day.

lower on mental and physical developmental tests. Some associations were statistically significant for 12-month Psychomotor Development Index (PDI) (BDE-47), 24-month Mental Development Index (MDI) (BDE-47, -99, and -100), 36-month MDI (BDE-100), 48-month full-scale and verbal IQ (BDE-47, -99, and -100), 36-month MDI (BDE-100), and 72-month performance IQ (BDE-100). A prospective cohort study in the Netherlands examined the association between neuropsychological functioning at 5 to 6 years and maternal blood organohalogens measured at 35 weeks of pregnancy (Roze et al., 2009). In this study, PBDEs correlated with worse fine manipulative abilities and attention, but with better visual perception and behavior.

Both short-term exposure of animals during the perinatal period and exposures throughout gestation to weaning commonly have resulted in alterations in motor activity and impaired learning and memory, with hyperactivity being most consistent (Driscoll et al., 2012). There is a question, however, of whether hyperactivity is permanent or only transient. One study suggests that BDE-209 reduces LTP and affects synaptic plasticity (Xing et al., 2009).

Table 17.1 shows the EPA RfDs for four BDE congeners. Note that the RfD for BDE-209 (the chlorine-saturated congener) is the greatest, which reflects its relatively lower toxicity. Confidence in the RfDs for all of these congeners, however, was listed as "low," reflecting the lack of human data and an inconsistency in animal data. To put these RfDs in perspective, the PBDE **no observed effect levels** (**NOELs**), determined in animal studies that examined either developmental neurotoxicity or TH changes, range from 140 to 1000 μg/kg-day (McDonald, 2005).

Mechanisms of action

Various animal studies of adult or prenatal and postnatal PBDE exposures have shown perturbation of the thyroid system and TH disruption, mostly reduced circulating levels of T4 or T3 (Costa and Giodano,

2007). The mechanism for this effect has not been elucidated. In a study of adult rats, a decrease in circulating T4 was found at 421 μg BDE-47/g lipid (Darnerud et al., 2007), which is about three orders of magnitude higher than levels measured in highly exposed humans. Although it has been proposed that PBDEs bind to the TH receptor (THR) because of their structural similarity to T4, in vitro studies have not revealed high affinity of PBDEs for the THR.

Human studies are still needed to confirm the potential effects on the TH system because rats and mice appear particularly sensitive (Herbstman et al., 2008). A recent epidemiologic study of PBDEs suggested a slight decrease of TSH in exposed pregnant women (Chevrier et al., 2010), but another study of electronic-waste recycling workers revealed higher TSH levels than in controls (Yuan et al., 2008). A study comparing maternal and fetal blood PBDE levels found no correlation with serum T4 concentrations (Mazdai et al., 2003). Clearly, well-designed studies investigating the relationship between body burden of PBDEs and child development are needed to validate the animal findings.

Additional mechanisms for PBDE-induced neurotoxicity are alterations in signal transduction pathways; induction of oxidative stress; interactions as antagonists or agonists at androgen, progesterone, and estrogen receptors;[7] induction of mixed-function monoxygenases (a family of enzymes that participate in many biochemical reactions); and inhibition of cytochrome P450 17 (CYP17), a key enzyme in the synthesis of testosterone (Canton et al., 2006).

Bisphenol A (BPA)

Bisphenyl A (BPA; 4,4-isopropylidenediphenol) is a synthetic monomer that is one of the highest production synthetic compounds worldwide. It is a semi-persistent organic pollutant (molecular weight, 228.3 g/mole) that is used primarily in the production of plastics, including polycarbonate plastics and epoxy resins. These materials are found in toys, compact disks, paints, food and beverage containers, dental sealants, and flooring (NTP, 2008). The chemical structure of BPA is shown in **Figure 17.11**.

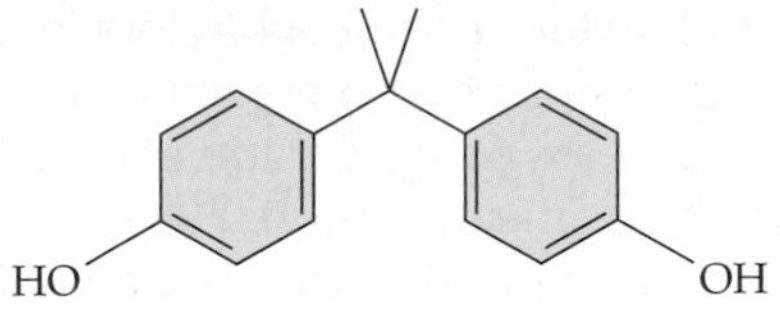

The primary source of exposure for the general population is through food and water. It has been estimated that human consumption of BPA from epoxy-lined food cans alone is over 6 μg/person-day (Chapin

Figure 17.11 Chemical structure of BPA

et al., 2008). The neonate is exposed to BPA through infant formula, maternal milk, or canned food. Concentrations in the range of 1 to 10 ng/ml have been reported in the serum of pregnant women, fetal amniotic fluid, and cord serum collected at birth (Diamanti-Kandarakis et al., 2009).

BPA is quickly absorbed from the gastrointestinal (GI) tract following oral exposure. Little free BPA, the biologically active form, remains following metabolism in the liver to BPA-glucuronide, the primary metabolite of BPA (NTP, 2008). The half-life of the glucuronide, which is excreted in the urine, is less than 6 hours.

Data from the 2005–2006 National Health and Nutrition Examination Survey (NHANES) database for the U.S. population reported the daily intake of BPA at the 95th percentile to be 195.8 ng/kg for women and 237.9 ng/kg for men (LaKind and Naimon, 2011), which corresponds to 11.7 μg/day for a 60-kg (132 pound) woman and 16.7 μg/day for a 70-kg (154 pound) man. The Centers for Disease Control and Prevention (CDC) reported that of 2517 Americans aged 6 years and older surveyed in 2003–2004, 92.6% had detectable BPA (including metabolites) in their urine (Calafat et al., 2008). Similarly, a Canadian study found that 91% of people 6 to 70 years of age had detectable levels of BPA (Bushnik et al., 2010). There were no reports of acute or chronic toxicity identified in human adults.

Neurotoxicity in children and the developing nervous system

The effect of BPA in humans with regard to developmental neurotoxicity is an area of intense debate because of the inconsistencies in published findings (Braun et al., 2009). One U.S. prospective birth cohort study of infants assessed at 5 weeks of age did not identify any significant associations between neurobehavior and maternal urinary BPA measured at about 16 and 26 weeks of gestation (Yolton et al., 2011). However, investigators did report a trend toward hypotonia (decreased muscle tone) associated with BPA exposure at 16 weeks of gestation. In another study of prenatal BPA exposure in which maternal urinary BPA also was measured at about 16 to 26 weeks of pregnancy and at birth, the BPA levels were

---

[7]Most PBDEs have antiandrogenic activity; tetra- to hexaBDEs have potent estrogenic activity in vitro; heptaBDE and 6-OH-BDE-47, a metabolite of BDE-47, have antiestrogenic activity (Hamers et al., 2006; Meerts et al., 2001).

associated with externalizing behaviors (e.g., hyperactivity and aggression) that were stronger for females than males at 2 years of age (Braun et al., 2009). At the 95th percentile, the mean maternal urinary BPA values across the sampling period were 7.8 and 8.0 µg BPA/g creatinine for male and female offspring, respectively. A case report arising from the same study population noted a woman with a urinary BPA concentration of 583 µg/g creatinine at 27 weeks of pregnancy (cohort mean was 2.0 µg/g) and 1.9 µg/g at parturition (Sathyanarayana et al., 2011). Her infant male was normal at birth but presented with neurobehavioral abnormalities at 1 month. The etiology is unclear because the child was normal at birth and at annual evaluations performed from 1 to 5 years of age.

Animal studies have shown an association between prenatal and early postnatal exposure to very low BPA doses (10 to 100 µg/kg-day) and neurobehavioral effects such as increased anxiety, cognitive deficits, altered sexually dimorphic behaviors, and changes in dopaminergic and NMDAergic systems (Palanza et al., 2008; Poimenova et al., 2010; Tian et al., 2010). Other studies have showed no effects on reproduction, development, or sexual differentiation at similarly low doses (2 to 200 µg/kg-day) (Ryan et al., 2010).

The National Toxicology Program reported "some concern" for BPA's effects on the brain, behavior, and prostate gland in fetuses, infants, and children at current exposure levels (NTP, 2008). "Some concern" represents the midpoint level of concern used by the NTP where there are insufficient data from human studies but there is limited evidence of developmental changes in some animal studies at doses potentially relevant to humans. In January 2010, the U.S. Food and Drug Administration (FDA) announced that it agreed there is reason for some concern about the potential effects of BPA (FDA, 2010). The interested reader is invited to read an Expert Panel Report by the NTP Center for the Evaluation of Risks to Human Reproduction (CERHR)[8] on the reproductive and developmental toxicity of BPA (Chapin et al., 2008).

Mechanisms of action

The primary mechanism of action for BPA is endocrine disruption related to its weak estrogenic properties and interaction on the nuclear estrogen receptor (ER) and the membrane ER. BPA is known to cross the placenta readily and to bind to α-fetoprotein, the estrogen-binding protein that normally prevents maternal estrogen from entering the fetal circulation.

By binding to α-fetoprotein, BPA could potentially decrease α-fetoprotein binding of endogenous estrogen and thus increase estrogen bioavailability to the fetus (Diamanti-Kandarakis et al., 2009).

BPA also has been shown to bind to the thyroid hormone receptor (THR) and to antagonize its activation by T3. As little as 1 µM BPA significantly inhibits THR-mediated gene activation (Diamanti-Kandarakis et al., 2009). Developmental exposure of rats to BPA produces normal TSH levels but elevated T4 levels, which is consistent with BPA inhibition of THR-mediated negative feedback.

Seiwa et al. (2004) showed that developmental exposure to BPA blocks T3-induced oligodendrocyte development from precursor cells. In addition, it has been proposed that there may be an association between thyroid resistance syndrome and ADHD in humans and rats. Well-designed human studies are needed to test this hypothesis.

Section Summary

- POPs, including semi-POPs, are ubiquitous contaminants that bioconcentrate in the food chain and are found in human blood and tissues.

- Mechanisms of toxicity for POPs include both direct action on nervous system components and indirect action through endocrine disruption.

- Acute high-level exposure to PCPs is associated with toxicity in adults; however, co-contamination with other halogenated hydrocarbons makes it impossible to isolate the effects inherent to PCPs.

- Chronic exposure of the developing human nervous system to PCBs is a concern, although results of epidemiological studies have been inconsistent. Animal studies have shown altered motor behavior and deficits in cognitive flexibility, working memory, and inhibitory control.

- Neurotoxicity resulting from exposure to PBDEs has little supporting evidence in the human literature; evidence is based on animal studies.

- BPA has no acute or chronic studies showing human toxicity. The only mechanism for neurotoxicity thus far identified from animal studies is endocrine disruption.

Insecticides

Insecticides encompass a variety of chemical classes and products. They are used both outdoors and indoors, and the majority of the U.S. population has

---

[8]The tasks carried out by CERHR (1998–2010) are now carried out by the NTP Office of Health Assessment and Translation (OHAT) (http://ntp.niehs.nih.gov/go/ohat).

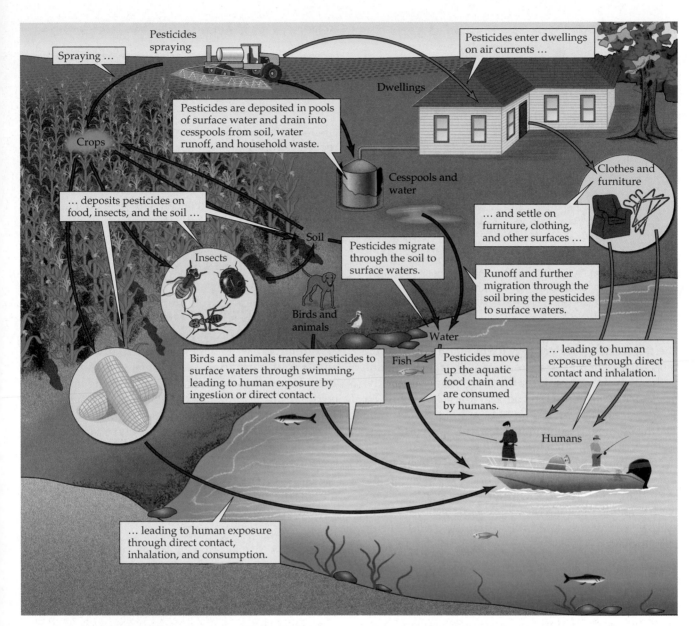

Figure 17.12 The pathways for human exposure to insecticides and other pesticides (After Sarkar, 2003.)

detectable concentrations of several insecticides and their metabolites in the urine (CDC, 2009, 2012a). Exposure of the general population to insecticides is primarily through contaminated food and water and home and garden products, as depicted in **Figure 17.12**. Other sources of exposure are also represented. Occupational exposures can be significant, especially for pest applicators, agricultural workers, ranchers, and farmers.

Two classes of insecticides—organophosphates and pyrethrins/pyrethroids—are discussed here. The interested reader is invited to read reviews of these and other pesticide health effects (Bjorling-Poulson et al., 2008; OCFP, 2012).

Organophosphate Insecticides

The organophosphate insecticides, referred to here as **organophosphates (OPs)**, usually are esters, amides, or thiol derivatives of phosphoric acid. Figure 17.13 shows the chemical formulas for a phosphate (**Figure 17.13A**) and a phosphorothioate (**Figure 17.13B**) compound. Organophosphates have a phosphorus with a double bond to a terminal oxygen (an oxon), as represented by dichlorvos, or to sulfur (a thion), as represented by parathion.

The organophosphates in general are well absorbed via the oral, dermal, and inhalation routes. Metabolism occurs primarily in the liver by hydrolysis at the ester linkage, but the rate is highly variable among OPs. The resulting metabolites have relatively low toxicity.

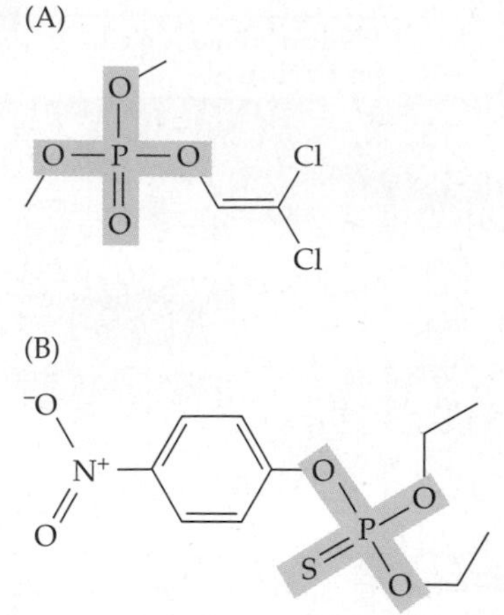

(A)

(B)

Figure 17.13 Organophosphates (OPs) (A) Dichlorvos (phosphoric acid, 2,2-dichloroethenyl dimethyl ester) is an example of a phosphate OP. (B) Parathion (phosphorothioic acid, O,O-diethyl O-[4-nitrophenyl] ester) is an example of a phosphorothioate OP.

The thions exhibit lower toxicity in mammals than the oxons and generally require metabolic transformation to the oxon form to inhibit the target enzyme, acetlycholinesterase (AChE). The normal acetylation of AChE by ACh is shown in **Figure 17.14**. In the presence of an OP, the enzyme is phosphorylated as opposed to being acetylated, as shown in **Figure 17.15**.

Not all OPs are capable of "aging" the enzyme. Only the phosphate and phosphonate OPs are capable of "aging" the enzyme, while the phosphinate OPs are incapable because they lack the possibility to be hydrolyzed at any site other than the AChE serine esteratic site.

Neurotoxicity in adults

OP inactivation of AChE causes accumulation of acetylcholine at cholinergic synapses and leads to over-stimulation of muscarinic and nicotinic receptors. The signs and symptoms of OP poisoning are cholinergic in nature, as would be expected, and are referred to as **cholinergic syndrome**, as depicted in **Figure 17.16** and listed in **Table 17.2**.

In adults, acute poisoning with high doses of an OP (brain AChE inhibition exceeding 70%)[9] develops within minutes to hours of exposure, depending on the route of exposure (Clegg and Gemert, 1999). Over-stimulation of the cholinergic system in both central and peripheral nervous systems is the primary form of toxicity exhibited with the OPs.

[9]Cholinesterase inhibition in red blood cells more closely reflects brain cholinesterase inhibition than plasma cholinesterase (pseudocholinesterase), although plasma cholinesterase is often used as an indicator of exposure.

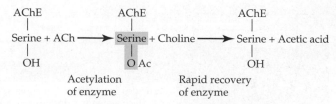

Figure 17.14 Acetylation of AChE by ACh and the rapid recovery of the enzyme following hydrolysis at the serine esteric site (highlighted in blue).

Prolonged effects can occur with irreversible inhibition of AChE. Death is usually the result of respiratory depression coupled with pulmonary secretions. Recovery is the result of new enzyme regeneration in critical tissues.

Following recovery (24 to 96 hours later) from an acute poisoning (cholinergic crisis), an intermediate syndrome has been described that is characterized by partial respiratory paralysis, reduced tendon reflexes, and muscular weakness (face, neck, proximal limbs) and lack of muscarinic symptoms (Christensen et al., 2009; Harper et al., 2009). This syndrome appears to be the result of pre- and post-synaptic dysfunction of neuromuscular transmission.

Some OPs also can induce a delayed neuropathy (OPIDN) that does not involve AChE inhibition, but rather, the inhibition of an enzyme called neuropathy target esterase (NTE). NTE deacetylates the major membrane phospholipid, phosphatidylcholine, and

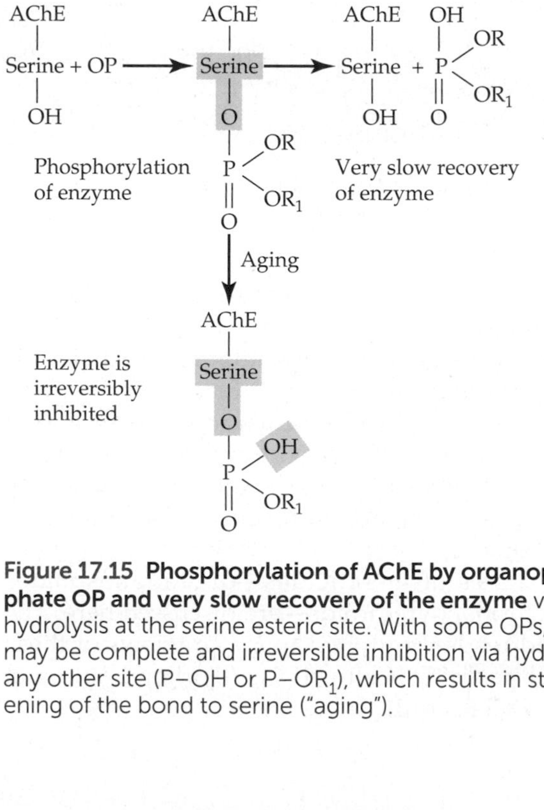

Figure 17.15 Phosphorylation of AChE by organophosphate OP and very slow recovery of the enzyme via hydrolysis at the serine esteric site. With some OPs, there may be complete and irreversible inhibition via hydrolysis at any other site (P–OH or P–OR₁), which results in strengthening of the bond to serine ("aging").

Figure 17.16 Cholinergic system Cholinergic system with receptor types that are overstimulated in the presence of AChE inhibition leading to acute cholinergic syndrome. NA, response is variable and not part of the classic cholinergic syndrome.

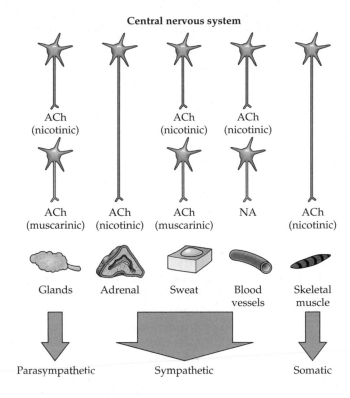

plays a major role in membrane homeostasis (Read et al., 2009). During neuronal differentiation, it regulates neurite outgrowth and process elongation. NTE inhibition results in axonal degeneration, which manifests chiefly as weakness or **paresthesia** (numbness and "pins-and-needles" feeling) and paralysis of the extremities, usually the legs.

Long-lasting behavioral effects have been reported in several human studies following recovery from intermediate syndrome or OPIDN (Bjorling-Poulsen, 2008). Although there has been concern for production of neurological effects following chronic, low exposure to OPs, the evidence is equivocal. In fact, chronic exposure may result in tolerance to AChE inhibition, as has been shown in animal studies, although the mechanism is unknown (Christensen et al., 2009; Harper et al., 2009).

TABLE 17.2 Clinical Signs and Symptoms of Acute OP Toxicity According to Receptor Type

| Central muscarinic and nicotinic | Peripheral | |
	Muscarinic	Nicotinic
Anxiety	Miosis	Muscle fasciculations
Ataxia	Blurred vision	Myoclonic jerks
Dysarthria (speech disorder)	Nausea	Muscle weakness
Confusion	Vomiting	Muscle rigidity
Headache	Diarrhea	Hyperreflexia
Fatigue	Salivation	Tremor
Drowsiness	Lacrimation	Paralysis
Difficulty concentrating	Rhinorrhea	Hypertension
Irritability	Bradycardia	Tachycardia
Emotional lability	Abdominal pain	Dysrhythmias
Delirium	Diaphoresis (profuse sweating)	Mydriasis (rare)
Toxic psychosis	Urinary incontinence	
Respiratory depression	Fecal incontinence	
Coma		
Seizures (occasional)		

Sources: ATSDR 2007a; Christensen et al., 2009; Harper et al., 2009; Kumar et al., 2010.

Neurotoxicity in children and the developing nervous system

Children with acute, high-dose poisoning can present with signs and symptoms somewhat different from those observed for adults (Sofer et al., 1989). In children, seizures, lethargy, and coma are more common.

Nineteen epidemiological studies of prenatal OP exposure reviewed by the Ontario College of Family Physicians (OCFP, 2012) included populations expected to be at higher risk for exposure; seven of the studies also examined another insecticide, which was usually a carbamate or pyrethrins (see OCFP, 2012 for summaries of individual studies). Most of the studies reviewed reported an association between OP exposure and impaired or delayed neurodevelopmental or behavioral outcomes. Prenatal OP exposure was associated with absent or hypotonic reflexes and deficits in attention to stimuli in neonates. In studies in which exposure was graded, more effects were observed with greater exposure. It was noted that deficits either were not measured or were not manifest at all time points in the longitudinal studies; thus it is difficult to evaluate the onset and persistence of some effects.

In studies from five countries of children over 3 years of age exposed postnatally to OPs, the neurological effects observed were inconsistent and were not related to OP exposure (OCFP, 2012). In what was deemed a high-quality study of Egyptian adolescent workers with high seasonal OP exposures, deficits were reported for all neurobehavioral measures evaluated compared with nonworker controls (Abdel Rasoul et al., 2008). Additionally, significantly more neurological symptoms were self-reported, such as difficulty concentrating, depression, and numbness. There was also a significant relationship between the years worked, the number of neurological symptoms reported, and performance on the Trails B test (an indicator of executive functioning). Other studies of children whose parents were exposed to pesticides, including OPs, showed a wide range of results from no effects to significant effects. These studies are largely uninterpretable because of study size and multiple confounding issues (OCFP, 2012).

In a study of 8- to 15-year-olds in which current exposure was evaluated, the increase in a urinary OP metabolite was associated with a significantly increased risk for the hyperactive/impulsive subtype of ADHD (Bouchard et al., 2010). The association with the combined subtypes was not statistically significant, but was in the same direction.

The developmental neurotoxicity of OPs is still relatively undefined in humans, in part because most studies reflect exposures to more than one pesticide. In California and New York City studies, an association was found between reflex abnormalities in neonates and increased concentrations of OP metabolites in maternal urine during pregnancy (Bjorling-Poulson et al., 2008). Similar associations between maternal urinary metabolites and reflex abnormalities were observed for an agricultural cohort from California (Young et al., 2005) and an inner city cohort from New York (Engel, 2007). Additionally, newborns of women who were slow OP metabolizers were more likely than newborns of normal or fast metabolizers to have abnormal reflexes.

Six cohort studies of prenatally exposed children examined up to 3 years of age in Ecuador, New York City, and California showed decreases in the Bayley Developmental Scales for Infant Development, which includes scores on the MDI and PDI scales. Most of the studies found that highly prenatally OP-exposed children scored lower on the Bayley MDI.

Studies of prenatally OP-exposed children at 3, 3.5, and 5 years show overall that high-exposure children were more likely to have attention problems. In one study, results reached statistical significance only for boys. Three studies examined the effects of prenatal OP exposure on the IQ of 6- to 9-year-olds using the Wechsler Intelligence Scale for children (WISC-IV). Two of the studies showed declines in full-scale IQ and the subscale of working memory. The third study showed nonsignificant trends toward lower IQ with higher OP exposure. Pesticide metabolite levels of urine in many of the studies have been reported to be similar to those measured in general populations in the United States and in E.U. countries (Bjorling-Poulson et al., 2008). Although the epidemiological evidence for the developmental neurotoxicity of OPs in humans is not without problems, there appears to be sufficient evidence that the OPs cause adverse effects. Additional well-controlled human studies are needed to define these neurotoxic effects.

The RfDs for the commonly used OPs range from about 10^{-2} mg/kg-day for less-toxic to about 10^{-5} mg/kg-day for more-toxic compounds.

Mechanisms of action

The primary mechanism for neurotoxicity is inhibition of AChE activity, as previously discussed. ACh, a neurotransmitter, has important functions during brain development that can be disrupted by inhibition of AChE. Other effects, as seen with chlorpyrifos (a phosphorothiate OP; **Figure 17.17**), suggest that mechanisms other than inhibition of AChE activity may, at least in part, be responsible for the

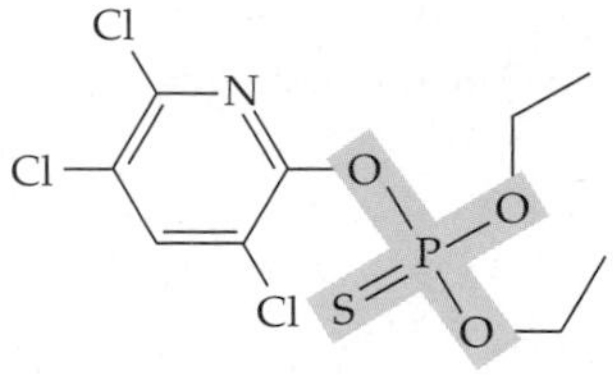

Figure 17.17 Chemical structure of chlorpyrifos (phosphorothioic acid, O,O-diethyl O-[3,5,6-trichloro-2-pyridinyl] ester)

developmental neurotoxicity of chlorpyrifos and possibly other OPs.

Chlorpyrifos is the most extensively studied OP with respect to developmental neurotoxicity in animals. Prenatal or neonatal exposure has resulted in a variety of behavioral abnormalities in rodents, including long-lasting effects on learning and memory (Aldridge et al., 2005; Canadas et al., 2005). These effects have been proposed to be the result of long-term alterations in 5-HT synaptic neurochemistry independent of AChE inhibition (Aldridge et al., 2005).

Prenatal exposure of rats to chlorpyrifos results in altered programming of synaptic development and deficits in brain cell numbers, neuritic projections, and synaptic communication (Qiao et al., 2003). The effects were first seen in adolescence and persisted into adulthood (i.e., the effects extend into relatively late stages of brain development). Neurobehavioral abnormalities can be induced as late as the second and third postnatal weeks in rats, which correspond to the neonatal stage of humans. Although this period occurs after the major phase of neurogenesis in most brain regions, it corresponds to the peak of gliogenesis and synaptogenesis. The developing glia are even more sensitive to chlorpyrifos than are the neurons. Antimitotic and pro-apoptotic mechanisms via directly targeted genes regulating the cell cycle and apoptosis during neurodifferentiation in the developing brain have been identified (Slotkin and Seidler, 2012). Deficits elicited by prenatal exposure to chlorpyrifos are seen even at exposures levels that do not inhibit AChE (Slotkin and Seidler, 2012).

Experiments with rat embryo cultures at concentrations relevant to humans have produced mitotic abnormalities and evidence of apoptosis during neural tube development (Ostrea et al., 2002). Significant effects have been seen at concentrations more than an order of magnitude *below* those present in human meconium (a fecal material that collects in the fetal intestine during development and is excreted shortly after birth) (Roy et al., 1998).

Pyrethrin and Pyrethroid Insecticides

The **pyrethroids** are synthetic analogs and derivatives of six naturally occurring **pyrethrins** from the *Chrysanthemum* genus of plants (ATSDR, 2003). This insecticidal class is quite diverse, but the pyrethroids have two common features—an acid moiety (e.g., a central ester) and an alcohol moiety. The pyrethrins and pyrethroids are generally classified into two groups (type I and type II) based on their structural and toxicological properties. Examples of type I and type II compounds are shown in **Figure 17.18**.

These compounds are readily degraded in the atmosphere, soil, and water and do not persist for longer than a few days to a few weeks. They are bound tightly to soil and do not "travel" or usually contaminate ground water. Likewise, they are not readily taken up by plant roots. They can bioconcentrate in aquatic organisms, however, and are toxic to fish. In spite of their lipophilicity, the pyrethroids do not bioaccumulate in human tissues because they are readily metabolized by hydrolases and cytochrome P450s (CYPs) (Soderlund et al., 2002).

These insecticides are used for both commercial and home applications. The general population is exposed to pyrethrins and pyrethroids primarily via foods, especially fruits and vegetables. Other sources of exposure include household insecticides, pet shampoos, and lice treatments. Occupational exposure can be the greatest, and dermal exposure is considered to be the most important (ATSDR, 2003). Several reviews are available for the interested reader (ATDSR, 2003; Breckenridge et al., 2009; Lautraite and Sargeant, 2009; Shafer et al., 2005; Soderlund et al., 2002).

Acute neurotoxicity

In rodents, type I pyrethroids typically induce aggressive behavior and increased sensitivity to external stimuli. At near lethal doses, fine tremor is observed followed by prostration and coarse whole body tremor, leading to coma and death. The term *T-syndrome*, for tremor, has been given to these type I responses (ATDSR, 2003).

The type II responses in rodents typically include pawing and burrowing behavior that is followed by profuse salivation, increased startle response, abnormal hand and limb movements and coarse whole body tremors that progress to serious writhing (choreoathetosis). Clonic seizures may be observed before death. The term *CS-syndrome*, for choreoathetosis and salivation, has been given to these type II responses. A few pyrethroids have demonstrated signs intermediate to the T- and CS-syndromes. Both syndromes are acute

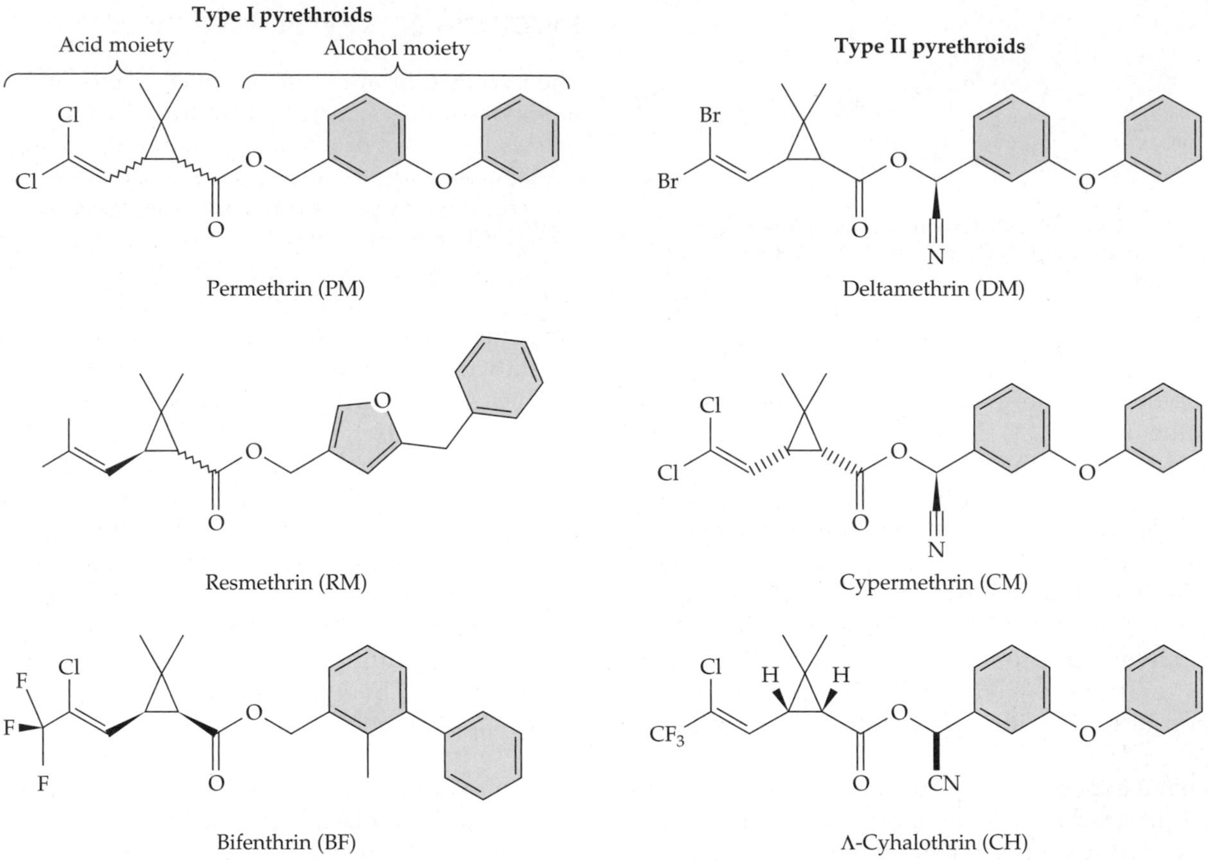

Figure 17.18 Representative structures of Type I and II pyrethroid pesticides

in nature, and chronic low-level exposures have not been reported to produce severe neurological effects (ATDSR, 2003).

Human pyrethroid poisoning is rare, and almost entirely involves type II pyrethroids. Occupational exposures have been the predominant source of pyrethroid poisoning. The main adverse effect of dermal exposure to type II pyrethroids is paresthesia, presumably due to a direct excitatory effect on small sensory nerve fibers in the skin (Lautraite and Sargeant, 2009). Dizziness, headache, and fatigue are common symptoms following ingestion and dermal exposure of type II pyrethroids. In severe cases, coma and convulsions are the principal life-threatening features (ATDSR, 2003). Increased acute peripheral nerve excitability has been reported for cotton workers exposed to deltamethrin over 3 days during spraying.

Developmental neurotoxicity

A series of 22 developmental neurotoxicity studies in animals have been summarized and critiqued by Shafer et al. (2005). The authors noted that there has been no systematic evaluation of exposure during various developmental periods, and no examination of the ontogeny of various behaviors and neurological endpoints. They also noted that there were inconsistencies in results even when similar neurobehavioral endpoints were evaluated. A few relatively consistent findings, however, were seen in studies in which the animals were evaluated following prenatal exposure: increased preweaning muscarinic ACh receptor (mAChR) expression in the cortex and increased motor activity and decreased habituation. Further work needs to be done to assess the potential for these insecticides to induce developmental toxicity in humans.

Mechanisms of action

The primary mechanism of action of the pyrethrins and pyrethroids is disruption of voltage-sensitive sodium channel (VSSC) function. The more potent the disruption of VSSC function, the more potent is the insecticidal and toxicological activity (Shafer et al., 2005). During development, perturbation of VSSC function impairs nervous system structure and function. VSSCs in mammals are composed of one α and two β subunits, with tissue specificity. The pyrethroids bind to the α subunit, which has been shown to have many variants in humans presumably contributing to the diversity seen in toxic responses.

(A)

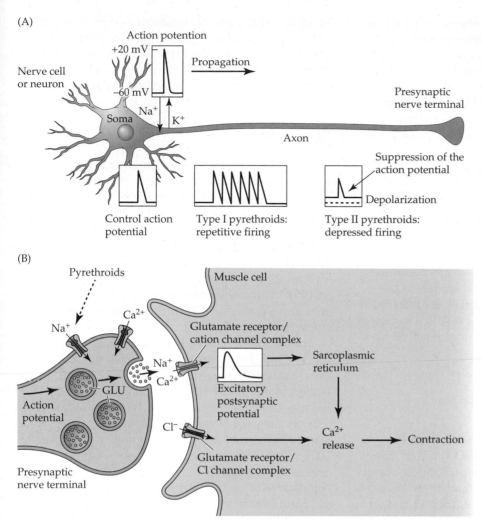

(B)

Figure 17.19 Neuromuscular transmission in the presence of pyrethroids (A) Depiction of propagation of an action potential down the presynaptic nerve axon. Under the axon the action potentials generated by type I and type II pyrethroids (i.e., repetitive firing and depressed firing) are shown relative to the control action potential (i.e., normal size and single action potential). The nerve terminal and muscle cell shown in (B) depict the normal release of glutamate (GLU, green circles) from the presynaptic terminal, their interaction with muscle cell receptor sites that open ion channels for the passage of Na^+, Ca^{2+}, and Cl^-, and the subsequent generation of the excitatory postsynaptic potential, the release of Ca^{2+} and contraction of the muscle cell. The site for action of the pyretheroids is shown at the presynaptic Na^+ ion channel. (After Bloomquist, 2009.)

The pyrethroids slow the opening (activation) and closing (inactivation) of VSSCs and shift the membrane potential at which they open to more hyperpolarized potentials; that is, the sodium channels open after smaller depolarizing changes in membrane potential. The result is that more sodium ions cross the neuronal membrane and depolarize it. Type I compounds prolong channel opening just long enough to induce repetitive firing of action potentials, and type II compounds hold the channels open such that depolarization occurs and prohibits generation of action potentials (Shafer et al., 2005) **(Figure 17.19)**.

The type II pyrethroids can bind to and block GABA receptors in in vitro mammalian brain preparations. Such blockade would be neuroexcititory in nature and is consistent with observed in vivo actions. Low potency, however, does not support this mechanism as a major role for acute toxicity (CS syndrome), although it could possibly be involved in developmentally induced neurotoxicity. It appears that pyrethrins and pyrethroids also affect calcium channel function; however, direct involvement in massive neurotransmitter release during pyrethroid intoxication has not been shown. There are some pyrethroids that have toxic effects that are intermediate between the two types.

Section Summary

- OPs produce acute neurotoxicity via inhibition of AChE and increased ACh concentrations at nicotinic and muscarinic receptors in the central and peripheral nervous systems.

- Prolonged toxicity with OPs occurs with irreversible inhibition of AChE, requiring the synthesis of new enzyme for normal function.

- OPIDN is produced by the irreversible inhibition of NTE, resulting in axonal degeneration and peripheral neuropathy.

- Studies of developmental neurotoxicity of OPs in humans are complicated by exposure to multiple pesticides. Effects on cognition and motor activity have been seen, although not consistently across studies. Prenatal chlorpyrifos exposure of rats at levels not causing AChE inhibition results in altered programming of synaptic development and deficits in brain cell numbers, neuritic projections, and synaptic communication.

- Pyrethrins and pyrethroids act through disruption of VSSC function, and severe poisonings of humans are seldom seen, but when they are, it is generally a type II compound. Neurotoxicity has not been reported following chronic low-level exposures.

- Developmental toxicity in humans has not been reported for pyrethroids. Animal studies of prenatal exposure have shown inconsistent effects except for increased preweaning mAChR expression in the cortex and increased motor activity and decreased habituation.

Toxic Metals

Lead, mercury, and arsenic are well-known environmental metals. (Arsenic is included in most discussions of toxic metals, but it is more appropriately referred to as a metalloid with properties in between those of metals and nonmetals.) Although the term *heavy metals* is often used in reference to the toxic environmental metals, it is an imprecise term that lacks a consistent and meaningful definition; thus the term *toxic metals* is more appropriately used.

Metals are naturally occurring and are among the oldest known toxicants. Hippocrates (460 to 377 BC) is credited with describing the symptoms of lead poisoning much as they are described today: "appetite loss, colic, pallor, weight loss, fatigue, irritability, and nervous spasm" (Lessler, 1988); however, it is questionable whether he recognized lead as the causative agent (Hernberg, 2000).

From an environmental perspective, metals are naturally redistributed in the environment by both geological and biological means, with human activity magnifying that distribution. The toxicity of many metals is determined by the oxidation state of the metal, its lipid solubility, the cellular dose achieved, the duration of exposure, and the extent of binding to the target biomolecule. The common mechanisms of metal-induced neurotoxicity are mediated through direct and indirect mitochondrial damage; oxidative stress and formation of ROS resulting in protein and lipid peroxidation; depletion of nonprotein sulfhydryls (e.g., glutathione, a naturally occurring antioxidant present in all cells); binding to protein sulfhydryl groups; substitution for key divalent cations, such as calcium (Ca^{2+}); and disruption of cellular signaling.

Lead (Pb)

Lead is found in the earth's crust primarily in areas with copper, silver, and zinc. Metallic (elemental) lead (zero oxidation state, Pb^0) is rare because it quickly oxidizes in the air. Lead is easy to extract and smelt and is highly malleable, which accounts for its extensive use through the millennia (Hernberg, 2000). Inorganic and organic compounds of lead are primarily in the +2 and +4 oxidation states, and Pb^{2+} is more common, being present in various ores around the world. In the environment, lead is strongly absorbed to soil.

In recent history, lead has been used in many products, including paints, gasoline, ceramics, pipes, solders, batteries, ammunition, and cosmetics. In the United States, lead exposure is most commonly from flaking and deteriorating lead-based paints used in older homes, contaminated soils and drinking water, lead crystal, and lead-glazed pottery (Sanders et al., 2009). The principal exposure source of lead for the general population is via food, and other sources are significant for certain populations. Contamination of soil from deteriorating lead-based paints and from the residual deposition of atmospheric lead from leaded gasoline is especially a concern for young children, who ingest soil and dust via their daily activities.

GI absorption of ingested water-soluble inorganic lead compounds is 3% to 10% in adults, and approximately 30% to 50% in infants and children (ATSDR, 2007b; Neal and Guilarte, 2012). Under circumstances where there is low dietary iron and calcium, lead absorption is significantly increased. In the blood, greater than 90% of the lead is contained in red blood cells, and less than 1% is in the plasma. From the blood, lead is distributed to the soft tissues and bone. It may be stored preferentially in the bone of adults because osteoclasts (the cells responsible for absorption of bone during normal turnover of bony tissues) can interchange Ca^{2+} and Pb^{2+}. Infants and children also store lead in bone, but their bone mass is small and the amount of stored lead as a percent of body burden is less than that of adults (73% versus 94%). Bone turnover due to skeletal growth in children and infants mobilizes Pb stores and may result in added exposure (Neal and Guilarte, 2012). Lead does not penetrate the blood–brain barrier of adults, but may penetrate the more poorly developed blood–brain barrier of children. For adults, the half-life of lead in blood is about 1 month, and in the skeleton 20 to 30 years (ATSDR, 2007b).

Lead exhibits neurotoxic effects in the central and peripheral nervous systems that are dependent on the developmental period and the level and duration of exposure.

Neurotoxicity in adults

In adults, acute high-dose lead poisoning can cause encephalopathy (brain damage or malfunction) that manifests as an altered mental state, seizures, ataxia, and coma. Severe encephalopathy generally is observed only at extremely high blood levels (460 µg/100 ml [460 µg/dl]) (ATSDR, 2007b); however, less severe, overt encephalopathy has been reported at blood levels as low as 100 µg/dl. Chronic occupational exposures are associated with symptoms ranging from forgetfulness and irritability to weakness and paresthesia at blood levels from 40 to 120 µg/dl. Chronic lead exposure also is associated with inattentiveness, distractibility, hyperactivity, frustration, and aggression at blood levels as low as 10 µg/dl in some studies. Peripheral neuropathy in adults is associated with chronic exposure at blood levels of 70 µg/dl and greater (ATSDR, 2007b).

Neurotoxicity in children and the developing nervous system

In children, high-dose lead poisoning can lead to significant neurotoxic sequelae similar to what are observed in adults, but at lower doses. Overt encephalopathy in children, for instance, is associated with blood lead levels as low as 70 µg/dl, compared with 100 µg/dl in adults (ATSDR, 2007b).

As more data were gathered during the 1960s and later, it became apparent that the greatest concern for environmental lead exposure was for the prenatally and postnatally developing nervous system. In addition to the high-dose encephalopathic effects of lead, it was recognized that lower doses over a prolonged exposure period resulted in significant toxic effects. Between 1960 and 1991, the CDC blood lead level recommendation for individual clinical intervention in children was lowered from 60 to 25 µg/dl and again from 25 to 15 µg/dl in 1991. At the same time, 10 µg/dl was set as a risk management tool (i.e., not as a threshold for toxicity) (Sanders et al., 2009). In 2012, the CDC lowered the blood lead threshold in children younger than 6 years of age from 10 to 5 µg/dl based on a shift in policy from that of a clinical intervention to that of a public health approach focused on prevention (CDC, 2012b).

Blood lead levels of 10 µg/dl and higher that are associated with chronic lead exposure in early childhood are detrimental to neurodevelopment. The recognized adverse effects include impaired cognitive function, behavioral disturbances, attention deficits, hyperactivity, conduct problems, antisocial behavior, delinquency, and violence (Bellinger, 2009; Neal and Guilarte, 2012; Needleman et al., 2002; Sanders et al., 2009; Wright et al., 2008). In children, lead exposure has also been associated with increased risk of ADHD (Braun et al., 2006). Blood lead levels in young school-age children also predict neurologic deficits in children and young adults (Hornung et al., 2009). Newly identified neuroanatomical changes in young adults exposed to lead in childhood include reduced gray matter in the prefrontal region and white matter changes indicative of effects on myelination (Brubaker et al., 2009).

After decades of study, a nonlinear relationship between lead exposure and IQ decline in children has been recognized. It appears that the greatest rate of decline in IQ comes with the initial 10 µg/dl increase in blood lead levels (Neal and Guilarte, 2012). A pooled analysis of internationally conducted epidemiology studies calculated that a blood lead level of 10 µg/dl was associated with a 6-point decline in IQ relative to children with a 1 µg/dl blood level (Lanphear et al., 2005). Another study reported a similar decline in IQ points (7.4) with 10 µg/dl (Canfield et al., 2003).

Mechanisms of action

Lead has many interrelated mechanisms that are involved in its observed neurotoxicity; however, the primary mechanism may well be its effect on calcium metabolism via substitution for calcium and disruption of calcium homeostasis. Although not necessarily all of the following are related to disruption of calcium metabolism, lead has been shown to promote apoptosis, produce excitotoxicity, affect neurotransmitter storage and release, damage mitochondria and cause oxidative stress resulting in peroxidative damage to lipids and proteins, deplete antioxidants by binding to sulfhydryls (e.g., glutathione), inactivate antioxidative enzymes (e.g., glutathione reductase), deregulate cell signaling (e.g., activation of protein kinase C [PKC]), alter cellular membranes (e.g., cerebrovascular endothelial cells), impair synaptic transmission, and alter neurotransmitter concentrations, alter neurotransmitter receptor channel properties, and affect protein and gene expression (ATSDR, 2007b; Neal and Guilarte, 2012; Sanders et al., 2009).

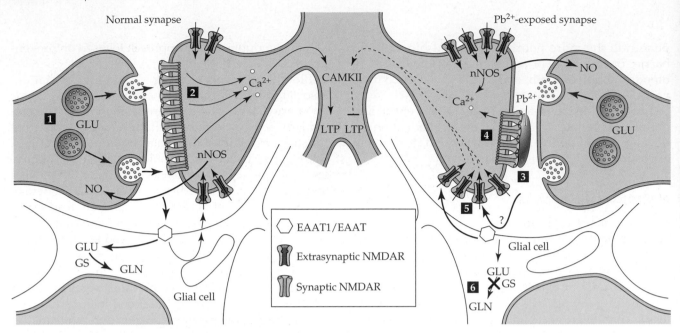

Figure 17.20 Pb^{2+} interaction at the synaptic level In a normal synapse, glutamate release (1), normal NMDAR density, and Ca^{2+} influx (2) through open NMDAR channels activate neuronal nitric oxide synthase (nNOS) and calcium/calmodulin kinase II (CAMKII), two enzymes involved in the induction and maintenance of long-term potentiation (LTP). Developmental exposure to Pb^{2+} leads to both reduced numbers of NMDARs and potential blockage of the receptors by Pb^{2+} (3). Reduced Ca^{2+} influx (4) may occur as a result of fewer receptors and receptor blockage resulting in altered activation of nNOS and CAMKII, which affects LTP. (5) Glutamine synthetase (GS) is inhibited by Pb^{2+} and may result in an accumulation of GLU in glial cells which then could be available to activate extrasynaptic NMDAR subunits. (6) An alternative mechanism for GLU activation of extrasynaptic NMDARs is Pb^{2+} inhibition of the GLU transporters (EAAT1/EAAT), which would result in increased extracelluar concentrations of GLU. GLN, glutamine. (After Toscano and Guilarte, 2005.)

The consequences of some of these mechanisms are briefly cited to give the reader a feel, albeit superficial, for the profound effect that lead can have on the developing organism. Perturbations in normal Ca^{2+} signaling affect synaptic development and plasticity. Lead impairs timed programming of cell–cell connections, resulting in modification of neuronal circuitry. Lead induces precocious differentiation of the glia, whereby cells migrate to their eventual positions during structuring of the CNS. Learning and memory deficits may be related to inhibition of the N-methyl-D-aspartate receptor (NMDAR) in the hippocampus (Neal and Guilarte, 2012). It has been hypothesized that Pb^{2+} also delays the normal ontogeny and alters the distribution of NMDAR (**Figure 17.20**). The interrelationships among and between these individual mechanisms are considerable, and the interested reader is invited to review several articles addressing various aspects of the mechanisms of lead neurotoxicity (ATSDR, 2007b; Hsiang and Diaz, 2011; Neal and Guilarte, 2012; Sanders et al., 2009).

Mercury (Hg)

Elemental mercury (Hg^0), also known as quick silver, is a naturally occurring shiny, silver-white metal that is a liquid at room temperature. Natural releases from volcanoes and the earth's crust put metallic mercury vapor into the atmosphere, as do anthropomorphic releases from mining ore deposits, coal-burning power plants, and the incineration of waste. An example of mercury entering the environment through human activity via the recent upsurge in gold mining is depicted in **Figure 17.21**. Mercury circulates in the atmosphere until it eventually returns to earth, where it may settle in aquatic sediments and may be fixed by bacteria or plankton as methylmercury (ATDSR, 1999).

Mercury compounds are primarily in the +1 and +2 oxidation states, referred to as mercurous (Hg$^+$) and mercuric (Hg^{2+}) mercury, respectively. Mercuric mercury can form stable organic mercury compounds, such as methylmercury (CH$_3$Hg$^+$), which is done in association with either a simple anion, such as Cl$^-$, or a large, charged molecule, such as a protein.

Mercury historically has been used in thermometers and barometers, as topical antiseptics and preservatives (**Box 17.1**), and more recently in fluorescent light bulbs, laptop monitors, cell phones, and printed circuit boards. Although individual electronic devices contain a small amount of mercury (1 g mercury was calculated for a cell phone vintage 2000–2005, while

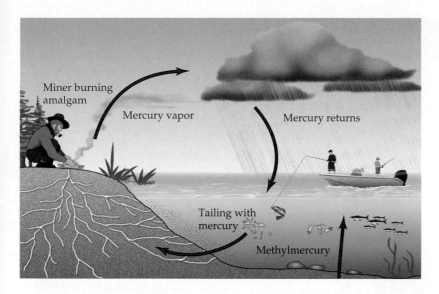

Figure 17.21 Release of mercury into the environment Mercury vapor enters the atmosphere as a result of mining activity where it can remain for some time before being deposited on land and surface waters (primarily through rainfall). Once mercury reaches surface water, it can settle into sediment, where it may be released through sediment resuspension, enter the food chain, or re-enter the atmosphere. (After UNIDO, 2006.)

other electronic devices cited contained 4 mg or more; EPA, 2007), their improper recycling has the potential to release elemental mercury vapor into the environment (Ramesh et al., 2007). This is especially a concern in third world countries, where environmental regulations are nonexistent or unenforced.

The primary source of human exposure to mercury is via methylmercury through consumption of fish and shellfish due to bioaccumulation because of its lipid solubility (EPA, 2012a). Consumption of large amounts of contaminated fish and/or shellfish can be sufficient to cause mercury poisoning in humans and animals. Although only a small percentage of metallic and mercuric mercury is absorbed from the adult human GI tract (approximately 0.01% and 15%, respectively), approximately 90% to 95% of methylmercury is absorbed (ATDSR, 1999). Methylmercury readily passes though the placenta, and infants can be exposed via the mother's milk. There appears to be very slow to no elimination of methylmercury for infants.

The tissue distribution of mercury is dependent on the speciation, lipid solubility, and route of exposure. Hg^0 is rapidly oxidized in red blood cells to inorganic mercury, and thus its distribution is similar to that of inorganic mercury. Hg^{2+} has a high affinity for sulfhydryl groups, and most all Hg^{2+} in the blood is bound to glutathione, cysteine, albumin, and other sulfhydryl-containing proteins.

Once methylmercury is absorbed, it can be transported across the blood–brain barrier via a carrier-mediated system (Aschner and Aschner, 1990). In the brain, methylmercury is metabolized to a limited extent to Hg^{2+}. Mercury toxicity in the brain is nonspecific in that it does not target a specific cell or receptor type. Its higher affinity for sulfhydryl groups, however, leads to its concentration in certain areas of the brain such as granule cells of the cerebellum and the calcarine region of the occipital cortex (Eto, 1997).

In 1995, the EPA lowered the allowable daily intake of methylmercury from 0.5 μg Hg/kg-day, a threshold established by the World Health Organization (WHO) in 1978, to 0.1 μg/kg-day based on adverse neurological effects in infants. The FDA and the EPA issued a joint advisory cautioning that "young children, women who are pregnant or who may become pregnant, and nursing mothers should avoid fish that contain high levels of methylmercury" (FDA, 2004). The species most likely to have these higher levels are shark, swordfish, king mackerel, and tilefish; shrimp, canned light tuna, salmon, Pollock, and catfish are the most common species to have low levels of mercury (EPA, 2012b; Neustadt and Pieczenik, 2007; NIEHS, 2012).

Neurotoxicity in adults

Neurotoxicity observed with mercury is similar for rodents, wild animals, and humans: ataxia, impaired gait, increased excitability, and tremors (ATSDR, 1999). Inhalation of metallic mercury vapor at high concentrations is associated with often acutely fatal interstitial pneumonitis. Acute high-level exposure of adults to mercury compounds via other routes generally results in paresthesia and ataxia that may be followed by visual field constriction and blindness. Lethal doses of organic mercury compounds have been estimated to range from 10 to 60 mg/kg for humans. For both inorganic and organic mercury, symptoms may not present for weeks to months after exposure. Neuropathology shows selective involvement of the cerebral and cerebellar cortices, focal necrosis, lysis, and phagocytosis in the visual cortex and cerebral granule cells (ATDSR, 1999). The neurons

BOX 17.1   Of Special Interest

Thimerosal in Vaccinations—Does It Cause Autism?

There has been controversy surrounding the use of thimerosal in childhood vaccines (Figure A). Thimerosal is a mercury-containing preservative that has been blamed for causing autism in children receiving the vaccines.

The controversy arose in the United States in the late 1990s and early 2000s with rising public concern about environmental mercury poisoning coupled with rising awareness of autism (the most severe of the autism spectrum disorders [ASDs]), rising incidence of autism, and an increase in the number of vocal advocacy groups of parents of autistic children. The tale of convergence of these factors is told by Baker (2008) in an article in the *American Journal of Public Health*.

In 1997, a rider was placed on the FDA Modernization Act that required the FDA to assess the mercury content of drug products. Assessment of vaccines in which thimerosal was used as a preservative began in early 1998. Thimerosal, as shown in Figure B, contains ethylmercury (CH_3CH_2Hg) attached to thiosalicylate; the mercury content is 49.6% by weight.

The FDA identified three vaccines routinely given to infants (diphtheria-tetanus-acellular pertussis, *Haemophilus influenzae* type b conjugate, and hepatitis B) that could potentially have thimerosal as a preservative. The analysis was completed in April 1999. The FDA had calculated that if infants received all the vaccines preserved with thimerosal over the first 6 months of life, the cumulative exposure could be 187.5 µg of ethylmercury, 200 µg if the influenza vaccine was also received (AAP, 1999). Moving rapidly, the American Academy of Pediatrics (AAP), the U.S. Public Health Service

(A)

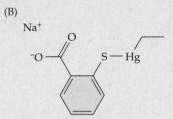

(B)

Thimerosal in vaccines (A) The only commonly recommended childhood vaccine that still contains thimerosal is the multidose vial of influenza vaccine. Single dose vials of the vaccine do not contain thimerosal. (B) The chemical structure of thimerosal (sodium ethylmercurithiosalicylate).

(PHS), and vaccine manufacturers decided in July 1999 that thimerosal should be removed from vaccines as a precautionary measure (CDC, 1999). This decision was reached in spite of the fact that thimerosal as a vaccine preservative had not caused any harm. The basis for the decision was the EPAs RfD for methylmercury (0.1 µg mercury/kg-day) since no standard for ethylmercury existed.

As chronicled in a review by Baker (2008), the efforts of activist parents of autistic children led to the publication of an article in *Medical Hypotheses* (Bernard et al., 2001) that compared various aspects associated with autism versus the signs and symptoms reported for mercury exposure. Although this article was not peer-reviewed, for many, especially the lay public, the publication legitimized the association between mercury and autism. Baker suggested that further complications

arose when litigation muddied the scientific waters with "expert witness testimony."

So, what was the basis for the claim of a causal relationship between thimerosal and development of autism? The assumptions underlying a causal relationship were as follows: (1) ethylmercury and methylmercury are equivalent in absorption, distribution, metabolism, and excretion (ADME); (2) the signs and symptoms of mercury poisoning and autism are the same, so there is biological plausibility; and (3) the rise in the incidence of autism was caused by thimerosal.

So what does the science say? The scientific weight of evidence does not support a causal relationship, and furthermore, the underlying assumptions for a causal relationship were false. First, ethylmercury is not methylmercury, and their ADME profiles are not equivalent. At the time of the original evaluation, because of lack of data, it was presumed that the half-life of ethylmercury was similar to that of methylmercury. The half-life of ethylmercury, however, was subsequently shown to be much

BOX 17.1 *(continued)*

shorter. Comparing blood levels, which are assumed to reflect the total body burden, the half-life of methylmercury is about 50 days, and the half-life of ethylmercury from thimerosal in vaccines is 7 to 10 days. Therefore, in the 2 months between vaccinations at birth and 2, 4, and 6 months, the mercury would have been excreted (i.e., 6 to 8.5 half-lives would have occurred).

Second, the signs and symptoms of mercury poisoning are not the same as those of autism, so there is little to no biological plausibility (Gerber and Offit, 2009; Nelson and Bauman, 2003). Children with mercury poisoning exhibit characteristic changes in head circumference and neurological motor, speech, sensory, psychiatric, and visual changes or deficits that are different from or not seen in autistic children.

Third, the incidence of autism did not decrease but continued to increase after removal of thimerosal from vaccines; therefore, thimerosal could not be the cause of the increased incidence.

Furthermore, since the controversy arose, about a dozen studies have been performed in the United States, Canada, the United Kingdom, and Denmark. A few studies concluded that there was an association between thimerosal and autism but those studies have been evaluated in multiple review articles, and all reviews detail significant design flaws that invalidate a conclusion of causality.

Today, the multidose vial of influenza vaccine is the only commonly recommended childhood vaccine that contains thimerosal in the United States and Canada. Despite all the scientific evidence that does not support the role of thimerosal in vaccines in the causation of autism, many articles in the lay press and on the Internet keep the controversy alive. The advocates sound convincing and offer "evidence" to support their claim; however, close scrutiny reveals the underlying unsupported assumptions. The lesson? Look at the underlying assumptions, and do not accept them without getting the facts. Look to the scientific community, not to individuals or the lay press, to examine all relevant aspects, not just those chosen to support a point of view.

---

are replaced by supporting glial cells. The overall acute effect is cerebral edema, but the long-term effect is cerebral atrophy that results from prolonged destruction of gray matter and subsequent gliosis.

With chronic exposure to mercury, the first manifestation of major CNS effects is paresthesia of the hands, feet, and sometimes around the mouth; impairment of coordination, such as waking or writing; muscle weakness; mental disturbances (e.g., mood swings, memory loss); and impairment of speech, hearing, and peripheral vision. The lower toxicity of mercurous compounds relative to mercuric compounds is most likely attributable to their lower solubility.

There are two well-known mass poisonings related to methylmercury: one in Minamata Bay, Japan, in the mid-1950s, and another in Iraq in 1971–1972. The Japanese episode is an example of chronic exposure and poisoning from contaminated seafood; the Iraqi episode is an example of a more acute exposure and poisoning from contaminated grain (ATSDR, 1999; Grandjean and Herz, 2011).

In Minamata, following an extended period of exposure, severe poisoning (called Minamata disease) presented as ataxia, numbness of the extremities, muscle weakness, narrowing of the visual field, and damaged hearing and speech. Within a short period following symptom onset, some victims exhibited psychoses, paralysis, coma, and death. In Iraq, seed grain treated with a methylmercury fungicide was consumed as food. Symptoms were similar to those observed with Minamata disease, with the exception that blindness was also reported. The difference in visual effects between Minamata and Iraq is thought to be most likely due to the different nature of the exposures.

Developmental neurotoxicity

The developmental effects observed following in utero exposure to methylmercury in Japan gave rise to the term "fetal Minamata disease." The first neurological signs were usually seen in infants at an early age and included delayed movements, failure to follow visual stimuli, and uncoordinated sucking and swallowing. These signs were followed by persisting primitive reflexes and markedly impaired coordination. In the few autopsies that were performed, characteristic neuropathological changes were observed: bilateral cerebral atrophy and hypoplasia (fewer cortical nerve cells and malformed cells or processes); cerebellar atrophy and hypoplasia (reduced granule cell layer); abnormal cytoarchitecture; hypoplasia of the corpus callosum; defective myelination of white matter; and hydrocephalus (Matsumoto et al., 1965). The most characteristic abnormality reported was the poorly developed and inappropriately located and positioned neurons in the

CNS, which is most likely the result of disrupted neuronal migration and maturation.

Neurodevelopmental effects with high-level exposures are undisputed. Questions have been raised about the neurodevelopmental effects of exposure to low to moderate levels of methylmercury, however, because of different findings in studies of the Faroe Islands and the Seychelles (Chen et al., 2011). An association was seen in the Faroe Islands study between prenatal methylmercury exposure (4 µg/g maternal hair; 23 µg/l cord blood) and deficits in motor function, attention, and verbal domains in children up to 14 years of age. The Seychelles study, on the other hand, did not show an association between neurodevelopmental endpoints and prenatal methylmercury exposure (7 µg/g maternal hair) (Davidson et al., 2010; Myers et al., 2009). Neither study showed an association with postnatal methylmercury exposures (Faroe Islands: 3 µg/g hair; 9 µg/l blood at 7 years of age) (Seychelles: 6 µg/g hair at 9 years of age).

When the Faroe Islands and Seychelles studies were analyzed with a cohort from New Zealand, however, the overall change in child IQ was calculated as –0.18 points for each 1-µg increase in methylmercury per gram maternal hair.

Although no threshold has been determined for neurotoxic effects with mercury, several studies suggest that very low levels are without significant effect. In the United States for 2-year-old children, background levels of methylmercury in whole blood were approximately 0.5 µg/l. This level of exposure was not associated with adverse neurodevelopmental outcomes in children evaluated at 2, 5, and 7 years of age (Cao et al., 2010).

Mechanisms of action

The mechanisms for producing neurotoxicity are believed to be similar for inorganic and organic mercury. The relative toxicities of the different forms of mercury (e.g., metallic, mercurous, mercuric, inorganic, and methyl and other organic mercury compounds) are related in part to differential accumulation in sensitive tissues. It appears that chronic exposure to methylmercury results in an accumulation of inorganic as well as organic mercury in the brain (ATSDR, 1999). In studies of monkeys, it was observed that the brain elimination half-life of methylmercury was 35 days, and that of inorganic mercury was on the order of years. The presence of inorganic mercury was thought to be due to the in vivo demethylation of methylmercury.

In the adult brain, the underlying neurotoxic mechanism may be disruption in protein synthesis, which is among the earliest biochemical effects seen in animal studies. Cells with greatest repair capacity survive, while others die.

Mercury also can disrupt signaling pathways involved in cellular communication throughout the CNS and peripheral nervous system. One example is the muscarinic ACh (mACh) signaling pathway, where Hg^{2+} (as $HgCl_2$) and methylmercury inhibit binding of ACh to the receptor in the cerebellum and cerebral cortex in several species, including humans (Basu et al., 2005). $HgCl_2$ is more potent than methylmercury, lending further support to speculation that neurotoxicity from methylmercury is the result of its demethylation to Hg^{2+}. $HgCl_2$ at sublethal concentrations is also implicated in selective inhibition of another neurochemical signaling pathway called the JAK-STAT pathway (Monroe and Halvorsen, 2006). The JAK-STAT pathway is involved in cytokine and growth factor signal transduction from the plasma membrane to the nucleus for regulation of cell differentiation and proliferation, thus inhibition of this pathway could be important for the developmental neurotoxicity of $HgCl_2$.

At the cellular level, $HgCl_2$ also interferes with mitochondrial respiration, resulting in oxidative stress. Because neurons have a high mitochondrial density, they are especially susceptible, and some neurons (e.g., motor neurons) have limited antioxidant capabilities.

Disruption of neuronal migration and neural cytoarchitecture by methylmercury is related to alteration of neural cell adhesion molecules (NCAMs) and disruption of the neurocytoskeleton (microtubules), both of which are important for cellular movements and kinetics.

Arsenic (As)

Arsenic is widely distributed in nature and occurs as a metalloid or semi-metallic element (As^0); as organic and inorganic arsenite (As^{3+}), arsenate (As^{5+}), and arsenide (As^{3-}) compounds; and as arsine (AsH_3), an inorganic gas. Arsenic is difficult to characterize because of its complex chemistry and ability to form many compounds.

The major source of arsenic exposure for the general population is via food and contaminated drinking water from natural geological sources (ATSDR, 2007c). Arsenic is one of the top environmental health threats in the United States and worldwide. In the United States and Europe, public water supplies have a regulatory limit of 10 parts per billion (ppb) arsenic; however, private water wells are unregulated, as are many water supplies worldwide. Thus, arsenic contamination affects hundreds of millions of people and is associated with an extensive list of disease risks.

Both As^{3+} and As^{5+} are well absorbed via inhalation and oral routes, and poorly absorbed via the dermal route. Water-soluble As^{3+} and As^{5+} compounds are 80% to 90% absorbed from the GI tract, but other arsenicals of lower solubility are less efficiently absorbed. Once absorbed, arsenates are partially reduced to arsenite, resulting in a mixture of As^{3+} and As^{5+} in the blood. As^{3+} compounds are the principal toxic forms; As^{5+} compounds are less toxic.

Metabolism of inorganic As^{3+} occurs in the liver, and some have speculated that the organic intermediary and end products formed by such metabolism may be more reactive and toxic than inorganic As^{3+} (Thomas et al., 2007). The biological half-life of orally ingested inorganic arsenic in the body is about 40 to 60 hours, and the half-life of arsenic metabolites is about 1 day (ATSDR, 2007c).

Although only the neurotoxic effects of arsenic are discussed here, it must be remembered that chronic arsenic exposure is associated with many diverse disease processes ranging from keratosis to cancer. The interested reader can examine a review that explores many aspects of arsenic neurotoxicity (Rodriguez et al., 2003).

Neurotoxicity in adults

Ingestion of large doses of arsenic in the range of 70 to 180 mg can induce encephalopathy and can cause death (ATSDR, 2007). If one recovers from severe acute toxicity, the most commonly observed neurological effect is sensory loss in the peripheral nervous system, which appears 1 to 2 weeks after the initial insult. The neuropathy results from degeneration of axons, which is potentially reversible if there is no additional exposure.

Acute inhalation exposure has been associated with severe nausea and vomiting, diarrhea, sleep disturbances, decreased concentration, disorientation, severe agitation, paranoid ideation, and emotional lability, which can be relieved by chelation therapy (ATSDR, 2007). Long-lasting effects such as severe impairment of learning and memory and mild impairment of visuoperception, visuomotor integration, psychomotor speed, and attention processes, however, have been observed even at 8 months post-exposure (Rodriguez et al., 2003).

Chronic exposure to inorganic arsenic compounds leading to neurotoxicity of both the peripheral and central nervous systems usually begins with sensory changes, paresthesia, and muscle tenderness, followed by weakness, progressing from proximal to distal muscle groups (ATSDR, 2007; Rodriguez et al., 2003). The sensory nerves are more sensitive, and neurons with large axons are more affected than those with short axons. Peripheral neuropathy is dose-dependent and may be progressive, involving both sensory and motor neurons and leading to demyelination of long axon nerve fibers.

In one report of chronic exposure to arsenic via contaminated well water, disturbances such as forgetfulness, confusion, and abnormal visual sensations were associated with a urinary arsenic of 488 µg/l, and peripheral neuropathy was diagnosed in another individual with 2260 µg As/l (Rodriguez et al., 2003). Occupational exposure to arsenic compounds has been associated with impairments of higher function, such as concentration, short-term memory, and learning (ATSDR, 2007; Rodriguez et al., 2003). Severity was associated with the duration of exposure, and most symptoms disappeared after exposure ceased.

Studies in rodents administered arsenic trioxide (As_2O_3) or sodium arsenite ($NaAsO_2$) orally have shown deficits in behavior, learning, and memory after 2 weeks to 3 months at doses that were not systemically toxic (Rodriguez et al., 2003).

Neurotoxicity in children and the developing nervous system

With acute exposures, children exhibit symptoms similar to those observed in adults. For chronic environmental exposures, children experience the same neurological effects as adults. In areas of endemically high arsenic in drinking water, arsenic concentrations in the human placental cord blood can be about as high as those in maternal blood (Concha et al., 1998), thus additional effects following exposure of the developing nervous system could be anticipated.

Several epidemiological studies of environmental arsenic exposure have evaluated neurotoxicity endpoints. A study of 720 children in China, aged 8 to 12 years, revealed decreased IQ scores with increased concentrations of arsenic in the drinking water (Wang et al., 2007). The mean IQ score in the control group (2 µg As/l water) was 105, and it was 101 and 95 for the medium (142 µg As/l) and high (190 µg As/l) arsenic exposed groups, respectively. These decreases were similar to those observed in a study of 201 10-year old children in Bangladesh (Wasserman et al., 2004) and in two small studies in Mexico (Calderon et al., 2001) and Taiwan (Tsai et al., 2003). Many factors affect IQ scores; decreasing scores from several studies are supportive but not conclusive evidence of a real effect. Other epidemiological studies of arsenic exposure via drinking water have not shown significant neurological effects, possibly as the result of confounding due to the inability to quantify past exposure (ATSDR, 2007). Hearing impairment has also been associated with airborne arsenic in chronically exposed 10-year-old children.

The physical malformations reported in animal studies have not been reported for humans exposed to equally high blood arsenic concentrations from contaminated drinking water. The differences between animal studies and the human experience may be due to the form of the arsenic. In humans, the organic arsenic metabolite dimethylarsenic acid (DMA) predominates with chronic exposure. DMA has been shown to be less toxic than inorganic As^{3+} compounds in developmental animal studies, which may explain the lack of malformations in humans.

Mechanisms of action

A number of mechanisms have been proposed for the ability of arsenic to cause such diverse adverse effects. These include alterations in cell signaling, cell cycle control, oxidative stress, DNA repair, and others. Arsenic binds to a number of sulfhydryl-containing proteins and enzymes, including mitochondrial enzymes, resulting in impaired tissue respiration, which is related to the cellular toxicity of arsenic. Arsenic also inhibits mitochondrial energy-linked functions by competition with phosphate during oxidative phosphorylation and inhibition of mitochondrial adenosine triphosphate (ATP) production, resulting in increased ROS generation (Hughes, 2002).

Disruption of hormone signaling may be a key component of arsenic-induced developmental effects. Arsenic alters steroid hormone receptor (SHR)-mediated gene regulation at very low, environmentally relevant concentrations in cell cultures and animal models (Bodwell et al., 2004, 2006; Davey et al., 2007). All five SHRs (i.e., glucocorticoid, androgen, progesterone, mineralocorticoid, and estrogen hormones) are affected in a similar manner, suggesting a broad effect on these pathways, and also suggesting a common mechanism for these effects. Additional work is needed to elucidate endocrine disruption effects in the etiology of arsenic-induced neurotoxicity.

Section Summary

- Lead produces neurotoxic effects ranging from fatigue and confusion to encephalopathy at acute high-level exposures. Chronic lower-level

exposures can result in cognitive deficits and peripheral neuropathy. Children are more sensitive than adults. Exposure of the developing nervous system can produce long-lasting neurological effects, including cognitive deficits.

- Mercury causes neurotoxic effects following acute high-level exposure and chronic low-level exposures in children and adults. The major source of exposure is from methylmercury in food. Paresthesia of the hands and feet is often the first manifestation of CNS effects in adults and children. Severe poisonings proceed to psychoses, paralysis, coma, and death. Neurodevelopmental effects at high exposure levels are undisputed. Neurodevelopmental effects following chronic low-level exposure are less conclusive but there are sufficient studies to suggest adverse effects on cognition, attention, and motor function.

- Arsenic causes acute neurotoxicity in adults and children at high exposures. Chronic exposure at significant levels is generally through contaminated drinking water and can induce neurotoxicity that first manifests as sensory changes that may progress to peripheral neuropathy. Neurodevelopmental studies of chronic exposure to low to moderate arsenic levels have been complicated by the inability to determine past exposure. There is suggestive evidence from several studies showing decreased IQ scores of children.

Go to the **COMPANION WEBSITE**

sites.sinauer.com/psychopharm2e
for Web Boxes, animations, flashcards, and other study resources.

Recommended Readings

Gilbert, S. (2012). *A Small Dose of Toxicology* (2nd ed.). Healthy World Press. Available online at: www.toxipedia.org/display/dose/A+Small+Dose+of+Toxicology

Walker, C. H., Sibly, R. M., Hopkin, S. P., and Peakall, D. B. (2012). *Principles of Ecotoxicology* (4th ed.). Boca Raton, FL: CRC Press.

Dong, M. H. (2012). *An Introduction to Environmental Toxicology* (2nd ed.). Elk Grove, CA: Lash and Temple.

Merrill, R. M. (2012). *Introduction to Epidemiology* (2nd ed.). Burlington, MA: Jones and Barlett Learning.

Feelings of fear, helplessness, and horror may lead to anxiety disorders such as posttraumatic stress disorder.

Anxiety Disorders: Sedative–Hypnotic and Anxiolytic Drugs

18

A NUMBER OF YEARS AGO, a psychologist was asked to make a house call to a woman having panic disorder with agoraphobia. Mrs. M. was 67 years old and lived in a lower-middle class section of the city. Her adult daughter was one of her few remaining contacts with the world and had requested the evaluation. Mrs. M. was friendly and was glad to see the clinician. He was the first person she had seen in 3 weeks. Mrs. M. had not set foot out of that apartment in 20 years, and she had suffered from panic disorder with agoraphobia for over 30 years.

As her story was told, she provided vivid images of the tragedy of a wasted life. Early in her very stressful marriage to a man who abused alcohol and her, Mrs. M. had her first panic attack and had gradually withdrawn from the world. Even areas of her apartment signaled the potential for terrifying panic attacks. She did not answer the door herself because she had not looked out in her hallway for the past 15 years. She reported that she could enter her kitchen and go into the areas containing her stove and refrigerator, but that she had not been to the back of her kitchen overlooking the backyard for the past 10 years. Thus her life for the past decade had revolved around her bedroom, her living room, and the front half of her kitchen. She relied on her daughter to bring in groceries and visit once a week. Her only remaining contact with the outside world was through the television and the radio. As long as she stayed within her apartment, she was relatively free of panic. In her mind, there were few reasons left in her life to venture out, and she declined treatment (adapted from Barlow and Durand, 1995).

Neurobiology of Anxiety

We turn now to a class of maladaptive behaviors that have *anxiety* as a major component. As a group, they produce an enormous amount of suffering, contribute to low productivity, and generate a poor quality of life for a large number of individuals. Although the incidence of each syndrome varies, it has been estimated that 10% to 30% of Americans will suffer from a significant anxiety disorder at some point in their lives. The ways in which that anxiety is expressed vary greatly and include episodes of panic, phobic avoidance of anxiety-eliciting stimuli, intrusive thoughts or compulsive behaviors, and damaging negative thinking patterns. In addition, anxiety is a factor commonly associated with other psychopathology, particularly clinical depression. The link between anxiety and depression is well documented: according to the National Comorbidity Survey, 58% of patients with major depression also show signs of anxiety disorder (Ninan, 1999). Furthermore, both neurobiological and pharmacological evidence support the idea of a common link between the two. Before describing in section two some of the psychiatric disorders in which anxiety is a major characteristic, let's look a little closer at the neurobiology of anxiety itself. The third section of this chapter will discuss the drugs that can be used to treat anxiety disorders—barbiturates, benzodiazepines, and second-generation anxiolytics[1]—as well as some of the potential new approaches to treatment.

What is anxiety?

Most anxiety manifests as a subjectively unsettling feeling of concern or worry that is displayed by behaviors including a worried facial expression as well as by bodily responses such as increased muscle tension, restlessness, impaired concentration, sleep disturbances, and irritability. In addition, activation of the sympathetic branch of the autonomic nervous system (ANS) produces increased heart rate, sweating, shortness of breath, and other signs of the "fight-or-flight" response (see Chapter 2). Anxiety can vary in intensity from feelings of vague discomfort to intense sensations of terror.

Evolutionarily, anxiety is important to survival since it warns us of danger and activates the fight-or-flight response, enabling us to cope with impending emergency. Unfortunately, many of the dangers we face in the modern world do not involve fighting off or running from predators like the saber-toothed tiger, when increased heart rate and blood pressure, elevated blood glucose, and surges of adrenaline would

be beneficial. Most of the anxiety-provoking situations that we face demand instead that we restrain our aggressive impulses (wanting to attack our hostile boss), think clearly (during a difficult exam), and remain in the anxiety-producing situation (giving a speech to a large group) until a resolution occurs. In these circumstances, the fight-or-flight response is not helpful and may impair our ability to perform at our best.

Nevertheless, despite its unpleasantness, anxiety in small doses is clearly a necessary stimulus for optimum performance in many everyday situations. If it is contextually appropriate, anxiety is a highly adaptive response to threat. Anxiety before an exam encourages more study; anxiety before public speaking forces us to practice our presentation one more time; anxiety before a first date prompts us to recheck our plans for the evening. Regardless of whether we are students, factory workers, or business people, it is anxiety that boosts our energy level and pushes us to work harder and longer. But sometimes we experience too much of a good thing. When anxiety increases beyond a certain level, performance deteriorates noticeably, particularly on complex tasks. What begins as increasing alertness and focus becomes preoccupation with our own agitation that distracts us from our task. The ANS prepares our bodies for emergency; our muscles are tense and we may suffer from digestive problems, sleep disturbances leading to fatigue, and psychosomatic illness. The overanxious student often cannot focus on an important exam because he is too preoccupied with thoughts of how awful it would be to fail. Worst of all, because high anxiety has damaged our performance, our failures provide more reason to be anxious, creating an escalating circular pattern (**Figure 18.1**). Once we begin to have negative feelings about ourselves and our lack of productivity, depression may develop.

Brief episodes of anxiety, even when rather intense, are not likely to be harmful and may be quite rational in many situations. Acute anxiety occurs in response to real-life stressors, and symptoms occur only in response to these events. Pharmacological treatment is very effective in providing relief from the anxiety associated with major life changes such as death of a loved one, divorce or permanent disability, or sudden stressors like major surgery that trigger intense anxiety. The anxiolytics in the benzodiazepine class are extremely effective for relieving this type of anxiety.

Although anxiety is related to the negative emotion fear, it is also somewhat different. Anxiety is apprehension about possible future events or misfortune and concern about the ability to predict or deal with these events. In contrast, fear is an emotional response to clear and current danger, as occurs when confronted by a threatening bear. It is characterized by a strong

---

[1]An anxiolytic is a drug that reduces anxiety.

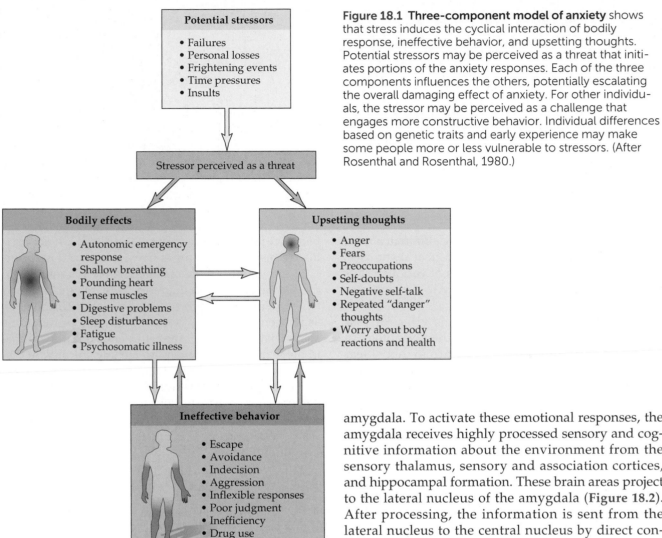

Potential stressors

- Failures
- Personal losses
- Frightening events
- Time pressures
- Insults

Stressor perceived as a threat

Bodily effects

- Autonomic emergency response
- Shallow breathing
- Pounding heart
- Tense muscles
- Digestive problems
- Sleep disturbances
- Fatigue
- Psychosomatic illness

Upsetting thoughts

- Anger
- Fears
- Preoccupations
- Self-doubts
- Negative self-talk
- Repeated "danger" thoughts
- Worry about body reactions and health

Ineffective behavior

- Escape
- Avoidance
- Indecision
- Aggression
- Inflexible responses
- Poor judgment
- Inefficiency
- Drug use

Figure 18.1 Three-component model of anxiety shows that stress induces the cyclical interaction of bodily response, ineffective behavior, and upsetting thoughts. Potential stressors may be perceived as a threat that initiates portions of the anxiety responses. Each of the three components influences the others, potentially escalating the overall damaging effect of anxiety. For other individuals, the stressor may be perceived as a challenge that engages more constructive behavior. Individual differences based on genetic traits and early experience may make some people more or less vulnerable to stressors. (After Rosenthal and Rosenthal, 1980.)

urge to escape, and it elicits a strong activation of the autonomic nervous system to mobilize the energy for "fight or flight." These two emotions differ not only in their temporal nature, but also in terms of psychological and neurobiological consequences.

The amygdala is important to emotion processing circuits

The amygdaloid complex, a structure deep within the temporal lobes, is a major component of several emotion processing circuits. These circuits have many components in addition to the amygdala and include structures of the limbic cortex (insula and anterior cingulate cortex [ACC]), hypothalamus, and hippocampus. The circuits evaluate environmental stimuli, contextual cues, and cognitions that have emotional relevance, and initiate appropriate responses via the

amygdala. To activate these emotional responses, the amygdala receives highly processed sensory and cognitive information about the environment from the sensory thalamus, sensory and association cortices, and hippocampal formation. These brain areas project to the lateral nucleus of the amygdala (**Figure 18.2**). After processing, the information is sent from the lateral nucleus to the central nucleus by direct connections, and by indirect connections via the basolateral nucleus. Fearful stimuli activate the amygdala in healthy human subjects as visualized with positron emission tomography (PET) scanning, and in laboratory animals, electrical stimulation of the amygdala produces signs of anxiety and fear.

The central nucleus of the amygdala orchestrates the components of fear: ANS activation, enhanced reflexes, increased vigilance, activation of the hypothalamic–pituitary–adrenal (HPA) axis, and other responses (LeDoux, 1996). Stimulation of the central nucleus has such widespread effects because of its multiple connections with brain areas that are responsible for how emotion is expressed. For example, projections to the lateral hypothalamus activate the sympathetic nervous system, those to the periaqueductal gray cause freezing, others that activate the locus coeruleus initiate arousal and vigilance, and so forth (refer to **Figure 18.3** for details). Damaging selected brain areas that receive projection neurons from the central nucleus can eliminate specific components of the anxiety response, and damaging

Figure 18.2 Flow diagram of connections of the amygdala This much simplified diagram shows how anxiety-related information processed by several brain areas inputs first to the lateral nucleus of the amygdala. From the lateral nucleus, it goes to the central nucleus (directly and indirectly) and the bed nucleus of the stria terminalis (BNST), which innervate widespread brain regions to orchestrate the components of emotion.

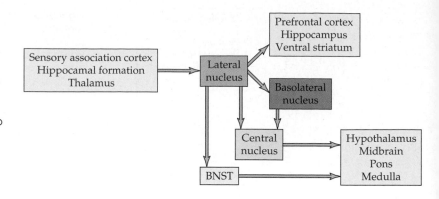

the central nucleus itself reduces or eliminates most emotional behaviors and physiological responses. Furthermore, intracerebral injection of various drugs into the amygdala reduces anxiety in a number of animal tests.

Although the central nucleus is vital for fear responses, evidence suggests that the physiology of anxiety may be somewhat different from that of fear (Walker et al., 2009). Although amygdaloid processing still plays a central role in the emotional circuit, the behavioral responses in anxiety may be initiated by a brain area referred to as the "extended amygdala," the

bed nucleus of the stria terminalis (BNST). It is possible that each of these areas may be involved in different types of anxiety disorders. The BNST is similar to the central nucleus in anatomy, cytoarchitecture, and neurochemistry. It projects to the same brain regions as the central nucleus (see Figure 18.2) but functions somewhat differently. The central nucleus plays a role in the fear response when threatening stimuli are distinct cues that appear suddenly and predict an aversive event, which also ends abruptly. This is modeled by conditioned fear-potentiated startle paradigm in rats (see Chapter 4). In contrast to the rapid response

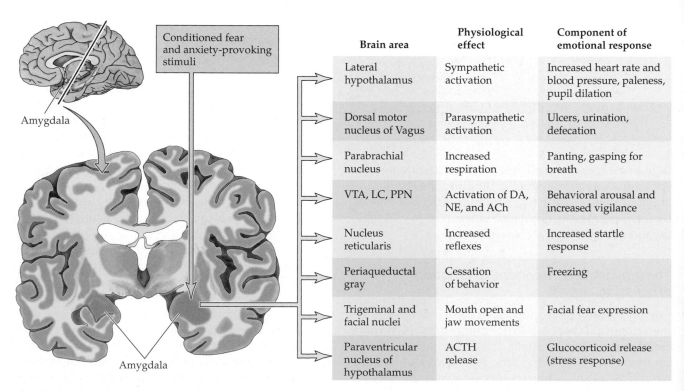

Figure 18.3 The amygdala coordinates components of emotion The amygdala has neuronal connections with all of these brain areas that produce individual pieces of emotional expression. ACh, acetylcholine; ACTH, adrenocorticotropic hormone; DA, dopamine; LC, locus coeruleus; NE, norepinephrine; PPN, pedunculopontine nucleus; VTA, ventral tegmental area.

system mediated by the central nucleus, the BNST initiates components of the emotional response when the stimuli are less precise predictors of a potentially dangerous situation. It produces a state of sustained preparedness for an unclear danger and a prolonged period of anticipation that something unpleasant might occur. In addition, this response persists long after the initial stimulus is ended and resembles the state of anxiety. Anxiety in the elevated plus-maze (see Chapter 4) is modulated by manipulations of the BNST. It is especially interesting to note that chronic restraint stress or chronic unpredictable stress increases dendritic length and branching, as well as volume of the BNST. This stress-induced plasticity was accompanied by increased anxiety in the elevated plus-maze. It is tempting to speculate that similar stress-induced plasticity may increase vulnerability to anxiety disorders. Additionally, the increased vulnerability is significant because BNST-dependent anxiety is modulated by sex hormones and may explain gender differences in anxiety disorders. Gender differences in stress response are discussed more fully later in this section.

In addition to identifying the emotional significance of events, the amygdala aids in the formation of emotional memories, sometimes called conditioned fear or conditioned emotional response (CER). An emotional memory, or CER, involves making an association between an environmental stimulus and an aversive stimulus, for example, the sound of a tone preceding the onset of a brief electrical shock. After only a few pairings, sounding the tone will lead to elevated heart rate, rapid breathing, secretion of stress hormones, and other signs of anxiety. Emotional memories are established quickly and are long lasting. Formation of the classically conditioned CER is significant for survival because it allows an animal to anticipate danger and to be prepared physiologically and behaviorally to cope with the situation. The association is formed in the lateral amygdala, which activates the central nucleus that in turn activates those brain areas responsible for individual components of the response. Although this emotional memory is important for survival, it is clear that if the emotional response generalizes to many similar stimuli, a chronic state of anxiety could result.

The amygdala also contributes to the enhancement of memory consolidation through its connections with the hippocampus (shown in Figure 18.2). Memories of events and their context are established in the hippocampus, and that memory consolidation is significantly improved for events with strong emotional relevance. In addition to memory consolidation, the hippocampus may have a role in some anxiety disorders because reciprocal connections with the amygdala modulate emotional responses on the basis

of context. The anxious behaviors of people suffering from anxiety disorders are not abnormal in character, but are expressed in contextually inappropriate situations (Davidson et al., 2000).

Although activation of the amygdala elicits emotional responses, the prefrontal cortex (PFC; particularly the orbitofrontal and medial prefrontal) and the subgenual anterior cingulate cortex exert inhibitory control over the more primitive responses of the subcortical regions. Without control by the PFC, which is responsible for planning, decision making, and evaluating consequences of behavior, the anxiety response produces more limited patterns of behavior that may not be suitable for coping with modern stressors that are not resolved by fighting or running away. Furthermore, the medial PFC is important for fear extinction, that is, for learning that a cue that once predicted danger no longer does so. Anxiety disorders are frequently considered to arise from an imbalance between emotion generating centers and higher cortical control (see the second section of this chapter, which describes the characteristics of anxiety). Neuroimaging has become increasingly important in generating neurocircuitry models of the disorders.

Multiple neurotransmitters mediate anxiety

Neurobiological hypotheses of anxiety disorders have been tested in animal studies and in clinical evaluation. The anatomical complexity of emotion and its importance to survival makes it highly likely that many neurotransmitters modulate the anxiety response.

ROLE OF CORTICOTROPIN-RELEASING FACTOR IN ANXIETY Corticotropin-releasing factor (CRF; sometimes called corticotropin-releasing hormone, or CRH) is a small neuropeptide that controls the neuroendocrine (HPA axis), autonomic, and behavioral responses to stress. As you know from Chapter 2, the HPA axis is activated by the release of CRF from the paraventricular nucleus of the hypothalamus in response to stress. CRF is responsible for inducing the anterior pituitary to release the stress hormone adrenocorticotropic hormone (ACTH) into the blood, which in turn increases the release of glucocorticoids such as cortisol from the adrenal cortex. These hormones induce a variety of physiological changes that provide the means to adapt to environmental challenges. In addition, elevated cortisol initiates a negative feedback loop by binding to receptors on the hippocampus, hypothalamus, and pituitary, which inhibits HPA axis function and brings cortisol levels back to normal. In addition to its role in stress hormone regulation, CRF acts as a neurotransmitter in neural circuits involved in the stress response including

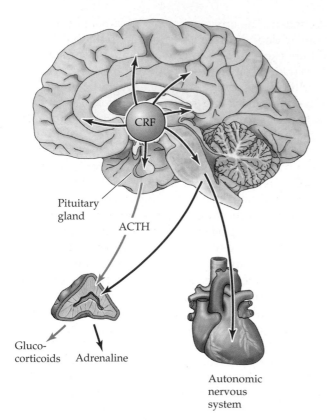

Pituitary
gland

ACTH

Gluco-
corticoids   Adrenaline

Autonomic
nervous
system

Figure 18.4 Dual role for CRF CRF is released by the
hypothalamus to act on the pituitary gland to control the
release of glucocorticoids from the adrenal cortex (HPA
axis) in response to stress (blue pathway). CRF also acts
as a neurotransmitter in multiple brain areas associated
with anxiety (indicated by purple) and is released following
threatening stimuli. Intracerebral CRF causes behavioral
signs of anxiety as well as altered autonomic nervous system function (red pathways). ACTH, adrenocorticotropic
hormone.

the amygdala (**Figure 18.4**). Therefore, the release of this
tiny peptide may help coordinate the mechanism needed
to adapt to stressful events and hence may contribute
to anxiety disorders.

Intraventricular administration of CRF stimulates
the sympathetic nervous system and causes increases in plasma adrenaline and increased heart rate and
blood pressure. These effects are not due to HPA axis
activation, because removing the adrenal gland does
not change this response to cerebral CRF. Therefore,
the effects must be mediated by extra-hypothalamic
neural control such as excitation of the locus coeruleus
(LC) (see the following section on the role of norepinephrine). CRF also has wide-ranging effects on feeding, gastrointestinal activity, and energy balance that
are consistent with preparation for dealing with environmental stressors. CRF causes increased anxiety as
seen in conflict tests, social interaction, exploration in

novel open fields, and the elevated plus-maze (these
and other tests of anxiety are described in Chapter 4).
Direct neuronal application of CRF produces strong
excitatory effects in many brain areas that contain significant numbers of CRF receptors, including the hippocampus, amygdala, LC, cortex, and hypothalamus,
all of which are parts of the neural circuit for anxiety. Of particular significance are the large numbers
of CRF nerve endings and CRF receptors found in the
amygdala. Further, individual differences in anxiety
level may be due to differences in the amount of CRF
in the amygdala (Davis, 1997). For example, rats that
show greater "freezing" responses to stress and show
enhanced physiological signs also have higher levels
of CRF mRNA in the central nucleus of the amygdala
compared with less anxious rat strains. Clinical studies show that CRF levels are higher in the cerebrospinal fluid of combat veterans with posttraumatic stress
disorder (PTSD) than in veterans without the anxiety
disorder.

Stressful stimuli such as physical restraint cause a
release of CRF in the amygdala, as measured by microdialysis. The increased extracellular CRF is accompanied by a variety of signs of anxiety. Many of these
effects can be prevented by pretreatment with the CRF
antagonist α-helical CRF_{9-41}. However, not all measures of anxiety are attenuated by intra-amygdaloid
infusion of the CRF antagonist, which suggests that
other areas within the central nervous system (CNS)
such as the LC must also mediate aspects of anxiety.

CRF neurons originating in the central nucleus of
the amygdala project to the LC and activate the adrenergic component of the stress response. Intracranial
injection of CRF increases the firing rate of cells in the
LC and increases the turnover of norepinephrine (NE),
as determined by the increase in the NE metabolite
MHPG in the amygdala (via reciprocal connections),
hypothalamus, hippocampus, and PFC. It should
be no surprise that infusion of CRF into the LC produces anxiety, as measured by time spent in the novel
open field. For all these reasons, the neuroendocrine
and CNS effects of CRF are generating a great deal
of research in neuroscience, and the neuropeptide is
a target for new drug development. **Web Box 18.1**
describes CRF antagonists and several other novel
approaches to treating anxiety.

ROLE OF NOREPINEPHRINE IN ANXIETY Reciprocal connections between the amygdala and the LC provide
a mechanism for generating arousal, orienting, and
responding to fear-evoking stimuli. The LC is a major
cluster of noradrenergic cell bodies in the dorsal pons that
send axons rostrally to several brain areas to increase vigilance and attention to physiologically relevant stimuli.
Several lines of evidence demonstrate the importance of

NE in anxiety. First, electrical recording in the LC shows increased firing when animals are presented with novel stimuli that signal threat or reward (Jacobs et al., 1995). The accompanying hypervigilance is similar to that occurring in PTSD and other anxiety disorders in humans. Electrical stimulation of the LC or administration of the α_2-autoreceptor antagonist yohimbine (which increases NE release) induces a wide range of alerting and fear responses accompanied by pupil dilation, piloerection, and increased heart rate in primates. Yohimbine likewise produces panic attacks in patients with panic disorder or PTSD, but not in normal subjects. Also, clonidine, an α_2-autoreceptor agonist (which reduces NE release), has antianxiety effects (Ninan, 1999).

Second, clinical studies of patients with a variety of anxiety disorders suggest that abnormal ANS response is a common key feature. NE is the neurotransmitter released at the target visceral organs, including the heart, during sympathetic activation. Additionally, the catecholamine adrenaline (epinephrine), released from the adrenal medulla, produces widespread effects that prepare the individual to respond to danger. Individuals with panic disorder and PTSD have especially dramatic body responses to anxiety-provoking stimuli. Furthermore, war veterans with PTSD have higher-than-normal circulating NE.

Third, both NE and epinephrine have a significant role in the formation of emotional memories that may contribute to anxiety disorders in which memories of past trauma or stress can influence future behavior (as in agoraphobia seen in the opening vignette, panic, and PTSD). The normal enhancement of memory by the catecholamines may be a way to help us remember what is emotionally significant and therefore important. However, in the case of individuals with PTSD, those memories become intrusive and they re-experience the extreme anxiety associated with their trauma over and over, both in the day as flashbacks and at night as nightmares. Fortunately, modifying NE function with drugs may represent a useful treatment for PTSD. Animal studies have shown that β-adrenergic agonists injected into the amygdala improve the consolidation of memory into long-term storage, and β-adrenergic antagonists impair the formation of emotional memories and associated physiological changes. This means that in humans, it may be possible to interfere with the formation of traumatic memories by blocking β-adrenergic receptors right after a severe trauma. It may also be possible to modify existing traumatic memories because in addition to helping consolidate new memories, β-adrenergic agonists may have a role in reconsolidation processes. It is believed that recalling or retrieving a memory makes it temporarily unstable and susceptible to interference that would prevent the reconsolidation needed to maintain the memory. On this basis, it was suggested that the use of β-adrenergic antagonists may disrupt the already consolidated traumatic memories and associated physiological responses of those suffering from PTSD. Although clinical findings are not entirely consistent, a number of reports show that the β-adrenergic antagonist propranolol reduces the initial consolidation of emotional memories. In one study, survivors of auto accidents who received propranolol in the emergency room and for the next 6 days developed fewer cases of PTSD, and those who developed PTSD had fewer symptoms compared with those individuals who declined the propranolol treatment (Vaiva et al., 2003). Propranolol treatment also was effective in disrupting emotional memories that have been previously consolidated and retrieved in response to a learned fear cue or personalized trauma scripts (i.e., specific reminders of the individual's traumatic experience). The β-blocker given before retrieval of the emotional memory does not seem to impair the declarative memory of the association of the conditioned and unconditioned stimuli, but it does seem to significantly diminish the emotional effects. This means that the individual would still remember the traumatic event but would not respond emotionally to associated cues (Shad et al., 2011).

Fourth, some of the therapeutic effects of anxiolytic drugs can be explained by modulation of LC firing (Sullivan et al., 1999). Noradrenergic cells in the LC are excited by CRF synaptic input and are inhibited by γ-aminobutyric acid (GABA) and serotonin (5-HT), as well as by stimulation of α_2-adrenergic somatodendritic autoreceptors (**Figure 18.5**). Since benzodiazepines enhance the inhibitory function of GABA, reduced LC firing may be responsible for at least some of the anxiolytic effects of these drugs. Serotonin reuptake blockade by selective serotonin reuptake inhibitors (SSRIs) and subsequent enhancement of serotonergic function would likewise reduce LC firing and explain some of their antianxiety effects. Tricyclic antidepressants such as desipramine and monoamine oxidase inhibitors that are used to treat selective anxiety disorders enhance NE function, which inhibits firing of LC neurons by acting on the α_2-autoreceptors (see Figure 18.5). In support of the therapeutic evidence, clinical studies have found abnormal autoreceptor response in individuals with generalized anxiety disorder (GAD) and social phobia (Sullivan et al., 1999).

ROLE OF GABA IN ANXIETY The inhibitory amino acid neurotransmitter GABA has a major role in modulating anxiety. As you recall from Chapter 8, GABA is the principal inhibitory neurotransmitter in the nervous system. The $GABA_A$ receptor complex comprises a chloride (Cl^-) channel that when opened following GABA binding

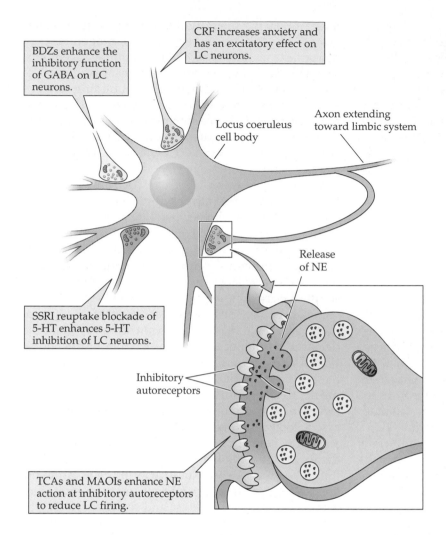

BDZs enhance the inhibitory function of GABA on LC neurons.

CRF increases anxiety and has an excitatory effect on LC neurons.

Locus coeruleus cell body

Axon extending toward limbic system

Release of NE

SSRI reuptake blockade of 5-HT enhances 5-HT inhibition of LC neurons.

Inhibitory autoreceptors

TCAs and MAOIs enhance NE action at inhibitory autoreceptors to reduce LC firing.

Figure 18.5 Drug effects on locus coeruleus (LC) cell firing Some of the anxiolytic effects of the benzodiazepines (BDZs), tricyclic antidepressants (TCAs), monoamine oxidase inhibitors (MAOIs), and selective serotonin reuptake inhibitors (SSRIs) may be explained by their inhibitory effect on LC neurons. On the other hand, corticotropin-releasing factor (CRF) increases anxiety and has excitatory effects on the LC. CRF antagonists may be effective in reducing anxiety.

tion was mapped in the rat brain using autoradiography, it became clear that benzodiazepine modulatory sites are widely distributed and are found on many, but not all, GABA receptor complexes. A PET scan of BDZ modulatory sites in the human brain shows their wide distribution (**Figure 18.6**). Their high concentration in the amygdala and in other parts of the limbic system that regulate fear/anxiety responses, and in the cerebral cortex (particularly the frontal lobe), which exerts control over limbic structures, provides the first clue to their function.

To clarify the role of the BDZ binding sites in neuropharmacological and behavioral experiments, a specific receptor antagonist, flumazenil, was developed. Flumazenil prevents the effects of BDZ binding but has no effect on the GABA receptor. A second group of substances have been

allows Cl⁻ to enter the cell, causing hyperpolarization. Several sedative–hypnotics enhance the function of GABA, causing sedation, reduced anxiety, and anticonvulsant effects. Benzodiazepines and barbiturates produce these effects by binding to distinct modulatory sites different from the GABA binding site on the receptor complex (further discussion of these drugs is found in section three of this chapter). Ethyl alcohol also enhances GABA function, although its precise mechanism remains unclear (see Chapter 10). Naturally occurring neurosteroids such as allopregnanalone additionally act as positive modulators at distinct sites on the receptor complex and also produce sedative–hypnotic and anxiolytic effects. The reader is directed to Figure 8.15 for a schematic diagram of the GABA receptor complex.

THE BENZODIAZEPINE (BDZ) BINDING SITE A great deal is known about the mechanism of action of the BDZs because they are the most clinically useful GABA modulators, and their neuropharmacology has told us a great deal about the neurochemistry of anxiety. The BDZ binding sites were identified in 1977. When their loca-

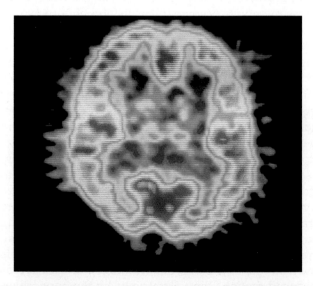

Figure 18.6 PET scan of benzodiazepine receptors in the human brain The highest concentrations are shown in orange and red. (Courtesy of Goran Sedvall.)

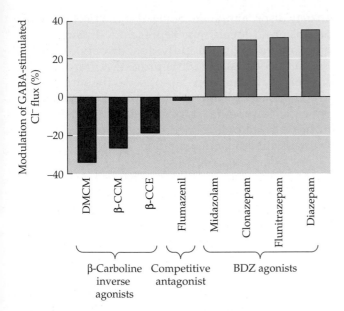

Figure 18.7 Modulation of GABA-induced chloride (Cl⁻) flux The anxiolytic BDZs are agonists (blue bars) and enhance the effects of GABA. The competitive antagonist flumazenil binds to the BDZ receptor but has no action of its own. However, it prevents either the BDZs or the inverse agonists from acting. The anxiety-producing β-carbolines (red bars) are inverse agonists at the BDZ receptor. They not only prevent the effect of GABA on Cl⁻ flux but produce the opposite effect, which leads to cell excitation. β-CCE, β-carboline-3-carboxylic acid ethylester; β-CCM, methyl-β-carboline-3-carboxylate; DMCM, methyl-6,7-dimethoxy-4-ethyl-β-carboline-3-carboxylate. (After Richards et al., 1991.)

found to bind to the BDZ sites and act as inverse agonists. They produce the opposite actions of the BDZ drugs, namely, increased anxiety, arousal, and seizures. One class of inverse agonists is the β-**carboline** family, which when administered to humans produce extreme anxiety and an overwhelming sense of panic. β-Carbolines have been very useful tools in the study of the neurobiology of anxiety. These inverse agonists are presumed to uncouple the GABA receptors from the Cl⁻ channels so that GABA is less effective in causing entry of Cl⁻ into the cells (**Figure 18.7**), leading to increased membrane excitability.

The importance of GABA is directly shown by the reduction in anxiety produced by local administration of GABA or the GABA agonist musimol into the amygdala. Intracranial administration of BDZs into the amygdala also has anxiolytic effects in several animal tests, including the light–dark crossing test, freezing response, elevated plus-maze, and operant conflict tests. The anticonflict effects indicative of reduced anxiety can be reversed by the benzodiazepine binding-site antagonist flumazenil and also by co-administration of the GABA antagonist bicuculline

into the amygdala. Furthermore, Sanders and Shekhar (1995) found that intra-amygdaloid injection of flumazenil or bicuculline also blocks *systemic* antianxiety effects of the benzodiazepine chlordiazepoxide in the social interaction test. The bicuculline effect demonstrates the necessity for GABA activity in the anxiolytic effects of BDZs. The amygdala, particularly the basolateral nucleus, is clearly an important site mediating the antianxiety effects of BDZs. However, since BDZs can still have anxiety-reducing effects following destruction of the amygdala, multiple redundant brain areas must be involved in the response to anxiety (see Davis, 2006, for an excellent summary).

Other evidence suggesting that BDZ binding sites mediate anxiety comes from studies that look at natural differences in animal anxiety in conflict situations such as the water-lick suppression test. In any group of animals, some (the "laid-back" type) become adapted to the tongue shock with repeated exposure and drink despite the shock, while their "uptight" littermates dramatically avoid drinking. The more emotional animals have fewer BDZ binding sites in several brain areas (Sepinwall and Cook, 1980). Other studies find a correlation between anxiety in the elevated plus-maze and decreased numbers of GABA and BDZ binding sites in mouse cerebral cortex (Rago et al., 1988).

Malizia and coworkers (1998) and others have shown with PET scans that patients with panic disorder show less benzodiazepine binding in the CNS, particularly in portions of the frontal lobes including the orbitofrontal cortex, medial prefrontal, and insula, as well as limbic structures involved in the anxiety neurocircuitry (**Figure 18.8**). These patients, compared with healthy individuals, are also less sensitive to BDZs on several psychophysiological measures such as eye movement to targets, and clinical evidence confirms that these patients require higher doses to reduce anxiety. Reductions in BDZ binding have also been found in selected brain areas of individuals with GAD and PTSD. It seems reasonable that reduced BDZ binding sites may result in failure of GABA inhibition leading to uncontrolled panic attacks, phobias, generalized anxiety, and the hyperarousal of PTSD. Refer to a review by Liberzon and colleagues (2003) for more detail on the relationship between GABA and anxiety disorders based on animal studies, molecular pharmacology, and brain imaging.

ROLE OF NEUROSTEROID MODULATION OF GABA IN ANXIETY Substantial evidence indicates that neuroactive steroids provide an additional modulatory role in anxiety. A family of neurosteroids, including pregnenolone, allopregnanolone, tetrahydrodeoxycorticosterone, and dehydroepiandrosterone (DHEA), are synthesized from cholesterol in both the central and peripheral nervous sys-

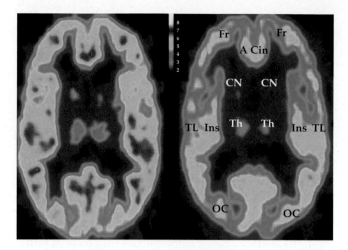

Figure 18.8 PET scans of a control subject (left) and a patient with panic disorder (right) The scans made in the horizontal plane with the frontal cortex at the top show decreased density of BDZ binding sites in the patient with panic disorder, particularly in the frontal cortex (Fr), anterior cingulate (A Cin), and insula (Ins), areas important in anxiety modulation. Other brain areas also show reduced numbers of BDZ binding sites. Warm colors indicate the most receptors; cool colors indicate fewer. Receptors were labeled with [^{11}C]flumazenil. CN, caudate nucleus; OC, occipital cortex; Th, thalamus; TL, temporal lobe. (From Malizia et al., 1998.)

anxiety disorder and generalized social phobia. Hence neurosteroid levels may represent a distinguishing biomarker among the individual anxiety disorders. Eser and colleagues (2006) provide a thorough discussion of the relationship of several neurosteroids to both anxiety disorders and depression and suggest potential therapeutic strategies such as creating synthetic neurosteroid-like agonists or manipulating their natural synthesis or degradation.

ROLE OF SEROTONIN IN ANXIETY There is a rich literature on the serotonergic link with mood, suicide, violence, and impulsivity (Apter et al., 1990). Likewise, 5-HT plays a large role in anxiety modulation, although the precise role has been difficult to delineate because of the large number of 5-HT receptor subtypes and its widespread innervation of brain structures in the complex neurocircuitry regulating anxiety. The neurotransmitter's role in anxiety is based to a large extent on the effectiveness of various drug treatments. The anxiolytic effects of 5-HT are demonstrated by the effectiveness of SSRIs, which enhance 5-HT function, in treating a variety of anxiety disorders. In a classic study, Blier and de Montigny (1999) found that SSRIs desensitize terminal 5-HT autoreceptors (but not 5-HT$_2$ receptors) in the orbitofrontal cortex only after a full 8 weeks of treatment, when improvement in symptoms of obsessive–compulsive disorder is seen. Desensitized autoreceptors indicate that more 5-HT is released to act on postsynaptic 5-HT$_2$ receptors. If a similar mechanism occurs in the LC, the enhanced serotonergic activity that gradually occurs may explain the progressive reduction in LC firing (Szabo et al., 1999) that is consistent with the slow onset of action in the treatment of panic attacks. Furthermore, SSRI efficacy can be prevented by reducing 5-HT synthesis with tryptophan depletion, indicating that 5-HT is needed for anxiolysis. However, in patients with a variety of anxiety disorders, tryptophan depletion does not consistently increase their anxiety as we might expect. Additionally, in anxious patients, evaluating 5-HT function by measuring hormonal response and by using behavioral measures has not revealed consistent differences in 5-HT function compared with control subjects.

Results from animal studies also show that 5-HT modulates anxiety, although it sometimes reduces anxiety and at other times increases it, depending on the anxiety model used (reviewed by Gordon and Hen, 2004). In general, in tasks requiring active coping with a stressor such as making an escape response, 5-HT agonists tend to be anxiolytic. In contrast, 5-HT agonists increase anxiety in tasks involving passive behavior or withholding a response to anticipated threat. These contrasting effects may be explained by the subtype of 5-HT receptor involved in the task, differences in acute and chronic treatment, or the specific

tems. They are elevated by physiological stressors such as forced swim and foot shock stress and have anxiolytic effects in animal models, including the light–dark test, open field, lick suppression, and elevated plus-maze. Additionally, they have potent anticonvulsant effects. The anxiolytic effects occur following both systemic and intraventricular administration. The importance of amygdala mediation of these effects was shown by direct infusion into the central nucleus. Neuroactive steroids bind to a site on the GABA$_A$ receptor that is different from those sites described thus far and potentiate the effect of GABA by increasing the duration of GABA-induced chloride channel opening.

Surprisingly, baseline levels of neurosteroids are *elevated* in individuals with panic disorder compared with controls. However, some have suggested that the higher levels may represent a natural self-defense mechanism that protects against spontaneous panic attacks. When a panic attack was induced in these patients, the levels dropped; this signals reduced GABA control of the anxiety. Since there was no change in control subjects even when they experienced similar levels of panic anxiety, it suggests that the reduction in neurosteroid is not caused by anxiety itself but may represent the underlying pathophysiology of the disorder. In contrast, neurosteroid levels tend to be lower in individuals treated for generalized brain regions involved in fear versus anxiety (active coping versus passive responding).

In addition to the effects of 5-HT in the adult, 5-HT has a neurotrophic effect during fetal development and is critical for normal development of the anxiety circuitry. This means that appropriate regulation of both pre- and postnatal serotonergic function is needed to prevent anatomical, functional, and behavioral abnormalities. The amygdala and the PFC are two brain areas that show serotonin-dependent developmental differences in morphology and activity. It is of interest that infants and adults having a polymorphism of the promoter region of the 5-HT reuptake transporter (SERT) gene show increased emotionality and anxiety. People with one or two short alleles had a significantly smaller volume of the amygdala and the subgenual anterior cingulate cortex. In addition, neuronal connectivity between the two regions was weaker. Similar reductions in white matter connections between the amygdala and several regions of the PFC were reported by others. It seems reasonable to assume that such differences may be responsible for variations in processing of emotional events. In fact, when anticipating public speaking, individuals with social phobia having one or two short alleles reported higher symptom severity and increased anxiety and showed greater neural activity in the amygdala than phobic individuals with two long alleles (Furmark et al., 2004).

Individuals having the short version of the 5-HT reuptake transporter gene express fewer reuptake transporters than those with long alleles, which means that more 5-HT remains in the synapse. Since elevated 5-HT in the adult is associated with enhanced mood and reduced impulsivity and aggression, it is likely that the polymorphism and the resulting elevation in synaptic 5-HT have their impact during early brain development, and that this causes abnormalities in brain structure and emotional traits. Animal studies support this conclusion since similar increases in anxiety occur in knockout mice lacking SERT or 5-HT_{1A} receptors, suggesting that the 5-HT_{1A} receptor mediates the neurodevelopmental effect. In addition, reducing 5-HT reuptake during the first 2 weeks of life in rodents increases anxious behaviors in the adults, indicating that the developmental effect of elevated 5-HT may extend to early postnatal periods as well. Since environmental events influence 5-HT function, it is possible that stress-induced alterations in 5-HT during pre- or early postnatal development may in part explain why early life stress predisposes some individuals to anxiety disorders and depression later in life (more detail is provided in the section on gene–environment interactions). For further information, the reader may refer to excellent reviews by Gross and Hen (2004) and Nordquist and Oreland (2010).

ROLE OF DOPAMINE IN ANXIETY   A modulatory role for dopamine (DA) is suggested by the significant DA projections from the ventral tegmental area (VTA) to the mPFC (mesocortical tract) and limbic regions including the amygdala (mesolimbic tract). Stress such as forced swimming or administration of the anxiety producing β-carboline FG7142 increases firing of mesocortical dopaminergic neurons and increases DA turnover in the prefrontal cortex. Further, the vicarious stress of observing another rat receiving foot shocks also increases DA turnover in the prefrontal neurons and elevates adrenal glucocorticoids. Enhancement of GABA function by the benzodiazepine diazepam blocks the anxiety responses to the stressors and to β-carboline treatment and also prevents the DA turnover (Kaneyuki et al., 1991).

Dopaminergic projections to the amygdala from the VTA apparently inhibit the normal descending inhibition from the mPFC and permit expression of adaptive anxiety responses. These mesolimbic DA cells are activated by stressful or threatening environmental stimuli. The released DA acting on D_1 and D_2 receptors in the amygdala reduces the inhibitory control of local GABA interneurons that are activated by the PFC. Decreasing inhibitory control increases amygdaloid activation. In support of this hypothesis, a variety of stressors increase release and turnover of DA in the central and basolateral nuclei of the amygdala, where D_2 and D_1 receptors, respectively, are most densely located. As would be expected, reducing dopaminergic transmission with neurotoxic lesions of the VTA–amygdala pathway reduces conditioned fear and fear-potentiated startle and impairs acquisition of avoidance behavior. Furthermore, intra-amygdaloid injection of D_1 receptor agonists increases anxiety responses in a variety of rodent models, and antagonists at the D_1 receptor produce anxiolytic effects. The effects of D_2 agonists and antagonists are more difficult to interpret since their effects vary depending on the type of fear/anxiety paradigm utilized, which may reflect the distinct role played by D_1 and D_2 receptors in fear and anxiety. De la Mora and colleagues (2010) provide an in-depth discussion of the structure and function of DA mechanisms in fear and anxiety.

Genes and environment interact to determine the tendency to express anxiety

Now that you have an appreciation for the complexities of the anatomy and neurochemistry of anxiety, we are left with the questions of why some individuals are more anxious than others, and why some develop anxiety disorders while others are resilient. It is quite clear that there are large individual differences in the level of trait anxiety (the enduring characteristic to experience anxiety in a variety of situations) among individuals, and that this characteristic is reasonably consistent over one's lifetime. For example, evidence suggests that behavioral inhibition in young children is associated with a CRF gene polymorphism, and these individuals are more likely than average to develop social phobia and panic disorder as adolescents. Rodents also can vary in innate anxiety level, and inbred strains of rodents can be used to study the neurobiology and treatment of anxiety. Several rodent lines have been bred for anxiety as well as abnormal regulation of the HPA axis. These differences in trait anxiety levels and hormone response indicate genetically determined brain differences, and these differences may predispose some individuals to anxiety disorders. As you will see, many of the anxiety disorders are more prevalent among individuals in the same family. Nevertheless studies of monozygotic twins with identical genes do not show a strong concordance for developing such disorders, which demonstrates that life experiences must interact with a genetic vulnerability in shaping the anxious individual. A large volume of evidence has shown that aversive childhood experiences have multiple damaging effects on the adult body and brain and predispose the individual to health problems such as cardiovascular disease, as well as to psychiatric disorders including depression, anxiety, schizophrenia, and others. Although the brain shows plasticity throughout the life span, animal studies suggest that adverse events occurring prenatally and during early development have the most profound effects because of maximal brain plasticity during that time.

Both animal and human studies have shown that early exposure to stress and neglect alters the developing brain and can produce a lifelong tendency to respond to stimuli with enhanced anxiety. Both pre- and postnatal stressors have been shown to produce behaviors resembling anxiety such as enhanced freezing, increased fear-potentiated startle, hyperarousal, reduced feeding and increased defecation under stress, avoidance of novel stimuli, and others. In addition, early stress alters the programming of the HPA axis, causing a hyperactive hormonal response to challenge that persists throughout adulthood. The stability of these changes suggests epigenetic factors at work. Evidence exists for changes in DNA methylation of promoter elements that control the expression of genes within the stress circuits (see Chapter 2 for a discussion on epigenetic effects). For example, Mueller and Bale (2008) found that male offspring of mice who had been exposed to chronic, variable stressors during early fetal development (days 1 through 7 of gestation), as adults not only showed heightened HPA axis responsivity to stress compared with controls (**Figure 18.9A**), but also showed long-term increases in the expression of CRF in the central nucleus of the amygdala (**Figure 18.9B,C**), indicating an enhancement of stress neurocircuitry. These adult male mice also showed decreased expression of glucocorticoid receptors in several regions of the hippocampus that are normally responsible for restoring HPA activation to normal via the negative feedback mechanism (**Figure 18.9D,E**). Epigenetic effects were associated with these changes, including reduced methylation of the CRF promoter region in the hypothalamus and central nucleus of the amygdala and increased methylation of the glucocorticoid receptor promoter region. These may be expected to contribute to stress circuit programming during fetal development. As you will see later, postnatal stress also is capable of programming the stress responsivity, and this effect is gender specific. **Web Box 18.2** highlights the impact of early maternal neglect in determining the emotional response and hormonal reactivity of offspring to stressful events.

We are now left with the question of how epigenetic changes in the stress response might increase the probability of developing anxiety disorders. The activation of the HPA axis is critical to the survival of an animal, and destruction of the adrenal gland ultimately leads to death. However, excessive HPA activation leads to damaging effects on the body, including changes in brain structure and synaptic transmission. Prolonged stress and the subsequent elevation in glucocorticoids impair the function of the hippocampus by reducing neurogenesis, failing to protect cells against cell death (apoptosis), and preventing the normal dendritic growth and elaboration that enhance synaptic connectivity. Loss of such hippocampal plasticity is reflected in a reduction in cognitive processing and memory consolidation. Glucocorticoids also influence other brain regions that do not support neurogenesis by preventing synaptic restructuring including dendritic elaboration and an increase in dendritic spines. Most significant to our discussion of anxiety are the changes to limbic structures that comprise the emotion regulating circuits including the hippocampus, amygdala, and PFC. Of interest is the finding that prolonged stress apparently produces opposite effects on the hippocampus, where synaptic structures atrophy, and on the amygdala, where dendritic growth, increased arborization, and increased spine connectivity are seen (McEwen, 2008). These differences are reflected in behavioral effects: impaired hippocampus-mediated contextual learning that helps an individual to distinguish between context-appropriate and context-inappropriate emotional responding, and enhanced amygdala-mediated fear conditioning. Furthermore, the medial prefrontal area that is responsible for extinguishing conditioned emotional responses shows a decrease in dendritic connections. The molecular

(A)

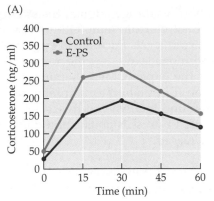

Figure 18.9 Stress pathway dysregulation following early prenatal stress
(A) Adult male mice exposed to early prenatal stress (E-PS) during the first 7 days of gestation showed elevated blood corticosterone (the principal glucocorticoid in rodents) levels after 15 minutes of restraint stress compared to controls, indicating an increased HPA axis function. (B,C) In situ hybridization showed significantly increased CRF expression in the central nucleus of the amygdala in adult male E-PS mice compared to controls, indicating an enhancement of stress neurocircuitry. (D,E) In situ hybridization showed glucocorticoid receptors were significantly lower in the CA3 and dentate gyrus (DG) regions of the hippocampus in E-PS adult male mice compared to controls, indicating a reduction in HPA axis negative feedback. Glucocorticoid receptor expression was less, but not significantly in the CA1 region and there was no difference in CA2. (After Mueller and Babe, 2008.)

(B)

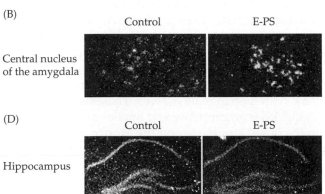

Central nucleus of the amygdala

(D)

Hippocampus

(C)

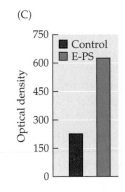

(E)

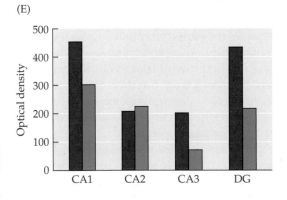

continues throughout gestation, and most structures continue to elaborate after birth. In fact, the PFC is not fully mature until adolescence and hence is highly vulnerable throughout this period.

Although most prenatal stress research has been done using rodents, several researchers in a series of studies have provided important data using nonhuman primates because their stages of gestation and early brain development are more similar to those of humans (see Schneider et al., 2002). In rhesus monkeys, repeated random noise blasts several times a day during pregnancy produced offspring that were lighter in weight at birth and showed impaired motor coordination. In addition to various motor deficits, when exposed to new stressors, the offspring showed a hyperresponsive HPA axis in the form of elevated ACTH and cortisol, heightened signs of anxiety during social separation, reduced exploration of their environment, limited play behavior, and more clinging to their peers than control monkeys. Additionally, the prenatally stressed animals showed deficits in learning a nonmatching-to-sample task that requires both working memory and attention shifting as they select the object that is different from the one previously presented to get a food reward. Furthermore, at adolescence, the stressed monkeys demonstrated an increasing preference for ethyl alcohol compared with controls. Both physiological and behavioral effects were most pronounced when the stressor occurred during the most intense period of neuronal migration early in gestation. Since these effects also occurred in the offspring of mothers who were administered ACTH, the elevation of stress hormones including glucocorticoids was the likely cause of the altered fetal development. Since such experiments cannot be performed on humans, alternative approaches must be used. One retrospective study was performed using volumetric magnetic

mechanism of these effects is less well studied than in the hippocampus, but as you will see in the next section, abnormal neural activity in these brain regions is characteristic of several clinical disorders.

The effects of early stress are dependent on timing and gender

Not only does stress impact various brain regions in a distinct fashion, but several other variables also help to determine the nature of the effects of early stress. As is true for any other teratogenic agent, an important factor is the timing of the exposure. It is apparent that periods of greatest brain development are the most sensitive to insult, but how the trajectory of brain development is altered will depend on the particular developmental stage. Nervous system development resonance imaging (MRI) of individuals who had been sexually abused during discrete stages of development. Their preliminary results showed that several brain regions had unique sensitive periods to the damaging effects of early stress. The findings suggest that hippocampal volume was reduced when childhood sexual abuse occurred during the ages of 3 to 5 and 11 to 15. The corpus callosum was reduced in women abused at 9 to 10 years of age, and the vulnerable period of the slowly developing prefrontal cortex occurred between 14 and 16 years of age (Andersen et al., 2008).

A second significant variable that determines the effects of stress on the brain is gender. Animal studies have shown that the behavioral and hormonal effects of prenatal stress depend on the sex of the offspring. Although it has been frequently assumed that male and female brains are identical, over the past 15 years, brain imaging has shown significant differences not only in structure but also in neurotransmitter systems and function. Many studies have shown gender differences in hormonal, physiological, and behavioral responses to stress, although the results are frequently contradictory because of the types of stressors used, timing of stress, brain regions examined, hormonal changes during stages of the estrous cycle, and methodological differences. Some have suggested that on the basis of the evolutionary roles of the sexes, it is reasonable to expect differences in the ways that males and females respond to stress. While the males of many species actively respond to acute danger in the environment by fighting or running, females frequently respond by engaging in social interaction such as organizing the herd and protecting the young. These differences are important to study because they may help to explain some of the differences in the incidence and symptomology of psychiatric disorders in men and women. Important to our discussion are the epidemiological studies showing that the lifetime male-to-female prevalence rate of having any anxiety disorder is 1:1.7. Women have higher rates for each of the disorders although the literature is not always consistent regarding social anxiety disorder. Also there are variations in comorbidity and in the overall burden of illness (McLean et al., 2011). Although some of the differences may be explained by sociocultural influences experienced by girls, such as the greater acceptance of women expressing fearfulness, it is apparent that several brain areas in the circuitry modulating emotion respond to stress in different ways. Using functional MRI (fMRI), Goldstein and colleagues (2010) found that brain activity in the stress response circuitry was dissimilar in men and in women when they were exposed to negative affect/high arousal pictures, but that difference was highly dependent on the phase of the women's menstrual cycle. This evidence suggests that women have a hormonal regulation of the stress response that is distinctive from men. Others have shown that glucocorticoid levels fluctuate in synchrony with changes in hormone levels over the menstrual cycle, demonstrating the impact of female hormones on HPA axis function. Both laboratory animal and human studies have found that when estrogen levels are elevated, sensitivity to stress is greater and glucocorticoid release is increased.

MORPHOLOGICAL DIFFERENCES IN RESPONSE TO STRESS In a series of studies, morphological and behavioral differences between the sexes were found in animal tests using chronic restraint stress, chronic foot shock stress, or glucocorticoid administration (reviewed in McLaughlin et al., 2009). Such stressors cause the previously described reduction in hippocampal neurogenesis, shrinking of the dendritic arbor, and loss of giant dendritic spines in the CA3 region in male rodents. These neurobiological changes are accompanied by spatial memory deficits in the radial arm maze and the Morris water maze. In contrast, similar treatment of females produced neither dendritic atrophy nor memory impairment unless they had had their ovaries removed, in which case dramatic shrinkage occurred. The relative resistance of the female hippocampal cells to stress-induced damage suggests a neuroprotective effect of female hormones. Of particular interest is that in rodents, synaptic complexity in the CA1 region of the hippocampus changes over the 5-day estrous cycle in such a way that synaptic complexity gradually increases over the days when estrogen is elevated and drops when progesterone levels rise. This type of change shows very rapid effects of female hormones on hippocampal plasticity.

Chronic stress also causes shrinking and simplification of dendritic arbors as well as loss of dendritic spines in the PFC of male rats, as mentioned earlier. These changes are associated with the expected deficits in extinction of fear conditioning. In contrast, in females, similar stress causes estrogen-dependent enhancement of dendritic trees of neurons that project to the amygdala.

Lastly, dendritic arborization in the amygdala of chronically stressed males is enhanced, and this is associated with enhanced conditioned fear acquisition. In humans, this enhanced fear conditioning is correlated with glucocorticoid levels in men but not in women. Although chronic stress impairs fear conditioning in women, the neural basis is not yet clear. In sum, it is quite clear that males and females respond to prenatal and postnatal stress in a distinct fashion, and those disparities may help to explain the differences in incidence and characteristics of a variety of clinical disorders including autism, attention deficit hyperactivity disorder (ADHD), depression, and anxiety. However, it is somewhat puzzling to find that women apparently have a diminished neurobiological response to stress yet show an *increased* incidence of anxiety and mood disorders. One possible resolution to this paradox is to consider male responsiveness as an adaptive mechanism that protects against some psychiatric disorders (Altemus, 2006). For example, stress-induced impairment of hippocampal memory consolidation may serve to limit memories of a trauma and associated stimuli, thereby enhancing recovery. Alternatively, it is perhaps significant that although males have a greater neurobiological response to stress, their receptor affinity for glucocorticoids in the hippocampus is almost twice as great as in females, suggesting that the negative feedback that returns stress hormone levels to normal is more effective. Perhaps the robust response followed by rapid recovery is key to their relative resilience to some disorders. Finally, one needs to consider that women face many significant reproductive hormonal changes over their lifetime, including during the prenatal period, puberty, the estrous cycle, pregnancy and lactation, and menopause, each of which may alter neural circuits of emotion regulation. Because of space limitations, we cannot review all the behavioral effects of gonadal hormones that might contribute to their vulnerability and resilience to anxiety disorders, but we suggest two review articles for consideration: Altemus, 2006, and Toufexis, 2007.

Section Summary

- Anxiety is a disturbing feeling of concern accompanied by bodily changes including activation of the "fight-or-flight" response that prepares the animal to cope with impending danger.

- Fear and anxiety differ in duration, psychological consequences, and neurobiology.

- Many brain regions (including the insula, cingulate cortex, hypothalamus, and hippocampus) are involved in emotion processing, but the amygdala plays a central role.

- The central nucleus of the amygdala and the BNST project widely and orchestrate the components of the emotional response. The central nucleus organizes the fear response when threatening stimuli appear suddenly and end abruptly. The BNST orchestrates components of emotion to produce sustained preparedness for unclear danger, a state resembling anxiety.

- The amygdala forms emotional memories and enhances semantic memory consolidation by the hippocampus.

- Regions of the prefrontal and cingulate cortices exert inhibitory control over the amygdala and mediate fear extinction.

- Anxiety disorders may arise from an imbalance between emotion generating brain regions and higher cortical control.

- CRF regulates stress hormone secretion and activates neuronal circuits of emotion that produce anxious behaviors in animal models.

- Noradrenergic neurons in the locus coeruleus are activated by threatening stimuli and produce hypervigilance and fearfulness. NE mediates the formation and reconsolidation of traumatic memories. Elevated adrenergic function is found in some anxiety disorders.

- Drugs that enhance GABA function (particularly in the amygdala) indirectly via modulatory sites on the GABA receptor for barbiturates, benzodiazepines, and neuroactive steroids reduce anxiety and seizures and produce sedation.

- Low levels of BDZ modulatory sites are associated with elevated anxiety in rodents and with panic disorder, PTSD, and GAD in human patients.

- Enhancing 5-HT function by blocking the reuptake transporter or stimulating 5-HT_{1A} receptors reduces anxiety.

- The neurotrophic effect of 5-HT during fetal development is needed for normal development of the anxiety circuitry. People with a polymorphism of the 5-HT transporter gene who have higher prenatal 5-HT show increased emotionality. They also have reduced volume of the amygdala and ACC and weaker connections between these structures as adults.

- Dopaminergic projections to the amygdala reduce the inhibitory control from the mPFC and increase emotional responses.

- The tendency to express anxiety is determined by both genes and environmental events. Pre- and early postnatal exposure to stress cause epigenetic changes that alter the stress circuitry and increase the behavioral and hormonal response to stressors in the adult. Stress-induced glucocorticoids damage the hippocampus and the PFC but increase synaptic connectivity in the amygdala.

- Stress-induced brain abnormalities depend on the timing and the developmental period. Significant gender differences in stress response are found in neural activity of the anxiety circuit, in HPA response, and in morphological differences after chronic stress.

Characteristics of Anxiety Disorders

Among the disorders that are recognized as anxiety syndromes by the American Psychiatric Association, this chapter will consider the five principal categories: generalized anxiety disorder, panic disorder, several types of phobias, posttraumatic stress disorder, and obsessive–compulsive disorder. These disorders vary significantly in the constellation of symptoms, the precipitating stimulus, and their time course, but all include high levels of anxiety that significantly impair the quality of life for those suffering with the disorder. Because of space limitations, this discussion will include only an introduction to each of the anxiety disorders. Students are directed to Martin et al., 2010 for an excellent review of neuroimaging, associated neurotransmitter signaling, and genetic contributions to each disorder.

GENERALIZED ANXIETY DISORDER   Although acute anxiety may at times need to be treated, it generally is not long-lasting and is not considered a clinical disorder. In contrast, for some people the symptoms of anxiety have no real focus, and they can be present for much of the day and can persist for months or years. These individuals suffer from **generalized anxiety disorder (GAD)**. Individuals with GAD show signs of constant worry and continuously predict, anticipate, or imagine dreadful events. For them, life is generally stressful, and even minor events provoke worry. Being late for an appointment, not completing a task, and making a minor mistake are all causes of worry. The most common physical symptoms include muscle tension and agitation that lead to fatigue, poor concentration, irritability, and sleep difficulties. As you might expect, the chronic anxiety reduces the individual's performance on many tasks and decreases the pleasure derived from his or her efforts. GAD is one of the more common anxiety disorders, afflicting an estimated 5% of the general population between the ages of 15 and 45 (Wittchen et al., 1994). Most cases begin gradually, usually in the teens or early adulthood, and persist throughout life.

Although some genetic contribution is suggested by the fact that GAD tends to run in families, twin studies are not consistent in supporting the role of heritability. It is perhaps not surprising that patients with GAD demonstrate an increased volume of the amygdala, which resembles the hypertrophy of that structure in laboratory animals exposed to repeated stressors. In addition, during PET scans, exposure to stimuli evoking negative emotions increases amygdala and insula activity to a greater extent in individuals with GAD than in healthy subjects. It is not entirely clear whether amygdala hyperactivity is secondary to too little inhibitory control by the prefrontal cortex, but the significant reduction in temporocortical GABA$_A$ receptors demonstrated in imaging studies would suggest that this is the case. Furthermore, symptoms of GAD are reduced by drugs that enhance GABA function, such as the benzodiazepines.

PANIC ATTACKS AND PANIC DISORDER WITH ANTICIPATORY ANXIETY   In contrast to anxiety, which is the anticipation of potential danger, fear is the physiological reaction to immediate danger that prepares us to fight or run away. When an individual experiences all the effects of a fear reaction without a threatening stimulus, he is having a **panic attack**. The sudden intense fearfulness is accompanied by strong arousal of the sympathetic ANS. The symptoms associated with panic include heart pounding or chest pain, sweating, shortness of breath, faintness, choking, and fear of losing control or dying (**Figure 18.10**). These symptoms, which last minutes or even hours, may occur (1) in response to a particular environmental cue (producing a phobia); (2) totally without warning in unexpected fashion; or (3) in a situation where an attack occurred previously, thus making it more likely to occur again. The latter two cases are the

Figure 18.10 The word panic comes from Pan, the Greek god of pastures and shepherds, who is represented as having the legs, horns, and ears of a goat. It was believed that if he were awakened from his nap by travelers, he would let out a bloodcurdling scream that would often scare them to death.

TABLE 18.1 Typical Situations Avoided by a Person with Agoraphobia
Shopping malls
Cars (as driver or passenger)
Buses
Trains
Subways
Wide streets
Tunnels
Restaurants
Theaters
Being far from home
Staying at home alone
Waiting in line
Supermarkets
Stores
Crowds
Planes
Elevators
Escalators

Source: Barlow and Durand, 1995.

basis for **panic disorder**. Panic disorder usually begins in the late twenties and may last for many years, with attacks occurring at different frequencies and intensities over that time. In panic disorder, the individual experiences both panic (in the form of individual attacks) and anxiety (called **anticipatory anxiety**) over the possibility that she may have an attack in a place that is not safe, for example, in the middle of a movie theater or during a church service, where it would be embarrassing or perhaps impossible to escape. The anxiety associated with being in an "unsafe" place leads to **agoraphobia**, a fear of public places, and subsequent avoidance of many common situations (**Table 18.1**). Individuals with agoraphobia often lead very limited lives because they never leave the safety of their own homes. You were introduced to such an individual in the opening vignette.

Unlike some of the other anxiety disorders, a genetic predisposition for panic is well documented. The concordance rate is significantly higher in monozygotic than in dizygotic twins. Furthermore, a significant number of patients with panic disorder have parents with the same diagnosis.

It has been suggested that panic attacks represent a normal physiological response that is not regulated by

appropriate feedback. It is also possible that the anxiety response is triggered too easily and may be initiated by environmental events that are not consciously processed. It is not entirely clear whether people with panic disorder have a more reactive ANS, but panic attacks can be triggered in individuals with the disorder by a variety of stimuli that activate the ANS. These include injecting lactic acid (a product of muscle exertion), caffeine, or yohimbine (an α_2-adrenergic autoreceptor antagonist) and breathing air with increased amounts of carbon dioxide. Because these same techniques do not elicit panic in normal individuals, they have been useful in studying panic disorder in the laboratory (see Nutt et al., 1998). The ability of these agents to induce ANS arousal suggests that dysregulation of noradrenergic function may occur in the disorder. During a panic attack, blood and urine levels of both NE and epinephrine are elevated. Additionally, not only does increasing the release of NE with the α_2-adrenergic autoreceptor antagonist yohimbine induce panic in these individuals, but reducing NE release with the α_2-adrenergic autoreceptor agonist clonidine produces an anxiolytic effect. Preliminary research also suggests that genetic variation in the norepinephrine transporter gene may increase susceptibility to panic disorder. Adrenergic dysfunction in the neurons originating in the locus coeruleus would produce widespread effects including arousal and vigilance.

Anatomically, the most consistent findings suggest that individuals suffering from panic disorder have abnormalities such as small white matter lesions in the temporal lobes and enlargement of the lateral ventricles, which suggests tissue reduction. The temporal lobes are overall smaller in a significant number of panic disorder patients, which may be accounted for by a reduction in amygdala volume and in some cases reduced hippocampal volume. As is frequently true in anxiety disorders, despite the reduced volume of the amygdala, it shows increased activity under challenge conditions. For example, during an induced panic attack, patients showed a significantly greater increase in activity of the amygdala, cingulate cortex, and insula compared with controls. Projections from the amygdala would contribute to the many bodily signs of panic, and the insula may make the individual more aware of the bodily sensations. In these panicked individuals, widespread areas of cerebral cortex including the PFC showed reduced function, indicating a lack of top-down control and failure of appropriate cognitive evaluation of the situation.

PHOBIAS **Phobias** involve fears that the individual recognizes as irrational. Fears may focus on specific objects or situations such as high places, closed-in

Figure 18.11 Cynophobia causes individuals to suffer signs of anxiety in the presence of dogs or even in response to items closely associated with the animals. Other animals like snakes, mice, or cats are also frequent bases for phobias and phobic avoidance.

TABLE 18.2 Some Common (*) and Less Common Phobias	
Phobia	Fear of
Acrophobia*	Heights
Aichmophobia	Sharp, pointed objects; knives
Ailurophobia	Cats
Algophobia	Pain
Astraphobia*	Storms, thunder, lightning
Claustrophobia*	Tight enclosures
Hematophobia*	Blood
Monophobia*	Being alone
Nyctophobia	Darkness, night
Ochlophobia	Crowds
Pyrophobia	Fire
Thanatophobia*	Death
Xenophobia*	Strangers

spaces, water, mice, or snakes, or they may relate to social or interpersonal situations such as speaking in public (see social anxiety disorder later). Phobias can affect the individual's daily existence and can reduce his quality of life. Although many of us have irrational fears of things like spiders, usually we can avoid those things with little modification of lifestyle (**Figure 18.11**). However, for some people, an irrational fear significantly alters their daily activities. One example of such an individual is John Madden, the well-known American sports announcer and former football coach. He suffers from claustrophobia and is overwhelmed with anxiety when traveling within the confined space of an airplane. Although he maintains a busy schedule of cross-country appearances for television, he travels only by train or on a bus designed for his use.

Although there is an almost infinite list of items that can elicit phobic anxiety (**Table 18.2**), what people fear is at least partially determined by culture. For instance, in the Chinese culture, *pa-leng* is a morbid fear of the cold and loss of body heat. This fear is based on the Chinese belief that yin represents the cold, dark, and energy-draining parts of life, which optimally should be balanced with yang, the warm, light, and sustaining elements. People with *pa-leng* often wear several layers of clothing even on extremely hot days.

Fortunately, phobias can usually be effectively treated with behavior therapy that involves presenting the fear-inducing stimulus in gradual increments, allowing the individual to maintain a relaxed state while confronting the source of her fear. This technique, called **behavioral desensitization**, is a common modern treatment method but may reflect an ancient Chinese proverb: "Go straight to the heart of danger, for there you will find safety." A more contemporary version utilizes exposure therapy in a virtual reality setting, which is easier than reproducing real-world situations and is more realistic than having the patient imagine the danger. Medication for phobias is rarely needed. Regardless of the method, effective treatment reduces the hyperactivity of the amygdala, the bed nucleus of the stria terminalis, anterior cingulate cortex, and insula.

SOCIAL ANXIETY DISORDER   Social anxiety disorder (SAD) or social phobia is among the most common anxiety disorders, with an estimated lifetime prevalence of approximately 12%. It is characterized by extreme fear of being evaluated or criticized by others. Those with social anxiety disorder tend to avoid most interpersonal situations or, if unavoidable, suffer extreme anxiety. The extreme anxiety may take the form of a panic attack. The disorder restricts many activities such as public speaking, attending parties, taking exams, and even eating in public places. Onset is typically at a young age with almost half of affected individuals developing symptoms by age 11. The disorder is slightly more common in women and in those individuals with low self-esteem and high levels of self-criticism. Evidence suggests that cognitive therapy that modifies negative thoughts such as the likelihood of looking foolish, plus social-skills training, is frequently highly beneficial.

The amygdala is once again central to this anxiety disorder, and numerous studies have shown that the level of activation of the amygdala in response to pictures of emotional faces correlates with the severity of symptoms. There is also a significantly greater elevation in blood flow in the amygdala during public speaking compared with control subjects, which is normalized after successful treatment. The neurobiology of social anxiety disorder is highly reminiscent of other anxiety disorders that show increased activity not only in the amygdala, but also in other limbic areas such as the insula and hippocampus, which in this case would lead to the anticipatory anxiety and autonomic response.

POSTTRAUMATIC STRESS DISORDER Severe and chronic emotional disorders can occur after traumatic events such as war, natural disasters like hurricanes or earthquakes, terrorist attacks such as 9/11, physical assault, or auto accidents. In each case, the individual involved feels not only fear but also a sense of helplessness and horror. As many as 10,000 individuals who witnessed the terrorist attack on the World Trade Center in New York City have developed **posttraumatic stress disorder (PTSD)**, and the soldiers returning from the wars in Iraq and Afghanistan show a particularly high rate of PTSD. Individuals with PTSD frequently experience nightmares and memories that may occur as sudden flashbacks of the traumatic event. In addition, they show increased physiological reactivity to reminders of the trauma, sleep disturbances, avoidance of stimuli associated with the trauma, and a numbing of emotional responses for many years after the original stress. Many exhibit sudden outbursts of irritability that can emotionally injure family and friends who are making an effort to be supportive. The individuals often feel detached from others and fail to experience the full range of emotions, which leads to diminished interest in life activities. In addition, the probability of attempting suicide is significantly greater in these individuals, as is the incidence of substance abuse and of marital problems, depression, and feelings of guilt and anger. Children also develop PTSD following trauma, although their symptoms are somewhat different.

Although statistics tell us that lifetime prevalence of PTSD ranges from 1% to 10% in the United States, the occurrence varies widely depending on the trauma.

For example, approximately 3% of people who have experienced a personal attack, 4% to 16% surviving a natural disaster, 30% of war veterans, as many as 50% of those who have experienced rape, and 50% to 75% of prisoners of war who were torture victims develop PTSD (Yehuda et al., 1998). Given the frequent occurrence of war, starvation, forced immigration, terrorist activities, and ethnic and religious conflict occurring globally in the recent past, it is painful to think of the number of cases of PTSD around the world.

Although PTSD is clearly related to the intensity of the traumatic event, some individuals seem far more susceptible than others. Clearly, not all war veterans in active combat develop PTSD, nor do all women who experience rape. Family studies of individuals who develop PTSD after trauma show that as many as 74% had a family history of psychopathology (PTSD, anxiety, depression, or antisocial behavior). The significantly higher concordance among monozygotic twins than dizygotic twins further supports the genetic vulnerability model. The interaction of family history and the magnitude of trauma is suggested by the fact that under conditions of high stress, people with a family history of PTSD may be only slightly more vulnerable to PTSD. However, when the magnitude of trauma is less intense, biologically vulnerable individuals are significantly more likely to show signs of the disorder. One possibility is that vulnerable individuals may perceive events as more traumatic than other individuals.

Children who have parents with PTSD have an increased risk for PTSD and also tend to have lower-than-normal blood cortisol. The hormonal difference may be a marker that predicts vulnerability. Although on the surface it seems odd to have low stress hormones associated with an anxiety disorder, it is possible that the normal feedback mechanism that turns off cortisol secretion is hypersensitive in PTSD. Yehuda and colleagues (2000) show that in the high-risk population of Holocaust survivor offspring, those who both developed PTSD themselves and had a parent with PTSD had the lowest levels of cortisol (**Figure 18.12**). Those whose parents had PTSD but did not themselves show PTSD had intermediate levels, and those who neither had a family history of PTSD nor had symptoms themselves had cortisol levels equal to controls. Although there is almost certainly a genetic contribution to this susceptibility, the extent of social support after the trauma may also be a significant factor. Women show an increased incidence of PTSD compared with men, and an additional factor that increases the risk of not only PTSD but also other anxiety disorders and associated depression is a history of chronic stress, abuse, or trauma.

Many neuroimaging studies have used patients with PTSD as subjects. The most consistent finding is a

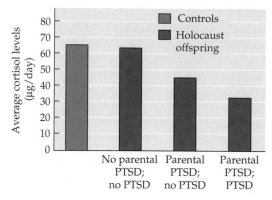

Figure 18.12 Average blood cortisol levels in several groups of offspring of Holocaust survivors and control subjects. Subjects with no parental history of PTSD and no PTSD themselves had similar cortisol levels to controls. A family history of PTSD was associated with reduced cortisol in the absence of symptoms. The lowest cortisol levels occurred in subjects with PTSD who also had a family history of the disorder. (After Yehuda et al., 2000.)

reduction in the volume of the hippocampus, although differences regarding laterality of the reduction have been reported. A smaller hippocampus might explain some of the cognitive symptoms of PTSD, including deficits in short-term memory, flashbacks, and amnesia for the traumatic events in those individuals with dissociative PTSD. Since the hippocampus plays a part in contextual learning, dysfunction might also explain why individuals with PTSD respond physiologically to cues that are not directly related to trauma. Situations resembling the trauma stimuli activate the amygdala and elicit emotional responses. Normally, the hippocampus would assist in determining whether the present context is safe or resembles the original dangerous context and would inhibit the emotional response of the amygdala in the safe context. Since reduced hippocampal volume is found so frequently and is associated with more severe symptoms, it is tempting to assume that it is a component of PTSD. However, several pieces of evidence suggest otherwise. First, reduced hippocampal volume has been reported in traumatized burn victims who do not have PTSD, suggesting that the brain change may be a consequence of trauma, not PTSD. Second, researchers have found the smaller hippocampus in individuals with PTSD a very short time after the traumatic event, which may mean that the smaller hippocampus was present before the trauma. A more direct evaluation utilized monozygotic twins, only one of whom suffered combat trauma and developed PTSD. The twin with PTSD had a smaller hippocampus than other traumatized GIs with no PTSD, but the identical twin with no trauma-induced PTSD also had a hippocampus with reduced volume, suggesting that the

abnormality represents a vulnerability factor for PTSD (Gilbertson et al., 2002).

Since the symptoms of PTSD resemble an unregulated activation of emotional memories, the increased neural activity of the amygdala to trauma cues would be expected along with reduced inhibitory control by PFC. In fact, both structural imaging studies and functional studies show smaller, less active anterior cingulate cortices and medial prefrontal cortices, which normally inhibit the amygdala and establish extinction of conditioned emotional responses.

OBSESSIVE–COMPULSIVE DISORDER   Have you ever made an attempt to forget some peculiar, sexual, or aggressive thought and found the thought recurring over and over? Have you ever checked your alarm clock before you got ready for bed and then felt compelled to check it again and again before you climbed into the sack even though you know you set it correctly? Having experienced those normal events will help you begin to understand **obsessive–compulsive disorder** (OCD). However, while these examples are trivial ones, OCD is anything but trivial. It is a severe, chronic psychiatric problem that may require hospitalization, or in the most extreme cases psychosurgery, to control the symptoms. The disorder is characterized by recurring, persistent, intrusive, and troublesome thoughts of contamination, violence, sex, or religion (**obsessions**) that the individual tries to resist but that cause a great deal of anxiety, guilt, and shame. **Compulsions** are repetitive rituals considered attempts to relieve the tremendous anxiety generated by the obsessive thoughts, although they may be directly related or totally unrelated to the obsessive ideas. In the first instance, an individual may wash his hands hundreds of times a day until the skin is raw and bleeding because of an obsession about contracting a fatal disease. Other compulsions are unrelated to obsessions; they may involve meaningless repetitive acts like counting each crack in the sidewalk, jumping through doorways, or chewing each bite of food 100 times because of the belief that a family member may otherwise become fatally ill. Regardless of the compulsion, the individual is convinced that unless the compulsive ritual is completed, disastrous consequences will occur. These activities are recognized by sufferers as inappropriate or irrational and consume most of their waking hours, yet they feel forced to do them against their will. The disorder causes intense emotional distress but is often left untreated because the individual is so ashamed of the symptoms that he recognizes as irrational or bizarre. Only when the symptoms become extreme is help sought. Although once considered rare, the lifetime prevalence of OCD is now estimated at 2% to 3%.

OCD is described as an anxiety disorder because patients experience extreme anxiety unless they perform their compulsive behaviors, but some researchers suggest that it is fundamentally an uncontrolled motor disorder. Rapoport (1989) and others believe that many of the symptoms involve behavior patterns that resemble species-typical behaviors of other animals such as grooming, nest building, and defensive behaviors. It is possible that these repetitive actions of OCD are behaviors that are "wired in" and are released because they are not adequately inhibited by the cerebral cortex. Furthermore, we find that

people with OCD often suffer from other movement disorders including Tourette's syndrome, Sydenham's chorea, and Parkinson's disease. Each of these has uncontrolled movements as a characteristic symptom, and each involves the function of the basal ganglia. PET scans show high levels of metabolic activity in the basal ganglia and other areas of the brain in OCD patients compared with controls. **Box 18.1** explains more about the neurobiology of OCD.

BOX 18.1   Clinical Applications

Neurobiological Model of OCD

Several lines of evidence support a neurobiological model of OCD (Saxena and Rauch, 2000; Stein, 2000) that includes abnormalities in a neural loop connecting the basal ganglia (caudate and globus pallidus), frontal lobe (particularly orbitofrontal), thalamus, and anterior cingulate cortex (Figure A). First, computerized tomography (CT) scans of the brains of OCD patients show significant differences in the caudate, an area that normally helps to sequence and elaborate behaviors. Abnormal function of the caudate might produce OCD symptoms such as stereotyped behavior and perseveration (the inability to turn one's attention to new situations). Further, the repetitive, aimless, and stereotypical behaviors observed in animals following amphetamine and cocaine administration provide empirical support for the importance of dopamine in the caudate–putamen (see Chapter 12).

Second, PET and single-photon emission computerized tomography (SPECT) studies show distinct patterns of glucose metabolism in the basal ganglia and frontal lobes (prefrontal and orbitofrontal) of patients with OCD that are correlated with the severity of symptoms (Rapoport, 1989). The abnormal cell activity increases when feared stimuli are presented to the patients.

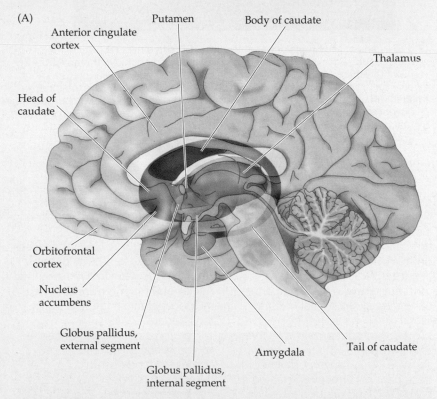

(A) The neural network involved in OCD includes the caudate (part of the basal ganglia), which lies under the cerebral cortex but has rich connections to the frontal lobe and the cingulate cortex as well as to the subcortical thalamus.

Since frontal lobes modulate functions such as planning, regulating, controlling, and evaluating behaviors, it seems plausible that dysfunction might be responsible for reduced response inhibition and inflexible behavior. Increased neural

activity of the anterior cingulate cortex also has been linked to compulsive behavior.

Third, pharmacotherapy with an SSRI or cognitive-behavioral

(Continued on next page)

BOX 18.1 *(continued)*

(B)

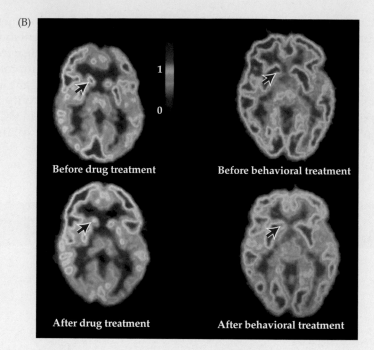

Before drug treatment

Before behavioral treatment

After drug treatment

After behavioral treatment

(C) Horizontal view

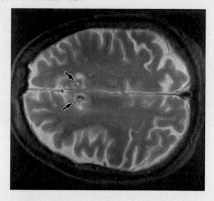

Sagittal view

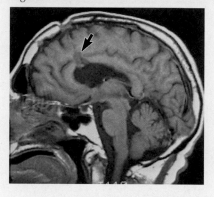

(B) PET scans of the brains of patients with OCD show hyperactivity in the head of the caudate. Both SSRI treatment (bottom left) and cognitive therapy (bottom right) reduce the hyperactivity in the caudate compared with pretreatment levels (top left and right). (From Baxter et al., 1992.) **(C)** Magnetic resonance image (MRI) of the brain of a patient with OCD The patient had neurosurgery to disrupt the neural connections of the cingulate cortex (see arrows) from the frontal cortex, basal ganglia, and thalamus. (From Martuza et al., 1990; courtesy of Robert L. Martuza.)

therapy that significantly decreases symptoms also decreases regional cerebral metabolism or blood flow. Those areas with the greatest change once again include the caudate, anterior cingulate, orbitofrontal cortex, and thalamus (Figure B). A total of 8 to 12 weeks of treatment with the SSRI paroxetine *decreased* striatal metabolism in OCD patients who showed symptom reduction of more than 25% compared with those who showed no improvement. In contrast, patients effectively treated for both OCD and major depression showed an *increase* in striatal activity compared with nonresponders.

These results suggest that SSRIs produce brain metabolic responses that are specific to both the disorder and the therapeutic response (Saxena et al., 2002). The SSRIs may be effective for OCD because they enhance the activity of the serotonergic neurons of the raphe nuclei, and this interrupts the neural loop by inhibiting cell firing in the caudate.

The most compelling evidence for the overactive-circuit model comes from neurosurgical procedures. Neurosurgery that destroys the anterior cingulate (Figure C) or severs the connection between the frontal cortex and subcortical areas,

including the basal ganglia and the thalamus, is successful in relieving symptoms in 50% to 70% of cases (Mindus et al., 1994). It appears that interrupting the circuitry at any one of several points may relieve symptoms of OCD. These results demonstrate the importance of considering the functional interaction of multiple brain areas when looking for the biological basis of any psychiatric disorder. Understanding the neural network associated with behavior also means that psychopharmacology can be used to target the symptoms at multiple sites by modulating the synaptic connections.

Section Summary

- Anxiety disorders vary in symptoms, incidence, and time course, but all include high levels of anxiety.

- The chronic anxiety experienced in GAD is associated with enlargement and hyperactivity of the

amygdala and too little inhibitory control by the PFC. Increasing inhibition with GABA agonists reduces symptoms.

- There is a genetic predisposition to sudden episodes of panic disorder. Dysregulation of adrenergic neurons in the autonomic nervous system and locus coeruleus may be involved. A genetic polymorphism of the NE transporter gene is associated with increased vulnerability to panic.

- In panic disorder, the volume of the amygdala and the hippocampus is reduced. During a panic attack, neural activity is increased in the amygdala, cingulate cortex, and insula and is reduced in the PFC.

- The individual with panic disorder experiences intense fearfulness with autonomic activation as well as anticipatory anxiety over the concern of being observed in a public place.

- Phobias involve irrational fears of objects or situations that are best treated with behavioral desensitization.

- Social anxiety disorder involves extreme fear of being evaluated in public and is associated with increased blood flow in the amygdala during challenge that normalizes after treatment.

- Not all trauma victims develop PTSD. Genetic vulnerability factors increase the probability that PTSD will occur following a less intense traumatic event. Other vulnerability factors include female gender, lack of social support after the trauma, and a history of chronic stress or abuse.

- Low blood cortisol is a marker of vulnerability for PTSD and may be due to a hypersensitive negative feedback mechanism.

- Neuroimaging shows a reduction in hippocampal volume in patients with PTSD. It may be a consequence of trauma itself rather than of PTSD, but others have found that the reduction preceded the trauma-induced PTSD, making it a vulnerability factor.

- In PTSD the amygdala shows increased neural activity, and the anterior cingulate and the medial PFC are less active and fail to inhibit the limbic structures.

- OCD is a severe, chronic psychiatric problem characterized by recurring, persistent, intrusive thoughts and repetitive rituals. The irrational acts of OCD must be performed to prevent extreme anxiety.

- Because of high levels of metabolic activity in the basal ganglia, some researchers consider OCD to be an uncontrolled motor disorder.

Drugs for Treating Anxiety

Drugs that are used to relieve anxiety are called **anxiolytics**. Many belong to the class of **sedative–hypnotics**, which is part of a still larger category, the **CNS**

depressants. CNS depressants include the barbiturates, the benzodiazepines, and alcohol, and all of these drugs reduce neuron excitability. As you may know, the oldest known anxiety-reducing drug is alcohol, and it is still popular as an over-the-counter remedy for stress (see Chapter 10). However, because it is difficult to administer in accurate doses and has a very poor therapeutic index, alcohol has no medical use.

To be considered an anxiolytic, a drug should relieve the feelings of tension and worry and signs of stress that are typical of the anxious individual with minimal side effects such as sedation. As we saw in animal models described in Chapter 4, drugs in this class increase behaviors that are normally suppressed by anxiety or punishment. **Figure 18.13** shows the strong correlation between the effectiveness of anxiolytic drugs from several classes in a conflict procedure and the potency of these drugs in clinical trials with human patients.

Drugs that relieve anxiety often also produce a calm and relaxed state, with drowsiness and mental clouding, incoordination, and prolonged reaction time. At higher doses, these drugs also induce sleep, and they are therefore sometimes called hypnotics. At the highest doses, CNS depressants induce coma and death,

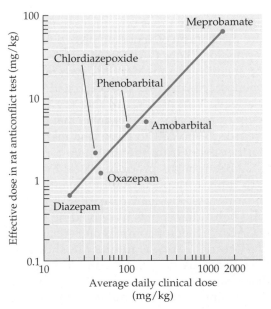

Figure 18.13 Correlation of drug potency in rat anticonflict test with clinical potency Drugs that increase punished behaviors in the operant conflict test at low doses are also clinically useful for treating anxiety in patients at low doses. Less potent anticonflict drugs also require higher doses to be effective for human anxiety. The drugs tested include benzodiazepines (diazepam, oxazepam, chlordiazepoxide), barbiturates (phenobarbital, amobarbital), and a barbiturate-like anxiolytic (meprobamate). (After Cook and Sepinwall, 1975.)

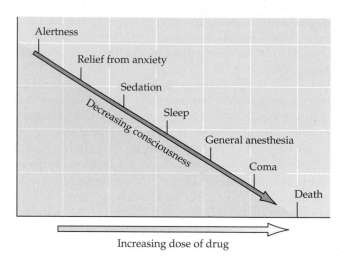

Figure 18.14 Dose-dependent effects of CNS depressants on levels of consciousness With increasing doses, the level of awareness and arousability gradually decreases along a continuum until death occurs.

antagonist flumazenil prevents the BDZ-induced enhancement of GABA action but does not affect GABA-induced hyperpolarization (**Figure 18.15B**). In contrast, the addition of a GABA antagonist prevents GABA from opening the channel, and the presence of a benzodiazepine has no further effect. It is generally assumed that the fact that BDZs do not enhance the maximum response to GABA is responsible for their high therapeutic index (i.e., clinical safety).

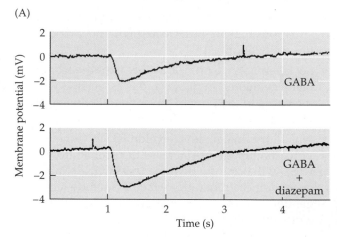

although even at therapeutic doses they can be fatal if combined with other drugs (**Figure 18.14**). Selected sedative–hypnotics also reduce seizures and may be used to treat epilepsy. Others produce muscle relaxation as needed to treat muscle spasms, for example, following an auto accident.

Although the classic sedative–hypnotic drugs affect the functioning of many types of neurons in the CNS, their primary mechanism of action involves enhancing GABA transmission. Since GABA is the major inhibitory neurotransmitter in the nervous system, it has receptors on most cells in the CNS to exert widespread inhibitory effects. You may recall that the $GABA_A$ receptor complex regulates a Cl^- channel that increases Cl^- current into the cell to move the membrane potential farther away from the threshold for firing. Therefore, GABA agonists produce a local hyperpolarization, or inhibitory postsynaptic potential, and inhibit cell firing. As you learned earlier, both barbiturates and benzodiazepines have binding sites as part of the $GABA_A$ receptor complex and enhance the inhibitory effects of GABA. **Figure 18.15A** shows the hyperpolarization caused by GABA and its enhancement by diazepam.

When BDZs bind to their modulatory sites on the $GABA_A$ complex, they enhance the effect of GABA by increasing the number of times the channel opens. However, in the absence of GABA, the benzodiazepines have no effect on Cl^- channel opening. Apparently the presence of a BDZ alters the physical state of the receptors, increasing the receptor affinity for GABA so that GABA opens the channels more easily, shifting the dose–response curve to the left. As you would expect, the addition of the competitive

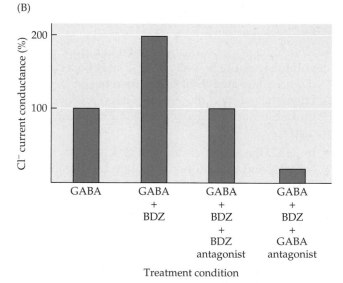

Figure 18.15 Effects of GABA and diazepam on membrane potentials and chloride (Cl^-) flux (A) Electrical recording of the hyperpolarizing effect of GABA and the enhanced hyperpolarization caused by the addition of diazepam to a mouse spinal cord neuron. Diazepam alone would produce little or no hyperpolarization. (B) GABA alone increases the conductance of Cl^- through its channel. Adding a BDZ enhances the amount of Cl^- movement into the cell. Blocking the BDZ binding site prevents the drug's enhancement of GABA but not the effect of GABA itself. A GABA antagonist prevents GABA from opening the Cl^- channel, and the presence of BDZ has no effect. (After Kandel, 2000.)

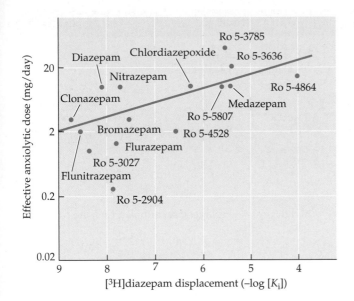

Figure 18.16 Correlation of benzodiazepine binding and antianxiety effect The ability of the benzodiazepines (including several experimental compounds having the "Ro" designation) to displace [³H]diazepam from the BDZ binding site is correlated with the doses required for anxiolytic action. The negative log scale on the *x*-axis reflects increasing concentrations from left to right. Therefore, the benzodiazepines that displace labeled diazepam at low concentrations (e.g., clonazepam and flunitrazepam) also tend to be those that require lower doses to reduce anxiety. Those that are less effective at binding (needing higher concentrations) to the diazepam site (e.g., Ro 5-4864) also need higher doses for antianxiety effects. (After Braestrup and Squires, 1978.)

Competition experiments that measured the effectiveness of various BDZs in displacing [³H]diazepam showed a positive correlation between the ability to displace the radioligand and the clinically effective dose for relieving anxiety (**Figure 18.16**). This means that the drugs that bind most readily to the BDZ receptor (i.e., require low concentrations to displace [³H] diazepam) are also clinically effective at low doses. Likewise, BDZs that bind less easily need higher doses to be effective.

Barbiturates also increase the affinity of the GABA$_A$ receptor for GABA; however, they increase the duration of the opening of GABA-activated Cl⁻ channels rather than the number of openings. In addition to enhancing GABA's action at the receptor, barbiturates

directly open the Cl⁻ channel without GABA. This additional action may explain why barbiturates can be lethal but benzodiazepines are not.

Barbiturates are the oldest sedative–hypnotics

Sodium amytal was the first barbiturate, but as many as 50 others with different profiles of bioavailability were developed. The pharmacokinetic factors of absorption, distribution, and metabolism described in Chapter 1 determine each drug's onset of effect and duration of action, and it is on this basis that the drugs are classified into three groups. Because the barbiturates have essentially been replaced by the benzodiazepines in the treatment of anxiety disorders, our discussion of these drugs will be brief.

PHARMACOKINETICS All of the barbiturates have a similar basic ring structure (**Figure 18.17**) but vary in the length and complexity of the side chain attached

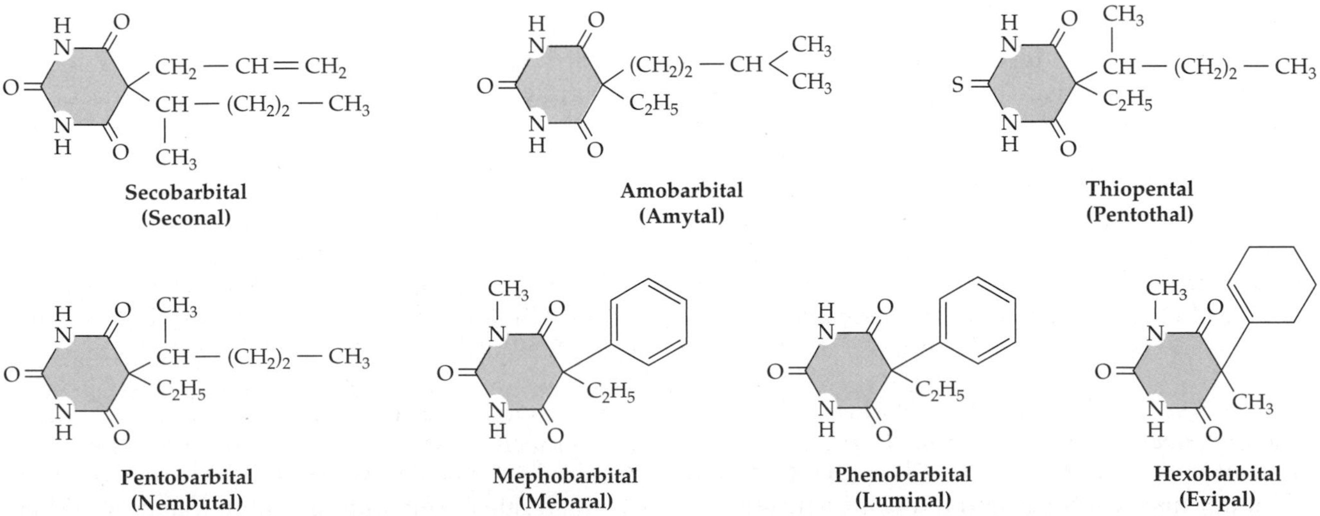

Secobarbital (Seconal) **Amobarbital (Amytal)** **Thiopental (Pentothal)**

Pentobarbital (Nembutal) **Mephobarbital (Mebaral)** **Phenobarbital (Luminal)** **Hexobarbital (Evipal)**

Figure 18.17 Chemical structure of the barbiturates The barbiturates all have a similar molecular ring structure (highlighted in orange) with distinct side chains that affect

their lipid solubility. Each drug's lipid solubility determines how quickly it enters the brain, binds to drug depots, and is metabolized.

Duration of action	Lipid solubility	Onset	Duration	Use
TABLE 18.3 Duration of Action and Uses of Major Barbiturates				
Ultrashort	High	10–20 s	20–30 min	IV anesthesia
Thiopental (Pentothal)				
Methohexital (Brevital)				
Short/intermediate	Moderate	20–40 min	5–8 h	Surgical anesthesia and sleep induction
Amobarbital (Amytal)				
Secobarbital (Seconal)				
Pentobarbital (Nembutal)				
Long	Low	Over 1 h	10–12 h	Prolonged sedation and seizure control
Phenobarbital (Luminal)				
Mephobarbital (Mebaral)				

to the ring. These molecular differences are responsible for their differences in lipid solubility. The **ultrashort-acting** barbiturates such as thiopental (Pentothal) and hexobarbital (Evipal) are highly lipid soluble and readily penetrate into the brain to put an individual to sleep within 10 to 20 seconds when intravenously administered. Consciousness returns in about 20 to 30 minutes because of the redistribution of drug to inactive drug depots in muscle and fat.

The **short/intermediate-acting** barbiturates are moderately lipid soluble and take longer to reach significant brain levels. They are likely to produce relaxation and sleep in about 20 to 40 minutes and last about 5 to 8 hours. Their moderate lipid solubility is also responsible for their longer duration of action because termination depends more on liver metabolism than on redistribution, which is characteristic of very lipid-soluble drugs. This group (including amobarbital [Amytal] and secobarbital [Seconal]) is most likely to be prescribed for insomnia but also includes those drugs most likely to be abused.

Finally, the **long-acting** drugs have poor lipid penetration, so their onset takes an hour or longer, but their slow metabolism produces prolonged action for 10 to 12 hours. These characteristics are optimal for treating seizure disorders because a stable blood level can be maintained. Phenobarbital (Luminal) is commonly used in this way. **Table 18.3** summarizes these characteristics and provides examples.

SIDE EFFECTS   First, although barbiturates readily induce sleep, it is not a normal, restful sleep. The drugs alter sleep architecture by reducing the amount of REM (rapid-eye-movement) sleep and causing a rebound in REM after withdrawal.

Second, the anxiolytic effects of these drugs are accompanied by pronounced cognitive side effects including mental clouding, loss of judgment, and slowed reflexes, making driving particularly dangerous. High doses also lead to gross intoxication, staggering, jumbled speech, and impaired thinking. Coma and death due to respiratory depression occur at 10 to 20 times the normal therapeutic dose. These drugs are extremely dangerous when combined with alcohol.

Third, when used repeatedly, barbiturates increase the number of liver microsomal enzymes. This increase enhances drug metabolism, producing lower blood levels (metabolic tolerance) and reduced effectiveness. Since the same liver enzymes metabolize many other drugs, cross-tolerance diminishes the effectiveness of other drugs as well. Further, pharmacodynamic tolerance occurs when CNS neurons adapt to the presence of the drug and become less responsive with chronic drug use. Mood changes and sedation seem to show the greatest and most rapid tolerance, but the lethal respiratory-depressant action of the drug does not show tolerance at all. Therefore, as one gradually increases the dose of drug needed to achieve a desired effect, the margin of safety (therapeutic index) becomes less (**Figure 18.18**).

Fourth, barbiturates produce significant physical dependence and potential for abuse. Terminating drug use after extended treatment produces a potentially fatal rebound hyperexcitability withdrawal syndrome similar to that for alcohol. Although gradual reduction in the dose of the drug will decrease the intensity of withdrawal because receptors are not suddenly deprived of the drug molecule, the withdrawal syndrome will be longer in duration. The potent reinforcing effect of barbiturates is demonstrated by the high rate of self-administration found in rats and monkeys in an operant chamber, although the shorter-acting agents sustain a higher response rate than longer-acting barbiturates. It was the concern about

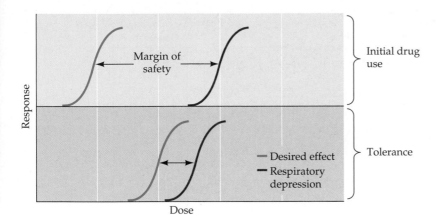

Figure 18.18 Margin of safety Dose–response curves for the barbiturate-induced desired effect (mood change or sedation) and lethal respiratory depression. The top panel shows that with early drug use (nontolerant), the individual experiences mood effects without significant respiratory depression. However, as tolerance develops with repeated use (bottom panel), larger amounts of drug are needed to experience the sedation (the curve shifts to the right), but no change in the dose causing depression of respiration occurs. The margin of safety shrinks dramatically in the tolerant individual.

abuse potential among patients as well as the diversion of the prescription medications to street use along with the high incidence of side effects, potential lethality, and rapid tolerance of barbiturates that prompted the search for a novel anxiolytic drug without these undesirable characteristics. The benzodiazepines were introduced in 1960 and in general have replaced the prescription of barbiturates. The decline in prescriptions for barbiturates over the years has made these drugs less available and has caused a parallel decline in abuse.

Benzodiazepines are highly effective for anxiety reduction

The first benzodiazepine (BDZ) to be introduced was chlordiazepoxide (Librium). It represented the first true anxiolytic that targeted anxiety without producing excessive sedation. It has a low incidence of tolerance, a less severe withdrawal syndrome than barbiturates, and a very safe therapeutic index. Within a few years, diazepam (Valium), oxazepam (Serax), flurazepam (Dalmane), and at least a dozen other chemically related drugs were developed.

PHARMACOKINETICS All BDZs have a common molecular structure (**Figure 18.19**) and a similar mechanism of action. As was true for the barbiturates, the choice of a particular benzodiazepine for a given therapeutic situation depends primarily on the speed of onset and the duration of drug action. The onset of action is determined by the drug's lipid solubility; the most soluble are quickest to be absorbed and moved through the blood–brain barrier to initiate the drug effect. Their duration of action is determined by (1) differences in their method of biotransformation and (2) the extent of redistribution to inactive depots such as skeletal muscle and fat. The long-acting BDZs undergo several metabolic steps to produce multiple active metabolites that may have half-lives of 60 hours or longer. These can be problematic for elderly individuals, who may

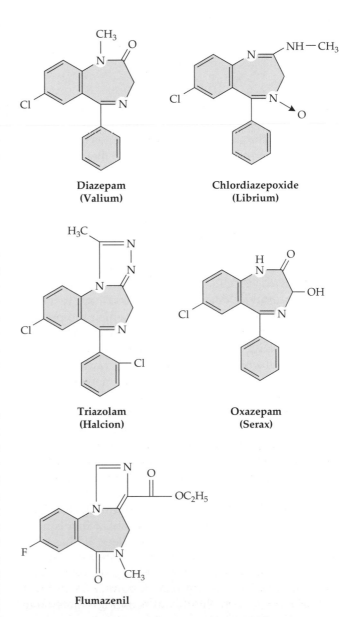

Figure 18.19 Molecular structure of several benzodiazepines and the benzodiazepine binding site antagonist flumazenil. The common BDZ structure is highlighted in blue.

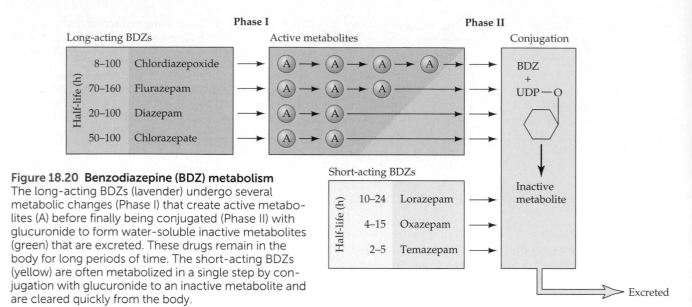

Figure 18.20 Benzodiazepine (BDZ) metabolism
The long-acting BDZs (lavender) undergo several metabolic changes (Phase I) that create active metabolites (A) before finally being conjugated (Phase II) with glucuronide to form water-soluble inactive metabolites (green) that are excreted. These drugs remain in the body for long periods of time. The short-acting BDZs (yellow) are often metabolized in a single step by conjugation with glucuronide to an inactive metabolite and are cleared quickly from the body.

rapidly accumulate drug in the body because of their reduced metabolic capacity, increasing the probability of side effects. The short-acting BDZs, such as temazepam (Restoril) and lorazepam (Ativan), are metabolized in one step into inactive metabolites by conjugation with glucuronide (**Figure 18.20**). Redistribution also contributes to the short duration of action by reducing the amount of drug available to act on the CNS. The slow release from inert depots back into circulation is responsible for any drug hangover effects that might occur.

THERAPEUTIC EFFECTS   Unlike barbiturates, the BDZs cannot be used for deep anesthesia, but they are useful for presurgical anesthesia, during which the patient is conscious but is less aware of his surroundings and is quite relaxed. They are also commonly used before major dental work as well as for a wide range of stressful diagnostic procedures. One of the newer BDZs is midazolam (Versed), used for rapid onset of relaxation and deep sleep during brief surgical procedures done with local anesthetics. Because it has a short half-life, recovery takes only a few hours without hangover. It also induces an anterograde amnesia that creates an illusion of anesthesia in some patients, which is considered a beneficial drug effect.

In other cases, however, the drug-induced amnesia is highly undesirable. Recently a BDZ that is marketed outside the United States as a sleep aid has been illegally imported and used as a "date rape" drug. Flunitrazepam (Rohypnol) is quite potent and, when combined with alcohol, impairs judgment and causes amnesia along with significant sedation. There have been a limited number of reports of women who have been sexually assaulted and found themselves in unfamiliar locations with no memory of the events

surrounding the attack. Although such situations produced serious concern on college campuses and at social establishments serving alcohol, the number of documented cases is quite small and the risk is low. However, because of the illicit use, the U.S. Drug Enforcement Administration has classified flunitrazepam as a Schedule I drug (i.e., a drug with high potential for abuse and no medical use).

The most popular use for BDZs is anxiety relief. Benzodiazepines relieve the sense of worry and fearfulness as well as the physical symptoms associated with anxiety with less mental clouding, loss of judgment, and motor incoordination than is typical of other sedative–hypnotics. The mild sedation that accompanies use of some of the BDZs decreases with repeated use over a week to 10 days, but little or no tolerance occurs for the antianxiety effects. Nevertheless, in older individuals with slower drug metabolism, excessive confusion and reduced cognitive function may be quite serious and may resemble senile dementia.

Several of the longer-acting benzodiazepines are useful **hypnotics**. BDZs shorten the time needed to fall asleep and increase the duration of sleep time, as well as reduce the number of nighttime awakenings. Despite their relative safety, all sleep medications pose potential problems, such as causing reduced alertness the next day and rebound withdrawal insomnia after prolonged use (see **Web Box 18.3**). Some BDZs are useful **muscle relaxants** and others are **anticonvulsants** for the management of particular forms of epilepsy. Intravenous diazepam is the treatment of choice for status epilepticus, a period of severe and persistent seizures that can be life-threatening. BDZs are also the drugs of choice in preventing acute **alcohol** or **barbiturate withdrawal** symptoms, including sei-zures. This action is based on the cross-dependence of these three drugs, hence withdrawal from any one of them can be terminated by administration of any of the others. Since withdrawal from heavy alcohol or barbi-turate use can produce a life-threatening situation, the treatment of choice is to substitute a long-acting ben-zodiazepine (usually Valium) to stop the abstinence syndrome and then to gradually lower the dose of the BDZ over several weeks to minimize the withdrawal.

ADVANTAGES OVER OTHER SEDATIVE–HYPNOTICS Ben-zodiazepines have several clear advantages over the older barbiturates. The most notable advantage is the high therapeutic index. Extremely high doses produce disorientation, cognitive impairment, and amnesia, and in some cases, a paradoxical increase in aggressiveness, irritability, and anxiety (Hobbs et al., 1996). However, since they have almost no effect on the respiratory center in the medulla, lethal overdose is extremely rare unless the drugs are taken in combination with other CNS depressants such as alcohol. Unfortunately, recreational use of BDZs is often combined with alcohol, opioids such as methadone, or other CNS depressants, which can produce highly toxic interactions. Although no specific antagonist is available for alcohol or barbiturate over-dose, the BDZ flumazenil (Romazicon) is a competitive antagonist for the BDZ receptor. Individuals brought to the emergency room unconscious can be treated with flumazenil, which quickly reverses the effects of the BDZ while the non-BDZ depressant is gradually eliminated from the body through normal metabolic processes.

Benzodiazepines are also safer than barbiturates because they do not increase the number of liver microsomal enzymes that normally metabolize the drugs. The lack of enzyme induction means there is reduced tolerance during repeated drug administra-tion and also fewer drug interactions.

Benzodiazepines have a reputation for lower prob-ability of physical dependence and abuse. Neverthe-less, chronic use and physical dependence do occur. The abstinence syndrome, which is milder than that of the barbiturates and is not life-threatening, devel-ops gradually over several weeks, especially for those drugs with a very long half-life. Symptoms may include insomnia, restlessness, headache, anxiety, mild depression, subtle perceptual distortions, muscle pain, and muscle twitches (Carvey, 1998). The most severe symptoms, which resemble those of other CNS depressants, include panic, delirium, and seizures. These occur in individuals who are abusing the drugs at high doses for prolonged periods, often in combina-tion with other drugs.

In initial research, laboratory animals did not read-ily self-administer benzodiazepines in an operant chamber, suggesting that the drugs have little reinforce-ment value and low abuse potential in humans. How-ever, BDZs with more rapid onset are more likely to be self-administered by animals. Furthermore, in animals that are first trained to self-administer a barbiturate, the reinforcing effects of BDZs are more apparent. In drug-discrimination tests (see Chapter 4) in which rats are taught to discriminate between barbiturates and saline by pressing a lever for reinforcement, BDZs will substi-tute for barbiturates. However, rats can also be trained to discriminate chlordiazepoxide from barbiturates and alcohol. These results indicate that the subjective drug-induced states of the three drugs must be similar if they substitute for each other in the discrimination test yet have some qualitative differences that can be distinguished. Overall, animal studies suggest that the reinforcement value of BDZs is much less than that of barbiturates (Griffiths et al., 1991).

Over the years, concern about the abuse potential of these drugs has led to fewer prescriptions. How-ever, studies with humans show that normal volun-teers prefer to take a placebo over diazepam, and that anxious subjects also choose the placebo unless they are seeking treatment for anxiety. Individuals who are experiencing withdrawal after termination of chronic diazepam or other sedative–hypnotics, however, do tend to self-administer a BDZ rather than placebo. These results suggest that BDZs have a relatively low risk of abuse, but that physical dependence and with-drawal may encourage continued use. Overall, the probability of abuse is almost always associated with polydrug use; that is, individuals who have a history of drug or alcohol abuse are those who most likely will abuse benzodiazepines (Woods et al., 1995).

BDZ PARTIAL AGONISTS A number of drugs such as imidazenil, etizolam, abecarnil, and bretazenil were developed to bind readily to the benzodiazepine modu-latory site but produce less of an effect than the BDZs. It was believed that the partial agonists would relieve anxiety with reduced side effects. In animal studies, these partial agonists were found to reduce anxiety with less sedation and muscle relaxation than the benzodiazepines. In addition, they did not seem to potentiate the effects of other CNS depressants, suggesting enhanced safety. Finally, they were associated with a low incidence of physical dependence (Costa and Guidotti, 1996). Unfor-tunately, in human patients, the initial clinical efficacy was not maintained over time so the partial agonists are of limited practical utility.

SUBUNIT-SELECTIVE DRUG DEVELOPMENT Studies using knockout mice suggest that drugs may be developed to act selectively on $GABA_A$ receptors with distinct α subunit isoforms. Such selectivity would permit targeting a specific GABA-associated symptom with minimal side effects. **Web Box 18.4** discusses the potential for these drugs.

Second-generation anxiolytics produce distinctive clinical effects

The drugs in this group were developed to provide anxiety reduction without some of the side effects of the benzodiazepines. The best known is **buspirone** (BuSpar), which has a novel structure and mechanism of action compared with the sedative–hypnotics. It is also unusual in that it does not necessarily increase punished behaviors as in the water-lick suppression test. Furthermore, in drug discrimination tests, it does not substitute for either barbiturates or BDZs. Clearly, buspirone has distinctive subjective effects as well as a distinctive mechanism of action.

In clinical tests, buspirone has significant anxiolytic actions, although it is much less effective in reducing the physical symptoms of anxiety than the cognitive aspects of worry and poor concentration. Some suggest that it may be best used in combination with other pharmacotherapies or along with cognitive-behavioral therapy (Harvey and Balon, 1995).

Buspirone has several advantages over the benzodiazepines, including its usefulness in treating depression that often accompanies anxiety. In addition, its anxiety reduction is not accompanied by sedation, confusion, or mental clouding. Buspirone does not enhance the CNS-depressant effects of alcohol or other CNS depressants, so it is still safer than the BDZs. It also has a minimum of severe side effects, and fatalities have not been reported. Further, it has little or no potential for recreational use or dependence. In fact, some patients report a dysphoric effect, described as a feeling of restlessness and malaise. Finally, no rebound withdrawal syndrome has been reported for buspirone. Figure 18.20 compares the effects of buspirone and diazepam in the light–dark exploration test. Mice treated for 14 days with either drug spent more time in the lighted box than saline-treated controls, demonstrating antianxiety effects. When the drugs were abruptly stopped, the mice that had been treated with buspirone showed a slow gradual return of anxiety (the time in the white box decreased) to control values, with no rebound in anxiety (**Figure 18.21A**). In contrast, mice treated with diazepam showed an abstinence-induced rebound to less than control levels of exploration (suggesting increased anxiety) followed by a slow recovery (**Figure 18.21B**).

One downside of buspirone use is that its onset of effectiveness in humans is quite long and its effectiveness in relieving anxiety is less than BDZs. In general, several weeks of daily use are required for significant

(A) Buspirone

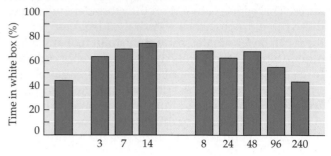

(B) Diazepam

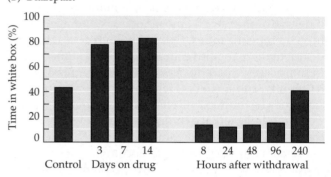

Figure 18.21 Abstinence effect after chronic diazepam but not buspirone Mice treated with buspirone (A) or diazepam (B) for 14 consecutive days and placed in the light–dark test on days 3, 7, and 14 showed reduced anxiety by exploring the bright box for a longer time than control mice. Neither drug produced tolerance over the 14 days. When the test was repeated at various times after drug withdrawal, the buspirone-treated mice showed a gradual return of anxiety. In contrast, mice treated with diazepam showed an abstinence-induced rebound in anxiety. This effect is shown by levels of exploration significantly less than control levels, followed by a slow recovery. (After Costall and Naylor, 1991.)

anxiolytic effects to be seen. This characteristic makes it less desirable for individuals who are accustomed to the immediate relief induced by BDZs. Also, its delayed action makes it less useful for patients who take the drug only when needed for situational anxiety. Second, buspirone, as well as other structurally related drugs (gepirone and ipsapirone), does not show cross-tolerance or cross-dependence with BDZs or sedative–hypnotics. This feature makes it inappropriate for use as a substitution in cases of alcohol or barbiturate withdrawal. Third, it lacks the hypnotic effects necessary to treat insomnia, has no muscle-relaxant effects, and does not control seizures.

Buspirone has unusual characteristics because, unlike the sedative–hypnotics, it does not enhance GABA function but instead acts as a partial agonist at serotonergic 5-HT$_{1A}$ receptors. These receptors are found in heavy concentration in the limbic system, including the amygdala and the frontal and entorhinal cortices. Although some of these receptors are thought to be located postsynaptically, autoradiographic and immunohistochemical studies also show 5-HT$_{1A}$ somatodendritic autoreceptors in the nucleus of the raphe. The neurochemical basis of the anxiolytic action is not fully explained, but Charney and colleagues (1990) suggest that down-regulation of the 5-HT receptors may be responsible for the delayed onset of action.

Antidepressants relieve anxiety and depression

Several of the anxiety disorders described in earlier sections are effectively treated with antidepressant drugs. These drugs are important because anxiety and depression very often occur in the same individual and a single drug can be used to treat both conditions. However, several antidepressants have beneficial effects in treating anxiety apart from their antidepressant action. For example, in OCD, the SSRIs clomipramine (Anafranil), fluoxetine (Prozac), fluvoxamine (Luvox), and sertraline (Zoloft) have been found effective in reducing symptoms, possibly because they enhance 5-HT function by blocking reuptake of the monoamine. The benefits are apparently unrelated to the antidepressant action of the SSRIs, as shown in the results of an experiment by Leonard et al. (1989). In this double-blind crossover experiment, investigators compared the effects of two antidepressants: desipramine (DMI), which blocks NE reuptake and has minimal effects on 5-HT, and clomipramine (CMI), which selectively blocks 5-HT reuptake. After 3 weeks of placebo treatment to establish a baseline of symptom severity, one group received DMI and the other CMI for a 5-week period. After 5 weeks, the drugs were switched for the two groups. **Figure 18.22** shows that the 5-HT agonist CMI was consistently more effective in relieving symptoms of OCD. Further, when patients on CMI switched to DMI, their symptoms reappeared; this shows the selective effect of the serotonergic antidepressant.

Tricyclic antidepressants such as imipramine (Tofranil) and MAOIs (e.g., phenelzine [Nardil] and

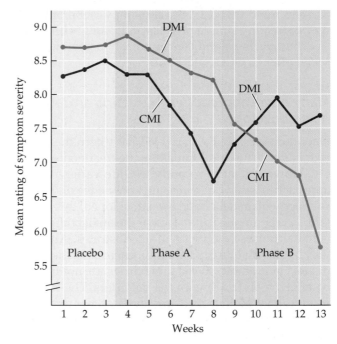

Figure 18.22 Mean rating of symptoms in patients with OCD when treated with desipramine (DMI) or clomipramine (CMI). In this crossover study, during drug treatment in phase A, the CMI group had fewer symptoms. In phase B, when the treatments were reversed for the two groups, the CMI-treated group again showed greater improvement. Patients who were treated with DMI during phase B showed a return of symptoms. (After Leonard et al., 1989.)

tranylcypromine [Parnate]) are also often effective in treating some anxiety disorders, including panic, phobic disorders, and GAD, although side effects are often troublesome (see Chapter 19). Since the side effects of SSRIs are sometimes less disturbing to patients and they have a more favorable therapeutic index, the serotonergic drugs are more often prescribed as a first choice. In addition, because abuse potential of the SSRIs is low, they may be used on occasions when benzodiazepine dependence is a concern. **Table 18.4** provides a summary of a variety of treatment options.

TABLE 18.4 Drugs Used to Treat Various Anxiety Disorders

Drug class	Trade name	Anxiety disorders
Benzodiazepines	Valium, Xanax	GAD, PTSD, panic disorder
Tricyclic antidepressants	Tofranil, Aventil	Panic disorder, GAD, OCD, PTSD
Monoamine oxidase inhibitors	Nardil, Parnate	Social phobia, panic disorder
Selective serotonin reuptake inhibitors	Prozac, Zoloft, Paxil	Social phobia, panic disorder, OCD, PTSD
Buspirone	BuSpar	GAD, panic disorder, OCD

Keep in mind that behavioral therapy is the principal way of treating simple phobias and, along with cognitive therapy, is a significant approach in treating GAD, social phobia, OCD, and PTSD.

Many novel approaches to treating anxiety are being developed

Over the years, GABA and 5-HT have been the primary focus of drug development in the treatment of anxiety. However, more recently, a wide variety of new approaches based on increasing knowledge of the neurobiology of anxiety have been developed. It is important to keep in mind that each of the anxiety disorders is likely to have distinct neural substrates. Although they all involve fear or anxiety, each has other quite distinct symptoms, so the same drugs are not likely to be effective in treating all the disorders. The fact that most animal models measure levels of fear or anxiety rather than modeling specific symptoms of the anxiety disorders means that preclinical effectiveness in the laboratory does not necessarily translate into clinical effectiveness for a particular disorder. New drug research into anxiolytics is further complicated by the high rate of comorbidity with clinical depression. There are numerous drugs in the development pipeline at various stages. Because of space limitations, we cannot review all the new developments; however, various neuropharmacological studies suggest that anxiolytic effects may be associated with modulation of CRF, glutamate, oxytocin, endocannabinoids, substance P, neuropeptide Y, galanin, orexin and others. **Web Box 18.1** describes just a few with potential promise. Mathew et al., (2008) provide an excellent overview, and several articles on potential new drug targets are provided in Recommended Readings at the end of the chapter.

Section Summary

- Anxiolytics are sedative–hypnotics that belong to the larger class of CNS depressants.
- Dose-dependent effects of sedative–hypnotics begin with reduction in anxiety and progress through stages of increasing sedation, incoordination, sleep, coma, and death.
- Sedative–hypnotics increase GABA-induced Cl⁻ current into the cell, causing enhanced hyperpolarization and inhibition of many cells.
- BDZs enhance GABA inhibition but have no effect of their own on chloride conductance. Flumazenil is a BDZ receptor competitive antagonist that reduces BDZ effects but has no effect on GABA-induced hyperpolarization. Since BDZs shift the GABA dose response to the left but do not increase the maximum GABA response, they are safer than barbiturates and other sedative–hypnotics.
- Barbiturates increase GABA-induced Cl⁻ conductance and directly open the Cl⁻ channel without GABA.
- The barbiturates are ultrashort acting, short/intermediate acting, and long acting, depending on their lipid solubility, which determines the rate of penetration into the brain and the extent of redistribution to drug depots and liver metabolism.
- Side effects of barbiturates include altered sleep architecture, mental clouding and cognitive impairment, low therapeutic index, rapid tolerance and cross-tolerance, physical dependence, and dangerous withdrawal.
- BDZs are prescribed on the basis of onset and duration. Lipid solubility determines onset. Redistribution to depots and metabolism determine duration. Many have active metabolites, making them long acting.
- Therapeutic uses of BDZs include presurgical anesthesia, anxiolysis, sleep induction, muscle relaxation, seizure control, and termination of alcohol withdrawal.
- Advantages of BDZs compared with other sedative–hypnotics include high therapeutic index, availability of a competitive antagonist to reverse overdose, reduced tolerance and drug interactions, less physical dependence and milder withdrawal, less reinforcement value, and lower abuse potential. Fatalities do not occur unless combined with another sedative–hypnotic.
- Multiple forms of the GABA$_A$ receptor subunits provide targets in drug development aimed at increasing therapeutic selectivity and reducing side effects.
- Buspirone is an anxiolytic that does not enhance GABA action but is a partial agonist at 5-HT$_{1A}$ receptors. Its advantages over BDZs are that it reduces both anxiety and depression without sedation or mental clouding, it does not enhance other sedative–hypnotics, and it has no withdrawal syndrome or abuse potential.
- The disadvantages of buspirone are its slow onset of anxiolytic effects, its ineffectiveness for relieving alcohol or barbiturate withdrawal, insomnia or seizures, and its lack of muscle-relaxant effects.
- Antidepressants including tricyclic antidepressants, MAOIs, and SSRIs may be used to reduce the anxiety accompanying depression. Some

antidepressants relieve symptoms of specific anxiety disorders. SSRIs are a drug class of first choice because they have fewer troubling side effects, a high therapeutic index, and low abuse potential.

Go to the **COMPANION WEBSITE**

sites.sinauer.com/psychopharm2e
for Web Boxes, animations, flashcards,
and other study resources.

Recommended Readings

Blanchard, R., Blanchard, D. C., Griebel, G., and Nutt, D. (Eds.). (2008). *Handbook of Anxiety and Fear*. San Diego, CA: Elsevier Academic Press.

Hamm, A. O. and Weike, A. I. (2005). The neuropsychology of fear learning and fear regulation. *Int. J. Psychophysiol.*, 57, 5–14.

Herpfer, I. and Lieb, K. (2005). Substance P receptor antagonists in psychiatry: Rationale for development and therapeutic potential. *CNS Drugs*, 19, 275–293.

LeDoux, J. E. (1996). *The Emotional Brain*. New York: Simon and Schuster.

Manning, M., Stoev, S., Chini, B., Durroux, T., Mouillac, B., and Guillon, G. (2008). Peptide and non-peptide agonists and antagonists for the vasopressin and oxytocin V1a, V1b, V2 and OT receptors: Research tools and potential therapeutic agents. *Prog. Brain Res.*, 170, 473–512.

Martin, E. I., Ressler, K. J., Binder, E., and Nemeroff, C. B. (2010). The neurobiology of anxiety disorders: Brain imaging, genetics, and psychoneuroendocrinology. *Clin. Lab. Med.*, 30, 865–891.

McEwen, B. S. (2010). Stress, sex, and neural adaptation to a changing environment: Mechanisms of neuronal remodeling. *Ann. N. Y. Acad. Sci.*, 1204 (Suppl. E), 38–59.

Rotzinger, S., Lovejoy, D. A., and Tan, L. A. (2010). Behavioral effects of neuropeptides in rodent models of depression and anxiety. *Peptides*, 31, 736–756.

Roy-Byrne, P. P. (2005). The GABA-benzodiazepine receptor complex: Structure, function, and role in anxiety. *J. Clin. Psychiatry*, 66 (Suppl. 2), 14–20.

Wang, J., Korczykowski, M., Rao, H., Fan, Y., Pluta, J., Gur, R. C., McEwen, B. S., and Detre, J. A. (2007). Gender difference in neural response to psychological stress. *Soc. Cogn. Affect. Neurosci.*, 2, 227–239.

Witkin, J. M., Tzavara, E. T., and Nomikos, G. G. (2005). A role for cannabinoid CB1 receptors in mood and anxiety disorders. *Behav. Pharmacol.*, 16, 315–331.

Our revered 16th president struggled with clinical depression at various times throughout his life.

Affective Disorders: Antidepressants and Mood Stabilizers

19

CLINICAL DEPRESSION CAN BE TOTALLY DEBILITATING, leaving the individual in absolute despair and feeling empty and worthless, unable to function, and preoccupied with his own death. But sometimes during breaks in their depression, people can accomplish important things. Consider Abraham Lincoln. Biographers have described him as the classic image of gloom. He often wept in public and cited maudlin poetry. He told jokes at odd times—he needed laughs, he said, for his survival. As a young man, he talked of suicide, and as he grew older, he said he saw the world as hard and grim. His law partner once said about Lincoln, "His melancholy dripped from him as he walked." There were times when the depression overwhelmed him and he remained in bed. On his wedding day, suffering from a severe depressive episode, he never showed up and left his bride and wedding party waiting for him at the ceremony. To quote Lincoln, "I am now the most miserable man living." Nevertheless, his lifelong illness shaped his character and helped him avoid the pitfalls of inappropriate optimism, making him a realist with vision. His troubles gave him wisdom and deeper humanity and prepared him for the painful tasks of his presidency. He possessed insight, fortitude, and moral will. His depression made him stronger, graced him with dignity, and gave him the courage and confidence to take the risks that made him one of our greatest and most beloved presidents (for more on Lincoln's story, readers can go to *Lincoln's Melancholy*, by Joshua Wolf Shenk, 2005).

Characteristics of Affective Disorders

The *Diagnostic and Statistical Manual of Mental Disorders*, Fourth Edition (*DSM-IV*), describes two principal types of affective disorder: **major depression** and **bipolar disorder**. Both of these are characterized by extreme and inappropriate exaggeration of mood (or affect). Major depression, also called unipolar depression, is characterized by recurring episodes of dysphoria and negative thinking that is also reflected in behavior. Bipolar disorder (also called bipolar depression) is also cyclical, but moods swing from depression to mania over time. The thinking and behavior of individuals with affective disorders are consistent with the exaggerated mood, but the mood does not reflect a realistic appraisal of the environment. Mood disorders are among the most common form of mental illness today and were described as early as 400 BC by Hippocrates. The Greeks called depression *melancholia*, meaning "black bile," and recognized that it was associated with anxiety and heavy alcohol use. However, only in the past 150 years has it been recognized as a disorder of brain function.

Major depression damages the quality of life

We are all familiar with the essential feelings associated with depression: feeling down and blue, feeling listless, and lacking energy to do even the fun things we normally enjoy. The state of sadness that occurs in response to situations such as the loss of a loved one, failure to achieve goals, or disappointment in love is called **reactive depression** and does not constitute mental illness unless symptoms are disproportionate to the event or are significantly prolonged. The fact that we all have experienced depression does not make the clinical condition any easier to understand. In clinical depression, the mood disorder is so severe that the individual withdraws from life and from all social interactions. The intense pain and loneliness may make suicide seem like the only option. Pathological depression resembles the emotional state that we have all experienced but differs significantly in both intensity and duration.

The dysphoric mood is characterized by a loss of interest in almost everything and an inability to experience pleasure in anything (anhedonia). Most depressed patients express feelings of hopelessness, worthlessness, sadness, guilt, and desperation. Frequently, patients exhibit loss of appetite, insomnia (characterized particularly by early morning awakening), crying, diminished sexual desire, loss of ambition, fatigue, and either motor retardation or agitation. Self-devaluation and loss of self-esteem are very common and are combined with a complete sense of hopelessness about the future. Individuals may stop eating or caring for themselves physically, sometimes remaining in bed for prolonged periods. Other physical symptoms may include localized pain, severe digestive disturbances, and difficulty breathing. Thoughts of suicide are common; one estimate of suicide rates suggests that 7% to 15% of depressed individuals commit suicide, in contrast to a rate of 1% to 1.5% of the overall population. **Table 19.1** summarizes the *DSM-IV* criteria for manic episodes and major depression.

Although there are some common features of clinical depression, symptom clusters do vary with the individual. Furthermore, particular patterns of symptoms suggest that there are depression subtypes that may be associated with distinct pathophysiologies and distinct causes. What has been well recognized since the time of Hippocrates (around 400 BC) is that there is an extensive overlap of depression with anxiety and alcohol dependence (see Chapter 10). Confirmation of the relationship has been shown by many epidemiological surveys that estimate comorbidity (i.e., when two or more disorders occur in the same individual) at almost 60%. When the disorders are comorbid, it is usually the anxiety disorder, particularly generalized anxiety disorder or social anxiety disorder (see Chapter 18), that precedes the onset of depression. Comorbidity of the disorders predicts more *severe* symptoms, causing impaired daily function in work or while attending school or social events. Comorbidity also predicts more *persistent* symptoms that are more difficult to treat. Further discussion of the relationship between anxiety and depression follows in the sections on the role of heredity and stress in depression etiology. Belzer and Schneier (2004) provide more information on diagnosis and treatment and theoretical explanatory models for the comorbidity of anxiety and depression.

If left untreated, most episodes of unipolar depression improve in about 6 to 9 months. However, the episodes usually recur throughout life, often increasing in frequency and intensity in later years. Although stress often precedes the first episodes of depression, later episodes are more likely to occur without the influence of psychosocial stress. Estimates of the incidence of depression vary significantly, but it is generally believed that 15% to 20% of the population experience depressive symptoms at any given time. The lifetime risk for a first episode of unipolar depression is between 3% and 4% for men and from 5% to 9% for women. The gender difference in the risk for depression is a topic of considerable interest and debate. The mean age of onset for depression is 27 years. This figure has decreased in recent years: **Figure 19.1** shows that among Americans born before 1905, only 1% developed depression by age 75, whereas among those born since 1955, 6% had become depressed by age 24.

TABLE 19.1 Symptoms of Manic Episodes and Major Depression

Diagnosis	Symptom
Manic episode	Inflated self-esteem or grandiosity
	Decreased need for sleep (e.g., feeling rested after only 3 hours of sleep)
	Greater talkativeness than usual or pressure to keep talking
	Flight of ideas or feeling that thoughts are racing
	Distractibility (i.e., attention too easily drawn to unimportant external stimuli)
	Increase in goal-directed activity (either socially, at work, or sexually); agitation
	Excess involvement in pleasurable activities that have a high potential for painful consequences (e.g., unrestrained buying sprees, sexual indiscretions, or foolish investments)
Major depressive episode	Depressed mood (or irritable mood in children and adolescents) most of the day, nearly every day
	Diminished interest or pleasure in most activities most of the day, every day
	Significant changes in body weight or appetite (gain or loss)
	Insomnia or hypersomnia nearly every day
	Psychomotor agitation (increased activity) or retardation (decreased activity)
	Fatigue or loss of energy
	Feelings of worthlessness or excessive or inappropriate guilt
	Diminished ability to think or concentrate; indecisiveness
	Recurrent thoughts of death, recurrent suicidal ideation without a specific plan, or a suicide attempt or specific plan for committing suicide

Source: American Psychiatric Association, 1994.

In bipolar disorder moods alternate from mania to depression

The second type of exaggerated mood is mania. Mania rarely occurs alone but rather alternates with periods of depression to form bipolar disorder. The primary symptom of mania is elation. Manic individuals feel faultless, full of fun, and bursting with energy. Their need for sleep is significantly reduced. They tend to be more talkative than usual and experience racing thoughts and ideas. In some individuals, the predominant mood is characterized by irritability, belligerence, and impatience because the rest of us are just too slow. They tend to make impulsive decisions of the grandiose sort and have unlimited confidence in themselves. The manic individual becomes involved in activities that have a high potential for negative consequences that often go unrecognized by the individual, such as foolish business investments, reckless driving, buying sprees, or sexual indiscretions. However, some individuals during a manic phase are capable of highly productive efforts when channeled appropriately. A high proportion of creative individuals in the arts and sciences have experienced bipolar disorder and find that during the manic periods, their thought processes quicken and they feel both creative and productive. Is creativity linked to mental illness? **Web Box 19.1** considers that possibility.

The incidence of bipolar disorder is the same in men and women: it occurs in approximately 1% of the population. The time of onset for bipolar illness is typically between 20 and 30 years of age, and episodes continue throughout the life span.

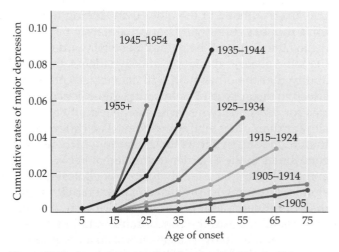

Figure 19.1 Age of onset of major depression Americans are developing major depression at higher rates and younger ages than previously, according to this analysis of data. The study evaluated 18,244 subjects at five sites, grouped in cohorts on the basis of year of birth. Cross-cultural surveys indicate a similar phenomenon worldwide. (After Barlow and Durand, 1995.)

Risk factors for mood disorders are biological and environmental

Most scientists agree that psychiatric disorders develop in a given individual because of the interaction of genes and environmental events. Individuals with particular clusters of genes inherit the tendency to express certain traits or behaviors that increase their vulnerability to specific disorders. Having those genes does not mean that you will develop the disorder, but exposure to particular environmental events is more likely to trigger the disorder in the vulnerable individual. Heredity, environmental stress, and altered biological rhythms are risk factors for affective disorders.

ROLE OF HEREDITY   Evidence for a genetic contribution to affective disorders comes from several sources. **Adoption studies** help to clarify the roles of genetics and family environment. In these studies, individuals with a firm diagnosis who were adopted at an early age are the focus of the research. If a heritable component exists, one would expect to see that, compared with controls, the individual with an affective disorder would have a greater number of biological relatives with the same disorder, despite being raised in a different environment. Although many adoption studies have found such a relationship and suggest a role for genetics, the results have not always been consistent.

The best evidence for a heritable component of affective illness comes from **twin studies**, which show a significant difference between monozygotic (identical) and dizygotic (fraternal) twins in the rate of concordance for the disorders. The data in **Figure 19.2** show that if one twin has a mood disorder, the concordance rate (i.e., the likelihood of the other twin sharing the trait) for a monozygotic twin is approximately 65%. This means that if one of the pair of identical twins (having the same genes) experiences affective illness, the probability that the other twin will also experience some affective disorder is 65%. In contrast, the concordance rate for dizygotic twins (who are genetically no more similar than other siblings) is 20%. The difference in these two rates suggests the extent to which genetics contributes to the disorder (estimated at between 40% and 50%), and that a family history of clinical depression is the strongest predictor of vulnerability to the disorder. Keep in mind that if genetics were the only determining factor, the concordance rate in identical twins would be 100%. The genetics of an individual can certainly make him more vulnerable, but whether or not he actually develops the disorder must also depend on other psychosocial or pathophysiological factors.

If you look again at Figure 19.2 you will see that the concordance rate is also dependent on the severity of clinical depression: more severe mood disorders

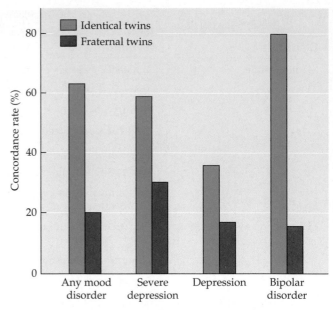

Figure 19.2 Concordance rate for mood disorders among identical and fraternal twins Identical twins are far more likely to share mood disorders than are fraternal twins, especially in the case of bipolar disorder. Concordance for clinical depression depends to some extent on severity. In this case, severe depression is defined as three or more episodes of depression. Data were derived from 110 pairs of twins. (After Bertelsen et al., 1977.)

may have a stronger genetic contribution than less severe disorders. Of additional interest is the finding that there are shared genetic risk factors for clinical depression and anxiety disorders, although the magnitude depends on the particular anxiety disorder. For instance, major depressive disorder is most closely related genetically to generalized anxiety disorder. Figure 19.2 also shows that the genetic contribution to bipolar disorder is significantly greater than that to major depression. Eighty percent concordance in monozygotic twins compared with 16% in dizygotic twins indicates a very strong role for heredity in bipolar disorder.

Despite **linkage studies**, which look for similarities in gene location on chromosomes in families with affected members, and other more sophisticated methods of molecular biology that examine DNA fragments, no single dominant gene for affective disorders is known. We may well find that the genes involved confer a general vulnerability to a host of mood and anxiety disorders. For example, linkage studies for major depressive disorder and associated personality traits like neuroticism have been attempted because high scores on neuroticism are a strong predictor of future depressive disorder and other psychiatric ailments. Individuals who score high on neuroticism experience more negative emotions including anxiety, anger, guilt, and depressed mood and are more bothered by psychosocial stress. The particular disorder that is expressed in such an individual may ultimately

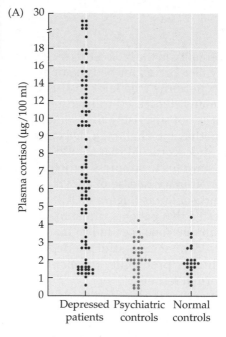

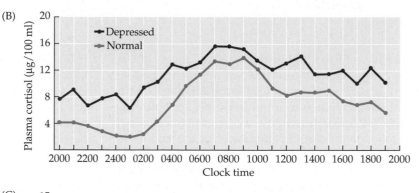

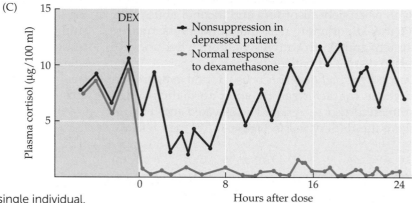

Figure 19.3 Abnormalities in glucocorticoids (A) Many (but not all) depressed patients have elevated cortisol levels compared with controls. Each dot represents a single individual. (B) Differences exist between the circadian changes in blood cortisol levels of depressed patients and healthy control subjects. The measures were made each hour over a 1-day period. The decline in cortisol that normally occurs in the early morning and evening occurs to a lesser extent in depressed patients. (C) Depressed individuals fail to respond with reduced cortisol levels after injection with 1 mg dexamethasone (DEX). The injected glucocorticoid also normally reduces both CRF release from the hypothalamus and pituitary release of ACTH. (B after Kandel, 1991; C after Klein, 2000.)

be determined by developmental or psychosocial factors. Discussion of several candidate genes associated with clinical depression will be found in the section on serotonin dysfunction and in the section on brain-derived neurotrophic factor (BDNF). It is important to keep in mind that in any complex psychiatric disorder, there will be many vulnerability genes, each of which contributes only a very modest amount.

ROLE OF STRESS Both neurobiological studies and family studies indicate that anxiety and depression are closely related. First, anxiety along with its associated physiological symptoms is a frequent accompaniment to depression. Second, intense environmental stress and anxiety often precede episodes of depression, particularly early on in the course of the disorder. Further, altered patterns of stress hormone levels are frequently found in depressed patients. Chapter 18 has already introduced the relationship between anxiety and depression. Despite the importance of environmental stress, keep in mind that identical life stresses may be perceived very differently by individuals. Many people seem resilient and capable of coping despite extraordinary stresses, while

others seem to succumb to relatively minor problems. It is likely that genetics plays a role in determining how one responds physically and behaviorally to daily traumas and stress. The dual importance of nature (genetics) and nurture (environment) can never be ignored.

The importance of stress to the etiology of depression and its mediation by the hypothalamic–pituitary–adrenal (HPA) axis is a significant focus in neuroscience. In response to stress, multiple neurotransmitters (including norepinephrine [NE], acetylcholine [Ach], and γ-aminobutyric acid [GABA]) regulate the secretion of corticotropin-releasing factor (CRF) from hypothalamic cells. CRF controls the release of adrenocorticotropic hormone (ACTH) from the pituitary into the blood. ACTH in turn acts on the adrenal gland to increase secretion of cortisol and other glucocorticoids, all of which play a role in the mobilization of energy to deal with stress (Box 2.4 shows the HPA axis). Normally, cortisol feeds back to shut down HPA activation, resulting in transient activity of the system and brief surges in cortisol.

Among the most consistent neuroendocrine abnormalities in depressed individuals is abnormal secretion of cortisol, which is demonstrated in several ways. First, many depressed patients have elevated levels of cortisol (**Figure 19.3A**) in response to a greater-than-normal release of ACTH. Although both the pituitary and adrenal glands are enlarged as a result of hypersecretion, evidence from several sources suggests that the abnormality is not in the glands but is in the brain. The hypersecretion is most likely due to abnormal regulation of CRF by the hypothalamus. Numerous studies have found higher-than-normal levels of CRF in the cerebrospinal fluid (CSF) of depressed patients and increased numbers of CRF-producing cells in the hypothalamus in postmortem brain tissue. This exaggerated HPA axis function may be explained in part by the impact of early life traumas on the vulnerable individual. Early life stress apparently alters the setpoint of the HPA axis, making it permanently overly responsive and increasing the risk for later depression as well as anxiety disorders and alcohol abuse (**Box 19.1**). It is important to note that antidepressant drug treatment and electroconvulsive therapy reduce CRF levels in depressed patients.

Second, the high level of cortisol found in depressed patients is characterized by an abnormal circadian rhythm in cortisol secretion. The elevated and relatively flat pattern (depicted in **Figure 19.3B**) may reflect a more general abnormality in the biological clock, since altered rhythmicity also occurs for body temperature changes and sleep patterns (see later in this chapter). Third, since many depressed individuals have elevated cortisol, it is not surprising that some fail to respond to dexamethasone challenge. **Dexamethasone** is a synthetic glucocorticoid that should act as a negative-feedback stimulus to suppress hypothalamic release of CRF and pituitary release of ACTH, resulting in decreased cortisol levels (**Figure 19.3C**). Several studies have suggested that patients who remain nonresponders to dexamethasone (i.e., fail to have cortisol release suppressed) after successful antidepressant treatment have a higher probability of relapse than those who show normal response.

Although usually adrenal glucocorticoids (including cortisol) are helpful in preparing an organism

BOX 19.1   Pharmacology in Action

Stress–Diathesis Model of Depression

Nemeroff and colleagues (1998) developed a model of mood disorders called the stress–diathesis model of depression, which refers to the interaction between early experience (stresses such as abuse or neglect) and genetic predisposition (diathesis). In essence, they propose that the genetic character of depression is expressed in lowered monoamine levels in the brain or in increased reactivity of the HPA axis to stress. These factors create a lower threshold for depression. In addition, they believe that negative, stressful events early in life may lower the threshold even further, leaving the individual more vulnerable to depression as an adult. To test the model, one would have to show that early stress not only produces immediate activity of the HPA axis but also causes persistent activation of CRF-containing neurons. If such were the case, these individuals would respond more strongly to stress as adults than control subjects.

The design to test the model used newborn rats that were stressed by being removed from their mothers for brief periods daily for 10 days of their first 21 days of life. They were then allowed to grow up under standard conditions. The results showed that as adults, the deprived rats had elevations in stress-induced ACTH and cortisol and increased CRF in the brain. A permanent increase in CRF gene expression explains the increase in CRF production. Despite the higher levels of CRF, the studies also found increased CRF receptor density, which might be expected to produce long-term enhancement of stress and CRF-induced depression. More recently, other researchers in the same group observed that antidepressant drug treatment prevented the increase in CRF and reduced the fearful behaviors (e.g., freezing in novel situations) normally exhibited by the rats. When treatment was terminated, all the abnormalities returned. How the blocking of 5-HT reuptake with the antidepressant modifies the CRF

axis is not immediately evident but is certainly the focus of future research.

The implications of this type of research are very clear. Several million children are abused or neglected in the United States each year. Based on the animal evidence, we would expect these children to be exposed to events that permanently modify their developing brains, leaving them more vulnerable to stress and depression as adults.

The research also suggests a new direction for antidepressant drug development and therapeutic regimens. The reemergence of biological abnormalities after termination of drug treatment suggests that treatment may need to be continued indefinitely to prevent the recurrence of depressive episodes. Also, the potential to develop a new class of antidepressants that block CRF receptors could lead to a new therapeutic approach to the treatment of at least some patients with depression.

(A) Sleep pattern of a patient with depression

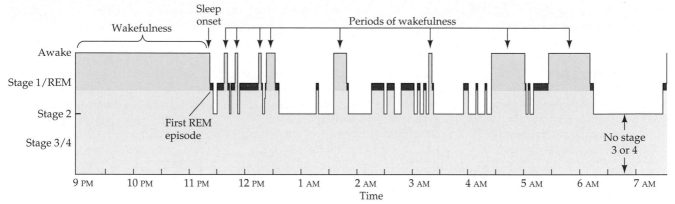

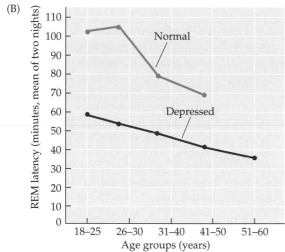

Figure 19.4 Altered sleep architecture in depression (A) In depressed patients, the onset of sleep is delayed and REM periods (colored red) get shorter rather than longer as the night goes on, which is typical in healthy adults. Also, notice the many awakenings that occur during the night because of failure to reach deep sleep (stages 3 and 4). (B) REM episodes begin sooner after the onset of sleep in depressed than in nondepressed individuals at every age.

for stress, when the levels are persistently elevated, several systems begin to show pathological changes. Besides having damaging effects on immune-system and organ function, glucocorticoids are associated with neuronal atrophy in the hippocampus, leading to cognitive impairment, imbalances in the serotonin (5-HT) system correlated with anxiety, and hormonal changes associated with depression (McEwen, 2008). The section on the neurobiological models of depression later in the chapter will provide more detail on the role of glucocorticoids in depression.

ALTERED BIOLOGICAL RHYTHMS Cortisol secretion is not the only biological rhythm that is disturbed in major depression. Altered sleep rhythms are among the most common and persistent symptoms of depression. Circa-

dian rhythm controls the onset, pattern, and termination of sleep. The normal sleep cycle is quite regular, having four stages of non-REM sleep (stages 1 to 4) lasting a total of 70 to 100 minutes followed by a 10- to 15-minute period of rapid-eye-movement (REM) sleep, during which time dreaming occurs. This cycle is repeated four or five times a night. Depressed individuals show several distinct abnormalities in their sleep rhythm (**Figure 19.4A**). First, there is a long period before sleep onset. Second, there is a significant decrease in the time spent in slow-wave sleep, or deep sleep (stages 3 and 4), which leads to repeated awakenings during the night. Third, the onset of REM sleep occurs much earlier after the onset of sleep. Although REM latency decreases with age, individuals who are depressed show a shorter latency at all ages (**Figure 19.4B**). In extreme cases, the individual may enter REM sleep almost immediately after falling asleep. Fourth, REM sleep is significantly increased during the first one third of the night in depressed individuals, but nondepressed individuals have proportionately more REM sleep in the final one third of sleep. Also, although normal REM periods tend to increase in duration during the night, depressed patients do not show such a pattern. Finally, when ocular movement is measured, depressed individuals show more frequent and vigorous eye movements during REM sleep, which suggests more-intense dreaming.

Although we don't know what the altered rhythms mean, the irregularities in sleep patterns found in depressed individuals resemble the sleep patterns of normal individuals who must alter their time of sleep by 12 hours. Since other indicators of biological rhythms, such as body temperature fluctuation and hormonal secretion (e.g., cortisol), are often also altered, one might consider the possibility that the biological clocks of people with depression are "phase-shifted." In some individuals, the three rhythms are out of harmony (called desynchronization) or are mismatched. Since it is well documented

BOX 19.2   Clinical Applications

Agomelatine

Sleep disruptions and multiple circadian dysfunctions are central features of clinical depression. Additionally, polymorphisms of genes of the biological clock in the suprachiasmatic nucleus of the hypothalamus represent a genetic predisposition to circadian irregularities in some depressed patients. One classic approach to resynchronizing endogenous rhythms and the sleep–wake cycle is administration of melatonin. Melatonin, a pineal gland hormone regulated by light exposure, induces sleep and regulates circadian function by acting at MT_1 and MT_2 melatonin receptors. Although melatonin has been shown to be effective in treating circadian sleep disorders such as those associated with jet lag and shift work, primary sleep disorders are not effectively improved because melatonin has a very short half-life in the blood circulation. In contrast, novel long-acting melatonin agonists such as **agomelatine** reset circadian rhythms by binding to both MT_1

and MT_2 receptors in the suprachiasmatic nucleus of the hypothalamus. Additionally, agomelatine blocks 5-HT_2 receptors with high affinity in several brain areas including the cerebral cortex, hippocampus, and amygdala. In addition to resynchronizing rhythms in various animal models that have disrupted circadian rhythms, agomelatine also has antidepressant-like activity in several animal models of depression. Paralleling the animal studies, multiple double-blind, placebo-controlled trials with depressed patients showed that agomelatine was effective in significantly reducing symptoms of moderate to severe major depressive disorder while normalizing sleep patterns. It is quite possible that the antidepressant effect is at least partially due to the resynchronization of the circadian rhythms of depressed patients. Data from studies that used a comparison antidepressant showed agomelatine to be similarly effective or more effective than the comparison drug, and its onset

of effectiveness was much more rapid. Furthermore, agomelatine demonstrated only mild adverse effects, not different from placebo, and it was tolerated better than established antidepressant drugs. Side effects included headache, symptoms of the common cold, fatigue, and gastrointestinal complaints. Unlike many current antidepressants, it does not impair sexual function and discontinuation leads to no rebound withdrawal syndrome. Effects of overdose are relatively mild. One potential problem is a transient increase in liver enzymes in about 1% of the patients; periodic liver function tests are required. Its distinct pharmacological profile and mechanism of action would make it a valuable treatment option. Long-term safety must still be evaluated, including effects on liver function and potential drug interactions. A brief review is provided by Sansone and Sansone (2011).

that neurotransmitters involved in emotion regulation such as 5-HT and NE show circadian rhythms in function, the importance of evaluating altered rhythms in mood disorders is clear. The implications of these irregularities in sleep cycles have led to several novel treatment strategies including the use of melatonin agonists described in **Box 19.2** and sleep deprivation therapy found in **Web Box 19.2**.

It is probably no surprise that bipolar patients also show altered sleep rhythms (Plante and Winkelman, 2008). Although their sleep during depressive episodes resembles that of unipolar depression with its shortened REM latency onset, one of the hallmark diagnostic symptoms of mania is the severely reduced need (sometimes almost absence) of sleep with no loss of energy. It is particularly interesting that in the nonsymptomatic bipolar individual, sleep deprivation that is intentional or is associated with environmental events such as experiencing jet lag, bereavement, or

late night studying can actually trigger an episode of mania. It is not clear whether the lack of sleep causes the onset of mania or represents an early occurring symptom. However, when manic patients are treated with a sleep-inducing benzodiazepine, the manic symptoms subside. Such sedatives are used as a common additive treatment along with a mood stabilizer such as lithium (see the last section of this chapter).

Animal Models of Affective Disorders

Animal models are used to study the neurobiology of depression and to evaluate the mechanism of antidepressant drugs, as well as to screen new drugs for effectiveness. Although the affective symptoms of depression, such as feelings of worthlessness and guilt, can really be described only in human terms, several animal models have provided important tools

Figure 19.5 Forced swim test After initial attempts to escape, the rat in the water-filled cylinder is shown in a posture reflecting a sense of futility. Antidepressant drugs reduce the amount of time spent in the immobile posture. (Courtesy of Porsolt and Partners Pharmacology.)

with which to evaluate drugs and neurochemistry. There is no available model that mimics all the symptoms of depression; instead they consider specific aspects of the disorder such as reductions in psychomotor activity, neuroendocrine responses, cognitive changes, or such functions as eating, sleeping, and deriving pleasure from everyday activities. Therefore, the usefulness of any single model in evaluating the complex etiology of depression is limited, and the ability of models to predict which new drugs will be effective for the clinical population is challenging.

One of the oldest methods used to identify clinically useful antidepressants is antagonism or reversal of **reserpine-induced sedation**. In terms of face validity, psychomotor slowing seems to be most similar to human depression, although other reserpine-induced effects can be used as readily. For example, reserpine-induced ptosis (drooping eyelids) and hypersecretion of tears and saliva provide ready measures and are frequently used in animal research. The validity of the model has been further demonstrated by the almost universal ability of clinically useful antidepressants to antagonize the effects of reserpine. The model is limited in that it is dependent on monoamine neurochemistry and does not identify novel approaches to therapeutics.

A more commonly used measure that permits rapid behavioral screening of novel antidepressants, called the **behavioral despair** or **forced swim test**, requires rats or mice to swim in a cylinder from which there is no escape. After early attempts to escape are unsuccessful, the animals assume an immobile posture except for the minimal movements needed to keep their heads above water (**Figure 19.5**). In a closely related test (**tail suspension test**), mice are suspended by the tail from a lever, and the duration of movements (a period of agitation followed by immobility) is recorded. These models are based on the idea that the immobility reflects a lowered mood in which the animals are resigned to their fate and have given up hope. Acute administration of effective antidepressants reduces the time spent in this "freezing" phase of immobility relative to untreated control animals. This test has similarities to the **learned helplessness** test, in which subjects are initially exposed to aversive events such as *unescapable* foot shock for several hours or for periods over several days. When the subjects are placed in a new situation in which a response could alter an aversive event, they fail to make the appropriate response. The animal behavior resembles clinical depression in that depressed humans frequently fail to respond to environmental changes and express feelings of hopelessness and the belief that nothing they do has an effect. Although these antidepressant screening tests are frequently used, all three have been criticized because the stress is only short-lived, the animals tested are normal rather than genetically vulnerable to depression, and the antidepressants reduce behavioral despair after acute drug treatment rather than after the chronic antidepressant administration that is needed to reverse symptoms in humans.

Several chronic stress procedures are more difficult to perform but are considered to have greater validity (Nestler and Hyman, 2010). The **chronic mild unpredictable stress** model exposes rodents to a series of physically stressful events such as cold temperatures, wet bedding, restraint, and sudden loud noise for several weeks. Following the stress, these animals show several behaviors reminiscent of depressed individuals including multiple cognitive impairments, increased anxiety-like behaviors, social withdrawal, and a reduced preference for sucrose that models human anhedonia. Of significance is that chronic rather than acute antidepressant treatment is required to reverse the behaviors. **Chronic social defeat stress** uses the resident-intruder paradigm to create intense stress. The animal is placed in another animal's cage of the same species, and this generates nonlethal aggression. Exposure to the conflict is repeated over several days, and between exposures the animal may be housed in a cage adjacent to the dominant animal to expose it further to visual and olfactory cues. Animals stressed in this manner show multiple depression-like behaviors including reductions in motor activity, exploration, sucrose preference, and copulatory behaviors, as well as social withdrawal. Chronic but not acute antidepressant administration reverses these behaviors.

To evaluate the importance of early life stress as a vulnerability factor in the development of depression, **maternal separation** can be used. Stress is induced by separating young animals (usually rats) from their mothers for brief periods daily during the first few weeks of life. Early stress provides the opportunity to evaluate long-term behavioral and neuroendocrine abnormalities in the animals as adults. Nemeroff (1998) used this model to evaluate the hypothesis that abuse or neglect early in life activates the stress response at the time, but also produces long-term changes in CRF function that may predispose the individual to clinical depression later in life (discussed in Box 19.1).

In general, researchers rely on the tests for screening antidepressants to model the depression phase of bipolar disorder and have focused more recently on developing models for mania. Attempts to develop models eliciting spontaneously cycling episodes of mania and depression are even more limited. Several models are based on the significance of the altered circadian rhythms observed in bipolar individuals. In one environmentally induced model, the animals are exposed to **sleep deprivation** for an extended period. At the end of the deprivation period, the rat does not immediately fall asleep but instead remains awake for about 30 minutes and demonstrates multiple manic-like symptoms including insomnia, hyperactivity, irritability, aggressiveness, hypersexuality, and stereotypical behaviors. This sleep deprivation–induced mania resembles that observed in individuals with bipolar disorder. If lithium (a drug commonly used to treat bipolar disorder) is added to the animal's food during the sleep deprivation, some but not all of the manic behaviors are reduced. Although it has face validity, this test is time consuming and provides only a 30-minute window of opportunity for investigation. A second approach utilizes mutant mice that target genes of the circadian clock such as the *Clock* gene. Mice lacking the Clock protein show manic-like behaviors such as less depression-like behavior in the forced swim test, reduced anxiety, hyperactivity, disrupted circadian rhythms, decreased sleep, and increased preference for rewarding stimuli including cocaine, sucrose, and electrical brain stimulation. Chronic lithium treatment restores most manic-like behaviors to control levels. More investigation into these behaviors and into pharmacological treatments that are effective and ineffective in altering manic-like behaviors is needed to establish validity. For the interested reader, Young and colleagues (2011) provide a review and assessment of pharmacological, environmental, and genetic models of bipolar disorder.

Section Summary

- Affective disorders including major depression and bipolar disorder are chronic disorders that recur in episodes over the life span. Symptoms are listed in Table 19.1.

- The incidence of depression is approximately 15% to 20% of the population at any one time. Depression is twice as common in women and is highly comorbid with anxiety and alcohol abuse.

- Bipolar disorder constitutes episodes of depression alternating with mania and occurs in about 1% of the population.

- On the basis of twin studies and adoption studies, genetic contribution to the occurrence of major depression is estimated at 45% and family history is the strongest predictor of vulnerability. Genetic contribution to bipolar disorder is significantly greater than that for depression.

- Depression is associated with abnormalities of HPA axis function: high plasma ACTH and cortisol, hypersecretion of CRF, flat circadian rhythm of cortisol, and failure of dexamethasone-induced negative feedback.

- In depression, sleep architecture is altered in the following ways: onset insomnia, reduced slow-wave sleep, early onset of REM sleep, more frequent and longer REM episodes early in the night, and more vigorous eye movement during REM.

- Individuals with mania sleep very little without loss of energy. In symptom-free patients, sleep deprivation initiates a manic episode.

- Animal models of depression are used to screen new treatments but mimic only a tiny portion of the clinical symptoms. Some models include reserpine-induced sedation, forced swim test, tail suspension test, learned helplessness, chronic mild unpredictable stress, chronic social defeat stress, and early maternal separation.

- Exposure to sleep deprivation and the creation of mutant mice that target genes of the biological clock are two means used to produce a model of mania in rodents.

Neurochemical Basis of Mood Disorders

The earliest attempt to develop a cohesive theory of the neurochemical basis of affective disorders was the **monoamine hypothesis**. The monoamine hypothesis originated with the observation that reserpine, a drug effective in reducing high blood pressure, induces depression as a side effect in a significant number of patients. The drug prevents the packaging of neurotransmitters into vesicles, leaving the molecules in the cytoplasm, where monoamine oxidase (MAO) degrades them. In this way, reserpine treatment produces empty vesicles and reduces the levels of dopamine (DA), NE, and 5-HT (all monoamines). Could it be that the reduced level of monoamines in the central nervous system (CNS) is responsible for the depressed mood? This possibility seemed increasingly likely when the mechanism of action of two types of antidepressants, monoamine oxidase inhibitors (MAOIs) and tricyclic antidepressants (TCAs), was considered. Despite their varied synaptic action, the antidepressant drugs acutely increase the function of NE or 5-HT or both. In addition, drugs in both classes reverse reserpine-induced reduction in motor activity—a classic animal model for testing antidepressant agents that was described earlier (**Figure 19.6**). The drug studies were combined with early data showing reduced levels of the NE metabolite 3-methoxy-4-hydroxyphenylglycol (MHPG; suggesting lowered NE synaptic activity) and reduced 5-hydroxyindole acetic acid (5-HIAA, suggesting lowered 5-HT synaptic activity) in the CSF, plasma, or urine of depressed patients. These measures suggest low utilization of the monoamines. In addition, the manic-like activity produced by amphetamine and cocaine is correlated with the increase in catecholamines in the synapse following enhanced release or blocked reuptake. Prolonged use of the drugs causes depletion of the amines, resulting in depression, lethargy, and craving. All of these pieces of evidence formed the basis of the monoamine hypothesis of affective disorders (Schildkraut, 1965).

Although many new questions have challenged the original hypothesis, when it was first proposed, the best evidence supported the idea that depression is associated with low levels of monoamines, whereas mania coincides with excess monoamine activity. Because reserpine acts on all monoamines and the early antidepressants also were nonselective in increasing NE and 5-HT, it really was not clear which of the neurotransmitters was most important in the etiology of depression. Unfortunately, we have not yet resolved this issue, and more and more researchers are coming to the conclusion that both of these amines are likely to play a role in clinical depression, and that other neurotransmitters may also contribute to the complex pattern of symptoms. Increasing evidence suggests that there is anatomical and functional interaction between noradrenergic neurons in the locus coeruleus and serotonergic neurons originating in the midbrain raphe. Each of the two transmitter systems seems to be capable of modulating the other. In the meantime, it is important to remember that neurotransmitter systems should be considered not in isolation but instead as a part of a complex network of interacting neurons.

Although we now know that the monoamine hypothesis is overly simple, it provided an important theoretical model that was the focus of enormous amounts of research over many years. It provided the basis for new drug development, for the creation and testing of new animal models, and for the formulation of new questions that could not be answered within

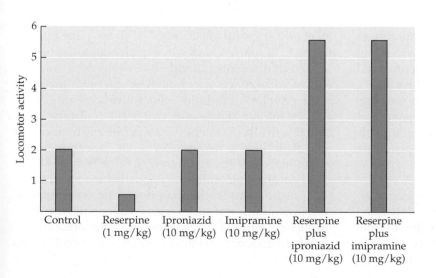

Figure 19.6 Effects of reserpine, the MAOI iproniazid, and the TCA imipramine on rat locomotor activity Reserpine clearly reduces motor activity of rats compared with control treatment. Neither of the antidepressants has any effect on motor activity when given alone. However, a dramatic increase in motor behavior occurs when reserpine is given in combination with either of the antidepressants. The reversal of reserpine-induced depression parallels the changes in brain amines and contributes to the monoamine hypothesis of affective disorders. (After Snyder, 1996.)

the old theory. As is always the case in good science, new and often conflicting evidence must be accounted for and old theories modified.

The monoamine hypothesis as originally stated was based heavily on acute antidepressant drug effects. It is too simplistic to account for the complex syndrome of affective disorders, and it fails to resolve several discrepancies. The most important of these is the discrepancy in time between the rapid neurochemical actions of antidepressants and the slow onset of clinical effects over several weeks. This disparity in time course clearly demonstrates that the acute enhancement of monoamine function is not the neurochemical basis for therapeutic activity. Newer testable models of the neurobiological basis of affective disorders still use three basic approaches: (1) developing animal models including gene manipulation models; (2) evaluating the mechanism of action of effective drug treatment; and (3) examining neurobiological differences in patient populations. The most common ways of evaluating groups of patients include measuring neurochemical differences in biological fluids or brain tissue postmortem, screening for genetic polymorphisms, evaluating response to drug challenge, and visualizing the brain with positron emission tomography (PET) or magnetic resonance imaging. Using patients is most problematic in that results are frequently inconsistent because of variability among patients in symptoms, history of drug use, lifestyle issues, and so forth. Nevertheless, clarifying the neurobiological mechanisms of major depression will ultimately pave the way for the discovery of new and more effective treatments (Belmaker and Agam, 2008).

Serotonin dysfunction contributes to mood disorders

Serotonin continues to be a focus of research because it has a significant influence on sensitivity to pain, emotionality, and response to negative consequences as well as to reward. The effects of 5-HT on sleep, eating, and thermoregulation are likewise well documented and intuitively seem to contribute to depressive symptoms. Rats with depleted stores of 5-HT are irritable and aggressive, appear overly sensitive to pain, and show altered patterns of eating and satiety. Parallels in humans suffering from major affective disorders can be easily seen.

MEASURING 5-HT IN HUMANS Although there is no solid evidence of abnormal 5-HT function in depressed patients, several measures can provide a clue to CNS function. First, the most common way to determine the level of 5-HT function (called **turnover**) is by measuring the principal metabolite of serotonin 5-HIAA. It is gener-

ally assumed that high 5-HIAA reflects increased function of serotonergic neurons, and low 5-HIAA the converse. Lower 5-HIAA levels have been found in postmortem brains of depressed individuals, most consistently in the brains of suicide victims. Several studies have also reported lower 5-HIAA levels in the CSF of depressed individuals. Measuring monoamine metabolites in other body fluids such as blood or urine is much easier, but the results may or may not indicate CNS function.

Second, blood level of tryptophan, the 5-HT precursor, is another measure of serotonergic function that frequently appears low in depressed patients compared with controls. One of the most effective ways to investigate the role of serotonin in depressive disorders is the **tryptophan depletion challenge**, in which subjects consume a tryptophan-deficient amino acid cocktail that transiently reduces 5-HT level in the brain by 70% to 80% because tryptophan is necessary for 5-HT synthesis. Tryptophan depletion of unmedicated patients in remission causes a relapse of depression symptoms. The same depletion leads to a depressed mood in healthy subjects who have a family history of depression, but not in healthy subjects without such a family history. These findings together indicate that merely having low levels of brain serotonin does not cause depression, except in vulnerable individuals. Hence sensitivity to reduced brain serotonin represents a *vulnerability factor* and may be considered a trait abnormality in depression.

Third, the identification of a relatively common gene variation, a polymorphism of the **serotonin reuptake transporter** (**SERT**) gene, has generated a good deal of interest. Referred to as the long (l) or short (s) allele, it is apparent that the short allele on one (s/l) or both (s/s) chromosomes is associated with significantly reduced level and function of the transporter. Although the short allele has been found by some researchers to be associated with depressive disorder, the relationship occurs only in association with increased stressful life events. The stress–gene interaction may help to explain why not all people experiencing stressful events ultimately develop depression. It also would explain why not all people with the short allele develop depression. Since stress elevates synaptic serotonin, more effective 5-HT reuptake associated with the l/l genotype may be more adept at modulating the extremes of synaptic function and the individual's sensitivity to stress. It has also been found that healthy women homozygous for the short allele (s/s) respond to tryptophan depletion with depressive symptoms, but those with two long alleles show no such response. Heterozygous (s/l) subjects showed depressive symptoms intermediate between the two other groups. Additionally, brain imaging indicates that healthy individuals with one or two short alleles

TABLE 19.2 Effects of Chronic Antidepressant Treatment on Serotonin Neurons

Antidepressant treatment	Effect on 5-HT$_2$ receptor binding[a]	Electrophysiological response to 5-HT
Tricyclics		
Amitriptyline	↓ or =	↑
Chlorimipramine	↓	↑
Desmethylimipramine	most ↓	↑
Imipramine	↓ or =	↑
Second-generation		
Fluoxetine	↓ or =	=
Iprindole	↓	↑
Mianserin	↓	↑
Trazodone	↓	↑
MAOIs		
Tranylcypromine	↓	↓
Clorgyline	↓	↓
ECT	= or ↑	↑

Source: Willner, 1995.

[a] ↑ enhancement; = no change; ↓ reduction.

show a much greater amygdala response to threatening visual stimuli than homozygous (l/l) subjects and score higher on the trait of negative emotionality. The greater neural response of the amygdala may be explained by the weakened connectivity between the amygdala and the dorsal anterior cingulate cortex, which normally serves to modulate amygdaloid activity. The reduced connectivity potentially increases the vulnerability to clinical depression (Pezawas et al., 2005). Whether the SERT polymorphism modulates stress-induced 5-HT function to determine vulnerability or resilience to stressors or is responsible for early developmental effects on maturation of the emotional circuitry in the brain (see Chapter 18 for a description of the neurodevelopmental effects of elevated 5-HT), effects of any genetic variation will contribute only a small amount to the vulnerability to depressive disorders.

Fourth, **receptor binding studies** in postmortem brain samples from unmedicated individuals with mood disorders have found *increased* density of postsynaptic 5-HT$_2$ receptors, which may be considered a compensatory response to low serotonergic activity. In accord with this finding, animal studies show that chronic antidepressant treatment leads to a fairly consistent decrease (down-regulation) in 5-HT$_2$ receptors. **Table 19.2** gives you some idea of the variety of antidepressant treatments that produce this

down-regulation. Only the clinically effective use of chronic electroconvulsive therapy (ECT) fails to reduce these receptors.

Fifth, **challenge studies** provide one additional way to evaluate receptor function indirectly in vivo by measuring the magnitude of a biological response to administered agonists or antagonists. For the serotonergic system, the biological response measured is most often hormonal, including changes in cortisol, prolactin, or growth hormone, although other physiological measures such as body temperature may also be used. The magnitude of the response is considered an indicator of the sensitivity or function of the receptor. Overall, the agonist-induced increase in prolactin suggests that 5-HT receptors are less sensitive in depressed patients. Sensitivity to 5-HT is restored by chronic administration of certain antidepressants.

Finally, we can use some of the newest **imaging techniques** to visualize changes in brain function and receptors in human subjects. PET imaging (**Figure 19.7**) provides the first look at blood flow changes in the brains of patients with depression compared with normal blood flow in control subjects. Increased activity in part of the medial orbitofrontal cortex and in the amygdala supports their role in the regulation of emotion.

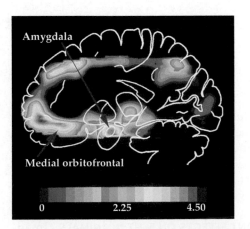

Figure 19.7 PET scan of blood flow in the brain of a patient with unipolar depression Increased metabolic activity occurs in the amygdala and the medial orbitofrontal cortex. Activation is shown in red and orange. (Courtesy of Wayne C. Drevets.)

(A) Acute effects of antidepressants

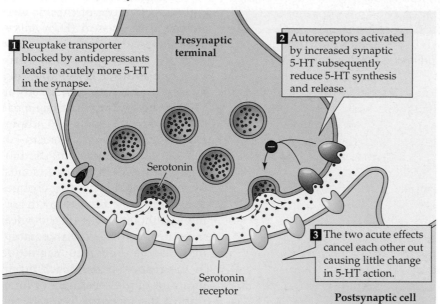

Figure 19.8 Effects of antidepressants on serotonergic cells (A) The initial effects of reuptake blockade include increased 5-HT in the synapse and activity at both postsynaptic receptors and autoreceptors. Autoreceptor activation reduces the rate of firing of the cell as well as the rate of synthesis and release of 5-HT and subsequently also reduces the rate of formation of 5-HIAA. (B) With repeated administration, the autoreceptors become less sensitive, and their inhibition of serotonergic neurons decreases, which leads to an increase in 5-HT function and 5-HIAA. The desensitization of the autoreceptors coincides with the onset of clinical effectiveness.

(B) Chronic effects of antidepressants

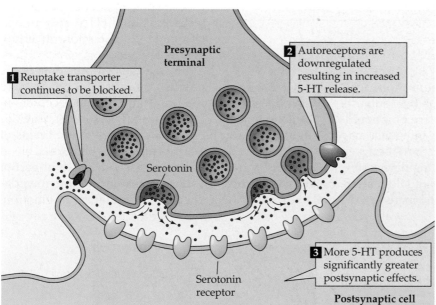

Increased metabolic activity in the amygdala is correlated with the severity of depression and returns to normal after antidepressant drug treatment. Increased activity of the orbitofrontal cortex may reflect the individual's effort to control unpleasant thoughts and emotions (Drevets, 2001).

ANTIDEPRESSANT EFFECTS ON 5-HT IN ANIMALS In addition to evaluating depressed patients, we can look at the long-term effects of antidepressant drugs on 5-HT by using animals. Animal studies have shown that most antidepressants increase 5-HT by blocking reuptake or inhibiting MAO. The increased synaptic 5-HT has postsynaptic action but also acts on 5-HT autoreceptors to slow the firing rate of cells and to reduce 5-HT synthesis as well as release. Therefore, the two effects tend to cancel one another out. Overall, lower neuronal activity reduces metabolism of 5-HT to 5-HIAA, indicating reduced turnover (**Figure 19.8**). However, chronic treatment results in tolerance and reduces the action of the autoreceptor (down-regulation) and in that way gradually increases the amount of 5-HT in the synapse. The reuptake transporter blockade is still effective, so at this point the two actions both produce an increase in 5-HT. Since the therapeutic effects of antidepressants take several weeks to develop, the delay in autoreceptor desensitization and subsequent enhanced 5-HT activity may be in part responsible for the delayed therapeutic onset (Blier et al., 1990). Ultimately the increased synaptic 5-HT also down-regulates postsynaptic $5-HT_{2A}$ receptors.

Further evidence for a role of 5-HT in antidepressant actions comes from studies showing that patients who are effectively treated with a serotonergic antidepressant (e.g., a selective serotonin reuptake inhibitor [SSRI]) show a temporary relapse when challenged with tryptophan depletion. Clearly 5-HT must be available for those drugs to work. In contrast, tryptophan depletion does not prevent effectiveness in individuals treated with NE reuptake inhibitors.

Animal studies also show that electrophysiological response to the application of 5-HT agonists is *enhanced* by long-term antidepressant treatment. De Montigny (1981) examined responses of single cells in rat forebrain to the application of 5-HT. Results showed that 2 days of antidepressant pretreatment produced no change in the sensitivity of the neurons to 5-HT, but that after 4 to 7 days of pretreatment, the response was moderately increased. Following 15 days of antidepressant administration, there was a large increase in sensitivity to 5-HT. The time course of this physiological change is related to the onset of clinical antidepressant effects. Although the argument for enhanced sensitivity of serotonergic neurons is among the most consistent (see Table 19.2), the fact that the enhanced physiological response occurs in brain areas where $5-HT_{2A}$ receptors are reduced is difficult to reconcile (Caldecott-Hazard et al., 1991). However, differences in pre- and postsynaptic receptors or the up-regulation of intracellular signaling may be responsible.

Norepinephrine activity is altered by antidepressants

Norepinephrine also continues to be a focus of research because it has a known role in neuroendocrine function, reward mechanisms, attention and arousal, and response to stress, each of which may contribute to the symptoms of the affective disorders. Regrettably, results of studies with depressed patients are difficult to interpret. Levels of the principal noradrenergic metabolite MHPG in the body fluids of depressed patients have been found to be higher, lower, and no different from those of controls. In general, MHPG is usually found to be elevated in patients undergoing treatment, suggesting an increase in turnover with antidepressant use. Although no consistent differences have been found in noradrenergic receptor binding in untreated depressed or bipolar patients, chronic antidepressant treatment

leads to down-regulation of both β-receptors and α_2-autoreceptors. Unfortunately, when both α_2- and β-receptors are down-regulated, they have opposite effects on adrenergic synapses. Since α_2-autoreceptors acutely reduce noradrenergic cell function by decreasing the rate of firing and reducing NE release, α_2-autoreceptor down-regulation increases both of these cell functions. With the use of α_2-challenge measures, the majority of experiments show that chronic, but not acute, antidepressant treatment produces a reduction in autoreceptor responsiveness that coincides with the increase in turnover described earlier.

One of the most consistent findings regarding catecholamine response to chronic antidepressant treatment is the down-regulation of β-receptors, which requires 7 to 21 days of treatment—a lag that parallels that seen in the onset of therapeutic response in depressed patients. Similar results occur with many of the antidepressant drugs tested, including TCAs, MAOIs, SSRIs, and second-generation antidepressants. ECT, lithium (used to treat bipolar disorder) under some conditions, and even REM sleep deprivation that has antidepressant action seem to reduce β-receptors. However, not all antidepressants reduce β-receptors, and yohimbine, an α_2-autoreceptor antagonist that enhances the antidepressant-induced down-regulation of β-receptors, does not enhance the antidepressant effects as would be expected.

Nevertheless, the importance of NE to the actions of antidepressant drugs can be demonstrated in patients treated with adrenergic antidepressants (i.e., NE reuptake inhibitors), who show relapse of symptoms if NE synthesis is prevented by depletion of the NE precursor tyrosine. Clearly NE is necessary for those drugs to be effective. A similar NE synthesis inhibition does not cause relapse in patients treated with the serotonergic reuptake inhibitors.

Norepinephrine and serotonin modulate one another

Because the most consistent chronic effects of antidepressants are down-regulation of β-receptors and $5-HT_2$ receptors and an enhanced physiological response to 5-HT, Sulser (1989) proposed a "serotonin–norepinephrine" hypothesis of depression. Both anatomical and functional interactions exist between the noradrenergic neurons originating in the locus coeruleus and the serotonergic neurons in the raphe nuclei (**Figure 19.9**), and each system is capable of modulating the other. Destroying 5-HT terminals with the neurotoxin 5,6-dihydroxytryptamine prevents the down-regulation of β-receptors that follows chronic antidepressant treatment. Others have shown that 5-HT agonists can indirectly stimulate the

(A) **Norepinephrine**

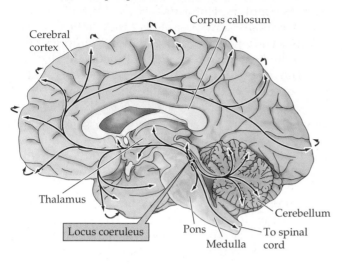

(B) **Serotonin**

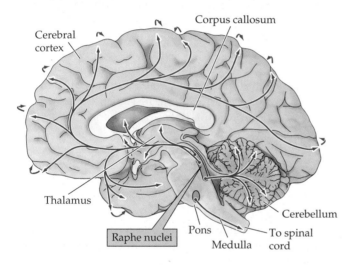

Figure 19.9 Two monoamine pathways in the human brain This schematic diagram shows noradrenergic pathways originating in the locus coeruleus (A) and serotonergic pathways originating in the raphe nuclei (B). The overlapping nature and interaction of the two neurotransmitter systems are very apparent.

hypothesis, focuses on the stress-related neuroendocrine abnormalities that are frequently found in depressed individuals (see the section on biological rhythms earlier in the chapter). McEwen (2008) provides an excellent discussion of how stress hormones and lifestyle behaviors interact to promote pathophysiology of the brain and rest of the body. In the depressed individual, the abnormal secretion of CRF from the hypothalamus is apparently responsible for the hypersecretion of ACTH from the pituitary and cortisol from the adrenal cortex. The hypothalamic CRF neurons are normally controlled by other areas of the CNS: the amygdala, which is central to emotional responses, normally stimulates the CRF circuit, and the hippocampus has inhibitory control (see Box 2.4). The hippocampus has receptors that when activated by high levels of glucocorticoids (such as cortisol) help to inhibit CRF release from the hypothalamus, subsequently returning glucocorticoid levels to normal. However, when stress is intense and/or prolonged, glucocorticoid levels remain high, and, as shown in animal studies, hippocampal neurons are damaged and no longer respond. The principal damage includes decreases in dendritic branches and loss of dendritic spines, both of which occur in the prefrontal cortex (PFC) as well as in the hippocampus. Additionally, the elevated cortisol reduces the formation of new hippocampal cells (neurogenesis). Cell loss in the hippocampus means reduced response to circulating cortisol and loss of inhibition of the HPA axis, inducing further glucocorticoid-mediated hippocampal cell loss.

One might speculate that the elevated cortisol levels found in depressed individuals contribute to cell death and to some of the cognitive symptoms of depression. Small reductions in hippocampal volume are found in magnetic resonance imaging scans of depressed patients. Further, antidepressant drugs and ECT reduce CRF levels in depressed patients. In animals, several types of antidepressant drugs also reverse the loss of dendrites in the hippocampus and other brain areas and increase neurogenesis in the hippocampus. Finally, intracerebroventricular (ICV) administration of CRF elicits stress-related behavioral and physiological responses in animals, including the expected enhancement of cortisol levels and sympathetic nervous system activity. CRF also elicits behaviors in animals that are closely correlated with symptoms of clinical depression in humans: arousal,

noradrenergic system, causing β-receptor down-regulation, and that increased noradrenergic function may also increase electrophysiological activity in the raphe nuclei. Sulser suggests that NE function involves multiple feedback loops that use a variety of neurotransmitters, including 5-HT, ACh, DA, GABA, and opioid peptides. For more information on the contribution of these neurotransmitters to the symptoms of depression, refer to several excellent reviews (Maletic and Raison, 2009; Ordway et al., 2002).

Neurobiological Models of Depression

In addition to the consideration of neurotransmitter function in depression, other hypotheses pose alternative neurobiological models that are now being tested. One such hypothesis, the **glucocorticoid** insomnia, decreased eating, reduced sexual activity, and anxiety.

The glucocorticoid hypothesis of affective disorders is the basis for the clinical tests of CRF receptor antagonists, which showed early promise as antidepressants. Preliminary clinical studies (Zobel et al., 2000) found significant improvement in both depression and anxiety scores using the CRF receptor antagonist R121919. Minimal side effects were found in this preliminary study; however, subsequent research showed that patients frequently showed elevations in liver enzymes, and further development of the drug was halted.

A second closely related neurobiological model looks at potential mechanisms underlying the hippocampal cell loss following stress-induced glucocorticoid elevation: deficits in neurotrophic factors such as **BDNF (brain-derived neurotrophic factor)**. Neurotrophic factors are important proteins that are needed during brain development but also regulate changes in synapses and cell survival in adult brains. The **neurotrophic hypothesis** suggests that low BDNF may be responsible for the loss of dendritic branches and spines in the hippocampus and PFC and for reduced neurogenesis in the hippocampus. Furthermore, antidepressants may protect vulnerable cells by preventing the decrease in BDNF. Evidence in support can be briefly summarized as follows: (1) chronic stress reduces BDNF in the hippocampus in rats; (2) chronic but not acute antidepressant treatment increases BDNF in both animals and humans; and (3) antidepressants prevent stress-induced reductions in BDNF and neuronal atrophy (**Figure 19.10**).

A *causal* connection between BDNF-enhanced neurogenesis and antidepressant effects is more difficult to determine. However, direct demonstration that enhanced neurogenesis is necessary for antidepressant action was initially provided by Santarelli and colleagues (2003) using mice and several animal models of depression. The 90% reduction in hippocampal cell proliferation following focused irradiation prevented both fluoxetine- and imipramine-induced neurogenesis as well as their antidepressant action in the chronic unpredictable stress model of depression. Although this finding is a critical component of the neurogenesis hypothesis, cautious interpretation is needed because irradiation does not act selectively to interfere with the production of neurons, and other damaging effects occur. Nevertheless, more recent studies supported the earlier work and indicated that antidepressants may impact neurons in several ways: by enhancing proliferation of new cells, by protecting them from apoptosis and atrophy, and by strengthening neuropil development by increasing the number and length of dendrites. Each of these changes is influenced by

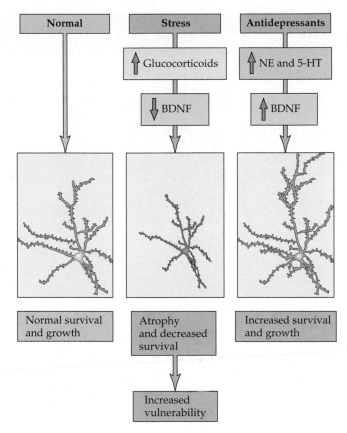

Figure 19.10 Effect of stress and antidepressant treatment on BDNF in hippocampal cells The box on the left shows a typical hippocampal cell in the CA3 area. Chronic stress (center) elevates glucocorticoids and decreases BDNF, which may be responsible for the loss of dendritic trees and may make the cells more vulnerable to a variety of detrimental factors. Chronic antidepressant treatment (right) not only alters monoamine transmission but also increases BDNF. BDNF may protect the cells from further damage and may help repair those already damaged. (After Duman et al., 1999.)

neurotrophins; however, how the cellular changes contribute to function at the circuit level and how that translates into changes in affect in depressed individuals remain unclear (Balu and Lucki, 2009). If neuroprotective effects are central to antidepressant action, an additional treatment approach might be to use modulation of epigenetic events (**Box 19.3**). As you learned earlier, environmental events including the stress of early abuse or neglect can cause long-lasting epigenetic changes that alter brain development and increase vulnerability to a variety of disorders. Hence early intervention to reverse the epigenetic effects of stress may enhance resilience.

Since the production of BDNF is dependent on the cyclic adenosine monophosphate (cAMP) second-messenger system, it is significant that *chronic* antidepressant drug treatment up-regulates several components

BOX 19.3   The Cutting Edge

Epigenetic Modifications in Psychopathology and Treatment

You learned in Chapter 18 that genes and environment interact to determine the tendency to express anxiety. Environmental stress, including parental abuse or neglect (see Web Box 18.2), causes long-lasting epigenetic changes to the genes of several components of the stress circuit, leading to enhanced CRF expression in the amygdala and hypothalamus and decreased glucocorticoid receptors in the hippocampus. These and other changes contribute to stress circuit programming during development, making it more sensitive, and increasing the vulnerability to both anxiety disorders and depression in the adult. Given the close relationship between stress and depression, this outcome is not surprising.

Other genes of significance are also modified by stress-induced chromatin remodeling. Chromatin remodeling or rearrangement occurs when the small proteins known as histones, which are complexed with DNA, are altered by any one of several chemical changes brought about by enzymes. These chemical changes including methylation, acetylation, phosphorylation, and others less well studied occur on the amino acid tails of the histone molecules. These changes either make the chromatin more tightly packed, which limits gene expression by physically limiting the access of transcription factors, or loosen the chromatin structure, enhancing transcription. A delicate balance of epigenetic factors maintains normal cell function. Dysregulation in the form of either too much expression of a gene or too little may be the basis of pathological conditions. Chronic social defeat stress (see the earlier section on animal models) causes long-lasting

(A)

(B)

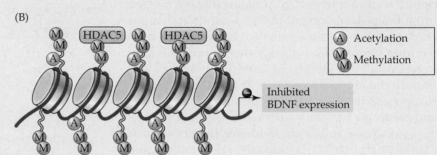

(C)

Chromatin remodeling (A) Under nonstress conditions, the chromatin of the BDNF gene has low levels of acetylation and virtually no methylation, providing a basal BDNF expression. (B) The histone methylation following prolonged episodes of defeat stress induces a tighter envelope of chromatin proteins and blocks BDNF gene expression. (C) Chronic antidepressants increase acetylation without altering the chronic stress-induced methylation, which produces a "relaxation" of the repressed chromatin, encouraging transcription of the BDNF gene, that which may be necessary for the antidepressant effects. (After Tsankova et al., 2007.)

reductions in BDNF expression by epigenetically increasing histone methylation more than four-fold. The methylation of histone induces a more "closed" chromatin state that reduces transcription of the gene for BDNF (see figure). Chronic, but not acute, antidepressant treatment with imipramine reverses the stress-induced depression-like symptoms, but somewhat surprisingly, does not reverse the

BOX 19.3 *(continued)*

stress-induced methylation of histone. Instead, it apparently reverses the suppression of BDNF expression by increasing the level of histone acetylation subsequent to the activation of histone acetylase. The acetylation of histone induces a more "open" chromatin state, resulting in an imipramine-induced increase in BDNF as reported earlier. Nemeroff and colleagues (as reported in Tsankova et al., 2007) further evaluated the underlying mechanism and found that in socially defeated mice, not only does imipramine cause hyperacetylation, but it additionally down-regulates histone deacetylase (HDAC), the enzyme that normally removes the acetyl groups. The

lack of these effects in nonstressed mice is particularly interesting because antidepressants rarely have any effect in healthy, nondepressed individuals. Furthermore, when the researchers caused overexpression of HDAC in the dentate gyrus of the hippocampus with genetic manipulation, they found total blockade of the antidepressant effects of imipramine.

The importance of down-regulation of HDAC to antidepressant action has been investigated further as a potential approach to treating mood disorders (see Machado-Vieira et al., 2010). If HDAC inhibitors could reverse dysfunctional epigenetic changes, neurotrophic proteins could be elevated and

could enhance the neural connectivity that is necessary for behavioral adaptation. Several preclinical studies have now demonstrated antidepressant effects in rodents after intracerebral injection of several different HDAC inhibitors. Further, the HDAC inhibitors have been shown to reverse oxidative stress–induced neuronal injury in vitro. Oxidative stress is characteristic of individuals with bipolar disorder, who often find lithium and valproate, drugs that reduce oxidative stress, to be therapeutic. Clearly this early research has promise, and the role of epigenetic acetylation in both pathophysiology of mood disorders and therapeutics deserves further study.

---

of the system in the hippocampus and frontal cortex. This up-regulation occurs despite the down-regulation of the β-adrenergic receptors (βARs) and 5-HT receptors that are coupled to the cAMP cascade (**Figure 19.11**). Up-regulation occurs in several stages of the cascade, including enhanced coupling between stimulatory G_s protein and adenylyl cyclase, an increase in activated cAMP-dependent protein kinase A (PKA), and an increase in phosphorylation of cAMP response element binding protein (CREB), which is a transcription factor that induces protein synthesis of BDNF and other proteins.

Although at present there is no way to directly inject BDNF into humans as a test for antidepressant activity, intracerebral injection of BDNF or CREB into the hippocampus in rodents produced antidepressant effects in the forced swim and learned helplessness tests (Shirayama et al., 2002). Brain levels of CREB are low in depressed patients and are increased by most antidepressant drugs after several weeks. It is tempting

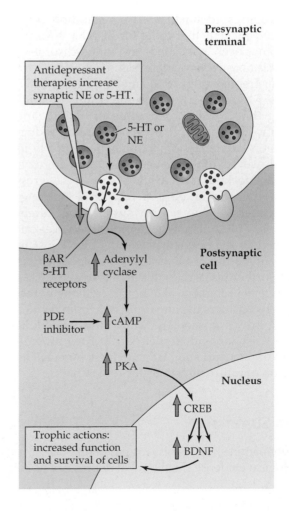

Figure 19.11 Up-regulation of second-messenger pathway by chronic antidepressant treatment The increase in NE and 5-HT caused by acute antidepressant treatment produces down-regulation of their receptors when treatment is chronic. In response to the reduction in receptors, the cAMP pathway is up-regulated, producing increases in adenylyl cyclase activity, cAMP, PKA, and the transcription factor within the nucleus, CREB. CREB increases the synthesis of several proteins, including BDNF. (After Duman et al., 1997.)

to try to develop therapeutic methods that might rapidly enhance CREB and the neurotrophic factors. One might consider that enhancing any portion of the cAMP cascade could ultimately enhance BDNF production and relieve depression. One approach involves inhibiting **phosphodiesterase** (**PDE**), the enzyme that normally degrades cAMP to 5'-AMP. By inhibiting phosphodiesterase, the cAMP cascade would be up-regulated in a prolonged fashion. One phosphodiesterase inhibitor, rolipram, reduced symptoms in a small trial of depressed patients, but side effects prohibit its regular use. More selective inhibitors may prove effective with reduced side effects. Although the possibilities are exciting, application to human therapeutics is clearly a long way off.

Although there is fairly convincing evidence that increased neurogenesis is needed for antidepressant effects, a causal role for neurogenesis in the etiology of depression remains more difficult to demonstrate. The reduction in hippocampal volume and the morphological changes found in depressed patients that are reversed by antidepressant treatment could be related to the reduced levels of BDNF found in the hippocampus and the PFC postmortem, although these findings are not consistent and are best documented in depressed suicides. Also a common polymorphism of the gene that codes for BDNF (*val66met*) has sometimes been associated with mood disorders, although it is not specific to depression but also occurs with higher frequency in Alzheimer's disease, OCD, and others. More convincing are the results of studies finding that *temporary* reduction of BDNF gene expression in *specific* regions of the forebrain produces depression-like behaviors in mice, particularly in females. However, others have found that heterozygous BDNF knockout mice display increased aggressiveness, hyperphagia, deficits in spatial learning, and subtle alterations in sensory systems, but rarely depressive-like behaviors. Whether the differences can be explained by the permanence of the BDNF loss in the knockout studies or the lack of brain specificity is not clear. Further research in this area is ongoing.

These two neurobiological hypotheses, along with a third, which considers the impairment of brain reward pathways, are discussed in detail in an excellent review by Krishnan and Nestler (2010). They provide both an overview and supporting evidence as well as a discussion of future directions for research.

Section Summary

- The monoamine hypothesis was based on pharmacological evidence showing that depression is associated with low levels of monoamines, whereas mania coincides with excess monoamine activity.

- Modifications of the hypothesis were needed to explain the discrepancy in time between the rapid increase in monoamines by antidepressant drugs and the slow onset of clinical effects over several weeks.

- A role for 5-HT in depression is suggested by the following: (1) lower 5-HIAA occurs in depressed individuals; (2) depletion of tryptophan causes depressed mood in patients in remission; (3) a polymorphism of the SERT gene is associated with depression; (4) increased postsynaptic 5-HT$_2$ receptors are found in patients postmortem; and (5) challenge studies suggest less prolactin response to 5-HT agonists.

- Chronic antidepressant treatment causes the down-regulation of 5-HT autoreceptors, which increases synaptic 5-HT and subsequent down-regulation of 5-HT$_{2A}$ receptors. Nevertheless, the electrophysiological response to 5-HT is enhanced.

- In depressed patients, chronic antidepressants increase NE turnover, which leads to down-regulation of β-adrenergic receptors and α$_2$-autoreceptors.

- Inhibiting the synthesis of 5-HT causes relapse in patients treated with serotonin reuptake inhibitors, but not in those treated with adrenergic antidepressants. Likewise, inhibiting NE synthesis produces relapse in patients treated with NE reuptake inhibitors, but not in those treated with serotonergic agents.

- Prolonged hypersecretion of CRF, ACTH, and glucocorticoids damages dendritic branching and spines in the hippocampus and PFC. It also reduces neurogenesis in the hippocampus, which further diminishes the negative feedback on HPA axis function. Chronic antidepressants reverse these effects.

- ICV CRF elicits stress-related behavior and hormone response and signs of depression in rodents. A clinical trial of a CRF antagonist improved depression and anxiety scores in patients.

- The neurotrophic hypothesis suggests that stress hormones that reduce BDNF may cause neuronal damage, and antidepressants may prevent it by elevating BDNF.

- Intrahippocampal BDNF has antidepressant action.

- Preventing hippocampal cell proliferation prevents antidepressant-induced neurogenesis and behavioral effects.

- Chronic antidepressants up-regulate the cAMP cascade, leading to increased phosphorylated CREB and subsequent expression of BDNF. Enhancing the cAMP cascade by inhibiting phosphodiesterase produced antidepressant effects in some patients.

- Evidence for BDNF in the etiology of depression includes the following: (1) BDNF is low in the hippocampus and the PFC of depressed patients postmortem; (2) a BDNF gene polymorphism may be associated with mood disorders; (3) modifying BDNF gene expression in mice leads to depressive behaviors.

Therapies for Affective Disorders

Three major classes of antidepressants have proved effective in reducing symptoms of mood disorders (**Table 19.3**). They are the monoamine oxidase inhibitors, the tricyclic antidepressants, and the second-generation antidepressants, which include the selective serotonin reuptake blockers. In addition, there are several atypical antidepressants as well as several nondrug therapies including sleep deprivation (see Web Box 19.2), electroconvulsive therapy, transcranial magnetic stimulation, vagal nerve stimulation, and deep brain stimulation. These brain stimulation treatments are discussed in **Web Box 19.3**. Drugs for treating the manic episodes of bipolar disorder will be considered separately.

The availability of a variety of antidepressant drugs means that many clinically depressed individuals can find significant relief. However, double-blind, placebo-controlled trials of antidepressants show that no one specific drug or drug type is more effective than any other, and there is no way to predict which patient will respond to a particular drug. Each drug is effective in reducing, but not necessarily eliminating, symptoms for about two thirds of cases of clinical depression. The different pharmacological characteristics of the agents mean that they will reduce different symptoms and will produce distinct but characteristic side effects. Each patient must usually undergo trials to find an antidepressant that optimally balances effectiveness and side effects. Frequently, outcomes are enhanced by the addition of a second drug to the treatment regimen. Every one of the treatment methods currently available requires chronic administration, suggesting that although we understand how each works acutely at the synapse, the clinical effect must depend on compensatory changes in function that require time to develop. Although significant changes in symptoms can occur during the first 1 to 3 weeks of drug treatment, maximum effectiveness may not be

TABLE 19.3	Major Classes of Antidepressants and Their Most Notable Side Effects	
Class	**Antidepressants**	**Side effects**
Monoamine oxidase inhibitors	Phenelzine (Nardil)	Insomnia, weight gain, hypertension, drug interactions, tyramine effect
	Tranylcypromine (Parnate)	
	Isocarboxazid (Marplan)	
Classic tricyclics	Imipramine (Tofranil)	Sedation, anticholinergic effects, cardiovascular toxicity
	Amitriptyline (Elavil)	
	Desipramine (Norpramine)	
Second-generation:		
Selective serotonin reuptake inhibitors	Fluoxetine (Prozac)	Insomnia, gastrointestinal disturbances, sexual dysfunction, serotonin syndrome
	Sertraline (Zoloft)	
	Paroxetine (Paxil)	
Atypical antidepressants	Maprotiline (Ludiomil)	Varies with individual mechanism of action
	Bupropion (Wellbutrin)	
	Mirtazapine (Remeron)	
Electroconvulsive shock and transcranial magnetic stimulation		Memory impairment, confusion, amnesia

achieved until after 4 to 6 weeks of therapy. This time lag is especially worrisome in patients who are severely depressed and suicidal. Some symptoms, including irregularities in sleep and appetite, are the first signs that show improvement, followed over the next few weeks by mood enhancement. Several long-term studies from the National Institute of Mental Health suggest a period of maintenance drug treatment of at least 6 to 8 months after symptoms are reduced. Because maintenance therapy significantly reduces the probability of relapse, treatment is extended indefinitely for some individuals.

Although we are treating antidepressant drugs and drugs used for anxiety (see Chapter 18) as separate entities, we would like to make it clear that the distinction is often more semantic than real. As we noted earlier, stress and anxiety are components of affective disorders, and the trend in drug treatment further blurs the distinction. Antidepressant drugs reduce the anxiety that accompanies depression, and they are increasingly being used to treat anxiety disorders unrelated to depression.

Monoamine oxidase inhibitors are the oldest antidepressant drugs

The first true antidepressant action was discovered quite by accident as the result of a lucky clinical observation. The drug iproniazid was used in the early 1950s to treat tuberculosis but had significant mood-elevating effects unrelated to its effects on the disease. Following that observation, iproniazid was found to inhibit monoamine oxidase (MAO). Although met with enthusiasm following their early introduction as antidepressants, the **MAO inhibitors** (**MAOIs**) fell into disfavor because of their reputation for having severe and dangerous side effects (see later). However, over the years it has become apparent that, with appropriate dietary restrictions, MAOIs can be used safely and often work well for patients who are treatment-resistant (those who do not respond to other drugs) and who reject the idea of electroconvulsive therapy. In addition to their use in affective disorders, MAOIs are used in the treatment of several anxiety states and have positive effects on the eating behavior and mood of patients with bulimia and anorexia nervosa. The currently available MAOIs include phenelzine (Nardil), tranylcypromine (Parnate), and isocarboxazid (Marplan).

MECHANISM OF ACTION   You will recall from Chapter 5 that MAO is an enzyme found inside the cells of many tissues, including neurons. The normal function of the enzyme is to metabolize the monoamine neurotransmitters in the presynaptic terminals that are not contained in protective synaptic vesicles. The inhibition of MAO increases the amount of neurotransmitter available for release. A single dose of an MAOI increases NE, DA, and 5-HT and thus increases the action of the transmitters at their receptors. It was initially assumed that enhanced neurotransmitter function was responsible for the antidepressant action; however, those biochemical changes occur within hours, but the antidepressant effects require weeks of chronic treatment. It is now apparent that neuron adaptation involving change in receptor density or second-messenger function must play an important part in these drug effects (**Figure 19.12**).

SIDE EFFECTS   The more common side effects of MAOIs include changes in blood pressure, sleep disturbances including insomnia, and overeating, especially of carbohydrates, which may lead to excessive weight gain. In addition to these side effects, three other types of side effects are significantly more dangerous. First, because inhibition of MAO elevates NE levels in peripheral nerves of the sympathetic branch of the autonomic nervous system as well as in the CNS, any prescription or over-the-counter drug that enhances NE function will have a much greater effect than normal. For example, nasal sprays, cold medications, antiasthma drugs, amphetamine, and cocaine will all have greater-than-expected effects and will produce elevated blood pressure, sweating, and increased body temperature. Second, some serious side effects are due to the inhibition of MAO in the liver as well as in the brain. The MAO in the liver is responsible for deaminating tyramine, which is a naturally occurring amine formed as a by-product of fermentation in many foods, including cheeses, certain meats, pickled products, and other foods. These foods must be avoided by individuals using MAOIs (**Table 19.4**). Elevated tyramine levels release the higher-than-normal stores of NE at nerve endings, causing a dramatic increase in blood pressure. Blood pressure may reach critical levels, and this is accompanied by headache, sweating, nausea, vomiting, and sometimes stroke. Third, MAOIs also inhibit other liver enzymes such as the cytochrome P450 enzymes (see Chapter 1), which normally degrade such drugs as barbiturates, alcohol, opioids, aspirin, and many others. The effects of these drugs are prolonged and intensified in the presence of MAOIs.

Tricyclic antidepressants block the reuptake of norepinephrine and serotonin

This class of antidepressant is named for its characteristic three-ring structure (**Figure 19.13**), which is closely related to that of the antipsychotic drugs in the phenothiazine class (see Chapter 20). Although the prototypical **tricyclic antidepressant** (**TCA**) imipramine (Tofranil) failed its original test for antipsychotic effects, it

(A)

MAO normally regulates the amount of neurotransmitter in the presynaptic terminal.

(B)

Inhibiting MAO increases the amount of neurotransmitter available for release.

(C)

After two weeks or more of MAO inhibition, neurotransmitter levels are still high but postsynaptic changes occur.

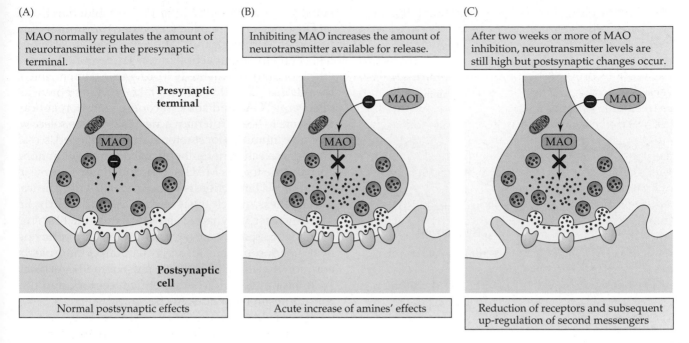

| Normal postsynaptic effects | Acute increase of amines' effects | Reduction of receptors and subsequent up-regulation of second messengers |

Figure 19.12 Acute and long-term effects of MAOIs on synaptic function (A) Presynaptic MAO degrades neurotransmitter molecules that are not in vesicles, to keep amines at "normal" levels. (B) MAOIs inhibit the enzyme, causing an elevation in available neurotransmitter for release, resulting in increased action at receptors. (C) After 10 days to 2 weeks of antidepressant treatment, the amount of neurotransmitter in the synapse is still elevated over control conditions, but neural adaptation has occurred: down-regulation of amine receptors and up-regulation of the cyclic adenosine monophosphate (cAMP) second-messenger system. Other antidepressant drugs produce similar adaptive changes in neurons.

did appear to have mood-elevating actions. Many other tricyclics were subsequently developed.

MECHANISM OF ACTION   The drugs in this class act by binding to the presynaptic transporter proteins and inhibiting reuptake of neurotransmitters into the presynaptic terminal. Inhibition of reuptake prolongs the duration of transmitter action at the synapse, ultimately producing changes in both pre- and postsynaptic receptors. Although many of the drugs in this class are

TABLE 19.4   Dietary Restrictions for Patients Taking MAOIs

Food group	Examples
Dairy	Unpasteurized milk and yogurt; aged cheese; other cheeses including blue, Boursault, brick, Brie, Camembert, cheddar, Colby, Emmenthaler, Gouda, Gruyere, mozzarella, Parmesan, provolone, Romano, Roquefort, and Stilton
Meat and meat alternatives	Aged game; liver; canned meats; yeast extracts; salami; dry sausage; salted, dried, smoked, or pickled fish such as herring, cod, and caviar; peanuts
Breads, cereals, and grains	Homemade yeast breads with substantial quantities of yeast; bread or crackers containing cheese
Vegetables and fruits	Italian broad beans, sauerkraut, bananas, red plums, avocados, raspberries
Miscellaneous	Alcoholic beverages including red and white table wines, ale, beer, champagne, sherry, and vermouth; yeast concentrates, soup cubes, commercial gravies, or meat extracts; soups containing items that must be avoided; soy sauce; soy bean curd (hoison)

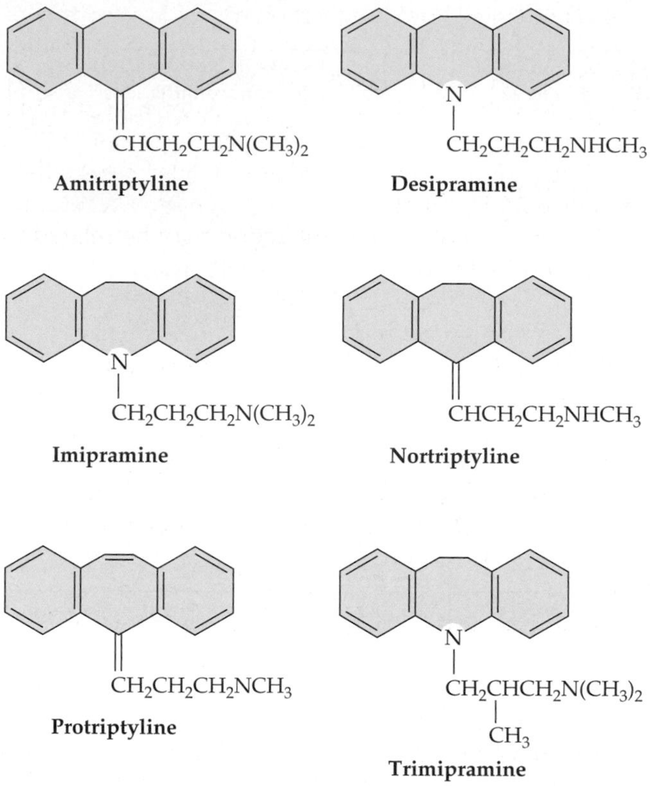

Figure 19.13 Tricyclic antidepressants are named for their characteristic three-ring structure.

equally effective in inhibiting the reuptake of NE and 5-HT, some are more effective on one transmitter than the other. Although this difference does not change their antidepressant action, it does determine the side effects of the drugs. **Table 19.5** provides a comparison of the relative NE and 5-HT reuptake-blocking potencies of several TCAs and some second-generation antidepressants as well. You may notice that just as selective reuptake inhibitors for serotonin were developed, so too are there selective norepinephrine reuptake inhibitors. As was true for the MAOIs, the immediate increase in NE and 5-HT function is not correlated with clinical effectiveness, which takes several weeks. Clearly, an acute increase in synaptic activity is only the first step in antidepressant action; neuronal adaptation, occurring over a period of time, also plays an important role. In addition to reuptake blockade, most of the TCAs block ACh, histamine, and α-adrenergic receptors, and this contributes to their side effects.

SIDE EFFECTS   Although we assume that TCA action is due to enhancement of monoamine activity followed by compensatory changes in the transmitter systems, the receptor-blocking activity contributes to side effects. Histamine receptor blockade is responsible for the sedation and fatigue that are frequent side effects that limit the drugs' usefulness in individuals who must remain alert. On the other hand, for patients who experience

TABLE 19.5   Relative Specificity of Antidepressant Drugs that Block Monoamine Reuptake

Drug name	Extent of reuptake inhibition[a]	
	Norepinephrine	Serotonin
Tricyclic Compounds		
Desipramine (Norpramin)	+++	+
Protriptyline (Vivactil)	+++	+
Amitriptyline (Elavil)	++	++
Imipramine (Tofranil)	++	++
Clomipramine (Anafranil)	++	++++
Selective serotonin reuptake inhibitors		
Fluoxetine (Prozac)	0	++++
Sertraline (Zoloft)	0	++++
Paroxetine (Paxil)	+	++++
Selective norepinephrine reuptake inhibitors		
Reboxetine (Edronax)	++++	0
Atomoxetine (Strattera)	++++	0

[a]0, no effect; +, mild effect; ++, moderate effect; +++, strong effect; ++++, maximal effect.

agitation, the sedative effects may be welcome. Anticholinergic side effects are troublesome for others and include dry mouth, constipation, urinary retention, dizziness, confusion, impaired memory, and blurred vision. The α_1 blockade in combination with the NE reuptake-blocking effects leads to several potentially dangerous cardiovascular side effects, including orthostatic hypotension, tachycardia, and arrhythmias. This particular set of side effects makes it especially difficult to treat depression in elderly patients with known cardiac disorders.

In addition, toxicity following overdose causes cardiovascular depression, delirium, convulsions, respiratory depression, and coma. Heart arrhythmias may produce cardiac arrest and fatalities. Since the fatalities associated with TCA treatment occur at approximately 10 times the normal dose, these drugs have a relatively low therapeutic index (TD_{50}/ED_{50}), particularly when used by patients demonstrating suicidal tendencies.

Second-generation antidepressants have different side effects

In an attempt to offer drugs with fewer side effects and more rapid onset of action, a host of new antidepressants have been developed. In general, they are designed to be more selective in their action with the hope of eliminating the anticholinergic and cardiovascular effects produced by the older drugs while still elevating levels of NE and/or 5-HT to provide antidepressant action. None are more effective, however, nor do they have a more rapid onset. The most significant difference is seen in the nature of their side effects, which are related to their neurochemical mechanisms of action. Many are considered safer than the older drugs if taken as an overdose.

The **selective serotonin reuptake inhibitors** (**SSRIs**) deserve special mention because they are often the first choice among antidepressants because of their greater relative safety. In addition to major depression, these drugs are also used to treat several distinct disorders: panic and anxiety disorders, obsessive–compulsive disorder, obesity, and alcoholism.

MECHANISM OF ACTION Drugs in this class, which include fluoxetine (Prozac), sertraline (Zoloft), and paroxetine (Paxil), are more selective than TCAs in enhancing serotonin function because they block the presynaptic reuptake transporter for 5-HT to a greater extent than the noradrenergic transporter. As is true for all of the antidepressants discussed, we assume that the antidepressant action requires compensatory changes in neurons that occur over several weeks as shown in Figure 19.11.

SIDE EFFECTS The side effects of the SSRIs are different from those of the TCAs because the drugs do not alter NE, histamine, or ACh. Hence, the frequent TCA-induced side effects of sedation, cardiovascular toxicity, and anticholinergic effects are absent. Nevertheless, SSRIs produce a different pattern of side effects because they enhance 5-HT function at all serotonergic receptors. Although the antidepressant action may be related to increased 5-HT function at some serotonergic receptors, increased 5-HT activity at other receptors causes side effects: anxiety, restlessness, movement disorders, muscle rigidity, nausea, headache, insomnia, and sexual dysfunction. The sexual dysfunction, which occurs in 40% to 70% of patients, is a frequent reason for terminating therapy, particularly among young male patients.

Although the SSRIs are generally safer than the older drugs, they have potentially life-threatening effects when combined with other serotonergic agonists or with drugs that interfere with the normal metabolism of the SSRIs. These effects, referred to as the **serotonin syndrome**, are characterized by severe agitation, disorientation and confusion, ataxia, muscle spasms, and exaggerated autonomic nervous system functions including fever, shivering, chills, diarrhea, elevated blood pressure, and increased heart rate (Lane and Baldwin, 1997).

One other distinctive characteristic of the SSRIs compared with the older antidepressants is their ability to cause physical dependence. As many as 60% of patients suffer withdrawal effects following drug termination, particularly with the short-acting SSRIs, unless the dose is tapered off gradually (Zajecka et al., 1997). These withdrawal symptoms, which can last for several weeks, include dizziness and ataxia, nausea, vomiting and diarrhea, fatigue, chills, sensory disturbances, insomnia, vivid dreams and increased anxiety, agitation, and irritability. Although the SSRIs avoid many of the dangerous side effects of the older drugs, caution in their use is still warranted.

Although the SSRIs are second-generation antidepressants, some of the newer antidepressants are once again **dual NE/5-HT modulators** because the most current thinking suggests that enhancing both NE and 5-HT function is more beneficial than acting on a single monoamine. The reuptake blocker duloxetine (Cymbalta) and mirtazapine (Remeron) are two such drugs. Mirtazapine is an antidepressant with a unique mechanism of action. It blocks α_2-autoreceptors, which increases synaptic NE and α_2-heteroreceptors on serotonergic cells, which increases 5-HT release. Additionally, to reduce side effects, the drug specifically blocks selected 5-HT receptors. Early trials showed clear clinical benefit in a broad range of patients when compared with placebo and equal effectiveness compared with the TCA amitriptyline, but with somewhat fewer (65%) adverse side effects compared with placebo (70%) or amitriptyline (87%).

Third-generation antidepressants have distinctive mechanisms of action

Third-generation antidepressants are currently in the development and testing stages. The goals for the newest drugs will be to continue to minimize side effects and toxicity as well as speed up the onset of effectiveness. Despite our best attempts, it is evident that neuropharmacology is still unsure about the cellular changes that produce effective antidepressant action, but it is clear that a series of molecular changes underlie the therapies. The two newest approaches—CRF receptor antagonism and enhancement of the cAMP intracellular second-messenger system and subsequent synaptic plasticity—were discussed earlier in the chapter, in the section on neurobiological models of depression. In addition to these approaches, regulation of chronobiology by agomelatine as discussed in Box 19.2 holds great promise. It has passed both Phase II and Phase III clinical trials, and is already approved for use in Europe. Several others that also attack depression symptoms from a novel direction include intravenous ketamine and galanin agonists.

INTRAVENOUS KETAMINE   Among the more troublesome problems in depression therapy is finding a way to reduce symptoms in the large number of treatment-resistant patients (i.e., those who do not respond to available medications or cannot tolerate them). One new approach has been the use of the N-methyl-D-aspartate (NMDA) receptor antagonist ketamine (reviewed by Murrough, 2012). Ketamine is a dissociative anesthetic that when administered intravenously at subanesthetic doses has been shown in multiple small clinical trials to produce a rapid (generally within hours) reduction in depression symptoms for 65% to 70% of treatment-resistant patients and in some cases has led to remission of all symptoms. The duration of the antidepressant effect varied among individuals and ranged from 1 to 3 weeks, although one individual remained symptom free for 3 months after a single infusion. The rapid onset and prolonged effect, lasting far longer than the drug's short half-life, have prompted investigation into other NMDA antagonists that do not cause the transient side effects of psychosis-like symptoms that last up to 2 hours and the dissociative effects produced by ketamine. An additional problem is that although ketamine does not produce physical dependence, it is an abused substance, which further limits its usefulness in treatment programs. Since other NMDA receptor antagonists have been shown to have antidepressant effects in a wide variety of animal models, the pressure to translate these findings to clinical use is

significant. Other means of modifying glutamate function such as blocking the NMDA receptor ion channel, inhibiting glutamate release, or enhancing glutamate reuptake transporter function are generating a good deal of research.

Additionally, glutamate α-amino-3-hydroxy-5-methyl-4-isoxazole-propionic acid (AMPA) receptor *agonists* are potentially useful because while ketamine reduces NMDA receptor function, it potentiates glutamate action at the AMPA receptor. This action may explain the increased neural activity in the anterior cingulate cortex that predicts antidepressant response to ketamine as well as other antidepressant drugs. Furthermore, the antidepressant effect of ketamine in the forced swim test was prevented by pretreatment with an AMPA antagonist, which demonstrates the importance of glutamate action at the AMPA receptor for this behavioral effect. Perhaps even more intriguing are the ketamine-induced changes in synaptic plasticity, including increased synaptic proteins and enhanced number and function of dendritic spines in the prefrontal cortex. These synaptic modifications are correlated with the antidepressant effects in several rodent models and can be prevented by AMPA antagonists. It is especially interesting that the rapid (overnight) antidepressant effect of sleep deprivation (see Web Box 19.2) also enhances AMPA-induced synaptic plasticity. How these antidepressants achieve such rapid synaptic changes is not clear, although ketamine has been shown to activate several important intracellular regulators of protein translation. As is true for other antidepressants, it apparently increases BDNF synthesis but in a much more rapid fashion than the typical drugs.

Another effective antidepressant that modulates glutamate function is **tianeptine**, a TCA in structure but with different and complex pharmacological actions (**Figure 19.14**). Its unique neurobiological properties may explain its effectiveness in reducing symptoms of depression and comorbid anxiety with only mild side effects and little sedation or cognitive impairment. The drug increases phosphorylation of glutamate receptor subtypes in selective brain areas. Given the current interest in ketamine's potentiation of AMPA receptor function, it is interesting to note that the phosphorylation of $GluR_1$ receptors by tianeptine potentiates AMPA receptor function. Its ability to enhance phosphorylation by intracellular kinases such as calcium-calmodulin–dependent protein kinase may further contribute to the synaptic plasticity characteristic of antidepressant drugs. Additionally, in animal studies, tianeptine prevents stress-induced changes in glutamate transmission (perhaps by adjusting the NMDA/AMPA balance) in hippocampus and amygdala, which contributes to its neuroprotective action.

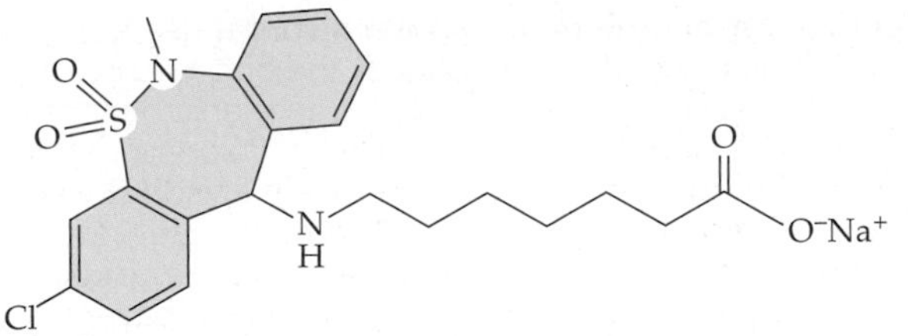

Figure 19.14 Chemical structure of tianeptine Note the three-ring structure (highlighted in blue). While tianeptine is similar in structure to the tricyclic antidepressants, it has very different pharmacological properties.

McEwen and colleagues (2010) provide a thorough description of the neurobiological effects of tianeptine.

GALANIN   Galanin is a 30 amino acid neuropeptide implicated in mood disorders as well as in regulating feeding, cognitive performance, sleep, sexual activity, and stress responses. It is widely distributed in the brain and is co-localized with 5-HT in the nucleus of the raphe and with NE in the locus coeruleus. It acts as an inhibitory modulator of the two monoamines by hyperpolarizing the cells and reducing neurotransmitter release at their projection areas in the limbic system and cerebral cortex. Contradictory evidence regarding whether intracerebral injections of galanin produce depressive or antidepressant effects may be explained by the existence of three distinct galanin G protein–coupled receptors that are differentially distributed in the brain and are coupled to distinct intracellular signaling mechanisms. Agonists at $GalR_1$ and $GalR_3$ cause depression-like behaviors in rodents, while agonists of $GalR_2$ have antidepressant effects in the same rodent models (Kuteeva et al., 2008). Hence galanin may have a role in the pathophysiology of depression and represents a potential target for novel antidepressant medications. Of particular interest is the finding that 14 days of treatment with the SSRI fluoxetine up-regulated galanin mRNA expression by 100% and $GalR_2$ (but not $GalR_1$) by 50% in the dorsal raphe (Lu et al., 2005). Electroconvulsive shock also increased galanin mRNA in the nucleus of the raphe, but sleep deprivation increased it in the locus coeruleus. These researchers also found that intraventricular injection of a nonselective galanin antagonist could prevent the antidepressant effects of fluoxetine in the forced swim test, indicating that galanin may mediate the drug's clinical effectiveness. Furthermore, galnon, a nonspecific, nonpeptide galanin receptor agonist, produced a dose-dependent reduction in immobilization in the forced swim test. These results suggest that $GalR_2$ agonists might augment standard antidepressant treatment. Additionally, on the basis of preclinical studies, antagonists at $GalR_1$ or $GalR_3$ would be expected to have clinically significant antidepressant effects, and several $GalR_3$

antagonists have recently been developed for testing. One final fascinating aspect is that evidence suggests that galanin has neuroprotective effects and increases hippocampal neurogenesis, providing further support for the neurotrophic hypothesis described earlier.

Drugs for treating bipolar disorder stabilize the highs and the lows

For the majority of patients with bipolar disorder, **lithium carbonate** (Carbolith, Eskalith) is the most effective medication and is the usual drug of choice. Although lithium has no effect on mood or behavior in healthy individuals, J. Cade in 1949 discovered that it had powerful effects on patients with mania. One to two weeks of lithium use eliminates or reduces symptoms in approximately 60% to 80% of manic episodes without causing depression or producing sedation. The drug is somewhat less effective in terminating episodes of depression, so it is often administered along with a TCA or other antidepressant drug. Most important is that it is useful for reducing the occurrence of future episodes of mania and depression. Additionally, it is particularly effective in reducing suicide in bipolar individuals. Patients who continue with lithium treatment have an average hospital stay of less than 2 weeks per year, but without lithium therapy patients spend an average of 8 to 13 weeks per year in the hospital. **Figure 19.15A** graphically demonstrates that without lithium maintenance, the typical bipolar patient has an episode of mania every 14 months and a period of depression every 17 months on average. Lithium maintenance reduces the recurrence of mania to once in 9 years and depressive episodes to about every 4 years (Lickey and Gordon, 1991).

Treatment of bipolar disorder with a mood stabilizer is a lifelong necessity for most patients. Either abrupt termination or gradual withdrawal of lithium results in recurring periods of mania and heightened suicide risk. Despite the risks, many patients stop taking the drug. In some cases, side effects are a significant problem for the patient, especially if they involve impaired memory and confusion. In other cases, patients stop taking the drug because they fail to experience normal mood changes, and this diminishes the richness of life. Finally, others object to the loss of the manic phase of bipolar disorder because this time is perceived as a period of heightened creativity and productiveness.

MECHANISM OF ACTION   It is probably not surprising to find that lithium enhances 5-HT actions: it elevates brain tryptophan, 5-HT, and 5-HIAA (the principal 5-HT metabolite) and increases 5-HT release, which ultimately alters receptor response in several brain areas. Lithium

(A)

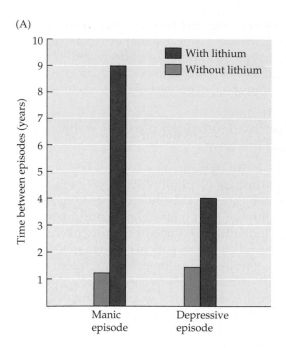

Figure 19.15 Effectiveness of lithium for bipolar disorder (A) Maintenance therapy with lithium significantly reduces the occurrence of manic episodes so that on average, the time between manic periods is 9 years, compared with 14 months without treatment. Depressive episodes also occur less often, averaging 4 years between episodes with lithium treatment and 17 months without. (B) The time course and extent of effectiveness of the newer drug carbamazepine are virtually identical to those of lithium in reducing manic symptoms in patients with bipolar disorder. (A after Lickey and Gordon, 1991; B after Post et al., 1984.)

(B)

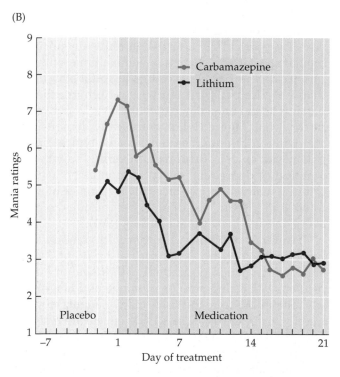

adenylyl cyclase, phosphoinositide cycling, G protein coupling, brain neurotrophic factors, and multiple cell survival cascades. Its ability to alter intracellular actions regardless of the triggering neurotransmitter may explain its effects in both mania and depression.

SIDE EFFECTS Lithium is not metabolized but is excreted by the kidney in its intact form. Sodium depletion due to extreme sweating, diarrhea, vomiting, dehydration, use of diuretic medication, or severely salt-restricted diets may lead to toxic levels of lithium because lithium is reabsorbed from kidney tubules instead of sodium. The effective therapeutic range of lithium concentration in the blood is 0.7 to 1.2 mM. Since toxic effects begin to occur at blood levels of 2.0 mM, the therapeutic index is very low, and a patient's blood level of lithium must be monitored on a regular basis. Side effects are generally quite mild at therapeutic doses but may include increased thirst and urination, impaired concentration and memory, fatigue, tremor, and weight gain. Toxic effects are more severe and include cramps, vomiting, diarrhea, kidney dysfunction, coarse tremor, confusion, and irritability. Levels of lithium above 3.0 mM may lead to seizures, coma, and death (Calabrese et al., 1995).

OTHER THERAPIES FOR BIPOLAR DISORDER Because only about 50% to 60% of patients show a good response to lithium, and because it has a significant potential for toxicity, alternative therapies have been developed. Of the alternatives, the anticonvulsant drugs carbamazepine (Tegretol) and valproate (Depakene) are the most common and will be described briefly. However, several newer drugs such as topiramate (Topamax) and tiagabine (Gabitril) are similarly effective when compared with lithium and have a different toxicity profile. Further discussion of these drugs is beyond the scope of this text and is left to others (Calabrese et al., 1995; Guay, 1995).

Valproate (Depakote), a simple branched-chain fatty acid was the first anticonvulsant approved by the U.S. Food and Drug Administration (FDA) for treatment of acute mania. Although valproate is readily absorbed after oral administration, it is low in potency so high doses are administered. It is highly bound

reduces catecholamine activity by enhancing reuptake and reducing release. Despite these neurochemical changes, it is unlikely that lithium acts on individual neurotransmitters to normalize mood swings of both mania and depression. Given that the drug flattens the extremes of emotion in both directions, it is more likely that it modifies synaptic transmission at points beyond the neurotransmitter receptors, for instance, in second-messenger function. Lithium has pronounced effects on to plasma proteins, and because of the high dosage requirements, the depots may become saturated. Toxicity can occur with continued administration after saturation of the depots or after consumption of other free fatty acids that displace valproate from them, raising the level of free drug in the blood. It is also capable of displacing other drugs bound to plasma protein, causing drug interactions. Its metabolism creates a number of active metabolites that contribute to valproate's action. Although its effectiveness is similar to lithium, one advantage of valproate is that it has a different side effect profile. Common side effects include drowsiness, lethargy, hand tremor, hair loss, weight gain, and gastrointestinal distress. Some evidence indicates that the drug can cause liver toxicity and pancreatitis, but the probability is low. However, overdose is potentially life-threatening. Since valproate is teratogenic and is associated with neural tube defects and with increased risk of polycystic ovary syndrome, its use in women of childbearing age is limited. For a review of its use in psychiatry, see Haddad and coworkers (2009).

Valproate has a complex mechanism of action. Valproate increases GABA levels by stimulating glutamic acid decarboxylase, which enhances synthesis, and inhibiting GABA transaminase, which decreases GABA degradation. Additionally, it has multiple actions on DA and glutamate neurotransmission. However, it also may have a common mechanism of action with other mood stabilizers on intracellular signaling including the regulation of several cell survival pathways involving neurotrophic factors.

Carbamazepine (Tegretol) is a structurally atypical anticonvulsant because it resembles tricyclic antidepressants, and this similarity allows it to inhibit NE reuptake. It also acutely blocks adenosine receptors and up-regulates them with chronic use. Its actions on intracellular signaling are similar to those of valproate and lithium. The time course and extent of effectiveness are similar to those of lithium (**Figure 19.15B**), but its side effects differ. The most common side effects, which usually diminish over time, include sedation, dizziness, somnolence, incoordination, nausea, and vomiting. More severe potential side effects include liver toxicity, severe skin rashes, and various blood diseases such as reduced white cell count, agranulocytosis, and aplastic anemia. The induction of several liver metabolizing enzymes in the cytochrome P450 family including CYP 3A4, CYP 1A2, and CYP 2C19 is also therapeutically significant because by increasing the amount of liver enzyme, it accelerates its own rate of metabolism and that of many other drugs (enzyme induction is discussed in Chapter 1). The more effective metabolism leads to reduced blood levels and the need to monitor and increase drug dosages to optimize treatment response and prevent drug interactions.

Section Summary

- Antidepressants of all classes reduce symptoms in about two thirds of individuals after 4 to 6 weeks of treatment. Total remission of symptoms occurs less often. Continued treatment prevents relapse.

- MAOIs elevate brain levels of monoamines by preventing their destruction in the presynaptic terminal by MAO and subsequently altering receptor number and intracellular signaling.

- The most common side effects of MAOIs include changes in blood pressure, sleep disturbances, and weight gain. More serious side effects are associated with enhanced response to sympathomimetics, hypertensive crisis following elevation of tyramine levels, and drug interactions due to liver enzyme inhibition.

- Tricyclic antidepressants block reuptake of NE or 5-HT or both, and this increases synaptic levels and produces subsequent compensatory changes in receptors and intracellular signaling.

- Side effects of TCAs include sedation, anticholinergic effects, and potentially dangerous cardiovascular effects.

- Second-generation antidepressants including the SSRIs are not more effective or more rapid in onset but are safer.

- Side effects of SSRIs are due to enhanced 5-HT function at multiple 5-HT receptors and include sexual dysfunction. Potentially fatal serotonin syndrome occurs when SSRIs are combined with other serotonergic drugs. Physical dependence occurs in 60% of cases.

- Mirtazapine enhances NE and 5-HT function by blocking α_2-autoreceptors and heteroreceptors on 5-HT cells. It also blocks selective 5-HT receptors to reduce side effects.

- Third-generation agents comprise CRF receptor antagonists, enhancers of the cAMP intracellular cascade, agomelatine, ketamine, and galanin agonists.

- Lithium carbonate reduces manic episodes without causing depression and reduces bipolar cycling. It is more effective than alternatives in reducing suicide rates.

- Side effects of lithium are relatively mild, but toxic effects at the highest doses lead to seizures, coma, and death. The therapeutic index is very small, so frequent monitoring of blood levels is needed.

- Lithium and other anti-manic drugs modulate several intracellular signaling pathways and neurotrophic factors.

- The anticonvulsant valproate is as effective as lithium and has different side effects but is teratogenic, so its use in women of childbearing age is limited.

- Carbamazepine has a time course and effectiveness similar to those of lithium with different side effects, some of which are liver toxicity and blood diseases. Induction of several cytochrome enzymes causes significant drug interactions.

Go to the **COMPANION WEBSITE**

sites.sinauer.com/psychopharm2e
for Web Boxes, animations, flashcards, and other study resources.

Recommended Readings

aan het Rot, M., Mathew, S. J., and Charney, D. S. (2009). Neurobiological mechanisms in major depressive disorder. *CMAJ.*, 180, 305–313.

Castrén, E. and Rantamäki, T. (2010). The role of BDNF and its receptors in depression and antidepressant drug action: Reactivation of developmental plasticity. *Dev. Neurobiol.*, 70, 289–297.

Connolly, K. R. and Thase, M. E. (2012). Emerging drugs for major depressive disorder. *Expert Opin. Emerg. Drugs*, 17, 105–126.

Jamison, K. R. (1993). *Touched with Fire: Manic-Depressive Illness and the Artistic Temperament*. New York: Free Press/ Macmillan.

Machado-Vieira, R., Manji, H. K., and Zarate, C. A., Jr. (2009). The role of lithium in the treatment of bipolar disorder: Convergent evidence for neurotrophic effects as a unifying hypothesis. *Bipolar Disord.*, 11 (Suppl. 2), 92–109.

McEwen, B. S. and Gianaros, P. J. (2010). Central role of the brain in stress and adaptation: Links to socioeconomic status, health, and disease. *Ann. N.Y. Acad. Sci.*, 1186, 190–222.

Southwick, S. M., Vythilingam, M., and Charney, D. S. (2005). The psychobiology of depression and resilience to stress: Implications for prevention and treatment. *Annu. Rev. Clin. Psychol.*, 1, 255–291.

The symptoms of schizophrenia frequently lead to personal isolation and failure to achieve a meaningful and productive lifestyle.

Schizophrenia: Antipsychotic Drugs 20

ARTHUR WAS 22 YEARS OLD WHEN HE WAS BROUGHT TO THE CLINIC because his parents were upset by his unusual behavior. He was an average student taking classes at a local junior college. He had taken a series of temporary jobs until he was laid off from the most recent one. It was then that he started talking about his blueprints to save all the starving children in the world. He said he had a secret plan that he would reveal only at the right time to the right person. His family became more distressed when he said he was going to the German embassy because they were the only ones who would listen to him. He said he would climb the fence at night and present his plan to the German ambassador. After several visits the psychiatrist finally saw the plan, which consisted of random thoughts (e.g., "The poor, starving souls" and "The moon is the only place") and drawings of rocket ships that would go to the moon, where Arthur would create a community for the poor children. As time went on, Arthur began to show dramatic changes in emotion, often crying and acting apprehensive. He stopped wearing socks and underwear and, despite the extremely cold weather, would not wear a jacket outdoors. He had moved into his mother's apartment, but he wouldn't sleep much at night and kept the family up until early morning. For his mother, it was a living nightmare because she felt so helpless to help her son (Barlow and Durand, 1995).

This chapter describes the characteristics of the devastating mental disorder known as schizophrenia and the drug therapies that are currently available to treat it. It also describes several models that attempt to explain the neuropathology that leads to its hallmark abnormal behavior and multiple symptoms.

Characteristics of Schizophrenia

Major mental disorders called psychoses are characterized by severe distortions of reality and disturbances in perception, intellectual functioning, affect (emotional expression), motivation, social relationships, and motor behavior. Schizophrenia is one relatively common form of psychosis. Other disorders that have psychosis as a component are schizophreniform disorder, schizoaffective disorder, delusional disorder, and bipolar disorder, which is classified as an affective disorder and was discussed in Chapter 19. Individuals with schizophrenia demonstrate many different symptoms, including hearing voices that are not there, holding unrealistic ideas and beliefs, and communicating in a way that is difficult to understand. They are frequently so incapacitated that voluntary or involuntary hospitalization is required.

Although drug use or environmental toxins may cause brief episodes of psychosis, schizophrenia is generally a chronic condition. Although its symptoms can usually be controlled to some extent, schizophrenia cannot at this time be cured or prevented. Despite therapy, approximately 30% of people with schizophrenia spend a significant portion of their lives in mental hospitals, accounting for a majority of the total hospital beds in these facilities. Approximately 1% to 1.5% of the world's population will suffer from schizophrenia during their lifetime. Another 2% to 3% will suffer from less severe schizophrenic symptoms but will not meet the diagnostic criteria.

Symptoms of schizophrenia most often begin during the late teenage years and early twenties, although the disorder may first occur in childhood. The early onset of the disorder means that the episodes recurring throughout life disrupt the individual's most productive years. Although epidemiological studies have indicated that schizophrenia affects men and women equally, a clear gender difference in the age of onset and the course of this disorder exists. **Figure 20.1** shows that the onset of schizophrenia among 470 patients is highest in early adulthood for both sexes. However, for men, the onset decreases rapidly with age. The onset for women is lower than for men until age 36. At that time, more women than men demonstrate a first episode, and this difference continues into old age (Howard et al., 1993). The implication of the gender difference for onset is not clear, but it may suggest the existence of two qualitatively distinct subtypes of the disorder. Schizophrenia can destroy lives and also cause a great deal of pain and suffering, not only for afflicted individuals but also for their families as they attempt to cope emotionally and financially with the disorder. On this basis, the direct (e.g., hospitalization and medication costs) and indirect (e.g., loss

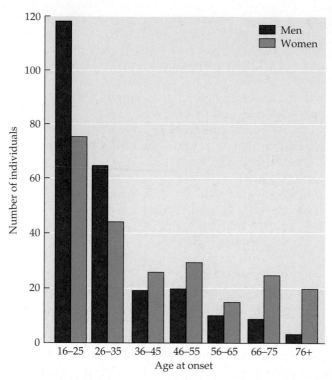

Figure 20.1 Gender differences in age at onset of schizophrenia Although both sexes show peak onset of symptoms between 16 and 25 years of age, this sample of 470 patients shows that more women than men experience their first episode after age 36, a difference that continues in every age bracket through old age. (After Howard et al., 1993.)

of productive employment, participation in society, and family stress) costs of schizophrenia have been estimated to be between $30 billion and $50 billion a year in the United States.

There is no defining cluster of schizophrenic symptoms

Schizophrenia is very clearly a thought disorder, characterized by illogical thinking, lack of reasoning, and inability to recognize reality; however, the specific symptoms show a great deal of individual variation. Disturbances in perception (hallucinations) are a frequent occurrence in schizophrenia. These hallucinations are most often auditory and generally consist of voices that are insulting or commanding. For a closer look at auditory hallucinations, turn to **Web Box 20.1**. Tactile hallucinations are often electrical, tingling, or burning sensations. Bizarre delusions (beliefs not based on reality) are also common. Particularly prevalent are delusions of persecution involving the individual's belief that others are spying on or planning to harm him. Also quite common is the delusion that one's thoughts are broadcast from one's head to the world, or that thoughts and feelings are not one's own but are imposed by an outside source, such as from outer space. Because the form of thought is disturbed, communication is confused and illogical and often does not even follow the rules of semantics. Speech may be vague or repetitive or may shift from one subject to another, totally unrelated subject.

In many individuals with schizophrenia, emotions are either absent or totally inappropriate to the situation. Inappropriate emotion is demonstrated, for example, by the individual who smiles or laughs while describing electrical tortures. Individuals who lack emotion show no expression, speak in a monotone, and report a lack of feeling. Sudden and unpredictable changes of emotion are also common.

People with schizophrenia are frequently withdrawn, preoccupied with their own thoughts and delusions. Extreme apathy and an inability to initiate activities (avolition) frequently mean that the individual has no interest in performing everyday activities, including maintaining personal hygiene, which further isolates the individual from the mainstream. A variety of cognitive deficits impair the individual's ability to function at home, school, and workplace. Motor activity is generally reduced and is characterized by inappropriate and bizarre postures, rigidity that resists efforts to be moved, or purposeless and stereotyped movements, for example, rocking or pacing. At times, people with schizophrenia, particularly the paranoid type, can be agitated and violent (Krakowski and Czobor, 1997).

DIAGNOSIS Although the symptoms described here seem to be easily recognizable, the diagnosis of schizophrenia is not so simple. One reason is that no two individuals show the identical pattern of symptoms, nor is there a single symptom that occurs in every patient with schizophrenia. Furthermore, symptoms increase and decrease over time, and the predominant symptoms or symptom clusters often change over the years in the same individual, which may lead to a change in diagnosis. The question of whether schizophrenia is a single disorder or a collection of disorders has never been fully resolved.

Historically, schizophrenia has been organized into subtypes, classified as **catatonic** (alternating periods of immobility and excited agitation), **paranoid** (characteristic delusions of grandeur or persecution), **disorganized** (silly and immature emotionality with disorganized behavior), and **undifferentiated** (cases not meeting the criteria of the other subtypes). These categories are based on the observations of Emil Kraepelin, a German psychiatrist who viewed these symptom patterns as manifestations of a single disorder in the early 1900s. Similar categories are used in the *Diagnostic and Statistical Manual of Mental Disorders* prepared by the American Psychiatric Association, now in its fourth revision (*DSM-IV-TR*, 2000).[1]

A second useful classification scheme, stemming from the work of Crow (1980) and modified more recently by Andreasen (1990), is that of **positive, negative**, and **cognitive symptoms**. The positive symptoms of schizophrenia include the more dramatic symptoms of the disorder, such as delusions and hallucinations, disorganized speech, unusual ways of thinking, and bizarre behavior. Patients who demonstrate predominantly positive symptoms tend to be older when they experienced a sudden onset of symptoms and appeared relatively normal in their younger years before the symptoms occurred. These patients respond well to conventional antipsychotic medications that block dopamine receptors (D_2), and their symptoms are made worse by drugs that enhance dopamine function. Current thinking suggests that neurochemical abnormalities are significant in this disorder (see the section on abnormal dopamine function).

Negative symptoms are characterized by a decline in normal function and include reduced speech (alogia), deficits in emotional responsiveness (flattened affect), loss of initiative and motivation (avolition), social withdrawal, and loss of ability to derive pleasure from normally pleasurable activities (anhedonia). These symptoms are harder to recognize and may be mistaken for other conditions such as major depression. The cognitive symptoms characteristic of schizophrenia include impaired working memory, executive functioning, and attention. Cognitive deficits are responsible for poorer functioning in the community and greater isolation. Unfortunately, the negative and cognitive symptoms are among the most resistant to antipsychotic drugs and make it difficult for the individual to perform tasks of daily living or to lead a normal life, even when medication reduces the positive symptoms. Unlike patients with prominent positive symptoms, patients with dominant negative and cognitive symptoms tend to show early onset of some symptoms and a long course of progressive deterioration, perhaps reflecting long-term neurodegeneration or developmental errors.

Long-term outcome depends on pharmacological treatment

Before the advent of drug therapy, the history of treatment for schizophrenia was rather dismal (**Figure 20.2A**). The mentally ill were maintained in huge mental hospitals, where treatment was limited to isolation or restraint, "shock" therapy using insulin-induced

---

[1]The fifth edition of the *DSM* is to be published in May, 2013.

(A)

(B)

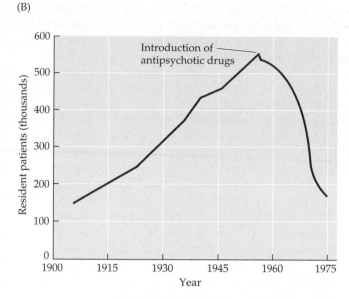

Figure 20.2 Treatment of the mentally ill (A) Drawing depicting one of the available methods of "treatment" of the mentally ill during the early 1800s. (B) Patient populations in public mental institutions in the United States increased from 1900 to 1956. At that point, a dramatic decline occurred in the number of institutionalized patients following the introduction of antipsychotic drugs. (After Bassuk and Gerson, 1978.)

seizures or electrical current, or surgery such as prefrontal lobotomy. **Figure 20.2B** shows a steady increase in the number of hospitalized psychiatric patients in the United States from 1900 to 1956 because such patients were usually permanently hospitalized. In 1956, the number of hospitalized patients began a sudden and steady decline despite a continued increase in initial admissions. This reduction coincided with the introduction of drug therapy, in particular the use of chlorpromazine (Thorazine). Chlorpromazine, a drug in the phenothiazine class, was initially used to enhance surgical anesthesia because it produces a sense of calmness and reduced awareness of environmental stimuli when administered before surgery. When tried with schizophrenic patients, chlorpromazine was especially effective because it calmed the excited patient and activated the patient who was profoundly withdrawn. Many modifications of the chlorpromazine molecule have already been made, and the development of new compounds to reduce symptoms with fewer side effects continues today.

Section Summary

- Schizophrenia is a chronic psychosis that occurs in 1% of the population worldwide.

- Symptoms begin during late adolescence and early adulthood. Men have an earlier onset than women.

- Schizophrenia is a thought disorder, characterized by illogical thinking, lack of reasoning, and failure to recognize reality. Specific symptoms show large variation among individuals, making diagnosis difficult.

- Patients can be classed as catatonic, paranoid, disorganized, and undifferentiated.

- Positive symptoms are dramatic and lead to diagnosis. They include hallucinations, delusions, disorganized speech, unusual ways of thinking, and bizarre behavior. These symptoms respond to antipsychotic drug treatment.

- Negative symptoms are the absence of normal functions and include reduced speech, flat affect, loss of motivation, social withdrawal, apathy, and anhedonia.

- Cognitive deficits include impaired working memory, executive function, and attention. Negative symptoms and cognitive deficits are resistant to current treatments.

Etiology of Schizophrenia

Scientists from several disciplines use a variety of strategies to uncover the causes of schizophrenia. The goal is to develop an integrated approach to psychopathology that considers anatomical, neurochemical, and functional factors. Schizophrenia is best understood as a disorder having a genetic component that makes the individual more vulnerable than the average person to particular environmental factors.

28-year-old male identical twins

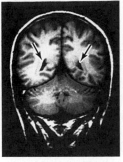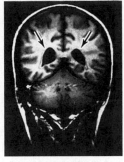

Well   Affected

Figure 20.3 Brain images of twins not concordant for schizophrenia The arrows in the figure point to the ventricles filled with cerebrospinal fluid. The healthy twin has normal-sized ventricles, and his schizophrenic twin has ventricles that are much enlarged. (Courtesy of Drs. E. Fuller Torrey and Daniel Weinberger.)

Abnormalities of brain structure and function occur in individuals with schizophrenia

Until recently, differences in the brains of individuals with schizophrenia compared with controls could not be detected. However, with the development of new techniques in neuroscience, differences of several kinds have been found, including structural differences, functional abnormalities, and irregularities in psychophysiological measures.

STRUCTURAL ABNORMALITIES Brain imaging techniques such as computerized tomography and magnetic resonance imaging continue to produce evidence of structural abnormalities in the brains of people with schizophrenia. Many studies show cerebral atrophy (shrinking or wasting away) and enlargement of fluid-filled ventricles following cell loss (**Figure 20.3**). Among the brain areas showing reduced volume are the basal ganglia, the temporal lobe, and several

limbic regions such as the hippocampus. The temporal lobe and hippocampal changes in people with chronic schizophrenia compared with controls are some of the most consistent magnetic resonance imaging findings (DeLisi et al., 1991). Structural differences in these areas also occur in monozygotic twins when only one has the disorder. Numerous studies show that hippocampal cells of patients with schizophrenia are more disorganized (**Figure 20.4A**) than those of healthy subjects (**Figure 20.4B**), and that selected cortical layers in the brains of patients with schizophrenia are atrophied. Additionally, many brain areas show shrinking of dendritic trees that would lead to failures of connectivity among neurons and abnormal neuronal processing. Involvement of the hippocampus and dopamine-rich basal ganglia may be related to the memory impairment and poor cognitive function found in most individuals with schizophrenia.

Investigators are always concerned that some brain changes may be due to progressive deterioration during the course of illness rather than causing the illness, or may be due to the effects of antipsychotic medication used chronically over many years. However, most brain changes, such as enlarged ventricles, are not correlated with either the duration of time since the onset of symptoms or the duration of time since

(A) Patient with schizophrenia   (B) Normal control

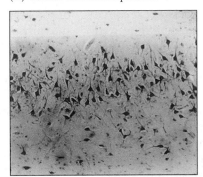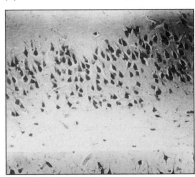

Figure 20.4 Disorganization of cells in the hippocampus Histological cross sections of hippocampus showing the disorganized cells in the brain of a patient with schizophrenia (A) compared with the brain of a normal control (B). Corresponding schematic diagrams showing the haphazard arrangement of pyramidal cells in the hippocampus of the patient with schizophrenia and the normal parallel organization in normal controls. (From Kovelman and Scheibel, 1984.)

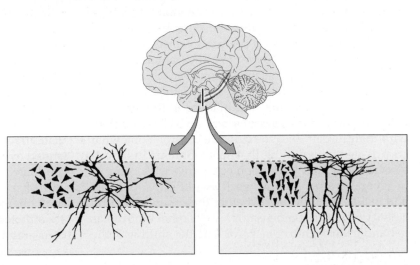

the first hospitalization. In contrast, a significant correlation does exist between ventricle size and age of the individual when symptoms were first diagnosed. On the basis of these results, researchers have concluded that ventricular enlargement is not due to progressive loss of brain cells, but may represent abnormalities of brain growth and development preceding the onset of symptoms. Additional evidence for this idea is the discovery that the more subtle abnormalities in cell structure are rarely accompanied by gliosis (multiplication of astrocytes and microglia). Since gliosis is a response to neuronal damage that occurs in the mature brain, but not in the immature brain, it is likely that the cell abnormalities occurred during the developmental process (Weinberger, 1995).

FUNCTIONAL ABNORMALITIES   In addition to structural abnormalities in the brains of individuals with schizophrenia, regional brain function in these individuals differs from that in controls. Measures of brain function include rate of cell metabolism, blood flow, electrical activity, and chemical changes. The most consistent difference is reduced function of the prefrontal cortex (PFC), called hypofrontality (Buchsbaum, 1990). Positron emission tomography (PET) and single-photon emission computerized tomography (SPECT) studies show less of an increase in cerebral blood flow in the frontal cortex of patients with schizophrenia than in normal subjects while they perform cognitive tasks of executive functioning, working memory, response inhibition, and problem solving that require planning and strategy, such as the Wisconsin Card Sorting Test (WCST; **Figure 20.5A**). Reduced blood flow is associated with less glucose use, which in turn is a good indicator of how active the brain cells are. **Figure 20.5B** shows that the frontal cortex is less active in a patient with schizophrenia compared to a nonschizophrenic twin both at rest and during the WCST. Nevertheless, further research indicates that the picture is not quite so simple. When performing several different executive tasks, healthy individuals and those with schizophrenia activated the same brain regions including the dorsolateral prefrontal cortex (DLPFC), ventrolateral prefrontal cortex (VLPFC), anterior cingulate cortex (ACC), and thalamus. However, schizophrenic patients showed much less activation in the left DLPFC, ACC, and left thalamus, and in areas in the inferior/posterior cortex during selective tasks, which is consistent with their impairment in cognitive control. Somewhat surprising is the finding that schizophrenic individuals showed *greater* activation compared with controls in several brain structures such as VLPFC, amygdala, and insula. It is not clear whether the enhanced neural activity reflects a compensatory use of other brain areas to handle the cognitive tasks, or whether shifting of the network of activity represents a disease-specific pattern (Minzenberg et al., 2009). Hypofrontality in schizophrenia is especially interesting because the negative and cognitive symptoms of schizophrenia resemble the deficits seen following surgical disconnection of the frontal lobes (prefrontal lobotomy). Included in these deficits are poor social functioning, loss of motivation, defective attention, emotional blunting, and inability to shift strategies during problem solving (Gur, 1995).

PSYCHOPHYSIOLOGICAL IRREGULARITIES   Several potential markers for schizophrenia have been evaluated and may be useful in diagnosis. A majority of patients with schizophrenia demonstrate eye-movement dysfunctions such as the inability to visually track an object. With their heads held still, they are unable to follow a moving pendulum with their eyes. This deficit is not related to drug treatment or institutionalization (Lieberman et al., 1993). Since failure to track is also found in many of the relatives of patients with schizophrenia, genetic research suggests that the defective eye-tracking gene may be inherited along with the genes for schizophrenia.

A second neurophysiological abnormality involves brain electrical activity measured by electroencephalography (EEG). The EEG records neural activity associated with the perception of an event and related cognitive processes. Healthy individuals show localized stimulus-induced electrical activity in a specific area of the brain depending on the nature of the stimulus. In contrast, individuals with schizophrenia respond to specific stimuli with widespread electrical activity across large portions of the brain. Differences in eye movement and EEG patterns suggest a defect in stimulus perception and psychological processing of the information (Baribeau and Laurent, 1991).

Genetic, environmental, and developmental factors interact

Although schizophrenia is an ancient disorder described as early as 1000 BC, its causes remain unknown. Schizophrenia is increasingly regarded as a neurodevelopmental disorder with a strong genetic component; however, psychological, biological, and sociological factors combine in a unique manner to contribute to its psychopathology, course, and outcome.

HEREDITY   The importance of heredity has been demonstrated by numerous family, twin, and adoption studies conducted by investigators who have taken advantage of the excellent record-keeping system of Denmark to show that relatives of individuals with schizophrenia are afflicted with the disorder much more frequently than members of the general population. In fact, the

(A)

(B)

At rest

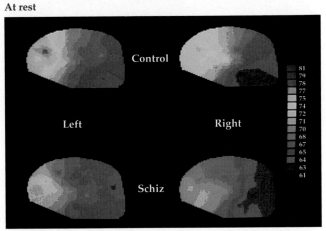

During card-sorting task

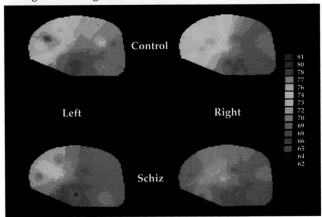

Figure 20.5 Hypofrontality in schizophrenia (A) The Wisconsin Card Sorting Test is used to evaluate the ability of a subject to shift response strategies on the basis of feedback from the tester. The subject is presented with stimulus cards having simple designs that differ in color, shape, and number of elements. The subject is asked to sort the remaining cards into piles. With each attempt, the subject is told whether the choice is correct or incorrect. Over the test period, the sorting principle may first be color and then may shift to form or number. Patients with schizophrenia and those with frontal lobe lesions fail to shift strategies and may continue to sort on the basis of the original stimulus (e.g., color) despite being told that color sorting is no longer correct. (B) PET scans comparing frontal lobe activity of a patient with schizophrenia and a nonschizophrenic twin. The sibling with schizophrenia has less frontal lobe activity at rest (top) as well as during a frontal lobe challenge with the Wisconsin Card Sorting Test (bottom). (B courtesy of Karen Berman.)

closer the genetic relationship, the greater is the probability of schizophrenia in the relative. Gottesman (1991) summarized a large number of family and twin studies of individuals with schizophrenia completed between 1920 and 1987 (**Figure 20.6**). These data demonstrate that the risk of having schizophrenia varies according to how many genes one shares with someone who has the disorder. Compared with the lifetime risk in the general population of about 1%, first-degree relatives such as parents, children, and siblings have an average lifetime risk 12 times greater (ranging from 6% to 17%), but more distant (second-degree) relatives, including uncles and aunts, nephews and nieces, grandchildren, and half-siblings, have an average risk of 4% (ranging

from 2% to 6%). Dizygotic twins, who have the genetic similarity of siblings but who share the prenatal environment, show a concordance of 17%, which means that if one twin of the pair develops schizophrenia, the probability of the second twin developing the disorder is 17%. In comparison, monozygotic (identical) twins, who have identical genes, have a concordance of 48%. This concordance exists even when the twins are reared apart in different environments, which further demonstrates the heritability of schizophrenia. However, although the concordance is striking, it is important to point out that other factors must be involved in the occurrence of the disorder, because if genetic abnormalities were totally responsible, concordance for identical twins would be

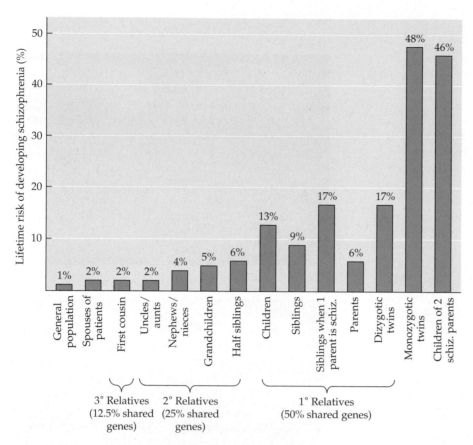

Figure 20.6 Lifetime risks of developing schizophrenia among relatives of an affected individual Data are summarized from about 40 family and twin studies conducted between 1920 and 1987. Compared with a 1% risk of developing schizophrenia in the general population, second-degree relatives have an average risk of 4%, first-degree relatives have a 6% to 17% risk, monozygotic twins have a 48% risk and children having 2 schizophrenic parents have an average 47% risk. (After Gottesman, 1991.)

100%. Hence individuals having a gene that predisposes them to schizophrenia do not necessarily develop the disorder. Equally striking is the high risk for children born to two parents with schizophrenia.

Current molecular genetic research is trying to identify the specific genes that predict vulnerability to schizophrenia, which would allow early intervention to prevent onset of the disorder and to identify molecular pathways involved in its etiology (Muglia, 2011). The task is difficult because multiple genes located at different **loci** (sites on our chromosomes) are involved. Multiple gene abnormalities would explain why the risk of having schizophrenia increases with the number of affected relatives in the family. It also might explain why the symptom clusters vary in nature and intensity from individual to individual. Despite the difficulties, loci on a dozen chromosomes have been identified as likely sites for genes that increase the risk

for developing schizophrenia, with the most promising being on chromosomes 13, 8, 22, and 6. Some have been identified by **linkage studies**, which look for similarities at the loci in families with affected members. A second approach considers **candidate genes**, genes that on prior physiological or theoretical grounds are suspected to be involved in disease development, progression, or clinical manifestation. In the case of schizophrenia, identification of candidate genes falls into three possible areas. First, genetic correlates of neurophysiological characteristics typical of the schizophrenic individual are evaluated, such as the defective filtering of auditory stimuli, eye-tracking dysfunction, ventricular enlargement, and so forth. Second, neurochemical models or studies of pharmacological response may provide an additional focus in the search for candidate genes. A productive line of research evaluates differences in alleles associated with neurotransmitters and receptors, including dopamine, glutamate, and γ-aminobutyric acid (GABA), and with second-messenger systems, including G proteins, adenylyl cyclase, and protein kinases. Third, because schizophrenia is considered a neurodevelopmental disorder, gene mutations that affect proteins needed for key events during brain development, such as growth factors, are significant. Early gene-induced errors could produce the major permanent modifications of brain structure seen in schizophrenia.

New developments in technology like **DNA microarray** provide the means for rapid screening of large quantities of genomic data. This method, described in Chapter 4, can identify complex gene expression patterns. For example, Mirnics et al. (2000) reported multiple defects in the gene groups related to presynaptic function in the PFC of individuals with schizophrenia compared with normal controls. In particular, they found the greatest and most consistent defects in proteins needed for normal maintenance of synaptic vesicles and in those needed for the release process. However, other differences in gene expression involve glutamate and GABA transmission, energy metabolism, and growth factors.

A modification of the standard microarray technology spurred the development of **genome-wide association screening**. This technique utilizes gene chips consisting of large sets of single-nucleotide polymorphisms (SNPs) (i.e., gene alleles that differ in only one nucleotide). DNA samples from people with the disorder and matched control subjects are assayed on the chips. If a particular allele is found more often in people with the disease, it is "associated" with the disorder. The method is data-driven rather than hypothesis-driven, meaning that researchers do not need to know anything about the function of the gene, although sometimes this makes the results difficult to interpret. Although originally limited to detecting common SNPs (i.e., those found in more than 5% of the population), it is now possible to identify rare SNPs, as well as more of the copy number variants (CNVs). CNVs are chromosomal abnormalities in which portions of a chromosome are duplicated, deleted, inverted, or translocated. The technology is highly accurate, relatively inexpensive, and very fast, and it uses powerful statistical methods that reduce the risk of finding false-positive associations between genotype and phenotype. For details on the history, rationale, and application of genome-wide association studies, the reader is directed to a paper by the Psychiatric GWAS Consortium Coordinating Committee (2009).

The new technology has led to a huge number of studies in an attempt to predict vulnerability to schizophrenia. The work has generated an enormous amount of enthusiasm among researchers because it holds such tremendous promise for understanding the neural basis for the disorder, developing better animal models for drug testing, and improving treatment options. However, others are more pessimistic because despite the great effort and cost, success has been quite modest. Although hundreds of new chromosomal loci linked to schizophrenia have been identified using the most powerful new genome-wide association screening, there have been considerable inconsistencies in efforts to replicate the findings using different patient populations (Rudan, 2010). Certainly one reason is that there is little precision in diagnosis of schizophrenia (as is true for other psychiatric disorders) because there is no objective measure (as there is for diabetes or cancer), and researchers cannot know whether their sampling population is homogeneous, or whether it contains multiple subsets of patients. Also compared with other, more common diseases such as diabetes, the size of the population sampled has been much smaller for schizophrenia.

It is unlikely that a single gene will be found that makes a large contribution to the susceptibility to such a complex disorder as schizophrenia. Instead it seems that there will be large numbers of genetic variants that each contributes only a small amount. It has been estimated that combining all the identified polymorphisms together would explain less than 5% of the variability in disease risk, which means that predicting the disorder for a given individual is very limited (Rudan, 2010). Alternatively, it has been suggested that one way to explain the evidence for a high level of heritability from family, twin, and adoption studies is to consider epigenetic modifications as the source (Crow, 2008). It is possible that environmental factors causing epigenetic changes modify developmental mechanisms not by altering the gene itself, but by altering the expression of the gene (**Box 20.1**). Another alternative is that some of the missing genetic component may be explained by rare chromosomal abnormalities in genes such as *DISC1*.

Chubb and colleagues (2008) summarize the evidence suggesting that mutations of the **DISC1 gene** (as many as 15 variants of the gene exist) increase the probability of developing schizophrenia and other mental disorders. The initial finding showed that a chromosomal abnormality, specifically, a translocation of pieces of DNA on chromosomes 1 and 11, was strongly linked to schizophrenia in a large Scottish family (St Clair et al., 1990). One gene that was disrupted by the translocation is *DISC1* (disrupted-in-schizophrenia), which codes for proteins essential for neuronal functions such as embryonic neurogenesis and neuronal migration, intracellular transport functions, and axon elongation. Each of these could contribute to the morphological abnormalities seen in the schizophrenic brain. Since DISC1 protein is found in cell bodies, axon terminals, the postsynaptic density, and dendritic spines, it is likely to have multiple roles in synaptic function, in addition to its known role in regulating mitochondrial function. Subsequently, *DISC1* has been implicated in several psychiatric disorders, including bipolar disorder, depression, and autism.

Individuals carrying the translocation show the reduced P300 event-related potential that is

BOX 20.1   The Cutting Edge

Epigenetic Modifications and Risk for Schizophrenia

Schizophrenia is likely due to the interaction of a large number of susceptibility genes, each contributing a small amount to overall risk, in combination with environmentally induced epigenetic modifications. As you previously saw, complications of labor and delivery, prenatal exposure to viral infection, malnutrition, and many other such events occur to a greater extent in people who develop schizophrenia. Although no single event will be predictive, all of these things as well as trauma later in life may be considered environmental stressors. Stress, especially early in life, produces epigenetic modifications that alter neurodevelopment. In earlier chapters (see Chapters 18 and 19), you learned that exposure to stress and neglect in the early years of life alters the development of the brain and endocrine stress circuits, leading to subsequent overarousal to stressors and an increased probability of psychopathology. Environmental stressors can also alter the expression of genes such as reelin (*RELN*).

Since abnormal neural connectivity characterizes schizophrenia, the discovery of epigenetic modification of the *RELN* gene has received a great deal of attention. Reelin is an extracellular glycoprotein secreted by neurons, and among its many functions is its role in guiding neuron positioning during fetal brain development. A reduction in reelin in the developing nervous system could explain the cell disorganization and morphological abnormalities typically

seen in postmortem neuroanatomical studies of schizophrenic patients. In adulthood, reelin seems to have a role in learning and memory by enhancing dendritic spine growth and synaptic plasticity. Consequently, low levels in the adult may reduce synaptic plasticity in hippocampus and PFC, leading to cognitive deficits typical of schizophrenia. In fact, a number of studies have found up to 50% less reelin and its mRNA in the brains of schizophrenic patients postmortem compared with controls, particularly in the PFC, but also in hippocampus, cerebellum, and basal ganglia.

At least some of the reduced reelin expression is due to epigenetic modulation, which has prompted some researchers to consider it a critical factor in psychosis (Guidotti and Grayson, 2011). Several postmortem studies have shown greater *RELN* hypermethylation (an epigenetic change described in Chapter 2) in several brain areas in schizophrenic patients compared with controls. The added methyl groups would cause a more "closed" chromatin state and reduce transcription of the gene so that less reelin is produced. The down-regulation of reelin may be due, at least in part, to an observed up-regulation of a methyltransferase enzyme responsible for the transfer of the methyl groups. Further evidence to support a role for epigenetic modification of *RELN* was noted when the amino acid methionine, which increases methylation, was given

to schizophrenic patients. It made the symptoms for more than 60% of them dramatically worse. Of special significance is the finding that there are differences in DNA methylation between monozygotic twins discordant for schizophrenia, which may explain how the differences in experientially induced epigenetic processes increase one individual's vulnerability despite the presence of identical genes.

These findings have several important ramifications. First, they suggest ways to create mouse models that mimic the cognitive deficits of schizophrenia with prenatal administration of methionine, stress, or viral infection. These models can then be used to identify drugs to reverse the cognitive symptoms that presently are not effectively treated. Second, unlike genetic impairments, epigenetic programming can be reversed, creating new treatment options. As you learned earlier (see Box 19.3), down-regulation of gene expression due to hypermethylation can be reversed by enhancing histone acetylation, either by activating histone acetylase or by inhibiting histone deacetylase. It is interesting that the mood stabilizer valproate, which is used to treat bipolar disorder (see Chapter 19), inhibits histone deacetylase and increases reelin expression in animals with suppressed reelin following methionine administration. It also enhances cognitive function and may be useful as an add-on treatment along with antipsychotic drugs (see Guidotti et al., 2011).

characteristic of those with schizophrenia and bipolar disorder. Various *DISC1* polymorphisms are also associated with impaired cognitive function in the areas of spatial working memory, verbal learning, sustained

attention, performance on the WCST, and activation of the hippocampus during working memory tasks. Brain volume reductions in those with *DISC1* polymorphisms have been found in several studies, although the specific brain regions vary. Regional differences in the hippocampus, cingulate gyrus, and PFC have been found along with those in other brain areas. Using *DISC1* mutant mice, researchers have reported brain volume reductions similar to those found in schizophrenia and bipolar disorder. Some but not all have found schizophrenic-like behaviors such as deficits in PPI (see **Web Box 20.2**) and working memory in adult animals, which were normalized by antipsychotic drugs. These animal models provide further support for the importance of *DISC1* in increasing the vulnerability for schizophrenia. Perhaps most important to psychopharmacologists, the genetic model will potentially aid in screening drugs to alleviate the cognitive symptoms. Surprisingly, although we now know a lot about the gene and the protein it codes for, there seems to be no difference in *DISC1* expression in the brains of schizophrenic individuals postmortem. Furthermore, antipsychotic medication does not alter its expression in these individuals. Hence although *DISC1* is strongly implicated in mental illness, the mechanism by which it contributes to the pathogenesis is not understood.

DEVELOPMENTAL ERRORS Many investigators now believe that genetic vulnerability increases the probability that events during perinatal (including prenatal and postnatal) brain development will contribute to the occurrence of schizophrenia (Lewis and Levitt, 2002). The abnormal pattern of cortical connections and other brain structure irregularities that exist in the brains of individuals with schizophrenia are likely to be due to disruptions in the normal processes of cell multiplication and cell loss that continue into adolescence. Evidence from several sources shows a higher occurrence of perinatal complications among individuals with schizophrenia than in the general population. Brain insult during pregnancy and delivery caused by oxygen deprivation, drug use, infection, endocrine disorders, or other factors occurs with higher frequency in individuals with schizophrenia. Exposure to viral infection (e.g., pneumonia, influenza, measles, or polio) during the second trimester of pregnancy significantly increases the risk of schizophrenia in the child. Severe malnutrition, as demonstrated in Holland during World War II, also represents an assault on the fetus that increases the probability of schizophrenia. Although none of these stresses alone may explain the occurrence of the illness, the assault may increase its probability in the individual who is genetically at risk. You have already seen in Chapter 18 and in Box 19.3 how environmental events that cause epigenetic modification of gene transcription may increase the risk for psychiatric disorders, which may include schizophrenia.

Further evidence for early developmental errors is provided by the observation of several behavioral characteristics of early infancy that may signal potential problems, particularly if the infant has other risk factors. The infant behaviors identified were passivity and apathy, reduced responsiveness to verbal commands, more difficult temperament, and poor sensorimotor performance. In later childhood, deficits in attentional and information-processing tasks, along with impairments in fine motor coordination, were the best predictors of psychiatric disorders.

Although evidence suggests that blind observers could identify subtle differences in the behavior of youngsters who later developed schizophrenia such as more negative facial expression, increased social withdrawal, and unusual motor movements, the more flamboyant symptoms that lead to diagnosis do not appear until adolescence, which is also a period of significant brain development. Keshavan and colleagues (1994) found significant abnormalities in the elimination of synapses (pruning) that normally occurs during puberty. Excessive synaptic pruning in the PFC (associated with negative symptoms) and failure of pruning in certain subcortical structures (associated with positive symptoms) occur more often in the brains of individuals with schizophrenia than in healthy individuals. Using different technology, Thompson and coworkers (2001) imaged the brains of early-onset patients compared with age-matched controls over several years with high-resolution magnetic resonance imaging (MRI). Although relatively rare, early-onset patients provide a unique opportunity to evaluate the timing and pattern of cortical gray matter changes to see how the disease emerges. What investigators found was that over the 5 years of the study, the patients lost twice as much cortical gray matter as the healthy controls. The excessive loss started in the parietal lobes and progressed anteriorly to the temporal lobes, to the DLPFC, and ultimately to the frontal eye fields (**Figure 20.7**). Of particular interest was that the extent of gray matter loss was correlated with the nature and severity of symptoms. Alterations in these normal developmental processes could be caused by genetic programming errors, early brain insults, and environmental factors. The nature and extent of interaction of these factors remain unclear.

BIOPSYCHOSOCIAL INTERACTION It is easy to imagine an interactive basis for schizophrenia that depends on genetic predisposition, structural brain-wiring errors, and subsequent biochemical abnormalities. Environmental or social factors that challenge the susceptible individual beyond his ability to deal with the stress further contribute to the development of the disorder. **Web Box 20.3** provides a

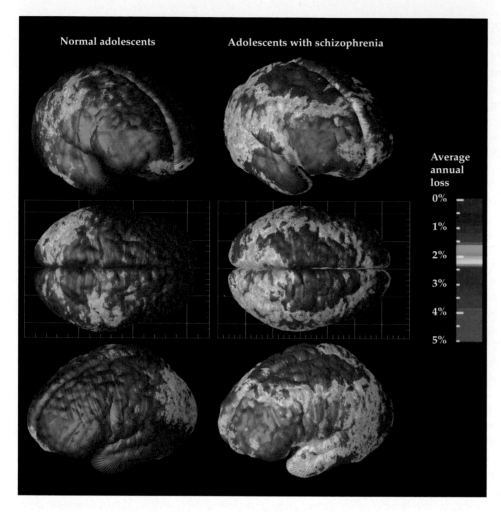

Figure 20.7 Cortical gray matter loss Three-dimensional maps of brain changes show the average annual rate of loss of cortical gray matter in normal adolescents (left) and in adolescents with schizophrenia (right). (From Thompson et al., 2001; courtesy of Paul Thompson.)

fascinating case study demonstrating the interaction of genetic and environmental factors in a set of quadruplets with schizophrenia. **Figure 20.8** summarizes the stages in the development of schizophrenia on the basis of material presented in the text.

Preclinical Models of Schizophrenia

Developing animal models for schizophrenia is especially difficult because the primary symptom is profound thought disorder, a cortical process not found in lower animals. No single animal model can mimic the complex symptomatology of schizophrenia, so each one tends to focus on one aspect of the disorder and experimentally induce homologous (similar) changes in animal behavior. It is assumed that subsequent attempts to manipulate the experimental response both neurochemically and neuroanatomically should

provide evidence for the neurobiological and genetic bases of human behavior.

Animal models are also used to screen new therapeutic drugs for effectiveness. These models may not resemble the psychiatric condition in any way and may instead depend on neurochemically induced behaviors that are known to respond to currently useful drugs. The disadvantage, of course, is that such screening devices often fail to identify drugs with novel mechanisms of action, which may be of greatest importance to the researcher.

There are multiple approaches to creating these models including pharmacological, developmental, and environmental manipulations as well as gene modification. In all cases, the models must be evaluated for face validity, construct validity, and predictive validity as discussed in Chapter 4. This section of the chapter will highlight just a few of the many techniques used, and recommended readings

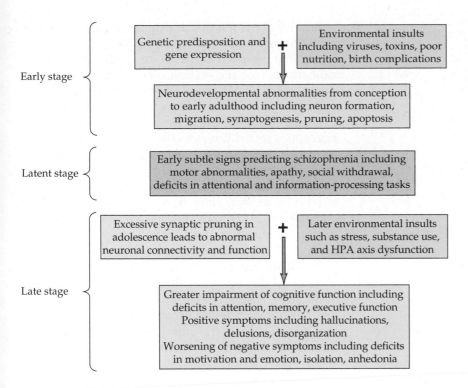

Early stage

Genetic predisposition and gene expression

+

Environmental insults including viruses, toxins, poor nutrition, birth complications

Neurodevelopmental abnormalities from conception to early adulthood including neuron formation, migration, synaptogenesis, pruning, apoptosis

Latent stage

Early subtle signs predicting schizophrenia including motor abnormalities, apathy, social withdrawal, deficits in attentional and information-processing tasks

Late stage

Excessive synaptic pruning in adolescence leads to abnormal neuronal connectivity and function

+

Later environmental insults such as stress, substance use, and HPA axis dysfunction

Greater impairment of cognitive function including deficits in attention, memory, executive function
Positive symptoms including hallucinations, delusions, disorganization
Worsening of negative symptoms including deficits in motivation and emotion, isolation, anhedonia

Figure 20.8 Etiology of schizophrenia This schematic diagram shows the importance of the interaction of genes and environmental factors in the development of schizophrenia based on material presented in the text. Genes and environment interact to cause abnormal development of the nervous system. The neurodevelopmental abnormalities such as errors in connectivity make the individual susceptible to later environmental events at adolescence, which exacerbates the cognitive deficits and negative symptoms and elicits the positive symptoms leading to diagnosis.

are provided at the end of the chapter for further consideration.

The toxic reaction to high doses of central nervous system (CNS) stimulants is a model that is still considered among the best. It was found quite accidentally when clinicians realized that people who abuse CNS stimulants (amphetamine and cocaine) frequently show signs of thought disorder. Addicts hospitalized with stimulant toxicity often have well-formed paranoid delusions; various stereotyped, compulsive behaviors; and either visual or auditory hallucinations. Even trained clinicians find the symptoms to be indistinguishable from those of paranoid schizophrenia. Also, when amphetamine is administered to patients with schizophrenia, the patients report that their existing symptoms get worse, not that new symptoms are produced. Finally, amphetamine-induced psychosis can be treated with the same drugs that are most effective in treating schizophrenia.

In animals, high doses of amphetamine produce a characteristic stereotyped sniffing, licking, and gnawing. Because stereotyped behavior also occurs in response to high doses of amphetamine in humans and is similar to the compulsive repetitions of meaningless behavior seen in schizophrenia, **amphetamine-induced stereotypy** is used in the laboratory as an animal model for schizophrenia. For many years, it has been a classic screening device to identify effective antipsychotic drugs. Because high doses of amphetamine release dopamine, the abnormal behaviors produced by the drug support the dopamine hypothesis

of schizophrenia (this hypothesis is described later in the chapter). The down side to this model is that it mimics only the positive symptoms, and since it depends on dopamine-regulated behavior, it is unlikely to identify drugs with novel mechanisms of action.

A second screening procedure compares the dose–response curve for the antipsychotic drug's inhibition of motor activity induced by apomorphine (a dopamine agonist) with the curve for the drug's effectiveness in producing catalepsy (maintenance of abnormal postures). Although the animal models for measuring drug-induced running and the peculiar posturing of catalepsy may not seem to reflect psychotic behavior and motor side effects, respectively, they have provided consistent preclinical results. Drugs that are effective in reducing psychotic symptoms in humans quite consistently also reduce apomorphine-induced running as well as amphetamine-induced stereotyped behaviors. Likewise, antipsychotics that do not produce catalepsy in rats have low incidences of motor side effects. **Figure 20.9** shows that for the classic antipsychotic haloperidol, the dose–response curves for inhibiting apomorphine-induced locomotion and producing catalepsy are very similar, suggesting that doses that are effective in reducing the locomotion are almost identical to those that induce catalepsy. For patients, the poor separation of the curves predicts a drug that is effective in reducing symptoms but that has a high incidence of motor side effects. In contrast, the dose–response curves for the atypical antipsychotic remoxipride show a much larger difference in

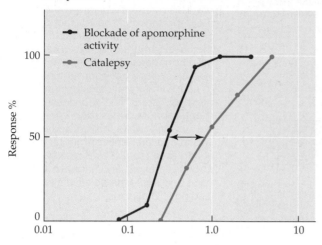

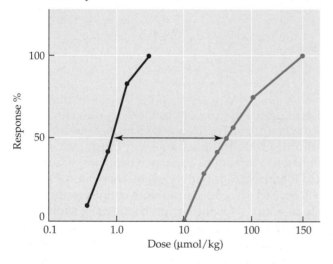

Figure 20.9 Dose–response curves for haloperidol and remoxipride for blocking apomorphine-induced hyperactivity and producing catalepsy in rats. The horizontal distance between the curves on each graph represents the difference in potency of the drug required to produce both of the effects. The wider the separation of the curves, the lower is the likelihood that the effective antipsychotic dose will produce motor side effects in humans.

doses required to inhibit hyperactivity and induce catalepsy. This type of preclinical screening predicts a lower incidence of motor side effects with the atypical drugs, and clinical evaluation with patients supports this conclusion.

An additional method used to distinguish between antipsychotic-induced therapeutic effects and side effects is the **paw test** (Geyer and Ellenbroek, 2003). The apparatus is a simple platform with four holes—two for the rear paws and two for the forepaws. The animal is injected with the test drug, and its paws are placed into the holes. The duration of time needed to remove the forelimbs and hind limbs is recorded. Since the striatum regulates forepaw retraction, deficits in that behavior serve as the analogue for motor side effects (see the section on classic antipsychotic drugs). The nucleus accumbens regulates rear paw retraction, and longer antipsychotic-induced retraction time correlates with therapeutic efficacy. All antipsychotics tested but not other classes of psychotropic drugs prolong rear paw retraction; this indicates their clinical effectiveness. More important, classical antipsychotics that produce significant motor side effects also prolong retraction of the forepaws, but the atypical antipsychotics that have a low incidence of motor side effects do not. This behavioral test is one of the few (along with prepulse inhibition of startle, see below) tests that can identify drugs that are effective without producing motor side effects.

Recently, cognitive symptoms have been an important focus for modeling because these symptoms are highly disruptive to the individual and to his ability to function in the community. Also the presently available antipsychotics are relatively ineffective in reversing the deficits. Some commonly used tasks that reflect deficits in schizophrenia were described in Chapter 4 and include tests of working memory, attention, and sensory processing. Of special interest is the development of a **rodent version of the WCST** (see Figure 20.5A). In the animal task, rodents are presented with pairs of bowls to dig into. Only one has a food reward. Unlike the human version, which requires sorting cards by color, shape, or number, the animals must choose the bowl on the basis of either odor or surface texture. Because of its similarity to the WCST, if this task is fully validated, it would be expected to have good translation to human behavior.

One very different type of model is based on evidence that schizophrenic individuals fail to "gate," or filter, most of the sensory stimuli they experience. Such a defect may lead to sensory overload and fragmented thinking because schizophrenic individuals are overwhelmed by sights and sounds and odors in the environment that they cannot filter out. The acoustic startle response is one of the most reliable and generalizable models used to study sensory-filtering deficits, and it can be used easily in both animals and human subjects. Reversal of induced sensory-filtering deficits predicts antipsychotic effects. Furthermore, when deficits are induced by administration of glutamate antagonists like phencyclidine (PCP), it is a screening device that distinguishes between classical and atypical antipsychotics. Web Box 20.2 describes the technique called **prepulse inhibition of startle** (**PPI**) and demonstrates the elegance of this model.

Since schizophrenia is a developmental disorder, models based on interfering with normal prenatal brain development have been developed. Many of the neurodevelopmental models are based on the epidemiological findings discussed earlier. That means that investigators subject pregnant rodents to inadequate diets, viral infections, elevated pro-inflammatory cytokines, or stressors that elevate glucocorticoids, or create complications during delivery such as hypoxia. Each of these methods alters development of brain circuitry, produces neurochemical aberrations, and causes behavioral deficits that mimic some of the pathophysiology of schizophrenia. Since several methods produce a developmental delay in the onset of abnormalities, they may be particularly important for understanding the etiology of the disorder. One such model, the **neonatal ventral hippocampal lesion model** (**NVHL**), is described in **Box 20.2**.

As you probably suspect, there is a good deal of interest in creating **genetic models** with the hope that by modifying a schizophrenia-susceptibility gene, abnormal behavior that is relevant to schizophrenia is produced. This may entail creating knockout, knock-in, or transgenic mice (see Chapter 4). For instance, when the gene for the dopamine reuptake transporter is deleted, the animals show hyperactivity in novel environments, deficits in PPI, stereotyped movements, and spatial learning impairments, each of which can be linked to schizophrenic behavior.

Section Summary

- Imaging shows cerebral atrophy, enlargement of ventricles, smaller basal ganglia, temporal lobe, and hippocampus in schizophrenic patients. Hippocampal cells are disorganized. Lack of gliosis indicates developmental error rather than degeneration.

- Brain function deficits include hypofrontality during tasks of working memory, executive function, response inhibition, and planning and strategy.

- Eye-movement dysfunctions and altered EEG patterns in response to stimulus presentation are biomarkers for schizophrenia.

- Family studies show that relatives of individuals with schizophrenia have increased risk for the disorder. The closer the genetic relationship, the greater is the risk.

- Concordance for schizophrenia is much higher in monozygotic than dizygotic twins, indicating significant genetic contribution.

- Linkage studies and genome-wide association studies have identified numerous gene variants that may each contribute a small amount to the increased risk for schizophrenia.

- Mutations of the *DISC1* gene increase the probability of developing schizophrenia. This gene codes for proteins necessary for embryonic brain development.

- Gene variants are associated with EEG abnormalities, impaired cognitive function, and brain volume reductions.

- Perinatal events such as stress during pregnancy and delivery, exposure to viral infection, and malnutrition may alter the trajectory of brain development and predispose the individual to schizophrenia.

- Behavioral abnormalities, apparent in young children who later develop schizophrenia, suggest early developmental errors. Other developmental errors during adolescence cause twice the cell loss in cortical areas compared with that seen in healthy teens.

- Animal models of schizophrenia created by pharmacological or environmental manipulations generally focus on one aspect of the disorder and induce similar changes in animal behavior. Neurodevelopmental models and genetic mutations are also used.

Neurochemical Models of Schizophrenia

To identify the neurochemical basis for any mental disorder, three general approaches can be taken. First, neurochemical correlates of animal and human models of the disorder can be studied. Second, the neuronal mechanisms of effective drug treatment are considered, keeping in mind that it is dangerous to assume that because the neurochemical effects of a drug reverse the symptoms, the drug is acting at the specific site of the disorder. Third, the functioning of neurotransmitter systems in patient populations is assessed by measuring neurochemicals in blood, cerebrospinal fluid (CSF), or urine, or in postmortem brain tissue. Brain imaging techniques provide the newest way of evaluating CNS function in patient populations. Based on these three approaches, evidence strongly suggests that although several neurotransmitters probably play a role in schizophrenic symptoms, malfunction of dopaminergic transmission is almost certainly involved.

Abnormal dopamine function contributes to schizophrenic symptoms

The finding that amphetamine can produce a psychotic reaction in healthy individuals that can be reversed

BOX 20.2   Pharmacology in Action

The Neonatal Ventral Hippocampal Lesion Model of Schizophrenia

The neonatal ventral hippocampal model (NVHL) was originally developed by Lipska and Weinberger and recently was reviewed extensively (Tseng et al., 2009). This model has been validated by a large number of studies. It is important because it demonstrates how a single neurobiological defect early in life can be responsible for producing later physiological and behavioral abnormalities reminiscent of the complex syndrome of schizophrenia, including some positive, negative, and cognitive symptoms. It involves lesioning the ventral hippocampus at postnatal day 7, a time corresponding to the human second trimester, a period of fetal hippocampal vulnerability.

Timeline of the behavioral syndrome of the NVHL model The upper timeline shows the emergence of behavioral changes in rats following neonatal ventral hippocampal lesioning in comparison with the occurrence of symptoms in schizophrenic individuals (lower timeline). As in human patients, negative-like symptoms and cognitive deficits appear early in rodents, whereas positive-like symptoms occur at a time corresponding to late human adolescence or early adulthood. (After Tseng et al., 2009.)

Although the young animals at day 35 behave normally, the lesion apparently alters the trajectory of brain development such that those same animals during post-adolescence (day 56) show significantly greater hyperactivity to stimuli such as mild stress, novelty, amphetamine, and apomorphine. The fact that these stimuli cause DA efflux suggests that the early lesion may produce an increased mesolimbic DA response as the animals mature—an effect supportive of the DA hypothesis of schizophrenia. Haloperidol and other antipsychotic drugs that block DA receptors can prevent the emergence of hyperactivity. Other parallels to the positive symptoms of the disorder such as abnormal PPI and increased sensitivity to glutamate antagonists also appear at this time.

It is especially interesting that those animals who did not show DA hyperresponsivity until day 56 did display analogues of negative symptoms at day 35 as well as day 56. Among the deficits is reduced social interaction, a hallmark feature of schizophrenia that occurs much earlier than the positive symptoms. Cognitive impairments are also evident in the animals, as demonstrated by deficits in the Morris water maze and tests of working memory. These deficits occur both early and later, and some may be analogous to the subtle impairments that schizophrenic individuals show before the onset of psychosis. It is of significance that injecting tetrodotoxin, which prevents action potentials by blocking voltage-gated sodium channels, into the hippocampus at day 7 produces a similar phenotype and timing of deficit onset without

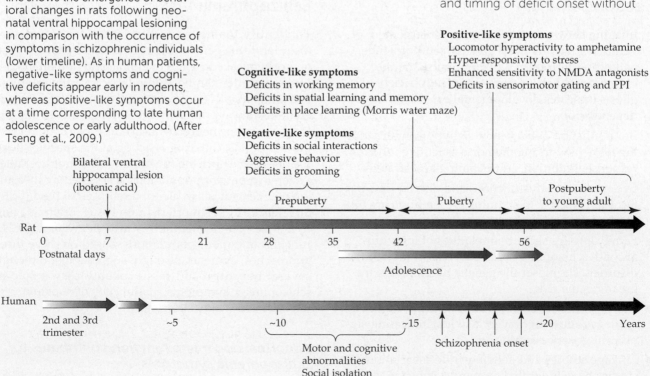

BOX 20.2 *(continued)*

causing a lesion. These results suggest that even temporary interruption of hippocampal function, if it occurs at a critical time of development, impairs further development of associated neural circuits. A timeline for the appearance of behavioral deficits is provided in the figure. Particularly fascinating is the observation that, just as symptoms vary among schizophrenic patients, the effects of lesions of the same size in various rat strains produce different phenotypes and differences in age at onset of the behavioral deficits. Of additional interest is that brief social isolation of young NVHL rats exaggerates the neurochemical, behavioral, and physiological outcomes. Other forms of stress produce similar enhancement.

A fascinating line of research has also shown that early hippocampal lesions affect the development of several other brain areas implicated in schizophrenia including the prefrontal cortex, the medial temporal lobe, and the nucleus accumbens. For instance, it is suspected that loss of hippocampal input to PFC is responsible for the decreased dendritic length and spine density that are characteristic of NVHL animals. A developmentally delayed change in the balance of dopamine–glutamate interactions also has been seen in the PFC of these animals, which might be expected to contribute to hypofrontality in patients (see later in this chapter).

---

by dopamine (DA) antagonists initially suggested the **dopamine hypothesis** of schizophrenia. Also, patients with schizophrenia who have been given amphetamine and cocaine say that the drugs make their symptoms worse but do not produce different symptoms. In addition, stereotyped behavior in rats can be elicited by intracerebral injection of amphetamine into forebrain DA areas and can be blocked by administration of DA receptor blockers, such as haloperidol.

As you will see in the following section, there is a strong correlation between D_2 receptor blockade and effectiveness in reducing schizophrenic symptoms. Finally, the finding that antipsychotic treatment induces changes in DA turnover, as determined by plasma levels of the dopamine metabolite homovanillic acid (HVA), further supports the DA hypothesis of schizophrenia, which suggests that excess DA function is related to the manifestation of the positive symptoms.

Of the approaches used to understand the neurochemistry of schizophrenia, evaluation of DA functioning in patient populations has been the least consistent. To substantiate the DA hypothesis, we would expect to see an increase in DA activity either through increased turnover (synthesis, release, metabolism) or by altered receptor number. Although the change in the dopamine metabolite HVA in response to antipsychotic treatment (i.e., an initial increase followed by a significant decrease over several weeks) predicts treatment outcome, under baseline (nondrug) conditions neither plasma nor CSF HVA levels are consistently different in patients with schizophrenia compared with control subjects. Nor are HVA levels correlated with symptom type or severity (Friedhoff and Silva, 1995). These data might be interpreted to mean that DA functioning is not increased in the brains of individuals with schizophrenia.

However, Laruelle and colleagues (1999) found that in patients with schizophrenia, a challenge dose of amphetamine elicited a significantly greater release of DA than was seen in control subjects. This effect was found at the onset of illness and in patients who had never taken antipsychotic drugs. Hence the hyperdopaminergic state is not due to prolonged illness, hospitalization, or chronic drug treatment. Further, a correlation was found between the exaggerated DA response and worsening of the positive symptoms. Other evidence for DA involvement comes from several studies that found increased D_2 receptors in the basal ganglia, nucleus accumbens, and substantia nigra of postmortem schizophrenic brains. PET scan quantification of DA receptors also suggests increased D_2 receptors in drug-free patients with schizophrenia, particularly in patients with positive symptoms as well as in those who are more acutely ill (Kahn and Davis, 1995).

Much of the evidence has been synthesized into a **DA imbalance hypothesis**, as described by Davis and colleagues (1991). They suggest that schizophrenic symptoms are due to reduced DA function in mesocortical neurons along with excess DA function in mesolimbic dopaminergic neurons. The negative symptoms and impaired thinking may be explained by impaired PFC function (low mesocortical activity). In contrast, positive symptoms seem to be improved by reducing DA function in mesolimbic neurons.

The neurodevelopmental model integrates anatomical and neurochemical evidence

Weinberger (1995) has developed a **neurodevelopmental model** that combines evidence of altered dopaminergic function with the loss of specific nerve cells (as described earlier in the section on etiology) and symptom clusters. The first part of the model is supported by several pieces of evidence that associate negative symptoms (flat affect, social withdrawal, lack of motivation, poor insight, and intellectual impairment) and cognitive symptoms (poor executive function, lack of attention, and so forth) with reduced frontal lobe function. First, the negative symptoms of schizophrenia resemble the characteristics of patients with lesions of the frontal lobe (e.g., following frontal lobotomy). Also, the severity of the negative symptoms is correlated with reduced prefrontal cell metabolism when evaluated by PET scan. In addition, neuropsychological testing in humans shows a relationship between poor performance on tasks requiring frontal lobe function, reduced cerebral blood flow in the PFC, and decreased DA function as determined by lowered CSF HVA. Further, in animal experiments, prefrontal lesions produce deficits in behaviors that require insight and strategy. Intracerebral injection of D_1 receptor antagonists impairs delayed-response performance and produces impulsivity and deficits in responding for delayed reward. Conversely, D_1 agonists improve cognitive deficits caused by injection of a DA neurotoxin into the PFC. These experiments indicate an important role for DA acting at the D_1 receptor in PFC in cognitive processes. Animal studies also implicate mesocortical cells in normal response to stress. Mesocortical cells are cells originating in the ventral tegmental area (VTA) that innervate the frontal cortex and other cortical areas. These cells respond with increased DA turnover not only to acute stress but also to learned stress, for instance, when an animal is returned to a previously stressful environment. In summary, these results suggest that the onset of negative symptoms of schizophrenia is due to the occurrence of early mesocortical failure. However, although the cell loss occurs relatively early in life, the abnormal behavior may not appear until the system would normally reach functional maturity (i.e., after puberty, when development, myelination, and synaptic pruning are complete). Thus complex cognitive functions, including insightful behavior and the ability to respond to the social stresses commonly occurring at adolescence, would be expected to be compromised.

The second part of the model attempts to explain positive symptoms of schizophrenia with evidence of hyperactive subcortical cells. In animal studies, lesioning of prefrontal dopaminergic neurons produces chronic subcortical DA hyperactivity, manifested by increased DA turnover (Kahn and Davis, 1995). In addition, when DA agonists such as apomorphine are injected into the PFC, DA metabolites are reduced in the striatum. Thus when the inhibitory cortical feedback is lost, mesolimbic cells increase their activity.

Furthermore, studies of epileptic patients suggest that psychotic experiences, hallucinations, perceptual distortions, and irrational fears are associated with electrical discharge in limbic regions. Thus Weinberger (1995) suggests that excessive mesolimbic DA activity following mesocortical cell loss could explain the more dramatic positive symptoms of schizophrenia. Those are the same symptoms that are most readily reversed by antipsychotic-induced DA receptor blockade.

The neurodevelopmental model makes no attempt to identify the cause of the proposed early mesocortical cell loss. The defect could be due to one of many factors, including genetically programmed errors, inadequate maternal nutrition, obstetrical complications, viral infection, and other possibilities discussed earlier in the chapter. Weinberger argues that such a lesion produces few symptoms early in life, but reveals itself later, at a time when social stresses demand maximum prefrontal cognitive function. Loss of the DA input prevents the individual from making appropriate responses and instead leads to confused thinking, perseveration of inappropriate behavior, and social withdrawal. The loss of inhibitory cortical feedback onto subcortical neurons plus the stress-induced increase in mesolimbic cell function leads to agitation, fearfulness, and hallucinations. The appeal of this model of schizophrenia is in its ability to incorporate many distinct pieces of the puzzle (neurochemical, anatomical, and developmental pieces, and social stress). It also provides several testable hypotheses on which future research can be designed.

Glutamate and other neurotransmitters contribute to symptoms

Since glutamate is known to have an important role in learning and memory as well as synaptic plasticity (see Chapter 8), glutamate hypofunction in schizophrenia may explain the negative symptoms, abnormal cognitive function, and impaired neural connectivity seen in schizophrenia. Since there is a great deal of similarity in the cognitive deficits caused by either D_1 or N-methyl-D-aspartate (NMDA) receptor blockade, it is clear that both receptors contribute to working memory processes. Inadequate glutamate may be a precursor to the DA dysfunction and may explain the apparent *increase* in mesolimbic DA and *decrease* in PFC. **Figure 20.10A** shows the relationship of the brain structures involved and how descending glutamatergic neurons influence both DA pathways. **Figure 20.10B** is a schematic diagram that shows the details of the glutamate–dopamine interaction. Descending excitatory glutamatergic cells (green) projecting from the PFC activate NMDA receptors on mesocortical DA cells (black) in the VTA. These mesocortical DA

(A)

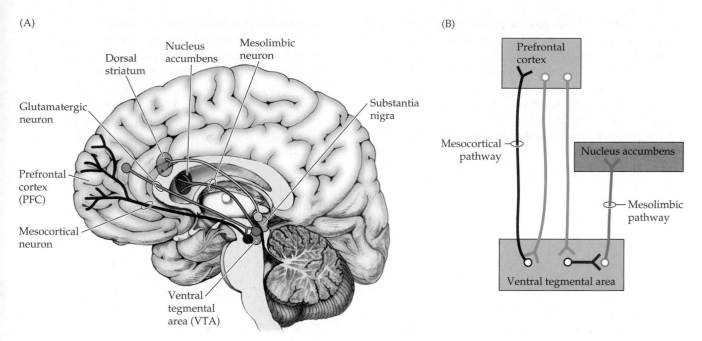

(B)

Figure 20.10 Hypoglutamate hypothesis of schizophrenia (A) Midsagittal view showing nigrostriatal (yellow), mesolimbic (blue), and mesocortical (black) dopaminergic neurons as well as the descending glutamatergic neurons (green) originating in the prefrontal cortex (PFC). (B) Since descending glutamate neurons (green) excite mesocortical DA neurons (black), poor glutamate signaling would produce low DA release in PFC, exacerbating negative and cognitive symptoms. Other glutamate neurons (green) excite inhibitory GABA neurons (red) that subsequently inhibit the dopaminergic mesolimbic pathway. (These tiny neurons within the VTA could not be depicted in part A.) In this case, low glutamate signaling would fail to inhibit mesolimbic firing, leading to excess DA release in the nucleus accumbens and positive symptoms.

cells reciprocally project back to the cortex. If glutamate levels are insufficient to activate mesocortical cells, low cortical DA neurotransmission and subsequent low D_1 receptor activation will lead to deficits in working memory and negative symptoms. In contrast, other PFC glutamatergic neurons acting on NMDA receptors have indirect *inhibitory* control of midbrain mesolimbic DA neurons (blue) that project to limbic regions. This happens because the glutamate neurons excite midbrain GABA cells (red; not shown in Part A) that have an inhibitory effect on mesolimbic DA neurons. In this case, low levels of glutamate signaling would fail to inhibit mesolimbic neurons and would produce excessive DA release and associated positive symptoms, which can be relieved with DA receptor blocking antipsychotic drugs. Evidence in support of this relationship was demonstrated in rats by blocking NMDA receptors in VTA, which resulted in an increase in DA release in the nucleus accumbens and

reduced release of DA in the PFC. Hence the PFC provides tonic inhibition of mesolimbic neurons and tonic excitatory regulation of mesocortical cells. A more detailed discussion of glutamate–dopamine interaction is provided by Winterer and Weinberger (2004).

Challenge studies consistently show that blocking the glutamatergic NMDA receptor with PCP ("angel dust") or ketamine produces a psychotic syndrome that closely resembles schizophrenia in healthy individuals and exacerbates symptoms in schizophrenic patients. Of special significance is the fact that PCP and ketamine produced both the positive and negative symptoms of schizophrenia. Some direct evidence for low CSF glutamate levels in patients with schizophrenia compared with controls has been found, although the differences are not consistent. More consistently, in postmortem studies, decreased levels are reported for both glutamate and aspartate in PFC and hippocampus compared with controls. Additionally, some studies have found that lower levels of the amino acid are correlated with greater brain atrophy and cognitive impairment. Also, in synaptosomes (i.e., preparation of isolated nerve terminals) prepared from the postmortem brains of patients with schizophrenia, depolarization-induced release of glutamate is reduced. Finally, changes in glutamate receptor subunit composition in several brain areas of individuals with schizophrenia have been described, and these may affect the quality of glutamate signaling (Ulas and Cotman, 1993). Of particular interest is that the antipsychotic drug clozapine interacts with the glutamate receptor and increases glutamate levels in the PFC of rats, which may explain the drug's unique ability to reduce negative and cognitive symptoms in patients (see the section on atypical antipsychotics). This characteristic of clozapine suggests that glutamate may be a new target for the development of antipsychotic drugs (see the final section of this chapter). For a more detailed discussion of the interaction of glutamate and DA in the production of schizophrenic symptoms and its potential therapeutic benefits, see Yang and Chen (2005).

Because the circuitry of the limbic structures and of the frontal cortex is complex, it is not surprising that many other neurotransmitters modulate or interact with DA transmission. Acetylcholine, GABA, norepinephrine, serotonin, and endorphins each may play a part in the presentation of individual symptoms of the disorder.

Section Summary

- To understand the neurobiology of any psychiatric disorder, researchers create animal models, evaluate mechanisms of effective drug treatment, and measure biological substances in patients or image their brains.

- The dopamine hypothesis suggests that positive symptoms are caused by excessive mesolimbic DA activity. Evidence includes the following: (1) amphetamine produces positive symptoms in healthy subjects and makes symptoms worse in schizophrenic patients; (2) intracerebral DA into the forebrain of rodents produces stereotyped behavior reversed by antipsychotics; (3) a strong correlation exits between D_2 receptor blockade and antipsychotic efficacy; (4) schizophrenic individuals show exaggerated DA release after amphetamine challenge as well as in basal conditions; and (5) there is some evidence for increased D_2 receptors in schizophrenia.

- Evidence that the negative and cognitive symptoms are due to reduced frontal lobe function includes the following: (1) the negative/cognitive symptoms resemble characteristics after frontal lobotomy; (2) the severity of negative symptoms is negatively correlated with prefrontal brain activity and decreased DA function; and (3) prefrontal brain lesions or D_1 receptor antagonists into PFC impair cognitive performance.

- The neurodevelopmental model suggests that early mesocortical deficits due to genetics or environmental events that alter brain development are followed by loss of inhibitory control of mesolimbic cells and the onset of positive symptoms.

- Poor glutamate signaling may be responsible for positive, negative, and cognitive symptoms and corresponding changes in DA activity.

- Descending glutamate neurons from PFC activate mesocortical neurons. Low glutamate (or NMDA receptor antagonist) reduces mesocortical function, causing negative/cognitive symptoms.

- Descending glutamate neurons from PFC activate midbrain inhibitory GABA cells that reduce mesolimbic DA cell firing. Low glutamate (or NMDA receptor antagonist) prevents the inhibition, leading to excessive mesolimbic firing and positive symptoms.

- The NMDA receptor antagonists PCP and ketamine produce psychotic symptoms and make psychosis in schizophrenic patients worse.

- Low levels of glutamate are found in hippocampus and PFC of schizophrenic patients postmortem, and low levels are correlated with greater brain atrophy. Glutamate release is lower in schizophrenic patients than in controls, and glutamate receptor subunits are different.

Classic Neuroleptics and Atypical Antipsychotics

Drugs useful in treating schizophrenia are called antipsychotic drugs or **neuroleptics**, an older term that refers to their ability to selectively reduce emotionality and psychomotor activity. A large number of drugs are included in this category, and they are commonly divided into two classes: traditional neuroleptics and the newer second-generation (often called "atypical") antipsychotics. Although none of the drugs is consistently more effective than the others, a particular individual may respond better to one drug than to another. Therefore, treatment may require testing several antipsychotic drugs to find the one that is most effective for a given patient. The classic antipsychotic drugs are the phenothiazines, such as chlorpromazine (Thorazine), and the butyrophenones, such as haloperidol (Haldol). The second-generation antipsychotics, such as clozapine (Clozaril), risperidone (Risperdal), and aripiprazole (Abilify) are noteworthy because they appear to produce fewer side effects involving abnormal movements (e.g., tremors, rigidity).

Phenothiazines and butyrophenones are traditional neuroleptics

Chlorpromazine was the first phenothiazine used in psychiatry, but many small changes in the shape of the drug molecule produced a family of related compounds that differ in potency, clinical effectiveness, and side effects. **Figure 20.11** shows the three-ring phenothiazine nucleus and the structural

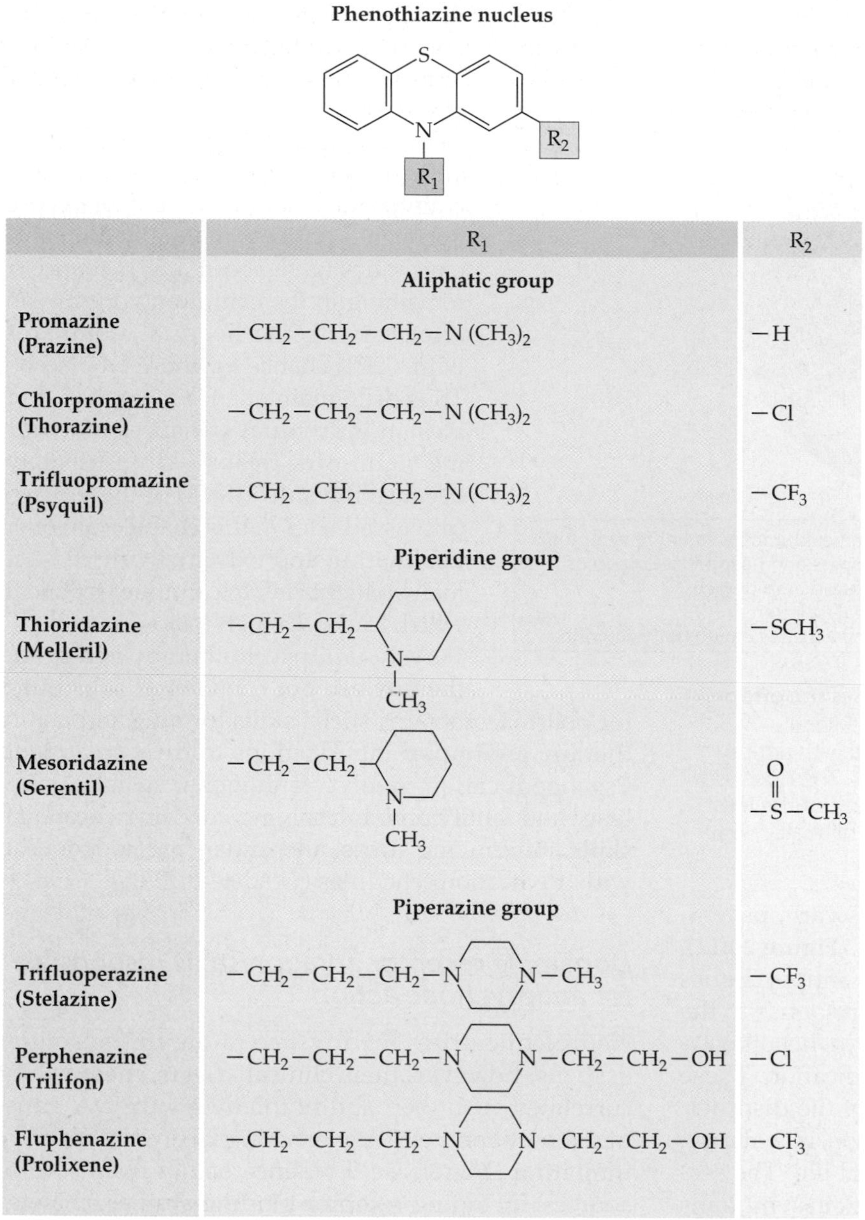

Phenothiazine nucleus

	R_1		R_2
	Aliphatic group		
Promazine (Prazine)	$-CH_2-CH_2-CH_2-N(CH_3)_2$		$-H$
Chlorpromazine (Thorazine)	$-CH_2-CH_2-CH_2-N(CH_3)_2$		$-Cl$
Trifluopromazine (Psyquil)	$-CH_2-CH_2-CH_2-N(CH_3)_2$		$-CF_3$
	Piperidine group		
Thioridazine (Melleril)	$-CH_2-CH_2-$ (piperidine, N–CH$_3$)		$-SCH_3$
Mesoridazine (Serentil)	$-CH_2-CH_2-$ (piperidine, N–CH$_3$)		$-S(=O)-CH_3$
	Piperazine group		
Trifluoperazine (Stelazine)	$-CH_2-CH_2-CH_2-N$ (piperazine) $N-CH_3$		$-CF_3$
Perphenazine (Trilifon)	$-CH_2-CH_2-CH_2-N$ (piperazine) $N-CH_2-CH_2-OH$		$-Cl$
Fluphenazine (Prolixene)	$-CH_2-CH_2-CH_2-N$ (piperazine) $N-CH_2-CH_2-OH$		$-CF_3$

Figure 20.11 Phenothiazine nucleus and related compounds Minor molecular modifications determine the three major subgroups of phenothiazines and change drug potency, pharmacological activity, and side effects.

relationships of several other drugs in this class. By changing the chemical groups at the R_1 and R_2 positions, many new compounds can be created that vary in their effects. For example, chlorpromazine (which has a chlorine at R_2) is much more potent than promazine (which has hydrogen at the R_2 position). By substituting at R_1, an antipsychotic (thioridazine [Melleril]) with fewer motor side effects is created. Further changes at R_1 and R_2 produce drugs (trifluoperazine [Stelazine], fluphenazine [Prolixene]) that further vary in potency and side effects. This structure–activity relationship provides clear evidence that molecular modifications alter the ability of the drugs to bind to specific receptor recognition sites in the cell membranes.

EFFECTIVENESS The introduction of antipsychotic drugs during the 1950s dramatically improved the treatment of schizophrenic patients. The effectiveness of these drugs has been demonstrated hundreds of times in double-blind, placebo-controlled trials. For a significant number of patients, the antipsychotics are more effective than placebo in reducing symptoms and decreasing the average length of hospitalization. After only a few doses, the hyperactive and manic symptoms usually disappear, whereas the positive symptoms of schizophrenia may gradually improve over several weeks. Delusions, hallucinations, and disordered thinking are reduced, and improvements in insight, judgment, self-care, and seclusiveness are seen. More resistant to treatment are the negative and cognitive symptoms of schizophrenia.

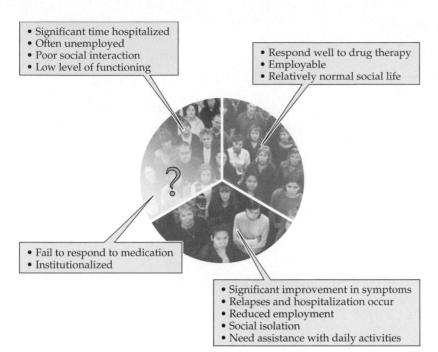

- Significant time hospitalized
- Often unemployed
- Poor social interaction
- Low level of functioning

- Respond well to drug therapy
- Employable
- Relatively normal social life

- Fail to respond to medication
- Institutionalized

- Significant improvement in symptoms
- Relapses and hospitalization occur
- Reduced employment
- Social isolation
- Need assistance with daily activities

Figure 20.12 The law of thirds approximates the effectiveness of antipsychotic drug treatment Overall, approximately two thirds of patients treated with antipsychotic drugs show significant improvement. The question mark indicates that some unspecified fraction of the least responsive third fails to respond to treatment at all.

Although estimates of effectiveness vary, psychiatrists often refer to the **law of thirds** (**Figure 20.12**). One third of the patients treated with antipsychotics show excellent symptom reduction in response to the drugs and may not experience subsequent hospitalizations even when they discontinue medication. These individuals show few residual signs of the disorder. They are employed outside the institution, may marry, and maintain a relatively normal social life. The second third show significant improvement in symptoms but may experience relapses that require hospitalization from time to time. These individuals may be employed, although usually at a reduced occupational level, and they may remain socially isolated. Some require significant help in day-to-day living, for example, in maintaining personal hygiene, preparing meals, or keeping scheduled appointments. The final third show a lesser degree of recovery and may spend a significant amount of time each year in a psychiatric institution. These patients need much more help in dealing with the stresses of everyday living. Since many of the behavioral abnormalities remain, these individuals are often unemployed, have few social relationships, and exist on the margins of society. Some portion of this final third fail to respond to any drug treatment and remain institutionalized. Estimates suggest that more

than 30% of the adult homeless population in the United States may suffer from unmedicated or inadequately medicated psychosis.

Following a patient's initial recovery, antipsychotic drugs are prescribed as maintenance therapy to prevent relapse. Recovered patients maintained on antipsychotics have about a 55% chance of remaining in the community for 2 years after leaving the hospital, compared with a 20% chance for those on placebo. Thus drug maintenance more than doubles an individual's chances of avoiding significant relapse. Unfortunately, because the side effects of these drugs (discussed later in this chapter) are often debilitating and extremely unpleasant, many patients fail to continue treatment, which leads to a high relapse rate.

Although psychotherapy and group therapy are not considered substitutes for pharmacotherapy, social skills training and family therapy are important additions to drug treatment. Psychoeducation involves enhancing social competence and family problem solving, teaching vocational skills, minimizing stress, and enhancing cooperation with medication schedules (Goldstein, 1995).

Dopamine receptor antagonism is responsible for antipsychotic action

Neuroleptic drugs modify several neurotransmitter systems; however, their clinical effectiveness is best correlated with their ability to antagonize DA transmission by competitively blocking DA receptors or by inhibiting DA release. Evidence comes from several sources, including receptor binding studies, changes in DA turnover, second-messenger function, and neuroendocrine effects.

RECEPTOR BINDING Both first- and second-generation antipsychotics block D_2 receptors. A strong positive correlation exists between the ability of antipsychotic drugs to displace a labeled ligand on DA receptors and average clinical daily dose (**Figure 20.13A**). Drugs that readily bind to the DA receptor at low concentration because of their high affinity also reduce symptoms at low doses. Likewise, antipsychotics that require higher concentrations to bind to DA receptors require higher doses to be clinically effective. Although antipsychotic drugs bind to other neurotransmitter receptors in addition to DA, there is no clear relationship between clinical effectiveness and binding to serotonin (**Figure**

Figure 20.13 Correlation between antipsychotic drug binding to neurotransmitter receptors and clinical effectiveness The receptor binding studies were accomplished by first labeling the receptors with an appropriate radioactive ligand for each neurotransmitter. The antipsychotic drug was added in increasing concentrations until it competed successfully for half of the labeled sites. That value (K_i) is plotted along the x-axis, and the corresponding average clinical daily dose for that drug is plotted on the y-axis. A clear positive correlation is found for dopamine receptor binding (A), but serotonin receptor binding shows no apparent correlation with effectiveness (B). Further experiments found no correlation between clinical effects and binding to either α-adrenergic or histamine receptors. (After Snyder, 1996.)

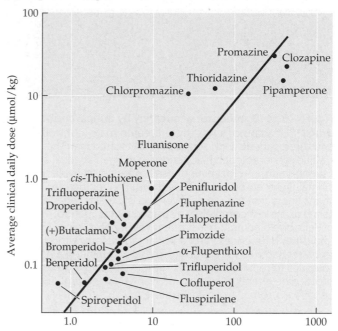

(A) Dopamine receptors

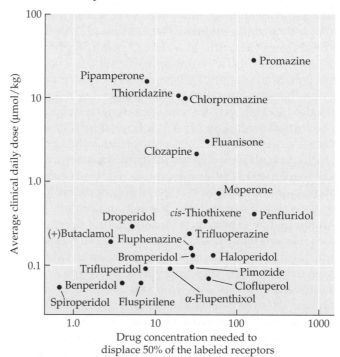

(B) Serotonin receptors

20.13B), α-adrenergic, or histamine receptors. Nor is there a correlation for D_1 receptor binding. Therefore, the correlation with DA_2 receptor binding establishes quite clearly the mechanism of antipsychotic drug action.

Neuroleptics have a particularly high affinity for D_2 receptors, which serve as both normal postsynaptic receptors and autoreceptors and are located in the basal ganglia, nucleus accumbens, amygdala, hippocampus, and cerebral cortex. **Figure 20.14** shows a series of PET images in which D_2 receptors in the basal ganglia were labeled with [^{11}C]raclopride. The bright areas show the binding of the labeled drug to D_2 receptors. The control is a scan of a healthy man injected only with the [^{11}C]raclopride to show maximum binding. The remaining scans are from schizophrenic patients given [^{11}C]raclopride in addition to one of the antipsychotic drugs. Reduction of radioactive ligand binding indicates competition for the sites. Striatal D_2 receptors were almost completely blocked by haloperidol and risperidone, but clozapine had less affinity. Although a drug's ability to bind to the D_2 receptor is closely correlated with its effectiveness in reducing psychotic symptoms, some of the atypical antipsychotics, such as clozapine, may produce their unique effects by acting on a combination of receptor types.

In addition to reducing dopaminergic transmission by blocking postsynaptic D_2 receptors, the antipsychotics also readily block D_2 autoreceptors. The inhibitory autoreceptors are responsible for controlling the rate of firing of the cell as well as the rate of synthesis and release of neurotransmitter. Applying a DA agonist, such as apomorphine, to the DA cell bodies in the substantia nigra (origin of nigrostriatal cells) or ventral tegmentum (origin of mesolimbic and mesocortical neurons) stimulates the autoreceptors and decreases the rate of firing of the dopaminergic neurons. This inhibition is antagonized by administration of an effective neuroleptic drug such as chlorpromazine, but not by an inactive phenothiazine. The increase in

firing rate after antipsychotic administration is accompanied by increased turnover (synthesis, release, and metabolism) of DA.

DA TURNOVER Clinical response to antipsychotic treatment is associated with an initial increase in dopamine metabolism, which is determined by measuring the

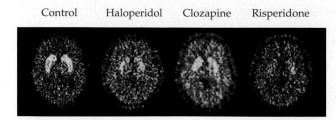

Control   Haloperidol   Clozapine   Risperidone

Figure 20.14 D₂ receptor occupancy by antipsychotic drugs PET scans of a healthy, untreated male (control) and three patients with schizophrenia treated with the traditional neuroleptic haloperidol or with an atypical antipsychotic drug—clozapine or risperidone. In all subjects, striatal D₂ receptors were labeled with [¹¹C]raclopride. The scans show that the radioactive label of striatal D₂ receptors was almost completely displaced by haloperidol and risperidone binding but less effectively by clozapine. These and other differences in receptor antagonism are thought to be responsible for the ability of the clozapine-like neuroleptics to reduce symptoms without producing serious motor side effects. (Courtesy of Svante Nyberg and Anna-Lena Nordstöm, Karolinska Institute.)

concentration of the principal DA metabolite, HVA. An increase in metabolism is assumed to reflect an increase in neurotransmitter release. The increase in DA utilization follows the acute blockade of autoreceptors on dopaminergic cells. If the dopamine hypothesis is correct, this enhanced synaptic DA should make the symptoms worse. However, recall that postsynaptic DA receptors are also blocked, so there is no worsening of symptoms. The initial increase in HVA is followed by a gradual decrease with chronic treatment because the chronic blockade with neuroleptics leads to supersensitivity (up-regulation) of the autoreceptors. The up-regulation once again allows them to respond appropriately to DA by reducing DA synthesis, release, and metabolism. An alternative explanation for the gradual decrease in turnover, originally posed by Grace (1992), suggests that after the initial neuroleptic-induced increase in DA turnover, dopaminergic cells have the ability to temporarily inactivate themselves. This temporary inactivation, called depolarization block, would reduce the release of DA and its subsequent metabolism. The time-dependent change in receptors and the depolarization block help to explain the gradual onset of effectiveness of antipsychotic drugs.

PROLACTIN RELEASE Further evidence for DA receptor blockade comes from neuroendocrine measures of prolactin. Under normal conditions, DA inhibits prolactin release. By blocking D₂ receptors in the pituitary gland, neuroleptics stimulate the secretion of prolactin, which leads to lactation and breast enlargement, even in males, disturbing side effects of antipsychotic drug use. Measuring serum prolactin in patients provides an easy measure of D₂ receptor function in the CNS.

SLOW HOMEOSTATIC CHANGES Although the clinical effectiveness of antipsychotics is closely correlated with dopamine receptor blockade, the time courses of the two events are significantly different. Since the receptor blockade is almost immediate, it is surprising that several weeks of treatment are necessary before symptoms begin to subside. This disparity in time course suggests that the drugs are not directly targeting the locus of the disorder but are gradually inducing the nervous system to make adaptive changes that lead to clinical improvement. Some of the slow homeostatic changes that occur over time are depolarization block, change in receptor number, and altered dopamine turnover.

Side effects are directly related to neurochemical action

Unfortunately, both traditional and atypical antipsychotic drugs frequently produce a large number of side effects, some of which are so disturbing that nonhospitalized patients stop taking the drug and suffer a relapse of psychiatric symptoms. Each drug may have different potential side effects based on the neurotransmitter receptors it binds to. Because patient compliance (cooperation in following the treatment schedule) is a large problem, clinicians most often choose the neuroleptic to prescribe on the basis of minimizing the side effects for a given patient. **Table 20.1** summarizes some of the benefits and side effects associated with the blockade of various receptors.

Neuroleptic-induced DA receptor antagonism occurs in each of the DA pathways described in Chapter 5 and is responsible not only for the clinical effectiveness of antipsychotics but also for many of their side effects. There are four dopamine pathways in the brain that are important for understanding antipsychotic drug action, three of which are illustrated in Figure 20.10A.

1. The mesolimbic pathway projects from the ventral tegmental area to the nucleus accumbens and other limbic areas. It is involved in many behaviors, as well as in the pleasure derived from drugs of abuse and the delusions and hallucinations of schizophrenia. It is reasonable to consider the mesolimbic pathway as the site for the drug-induced reduction of positive symptoms.

2. The mesocortical pathway also projects from the ventral tegmental area but sends axons to the prefrontal and limbic cortex, where it may have a role in the cognitive effects and negative symptoms of schizophrenia.

3. The nigrostriatal pathway begins in the substantia nigra and projects to the striatum, where it contributes to the modulation of movement. Parkinsonian

TABLE 20.1 Clinical Implications of the Blockade of Various Receptors by Antipsychotics

Receptor	Possible benefits	Possible side effects
Dopamine D_2	Reduces positive symptoms	Extrapyramidal side effects (EPS) including parkinsonism, akathisia, tardive dyskinesia; endocrine effects such as prolactin secretion, menstrual changes, sexual dysfunction
Serotonin $5\text{-}HT_{2A}$	Reduced EPS?	Sexual dysfunction
Serotonin $5\text{-}HT_{2C}$	Unknown	Weight gain
Histamine H_1	Sedation	Sedation, increased appetite, weight gain, hypotension
Muscarinic cholinergic	Reduced EPS	Autonomic side effects such as blurred vision, dry mouth, constipation, urinary retention, tachycardia; memory dysfunction
α_1-adrenergic	Unknown	Orthostatic hypotension, dizziness, reflex tachycardia
α_2-adrenergic	Unknown	Drug interactions

symptoms are caused by insufficient DA binding to receptors in the striatum. Therefore, neuroleptic effects on nigrostriatal DA are likely to be responsible for parkinsonian tremors and other motor side effects.

4. Projecting from the hypothalamus to the pituitary gland are the short neurons that constitute the tuberohypophyseal pathway, which regulates pituitary hormone secretion. Blockade of DA receptors in this pathway is the likely source of the neuroendocrine side effects.

PARKINSONISM The most serious and troublesome side effects of classic antipsychotics are the movement disorders that resemble the symptoms of Parkinson's disease (see Chapter 21) and involve the extrapyramidal motor system (collectively called extrapyramidal side effects [EPS]). **Parkinsonian symptoms** include tremors, akinesia (slowing or loss of voluntary movement), muscle rigidity, akathisia (a strong feeling of discomfort in the legs and an inability to sit still, which compels the patient to get up and walk about), and loss of facial expression. We know that Parkinson's disease is caused by a loss of cell bodies in the substantia nigra, which gives rise to the nigrostriatal pathway (see Figure 20.10A). The lack of inhibitory dopamine function in the striatum (a subcortical brain area that modulates movement) causes excess cholinergic neural activity (**Figure 20.15**). Knowing that the classic antipsychotic drugs block dopamine receptors, we assume that drug-induced parkinsonism is due to dopamine blockade in that area

of the brain. To verify this hypothesis, experiments using PET showed that neuroleptic-treated patients with parkinsonian symptoms had *more* dopamine receptors of the D_2 type in the striatum than did those without those side effects (Farde et al., 1992). Such compensatory receptor up-regulation is likely to occur after reduced dopamine transmission. Therefore, it is assumed that the antipsychotic-induced tremors are due to the blockade of dopamine receptors in the striatum, the projection region of the nigrostriatal dopaminergic neurons. Since one way to treat the symptoms of Parkinson's disease is to reduce excess acetylcholine activity, neuroleptic drugs that have anticholinergic action were developed to minimize the parkinsonian side effects. One such example is thioridazine. Alternatively, combining antipsychotic drug treatment with an anticholinergic drug such as benztropine (Cogentin) is also a common treatment approach. In addition, several of the atypical antipsychotics, such as clozapine and risperidone, produce a lower-than-normal incidence of extrapyramidal side effects (see the section on atypical antipsychotics).

TARDIVE DYSKINESIA A second type of motor side effect associated with prolonged use of antipsychotic drugs is **tardive dyskinesia (TD)**. TD is characterized by stereotyped involuntary movements, particularly of the face and jaw, such as sucking and lip smacking, lateral jaw movements, and "fly-catching" movements of the tongue. There may also be purposeless, quick, and uncontrolled movements of the arms and legs or slow squirming movements of the trunk, limbs, and neck. Estimates suggest that

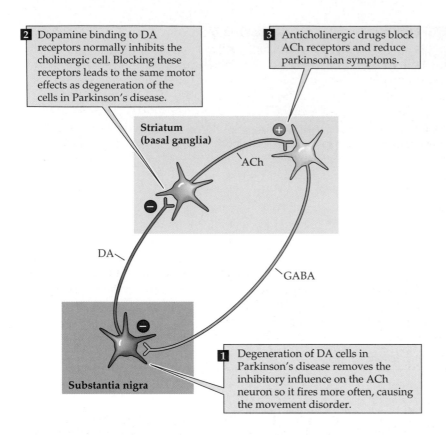

2 Dopamine binding to DA receptors normally inhibits the cholinergic cell. Blocking these receptors leads to the same motor effects as degeneration of the cells in Parkinson's disease.

3 Anticholinergic drugs block ACh receptors and reduce parkinsonian symptoms.

Striatum (basal ganglia)

ACh

DA

GABA

Substantia nigra

1 Degeneration of DA cells in Parkinson's disease removes the inhibitory influence on the ACh neuron so it fires more often, causing the movement disorder.

Figure 20.15 Schematic diagram showing the neurotransmitters involved in parkinsonian symptoms Parkinson's disease is caused by degeneration of the nigrostriatal dopaminergic neurons, which begin in the substantia nigra. The reduced dopaminergic cell function causes a loss of inhibitory control of the cholinergic cells in the striatum, so the cholinergic cells fire at higher rates. Drug-induced parkinsonian symptoms follow DA receptor blockade in the striatum and subsequent excess acetylcholine activity, which is functionally similar to the loss of dopaminergic cells in Parkinson's disease. Anticholinergic drugs reduce the symptoms of Parkinson's disease and the side effects of antipsychotic drug treatment.

TD appears in about 10% to 20% of patients treated with neuroleptics overall. Although TD may appear in any age group, the incidence increases to 50% in patients older than 60 years and may exceed 70% in geriatric patients. It is generally assumed that the dose of neuroleptic and the duration of treatment are related to the occurrence of TD. To demonstrate the importance of treatment duration, **Figure 20.16** shows the cumulative incidence of TD in a group of 362 chronic psychiatric patients who were maintained on antipsychotic drugs. The conclusion that two out of three patients maintained on antipsychotics for a period of 25 years will develop TD is a sobering one that should encourage further research into treatment strategies that minimize such side effects. Although the symptoms are considered to be irreversible in some patients, for many individuals improvement does gradually occur. However, in many cases, the symptoms are much worse when the drug is first terminated and persist for long periods after the withdrawal of neuroleptics. Reversal of TD occurs most readily in younger patients. Despite a good deal of research with both animal and human models, the underlying neuropathology responsible for TD is not known.

NEUROENDOCRINE EFFECTS   Blockade of receptors in the dopamine pathway that regulates pituitary function produces a variety of neuroendocrine effects. These effects include breast enlargement and tenderness, decreased sex drive, lack of menstruation, increased release of prolactin (frequently producing lactation), and inhibition of growth hormone release. Reduced growth hormone release represents a significant therapeutic issue when

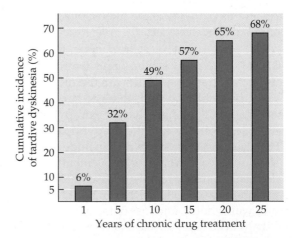

Figure 20.16 Cumulative incidence of tardive dyskinesia in a group of psychiatric patients maintained on antipsychotic medication. Evaluation of the patients showed an average incidence of approximately 6% for each of the first 5 years, with a cumulative incidence of 30% at the end of 5 years of chronic medication. By combining data, investigators estimated the 10-year and 25-year risks. Clearly, long-term treatment increases the probability of developing tardive dyskinesia.

children and adolescents are medicated. In addition, significant weight gain and the inability to regulate body temperature can be disturbing side effects, particularly for young people who are concerned with body image.

NEUROLEPTIC MALIGNANT SYNDROME   Of the possible side effects, **neuroleptic malignant syndrome (NMS)** is the most serious and life-threatening. NMS is characterized by fever, rigidity, altered consciousness, and autonomic nervous system instability (including rapid heart rate and fluctuations in blood pressure). NMS is potentially lethal, but rapid diagnosis and immediate action have significantly reduced the mortality risk.

ADDITIONAL SIDE EFFECTS   Many of the older and newer antipsychotic drugs have not only dopamine-blocking effects but also anticholinergic and antiadrenergic actions. These complex interactions produce widespread effects on the autonomic nervous system. For example, blocking cholinergic synapses produces effects such as dry mouth, blurred vision, constipation, difficulty in urination, and decreased gastric secretion and motility. You may notice that although anticholinergic effects in the autonomic

nervous system are problematic, anticholinergic effects in the striatum reduce parkinsonian side effects. Orthostatic hypotension (low blood pressure when an individual stands upright) from the antiadrenergic action of antipsychotics leads to dizziness, faintness, or blacking out. Many of these drugs produce significant sedation, which may be very troublesome for some patients but useful for those who suffer from agitation and restlessness.

In general, the particular drug chosen for a patient depends on its side effects. For example, chlorpromazine or thioridazine may be used because they tend to minimize the extrapyramidal side effects, although their sedative effects may be undesirable and the probability of autonomic side effects is relatively high. Haloperidol, in contrast, tends to produce less sedation and fewer autonomic side effects but is associated with a greater probability of movement disorders. Many of the newer antipsychotic drugs have been developed to provide professionals with more options for matching a particular patient and the side effects that he can tolerate. **Table 20.2** compares a number of traditional and atypical antipsychotic drugs and rates the incidence of specific side effects for each drug.

TABLE 20.2   Relative Benefits and Risks of Atypical and Conventional Antipsychotic Drugs[a]

Property	Atypical Antipsychotic Agents						Conventional Antipsychotic Agents by Potency[b]		
	Aripip-razole	Clozap-ine	Olan-zapine	Que-tiapine	Risper-idone	Zipra-sidone	High	Moderate	Low
Efficacy in terms of:									
Positive symptoms	++	++++	+++	++	+++	+++	+++	+++	+++
Negative symptoms	+	++	+	+	+	+	+	+	+
Relapse[c]	++	++++	+++	?	+++	+	++	++	++
Adverse effects									
Anticholinergic	0	+++	+	0	0	0	0	++	+++
Hypotension	+	+++	++	++	+++	+	+	++	+++
Hyperprolactinemia	0	0	+	0	++	+	++	++	++
Diabetes mellitus	+	++	++	+	+	+	+	+	+
Sexual dysfunction	+	++	++	+	++	+	++	++	+++
Weight gain	0	+++	+++	++	+	0	0	+	++
Extrapyramidal symptoms	+	0	+	0	++	+	++++	+++	++
Neuroleptic malignant syndrome	?	+	+	+	+	+	+++	++	+

Source: Gardner et al., 2005.

[a]Benefit or risk: ++++, very high; +++, high; ++, moderate; +, low; 0, negligible; ?, not defined.

[b]High potency agents are flupenthixol, fluphenazine, haloperidol, trifluoperazine; moderate potency agents are lozapine and zuclopenthixol; low potency are chlorpromazine, methotrimeprazine, thioridazine.

[c]Relapse was compared to placebo after one year.

TOLERANCE AND DEPENDENCE Clinically, the antipsychotic drugs cause little or no tolerance, physical dependence, or abuse potential (psychological dependence). Patients can take the same dose of these drugs for years without seeing a reduction in the effectiveness in reducing psychotic symptoms. However, some tolerance to the sedative, hypotensive, and anticholinergic effects develops gradually over a period of weeks. The lack of physical dependence is demonstrated by the absence of withdrawal symptoms following abrupt cessation of these drugs even after years of administration. The lack of abstinence syndrome may be due to the long half-life of the drugs and the prolonged presence of the drugs and their active metabolites in the body before excretion. However, abrupt termination of the drugs may unmask signs of TD.

Since the neuroleptics do not produce euphoria and have subjectively unpleasant effects, these drugs are rarely abused. Animal studies also demonstrate a low incidence of self-administration and a tendency to avoid these drugs. Despite the drugs' unpleasant nature and disagreeable side effects, the antipsychotics are not lethal and have a high therapeutic index, which makes them unlikely candidates for drug overdose.

Atypical antipsychotics are distinctive in several ways

Presently, the designation of "atypical" or "second-generation" is reserved for antipsychotics that reduce positive symptoms of schizophrenia as well as the classical drugs, but without causing significant extrapyramidal side effects. In addition, some of the newer agents fail to increase serum prolactin and have a low incidence of tardive dyskinesia. Three general approaches have been taken to develop these second-generation drugs: selective D_2 receptor antagonists, DA system stabilizers, and broad-spectrum antipsychotics.

SELECTIVE D_2 RECEPTOR ANTAGONISTS Since effective antipsychotic drugs block D_2 receptors, the first attempts to develop new drugs with fewer side effects evaluated **selective D_2 receptor antagonists**. Examples of such drugs include sulpiride and amisulpride. These drugs bind specifically to D_2 receptors and have a slight affinity for D_3 receptors (**Table 20.3**), which may explain why their behavioral effects differ to some extent from those of traditional neuroleptics. Their selectivity for DA receptors also means that effects on the autonomic nervous

TABLE 20.3 Relative Neurotransmitter Receptor Affinities for Selected Antipsychotics at Therapeutic Dose[a]

	Broad Spectrum						Selective D_2		Stabilizer	Classical
Receptor[b]	Clo-zapine	Risperi-done	Olan-zapine	Que-tiapine	Zipra-sidone	Sertin-dole	Sul-piride	Amis-ulpride	Aripipra-zole	Halo-peridol
D_1	+	+	++	–	+	++	–	–	–	+
D_2	+	+++	++	+	+++	+++	++++	++++	++++	++++
D_3	+	++	+	–	++	++	++	++	++	+++
D_4	++	–	++	–	++	+	–	–	+	+++
5-HT_{1A}	–	–	–	–	+++	ND	ND	ND	++	–
5-HT_{1D}	–	+	–	–	+++	ND	ND	ND	+	–
5-HT_{2A}	+++	++++	+++	++	++++	++++	–	–	+++	+
5-HT_{2C}	++	++	++	–	++++	++	–	–	+	–
5-HT_6	++	–	++	–	+	ND	ND	ND	+	–
5-HT_7	++	+++	–	–	++	ND	ND	ND	++	–
α_1	+++	+++	++	+++	++	++	–	–	+	+++
α_2	+	++	+	–	–	+	–	–	+	–
H_1	+++	–	+++	++	–	+	–	–	+	–
m_1	++++	–	+++	++	–	–	–	–	–	–

Source: Miyamoto et al., 2005.
[a]–, minimal to none; +, low; ++, moderate; +++, high; ++++, very high; ND, no data.
[b]D, dopamine; 5-HT, serotonin; α, adrenergic; H, histamine; m, muscarinic cholinergic.

system and the cardiovascular system are minimal and sedation is mild. However, hormonal side effects tend to be common, and the risk of fatal blood disorders reduces the utility of the drugs.

DOPAMINE SYSTEM STABILIZERS Among the newer of the atypical antipsychotics are the **dopamine system stabilizers**. The prototypical drug aripiprazole (Abilify) is a DA partial agonist, which means that the drug readily binds to DA receptors but produces less of an effect than DA itself. Hence aripiprazole competes with DA for DA receptors in overactive synapses, reducing the effect of DA for as long as the drug is bound. By reducing excessive DA activity, the positive symptoms are reduced. In contrast, the same drug stimulates DA receptors (but to a lesser extent than DA) in brain areas where there may be too little DA, thus in principle reducing negative symptoms. In clinical trials, the drug had a relatively low incidence of side effects (see Table 20.2). There was little evidence of cardiotoxicity, weight gain, or motor side effects. Reported adverse effects such as headache, agitation, insomnia, and nervousness were minor. Aripiprazole may represent a new class of antipsychotics that is more readily accepted because of fewer unpleasant side effects.

BROAD-SPECTRUM ANTIPSYCHOTICS A second trend in neuropharmacology is to evaluate **broad-spectrum antipsychotics** that block other receptor types in addition to D_2 receptors. The rationale for this work is the clinical effectiveness of clozapine, a drug that has relatively weak affinities for D_1 and D_2 and substantial serotonergic, muscarinic, and histaminergic affinities, as well a high affinity for the D_4 receptor (see Table 20.3). Clozapine is the best-known atypical antipsychotic. Preclinical animal testing shows that it blocks apomorphine-induced hyperactivity but does not produce catalepsy except at high doses. The wide separation of the dose-response curves for these two behavioral effects predicts a low incidence of motor side effects. Although clozapine is no more effective than standard neuroleptics in treating the positive symptoms of schizophrenia, it is often effective in patients who are treatment resistant. Clozapine produces significant improvement in 60% of patients who do not respond to typical neuroleptics. Clozapine is also the first antipsychotic that can reduce some of the negative and cognitive symptoms as well as reduce anxiety and tension. Unfortunately, the drug has a wide variety of side effects because of its action on multiple receptors. Clozapine reduces the seizure threshold, making seizures more likely in the vulnerable individual. It can also produce hypersalivation, weight gain, and cardiovascular problems. A more dangerous side effect is the occurrence of agranulocytosis, a serious blood abnormality that can be detected only with frequent

(i.e., weekly or biweekly) blood screening tests. The increased expense of testing and the seriousness of side effects restrict the use of clozapine to selected patients.

The initial discovery of the effectiveness of clozapine led to a great deal of excitement and efforts to design a new class of antipsychotic with similar efficacy but without dangerous side effects. These atypical drugs, which include risperidone, olanzapine, quetiapine, ziprasidone, and sertindole, bind with varying affinities for multiple neurotransmitter receptor subtypes. Table 20.3 allows you to compare binding affinities of these agents with those of the selective D_2 antagonists, the DA system stabilizer aripiprazole, and the classic drug haloperidol. Keep in mind that these atypical drugs are a heterogeneous group neurochemically and in clinical profiles, making it difficult to allow broad generalizations about the class, but you can predict side effects on the basis of receptor affinity (refer to Table 20.1). You can compare clinical benefits and risks of these drugs by examining Table 20.2. Although they all reduce positive symptoms better than placebo, there is little evidence to suggest *superiority* of the atypical drugs over conventional drugs. Keep in mind that clinical studies are difficult to perform, and that variability in results may be explained by differences in sampling of patient populations, durations of treatment, high dropout rates, inappropriate dose comparisons, and small outcome measures that may be statistically significant but not significant to the patient (Gardner et al., 2005). Superiority of the newer agents in treating negative symptoms is even more difficult to demonstrate because evaluating behavior such as social and emotional withdrawal and lack of motivation is problematic with the usual measuring devices. Although a number of clinical studies and meta-analyses suggest that cognitive deficits such as verbal memory, attention, psychomotor processing, and verbal fluency frequently show improvement with some atypical drugs such as risperidone compared with haloperidol, other studies and meta-analyses report no difference.

Most significant for atypical status is the low incidence of motor side effects (called extrapyramidal side effects or EPS) described earlier. Clozapine does not appear to cause EPS even at high doses, and reports of TD are uncommon. Although all of the newer drugs are generally considered less likely to cause EPS, keep in mind that the occurrence of motor side effects varies significantly for each of the atypical agents (see Table 20.2). Furthermore, the occurrence of EPS is frequently dose-dependent, which means that a drug may act as an atypical antipsychotic at low doses but become more conventional at higher doses. A prominent endocrine side effect with the classical antipsychotics is hyperprolactinemia and associated sexual dysfunction. Several of the newer agents including quetiapine and the dopamine system stabilizer aripiprazole lack this effect entirely, although some of the newer drugs such as risperidone elevate prolactin to the same moderate level as the older agents. Finally, some cases of neuroleptic malignant syndrome have been reported for the atypical drugs.

Metabolic side effects including weight gain, hyperglycemia, and elevated plasma cholesterol are troublesome characteristics for at least some of the atypical antipsychotics, although these side effects also occur with some of the older drugs. Significant weight gain is common with atypical antipsychotics and with some classical agents and is most robustly correlated with the extent of histamine H_1 receptor binding, although 5-HT_{2C} receptor antagonism may also contribute to this effect. Adolescents tend to gain even more weight than adults. Clozapine and olanzapine seem to cause the most weight gain, probably through suppression of the satiety response, and the most prolonged weight gain over time. Clozapine-induced weight gain was also most persistent despite efforts to behaviorally reverse the gain with diet and exercise. Some of the atypical antipsychotics cause sometimes severe elevations in blood sugar and insulin resistance leading to type 2 diabetes. The risk of developing diabetes is 9% to 14% greater in patients taking atypical antipsychotics compared with the first-generation drugs. The elevated plasma lipids caused by some of the drugs increases risk for high blood pressure and heart disease.

Several traditional and second-generation drugs cause alterations in the electrical activity of the heart in some individuals. If severe enough, these arrhythmias can cause sudden death. Several antipsychotics have been removed from the market because of this side effect. Because of these cardiac changes, "off-label" use (i.e., for a condition not approved by the Food and Drug Administration [FDA]) for the treatment of behavioral disorders in the elderly with dementia has been evaluated. The FDA reported a two-fold increase in sudden death in this population caused by cerebral ischemia, stroke, cerebrovascular events, or infection. Subsequent evaluation suggests as much as a tenfold increased risk for sudden death in elderly patients taking the drug for 1 week, which gradually decreases to control levels after 3 months. Nevertheless, the FDA (2008) has recommended a boxed warning on drug labels describing the potential risks. As is always the case, the potential risks and benefits along with the costs must be weighed for each patient.

Although there is general agreement that D_2 receptors are important in antipsychotic effects for all

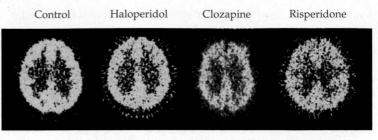

Control   Haloperidol   Clozapine   Risperidone

Figure 20.17 5-HT_2 receptor binding by atypical antipsychotics PET scans of a healthy, untreated male (control) and three patients with schizophrenia treated with the traditional neuroleptic haloperidol or with an atypical antipsychotic drug—clozapine or risperidone. In all subjects, neocortical 5-HT_2 receptors were labeled with [^{11}C] N-methylspiperone ([^{11}C]NMSP). The scans show that both atypical antipsychotics but not haloperidol reduced 5-HT_2 binding. These and other differences in receptor antagonism are thought to be responsible for the ability of clozapine to reduce schizophrenic symptoms (negative as well as positive) with a minimum of motor side effects. (Courtesy of Svante Nyberg and Anna-Lena Nordstöm, Karolinska Institute.)

neuroleptics, we have to wonder what is different about clozapine that explains its efficacy for reducing negative symptoms and its low potential for EPS. Some laboratories hypothesize that typical and atypical neuroleptics can be differentiated by their ratio of antagonism for various receptors. For instance, a high degree of binding to D_4 receptors, found in high concentration in the mesolimbic system and the frontal cortex, may enhance the therapeutic effect but minimize the nigrostriatal motor symptoms associated with D_2 occupation. Other evidence suggests the importance of antagonism of the 5-HT_2 receptor in combination with D_2 blockade. **Figure 20.17** shows that the atypical neuroleptics clozapine and risperidone readily bind to 5-HT_2 receptors, but haloperidol does not. In contrast, haloperidol almost completely blocks D_2 receptors (see Figure 20.13), but the clozapine shows only a partial effect on D_2. Because 5-HT_2 receptors modulate DA release, it has been suggested that this difference in receptor antagonism is responsible for increasing DA efflux in cortex and hippocampus, potentially improving cognitive symptoms while producing less DA release in striatum, which would be expected to reduce EPS. For this reason, extensive research is being conducted into the potential enhancement of cognitive function by modulating 5-HT at the 5-HT_{2A} and several other 5-HT receptor subtypes (Meltzer and Massey, 2011). In contrast, other researchers believe that atypicality can be explained solely by low D_2 receptor binding affinity, regardless of any other receptor type function (Seeman, 2002). Receptor affinity (K_d) is the ratio of how readily the drug moves off the receptor compared with how readily it binds (see Chapter 4 for radioligand binding). Hence, a drug with low affinity could be one that binds slowly or that after binding moves off the receptor rapidly. Most antipsychotic drugs bind at similar rates, but there are large differences in how quickly they unbind. For example, clozapine binds to and unbinds from the D_2 receptor 100 times faster than haloperidol. Low affinity means that the drug is not constantly bound to the receptor, during which time normal DA transmission can occur. This characteristic might prevent EPS, maintain prolactin levels, and protect cognitive function.

Practical clinical trials help clinicians make decisions about drugs

Since their inception, the second-generation antipsychotics have been the first line of treatment and have been prescribed in about 90% of cases, despite no conclusive evidence that they are superior to the first-generation drugs. In many instances, the clinical effects seen in the "real-world" applications have been less robust than the results from randomized, placebo-controlled trials performed as part of drug development. There can be several reasons for this disparity such as differences in the duration of drug treatment. Others have suggested that the drug development trials are biased toward the atypical agents because they use as the comparator a high-potency classical drug like haloperidol, which is known to have significant EPS. Bias would also occur when first-generation drugs are used at higher than necessary doses, which increases the potential for side effects. Often an older drug is used to compare outcomes without the usual co-administration of an anticholinergic agent that would reduce the appearance of EPS. At other times, the outcome measures, although statistically significant, are insufficient to make the patient himself feel better. Finally, well-controlled trials, by necessity, exclude patients with comorbid medical or psychiatric conditions, although these excluded individuals are more typical of the usual schizophrenic patient in the real world. Furthermore, drug development trials generally select a carefully defined and limited subset of patients who do not reflect the heterogeneous schizophrenic population. For these reasons, drug trial results comparing antipsychotic drugs may not be generalizable to the larger population. Because the newer drugs generally cost about 10 times what older generic agents cost, cost–benefit considerations are important in clinical decisions.

For all these reasons, the National Institute of Mental Health (NIMH) between January 2001 and December 2004 initiated the Clinical Antipsychotic Trials of Intervention Effectiveness (CATIE), a blinded and controlled study, to compare effectiveness, tolerability, and cost-effectiveness of treatments. These variables were determined by measuring the duration of use before discontinuation of treatment by a patient (Lieberman et al., 2005). Discontinuation of treatment (i.e., switching to another drug) was chosen as a critical measure because it combined several factors, including *both* the patients' and the clinicians' judgments of effectiveness, safety, and side effects, into an overall measure of effectiveness that balances benefits and undesirable effects. Secondary measures of outcome included the specific reasons for discontinuation of treatment and scores on two symptom scales. Additional secondary measures of safety and tolerability were made every 3 months for 18 months. These measures included the incidence of serious adverse effects, the incidence of serious neurological effects, and changes in body weight, electrocardiographic (EKG or ECG) findings, and lab blood analyses. At 57 sites in a variety of treatment settings in the United States, almost 1500 patients were recruited and randomly assigned to receive the classical neuroleptic perphenazine or one of the atypical agents, olanzapine, quetiapine, risperidone, or ziprasidone. The goal of the study was to replicate the "real-world" prescription of these drugs to patients who are more representative of the typical outpatient population, without the normally extensive exclusion criteria required in clinical studies. Hence the results of this practical clinical trial are intended to serve as a guide for clinical practice and to allow patients to make more informed decisions. The biggest surprise of the study results, counter to the hypothesis, was that the newer drugs were no more effective than the first-generation drug perphenazine. Overall rates of discontinuation (74%) were high, which means that the majority of patients had to switch to another drug either because of lack of effectiveness or because they could not tolerate the side effects. Among all the drugs, olanzapine had the longest duration before discontinuation and produced the greatest improvement initially, although this advantage decreased over the 18 months. Also, olanzapine showed the highest discontinuation rate as the result of adverse side effects, particularly weight gain and metabolic effects. To the researchers' surprise, there were no differences among the drugs in terms of effectiveness for reducing negative symptoms or cognitive deficits. Further, the incidence of EPS was the same for all agents, and this may be attributed to the low but effective dose of perphenazine used. This study was important because it showed that drug effectiveness is quite different under conditions similar to routine clinical practice compared with tightly controlled trials. The database has been used in subsequent studies looking at other factors including cost-effectiveness, quality of life, patient characteristics that predict response, and other variables (see Lieberman and Stroup, 2011, for a list of references). Subsequent naturalistic research, such as the Cost Utility of the Latest Antipsychotic Drugs in Schizophrenia Study (CUtLASS) performed in the United Kingdom, supported the findings from CATIE and found no difference among the first- and second-generation drugs, except that clozapine was superior (see Lewis and Lieberman, 2008, for a brief review). It would seem that only clozapine is truly "atypical." These findings should encourage the use of older first-generation drugs, which are effective at a significantly lower cost. For the patient, this means more treatment options are available to optimize benefits and side effects for the individual.

There are renewed efforts to treat the cognitive symptoms

It is quite clear that the cognitive symptoms along with the negative symptoms represent aspects of the disorder that most damage the quality of life of the schizophrenic individual. These sysmptoms prevent integration into the community and reduce the probability of functioning in a productive manner. Since neither the first- nor second-generation antipsychotics improve the cognitive impairments of schizophrenia, several new pharmacological approaches are being considered (Buchanan et al., 2007).

ACETYLCHOLINE Because acetylcholine (ACh) has a role in attention, sensory processing, and several aspects of memory, enhancing ACh is one reasonable approach. Furthermore, this neurotransmitter is an appropriate target because postmortem and imaging studies have shown cholinergic deficits in schizophrenic patients. It is interesting that the only antipsychotic drug currently available that enhances cognitive deficits, clozapine, increases the release of ACh in the hippocampus and DA in the PFC. Acute administration of nicotine produces some cognitive improvement, particularly enhancing selective attention; however, the rapid development of tolerance prevents its therapeutic use. Several subtype-specific nicotinic partial agonists were found to normalize auditory gating deficits in rodents, as well as in early trials with schizophrenic patients. Surprisingly, enhancing ACh function by inhibiting its synaptic breakdown by acetylcholinesterase does not seem to have similar cognitive-enhancing effects.

DOPAMINE In the previous section, you saw that negative symptoms and cognitive deficits including hypofrontality are associated with reduced DA function in PFC, particularly at D_1 receptors, which are the most common receptor subtype in that region. It is well known that increasing synaptic DA with amphetamine improves cognitive deficits in schizophrenic patients; however, since the positive symptoms are due to excessive DA release from mesolimbic neurons, those symptoms worsen. The goal then is to selectively enhance D_1 receptor signaling in PFC with D_1 agonists. The first agent, dihydrexidine, was found to reverse cognitive performance deficits in aged primates and in other animals after neurotoxin-induced lesions of DA cells. In a small number of schizophrenic patients, the drug increased blood flow in prefrontal regions but unfortunately failed to improve task performance in delayed recall or working memory. Recent research showed that very high plasma concentrations are needed to reach detectable D_1 receptor occupancy of the brain. Because of poor bioavailability of the drug, insufficient dosage may in part explain the failure to improve cognitive function.

A second approach to enhancing PFC DA function is to inhibit the enzyme catechol-O-methyltransferase (COMT), which degrades DA in the synapse, ending its signaling. Inhibition of the enzyme with a drug such as tolcapone causes a relatively selective increase of DA in PFC because there are few reuptake transporters in that region; hence, metabolism is the principal way in which synaptic DA in the PFC is inactivated. In COMT knockout mice, DA levels are increased in PFC but not in striatum, and performance on memory tasks is improved. In patients with advanced Parkinson's disease, tolcapone improved performance on attentional tasks, verbal short-term memory, and visuospatial recall. Others found tolcapone-induced improvement in executive function and verbal episodic memory in healthy volunteers that was accompanied by improvement in information processing in PFC, as visualized with functional MRI (fMRI). Given that COMT polymorphisms influence frontal lobe function and performance on tasks of working memory, the genetic variation may represent a predictive marker for effective pharmacotherapy. Unfortunately, tolcapone can produce serious liver dysfunction, which requires frequent liver enzyme testing; it has already been withdrawn from the market in Canada and Europe. Gupta and colleagues (2011) provide a review of COMT function and its significance as a therapeutic target for cognitive disorders.

GLUTAMATE In a previous section, you learned that glutamate antagonists such as PCP and ketamine produce behaviors that resemble the positive, negative, and cognitive symptoms of schizophrenia. Figure 20.10 showed that low glutamate signaling could explain the decrease in mesocortical activity that is believed to cause negative and cognitive symptoms. On the basis of this notion, enhancing glutamate activity at NMDA receptors might reverse these symptoms. Although administering an NMDA receptor agonist seems reasonable, it is not possible because these drugs produce neuronal hyperexcitability and seizures. Instead, glycine site agonists can be used to enhance NMDA signaling because glycine is an obligatory co-agonist at this receptor and is as necessary as glutamate for receptor activation (see Chapter 8). The glycine receptor agonists glycine, D-cycloserine, and D-serine, when combined with antipsychotics, reduced negative and cognitive symptoms in some but not all clinical trials. An alternative way to increase synaptic glycine is to administer an inhibitor of the glycine transporter that moves synaptic glycine from the synapse to neurons and glial cells. A recent clinical trial administering the glycine transporter/inhibitor sarcosine, along with atypical antipsychotics shows that sarcosine has greater efficacy than the glycine agonist D-serine in overall symptom reduction, reduction of negative symptoms, and improvement in quality of life ratings of social activity, sense of purpose, motivation, anhedonia, capacity for empathy, aimless inactivity, and emotional interaction (Lane et al., 2010). Both were superior to placebo. New glycine transporter inhibitors are being developed, and only with time will we know whether NMDA enhancement lives up to its promise.

Section Summary

- All antipsychotics are significantly better than placebo in reducing positive symptoms and decreasing length of hospitalization.
- The Law of Thirds says one third of patients treated with antipsychotics improve dramatically and return to normal lives. A second third show some improvement but experience relapses and need help with day-to-day living. The final third show little improvement and have significant periods of hospitalization.
- Prolonged maintenance therapy doubles the odds of avoiding relapse.
- There is a strong positive correlation between antipsychotic binding to D_2 receptors and clinical effectiveness.
- Antipsychotic blocking of D_2 autoreceptors causes an initial increase in DA neuron firing and increased turnover of DA, followed by a gradual decrease as the autoreceptors up-regulate. Depolarization block may contribute to the decrease in turnover. These adaptive changes may explain the gradual onset of effectiveness.
- Parkinsonian-like symptoms are the most troubling side effects with traditional antipsychotic

treatment. Combining the drugs with anticholinergic agents reduces risk. Second-generation drugs have a lower incidence of motor side effects.
- Tardive dyskinesia involves involuntary movement of face, jaw, tongue, neck, or extremities, which may be irreversible in some patients.
- Neuroendocrine side effects are caused by DA receptor blockade of tuberoinfundibular neurons that project to the pituitary.
- Neuroleptic malignant syndrome is a potentially life-threatening effect of antipsychotics.
- Anticholinergic effects of antipsychotics produce widespread effects on autonomic nervous system function.
- Antipsychotics cause little tolerance or physical dependence, and have no addiction potential.
- Atypical antipsychotics may be selective D_2 antagonists, DA partial agonists (DA system stabilizers), or broad-spectrum antipsychotics.
- The atypical drugs are heterogeneous neurochemically and clinically but overall cause fewer motor side effects than the older drugs.
- Several of the atypical drugs are especially problematic in causing weight gain, hyperglycemia, cardiotoxicity, elevated cholesterol, and increased risk for diabetes.
- Only clozapine improves negative and cognitive symptoms without motor side effects and is often effective for treatment-resistant patients. Serious side effects limit its use.
- The neurochemical property that makes clozapine unique is not known. It may be high affinity for D_4 receptors, antagonism of 5-HT_2 receptors, or low D_2 affinity.
- A practical clinical trial (CATIE) using 1500 patients under "real-world" conditions showed that the atypical drugs were no more effective than the traditional agents in reducing positive, negative, or cognitive symptoms. Occurrence of EPS was the same for both. Only clozapine is superior.
- Nicotinic partial agonists, D_1 agonists, COMT inhibitors, glycine agonists, and glycine transporter inhibitors improve cognitive processing and are under development.

Go to the **COMPANION WEBSITE**

sites.sinauer.com/psychopharm2e
for Web Boxes, animations, flashcards, and other study resources.

Recommended Readings

Abi-Dargham, A. (2004). Do we still believe in the dopamine hypothesis? New data bring new evidence. *Int. J. Neuropsychopharmacol.*, 7 (Suppl. 1), S1–S5.

Gray, J. A. and Roth, B. L. (2007). Molecular targets for treating cognitive dysfunction in schizophrenia. *Schizophr. Bull.*, 33, 1100–1119.

Horacek, J., Bubenikova-Valesova, V., Kopecek, M., Palenicek, T., Dockery, C., Mohr, P., and Höschl, C. (2006). Mechanism of action of atypical antipsychotic drugs and the neurobiology of schizophrenia. *CNS Drugs*, 20, 389–409.

Lewis, D. A., and Levitt, P. (2002). Schizophrenia as a disorder of neurodevelopment. *Annu. Rev. Neurosci.*, 25, 409–432.

Margolis, R. L. (2009). Neuropsychiatric disorders: The choice of antipsychotics in schizophrenia. *Nat. Rev. Neurol.*, 5, 308–310.

Meyer, U. and Feldon, J. (2010). Epidemiology-driven neurodevelopmental animal models of schizophrenia. *Prog. Neurobiol.*, 90, 285–326.

Papaleo, F., Lipska, B. K., and Weinberger, D. R. (2012). Mouse models of genetic effects on cognition: Relevance to schizophrenia. *Neuropharmacology*, 62, 1204–1220.

Powell, C. M. and Miyakawa, T. (2006). Schizophrenia-relevant behavioral testing in rodent models: A uniquely human disorder? *Biol. Psychiatry*, 59, 1198–1207.

Rosenthal, D. (Ed.). (1963). *The Genain Quadruplets: A Case Study and Theoretical Analysis of Heredity and Environment in Schizophrenia*. New York: Basic Books.

Exercise can help alleviate some of the symptoms of Parkinson's disease.

Neurodegenerative Diseases

21

WHILE RETURNING FROM A VISIT WITH FRIENDS, 54-year-old Ms. S. noticed a familiar sensation, a creeping heaviness throughout her body. As she parked her car at her apartment complex, she found herself "frozen" in the driver's seat. She called a friend for help getting out of her car and then pondered how to get her unmoving muscles to carry her to her third floor apartment. Her solution? To sing her way upstairs. Singing her favorite song allowed her muscles to move with the beat of the music. With her friend helping by opening her apartment door, Ms. S. was able to get into her apartment and collapse on her couch before freezing again.

Like the "frozen addicts" that you read about in Chapter 4, Ms. S. is suffering from a deficiency of dopamine signaling in her brain. She has Parkinson's disease. The creeping heaviness that she experiences signals the wearing off of her dopamine-enhancing medication. As the medication leaves her system, she has difficulty with limb movement (as for many with Parkinson's, this is an asymmetrical effect; for Ms. S., it happens more on the right side), her muscles become stiff, and she has difficulty lifting her feet (this results in a shuffling gait). She has a tendency to lean forward and has a corresponding anterior lean of her head. With medication, her body feels lighter, and movement feels normal and natural; her motivation to move is automatically translated to the movement. There is a noticeable change in her thinking when the medication takes effect. Limitations in movement as her Parkinson's disease progressed caused Ms. S. to have to give up her career as a chiropractor, but she is still able to swim for 30 minutes three times a week.

Parkinson's disease is one of several disorders in which the primary pathological mechanism is loss of cells in the nervous system. Other disorders that are classified this way and discussed in this chapter are Alzheimer's disease, Huntington's disease, amyotrophic lateral sclerosis, and multiple sclerosis.

Parkinson's Disease and Alzheimer's Disease

Parkinson's Disease

Parkinson's disease (**PD**), the disorder suffered by Ms. S. in the opening vignette, is a chronic, progressive, neurodegenerative disorder (Davie, 2008). The symptoms of the disorder are not reversible and get worse as the degeneration of neurons progresses. Although there are genetic and environmental risk factors, a definitive cause of the disorder has not yet been discovered. Treatments are symptomatic in nature; no treatments are known to affect disease progression. Generally, age is the most significant risk factor for development of PD, and the incidence of the disorder increases with age. But there is an early-onset variant of the disease in which symptom onset occurs before the age of 40. Perhaps the most famous case of early-onset PD is Michael J. Fox (**Figure 21.1**), whose disclosure of his diagnosis came the day before it was to be reported in a tabloid newspaper. He has since become a vocal and dedicated advocate for research on PD and care for those with the disorder.

Figure 21.1 Among the most public faces of Parkinson's disease are Michael J. Fox and Muhammed Ali In addition to educating the public and federal leaders (shown here testifying before the U.S. Senate health committee), Fox created and advocates for the Michael J. Fox Foundation for Parkinson's Research.

The clinical features of PD are primarily motor related

Often the most visible outward sign of PD is a 4- to 6-hertz **resting tremor**, which occurs in about 70% of patients with PD. It generally starts in the hand (where it is called a "pill-rolling" tremor for its characteristic motion) or foot on one side of the body, although it can also happen in the jaw or face. The tremor is present when the limb is relaxed and generally disappears with intentional movement. The tremor can be exacerbated by stress or excitement and can spread to the other side of the body with disease progression (although the initially affected limb generally shows a more severe tremor throughout the disease process).

Parkinson's disease is characterized by both difficulty in initiating movement (**akinesia**) and slowing of movement in general. This slowing, called **bradykinesia** (from the Greek *bradys*, "slow," and *kinesis*, "motion"), leads to several seemingly unrelated symptoms. Many patients with PD are described as "stone-faced" because their facial muscles do not move as much and therefore don't allow the range of facial expression that was previously achievable. Perhaps less obvious as consequences of slowed/reduced movement are the micrographia (smaller handwriting), hypophonia (decreased volume of speaking), and monotonous speech (decreased prosody in the voice) that accompany PD.

Rigidity, or stiffness and inflexibility in the joints, is another common symptom of PD. This difficulty in joint movement often manifests (together with bradykinesia) as lack of arm swing when walking. This contributes to the "Parkinson's shuffle" gait often seen in patients. The two particular types of rigidity that may be seen with PD are described as "lead-pipe" rigidity, a state where the inflexibility of the joint is maintained consistently through a range of passive movement, and "cog-wheel" rigidity, which is characterized by ratchet-like interruptions in muscle tone. "Cog-wheel" rigidity is likely the result of a superimposition of a tremor over the rigidity.

Postural instability—impaired balance and coordination—causes patients to exhibit a forward or backward lean in their upright posture. This leads to **retropulsion** in some patients. When bumped from the front or when starting to walk, patients with a backward lean have a tendency to step backward. Postural instability can cause patients to have a stooped posture, in which the head is bowed and the shoulders are drooped (**anteropulsion**). Both anteropulsion and retropulsion can manifest as counterintuitive symptoms of **festination**, which is defined as an uncontrollable acceleration of gait. This is likely what Ms. S. was experiencing as she entered her apartment in our opening vignette. Unwanted acceleration of movement can also happen in a patient's speech, a condition called tachyphemia.

Another early sign of motor dysfunction is evident in eye movement, primarily as difficulty in tracking moving objects. This occurs in both medicated and nonmedicated patients with PD and may be useful in the differential diagnosis of PD. Other motor symptoms also occur but are less consistently seen, including **dystonia** (persistent involuntary muscle contractions), impaired gross and fine motor control, **akathisia** (a constant urge to move certain body parts), speech problems, difficulty swallowing, sexual dysfunction, cramping, and drooling.

Although the symptoms of PD are primarily motor related, other difficulties accompany the disorder. Early signs include loss of the sense of smell, constipation, REM (rapid-eye-movement) behavior disorder (lack of normal loss of muscle tone during REM sleep), mood disorders, and orthostatic hypotension (also known as postural hypotension—the sudden drop in a person's blood pressure upon standing, resulting in dizziness or fainting). As the disease progresses, patients may also experience sleep disturbances, bladder problems, weight loss or gain, vision problems, dental issues, fatigue or loss of energy, skin problems, and medication side effects (see Box 21.1).

Several other disorders can mimic the effects of PD. Symptoms of Parkinson's disease in the absence of the hallmark pathology of PD are referred to as parkinsonism. Some disorders that may bring about parkinsonian symptoms are strokes, encephalitis, and repeated brain trauma. Additionally, medications, including many antipsychotic drugs (e.g., haloperidol), some drugs used to treat high blood pressure (e.g., reserpine), and some mood stabilizers (e.g., Valproate and lithium) can cause parkinsonian symptoms as side effects.

Parkinson's patients may also develop dementia

Parkinson's disease dementia (**PDD**) is diagnosed when one or more cognitive functions are impaired to the point of interfering with the ability of the patient to navigate everyday life. Prevalence estimates vary, but it is likely between 15% and 40% and increases to closer to 70% after 15 years of disease progression. The tricky part of the diagnosis of PDD is differentiating it from comorbid Alzheimer's disease (AD) or **Lewy body dementia** (**LBD**). Generally, AD and PDD share symptoms, but they tend to occur in a different order. Early PDD may be characterized by **bradyphrenia** (slowed answers), although patients may still be capable of giving correct answers if allowed adequate time. They may also show mental inflexibility and changes in visuospatial function. Hallucinations are fairly common in PDD early on in the dementia process, but they don't show up in AD until very late in the disease progression. Patients may show improvement on cognitive tests of dementia severity (e.g., the **Mini-Mental State Exam** [**MMSE**] and others) with cholinesterase inhibitors, particularly Exelon (rivastigmine) (Emre et al., 2004), a medication that is also used to treat symptoms of AD.

The primary pathology of PD is a loss of dopaminergic neurons in the substantia nigra

The **substantia nigra** is generally considered part of the **basal ganglia**, a group of structures that are instrumental in translating motivation into action (see Chapter 2). A common model is to think of them as the accelerator and the brake for voluntary movements. But these neurons are not the start of the pathology in PD. In 2003, Braak et al. described stages of pathological changes that happen in PD. The degeneration starts in the dorsal motor nucleus of the vagus and the anterior olfactory structures. This loss of olfactory processing accounts for the **anosmia** experienced by many of those with PD. The degeneration then moves to two sets of brainstem nuclei: the raphe and the locus coeruleus (**Figure 21.2**). Only in the third stage do we start to see degeneration of the substantia nigra (**Figure 21.3**), along with the amygdala and the nucleus basalis of Meynert. It is in this third stage that clinical diagnosis generally occurs with the onset of motor symptoms. Degeneration of the temporal lobe mesocortex (an area of cortex where layers 3, 4, and 5 are fused into one; e.g., the parahippocampal cortex) follows in stage 4, followed by degeneration of the neocortex in the temporal lobe along with neocortex sensory association and premotor areas in stage 5. Finally, the neocortex areas of primary sensory function and motor areas show degeneration in the final stage, 6.

Motor symptoms, other than the resting tremor, are generally explained by the loss of dopaminergic substantia nigra cells. Loss of these cells results in less dopaminergic input to the striatum (the putamen and the caudate nucleus) of the basal ganglia. This loss

(A) Parkinson's disease (PD)

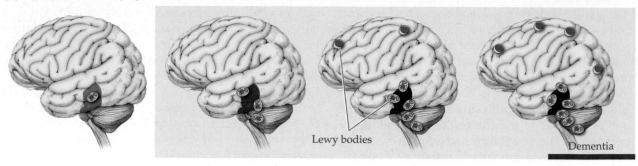

Lewy bodies

Dementia

(B) Parkinson's disease with dementia (PDD)

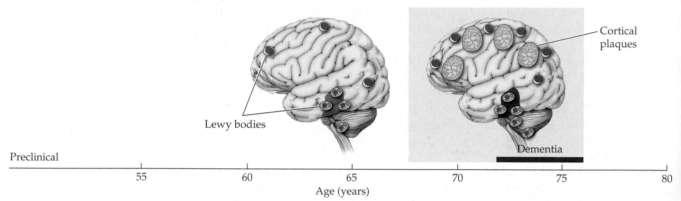

Cortical plaques

Lewy bodies

Dementia

Preclinical

| 55 | 60 | 65 | 70 | 75 | 80 |

Age (years)

Figure 21.2 Disease progression in early- and late-onset Parkinson's disease Cellular degeneration (represented by progressively darker red shading in the midbrain) and the accumulation of Lewy bodies spread at different rates through the brainstem nuclei and midbrain depending on the age of onset. Compared to those with earlier-onset PD (A), more pronounced pathology earlier in disease progression is seen in those with later-onset PD (B). Latency to dementia onset from disease onset is also faster in later-onset cases. (After Obeso, et al., 2010.)

increases excitation to the subthalamic nucleus and the internal globus pallidus through direct and indirect pathways of the basal ganglia. Excitation of inhibitory neurons leads to inhibition of the thalamus and subsequent inhibition of motor structures in the cortex (**Figure 21.4**). This results in the akinesia and bradykinesia of PD.

Figure 21.3 Selective loss of pigmented dopaminergic cells occurs in the substantia nigra (red arrows) of those with Parkinson's disease, compared to the same area in a normal subject. (Courtesy of the Harvard Brain Tissue Resource Center at McLean Hospital.)

In most cases, the onset of PD is a sporadic event. Estimates of the percentage of cases resulting from familial inheritance generally are around 10%. Age is the most significant risk factor for PD; the incidence increases as the population ages. Environmental contributors are also suspected in the development of PD (a result of the observation of MPTP addicts as discussed in Chapter 4). Although research has not identified any one specific cause, it has supported the idea that pesticides and other toxins may contribute to PD onset (Tanner et al., 2011).

Regardless of the cause of PD, several processes contribute to the degeneration of neurons, including mitochondrial dysfunction, oxidative stress, inflammation, excitotoxicity, protein misfolding, and proteosomal dysfunction (Davie, 2008). These mechanisms then lead to **Lewy body** formation (see later in this chapter), other protein accumulation, and ultimately apoptosis of the cells (see Chapter 8 for a discussion of apoptosis).

Supporting evidence for these mechanisms comes from many different places. Mitochondrial dysfunction is indicated from the process by which **MPTP**

Parkinson's disease (hypokinetic)

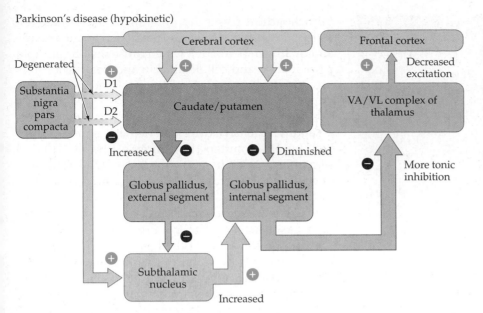

Figure 21.4 The effects of Parkinson's disease on motor control pathways With the degeneration of the substantia nigra, the balance of signals in the direct and indirect pathways is changed such that there is less inhibition from the caudate and putamen into the globus pallidus. This keeps the thalamus inhibited by the globus pallidus, thus decreasing activation of the motor cortex by the thalamus. (From Purves et al., 2012.)

(1-methyl-4-phenyl-1,2,3,6-tetrahydropyridine) destroys cells. Actually, it is not the MPTP itself that damages the cells, but the oxidation product MPP⁺. MPP⁺ is formed by the activity of monoamine oxidase-B (MAO-B) in astrocytes and serotonergic neurons, and is transported by the dopamine (DA) transporter into substantia nigra cells. Once inside the cells, MPP⁺ accumulates in mitochondria, blocking mitochondrial respiration (i.e., oxygen-dependent energy production). Mutations in genes supporting mitochondrial function have been identified in familial forms of PD. The "MitoPark" mouse model was designed to test the hypothesis that mitochondrial dysfunction is particularly important in the pathogenesis of PD. In this mouse, mitochondrial transcription factor alpha (TFAM) was inactivated in substantia nigra dopaminergic neurons. The results of this inactivation is depletion of mitochondrial DNA (mtDNA), loss of gene transcripts, and deficiency in the respiratory chain, the end result of which is cell death (Sorensen et al., 2001). The behavioral outcomes in these mice were similar in manner and scope to PD and were reversed by L-DOPA treatment, one of the most common therapies for PD (discussed in detail later in this chapter).

Oxidative stress is indicated as a contributor to the pathology of PD by postmortem analysis of patient brain tissue, which shows oxidative damage, accumulation of iron, glutathione (GSH) depletion (Martin and Teismann, 2009), and a decrease in GSH peroxidase (Kish et al., 1985). Additionally, in an experimental model, the use of **6-hydroxydopamine (6-OHDA)** destroys dopaminergic neurons by producing reactive oxygen species (see Chapter 5 for discussion of DA neurotoxins). This destruction produces symptoms of parkinsonism. A caveat is required when discussing

oxidative stress because antioxidants such as tocopherol, more commonly known as Vitamin E (The Parkinson Study Group, 1993) and coenzyme Q (Shults et al., 2002; Storch et al., 2007) have not been shown to be consistently effective against the degeneration and symptomatology of PD.

The roles of inflammation and excitotoxicity in the pathology of PD are primarily supported by the fact that therapeutic effects of agents block them in some animal models and in some clinical trials. In particular, some evidence suggests a protective effect of nonsteroidal anti-inflammatory drugs (NSAIDs) (Gagne and Power, 2010). Glutamate excitotoxicity can also be blocked with some therapeutic benefit in both animal models and patients. *N*-methyl-D-aspartate (NMDA) receptor modulators and antagonists can be beneficial because of their glutamatergic connections to the DA-containing neurons of the substantia nigra (Koutsilieri and Riedererer, 2007).

One of the key components of PD degeneration though, is protein aggregation, which makes PD similar in pathology to AD. In particular, Lewy bodies are formed in the cells that are affected by PD (**Figure 21.5**). Lewy bodies are primarily composed of the **α-synuclein** protein, along with associated proteins such as ubiquitin, neurofilament protein, and alpha B crystalline. The purported role of α-synuclein in healthy cells involves interactions with membranes, particularly those of vesicles. In these interactions, the protein mediates vesicle movement at the axon terminal (the name *synuclein* comes from its role at the *syn*apse). For a comprehensive review of α-synuclein function and dysfunction, see Auluck et al., 2010. There can also be tau proteins and surrounding neurofibrillary tangles that are more often associated with Alzheimer's

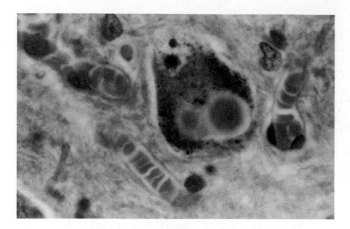

Figure 21.5 Lewy bodies are formed by abnormal accumulations of proteins They are composed mostly of α-synuclein, but also contain ubiquitin, tau, and other proteins.

disease. These Lewy body protein accumulations result from a combination of pathological processes, including protein misfolding and proteosomal dysfunction. Proteins require a precise three-dimensional (3D) conformation to function correctly. Those that are misfolded should be destroyed by proteosomes in the cells, but this process does not happen effectively, resulting in aggregation of these proteins and the formation of Lewy bodies. These protein aggregations interrupt normal cellular functions and trigger apoptotic cell death. In fact, the Braak stages discussed earlier are based on the accumulation of α-synuclein in the cells of the listed brain areas, not on neuronal death. Selective vulnerability has been noted in low-speed, long, nonmyelinated neurons in the brain.

Animal models of PD have strengths and limitations

We've already mentioned a couple of useful animal models, the use of MPTP (in mice or nonhuman primates) or 6-OHDA to make lesions, and the genetic model of the "MitoPark" mouse. These represent two classes of animal models: toxins and genetic manipulations. Another substance that falls into the category of toxin administration is rotenone. Rotenone is a compound obtained from the roots, seeds, and stems of several plants and is used as a pesticide, both as an insecticide and as a piscicide (fish poison). When administered to a mammal, this compound produces a pattern of pathology that is very similar to PD in humans. It triggers the accumulation and aggregation of α-synuclein and ubiquitin, and causes oxidative damage and apoptosis (Li et al., 2003). It is thought that it produces this effect by blocking complex I in the mitochondrial respiratory chain. Blocking

mitochondrial respiration results in the production of reactive oxygen species (particularly superoxide and hydrogen peroxide), which cause membrane lipid peroxidation and cell death (Lin and Beal, 2006). This provides further evidence for mitochondrial dysfunction as a mechanism in PD.

A pharmacological model uses the drug reserpine, an antihypertensive drug that depletes stores of three key neurotransmitters (DA, norepinephrine [NE], and serotonin [5-HT]), to mimic the lack of DA release and effects on NE neurons in PD, including cell death in the locus coeruleus. Lesion models include intentional damage of the nigrostriatal tract (cutting the dopaminergic axons as they run from the substantia nigra to the striatum), usually at the level of the medial forebrain bundle (a collection of ascending fiber tracts that include the nigrostriatal tract). Generally, these are good models of the motor dysfunction that occurs with PD, but there are certainly some limitations. Some of the models have problems with specificity. It is impossible to target only the DA neurons in the substantia nigra with 6-OHDA or reserpine. Many of these models are not degenerative in a progressive way as PD is, particularly the drug and lesion models. Most of the animal models are limited in the scope of the PD phenotype they exhibit and may not mimic the specific cellular changes seen in PD (e.g., Lewy bodies, α-synuclein accumulation, apoptosis).

Pharmacological treatments for PD are primarily symptomatic, not disease-altering

Generally, there are five categories of drugs for PD. These include:

1. Drugs that prevent clinical progression of the disease
2. Drugs that are symptomatic monotherapies (i.e., given alone for treatment of a particular symptom)
3. Drugs that are given as adjunct treatments to levodopa (L-DOPA) therapy
4. Drugs that prevent motor complications
5. Drugs that treat motor complications

We are going to address primarily those that are symptomatic treatments given alone or in conjunction with the most common pharmacological treatment, levodopa.

LEVODOPA Levodopa (L-DOPA), a metabolite of the amino acid tyrosine, immediately precedes the production of DA in its metabolic pathway (see Chapter 5). Because the pathway continues on to form NE and epinephrine (EPI), it is also a precursor to those neurotransmitters. The reason L-DOPA is given as a treatment rather than DA itself is that L-DOPA is capable of crossing the blood–brain barrier, where DA does not cross. Once L-DOPA has reached the brain, it can be converted to DA by cells that contain the enzyme **aromatic amino acid decarboxylase**. Because aromatic amino acid decarboxylase is also present in the periphery, L-DOPA is often administered with a peripheral inhibitor of this enzyme such as **carbidopa**, which allows more of the compound to reach the brain. L-DOPA is very effective, even compared to other dopamine agonist drugs (**Figure 21.6**), but this treatment is prone to several side effects. In the short term, L-DOPA therapy can result in nausea, hypotension, and neuropsychiatric side effects (e.g., hallucinations, confusion and anxiety). The long term can bring motor fluctuations (the on-off periods described in the opening vignette) and **dyskinesias**. Dyskinesias are generally unwanted movements like severe tics or choreic movements. You've heard this term before in the context of side effects of antipsychotics that result in tardive (delayed) dyskinesias (see Chapter 20).

MAOIs, COMT INHIBITORS, AND DA AGONISTS Other treatments are also aimed at increasing dopamine signaling in the brain. Three classes of drugs used for this purpose are the **monoamine oxidase inhibitors** (**MAOIs**), the **catechol-*O*-methyltransferase** (**COMT**) inhibitors, and dopamine agonists. The two most common MAOIs used for this purpose are selegiline (Eldepryl) and rasagiline (Azilect). These can be given as monotherapies or as adjuncts to levodopa treatment. As in their use in depression, MAOIs prevent the breakdown of DA, NE, and EPI before their repackaging into vesicles, allowing these neurotransmitters to be released in greater quantities with cell stimulation, which increases the opportunity to connect with postsynaptic receptors and bring about signaling between neurons. Because PD is often comorbid with depression, it is important to watch for interactions between MAOIs and other antidepressants like **selective serotonin reuptake inhibitors** (**SSRIs**) or **tricyclic antidepressants** (**TCAs**), and to adhere to the strict dietary restrictions that come with MAOIs to avoid side effects such as severe hypertension (see Chapter 19). COMT inhibitors also prevent the breakdown of DA in the synapse but are given only as adjuncts to L-DOPA. The most common COMT inhibitor used is a drug called entacapone. There is a single-drug treatment (Stalevo) that combines carbidopa, levodopa, and entacapone into one pill for ease of dosing. Several side effects are associated with entacapone, including dyskinesia, dizziness, nausea, diarrhea, and urine discoloration.

Dopamine receptor agonists may also be used for the treatment of PD. The three most popular options are pramipexole (Mirapex), ropinirole (Requip), and rotigotine (Neupro). These drugs all have longer

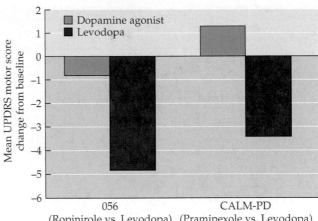

Figure 21.6 One measure of the severity of PD symptoms is the Unified Parkinson's Disease Rating Scale (UPDRS) Two large scale studies, the Comparison of Agonist Pramipexole versus Levodopa on Motor Complication of Parkinson's Disease (CALM-PD) and the 056 compared long-term UPDRS scores (a higher rating on this scale denotes more severe disability) in patients receiving levodopa or the dopamine agonists ropinirole (056) and pramipexole (CALM-PD). Levodopa was more effective over time than either ropinirole or pramipexole. (After Poewe et al., 2010.)

half-lives than L-DOPA (5 to 8 hours versus 0.75 to 1.5 hours for L-DOPA); however, with carbidopa co-administration, the half-life is on the longer end of the window. These drugs also carry lower risks for dyskinesias and "off-periods." However, several side effects of these medications decrease their usefulness, including nausea, sedation, insomnia, orthostatic hypertension, hallucinations, leg edema, and impulse control disorders (**Box 21.1**).

AMANTADINE Another approach to pharmacological treatment comes in the use of the drug amantadine (Symmetrel) as monotherapy or to decrease dyskinesias related to the use of L-DOPA. Amantadine was originally approved and used to treat and prevent infection caused by influenza A virus. The mechanism of the drug is anticholinergic and antiglutamatergic (an NMDA receptor antagonist). These actions lead to an increase in dopamine release in the nigrostriatal pathway and in other areas of the brain.

STATIN DRUGS Newer evidence has shown that people may be able to reduce the risk of developing Parkinson's by taking statin drugs for lowering cholesterol. This protection is likely provided by a decrease in cholesterol that subsequently improves heart health and increases anti-inflammatory effects. Additionally, evidence suggests that DA receptors are up-regulated by statin therapy (Wang et al., 2011).

BOX 21.1   Pharmacology in Action

Betting with Parkinson's Disease

In 2000, two independent reports were published showing a relationship among PD, its treatment, and impulse control disorders (Molina et al., 2000; Seedat et al., 2002. Molina and colleagues found an increase in compulsive gambling in these patients and reported that gambling was more often (or exclusively in some patients) found during the "on" periods of L-DOPA treatment. The gambling disorder started after the onset of PD and worsened with increasing L-DOPA therapy.

In the years since that time, more than 250 articles have been published on the development of impulse control disorders in PD patients. In addition to gambling, these disorders take the form of compulsive sexual behavior, binge eating, punding (a fascination with repetitive, meaningless, although not necessarily purposeless, movements like cleaning or pulling the arm of a slot machine), excessive hobbying, or compulsive shopping. The overall prevalence rate in PD patients is 14% for these compulsive behaviors (Djamsidian et al., 2011a), with 6% prevalence in nonmedicated PD patients and 17% prevalence in those treated with dopamine agonists (L-DOPA, ropinirole, pramipexole).

Recent reviews indicate that there is an inverse relationship between compulsive behaviors in PD and age of onset of motor symptoms (Singh et al., 2007; Ahearn et al., 2012). The earlier the age of onset of symptoms, the more likely one is to develop these issues. Generally, males are more likely than females to experience these issues. Those with a history of drug abuse before the development of PD are also at greater risk (Djamsidian et al., 2011a).

Although initial reports were focused on L-DOPA treatment, recent indicators are that DA agonists are actually more problematic in the induction of these behaviors (Kelley et al., 2012). In particular, the high affinity that ropinirole and pramipexole have for the D_3 receptor subtype seems to contribute. After cessation of these medications, the symptoms of impulse control disorders dissipate. It is possible even to reintroduce L-DOPA treatment for the motor fluctuations in some patients (Djamsidian et al., 2011b).

Several hypotheses have been put forth for the basis of this effect. In a comprehensive review, Leeman and Potenza (2011) discussed possible contributors, including loss of DA signaling (and therefore reward processing), which may drive compulsive behaviors. It would take significantly more signaling to reach normal levels; therefore, compulsive repetition of acts that are normally rewarding (gambling, sex, shopping, hobbies) brings signaling to a more normal level. Additionally, it may be that cognitive decline leads to perseveration (the recurrence of a word or thought in the mind), which then leads to behavior that follows the repeated thought. Despite changes in DA signaling, rewarding behavior, and cognition, there do not seem to be changes in genes associated with DA signaling, including the D_2 DA receptors, catechol-O-methyltransferase (COMT), and the dopamine transporter (DAT; Vallelunga et al., 2011).

Neurobiologically, there are indications not only of striatal DA abnormalities, but also of midbrain and cingulate cortex. In the midbrain, there is dysfunctional activation of autoreceptors and DA tone in the anterior cingulate cortex is low (Ray et al., 2012). The contribution of these alterations to the manifestation of impulse control disorders is not yet clear.

Treatment for these compulsive behaviors usually begins with reduction of the dose of DA agonist. Other possibilities are cognitive-behavioral therapy, which has shown success against impulse control disorders in general; opioid antagonists, given to reduce the rewarding aspects of these behaviors; and perhaps neuroleptics, but, of course, the danger in the use of neuroleptics is that they may intensify PD motor symptoms.

There are several unmet needs in PD diagnosis and treatment

Although researchers have made great strides in understanding the etiology of PD and in developing new treatments, more research and knowledge is needed in several areas. Since a definitive diagnosis of PD is currently not possible until death, a biomarker or diagnostic test that reliably indicates PD pathology that could be done with minimal expense would be of great use in determining treatment options and regimens. New imaging technologies for DA transporter visualization (Seibyl et al., 2012; Stoessl, 2012) may fill this need and increase diagnostic and treatment efficiency (**Figure 21.7**), but they are currently

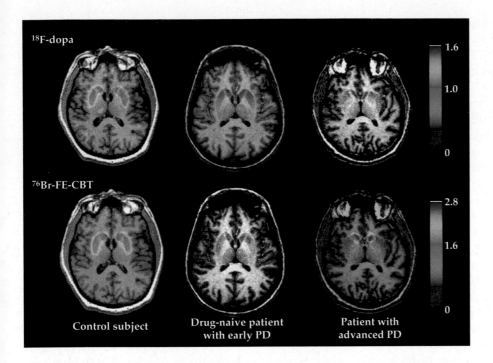

Figure 21.7 PET scan visualization of ^{18}F-dopa and ^{76}Br-FE-CBT uptake at the level of the striatum in a control subject, a drug-naive patient with early Parkinson disease (PD), and a patient with advanced PD. Uptake of both tracers is asymmetrically decreased in patients with PD and is less in the posterior than in the anterior striatum indicating decreased dopaminergic cells. The decrease is more severe in more advanced disease. (From Ribeiro et al., 2002.)

cost-prohibitive for regular use. Although symptomatic treatments are available, none have yet convincingly showed slowing of the disease process. A treatment that could interrupt this process would be most useful. Treatment options for gait freezing to help patients avoid falls and for nonmotor symptoms, particularly the cognitive and behavioral changes, of PD should be explored. Finally, treatment options that promote regeneration and restoration of structure and function should also be actively pursued.

Section Summary

- Parkinson's disease is a chronic, progressive neurodegenerative disorder.
- The primary symptoms of PD are motor disturbances that result in a visible resting tremor and slowing of movement (bradykinesia). Other motor symptoms of the disorder include rigidity and postural instability.
- Nonmotor effects of the disorder start with loss of the sense of smell and include REM behavior disorder and mood disorders.
- Cognitive disturbance can be a result of PD and is called Parkinson's disease dementia (PDD). The slowing of thought and verbal responses (bradyphrenia) is a cardinal symptom.
- These motor and cognitive symptoms are traced to loss of dopaminergic neurons in the substantia nigra, a major input pathway to the basal ganglia.

- PD is most commonly a sporadic event, although about 10% of cases have an inherited genetic cause.
- Pathology in PD is likely due to mitochondrial dysfunction and resulting oxidative stress. Additionally, protein aggregation in cells causes the formation of Lewy bodies, which trigger apoptotic cell death.
- Several animal models of PD allow investigation of various aspects of PD pathology, including the MPTP model, 6-OHDA lesions, and administration of the pesticide rotenone or the drug reserpine.
- The primary therapies in PD aim to increase DA signaling and include L-DOPA, a DA precursor, MAOIs, COMT inhibitors, and DA agonists such as pramipexole, ropinirole, and rotigotine.

Alzheimer's Disease

Alzheimer's disease (AD) is a chronic, progressive dementia disorder that is much more widespread than PD. Among the 25 million patients worldwide who suffer from dementia, 50% to 70% are afflicted with AD. The disorder affects approximately 4.4% of people over the age of 65 and 9.7% of those over 70, and is said to roughly double in prevalence for each 5 years over age 65 (Qui et al., 2009). With the aging of the population, incidence of AD will continue to grow (**Figure 21.8**). Although the typical course of the disease includes an increase in risk as one ages, there is an early-onset form of the disease that begins before age

60, progresses more quickly, and has a genetic basis. Alzheimer's disease is preceded by a disorder called **mild cognitive impairment** (**MCI**). And while all cases of AD are preceded by MCI, not all cases of MCI develop into AD. MCI is marked by difficulty in performing more than one task at a time, difficulty solving problems, and forgetting of recent events or conversations. Those with MCI generally take longer to perform more difficult tasks than they took previously. In work presented at the 2012 American Academy of Neurology annual meeting, Geda and colleagues reported doubling of the risk for MCI in people over the age of 70 who take in between 2100 and 6000 calories per day.

As MCI progresses to AD, several prominent cognitive symptoms appear. The first to appear is general forgetfulness, which leads to progressive loss of memory function. Impairments in other cognitive domains, including emotional behavior, personality, language, perception, thinking, and judgment, are also seen. Patients and caregivers may notice that tasks that used to be relatively easy are now more difficult, particularly more complex cognitive tasks. Anhedonia (loss of enjoyment of previously pleasurable things) is also common. Some anomia or anomic aphasia may be experienced, in which the ability to name familiar objects or people is impaired. Additionally, problems with misplacing or not finding items or getting lost on familiar routes occur with increasing frequency. For a comprehensive discussion of the symptoms of AD, see the Alzheimer's Association website (www.alz.org).

As the disease progresses, these issues get worse, and other behavioral and cognitive changes occur. Changes in physiological processes such as disrupted sleep, incontinence, and difficulty swallowing are seen. Psychiatric symptoms such as delusions, hallucinations, depressed mood, and agitation (including violent outbursts) may occur. Tasks that allow for basic self-sufficiency may suffer, including the ability to prepare food, to choose appropriate clothing, and, particularly, to drive. Additionally, the person's ability to recognize danger and to accurately and appropriately judge a situation is diminished. Reading and writing become more difficult, and strategies such as leaving lists and notes for memory cues may become less effective. Verbal communication also suffers as the disease progresses and language becomes confused, with incorrect word usage and mispronunciation of words. Much of our sense of "self" comes from our memory and cognitive function, and this commonly is lost in those with advancing AD. The loss of personal episodic memories contributes to this. With loss of these functions comes withdrawal from social contact with family and friends. AD will eventually take away completely the ability to use language, interact with or even recognize family or friends, and live independently.

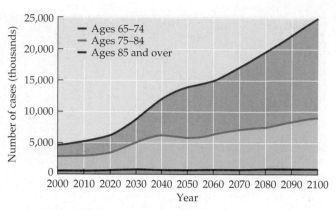

Figure 21.8 Past and projected rates of Alzheimer's disease (AD) With the aging population, cases of AD are expected to increase by approximately five-fold over the next 90 years. (After PhRMA, 2006.)

AD is defined by several pathological cellular disturbances

The cardinal cellular pathologies in AD are amyloid plaques and neurofibrillary tangles. These changes, described in detail in the following sections, result in degeneration of cells throughout the cortex, but primarily in the frontotemporal association cortex (Perl, 2010) as seen in **Figure 21.9**. Additionally, a significant loss of synapses (up to 45%) may be the basis for the significant cognitive deficits seen in AD (Perl, 2010).

AMYLOID PLAQUES The accumulation of the **beta-amyloid protein** (β-amyloid, or **A-beta** [Aβ]) between neurons in the brain results in the formation of amyloid plaques. Aβ is a protein fragment normally produced by the brain by enzymatic cleavage of **amyloid precursor protein** (**APP**). APP is first cleaved by a β-secretase, most commonly BACE1, although BACE2 may also play a role in AD pathology. The cleavage product, APP-CTFβ is then further cleaved by γ-secretase to generate either the 40 amino acid (Aβ40) or the 42 amino acid (Aβ42) form of Aβ (Goedert and Spillantini, 2006; Zhang et al., 2011) (**Figure 21.10**). In healthy brains, there are several proposed functions of the fragments of APP (including soluble APPα which is formed by APP cleaving by α-secretase) including kinase activation, facilitation of gene transcription, cholesterol transport regulation, and pro-inflammatory actions and antimicrobial activities. After use, these fragments are degraded and cause no harm. In the brains of those with AD, these protein fragments, particularly Aβ42, accumulate to form plaques. Several different subtypes of plaques exist and they include the senile or neuritic plaque, which has a core of the amyloid protein surrounded by abnormal neurites (dendrites or axons). Often, microglial cells or reactive astrocytes are found in the periphery of these plaques. A second form of the plaque has focal diffuse deposits

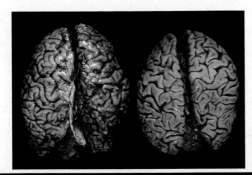

Figure 21.9 Pathological changes in the brain of an individual with advanced Alzheimer's disease (AD) as compared to a normal age-matched individual. The brain of the individual with AD shows significant atrophy, narrowing of the gyri, widening of the sulci, and enlargement of the ventricles. (Courtesy of Ann C. McKee, MD, Boston University School of Medicine/VA Boston Healthcare System.)

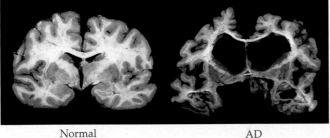

Normal   AD

of amyloid with no neurites surrounding the core. The third form has a dense core of amyloid without neurites. These are generally considered the long-term outcome of neuritic plaques, after the neurites have died off.

NEUROFIBRILLARY TANGLES   Neurofibrillary tangles (NFTs) are fibrous inclusions that are abnormally located in the cytoplasm of neurons. The neurons particularly susceptible to NFTs are pyramidal neurons—those with a pyramid-shaped cell body. The primary component of these tangles is the protein **tau**, which is a protein associated with microtubules (long filaments that help maintain cellular structure and also participate in axonal transport; see Chapter 2). As a component of these

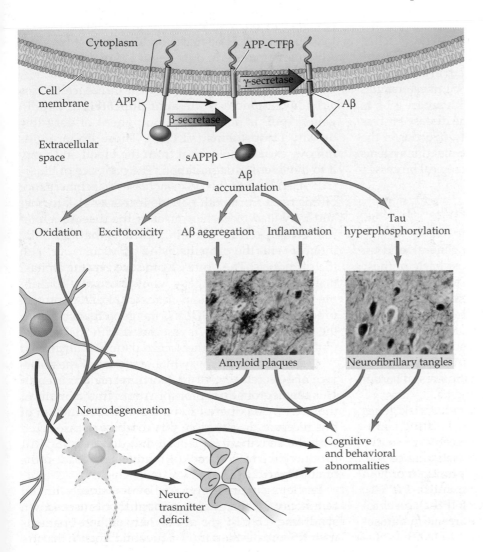

Amyloid plaques   Neurofibrillary tangles

Figure 21.10 Formation of amyloid plaques Amyloid-β (Aβ) is formed by the sequential cleavage of amyloid precursor protein (APP) by β-secretase and γ-secretase. The accumulation of Aβ results in several different pathological changes which, in turn, result in neural degeneration and cognitive and behavioral symptoms. sAPPβ, soluble APPβ. (After Cummings, 2004.)

(A)   Neurofibrillary tangle   (B)

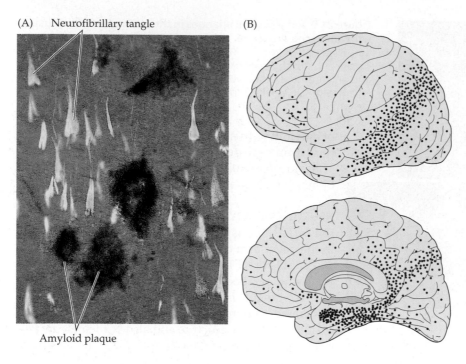

Amyloid plaque

Figure 21.11 Cellular pathology in Alzheimer's disease In Alzheimer's disease, amyloid plaques and neurofibrillary tangles (A) accumulate in the brain (B) with dot density indicating degree of pathology. (A from Roses, 1995, courtesy of Gary W. Van Hoesen; B after Blumenfeld, 2002, based on Brun and Englund, 1981.)

tangles, the tau is abnormally phosphorylated. Other proteins, including ubiquitin, are also found in NFTs. The accumulation of these tangles follows a relatively typical pattern of trans-synaptic spread. In early stages of the disease (Braak and Braak, 1995), these tangles are found in the entorhinal cortex, with progression to the hippocampus and neocortex as the disease process continues (**Figure 21.11**). Additionally, neurons in the basal forebrain cholinergic and monoaminergic systems are susceptible to damage by AD pathological processes.

There are several behavioral, health, and genetic risk factors for AD

Several risk factors for dementia in general, and for AD specifically, are known. The most basic of these risk factors are advancing age and a family history of dementia or AD. Several of these risks are similar to those for the development of heart disease (e.g., diabetes, obesity, untreated hyptertension, high cholesterol, stress, and a sedentary lifestyle). In addition, a history of head trauma or hypoxic brain injury, depression, bipolar disorder, or posttraumatic stress disorder (PTSD) can increase the risk for dementia.

Genetic contributors to AD consist of risk genes and deterministic genes (Zetzsche et al., 2010). Deterministic genes are those that can directly cause disease. Three genes are known to directly cause AD. These include the genes for amyloid precursor protein (APP), found on chromosome 21, **presenilin-1 (PS-1)**, on chromosome 14, and **presenilin-2 (PS-2)**, on chromosome 1. Mutations of these genes result in **autosomal dominant Alzheimer's disease (ADAD)**. In this

familial version of the disease, symptom onset is likely to occur before age 60 (it can occur as early as the 30s). Although of concern, only about 5% of AD cases are familial.

The risk gene with the greatest influence on disease development is the **apolipoprotein E (ApoE)** gene. ApoE is normally a component of very low density lipoproteins (VLDLs). These lipoproteins remove excess cholesterol from the blood and carry it to the liver for degradation. The presence of the E4 (APOEε4) form of this gene increases risk; inheritance of this form from both parents increases risk further and may lead to earlier onset of the disease. Other risk genes produce protein products that normally interact with the proteins listed previously, or with their products. The protease produced by the alpha-2 macroglobulin (A2M) gene would normally contribute to the degradation and clearance of the Aβ protein produced by APP. *UBQLN1*, the gene that codes for the protein ubiquitin 1, is associated with AD because ubiquitin 1 promotes the accumulation of uncleaved PS-1 and PS-2 proteins, which are part of the structure of γ-secretase. SORL1 (sortilin-related receptor 1) is the neuronal receptor for ApoE. In the brains of those with AD, there can be a marked reduction of this receptor. In addition, this receptor is associated with the activity of APP such that decreased SORL1 production is correlated with higher Aβ load in the brain (**Figure 21.12**).

Perhaps surprisingly, AD is also closely linked to trisomy 21, the genetic variant that causes Down syndrome (DS). By the age of 30 to 40, most patients with DS will develop the plaques and tangles that are

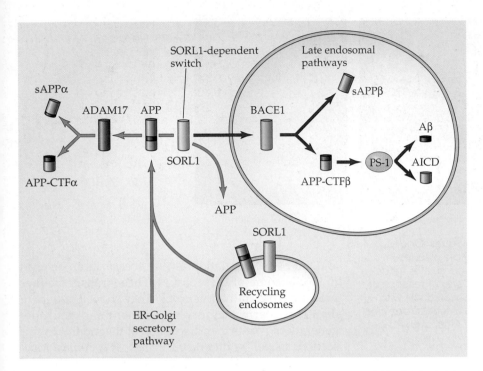

Figure 21.12 The APP processing pathway illustrates the important role SORL1 plays as a switch in this process. After synthesis in the endoplasmic reticulum (ER), APP can be cleaved by ADAM17 (an α-secretase) to form soluble APPα (sAPPα) and a cytoplasmic fragment (APP-CTFα). Alternatively, SORL1 can bind APP and sort it into a recycling pathway. If SORL1 is absent, the APP is directed into β-secretase processing (e.g., by BACE1). BACE1 cleavage forms an N-terminal fragment (sAPPβ) and APP-CTFβ, which is cleaved again by presenilin-dependent γ-secretase to form Aβ and amyloid intracellular domain (AICD). A similar effect can be produced by inhibition of APP recycling from endosomes within the cell. (After Rogaeva et al., 2007.)

associated with AD. These changes are nearly universal among DS patients who reach this age, and although the severity of plaque and tangle accumulation mimics that found in AD, not all such individuals will develop AD. One of the possibilities for the connection is that DS patients have three copies of the *APP* gene, which is located on chromosome 21.

Alzheimer's disease cannot be definitively diagnosed until postmortem analysis

Alzheimer's disease is defined by changes that happen in the brain during degenerative processes, as in the plaques and tangles described previously. These processes generally are not visible without direct examination of the brain. So AD is a diagnosis of elimination rather than confirmation. There is no definitive test to rule *in* AD, but there are several tests that will rule *out* other sources of dementia. By performing physical and neurological exams, taking a thorough medical history, and doing a mental state exam (generally the Mini Mental State Exam, 2nd Edition [MMSE-2]) along with other tests, doctors can rule out anemia, brain

tumor, chronic infection, medication intoxication, severe depression, stroke, thyroid disease, and vitamin deficiency. Only when other causes of dementia have been ruled out can a differential diagnosis of AD be given to a living patient. Several newer technologies allow visualization of the plaques formed around deposits of Aβ protein. One, called Amyvid (florbetapir) is a [18F] tagged small molecule which binds β-amyloid and was developed by Eli Lilly and is used with a positron emission tomography (PET) scanner to examine those who already show signs of cognitive decline. It is a tool of elimination rather than confirmation for AD because amyloid plaques can be present without AD. Another imaging technique with a similar mechanism, also used with a PET scanner, is called florbetaben. This technique has a small but significant false-positive rate. The risk of a false-positive ("You might have Alzheimer's") when a person doesn't have the disease is the reason for its use exclusively in those in whom cognitive decline has already occurred. A third technique, based on work by Wolk et al. (2009), uses [18F] flutemetamol (Pittsburgh Blue [PiB]), which accumulates in the amyloid plaques (**Figure 21.13**).

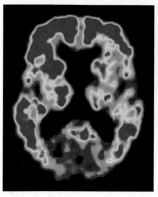
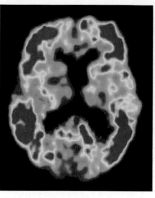
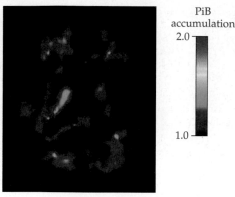

Alzheimer's disease   Cognitive impairment   Control subject

PiB accumulation
2.0
1.0

Figure 21.13 Visualization of amyloid plaques One of several new methods for visualizing amyloid plaques in living brains, Pittsburgh Blue (PiB) dye accumulates in the plaques and can be visualized using PET scan. Presence of these plaques is more common in those individuals with Alzheimer's or significant cognitive impairment. (From Wolk et al., 2009, courtesy of the University of Pittsburgh Amyloid Imaging Group.)

Despite these advancements, definitive diagnosis still requires postmortem analysis to look for the trademark neuronal changes that happen in AD.

Postmortem analysis of brain tissue is performed to look for the presence of two key indicators: NFTs and amyloid plaques. If these two pathologies are present, a diagnosis of AD is made; if these plaques are not detected, another explanation is put forth for the cognitive deficits seen in the patient. While postmortem diagnosis can confirm AD in the deceased, it is not useful in developing treatment strategies in those who are still alive. It is only through advancement of the amyloid imaging techniques discussed above that more informed treatment decisions can be made.

Several different animal models contribute to our understanding of AD

As with other disorders, the primary goal of animal models is to closely approximate one or more aspects of the human condition of AD. Several transgenic mouse models aim to get the progressive neuropathology that is seen with AD. Two common models (the APP/PSδE9 and APPswe/PS1δE9 models) are mutations on the *APP* gene. Each of these mutations results in memory deficits, high levels of Aβ42 in the brain, and amyloid deposits. The APPswe/PSδE9 model also shows the formation of neuritic plaques. The senescence-accelerated prone (SAMP8) mouse shows early learning and memory deficits along with the accumulation of Aβ protein, oxidative damage,

and tau phosphorylation. Even *Drosophila* can be used to model some of these issues. These transgenic flies produce Aβ42 in their neurons. They show age-dependent short-term memory impairment and neurodegeneration. For further discussion of the models in this section, as well as others, see *Handbook of Animal Models in Alzheimer's Disease* (2011), edited by Casadesus.

A more natural (nontransgenic) model may be found in the beagle. Aged beagles can develop learning and memory deficits, as well as problems with executive function. This naturally occurring pathology shows similarity to the human condition in cortical atrophy, neuron loss, lack of neurogenesis, β-amyloid plaques, and other damage. The pathological changes correlate with the deficits in function. The progressive nature of the disorder in these animals is beneficial for longitudinal study.

Sometimes, models of other pathological processes can inadvertently bring about neuropathology. Originally models of coronary artery disease, cholesterol-fed rabbits also developed Aβ deposits, neurofibrillary tangles, and cognitive deficits at rates higher than those seen in rabbits that ate a normal diet. If the cholesterol feeding was paired with the administration of copper, outcomes were even worse. This is likely a result of copper interfering with clearance of Aβ from the brain by LDL receptor–related protein 1 (LRP). Like humans with AD, these rabbits are deficient in eyeblink conditioning and show neuronal loss in the frontal cortex, hippocampus, and cerebellum.

Symptomatic treatments are available and several others are under study for slowing disease progression

Current treatments fall into two categories: **cholinesterase inhibitors** and an **N-methyl-D-aspartate (NMDA)** glutamate receptor antagonist. Because AD seems to target cholinergic cells involved in cognition, the cholinesterase inhibitors improve cognition by increasing the presence of acetylcholine in the synapse by lessening its breakdown. The first cholinesterase inhibitor approved for use in AD was tacrine (Cognex) for the treatment of mild to moderate AD. Soon after (in 1996) came donepezil (Aricept). Like Cognex and the cholinesterase inhibitors that followed, it was initially prescribed for mild to moderate AD, but newer evidence suggests that staying on the drug through the moderate stage (when previously the drug would have been stopped) may slow memory decline. After donepezil (in 2000) came rivastigmine (Exelon), which can be given in pill or transdermal patch form, and (in 2001) galantamine (Razadyne).

After it was observed that damaged neurons release significant amounts of glutamate, the drug memantine (**Namenda**) was introduced to prevent further excitotoxic neuron damage. Approved in 2003, memantine works by blocking current flow through the NMDA subtype of glutamate receptor. This prevents the drastic increase in cell firing that leads to excitotoxicity, without producing significant side effects. As a result of binding to two sites on the receptor, modulation of the receptor is less severe than with other NMDA receptor antagonists like MK-801 and ketamine (Johnson and Kotermanski, 2006). Namenda is the only drug specifically approved for use in moderate to severe cases of AD.

Because of the devastating effects of AD, its increase in incidence and prevalence among those over age 65, and the increasing age of the population (at least in the United States), there is an urgent need for more effective AD therapies. Several recent studies have indicated promise for new types of therapies. In what certainly must have started as an anecdotal observation in Alzheimer's patients who had comorbid cancer, researchers at Case Western Reserve University in Cleveland, Ohio, found that the chemotherapy drug Epothilone D (EpoD) can reduce the presence of tau protein tangles in mice (Zhang et al., 2012).

Two antibodies are currently in preclinical development for AD, with the promise of upcoming clinical trials. The first antibody, bapineuzumab, decreases levels of phosphorylated tau protein in the brains of mice, although its target is β-amyloid (which it does not decrease). The second antibody, crenezumab, is in two current U.S. trials as well as a clinical trial starting in 2013 in a large Columbian family of 3000 people who carry the *PSEN-1* gene. Early indications from preclinical work and from early-stage clinical trials are that it may be useful in preventing the onset of familial AD (Adolfsson et al., 2012).

A potential therapy that is in a much earlier stage of development consists of a class of compounds called spin-labeled fluorene compounds. These compounds reduce amyloid plaque formation in cultured neurons and can cross the blood–brain barrier (Petrlova et al., 2012). The next step is to test these compounds in animal models of AD. Perhaps the most anticipated potential new therapy is the "Alzheimer's vaccine." This therapy is discussed in greater detail in **Box 21.2**.

Section Summary

- Alzheimer's disease is a dementia disorder that affects increasing numbers of people in the United States.

- The onset of AD is preceded by MCI, but not all cases of MCI develop into AD.

- Early symptoms of AD include forgetfulness and impairment in other cognitive functions, including language, thinking, and judgment. Physiological changes include difficulty swallowing and disrupted sleep. Psychiatric difficulties come in the form of delusions, hallucinations, depression, and agitation. As the disease progresses, communication becomes increasingly difficult because of reading, writing, and verbal communication problems.

- Two pathological findings hallmark disease progression in AD: amyloid plaques and NFTs. Amyloid plaques are formed by accumulation of Aβ (primarily Aβ42) after production by secretase cutting of the amyloid precursor protein (APP). NFTs are composed primarily of abnormally phosphyorylated tau, a microtubule-associated protein, and other proteins like ubiquitin. Accumulation of NFTs results in disruption of cellular processes and eventually apoptotic cell death.

- Risk factors for development of AD include advancing age and poor cardiovascular health. Previous head injury or psychopathology can also increase risk.

- Several genes are associated with the development of autosomal dominant AD (ADAD) and include APP, presenilin-1, and presenilin-2.

- Several other genes impart increased risk for AD, including the APOEε4 allele, alpha-2 macroglobulin, *UBQLN1*, and SORL1.

- Because of the location of risk genes on chromosome 21, AD has a strong association with Down syndrome (trisomy 21).

- AD generally is not diagnosed until after death, although newer imaging technologies may allow earlier diagnosis in the future.

- Animal models for AD include transgenic mice, with alterations in the genes listed above, a natural aged beagle model, and a cholesterol-fed rabbit model.

BOX 21.2   The Cutting Edge

Measles, Mumps, and ... Alzheimer's Vaccines?

For several years, attention has been focused on the possibility of a vaccine to combat the Aβ buildup in AD. Early efforts were focused on AN1792, which, in addition to the desired antibody response, brought about a T-cell response specific to Aβ. This T-cell response was thought to be the reason for a significant adverse event (and the cessation of a clinical trial)—the development of meningoencephalitis (an inflammation of the brain and meninges; Orogozo, et al., 2003). The reason for this cross-activation is likely that in the full-length Aβ42, which was used to generate AN1792, there are many epitopes (the part of an antigen that is recognized by the immune system) to which T cells bind (Cribbs et al., 2003; Nicoll et al., 2003). Although adverse events occurred, indications suggested that the antibody response generated by the vaccine was effective in reducing functional decline and reducing dependence on caregivers (Gilman et al., 2005; Vellas et al., 2009), although significant effects on cognitive function were not seen. These changes were attributed to an observed reduction in the number of amyloid plaques (Ferrer et al., 2004; Holmes et al., 2008). A reduction was also seen in the amount of tau protein found in the CSF of vaccinated patients (Gilman et al., 2005; Vellas et al., 2009).

Recently, another attempt was made to induce an antibody reaction to Aβ without also activating T cells (Weisner et al., 2011; Wingblad et al., 2012). Instead of the whole Aβ protein, a smaller fragment, $A\beta_{1-6}$, was used to generate the CAD106 vaccine. The CAD106 vaccine was tested in two different transgenic mouse models and resulted in the reduction of plaques in those animals (Weisner et al., 2011); antibodies were produced, but no T-cell activation was seen. The amount of amyloid deposited in the brain was quite significantly reduced, seen as both a reduction in plaque area and a reduction in the number of plaques. A Phase I clinical trial of CAD106, conducted primarily to evaluate safety and side effects, was conducted in Sweden. Published reports of this trial (Wingblad et al., 2012) indicate that 67% of patients in a low-dose condition and 82% given a higher dose produced antibodies to Aβ, and among enrolled patients, no cases of meningoencephalitis were reported. With these promising results, further trials are planned to investigate the efficacy of this antibody response.

- Current treatments for AD are primarily cholinesterase inhibitors and an NMDA receptor modulator.
- Research indicates that Aβ antibodies, chemotherapy drugs, and perhaps even an AD vaccine may be effective treatments that will become available in the future.

Other Major Neurodegenerative Diseases

Huntington's Disease

Mr. R. was working for a large international bank in England—his dream job. When he forgot his password to the company banking system, he feared the worst. While most of us would attribute that slip to a rough day, he suspected that it was the beginning of a long, painful process that he had seen in his mother and grandmother. Anger and time management issues followed the memory lapses. These eventually led to loss of his job and the need to move back to the United States. He started a roofing business, but quickly, physical symptoms such as loss of balance prevented him from doing the job, and cognitive and psychiatric symptoms interfered with his ability to run the business. A genetic test for a clinical trial confirmed fears that Mr. R. had inherited the **Huntington's disease (HD)** gene from his mother. His focus became raising awareness of issues surrounding HD, receiving treatment for his increasing symptoms, and recognizing his fear for the future of his children, who have a 50% chance of developing the disorder, just as he and his siblings had. Mr. R. now faces progressive loss of cognitive and physical abilities and ongoing psychiatric problems. This will end with his death from Huntington's disease.

Huntington's disease is one of a few neurodegenerative disorders with a clear, singular genetic cause. A **trinucleotide repeat** (a CAG sequence) results in a gain-of-function mutation in the ***huntingtin*** **gene**. *Huntingtin* is a highly penetrant mutation (meaning that, if the gene is a certain form, the chance of developing the disease is very high or is guaranteed). In this case, the likelihood of developing HD is dependent on the number of CAG repeats in the gene. There is essentially complete **penetrance** at 40 repeats, but lesser penetrance at smaller numbers of repeats, and no development of the disease at fewer than 35 copies. There is 90% penetrance at 39 copies, meaning that 90% of those with 39 copies of the CAG repeat will develop the disease, and 10% will not. There is 75% penetrance at 38, 50% at 37, and 25% at 36 (Myers, 2011, personal communication). Although those with 27 to 35 copies do not develop the disease themselves, because of the instability of the gene men can pass on a longer version of the gene to their offspring and increase their risk of developing the disorder. The number of repeats generally correlates with the age of onset such that more repeats result in earlier disease development. Age of onset can range from 4 to 65 years of age, but generally comes in middle age.

The "normal" version of the gene has about 20 CAG repeats at this location. The extra repeats in the gene cause a toxic gain-of-function resulting in protein aggregation and cell death.

Symptoms

Huntington's disease tends to be grouped with motor disorders when it is classified, but significant cognitive and psychiatric symptoms have been noted as well (Novak and Tabrizi, 2011). The motor symptoms result from degenerative effects on the basal ganglia (**Figure 21.14**) and reduced ability to suppress unwanted movement. Originally named "**Huntington's chorea**" these involuntary movements are jerky or writhing, "dance-like" movements of the limbs. In addition to these gross motor function changes, fine movement is significantly impaired in speed and coordination. Other issues in motor function include rigidity, dystonia, problems with speech and swallowing, and gait problems. Generally, the cause of death in HD is associated with these changes in motor function. Many with HD die from pneumonia and other complications of the inability to swallow or of injuries related to falls.

Motor symptoms, however, are not the only consequences of the significant degeneration in this disorder. Cognitively, patients with HD often find that they have difficulty with higher-order functions like planning and organizing. There are perseveration issues, where thoughts or behaviors are repeated over and over. There are issues with learning and memory, attention, and language usage. While this may seem unrelated to a movement disorder, these cognitive issues also result from damage to basal ganglia circuits. In addition to circuits initiating movement, the basal ganglia initiate cognitive and emotional processes through connections to the dorsolateral prefrontal cortex, the orbitofrontal cortex, and the cingulate cortex (Middleton and Strick, 2000). One of the more interesting consequences of this disorder is difficulty

(A)

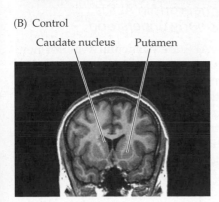

(B) Control

Caudate nucleus   Putamen

Patient with Huntington's disease

Lateral ventricles

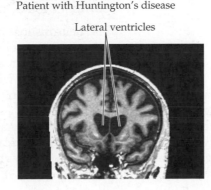

Figure 21.14 Neuropathology in Huntington's disease (A) Significant degeneration is seen in the brain of a patient with Huntington's disease compared to a control patient. In particular, the size of the caudate and putamen (the striatum) is decreased due to neurodegeneration of cells found there. (B) On MRI, the degeneration of the caudate and putamen can be seen in the enlargement of the lateral ventricles in patients with HD (right) compared with those of a control subject (left). (A courtesy of Harvard Brain Tissue Resource Center; B courtesy of Terry L. Jernigan and C. Fennema Notestine.)

with or refusal to be aware of their own symptoms, despite their obvious nature to others.

HD is also comorbid with several psychiatric symptoms and disorders. These comorbidities include obsessive–compulsive disorder (OCD), bipolar disorder, and mania. Several symptoms of depression, including changes in sleep patterns and energy, sadness, and thoughts of death, are also common in those with HD. Personality characteristics may change in HD, bringing about irritability, impulsivity, and anxiety.

Only symptomatic treatments are available for HD, none alter disease progression

No treatments yet tested can alter the course of Huntington's disease; all of the treatments are symptomatic in nature. Tetrabenazine (Xenazine) is the only drug specifically approved by the Food and Drug Administration (FDA) for HD. This drug is useful in decreasing the excessive movement found in the disorder. The mechanism of this decrease in motor function is a decrease in monoamine vesicle packaging. Tetrabenazine is a reversible antagonist of the type 2 vesicular monoamine transporter (VMAT2) (see Chapter 5). The half-life of tetrabenazine is 4 to 8 hours, and the duration of effect of a dose is approximately 5.5 hours. Because of the depletion of monoamines, the drug may increase psychiatric symptoms, particularly those associated with depression. Other side effects include parkinsonism and sedation.

Dopamine antagonist drugs, such as those usually used to treat schizophrenia, are also used to suppress the unwanted movements. Anticonvulsants and anxiolytic drugs are often used to combat both the choreic movements and the dystonia or rigidity that may accompany HD. To combat the psychiatric symptoms of the disorder, antidepressants, particularly the SSRIs are used, as are the typical antipsychotics and mood stabilizers. More information about the mechanisms of these drugs is available in Chapters 18, 17, and 19, respectively.

Nondrug treatments that may be included in a treatment plan for someone with HD include physical and occupational therapy to combat changes in fine motor control, speech therapy, and psychotherapy.

Amyotrophic Lateral Sclerosis

Certainly the most famous patient with amyotrophic lateral sclerosis (ALS) was Lou Gherig, a New York Yankee who, in 1939, retired from baseball after he was diagnosed with the disorder. Today, the disorder often bears his name. ALS is another degenerative disorder with principally motor symptoms. The degeneration of upper and lower motor neurons results in a progressive loss of fine and then gross motor function (Hardiman et al., 2011). The disorder leads to death from respiratory failure, generally within 5 years.

The incidence of ALS is around 1 to 3 cases per 100,000 people. Both familial and nonfamilial cases have been reported. Those that are nonfamilial in origin show more men affected than women. Risk factors may include exposure to some chemicals (such as insecticides and pesticides, which may also contribute to the development of PD). Those who smoke are at higher risk, as are those who have served in the military.

The symptoms and disease progression in ALS are devastating

In the early stages of ALS, with degeneration of spinal motor neurons, focal muscle weakness may manifest as tripping, clumsiness (particularly dropping things), and abnormal fatigue in the arms or legs. As the muscles are denervated, fasciculations (muscle twitches) and cramping may be noted. If the motor neurons most affected early on are those that give rise to the corticobulbar tract (the tract that runs from the cortex to the brainstem to control cranial nerve functions), the disease may start with difficulty chewing and swallowing and general facial weakness. Strangely, this degeneration may also be associated with involuntary exaggeration of emotional reflexes, including uncontrolled laughing or crying. Other manifestations of loss of these cells include slurred speech and difficulty projecting the voice.

Despite the start of symptoms in focal, distinct areas, eventually nearly all of the motor neurons are affected. This will lead to difficulty in breathing, which eventually will require ventilatory support for survival. Motor neurons are spared in only a couple of systems: eye movements are not compromised, nor is bladder and bowel function.

The loss of motor neurons in ALS is complicated and poorly understood

The neurons lost in ALS are particularly motor neurons. In these neurons, one would see disruption of the cytoskeleton and aggregates of the component neurofilaments with other proteins to form "spheroids." This pathology also leads to the activation and proliferation of astrocytes and microglia, resulting in neuroinflammation. The name "lateral sclerosis" comes from the scarred appearance of the spinal cord caused by the loss of the lateral corticospinal tract neurons (**Figure 21.15**).

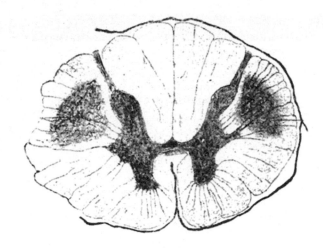

Figure 21.15 Amyotrophic lateral sclerosis is characterized by scarring of the spinal cord (dark pink areas) that is caused by the loss of lateral corticospinal tract neurons.

Multiple Sclerosis

Multiple sclerosis (MS) is perhaps the least predictable of the disorders discussed in this chapter. Thought to be primarily an autoimmune disorder, MS is the result of a chronic attack on the brain, spinal cord, and optic nerves. In particular, the autoimmune target is the protein in the myelin produced by **oligodendrocytes** (as opposed to that produced by **Schwann cells** in the peripheral nervous system; see Chapter 2). Multiple sclerosis might take one of four courses: (1) relapsing-remitting MS (RRMS), (2) primary-progressive MS (PPMS), (3) secondary-progressive MS (SPMS), or (4) progressive-relapsing MS (PRMS) (**Table 21.1**). Disease progression is evaluated in several ways:

- Lesions in the central nervous system (CNS) can be visualized on magnetic resonance imaging (MRI); doctors will look for scarred lesions and gadolinium-enhanced new lesions (when given during an MRI, gadolinium is a contrast material that indicates areas of active inflammation).

How and why these cells die is a subject of much research. Several mechanisms seem to contribute to this loss (Joyce et al., 2011). Excitotoxicity from excessive glutamate signaling is one component of the damage. Other mechanisms include aggregation of proteins, breakdown of axonal transport with loss of neurofilament structure, reduced production of adenosine triphosphate (ATP), neuroinflammation, and triggering of cell death pathways. Indications suggest that some RNA binding proteins are mutated in some ALS cases. How problems in these proteins might lead to the death of motor neurons is not clear.

Only one medication is FDA-approved for use in ALS

Only one treatment has been approved by the FDA specifically for the treatment of ALS. That drug, riluzole (Rilutek), has a modest disease-modifying effect such that the average survival time in treated patients is 2 to 3 months longer than in those who are untreated. The drug acts as a presynaptic inhibitor of glutamate release. Because excitotoxic damage to neurons occurs in the pathological processes of ALS, this drug is thought to provide benefit by blocking this glutamate-mediated excitotoxicity (**Figure 21.16**). Some small benefit is associated with riluzole therapy in terms of symptom severity (including bulbar and limb function), but no benefit has been noted for muscle strength. Other indications suggest that the drug may delay the need for intubation and ventilatory support.

Other treatments are largely symptomatic and are not pharmacological. These might include splinting of affected limbs and, at the patient's choice, measures to augment breathing function. When swallowing function is lost, patients might be fed through a gastronomy tube.

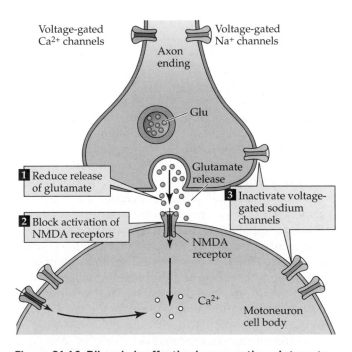

Figure 21.16 Riluzole is effective in preventing glutamate transmission by three mechanisms It can reduce release of glutamate (1), block activation of NMDA receptors (2), and inactivate voltage-gated sodium channels thereby preventing the transmission of action potentials (3). (After Charité Campus Virchow-Klinikum Neurological Clinic, 2009.)

TABLE 21.1	MS Can Take One of Four Courses	
Type	**Incidence**	**Course**
Relapsing-Remitting	85%	Clearly defined attacks of neurological deficits, which are followed by times of partial or complete recovery. During the remissions, disease progression is halted.
Primary-Progressive	10%	Neurological deficits are experienced slowly, but progressively worsen over time. The rate of progression varies across cases and even for a given patient such that there can be plateaus or brief periods of minor improvement.
Secondary-Progressive	Approximately 50% of those with relapsing-remitting MS (RRMS) developed this before disease-modifying medications were available. Long-term data are not yet available on whether this number has declined.	After first presenting with RRMS, these patients start a period of steady decline. There may still be periods of relapse and minor improvement (remissions) or plateaus in progression.
Progressive-Relapsing	5%	The worst of the possibilities, this course includes steady decline from disease onset along with clear attacks of worsening function. While there may be some recovery from these attacks, there are no periods of remission from disease symptoms.

- Sensory-evoked potentials can indicate deficits in signaling through sensory pathways.
- Neurological and functional exams can be used to assess physical and cognitive function.

For more information about these and other aspects of MS, see the National MS Society website (www.nationalmssociety.org).

The symptoms of MS are variable and unpredictable

The symptoms experienced by any one person with MS vary widely across the disease course and vary to an even greater extent across patients. The more common symptoms include **fatigue**, numbness, walking/balance/coordination problems, bladder and/or bowel dysfunction, vision problems, dizziness and vertigo, sexual dysfunction, pain, cognitive dysfunction, emotional changes, and **spasticity**. Other, less common symptoms include speech disorders, swallowing problems, persistent headache, hearing loss, seizures, tremor, breathing problems, and itching.

The symptoms listed here can lead to secondary and tertiary symptoms of the disease. If a person with MS is experiencing bladder dysfunction, she may be at significant risk for repeated urinary tract infections (UTIs)—an example of a secondary symptom. Other examples of secondary symptoms include prolonged periods of inactivity due to motor symptoms that may cause muscle weakness, pressure sores, and decreased bone density. Tertiary symptoms are those that are a result of the disease's impact on the person's life; job

loss or limitations, stress, failure of relationships, and social isolation are some examples.

Depression is more common in those with MS than in the general population; the lifetime risk is approximately 50% in people with MS versus about 12% to 15% in those without MS (Siegert and Abernethy, 2005). It is likely that this condition can be either a primary symptom or a tertiary symptom of MS. Studies of lesion location and symptom severity reveal variation in the association of depression with lesion location, although there may be a relationship between some frontal and temporal region lesions and depression. Significant concern arises when rates of suicidal ideation are investigated in those with MS, along with the impact of depression, in general, on quality of life and on participation in therapeutic interventions. **Table 21.2** summarizes the symptoms of MS and the other neurodegenerative diseases discussed in this chapter.

Diagnosis

The diagnosis of MS is an inexact science and often takes some time. This is the case because the symptoms of MS can result from several disorders. To receive a diagnosis of MS, one must have lesions in at least two distinct areas of the CNS (or optic nerves). Evaluation must indicate that these lesions happened at least 1 month apart. Perhaps most important, other causes of the symptoms (such as viral infections, exposure to toxic chemicals, vitamin B12 deficiency, and Guillain-Barré syndrome) must be ruled out.

Lesions are visualized using MRI. To differentiate between older and more current lesions, gadolinium

TABLE 21.2   Neurodegenerative Disorders Can Have a Variety of Symptoms

Disorder	Motor	Sensory	Cognitive	Psychiatric
		Symptoms		
Parkinson's disease	Resting tremor; akinesia; bradykinesia; rigidity; postural instability; retropulsion: anteropulsion; festination; dystonia; akathisia	Loss of smell	PD dementia; bradyphrenia; mental inflexibility; visuospatial deficits	PD dementia; hallucinations
Alzheimer's disease	Inability to perform self-care activities such as bathing, cooking, and driving	—	Forgetfulness; progressive memory loss; verbal communication deficits; anomia; poor judgment; slowed thinking	Altered emotional processing; personality changes; anhedonia; sleep disturbance; agitation; delusions; hallucinations
Huntington's disease	Choreic movements; rigidity; dystonia; swallowing and speech difficulties; gait problems	—	Planning and organization difficulties; perseveration; attention deficits; memory difficulties; language use issues	OCD; bipolar disorder; mania; depression; irritability; impulsivity; anxiety; other personality changes
Amyotrophic lateral sclerosis	Focal and progressive muscle weakness; tripping; clumsiness; abnormal fatigue; muscle fasciculation; slurred speech; difficulty with voice projection, breathing, and chewing and swallowing	—	—	Exaggerated emotional responses such as uncontrolled laughing or crying
Multiple sclerosis	Fatigue; problems with coordination and gait; sexual, bladder, and bowel dysfunction; spasticity; difficulty swallowing	Vision loss; dizziness/ vertigo; persistent headache; pain	Memory and attention deficits	Emotional changes

can be used as a contrast agent to reveal active inflammation. This can help with the timing of lesions for diagnosis. However, about 5% of those who have MS do not have lesions visible on MRI in the early stages of symptoms. Other tests that can be done to support a diagnosis of MS are visual evoked potentials (VEPs). These potentials measure the speed at which information passes through the visual system to reach the appropriate processing area of the brain. To do this, brief visual stimuli are presented. Electrodes on the scalp overlying the visual cortex in the occipital lobe measure resulting brain activity. Another indicator of MS, but unfortunately also of other immune-activating issues in the brain, is the presence of **oligoclonal bands** in the cerebrospinal fluid (CSF) (without presence in the blood). These bands, visualized with protein electrophoresis methods, are actually immunoglobulins that indicate inflammatory processes within the CNS. When combined with MRI and VEP data, they strengthen confidence in a diagnosis of MS.

Causes of MS

The causes of MS are still unknown, but researchers have identified several factors that may contribute to the development the disease.

IMMUNOLOGICAL   MS is generally thought of as an autoimmune disease because of the presence of autoreactive **T cells**, which recognize oligodendrocyte myelin-specific antigens. Although the exact antigens have yet to be definitively identified, it is known that T cells cross the blood–brain barrier and secrete molecules that are damaging to neurons and release pro-inflammatory cytokines. While the brain is generally considered immunoprivileged (meaning that there is little interaction with the immune system), some immune cells enter the brain to surveil the environment. If they do not find a target, they die in the unwelcoming brain environment. If they do find their target, they recruit more cells to the area.

World Distribution of Multiple Sclerosis

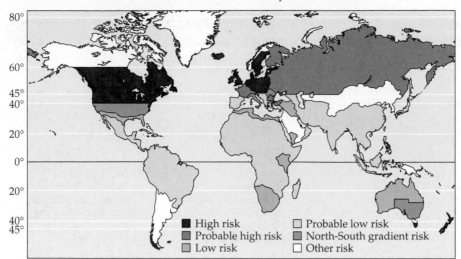

Figure 21.17 Geographic patterns to the distribution of multiple sclerosis (MS) cases In general, colder climates bring increased risk for the development of MS. (After Rose et al., 2000.)

ENVIRONMENTAL   Some of the evidence for an environmental contributor to the development of MS is the interesting trend toward a geographical risk map (Simpson et al., 2011). Generally, the risk for MS is very much greater in those who live above 40° latitude in the Northern hemisphere (**Figure 21.17**). The risk for development of MS seems to be determined by the location of residence up to about age 15. Those who move to a temperate climate from a tropical one before the age of 15 take on the increased risk of a temperate climate. Those who make this move after age 15 keep the risk level from the tropical climate. There are several risk factors for MS that might also be linked to this geographical anomaly. One is that vitamin D may be protective. Those who live in more tropical climates tend to spend more time in the sun and therefore produce more vitamin D.

Interestingly, the warmer months in both the United States and Italy tend to increase relapses of MS in diagnosed patients. The risk in the United States, particularly in Massachusetts, was found to be highest between May and August (Meier et al., 2010). In the study conducted in Italy, the highest risk was between May and June, with a smaller peak in November and December. Although these studies are small, they do indicate an interesting seasonal pattern that may invite further study.

As with PD and ALS, there may be a role for environmental toxins and metals in disease onset. There are clusters, or areas, where the rate of MS is higher than would normally be expected that are currently being investigated for the presence of a toxin or toxins that may influence the development of the disease.

INFECTIOUS   Infectious processes can also increase the likelihood of developing MS. Infection with measles, human herpes virus-6, Epstein-Barr (E-B) virus, and *Chlamydia pneumoniae* may increase one's risk (about 90% of all those with MS have also had E-B virus infec-

tion such as mononucleosis). These infections are more likely (and spread more easily) in colder climates, where residents are likely to spend more time inside.

GENETIC   MS is not a strictly hereditary disease. There has been no identified "MS gene," as there was for Huntington's disease. But indications suggest that some genes may increase a person's risk for developing this disorder. This conclusion comes from the fact that first-degree relatives of those with MS are at greater risk for development of MS than are people in the general population. It is likely that there are gene variants that make one more likely to react to certain environmental or immune triggers with the development of autoimmunity.

Treatments fall into several categories for MS and can be very effective

Treatments for MS may be disease modifying or intended to treat an acute exacerbation. Still others may be used to treat specific symptoms.

DISEASE-MODIFYING TREATMENTS   In contrast to many of the other disorders discussed in this chapter, several drugs are able to reduce the frequency and severity of relapses and the accumulation of lesions, and appear to slow the accumulation of disability in MS.

The first class of drugs approved for use in MS was the interferons. **Interferon beta** (**1a** and **1b**) likely works in MS by increasing **suppressor T-cell** function. These T cells modulate the immune system and maintain tolerance to self-antigens in contrast or opposition to the myelin-reactive T cells described previously. Thus, they decrease the self-attack in MS. The four interferon drugs are Avonex and Rebif (interferon beta-1a) and Betaseron and Extavia (interferon beta-1b). Each is administered by injection—Avonex once per week by IM injection, the rest every other day or three times per week by SC injection. The side effects of these drugs are flulike symptoms and injection site reactions. Evidence suggests the possibility of a relationship between therapy and depression with these drugs, but it remains unclear whether this is an increased risk for depression above MS itself.

Copaxone (glatiramer acetate) is a synthetic protein that simulates myelin basic protein, a component of myelin that may be one of the antigenic targets of autoimmunity. It is thought to work by blocking myelin-damaging T cells, but it is unclear how it achieves this effect. Side effects of Copaxone generally resolve on their own and include injection site reactions, runny nose, tremor, unusual tiredness or weakness, and weight gain. About 13% of patients taking the drug have a one-time (although not necessarily a first-time) reaction, which includes very short-lived (around 15 minutes) flushing, chest tightness, palpitations, anxiety, and difficulty breathing.

Novantrone (mitoxantrone) is the only MS drug currently available as a generic drug and as an antineoplastic agent. Therefore, before its use for MS, it had been used only to treat cancers. Novantrone works in MS because it suppresses several components of the immune system, including T cells, B cells, and macrophages. This is the only drug that is approved for subtypes of MS other than RRMS. It is approved for use in worsening RRMS, SPMS, and PRMS, but not in PPMS. Four injections are administered across a year (injected once every 3 months). Risks are similar to those of other chemotherapy drugs and include cardiotoxicity and secondary acute myelogenous leukemia.

Following its original approval, Tysabri (natalizumab) was briefly removed from the market by the FDA because of an increased incidence of progressive multifocal leukoencephalopathy (PML). An IV infusion that is administered four times per year, Tysabri is a monoclonal antibody that hampers movement of damaging immune cells from the bloodstream across the blood–brain barrier. Further study revealed that the risk for PML is increased in those who have been exposed to **John Cunningham (JC) virus** and have JC virus antibodies. JC virus causes PML in those with suppressed immune systems (e.g., individuals with acquired immunodeficiency syndrome [AIDS] or those receiving treatment with immunosuppressants).

The goal in the field of MS therapy research has long been to develop a disease-modifying medication that can be administered orally. Recent advancements have actually led to two such medications. Gilenya (fingolimod) is a sphingosine 1-phosphate receptor modulator. This therapy causes retention of lymphocytes in lymph nodes, thereby preventing their entry to the CNS through the blood–brain barrier. This, in turn, prevents inflammatory damage to neurons. The side effects are relatively mild and include headache, flu, diarrhea, back pain, and cough. The side effect of abnormal liver tests is a little more serious.

The most recent MS disease-modifying medication is also a drug that is administered orally. Augbagio (teriflunomide) is a pyrimidine synthesis inhibitor that inhibits the function of specific immune cells. It is closely related to a therapy for another autoimmune disorder, rheumatoid arthritis. Augbagio reduces the proliferation of both T and B cells. It also reduces T-cell cytokine release. The side effects are similar to those seen with Gilenya and include diarrhea, nausea, flu, alopecia (thinning/loss of the hair), and abnormal liver tests.

TREATING EXACERBATIONS   The most common mechanism for treating acute exacerbations that are affecting someone's ability to perform at home or at work is the administration of corticosteroids. Three are commonly used on a short-term basis, generally for 3 to 5 days, to treat a relapse: prednisone (administered PO), methylprednisolone (MP; given as an IV), and dexamethasone (also administered by IV means). MP is also used for acute optic neuritis. These drugs work through their powerful anti-inflammatory effects. The side effects of these drugs prohibit their long-term use in the management of MS and include stomach irritation, elevated blood sugar, water retention, restlessness, insomnia, and mood swings.

MANAGING SYMPTOMS   Many medications are used to minimize the symptoms of MS, in addition to the disease-modifying and exacerbation-treating medications. Antidepressants, pain medications, and drugs for bladder and bowel dysfunction are common. Ampyra (dalfampridine) has been approved for the treatment of walking dysfunction in those with MS. A potassium channel blocker, Amypyra, allows transmission through demyelinated fibers in motor pathways. This medication has several side effects, including UTI, difficulty sleeping, dizziness, headache, nausea, weakness, back pain, problems with balance, MS relapse, burning, tingling/itching of the skin, irritation of the nose and throat, constipation, indigestion, and throat pain. Recently, the FDA added a notice to the prescribing information for Ampyra, indicating risk for seizures associated with this medication in those who have reduced kidney function.

Several nonmedication treatments are also used in the management of MS symptoms. These include participation in physical or occupational therapy, visits to a speech/language pathologist, cognitive rehabilitation, and assistive devices used inside and outside the home.

Section Summary

- Huntington's disease (HD) is an inherited, single-gene, neurodegenerative disorder that leads to significant motor, cognitive, and psychiatric symptoms.

- The *huntingtin* gene contains a CAG trinucleotide repeat, and the disease is tied to an abnormal number of repeats (generally 40 repeats).

- Motor function deficits are characterized by choreic movements, which are jerky, writhing movements that are present during waking hours. Additionally, speech, swallowing, and gait problems are noted in patients. Psychiatric symptoms associated with HD include OCD, bipolar disorder, depression, and mania.

- No disease-modifying treatments are available for HD, but one drug, tetrabenazine, is approved for treatment of the excessive movement found in HD. Tetrabenazine works by decreasing monoamine vesicle packaging, thereby reducing dopamine signaling. The decreased DA signaling, however, can bring about depressive and parkinsonian side effects.

- Amyotrophic lateral sclerosis (ALS) is a degenerative disorder that affects motor function but spares most other cognitive and mood function.

- Degeneration of upper and lower motor neurons results in a progressive loss of motor function that generally starts with the far extremities and moves "inward" until muscles of breathing are finally affected. Some motor groups are spared, including bladder and bowel function and eye movements. A strange side effect of this degeneration is an exaggeration of emotional behavioral responses, including laughing and crying.

- The mechanism of degeneration of the motor neurons is still poorly understood but seems to involve protein aggregation in the cells and inflammation. These processes cause the triggering of apoptotic cell death pathways.

- One FDA-approved therapy is available for ALS, riluzole, but it's disease-modifying effects are modest, generally increasing life expectancy by about 2 to 3 months. Reliance on mechanical breathing support may also be delayed in patients on riluzole.

- Multiple sclerosis is widely believed to be the result of an autoimmune attack on central nervous system myelin.

- Four subtypes of MS are defined by their course: relapsing-remitting MS, primary-progressive MS, secondary-progressive MS, and progressive-relapsing MS.

- Symptoms of MS vary widely and are largely unpredictable. Depending on the location of the immune attack, symptoms may include motor, sensory, gait, emotional, cognitive, or vision problems. Depression is often comorbid with MS, at rates that are not explained entirely by the stress of having a neurological disorder.

- MS is diagnosed by MRI, neurological exam, and evidence of neuroinflammation.

- Immunological, environmental, infectious, and genetic contributors may play a role in the development of MS, but no clear-cut cause has been identified.

- Treatments fall into disease-modifying and symptomatic categories.

- Disease-modifying treatments include several interferon drugs (Avonex, Rebif, Betaseron, and Extavia), Copaxone (a protein that stimulates myelin basic protein), Novantrone (a cancer drug), Tysabri (an antibody that prevents immune cells from entering the brain), Gilenya (a drug that keeps immune cells from leaving the lymph system), and Augbagio (which inhibits immune cell function).

- Symptomatic treatments include corticosteroids for treating acute exacerbations and antidepressants, drugs for bowel and bladder function, and Ampyra (a drug that treats gait and walking dysfunction).

Go to the **COMPANION WEBSITE**

sites.sinauer.com/psychopharm2e
for Web Boxes, animations, flashcards, and other study resources.

Recommended Readings

Alzheimer's Association website. www.alz.org

Hardiman, O., van den Berg, L. H., Kiernan, M. C. (2011). Clinical diagnosis and management of amyotrophic lateral sclerosis. *Nat. Rev. Neurol.*, 7, 639–649.

National Multiple Sclerosis Society website. www.nmss.org

Novak, M. J. and Tabrizi, S. J. (2011). Huntington's disease: Clinical presentation and treatment. *Int. Rev. Neurobiol.*, 98, 297–323.

Perl, D. P. (2010). Neuropathology of Alzheimer's Disease. *Mount Sinai Journal of Medicine*, 77, 32–42.

Glossary

A

AADC See *aromatic amino acid decarboxylase.*

absolute refractory period Short period of time after an action potential characterized by the inability to open Na⁺ channels and the inability to respond to subsequent stimuli.

absorption Movement of a drug from the site of administration to the circulatory system.

abstinence syndrome Condition characterized by unpleasant symptoms when an individual tries to cease drug use.

acamprosate Partial antagonist at NMDA receptors used for the treatment of alcoholism.

acetaldehyde dehydrogenase (ALDH) Enzyme in the liver that metabolizes the acetaldehyde intermediate formed by alcohol oxidation into acetic acid.

acetyl coenzyme A (acetyl CoA) Precursor necessary for ACh synthesis.

acetylcholine (ACh) Neurotransmitter involved with the central and peripheral nervous system and synthesized by the cholinergic neurons. It is the target of many of the deadliest neurotoxins.

acetylcholinesterase (AChE) Enzyme that controls levels of ACh by breaking it down into choline and acetic acid.

ACTH See *adrenocorticotropic hormone.*

action potential Rapid change in electrical signal that is transmitted down the axon.

active zone Area along the axon terminal, near the postsynaptic cell, that is specialized for neurotransmitter release.

acute tolerance Rapid tolerance formed during a single administration of a drug, as is the case with alcohol.

ADAD See *autosomal dominant Alzheimer's disease.*

additive effects Drug interactions characterized by the collective sum of the two individual drug effects.

adenosine Blockade of receptors for this substance is responsible for caffeine's stimulant effects.

adoption study Study used to understand how heredity contributes to a disorder by comparing the incidence of the disorder in the biological and adoptive parents of people adopted at an early age who have the disorder. A higher incidence of the disorder among biological parents than adoptive parents suggests a hereditary influence.

adrenal cortex Outer portion of the adrenal gland that secretes glucocorticoids.

adrenal gland An endocrine gland that is located above the kidney and secretes EPI, NE, and glucocorticoids. It is composed of the adrenal medulla and the adrenal cortex.

adrenal medulla Inner portion of the adrenal gland that secretes the catecholamines EPI and NE.

adrenergic Adjectival form of adrenaline, also called epinephrine (EPI). May be used broadly to include both NE- and EPI-related features.

adrenoceptor Receptor to which NE and EPI bind; part of the metabotropic receptor family. Also known as an adrenergic receptor.

adrenocorticotropic hormone (ACTH) Hormone secreted by the anterior pituitary that stimulates glucocorticoid synthesis and release from the adrenal cortex.

aerosols Class of inhalants characterized by sprays, such as hair or deodorant sprays, containing various chemicals used as solvents and propellants.

affinity Attraction between a molecule and a receptor.

agomelatine Long acting melatonin agonist that has antidepressant effects.

agonist Substance that binds to a receptor causing stimulation.

agoraphobia Fear of public places.

akathisia Constant urge to move certain body parts.

akinesia Difficulty in initiating movement.

albuterol Drug that selectively stimulates the β-adrenoceptor. It is used in asthma treatments.

alcohol Ethyl alcohol is an organic compound that is a product of fermentation and belongs to the class of sedative–hypnotics.

alcohol abuse Excessive use of alcohol or alcohol use in inappropriate ways.

alcohol dehydrogenase (ALDH) Enzyme in the liver and stomach that oxidizes alcohol into acetaldehyde.

alcohol dependence Heavy alcohol use, characterized by a physical reliance on alcohol.

alcohol or barbiturate withdrawal Symptoms associated with the termination of alcohol, barbiturate, or benzodiazepine use. The three drugs are cross dependent; administration of one alleviates withdrawal symptoms of the other.

alcohol poisoning Toxic effects associated with the ingestion of excess alcohol, characterized by unconsciousness, vomiting, irregular breathing, and cold, clammy skin.

alcoholic cirrhosis Condition seen in chronic alcohol abusers caused by accumulation of acetaldehyde in the liver that kills cells, stimulates scar tissue formation, and promotes cell death as scar tissue cuts off blood supplies.

alcoholic hepatitis Condition seen in chronic alcohol abusers caused by accumulation of acetaldehyde in the liver and characterized by inflammation of the liver, fever, jaundice, and pain.

alcoholism A form of substance abuse characterized by compulsive alcohol seeking and use despite damaging social and health effects.

ALDH See *alcohol dehydrogenase.*

allele Alternative form of a gene. Multiple alleles of a gene differ by one or more nucleotides in the gene's DNA sequence and may code for proteins with slightly different amino acid sequences.

allostasis Adaptive biological process in which an organism's response to repeated threats or challenges results in long-lasting physiological or behavioral changes. This concept is distinguished from homeostasis, which refers to the tendency of an organism to maintain physiological or behavioral stability in the face of threats or challenges (i.e., to remain unchanged).

allylglycine Drug that blocks GABA synthesis, inducing convulsions.

α-methyl-para-tyrosine (AMPT) Drug that inhibits TH activity, thereby reducing catecholamine synthesis.

ALS See *amyotrophic lateral sclerosis.*

Altered States of Consciousness (ASC) rating scale Psychometric scale developed to quantify the subjective effects of hallucinogenic agents.

amino acids Essential building blocks of proteins, some of which also act as neurotransmitters.

amotivational syndrome Symptoms of cannabis use that relate to poor educational achievement and motivation.

AMPA receptor An ionotropic glutamate receptor selective for the synthetic amino acid agonist AMPA.

ampakines Class of cognitive enhancing drugs that work by inhibiting the desensitization of glutamate AMPA receptors.

amphetamine Psychostimulant that acts by increasing catecholamine release in nerve cells.

amphetamine-induced stereotypy Model for schizophrenia induced by giving animals high doses of amphetamine to produce repetitive, stereotyped behavior.

AMPT See *α-methyl-para-tyrosine.*

amygdala Part of the limbic system that helps to modulate emotional behavior.

amyloid precursor protein (APP) Transmembrane protein. Cleavage by secretases forms Aβ.

amyotrophic lateral sclerosis (ALS) Neurological disorder characterized by degeneration of the motor neurons of the spinal cord and cortex. Also known as Lou Gehrig's disease.

anabolic–androgenic steroids Group of performance enhancers characterized by their ability to increase muscle mass and produce masculine qualities. The name may be shortened to anabolic steroids.

analeptics Drugs that act as circulatory, respiratory, or general CNS stimulants.

anandamide Common chemical name of the arachidonic acid derivative that functions as an endogenous ligand for cannabinoid receptors in the brain.

androgen receptor Target site of testosterone and other androgens, located within the cytoplasm of the cell and present in many tissues.

androgens Male sex hormones secreted by the testes.

anesthetic General anesthetics are substances that depress the CNS, decreasing all sensations in the body and causing unconsciousness. Local anesthetics do not cause unconsciousness, but prevent pain signals by blocking Na$^+$ channels.

anhedonia Difficulty or lack of the ability to experience pleasure. Such a state is characteristic of many depressed patients and may also occur during drug withdrawal in an addicted person.

anosmia Inability to perceive odors.

Antabuse See *disulfiram.*

antagonist Substance that reduces the effect of an agonist by binding to the receptor and inhibiting the subsequent binding of active ligands.

anterior pituitary Portion of the pituitary gland that secretes the hormones TSH, ACTH, FSH, LH, GH, and PRL.

anterior Located near the front or head of an animal.

anteropulsion Feeling of being pushed forward.

anti-reward system Neural system that is thought to be engaged during the transition from impulsive to compulsive drug use. This system is an important contributor to the negative mood state induced by withdrawal from abused drugs.

antibody Protein produced by the immune system for the purpose of recognizing, attacking, and destroying a specific foreign substance (i.e., an antigen).

anticipatory anxiety Feeling of extreme worry over the possibility that a certain unpleasant event will occur in a particular, often public, situation.

anticonvulsants Drugs, such as benzodiazepines, that prevent or control seizures. They are used to treat epilepsy.

antisense nucleotide A nucleotide that binds to a particular mRNA sequence, delaying translation and increasing mRNA degradation. Antisense nucleotides are used to create reversible suppression of gene expression.

antitussives Drugs that suppress the coughing reflex.

anxiolytics Drugs that alleviate feelings of anxiety in humans and that reduce anxiety-related behaviors in animals.

apolipoprotein E (ApoE) Protein that helps break down amyloid. Individuals carrying the E4 allele of the gene encoding this protein develop AD.

apomorphine Drug that is a D$_1$ and D$_2$ receptor agonist and causes behavioral activation. It may also be used to treat erectile dysfunction by acting through DA receptors in the brain to increase penile blood flow.

apoptosis Cell death resulting from a programmed series of biochemical events designed to eliminate unnecessary cells. It may also be called programmed cell death.

APP See *amyloid precursor protein.*

arachidonoyl ethanolamide Formal chemical name of *anandamide.*

2-arachidonoylglycerol (2-AG) An arachidonic acid derivative that functions as an endogenous ligand for brain cannabinoid receptors.

arachnoid Membrane consisting of a weblike sublayer that covers the brain and spinal cord. One of the three meninges.

area postrema Area in the medulla of the brain stem that is not isolated from chemicals in the blood. It is responsible for inducing a vomiting response when a toxic substance is present in the blood.

arecoline Chemical from the seeds of the betel nut palm *Areca catechu* that stimulates muscarinic receptors.

aromatic amino acid decarboxylase (AADC) Enzyme that catalyzes the removal of a carboxyl group from certain amino acids. It is responsible for the conversion of DOPA to DA in catecholaminergic neurons and the conversion of 5-HTP to 5-HT in serotonergic neurons.

Artane See *trihexyphenidyl*.

ASC See *Altered States of Consciousness rating scale*.

aspartate Ionized form of aspartic acid. It is an excitatory amino acid neurotransmitter of the CNS.

association model Model relating two variables that proposes that the variables occur together without any causal connection between them.

astrocytes Star-shaped cells of the nerve tissue that have numerous extensions and that modulate the chemical environment around neurons, metabolically assist neurons, and provide phagocytosis for cellular debris.

atomoxetine Selective norepinephrine uptake inhibitor used in the treatment of ADHD.

atropine Drug found in nightshade, *Atropa belladonna*, and henbane, *Hyoscyamus niger*, that blocks muscarinic receptors.

autoimmune disorder Condition in which the immune system attacks part of one's own body.

autoradiography Process used to detect the amount and location of bound radioligand by using a specialized film to create an image of where the radioligand is located within a tissue slice.

autoreceptors Neuronal receptors in a cell that are specific for the same neurotransmitter released by that cell. They typically inhibit further neurotransmitter release.

autosomal dominant Alzheimer's disease (ADAD) Familial version of AD caused by mutations in the genes for presenelin-1, presenilin-2, and amyloid precursor protein.

axoaxonic synapse Junction used for communication between the axon terminals of two neurons, permitting the presynaptic cell to control neurotransmitter release from the postsynaptic cell at the terminals.

axodendritic synapse Junction used for communication between the axon terminal of a presynaptic neuron and a dendrite of a postsynaptic neuron.

axon Long tubular extention from the soma of the nerve cell that conducts electrical signals away from the cell body and toward the axon terminals.

axon collaterals Branches formed when an axon splits, giving the neuron the ability to signal more cells.

axon terminal End of the axon where the signal may be passed to the dendrites of the next nerve cell.

axoplasmic transport Method of transporting proteins along the microtubules of the cytoskeleton to designations throughout a neuron.

axosomatic synapse Junction used for communication between a nerve terminal and a nerve cell body.

B

BAC See *blood alcohol concentration*.

baclofen (Lioresal) Drug that is a selective agonist for the $GABA_B$ receptors. It is used as a muscle relaxant and an antispastic agent.

barbiturate withdrawal See *alcohol or barbituate withdrawal*.

barbiturates Drugs that act as a CNS depressant, in part by enhancing $GABA_A$ receptor activity.

basal forebrain cholinergic system (BFCS) Collection of cholinergic nerve cells that innervates the cerebral cortex and limbic system structures. Damage to this system contributes to the symptoms of Alzheimer's disease.

basal ganglia Nuclei of the telencephalon that includes the caudate, putamen, and globus pallidus. The structures help regulate motor control.

BDNF See *brain-derived neurotrophic factor*.

BDZ See *benzodiazapine*.

beam walking Device resembling a human gymnastics balance beam used to evaluate rodent fine motor coordination and balance.

behavioral desensitization Technique used to treat phobias by introducing the fear-inducing stimulus in increments, allowing the patient to maintain a relaxed feeling in its presence.

behavioral despair Technique used to measure depression in animals by placing them in a cylinder of water from which they cannot escape and recording the time it takes for them to abandon attempts to escape.

behavioral supersensitivity An increased response to a drug treatment as a direct result of previous drug history or drug intake.

behavioral tolerance The reduced effectiveness of a drug administered chronically that involves learning: either instumental or classical conditioning.

benzodiazepine (BDZ) Drug that acts as a CNS depressant in part by enhancing $GABA_A$ receptor activity.

benztropine mesylate (Cogentin) Anticholinergic drug used to treat early symptoms of Parkinson's disease.

beta-amyloid protein (β-amyloid) Protein fragment derived from enzymatic cleavage of amyloid precursor protein. Primary component of the plaques characteristic of Alzheimer's disease. Also called A-beta and Aβ.

BFCS See *basal forebrain cholinergic system*.

bicuculline Drug that blocks the binding of GABA to the $GABA_A$ receptor and acts as a convulsant.

binge drinking Consumption of five or more alcoholic drinks within a 2-hour period.

bioaccumulation The progressive increase in the concentration of a substance in an organism's body. Occurs when the rate of intake exceeds the rate of excretion.

bioavailability Concentration of drug present in the blood that is free to bind to specific target sites.

bioconcentration The sequential process whereby tissue concentration of a contaminant increases up the food chain through consumption of contaminant-containing prey.

biogenic amine A transmitter that is made by a living organism and contains at least one amine group.

biopsychosocial model   Model of addiction that attempts to give a full account of addiction by incorporating biological, psychological, and sociological factors.

biotransformation   Inactivation of a drug through a chemical change, usually by metabolic processes in the liver.

bipolar disorder   Type of affective disorder characterized by extreme mood swings between depression and mania.

bisphenyl A (BPA)   An industrial chemical used in the production of certain plastics and epoxy resins.

blackout   Amnesia directly associated with heavy alcohol consumption.

blood alcohol concentration (BAC)   The amount of alcohol in a given unit of blood, usually given as a percent representing milligrams of alcohol per 100 milliliters of blood.

bradykinesia   General slowing of movement that is characteristic of Parkinson's disease. Examples include slowed movement of facial muscles leading to "stone-faced" expression and reduced hand movement resulting in micrographia (smaller handwriting).

bradyphrenia   Slowed response to questioning.

brainstem   Portion of the brain, consisting of the medulla, pons, and midbrain.

brain-derived neurotrophic factor (BDNF)   Protein of the CNS that stimulates cell proliferation, aids in cell survival and synaptic restructuring. It is also implicated in the neurotrophic hypothesis of depression.

breaking point   The point at which an animal will no longer expend the effort required to receive the reward (e.g., in a drug self-administration paradigm).

breakpoint   See *breaking point*.

broad-spectrum antipsychotics   Class of drugs used to treat schizophrenia by blocking a wide range of receptors in addition to the D_2 receptor.

buprenorphine (Buprenex)   An opioid agonist–antagonist used in opioid treatment programs that may be substituted for methadone and yields similar treatment results.

buspirone (Buspar)   Drug that stimulates $5-HT1_A$ receptors. Symptoms include increased appetite, reduced anxiety, reduced alcohol cravings, and a lower body temperature. It is prescribed as an antianxiety medication.

C

c-fos   Transcription factor that rises rapidly within cells and increased neural activity.

caffeinism   Syndrome caused by taking excessive amounts of caffeine and characterized by restlessness, insomnia, anxiety, and physiological disturbances.

calcium/calmodulin kinase (CaMK)   Enzyme stimulated by calcium and calmodulin that phosphorylates specific proteins in a signaling pathway.

cAMP   See *cyclic adenosine monophosphate*.

candidate gene   A gene that is suspected of involvement in the development, progression, or manifestation of a disease.

cannabinoid receptor   Receptor for cannabinoids, including THC and anandamide. In the CNS, they are concentrated in the basal ganglia, cerebellum, hippocampus, and cerebral cortex.

cannabinoids   Collection of over 60 compounds found uniquely in cannabis plants.

carbamazepine (Tegretol)   An anticonvulsant drug used to treat bipolar disorder.

carbidopa   A decarboxylase inhibitor that cannot cross the blood–brain barrier. Increases the availability of L-DOPA to the brain.

carbon monoxide (CO)   Gas that acts as a signaling molecule in the brain and is deadly in high concentrations.

case-control method   Technique used to identify genes associated with a disorder by comparing the genes of unrelated affected and unaffected people to determine if those who are affected are more likely to possess a particular allele.

catalepsy   State characterized by a lack of spontaneous movement. It is usually associated with D_2 receptor blockers (a DA receptor subtype), but can also be induced with a D_1 blocker.

Catapres   See *clonidine*.

catatonic schizophrenia   Subtype characterized by alternating periods of activity and inactivity.

catechol-*O*-methyltransferase (COMT)   One of the enzymes responsible for metabolic breakdown of catecholamines.

catecholamines   Group of neurotransmitters and hormones characterized by two chemical similarities: a core structure of catechol and a nitrogen-containing amine. They belong to a wider group of transmitters called monoamines or biogenic amines.

caudal   The tail end of the nervous sytem is caudal or posterior.

causal model   Model relating two variables that proposes that one of the variables causes the other.

CB1   Cannabinoid receptor of the metabotropic receptor family located in the CNS.

CB2   Cannabinoid receptor located primarily in the immune system.

central canal   Channel within the center of the spinal cord filled with CSF.

cerebellar peduncles   Large bundles of axons that connect the cerebellum to the pons, midbrain, or medulla oblongata.

cerebellum   Large structure of the metencephalon that is located on the dorsal surface of the brain and that is connected to the pons by the cerebellar peduncles. It is an important sensorimotor control center of the brain.

cerebral ventricles   Cavities within the brain filled with CSF.

cerebrospinal fluid (CSF)   Fluid that surrounds the brain and spinal cord, providing cushioning that protects against trauma.

cGMP   See *cyclic guanosine monophosphate*.

cGMP phosphodiesterase   Enzyme that catalyzes the breakdown of cGMP.

challenge study   Method to indirectly measure receptor function by recording the magnitude of a biological response to an agonist or antagonist.

choline   Precursor necessary for ACh synthesis.

choline acetyltransferase (ChAT)   Enzyme that catalyzes the synthesis of ACh from acetyl CoA and choline.

choline transporter   Protein in the membrane of the cholinergic nerve terminal involved with the uptake of choline from the synaptic cleft.

cholinergic syndrome   Syndrome that results from excessive stimulation of acetylcholine receptors. It is characterized by muscle weakness, changes in mental status, and excessive secretory activity.

cholinergic   Adjectival form of ACh.

cholinesterase inhibitors   Drugs that improve cognitive symptoms by increasing the presence of acetylcholine in the synapse by lessening breakdown of ACh. One of two categories of treatment for AD.

chromaffin cells   The cells of the adrenal medulla.

chromatin remodeling   One type of environmentally-induced epigenetic modification that increases or decreases gene transcription.

chromosomes   Linear strands of DNA that carry genes.

chronic mild unpredictable stress   Rodent model of depression created by exposing animals to a series of stressful events in an unpredictable fashion.

chronic obstructive pulmonary disease (COPD)   Disorder of the respiratory system characterized by shortness of breath, wheezing, chronic coughing, and chest tightness. Two main conditions comprise COPD, namely emphysema and bronchitis.

chronic social defeat stress   Rodent model of depression created by the intense stress of being repeatedly placed as an intruder in a cage with a resident animal.

classical conditioning   Repeated pairing of a neutral stimulus with an unconditioned stimulus. Eventually the neutral stimulus becomes a conditioned stimulus and elicits a (conditioned) response that is similar to the original unconditioned response.

clonidine   An α_2-adrenergic agonist that stimulates autoreceptors and inhibits noradrenergic cell firing. It is used to reduce symptoms of opioid withdrawal.

cloning   Method used to produce large numbers of genetically identical cells.

clozapine (Clozaril)   Drug that inhibits 5-HT$_{2A}$ and D$_2$ dopamine receptors. It is used to treat schizophrenia.

club drug   Street name for GHB, as well as MDMA and ketamine, coined as a result of their popularity at nightclubs.

CNS depressants   Large category of drugs that inhibit nerve cell firing within the central nervous system. They include sedative–hypnotics and are used to induce sleep and to treat symptoms of anxiety.

co-agonists   Substances needed simultaneously to activate a specific receptor.

CO   See *carbon monoxide*.

cocaethylene   Metabolite formed from the interaction of cocaine and alcohol. It produces biological effects similar to those of cocaine.

cocaine binges   Periods of cocaine use lasting hours or days with little or no sleep.

cocaine   Stimulant drug that blocks reuptake of DA, NE, and 5-HT by neurons, thereby increasing their concentration in the synaptic cleft.

coding region   Portion of the gene that codes for the amino acid sequence of a protein.

Cogentin   See *benztropine mesylate*.

cognitive symptoms   A category of symptoms of schizophrenia that includes impaired working memory, poor executive function, and attention deficits.

comorbidity   Diagnosis of simultaneous but distinct disease processes in an individual, such as the propensity for drug abusers to be diagnosed with other psychiatric problems.

competitive antagonist   Drug that binds to a receptor but has little or no efficacy. When it competes with an agonist for receptor sites, it reduces the effect of the agonist.

compulsions   Repetitive tasks that an individual feels obligated to complete in an effort to quell the anxiety caused by obsessive thoughts.

computerized tomography (CT)   X-ray based technique that provides computer-generated "slices" through the brain or body part that can be computer reconstructed into 3-dimensional images.

COMT   See catechol-*O*-methyltransferase.

Comtan   See *entacapone*.

concentration gradient   Difference in the amount or concentration of a substance on each side of a biological barrier, such as the cell membrane.

conditioned emotional response   Learned response to a neutral stimulus given just prior to a negative stimulus (e.g., an electric shock) in an effort to create a fear association to the neutral stimulus.

conditioned place preference   Method used to determine the rewarding effects of a drug by allowing an animal to associate the drug with a specific environment and measuring its subsequent preference for that environment.

conflict procedure   Method that creates a dilemma for an animal by giving it the choice of selecting a reward that is accompanied by a negative stimulus. Conflict procedures screen drugs for antianxiety effects.

congeners   Compounds with similar structures and chemical properties.

construct validity   Term that represents the extent to which the animal measurement tool actually measures the human characteristic of interest.

contextual fear conditioning   Experimental paradigm in which the subject learns to fear the environmental stimuli (i.e., context) associated with the testing chamber.

contingency management program   Type of addiction treatment program in which the client's drug taking is monitored by regular urine testing and abstinence is reinforced with vouchers redeemable locally for consumer products or services.

convergence   Process by which neurons receive and integrate the numerous signals from other cells.

COPD   See *chronic obstructive pulmonary disease*.

coronal   Sections cut parallel to the face.

corpus callosum   Large pathway connecting corresponding areas of the two brain hemispheres, allowing communication between each half of the brain.

correlational relationship   Connection between two events that appear related, but cannot be assumed to be cause and effect.

corticosterone   Glucocorticoid secreted by the adrenal cortex of rats and mice.

corticotropin-releasing hormone (CRH)   Hormone synthesized by neurons of the hypothalamus that stimulates ACTH release. Also known as corticotrophin-releasing factor (CRF).

cortisol   Specific glucocorticoid secreted by the adrenal cortex of primates.

cotinine   Principal product of nicotine metabolism by the liver.

crack   Form of cocaine made by adding baking soda to a solution of cocaine HCl, heating the mixture, and drying the solid.

craving   Strong urge addicts feel, compelling them to take a drug.

CRF   See *corticotropin-releasing hormone.*

CRF₁ antagonist   A drug that binds to CRF$_1$ receptors and produces little or no conformational change. In the presence of a CRF agonist, the agonist effect is reduced.

CRH   See *corticotropin-releasing hormone.*

cross-dependence   Withdrawal signs occurring in a dependent individual can be terminated by administering drugs in the same class.

cross-tolerance   Tolerance to a specific drug can reduce the effectiveness of a another drug in the same class.

CSF   See *cerebrospinal fluid.*

CT   See *computerized tomography.*

cyclic adenosine monophosphate (cAMP)   Second messenger that activates PKA and is controlled by DA, NE, 5-HT, and endorphins.

cyclic guanosine monophosphate (cGMP)   Second messenger that activates PKG and is controlled in part by NO.

cycling   Pattern of steroid use characterized by 6 to 12 weeks of drug use, followed by a period of abstinence before repeating the drug use pattern.

cytochrome P450 (CYP450)   Class of liver enzymes, in the microsomal enzyme group, responsible for both phase 1 and phase 2 biotransformation of psychoactive drugs.

cytochrome P450 2A6 (CYP2A6)   Specific type of cytochrome P450 that metabolizes nicotine into cotinine.

cytoplasm   Salty gelatinous fluid of the cell, outside of the nucleus and bounded by the cell membrane.

cytoskeleton   Structural matrix of a cell that is composed of tubular materials.

D

DA   See *dopamine.*

DAG   See *diacylglycerol.*

DA imbalance hypothesis of schizophrenia   Theory that altered DA function, reduced in mesocortical dopaminergic neurons and increased in mesolimbic dopaminergic neurons, leads to the symptoms observed in individuals with schizophrenia.

DA transporter (DAT)   Protein in the membrane of dopaminergic neurons that is responsible for DA uptake from the synaptic cleft.

DBH   See *dopamine β-hydroxylase.*

deiodinases   Enzymes that remove iodine. Deiodinases are involved in the synthesis and inactivation of thyroid hormones.

delirium tremens   Severe effects of alcohol withdrawal characterized by irritability, headaches, agitation, hallucinations, and confusion.

ΔFosB   Member of the Fos family of transcription factors. This protein accumulates in some brain areas after repeated exposure to various drugs of abuse and is hypothesized to contribute to the development of an addicted state.

Δ⁹-tetrahydrocannabinol (THC)   Psychoactive chemical found in cannabis plants; a cannabinoid.

δ-receptor   A type of opioid receptor primarily in the forebrain that may help regulate olfaction, motor integration, reinforcement, and cognitive function.

dendrites   Projections from the soma that receive signals and information from other cells.

dendritic spines   Projections from dendrites that increase the receiving surface area.

denial   Characteristic of alcoholics who insist that alcohol is not the source of their problems.

Depakote   See *valproate.*

depolarization   Change in membrane potential making the inside of the cell more positive.

depolarization block   Process in which the resting potential across the cell membrane is lost. The neuron cannot be excited until the membrane is repolarized.

depot binding   Type of drug interaction involving binding to an inactive site, such as to proteins in the plasma, to bone, or to fat.

deprivation reversal model   Theory that smoking is maintained by mood enhancement and increased concentration that occur when nicotine withdrawal symptoms are alleviated.

descending modulatory pathways   Bundles of nerve fibers originating at higher brain regions that influence lower brain or spinal cord function. One arises from the PAG in the the midbrain and influences pain signals carried by the spinal cord neurons.

desensitized   Altered receptor state characterized by a lack of response to an agonist.

detoxification   Procedure used to treat addicted individuals in which the drug is stopped and withdrawal symptoms are treated until the abstinence syndrome has ended.

detoxified   A drug user undergoing detoxification is considered to be detoxified when signs of the abstinence syndrome end.

dexamethasone   A synthetic corticosteroid used to test the function of the negative feedback mechanism regulating the HPA axis.

dexmedetomidine (Precedex)   Drug that stimulates α$_2$-receptors, characterized by its sedative, anxiolytic, and analgesic effects. It is used to treat surgical patients in intensive care.

dextromethorphan   Opioid-like drug that is the major antitussive agent in most over-the-counter cough medicine.

diacylglycerol (DAG)   Second messenger generated by the phosphoinositide second messenger system; stimulates protein kinase C (PKC).

diazepam (Valium)   A BDZ that binds to the BDZ receptor, increasing the effectiveness of GABA to open the GABA$_A$ receptor channel.

5,7-dihydroxytryptamine (5,7-DHT)   Neurotoxin that selectively damages serotonergic neurons.

1-(2,5-dimethoxy-4-iodophenyl)-2-aminopropane (DOI)   Drug that stimulates 5-HT$_{2A}$ receptors, producing "head-twitch" in rodents and hallucinations in humans.

dimethyltryptamine (DMT)   Hallucinogenic drug found in several South American plants.

DISC1 gene   *DISC1* variants may increase the probability of developing schizophrenia.

disease model   Model of addiction that treats addiction as a distinct medical disorder or disease.

disorganized schizophrenia Subtype of schizophrenia characterized by disorganized behavior and moods that are silly and immature.

dissociative anesthesia An unusual type of anesthetic state characterized by environmental detachment. It is produced by certain noncompetitive NMDA receptor antagonists such as ketamine and PCP.

disulfiram (Antabuse) A drug used to treat alcoholism by causing the buildup of toxic metabolites producing illness after alcohol intoxication.

divergence Process by which neurons transmit their integrated signals back out to many neurons.

dizocilpine (MK-801) Drug that binds to the PCP site and acts as a noncompetitive antagonist of the NMDA receptor.

DMT See *dimethyltryptamine*.

DNA methylation Environmentally-induced epigenetic covalent attachment of methyl groups to a gene decreases its expression.

DNA microarray Method used to screen tissue or cell extracts for changes in the expression of many genes at the same time.

DOI See *1-(2,5-dimethoxy-4-iodophenyl)-2-aminopropane*.

domoic acid Amino acid found in certain seafoods that causes excitotoxicity in organisms that consume it.

dopamine (DA) Neurotransmitter, related to NE and EPI, that belongs to a group called catecholamines.

dopamine hypothesis of schizophrenia Theory that excessive DA function of mesolimbic neurons produces postive symptoms and insufficient DA function of mesocortical neurons produces negative and cognitive symptoms of schizophrenia.

dopamine system stabilizer Antipsychotic drug that is a DA partial agonist which increases DA function where it is too low and reduces DA function where it is excessive.

dopamine β-hydroxylase (DBH) Enzyme that catalyzes the third step of NE synthesis in neurons, the conversion of DA to NE.

dopaminergic Adjectival form of DA.

doping agent A substance such as an anabolic steroid that is used to enhance athletic performance despite being banned by sports organizations.

dorsal raphe nucleus Structure located in the area of the caudal midbrain and rostral pons that contains a large number of serotonergic neurons. In conjunction with the median raphe nucleus, it is responsible for most of the serotonergic fibers in the forebrain. Together they regulate sleep, aggression, impulsiveness, and emotions.

dorsal Located toward the top of the brain and back of the body in humans.

dose–response curve Graph used to display the amount of biological change in relation to a given drug dose.

double-blind experiment Type of experiment in which neither the patient nor the observer knows the treatment received by the patient.

down-regulation Decrease in the number of receptors, which may be a consequence of chronic agonist treatment.

dronabinol Drug that is a synthetic form of THC, sold under the trade name Marinol, used to treat nausea symptoms in chemotherapy patients.

drug action Molecular changes associated with a drug binding to a particular target site or receptor.

drug competition Interaction between two drugs that share a metabolic system and compete for the same metabolic enzymes. Bioavailability of one or both increases.

drug depots Inactive sites where drugs accumulate. There is no biological effect from drugs binding at these sites, nor can they be metabolized.

drug detoxification Process whereby an individual eliminates a drug from the body and goes through an abstinence syndrome.

drug disposition tolerance See *metabolic tolerance*.

drug effects Alterations in physiological or psychological functions associated with a specific drug.

drug priming Delivery of a small dose of a drug by the experimenter for the purpose of eliciting drug-seeking behavior, typically in an animal whose drug self-administration responding was previously extinguished.

drug reward A positively-motivating subjective response to a drug, often experienced by humans as a euphoric feeling or "high."

drug-seeking behavior Performance of an operant response such as a lever-press or a nose-poke with the expectation of receiving delivery of a drug dose.

dry-mouth effect State characterized by a reduction in saliva production as a result of muscarinic antagonism. Its technical name is xerostomia.

D-serine Amino acid that is a co-agonist with glutamate for the NMDA receptor.

D-tubocurarine Poison that targets muscle nicotinic receptors, blocking cholinergic transmission.

DTs See *delerium tremens*.

dual NE/5-HT modulators Antidepressants that enhance both NE and 5-HT function.

dura mater The outer layer of the meninges. It is the strongest of the three meninges layers.

dyskinesia Abnormal or impaired movement such as severe tics or choreic movements.

dystonia Persistent invuluntary muscle contractions.

E

EAAT See *excitatory amino acid transporter*.

early LTP (E-LTP) Type of long-term potentiation that lasts no longer than a few hours.

ED See *endocrine disruptor*.

Edronax See *reboxetine*.

effector enzymes Enzymes of the cell membrane that may be regulated by G proteins and that cause biochemical and physiological effects in postsynaptic cells (e.g., by means of second messengers).

efficacy The extent to which a ligand-receptor binding initiates a biological action (e.g., the ability of an agonist to activate its receptor).

electrical self-stimulation A procedure whereby an animal self-administers a weak electrical shock to a specific brain area due to the reinforcing properties of the stimulation.

electroencephalography (EEG) Technique used to measure brain activity by using electrodes taped on the scalp to obtain electrical recordings in humans.

electrostatic pressure Force drawing an ion to either side of the cell membrane in an attempt to balance or neutralize ionic charges.

elevated plus-maze   Maze type that involves a cross-shaped maze that has two open arms, two enclosed arms, and has been raised 50 cm off the floor. It is used to test a rodent's level of anxiety.

empirical validity   Term used to describe the relationship between a testing procedure done on animals and its ability to predict clinical effects on humans, regardless of the similarity between their test responses.

enablers   Friends and family members who assist an alcoholic, allowing the individual to continue to function in society without getting treatment.

endocannabinoids   Lipid-like substances that activate CB receptors. They are produced from arachidonic acid in the body.

endocrine disruptors (EDs)   Natural or synthetic substances that interfere with the endocrine system. EDs may cause adverse effects in development, or in the reproductive, nervous, or immune system.

endocrine gland   Specialized organ that secretes hormones into the bloodstream.

endomorphins   Group of endogenous opioid peptides in the CNS that selectively bind to the opioid receptor, and eliminate pain.

endorphins   Group of endogneous peptides in the brain that stimulate mu and delta opioid receptors, reducing pain and enhancing one's general mood.

entacapone (Comtan)   COMT inhibitor used in conjunction with L-DOPA to treat Parkinson's disease.

enteral   Drug administration by oral or rectal routes.

enzyme induction   Increase in liver drug-metabolizing enzymes associated with repeated drug use.

enzyme inhibition   Reduction in liver enzyme activity associated with a specific drug.

enzyme   A protein that functions as a biochemical catalyst.

EPI   See *epinephrine*.

epidural   Method that involves administration of a drug into the cerebrospinal fluid surrounding the spinal cord.

epinephrine (EPI)   Hormone related to NE that belongs to a group called catecholamines. It is secreted by the chromaffin cells of the adrenal medulla, and it produces the "fight-or-flight" response by regulating the diversion of energy and blood to muscles. Also known as adrenaline.

EPSP   See *excitatory postsynaptic potential*.

equilibrium potential   Point at which the electrostatic forces and the concentration gradient for an ion are balanced.

ergot   Fungus, *Claviceps purpurea*, that infects certain grains and that contains several important alkaloids from which the structure of LSD was derived.

ergotism   Disease caused by ergot-contaminated grains that can lead to death.

Eserine   See *physostigmine*.

estradiol   Specific estrogen and a powerful female sex hormone.

estrogens   Female sex hormones secreted by the ovaries.

ethanol   Proper chemical name for the type of alcohol consumed by humans. Similar to BDZs, it acts as a CNS-depressant in part by enhancing $GABA_A$ receptor activity.

event-related potentials   Electrical changes in neuron activity in response to a sensory stimulus.

excitatory amino acid neurotransmitters   Transmitters, including glutamate, aspartate, and some other amino acids, that cause an excitatory response in most neurons of the brain or spinal cord.

excitatory amino acid transporter (EAAT)   Protein that transports glutamate and aspartate across the plasma membrane. There are five such transporters, designated EAAT1 to EAAT5.

excitatory postsynaptic potential (EPSP)   Small localized membrane depolarization of a postsynaptic neuron that results from neurotransmitters binding to specific receptors on the cell. EPSPs move the membrane potential closer to the threshold for firing.

excitotoxicity hypothesis   Theory that excessive glutamate or other excitatory amino acid exposure results in prolonged depolarization of receptive neurons, leading to their damage or death.

executive function   Collection of higher-order cognitive abilities including planning, organization, problem solving, mental flexibility, and valuation of incentives. The prefrontal cortex plays an important role in executive function.

exocytosis   Method by which vesicles release substances and neurotransmitters, characterized by fusion of the vesicle and the cell membrane, specifically the axon terminal membrane in the case of neurotransmitters. The vesicle opens toward the synaptic cleft allowing neurotransmitter molecules to diffuse out.

expectancy   Term used to describe the anticipated effect of a drug and its role in drug action or perceived drug action.

expression phase   The period of time after a tetanic stimulation is given, characterized by enhanced synaptic strength (i.e., LTP).

expression   Process that leads to manifestation of a sensitized response and that requires enhanced reactivity of DA nerve terminals in the nucleus accumbens.

extracellular fluid   Salty fluid surrounding nerve cells that provides oxygen, nutrients, and chemical signals, and that removes secreted cell waste.

extracellular recording   Method of taking measurements of cell firing by inserting a fine-tipped electrode into the extracellular fluid surrounding the cell.

F

face validity   Term used to describe the relationship between a testing procedure done on animals and its direct correlation to human test results or behavior.

FAS   See *fetal alcohol syndrome*.

fatigue   State of weariness that diminishes an individual's energy and mental capacity.

fatty acid amide hydrolase (FAAH)   Enzyme that metabolizes endocannabinoids.

fatty liver   Damaging effect of alcohol characterized by the accumulation of triglycerides inside liver cells.

fear-potentiated startle   Enhancement of a startle response when the stimulus is preceded by the presentation of a conditioned fear stimulus.

fenestrations   Large pores in endothelial cells allowing rapid exchange between blood vessels and tissue.

fenfluramine   Drug similar in structure to amphetamine that stimulates 5-HT release. It is an appetite suppressor formerly used as a treatment for obesity.

festination   Uncontrollable acceleration of gait.

fetal alchol syndrome (FAS)   The damaging developmental effects of prenatal alcohol exposure.

fetal solvent syndrome   Group of symptoms, typically including cognitive deficits and craniofacial (i.e., head and face) abnormalities, seen in some newborn infants of inhalant-abusing women.

first-order kinetics   Term used to describe exponential elimination of drugs from the bloodstream.

first-pass metabolism   Phenomenon in which the liver metabolizes some of a drug before it can circulate through the body, particularly when the drug has been taken orally.

fissures   Deep grooves of the cerebral cortex.

flashback   Reexperience of the perceptual drug effects, specifically those of a hallucinogen, following termination of drug use.

fluoxetine (Prozac)   Drug that selectively blocks the 5-HT transporter. It is used as an antidepressant.

fMRI   See *functional MRI*.

focused stereotypies   Behaviors produced by high doses of psychostimulants (e.g., cocaine and amphetamine) and characterized by repetitive and aimless movement.

follicle-stimulating hormone (FSH)   Hormone secreted by the anterior pituitary that helps control gonad growth and function.

forced swim test   Technique used to measure depression in animals by placing them in a cylinder of water from which they cannot escape and recording the time it takes for them to abandon attempts to escape.

freebasing   Smoking the freebase form of cocaine obtained by dissolving cocaine HCl in water, adding an alkaline solution, and then extracting with an organic solvent.

frontal lobe   One of four lobes of the cerebral cortex. It is responsible for movement and executive planning.

frontal   Tissue sections cut parallel to the face.

FSH   See *follicle-stimulating hormone*.

functional MRI (fMRI)   Technique used to regionally visualize brain activity by detecting the increase in blood oxygen levels through magnetic resonance measurements of oxygenated and oxygen-depleted hemoglobin.

G

G protein–coupled receptor   Slow acting receptor type composed of a single large protein in the cell membrane that activates G proteins. It may also be called a metabotropic receptor.

G proteins   Specific membrane proteins that are necessary for neurotransmitter signaling by metabotropic receptors. They operate by regulating ion channels or effector enzymes involved in the synthesis or breakdown of second messengers, ultimately causing biochemical or physiological changes in the postsynaptic cell.

GABA aminotransferase (GABA-T)   Enzyme that breaks down GABA in GABAergic neurons and astrocytes.

GABA$_A$ receptor   Ionotropic receptor for GABA that allows Cl$^-$ ions to enter the cell, thereby inhibiting cell firing.

GABA$_B$ receptor   Metabotropic receptor for GABA.

GABA transporter   Transporters responsible for GABA uptake from the synaptic cleft into nerve cells and glia. There are three such transporters designated GAT-1, GAT-2, GAT-3.

Gabitril   See *tiagabine*.

GAD   See *general anxiety disorder* or *glutamic acid decarboxylase*.

gait   Pattern of limb movement during locomotion over a solid surface.

γ-aminobutyric acid (GABA)   Amino acid that is the principal inhibitory neurotransmitter in the CNS.

γ-hydroxybutyrate (GHB)   Chemical similar in structure to GABA that produces sedative and anesthetic effects in users and that is used medicinally as well as recreationally.

ganglia   A cluster of cell bodies outside the CNS.

gaseous transmitter   Substance in the gas phase that acts as a neurotransmitter in the body.

gases   Class of inhalants, such as propane and nitrous oxide, that are obtained in their gaseous form from domestic or commercial products.

GAT-1   Member of the family of plasma membrane GABA transporters that is expressed in both neurons and astrocytes.

GAT-2   Member of the family of plasma membrane GABA transporters that is expressed in both neurons and astrocytes.

GAT-3   Member of the family of plasma membrane GABA transporters that is expressed only in astrocytes.

gated channels   Ion channels that are normally in a closed configuration that can be opened momentarily by specific stimuli.

Gateway Theory   Theory proposing that use of certain drugs of abuse, particularly during childhood or adolescence, increases the risk of progressing to other substances. For example, tobacco or alcohol have been proposed as gateways to marijuana use, and in turn marijuana has been proposed as a gateway to so-called "hard drugs" like cocaine and heroin.

Geller-Seifter conflict test   An operant procedure involving alternate periods of lever pressing for reinforcement and lever pressing for reinforcement accompanied by foot shock; a classic method to screen antianxiety drugs.

gene   Portion of a chromosome that codes for a particular protein.

gene therapy   Application of DNA that encodes a specific protein to increase or block expression of the gene product to correct a clinical condition.

general anxiety disorder   An anxiety disorder characterized by excessive worrying that does not have a specific cause.

genetic models   Creation of knockout, knockin, or transgenic mice to produce a phenotype analagous to the human clinical disorder of interest.

genetic polymorphisms   Genetic variations in a population resulting in multiple forms of a particular protein.

genome-wide association screening   A modification of microarray technology used to compare the incidence of single-nucleotide polymorphisms and copy number variants in DNA samples from people with a given disorder and matched controls.

GH   See *growth hormone*.

GHB   See *γ-hydroxybutyrate*.

glial cells   Supporting cells of the nervous system that insulate, protect, and metabolically support neurons.

glucagon   Hormone secreted by the islets of Langerhans that, along with insulin, regulates metabolic energy sources in the body.

glucocorticoid   Hormone belonging to the steroid family that is secreted by the adrenal cortex and helps maintain blood glucose levels in the body.

glucocorticoid hypothesis   Theory that elevated glucocorticoid levels accelerate cell damage and lead to the cognitive symptoms of depression.

glutamate   The ionized form of glutamic acid. It is an excitatory amino acid neurotransmitter of the CNS.

glutamatergic neurons   Neurons that use glutamate as a transmitter.

glutamic acid decarboxylase (GAD)   Enzyme that transforms glutamate into GABA.

glutaminase   Enzyme that transforms glutamine into glutamate.

glutamine   Precursor of the transmitter-related glutamate.

glutamine synthetase   Enzyme in astrocytes that converts glutamate into glutamine.

glycine   Amino acid characterized by the lack of a functional group. It is a co-agonist with glutamate for the NMDA receptor.

gonadotropin-releasing hormone (GnRH)   Hormone that stimulates FSH and LH release. It is synthesized by neurons of the hypothalamus.

gonads   Glands that secrete sex-specific steroid hormones.

graded   Term used to describe the observation that the larger a stimulus, the greater the magnitude of hyperpolarization or depolarization in neurons.

growth hormone (GH)   Hormone secreted by the anterior pituitary that increases production of IGF-I in peripheral organs.

guanfacine (Intuniv) α_{2A}-adrenergic agonist prescribed for the treatment of ADHD. Guanfacine is believed to improve attention and memory by stimulating α_{2A}-adrenergic receptors in the prefrontal cortex.

gyrus (pl. gyri)   Bulge of tissue between the grooves in the cerebral cortex.

H

half-life   Time required to remove half of the drug from the blood. It is referred to as $t_{1/2}$.

hallucinogen   Substance that evokes hallucinations when consumed.

Hallucinogen Rating Scale   Psychometric scale developed to quantify the subjective effects of hallucinogenic agents.

hallucinogenic   Adjectival form of hallucinogen.

haloperidol (Haldol)   A D_2 receptor blocker that can induce catalepsy in animals when administered in high doses. It is used clinically as an antipsychotic agent.

hangover   Effect of heavy alcohol consumption that may be a sign of withdrawal, acute toxicity, or other negative effects on body regulation.

hash oil   Potent oil that is derived from hashish and contains a high concentration of cannabinoids.

hashish   Type of cannabis derivative that is smoked or eaten.

HD   See *Huntington's disease*.

hemicholinium-3 (HC-3)   Drug that blocks the choline transporter in cholinergic nerve terminals.

heritability   The relative contribution of genetics to the variability of a trait within a population.

heteroreceptors   Axon receptors that are specific for neurotransmitters released by other cells at axoaxonic synapses. They may either decrease or increase further neurotransmitter release.

hippocampus   Subcortical structure of the limbic system that helps to establish long-term and spatial memories. The hippocampus is where LTP was first discovered and is also one of the brain areas damaged in Alzheimer's disease.

homovanillic acid (HVA)   Major metabolite formed in the breakdown of DA.

horizontal   Brain sections cut parallel to the horizon.

hormone   Chemical substance secreted by endocrine glands into the bloodstream, where it travels to target locations in the body.

HPLC   Abbreviation for high-performance liquid chromatography, a sensitive technique for measuring small amounts of substances (e.g., neurotransmitters or drugs) in biological samples.

5-HT transporter (SERT)   Protein in the membrane that is responsible for 5-HT reuptake from the synaptic cleft.

5-HT   See serotonin.

huntingtin gene   Gene containing a CAG trinucleotide repeat. A mutation resulting in more than 40 repeats of the CAG sequence results in Huntington's disease.

Huntington's chorea   Involuntary jerky, writhing movements of the limbs.

Huntington's disease (HD)   An inherited disorder caused by a genetic defect on chromosome 4. The defect results in the abnormal repetition of a CAG sequence. The disorder causes progressive degeneration of nerve cells in the brain resulting in movement, cognitive, and psychiatric symptoms.

HVA   See *homovanillic acid*.

8-hydroxy-2-(di-*n*-propylamino)tetralin (8-OH-DPAT)   Drug that stimulates 5-HT_{1A} receptors. Effects include increased appetite, reduced anxiety, reduced alcohol cravings, and a lower body temperature.

6-hydroxydopamine (6-OHDA)   Neurotoxin similar in structure to DA that damages catecholaminergic nerve terminals and is used to study catecholamine pathways.

5-hydroxyindoleacetic acid (5-HIAA)   Major metabolite of 5-HT that is produced by the action of MAO.

5-hydroxytryptamine (5-HT)   Neurotransmitter present in the central and peripheral nervous system and synthesized by the serotonergic neurons. Also known as serotonin.

5-hydroxytryptophan (5-HTP)   Intermediate formed in the synthesis of 5-HT.

hyperalgesia   Condition characterized by an increased sensitivity to pain.

hyperphagia   Condition characterized by overeating. It is one of the effects of 5-HT_{1A} reception stimulation.

hyperpolarization   Act of making the inside of a cell more negative relative to the resting potential, reducing the likelihood that the cell will fire an action potential.

hypnotics   Drugs, such as benzodiazepines, that help a patient to fall asleep and stay asleep.

hypophagia   Decrease in food consumption due to loss of appetite.

hypothalamic-releasing hormones   Neuropeptide hormones synthesized by neurons of the hypothalamus and carried by blood vessels to the anterior pituitary, where they control the release of many of the pituitary hormones.

hypothalamus   Structure of the diencephalon located at the base of the brain, ventral to the thalamus. It provides many functions important for survival, including the maintenance of body temperature and salt balance, regulation of hunger and thirst, control of the ANS and pituitary gland, and modulation of emotional responses.

I

192 IgG–saporin   Neurotoxin containing the monoclonal antibody 192 IgG, which binds to cholinergic neurons in the forebrain, and the cellular toxin saporin. It is used to selectively kill cholinergic neurons.

IM   See *intramuscular*.

imaging techniques   Technology that permits the visualization of the living human brain, including CT, MRI, PET, fMRI, and SPECT.

immunocytochemistry (ICC)   Technique that uses antibodies to determine the brain areas or neurons that contain a specific antigen such as a protein, neuropeptide, or neurotransmitter.

impaired response inhibition and salience attribution (iRISA)   Theory of addiction that emphasizes prefrontal cortical deficits leading to difficulty in refraining from drug use (impaired response inhibition) and the development of an abnormal psychological state in which drugs have much greater motivational power than normal reinforcers (impaired salience attribution).

in situ hybridization (ISH)   Technique used to locate cells that manufacture a specific protein or peptide by detecting the specific mRNA sequence coding for that substance. It can also be used to study changes in regional mRNA levels (i.e., gene expression).

in vitro   Refers to measurements performed outside the living body (traditionally in a test tube).

in vivo voltammetry   Technique used to measure neurotransmitter release in the brain of an awake, freely moving animal by using a microelectrode to measure electrochemical responses to an applied electrical signal.

in vivo   Refers to measurements observed in the living organism.

incentive salience   Psychological process by which drug-related stimuli gain increased prominence and attractiveness. It is an important component of the incentive-sensitization model of addiction.

incentive-sensitization model   Model of addiction based on the theory that repeated drug use leads to an increase in "wanting" the drug (i.e., craving) but no increase in drug "liking" (reward or euphoria) because only the neural system underlying drug "wanting" becomes sensitized.

incubation   Time-dependent increase in drug craving and drug seeking behavior during abstinence.

Inderal   See *propranolol*.

indicator-variable model   Explanatory model in which one or more factors lead to multiple outcomes that occur together. This is one of the models proposed to account for the statistical association between early heavy cannabis use and later development of psychosis.

indoleamines   Indole derivatives containing an amine group. They include serotonin and the hallucinogens LSD, psilocybin, psilocin, DMT, and 5-MeO-DMT.

induction phase   Phase of LTP, during and immediately after a tetanic stimulation is given, which requires activation of NMDA receptors.

induction   1. Increase in liver enzymes specific for drug metabolism in response to repeated drug use. 2. Process that establishes psychostimulant sensitization by activating

glutamate NMDA receptors and, in some cases, D_1 receptors.

inferior   Located toward the underside of the brain in humans.

infusion pump   Drug delivery via an implanted pump (e.g., subcutaneous) that delivers regular, constant doses to the body or into the cerebral ventricles.

inhalants   Group of volatile substances, such as glue, that may be abused as a drug by inhaling the fumes.

inhalation   Method that involves administration of a drug through the lungs.

inhibitory postsynaptic potentials (IPSPs)   Hyperpolarizing responses of a postsynaptic cell that result from neurotransmitters binding to specific receptors on the cell. IPSPs move the membrane potential farther from threshold for firing, hence decrease the likelihood of an action potential.

inositol triphosphate   See *diacylglycerol* (*DAG*).

insulin   Polypeptide hormone that is secreted by the islets of Langerhans and, along with glucagon, regulates glucose and metabolic energy sources in the body. It regulates glucose uptake from the bloodstream into tissues and stimulates the uptake of certain amino acids.

integration   Process at the axon hillock whereby several small depolarizations or hyperpolarizations will add together to create one large change in membrane potential. Similarly, simultaneous depolarizations and hyperpolarizations will cancel each other out.

intercellular clefts   Small gaps between adjacent cells.

interferon-beta 1a and 1b   Drugs used in the treatment of relapsing forms of MS.

interictal period   Time interval between seizures in an epileptic patient.

interneurons   Nerve cells in the CNS that possess short axons and mediate local information transmission.

intracellular recording   Method of taking measurements of cell firing by inserting a fine-tipped electrode into the cell.

intracerebroventricular   Method that involves administration of a drug into the cerebrospinal fluid of the ventricles.

intracranial   Method that involves administration of a drug into the brain tissue.

intramuscular (IM)   Method that involves administration of a drug into a muscle.

intranasal administration   Topical administration of a drug to the nasal mucosa.

intraperitoneal (IP)   Injection technique that is the most common route of administration for small laboratory animals. The drug is injected through the abdominal wall into the peritoneal cavity—the space that surrounds the abdominal organs.

intravenous (IV)   Method that involves administration of a drug directly into the bloodstream by means of a vein.

Intuniv   See *guanfacine*.

inverse agonist   Substance that activates a receptor but produces the opposite effect of a typical agonist at that receptor.

ion channel   Protein that traverse the cell membrane and possess a water-filled pore, regulating ion movement into and out of the cell.

ionization   Process involving the dissociation of an electrically neutral molecule into charged particles (ions).

ionotropic receptor Fast acting receptor type comprised of several subunits that come together in the cell membrane. The receptor has an ion channel at its center, which is regulated by neurotransmitters binding to specific sites on the receptor causing the channel to open. It may also be called a ligand-gated channel receptor.

IP See *intraperitoneal*.

ipsapirone Drug that stimulates 5-HT$_{1A}$ receptors. Some of its effects include increased appetite, reduced anxiety, reduced alcohol cravings, and a lower body temperature.

IPSP See *inhibitory postsynaptic potential*.

iRISA See *impaired response inhibition and salience attribution*.

ischemia Condition characterized by an interruption of blood flow to the brain.

ISH See *in situ hybridization*.

islets of Langerhans Endocrine gland in the pancreas that secretes insulin and glucagons.

isoproterenol An agonist at β-adrenergic receptors.

IV See *intravenous*.

J

John Cunningham (JC) virus Common virus that is present in more than 50% of the population. Most people acquire it sometime during childhood. It lives in a latent harmless state in the kidneys and the gastrointestinal tract in individuals with healthy immune systems, but becomes life-threatening in those whose immune systems are compromised. The virus causes progressive multifocal leukoencephalopathy (PML), a rare, but frequently deadly condition that destroys myelin, a protective covering of nerve cells in the brain.

K

kainate receptor An ionotropic glutamate receptor selective for the agonist kainic acid.

κ-receptor An opioid receptor located in the striatum, amygdala, hypothalamus, and pituitary gland that may help regulate pain, perception, gut motility, dysphoria, water balance, hunger, temperature, and neuroendocrine function.

ketamine Drug that binds to the PCP site and acts as a noncompetitive antagonist of the NMDA receptor. It is a dissociative anesthetic used in both human and veterinary medicine, and it is also used recreationally.

ketanserin Drug that inhibits 5-HT$_{2A}$ receptors.

knockin mice Mice that have a specific gene inserted into their DNA, so they produce a slightly different protein than is produced by wild-type mice.

knockout mice Mice that are homozygous for the targeted deletion of a specific gene. They are used to study the normal function of that gene as well as the involvement of the gene in behavioral and physiological responses to various psychoactive drugs.

L

LAAM (Orlamm) Abbreviation for L-α-acetylmethadol. LAAM is an opioid agonist that may be substituted for methadone and has similar therapeutic results.

L-2-amino-4-phosphonobutyrate (L-AP4) Synthetic amino acid that is an agonist selective for glutamate autoreceptors.

L-DOPA Precursor necessary for the synthesis of DA. L-DOPA is formed by the addition of a hydroxyl group to tyrosine by the enzyme TH. It is used to treat Parkinson's disease by increasing DA formation.

late LTP (L-LTP) Type of LTP that is dependent on protein synthesis and that can last for much longer periods of time than early LTP.

lateral Located to either side of the body or brain.

laterodorsal tegmental nucleus (LDTg) Structure within the dorsal lateral pons containing cholinergic neurons that project to the ventral tegmental area (important for stimulating VTA dopamine neurons) and others that project to the brainstem and thalamus (important for behavioral arousal, sensory processing, and inititation of rapid-eye-movement sleep).

law of thirds Observation that schizophrenic patients' response to antipsychotic drugs falls into one of three categories in approximately a 1:1:1 ratio: The patient may show minor symptoms and lead a relatively normal life; the patient may show symptoms at various times and need help with tasks of daily living; or the patient may show major symptoms, spend significant time in mental hospitals, and need constant help in daily life.

LC See *locus coeruleus*.

LDTg See *laterodorsal tegmental nucleus*.

learned helplessness A classic screening device for antidepressant drugs. After being subjected to periods of unescapable foot shock, rodents fail to respond when given the opportunity to alter an aversive event. Antidepressant drugs increase appropriate responding.

lesioning Process whereby brain cells are destroyed using an electrode to administer a high radio frequency current, or by injecting a neurotoxin that kills cells.

levodopa See L-DOPA.

Lewy body dementia (LBD) Progressive form of dementia that is similar in symptomology to Parkinson's disease and Alzheimer's disease. Characterized by abnormal accumulations of proteins (Lewy bodies) in the nuclei of neurons in the brain that control memory and movement.

LH See *luteinizing hormone*.

ligand-gated channel Type of ion channel that is regulated by an active ligand binding to a receptor site associated with the channel.

ligand-gated channel receptor See *ionotropic receptor*.

ligand Molecule that selectively binds to a receptor.

light–dark crossing task Test used to determine a rodent's level of anxiety by placing it in a two-compartment box, one side lit and the other side dark. Fewer crossings and less time spent in the lighted side indicate anxiety.

limbic cortex Part of the limbic system located on the medial and interior surface of the cerebral hemispheres. The limbic cortex includes the cingulate.

limbic system Neural network that integrates emotional responses and regulates behavior and learning. Some major structures include the limbic cortex, amygdala, nucleus accumbens, and hippocampus.

linkage study Method used to locate genes responsible for a disorder, such as alcoholism or schizophrenia, by comparing similarities in the genetic loci of families with affected members.

Lioresal See *baclofen*.

lipids Fatty molecules in the body. Lipids are a major component of cell membranes, and some of them also act as neurotransmitters.

lithium carbonate   Drug that stabilizes moods, preventing episodes of mania and depression, in people with bipolar disorder.

local potential   Small localized short-lived change in voltage across the cell membrane.

locus (pl. loci)   The location of a gene on a chromosome.

locus coeruleus (LC)   Collection of noradrenergic neurons in the reticular formation of the pons that supplies most of the NE to the cortex, limbic system, thalamus, and hypothalamus. These cells cause arousal and increased attention when active.

long-acting drug   Drug that has low lipid solubility, taking more than an hour to reach the brain. Slow metabolism or presence of active metabolites allows for prolonged effects that persist for long periods.

long-term potentiation (LTP)   Phenomenon whereby synaptic connections are strengthened for a period of at least an hour. It requires activation of NMDA receptors for its induction and AMPA receptors for its expression.

Lopressor   See *metoprolol*.

LSD   See *lysergic acid diethylamide*.

luteinizing hormone (LH)   Hormone secreted by the anterior pituitary that helps control gonad growth and function, and increases estrogen and androgen secretion.

lysergic acid diethylamide (LSD)   Hallucinogenic drug that is synthesized from lysergic acid and based on alkaloids found in ergot fungus. It is thought to produce its effects mainly by stimulating 5-HT$_{2A}$ receptors in the brain.

lysergic acid   Core structural unit of all ergot alkaloids.

lysis   Bursting of a cell.

M

macroelectrode   Device used to electrically stimulate deep brain regions while monitoring behavior or recording the summated electrical response of thousands of neurons.

MAGL   See *monoacylglycerol lipase*.

magnetic resonance imaging (MRI)   Technique used to visualize in high resolution, detailed slices through the brain or other organ by taking computerized measurements of the signals emitted by atoms in the tissue as they are exposed to a strong magnetic field. Computer technology permits recreation of the structure in 3-dimensions.

major depression   Type of affective disorder characterized by extreme recurring episodes of dysphoria and negative thinking that are reflected in behavior.

MAO inhibitors (MAOIs)   Class of drugs that inhibit monoamine oxidase (MAO), thereby causing an accumulation of catecholamines and serotonin in the brain. They are often used to treat clinical depression.

MAO   See *monoamine oxidase*.

maternal separation   Technique used to test the role of early-life stress as a factor in the development of depression, substance abuse, and other psychopathology. Week-old animals are separated from their mothers for brief periods daily.

MCI   See *mild cognitive impairment*.

MDMA   See *3,4-methylenedioxymethamphetamine*.

mecamylamine   Drug that is an antagonist for nicotinic receptors.

medial   Located near the center or midline of the body or brain.

median eminence   Area in the hypothalamus that is not isolated from chemicals in the blood and where hypothalamic-releasing hormones are secreted for transport to the anterior pituitary gland.

median raphe nucleus   Structure located in the area of the caudal midbrain and rostral pons that contains a large number of serotonergic neurons. In conjunction with the dorsal raphe nucleus, it is responsible for most of the serotonergic fibers in the forebrain. Together they regulate sleep, aggression, impulsiveness, and emotions.

medical model   See *disease model*.

medulla   Structure located in the caudal brain stem responsible for regulating heart rate, digestion, respiration, blood pressure, coughing, and vomiting.

melatonin   Hormone that regulates rhythmic functions in the body. It is secreted by the pineal gland.

meninges   Layers of protective tissue located between the bones of the skull and vertebrae and the tissue of the brain and spinal cord.

MEOS   See *microsomal ethanol oxidizing system*.

mephedrone   Cathinone derivative (4-methylmethcathinone) that is an emerging abused stimulant drug. It is a member of a group of compounds sometimes called "legal highs."

3-mercaptopropionic acid   Drug that blocks GABA synthesis, inducing convulsions.

mescal button   Crown of the peyote cactus, *Lophophora williamsii*, which can be dried and ingested to obtain the hallucinogenic drug mescaline.

mescaline   Hallucinogenic drug produced by several cacti species, especially that of the peyote cactus, *Lophophora williamsii*.

mesocortical dopamine pathway   Group of dopaminergic axons that originates in the VTA and travels to the cerebral cortex, including the prefrontal, cingulated, and entorhinal cortices. It may also be called the mesocortical tract.

mesolimbic dopamine pathway   Group of dopaminergic axons that originates in the VTA and travels to structures of the limbic system, including the nucleus accumbens, septum, amygdala, and hippocampus. It may also be called the mesolimbic tract.

Mestinon   See *pyridostigmine*.

metabolic tolerance   Type of tolerance to a drug that is characterized by a reduced amount of drug available at the target tissue, often as a result of more-rapid drug metabolism. It is sometimes also called drug disposition tolerance.

metabolites   Byproducts of biochemical pathways, such as those involved in neurotransmitter or drug inactivation.

metabotropic receptors   Slow-acting receptor type composed of a single large protein in the cell membrane that activates G proteins. It may also be called a G protein–coupled receptor.

methadone   A long-acting opioid drug that may be substituted for other opioids in order to prevent withdrawal symptoms.

methadone maintenance program   Most effective treatment program for opioid addicts that involves the substitution of the opioid with methadone to prevent withdrawal symptoms and avoid a relapse.

methamphetamine   Psychostimulant that acts by increasing catecholamine release from nerve terminals. It can also cause neurotoxicity at high doses.

3-methoxy-4-hydroxy-phenylglycol (MHPG)   A metabolite of NE, formed primarily as a result of NE breakdown in the brain.

5-methoxy-dimethyltryptamine (5-MeO-DMT)   Hallucinogenic drug found in certain South American plants. Its street name is "foxy" or "foxy methoxy."

1-methyl-4-phenyl-1,2,3,6-tetrahydropyridine (MPTP)   Dopamine neurotoxin sometimes used to produce an animal model of Parkinson's disease.

3,4-methylenedioxymethamphetamine (MDMA)   Drug similar in structure to amphetamine that stimulates 5-HT release and is neurotoxic at high doses. It is a recreational drug that is often abused.

metoprolol   Drug that selectively blocks the β_1-receptor, limiting contraction of the heart muscles. It is useful for treating hypertension.

Metrazol   See *pentylenetetrazol*.

mGluR1–mGluR8   Eight metabotropic glutamate receptors of the nervous system. They can inhibit cyclic adenosine monophosphate synthesis, activate the phosphoinositide second-messenger system, or inhibit glutamate release into the synaptic cleft.

MHPG   See *3-methoxy-4-hydroxy-phenylglycol*.

microdialysis   Technique used to measure neurotransmitter release in the brain of an awake, freely moving animal by collecting samples of extracellular fluid and then analyzing the samples biochemically using sensitive methods such as HPLC. Chemicals can also be applied to precise brain sites with the same technique.

microelectrode   Device used to electrically stimulate or record the response of a single cell intracellularly or extracellularly.

microglia   Small nonneuronal cells in the CNS that collect at points of cell damage or inflammation and demonstrate phagocytic behavior.

microsomal enzymes   Enzymes in liver cells responsible for metabolizing exogenous substances such as drugs.

microsomal ethanol oxidizing system (MEOS)   The cytochrome P450 enzyme CYP 2E1 that metabolizes ethanol and many other drugs.

microtubles   Tubular structures composed of proteins that form both a structural scaffold and a stationary track in the cytoplasm of cells, suitble for movement of materials along its length.

midsagittal   Section taken of the brain that divides it into left and right symmetrical pieces.

mild cognitive impairment (MCI)   Conditions characterized by difficulty in performing more than one task at a time, difficulty in solving problems, and forgetting of recent events or conversations. All cases of Alzheimer's disease are preceded by MCI, but not all cases of MCI develop into Alzheimer's disease.

Mini-Mental State Exam (MMSE)   Cognitive test for measuring the severity of dementia.

Minipress   See *prazosin*.

mitochondrion (pl. mitochrondria)   Organelle of the cell that produces energy, in the form of ATP, from glucose.

MK-801   See *dizocilpine*.

monoacylglycerol lipase (MAGL)   Enzyme primarily responsible for metabolism of the endocannabinoid 2-arachidonoylglycerol.

monoamine hypothesis   Theory that a reduced level of monoamines in the CNS will cause depressed moods, including clinical depression.

monoamine oxidase (MAO)   Enzyme responsible for metabolic breakdown of catecholamines and serotonin.

monoamine   Refers to a compound or transmitter that contains a single amine group.

moral model   Model of addiction that treats addiction as a personal and moral problem.

Morris water maze   Maze type that involves repeatedly placing the animal in a pool of opaque water and testing its ability to use visual cues from outside the pool to find the escape platform. It is used to test spatial learning.

motor efferents   Nerve fibers originating at the ventral horn of the spinal cord and traveling to the skeletal muscles, controlling voluntary movements.

motor neuron   Nerve cell that transmits electrical signals from the CNS to muscles.

MPTP   See *1-methyl-4-phenyl-1,2,3,6-tetrahydropyridine*.

MRI   See *magnetic resonance imaging*.

MS   See *multiple sclerosis*.

multidimensional approach   Treatment that involves a combination of methods to prevent drug abuse relapse, including detoxification, pharmacological support, and counseling.

multiple sclerosis (MS)   Disorder caused by autoimmune destruction of the myelin covering neurons in the brain and spinal cord. MS affects movement, sensation, and bodily functions.

multiple T-maze   Maze type that contains many alleys ending in a "T" shape, which gives the animal two possible directions at each choice point.

μ-receptor   A subtype of opioid receptor located in the brain and spinal cord that has a high affinity for morphine and certain other opiate drugs.

muscarinic receptors   Family of metabotropic cholinergic receptors that are selectively stimulated by muscarine.

muscimol   Drug found in the mushroom *Amanita muscaria* that is an agonist for the $GABA_A$ receptor.

muscle dysmorphia   Psychological disorder characterized by a false perception that the sufferer is weak and small, constant checking of one's appearance, concealing one's body shape, and a preoccupation with working out and using steroids to enhance muscle growth.

muscle relaxants   Drugs, such as benzodiazepines, that reduce muscle tension in a patient.

myasthenia gravis   Neuromuscular disorder involving an attack on the muscle cholinergic receptors by one's own immune system.

myelin   A fatty insulating sheath surrounding many axons that increases the speed of nerve conduction. It is produced by oligodendrocytes in the CNS and by Schwann cells in the peripheral nervous system.

N

Na⁺–K⁺ pump   Protein pump that helps to maintain the resting membrane potential by removing Na^+ from inside the cell. Three Na^+ ions are exchanged for two K^+ ions, maintaining a negative charge inside the cell. It also forces the ions against their concentration gradients following an action potential.

nabilone   Drug that is an analog of THC, sold under the trade name Cesamet, used to treat nausea in chemotherapy patients.

nabiximols (Sativex)   Cannabis extract containing THC and cannabidiol that is taken as an oral spray and is used therapeutically to treat neuropathic pain and spasticity in multiple sclerosis patients.

NAcc   See *nucleus accumbens*.

nAChRs   See *nicotinic cholinergic receptors*.

nalmefene   A dual κ/μ-opioid antagonist effective in reducing lever pressing for alcohol in rodent studies, particularly in alcohol-dependent animals.

naloxone   A pure opioid antagonist used to reverse opioid overdose and in opioid addiction treatment for highly motivated addicts.

naltrexone   A μ-receptor antagonist that reduces consumption and craving in some alcoholic individuals, perhaps by reducing the positive feeling caused by alcohol.

narcolepsy   Sleep disorder characterized by repeated bouts of extreme sleepiness during the daytime. Symptoms include sudden cataplexy, sleep paralysis, and dream-like hallucinations.

narcotic analgesics   Class of drugs originally derived from the opium poppy that reduce pain but do not cause unconsciousness. They create a feeling of relaxation and sleep in an individual, but in high doses can cause coma or death.

Nardil   See *phenelzine*.

natural recovery   Recovery from drug addiction without the aid of treatment.

NBQX   Antagonist that blocks both AMPA and kainate receptors, but has no effect on NMDA receptors.

NE   See *norepinephrine*.

NE transporter   Protein in the membrane of noradrenergic neurons that is responsible for NE reuptake from the synaptic cleft.

necrosis   Cell death resulting from exposure to a chemical agent (such as glutamate), disease, or other injury. It differs in several important ways from apoptosis (programmed cell death).

negative symptoms   Characteristics of schizophrenia that are observed as a decline in normal function, such as reduced speech, loss of motivation, social withdrawal, and anhedonia.

neonatal ventral hippocampal lesion model   Neuro-developmental model of schizophrenia that relies on early damage to the hippocampus in rodents. Hippocampal lesioning leads to some behaviors analogous to the early negative symptoms of schizophrenia. Behaviors similar to the positive symptoms of psychosis appear only at post-adolescence.

neostigmine (Prostigmin)   Synthetic analog of the drug physostigmine that cannot cross the blood–brain barrier. It is used to treat myasthenia gravis due to its ability to block AChE activity in muscle tissue.

nerves   Bundles of neurons that transmit electrical signals for nervous system function.

neuraxis   Imposed line through the body that starts at the base of the spinal cord and ends at the front of the brain.

neuroadaptation   Changes in brain functioning that attempt to compensate for the effects of repeated substance use.

neurodevelopmental model of schizophrenia   Theory that genetic vulnerability in combination with environmental stressors alters the trajectory of brain development resulting in the symptoms observed in schizophrenics.

neurofibrillary tangles (NFTs)   Fibrous inclusions, composed primarily of tau protein, that are abnormally located in the cytoplasm of neurons. Pyramidal neurons are particularly susceptible to NFTs.

neuroleptic malignant syndrome (NMS)   Undesired response to antipsychotic drugs characterized by fever, instability of the autonomic nervous system, rigidity, and altered consciousness.

neuroleptics   Drugs useful in treating schizophrenia; an older term that refers to their ability to selectively reduce emotionality and psychomotor activity.

neuromodulators   Chemicals that don't follow the typical neurotransmitter model. They may regulate neurotransmitter activity or act at distant sites from their point of release.

neuromuscular junction   Connection point between neurons and muscle cells. It has some of the characteristics of a synapse.

neurons   Nerve cells that form the brain, spinal cord, and nerves and that transmit electrical signals throughout the body.

neuropeptides   Small proteins (3 to 40 amino acids long) in the nervous system that act as neurotransmitters.

neuropharmacology   Area of pharmacology specializing in drug-induced changes to the function of cells in the nervous system.

neuropsychopharmacology   Area of pharmacology focusing on chemical substances that interact with the nervous system to alter behavior, emotions, and cognition.

neurosteroids   Family of substances that are synthesized in the brain from cholesterol and that have a steroid structure. They act as local signaling agents.

neurotoxicant   An element or compound that produces an adverse change in the structure or function of one or more components of the central or peripheral nervous system.

neurotoxin   Chemical that damages or kills nerve cells.

neurotransmitter   Chemical substance released by a neuron to communicate with another cell, which may be a different neuron, a muscle cell, or a hormone-producing cell in an endocrine gland.

neurotrophic factors   Proteins that encourage the growth, development, and survival of neurons. They are also involved in neuronal signaling.

NFTs   See *neurofibrillary tangles*.

nicotine   Alkaloid that is a behavioral stimulant. It is found in the tobacco plant.

nicotine replacement   Method to stop smoking that involves giving the smoker a safer nicotine source, thereby maintaining a level of nicotine in the body and reducing nicotine withdrawal symptoms.

nicotine resource model   Theory that smoking is maintained due to positive effects of nicotine such as increased concentration and greater mood control.

nicotinic cholinergic receptors (nAChRs)   Family of ionotropic receptors that are activated by ACh and selectively stimulated by nicotine. They may also be called nicotinic receptors.

nicotinic receptors   See *nicotinic cholinergic receptors*.

nigrostriatal tract   Dopaminergic nerve tract originating at the substantia nigra and terminating in the stratum. It is important for regulation of movement and is severely damaged in Parkinson's disease.

nitric oxide (NO)   Gas that acts as a signaling molecule in the brain. Unlike typical neurotransmitters, it is not stored or released from synaptic vesicles. It may function as a retrograde messenger in LTP.

nitric oxide synthase (NOS)   Enzyme that catalyzes the formation of NO from arginine.

nitrites   Class of inhalants that are characterized by the presence of an NO_2 group and that heighten sexual arousal and pleasure.

NMDA receptor   Ionotropic glutamate receptor selective for the agonist NMDA.

NMS   See *neuroleptic malignant syndrome*.

no observed effect level (NOEL)   Level of exposure at which there are no detectable adverse health effects.

NO   See *nitric oxide*.

nodes of Ranvier   Gaps in the myelin sheath that expose the axon to the extracellular fluid.

noncompetitive antagonist   Drug that reduces the effect of an agonist, but does not compete at the receptor site. The drug may bind to an inactive portion of the receptor, disturb the cell membrane around the receptor, or interrupt the intercellular processes initiated by the agonist–receptor association.

nonspecific drug effects   Physical or behavioral changes not associated with the chemical activity of the drug–receptor interaction but with certain unique characteristics of the individual such as present mood or expectations of drug effects.

NOP-R   One of the four opioid receptors. It is widely distributed in the CNS and the peripheral nervous system and is activated by the neuropeptide nociceptin/orphanin FQ.

nor-binaltorphimine   A selective κ-opioid antagonist. Because it reduces the self-administration of alcohol only in animals dependent on alcohol, a role for the κ receptor in alcohol abuse is suspected.

noradrenergic   Adjectival form of noradrenaline (norepinephrine).

norepinephrine (NE)   Neurotransmitter related to DA that belongs to a group called catecholamines. It also functions as a hormone secreted by the chromaffin cells of the adrenal medulla. Also known as noradrenaline.

Norflex   See *orphenadrine*.

NOS   See *nitric oxide synthase*.

novel object recognition   Test of short-term memory in rodents based on the tendency of the animal to explore a novel object in preference to a familiar one.

nuclei   Localized cluster of nerve cell bodies in the brain or spinal cord.

nucleus accumbens (NAcc)   Structure of the limbic system that helps to modulate emotional behavior and also plays an important role in the reinforcing and incentive salience effects of many abused drugs.

NVHL   See *neonatal ventral hippocampal lesion model*.

O

obsessions   Worrying thoughts or ideas that an individual cannot easily ignore.

obsessive–compulsive disorder (OCD)   Psychiatric anxiety disorder characterized by persistent thoughts of contamination, violence, sex, or religion that the individual cannot easily ignore, and that cause the individual anxiety, guilt, or shame, etc. and may be accompanied by compulsive repetitive behaviors.

occipital lobe   One of four lobes of the cerebral cortex. It contains the primary visual cortex and helps integrate visual information.

oligoclonal bands   Immunoglobins that indicate inflammatory processes within the central nervous system.

oligodendroglia   Glial cells that myelinate nerve axons of the CNS. Also known as oligodendrocytes.

open field test   Technique used to measure locomotor activity and exploratory behavior by placing the animal on a grid and recording the number of squares traversed in a unit of time.

operant analgesia testing   Technique used to test analgesic drugs. Once an animal is trained to lever press to terminate foot shock, the researchers gradually increase shock stimulation from very low levels until the animal responds by lever pressing, to indicate threshold. Analgesic drugs would be expected to raise that threshold.

operant conditioning   Type of learning in which animals learn to repond to obtain rewards and avoid punishment.

opponent-process model   Model of addiction in which the initial positive response to a drug is followed by an opposing withdrawal response as the drug wears off.

optogenetics   New neurobiological technique based on the ability of certain light-sensitive proteins, when expressed in a specific subset of neurons, to either excite or inhibit the cells when exposed to light of the appropriate wavelength.

oral administration (PO)   Method that involves administering a drug through the mouth.

organophosphate (OP)   General name for esters of phosphoric acid. OPs are the basis for many insecticides, herbicides, and nerve gases.

orphan receptor   Receptor that is not activated by any known neurotransmitter.

orphenadrine (Norflex)   Anticholinergic drug used to treat early symptoms of Parkinson's disease.

osmotic minipump   Device placed just under the skin of an animal that allows a drug to be administered continuously over a set period of time.

ovaries   Female-specific gonads that secrete the sex hormones estrogen and progesterone.

oxytocin   Peptide hormone synthesized by certain hypothalamic neurons and secreted into the bloodstream at the posterior lobe of the pituitary gland. Circulating oxytocin induces uterine contractions during childbirth and milk letdown during lactation. Other oxytocin neurons form synapses within the brain and play an important role in social, including maternal, behaviors in some species.

P

PAG   See *periaqueductal gray*.

panic attack   Feeling of extreme fear that was not preceded by a threatening stimulus.

panic disorder   Disease involving repeated attacks of extreme fear, occurring either without warning or in an environment similar to where previous panic attacks occurred.

para-chloroamphetamine Drug similar in structure to amphetamine that stimulates 5-HT release. It is also neurotoxic at high doses.

para-chlorophenylalanine (PCPA) Drug that irreversibly inhibits tryptophan hydroxylase, blocking 5-HT synthesis.

paranoid schizophrenia Subtype of schizophrenia distinguished by delusions of persecution.

parasympathetic Division of the autonomic nervous system responsible for conserving energy, digestion, glucose and nutrient storage, slowing the heart rate, and decreasing respiration.

parasympatholytic agents Drugs that block muscarinic receptors, inhibiting the parasympathetic system. They are deadly at high doses, but at low doses they are used medicinally to dilate pupils, relax airways, counteract cholinergic agonists, and induce drowsiness.

parenteral Methods of drug administration that do not use the gastrointestinal system, such as intravenous, inhalation, intramuscular, transdermal, etc.

paresthesia Condition characterized by numbness and a "pins-and-needles" feeling.

parietal lobe One of four lobes of the cerebral cortex. It contains the primary somatosensory cortex and helps integrate information about body senses.

Parkinson's disease Chronic, progressive, neurodegenerative disorder characterized by tremor, rigidity, difficulty in initiating movement, slowing of movement, and postural instability.

Parkinson's disease dementia (PDD) Condition in which one or more cognitive functions are impaired to the point of interfering with the ability of the individual to navigate everyday life.

Parkinsonian symptoms Undesired response to antipsychotic drugs that resembles Parkinson's disease, including tremors, akinesia, muscle rigidity, akathesia, and lack of mood expression.

Parnate See *tranylcypromine*.

paroxysmal depolarization shift (PDS) Periodic episodes of prolonged neuronal depolarization occurring during the interictal period in the brain of epileptic patients.

partial agonists Drugs that bind to a receptor but have low efficacy, producing weaker biological effects than a full agonist. Hence they act as agonists at some receptors and antagonists at others, depending on the regional concentration of full agonist. These were previously called mixed agonist-antagonists.

partial antagonist Drug that acts as an agonist to some receptors, but an antagonist to others. Some opioid drugs have this property.

partition coefficient An experimentally-derived measure of a drug's lipid solubility used to predict its relative rate of movement across cell membranes.

passive avoidance learning Type of learning task in rats and mice in which the animal is trained to avoid a location that it would normally enter (e.g., going into a dark compartment from one that is brightly lit) by administration of a brief electric footshock when it enters the location. The word "passive" in the name of the task reflects the fact that the animal must withhold its usual response of moving into the dark compartment.

passive diffusion Movement of lipid-soluble materials across a biological barrier without assistance based on its concentration gradient, from higher to lower concentration.

patch clamp electrophysiology Technique used to measure the function of a single ion channel by using a micropipette to isolate the ion channel and obtain an electrical recording.

Pavlovian Reflexive and unconscious response to a stimulus.

paw test Animal research method used to distinguish between antipsychotic-induced therapeutic effects and side effects

PCP See *phencyclidine*.

PCPA See *para-chlorophenylalanine*.

PDD See *Parkinson's disease dementia*.

PDR See *phosphodiesterase*.

PDS See *paroxysmal depoarization shift*.

pedunculopontine tegmental nucleus (PPTg) Structure within the dorsal lateral pons containing cholinergic neurons that project to the substantia nigra (important for stimulating nigral dopamine neurons) and others that project to the brainstem and thalamus (important for behavioral arousal, sensory processing, and inititation of rapid-eye-movement sleep).

penetrance Frequency with which a particular gene produces its main effect.

pentylenetetrazol (Metrazol) Convulsant drug that acts by blocking the function of $GABA_A$ receptors.

periaqueductal gray (PAG) Structure of the tegmentum located around the cerebral aqueduct and connecting the third and fourth ventricles. It is important for regulating pain; stimulation produces an analgesic effect.

persistent organic pollutants (POPs) Synthetic organic compounds that are resistant to environmental degradation through chemical, biological, and photolytic processes. Physiochemical properties include low water solubility, high lipid solubility, semi-volatility, and relatively high molecular mass.

PET See *positron emission tomography*.

peyote button Crown of the peyote cactus, *Lophophora williamsii*, that can be dried and ingested to obtain the hallucinogenic drug mescaline.

peyote cactus Species of cactus, *Lophophora williamsii*, that produces mescaline.

pharmacodynamics Study of physiological and biochemical interactions of a drug with the target tissue responsible for the drug's effects.

pharmacodynamic tolerance Type of tolerance formed by changes in nerve cell functions in response to the continued presence of a drug.

pharmacogenetics The study of the genetic basis for variability in drug response among individuals (sometimes called pharmacogenomics).

pharmacokinetic Factors that contribute to bioavailability: the administration, absorption, distribution, binding, inactivation, and excretion of a drug.

pharmacological MRI (phMRI) A spin-off of functional MRI (fMRI), is a technique used in drug development to investigate the mechanism of drug action by visualizing changes in brain function following drug administration.

pharmacology Study of the actions of drugs and their effects on living organisms.

pharmacotherapeutic treatment Method of disease treatment that uses drugs to modify a clinical condition.

phencyclidine (PCP) Drug that binds to the PCP site and acts as a noncompetitive antagonist of the NMDA receptor. It is a dissociative anesthetic that was once used medicinally but is now only taken recreationally.

phenelzine (Nardil)   MAO inhibitor used to treat clinical depression.

phenethylamine   Class of drugs that includes mescaline as well as NE- and amphetamine-related substances.

phenylephrine α_1-receptor agonist that causes behavioral stimulation.

phMRI   See *pharmacological MRI*.

phobias   Fears of specific objects or situations that are recognized as irrational.

phosphodiesterase (PDE)   the enzyme that normally degrades cAMP to 5′-AMP.

phosphoinositide second-messenger system   Neurotransmitter signaling mechanism that activates PKC and is controlled by certain receptors for ACh, NE, and 5-HT.

phospholipid bilayer   Fatty sheet surrounding a cell that prevents most substances from passing, but allows lipid-soluble materials to pass. The sheet is composed of phospholipids aligned linearly head-to-tail, forming a tail-to-tail bilayer with the water-soluble heads facing toward the inside and outside of the cell.

phospholipids   Lipid molecules that are major constituents of the cell membrane. They are composed of a polar head and two lipid tails.

physical dependence   Developed need for a drug, such as alcohol or opioids, by the body as a result of prolonged drug use. Termination of drug use will lead to withdrawal symptoms (abstinence).

physiological antagonism   Drug interaction characterized by two drugs reducing each other's effectiveness in the body.

physostigmine (Eserine)   Drug that blocks AChE activity. Its symptoms include slurred speech, mental confusion, hallucinations, loss of reflexes, convulsions, coma, and death. It is isolated from Calabar beans.

pia mater   The innermost of the meninges. The pia mater is a thin tissue immediately surrounding the brain and spinal cord.

picrotoxin   Convulsant drug that acts by blocking the function of $GABA_A$ receptors.

pilocarpine   Extract of the shrub *Pilocarpus jaborandi* known for its ability to stimulate muscarinic receptors.

pineal gland   Specific endocrine gland that is located above the brain stem, covered by the cerebral hemispheres. It secretes melatonin.

pinocytotic vesicles   Type of vesicles that envelop and transport large molecules across the capillary wall.

pituitary gland   Endocrine gland that is located under the hypothalamus and connects to the brain by a thin stalk. It secretes TSH, ACTH, FSH, LH, GH, PRL, vasopressin, and oxytocin.

PKA   See *protein kinase A*.

PKC   See *protein kinase C*.

PKG   See *protein kinase G*.

PKMzeta   See *protein kinase Mzeta*.

place conditioning   Pavlovian conditioning procedure used to test the rewarding effects of drugs in rats and mice.

placebo   Substance that is pharmacologically inert, yet in many instances produces both therapeutic and side effects.

PO   See *oral administration*.

polarized   Possessing an electrical charge.

polybrominated diphenyl ethers (PBDEs)   Synthetic brominated compounds that are used as flame retardants.

polychlorinated biphenyls (PCBs)   Synthetic chlorinated compounds that were used in industrial and consumer products. Production of PCBs was banned in the United States in the late 1970s.

polypharmacy   Use of multiple pharmacological agents at the same time.

POMC   See *pro-opiomelanocortin*.

positive reinforcer   Something (e.g., an abused drug) that, when provided to an organism, increases the strength of the response that was used to obtain the item. In studies of addiction, the positive reinforcing quality of a drug is usually measured by means of a self-administration procedure.

positive symptoms   Characteristics of schizophrenia that include delusions, hallucinations, disorganized speech, and bizarre behavior. They are often the more dramatic symptoms.

positron emission tomography (PET)   Imaging technique used to determine the distribution of a radioactively labeled substance in the body. It can be used to measure drug binding to neurotransmitter receptors or transporters in the brain as well as measuring changes in metabolic activity reflecting neuron function.

posterior   Located near the back or rear of an animal.

posterior pituitary   Part of the pituitary gland in which vasopressin and oxytocin are secreted.

postsynaptic cell   Neuron at a synapse that receives a signal from the presynaptic cell.

posttraumatic stress disorder (PTSD)   Emotional disorder that develops in response to a traumatic event, leaving the individual feeling a sense of fear, helplessness, and terror. Symptoms include sleep disturbances, avoidance of stimuli associated with the trauma, intrusive thoughts reliving the event, and a numbing of general emotional responses. An increase in suicidal thoughts has also been observed.

postural instability   Impaired balance and coordination. In Parkinson's disease, manifests as a pronounced forward or backward lean in upright position.

potency   Measure of the amount of drug necessary to produce a specific response.

potentiation   Drug interaction characterized by an increase in effectiveness greater than the collective sum of the individual drugs.

PPI   See *prepulse inhibition of startle*.

PPTg   See *pedunculopontine tegmental nucleus*.

prazosin (Minipress) α_1-receptor antagonist that causes dilation of blood vessels and is useful for treating hypertension.

Precedex   See *dexmedetomidine*.

precipitated withdrawal   Method used to test dependence and withdrawal by administering an antagonist to block drug effects rapidly.

precursor   Chemical that is used to make the product formed in a biochemical pathway (e.g., tyrosine is the precursor of DOPA in the pathway for catecholamine synthesis).

predictive validity   A measure of how closely the results from animal tests predict clinically useful effects in humans.

prepulse inhibition of startle (PPI)   Method to study the ability of an individual to filter out sensory stimuli by applying a weak "prepulse" stimulus shortly before the startle-inducing stimulus. Well validated model of information-processing deficits in schizophrenia.

presenilin-1 (PS-1) and presenilin-2 (PS-2)   Proteins involved in the processing of APP.

presynaptic cell   Neuron at a synapse that transmits a signal to the postsynaptic cell.

presynaptic facilitation   Signaling by the presynaptic cell to increase neurotransmitter release by the axon terminal of the postsynaptic cell.

presynaptic inhibition   Signaling by the presynaptic cell to reduce neurotransmitter release by the axon terminal of the postsynaptic cell.

primary cortex   The part of each lobe of the cortex that provides conscious awareness of sensory experience and the initial cortical processing of sensory qualities.

primers   Drug-like effects caused by stress or drug-conditioned stimuli that reinstate drug use after abstinence.

PRL   See *prolactin*.

prodynorphin   One of the four large opioid propeptide precursors that are broken down by proteases to form smaller active opioids (dynorphins) in the brain.

proenkephalin   One of the four large opioid propeptide precursors that are broken down by proteases to form smaller active opioids (enkephalins) in the brain.

progesterone   Female sex hormone secreted by the ovaries that is present at high levels during pregnancy.

progestins   Group of female sex hormones that are important for the maintenance of pregnancy. The principal naturally occurring progestin is progesterone.

programmed cell death   Cell death resulting from a programmed series of biochemical events in the cell designed to eliminate unnecessary cells. Also called apoptosis.

progressive-ratio procedure   Method used to measure the relative power of drug reinforcement by steadily increasing the response to reward ratio.

prolactin (PRL)   Hormone secreted by the anterior pituitary that promotes milk production by the mammary glands.

promoter region   Section of a gene, adjacent to the coding region, that controls the rate of transcription.

pronociceptin/orphanin FQ   One of the four large opioid propeptide precursors, that is broken down by proteases to form smaller active opioids (nociceptin, orphanin FQ) in the brain.

pro-opiomelanocortin (POMC)   One of the four large opioid propeptide precursors that are broken down by proteases to form smaller active opioids (endorphins) in the brain.

propranolol (Inderal)   β-receptor antagonist. It is useful for treating hypertension due to its ability to block β-receptors in the heart, thereby limiting contraction of the heart muscles.

Prostigmin   See *neostigmine*.

protein kinase A (PKA)   Enzyme that is stimulated by cAMP and that phosphorylates specific proteins as part of a neurotransmitter signaling pathway.

protein kinase C (PKC)   Enzyme that is stimulated by diacylglycerol and Ca^{2+} and that phosphorylates specific proteins as part of a neurotransmitter signaling pathway.

protein kinase G (PKG)   Enzyme that is stimulated by cGMP and that phosphorylates specific proteins, including proteins involved in cell growth and differentiation.

protein kinase Mzeta (PKMzeta)   Novel form of protein kinase C that is hypothesized to play an important role in stabilizing the extra AMPA receptors inserted in the dendritic membrane in late-LTP.

protein kinases   Enzymes that catalyze the phosphorylation of other proteins.

Prozac   See *fluoxetine*.

psilocin   Metabolite of psilocybin. Psilocin is the actual psychoactive agent.

psilocybin   Hallucinogenic drug found in several mushroom species.

psychedelic   Substance that alters perceptions, state of mind or awareness.

psychedelic therapy   Therapeutic method that involved giving patients a single high dose of LSD to help them understand their problems by reaching a drug-induced spiritual state.

psychoactive drugs   Those drugs that have an effect on thinking, mood, or behavior.

psycholytic therapy   Therapeutic method that employed LSD in low doses, gradually increasing the dose, in attempts to recover repressed memories or increase communication with the therapist.

psychopharmacology   Area of pharmacology specializing in drug-induced changes in mood, thinking, and behavior.

psychosocial rehabilitation program   See *psychosocial treatment program*.

psychosocial treatment programs   Counseling programs that involve educating the user, promoting behavioral change and alleviating problems caused by drug use.

psychotomimetic   Substance that mimics psychosis in a subject, such as by inducing hallucinations or delusions.

PTSD   See *posttraumatic stress disorder*.

pure antagonist   Drug that produces no pharmacological activity (i.e., no efficacy) and that can prevent or reverse the effects of a drug agonist by occupying the receptor site.

pyramiding   Pattern of steroid use characterized by gradually increasing the drug dose until the middle of the cycle, then gradually decreasing the drug dose until the cycle is complete.

pyridostigmine (Mestinon)   Synthetic analog of the drug physostigmine that cannot cross the blood–brain barrier. It is used to treat myasthenia gravis due to its ability to block AChE activity in muscle tissue.

R

radial arm maze   Maze type composed of multiple arms leading from a central choice point. Radial arm mazes are used to test spatial learning.

radioimmunoassay (RIA)   A very sensitive method that uses antibodies to measure moelcules in body fluids or tissue extracts. The essay depends on competitive binding of an antibody to the antigen of interest.

radioligand binding   Technique used to measure the affinity and relative density of receptors in a particular brain area by using a radioactively labeled ligand for the receptor.

raphe nuclei   Network of cell clusters in the CNS that contain the cell bodies of serotonergic neurons. They are found almost exclusively along the midline of the brain stem.

rate-limiting enzyme   Enzyme that catalyzes the slowest step in a biochemical pathway. It determines the overall rate of product formation.

reactive depression   State of sadness that is appropriate and of a reasonable level in response to a given aversive situation. Not usually considered a clinical condition.

reboxetine   Antidepressant that selectively blocks the NE transporter, thereby increasing NE concentration in the synaptic cleft.

receptor agonist   A neurochemical or drug that can bind to a particular receptor protein and alter the shape of the receptor to initiate a cellular response.

receptor antagonist   A molecule that interacts with a receptor protein and produces no cellular effect after binding, and also prevents an "active" ligand from binding.

receptor binding studies   See *radioligand binding*.

receptor cloning   Process used to produce large amounts of identical receptor proteins in a cell line.

receptor subtypes   Group of receptors that respond to the same neurotransmitter but that differ from each other to varying degrees with respect to their structure, signaling mechanisms, and pharmacology.

receptor trafficking   Normal process in which the receptors for a particular neurotransmitter are shuttled into and out of the cell membrane to regulate sensitivity of the cell to that transmitter.

receptor up-regulation   Increase in the number of receptors produced and maintained in a target cell.

receptors   Proteins located on the surface of or within cells that bind to specific ligands to initiate biological changes within the cell.

rectal administration   Drug delivery method, such as a suppository, used to deliver drugs via the lower intestine.

reference dose (RfD)   The maximum oral dose of a toxic substance that is not likely to cause adverse effects. RfDs are set by the U.S. Environmental Protection Agency.

relapse prevention therapy   Treatment program for drug abusers that teaches an individual how to avoid and cope with high-risk situations.

relapse   Recurrence of drug use following a period of abstinence.

relative refractory period   Short hyperpolarizing phase after an action potential during which a more intense excitatory stimulus is necessary to obtain an action potential.

reliability   Term used to indicate how dependable test results are and how likely the same test results will be found in subsequent trials.

remission   Period in which an addict is drug free.

resensitize   Receptor state characterized by the return of receptor function and a normal response to agonist stimulation.

reserpine-induced sedation   Animal testing method used to identify clinically useful antidepressant drugs.

reserpine   Drug extracted from *Rauwolfia serpentina* (snake root) roots. It inhibits vesicular monoamine uptake by VMAT, thereby reducing monoamine levels in the central and peripheral nervous system.

resting membrane potential   The difference in the electrical charge inside a neuron at rest compared to the outside. The inside of the cell is more negative, and that potential is –70 mV.

resting tremor   Tremor that is present when the limb is relaxed. Can be present in the hand, foot, jaw or face. Generally disappears with intentional movement.

reticular formation   Collection of nuclei within the core of the pons forming a network that extends into the midbrain and medulla. These nuclei are important for arousal, attention, sleep, muscle tone, and some cardiac and respiratory reflexes.

retrograde axonal transport   Process by which waste materials are transported in vesicles along microtubules from the axon terminal to the soma for recycling.

retrograde messenger   Chemical synthesized and released by a postsynaptic cell that diffuses into the nerve terminal of the presynaptic cell, often for the purpose of altering neurotransmitter release by the terminal.

retropulsion   The need to take a step backward when starting to walk.

reuptake   Process that involves transport of neurotransmitters out of the synaptic cleft by the same cell that released them.

reward ciruit   Circuit of neurons that, when activated, mediates the rewarding effects of both natural rewards (e.g., food, water, sex) and drugs of abuse.

RIA   See *radioimmunoassay*.

ribosome   Organelles in the cytoplasm that, using the coding from messenger RNA (mRNA), link together appropriate amino acids to create a protein. This is the translation stage of protein synthesis.

rigidity   Stiffness and inflexibility in the joints. Two types are present in Parkinson's disease: "lead-pipe" rigidity, which is characterized by maintenance of inflexibility of the joint through the entire range of movement, and "cogwheel" rigidity, which is characterized by a ratchet-like interruption in movement.

rimonabant   Antagonist selective for the CB_1 receptor. It is also called SR 141716.

risperidone (Risperdal)   Drug that inhibits $5-HT_{2A}$ and D_2 dopamine receptors. It is used to treat schizophrenia.

rodent version of the WCST   A variation of the Wisconsin Card Sorting Test (WCST) developed for use on animals to evaluate working memory, attention, and problem solving.

rostral   Located near the front or head of an animal.

rotarod   An animal test technique using a horizontally-oriented cylinder that is mechanically rotated at set speeds. Researchers time latency to fall (e.g., how long mice remain balanced on the rod).

S

Sabril   See *vigabatrin*.

sagittal   Section that is taken parallel to the plane bisecting the nervous system into right and left halves.

saltatory conduction   Mode of action potential conduction along a myelinated neuron characterized by jumps from one node of Ranvier to the next.

salvinorin A   Active compound in the hallucinogenic plant *Salvia divinorum*; acts as a κ-opioid receptor agonist.

SC   See *subcutaneous*.

SCH 23390 D_1 receptor antagonist that may induce catalepsy when administered in high doses.

Schedule of Controlled Substances System established by the Controlled Substances Act in 1970 that classifies most substances with abuse potential into one of five schedules. Schedules I and II have the strictest guidelines.

schedule of reinforcement Predetermined schedule used to determine when an animal will be rewarded for performing a specific behavior. A fixed ratio (FR) schedule refers to rewards given after a set number of responses; a fixed interval (FI) schedule refers to rewards given to the first response that occurs after a set amount of time has elapsed.

Schwann cells Glial cells that myelinate peripheral nerve axons.

scopolamine Drug that blocks muscarinic receptors. It is found in nightshade, *Atropa belladonna*, and in henbane, *Hyoscyamus niger*.

second messenger Substance that, when activated by signaling molecules bound to receptors in the cell membrane, will initiate biochemical processes within the cell.

second-messenger systems Biochemical pathways that use second messengers to mediate intercellular signaling.

secondary cortex Section of the cerebral cortex containing the neuronal circuits responsible for analyzing and recognizing information from the primary cortex, and for memory storage.

section Tissue slice showing structures of the body or nervous system.

sedative–hypnotics Class of drugs that depresses nervous system activity. They are used to produce relaxation, reduce anxiety, and induce sleep.

selective D$_2$ receptor antagonists Drugs that selectively block D$_2$ receptors, including sulpiride, raclopride, and remoxipride.

selective serotonin reuptake inhibitors (SSRIs) Antidepressants used to treat major depression, panic and anxiety disorders, obsessive-compulsive disorder, obesity, and alcoholism by blocking the presynaptic membrane transporter for 5-HT.

self-administration method Test used to measure the abuse potential of a drug by allowing an animal to give itself the drug doses.

self-medication hypothesis Theory that addiction is based on an effort by the individual to treat oneself for mood or other ill feelings.

semi-persistent organic pollutants (semi-POPs) Similar to POPs, but generally lower in molecular mass with physicochemical properties that make them more vulnerable to degradation and thus less persistent in the environment.

sensitive Term used to indicate that a test uses drug doses within the normal therapeutic range.

sensitization Enhanced response to a particular drug after repeated drug exposure.

sensory afferents Neurons carrying sensory information from the body surface or internal organs into the CNS.

sensory neurons Nerve cells that are sensitive to environmental stimuli and convert the physical stimuli into electrical signals.

serotonergic Adjectival form of serotonin (5-HT).

serotonergic neurons Neurons that use serotonin as their transmitter.

serotonin syndrome Effects associated with an overdose of SSRIs or serotonergic agonists, including severe agitation, disorientation, confusion, ataxia, muscle spasms, fever, shivering, chills, diarrhea, elevated blood pressure, and increased heart rate.

serotonin (5-HT) Neurotransmitter found in the central and peripheral nervous system and synthesized by serotonergic neurons.

SERT See *5-HT transporter*.

shared etiology Situation in which multiple disorders are caused by the same set of factors.

short/intermediate-acting drugs Drugs that are moderately lipid-soluble, reaching the brain within 20 to 40 minutes. The drugs lose effectiveness over time due to liver metabolism.

side effect Undesired physical or behavioral change associated with a particular drug.

single-photon emission computerized tomography (SPECT) Imaging technique used to view changes in regional blood flow or drug binding by using radioactively labeled compounds injected or inhaled into the body.

sinsemilla The potent marijuana produced by preventing pollination and seed production in the female cannabis plants.

sleep deprivation Lack of proper sleep, either unintentional (e.g., jet lag), or intentional (such as can be used to relieve clinical depression in human patients).

social interaction test Test used to measure the level of anxiety in rodents by recording the time spent investigating other animals.

soma Cell body of a neuron, containing all of the organelles needed to maintain the cell.

soman Toxin that causes irreversible inhibition of AChE. It is used as a nerve gas for chemical warfare.

somatodendritic autoreceptors Autoreceptors located on the dendrites or cell body that slow the rate of cell firing when activated.

spasticity Constant unwanted contraction of one or more muscle groups.

specific Term referring to the fact that drug screening tests should identify only those drugs in a particular class.

specific drug effects Physical or behavioral changes associated with biochemical interactions of a drug with the target site.

specific neurotoxin Chemical that damages a specific neural pathway leaving others intact.

SPECT See *single-photon emission computerized tomography*.

spinal interneurons Nerve cells with short axons within the spinal cord.

SR 141716 See *rimonabant*.

SSRIs See *selective serotonin reuptake inhibitors*.

stacking Pattern of anabolic steroid use characterized by the simultaneous use of multiple steroids, such as a short- and a long-acting steroid.

state-dependent learning Condition characterized by better performance of a particular task that was learned in a drugged state in the same drugged state, rather than in a nondrugged state. Tasks learned in a nondrugged state are likewise performed better in a nondrugged state.

status epilepticus Dangerous condition characterized either by continuous epileptic seizures or a sufficiently short period between seizures so that the patient has insufficient time to recover.

steady state plasma level   The desired blood concentration of drug achieved when the absorption/distribution phase is equal to the metabolism/excretion phase.

stereotyped behaviors   Repeated, relatively invariant behaviors associated with a particular situation or drug treatment. They often occur following a high dose of a psychostimulant such as cocaine or amphetamine.

steroids   Class of hormones that are derived from cholesterol and regulate a variety of biochemical pathways.

stop-signal task   Test used to evaluate impulsivity (e.g., lack of behavior control). It requires the subject (human or otherwise) to rapidly press one button or lever when a square is displayed, and the other button or lever when any other shape appears. Periodically, a tone, which is the "stop" signal, is sounded following the visual presentation. The tone indicates that the subject should withhold responding.

Strattera   See *atomoxetine*.

subcutaneous (SC)   Method that involves injection of a drug just below the skin.

substance abuse   Disorder involving the overuse of a drug by an individual. It may or may not lead to substance dependence.

substance dependence   Disorder involving excessive and harmful drug use by an individual, corresponding to addiction.

substance use disorder   New *DSM-5* designation for a psychiatric disorder with features typically associated with addiction. This designation replaces both substance abuse and substance dependence categories in *DSM-IV*.

substantia nigra   Collection of dopaminergic cell bodies within the tegmentum of the mesencephalon that innervate the striatum by way of the nigrostriatal tract. Damage to cells in this region leads to Parkinson's disease.

subunits   Individual protein components that must join in the cell membrane to form a complete receptor.

succinylcholine   Chemical similar to ACh that is resistant to metabolism by AChE. It is used as a muscle relaxant during some surgical procedures.

sudden sniffing death syndrome   Fatal cardiac arrhythmia associated with inhalant use.

sulcus (pl. sulci)   Small grooves of the cerebral cortex.

superior   Located near the top of the brain in humans.

supraspinal   Located above the spinal cord or spine.

supressor T cell   Type of T cell that reduces or suppresses the immune response of other T cells (or B cells) to an antigen.

swimming performance   A rodent test of coordination used in the study of motor deficit diseases.

sympathetic   Division of the autonomic nervous system responsible for providing energy expenditure to deal with a challenge by triggering the "fight-or-flight" response: increasing heart rate, increasing blood pressure, stimulating adrenaline secretion, and increasing blood flow to skeletal muscles.

sympathomimetic   Substance that produces symptoms of sympathetic nervous system activation.

synapse   Structural unit of information transmission between two nerve cells. It consists of the presynaptic nerve terminal, the synaptic cleft, and a small area of the postsynaptic cell (typically associated with a dendrite or region of the cell body) that receives the incoming signal.

synaptic cleft   Small gap, about 20 nm wide, between the presynaptic and postsynaptic cells.

synaptic plasticity   Ability of synapses to change structurally (i.e., growth of new synapses or loss of existing ones) and functionally (i.e., increased or decreased strength of existing synapses). In the adult nervous system, synaptic plasticity is particularly important for learning and memory and for the development of addiction following repeated exposure to abused drugs.

synaptic vesicles   Sac-like structures located in the axon terminal that are filled with molecules of neurotransmitter.

synesthesia   Mixing of sensations such that one kind of sensory stimulus creates a different kind of sensation, such as a color producing the sensation of sound.

T

T cell   A type of white blood cell.

T-maze   Maze type that involves an alley ending in a "T" shape, giving the animal two path choices to reach food in goal box.

T3   See *triiodothyronine*.

T4   See *thyroxine*.

tail suspension test   Used in the study of animal models for affective disorders; mice are suspended by the tail from a lever, and the duration of movements (a period of agitation followed by immobility) is recorded. Antidepressant drugs prolong the active struggling.

tail-flick test   Technique used to measure pain sensitivity in an animal by placing a hot beam of light on the animal's tail and recording the time it takes for the animal to remove its tail from the beam.

tar   Mixture of hydrocarbons created by the vaporization of nicotine in tobacco. Tar is a major component of cigarette smoke.

tardive dyskinesia (TD)   Undesired response to antipsychotic drugs characterized by involuntary muscle movements, particularly of the face, head, and neck, that may be irreversible in some patients.

Tasmar   See *tolcapone*.

tau   Protein associated with NFTs.

TCA   See *tricyclic antidepressant*.

tegmentum   Division of the midbrain. The tegmentum is composed of several important structures including the PAG, substantia nigra, and the VTA.

Tegretol   See *carbamazepine*.

temporal lobe   One of four lobes of the cerebral cortex. It contains the primary auditory cortex and helps integrate auditory information.

temporal lobe sclerosis   Cell death in temporal lobe structures (especially the hippocampus) of an epileptic patient that is believed to be due to seizure-induced excitotoxicity.

teratogen   Any agent including a virus, drug, or radiation that induces abnormal fetal development, causing birth defects.

terminal autoreceptors   Autoreceptors that are located on axon terminals and that inhibit neurotransmitter release.

terminal buttons   Small enlargements at the axon terminal, in close proximity to the dendrites of the postsynaptic cell, containing synaptic vesicles. Also known as boutons.

tertiary association areas   Section of the cerebral cortex where the three sensory lobes can interact, providing a higher order of perception and memory.

testes   Male specific gonads that secrete androgens.

testosterone   The principal androgen (male sex steroid) secreted by the testes.

tetanic stimulus   Electrical stimuli delivered repeatedly, in a brief train of electrical bursts. Also referred to as tetanus.

tetanus   A train of electrical stimuli that is used experimentally to induce LTP. Also referred to as a tetanic stimulus.

TH   See *tyrosine hydroxylase*.

thalamus   Structure of the diencephalon that is responsible for processing and distributing sensory and motor signals to the appropriate section of the cerebral cortex.

therapeutic drug monitoring   Taking multiple blood samples to directly measure plasma levels of a drug after administration, to identify the optimum dosage for maximum therapeutic potential and minimal side effects.

therapeutic effects   Desired physical or behavioral changes associated with a particular drug.

therapeutic index   The relationship between the drug dose that results in a toxic response compared to the dose required for the desired biological response. It is represented by the equation $TI = TD_{50}/ED_{50}$ where TD_{50} is the dose that is toxic for 50% of the population and ED_{50} is the effective dose for 50%.

thiosemicarbazide   Drug that blocks GABA synthesis, inducing convulsions.

threshold   Membrane potential, typically −50 mV, at which voltage-gated Na^+ channels will open, generating an action potential.

thyroid gland   Specific endocrine gland that is located in the throat and secretes T3 and T4.

thyroid-stimulating hormone (TSH)   Hormone that stimulates the thyroid gland. It is secreted by the anterior pituitary.

thyrotropin-releasing hormone (TRH)   Hormone that stimulates TSH release. It is synthesized by neurons of the hypothalamus.

thyroxine (T4)   Hormone that is synthesized from tyrosine and helps control normal energy and metabolism in the body. It is secreted by the thyroid gland.

tiagabine (Gabitril)   Drug that is a selective inhibitor of GAT-1. It is used in pharmacological studies and to treat patients with partial seizures who are resistant to standard antiepileptic drugs.

tianeptine   Tricyclic antidepressant (TCA) that modulates glutamate function.

tight junctions   Connection between cells characterized by a fusing of adjoining cell membranes.

tolcapone (Tasmar)   COMT inhibitor used in conjunction with L-DOPA to treat Parkinson's disease.

tolerance   Decreased response to a drug as a direct result of repeated drug exposure.

topical   Method that involves administration of a drug through a mucous membrane such as the oral cavity, nasal mucosa, or vagina.

tracts   Bundles of nerve axons in the CNS sharing a common origin and target.

transcription   Process whereby mRNA is produced as a complementary copy of an active gene.

transcription factors   Nuclear proteins that regulate gene transcription within a cell.

transdermal   Method that involves administration of a drug through the skin (e.g., with a patch).

transfection   Process used to introduce genetic material into a cell by injecting it with a DNA sequence coding for the desired protein product.

transgenic mice   Mice bred to replace one gene with another (e.g., a normal gene with a mutant version of that gene). They are used to study genetic disorders.

translation   Process whereby proteins are produced using mRNA code to direct the amino acid sequence. Translation is performed by ribosomes.

transporter proteins   Specific proteins in the cell membrane that transport molecules into and out of the cell (e.g., proteins that remove neurotransmitters from the synaptic cleft following their release). They are sometimes just called transporters.

tranylcypromine (Parnate)   MAO inhibitor used to treat clinical depression.

TRH   See *thyrotropin-releasing hormone*.

tricyclic antidepressants (TCAs)   Class of antidepressants characterized by a three-ring structure. They block reuptake of NE and 5-HT, thereby increasing their concentration in the synaptic cleft.

trihexyphenidyl (Artane)   Anticholinergic drug used to treat early symptoms of Parkinson's disease.

triiodothyronine (T3)   Hormone that is synthesized from tyrosine and helps control normal energy and metabolism in the body. It is secreted by the thyroid gland.

trinucleotide repeat   Sequence of three nucleotides repeated a number of times in tandem on the same chromosome. In Huntington's disease, the CAG sequence is repeated more than 40 times.

trkA–trkC   Types of tyrosine kinase receptors that are activated by neurotrophic factors: trkA by NGF, trkC by NT-3, and trkB by BDNF and NT4. Two activated trk receptors are needed to phosphorylate each other and trigger subsequent signaling events.

tryptophan   Amino acid characterized by the presence of an indole group. It is a precursor to 5-HT.

tryptophan depletion challenge   Research method used to investigate the role of serotonin in depressive disorders, in which subjects consume a tryptophan-deficient amino acid cocktail that transiently reduces 5-HT level in the brain.

tryptophan hydroxylase   Enzyme that catalyzes the conversion of tryptophan into 5-HTP.

TSH   See *thyroid-stimulating hormone*.

tuberohypophyseal dopamine pathway   Pathway that controls the secretion of the hormone prolactin by the pituitary gland.

turnover   Index of neurotransmitter activity, typically obtained by determining the level or rate of production of one or more metabolites for that transmitter.

twin studies   Studies used to understand how heredity contributes to a disorder by comparing the concordance rate for the disorder in pairs of monozygotic and dizygotic twins.

tyrosine   Amino acid characterized by a phenol group. It is necessary for the synthesis of the catecholamine neurotransmitters.

tyrosine hydroxylase (TH)   Enzyme that catalyzes the first step of catecholamine synthesis in neurons, the conversion of tyrosine to DOPA.

tyrosine kinase receptors   Family of receptors that mediate neurotrophic factor signaling.

U

ultrashort-acting   Drugs that are highly lipid-soluble, reaching the brain within seconds when administered intravenously. They lose effectiveness quickly, as they rapidly redistribute to inactive drug depots in fat, bone, and muscle.

ultrasonic vocalizations   High-frequency rodent calls typically emitted by juveniles as when separated from their mothers, indicating distress.

undifferentiated schizophrenia   Subtype of schizophrenia characterized by symptoms that do not match other subtypes.

up-regulation   Increase in the number of receptors, which may be a consequence of denervation or of chronic antagonist treatment.

V

VaChT   See *vesicular ACh transporter.*

Valium   See *diazepam.*

valproate (Depakote)   Simple branched-chain fatty acid that was the first anticonvulsant approved by the U.S. FDA for treatment of acute mania.

vanillymandelic acid (VMA)   Metabolite of NE, formed primarily by NE breakdown in the peripheral nervous system.

vasopressin   Peptide hormone secreted by the posterior pituitary that increases water retention by the kidneys.

Ventolin   See *albuteral.*

ventral tegmental area (VTA)   Region containing dopaminergic cell bodies within the tegmentum of the mesencephalon (midbrain) that form the mesolimbic and mesocortical tracts.

ventral   Located toward the underside of the brain or front of the body in humans.

vesicular ACh transporter (VaChT)   Vesicle membrane protein that transports ACh into synaptic vesicles.

vesicular GABA transporter (VGAT)   Vesicle membrane protein that transports both GABA and glycine into synaptic vesicles; also known as VIAAT.

vesicular glutamate transporter (VGLUT)   Vesicle membrane protein that transports glutamate into synaptic vesicles. There are three such proteins, designated VGLUT1–VGLUT3, which differ in their location within the brain.

vesicular inhibitory amino acid transporter (VIAAT)   See *vesicular GABA transporter.*

vesicular monoamine transporter (VMAT)   Vesicle membrane protein that transports monoamines (i.e., catecholamines and 5-HT) into synaptic vesicles. Monoamine neurons express a particular form of VMAT called VMAT2, whereas the epinephrine- and norepinephrine-secreting chromaffin cells of the adrenal medulla express a different form called VMAT1.

vigabatrin (Sabril)   Drug that irreversibly inhibits GABA-T. It is used to treat epilepsy.

viral vector   Use of a virus as a delivery system (called a vector) to carry a gene into the nuclei of target cells to alter protein synthesis.

VMA   See *vanillymandelic acid.*

Vogel test   Water-lick suppression test (a conflict procedure) that reliably screens anxiety-reducing drugs in rodents.

volatile solvents   Class of inhalants characterized by chemicals, such as adhesives, ink, and paint thinner, that are liquid at room temperature, but readily give off fumes that can be easily inhaled.

voltage-gated channels   Type of ion channels that are regulated by voltage differences across the membrane.

volume transmission   Phenomenon characterized by the diffusion of a chemical signal (e.g., a neurotransmitter) through the extracellular fluid to reach target cells at some distance from the point of release.

VTA   See *ventral tegmental area.*

W

water-lick suppression test   Technique used to measure anxiety in rodents by recording their propensity to lick a drinking spout that will also deliver a mild electric shock. Also called Vogel test.

WAY 100635   Drug that selectively inhibits 5-HT_{1A} receptors.

Wernicke–Korsakoff syndrome   Symptom of thiamine deficiency characterized by confusion, disorientation, tremors, poor coordination, ataxia, and in later stages, short-term memory loss.

wiring transmission   Point-to-point communication between neurons in which the neurotransmitter acts locally within the synapse to affect the target cell. The opposite of wiring transmission is volume transmission.

withdrawal   See *abstinence syndrome.*

Y

yohimbine α_2-antagonist that blocks autoreceptors and increases noradrenergic cell firing. It enhances symptoms of opioid withdrawal.

Z

zero-order kinetics   Term used to describe a constant rate of drug removal from the body, regardless of drug concentration in the blood.

Illustration Credits

Chapter 1   *Opener*: © Bettmann/Corbis.

Chapter 2   *Opener*: ©Dr. Thomas Deerinck/Visuals Unlimited, Inc. Box 2.1: © Dr. Yorgos Nikas/Science Source. Box 2.2: S. Mark Williams and Dale Purves, Duke University Medical Center.

Chapter 3   *Opener*: Data from PDB 3KG2, Sobolevsky et al., 2009. *Nature* 462: 745.

Chapter 4   *Opener*: Courtesy of the Oak Ridge National Laboratory. 4.21B: © Zephyr/SPL/Science Source. 4.22: © S. Mark Williams (Pyramis Studios), and Leonard E. White and James Voyvodic (Duke University). 4.24: Courtesy of Neuroscan Labs, a division of Neurosoft, Inc. Box 4.3B: Courtesy of Susan Urmy, Vanderbilt University.

Chapter 5   *Opener*: © i love images/Alamy.

Chapter 6   *Opener*: © Tessa Hirschfeld-Stoler.

Chapter 7   *Opener*: © Pete Oxford/Naturepl.com. 7.11: © Science Photo Library/Alamy.

Chapter 8   *Opener*: Courtesy of the Office of Communications, Princeton University. 8.16: © Arie v.d. Wolde/Shutterstock.

Chapter 9   *Opener*: © Aj Wilhelm/National Geographic Society/Corbis.

Chapter 10   *Opener*: © David Kadlubowski/DIT/Corbis. 10.1: Courtesy of the National Library of Medicine. 10.11: © Arthur Glauberman/Science Source. 10.12A: © Rick's Photography/Shutterstock.

Chapter 11   *Opener*: © WpN/UPPA/Photoshot. 11.1: © Heather Angel/Alamy Images.

Chapter 12   *Opener*: Courtesy of the National Library of Medicine. 12.2: © Jean-Philippe Soule/Alamy Images. 12.5: Courtesy of the U.S. DEA. 12.19: © Stephen Psallidas/Alamy images. 12.22: Courtesy of the Multnomah County Sheriff's Office.

Chapter 13   *Opener*: © Archive Images/Alamy. 13.2: David McIntyre.

Chapter 14   *Opener*: © Alex Milan Tracy/Demotix/Corbis. 14.2: © Science Photo Library/Alamy. 14.3: Courtesy of the U.S. DEA.

Chapter 15   *Opener*: © Willfried Gredler/AGE Fotostock. 15.2: © Nigel Bean/Naturepl.com. 15.3: The Tina & R. Gordon Wasson Ethnomycological Collection Archives, Harvard University, Cambridge, MA 02138. 15.4: © Ted Kinsman/Science Source. 15.11: © Ace Stock Limited/Alamy Images. 15.13: Courtesy of Coaster420/Wikipedia. Box 15.1: © Ken Wagner/Visuals Unlimited, Inc.

Chapter 16   *Opener*: © Jan Sochor/Alamy. 16.6: © David Hoffman Photo Library/Alamy Images. Box 16.1: David McIntyre.

Chapter 17   *Opener*: © Kristian Buus/In Pictures/Corbis. 17.1: © Alain Nogues/Sygma/Corbis. Box 17.1: © Science Photo Library/Alamy.

Chapter 18   *Opener*: © SuperStock/AGE Fotostock. 18.10: Nicolas Poussin. 18.11: Courtesy of Amy Bedell.

Chapter 19   *Opener*: © Corbis.

Chapter 20   *Opener*: © Grunnitus Studio/Science Source. 20.2A: Courtesy of the National Library of Medicine.

Chapter 21   *Opener*: © Epicscotland/Alamy. 21.1: © Reuters/Corbis. 21.3: Courtesy of the Harvard Brain Tissue Resource Center at McLean Hospital. 21.5: © Biophoto Associates/Science Source. 21.10: © Dr. Thomas Deerinck/Visuals Unlimited, Inc. 21.14A: Courtesy of the Harvard Brain Tissue Resource Center at McLean Hospital. 21.15: From Bramwell, B. (1886). *Diseases of the Spinal Cord*. Young J. Pentland, Edinburgh.

References

Abanades, S., Farré, M., Segura, M., Pichini, S., Barral, D., Pacifici, R., et al. (2006). γ-Hydroxybutyrate (GHB) in humans: Pharmacodynamics and pharmacokinetics. *Ann. N.Y. Acad. Sci.*, 1074, 559–576.

Abdel Rasoul, G. M., Abou Salem, M. E., Mechael, A. A., Hendy, O. M., Rohlman, D. S., and Ismail, A. A. (2008). Effects of occupational pesticide exposure on children applying pesticides. *Neurotoxicol.*, 29, 833–838.

Abreu-Villaça, Y., Seidler, F. J., Qiao, D., Tate, C. A., Cousins, M. M., Thillai, I., et al. (2003). Short-term adolescent nicotine exposure has immediate and persistent effects on cholinergic systems: Critical periods, patterns of exposure, dose thresholds. *Neuropsychopharmacology*, 28, 1935–1949.

Absalom, N., Eghorn, L. F., Villumsen, I. S., Karim, N., Bay, T., Olsen, J. V., et al. (2012). α4βδ GABA$_A$ receptors are high-affinity targets for γ-hydroxybutyric acid (GHB). *Proc. Natl. Acad. Sci. U.S.A.*, 109, 13404–13409.

Ackerman, J. P., Riggins, T., and Black, M. M. (2010). A review of the effects of prenatal cocaine exposure among school-aged children. *Pediatrics*, 125, 554–565.

Adhikari, B., Kahende, J., Malarcher, A., Pechacek, T., and Tong, V. (2008). Smoking-attributable mortality, years of potential life lost, and productivity losses—United States, 2000–2004. *MMWR Morb. Mortal. Wkly. Rep.*, 57, 1226–1228.

Adolfsson, O., Pihlgren, M., Toni, N., Varisco, Y., Buccarello, A. L., Antoniello, K., et al. (2012). An effector-reduced anti-β-amyloid (Aβ) antibody with unique Aβ binding properties promotes neuroprotection and glial engulfment of Aβ. *Neurobiol. Dis.*, 32, 9677–9689.

Agency for Toxic Substances and Disease Registry (ATSDR). (1999). *Toxicological Profile for Mercury*. Atlanta, GA: U.S. Department of Health and Human Services, Public Health Service.

Agency for Toxic Substances and Disease Registry (ATSDR). (2003). *Toxicological Profile for Pyrethrins and Pyrethroids*. Atlanta, GA: U.S. Department of Health and Human Services, Public Health Service.

Agency for Toxic Substances and Disease Registry (ATSDR). (2004). *Toxicological Profile for Polybrominated Bipheynyls and Polybrominated Diphenyl Ethers*. Atlanta, GA: U.S. Department of Health and Human Services, Public Health Service.

Agency for Toxic Substances and Disease Registry (ATSDR). (2007a). *Case Studies in Environmental Medicine. Cholinesterase Inhibitors: Including Pesticides and Chemical Warfare Nerve Agents*. Course: WB1102. U.S. Department of Health and Human Services Agency for Toxic Substances and Disease Registry Division of Toxicology and Environmental Medicine, Environmental Medicine and Educational Services Branch. Available online at: www.atsdr.cdc.gov/csem/cholinesterase/docs/cholinesterase.pdf, accessed 11/26/12.

Agency for Toxic Substances and Disease Registry (ATSDR). (2007b). *Toxicological Profile for Lead*. Atlanta, GA: U.S. Department of Health and Human Services, Public Health Service.

Agency for Toxic Substances and Disease Registry (ATSDR). (2007c). *Toxicological Profile for Arsenic*. Atlanta, GA: U.S. Department of Health and Human Services, Public Health Service.

Aghajanian, G. K. and Marek, G. J. (1999). Serotonin and hallucinogens. *Neuropsychopharmacology*, 21, 16S–23S.

Aghajanian, G. K. and Marek, G. J. (2000). Serotonin model of schizophrenia: Emerging role of glutamate mechanisms. *Brain Res. Rev.*, 31, 302–312.

Agrawal, A., Verweij, K. J. H., Gillespie, N. A., Heath, A. C., Lessov-Schlaggar, C. N., Martin, N. G., et al. (2012). The genetics of addiction—A translational perspective. *Transl. Psychiatry*, 2, e140; doi:10.1038/tp.2012.54.

Agurell, S., Halldin, M., Lindgren, J.-E., Ohlsson, A., Widman, M., Gillespie, H., et al. (1986). Pharmacokinetics and metabolism of Δ⁹-tetrahydrocannabinol and other cannabinoids with emphasis on man. *Pharmacol. Rev.*, 38, 21–43.

Ahearn, D. J., McDonald, K., Barraclough, M., and Leroi, I. (2012). An exploration of apathy and impulsivity in Parkinson disease. *Curr. Gerontol. Geriatr. Res.*, 2012, 1–10.

Ahlquist, R. P. (1948). A study of adrenotropic receptors. *Am. J. Physiol.*, 153, 586–600.

Ahlquist, R. P. (1979). Adrenoreceptors. *Trends Pharmacol. Sci.*, 1, 16–17.

Ahmed, S. H. (2010). Validation crisis in animal models of drug addiction: Beyond non-disordered drug use toward drug addiction. *Neurosci. Biobehav. Rev.*, 35, 172–184.

Ahmed, S. H. (2012). The science of making drug-addicted animals. *Neuroscience*, 211, 107–125.

Ahmed, S. H. and Koob, G. F. (1998). Transition from moderate to excessive drug intake: Change in hedonic set point. *Science*, 282, 298–300.

Ahmed, S. H., Kenny, P. J., Koob, G. F., and Markou, A. (2002). Neurobiological evidence for hedonic allostasis associated with escalating cocaine use. *Nat. Neurosci.*, 5, 625–626.

Aigner, T. G. and Balster, R. L. (1978). Choice behavior in rhesus monkeys: Cocaine versus food. *Science*, 201, 534–535.

Akimova, E., Lanzenberger, R., and Kasper, S. (2009). The serotonin-1A receptor in anxiety disorders. *Biol. Psychiatry*, 66, 627–635.

Albertson, D. N. and Grubbs, L. E. (2009). Subjective effects of *Salvia divinorum*: LSD- or marijuanalike? *J. Psychoactive Drugs*, 41, 213–217.

Albuquerque, E. X., Pereira, E. F. R., Alkondon, M., and Rogers, S. W. (2009). Mammalian nicotinic acetylcholine receptors: From structure to function. *Physiol. Rev.*, 89, 73–120.

Aldridge, J. D., Levin, E. D., Seidler, F. J., and Slotkin, T. A. (2005). Developmental exposure of rats to chlorpyrifos leads to behavioral alterations in adulthood, involving serotonergic mechanisms and resembling animal models of depression. *Environ. Health Perspect.*, 113, 527–531.

Alford, C., Cox, H., and Wescott, R. (2001). The effects of Red Bull Energy Drink on human performance and mood. *Amino Acids*, 21, 139–150.

Allen, G. F. G., Land, J. M., and Heales, S. J. R. (2009). A new perspective on the treatment of aromatic L-amino acid decarboxylase deficiency. *Mol. Gen. Metab.*, 97, 6–14.

Altemus, M. (2006). Sex differences in depression and anxiety disorders: Potential biological determinants. *Horm. Behav.*, 50, 534–538.

Alvarez, J. A. and Emory, E. (2006). Executive function and the frontal lobes: A meta-analytic review. *Neuropsychol. Rev.*, 16, 17–42.

Alzado, L. (1991). I'm sick and I'm scared. Available online at: http://sportsillustrated.cnn.com/vault/article/magazine/MAG1139729/index.htm, accessed 8/26/12.

Alzheimer's Association. Available online at: www.alz.org, accessed 1/15/13.

Amaladoss, A. and O'Brien, S. (2011). Cough syrup psychosis. *CJEM*, 13, 53–56.

American Academy of Pediatrics (AAP). (1999). Thimerosal in vaccines—An interim report to clinicians. American Academy of Pediatrics. Committee on Infectious Diseases and Committee on Environmental Health. *Pediatrics* 104, 570–574.

American Association for Clinical Chemistry. (2011). *Therapeutic Drug Monitoring*. Available online at: http://www.labtestsonline.org/understanding/analytes/therapeutic_drug/glance.html

American Psychiatric Association. (1994). *Diagnostic and Statistical Manual of Mental Disorders* (4th ed.). Washington: American Psychiatric Association.

American Psychiatric Association. (2000). *Diagnostic and Statistical Manual of Mental Disorder* (4th ed., Text Revision). Washington: American Psychiatric Association.

Andari, E., Duhamel, J. R., Zalla, T., Herbrecht, E., Leboyer, M., and Sirigu A. (2010). Promoting social behavior with oxytocin in high-functioning autism spectrum disorders. *Proc. Natl. Acad. Sci.*, 107, 4389–4394.

Andersen, S. L. (2003). Trajectories of brain development: Point of vulnerability or window of opportunity? *Neurosci. Biobehav. Rev.*, 27, 3–18.

Andersen, S. L., Tomada, A., Vincow, E. S., Valente, E., Polcari, A., and Teicher, M. H. (2008). Preliminary evidence for sensitive periods in the effect of childhood sexual abuse on regional brain development. *J. Neuropsychiatry Clin. Neurosci.*, 20, 292–301.

Anderson, A. L., Reid, M. S., Li, S.-H., Holmes, T., Shemanski, L., Slee, A., et al. (2009). Modafinil for the treatment of cocaine dependence. *Drug Alcohol Depend.*, 104, 133–139.

Anderson, R. (2010). A tortured path: Curare's journey from poison darts to paralysis by design. *Mol. Interv.*, 10, 252–258.

Andreasen, N. C. (1990). Positive and negative symptoms: Historical and conceptual aspects. In T. A. Ban, A. M. Freedman, C. G. Gottfries, R. Levy, P. Pinchot, and W. Poldinger (Eds.), *Mod. Probl. Pharmacopsychiatry*, pp. 1–42. Basel, Switzerland: Karger.

Andresen, H., Aydin, B. E., Mueller, A., and Iwersen-Bergmann, S. (2011). An overview of gamma-hydroxybyric acid: Pharmacodynamics, pharmacokinetics, toxic effects, addiction, analytical methods, and interpretation of results. *Drug Test. Analysis*, 3, 560–568.

Andriamampandry, C., Taleb, O., Kemmel, V., Humbert, J.-P., Aunis, D., and Maitre, M. (2007). Cloning and functional characterization of a gamma-hydroxybutyrate receptor identified in the human brain. *FASEB J.*, 21, 885–895.

Andriamampandry, C., Taleb, O., Viry, S., Muller, C., Humbert, J. P., Gobaille, S., et al. (2003). Cloning and characterization of a rat brain receptor that binds the endogenous neuromodulator γ-hydroxybutyrate. *FASEB J.*, 17, 1691–1693.

Angell, P., Chester, N., Green, D., Somauroo, J., Whyte, G., and George, K. (2012) Anabolic steroids and cardiovascular risk. *Sports Med.*, 42, 119–134.

Anton, R. F., O'Malley, S. S., Ciraulo, D. A., Cisler, R. A., Couper, D., Donovan, D. M., et al. (2006). Combined pharmacotherapies and behavioral interventions for alcohol dependence: The COMBINE study: A randomized controlled trial. *JAMA*, 295, 2003–2017.

Appel, J. B., West, W. B., and Buggy, J. (2004). LSD, 5-HT (serotonin), and the evolution of a behavioral assay. *Neurosci. Biobehav. Rev.*, 27, 693–701.

Applegate, M. (1999). Cytochrome P450 isoenzymes: Nursing considerations. *Am. Psychiatr. Nurs. Assoc.*, 5, 15–22.

Apter, A., van Praag, H. M., Plutchik, R., Sevy, S., Korn, M., and Brown, S. L. (1990). Interrelationships among anxiety, aggression, impulsivity, and mood: A serotonergically linked cluster? *Psychiatry Res.*, 32, 191–199.

Arai, A. C. and Kessler, M. (2007). Pharmacology of ampakine modulators: From AMPA receptors to synapses and behavior. *Curr. Drug Targets*, 8, 583–602.

Armijo, J. A., Shushtarian, M., Valdizan, E. M., Cuadrado, A., de las Cuevas, I., and Adin, J. (2005). Ion channels and epilepsy. *Curr. Pharm. Des.*, 11, 1975–2003.

Arnold, J. C. (2005). The role of endocannabinoid transmission in cocaine addiction. *Pharmacol. Biochem. Behav.*, 81, 396–406.

Arnsten, A. F. T. (2007). Catecholamine and second messenger influences on prefrontal cortical networks of "representational knowledge": A rational bridge between genetics and the symptoms of mental illness. *Cereb. Cortex*, 17, i6-i15.

Arnsten, A. F. T. (2009). Toward a new understanding of attention-deficit hyperactivity disorder pathophysiology: An important role for prefrontal cortex dysfunction. *CNS Drugs*, 23 (Suppl. 1), 33–41.

Arranz, M. J. and Kapur, S. (2008). Pharmacogenetics in psychiatry: Are we ready for widespread clinical use? *Schizophr. Bull.*, 34, 1130–1144.

Aryana, A. and Williams, M. A. (2007). Marijuana as a trigger of cardiovascular events: Speculation or scientific certainty? *Int. J. Cardiol.*, 118, 141–144.

Aschner, M. and Aschner, J. L. (1990). Mercury neurotoxicity: Mechanisms of blood-brain barrier transport. *Neurosci. Biobehav. Rev.*, 14, 169–176.

Astorino, T. A. and Roberson, D. W. (2010). Efficacy of acute caffeine ingestion for short-term high-intensity exercise performance: A systematic review. *J. Strength Cond. Res.*, 24, 257–265.

Ator, N. A. and Griffiths, R. R. (2003). Principles of drug abuse liability assessment in laboratory animals. *Drug Alcohol Depend.*, 70, S55–S72.

Atwood, B. K. and Mackie, K. (2010). CB$_2$: A cannabinoid receptor with an identity crisis. *Br. J. Pharmacol.*, 160, 467–479.

Audrain-McGovern, J. and Benowitz, N. L. (2011). Cigarette smoking, nicotine, and body weight. *Clin. Pharmacol. Ther.*, 90, 164–168.

Auluck, P. K., Caraveo, G., and Lindquist, S. (2010). α-Synuclein: Membrane interactions and toxicity in Parkinson's disease. *Annu. Rev. Cell Dev. Biol.*, 26, 211–233.

Avena, N. M., Bocarsly, M. E., Hoebel, B. G., and Gold, M. S. (2011). Overlaps in the nosology of substance abuse and overeating: The translational implications of "food addiction." *Curr. Drug Abuse Rev.*, 4, 133–139.

Bachtell, R. K., Whisler, K., Karanian, D., and Self, D. W. (2005). Effects of intranucleus accumbens shell administration of dopamine agonists and antagonists on cocaine-taking and cocaine-seeking behaviors in the rat. *Psychopharmacology*, 183, 41–53.

Baker, J. P. (2008). Mercury, vaccines, and autism. One controversy, three histories. *Am. J. Public Health*, 98, 244–253.

Balda, M. A., Anderson, K. L., and Itzhak, Y. (2008). Differential role of the nNOS gene in the development of behavioral sensitization to cocaine in adolescent and adult B6;129S mice. *Psychopharmacology*, 200, 509–519.

Balda, M. A., Anderson, K. L., and Itzhak, Y. (2009). Development and persistence of long-lasting behavioral sensitization to cocaine in female mice: Role of the nNOS gene. *Neuropharmacology*, 56, 709–715.

Bales, R. F. (1946). Cultural differences in rates of alcoholism. *Q. J. Studies Alcohol*, 6, 480–499.

Ball, K. T., Wellman, C. L., Fortenberry, E., and Rebec, G. V. (2009). Sensitizing regimens of (±)3,4-methylenedioxymethamphetamine (Ecstasy) elicit enduring and differential structural alterations in the brain motive circuit of the rat. *Neuroscience*, 160, 264–274.

Balster, R. L. and Woolverton, W. L. (1980). Continuous-access phencyclidine self-administration by rhesus monkeys leading to physical dependence. *Psychopharmacology*, 70, 5–10.

Balster, R. L. and Woolverton, W. L. (1981). Tolerance and dependence to phencyclidine. In E. F. Domino (Ed.), *PCP (Phencyclidine): Historical and Current Perspectives*, pp. 293–306. Ann Arbor, MI: NPP Books.

Balu, D. T. and Lucki, I. (2009). Adult hippocampal neurogenesis: Regulation, functional implications, and contribution to disease pathology. *Neurosci. Biobehav. Rev.*, 33, 232–252.

Bamberger, M. and Yaeger, D. (1997). Over the edge: Aware that drug testing is a sham, athletes seem to rely more than ever on banned performance enhancers. Available online at: http://sportsillustrated.cnn.com/vault/article/magazine/MAG1009868/index.htm, accessed 8/9/12.

Bandstra, E. S., Morrow, C. E., Mansoor, E., and Accornero, V. H. (2010). Prenatal drug exposure: Infant and toddler outcomes. *J. Addict. Dis.*, 29, 245–258.

Banga, A. K. (2009). Microporation applications for enhancing drug delivery. *Expert Opin. Drug Deliv.*, 6, 343–354.

Banken, J. A. and Foster, H. (2008). Dextromethorphan: An emerging drug of abuse. *Ann. N.Y. Acad. Sci.*, 1139, 402–411.

Barbano, M. F. and Cador, M. (2007). Opioids for hedonic experience and dopamine to get ready for it. *Psychopharmacology*, 191, 497–506.

Barch, D. M., Carter, C. S., Arnsten, A., Buchanan, R. W., Cohen, J. D., Geyer, M., et al. (2009). Selecting paradigms from cognitive neuroscience for translation into use in clinical trials: Proceedings of the third CNTRICS meeting. *Schizophr. Bull.*, 35, 109–114.

Barclay, J. W., Graham, M. E., Edwards, M. R., Johnson, J. R., Morgan, A., and Burgoyne, R. D. (2010). Presynaptic targets for acute ethanol sensitivity. *Biochem. Soc. Trans.*, 38, 172–176.

Bardo, M. T., Donohew, R. L., and Harrington, N. G. (1996). Psychobiology of novelty seeking and drug seeking behavior. *Behav. Brain Res.*, 77, 23–43.

Bargu, S., Silver, M. W., Ohman, M. D., Benitez-Nelson, C. R., and Garrison, D. L. (2012). Mystery behind Hitchcock's birds. *Nat. Geosci.*, 2–3.

Bari, A., Dalley, J. W., and Robbins, T. W. (2008). The application of the 5-choice serial reaction time task for the assessment of visual attentional processes and impulse control in rats. *Nat. Protoc.*, 3, 759–767.

Bari, M., Battista, N., Pirazzi, V., and Maccarrone, M. (2011). The manifold actions of endocannabinoids on female and male reproductive events. *Front. Biosci.*, 16, 498–516.

Baribeau, J. and Laurent, J. P. (1991). Longitudinal studies of clinical and ERP correlates of thought disorder and positive/negative symptoms in schizophrenia. In T. Nakazawa (Ed.), *Biological Basis of Schizophrenic Disorders*, pp. 19–30. New York: Karger.

Barlow, D. H. and Durand, V. M. (1995). *Abnormal Psychology: An Integrative Approach.* New York: Brooks/Cole.

Barrós-Loscertales, A., Garavan, H., Bustamante, J. C., Ventura-Campos, N., Llopis, J. J., Belloch, V., et al. (2011). Reduced striatal volume in cocaine-dependent patients. *NeuroImage*, 56, 1021–1026.

Bartus, R. T., Dean, R. L., III, Beer, B., and Lippa, A. S. (1982). The cholinergic hypothesis of geriatric memory dysfunction. *Science*, 217, 408–414.

Basile, A. S., Fedorova, I., Zapata, A., Liu, X., Shippenberg, T., Duttaroy, A., et al. (2002). Deletion of the M_5 muscarinic acetylcholine receptor attenuates morphine reinforcement and withdrawal but not morphine analgesia. *Proc. Natl. Acad. Sci. U.S.A.*, 99, 11452–11457.

Bassuk, E. L. and Gerson, S. (1978). Deinstitutionalization and mental health services. *Sci. Am.*, 444, 332–358.

Basu, N., Stamler C. J., Loua, K. M., and Chan, H. M. (2005). An interspecies comparison of mercury inhibition on muscarinic acetylcholine receptor binding in the cerebral cortex and cerebellum. *Toxicol. Appl. Pharmacol.*, 205, 71–6.

Battle, C. (2010). Students consume study drugs to focus on exams. Available online at: http://www.thehilltoponline.com/life-style/students-consume-study-drugs-to-focus-on-exams-1.2405750, accessed 11/20/12.

Baxter, J. D. and Webb, P. (2009). Thyroid hormone mimetics: Potential applications in atherosclerosis, obesity and type 2 diabetes. *Nat. Rev. Drug Disc.*, 8, 308–320

Baxter, L. R., Jr., Schwartz, J. M., Bergman, K. S., Szuba, M. P., Guze, B. H., Mazziotta, J. C., et al. (1992). Caudate glucose metabolic rate changes with both drug and behavior therapy for obsessive-compulsive disorder. *Arch. Gen. Psychiatry*, 49(9), 681–689.

Baxter, M. G. (2001). Effects of selective immunotoxic lesions on learning and memory. In W. A. Hall (Ed.), *Methods in Molecular Biology*, Vol. 166: *Immunotoxin Methods and Protocols*, pp. 249–265. Totowa: Humana Press.

Bear, M. F., Connors, B. W., and Paradiso, M. A. (2001). *Neuroscience: Exploring the Brain* (2nd ed.). Philadelphia: Lippincott, Williams, and Wilkins.

Bear, M. F., Connors, B. W., and Paradiso, M. A. (2007). *Neuroscience: Exploring the Brain* (3rd ed.). New York: Lippincott Williams and Wilkins.

Beart, P. M. and O'Shea, R. D. (2007). Transporters for L-glutamate: An update on their molecular pharmacology and pathological involvement. *Br. J. Pharmacol.*, 150, 5–17.

Beaver, K. M., Vaughn, M. G., DeLisi, M., and Wright, J. P. (2008). Anabolic-androgenic steroid use and involvement in violent behavior in a nationally representative sample of young adult males in the United States. *Am. J. Pub. Health*, 98, 2185–2187.

Becker, J. B. and Hu, M. (2008). Sex differences in drug abuse. *Front. Neuroendocrinol.*, 29, 36–47.

Béïque, J.-C., Imad, M., Mladenovic, L., Gingrich, J. A., and Andrade, R. (2007). Mechanism of the 5-hydroxytryptamine 2A receptor-mediated facilitation of synaptic activity in prefrontal cortex. *Proc. Natl. Acad. Sci.*, 104, 9870–9875.

Belelli, D., Harrison, N. L., Maguire, J., Macdonald, R. L., Walker, M. C., and Cope, D. W. (2009). Extrasynaptic $GABA_A$ receptors: Form, pharmacology, and function. *J. Neurosci.*, 29, 12757–12763.

Belin, D., Berson, N., Balado, E., Piazza, P. V., and Deroche-Gamonet, V. (2011). High-novelty-preference rats are predisposed to compulsive cocaine self-administration. *Neuropsychopharmacology*, 36, 569–579.

Belin, D., Mar, A. C., Dalley, J. W., Robbins, T. W., and Everitt, B. J. (2008). High impulsivity predicts the switch to compulsive cocaine-taking. *Science*, 320, 1352–1355.

Bellinger, D. C. (2009). Interpreting epidemiologic studies of developmental neurotoxicity: Conceptual and analytic issues. *Neurotox. Teratol.*, 31, 267–274.

Bello, E. P., Mateo, Y., Gelman, D. M., Noaín, D., Shin, J. H., Low, M. J., et al. (2011). Cocaine supersensitivity and enhanced motivation for reward in mice lacking dopamine D_2 autoreceptors. *Nat. Neurosci.*, 14, 1033–1038.

Belmaker, R. H. and Agam, G. (2008). Major depressive disorder. *N. Engl. J. Med.*, 358, 55–68.

Belzer, K. and Schneier, F. R. (2004). Comorbidity of anxiety and depressive disorders: Issues in conceptualization, assessment, and treatment. *J. Psychiatr. Pract.*, 10, 296–306.

Benowitz, N. L. (2010). Nicotine addiction. *N. Engl. J. Med.*, 362, 2295–2303.

Benzenhöfer, U. and Passie, T. (2010). Rediscovering MDMA (ecstasy): The role of the American chemist Alexander T. Shulgin. *Addiction*, 105, 1355–1361.

Bergman, J. and Paronis, C. A. (2006). Measuring the reinforcing strength of abused drugs. *Mol. Interv.*, 6, 273–283.

Bergman, J., Kamien, J. B., and Spealman, R. D. (1990). Antagonism of cocaine self-administration by selective dopamine D_1 and D_2 antagonists. *Behav. Pharmacol.*, 1, 355–363.

Bernard, S., Enayati, A., Redwood, L., and Roger, H., and Binstock, T. (2001). Autism: A novel form of mercury poisoning. *Med. Hypoth.*, 56, 462–471.

Berridge, C. W. (2008). Noradrenergic modulation of arousal. *Brain Res. Rev.*, 58, 1–17.

Berridge, C. W., Isaac, S. O., and Espana, R. A. (2003). Additive wake-promoting actions of medial basal forebrain noradrenergic α_1- and β-receptor stimulation. *Behav. Neurosci.*, 117, 350–359.

Berridge, K. C. (2007). The debate over dopamine's role in reward: The case for incentive salience. *Psychopharmacology*, 191, 391–431.

Berridge, K. C. and Kringelbach, M. L. (2008). Affective neuroscience of pleasure: Reward in humans and animals. *Psychopharmacology*, 199, 457–480.

Berridge, K. C. and Robinson, T. E. (2003). Parsing reward. *Trends Neurosci.*, 26, 507–513.

Berridge, K. C., Robinson, T. E., and Aldridge, J. W. (2009). Dissecting components of reward: "Liking," "wanting," and learning. *Curr. Opin. Pharmacol.*, 9, 65–73.

Bertelsen, A., Harvald, B., and Hauge, M. (1977). A Danish twin study of manic-depressive disorders. *Br. J. Psychiatry*, 130, 330–351.

Bertschy, G. (1995). Methadone maintenance treatment: An update. *Eur. Arch. Psychiatr. Clin. Neurosci.*, 245, 114–124.

Bettler, B. and Tiao, J. Y-H. (2006). Molecular diversity, trafficking and subcellular localization of GABA_B receptors. *Pharmacol. Ther.*, 110, 533–543.

Beveridge, T. J. R., Gill, K. E., Hanlon, C. A., and Porrino, L. J. (2008). Parallel studies of cocaine-related neural and cognitive impairment in humans and monkeys. *Phil. Trans. R. Soc. Lond. B. Biol. Sci.*, 363, 3257–3266.

Bhasin, S., Storer, T. W., Berman, N., Callegari, C., Clevenger, B. A., Phillips, J., et al. (1996). The effects of supraphysiological doses of testosterone on muscle size and strength in men. *New Engl. J. Med.*, 335, 1–7.

Bhasin, S., Woodhouse, L., Casaburi, R., Singh, A. B., Bhasin, D., Berman, N., et al. (2001). Testosterone dose-response relationships in healthy young men. *Am. J. Physiol. Endocrinol. Metab.*, 281, E1172–E1181.

Biezonski, D. K. and Meyer, J. S. (2011). The nature of 3,4-methylenedioxymethamphetamine (MDMA)-induced serotonergic dysfunction: Evidence for and against the neurodegeneration hypothesis. *Curr. Neuropharmacol.*, 9, 84–90.

Binienda, Z. K., Beaudoin, M. A., Thorn, B. T., and Ali, S. F. (2011). Analysis of electrical brain waves in neurotoxicology: Gamma-hydroxybutyrate. *Curr. Neuropharmacol.*, 9, 236–239.

Bischof, G., Rumpf, H.-J., Hapke, U., Meyer, C., and John, U. (2001). Factors influencing remission from alcohol dependence without formal help in a representative population sample. *Addiction*, 96, 1327–1336.

Bjorling-Poulsen, M., Andersen, H. R., and Grandjean, P. (2008). Potential developmental neurotoxicity of pesticides used in Europe. *Environ. Health*, 7, 50. 22 pages.

Blier, P. and de Montigny, C. (1999). Serotonin and drug-induced therapeutic responses in major depression, obsessive-compulsive and panic disorders. *Neuropsychopharmacology*, 21, 91S–98S.

Blier, P., de Montigny, C., and Chaput, Y. (1990). A role for the serotonin system in the mechanism of action of antidepressant treatments: Preclinical evidence. *J. Clin. Psychiatry*, 51 (Suppl. 4), 4–20.

Blokhina, E. A., Dravolina, O. A., Bespalov, A. Y., Balster, R. L., and Zvartau, E. E. (2004). Intravenous self-administration of abused solvents and anesthetics in mice. *Eur. J. Pharmacol.*, 485, 211–218.

Bloomquist, J. R. (2009). *Insecticides: Chemistries and Characteristics*. IPM World Textbook. Available online at: http://ipmworld.umn.edu/chapters/bloomq.htm, last modified 12/3/09.

Blume, S. (1991). Sexuality and stigma. *Alcohol Health Res. World*, 15, 139–145.

Bock, N., Gerlach, M., and Rothenberger, A. (2010). Postnatal brain development and psychotropic drugs: Effects on animals and animal models of depression and attention-deficit/hyperactivity disorder. *Curr. Pharm. Des.*, 16, 2474–2483.

Bodwell, J. E., Gosse, J. A., Nomikos, A. P., and Hamilton, J. W. (2006). Arsenic disruption of steroid receptor gene activation: Complex dose-response effects are shared by several steroid receptors. *Chem. Res. Toxicol.*, 19, 1619–1629.

Bodwell, J. E., Kingsley, L. A., and Hamilton, J. W. (2004). Arsenic at very low concentrations alters glucocorticoid receptor (GR)-mediated gene activation but not GR-mediated gene repression: Complex dose-response effects are closely correlated with levels of activated GR and require a functional GR DNA binding domain. *Chem. Res. Toxicol.*, 17, 1064–1076.

Bogle, K. E. and Smith, B. H. (2009). Illicit methylphenidate use: A review of prevalence, availability, pharmacology, and consequences. *Curr. Drug Abuse Rev.*, 2, 157–176.

Boileau, I., Dagher, A., Leyton, M., Gunn, R. N., Baker, G. B., Diksic, M., et al. (2006). Modeling sensitization to stimulants in humans. An [^{11}C]raclopride/positron emission tomography study in healthy men. *Arch. Gen. Psychiatry*, 63, 1386–1395.

Booij, L., Van der Does, A. J. W., and Riedel, W. J. (2003). Monoamine depletion in psychiatric and healthy populations: Review. *Mol. Psychiatry*, 8, 951–973.

Bora, E., Yucel, M., and Allen, N. B. (2009). Neurobiology of human affiliative behavior: Implications for psychiaric disorders. *Curr. Opin. Psychiatry*, 22, 320–325.

Boscolo-Berto, R., Viel, G., Montagnese, S., Raduazo, D. I., Ferrara, S. D., and Dauvilers, Y. (2012). Narcolepsy and effectiveness of gamma-hydroxybutyrate (GHB): A systematic review and meta-analysis of randomized controlled trials. *Sleep Med. Rev.*, 16, 431–443.

Bossert, J. M., Ghitza, U. E., Lu, L., Epstein, D. H., and Shaham, Y. (2005). Neurobiology of relapse to heroin and cocaine seeking: An update and clinical implications. *Eur. J. Pharmacol.*, 526, 36–50.

Bouchard, M. F., Bellinger, D. C., Wright, R. O., and Weisskopf, M. G. (2010). Attention-deficit/hyperactivity disorder and urinary metabolites of organophosphate pesticides. *Pediatrics* 125, e1270–e1277.

Boucher, O., Muckle, G., and Bastien, C. H. (2009). Prenatal exposure to polychlorinated biphenyls: A neuropsychologic analysis. *Environ. Health Perspect.*, 117, 7–16.

Bowen, S. E. (2011). Two serious and challenging medical complications associated with volatile substance misuse: Sudden sniffing death and fetal solvent syndrome. *Subst. Use Misuse*, 46, 68–72.

Bowen, S. E., Batis, J. C., Paez-Masrtinez, N., and Cruz, S. L. (2006). The last decade of solvent research in animal models of abuse: Mechanistic and behavioral studies. *Neurotoxicol. Teratol.*, 28, 636–647.

Braak, H. and Braak, E. (1995). Staging of Alzheimer's disease-related neurofibrillary changes. *Neurobiol. Aging*, 16, 271–278.

Braak, H., Del Tredici, K., Rub, U., de Vos, R. A. I., Jansen Steur, E. N. H., and Braak, E. (2003). Staging of brain pathology related to sporadic Parkinson's disease. *Neurobiol. Aging*, 24, 197–211.

Bradley, C. (1937) The behavior of children receiving benzedrine. *Am. J. Psychiatry*, 94, 577–585.

Brady, K. T. and Sonne, S. C. (1999). The role of stress in alcohol use, alcoholism treatment, and relapse. *Alcohol Res. Health*, 23, 263–271.

Braestrup, C. and Squires, R. F. (1977). Specific benzodiazepine receptors in rat brain characterized by high-affinity [^{3}H]diazepam binding. *Proc. Natl. Acad. Sci. U.S.A.*, 74, 3805–3809.

Bramwell, B. (1882). *The diseases of the spinal cord*. New York, New York: William Wood and Company.

Brandt, S. D., Freeman, S., Sumnall, H. R., Measham, F., and Cole, J. (2011). Analysis of NRG "legal highs" in the UK: Identification and formation of novel cathinones. *Drug Test. Anal.*, 3, 569–575.

Brauer, L. H. and de Wit, H. (1995). Role of dopamine in *d*-amphetamine-induced euphoria in normal, healthy volunteers. *Exp. Clin. Psychopharmacol.*, 3, 371–381.

Brauer, L. H. and de Wit, H. (1997). High dose pimozide does not block amphetamine-induced euphoria in normal volunteers. *Pharmacol. Biochem. Behav.*, 56, 265–272.

Braun, J. M., Kahn, R. S., Froehlich, T., Auinger, P., and Lanphear, B. P. (2006). Exposures to environmental toxicants and attention deficit hyperactivity disorder in U.S. children. *Environ. Health Perspect.*, 114, 1904–1909.

Braun, J. M., Yolton, K., Dietrich, K. N., Hornung, R., Ye, X., Calafat, A. M., et al. (2009). Prenatal bisphenol A exposure and early childhood behavior. *Environ. Health Perspect.*, 117, 1945–1952.

Breckenridge, C. B., Holden, L., Sturgess, N., Weiner, M., Sheets, L., Sargent, D., et al. (2009). Evidence for a separate mechanism of toxicity for the Type I and the Type II pyrethroid insecticides. *Neurotoxicology*, 30 Suppl. 1, S17–S31.

Breedlove, S. M., Watson, N. V., and Rosenzweig, M. R. (2010). *Biological Psychology* (6th ed.). Sunderland, MA: Sinauer.

Breivogel, C. S., Childers, S. R., Deadwyler, S. A., Hampson, R. E., Vogt, L. J., and Sim-Selley, L. J. (1999). Chronic Δ^9-tetrahydrocannabinol treatment produces a time-dependent loss of cannabinoid receptors and cannabinoid receptor-activated G proteins in rat brain. *J. Neurochem.*, 73, 2447–2459.

Brondum, J. (2011). ADHD, lead, and PCBs: Appropriate comparison studies. Letter to the Editor. *Environ. Health Perspect.*, 119, A282.

Bronstein, A. C., Spyker, D. A., Cantilena, L. R., Green, J. L., Rumack, B. H., and Dart, R. C. (2011). 2010 Annual Report of the American Association of Poison Control

Centers' National Poison Data System (NPDS): 28th Annual Report. *Clin. Toxicol.*, 49, 910–941.

Brook, J. S., Stimmel, M. A., Zhang, C., and Brook, D. W. (2008). The association between earlier marijuana use and subsequent academic achievement and health problems: A longitudinal study. *Am. J. Addict.*, 17, 155–160.

Brook, J. S., Zhang, C., and Brook, D. W. (2011). Developmental trajectories of marijuana use from adolescence to adulthood: Personal predictors. *Arch. Pediatr. Adolesc. Med.*, 165, 55–60.

Brooks, J. S., Kessler, R. C., and Cohen, P. (1999). The onset of marijuana use from preadolescence and early adolescence to young adulthood. *Dev. Psychopathol.*, 11, 901–914.

Brower, K. J. (2009). Anabolic steroid abuse and dependence in clinical practice. *Phys. Sportsmed.*, 37, 131–140.

Brower, K. J., Blow, F. C., Young, J. P., and Hill, E. M. (1991). Symptoms and correlates of anabolic-androgenic steroid dependence. *Br. J. Addict.*, 86, 759–768.

Brower, K. J., Eliopulos, G. A., Blow, F. C., Catlin, D. H., and Beresford, T. P. (1990). Evidence for physical and psychological dependence on anabolic androgenic steroids in eight weight lifters. *Am. J. Psychiatry*, 147, 510–512.

Brown, W. A. (1998). The placebo effect. *Sci. Am.*, 278, 90–95.

Browndyke, J. N., Tucker, K. A., Woods, S. P., Beauvals, J., Cohen, R. A., Gottschalk, P. C., et al. (2004). Examining the effect of cerebral perfusion abnormality magnitude on cognitive performance in recently abstinent chronic cocaine abusers. *J. Neuroimaging*, 14, 162–169.

Browne, T. R. and Holme, G. L. (2008). *Handbook of Epilepsy* (3rd ed.). Philadelphia: Wolters Kluwer.

Brubaker, C. J., Schmithorst, V. J., Haynes, E. N., Dietrich, K. N., Egelhoff, J. C., Lindquist, D. et al. (2009). Altered myelination and axonal integrity in adults with childhood lead exposure: A diffusion tensor imaging study. *Neurotoxicology*, 30, 867–875.

Bruhn, J. G., De Smet, P. A. G. M., El-Seedi, H. R., and Beck, O. (2002). Mescaline use for 5700 years. *Lancet*, 359, 1866.

Bruijnzeel, A. W., Ford, J., Rogers, J. A., Scheick, S., Ji, Y., Bishnoi, M., et al. (2012). Blockade of CRF1 receptors in the central nucleus of the amygdala attenuates the dysphoria associated with nicotine withdrawal in rats. *Pharmacol. Biochem. Behav.*, 101, 62–68.

Brunzell, D. H. (2012). Preclinical evidence that activation of mesolimbic alpha 6 subunit containing nicotinic acetylcholine receptors supports nicotine addiction phenotype. *Nic. Tob. Res.*, 14, 1258–1269.

Brüstle, O., Jones, K. N., Learish, R. D., Karram, K., Choudhary, K., Wiestler, O. D., et al. (1999). Embryonic stem cell-derived glial precursors: A source of myelinating transplants. *Science*, 285, 754–756.

Buchanan, R. W., Freedman, R., Javitt, D. C., Abi-Dargham, A., and Lieberman, J. A. (2007). Recent advances in the development of novel pharmacological agents for the treatment of cognitive impairments in schizophrenia. *Schizophr. Bull.*, 33, 1120–1130.

Buchsbaum, M. S. (1990). The frontal lobes, basal ganglia, and temporal lobes as sites for schizophrenia. *Schizophr. Bull.*, 16, 379–390.

Buckholtz, N. S., Zhou, D., Freedman, D. X., and Potter, W. Z. (1990). Lysergic acid diethylamide (LSD) administration selectively downregulates serotonin$_2$ receptors in rat brain. *Neuropsychopharmacology*, 3, 137–148.

Buckley, N. E. (2008). The peripheral cannabinoid receptor knockout mice: An update. *Br. J. Pharmacol.*, 153, 309–318.

Budney, A. J., Moore, B. A., Vandrey, R. G., and Hughes, J. R. (2003). The time course and significance of cannabis withdrawal. *J. Abnorm. Psychol.*, 112, 393–402.

Budney, A. J., Roffman, R., Stephens, R. S., and Walker, D. (2007). Marijuana dependence and its treatment. *Addict. Sci. Clin. Pract.*, 4, 4–16.

Burglass, M. E. and Shaffer, H. (1984). Diagnosis in the addictions I: Conceptual problems. *Adv. Alcohol Subst. Abuse*, 3, 19–34.

Burke, L. M. (2008). Caffeine and sports performance. *Appl. Physiol. Nutr. Metab.*, 33, 1319–1334.

Burns, E. (2007). *The Smoke of the Gods. A Social History of Tobacco*. Philadelphia, PA: Temple University Press.

Bushnik, T., Haines, D., Levallois, P., Levesque, J., Van Oostdam, J., and Viau, C. (2010). Lead and bisphenol A concentrations in the Canadian population. *Health Reports*, 21, 7–18.

Byck, R. (Ed.) (1974). *The Cocaine Papers by Sigmund Freud*. New York: Stonehill.

Cabral, G. A. and Pettit, D. A. D. (1998). Drugs and immunity: Cannabinoids and their role in decreased resistance to infectious disease. *J. Neuroimmunol.*, 83, 116–123.

Cabýoglu, M. T., Ergene, N., and Tan, U. (2006). The mechanism of acupuncture and clinical applications. *Int. J. Neurosci.*, 116, 115–125.

Cadet, J. L. and Krasnova, I. N. (2009). Molecular bases of methamphetamine-induced neurodegeneration. *Int. Rev. Neurobiol.*, 88, 101–119.

Caine, S. B., Negus, S. S., Mello, N. K., Patel, S., Bristow, L., Kulagowski, J., et al. (2002). Role of dopamine D$_2$-like receptors in cocaine self-administration: Studies with D$_2$ receptor mutant mice and novel D$_2$ receptor antagonists. *J. Neurosci.*, 22, 2977–2988.

Caine, S. B., Thomsen, M., Gabriel, K. I., Berkowitz, J. S., Gold, L. H., Koob, G. F., et al. (2007). Lack of self-administration of cocaine in dopamine D$_1$ receptor knockout mice. *J. Neurosci.*, 27, 13140–13150.

Calabrese, J. R., Bowden, C., and Woyshville, M. J. (1995). Lithium and the anticonvul-

sants in the treatment of bipolar disorder. In F. E. Bloom and D. J. Kupfer (Eds.), *Psychopharmacology: The Fourth Generation of Progress*, pp. 1099–1111. New York: Raven Press.

Calafat, A. M., Ye, X., Wong, L-Y., Reidy, J. A., and Needham, L. L. (2008). Exposure of the U.S. population to bisphenol A and 4-tertiary-octylphenol: 2003–2004. *Environ. Health Perspect.*, 116, 39–44.

Caldecott-Hazard, S., Morgan, D. G., DeLeon-Jones, F., Overstreet, D. H., and Hanowsky, D. (1991). Clinical and biochemical aspects of depressive disorders: II. Transmitter/receptor theories. *Synapse*, 9, 251–301.

Calderon, J., Navarro, M. E., Jimenez-Capdeville, M. E., Santos-Diaz, M. A., Golden, A., Rodriguez-Leyva, I., et al. (2001). Exposure to arsenic and lead and neuropsychological development in Mexican children. *Environ. Res.*, 85, 69–76.

Calignano, A., La Rana, G., Giuffrida, A., and Piomelli, D. (1998). Control of pain initiation by endogenous cannabinoids. *Nature*, 394, 277–281.

Camarini, R., Pautassi, R. M., Méndez, M., Quadros, I. M., Souza-Formigoni, M. L., and Boerngen-Lacerda, R. (2010). Behavioral and neurochemical studies in distinct animal models of ethanol's motivational effects. *Curr. Drug Abuse Rev.*, 3, 205–221.

Campbell, U. C., Rodefer, J. S., and Carroll, M. E. (1999). Effects of dopamine receptor antagonists (D$_1$ and D$_2$) on the demand for smoked cocaine base in rhesus monkeys. *Psychopharmacology*, 144, 381–388.

Campbell, W. G. and Hodgins, D. C. (1993). Alcohol-related blackouts in a medical practice. *Am. J. Drug Alcohol Abuse*, 19, 369–376.

Canadas, F., Cardona, D., Davila, E., and Sanchez-Santed, F. (2005). Long-term neurotoxicity of chlorpyrifos: Spatial learning impairment on repeated acquisition in a water maze. *Tox. Sci.*, 85, 944–951.

Canal, C. E. and Morgan, D. (2012). Head-twitch response in rodents induced by the hallucinogen 2,5-dimethoxy-4-iodo-amphetamine: A comprehensive history, a re-evaluation of mechanisms, and its utility as a model. *Drug Test. Analysis*, 4, 556–576.

Canfield, R. L., Henderson, C. R., Cory-Slechta, D. A., Cox, C., Jusko, T. A., and Lanphear, B. P. (2003). Intellectual impairment in children with blood lead concentrations below 10 µg/dL. *N. Engl. J. Med.*, 348, 1517–1526.

Cannon, M. E., Cooke, C. T., and McCarthy, J. S. (2001). Caffeine-induced cardiac arrhythmia: An unrecognised danger of healthfood products. *Med. J. Aust.*, 174, 520–521.

Cantin, L., Lenoir, M., Augier, E., Vanhille, N., Dubreucq, S., Serre, F., et al. (2010). Cocaine is low on the value ladder of rats: Possible evidence for resilience to addiction. *PLoS ONE* 5(7): e11592. doi:10.1371/journal.pone.0011592

Canton, R. F., Sanderson, J. T., Nijmeijer, S., Bergman, A., Letcher, R. J., and van den Berg, M. (2006). In vitro effects of brominated flame retardants and metabolites on CYP17 catalytic activity: A novel mechanism of action? *Toxicol. Appl. Pharmacol.*, 216, 274–281.

Cao, Y., Chen, A., Jones, R. L., Radcliffe, J., Caldwell, K. L., Dietrich, K. N., et al. (2010). Does background postnatal methyl mercury exposure in toddlers affect cognition and behavior? *Neurotoxicology*, 31, 1–9.

Caputo, F., Vignoli, T., Maremmani, I., Bernardi, M., and Zoli, G. (2009). Gamma hydroxybutyric acid (GHB) for the treatment of alcohol dependence: A review. *Int. J. Environ. Res. Public Health*, 6, 1917–1929.

Cárdenas, L., Houle, S., Kapur, S., and Busto, U. E. (2004). Oral D-amphetamine causes prolonged displacement of [^{11}C]raclopride as measured by PET. *Synapse*, 51, 27–31.

Carlezon, W. A., Jr. and Wise, R. A. (1996). Rewarding actions of phencyclidine and related drugs in nucleus accumbens shell and frontal cortex. *J. Neurosci.*, 16, 3112–3122.

Carlezon, W. A. Jr., Devine, D. P., and Wise, R. A. (1995). Habit-forming actions of nomifensine in nucleus accumbens. *Psychopharmacology*, 122, 194–197.

Carlsson, A. (2001). A paradigm shift in brain research. *Science*, 294, 1021–1024.

Carlsson, A., Lindqvist, M., and Magnusson, T. (1957). 3,4-Dihydrozypheylalanine and 5-hydroxytryptophan as reserpine antagonists. *Nature*, 180, 1200.

Carlton, P. L. (1983). *A Primer of Behavioral Pharmacology*. New York: Freeman.

Carpenter, C. M., Wayne, G. F., and Connolly, G. N. (2007). The role of sensory perception in the development and targeting of tobacco products. *Addiction*, 102, 136–147.

Carrillo, M., Ricci, L. A., Coppersmith, G. A., and Melloni, R. H. Jr. (2009). The effect of increased serotonergic neurotransmission on aggression: A critical meta-analytical review of preclinical studies. *Psychopharmacology*, 205, 349–368.

Carroll, C. R. (1996). *Drugs in Modern Society* (4th ed.). Guilford, CT: Brown and Benchmark.

Carroll, M. E. and Anker, J. J. (2010). Sex differences and ovarian hormones in animal models of drug dependence. *Horm. Behav.*, 58, 44–56.

Carroll, M. E., Krattiger, K. L., Gieske, D., and Sadoff, D. A. (1990). Cocaine-base smoking in rhesus monkeys: Reinforcing and physiological effects. *Psychopharmacology*, 102, 443–450.

Carter, L. P., Koek, W., and France, C. P. (2009a). Behavioral analyses of GHB: Receptor mechanisms. *Pharmacol. Ther.*, 121, 100–114.

Carter, L. P., Pardi, D., Gorsline, J., and Griffiths, R. R. (2009b). Illicit gamma-hydroxybutyrate (GHB) and pharmaceutical sodium oxybate (Xyrem): Differences in characteristics and misuse. *Drug Alcohol Depend.*, 104, 1–10.

Carter, L. P., Richards, B. D., Mintzer, M. Z., and Griffiths, R. R. (2006). Relative abuse liability of GHB in humans: A comparison of psychomotor, subjective, and cognitive effects of supratherapeutic doses of triazolam, pentobarbital, and GHB. *Neuropsychopharmacology*, 31, 2537–2551.

Carter, R. J., Lione, L. A., Humby, T., Mangiarini, L., Mahal, A., Bates, G. P., et al. (1999). Characterization of progressive motor deficits in mice transgenic for the human Huntington's disease mutation. *J. Neurosci.*, 19, 3248–3257.

Carvey, P. M. (1998). *Drug Action in the Central Nervous System*. New York: Oxford University Press.

Casadeus, G. (Ed.). (2011). *Handbook of Animal Models in Alzheimer's Disease*. Amsterdam, Netherlands: IOS Press.

Castañé, A., Berrendero, F., and Maldonado, R. (2005). The role of the cannabinoid system in nicotine addiction. *Pharmacol. Biochem. Behav.*, 81, 381–386.

Castelli, M. P. (2008). Multi-faceted aspects of gamma-hydroxybutyric acid: A neurotransmitter, therapeutic agent and drug of abuse. *Mini Rev. Med. Chem.*, 8, 1188–1202.

Castelli, M. P., Pibiri, F., Carboni, G., and Piras, A. P. (2004). A review of pharmacology of NCS-382, a putative antagonist of γ-hydroxybutyric acid (GHB) receptor. *CNS Drug Rev.*, 10, 243–260.

Centers for Disease Control and Prevention (CDC). (1999). Thimerosal in vaccines: A joint statement of the American Academy of Pediatrics and the Public Health Service. *Morb. Mortal Wkly. Rep.*, 48, 563–565.

Centers for Disease Control and Prevention (CDC). (2009). *Fourth National Report on Human Exposure to Environmental Chemicals*, p. 519. Atlanta, GA: U.S. Department of Health and Human Services.

Centers for Disease Control and Prevention (CDC). (2012a). *Fourth National Report on Human Exposure to Environmental Chemicals*. Updated tables, p. 307. Atlanta, GA: U.S. Department of Health and Human Services.

Centers for Disease Control and Prevention (CDC). (2012b). CDC Response to Advisory Committee on Childhood Lead Poisoning Prevention Recommendations in "Low Level Lead Exposure Harms Children: A Renewed Call of Primary Prevention," revised June 7, 2012. Available online at: http://www.cdc.gov/nceh/lead/ACCLPP/CDC_Response_Lead_Exposure_Recs.pdf, accessed 10/15/12.

Center for Substance Abuse Research, University of Maryland, College Park. (2011). Number of U.S. emergency department visits related to the nonmedical use of buprenorphine more than triples since 2006. *CESAR Fax*, 20, Issue 25.

Ceylan-Isik, A. F., McBride, S. M., and Ren, J. (2010). Sex difference in alcoholism: Who is at a greater risk for development of alcoholic complications? *Life Sci.*, 87, 133–138.

Chait, L. D. and Burke, K. A. (1994). Preference for high- versus low-potency marijuana. *Pharmacol. Biochem. Behav.*, 49, 643–647.

Chait, L. D. and Zacny, J. P. (1992). Reinforcing and subjective effects of oral Δ^9-THC and smoked marijuana in humans. *Psychopharmacology*, 107, 255–262.

Chanda, P. K., Gao, Y., Mark, L., Btesh, J., Strassle, B. W., Lu, P., et al. (2010). Monoacylglycerol lipase activity is a critical modulator of the tone and integrity of the endocannabinoid system. *Mol. Pharmacol.*, 78, 996–1003.

Changeux, J.-P. (2010). Nicotine addiction and nicotinic receptors: Lessons from genetically modified mice. *Nat. Rev. Neurosci.*, 11, 389–401.

Chao, H. R., Wang, S. L., Lee, W. J., Wang, Y. F., and Papke, O. (2007). Levels of polybrominated diphenyl ethers (PBDEs) in breast milk from central Taiwan and their relation to infant birth outcome and maternal menstruation effects. *Environ. Int.* 33, 239–245.

Chapin, R. E., Adams, J., Boekelheide, K., Gray, Jr., L. E., Hayward, S. W., Lees, P. S. J., et al. (2008). NTP-CERHR expert panel report on the reproductive and developmental toxicity of bisphenol A. *Birth Defects Res. B Dev. Reprod. Toxicol.*, 83, 157–395.

Charité Campus Virchow-Klinikum Neurological Clinic. (2009.) Available online at: http://www.english.als-charite.de/VM/ALS/Therapy/Neuroprotectivetherapy/tabid/1244/Default.aspx, accessed 12/12/12.

Charney, D. S., Grillon, C. C. G., and Bremner, J. D. (1998). The neurobiological basis of anxiety and fear: Circuits, mechanisms, and neurochemical interactions (part II). *Neuroscientist*, 4, 122–132.

Charney, D. S., Krystal, J. H., Delgado, P. L., and Heninger, G. R. (1990). Serotonin-specific drugs for anxiety and depressive disorders. *Ann. Rev. Med.*, 41, 437–446.

Chausmer, A. L., Elmer, G. I., Rubinstein, M., Low, M. J., Grandy, D. K., and Katz, J. I. (2002). Cocaine-induced locomotor activity and cocaine discrimination in dopamine D$_2$ receptor mutant mice. *Psychopharmacology*, 163, 54–61.

Chen, A., Dietrich, K. N., Huo, X., and Ho, S-M. (2011). Developmental neurotoxicants in E-waste: An emerging health concern. *Environ. Health Perspect.* 119, 431–438.

Chen, J.-F., Yu, L., Shen, H.-Y., He, J.-C., Wang, X., and Zheng, R. (2010). What knock-out animals tell us about the effects of caffeine. *J. Alzheimers Dis.*, 20, S17–S24.

Chen, K. and Kandel, D. B. (1995). The natural history of drug use from adolescence to the mid-thirties in a general population sample. *Am. J. Public Health*, 85, 41–47.

Cherblanc, F., Chapman-Rothe, N., Brown, R., and Fuchter, M. J. (2012). Current limitations and future opportunities for epigenetic therapies. *Future Med. Chem.*, 4, 425–446.

Chevaleyre, V., Takahashi, K. A., and Castillo, P. E. (2006). Endocannabinoid-mediated synaptic plasticity in the CNS. *Annu. Rev. Neurosci.*, 29, 37–76.

Chevrier, J., Harley, K. G., Bradman, A., Gharbi, M., Sjodin, A., and Eskenazi, B. (2010) Polybrominated Diphenyl Ether (PBDE) Flame Retardants and Thyroid Hormone during Pregnancy. *Environ. Health Perspect.*, 118, 1444–1449.

Chia, L-G. and Chu, F-L. (1985). A clinical and electrophysiological study of patients with polychlorinated biphenyl poisoning. *J. Neurol. Neurosurg. Psych.*, 48, 894–901.

Childers, S. R. and Breivogel, C. S. (1998). Cannabis and endogenous cannabinoid systems. *Drug Alcohol Depend.*, 51, 173–187.

Childress, A. R., McLellan, T., and O'Brien, C. P. (1986). Abstinent opiate abusers exhibit conditioned craving, conditioned withdrawal and reductions in both through extinction. *Br. J. Addict.*, 81, 655–660.

Childress, A. R., Mozley, P. D., McElgin, W., Fitzgerald, J., Reivich, M., and O'Brien, C. P. (1999). Limbic activation during cue-induced cocaine craving. *Am. J. Psychiatry*, 156, 11–18.

Christensen, K., Harper, B., Luukinen, B., Buhl, K., and Stone, D. (2009). *Chlorpyrifos Technical Fact Sheet*. National Pesticide Information Center, Oregon State University Extension Services. Available online at: http://npic.orst.edu/factsheets/chlorptech.pdf.

Chubb, J. E., Bradshaw, N. J., Soares, D. C., Porteous, D. J., and Millar, J. K. (2008). The DISC locus in psychiatric illness. *Mol. Psychiatry*, 13, 36–64.

Clarke, T. K. and Schumann, G. (2009). Gene-environment interactions resulting in risky alcohol drinking behaviour are mediated by CRF and CRF$_1$. *Pharmacol. Biochem. Behav.*, 93, 230–236.

Clegg, D. J., and van Gemert, M. (1999). Determination of the reference dose for chlorpyrifos: Proceedings of an expert panel. *J. Toxicol. Environ. Health B Crit. Rev.*, 2, 211–255.

Cloninger, C. R. (1987). Neurogenetic adaptive mechanisms in alcoholism. *Science*, 236, 410–416.

Cluny, N. L., Vemuri, V. K., Chambers, A. P., Limebeer, C. L., Bedard, H., Wood, J. T., et al. (2010). A novel peripherally restricted cannabinoid receptor antagonist, AM6545, reduces food intake and body weight, but does not cause malaise, in rodents. *Br. J. Pharmacol.*, 161, 629–642.

Cohen, I., Navarro, V., Clemenceau, S., Baulac, M., and Miles, R. (2002). On the origin of interictal activity in human temporal lobe epilepsy in vitro. *Science*, 298, 1418–1421.

Cohen, J. Y., Haesler, S., Vong, L., Lowell, B. B., and Uchida, N. (2012). Neuron-type-specific signals for reward and punishment in the ventral tegmental area. *Nature*, 482, 85–88.

Cohen, P. J. (2009a). Medical marijuana: The conflict between scientific evidence and political ideology. Part one of two. *J. Pain Palliat. Care Pharmacother.*, 23, 4–25.

Cohen, P. J. (2009b). Medical marijuana: The conflict between scientific evidence and political ideology. Part two of two. *J. Pain Palliat. Care Pharmacother.*, 23, 120–140.

Cohen, S. P., Liao, W., Gupta, A., and Plunkett, A. (2011). Ketamine in pain management. In M. R. Clark and G. J. Treisman (Eds.), *Chronic Pain and Addiction. Advances in Psychosomatic Medicine*, Vol. 30, pp. 139–161. Basel, Switzerland: Karger.

Colby, S. M., Tiffany, S. T., Shiffman, S., and Niaura, R. S. (2000). Are adolescent smokers dependent on nicotine? A review of the evidence. *Drug Alc. Depend.*, 59 (Suppl. 1), S83–S95.

Collins, E. D., Vosburg, S. K., Hart, C. L., Haney, M., and Foltin, R. W. (2003). Amantadine does not modulate reinforcing, subjective, or cardiovascular effects of cocaine in humans. *Pharmacol. Biochem. Behav.*, 76, 401–407.

Colombo, G., Serra, S., Vacca, G., Carai, M. A. M., and Gessa, G. L. (2005). Endocannabinoid system and alcohol addiction: Pharmacological studies. *Pharmacol. Biochem. Behav.*, 81, 369–380.

Comer, S. D., Ashworth, J. B., Foltin, R. W., Johanson, C. E., Zacny, J. P., and Walsh, S. L. (2008). The role of human drug self-administration procedures in the development of medications. *Drug Alcohol Depend.*, 96, 1–15.

Committee on Nutrition and the Council on Sports Medicine and Fitness. (2011). Sports drinks and energy drinks for children and adolescents: Are they appropriate? *Pediatrics*, 127, 1182–1189.

Concha, G., Vogler, G., Lezcano, D., Nermell, B., and Vahter, M. (1998). Exposure to inorganic arsenic metabolites during early human development. *Toxicol. Sci.* 44, 185–190.

Conti, A. A. (2010). Doping in sports in ancient and recent times. *Med. Secoli*, 22, 181–190.

Cooper, A. (2011). College students take ADHD drugs for better grades. Available online at: http://www.cnn.com/2011/09/01/health/drugs-adderall-concentration/index.html?iref=allsearch, accessed 10/27/12.

Cooper, Z. D. and Haney, M. (2008). Cannabis reinforcement and dependence: Role of the cannabinoid CB1 receptor. *Addict. Biol.*, 13, 188–195.

Cooper, Z. D. and Haney, M. (2009). Actions of delta-9-tetrahydrocannabinol in cannabis: Relation to use, abuse, dependence. *Int. Rev. Psychiatry*, 21, 104–112.

Copeland, J. and Swift, W. (2009). Cannabis use disorder: Epidemiology and management. *Int. Rev. Psychiatry*, 21, 96–103.

Corrigall, W. A., Franklin, K. B., Coen, K. M., and Clarke, P. B. (1992). The mesolimbic dopaminergic system is implicated in the reinforcing effects of nicotine. *Psychopharmacology*, 107, 285–289.

Costa, E. and Guidotti, A. (1996). Benzodiazepines on trial: A research strategy for their rehabilitation. *Trends Pharmacol. Sci.*, 17, 192–2000.

Costa, L. G. and Giordano, G. (2007). Developmental neurotoxicity of polybrominated diphenyl ether (PBDE) flame retardants. *Neurotoxicity* 28, 1047–1067.

Costall, B. and Naylor, R. J. (1991). Anxiolytic effects of 5-H$_3$ antagonists in animals. In R. J. Rodgers and S. J. Cooper (Eds.), *5-HT$_{1A}$ Agonists, 5-HT$_3$ Antagonists and Benzodiazepines: Their Comparative Behavioral Pharmacology*, pp. 133–157. New York: Wiley.

Crabbe, J. C., Phillips, T. J., and Belknap, J. K. (2010). The complexity of alcohol drinking: Studies in rodent genetic models. *Behav. Genet.*, 40, 737–750.

Crawley, J. N. (1996). Unusual behavioral phenotypes of inbred mouse strains. *Trends Neurosci.*, 19, 181–182.

Crean, R. D., Crane, N. A., and Mason, B. J. (2011). An evidence-based review of acute and long-term effects of cannabis use on executive cognitive functions. *J. Addict. Med.*, 5, 1–8.

Crews, D., Gore, A. C., Hsu, T. S., Dangleben, N. L., Spinetta, M., Schallert, T., et al. (2007). Transgenerational epigenetic imprints on mate preference. *Proc. Natl. Acad. Sci. U.S.A.* 104, 5942–5946.

Cribbs, D. H., Ghochikyan, A., Vasilevko, V., Tran, M., Petrushina, I., Sadzikava, N., et al. (2003). Adjuvant-dependent modulation of Th1 and Th2 responses to immunization with beta-amyloid. *Int. Immunol.*, 15, 505–514.

Crombag, H. S., Bossert, J. M., Koya, E., and Shaham, Y. (2008). Review. Context-induced relapse to drug seeking: A review. *Phil. Trans.R. Soc. Lond. B. Biol. Sci.*, 363, 3233–3243.

Crow, T. J. (1980). Molecular pathology of schizophrenia: More than one disease process? *Br. Med. J.*, 280, 66–68.

Crow, T. J. (2008). The emperors of the schizophrenia polygene have no clothes. *Psychol. Med.*, 38, 1681–1685.

Cruickshank, C. C. and Dyer, K. R. (2009). A review of the clinical pharmacology of methamphetamine. *Addiction*, 104, 1085–1099.

Crunelli, V., Emri, Z., and Leresche, N. (2006). Unraveling the brain targets of γ-hydroxybutyric acid. *Curr. Opin. Pharmacol.*, 6, 44–52.

Cruz, S. L. and Domínguez, M. (2011). Misusing volatile substances for their hallucinatory effects: A qualitative pilot study with Mexican teenagers and a pharmacological discussion of their hallucinations. *Subst. Use Misuse*, 46, 84–94.

Cryan, J. F. and Sweeney, F. F. (2011). The age of anxiety: Role of animal models of anxiolytic action in drug discovery. *Br. J. Pharmacol.*, 164, 1129–1161.

Cui, C. L., Wu, L. Z., and Luo, F. (2008). Acupuncture for the treatment of drug addiction. *Neurochem. Res.*, 33, 2013–2022.

Cummings, J. L. (2004). Alzheimer's disease. *N. Engl. J. Med.*, 351, 56–67.

Cunningham, C. W., Rothman, R. B., and Prisinzano, T. E. (2011). Neuropharmacology of the naturally occurring κ-opioid hallucinogen salvinorin A. *Pharmacol. Rev.*, 63, 316–347.

Curran, H. V., Brignell, C., Fletcher, S., Middleton, P., and Henry, J. (2002). Cognitive and subjective dose-response effects of acute oral Δ^9-tetrahydrocannabinol (THC) in infrequent cannabis users. *Psychopharmacology*, 164, 61–70.

D'Addario, D. (2010). High on study drugs. Available online at: http://www.thedailybeast.com/blogs-and-stories/2010-05-09/high-on-study-drugs/, accessed 11/20/10.

Dahchour, A. and DeWitte, P. (2000). Ethanol and amino acids in the central nervous system: Assessment of the pharmacological actions of acamprosate. *Prog. Neurobiol.*, 60, 343–362.

Dahlström, A. and Fuxe, K. (1964). Evidence for the existence of monoamine-containing neurons in the central nervous system. I. Demonstration of monoamines in the cell bodies of brainstem neurons. *Acta Physiol. Scand.*, 62 (Suppl. 232), 1–55.

Dalgarno, P. (2007). Subjective effects of *Salvia divinorum*. *J. Psychoactive Drugs*, 39, 143–149.

Dalgarno, P. J. and Shewan, D. (1996). Illicit use of ketamine in Scotland. *J. Psychoactive Drugs*, 28, 191–199.

Daly, J. W. (2007). Caffeine analogs: Biomedical impact. *Cell. Mol. Life Sci.*, 64, 2153–2169.

Daly, J. W. and Fredholm, B. B. (1998). Caffeine—An atypical drug of dependence. *Drug Alcohol Depend.*, 51, 199–206.

Damasio, H., Grabowski, T., Frank, R., Galaburga, A. M., and Damasio, A. R. (1994). The return of Phineas Gage: Clues about the brain from the skull of a famous patient. *Science*, 264, 1102–1105.

Dar, R. and Frenk, H. (2010). Can one puff really make an adolescent addicted to nicotine? A critical review of the literature. *Harm Reduct. J.*, 7, 28.

Dar, R., Rosen-Korakin, N., Shapira, O., Gottlieb, Y., and Frenk, H. (2010). The craving to smoke in flight attendants: Relations with smoking deprivation, anticipation of smoking, and actual smoking. *J. Abn. Psychol.*, 119, 248–253.

Darke, S., Kaye, S., McKetin, R., and Duflou, J. (2008). Major physical and psychological harms of methamphetamine use. *Drug Alcohol Rev.*, 27, 253–262.

Darnerud, P. O., Aune, M., Larsson, L., and Hallgren, S. (2007). Plasma PBDE and thyroxine levels in rats exposed to Bromkal or BDE-47. *Chemosph.*, 67, S386–S392.

Davey, J. C., Bodwell, J. E., Gosse, J. A., and Hamilton, J. W. (2007). Arsenic as an endocrine disruptor: Effects of arsenic on estrogen receptor-mediated gene expression in vivo and in cell culture. *Toxicol. Sci.* 98, 75–86.

Davidson, P. W., Leste, A., Benstrong, E., Burns, C. M., Valentin, J., Sloane-Reeves, J., et al. (2010). Fish consumption, mercury exposure, and their associations with scholastic achievement in the Seychelles Child Development Study. *Neurotoxicol.*, 31, 439–447.

Davidson, R. J., Jackson, D. C., and Kalin, N. H. (2000). Emotion, plasticity, context,and regulation: Perspectives from affective neuroscience. *Psychol. Bull.*, 126, 890–909.

Davie, C. A. (2008). A review of Parkinson's disease. *Br. Med. Bull.*, 86, 109–127.

Davis, K. L., Kahn, R. S., Ko, G., and Davidson, M. (1991). Dopamine in schizophrenia: A review and reconceptualization. *Am. J. Psychiatry*, 148, 1474–1486.

Davis, M. (1997). Neurobiology of fear responses: The role of the amygdala. *J. Neuropsychiatry Clin. Neurosci.*, 9, 382–402.

Davis, M. (2006). Neural systems involved in fear and anxiety measured with fear-potentiated startle. *Am. Psychol.*, 61, 741–756.

Davis, W. (1985). *The Serpent and the Rainbow*. New York: Warner Books.

de la Mora, M. P., Gallegos-Cari, A., Arizmendi-García, Y., Marcellino, D., and Fuxe, K. (2010). Role of dopamine receptor mechanisms in the amygdaloid modulation of fear and anxiety: Structural and functional analysis. *Prog. Neurobiol.*, 90, 198–216.

de Montigny, C. (1981). Enhancement of the 5-HT neurotransmission by antidepressant treatments. *J. Physiol.*, 77, 455–461.

de Souza, G. L. and Hallak, J. (2011). Anabolic steroids and male infertility: A comprehensive review. *BJU Int.*, 108, 1860–1865.

Deakin, J. F. W., Lees, J., McKie, S., Hallak, J. E. C., Williams, S. R., and Dursun, S. M. (2008). Glutamate and the neural basis of the subjective effects of ketamine. *Arch. Gen. Psychiatry*, 65, 154–164.

DeLisi, L. E., Hoff, A. L., Schwartz, J. E., Shields, G. W., Halthore, S. N., Gupta, S. M., et al. (1991). Brain morphology in first-episode schizophrenic-like psychotic patients: A quantitative magnetic resonance imaging study. *Biol. Psychiatry*, 29, 159–175.

DeMicco, A., Cooper, K. R., Richardson, J. R., and White, L. A. (2009). Developmental neurotoxicity of pyrethroid insecticides in Zebrafish embryos. *Toxicol. Sci.* 113, 177–186.

Deroche-Gamonet, V., Belin, D., and Piazza, P. V. (2004). Evidence for addiction-like behavior in the rat. *Science*, 305, 1014–1017.

Devane, W. A., Dysarz, F. A., III, Johnson, M. R., Melvin, L. S., and Howlett, A. C. (1988). Determination and characterization of a cannabinoid receptor in rat brain. *Mol. Pharmacol.*, 34, 605–613.

Devane, W. A., Hanus, L., Breuer, A., Pertwee, R. G., Stevenson, L. A., Griffin, G., et al. (1992). Isolation and structure of a brain constituent that binds to the cannabinoid receptor. *Science*, 258, 1946–1949.

Dews, P. B. (1982). Caffeine. *Ann. Rev. Nutr.*, 2, 323–341.

Diamanti-Kandarakis, E., Bourguignon, J-P., Giudice, L. C., Hauser, R., Prins, G. S., Soto, A. M., et al. (2009). Endocrine-disrupting chemicals: An endocrine society scientific statement. *Endocr. Rev.* 30, 293–342.

Diamond, I. and Gordon, A. (1997). Cellular and molecular neuroscience of alcoholism. *Physiol. Rev.*, 77, 1–20.

Diana, M., Pistis, M., Carboni, S., Gessa, G. L., and Rossetti, Z. L. (1993). Profound decrement of mesolimbic dopaminergic neuronal activity during ethanol withdrawal syndrome in rats: Electrophysiological

and biochemical evidence. *Proc. Natl. Acad. Sci. U.S.A.*, 90, 7966–7969.

DiChiara, G. (1997). Alcohol and dopamine. *Alcohol Health Res. World*, 21, 108–114.

DiChiara, G. and North, R. A. (1992). Neurobiology of opiate abuse. *Trends Pharmacol. Sci.*, 13, 185–193.

Didato, G. and Nobili, L. (2009). Treatment of narcolepsy. *Expert Rev. Neurother.*, 9, 897–910.

DiFranza, J. R. (2010). Thwarting science by protecting the received wisdom on tobacco addiction from the scientific method. *Harm Reduct. J.*, 7, 26.

DiFranza, J. R., Rigotti, N. A., McNeill, A. D., Ockene, J. K., Savageau, J. A., St. Cyr, D., et al. (2000). Initial symptoms of nicotine dependence in adolescents. *Tob. Control*, 9, 313–319.

DiFranza, J. R., Savageau, J. A., Fletcher, K., O'Loughlin, J., Pbwert, L, Ockene, J. K., et al. (2007). Symptoms of tobacco dependence after brief intermittent use: The development and assessment of nicotine dependence in Youth-2 study. *Arch. Pediatr. Adolesc. Med.*, 161, 704–710.

DiFranza, J. R., Savageau, J. A., Fletcher, K., Ockene, J. K., Rigotti, N. A., McNeill, A. D., et al. (2002a). Measuring the loss of autonomy over nicotine use in adolescents: The DANDY (Development and Assessment of Nicotine Dependence in Youths) study. *Arch. Pediatr. Adolesc. Med.*, 156, 397–403.

DiFranza, J. R., Savageau, J. A., Rigotti, N. A., Fletcher, K., Ockene, J. K., McNeill, A. D., et al. (2002b). Development of symptoms of tobacco dependence in youths: 30 month follow up data from the DANDY study. *Tob. Control*, 11, 228–235.

Dingwall, K. M. and Cairney, S. (2011). Recovery from central nervous system changes following volatile substance misuse. *Subst. Use Misuse*, 46, 73–83.

Dinwiddie, S. H. (1994). Abuse of inhalants: A review. *Addiction*, 89, 925–939.

DiPatrizio, N. V., Astarita, G., Schwartz, G., Li, X., and Piomelli, D. (2011). Endocannabinoid signal in the gut controls dietary fat intake. *Proc. Natl. Acad. Sci. U.S.A.*, 108, 12904–12908.

Dittrich, A. (1998). The standardized psychometric assessment of altered states of consciousness (ASCs) in humans. *Pharmacopsychiatry*, 31 (Suppl.), 80–84.

Djamsidian, A., Averbeck, B. B., Lees, A. J., O'Sullivan, S. S. (2011a). Clinical aspects of impulsive compulsive behaviors in Parkinson's disease. *J. Neurol. Sci.*, 310, 183–188.

Djamsidian, A., Cardoso, F., Grosset, D., Bowden-Jones, H., and Lees, A. J. (2011b). Pathological gambling in Parkinson's disease—A review of the literature. *Movement Disorders*, 26, 1976–1984.

Dluzen, D. E. and Liu, B. (2008). Gender differences in methamphetamine use and responses: A review. *Gender Med.*, 5, 24–35.

Dohan, O., De la Vieja, A., Paroder, V., Riedel, C., Artani, M., Reed, M., et al. (2003). The sodium/iodide Symporter (NIS): Characterization, regulation, and medical significance. *Endocr. Rev.*, 24, 48–77.

Dole, V. P. and Nyswander, M. E. (1965). A medical treatment for diacetylmorphine (heroin) addiction. *JAMA*, 193, 646–650.

Domino, E. F. and Luby, E. D. (2012). Phencyclidine/schizophrenia: One view toward the past, the other to the future. *Schizophr. Bull.*, 38, 914–919.

Doubeni, C. A., Reed, G., and DiFranza, J. R. (2010). Early course of nicotine dependence in adolescent smokers. *Pediatrics*, 125, 1127–1133.

Dragt, S., Nieman, D. H., Becker, H. E., van de Fliert, R., Dingemans, P. M., de Haan, L., et al. (2010). Age of onset of cannabis use is associated with age of onset of high-risk symptoms for psychosis. *Can. J. Psychiatry*, 55, 165–171.

Dragt, S., Nieman, D. H., Schultze-Lutter, F., van der Meer, F., Becker, H., de Haan, et al. (2012). Cannabis use and age at onset of symptoms in subjects at clinical high risk for psychosis. *Acta Psychiatr. Scand.*, 125, 45–53.

Drasbek, K. R., Christensen, J., and Jensen, J. (2006). Gamma-hydroxybutyrate—A drug of abuse. *Acta Neurol. Scand.*, 114, 145–156.

Drevets, W. C., Gautier, C., Price, J. C., Kupfer, D. J., Kinahan, P. E., Grace, A. A., et al. (2001). Amphetamine-induced dopamine release in human ventral striatum correlates with euphoria. *Biol. Psychiatry*, 49, 81–96.

Driscoll, L. L., Kaplan J., Bucuvalas E., Allen, H., Kraut, J., and Fitzpatrick, J. (2012). Acute postnatal exposure to the pentaBDE commercial mixture DE-71 at 5 or 15 mg/kg/day does not produce learning or attention deficits in rats. *Neurotoxicol. Teratol.* 34, 20–26.

Duman, R. S., Heninger, G. R., and Nestler, E. J. (1997). A molecular and cellular theory of depression. *Arch. Gen. Psychiatry.*, 54, 597–606.

Duman, R. S., Malberg, J., and Thome. J. (1999). Neural plasticity to stress and anitdepressant treatment. *Biol. Psychiatry*, 46, 1181–1191.

Dyck, E. (2005). Flashback: Psychiatric experimentation with LSD in historical perspective. *Can. J. Psychiatry*, 50, 381–388.

Dyer, J. E. (1991). γ-Hydroxybutyrate: A health-food product producing coma and seizure-like activity. *Am. J. Emerg. Med.*, 9, 321–324.

Dyer, J. E., Roth, B., and Hyma, B. A. (2001). Gamma-hydroxybutyrate withdrawal syndrome. *Ann. Emerg. Med.*, 37, 147–153.

Eagle, D. M., Bari, A., and Robbins, T. W. (2008). The neuropsychopharmacology of action inhibition: Cross-species translation of the stop-signal and go/no-go tasks. *Psychopharmacology*, 199, 439–456.

El Mestikawy, S., Wallén-Mackenzie, Å., Fortin, G. M., Descarries, L., and Trudeau, L.-E. (2011). From glutamate co-release to vesicular synergy: Vesicular glutamate transporters. *Nat. Rev. Neurosci.*, 12, 204–216.

ElSohly, M. A. and Slade, D. (2005). Chemical constituents of marijuana: The complex mixture of natural cannabinoids. *Life Sci.*, 78, 539–548.

Elsworth, J. D., Hajszan, T., Leranth, C., and Roth, R. H. (2011a). Loss of asymmetric spine synapses in dorsolateral prefrontal cortex of cognitively impaired phencyclidine-treated monkeys. *Int. J. Neuropsychopharmacol.*, 14, 1411–1415.

Elsworth, J. D., Morrow, B. A., Hajszan, T., Leranth, C., and Roth, R. H. (2011b). Phencyclidine-induced loss of asymmetric spine synapses in rodent prefrontal cortex is reversed by acute and chronic treatment with olanzapine. *Neuropsychopharmacology*, 36, 2054–2061.

Emre, M., Aarsland, D., Albanese, A., Byrne, E. J., Deuschl, G., De Deyn, P. P., et al. (2004). Rivastigmine for dementia associated with Parkinson's disease. *N. Engl. J. Med.*, 351, 2509–2518.

Engel, S. M., Berkowitz, G. S., Barr, D. B., Teitelbaum, S. L., Siskind, J., Meisel S. J., et al. (2007). Prenatal organophosphate metabolite and organochlorine levels and performance on the Brazelton Neonatal Behavioral Assessment Scale in a multiethnic pregnancy cohort. *Am. J. Epidemiol.* 165, 1397–1404.

Enoch, M.-A. and Goldman, D. (1999). Genetics of alcoholism and substance abuse. *Psychiatr. Clin. North Am.*, 22, 289–299.

Environmental Protection Agency (EPA). (1998). *Guidelines for Neurotoxicity Risk Assessment.* Washington, DC: U.S. Environmental Protection Agency, Risk Assessment Forum, EPA/630/R-95/001F.

Environmental Protection Agency (EPA). (2007). *Management of Electronic Waste in The United States: Approach Two.* Draft Final Report. EPA530-R-07-004b.

Environmental Protection Agency (EPA). (2008a). 2,2′,4,4′-Tetrabromodiphenyl ether (BDE-47) Quickview (CASRN 5436-43-1). Integrated Risk Information System. U.S. Environmental Protection Agency. Available online at: http://cfpub.epa.gov/ncea/iris/index.cfm?fuseaction=iris.showQuickView&substance_nmbr=1010, accessed 11/26/12.

Environmental Protection Agency (EPA). (2008b). 2,2′,4,4′,5-Pentabromodiphenyl ether (BDE-99) Quickview (CASRN 60348-60-9). Integrated Risk Information System. U.S. Environmental Protection Agency. Available online at: http://cfpub.epa.gov/ncea/iris/index.cfm?fuseaction=iris.showQuickView&substance_nmbr=1008, accessed 11/26/12.

Environmental Protection Agency (EPA). (2008c). 2,2′,4,4′,5,5′-Hexabromodiphenyl ether (BDE-153) Quickview (CASRN 68631-49-2). Integrated Risk Information System. U.S. Environmental Protection Agency. Available online at: http://cfpub.epa.gov/ncea/iris/index.cfm?fuseaction=iris.showQuickView&substance_nmbr=1009, accessed 11/26/12.

Environmental Protection Agency (EPA). (2008d). 2,2′,3,3′,4,4′,5,5′,6,6′-Decabro-modiphenyl ether (BDE-209) Quickview (CASRN 1163-19-5). Integrated Risk Information System. U.S. Environmental Protection Agency. Available online at: http://cfpub.epa.gov/ncea/iris/index.cfm?fuseaction=iris.showQuickView&substance_nmbr=0035, accessed 11/26/12.

Environmental Protection Agency (EPA). (2012a). Risk assessment glossary. U.S. Environmental Protection Agency. Available online at: http://www.epa.gov/risk_assessment/glossary.htm#r, accessed 11/26/12.

Environmental Protection Agency (EPA). (2012b). Mercury: Human exposure. U.S. Environmental Protection Agency. Available online at: http://www.epa.gov/mercury/exposure.htm, accessed 11/26/12.

Epilepsy Foundation. (2011). Available online at: http://www.epilepsyfoundation.org/about/statistics.cfm, accessed 8/18/11.

Epping-Jordan, M. P., Watkins, S. S., Koob, G. F., and Markou, A. (1998). Dramatic decreases in brain reward function during nicotine withdrawal. *Nature*, 393, 76–79.

Ersche, K. D. and Sahakian, B. J. (2007). The neuropsychology of amphetamine and opiate dependence: Implications for treatment. *Neuropsychol. Rev.*, 17, 317–336.

Escobar-Chávez, J. J., Dominguez-Delgado, C. L., and Rodriguez-Cruz, I. M. (2011). Targeting nicotine addiction: The possibility of a therapeutic vaccine. *Drug Des. Dev. Ther.*, 5, 211–224.

Eser, D., Schüle, C., Romeo, E., Baghai, T. C., di Michele, F., Pasini, A., et al. (2006). Neuropsychopharmacological properties of neuroactive steroids in depression and anxiety disorders. *Psychopharmacology*, 186, 373–387.

Esposito, R. U., Porrino, L. J., and Seeger, T. F. (1989). Brain stimulation reward measurement and mapping by psychophysical techniques and quantitative 2-(^{14}C) deoxyglucose autoradiography. In M. A. Bozartth (Ed.), *Methods of Assessing the Reinforcing Properties of Abused Drugs*, pp. 421–447. New York: Springer-Verlag.

Etkin, A. (2009). Functional neuroanatomy of anxiety: A neural circuit perspective. *Curr. Top. Behav. Neurosci.*, 2, 251–277.

Eto, K. (1997). Pathology of Minamata disease. *Toxicol. Pathol.* 25, 614–623.

Eubig, P. A., Aguiar, A., and Schantz, S. L. (2010). Lead and PCBs as risk factors for attention deficit/hyperactivity disorder. *Environ. Health Perspect.* 118, 1654–1667.

Evans, A. C. and Raistrick, D. (1987). Phenomenology of intoxication with toluene-based adhesives and butane gas. *Br. J. Psychiatry*, 150, 769–773.

Evans, C. J., Keith, D. E., Jr., Morrison, H., Magendzo, K., and Edwards, R. H. (1992). Cloning of a delta opioid receptor by functional expression. *Science*, 258, 1952–1955.

Evans, D. A. P., Manley, K. A., and McKusick, V. C. (1960). Genetic control of isoniazid metabolism in man. *Brit. Med. J.*, 2, 485–491.

Evans, D. E. and Drobes, D. J. (2008). Nicotine self-medication of cognitive-attentional processing. *Addict. Biol.*, 14, 32–42.

Evans, S. M. and Foltin, R. W. (2010). Does the response to cocaine differ as a function of sex or hormonal status in human and non-human primates? *Horm. Behav.*, 58, 13–21.

Everitt, B. J., Belin, D., Economidou, D., Pelloux, Y., Dalley, J. W., and Robbins, T. W. (2008). Neural mechanisms underlying the vulnerability to develop compulsive drug-seeking habits and addiction. *Phil. Trans. R. Soc. B*, 363, 3125–3135.

Exley, R., Maubourguet, N., David, V., Eddine, R., Evrard, A., Pons, S., et al. (2011). Distinct contributions of nicotinic acetylcholine receptor subunit α4 and subunit α6 to the reinforcing effects of nicotine. *Proc. Natl. Acad. Sci. U.S.A.*, 108, 7577–7582.

Fà, M., Carcangiu, G., Passino, N., Ghiglieri, V., Gessa, G. L., and Mereu, G. (2000). Cigarette smoke inhalation stimulates dopaminergic neurons in rats. *NeuroReport*, 11, 3637–3639.

Fadda, F. and Rossetti, Z. (1998). Chronic ethanol consumption: From neuroadaptation to neurodegeneration. *Prog. Neurobiol.*, 56, 385–431.

Falls, B. J., Wish, E. D., Garnier, L. M., Caldeira, K., O'Grady, K. E., Vincent, K. B., et al. (2011). The association between early conduct problems and early marijuana use in college students. *J. Child Adolesc. Subst. Abuse*, 20, 221–236.

Fantegrossi, W. E., Murnane, K. S., and Reissig, C. J. (2008). The behavioral pharmacology of hallucinogens. *Biochem. Pharmacol.*, 75, 17–33.

Farde, L. (1996). The advantage of using positron emission tomography in drug research. *Trends Neurosci.*, 19, 211–214.

Farde, L., Nordstrom, A.-L., Wiesel, F.-A., Pauli, S., Halldin, C., and Sedvall, G. (1992). Positron emission tomographic analysis of central D_1 and D_2 dopamine receptor occupancy in patients treated with classical neuroleptics and clozapine. *Arch. Gen. Psychiatry*, 49, 538–544.

Farkas, G. and Rosen, R. C. (1976). The effects of ethanol on male sexual arousal. *J. Stud. Alcohol*, 37, 265–272.

Fattore, L., Cossu, G., Martellotta, C. M., and Fratta, W. (2001). Intravenous self-administration of the cannabinoid CB_1 receptor agonist WIN 55,212-2 in rats. *Psychopharmacology*, 156, 410–416.

Fattore, L., Deiana, S., Spano, S. M., Cossu, G., Fadda, P., Scherma, M., et al. (2005). Endocannabinoid system and opioid addiction: Behavioural aspects. *Pharmacol. Biochem. Behav.*, 81, 343–359.

Faulkner, J. M. (1933). Nicotine poisoning by absorption through the skin. *JAMA*, 100, 1664–1665.

Felder, C. C. and Glass, M. (1998). Cannabinoid receptors and their endogenous agonists. *Annu. Rev. Pharmacol.*, 38, 179–200.

Fell, M. J., Svensson, K. A., Johnson, B. G., and Schoepp, D. D. (2008). Evidence for the role of metabotropic glutamate (mGlu)2 not mGlu3 receptors in the preclinical antipsychotic pharmacology of the mGlu2/3 receptor agonist (-)-(1R,4S,5S,6S)-4-amino-2-sulfonylbicyclo[3.1.0]hexane-4,6-dicarboxylic acid (LY404039). *J. Pharmacol. Exp. Ther.*, 326, 209–217.

Feng, Q., Lu, S. J., Klimanskaya, I., Gomes, I., Kim, D., Chung, Y., et al. (2010). Hemangioblastic derivatives from human induced pluripotent stem cells exhibit limited expansion and early senescence. *Stem Cells*, 28, 704–712.

Ferguson, S. M., Bazalakova, M., Savchenko, V., Tapia, J. C., Wright, J., and Blakely, R. D. (2004). Lethal impairment of cholinergic neurotransmission in hemicholinium-3-sensitive choline transporter knockout mice. *Proc. Natl. Acad. Sci. U.S.A.*, 101, 8762–8767.

Fergusson, D. M., Horwood, L. J., and Beautrais, A. L. (2003a). Cannabis and educational achievement. *Addiction*, 98, 1681–1692.

Fergusson, D. M., Horwood, L. J., Lynskey, M. T., and Madden, P. A. F. (2003b). Early reactions to cannabis predict later dependence. *Arch. Gen. Psychiatry*, 60, 1033–1039.

Fernstrom, J. D. and Wurtman, R. J. (1972). Brain serotonin content: Physiological regulation by plasma neutral amino acids. *Science*, 178, 149–152.

Ferrari, P., Palanza, P., Parmigiani, S., de Almeida, R. M. M., and Miczek, K. A. (2005). Serotonin and aggressive behavior in rodents and nonhuman primates: Predispositions and plasticity. *Eur. J. Pharmacol.*, 526, 259–273.

Ferré, S. (2008). An update on the mechanisms of the psychostimulant effects of caffeine. *J. Neurochem.*, 105, 1067–1079.

Ferrer, I., Boada Rovira, M., Sanchez Guerra, M. L., Ray, M. J., and Costa-Jussa, F. (2004). Neuropathology and pathogenesis of encephalitis following amyloid-beta immunization in Alzheimer's disease. *Brain Pathol.*, 14, 11–20.

Fibiger, H. C., Phillips, A. G., and Brown, E. E. (1992). The neurobiology of cocaine-induced reinforcement. *Ciba Found. Symp.*, 166, 96–111.

Fink, D. J., Wechuck, J., Mata, M., Glorioso, J. C., Goss, J., Krisky, D., et al. (2011). Gene therapy for pain: Results of a phase I clinical trial. *Ann. Neurol.*, 70, 207–212.

Finney, J. W., Hahn, A. C., and Moos, R. H. (1996). The effectiveness of inpatient and outpatient treatment for alcohol abuse: The need to focus on mediators and moderators of setting effects. *Addiction*, 91, 1773–1796.

Fischer, M., Kaech, S., Knutti, D., and Matus, A. (1998). Rapid actin-based plasticity in dendritic spines. *Neuron*, 20, 847–854.

Foltin, R. W., Fischman, M. W., and Byrne, M. F. (1988). Effects of smoked marijuana on food intake and body weight of humans living in a residential laboratory. *Appetite*, 11, 1–14.

Fone, K. C. F. (2008). An update on the role of the 5-hydroxytryptamine$_6$ receptor in cognitive function. *Neuropharmacology*, 55, 1015–1022.

Fonnum, F. (1987). Biochemistry, anatomy, and pharmacology of GABA neurons. In H. Y. Meltzer (Ed.), *Psychopharmacology: The Third Generation of Progress*, pp. 173–182. New York: Raven Press.

Food and Drug Administraion (FDA). (2004). FDA and EPA Announce the Revised Consumer Advisory on Methylmercury in Fish. News Release, 03/19/04. U.S. Food and Drug Administration. Available online at: http://www.fda.gov/NewsEvents/Newsroom/PressAnnouncements/2004/ucm108267.htm, accessed 11/26/12.

Federal Drug Administration (FDA). (2008). FDA issues public health advisory for antipsychotic drugs used for treatment of behavioral disorders in elderly patients [FDA Talk Paper]. Rockville, MD: US Food and Drug Administration. Available online at: http://www.fda.gov/Drugs/DrugSafety/PostmarketDrugSafetyInformationforPatientsandProviders/DrugSafetyInformationforHeathcareProfessionals/PublicHealthAdvisories/ucm053171.htm, accessed 7/17/12.

Food and Drug Administration (FDA). (2010). Update on Bisphenol A for Use in Food Contact Applications. U.S. Food and Drug Administration. Available online at: http://www.fda.gov/downloads/NewsEvents/PublicHealthFocus/UCM197778.pdf, accessed 11/26/12.

Forey, B. A., Thornton, A. J., and Lee, P. N. (2011). Systematic review with meta-analysis of the epidemiological evidence relating smoking to COPD, chronic bronchitis, and emphysema. *BMC Pulmonary Med.*, 11, 36. doi:10.1186/1471-2466-11-36

Foulds, J., Stapleton, J. A., Bell, N., Swettenham, J., Jarvis, M. J., and Russell, M. A. H. (1997). Mood and physiological effects of subcutaneous nicotine in smokers and never-smokers. *Drug Alcohol Depend.*, 44, 105–115.

Fowler, C. D., Lu, Q., Johnson, P. M., Marks, M. J., and Kenny, P. J. (2011). Habenular α5 nicotinic receptor subunit signaling controls nicotine intake. *Nature*, 471, 597–601.

Fowler, J. S., Logan, J., Wang, G. J., Volkow, N. D., Telang, F., Zhu, W., et al. (2003). Low monoamine oxidase B in peripheral organs in smokers. *Proc. Natl. Acad. Sci. U.S.A.*, 100, 11600–11605.

Franke, W. W. and Berendonk, B. (1997). Hormonal doping and androgenization of athletes: A secret program of the German Democratic Republic government. *Clin. Chem.*, 43, 1262–1279.

Franklin, T. R., Acton, P. D., Maldjian, J. A., Gray, J. D., Croft, J. R., Dackis, C. A., et al. (2002). Decreased gray matter concentration in the insular, orbitofrontal, cingulate, and temporal cortices of cocaine patients. *Biol. Psychiatry*, 51, 134–142.

Frascella, J., Potenza, M. N., Brown, L. L., and Childress, A. R. (2010). Shared brain vulnerabilities open the way for nonsubstance addictions: Carving addiction at a new joint? *Ann. N.Y. Acad. Sci.*, 1187, 294–315.

Freeza, M., Padova, C., Terpin, M., Baranona, E., and Lieber, C. (1990). High blood alcohol levels in women: The role of decreased gastric alcohol dehydrogenase activity and first-pass metabolism. *N. Engl. J. Med.*, 322, 95–99.

Freudenmann, R. W., Öxler, F., and Bernschneider-Reif, S. (2006). The origin of MDMA (ecstasy) revisited: The true story reconstructed from the original documents. *Addiction*, 101, 1241–1245.

Friedhoff, A. J. and Silva, R. R. (1995). The effects of neuroleptics on plasma homovanillic acid. In F. E. Bloom and D. J. Kupfer (Eds.), *Psychopharmacology: The Fourth Generation of Progress*, pp. 1229–1234. New York: Raven Press.

Froelich, J. C. (1997). Opioid peptides. *Alcohol Health Res. World*, 21, 132–143.

Fuller, R. K. and Hiller-Sturmhofel, S. (1999). Alcoholism treatment in the United States. *Alcohol Health Res. World*, 23, 69–77.

Funada, M., Sato, M., Makino, Y., and Wada, K. (2002). Evaluation of rewarding effect of toluene by the conditioned place preference procedure in mice. *Brain Res. Protocols*, 10, 47–54.

Furmark, T., Tillfors, M., Garpenstrand, H., Marteinsdottir, I., Långström, B., Oreland, L., et al. (2004). Serotonin transporter polymorphism related to amygdala excitability and symptom severity in patients with social phobia. *Neurosci. Lett.*, 362, 189–192.

Fuxe, K., Dahlström, A. B., Jonsson, G., Marcellino, D., Guescini, M., Dam, M., et al. (2010). The discovery of central monoamine neurons gave volume transmission to the wired brain. *Prog. Brain Res.*, 90, 82–100.

Gagne, J. J. and Power, M. C. (2010). Anti-inflammatory drugs and risk of Parkinson disease: A meta-analysis. *Neurology*, 74, 995–1002.

Gamo, N. J., Wang, M., and Arnsten, A. F. T. (2010). Methylphenidate and atomoxetine enhance prefrontal function through α_2-adrenergic and dopamine D_1 receptors. *J. Am. Acad. Child Adolesc. Psychiatry*, 49, 1011–1023.

Ganio, M. S., Klau, J. F., Casa, D. J., Armstrong, L. E., and Maresh, C. M. (2009). Effect of caffeine on sport-specific endurance performance: A systematic review. *J. Strength Cond. Res.*, 23, 315–324.

Garavan, H. and Hesster, R. (2007). The role of cognitive control in cocaine dependence. *Neuropsychol. Rev.*, 17, 337–345.

Garbutt, J. C., West, S. L., Carey, T. S., Lohr, K. N., and Crews, F. T. (1999). Pharmacological treatment of alcohol dependence: A review of the evidence. *JAMA*, 281, 1318–1325.

Garcia, F. D. and Thibaut, F. (2010.) Sexual addictions. *Am. J. Drug Alcohol Abuse*, 36, 254–260.

Gardner, D. M., Baldessarini, R. J., and Waraich, P. (2005) Modern antipsychotic drugs: A critical overview. *CMAJ*, 172, 1703–1711.

Garfield, A. S. and Heisler, L. K. (2009). Pharmacological targeting of the serotonergic system for the treatment of obesity. *J. Physiol.*, 587, 49–60.

Garland, E. L. and Howard, M. O. (2010). Phenomenology of adolescent inhalant intoxication. *Exp. Clin. Psychopharmacol.*, 18, 498–509.

Garnier-Dykstra, L. M., Caldeira, K. M., Vincent, K. B., O'Grady, K. E., and Arria, A. M. (2012). Nonmedical use of prescription stimulants during college: Four-year trends in exposure opportunity, use, motives, and sources. *J. Am. Coll. Health*, 60, 226–234.

Garrett, B. E. and Griffiths, R. R. (1998). Physical dependence increases the relative reinforcing effects of caffeine versus placebo. *Psychopharmacology*, 139, 195–202.

Gaval-Cruz, M. and Weinshenker, D. (2009). Mechanisms of disulfiram-induced cocaine abstinence: Antabuse and cocaine relapse. *Mol. Interv.*, 9, 175–187.

Gawin, F. H. and Kleber, H. D. (1986). Abstinence symptomatology and psychiatric diagnosis in cocaine abusers. Clinical observations. *Arch. Gen. Psychiatry*, 43, 107–113.

Gawin, F. H. and Kleber, H. D. (1988). Evolving conceptualizations of cocaine dependence. *Yale J. Biol. Med.*, 61, 123–136.

Gaziano, J. M. and Hennekens, C. (1995). Moderate alcohol intake, increased levels of high density lipoprotein and its subfractions, and decreased risk of myocardial infarction. *N. Engl. J. Med.*, 329, 1829–1834.

Geda, Y., Ragossnig, M., Roberts, L. K., Roberts, R., Pankratz, V., Christianson, T., et al. (2012). Caloric intakem aging, and mild cognitive impairment: A population-based study. *J. Alzheimers Dis.*, in press.

Gehlbach, S. H., Williams, W. A., Perry, L. D., and Woodall, J. S. (1974). Green-tobacco sickness. An illness of tobacco harvesters. *JAMA*, 229, 1880–1883.

Genro, J. P., Hutz, M. H., Kieling, C., and Rohde, L. A. (2010). Attention-deficit / hyperactivity disorder and the dopaminergic hypotheses. *Expert Rev. Neurother.*, 10, 587–601.

George, T. P. and O'Malley, S. S. (2004). Current pharmacological treatments for nicotine dependence. *Trends Pharmacol. Sci.*, 25, 42–48.

George, W. H. and Norris, J. (1991). Alcohol, disinhibition, sexual arousal, and deviant sexual behavior. *Alcohol Health Res. World*, 15, 133–138.

Gerasimov, M. R., Ferrieri, R. A., Schiffer, W. K., Logan, J., Gatley, S. J., Gifford, A. N., et al. (2002). Study of brain uptake and biodistribution of [^{11}C]toluene in non-human primates and mice. *Life Sci.*, 70, 2811–2828.

Gerber, J. S. and Offit, P. A. (2009). Vaccines and autism: A tale of shifting hypotheses. *Clin. Infect. Dis.* 48, 456–461.

Gereben, B., Zavacki, A. M., Ribich, S., Kim, B. W., Huang, S. A, Simonides, W. S., et al. (2008). Cellular and molecular basis of deiodinase-regulated thyroid hormone signaling. *Endocr. Rev.* 29, 898–938.

Gerlai, R. (1996). Gene-targeting studies of mammalian behavior: Is it the mutation or the background genotype? *Trends Neurosci.*, 19, 177–181.

Gerrits, M. and Vanree, J. (1996). Effects of nucleus accumbens dopamine depletion on motivational aspects involved in initiation of cocaine and heroin self-administration in rats. *Brain Res.*, 713, 114–124.

Geyer, M. A. and Ellenbroek, B. (2003). Animal behavior models of the mechanisms underlying antipsychotic atypicality. *Prog. Neuropsychopharmacol. Biol. Psychiatry*, 27, 1071–1079.

Gibbons, B. (1992). Alcohol: The legal drug. *Natl. Geogr. Mag.*, 181 (2), 3–35.

Gilbert, M. E., Rovet, J., Chen, Z., and Koibuchi, N. (2012). Developmental thyroid hormone disruption: Prevalence, environmental contaminants and neurodevelopmental consequences. *Neurotoxicol.* 33, 842–852.

Gilbertson, M. W., Shenton, M. E., Ciszewski, A., Kasai, K., Lasko, N. B., Orr, S. P., et al. (2002). Smaller hippocampal volume predicts pathologic vulnerability to psychological trauma. *Nat. Neurosci.*, 5, 1242–1247.

Gilman, S, Koller, M., Black, R. S., Jenkins, L., Griffith, S. G., Fox, N. C., et al. (2005). Clinical effects of Aβ immunization (AN1792) on MRI measures of cerebral volume in Alzheimer disease. *Neurology*, 61, 1563–1572.

Giros, B., Jaber, M., Jones, S. R., Wightman, R. M., and Caron, M. G. (1996). Hyperlocomotion and indifference to cocaine and amphetamine in mice lacking the dopamine transporter. *Nature*, 379, 606–612.

Glade, M. J. (2010). Caffeine—Not just a stimulant. *Nutrition*, 26, 932–938.

Goedert, M. and Spillantini, M. S. (2006). A Century of Alzheimer's Disease. *Science*, 314, 777–781.

Gold, L. H., Geyer, M. A., and Koob, G. F. (1989). Neurochemical mechanisms involved in behavioral effects of amphetamines and related designer drugs. *NIDA Res. Monogr.*, 104, 101–126.

Gold, M. S. (1989). Opiates. In A. J. Giannini and A. E. Slaby (Eds.), *Drugs of Abuse*, pp. 127–145. Oradell, NJ: Medical Economics Books.

Gold, P. E. and van Buskirk, R. B. (1975). Facilitation of time-dependent memory processes with posttrial epinephrine injections. *Behav. Biol.*, 13, 145–153.

Goldman-Rakic, P. S. (1987). Circuitry of the prefrontal cortex and the regulation of behavior by representational memory. In F. Plum (Ed.), *Handbook of Physiology*, Section 1, The Nervous System, Vol. 5, Higher Functions of the Brain, Part I, pp. 373–417. Bethesda, MD: American Physiological Society.

Goldstein, A. (1989). *Molecular and Cellular Aspects of the Drug Addictions*. New York: Springer-Verlag.

Goldstein, D. B. (1972). Relationship of alcohol dose to intensity of withdrawal signs in mice. *J. Pharmacol. Exp. Ther.*, 180, 203–210.

Goldstein, J. M., Jerram, M., Abbs, B., Whitfield-Gabrieli, S., and Makris, N. (2010). Sex differences in stress response circuitry activation dependent on female hormonal cycle. *J. Neurosci.*, 30, 431–438.

Goldstein, M. J. (1995). Psychoeducation and relapse prevention. An update. In N. Brunello, G. Racagni, S. Z. Langer, and J. Mendlewicz (Eds.), *Critical Issues in the Treatment of Schizophrenia*, pp. 134–141. New York: Karger.

Goldstein, R. A., DesLauriers, C., and Burda, A. M. (2009). Cocaine: History, social implications, and toxicity—A review. *Dis. Mon.*, 55, 6–38.

Goldstein, R. Z. and Volkow, N. D. (2011). Dysfunction of the prefrontal cortex in addiction: Neuroimaging findings and clinical implications. *Nat. Rev. Neurosci.*, 12, 652–669.

Gonzales, R., Mooney, L., and Rawson, R. A. (2010). The methamphetamine problem in the United States. *Annu. Rev. Public Health*, 31, 385–398.

González, D., Riba, J., Bouso, J. C., Gómez-Jarabo, G., and Barbanoj, M. J. (2006). Pattern of use and subjective effects of *Salvia divinorum* among recreational users. *Drug Alcohol Depend.*, 85, 157–162.

González, S., Cebeira, M., and Fernández-Ruiz, J. (2005). Cannabinoid tolerance and dependence: A review of studies in laboratory animals. *Pharmacol. Biochem. Behav.*, 81, 300–318.

Goode, E. (1993). *Drugs in American Society*. New York: McGraw-Hill.

Goodman, M., Squibb, K., Youngstrom, E., Anthony, L. G., Kenworthy, L., Lipkin, P. H., (2011). Clinical effects of Aβ immunization (AN1792) on MRI measures of cerebral volume in Alzheimer disease. Using systematic reviews and meta-analyses to support regulatory decision making for neurotoxicants: Lessons learned from a case study of PCBs. *Ciencia & Saude Coletiva*, 16, 3207–3220.

Gordon, J. A. and Hen, R. (2004). The serotonergic system and anxiety. *Neuromolecular Med.*, 5, 27–40.

Gordon, N. (2007). Segawa's disease: Dopa-responsive dystonia. *Int. J. Clin. Pract.*, 62, 943–946.

Gorelick, D. A. and Heishman, S. J. (2006). Methods for clinical research involving cannabis administration. In E. S. Onavi (Ed.), *Methods in Molecular Medicine: Marijuana and Cannabinoid Research: Methods and Protocols*, pp. 235–253. Totowa, NJ: Humana.

Gottesman, I. I. (1991). *Schizophrenia Genesis*. New York: W.H. Freeman.

Gourlay, S. G. and Benowitz, N. L. (1997). Arteriovenous differences in plasma concentration of nicotine and catecholamines and related cardiovascular effects after smoking, nicotine nasal spray, and intravenous nicotine. *Clin. Pharmacol. Ther.*, 62, 453–463.

Govind, A. P., Vezina, P., and Green, W. N. (2009). Nicotine-induced upregulation of nicotinic receptors: Underlying mechanisms and relevance to nicotine addiction. *Biochem. Pharmacol.*, 78, 756–765.

Grace, A. A. (1992). The depolarization block hypothesis of neuroleptic action: Implications for the etiology and treatment of schizophrenia. *J. Neural Transm.*, 36 (Suppl.), 91–131.

Grandjean, P. and Herz, K. T. (2011). Brain development and methylmercury: Underestimation of neurotoxicity. *Mt. Sinai J. Med.*, 78, 107–118.

Grant, J. E., Potenza, M. N., Weinstein, A., and Gorelick, D. A. (2010). Introduction to behavioral addictions. *Am. J. Drug Alcohol Abuse*, 36, 233–241.

Green, A. I. and Brown, W. A. (1988). Prolactin and neuroleptic drugs. *Neurol. Clin.*, 6, 213–223.

Green, B., Kavanagh, D., and Young, R. (2003). Being stoned: A review of self-reported cannabis effects. *Drug Alcohol Rev.*, 22, 453–460.

Green, S. M. and Coté, C. J. (2009). Ketamine and neurotoxicity: Clinical perspectives and implications for emergency medicine. *Ann. Emerg. Med.*, 54, 181–190.

Greider, T. E., Sellings, L. H., Vargas-Perez, H., Ting-A-Kee, R., Siu, E. C., Tyndale, R. F., et al. (2010). Dopaminergic signaling mediates the motivational response underlying the opponent process to chronic but not acute nicotine. *Neuropsychopharmacology*, 35, 943–954.

Griffiths, R. R. and Mumford, G. K. (1995). Caffeine: A drug of abuse? In F. E. Bloom and D. J. Kupfer (Eds.), *Psychopharmacology: The Fourth Generation of Progress*, pp. 1699–1713. New York: Raven Press.

Griffiths, R. R., Bigelow, G. E., and Henningfield, J. E. (1980). Similarities in animal and human drug taking behavior. In N. K. Mello (Ed.), *Advances in Substance Abuse*, Vol 1, pp. 1–90. Greenwich, CT: JAI Press.

Griffiths, R. R., Evans, S. M., Heishman, S. J., Preston, K. L., Sannerud, C. A., Wolf, B., et al. (1990). Low-dose caffeine physical dependence in humans. *J. Pharmacol. Exp. Ther.*, 255, 1123–1132.

Griffiths, R. R., Lamb, R. J., Sannerud, C. A., Ator, N., and Brady, J. V. (1991). Self-injection of barbiturates and benzodiazepines. *Psychopharmacology*, 103, 154–161.

Grimaldi, C. and Capasso, A. (2011). The endocannabinoid system in the cancer therapy: An overview. *Curr. Med. Chem.*, 18, 1575–1583.

Grobin, A. C., Matthews, D. B., Devaud, L. L., and Morrow, A. L. (1998). The role of GABA$_A$ receptors in the acute and chronic effects of ethanol. *Psychopharmacology*, 139, 2–19.

Gross, C. and Hen, R. (2004). The developmental origins of anxiety. *Nat. Rev. Neurosci.*, 5, 545–552.

Gross, C., Zhuang, X., Stark, K., Ramboz, S., Oosting, R., Kirby, L., et al. (2002). Serotonin$_{1A}$ receptor acts during development to establish normal anxiety-like behaviour in the adult. *Nature*, 416, 396–400.

Gruber, A. J. and Pope, H. G., Jr. (2002). Marijuana use among adolescents. *Pediatr. Clin. North Am.*, 49, 389–413.

Gruber, S. A., Rogowska, J., and Yurgelun-Todd, D. A. (2009). Altered affective response in marijuana smokers: An fMRI study. *Drug Alcohol Depend.*, 105, 139–153.

Guay, D. R. (1995). The emerging role of valproate in bipolar disorder and other psychiatric disorders. *Pharmacotherapy*, 15, 631–647.

Guidotti, A. and Grayson, D. R. (2011). A neurochemical basis for an epigenetic vision of psychiatric disorders (1994–2009). *Pharmacol. Res.*, 64, 344–349.

Guidotti, A., Auta, J., Chen, Y., Davis, J. M., Dong, E., Gavin, D. P., et al. (2011). Epigenetic GABAergic targets in schizophrenia and bipolar disorder. *Neuropharmacology*, 60, 1007–1016.

Gunduz-Bruce, H. (2009). The acute effects of NMDA antagonism: From the rodent to the human brain. *Brain Res. Rev.*, 279–286.

Gunduz-Cinar, O., MacPherson, K. P., Cinar, R., Gamble-George, J., Sugden, K., Williams, B., et al. (2012). Convergent translational evidence for a role for anandamide in amygdala-mediated fear extinction, threat processing and stress-reactivity. *Mol. Psychiatry*, in press.

Gunja, N. and Brown, J. A. (2012). Energy drinks: Health risks and toxicity. *Med. J. Aust.*, 196, 46–49.

Guo, Y. L., Lambert, G. H., Hsu, C. C., and Hsu, M. M. L. (2004). Yucheng: Health effects of prenatal exposure to polychlorinated biphenyls and dibenzofurans. *Int. Arch. Occup. Environ. Health* 77, 153–158.

Guo, Y. L., Yu, M-L., Hsu, C-C., and Rogan, W. J. (1999). Chloracne, goiter, arthritis, and anemia after polychlorinated biphenyl poisoning: 14-year follow-up of the Taiwan Yucheng cohort. *Environ. Health Persp.*, 107, 715–719.

Gupta, M., Kaur, H., Jajodia, A., Jain, S., Satyamoorthy, K., Mukerji, M., et al. (2011). Diverse facets of COMT: From a plausible predictive marker to a potential drug target for schizophrenia. *Curr. Mol. Med.*, 11, 732–743.

Gur, R. E. (1995). Functional brain-imaging studies in schizophrenia. In F. E. Bloom and D. J. Kupfer (Eds.), *Psychopharmacology: The Fourth Generation of Progress*, pp. 1185–1192. New York: Raven Press.

Haber, S. N. and Knutson, B. (2010). The reward circuit: Linking primate anatomy and human imaging. *Neuropsychopharmacology*, 35, 4–26.

Haddad, P. M., Das, A., Ashfaq, M., and Wieck, A. (2009). A review of valproate in psychiatric practice. *Expert Opin. Drug Metab. Toxicol.*, 5, 539–551.

Hadlock, G. C., Webb, K. M., McFadden, L. M., Chu, P. W., Ellis, J. D., Allen, S. C., et al. (2011). 4-Methylmethcathinone (mephedrone): Neuropharmacological effects of a designer stimulant of abuse. *J. Pharmacol. Exp. Ther.*, 339, 530–536.

Hahn, B., Shoaib, M., and Stolerman, I. P. (2011). Selective nicotinic receptor antagonists: Effects on attention and nicotine-induced attentional enhancement. *Psychopharmacology*, 217, 75–82.

Halberstadt, A. L. and Geyer, M. A. (2011). Multiple receptors contribute to the behavioral effects of indoleamine hallucinogens. *Neuropharmacology*, 61, 364–381.

Halberstadt, A. L. and Nichols, D. E. (2010). Serotonin and serotonin receptors in hallucinogen action. In C. P. Müller and B. L. Jacobs (Eds.), *Handbook of the Behavioral Neurobiology of Serotonin*, pp. 621–636. London: Academic Press.

Halpern, J. H. and Pope, H. G., Jr. (2003). Hallucinogen persisting perception disorder: What do we know after 50 years? *Drug Alcohol Depend.*, 69, 109–119.

Hamel, D. (2007). Serotonin and migraine: Biology and clinical implications. *Cephalalgia*, 27, 1295–1300.

Hamers, T., Kamstra, J. H., Sonneveld, E., Murk, A. J., Keter, M. H. A., Andersson, P. L., et al. (2006). In vitro profiling of the endocrine-disrupting potency of brominated flame retardants. *Toxicol. Sci.* 92, 157–173.

Hamilton, L. W. and Timmons, C. R. (1990). *Principles of Behavioral Pharmacology: A Biopsychological Perspective.* Englewood Cliffs, NJ: Prentice Hall.

Hamner, M. (2002). The effects of atypical antipsychotics on serum prolactin levels. *Ann. Clin. Psychiatry*, 14, 163–173.

Hampson, R. E., España, R. A., Rogers, G. A., Porrino, L. J., and Deadwyler, S. A. (2009). Mechanisms underlying cognitive enhancement and reversal of cognitive deficits in nonhuman primates by the ampakine CX717. *Psychopharmacology*, 202, 355–369.

Han, J. S. (2004). Acupuncture and endorphins. *Neurosci. Lett.*, 361, 258–261.

Haney, M. (2009). Self-administration of cocaine, cannabis and heroin in the human laboratory: Benefits and pitfalls. *Addict. Biol.*, 14, 9–21.

Haney, M., Ward, A. S., Comer, S. D., Foltin, R. W., and Fischman, M. W. (1999a). Abstinence symptoms following smoked marijuana in humans. *Psychopharmacology*, 141, 395–404.

Haney, M., Ward, A. S., Comer, S. D., Foltin, R. W., and Fischman, M. W. (1999b). Abstinence symptoms following oral THC administration to humans. *Psychopharmacology*, 141, 385–394.

Haney, M., Ward, A. S., Foltin, R. W., and Fischman, M. W. (2001). Effects of ecopipam, a selective D_1 antagonist, on smoked cocaine self-administration by humans. *Psychopharmacology*, 155, 330–337.

Hannigan, J. H. and Bowen, S. E. (2010). Reproductive toxicology and teratology of abused toluene. *Syst. Biol. Reprod. Med.*, 56, 184–200.

Hardiman, O., van den Berg, L. H., Kiernan, M. C. (2011). Clinical diagnosis and management of amyotrophic lateral sclerosis. *Nat. Rev. Neurol.*, 7, 639–649.

Hardman, H. F., Haavik, C. O., and Seevers, M. H. (1973). Relationship of the structure of mescaline and seven analogs to toxic-ity and behavior in five species of laboratory animals. *Toxicol. Appl. Pharmacol.*, 25, 299–309.

Harney, J., Scarbrough, K., Rosewell, K. L., and Wise, P. M. (1996). In vivo antisense antagonism of vasoactive intestinal peptide in the suprachiasmatic nuclei causes aging-like changes in the estradiol-induced luteinizing hormone and prolactin surges. *Endocrinology*, 137, 3696–3701.

Harper, B., Luukinen, B. Gervais, J. A., Buhl, K., and Stone, D. (2009). Diazinon technical fact sheet. National Pesticide Information Center, Oregon State University Extension Services. Available online at: http://npic.orst.edu/factsheets/diazinontech.pdf.

Hart, C. L., van Gorp, W., Haney, M., Foltin, R. W., and Fischman, M. W. (2001). Effects of acute smoked marijuana on complex cognitive performance. *Neuropsychopharmacology*, 25, 757–765.

Harvey, D. M., Yasar, S., Heishman, S. J., Panlilio, L. V., Henningfield, J. E., and Goldberg, S. R. (2004). Nicotine serves as an effective reinforcer of intravenous drug-taking behavior in human cigarette smokers. *Psychopharmacology*, 175, 134–142.

Harvey, K. V. and Balon, R. (1995). Augmentation with buspirone: A review. *Ann. Clin. Psychiatry*, 7, 143–147.

Hasselmo, M. E. and Sarter, M. (2011). Modes and models of forebrain cholinergic neuromodulation of cognition. *Neuropsychopharmacology*, 36, 52–73.

Hattoff, Q. D. (2012). As crunch time hits, some students turn to dangerous study drug. Available online at: http://www.thecrimson.com/article/2012/5/2/adderall-study-drug-misuse/?, accessed 10/26/12.

Hatzidimitriou, G., McCann, U. D., and Ricaurte, G. A. (1999). Altered serotonin innervation patterns in the forebrain of monkeys treated with (±)3,4-methylenedioxymethamphetamine seven years previously: Factors influencing abnormal recovery. *J. Neurosci.*, 19, 5096–5107.

Hays, S. R. and Deshpande, J. K. (2011). Newly postulated neurodevelopmental risks of pediatric anesthesia. *Curr. Neurol. Neurosci. Rep.*, 11, 205–210.

Heatherley, S. V. (2011). Caffeine withdrawal, sleepiness, and driving performance: What does the research really tell us? *Nutr. Neurosci.*, 14, 89–95.

Hedges, D. W., Woon, F. L., and Hoopes, S. P. (2009). Caffeine-induced psychosis. *CNS Spectr.*, 14, 127–129.

Heidbreder, C. A. and Newman, A. H. (2010). Current perspectives on selective dopamine D3 receptor antagonists as pharmacotherapeutics for addictions and related disorders. *Ann. N.Y. Acad. Sci.*, 1187, 4–34.

Heilig, M. and Koob, G. F. (2007). A key role for corticotropin-releasing factor in alcohol dependence. *Trends Neurosci.*, 30, 399–406.

Heilig, M., Thorsell, A., Sommer, W. H., Hansson, A. C., Ramchandani, V. A., George, D. T., et al. (2010). Translating the neuroscience of alcoholism into clinical treatments: From blocking the buzz to curing the blues. *Neurosci. Biobehav. Rev.*, 35, 334–344.

Heinz, A., Reimold, M., Wrase, J., Hermann, D., Croissant, B., Mundle, G., et al. (2005). Correlation of stable elevations in striatal mu-opioid receptor availability in detoxified alcoholic patients with alcohol craving: A positron emission tomography study using carbon 11-labeled carfentanil. *Arch. Gen. Psychiatr.*, 62, 57–64.

Heinzen, E. L. and Pollack, G. M. (2004). The development of morphine antinociceptive tolerance in nitric oxide synthase-deficient mice. *Biochem. Pharmacol.*, 67, 735–741.

Heishman, S. J., Kleykamp, B. A., and Singleton, E. G. (2010). Meta-analysis of the acute effects of nicotine and smoking on human performance. *Psychopharmacology*, 210, 453–469.

Heisler, L. K., Chu, H.-M., Brennan, T. J., Danao, J. A., Bajwa, P., Parsons, L. H., et al. (1998). Elevated anxiety and antidepressant-like responses in serotonin 5-HT_{1A} receptor mutant mice. *Proc. Natl. Acad. Sci. U.S.A.*, 95, 15049–15054.

Heisler, L. K., Zhou, L., Bajwa, P., Hsu, J., and Tecott, L. H. (2007). Serotonin 5-HT_{2C} receptors regulate anxiety-like behavior. *Genes Brain Behav.*, 6, 491–496.

Helton, D. R., Modlin, D. L., Tizzano, J. P., and Rasmussen, K. (1993). Nicotine withdrawal: A behavioral assessment using schedule controlled responding, locomotor activity, and sensorimotor reactivity. *Psychopharmacology*, 113, 205–210.

Hendershott, J. (1969). Steroids: Breakfast of champions. *Track and Field News*, I April, 3.

Hendrickson, R. G. and Cloutier, R. L. (2007). "Crystal Dex": Free-base dextromethorphan. *J. Emerg. Med.*, 32, 393–396.

Herbst, A. L., Ulfelder, H., and Poskanzer, D. C. (1971). Adenocarcinoma of the vagina: Association of maternal stilbestrol therapy with tumor appearance in young women. *N. Engl. J. Med.* 284, 878–881.

Herbstman, J. B., Sjodin, A., Apelberg, B. J., Witter, F. R., Halden, R. U., Patterson, D. G., et al. (2008). Birth delivery mode modifies the associations between prenatal polychlorinated biphenyl (PCB) and polybrominated diphenyl ether (PBDE) and neonatal thyroid hormone levels. *Environ. Health Perspect.* 116:1376–1382.

Herbstman, J. B., Sjodin, A., Kurzon, M., Lederman, S. A., Jones, R. S., Rauh, V., et al. (2010). Prenatal exposure to PBDEs and neurodevelopment. *Environ. Health Perspect.* 118, 712–719.

Hering-Hanit, R. and Gadoth, N. (2003). Caffeine-induced headache in children and adolescents. *Cephalagia*, 23, 332–335.

Hernberg, S. (2000). Lead poisoning in a historical perspective. *Am. J. Ind. Med.* 38, 244–254.

Herz, A. (1997). Endogenous opioid systems and alcohol addiction. *Psychopharmacology*, 129, 99–111.

Heuser, I. and Lammers, C.-H. (2003). Stress and the brain. *Neurobiol. Aging*, 24, S69–S76.

Heyman, G. M. (2009). *Addiction: A Disorder of Choice*. Cambridge: Harvard University Press.

Higgins, S. T., Bickel, W. K., and Hughes, J. R. (1994). Influence of an alternative reinforcer on human cocaine self-administration. *Life Sci.*, 55, 179–197.

Higgins, S. T., Delaney, D. D., Budney, A. J., Bickel, W. K., Hughes, J. R., Foerg, F., et al. (1991). A behavioral approach to achieving initial cocaine abstinence. *Am. J. Psychiatry*, 148, 1218–1224.

Hildebrand, B. E., Nomikos, G. G., Bondjers, C., Nisell, M., and Svensson, T. H. (1997). Behavioral manifestations of the nicotine abstinence syndrome in the rat: Peripheral versus central mechanisms. *Psychopharmacology*, 129, 348–356.

Hill, M. N., Hillard, C. J., Bambico, F. R., Patel, S., Gorzalka, B. B., and Gobbi, G. (2009). The therapeutic potential of the endocannabinoid system for the development of a novel class of antidepressants. *Trends Pharmacol. Sci.*, 30, 484–493.

Himmelsbach, C. K. (1943). Can the euphoric, analgesic and physical dependence effects of drugs be separated? With reference to physical dependence. *Fed. Proc.*, 2, 201–203.

Hingson, R. W. and Zha, W. (2009). Age of drinking onset, alcohol use disorders, frequent heavy drinking, and unintentionally injuring oneself and others after drinking. *Pediatrics*, 123, 1477–1484.

Hingson, R. W., Zha, W., and Weitzman, E. R. (2009). Magnitude of and trends in alcohol-related mortality and morbidity among U.S. college students ages 18–24, 1998–2005. *J. Stud. Alcohol Drugs Suppl.*, 16, 12–20.

Hirvonen, J., Goodwin, R. S., Li, C.-T., Terry, G. E., Zoghbi, S. S., Morse, C., et al. (2012). Reversible and regionally selective downregulation of brain cannabinoid CB$_1$ receptors in chronic daily cannabis smokers. *Mol. Psychiatry*, 17, 642–649.

Hobbs, W. R., Rall, T. W., and Verdoorn, T. A. (1996). Hypnotics and sedatives: Ethanol. In A. G. Gilman, L. S. Goodman, J. G. Hardman, L. E. Limbird, P. B. Molinoff, and R. W. Rudon (Eds.), *The Pharmacological Basis of Therapeutics*, pp. 361–396. New York: McGraw-Hill.

Hodges, M. R. and Richerson, G. B. (2010). The role of medullary serotonin (5-HT) neurons in respiratory control: Contributions to eupneic ventilation, CO$_2$ chemoreception, and thermoregulation. *J. Appl. Physiol.*, 108, 1425–1432.

Hoebel, B. G., Monaco, A. P., Hernandez, L., Aulisi, E. F., Stanley, B. G., and Lenard, L. (1983). Self-injection of amphetamine directly into the brain. *Psychopharmacology*, 81, 158–163.

Hollinger, M. A. (1995). The criminalization of drug use in the United States. A brief historical perspective. *Res. Commun. Alcohol Subst. Abuse*, 16, 1–23.

Hollinger, M. A. (2008). Animals in research. In *Introduction to Pharmacology* (3rd ed.), pp. 333–353. New York: CRC Press.

Holmes, A., Lachowicz, J. E., and Sibley, D. R. (2004). Phenotypic analysis of dopamine receptor knockout mice; recent insights into the functional specificity of dopamine receptor subtypes. *Neuropharmacology*, 47, 1117–1134.

Holmes, A., Murphy, D. L., and Crawley, J. N. (2002). Reduced aggression in mice lacking the serotonin transporter. *Psychopharmacology*, 161, 160–167.

Holmes, C., Boche, D., Wilkinson, D., Yadegearfar, G., Hopkins, V., Bayer, A., et al. (2008). Long-term effects of Aβ42 immunisation in Alzheimer's disease: Follow-up of a randomized, placebo-controlled phase I trial. *Lancet*, 372, 216–223.

Holsboer, F. and Ising, M. (2008). Central CRH system in depression and anxiety—Evidence from clinical studies with CRH1 receptor antagonists. *Eur. J. Pharmacol.*, 583, 350–357.

Holtmaat, A. and Svoboda, K. (2009). Experience-dependent structural synaptic plasticity in the mammalian brain. *Nat. Rev. Neurosci.*, 10, 647–658.

Hornung, R. W., Lanphear, B. P., and Dietrich, K. N. (2009). Age of greatest susceptibility to childhood lead exposure: A new statistical approach. *Environ. Health Perspect.* 117, 1309–1312.

Howard, M. O., Bowen, S. E., Garland, E. L., Perron, B. E., and Vaughn, M. G. (2011). Inhalant use and inhalant use disorders in the United States. *Addict. Sci. Clin. Pract.*, 6, 18–31.

Howard, R., Castle, D., Wessely, S., and Murray, R. (1993). A comparative study of 470 cases of early-onset and late-onset schizophrenia. *Br. J. Psychiatry*, 163, 352–357.

Howden, M. L. and Naughton, M. T. (2011). Pulmonary effects of marijuana inhalation. *Expert Rev. Respir. Med.*, 5, 87–92.

Howlett, A. C. (2005). Cannabinoid receptor signaling. *Handb. Exp. Pharmacol.*, 168, 53–79.

Hsiang, J. and Diaz, E. (2011). Lead and developmental neurotoxicity of the central nervous system. *Curr. Neurobiol.* 2, 35–42.

Hu, M.-C., Muthén, B., Schaffran, C., Griesler, P. C., and Kandel, D. B. (2008). Developmental trajectories of criteria of nicotine dependence in adolescence. *Drug Alcohol Depend.*, 98, 94–104.

Huberfeld, G., Wittner, L., Clemenceau, S., Baulac, M., Kaila, K., Miles, R., et al. (2007). Perturbed chloride homeostasis and GABAergic signaling in human temporal lobe epilepsy. *J. Neurosci.*, 27, 9866–9873.

Huestis, M. A., Boyd, S. J., Heishman, S. J., Preston, K. L., Bonnet, D., Le Fur, G., et al. (2007). Single and multiple doses of rimonabant antagonize acute effects of smoked cannabis in male cannabis users. *Psychopharmacology*, 194, 505–515.

Huestis, M. A., Gorelick, D. A., Heishman, S. J., Preston, K. L., Nelson, R. A., Moolchan, E. T., et al. (2001). Blockade of effects of smoked marijuana by the CB$_1$-selective cannabinoid receptor antagonist SR141716. *Arch. Gen. Psychiatry*, 58, 322–328.

Hughes, J. (1975). Search for the endogenous ligand of the opiate receptor. *Neurosci. Res. Prog. Bull.*, 13, 55–58.

Hughes, J. R., Gust, S. W., Skoog, K., Keenan, R. M., and Fenwick, J. W. (1991). Symptoms of tobacco withdrawal. A replication and extension. *Arch. Gen. Psychiatry*, 48, 52–59.

Hughes, J. R., Peters, E. N., and Naud, S. (2011). Effectiveness of over-the-counter nicotine replacement therapy: A qualitative review of nonrandomized trials. *Nic. Tob. Res.*, 13, 512–522.

Hughes, M. F. (2002). Arsenic toxicity and potential mechanisms of action. *Toxicol. Lett.* 133, 1–16.

Hunt, G. M. and Azrin, N. H. (1973). A community-reinforcement approach to alcoholism. *Behav. Res. Ther.*, 11, 91–104.

Ikonomidou, C., Bittigau, P., Ishimaru, M., Wozniak, D., Koch, C., Genz, K., et al. (2000). Ethanol-induced apoptotic neurodegeneration and fetal alcohol syndrome. *Science*, 287, 1056–1060.

Inada, T., Polk, K., Purser, C., Hume, A., Hoskins, B., Ho, I. K., et al. (1992). Behavioral and neurochemical effects of continuous infusion of cocaine in rats. *Neuropharmacology*, 31, 701–708.

Inturrisi, C. E. (1997). Preclinical evidence for a role of glutamatergic systems in opioid tolerance and dependence. *Semin. Neurosci.*, 9, 110–119.

Ip, E. J., Barnett, M. J., Tenerowicz, M. J., and Perry, P. J. (2011). The anabolic 500 survey: Characteristics of male users versus nonusers of anabolic-androgenic steroids for strength training. *Pharmacotherapy*, 31, 757–766.

Itzhak, Y. and Ali, S. F. (2002). Repeated administration of gamma-hydroxybutyric acid (GHB) to mice. Assessment of the sedative and rewarding effects of GHB. *Ann. N. Y. Acad. Sci.*, 965, 451–460.

Itzhak, Y. and Anderson, K. L. (2008). Ethanol-induced behavioral sensitization in adolescent and adult mice: Role of the nNOS gene. *Alcohol. Clin. Exp. Res.*, 32, 1839–1848.

Iversen, L. L. (2000). *The Science of Marijuana*. New York: Oxford University Press.

Iversen, L. L. (2003). Cannabis and the brain. *Brain*, 126, 1252–1270.

Jacobs, I. G., Roszler, M. H., Kelly, J. K., Klein, M. A., and Kling, G. A. (1989). Cocaine abuse: Neurovascular complications. *Radiology*, 170, 223–227.

Jacobs, M. J., Zigmond, M. J., Finlay, J. M., and Sved, A. F. (1995). Neurochemical studies of central noradrenergic responses to acute and chronic stress. In M. J. Friedman, D. S. Charney, and A. Y. Deutch (Eds.), *Neurobiological and Clinical Consequences of Stress: From Normal Adaptation to PTSD*, pp. 45–60. Philadelphia: Lippincott-Raven.

Jacobson, S. (1972). Neurocytology. In B. A. Curtis, S. Jacobson, and E. M. Marcus (Eds.), *An Introduction to the Neurosciences*, pp. 36–71. Philadelphia: Saunders.

Jacobus, J., Bava, S., Cohen-Zion, M., Mahmood, O., and Tapert, S. F. (2009). Functional consequences of marijuana use in adolescents. *Pharmacol. Biochem. Behav.*, 92, 559–565.

Jansen, K. L. R. (2000). A review of the non-medical use of ketamine: Use, users and consequences. *J. Psychoactive Drugs*, 32, 419–433.

Jansen, K. L. R. (2001). *Ketamine: Dreams and Realities*. Sarasota, FL: Multidisciplinary Association for Psychedelic Studies.

Jansen, K. L. R. and Darracot-Cankovic, R. (2001). The nonmedical use of ketamine, part two: A review of problem use and dependence. *J. Psychoactive Drugs*, 33, 151–158.

Jayawant, S. S. and Balkrishnan, R. (2005). The controversy surrounding OxyContin abuse: Issues and solutions. *Ther. Clin. Risk Manag.*, 1, 77–82.

Jellinek, E. M. (1960). *The Disease Concept of Alcoholism*. New Haven, CT: Hillhouse Press.

Johnson, J. W. and Kotermanski, S. E. (2006). Mechanism of action of memantine. *Curr. Opin. Pharmacol.*, 6, 61–67.

Johnson, M. W., MacLean, K. A., Reissig, C. J., Prisinzano, T. E., and Griffiths, R. R. (2011). Human psychopharmacology and dose-effects of salvinorin A, a kappa opioid agonist hallucinogen present in the plant *Salvia divinorum*. *Drug Alcohol Depend.*, 115, 150–155.

Jones-Otazo, H. A., Clarke, J. P., Diamond, M. L., Archbold, J. A., Ferguson, G., Harner, T., et al. (2005). Is house dust the missing exposure pathway for PBDEs? An analysis of the urban fate and human exposure to PBDEs. *Environ. Sci.Technol.* 39, 5121–5130.

Jones, R. T. (1990). The pharmacology of cocaine smoking in humans. *NIDA Res. Monogr.*, 99, 30–41.

Joyce, P. I., Fratta, P., Fisher, E. M., and Acevedo-Arozena, A. (2011). SOD1 and TDP-43 animal models of amyotrophic lateral sclerosis: Recent advances in understanding disease toward the development of clinical treatments. *Mamm. Genome*, 22, 420–448.

Juliano, L. M. and Griffiths, R. R. (2004). A critical review of caffeine withdrawal: Empirical validation of symptoms and signs, incidence, severity, and associated features. *Psychopharmacology*, 176, 1–29.

Jung, J. (2001). *Psychology of Alcohol and Other Drugs: A Research Perspective*. London: Sage.

Justinová, Z., Munzar, P., Panlilio, L. V., Yasar, S., Redhi, G. H., Tanda, G., et al. (2008). Blockade of THC-seeking behavior and relapse in monkeys by the cannabinoid CB$_1$-receptor antagonist rimonabant. *Neuropsychopharmacology*, 33, 2870–2877.

Justinová, Z., Yasar, S., Redhi, G. H., and Goldberg, S. R. (2011). The endogenous cannabinoid 2-arachidonoylglycerol is intravenously self-administered by squirrel monkeys. *J. Neurosci.*, 31, 7043–7048.

Kaati, G., Bygren, L. O., Pembrey, M., and Sjöström, M. (2007). Transgenerational response to nutrition, early life circumstances and longevity. *Eur. J. Hum. Genet.*, 15, 784–790.

Kadden, R. M., Litt, M. D., Kabela-Cormier, E., and Petrya, N. M. (2007). Abstinence rates following behavioral treatments for marijuana dependence. *Addict. Behav.*, 32, 1220–1236.

Kadi, F. (2008). Cellular and molecular mechanisms responsible for the action of testosterone on human skeletal muscle: A basis for illegal performance enhancement. *Br. J. Pharmacol.*, 154, 522–528.

Kahn, R. S. and Davis, K. L. (1995). New developments in dopamine and schizophrenia. In F. E. Bloom and D. J. Kupfer (Eds.), *Psychopharmacology: The Fourth Generation of Progress*, pp. 1193–1204. New York: Raven Press.

Kalant, H. (2009). What neurobiology cannot tell us about addiction. *Addiction*, 105, 780–789.

Kalivas, P. W. (2009). The glutamate hypothesis of addiction. *Nat. Rev. Neurosci.*, 10, 561–572.

Kalivas, P. W. and O'Brien, C. (2008). Drug addiction as a pathology of staged neuroplasticity. *Neuropsychopharmacology*, 33, 166–180.

Kalivas, P. W., Peters, J., and Knackstedt, L. (2006). Animal models and brain circuits in drug addiction. *Mol. Interv.*, 6, 339–344.

Kalman, D. (2002). The subjective effects of nicotine: Methodological issues, a review of experimental studies, and recommendations for future research. *Nicotine Tobacco Res.*, 4, 25–70.

Kampman, K. M. (2010). What's new in the treatment of cocaine addiction? *Curr. Psychiatry Rep.*, 12, 441–447.

Kanayama, G., Brower, K. J., Wood, R. I., Hudson, J. I., and Pope, H. G., Jr. (2009). Anabolic-androgenic steroid dependence: An emerging disorder. *Addiction*, 104, 1966–1978.

Kanayama, G., Hudson, J. I., and Pope, H. G., Jr. (2008). Long-term psychiatric and medical consequences of anabolic-androgenic steroid abuse: A looming public health concern? *Drug Alcohol Depend.*, 98, 1–12.

Kanayama, G., Brower, K. J., Wood, R. I., Hudson, J. I., and Pope, H. G., Jr. (2010a). Treatment of anabolic-androgenic steroid dependence: Emerging evidence and its implications. *Drug Alcohol Depend.*, 109, 6–13.

Kanayama, G., Hudson, J. I., and Pope, H. G. Jr. (2010b). Illicit anabolic-androgenic steroid use. *Horm. Behav.*, 58, 111–121.

Kandel, E. R. (2000). Disorders of mood: Depression, mania, and anxiety disorders. In E. R. Kandel, J. H. Schwartz, and T. M. Jessell (Eds.), *Principles of Neural Science* (4th ed.), pp. 1209–1226. New York: McGraw-Hill.

Kane, H. H. (1880). *The Hypodermic Injection of Morphia: Its History, Advantages and Dangers*. New York: Bermingham Medical Publishers.

Kaneyuki, H., Yokoo, H., Tsuda, A., Yoskida, M., Mizuki, Y., Yamada, M., et al. (1991). Psychological stress increases dopamine turnover selectively in mesoprefrontal dopamine neurons of rats: Reversal by diazepine. *Brain Res.*, 557, 154–161.

Kantak, K. M. and Hofmann, S. G. (2011). Cognitive enhancers for the treatment of neuropsychiatric disorders: Clinical and preclinical investigations. *Pharmacol. Biochem. Behav.*, 99, 113–115.

Kapelewski, C. H., Vandenbergh, J. D., and Klein, L. C. (2011). Effect of the monoamine oxidase inhibition on rewarding effects of nicotine in rodents. *Curr. Drug Abuse Rev.*, 4, 110–121.

Kaplan, G. and Newcorn, J. H. (2011). Pharmacotherapy for child and adolescent attention-deficit hyperactivity disorder. *Pediatr. Clin. North Am.*, 58, 99–120.

Karila, L., Gorelick, D., Weinstein, A., Noble, F., Benyamina, A., Coscas, S., et al. (2008). New treatments for cocaine dependence: A focused review. *Int. J. Neuropsychopharmacol.*, 11, 425–438.

Karlsen, S. N., Spigset, O., and Slørdal, L. (2007). The dark side of Ecstasy: Neuropsychiatric symptoms after exposure to 3,4-methylenedioxymethamphetamine. *Bas. Clin. Pharmacol. Toxicol.*, 102, 15 24.

Karp, I., O'Loughlin, J., Paradis, G., Hanley, J., and DiFranza, J. (2005). Smoking trajectories of adolescent novice smokers in a longitudinal study of tobacco use. *Ann. Epidemiol.*, 15, 445–452.

Kasai, H., Fukuda, M., Watanabe, S., Hayashi-Takagi, A., and Noguchi, J. (2010). Structural dynamics of dendritic spines in memory and cognition. *Trends Neurosci.*, 33, 121–129.

Katz, D. L. and Pope, H. G., Jr. (1990). Anabolic-androgenic steroid-induced mental status changes. *NIDA Res. Monogr.*, 102, 215–223.

Kaupmann, K., Cryan, J. F., Wellendorph, P., Mombereau, C., Sansig, G., Klebs, K., et al. (2003). Specific γ-hydroxybutyrate-binding sites but loss of pharmacological effects of γ-hydroxybutyrate in GABA$_{B(1)}$-deficient mice. *Eur. J. Neurosci.*, 18, 2722–2730.

Kebabian, J. W. and Calne, D. B. (1979). Multiple receptors for dopamine. *Nature*, 277, 93–96.

Kehr, J., Ichinose, F., Yoshitake, S., Goiny, M., Sievertsson, T., Nyberg, F., et al. (2011). Mephedrone, compared to MDMA (ecstasy) and amphetamine, rapidly increases both dopamine and serotonin levels in nucleus accumbens of awake rats. *Br. J. Pharmacol.*, in press.

Kelley, B. J., Duker, A. P., and Chiu, P. (2012). Dopamine agonists and pathologic behaviors. *Parkinson's Dis.*, 2012, 1–5.

Kelly, Y., Sacker, A., Gray, R., Kelly, J., Wolke, D., and Quigley, M. A. (2009). Light drinking in pregnancy, a risk for behavioural problems and cognitive deficits at 3 years of age? *Int. J. Epidemiol.*, 38, 129–140.

Keshavan, M. S., Anderson, S., and Pettegrew, J. W. (1994). Is schizophrenia due to excessive synaptic pruning in the prefrontal cortex? The Feinberg hypothesis revisited. *J. Psychiatr. Res.*, 28, 239–265.

Kieffer, B. L., Befort, K., Gaveriaux-Ruff, C., and Hirth, C. G. (1992). The "mu"-opioid receptor: Isolation of a cDNA by expression cloning and pharmacological characterization. *Proc. Natl. Acad. Sci. U.S.A.*, 89, 12048–12052.

King, M. V., Marsden, C. A., and Fone, K. C. F. (2008). A role for the 5-HT$_{1A}$, 5-HT$_4$, and 5-HT$_6$ receptors in learning and memory. *Trends Pharmacol. Sci.*, 29, 482–492.

Kinney, H. C., Richerson, G. B., Dymecki, S. M., Darnall, R. A., and Nattie, E. E. (2009). The brainstem and serotonin in the sudden infant death syndrome. *Annu. Rev. Pathol.*, 4, 517–550.

Kinon, B. J., Zhang, L., Millen, B. A., Osuntokun, O. O., Williams, J. E., Kollack-Walker, S., et al. (2011). A multicenter, inpatient, phase 2, double-blind, placebo-controlled dose-ranging study of LY2140023 monohydrate in patients with *DSM-IV* schizophrenia. *J. Clin. Psychopharmacol.*, 31, 349–355.

Kinsey, B. M., Kosten, T. R., and Orson, F. M. (2010). Anti-cocaine vaccine development. *Expert Rev. Vaccines*, 9, 1109–1114.

Kirk, J. M. and de Wit, H. (1999). Responses to oral Δ^9-tetrahydrocannabinol in frequent and infrequent marijuana users. *Pharmacol. Biochem. Behav.*, 63, 137–142.

Kirk, J. M., Doty, P., and de Wit, H. (1998). Effects of expectancies on subjective responses to oral Δ^9-tetrahydrocannabinol. *Pharmacol. Biochem. Behav.*, 59, 287–293.

Kirkham, T. C. (2009). Cannabinoids and appetite: Food craving and food pleasure. *Int. Rev. Psychiatry*, 21, 163–171.

Kish, S. J., Morito, C., and Hornykiewicz, O. (1985). Glutathione peroxidase activity in Parkinson's disease brain. *Neurosci. Lett.*, 58, 343–346.

Klein, S. B. (2000). *Biological Psychology.* Upper Saddle River, NJ: Prentice-Hall.

Klingemann, H., Sobell, M. B., and Sobell, L. C. (2009). Continuities and changes in self-change research. *Addiction*, 105, 1510–1518.

Klinkenberg, I. and Blokland, A. (2010). The validity of scopolamine as a pharmacological model for cognitive impairment: A review of animal behavioral studies. *Neurosci. Biobehav. Rev.*, 34, 1307–1350.

Knouse, L. E. and Safren, S. A. (2010). Current status of cognitive behavioral therapy for adult attention-deficit hyperactivity disorder. *Psychiatr. Clin. N. Am.*, 33, 3497–3509.

Knutson, B., Taylor, J., Kaufman, M., Peterson, R., and Glover, G. (2005). Distributed neural representation of expected value. *J. Neurosci.*, 25, 4806–4812.

Kobayashi, K. and Nagatsu, T. (2005). Molecular genetics of tyrosine 3-monooxygenase and inherited diseases. *Biochem. Biophys. Res. Commun.*, 338, 267–270.

Kobayashi, M., Iaccarino, C., Saiardi, A., Heidt, V., Bozzi, Y., Picetti, R., et al. (2004). Simultaneous absence of dopamine D$_1$ and D$_2$ receptor-mediated signaling is lethal in mice. *Proc. Natl. Acad. Sci. U.S.A.*, 101, 11465–11470.

Kobayashi, Y. and Isa, T. (2002). Sensory-motor gating and cognitive control by the brainstem cholinergic system. *Neural Netw.*, 15, 731–741.

Kohtz, A. S. and Frye, C. A. (2012). Dissociating behavioral, autonomic, and neuroendocrine effects of androgen steroids in animal models. In F. H. Kobeissy (Ed.), *Psychiatric Disorders: Methods and Protocols. Methods in Molecular Biology*, Vol. 829, pp. 397–431. New York: Humana Press.

Kolb, B. and Whishaw, I. Q. (1989). Plasticity in the neocortex: Mechanisms underlying recovery from early brain damage. *Prog. Neurobiol.*, 32, 242.

Konghom, S., Verachai, V., Srisurapanont, M., Suwanmajo, S., Ranuwattananon, A., Kimsongneun, N., et al. (2010). Treatment for inhalant dependence and abuse. *Cochrane Database Syst. Rev.*, 12, CD007537.

Koob, G. F. (2009). Dynamics of neuronal circuits in addiction: Reward, antireward, and emotional memory. *Pharmacopsychiatry*, 42 (Suppl. 1), S32–S41.

Koob, G. F. and Le Moal, M. (2005). Plasticity of reward neurocircuitry and the "dark side" of drug addiction. *Nat. Neurosci.*, 8, 1442–1444.

Koob, G. F. and Le Moal, M. (2008a). Addiction and the brain antireward system. *Annu. Rev. Psychol.*, 59, 29–53.

Koob, G. F. and Le Moal, M. (2008b). Neurobiological mechanisms for opponent motivational processes in addiction. *Phil. Trans. R. Soc. B*, 363, 3113–3123.

Koob, G. F. and Volkow, N. D. (2010). Neurocircuitry of addiction. *Neuropsychopharmacology*, 35, 217–238.

Koob, G. F. and Zorrilla, E. P. (2010). Neurobiological mechanisms of addiction: Focus on corticotropin-releasing factor. *Curr. Opin. Investig. Drugs*, 11, 63–71.

Koob, G. F., Maldonado, R., and Stinus, L. (1992). Neural substrates of opiate withdrawal. *Trends Neurosci.*, 15, 186–191.

Koukkou, M. and Lehmann, D. (1976). Human EEG spectra before and during cannabis hallucinations. *Biol. Psychiatry*, 11, 663–677.

Koutsilieri, E. and Riederer, P. (2007). Excitotoxicity and new antiglutamatergic strategies in Parkinson's disease and Alzheimer's disease. *Parkinsonism Relat. Disord.*, 13, S329–S331.

Kovelman, J. A. and Scheibel, A. B. (1984). A neurohistologic correlate of schizophrenia. *Bio. Psychiatry*, 19, 1601–1621.

Krakowski, M. and Czobor, P. (1997). Violence in psychiatric patients: The role of psychosis, frontal lobe impairment, and ward turmoil. *Compr. Psychiatry*, 38, 230–236.

Krauss, B. and Green, S. M. (2000). Sedation and analgesia for procedures in children. *N. Engl. J. Med.*, 342, 938–945.

Krishnan, V. and Nestler, E. J. (2010). Linking molecules to mood: New insight into the biology of depression. *Am. J. Psychiatr.*, 167, 1305–1320.

Krystal, J. H., Mathew, S. J., D'Souza, D. C., Garakani, A., Gunduz-Bruze, H., and Charney, D. S. (2010). Potential psychiatric applications of metabotropic glutamate receptor agonists and antagonists. *CNS Drugs*, 24, 669–693.

Kumar, S. V., Fareedullah, Md., Sudhakar, Y., Venkateswarlu, B., and Kumar, E. A. (2010). Current review on organophosphorus poisoning. *Arch. Appl. Sci. Res.* 2, 199–215.

Kuteeva, E., Hökfelt, T., Wardi, T., and Ogren, S. O. (2008). Galanin, galanin receptor subtypes and depression-like behaviour. *Cell Mol. Life Sci.*, 65, 1854–1863.

LaKind, J. S. and Naimon, D. Q. (2011). Daily intake of bisphenol a and potential sources of exposure: 2005–2006 national health and nutrition examination survey. *J. Expo. Sci. Environ. Epidemiol.* 21, 272–279.

Lane, H. Y., Lin, C. H., Huang, Y. J., Liao, C. H., Chang, Y. C., and Tsai, G. E. (2010). A randomized, double-blind, placebo-controlled comparison study of sarcosine (N-methylglycine) and D-serine add-on treatment for schizophrenia. *Int. J. Neuropsychopharmacol.*, 13, 451–460.

Lane, R. and Baldwin, D. (1997). Selective serotonin reuptake inhibitor-induced serotonin syndrome: Review. *J. Clin. Psychopharmacol.*, 17, 208–221.

Langer, R. (2003). Where a pill won't reach. *Sci. Am.*, 288, 50–57.

Langlais, P. J. and Savage, L. M. (1995). Thiamine deficiency in rats produces cognitive and memory deficits on spatial tasks correlated with tissue loss in diencephalon, cortex and white matter. *Behav. Brain Res.*, 68, 75–89.

Lanphear, B. P., Hornung, R., Khoury, J., Yolton, K., Baghurst, P., Bellinger, D. C., et al. (2005). Low-level environmental lead exposure and children's intellectual function: An international pooled analysis. *Environ. Health Perspect.*, 113, 894–899.

Laruelle, M. Abi-Dargham, A., Gile R., Kegeles, L., and Innis, R. (1999). Increased dopamine transmission in schizophrenia: Relationship to illness phases. *Biol. Psychiatry*, 46, 56–72.

Laskowski, K., Stirling, A., McKay, W. P., and Lim, H. J. (2011). A systematic review of intravenous ketamine for postoperative analgesia. *Can. J. Anaesth.*, 58, 911–923.

Lathe, R. (1996). Mice, gene targeting and behaviour: More than just genetic background. *Trends Neurosci.*, 19, 183–186.

Latsari, M., Antonopoulos, J., Dori, I., Chiotelli, M., and Dinopoulos, A. (2004). Postnatal development of the noradrenergic system in the dorsal lateral geniculate nucleus of the rat. *Dev. Brain Res.*, 149, 79–83.

Lau, A. and Tymianski, M. (2010). Glutamate receptors, neurotoxicity and neurodegeneration. *Pflugers Arch.*, 460, 525–542.

Lautraite, S. and Sargeant, D. (2009). Pyrethroids toxicology–A review of attributes and current issues. *Bayer Crop Sci. J. 62*, 195–210.

Le, A. D., Poulos, C. X., and Cappell, H. (1979). Conditioned tolerance to the hypothermic effect of ethyl alcohol. *Science*, 206, 1109–1110.

Leary, T. (1984). Personal computers/personal freedom. In S. Ditlea (Ed.), *Digital Deli*, pp. 359–361. New York: Workman.

Leatherman, S. T. and McDonald, P. W. (2006). Are the recommended taxonomies for the stages of youth smoking onset consistent with youth's perceptions of their smoking status? *Can. J. Public Health*, 97, 316–319.

LeBlanc, A. E., Lalant, H., and Gibbins, R. J. (1975). Acute tolerance to ethanol in the rat. *Psychopharmacologia*, 41, 43–46.

LeBlanc, A. E., Lalant, H., and Gibbins, R. J. (1976). Acquisition and loss of behaviorally augmented tolerance to ethanol in the rat. *Psychopharmacology*, 48, 153–158.

LeDoux, J. E. (1996). *The Emotional Brain*. New York: Simon and Schuster.

Lee, D. E., Gerasimov, M. R., Schiffer, W. K., and Gifford, A. N. (2006). Concentration-dependent conditioned place preference to inhaled toluene vapors in rats. *Drug Alcohol Depend.*, 85, 87–90.

Lee, H.-K., Choi, E. B., and Pak, C. S. (2009). The current status and future perspectives of studies of cannabinoid receptor 1 antagonists as anti-obesity agents. *Curr. Top. Med. Chem.*, 9, 482–503.

Lee, M. A. and Shlain, B. (1992). *Acid Dreams. The Complete Social History of LSD: The CIA, the Sixties, and Beyond*. New York: Grove Press.

Leeman, R. F. and Potenza, M. N. (2011). Impulse control disorders in Parkinson's disease: Clinical characteristics and implications. *Neuropsychiatry*, 1, 133–147.

Lejoyeux, M. and Weinstein, A. (2010). Compulsive buying. *Am. J. Drug Alcohol Abuse*, 36, 248–253.

Lenoir, M., Serre, F., Cantin, L., and Ahmed, S. H. (2007). Intense sweetness surpasses cocaine reward. *PLoS ONE* 2(8): e698. doi:10.1371/journal.pone.0000698

Leonard, H. L., Swedo, S. E., Rapoport, J. L., Koby, E. V., Lenane, M. C., Cheslow, D. L., et al. (1989). Treatment of obsessive-compulsive disorder with clomipramine and desipramine in children and adolescents: A double blind crossover comparison. *Arch. Gen. Psychiatry*, 46, 1088–1092.

Leoni, M. A., Vigna-Taglianti, F., Avanzi, G., Brambilla, R., and Faggiano, F. (2010). Gamma-hydroxybutyrate (GHB) for the treatment of alcohol withdrawal and prevention of relapses. *Cochrane Database Syst. Rev.*, 2, CD006266.

Leshner, A. I. (1997). Addiction is a brain disease, and it matters. *Science*, 278, 45–47.

Lessler, M. A. (1988). Lead and lead poisoning from antiquity to modern times. *Ohio J. Sci.*, 88, 78–84.

Levin, E. D., Conners, C. K., Silva, D., Hinton, S. C., Meck, W. H., March, J., et al. (1998). Transdermal nicotine effects on attention. *Psychopharmacology*, 140, 135–141.

Levin, J. D. (1989). *Alcoholism: A Bio-psychosocial Approach*. New York: Hemisphere.

Levine, R. R. (1973). *Pharmacology: Drug Actions and Reactions*. Boston: Little, Brown, and Co.

Lewis, A., Miller, J. H., and Lea, R. A. (2007). Monoamine oxidase and tobacco dependence. *NeuroToxicology*, 28, 182–195.

Lewis, D. A. and Levitt, P. (2002). Schizophrenia as a disorder of neurodevelopment. *Annu. Rev. Neurosci.*, 25, 409–432.

Lewis, S. and Lieberman, J. (2008). CATIE and CUtLASS: Can we handle the truth? *Br. J. Psychiatry*, 192, 161–163.

Leyton, M., Casey, K. F., Delaney, J. S., Kolivakis, T., and Benkelfat, C. (2005). Cocaine craving, euphoria, and self-administration: A preliminary study of the effect of catecholamine precursor depletion. *Behav. Neurosci.*, 119, 1619–1627.

Li, C.-Y., Mao, X., and Wei, L. (2008). Genes and (common) pathways underlying drug addiction. *PLoS Comput. Biol.* 4(1), e2; doi:10.1371/journal.pcbi.0040002

Li, J. Y., Popovic, N., and Brundin, P. (2005). The use of the R6 transgenic mouse models of Huntington's disease in attempts to develop novel therapeutic strategies. *NeuroRx*, 2, 447–464.

Li, N., Ragheb, K., Lawler, G., Sturgis, J., Rajwa, B., Melendez, J. A., et al. (2003). Mitochondrial complex I inhibitor rotenone induces apoptosis through enhancing mitochondrial reactive oxygen specid production. *J. Biol. Chem.*, 278, 8516–8525.

Liao, Y., Tang, J., Corlett, P. R., Wang, X., Yang, M., Chen, H., et al. (2011). Reduced dorsal prefrontal gray matter after chronic ketamine use. *Biol. Psychiatry*, 69, 42–48.

Liao, Y., Tang, J., Ma, M., Wu, Z., Yang, M., Wang, X., et al. (2010). Frontal white matter abnormalities following chronic ketamine use: A diffusion tensor imaging study. *Brain*, 133, 2115–2122.

Liberzon, I., Phan, K. L., Khan, S. and Abelson, J. L. (2003). Role of the $GABA_A$ receptor in anxiety: Evidence from animal models, molecular and clinical psychopharmacology, and brain imaging studies. *Curr. Neuropharmacol.*, 1, 267–283.

Lickey, M. E. and Gordon, B. (1991). *Medicine and Mental Illness*. New York: W. H. Freeman.

Lieberman, J. A. and Stroup, T. S. (2011). The NIMH-CATIE Schizophrenia Study: What did we learn? *Am. J. Psychiatry*, 168, 770–775.

Lieberman, J. A., Jody, D., Alvir, J. M. J., Ashtari, M., Levy, D. L., Bogerts, B., et al. (1993). Brain morphology, dopamine, and eye-tracking abnormalities in first-episode schizophrenia. *Arch. Gen. Psychiatry*, 50, 357–368.

Lieberman, J. A., Stroup, T. S., McEvoy, J. P., Swartz, M. S., Rosenheck, R. A., Perkins, D. O., et al.; Clinical Antipsychotic Trials of Intervention Effectiveness (CATIE) Investigators. (2005). Effectiveness of antipsychotic drugs in patients with chronic schizophrenia. *N. Engl. J. Med.*, 353, 1209–1223.

Lile, J. A., Kelly, T. H., and Hays, L. R. (2012). Separate and combined effects of the $GABA_B$ agonist baclofen and Δ^9-THC in humans discriminating Δ^9-THC. *Drug Alcohol Depend.*, 126, 216–223.

Lim, K. O., Wozniak, J. R., Mueller, B. A., Franc, D. T., Specker, S. M., Rodriguez, C. P., et al. (2008). Brain macrostructural and microstructural abnormalities in cocaine dependence. *Drug Alcohol Depend.*, 92, 164–172.

Lim, M. M. and Young, L. J. (2006). Neuropeptidergic regulation of affiliative behavior and social bonding in animals. *Horm. Behav.*, 50, 506–517.

Lim, S. T., Airavaara, M., and Harvey, B. K. (2010). Viral vectors for neurotrophic factor delivery: A gene therapy approach for neurodegenerative diseases of the CNS. *Pharmacol. Res.*, 61, 14–26.

Lin, M. T. and Beal, M. F. (2006). Mitochondrial dysfunction and oxidative stress in neurodegenerative diseases. *Nature*, 443, 787–795.

Lindgren, J. E., Ohlsson, A., Agurell, S., Hollister, L., and Gillespie, H. (1981). Clinical effects and plasma levels of Δ^9-tetrahydrocannabinol (Δ^9-THC) in heavy and light users of cannabis. *Psychopharmacology*, 74, 208–212.

Lingford-Hughes, A., Potokar, J., and Nutt, D. (2002). Treating anxiety complicated by substance misuse. *Adv. Psychiatric Treat.*, 8, 107–116.

Lippi, G., Franchini, M., and Banfi, G. (2011). Biochemistry and physiology of anabolic androgenic steroids doping. *Mini Rev. Med. Chem.*, 11, 362–373.

Lipska, B. K. and Weinberger, D. R. (2002). A neurodevelopmental model of schizophrenia: Neonatal disconnection of the hippocampus. *Neurotox. Res.*, 4, 469–475.

Liu, K. G. and Robichaud, A. J. (2009). $5-HT_6$ antagonists as potential treatment for cognitive dysfunction. *Drug Dev. Res.*, 70, 145–168.

Loewi, O. (1960). An autobiographical sketch. *Persp. Biol. Med.*, 4, 3–25.

Logan, B. K., Goldfogel, G., Hamilton, R., and Kuhlman, J. (2009). Five deaths resulting from abuse of dextromethorphan sold over the internet. *J. Anal. Toxicol.*, 33, 99–103.

Logan, B. K., Yeakel, J. K., Goldfogel, G., Frost, M. P., Sandstrom, G., and Wickham, D. J. (2012). Dextromethorphan abuse leading to assault, suicide, or homicide. *J. Forensic Sci.*, 57, 1388–1394.

Lopez-Garcia, J. A. (2006). Serotonergic modulation of spinal sensory circuits. *Curr. Top. Med. Chem.*, 6, 1987–1996.

Lopez-Quintero, C., de los Cobos J. P., Hasin, D. S., Okuda, M., Wang, S., Grant, B. F., et al. (2011). Probability and predictors of transition from first use to dependence on nicotine, alcohol, cannabis, and cocaine: Results of the National Epidemiologic Survey on Alcohol and Related Conditions (NESARC). *Drug Alcohol Depend.*, 115, 120–130.

Lorenzetti, V., Lubman, D. I., Whittle, S., Solowij, N., and Yücel, M. (2010). Structural MRI findings in long-term cannabis users: What do we know? *Subst. Use Misuse*, 45, 1787–1808.

Louhiala, P. (2009). The ethics of the placebo in clinical trials revisited. *J. Med. Ethics*, 35, 407–409.

Lu, L., Grimm, J. W., Hope, B. T., and Shaham, Y. (2004). Incubation of cocaine craving after withdrawal: A review of preclinical data. *Neuropharmacology*, 47 (Suppl. 1), 214–226.

Lu, X., Barr, A. M., Kinney, J. W., Sanna, P., Conti, B., Behrens, M. M., et al. (2005). A role for galanin in antidepressant actions with a focus on the dorsal raphe nucleus. *Proc. Natl. Acad. Sci. U.S.A.*, 102, 874–879.

Lubman, D. I., Yücel, M., and Lawrence, A. J. (2008). Inhalant abuse among adolescents: Neurobiological considerations. *Br. J. Pharmacol.*, 154, 316–326.

Lucas, D. R. and Newhouse, J. P. (1957). The toxic effect of sodium L-glutamate on the inner layers of the retina. *Arch. Ophthalmol.*, 58, 193–201.

Lundahl, L. H. and Johanson, C.-E. (2011). Cue-induced craving for marijuana in cannabis-dependent adults. *Exp. Clin. Psychopharmacol.*, 19, 224–230.

Luo, Z. and Geschwind, D. (2001). Microarray applications in neuroscience. *Neurobiol. Dis.*, 8, 183–193.

Lynskey, M. and Hall, W. (2000). The effects of adolescent cannabis use on educational attainment: A review. *Addiction*, 95, 1621–1630.

Lynskey, M. T., Coffey, C., Degenhardt, L., Carlin, J. B., and Patton, G. (2003). A longitudinal study of the effects of adolescent cannabis use on high school completion. *Addiction*, 98, 685–692.

MacAndrew, C. and Edgerton, R. B. (1969). *Drunken Comportment: A Social Explanation.* Chicago: Aldine.

Maccarone, M. and Wenger, T. (2005). Effects of cannabinoids on hypothalamic and reproductive function. *Handb. Exp. Pharmacol.*, 168, 555–571.

Macdonald, K. and Macdonald, T. M. (2010). The peptide that binds: A systematic review of oxytocin and its prosocial effects in humans. *Harv. Rev. Psychiatry*, 18, 1–21.

Macdonald, R. L., Gallagher, M. J., Feng, H.-J., and Kang, J. (2004). GABA$_A$ receptor epilepsy mutations. *Biochem. Pharmacol.*, 68, 1497–1506.

Machado-Vieira, R., Ibrahim, L., and Zarate, C. A., Jr. (2010). Histone deacetylases and mood disorders: Epigenetic programming in gene-environment interactions. *CNS Neurosci. Ther.*, 17, 699–704.

Machado-Vieira, R., Salvadore, G., DiazGranados, N., and Zarate Jr., C. A. (2009). Ketamine and the next generation of antidepressants with a rapid onset of action. *Pharmacol. Ther.*, 123, 143–150.

Mackie, K. (2007). From active ingredients to the discovery of the targets: The cannabinoid receptors. *Chem. Biodiversity*, 4, 1693–1706.

Maddux, J. F. and Desmond, D. P. (1981). *Careers of Opioid Users.* New York: Praeger Publishers.

Madhusoodanan, S., Parida, S., and Jimenez, C. (2010). Hyperprolactinemia associated with psychotropics—A review. *Hum. Psychopharmacol. Clin. Exp.*, 25, 281–297.

Magalhães, C. P., de Freitas, M. F. L., Nogueira, M. I., de Farias Campina, R. C., Takase, L. F., de Souza, S. L., et al. (2010). Modulatory role of serotonin on feeding behavior. *Nutr. Neurosci.*, 13, 246–255.

Mahoney, J. J. III, Kalechstein, A. D., De La Garza, R. II, and Newton, T. F. (2007). A qualitative and quantitative review of cocaine-induced craving: The phenomenon of priming. *Prog. Neuro-Psychopharmacol. Biol. Psychiatry*, 31, 593–599.

Maldonado, R. and Berrendero, F. (2010). Endogenous cannabinoid and opioid systems and their role in nicotine addiction. *Curr. Drug Targ.*, 11, 440–449.

Maletic, V. and Raison, C. L. (2009). Neurobiology of depression, fibromyalgia and neuropathic pain. *Front. Biosci.*, 14, 5291–5338.

Malinauskas, B. M., Aeby, V. G., Overton, R. F., Carpenter-Aeby, T., and Barber-Heidal, K. (2007). A survey of energy drink consumption patterns among college students. *Nutr. J.*, 6:35. doi:10.1186/1475-2891-6-35.

Malizia, A. L., Cunningham, V. J., Bell, C. J., Liddle, P. F., Jones, T., et al. (1998). Decreased brain GABA(A)-benzodiazepine receptor binding in panic disorder: Preliminary results from a quantitative PET study. *Arch. Gen. Psychiatry*, 55, 715–720.

Malvaez, M., Sanchis-Segura, C., Vo, D., Lattal, K. M., and Wood, M. A. (2010). Modulation of chromatin modification facilitates extinction of cocaine-induced conditioned place preference. *Biol. Psychiatry*, 67, 36–43.

Mancinelli. R., Vitali. M., and Ceccanti, M. (2009). Women, alcohol and the environment: An update and perspectives in neuroscience. *Funct. Neurol.*, 24, 77–81.

Mann, J. (2000). *Murder, Magic & Medicine* (2nd ed.). Oxford: Oxford University Press.

Mansour, A. and Watson, S. J. (1993). Anatomical distribution of opioid receptors in mammalians: An overview. In A. Herz (Ed.), *Opioids I, Volume 104: Handbook of Experimental Pharmacology*, pp. 79–106. New York: Springer-Verlag.

Mansour, A., Khachaturian, H., Lewis, M. E., Akil, H., and Watson, S. J. (1988). Anatomy of CNS opioid receptors. *Trends Neurosci.*, 7, 308–314.

Mao, J., Price, D. D., Phillips, L. L., Lu, J., and Mayer, D. J. (1995). Increases in protein kinase C immunoreactivity in the spinal cord of rats associated with tolerance to the analgesic effects of morphine. *Brain Res.*, 677, 257–267.

Marco, E. M., García-Gutiérrez, M. S., Bermúdez-Silva, F.-J., Moreira, F. A., Guimarães. F., Manzanares, J., et al. (2011). Endocannabinoid system and psychiatry: In search of a neurobiological basis for detrimental and potential therapeutic effects. *Front. Behav. Neurosci.*, 5:63. doi:10.3389/fnbeh.2011.00063.

Marcotte, E., Srivastava, L., and Quirion, R. (2001). DNA microarrays in neuropsychopharmacology. *Trends Pharmacol. Sci.*, 22, 426–436.

Marczinski, C. A. and Fillmore, M. T. (2009). Acute alcohol tolerance on subjective intoxication and simulated driving performance in binge drinkers. *Psychol. Addict. Behav.*, 23, 238–247.

Marlatt, G. A. and Rohsenow, D. J. (1980). Cognitive processes in alcohol use: Expectancy and the balanced placebo design. In N. K. Mello (Ed.), *Advances in Substance Abuse: Behavioral and Biological Research*, pp. 159–199. Greenwich, CT: JAI.

Marshall, B. D. L. and Werb, D. (2010). Health outcomes associated with methamphetamine use among young people: A systematic review. *Addiction*, 105, 991–1002.

Marsicano, G., Wotjak, C. T., Azad, S. C., Bisogno, T., Rammes, G., Cascio, M. G., et al. (2002). The endogenous cannabinoid system controls extinction of aversive memories. *Nature*, 418, 530–534.

Martel, P., Leo, D., Fulton, S., Bérard, M., and Trudeau, L.-E. (2011). Role of Kv1 potassium channels in regulating dopamine release and presynaptic D2 receptor function. *PLoS ONE*, 6(5): e20402. doi:10.1371/journal.pone.0020402

Martellotta, M. C., Cossu, G., Fattore, L., Gessa, G. L., and Fratta, W. (1998a). Self-administration of the cannabinoid receptor agonist WIN 55,212-2 in drug-naive mice. *Neuroscience*, 85, 327–330.

Martellotta, M. C., Cossu, G., Fattore, L., Gessa, G. L., and Fratta, W. V. (1998b). Intravenous self-administration of gamma-hydroxybutyric acid in drug-naive mice. *Eur. Neuropsychopharmacology*, 8, 293–296.

Martin, E. I., Ressler, K. J., Binder, E., and Nemeroff, C. B. (2010). The neurobiology of anxiety disorders: Brain imaging, genetics, and psychoneuroendocrinology. *Clin. Lab. Med.*, 30, 865–891.

Martin, H. L. and Teismann, P. (2009). Glutathione—A review on its role and significance in Parkinson's disease. *FASEB J.*, 23, 3263–3272.

Martin, W. R., Eades, C. G., Thompson, J. A., Huppler, R. E., and Gilbert, P. E. (1976). The effects of morphine and naloxone-like drugs in the non-dependent and morphine dependent chronic spinal dog. *J. Pharmacol. Exp. Ther.*, 197, 517–532.

Martinez-Clemente, J., Escubedo, E., Pubill, D., and Camarsa, J. (2012). Interaction of mephedrone with dopamine and serotonin targets in rats. *Eur. Neuropsychopharmacol.*, 22, 231–236.

Martínez-Raga, J., Knecht, C., and Cepeda, S. (2008). Modafinil: A useful medication for cocaine addiction? Review of the evidence from neuropharrmacological, experimental and clinical studies. *Curr. Drug Abuse Rev.*, 1, 213–221.

Martuza, R. L., Chiocca, E. A., Jenike, M. A., Giriunas, I. E., and Ballantine, H. T. (1990). Stereotactic radoiofrequency thermal cingulotomy for obsessive compulsive disorder. *J. Neuropsychiatry Clin. Neurosci.*, 2, 331–336.

Maskell, P. D., de Paoli, G., Seneviratne, C., and Pounder, D. J. (2011). Mephedrone (4-methylmethcathinone)-related deaths. *J. Anal. Toxicol.*, 35, 188–191.

Maskos, U. (2008). The cholinergic mesopontine tegmentum is a relatively neglected nicotinic master modulator of the dopaminergic system: Relevance to drugs of abuse and pathology. *Br. J. Pharmacol.*, 153, S438–S445.

Masuda, Y. (2003). Health effect of polychlorinated biphenyls and related compounds. *J. Health Sci.*, 49, 333–336.

Mathew, S. J., Price, R. B., and Charney, D. S. (2008). Recent advances in the neurobiology of anxiety disorders: Implications for novel therapeutics. *Am. J. Med. Genet. Part C (Semin. Med. Genet.)*, 148C, 89–98.

Matsuda, L. A., Lolait, S. J., Brownstein, M. J., Young, A. C., and Bonner, T. I. (1990). Structure of a cannabinoid receptor and functional expression of the cloned cDNA. *Nature*, 346, 561–564.

Matsumoto, H., Koya, G., and Takeuchi, T. (1965). Fetal Minamata disease—A neuropathological study of two cases of intrauterine intoxication by a methylmercury compound. *J. Neuropathol. Exp. Neurol.* 24, 563–574.

Maxwell, J. C. and Rutkowski, B. A. (2008). The prevalence of methamphetamine and amphetamine abuse in North America: A review of the indicators, 1992–2007. *Drug Alcohol Rev.*, 27, 229–235.

Mayberg, H. S. and Frost, J. J. (1990). Opiate receptors. In J. J. Frost and H. N. Wagner, Jr. (Eds.), *Quantitative Imaging: Neuroreceptors, Neurotransmitters, and Enzymes*, pp. 81–95. New York: Raven Press.

Mayet, A., Legleye, S., Falissard, B., and Chau, N. (2012). Cannabis use stages as predictors of subsequent initiation with other illicit drugs among French adolescents: Use of a multi-state model. *Addict. Behav.*, 37, 160–166.

Mayhew, K. P., Flay, B. R., and Mott, J. A. (2000). Stages in the development of adolescent smoking. *Drug Alcohol Depend.*, 59 (Suppl. 1), S61–S81.

Mazdai, A., Dodder, N. G., Abernathy, M. P., Hites, R. A., and Bigsby, R. M. (2003). Polybrominated diphenyl ethers in maternal and fetal blood samples. *Environ. Health Perspect.*, 111, 1249–1252.

McCann, U. D., Wong, D. F., Yokoi, F., Villemagne, V., Dannals, R. F., and Ricaurte, G. A. (1998). Reduced striatal dopamine transporter density in abstinent methamphetamine and methcathinone users: Evidence from positron emission tomography studies with [^{11}C]WIN-35,428. *J. Neurosci.*, 18, 8417–8422.

McCarley, R. W. (2007). Neurobiology of REM and NREM sleep. *Sleep Med.*, 8, 302–330.

McCarthy, D. M., Mycyk, M. B., and DesLauriers, C. A. (2008). Hospitalization for caffeine abuse is associated with abuse of other pharmaceutical agents. *Am. J. Emerg. Med.*, 26, 799–802.

McDonald, T. A. (2005). Polybrominated diphenylether levels among United States residents: Daily intake and risk of harm to the developing brain and reproductive organs. *Integr. Environ. Assess. Manag.*, 1, 343–54.

McEwen, B. S. (2008). Central effects of stress hormones in health and disease: Understanding the protective and damaging effects of stress and stress mediators. *Eur. J. Pharmacol.*, 583, 174–185.

McEwen, B. S. (2010). Stress, sex, and neural adaptation to a changing environment: Mechanisms of neuronal remodeling. *Ann. N.Y. Acad. Sci.*, 1204 (Suppl. E), 38–59.

McEwen, B. S., Chattarji, S., Diamond, D. M., Jay, T. M., Reagan, L. P., Svenningsson, P., et al. (2010). The neurobiological properties of tianeptine (Stablon): From monoamine hypothesis to glutamatergic modulation. *Mol. Psychiatr.*, 15, 237–249.

McGaugh, J. L. (2004). The amygdala modulates the consolidation of memories of emotionally arousing experiences. *Annu. Rev. Neurosi.*, 27, 1–28.

McIntyre, C. K., Power, A. E., Roozendaal, B., and McGaugh, J. L. (2003). Role of the basolateral amygdala in memory consolidation. *Ann. N.Y. Acad. Sci.*, 985, 273–293.

McLaren, J. A., Silins, E., Hutchinson, D., Mattick, R. P., and Hall, W. (2010). Assessing evidence for a causal link between cannabis and psychosis: A review of cohort studies. *Int. J. Drug Policy*, 21, 10–19.

McLaughlin, K. J., Baran, S. E., and Conrad, C. D. (2009). Chronic stress- and sex-apecific neuromorphological and functional change in limbic structures. *Mol. Neurobiol.*, 40, 166–182.

McLean, C. P., Asnaani, A., Litz, B. T., and Hofmann, S. G. (2011). Gender differences in anxiety disorders: Prevalence, course of illness, comorbidity and burden of illness. *J. Psychiatr. Res.*, 45, 1027–1035.

McNeece, C. A. and DiNitto, D. M. (1998). *Chemical Dependency.* Boston: Allyn and Bacon.

McQuown, S. C. and Wood, M. A. (2010). Epigenetic regulation in substance use disorders. *Curr. Psychiatry Rep.*, 12, 145–153.

Meerts, I. A. T. M., Letcher, R. J., Hoving, S., Marsh, G., Bergman, A., Lemmen, J. G., et al. (2001). *In vitro* estrogenicity of polybrominated diphenyl ethers, hydroxylated PBDEs, and polybrominated bisphenol A compounds. *Environ. Health Perspect.*, 109, 399–407.

Mehra, R., Moore, B. A., Crothers, K., Tetrault, J., and Fiellin, D. A. (2006). The association between marijuana smoking and lung cancer. A systematic review. *Arch. Intern. Med.*, 166, 1359–1367.

Meier, D. S., Balashov, K. E., Healy, B., Weiner, H. L., and Guttman, C. R. G. (2010). Seasonal prevalence of MS disease activity. *Neurology*, 75, 799–806.

Meier, M. H., Caspi, A., Ambler, A., Harrington, H., Houts, R., Keefe, R. S. E., et al. (2012). Persistent cannabis users show neuropsychological decline from childhood to midlife. *Proc. Natl. Acad. Sci., U.S.A.*, 109, E2657–E2664.

Melichar, J. K., Daglish, M. R. C., and Nutt, D. J. (2001). Addiction and withdrawal—Current views. *Curr. Opin. Pharmacol.*, 1, 84–90.

Melloni Jr., R. H. and Ricci, L. A. (2010). Adolescent exposure to anabolic/androgenic steroids and the neurobiology of offensive aggression: A hypothalamic neural model based on findings in pubertal Syrian hamsters. *Horm. Behav.*, 58, 177–191.

Melnik, B., Jansen, T., and Grabbe, S. (2007). Abuse of anabolic-androgenic steroids and bodybuilding acne: An underestimated health problem. *J. Dtsch. Dermatol. Ges.*, 5, 110–117.

Meltzer, H. Y. and Massey, B. W. (2011). The role of serotonin receptors in the action of atypical antipsychotic drugs. *Curr. Opin. Pharmacol.*, 11, 59–67.

Meyer, R. E. (1996). The disease called addiction: Emerging evidence in a 200-year debate. *Lancet*, 347, 162–166.

Micevych, P. and Dominguez, R. (2009). Membrane estradiol signaling in the brain. *Front. Neuroendocrinol.*, 30, 315–327.

Miczek, K. A. and de Wit, H. (2008). Challenges for translational psychopharmacology research—Some basic principles. *Psychopharmacol.*, 199, 291–301.

Middleton, F. A. and Strick, P. L. (2000). Basal ganglia and cerebellar loops: Motor and cognitive circuits. *Brain Res. Rev.*, 31, 236–250.

Mihic, S. J. and Harris, R. A. (1997). GABA and the GABA$_A$ receptor. *Alcohol Health Res. World*, 21, 127–131.

Miller, A. M. and Stella, N. (2008). CB$_2$ receptor-mediated migration of immune cells: It can go either way. *Br. J. Pharmacol.*, 153, 299–308.

Miller, S. C. (2005). Dextromethorphan psychosis, dependence and physical withdrawal. *Addict. Biol.*, 10, 325–327.

Mindus, P., Rasmussen, S. A., and Lindquist, C. (1994). Neurosurgical treatment for refractory obsessive-compulsive disorder: Implications for understanding frontal lobe function. *J. Neuropsychiatry*, 6, 467–477.

Minnes, S., Lang, A., and Singer, L. (2011). Prenatal tobacco, marijuana, stimulant, and opiate exposure: Outcomes and practical implications. *Addict. Sci. Clin. Pract.*, 6, 57–70.

Minozzi, S., Davoli, M., Bargagli, A. M., Amato, L., Vecchi, S., and Perucci, C. A. (2010). An overview of systematic reviews on cannabis and psychosis: Discussing apparently conflicting results. *Drug Alcohol Rev.*, 29, 304–317.

Minzenberg, M. J., Laird, A. R., Thelen, S., Carter, C. S., and Glahn, D. C. (2009). Meta-analysis of 41 functional neuroimaging studies of executive function in schizophrenia. *Arch. Gen. Psychiatry*, 66, 811–822.

Miotto, K., Darakjian, J., Basch, J., Murray, S., Zogg, J., and Rawson, R. (2001). Gammahydroxybutyric acid: Patterns of use, effects and withdrawal. *Am. J. Addict.*, 10, 232–241.

Mirnics, K., Middleton, F. A., Marquez, A., Lewis, D. A., and Levitt, P. (2000). Molecular characterization of schizophrenia viewed by microarray analysis of gene expression in prefrontal cortex. *Neuron*, 28, 53–67.

Mirsky, I. E., Piker, P., Rosenbaum, M., and Lederer, H. (1941). "Adaptation" of the central nervous system to various concentrations of alcohol in the blood. *Q. J. Studies Alcohol*, 2, 35–45.

Mithoefer, M. C., Wagner, M. T., Mithoefer, A. T., Jerome, L., and Doblin, R. (2010). The safety and efficacy of ±3,4-methylenedioxymethamphetamine-assisted psychotherapy in subjects with chronic, treatment-resistant posttraumatic stress disorder: The first randomized controlled pilot study. *J. Psychopharmacology*, 25, 439–452.

Miyamoto, S., Duncan, G. E., Marx, C. E., and Lieberman, J. A., (2005). Treatments for schizophrenia: A critical review of pharmacology and mechanisms of action of antipsychotic drugs. *Mol. Psychiatry*, 10, 79–104.

Molina, J. A., Sainz-Artiga, M. J., Faile, A., Jimenez-Jimenez, F. J., Villanueva, C., Orti-Pareja, M., et al. (2000). Pathologic gambling in Parkinson's disease: A behavioral manifestation of pharmacologic treatment? *Mov. Disord.*, 15, 869–872.

Monroe, R. K. and Halvorsen, S. W. (2006). Mercury abolishes neurotrophic factor–stimulated Jak-STAT signaling in nerve cells by oxidative stress. *Toxicol. Sci.* 94, 129–138.

Moore, T. H. M., Zammit, S., Lingford-Hughes, A., Barnes, T. R. E., Jones, P. B., Burke, M., et al. (2007). Cannabis use and risk of psychotic or affective mental health outcomes: A systematic review. *Lancet*, 370, 319–328.

Moreira, F. A. and Wotjak, C. T. (2009). Cannabinoids and anxiety. *Curr. Top. Behav. Neurosci.*, 2, 429–450.

Morgan, C. J. A. and Curran, H. V. (2006). Acute and chronic effects of ketamine upon human memory: A review. *Psychopharmacology*, 188, 408–424.

Morgan, C. J. A., Muetzelfeldt, L., and Curran, H. V. (2009). Consequences of chronic ketamine self-administration upon neurocognitive function and psychological well-being: A 1-year longitudinal study. *Addiction*, 105, 121–133.

Morgan, H. W. (1981). *Drugs in America. A Social History, 1800–1980*. Syracuse: Syracuse University Press.

Moszczynska, A., Fitzmaurice, P., Ang, L., Kalasinsky, K. S., Schmunk, G. A., Peretti, F. J., et al. (2004). Why is parkinsonism not a feature of human methamphetamine users? *Brain*, 127, 363–370.

Mottram, D. R. and George, A. J. (2000). Anabolic steroids. *Baillieres Best Pract. Res. Clin. Endocrinol. Metab.*, 14, 55–69.

Moussawi, K. and Kalivas, P. W. (2010). Group II metabotropic glutamate receptors (mGlu$_{2/3}$) in drug addiction. *Eur. J. Pharmacol.*, 639, 115–122.

Moyer, K. E. (1968). Kinds of aggression and their physiological basis. *Commun. Behav. Biol. A*, 2, 65–87.

Mueller, B. R. and Bale, T. L. (2008). Sex-specific programming of offspring emotional-

ity after stress early in pregnancy. *J. Neurosci.*, 28, 9055–9065.

Muglia, P. (2011). From genes to therapeutic targets for psychiatric disorders: What to expect? *Curr. Opin. Pharmacol.*, 11, 563–571.

Mulcahey, M.K, Schiller, J. R., and Hulstyn, M. J. (2010). Anabolic steroid use in adolescents: Identification of those at risk and strategies for prevention. *Phys. Sportsmed.*, 38, 105–113.

Müller, C. P. and Huston, J. P. (2006). Determining the region-specific contributions of 5-HT receptors to the psychostimulant effects of cocaine. *Trends Pharmacol. Sci.*, 27, 105–112.

Muller, C., Viry, S., Miehe, M., Andriamampandry, C., Aunis, D., and Maitre, M. (2002). Evidence for a γ-hydroxybutyrate (GHB) uptake by rat brain synaptic vesicles. *J. Neurochem.*, 80, 899–904.

Munir, V. L., Hutton, J. E., Harney, J. P., Buykx, P., Weiland, T. J., and Dent, A. W. (2008). Gamma-hydroxybutyrate: A 30 month emergency department review. *Emerg. Med. Australas.*, 20, 521–530.

Murphy, D. L. and Lesch, K.-P. (2008). Targeting the murine serotonin transporter: Insights into human neurobiology. *Nat. Rev. Neurosci.*, 9, 85–96.

Murphy, D. L., Fox, M. A., Timpano, K. R., Moya, P. R., Ren-Patterson, R., Andrews, A. M., et al. (2008). How the serotonin story is being rewritten by new gene-based discoveries principally related to *SLC6A4*, the serotonin transporter gene, which functions to influence all cellular serotonin systems. *Neuropharmacology*, 55, 932–960.

Murphy, K. G. (2005). Dissecting the role of cocaine- and amphetamine-regulated transcript (CART) in the control of appetite. *Brief. Funct. Genomics Proteomic.*, 4, 95–111.

Murray, R. M., Morrison, P. D., Henquet, C., and Di Forti, M. (2007). Cannabis, the mind and society: The harsh realities. *Nat. Rev. Neurosci.*, 8, 885–895.

Murrough, J. W. (2012). Ketamine as a novel antidepressant: From synapse to behavior. *Clin. Pharmacol. Ther.*, 91, 303–309.

Myers, G. J., Thurston, S. W., Pearson, A., Davidson, P. W., Cox, C., Shamlaye, C. F., et al. (2009). Postnatal exposure to methyl mercury from fish consumption: A review and new data from the Seychelles child development study. *NeuroToxicol.* 30, 338–349.

Nahas, G. G. (1975). *Marijuana—Deceptive Weed*. New York: Raven Press.

Naranjo, C., Shulgin, A. T., and Sargent, T. (1967). Evaluation of 3,4-methylenedioxyamphetamine (MDA) as an adjunct to psychotherapy. *Med. Pharmacol. Exp.*, 17, 359–364.

Narendran, R. and Martinez, D. (2008). Cocaine abuse and sensitization of striatal dopamine transmission: A critical review of the preclinical and clinical imaging literature. *Synapse*, 62, 851–869.

Narendran, R., Frankle, W. G., Keefe, R., Gil, R., Martinez, D., Slifstein, M., et al. (2005).

Altered prefrontal dopaminergic function in chronic recreational ketamine users. *Am. J. Psychiatry*, 162, 2352–2359.

Nascimento, J. H. M. and Medei, E. (2011). Cardiac effects of anabolic steroids: Hypertrophy, ischemia and electrical remodelling as potential triggers of sudden death. *Mini Rev. Med. Chem.*, 11, 425–429.

National Institute of Environmental Health Sciences (NIEHS). (2012). *Mercury*. National Institutes of Health, U.S. Department of Health and Human Services. Available online at: http://www.niehs.nih.gov/health/topics/agents/mercury/index.cfm, last reviewed 9/10/12.

National Institute on Alcoholism and Alcohol Abuse (NIAAA). (1983). *Fifth Special Report to the U.S. Congress on Alcohol and Health*. Washington, DC: Government Printing Office.

National Multiple Sclerosis Society. Available online at: www.nationalmssociety.org/

National Toxicology Program (NTP). (2001). *National Toxicology Program's Report of the Endocrine Disruptors Low-Dose Peer Review*. Research Triangle Park, NC: National Institute of Environmental Health Sciences, National Institutes of Health. U.S. Department of Health and Human Services.

National Toxicology Program (NTP). (2008). *NTP-CERHR Monograph on the Potential Human Reproductive and Developmental Effects of Bisphenol A*. Center for the Evaluation of Risks to Human Reproduction. NIH Publication No. 08–5994. National Toxicology Program, U.S. Department of Health and Human Services.

Neal, A. P. and Guilarte, T. R. (2012). Mechanisms of heavy metal neurotoxicity: Lead and manganese. *J. Drug Metab. Toxicol.*, S5:002.

Needleman, H. L., McFarland, C., Ness, R. B., Fienberg, S. E., and Tobin, M. J. (2002). Bone lead levels in adjudicated delinquents. A case control study. *Neurotoxicol. Teratol.*, 24, 711–717.

Nees, F., Tzschoppe, J., Patrick, C. J., Vollstädt-Klein, S., Steiner, S., Poustka, L., et al. (2012). Determinants of early alcohol use in healthy adolescents: The differential contribution of neuroimaging and psychological factors. *Neuropsychopharmacology*, 37, 986–995.

Negishi, T., Kawasaki, K., Sekiguchi, S., Ishii, Y., Kyuwa, S., Kuroda, Y., et al. (2005). Attention-deficit and hyperactive neurobehavioral characteristics induced by perinatal hypothyroidism in rats. *Behav. Brain Res.*, 159, 323–331.

Nehlig, A. (2010). Is caffeine a cognitive enhancer? *J. Alzheimers Dis.*, 20 (Suppl. 1), S85–S94.

Nelson, K. B. and Bauman, M. L. (2003). Thimerosal and autism? *Pediatrics* 111, 674–679.

Nelson, R. J. and Chiavegatto, S. (2001). Molecular basis of aggression. *Trends Neurosci.*, 24, 713–719.

Nelson, R. J. and Trainor, B. C. (2007). Neural mechanisms of aggression. *Nat. Rev. Neurosci.*, 8, 536–546.

Nemeroff, C. B. (1998). The neurobiology of depression. *Sci. Am.*, 278, 42–49.

Németh, Z., Kun, B., and Demetrovics, Z. (2010). The involvement of gamma-hydroxybutyrate in reported sexual assaults: A systematic review. *J. Psychopharmacol.*, 24, 1281–1287.

Neri, M., Bello, S., Bonsignore, A., Cantatore, S., Riezzo, I., Turillazzi, E., et al. (2011). Anabolic androgenic steroids abuse and liver toxicity. *Mini Rev. Med. Chem.*, 11, 430–437.

Nestler, E. J. (2008). Transcriptional mechanisms of addiction: Role of ΔFosB. *Phil. Trans. R. Soc. B*, 363, 3425–3255.

Nestler, E. J. and Hyman, S. E. (2010). Animal models of neuropsychiatric disorders. *Nat. Neurosci.*, 13, 1161–1169.

Nestler, E. J., Alreja, M., and Aghajanian, G. K. (1994). Molecular and cellular mechanisms of opiate action: Studies in the rat locus coeruleus. *Brain Res. Bull.*, 35, 521–528.

Neustadt, J. and Pieczenik, S. (2007). Heavy-metal toxicity-with emphasis on mercury. *Integ. Med.*, 6, 26–32.

Newell, K. A., Zavitsanou, K., and Huang, X.-F. (2007). Short and long term changes in NMDA receptor binding in mouse brain following chronic phencyclidine treatment. *J. Neural Transm.*, 114, 995–1001.

Newhouse, P. A., Potter, A., and Singh, A. (2004). Effects of nicotinic stimulation on cognitive performance. *Curr. Opin. Pharmacol.*, 4, 36–46.

Nichols, D. E. (1997). Role of serotoninergic neurons and 5-HT receptors in the action of hallucinogens. In H. G. Baumgarten and M. Göthert (Eds.), *Serotoninergic Neurons and 5-HT Receptors in the CNS*. Handbook of Experimental Pharmacology, Vol. 129, pp. 563–585. Springer-Verlag, Berlin.

Nichols, D. E. (2004). Hallucinogens. *Pharmacol. Ther.*, 101, 131–181.

Nicholson, K. L. and Balster, R. L. (2001). GHB: A new and novel drug of abuse. *Drug Alcohol Depend.*, 63, 1–22.

Nicoll, J. A., Wilkinson, D., Holmes, C., Steart, P., Markham, H., and Weller, R. O. (2003). Neuropathology of human Alzheimer disease after immunization with amyloid-beta peptide: A case report. *Nat. Med.*, 9, 448–452.

Nie, H., Rewal, M., Gill, T. M., Ron, D., and Janak, P. H. (2011). Extrasynaptic delta-containing GABA$_A$ receptors in the nucleus accumbens dorsomedial shell contribute to alcohol intake. *Proc. Natl. Acad. Sci.*, 108, 4459–4464.

Ninan, P. T. (1999). The functional anatomy, neurochemistry, and pharmacology of anxiety. *J. Clin. Psychiatry*, 60 (Suppl. 22), 12–17.

Nishino, S. (2007). Clinical and neurobiological aspects of narcolepsy. *Sleep Med.*, 8, 373–399.

Noble, F. and Roques, B. P. (2007). Protection of endogenous enkephalin catabolism as natural approach to novel analgesic and antidepressant drugs. *Expert Opin. Ther. Targets*, 11, 145–159.

Nonnemaker, J. M., Crankshaw, E. C., Shive, D. R., Hussin, A. H., and Farrelly, M. C. (2011). Inhalant use initiation among U.S. adolescents: Evidence from the National Survey of Parents and Youth using discrete-time survival analysis. *Addict. Behav.*, 36, 878–881.

Noppers, I., Niesters, M., Aarts, L., Smith, T., Sarton, E., and Dahan, A. (2010). Ketamine for the treatment of chronic noncancer pain. *Expert Opin. Pharmacother.*, 11, 2417–2429.

Nordquist, N. and Oreland, L. (2010). Serotonin, genetic variability, behaviour, and psychiatric disorders—A review. *Ups. J. Med. Sci.*, 115, 2–10.

Nordstrom, A.-L. and Farde, L. (1998). Plasma prolactin and central D2 receptor occupancy in antipsychotic drug-treated patients. *J. Clin. Psychopharmacol.*, 18, 305–310.

Novak, M. J. and Tabrizi, S. J. (2011). Huntington's disease: Clinical presentation and treatment. *Int. Rev. Neurobiol.*, 98, 297–323.

Nowinski, J. (1996). Facilitating 12-step recovery from substance abuse and addiction. In F. Rotgers, D. S. Keller, and J. Morgenstern (Eds.), *Treating Substance Abuse: Theory and Technique*, pp. 37–67. New York: Guilford Press.

Nutt, D. J., Bell, C. J., and Malizia, A. L. (1998). Brain mechanisms of social anxiety disorder. *J. Clin. Psychiatry*, 59 (Suppl. 17), 4–9.

O'Brien, C. P. (1993). Opioid addiction. In A. Herz (Ed.), *Opioids II*, Volume 104: *Handbook of Experimental Pharmacology*, pp. 803–824. New York: Springer-Verlag.

O'Brien, C. P. (1994). Treatment of alcoholism as a chronic disorder. In B. Jansson, H. Jönvall, U. Rydberg, L. Terenius, and B. L. Vallee (Eds.), *Toward a Molecular Basis of Alcohol Use and Abuse*, pp. 349–359. Switzerland: Birkhäuser, Verlag, Basel.

O'Brien, C. P. and Gardner, E. L. (2005). Critical assessment of how to study addiction and its treatment: Human and non-human animal models. *Pharmacol. Ther.*, 108, 18–58.

O'Brien, M. S. and Anthony, J. C. (2005). Risk of becoming cocaine dependent: Epidemiological estimates for the United States, 2000–2001. *Neuropsychopharmacology*, 30, 1006–1018.

O'Connor, R. M., Finger, B. C., Flor, P. J., and Cryan, J. F. (2010). Metabotropic glutamate receptor 7: At the interface of cognition and emotion. *Eur. J. Pharmacol.*, 639, 123–131.

Oberlander, J. G. and Henderson, L. P. (2012). The *Sturm und Drang* of anabolic steroid use: Angst, anxiety, and aggression. *Trends Neurosci.*, 35, 382–392.

Obeso, J. A., Rodriguez-Oroz, M. C., Goetz, C. G., Marin, C., Kordower, J. H., Rodriguez, M., et al. (2010). Missing pieces in the Parkinson's disease puzzle. *Nat. Med.*, 16, 653–661.

Oddy, W. H. and O'Sullivan, T. A. (2010). Energy drinks for children and adolescents: Erring on the side of caution may reduce long term health risks. *BMJ*, 339, b5268.

OECD. (1978). *Road research: New research on the role of alcohol and drugs in road accidents*. A report prepared by an Organization for Economic Co-operation and Development (OECD) Road Research Group.

Office of Applied Studies. (2009). *Results from the 2008 National Survey on Drug Use and Health: National findings* (HHS Publication No. SMA 09-4434, NSDUH Series H-36). Rockville, MD: Substance Abuse and Mental Health Services Administration.

Ögren, S. O., Eriksson, T. M., Elvander-Tottie, E., D'Addario, C., Ekström, J. C., Svenningsson, P., et al. (2008). The role of 5-HT$_{1A}$ receptors in learning and memory. *Behav. Brain Res.*, 195, 54–77.

Oldendorf, W. H. (1975). Permeability of the blood–brain barrier. In D. B. Tower (Ed.), *The Nervous System*, Vol. 1, pp. 279–289. New York: Raven Press.

Olney, J. W. (1969). Brain lesions, obesity, and other disturbances in mice treated with monosodium glutamate. *Science*, 164, 719–721.

Olney, J. W., Ho, O. L., and Rhee, V. (1971). Cytotoxic effects of acidic and sulphur containing amino acids on the infant mouse central nervous system. *Exp. Brain Res.*, 14, 61–76.

Olszewski, D. (2009). Sexual assaults facilitated by drugs or alcohol. *Drugs: Educ. Prev. Policy*, 16, 39–52.

Ontario College of Family Physicians (OCFP). (2012). *2012 Systematic Review of Pesticide Health Effects*. Toronto: Ontario College of Family Physicians.

Ordway, G. A., Klimek, V., and Mann, J. J. (2002). Neurocircuitry of mood disorders. In K. L. Davis, D. Charney, J. T. Coyle, and C. Nemeroff (Eds.), *Neuropsychopharmacology: The Fifth Generation of Progress*, pp. 1051–1064. New York: Lippincot Williams & Wilkins.

Orogozo, J. M., Gilman, S., Dartigues, J. F., Laurent, B., Puel, M., Kirby, L. C., et al. (2003). Subacute meningoencephalitis in a subset of patients with AD after Aβ42 immunization. *Neurology*, 61, 46–54.

Osborn, E., Grey, C., and Reznikoff, M. (1986). Psychosocial adjustment, modality choice, and outcome in naltrexone versus methadone treatment. *Am. J. Drug Alcohol Abuse*, 12, 383–388.

Ostrea, E. M., Morales, V., Ngoumgna, E., Prescilla, R., Tan, E., Hernandez, E., et al. (2002). Prevalence of fetal exposure to environmental toxins as determined by meconium analysis. *Neurotoxicol.*, 23, 329–339.

Overton, D. A. (1984). State dependent learning and drug discriminations. In L. L. Iversen, S. D. Iversen, and S. H. Snyder (Eds.), *Handbook of Psychopharmacology*, Vol. 18, pp. 59–112. New York: Plenum Press.

Pagonis, T. A., Angelopoulos, N. V., Koukoulis, G. N., and Hadjichristodoulou, C. S. (2006a). Psychiatric side effects induced by supraphysiological doses of combinations of anabolic steroids correlate to the severity of abuse. *Eur. Psychiatry*, 21, 551–562.

Pagonis, T. A., Angelopoulos, N. V., Koukoulis, G. N., Hadjichristodoulou, C. S., and Toli, P. N. (2006b). Psychiatric and hostility factors related to use of anabolic steroids in monozygotic twins. *Eur. Psychiatry*, 21, 563–569.

Palanza, P., Gioiosa, L., vom Saalb, F. S., and Parmigiani, S. (2008). Effects of developmental exposure to bisphenol A on brain and behavior in mice. *Environ. Res.*, 108, 150–157.

Panagis, G., Vlachou, S., and Nomikos, G. G. (2008). Behavioral pharmacology of cannabinoids with a focus on preclinical models for studying reinforcing and dependence-producing properties. *Curr. Drug Abuse Rev.*, 1, 350–374.

Panlilio, L. V., Justinova, Z., and Goldberg, S. R. (2010). Animal models of cannabinoid reward. *Br. J. Pharmacol.*, 160, 499–510.

Paolini, M. and De Biasi, M. (2011). Mechanistic insights into nicotine withdrawal. *Biochem. Pharmacol.*, 82, 996–1007.

Parent, A-S., Naveau, E., Gerard, A., Bourguignon, J-P., and Westbrook, G. L. (2011). Early developmental actions of endocrine disruptors on the hypothalamus, hippocampus and cerebral cortex. *J. Toxicol. Environ. Health B Crit. Rev.*, 14, 328–345.

Parker, D. A., Harford, T. C., and Rosenstock, I. M. (1994). Alcohol, other drugs, and sexual risk-taking among young adults. *J. Subst. Abuse*, 6, 87–93.

Parrott, A. C. (2006). Nicotine psychobiology: How chronic-dose prospective studies can illuminate some of the theoretical issues from acute-dose research. *Psychopharmacology*, 184, 567–576.

Patandin, S., Lanting, C. I., Mulder, P. G., Boersma, E. R., Sauer, P. J., and Weisglas-Kuperus, N. (1999). Effects of environmental exposure to polychlorinated biphenyls and dioxins on cognitive abilities in Dutch children at 42 months of age. *J. Pediatr.*, 134, 33–41.

Patil, S. T., Zhang, L., Martenyi, F., Lowe, S. L., Jackson, K. A., Andreev, B. V., et al. (2007). Activation of mGlu2/3 receptors as a new approach to treat schizophrenia: A randomized Phase 2 clinical trial. *Nat. Med.*, 13, 1102–1107.

Paulson, P. E., Camp, D. M., and Robinson, T. E. (1991). Time course of transient behavioral depression and persistent behavioral sensitization in relation to regional brain monoamine concentrations during amphetamine withdrawal in rats. *Psychopharmacology*, 103, 480–492.

Paulzen, M. and Gründer, G. (2008). Toxic psychosis after intake of the hallucinogen salvinorin A. *J. Clin. Psychiatry*, 69, 1501–1502.

Peciña, S. and Smith, K. S. (2010). Hedonic and motivational roles of opioids in food reward: Implications for overeating disorders. *Pharmacol. Biochem. Behav.*, 97, 34–46.

Pedraza, C., García, F. B., and Navarro, J. F. (2009). Neurotoxic effects induced by gammahydroxybutyric acid (GHB) in

male rats. *Int. J. Neuropsychopharmacol.*, 12, 1165–1177.

Penberthy, J. K., Ait-Daoud, N., Vaughan, M., and Fanning, T. (2010). Review of treatments for cocaine dependence. *Curr. Drug Abuse Rev.*, 3, 49–62.

Pentney, A. R. (2001). An exploration of the history and controversies surrounding MDMA and MDA. *J. Psychoactive Drugs*, 33, 213–221.

Perkins, K. A., Donny, E., and Cagguila, A. R. (1999). Sex differences in nicotine effects and self-administration: Review of human and animal evidence. *Nicotine Tobacco Res.*, 1, 301–305.

Perkins, K. A., Gerlach, D., Broge, M., Grobe, J. E., Sanders, M., Fonte, C., et al. (2001). Dissociation of nicotine tolerance from tobacco dependence in humans. *J. Pharmacol. Exp. Ther.*, 296, 849–856.

Perl, D. P. (2010). Neuropathology of Alzheimer's disease. *Mount Sinai Journal of Medicine*, 77, 32–42.

Perron, B. E., Glass, J. E., Ahmedani, B. K., Vaughn, M. G., Roberts, D. E., and Wu, L.-T. (2011). The prevalence and clinical significance of inhalant withdrawal symptoms among a national sample. *Subst. Abuse Rehabil.*, 2011(2), 69–76.

Perron, B. E., Howard, M. O., Maitra, S., and Vaughn, M. G. (2009a). Prevalence, timing, and predictors of transition from inhalant use to inhalant use disorders. *Drug Alcohol Depend.*, 100, 277–284.

Perron, B. E., Howard, M. O., Vaughn, M. G., and Jarman, C. N. (2009b). Inhalant withdrawal as a clinically significant feature of inhalant dependence disorder. *Med. Hypotheses*, 73, 935–937.

Perry, D. C., Dávila-Garcia, M. I., Stockmeier, C. A., and Kellar, K. J. (1999). Increased nicotinic receptors in brains from smokers: Membrane binding and autoradiography studies. *J. Pharmacol. Exp. Ther.*, 289, 1545–1552.

Pert, C. B. and Snyder, S. H. (1973). Properties of opiate receptor binding in rat brain. *Proc. Natl. Acad. Sci. U.S.A.*, 70, 2243–2247.

Pertwee, R. G. (2008). The diverse CB_1 and CB_2 receptor pharmacology of three plant cannabinoids: Δ^9-tetrahydrocannabinol, cannabidiol and Δ^9-tetrahydrocannabivarin. *Br. J. Pharmacol.*, 153, 199–215.

Peters Jr., R. J., Williams, M., Ross, M. W., Atkinson, J., and McCurdy, S. A. (2008). The use of fry (embalming fluid and PCP-laced cigarettes or marijuana sticks) among crack cocaine smokers. *J. Drug Educ.*, 38, 285–295.

Peters, A., Palay, S. L., and Webster, H. deF. (1991). *The Fine Structure of the Nervous System: Neurons and Their Supporting Cells* (3rd ed.). New York: Oxford University Press.

Petersen, R. C. (1977). Cocaine: An overview. *NIDA Res. Monogr.*, 13, 17–34.

Petrlova, J., Kalai, T., Maezawa, I., Altman, R., Harishchandra, G., Hong, H-S., et al. (2012). The influence of spin-labeled fluorene compounds on the assembly and toxicity of the Aβ peptide. *PLOS One*, 7, 1–10.

Pezawas, L., Meyer-Lindenberg, A., Drabant, E. M., Verchinski, B. A., Munoz, K. E., Kolachana, B. S., et al. (2005). 5-HTTLPR polymorphism impacts human cingulate-amygdala interactions: A genetic susceptibility mechanism for depression. *Nat. Neurosci.*, 8, 828–834.

Pfefferbaum, A. and Sullivan, E. V. (2004). Diffusion MR imaging in psychiatry and ageing. In J. Gillard, A. Waldman, and P. Barker (Eds.), *Physiological Magnetic Resonance in Clinical Neuroscience*, Chapter 33. Cambridge: Cambridge University Press.

Phatak, D. R. and Walterscheid, J. (2012). Huffing air conditioner fluid: A cool way to die? *Am. J. Forensic Med. Pathol.*, 33, 64–67.

Philippu, A. (1984). Use of push–pull cannulae to determine the release of endogenous neurotransmitters in distinct brain areas of anaesthetized and freely moving animals. In C. A. Marsden (Ed.), *Measurement of Neurotransmitter Release In Vivo*, pp. 3–38. New York: Wiley.

Picciotto, M. R., Addy, N. A., Mineur, Y. S., and Brunzell, D. H. (2008). It is not "either/or": Activation and desensitization of nicotinic acetylcholine receptors both contribute to behaviors related to nicotine addiction and mood. *Prog. Neurobiol.*, 84, 329–342.

Pidoplichko, V. I., DeBiasi, M., Williams, J. T., and Dani, J. A. (1997). Nicotine activates and desensitizes midbrain dopamine neurons. *Nature*, 390, 401–404.

Piomelli, D. (2003). The molecular logic of endocannabinoid signaling. *Nat. Rev. Neurosci.*, 4, 873–884.

Piscitelli, F. and Di Marzo, V. (2012). "Redundancy" of endocannabinoid inactivation: New challenges and opportunities for pain control. *ACS Chem. Neurosci.*, 3, 356–363.

Plante, D. T. and Winkelman, J. W. (2008). Sleep disturbance in bipolar disorder: Therapeutic implications. *Am. J. Psychiatr.*, 165, 830–843.

Platt, D. M., Rowlett, J. K., and Spealman, R. D. (2001). Discriminative stimulus effects of intravenous heroin and its metabolites in rhesus monkeys: Opioid and dopaminergic mechanisms. *J. Pharmacol. Exp. Ther.*, 299, 760–767.

Platt, D. M., Rowlett, J. K., and Spealman, R. D. (2002). Behavioral effects of cocaine and dopaminergic strategies for preclinical medication development. *Psychopharmacology*, 163, 265–282.

Ploner, M., Gross, J., Timmermann, L., and Schnitzler, A. (2002). Cortical representation of first and second pain sensation in humans. *Proc. Natl. Acad. Sci. U.S.A.*, 99, 12444–12448.

Poewe, W., Antonini, A., Zijlmans, J. C. M., Burkhard, P. R., Vingerhoets, F. (2010). Levodopa in the treatment of Parkinson's disease: An old drug still going strong. *Clin. Interv. Aging*, 5, 229–238.

Poimenova, A., Markaki, E., Rahiotis, C., and Kitraki, E. (2010). Corticosterone-regulated actions in the rat brain are affected by perinatal exposure to low dose of bisphenol A. *Neuroscience*, 167, 741–749.

Polosa, R. and Benowitz, N. L. (2011). Treatment of nicotine addiction: Present therapeutic options and pipeline developments. *Trends Pharmacol. Sci.*, 32, 281–289.

Pons, R., Ford, B., Chiriboga, C. A., Clayton, P. T., Hinton, V., Hyland, K., et al. (2004). Aromatic L-amino acid decarboxylase deficiency. Clinical features, treatment, and prognosis. *Neurology*, 62, 1058–1065.

Porrino, L. J., Daunais, J. B., Rogers, G. A., Hampson, R. E., and Deadwyler, S. A. (2005). Facilitation of task performance and removal of the effects of sleep deprivation by an ampakine (CX717) in nonhuman primates. *PLoS Biol.*, 3(9), e299.

Posner, M. I. and Raichle, M. E. (1994). *Images of Mind*. New York: Freeman.

Post, R. M. and Contel, N. R. (1983). Human and animal studies of cocaine: Implications for the development of behavioral pathology. In I. Creese (Ed.), *Stimulants: Neurochemical, Behavioral, and Clinical Perspectives*, pp. 169–203. New York: Raven Press.

Post, R. M. and Weiss, S. R. B. (1988). Psychomotor stimulant vs. local anesthetic effects of cocaine: Role of behavioral sensitization and kindling. *NIDA Res. Monogr.*, 88, 217–238.

Post, R. M., Ballenger, J. C., Uhde, T., and Bunney, W. (1984). Efficacy of carbamazapine in manic-depressive illness: Implications for underlying mechanisms. In R. M. Post and J. C. Ballenger (Eds.), *Neurobiology of Mood Disorders*, pp. 777–816. Baltimore, MD: Williams and Wilkins.

Prager, E. M. and Johnson, L. R. (2009). Stress at the synapse: Signal transduction mechanisms of adrenal steroids at neuronal membranes. *Sci. Signal.*, 2, re5. doi: 10.1126/scisignal.286re5

Prescot, A. P., Locatelli, A. E., Renshaw, P. F., and Yurgelun-Todd, D. A. (2011). Neurochemical alterations in adolescent chronic marijuana smokers: A proton MRS study. *NeuroImage*, 57, 69–75.

Prescott, F., Organe, G., and Rowbotham, S. (1946). Tubocurarine chloride as an adjunct to anesthesia. *Lancet*, 248, 80–84.

Prommer, E. E. (2012). Ketamine for pain: An update of uses in palliative care. *J. Palliat. Med.*, 15, 474–483.

Psychiatric GWAS Consortium Coordinating Committee, Cichon, S., Craddock, N., Daly, M., Faraone, S. V., Gejman, P. V., et al. (2009). Genomewide association studies: History, rationale, and prospects for psychiatric disorders. *Am. J. Psychiatry*, 166, 540–556.

Punch, L. J., Self, D. W., Nestler, E. J., and Taylor, J. R. (1997). Opposite modulation of opiate withdrawal behaviors on microinfusion of a protein kinase A inhibitor versus activator into the locus coeruleus or periaqueductal gray. *J. Neurosci.*, 17, 8520–8527.

Purves, D., Augustine, G. J., Fitzpatrick, D., Hall, W. C., LaMantia, A.-S., and White, L. E. (2012). *Neuroscience* (5th ed.). Sunderland, MA: Sinauer.

Purves, W. K., Oriens, G. H., Sadava, D., and Heller, H. C. (1998). *Life: The Science of Biology*. (5th ed.). New York: W. H. Freeman.

Qiao, D., Seidler, F. J., Tate, C. A., Cousins, M. M., and Slotkin, T. A. (2003). Fetal chlorpyrifos exposure: Adverse effects on brain cell development and cholinergic biomarkers emerge postnatally and continue into adolescence and adulthood. *Environ. Health Perspect.*, 111, 536–544

Quednow, B. B., Geyer, M. A., and Halberstadt, A. L. (2010). Serotonin and schizophrenia. In C. P. Müller and B. L. Jacobs (Eds.), *Handbook of the Behavioral Neurobiology of Serotonin*, pp. 585–620. London: Academic Press.

Qui, C., Kivipelto, M., and von Strauss, E. (2009). Epidemiology of Alzheimer's disease: Occurrence, determinants, and strategies toward intervention. *Dialogues Clin. Neurosci.*, 11, 111–128.

Quinones-Jenab, V. and Jenab, S. (2010). Progesterone attenuates cocaine-induced responses. *Horm. Behav.*, 58, 22–32.

Quirion, R. and Pilapil, C. (1991). Distribution of multiple opioid receptors in the human brain. In F. A. O. Mendelsohn (Ed.), *Receptors in the Human Nervous System*, pp. 103–121. New York: Academic Press.

Radek, R. J., Kohlhaas, K. L, Rueter, L. E., and Mohler, E. G. (2010). Treating the cognitive deficits of schizophrenia with α4β2 neuronal nicotinic receptor agonists. *Curr. Pharm. Des.*, 16, 309–322.

Rago, L., Kiivet, R. A., Harro, J., and Pold, M. (1988). Behavioral differences in an elevated plus maze: Correlation between anxiety and decreased number of GABA and benzodiazepine receptors in mouse cerebral cortex. *Naunyn-Schmiedeberg's Arch. Pharmacol.*, 337, 3675–3678.

Rainville, P. (2002). Brain mechanisms of pain affect and pain modulation. *Curr. Opinion Neurobiol.*, 12, 195–204.

Rainville, P., Duncan, G. H., Price, D. D., Carrier, B., and Bushnell, M. C. (1997). Pain affect encoded in human anterior cingulate but not somatosensory cortex. *Science*, 277, 968–971.

Rajput, A. H., Gibb, W. R. G., Zhong, X. H., Shannak, K. S., Kish, S., Chang, L. G., et al. (1994). Dopa-responsive dystonia: Pathological and biochemical observations in a case. *Ann. Neurol.*, 35, 396–402.

Ramaekers, J. G., Berghaus, G., van Laar, M., and Drummer, O. H. (2004). Dose related risk of motor vehicle crashes after cannabis use. *Drug Alcohol Depend.*, 73, 109–119.

Ramesh, B. B., Parande, A. K., and Ahmed, B. C. (2007). Electrical and electronic waste: A global environmental problem. *Waste Manag. Res.*, 25, 307–318.

Ramos, B. P. and Arnsten, A. F. T. (2007). Adrenergic pharmacology and cognition: Focus on the prefrontal cortex. *Pharmacol. Ther.*, 113, 523–536.

Ramshaw, E. (2010). Under pressure, insurer agrees to fully cover vaccine. Available online at: http://www.texastribune.org/texas-health-resources/health-reform-and-texas/under-pressure-insurer-agrees-to-cover-vaccine, accessed 12/6/12.

Randall, C. L., Ekblad, U., and Anton, R. F. (1990). Perspectives on the pathophysiology of fetal alcohol syndrome. *Alcohol. Clin. Exp. Res.*, 14, 807–812.

Ranganathan, M. and D'Souza, D. C. (2006). The acute effects of cannabinoids on memory in humans: A review. *Psychopharmacology*, 188, 425–444.

Rapoport, J. L. (1989). The biology of obsessions and compulsions. *Sci. Am.*, 260, 83–89.

Rapport, R. (2005). *Nerve Endings. The Discovery of the Synapse*. New York: Norton.

Rattray, M. and Bendotti, C. (2006). Does excitotoxic cell death of motor neurons in ALS arise from glutamate transporter and glutamate receptor abnormalities? *Exp. Neurol.*, 201, 15–23.

Ray, N. J., Myasaki, J. M., Zurowski, M., Ko, J. H., Cho, S. S., Pellachia, G., et al. (2012). Extrastriatal dopaminergic abnormalities of DA homeostasis in Parkinson's patients with medication-induced pathological gambling: A [^{11}C] FLB-457 and PET study. *Neurobiol. Dis.*, 48, 519–525.

Read, D. J., Li, Y., Chao, M. V., Cavanagh, J. B., and Glynn, P. (2009). Neuropathy target esterase is required for adult vertebrate axon maintenance. *J. Neurosci.*, 29, 11594–11600.

Reissig, C. J., Carter, L. P., Johnson, M. W., Mintzer, M. Z., Klinedinst, M. A., and Griffiths, R. R. (2012). High doses of dextromethorphan, an NMDA antagonist, produce effects similar to classic hallucinogens. *Psychopharmacology*, 223, 1–15.

Reissig, C. J., Strain, E. C., and Griffiths, R. R. (2009). Caffeinated energy drinks—A growing problem. *Drug Alcohol Depend.*, 99, 1–10.

Ren, H., Du, C., Yuan, Z., Park, K., Volkow, N. D., and Pan, Y. (2012). Cocaine-induced cortical microischemia in the rodent brain: Clinical implications. *Mol. Psychiatry*, 17, 1017–1025.

Research Advisory Committee on Gulf War Veterans' Illnesses. (2008). *Gulf War Illness and the Health of Gulf War Veterans: Scientific Findings and Recommendations*. Washington, DC: U.S. Government Printing Office.

Rewal, M., Donahue, R., Gill, T. M., Nie, H., Ron, D., and Janak, P. H. (2012). Alpha4 subunit-containing GABA$_A$ receptors in the accumbens shell contribute to the reinforcing effects of alcohol. *Addict. Biol.*, 17, 309–321.

Ribeiro, J. A. and Sebastião, A. M. (2010). Caffeine and adenosine. *J. Alzheimers Dis.*, 20, S3–S15.

Ribeiro, M-J., Vidailhet, M., Loc'h, C., Dupel, C., Nguyen, J. P., Ponchant, M., et al. (2002). Dopaminergic function and dopamine transporter binding assessed with positron emission tomography in Parkinson disease. *Arch. Neurol.*, 59, 580–586.

Richards, J. G., Schoch, P., and Jenck, F. (1991). Benzodiazepine receptors and their ligands. In R. J. Rogers and S. J. Cooper (Eds.), *5-HT$_{1A}$ Agonists, 5-HT$_3$ Antagonists and Benzodiazepines: Their Comparative Behavioural Pharmacology*, pp. 1–30. New York: Wiley.

Riedel, G. and Davies, S. N. (2005). Cannabinoid function in learning, memory and plasticity. *Handb. Exp. Pharmacol.*, 168, 445–477.

Riegel, A. C. and French, E. D. (2002). Abused inhalants and central reward pathways. *Ann. N. Y. Acad. Sci.*, 965, 281–291.

Riegel, A. C., Zapata, A., Shippenberg, T. S., and French, E. D. (2007). The abused inhalant toluene increases dopamine release in the nucleus accumbens by directly stimulating ventral tegmental area neurons. *Neuropsychopharmacology*, 32, 1558–1569.

Ripley, T. L. and Stephens, D. N. (2011). Critical thoughts on current rodent models for evaluating potential treatments of alcohol addiction and withdrawal. *Br. J. Pharmacol.*, 164, 1335–1356.

Risinger, R. C., Salmeron B. J., Ross, T. J., Amen, S. L., Sanfilipo, M., Hoffmann, R. G., et al. (2005). Neural correlates of high and craving during cocaine self-administration using BOLD fMRI. *NeuroImage*, 26, 1097–1108.

Ritchie, J. M. (1975). Central nervous system stimulants. In L. Goodman and A. Gilman (Eds.), *The Pharmacological Basis of Therapeutics* (5th ed.), pp. 367–378. New York: Macmillan.

Ritter, L., Solomon, K. R., Forget, J., Stemeroff, M., and O'Leary, C. (1995). Persistent organic pollutants. Assessment Report on: DDT-Aldrin-Dieldrin-Endrin-Chlordane, Heptachlor-Hexachlorobenzene, Mirex-Toxaphene, Polychlorinated Biphenyls, Dioxins and Furans. United Nations Environment Programme. Available online at: http://www.chem.unep.ch/pops/ritter/en/ritteren.pdf, accessed 10/1/12.

Ritter, R., Scheringer, M., MacLeod, M., Moeckel, C., Jones, K. C., and Hungerbühler K. (2011). Intrinsic human elimination half-lives of polychlorinated biphenyls derived from the temporal evolution of cross-sectional biomonitoring data from the United Kingdom. *Environ. Health Perspect.*, 119, 225–231.

Ritz, M. C., Cone, E. J., and Kuhar, M. J. (1990). Cocaine inhibition of ligand binding at dopamine, norepinephrine and serotonin transporters: A structure-activity study. *Life Sci.*, 46, 635–645.

Roberts, A. J., McDonald, J. S., Heyser, C. J., Kieffer, B. L., Matthes, H. W. D., Koob, G. F., et al. (2000). μ-Opioid receptor knockout mice do not self-administer alcohol. *J. Pharmacol. Exp. Ther.*, 293, 1002–1008.

Roberts, D. C. S., Morgan, D., and Liu, Y. (2007). How to make a rat addicted to cocaine. *Prog. Neuro-Psychopharmacol. Biol. Psychiatry*, 31, 1614–1624.

Robertson, S. D., Matthies, H. J. G., and Galli, A. (2009). A closer look at amphetamine-induced reverse transport and trafficking of the dopamine and norepinephrine transporters. *Mol. Neurobiol.*, 39, 73–80.

Robinson, D. M. and Keating, G. M. (2007). Sodium oxybate: A review of its use in the management of narcolepsy. *CNS Drugs*, 21, 337–354.

Robinson, T. E. and Berridge, K. C. (1993). The neural basis of drug craving: An incentive-sensitization theory of addiction. *Brain Res. Rev.*, 18, 247–291.

Robinson, T. E. and Berridge, K. C. (2000). The psychology and neurobiology of addiction: An incentive-sensitization view. *Addiction*, 95 (Suppl. 2), S91–S117.

Robinson, T. E. and Berridge, K. C. (2001). Incentive-sensitization and addiction. *Addiction*, 96, 103–114.

Robinson, T. E. and Berridge, K. C. (2008). The incentive sensitization theory of addiction: Some current issues. *Phil. Trans. R. Soc. B*, 363, 3137–3146.

Robison, A. J. and Nestler, E. J. (2011). Transcriptional and epigenetic mechanisms in addiction. *Nat. Rev. Neurosci.*, 12, 623–637.

Robledo, P., Berrendero, F., Ozaita, A., and Maldonado, R. (2008). Advances in the field of cannabinoid-opioid cross-talk. *Addict. Biol.*, 13, 213–224.

Rocha, B. A., Fumagalli, F., Gainetdinov, R. R., Jones, S. R., Ator, R., Giros, B., et al. (1998). Cocaine self-administration in dopamine-transporter knockout mice. *Nat. Neurosci.*, 1, 132–137.

Rodriguez, V. M., Jimenez-Capdeville, and M. E., Giordano, M. (2003). The effects of arsenic exposure on the nervous system. *Toxicol. Lett.*, 145, 1–18.

Roehrs, T. and Roth, T. (2008). Caffeine: Sleep and daytime sleepiness. *Sleep Med. Rev.*, 12, 153–162.

Rog, D. J. (2010). Cannabis-based medicines in multiple sclerosis—A review of clinical studies. *Immunobiology*, 215, 658–672.

Rogaeva, E., Meng, Y., Lee, J. H., Gu1, Y., Kawarai, T., Zou, F., et al. (2007). The neuronal sortilin-related receptor SORL1 is genetically associated with Alzheimer disease. *Nat. Genet.*, 39, 168–177.

Rogers, P. J. and Dernoncourt, C. (1998). Regular caffeine consumption: A balance of adverse and beneficial effects for mood and psychomotor performance. *Pharmacol. Biochem. Behav.*, 59, 1039–1045.

Rohman, L. (2009). The relationship between anabolic androgenic steroids and muscle dysmorphia: A review. *Eat. Disord.*, 17, 187–199.

Roine, R., Gentry, T., Hernandez-Munoz, R., Baraona, E., and Lieber, C. (1990). Aspirin increases blood alcohol concentrations in humans after ingestion of ethanol. *JAMA*, 264, 2406–2408.

Romach, M. K., Glue, P., Kampman, K., Kaplan, H. L., Somer, G. R., Poole, S., et al. (1999). Attenuation of the euphoric effects of cocaine by the dopamine D_1/D_5 antagonist ecopipam (SCH 39166). *Arch. Gen. Psychiatry*, 56, 1101–1106.

Romanelli, F. and Smith, K. M. (2009). Dextromethorphan abuse: Clinical effects and management. *Pharmacy Today*, 15, 48–55.

Rorick-Kehn, L. M., Johnson, B. G., Knitowski, K. M., Salhoff, C. R., Witkin, J. M., Perry, K. W., et al. (2007). In vivo pharmacological characterization of the structurally novel, potent, selective mGlu2/3 receptor agonist LY404039 in animal models of psychiatric disorders. *Psychopharmacology*, 193, 212–136.

Rose, J. E. (2006). Nicotine and nonnicotine factors in cigarette addiction. *Psychopharmacology*, 184, 274–285.

Rose, J. W., Houtchens, M., and Lynch, S. G. (2000). Multiple sclerosis. Available online at: http://library.med.utah.edu/kw/ms/mml/ms_worldmap.html, accessed 12/29/12.

Rosenbaum, M. (2002). Ecstasy: America's new "reefer madness." *J. Psychoactive Drugs*, 34, 137–142.

Rosenberg, N. L., Grigsby, J., Dreisbach, J., Busenbark, D., and Grigsby, P. (2002). Neuropsychologic impairment and MRI abnormalities associated with chronic solvent abuse. *Clin. Toxicol.*, 40, 21–34.

Roser, P., Vollenweider, F. X., and Kawohl, W. (2010). Potential antipsychotic properties of central cannabinoid (CB_1) receptor antagonists. *World J. Biol. Psychiatry*, 11, 208–219.

Rossato, M., Pagano, C., and Vettor, R. (2008). The cannabinoid system and male reproductive functions. *J. Neuroendocrinol.*, 20 (Suppl. 1), 90–93.

Rotgers, F. (1996). Behavioral theory of substance abuse treatment: Bringing science to bear on practice. In F. Rotgers, D. S. Keller, and J. Morgenstern (Eds.), *Treating Substance Abuse: Theory and Technique*, pp. 174–201. New York: Guilford Press.

Rothman, K. J. and Michels, K. B. (1994). The continuing unethical use of placebo controls. *N. Engl. J. Med.*, 331, 394–398.

Rottlaender, D., Motloch, L. J., Reda, S., Larbig, R., and Hoppe, U. C. (2012). Cardiac arrest due to long QT syndrome associated with excessive consumption of energy drinks. *Int. J. Cardiol.*, 158, e51–e52.

Roy, A. (2012). How the FDA stifles new cures, Part I: The rising cost of clinical trials. *Forbes*. Available online at http://www.forbes.com/sites/aroy/2012/04/24/how-the-fda-stifles-new-cures-part-i-the-rising-cost-of-clinical-trials/, accessed 12/17/12.

Roy, T. S., Andrews, J. E., Seidler, F. J., and Slotkin, T. A. (1998). Chlorpyrifos elicits mitotic abnormalities and apoptosis in neuroepithelium of cultured rat embryos. *Teratology*, 58, 62–68.

Roze, E., Meijer, L., Bakker, A., Van Braeckel, K. N. J. A., Sauer, P. J. J., and Bos, A. F. (2009). Prenatal exposure to organohalogens, including brominated flame retardants, influences motor, cognitive, and behavioral performance at school age. *Environ. Health Perspect.* 117, 1953–1958.

Rucklidge, J. J. (2010). Gender differences in attention-deficit/hyperactivity disorder. *Psychiatr. Clin. N. Am.*, 33, 357–373.

Rudan, I. (2010). New technologies provide insights into genetic basis of psychiatric disorders and explain their co-morbidity. *Psychiatr. Danub.*, 22, 190–192.

Rudgley, R. (1999). *The Encyclopaedia of Psychoactive Substances*. New York: St. Martin's Press.

Rudy, J. W. (2008). *The Neurobiology of Learning and Memory*. Sunderland, MA: Sinauer.

Ruiz de Azua, I., Gautam, D., Guettier, J.-M., and Wess, J. (2011). Novel insights into the function of β-cell M₃ muscarinic acetylcholine receptors: Therapeutic implications. *Trends Endocrinol. Metab.*, 22, 74–80.

Russo, E. B. (2007). History of cannabis and its preparations in saga, science, and sobriquet. *Chem. Biodiversity*, 4, 1614–1648.

Rusted, J. M., Caulfield, D., King, L., and Goode, A. (2000). Moving out of the laboratory: Does nicotine improve everyday attention? *Behav. Pharmacol.*, 11, 621–629.

Ryan, B. C., Hotchkiss, A. K., Crofton, K. M., Gray, L. E., Jr. (2010). In utero and lactational exposure to bisphenol A, in contrast to ethinyl estradiol, does not alter sexually dimorphic behavior, puberty, fertility, and anatomy of female LE rats. *Toxicol. Sci.*, 114, 133–148.

Sable, H. and Schantz, S. (2006). Executive function following developmental exposure to polychlorinated biphenyls (PCBs): What animal models have told us. In E. D. Levin and J. J. Buccafusco (Eds.), *Animal Models of Cognitive Impairment (Frontiers in Neuroscience)*, pp. 147–167. New York: CRC Press.

Sacktor, T. C. (2008). PKMzeta, LTP maintenance, and the dynamic molecular biology of memory storage. *Prog. Brain Res.*, 169, 27–40.

Sagar, D. R., Gaw, A. G., Okine, B. N., Woodhams, S. G., Wong, A., Kendall, D. A., et al. (2009). Dynamic regulation of the endocannabinoid system: Implications for analgesia. *Mol. Pain*, 5:59 doi:10.1186/1744-8069-5-59

Sale, S. M. (2010). Neonatal apnoea. *Best Pract. Res. Clin. Anaesthesiol.*, 24, 323–336.

Sanchez, E. S., Bigbee, J. W., Fobbs, W., Robinson, S. E., and Sato-Bigbee, C. (2008). Opioid addiction and pregnancy: Perinatal exposure to buprenorphine affects myelination in the developing brain. *Glia*, 56, 1017–1027.

Sanders, S. K. and Shekhar, A. (1995). Anxiolytic effects of chlordiazepoxide blocked by injection of GABA_A and benzodiazepine receptor antagonists in the region of the anterior basolateral amygdala of rats. *Biol. Psychiatry*, 37, 473–476.

Sanders, T., Liu, Y., Buchner, V., Tchounwou, P. B. (2009). Neurotoxic effects and biomarkers of lead exposure: A review. *Rev. Environ. Health*, 24, 15–45.

Sansone, R. A. and Sansone, L. A. (2011). Agomelatine: A novel antidepressant. *Innov. Clin. Neurosci.*, 8, 10–14.

Santamarta, M. T., Ulibarri, I., and Pineda, J. (2005). Inhibition of neuronal nitric oxide synthase attenuates the development of morphine tolerance in rats. *Synapse*, 57, 38–46.

Santarelli, L., Saxe, M., Gross, C., Surget, A., Battaglia, F., Dulawa, S., et al. (2003). Requirement of hippocampal neurogenesis for the behavioral effects of antidepressants. *Science*, 301, 805–809.

Sarkar, P. (2003). The dirty dozen. A toxics link report on persistent organic pollutants and the challenges for India. San Diego, CA: India Together. Available online at: http://www.indiatogether.org/2003/dec/env-pops.htm, accessed 12/6/12.

Sartar, M. and Parikh, V. (2005). Choline transporters, cholinergic transmission and cognition. *Nat. Rev. Neurosci.*, 6, 48–56.

Satel, S. (2006). Is caffeine addictive? A review of the literature. *Am. J. Drug Alcohol Abuse*, 32, 493–502.

Sathyanarayana, S., Braun, J. M., Yolton, K., Liddy, S., and Lanphear, B. P. (2011). Case Report: High prenatal bisphenol A exposure and infant neonatal neurobehavior. *Environ. Health Perspect.*, 119, 1170–1175.

Sato, S. M., Schulz, K. M., Sisk, C. L., and Wood, R.I (2008). Adolescents and androgens, receptors and rewards. *Horm. Behav.*, 647–658.

Savageau, J. A., Mowery, P. D., and DiFranza, J. R. (2009). Symptoms of diminished autonomy over cigarettes with non-daily use. *Int. J. Environ. Res. Public Health*, 6, 25–35.

Saxena, S. and Rauch, S. L. (2000). Functional neuroimaging and the neuroanatomy of obsessive-compulsive disorder. *Psychiatr. Clin. North Am.*, 23, 563–586.

Saxena, S., Brody, A. L., Ho, M. L., Alborzian, S., Maidment, K. M., Zohrabi, N., et al. (2002). Differential cerebral metabolic changes with paroxetine treatment of obsessive-compulsive disorder vs. major depression. *Arch. Gen. Psychiatry*, 59, 250–261.

Schaler, J. A. (2000). *Addiction Is a Choice*. Peru, IL: Open Court.

Schantz, S. L., Gasior, D. M., Polverejan, E., McCaffrey, R. J., Sweeney, A. M., Humphrey, H. E. B., et al. (2001). Impairments of memory and learning in older adults exposed to polychlorinated biphenyls via consumption of Great Lakes fish. *Environ. Health Perspect.*, 109, 605–611.

Schantz, S. L., Widholm, J. J., and Rice, D. C. (2003). Effects of PCB exposure on neuropsychological function in children. *Environ. Health Perspect.*, 111, 357–376.

Schecter, A., Papke, O., Harris, T. R., Tung, K. C., Musumba, A., Olson, J., et al. (2006). Polybrominated diphenyl ether (PBDE) levels in expanded market basket survey of U.S. food and estimated PBDE dietary intake by age and sex. *Environ. Health Perspect.*, 114, 1515–1520.

Schico, R. and Storr, M. (2011). Alternative targets within the endocannabinoid system for future treatment of gastrointestinal diseases. *Can. J. Gastroenterol.*, 25, 377–383.

Schifano, F., Albanese, A., Fergus, S., Stair, J. L., DeLuca, P., Corazza, O., et al. (2011). Mephedrone (4-methylmethcathinone; 'meow meow'): Chemical, pharmacological and clinical issues. *Psychopharmacology*, 214, 593–602.

Schildkraut, J. J. (1965). The catecholamine hypothesis of affective disorders: A review of supporting evidence. *Am. J. Psychiatry*, 122, 509–522.

Schmidt, H. D., Anderson, S. M., and Pierce, R. C. (2006). Stimulation of D₁-like or D₂ dopamine receptors in the shell, but not the core, of the nucleus accumbens reinstates cocaine-seeking behaviour in the rat. *Eur. J. Neurosci.*, 23, 219–228.

Schneider, M. L., Moore, C. F., Kraemer, G. W., Roberts, A. D., and DeJesus, O. T. (2002). The impact of prenatal stress, fetal alcohol exposure, or both on development: Perspectives from a primate model. *Psychoneuroendocrinology*, 27, 285–298.

Scholey, A. B. and Kennedy, D. O. (2004). Cognitive and physiological effects of an "energy drink": An evaluation of the whole drink and of glucose, caffeine and herbal flavouring fractions. *Psychopharmacology*, 176, 320–330.

Schosser, A. and Kasper, S. (2009). The role of pharmacogenetics in the treatment of depression and anxiety disorders. *Int. Clin. Psychopharmacol.*, 24, 277–288.

Schottenfeld, R., Carroll, K., and Rounsaville, B. (1993). Cormorbid psychiatric disorders and cocaine abuse. *NIDA Res. Monogr.*, 135, 31–47.

Schuckit, M. A. (1994). Low level of response to alcohol as predictor of alcoholism. *Am. J. Psychol.*, 151, 184–189.

Schuckit, M. A. (2000). Genetics of the risk for alcoholism. *Am. J. Addict.*, 9, 103–112.

Schulteis, G., Markou, A., Cole, M., and Koob, G. F. (1995). Decreased brain reward produced by ethanol withdrawal. *Proc. Natl. Acad. Sci. U.S.A.*, 92, 5880–5884.

Schultz, W. (2007). Behavioral dopamine signals. *Trends Neurosci.*, 30, 203–210.

Schultz, W. (2010). Dopamine signals for reward value and risk: Basic and recent data. *Behav. Brain Funct.*, 6, 24. Available online at: http://www.behavioralandbrainfunctions.com/content/6/1/24

Schwartz, R. H. (2005). Adolescent abuse of dextromethorphan. *Clin. Pediatr.*, 44, 565–568.

Schwartz, R. H., Milteer, R., and LeBeau, M. A. (2000). Drug-facilitated sexual assault ("date rape"). *South. Med. J.*, 93, 558–561.

Schweinsburg, A. D., Brown, S. A., and Tapert, S. F. (2008). The influence of marijuana use on neurocognitive functioning in adolescents. *Curr. Drug Abuse Rev.*, 1, 99–111.

Scotter, E. L., Abood, M. E., and Glass, M. (2010). The endocannabinoid system as a target for the treatment of neurodegenerative diseases. *Br. J. Pharmacol.*, 160, 480–498.

Scragg, R., Wellman, R. J., Laugesen, M., and DiFranza, J. R. (2008). Diminished autonomy over tobacco can appear with the first cigarettes. *Addict. Behav.*, 33, 689–698.

Seal, R. P., Akil, O., Yi, E., Weber, C. M., Grant, L., Yoo, J., et al. (2008). Sensorineural deafness and seizures in mice lacking vesicular glutamate transporter 3. *Neuron*, 57, 263–275.

Seedat, S., Kesler, S., Niehaus, D. J., and Stein, D. J. (2002). Pathological gambling behaviour: Emergence secondary to treatment of Parkinson's disease with dopaminergic agents. *Depress. Anxiety*, 11, 185–186.

Seely, K. A., Prather, P. L., James, L. P., and Moran, J. H. (2011). Marijuana-based drugs: Innovative therapeutics or designer drugs of abuse? *Mol. Interv.*, 11, 36–50.

Seeman, P. (2002). Atypical antipsychotics: Mechanism of action. *Can. J. Psychiatry*, 47, 27–38.

Segawa, M. (2010). Hereditary progressive dystonia with marked diurnal fluctuation. *Brain Dev.*, 33, 195–201.

Segawa, M., Hosaka, A., Miyagawa, F., Nomura, Y., and Imai, H. (1976). Hereditary progressive dystonia with marked diurnal fluctuation. *Adv. Neurol.*, 14, 215–233.

Seibyl, J., Russel, D., Jennings, D., and Marek, K. (2012) Neuroimaging over the course of Parkinson's disease: From early detection of the at-risk patient to improving pharmacotherapy of later-stage disease. *Semin. Nucl. Med.*, 42, 406–414.

Seifert, S. M., Schaechter, J. L., Hershorin, E. R., and Lipshultz, S. E. (2011). Health effects of energy drinks on children, adolescents, and young adults. *Pediatrics*, 127, 511–528.

Seiwa, C., Nakahara, J., Komiyama, T., Katsu, Y., Iguchi, T., and Asou, H. (2004). Bisphenol-A exerts thyroid-hormone like effects on mouse oligodendrocyte precursor cells. *Neuroendocrinol.*, 80, 21–30.

Self, D. W. and Nestler, E. J. (1995). Molecular mechanisms of drug reinforcement and addiction. *Annu. Rev. Neurosci.*, 18, 463–495.

Semenova, S., Stolerman, I. P., and Markou, A. (2007). Chronic nicotine administration improves attention while nicotine withdrawal induces performance deficits in the 5-choice serial reaction time task in rats. *Pharmacol. Biochem. Behav.*, 87, 360–368.

Senard, J.-M. and Rouet, P. (2006). Dopamine beta-hydroxylase deficiency. *Orphanet J. Rare Dis.*, 1, 7. doi:10.1186/1750-1172-1-7

Sener, S., Yamanel, L., and Comert, B. (2005). A fatal case of severe serotonin syndrome accompanied by moclobemide and paroxetine overdose. *Indian J. Crit. Care Med.*, 9, 173–175.

Sepinwall, J. and Cook, L. (1980). Mechanism of action of the benzodiazepines: Behavioral aspect. *Fed. Proc.*, 39, 3024–3031.

Sewell, R. A. and Petrakis, I. L. (2011). Does gamma-hydroxybutyrate (GHB) have a role in the treatment of alcoholism? *Alcohol Alcohol.*, 46, 1–2.

Sewell, R. A., Ranganathan, M., and D'Souza, D. C. (2009). Cannabinoids and psychosis. *Int. Rev. Psychiatry*, 21, 152–162.

Shad, M. U., Suris, A. M., North, C. S. (2011). Novel combination strategy to optimize treatment for PTSD. *Hum. Psychopharmacol.*, 26, 4–11.

Shafer, T. J., Meyer, D. A., and Crofton, K. M. (2005). Developmental neurotoxicity of pyrethroid insecticides: Critical review and future research needs. *Environ. Health Perspect.*, 113, 123–136.

Shah, R. S. and Cole, J. W. (2010). Smoking and stroke: The more you smoke the more you stroke. *Expert Rev. Cardiovasc. Ther.*, 8, 917–932.

Shannon, J. R., Flattem, N. L., Jordan, J., Jacob, G., Black, B. K., Biaggioni, I., et al. (2000). Orthostatic intolerance and tachycardia associated with norepinephrine transporter deficiency. *N. Engl. J. Med.*, 342, 541–549.

Shapiro, R. E. (2008). Caffeine and headaches. *Curr. Pain Headache Rep.*, 12, 311–315.

Sharma, S. K., Klee, W. A., and Nirenberg, M. (1975). Dual regulation of adenylate cyclase accounts for narcotic dependence and tolerance. *Proc. Natl. Acad. Sci. U.S.A.*, 72, 3092–3096.

Shaw, G. K., Waller, S., Majumdar, S. K., Alberts, J. L., Latham, C. J., and Dunn, G. (1994). Tiapride in the prevention of relapse in recently detoxified alcoholics. *Br. J. Psychiatry*, 165, 515–523.

Sheldon, A. L. and Robinson, M. B. (2007). The role of glutamate transporters in neurodegenerative diseases and potential opportunities for intervention. *Neurochem. Int.*, 51, 333–355.

Shenk, J. W. (2005). *Lincoln's Melancholy: How Depression Challenged a President and Fueled His Greatness*. Boston: Houghton Mifflin Harcourt.

Sherwood, N. (1993). Effects of nicotine on human psychomotor performance. *Hum. Psychopharmacol.*, 8, 155–184.

Shiffman, S. and Paty, J. (2006). Smoking patterns and dependence: Contrasting chippers and heavy smokers. *J. Abn. Psychol.*, 115, 509–523.

Shippenberg, T. S. (1993). Motivational effects of opioids. In A. Herz (Ed.), *Opioids II*, Volume 104: *Handbook of Behavioral Neurology*, pp. 633–650. New York: Springer-Verlag.

Shippenberg, T. S., Herz, A., Spangel, R., and Bals-Kubik, R. (1991). Neural substrates mediating the motivational effects of opioids. *Biol. Psychiatry*, 2, 33–35.

Shirayama, Y., Chen, A. C.-H., Nakagawa, S., Russell, D. S., and Duman, R. S. (2002). Brain derived neurotrophic factor produces antidepressant effects in behavioral models of depression. *J. Neurosci.*, 22, 3251–3261.

Shulgin, A. T. and Nichols, D. E. (1978). Characterization of three new psychotomimetics. In R. C. Stillman and R. E. Willette (Eds.), *The Psychopharmacology of Hallucinogens*, pp. 74–83. New York: Pergamon.

Shults, C. W., Oakes, D., Kieburtz, K., Beal, M. F., Haas, R., Plumb, S., et al. (2002). Effects of coenzyme Q10 in early Parkinson disease: Evidence of slowing of the functional decline. *Arch. Neurol.*, 59, 1541–1550.

Siebert, D. J. (1994). *Salvia divinorum* and Salvinorin A new pharmacologic findings. *J. Ethnopharmacol.*, 43, 53–56.

Siegel, R. K. (1989). *Intoxication: Life in Pursuit of Artificial Paradise*. New York: Pocket Books.

Siegel, S. (1978). A pavlovian conditioning analysis of morphine tolerance. In N. A. Krasnegor (Ed.), *Behavioral Tolerance: Research and Treatment Implications*. NIDA Research Monograph 18, U.S. Department of Health, Education and Welfare, Public Health Service, National Institute of Drug Abuse, Washington, D.C.

Siegel, S. (1985). Drug-anticipatory responses in animals. In L. White, B. Tursky, and B. Schwartz (Eds.), *Placebo: Theory, Research and Mechanisms*, pp. 288–305. New York: Guilford Press.

Siegel, S. and Ramos, B. M. C. (2002). Applying laboratory research: Drug anticipation and the treatment of drug addiction. *Exp. Clin. Psychopharmacol.*, 10, 162–183.

Siegelbaum, S. A. and Koester, J. (1991). Ion channels. In E. R. Kandel, J. H. Schwartz, and T. M. Jessell (Eds.), *Principles of Neural Science* (3rd ed.), pp. 66–79. New York: Elsevier.

Siegert, R. J. and Abernethy, D. A. (2005). Depression in multiple sclerosis: A review. *J. Neurol. Neurosurg. Psychiatry*, 76, 469–475.

Sieghart, W. and Sperk, G. (2002). Subunit composition, distribution and function of $GABA_A$ receptor subtypes. *Curr. Top. Med. Chem.*, 2, 795–816.

Siever, L. J. (2008). Neurobiology of aggression and violence. *Am. J. Psychiatry*, 165, 429–442.

Simon, E. J. (1991). Opioid receptors and endogenous opioid peptides. *Med. Res. Rev.*, 11, 357–374.

Simonyi, A., Schachtman, T. R., and Christoffersen, G. R. J. (2010). Metabotropic glutamate receptor subtype 5 antagonism in learning and memory. *Eur. J. Pharmacol.*, 639, 17–25.

Simpson Jr., S., Blizzard, L., Otahal, P., Vander Mei, I., and Taylor, B. (2011). Latitude is significantly associated with the prevalence of multiple sclerosis: A meta-analysis. *J. Neurol. Neurosurg. Psychiatry*, 82, 1132–1141.

Simpson, D. D., Joe, G. W., and Bracy, S. A. (1982). Six-year follow-up of opioid addicts after administration to treatment. *Arch. Gen. Psychiatry*, 39, 1318–1326.

Singh, A., Kandimala, G., Dewey, R. B., and O'Suilleabhain, P. (2007). Risk factors for pathologic gambling and other compulsions among Parkinson's disease patients taking dopamine agonists. *J. Clin. Neurosci.*, 14, 1178–1181.

Sinha-Hikim, I., Artaza, J., Woodhouse, L., Gonzalez-Cadavid, N., Singh, A. B., Lee, M. I., et al. (2002). Testosterone-induced increase in muscle size in healthy young men is associated with muscle fiber hypertrophy. *Am. J. Physiol. Endocrinol. Metab.*, 283, E154–E164.

Sinha, R. (2008). Chronic stress, drug use, and vulnerability to addiction. *Ann. N.Y. Acad. Sci.*, 1141, 105–130.

Sircar, R., Basak, A., Sircar, D., and Wu, L.-C. (2010). Effects of γ-hydroxybutyric acid on spatial learning and memory in adolescent and adult female rats. *Pharmacol. Biochem. Behav.*, 96, 187–193.

Sircar, R., Wu, L.-C., Reddy, K., Sircar, D., and Basak, A. K. (2011). GHB-induced cognitive deficits during adolescence and the role of NMDA receptor. *Curr. Neuropharmacol.*, 9, 240–243.

Sjodin, A., Wong, L. Y., Jones, R. S., Park, A., Zhang, Y., Hodge, C., et al. (2008). Serum concentrations of polybrominated diphenyl ethers (PBDEs) and polybrominated biphenyl (PBB) in the United States population: 2003–2004. *Environ. Sci. Technol.*, 42, 1377–1384.

Sjöqvist, F., Garle, M., and Rane, A. (2008). Use of doping agents, particularly anabolic steroids, in sports and society. *Lancet*, 371, 1872–1882.

Slotkin, T. A. and Seidler, F. J. (2012) Developmental neurotoxicity of organophosphates targets cell cycle and apoptosis, revealed by transcriptional profiles in vivo and in vitro. *Neurotoxicol. Teratol.*, 34, 232–241.

Small, A. C., Kampman, K. M., Plebani, J., De Jesus Quinn, M., Peoples, L., and Lynch, K. G. (2009). Tolerance and sensitization to the effects of cocaine use in humans: A retrospective study of long-term cocaine users in Philadelphia. *Subst. Use Misuse*, 44, 1888–1898.

Smit, H. J., Cotton, J. R., Hughes, S. C., and Rogers, P. J. (2004). Mood and cognitive performance effects of "energy" drink constituents: Caffeine, glucose and carbonation. *Nutr. Neurosci.*, 7, 127–139.

Smith, A. P., Christopher, G., and Sutherland, D. (2006). Effects of caffeine in overnight-withdrawn consumers and non-consumers. *Nutr. Neurosci.*, 9, 63–71.

Smith, K. A., Fairburn, C. G., and Cowen, P. J. (1997). Relapse of depression after rapid depletion of tryptophan. *Lancet*, 349, 915–919.

Smith, S. M., Brown, H. O., Toman, E. P., and Goodman, L. S. (1947). The lack of cerebral effects of *d*-tubocurarine. *Anesthesiology*, 8, 1–14.

Smith, S. S. and Fiore, M. C., (1999). The epidemiology of tobacco use, dependence, and cessation in the United States. *Primary Care*, 26, 433–461.

Snyder, S. H. (1977). Opiate receptors and internal opiates. *Sci. Am.*, 236, 44–56.

Snyder, S. H. (1996). *Drugs and the Brain*, p. 80. New York: Scientific American Library.

Sobell, L. C., Ellingstad, T. P., and Sobell, M. B. (2000). Natural recovery from alcohol and drug problems: Methodological review of the research with suggestions for future directions. *Addiction*, 95, 749–764.

Soderlund, D. M., Clark, J. M., Sheets, L. P., Mullin, L. S., Piccirillo, V. J., Sargent, D., et al. (2002). Mechanisms of pyrethroid neurotoxicity: Implications for cumulative risk assessment. *Toxicology*, 171, 3–59.

Sofer, S., Tal, A., and Shahak, E. (1989). Carbamate and organophosphate poisoning in early childhood. *Ped. Emerg. Care*, 5, 222–225.

Sofuoglu, M. and Sewell, R. A. (2009). Norepinephrine and stimulant addiction. *Addict. Biol.*, 14, 119–129.

Sofuoglu, M., Sugarman, D. E., and Carroll, K. M. (2010). Cognitive function as an emerging treatment target for marijuana addiction. *Exp. Clin. Psychopharmacol.*, 18, 109–119.

Solinas, M., Goldberg, S. R., and Piomelli, D. (2008). The endocannabinoid system in brain reward processes. *Br. J. Pharmacol.*, 154, 369–383.

Solinas, M., Panlilio, L. V., Justinova, Z., Yasar, S., and Goldberg, S. R. (2006). Using drug-discrimination techniques to study the abuse-related effects of psychoactive drugs in rats. *Nat. Protoc.*, 1, 1194–1206.

Solomon, R. L. (1977). An opponent-process theory of acquired motivation: The affective dynamics of addiction. In J. D. Maser and M. E. P. Seligman (Eds.), *Psychopathology: Experimental Models*, pp. 66–103. San Francisco: W. H. Freeman.

Solomon, R. L. and Corbit, J. D. (1974). An opponent-process theory of motivation. I. Temporal dynamics of affect. *Psych. Rev.*, 81, 119–145.

Song, R., Yang, R.-F., Wu, N., Su, R.-B., Li, J., Peng, X.-Q., et al. (2012). YQA14: A novel dopamine D_3 receptor antagonist that inhibits cocaine self-administration in rats and mice but not in D_3 receptor-knockout mice. *Addict. Biol.*, 17, 259–273.

Sora, I., Wichems, C., Takahashi, N., Li, X.-F., Zeng, Z., Revay, R., et al. (1998). Cocaine reward models: Conditioned place preference can be established in dopamine- and in serotonin-transporter knockout mice. *Proc. Natl. Acad. Sci. U.S.A.*, 95, 7699–7704.

Sorensen, L., Ekstrand, M., Silva, J. P., Lindqvist, E., Xu, B., Rustin, P., et al. (2001). Late-onset corticohippocampal neurodepletion attributable to catastrophic failure of oxidative phosphorylation in MILON mice. *J. Neurosci.*, 21, 8082–8090.

Sperk, G., Furtinger, S., Schwarzer, C., and Pirker, S. (2004). GABA and its receptors in epilepsy. In D. K. Binder and H. E. Scharfman (Eds.), *Advances in Experimental Medicine and Biology*, Vol. 548, *Recent Advances in Epilepsy Research*, pp. 92–103. New York: Kluwer/Plenum.

Sprow, G. M. and Thiele, T. E. (2012). The neurobiology of binge-like ethanol drinking: Evidence from rodent models. *Physiol. Behav.*, 106, 325–331.

St Clair, D., Blackwood, D., Muir, W., Carothers, A., Walker, M., Spowart, G., et al. (1990). Association within a family of a balanced autosomal translocation with major mental illness. *Lancet*, 336, 13–16.

Stein, D. J. (2000). Advances in the neurobiology of obsessive-compulsive disorder. *Psychiatr. Clin. North Am.*, 23, 545–561.

Steketee, J. D. (2005). Cortical mechanisms of cocaine sensitization. *Crit. Rev. Neurobiol.*, 17, 69–86.

Sterling, P. and Eyer, J. (1988). Allostasis: A new paradigm to explain arousal pathology. In S. Fisher and J. Reason (Eds.), *Handbook of Life Stress, Cognition and Health*, pp. 629–649. New York: Wiley.

Stewart, J. (2000). Pathways to relapse: The neurobiology of drug- and stress-induced relapse to drug-taking. *J. Psychiatry Neurosci.*, 25, 125–136.

Stewart, J. (2008). Psychological and neural mechanisms of relapse. *Phil. Trans. R. Soc. B*, 363, 3147–3158.

Stewart, P. W., Reihman, J., Lonky, E., Pagano, J. (2012). Issues in the interpretation of associations of PCBs and IQ. *Neurotoxicol. Teratol.*, 34, 96–107.

Stewart, R. B. and Li, T.-K. (1997). The neurobiology of alcoholism in genetically selected rat models. *Alcohol Health Res. World*, 21, 169–176.

Stine, S. M., Southwick, S. M., Petrakis, I. L., Kosten, T. R., Charney, D. S., and Krystal, J. H. (2002). Yohimbine-induced withdrawal and anxiety symptoms in opioid-dependent patients. *Biol. Psychiatry*, 51, 642–651.

Stoessl, A. J. (2012). Neuroimaging in the early diagnosis of neurodegenerative disease. *Transl Neurodegener.*, 1, 1–6.

Stolerman, I. (1992). Drugs of abuse: Behavioural principles, methods and terms. *Trends Pharmacol. Sci.*, 13, 170–176.

Stolerman, I. P., Mirza, N. R., Hahn, B., and Shoaib, M. (2000). Nicotine in an animal model of attention. *Eur. J. Pharmacol.*, 393, 147–154.

Stone, A. L., O'Brien, M. S., de la Torre, A., and Anthony, J. C. (2007). Who is becoming hallucinogen dependent soon after hallucinogen use starts? *Drug Alcohol Depend.*, 87, 153–163.

Stone, A. L., Storr, C. L., and Anthony, J. C. (2006). Evidence for a hallucinogen dependence syndrome developing soon after onset of hallucinogen use during adolescence. *Int. J. Methods Psychiatr. Res.*, 15, 116–130.

Stone, J. M., Dietrich, C., Edden, R., Mehta, M. A., De Simoni, S., Reed, L. J., et al. (2012). Ketamine effects on brain GABA and glutamate levels with 1H-MRS: Relationship to ketamine-induced psychopathology. *Mol. Psychiatry*, 17, 664–668.

Storch, A., Jost, W. H., Vieregge, P., Spiegel, J., Greulich, W., Durner, J., et al. (2007). Randomized, double-blind, placebo-controlled trial on symptomatic effects of coenzyme Q10 in Parkinson disease. *Arch. Neurol.*, 64, 938–944.

Stowe, G. N., Vendruscolo, L. F., Edwards, S., Schlosburg, J. E., Misra, K. K., Schulteis, G., et al. (2011). A vaccine strategy that induces protective immunity against heroin. *J. Med. Chem.*, 54, 5195–5204.

Strassman, R. J., Qualls, C. R., Uhlenhuth, E. H., and Kellner, R. (1994). Dose-response study of N,N-dimethyltryptamine in humans. II. Subjective effects and preliminary results of a new rating scale. *Arch. Gen. Psychiatry*, 51, 98–108.

Substance Abuse and Mental Health Services Administration. (2010). *Results from the 2009 National Survey on Drug Use and Health: Volume I. Summary of National Findings* (Office of Applied Studies, NSDUH Series H-38A, HHS Publication No. SMA 10–4586 Findings). Rockville, MD: Substance Abuse and Mental Health Services Administration.

Substance Abuse and Mental Health Services Administration. (2011). *Results from the 2010 National Survey on Drug Use and Health: Summary of National Findings*, NSDUH Series H-41, HHS Publication No. (SMA) 11–4658. Rockville, MD: Substance Abuse and Mental Health Services Administration.

Substance Abuse and Mental Health Services Administration. (2012). *Results from* the 2011 National Survey on Drug Use and Health: Summary of National Findings, NS-DUH Series H-44, HHS Publication No. (SMA) 12-4713. Rockville, MD: Substance Abuse and Mental Health Services Administration.

Sugiura, T. (2009). Physiological roles of 2-arachidonoylglycerol, an endogenous cannabinoid receptor ligand. BioFactors, 35, 88–97.

Sulik, K. K., Johnston, M. C., and Webb, M. A. (1981). Fetal alcohol syndrome: Embryogenesis in a mouse model. Science, 214, 936–938.

Sullivan, E. V. (2000). Human brain vulnerability to alcoholism: Evidence from neuroimaging studies. NIAAA Res. Monogr., 34, 477–508.

Sullivan, G. M., Coplan, J. D., Kent, J. M., and Gorman, J. M. (1999). The noradrenergic system in pathological anxiety: A focus on panic with relevance to generalized anxiety and phobias. Biol. Psychiatry, 46, 1205–1218.

Sulser, F. (1989). New perspectives on the molecular pharmacology of affective disorders. Eur. Arch. Psychiatr. Neurol. Sci., 238, 231–239.

Sun, X. and Dey, S. K. (2012). Endocannabinoid signaling in female reproduction. ACS Chem. Neurosci., 3, 349–355.

Sussman, S., Lisha, N., and Griffiths, M. (2011). Prevalence of the addictions: A problem of the majority of the minority? Eval. Health Prof., 34, 3–56.

Svíženská, I., Dubový, P., and Šulcová, A. (2008). Cannabinoid receptors 1 and 2 (CB_1 and CB_2), their distribution, ligands and functional involvement in nervous system structures—A short review. Pharmacol. Biochem. Behav., 90, 501–511.

Swan, G. E. and Lessov-Schlaggar, C. N. (2007). The effects of tobacco smoke and nicotine on cognition and the brain. Neuropsychol. Rev., 17, 259–273.

Swendsen, J. and Le Moal, M. (2011). Individual vulnerability to addiction. Ann. N.Y. Acad. Sci., 1216, 73–85.

Swendsen, J., Conway, K. P., Degenhardt, L., Dierker, L., Glantz, M., Jin, R., et al. (2009). Socio-demographic risk factors for alcohol and drug dependence: The 10-year follow-up of the national comorbidity survey. Addiction, 104, 1346–1355.

Swift, R. M. (1999). Drug therapy for alcohol dependence. N. Engl. J. Med., 340, 1482–1490.

Sydserff, S., Sutton, E. J., Song, D., Quirk, M. C., Maciag, C., Li, C., et al. (2009). Selective α7 nicotinic receptor activation by AZD0328 enhances cortical dopamine release and improves learning and attentional processes. Biochem. Pharmacol., 78. 880–888.

Takagi, M., Lubman, D. I., and Yücel, M. (2011). Solvent-induced leukoencephalopathy: A disorder of adolescence? Subst. Use Misuse, 46, 95–98.

Tanaka, K., Watase, K., Manabe, T., Yamada, K., Watanabe, M., Takahashi, K., et al. (1997). Epilepsy and exacerbation of brain injury in mice lacking the glutamate transporter GLT-1. Science, 276, 1699–1702.

Tanasescu, R. and Constantinescu, C. S. (2010). Cannabinoids and the immune system: An overview. Immunobiology, 215, 588–597.

Tanda, G., Munzar, P., and Goldberg, S. R. (2000). Self-administration behavior is maintained by the psychoactive ingredient of marijuana in squirrel monkeys. Nat. Neurosci., 3, 1073–1074.

Tanda, G., Newman, A. H., and Katz, J. L. (2009). Discovery of drugs to treat cocaine dependence: Behavioral and neurochemical effects of atypical dopamine transport inhibitors. Adv. Pharmacol., 57, 253–289.

Tang, Y.-P., Shimizu, E., Dube, G. R., Rampon, C., Kerchner, G. A., Zhuo, M., et al. (1999). Genetic enhancement of learning and memory in mice. Nature, 401, 63–69.

Tanner, C. M., Kamel, F., Ross, G. W., Hoppin, J. A., Goldman, S. M., Korell, M., et al. (2011). Rotenone, paraquat and Parkinson's disease. Environ. Health Perspect., 119, 866–872.

Tarnopolsky, M. A. (2008). Effect of caffeine on the neuromuscular system—potential as an ergogenic aid. Appl. Physiol. Nutr. Metab., 33, 1284–1289.

Tashkin, D. P., Baldwin, G. C., Sarafian, T., Dubinett, S., and Roth, M. D. (2002). Respiratory and immunologic consequences of marijuana smoking. J. Clin. Pharmacol., 42 (Suppl. 11), 71S–81S.

Terenius, L. and Wahlstrom, A. (1974). Inhibitor(s) of narcotic receptor binding in brain extracts and cerebrospinal fluid. Acta Pharmacol. Toxicol., 35 (Suppl. 1), 87 (Abst.).

Tetrault, J. M., Crothers, K., Moore, B. A., Mehra, R., Concato, J., and Fiellin, D. A. (2007). Effects of marijuana smoking on pulmonary function and respiratory complications: A systematic review. Arch. Intern. Med., 167, 221–228.

Thannickal, T. C., Moore, R. Y., Nienhuis, R., Ramanathan, L., Gulyani, S., Aldrich, M., et al. (2000). Reduced number of hypocretin neurons in human narcolepsy. Neuron, 27, 469–474.

The Parkinson Study Group. (1993). Effects of tocopherol and deprenyl on the progression of disability in early Parkinson's disease. N. Engl. J. Med., 328, 176–183.

Thomas, C. L. (Ed.) (1993). Taber's Cyclopedic Medical Dictionary. Philadelphia: F. A. Davis.

Thomas, D. J., Li, J., Waters, S. B., Xing, W., Adair, B. M., Drobna, Z., et al. (2007). Arsenic (+3 Oxidation State) methyltransferase and the methylation of arsenicals. Exp. Biol. Med., 232, 3–13.

Thombs, D. L. (1999). Introduction to Addictive Behaviors (2nd ed.). New York: Guilford Press.

Thompson, P. M., Vidal, C., Giedd, J. N., Gochman, P., Blumenthal, J., Nicolson, R., et al. (2001) Mapping adolescent brain change reveals dynamic wave of accelerated gray matter loss in very early-onset schizophrenia. Proc. Natl. Acad. Sci. U.S.A., 98, 11650–11655.

Thomsen, M. S., Hansen, H. H., Timmerman, D. B., and Mikkelsen, J. D. (2010). Cognitive improvement by activation of α7 nicotinic acetylcholine receptors: From animal models to human pathophysiology. Curr. Pharm. Des., 16, 323–343.

Thomsen, M., Han, D. D., Gu, H. H., and Caine, S. B. (2009). Lack of cocaaine self-administration in mice expressing a cocaine-insensitive dopamine transporter. J. Pharmacol. Exp. Ther., 331, 204–211.

Tian, Y-H., Baek, J-H., Lee, S-Y. and Jang, C-G. (2010). Prenatal and postnatal exposure to bisphenol A. Synapse, 64, 432–439.

Ticku, M. K. and Mehta, A. K. (2008). Characterization and pharmacology of the GHB receptor. Ann. N.Y. Acad. Sci., 1139, 374–385.

Tiffany, S. T., Drobes, D. J., and Cepeda-Benito, A. (1992). Contribution of associative and nonassociative processes to the development of morphine tolerance. Psychopharmacology, 109, 185–190.

Timpone, J. G., Wright, D. J., Li, N., Egorin, M. J., Enama, M. E., Mayers, J., et al. (1997). The safety and pharmacokinetics of single-agent and combination therapy with megestrol acetate and dronabinol for the treatment of HIV wasting syndrome. The DATRI 004 Study Group. Division of AIDS Treatment Research Initiative. AIDS Res. Hum. Retroviruses, 13, 305–315.

Todorow, M., Moore, T. E., and Koren, G. (2010). Investigating the effects of low to moderate levels of prenatal alcohol exposure on child behaviour: A critical review. J. Popul. Ther. Clin. Pharmacol., 17, e323–330.

Toomey, R., Lyons, M. J., Eisen, S. A., Xian, H., Chantarujikapong, S., Seidman, L. J., et al. (2003). A twin study of the neuropsychological consequences of stimulant abuse. Arch. Gen. Psychiatry, 60, 303–310.

Toscano, C. C. and Guilarte, T. R. (2005). Lead neurotoxicity: From exposure to molecular effects. Brain Res Rev., 49, 529–554.

Toufexis, D. (2007). Region- and sex-specific modulation of anxiety behaviours in the rat. J. Neuroendocrinol., 19, 461–473.

Townsend, L., Flisher, A. J., and King, G. (2007). A systemic review of the relationship between high school dropout and substance use. Clin. Child Fam. Psychol., 10, 295–317.

Treadwell, S. D. and Robinson, T. G. (2007). Cocaine use and stroke. Postgrad. Med. J., 83, 389–394.

Treiman, D. M. (2001). GABAergic mechanisms in epilepsy. Epilepsia, 42 (Suppl. 3), 8–12.

Treit, D. (1985). Animal models for the study of anti-anxiety agents: A review. Neurosci. Biochem. Rev., 9, 203–222.

Trenton, A. J. and Currier, G. W. (2005). Behavioural manifestations of anabolic steroid use. CNS Drugs, 19, 571–596.

Trigo, J. M., Martin-García, E., Berrendero, F., Robledo, P., and Maldonado, R. (2010). The endogenous opioid system: A common substrate in drug addiction. Drug Alcohol Depend., 108, 183–194.

Trudeau, M. (2009). More students turning illegally to "smart" drugs. Available online at: http://www.npr.org/templates/story/story.php?storyId=100254163, accessed 11/20/10.

Trujillo, K. A. (2000). Are NMDA receptors involved in opiate-induced neural and behavioral plasticity? *Psychopharmacology*, 151, 121–141.

Tsai, S. Y., Chou, H. Y., The, H. W., Chen, C. M., and Chen, C. J. (2003). The effects of chronic arsenic exposure from drinking water on the neurobehavioral development in adolescence. *Neurotoxicol.*, 24, 747–753.

Tsankova, N., Renthal, W., Kumar, A., and Nestler, E. J. (2007). Epigenetic regulation in psychiatric disorders. *Nat. Rev. Neurosci.*, 8, 355–367.

Tseng, K. Y., Chambers, R. A., and Lipska, B. K. (2009). The neonatal ventral hippocampal lesion as a heuristic neurodevelopmental model of schizophrenia. *Behav. Brain Res.*, 204, 295–305.

Tuesta, L. M., Fowler, C. D., and Kenny, P. J. (2011). Recent advances in understanding nicotinic receptor signaling mechanisms that regulate drug self-administration behavior. *Biochem. Pharmacol.*, 82, 984–995.

Turillazzi, E., Perilli, G., Di Paolo, M., Neri, M., Riezzo, I., and Fineschi, V. (2011). Side effects of AAS abuse: An overview. *Mini Rev. Med. Chem.*, 11, 374–389.

Tyndale, R. F. and Sellers, E. M. (2001). Variable CYP2A6-mediated nicotine metabolism alters smoking behavior and risk. *Drug Metab. Dispos.*, 29, 548–552.

Ueda, N., Tsuboi, K., Uyama, T., and Ohnishi, T. (2010). Biosynthesis and degradation of the endocannabinoid 2-arachidonoylglycerol. *BioFactors*, 37, 1–7.

Uhart, M. and Wand, G. S. (2009). Stress, alcohol and drug interaction: An update of human research. *Addict. Biol.*, 14, 43–64.

Uhl, G. R., Drgon, T., Johnson, C., Fatusin, O. O., Liu, Q.-R., Contoreggi, C., et al. (2008). "Higher order" addiction molecular genetics: Convergent data from genome-wide association in humans and mice. *Biochem. Pharmacol.*, 75, 98–111.

Ulas, J. and Cotman, C. W. (1993). Excitatory amino acid receptors in schizophrenia. *Schizophr. Bull.*, 19, 105–117.

Ungerstedt, U. (1984). Measurement of neurotransmitter release by intracranial dialysis. In C. A. Marsden (Ed.), *Measurement of Neurotransmitter Release In Vivo*, pp. 81–106. New York: Wiley.

United Nations Industrial Development Organization (UNIDO). (2006). *Manual for Training Artisanal and Small-Scale Gold Miners*. Vienna, Austria: Global Mercury Project. Available online at: http://suriname.wedd.de/modules.php?op=modload&name=News&file=article&sid=409, accessed 11/26/12.

United States Department of Health and Human Services. (2010). *How Tobacco Smoke Causes Disease: The Biology and Behavioral Basis for Smoking-Attributable Disease: A Report of the Surgeon General*. Atlanta, GA:

U.S. Department of Health and Human Services, Centers for Disease Control and Prevention, National Center for Chronic Disease Prevention and Health Promotion, Office on Smoking and Health.

United States Department of Health, Education, and Welfare. Public Health Service. National Institute of Mental Health. (1968). *1943–1966 Bibliography on Psychotomimetics*. Washington, DC: U.S. Government Printing Office.

UNODC. (2012). *World Drug Report 2012*. United Nations publication, Sales No. E.12.XI.1.

Urban, N. B., Kegeles, L. S., Slifstein, M., Xu, X., Martinez, D., Sakr, E., et al. (2010). Sex differences in striatal dopamine release in young adults after oral alcohol challenge: A positron emission tomography imaging study with [^{11}C]raclopride. *Biol. Psychiatry*, 68, 689–696.

Urbanoski, K. A. and Kelly, J. F. (2012). Understanding genetic risk for substance use and addiction: A guide for non-geneticists. *Clin. Psychol. Rev.*, 32, 60–70.

Uys, J. D. and LaLumiere, R. T. (2008). Glutamate: The new frontier in pharmacotherapy for cocaine addiction. *CNS Neurol. Disord. Drug Targets*, 7, 482–491.

Vaillant, G. E. (1995). *The Natural History of Alcoholism Revisited*. Cambridge, MA: Harvard University Press.

Vaiva, G., Ducrocq, F., Jezequel, K., Averland, B., Lestavel, P., Brunet, A., et al. (2003). Immediate treatment with propranolol decreases posttraumatic stress disorder two months after trauma. *Biol. Psychiatry*, 54, 947–949.

Valenstein, E. S. (2005). *The War of the Soups and the Sparks. The Discovery of Neurotransmitters and the Dispute Over How Nerves Communicate*. New York: Columbia University Press.

Valjent, E. and Maldonado, R. (2000). A behavioural model to reveal place preference to Δ^9-tetrahydrocannabinol in mice. *Psychopharmacology*, 147, 436–438.

Vallelunga, A., Flaibani, R., Formento-Dojot, P., Biundo, R., Facchini, S., and Antonini, A. (2011). Role of genetic polymorphisms of the dopaminergic system in Parkinson's disease patients with impulse control disorders. *Parkinsonism Relat. Disord.*, 18, 397–399.

Valverde, O., Karsak, M., and Zimmer, A. (2005). Analysis of the endocannabinoid system by using CB$_1$ cannabinoid receptor knockout mice. *Handb. Exp. Pharmacol.*, 168, 117–145.

Van Dyke, C. and Byck, R. (1982). Cocaine. *Sci. Am.*, 246(3), 128–141.

van Leeuwen, A. P., Verhuist, F. C., Reijneveld, S. A., Vollebergh, W. A. M., Ormel, J., and Huizink, A. C. (2011). Can the gateway hypothesis, the common liability model and/or the route of administration model predict initiation of cannabis use during adolescence? A survival analysis—The TRAILS study. *J. Adolesc. Health*, 48, 73–78.

Vandenberg, L. N., Colborn, T., Hayes, T. B., Heindel, J. J., Jacobs, D. R. Jr., Lee, D. H., et al. (2012). Hormones and endocrine-disrupting chemicals: Low-dose effects and nonmonotonic dose responses. *Endocr. Rev.*, 33, 378–455.

Vardakou, I., Pistos, C., and Spiliopoulou, Ch. (2011). Drugs for youth via Internet and the example of mephedrone. *Toxicol. Lett.*, 201, 191–195.

Vellas, B., Black, R., Thal, L. G., Fox, N. C., Daniels, M., McLennan, G., et al. (2009). Long-term follow-up of patients immunized with AN1702: Reduced functional decline in antibody responders. *Curr. Alzheimer Res.*, 6, 144–151.

Verheul, R. and van den Brink, W. (2000). The role of personality pathology in the aetiology and treatment of substance use disorders. *Curr. Opinion Psychiatry*, 13, 163–169.

Verster, J. C., Aufricht, C., and Alford, C. (2012). Energy drinks mixed with alcohol: Misconceptions, myths, and facts. *Int. J. Gen. Med.*, 5, 187–198.

Vezina, P. (2004). Sensitization of midbrain dopamine reactivity and the self-administration of psychomotor stimulant drugs. *Neurosci. Biobehav. Rev.*, 27, 827–839.

Vilarim, M. M., Rocha Araujo, D. M., and Nardi, A. E. (2011). Caffeine challenge test and panic disorder: A systematic literature review. *Expert Rev. Neurother.*, 11, 1185–1195.

Vogel-Sprott, M. (1997). Is behavioral tolerance learned? *Alc. Health Res. World*, 21, 161–168.

Volkow, N. D., Fowler, J. S., and Wang, G.-J. (1999a). Imaging studies on the role of dopamine in cocaine reinforcement and addiction in humans. *J. Psychopharmacol.*, 13, 337–345.

Volkow, N. D., Fowler, J. S., Wang, G. J., Baler, R., and Telang, F. (2009). Imaging dopamine's role in drug abuse and addiction. *Neuropharmacology*, 56, 3–8.

Volkow, N. D., Wang, G.-J., Fischman, M. W., Foltin, R., Fowler, J. S., Franceschi, D., et al. (2000). Effects of route of administration on cocaine induced dopamine transporter blockade in the human brain. *Life Sci.*, 67, 1507–1515.

Volkow, N. D., Wang, G.-J., Fowler, J. S., and Tomasi, D. (2012). Addiction circuitry in the human brain. *Annu. Rev. Pharmacol. Toxicol.*, 52, 321–336.

Volkow, N. D., Wang, G.-J., Fowler, J. S., Gatley, S. J., Logan, J., Ding, Y.-S., et al. (1998). Dopamine transporter occupancies in the human brain induced by therapeutic doses of oral methylphenidate. *Am. J. Psychiatry*, 155, 1325–1331.

Volkow, N. D., Wang, G.-J., Fowler, J. S., Gatley, S. J., Logan, J., Ding, Y.-S., et al. (1999b). Blockade of striatal dopamine transporters by intravenous methylphenidate is not sufficient to induce self-reports of "high." *J. Pharmacol. Exp. Ther.*, 288, 14–20.

Volkow, N. D., Wang, G.-J., Fowler, J. S., Logan, J., Gatley, S. J., Gifford, A., et al. (1999c). Prediction of reinforcing responses to psychostimulants in humans by brain dopamine D_2 receptor levels. *Am. J. Psychiatry*, 156, 1440–1443.

Volkow, N. D., Wang, G.-J., Fowler, J. S., Logan, J., Gatley, S. J., Hitzemann, R., et al. (1997). Decreased striatal dopaminergic responsiveness in detoxified cocaine-dependent subjects. *Nature*, 386, 830–833.

Volkow, N. D., Wang, G.-J., Fowler, J. S., Logan, J., Gatley, S. J., Wong, C., et al. (1999). Reinforcing effects of psychostimulants in humans are associated with increases in brain dopamine and occupancy of D_2 receptors. *J. Pharmacol. Exp. Ther.*, 291, 409–415.

Volkow, N. D., Wang, G.-J., Fowler, J. S., Thanos, P., Logan, J., Gatley, S. J., et al. (2002). Brain DA D_2 receptors predict reinforcing effects of stimulants in humans: Replication study. *Synapse*, 46, 79–82.

Volkow, N. D., Wang, G.-J., Fowler, J. S., Tomasi, D., and Telang, F. (2011). Addiction: Beyond dopamine reward circuitry. *Proc. Natl. Acad. Sci. U.S.A.*, 108, 15037–15042.

Volkow, N. D., Wang, G.-J., Telang, F., Fowler, J. S., Logan, J., Childress, A.-R., et al. (2006). Cocaine cues and dopamine in dorsal striatum: Mechanism of craving in cocaine addiction. *J. Neurosci.*, 26, 6583–6588.

Volkow, N. D., Wang, G.-J., Telang, F., Fowler, J. S., Logan, J., Childress, A.-R., et al. (2008). Dopamine increases in striatum do not elicit craving in cocaine abusers unless they are coupled with cocaine cues. *NeuroImage*, 39, 1266–1273.

Vollenweider, F. X. and Geyer, M. A. (2001). A systems model of altered consciousness: Integrating natural and drug-induced psychoses. *Brain Res. Bull.*, 56, 495–507.

Vollenweider, F. X. and Kometer, M. (2010). The neurobiology of psychedelic drugs: Implications for the treatment of mood disorders. *Nat. Rev. Neurosci.*, 11, 642–651.

Vollenweider, F. X., Vollenweider-Scherpenhuyzen, M. F. I., Bäbler, A., Vogel, H., and Hell, D. (1998). Psilocybin induces schizophrenia-like psychosis in humans via a serotonin-2 agonist action. *NeuroReport*, 9, 3897–3902.

Vorel, S. R., Ashby, C. R., Jr., Paul, M., Liu, X., Hayes, R., Hagan, J. J., et al. (2002). Dopamine D_3 receptor antagonism inhibits cocaine-seeking and cocaine-enhanced brain reward in rats. *J. Neurosci.*, 22, 9595–9603.

Waldorf, D. (1983). Natural recovery from opiate addiction: Some social-psychological processes of untreated recovery. *J. Drug Issues*, 13, 237–280.

Walker, B. M. and Koob, G. F. (2008). Pharmacological evidence for a motivational role of kappa-opioid systems in ethanol dependence. *Neuropsychopharmacology*, 33, 643–652.

Walker, D. L., Miles, L. A., and Davis, M. (2009). Selective participation of the bed nucleus of the stria terminalis and CRF in sustained anxiety-like versus phasic fear-like responses. *Prog. Neuropsychopharmacol. Biol. Psychiatry*, 33, 1291–1308.

Wall, T. L. and Ehlers, C. L. (1995). Genetic influences affecting alcohol use among Asians. *Alcohol Health Res. World*, 19, 184–189.

Wallén-Mackenzie, Å., Wootz, H., and Englund, H. (2010). Genetic inactivation of the vesicular glutamate transporter 2 (VGLUT2) in the mouse: What have we learnt about functional glutamatergic neurotransmission? *Ups. J. Med. Sci.*, 115, 11–20.

Walters, G. D. (2000). Spontaneous remission from alcohol, tobacco, and other drug abuse: Seeking quantitative answers to qualitative questions. *Am. J. Drug Alcohol Abuse*, 26, 443–460.

Walters, G. D. and Gilbert, A. (2000). Defining addiction: Contrasting views of clients and experts. *Addiction Res.*, 8, 211–220.

Wang, G. B., Wu, L. Z., Yu, P., Li, Y. J., Ping, X. J., and Cui, C. L. (2011). Multiple 100 Hz electroacupuncture treatments produced cumulative effect on the suppression of morphine withdrawal syndrome: Central preprodynorphin mRNA and p-CREB implicated. *Peptides*, 32, 713–721.

Wang, G.-J., Volkow, N. D., Hitzemann, R. J., Wong, C., Angrist, B., Burr, G., et al. (1997). Behavioral and cardiovascular effects of intravenous methylphenidate in normal subjects and cocaine abusers. *Eur. Addict. Res.*, 3, 49–54.

Wang, Q., Yan, J., Chen, X., Li, J., Yang, Y., Weng, J. P., et al. (2011). Statins: Multiple neuroprotective mechanisms in neurodegenerative diseases. *Exp. Neurol.*, 230, 27–34.

Wang, S-X., Wang, Z-H., Cheng, X-T., Li, J., Sang, Z-P., Zhang, X-D., et al. (2007). Arsenic and fluoride exposure in drinking water: Children's IQ and growth in Shanyin County, Shanxi Province, China. *Environ. Health Perspect.*, 115, 643–647.

Wang, S. H. and Morris, R. G. (2010). Hippocampal-neocortical interactions in memory formation, consolidation, and reconsolidation. *Annu. Rev. Psychol.*, 61, 49–79.

Wareham, J. D. and Potenza, M. N. (2010). Pathological gambling and substance use disorders. *Am. J. Drug Alcohol Abuse*, 36, 242–247.

Warner, M., Chen, L. H., and Makuc, D. M. (2009). Increase in fatal poisonings involving opioid analgesics in the United States, 1999–2006. *NCHS Data Brief*, 22, 1–8.

Wassanaar, C. A., Dong, Q., Wei, Q., Amos, C. I., Spitz, M. R., and Tyndale, R. F. (2011). Relationship between *CYP2A6* and *CHRNA5-CHRNA3-CHRNB4* variation and smoking behaviors and lung cancer risk. *J. Natl. Cancer Inst.*, 103, 1342–1346.

Wasserman, G. A., Liu, X., Parvez, F., Ahsan, H., Factor-Litvak, P., van Geen, A., et al. (2004). Water arsenic exposure and children's intellectual function in Araihazar, Bangladesh. *Environ. Health Perspect.*, 112, 1329–1333.

Wasson, R. G. (1957). Seeking the magic mushroom. *Life*, 42 (19), 100–115.

Watson, J., Guzzetti, S., Franchi, C., Di Clemente, A., Burbassi, S., Emri, Z., et al. (2010). Gamma-hydroxybutyrate does not maintain self-administration but induces conditioned place preference when injected in the ventral tegmental area. *Int. J. Neuropsychopharmacol.*, 13, 143–153.

Wechsler, H., Dowdall, G. W., Davenport, A., and Castillo, S. (1995a). Correlates of college student binge drinking. *Am. J. Public Health*, 85, 921–926.

Wedin, G. P., Hornfeldt, C. S., and Ylitalo, L. M. (2006). The clinical development of γ-hydroxybutyrate (GHB). *Curr. Drug Safety*, 1, 99–106.

Weeks, J. R. and Collins, R. J. (1987). Screening for drug reinforcement using intravenous self-administration in the rat. In M. A. Bozarth (Ed.), *Methods of Assessing the Reinforcing Properties of Abused Drugs*, pp. 35–43. New York: Springer-Verlag.

Wei, F., Wang, G. D., Kerchner, G. A., Kim, S. J., Xu, H. M., Chen, Z. F., et al. (2001). Genetic enhancement of inflammatory pain by forebrain NR2B overexpression. *Nat. Neurosci.*, 4, 164–169.

Weinberger, D. R. (1995). Neurodevelopmental perspectives on schizophrenia. In F. E. Bloom and D. J. Kupfer (Eds.), *Psychopharmacology: The Fourth Generation of Progress*, pp. 1171–1183. New York: Raven Press.

Weinstein, A. and Lejoyeux, M. (2010). Internet addiction or excessive internet use. *Am. J. Drug Alcohol Abuse*, 36, 277–283.

Weisner, C., Wiederhold, K-H., Tissot, A. C., Frey, P., Danner, S., Jacobson, L. H., et al. (2011). The second-generation active Aβ immunotherapy CAD106 reduces amyloid accumulation in APP transgenic mice while minimizing potential side effects. *J. Neurosci.*, 31, 9323–9331.

Weisstaub, N. V., Zhou, M., Lira, A., Lambe, E., Gonález-Maeso, J., Hornung, J.-P., et al. (2006). Cortical $5HT_{2A}$ receptor signaling modulates anxiety-like behaviors in mice. *Science*, 313, 536–540.

Wenger, J. R., Tiffany, T. M., Bombardier, C., Nicoins, K., and Woods, S. C. (1981). Ethanol tolerance in the rat is learned. *Science*, 213, 575–576.

Wess, J., Eglen, R. M., and Gautam, D. (2007). Muscarinic acetylcholine receptors: Mutant mice provide new insights for drug development. *Nat. Rev. Drug Discov.*, 6, 721–733.

Wevers, R. A., de Rijk-van Andel, J. F., Bräutigam, C., Geurtz, B., van den Heuvel, L. P. W. J., Steenbergen-Spanjers, G. C. H., et al. (1999). A review of biochemical and molecular genetic aspects of tyrosine hydroxylase deficiency including a novel mutation (291delC). *J. Inher. Metab. Dis.*, 22, 364–373.

White, A. M., Hingson, R. W., Pan, I. J., and Yi, H. Y. (2011). Hospitalizations for alcohol and drug overdoses in young adults ages 18–24 in the United States, 1999–2008: Results from the Nationwide Inpatient Sample. *J. Stud. Alcohol Drugs*, 72, 774–786.

Wichterle, H., Lieberam, I., Porter, J. A., and Jessell, T. M. (2002). Directed differentiation of embryonic stem cells into motor neurons. *Cell*, 110, 385–397.

Wikler, A. (1973). Dynamics of drug dependence: Implications of a conditioning theory for research and treatment. *Arch. Gen. Psychiatry*, 28, 611–616.

Wikler, A. (1980). *Opioid Dependence*. New York: Plenum Press.

Wilder, R. T. (2010). Is there any relationship between long-term behavior disturbance and early exposure to anesthesia? *Curr. Opin. Anaesthesiol.*, 23, 332–336.

Wilens, T. E., Adler, L. A., Adams, J., Sgambati, S., Rotrosen, J., Sawtelle, R., et al. (2008). Misuse and diversion of stimulants prescribed for ADHD: A systematic review of the literature. *J. Am. Acad. Child Adolesc. Psychiatry*, 47, 21–31.

Wilhelm, M., Wittsiepe, J., Lemm, F., Ranft, U., Kramer, U., Furst, P., et al. (2008). The Duisburg birth cohort study: Influence of the prenatal exposure to PCDD/Fs and dioxin-like PCBs on thyroid hormone status in newborns and neurodevelopment of infants until the age of 24 months. *Mutat. Res.*, 659, 83–92.

Williams, B. F., Howard, V. F., and McLaughlin, T. F. (1994). Fetal alcohol syndrome: Developmental characteristics and directions for further research. *Educ. Treatment Child.*, 17, 86–97.

Williams, C. M., Rogers, P. J., and Kirkham, T. C. (1998). Hyperphagia in pre-fed rats following oral Δ^9-THC. *Physiol. Behav.*, 65, 343–346.

Williams, J. F., Storck, M., Committee on Substance Abuse, Committee on Native American Child Health. (2007). Inhalant abuse. *Pediatrics*, 119, 1009–1017.

Willner, P. (1995). Dopaminergic mechanisms in depression and mania. In F. E. Bloom and D. J. Kupfer (Eds.), *Psychopharmacology: The Fourth Generation of Progress*, pp. 921–932. New York: Raven Press.

Wilson, G. T. and Lawson, D. W. (1976). The effects of alcohol on sexual arousal in women. *J. Abnorm. Psychol.*, 85, 489–497.

Wilson, M. D., Ferguson, R. W., Mazer, M. E., and Litovitz, T. L. (2011). Monitoring trends in dextromethorphan abuse using the National Poison Data System: 2000–2010. *Clin. Toxicol.*, 49, 409–415.

Wilson, R. I. and Nicoll, R. A. (2002). Endocannabinoid signaling in the brain. *Science*, 296, 678–682.

Windle, M. and Davies, P. T. (1999). Developmental theory and research. In K. E. Leonard and H. T. Blane (Eds.), *Psychological Theories of Drinking and Alcoholism* (2nd ed.), pp. 164–202. New York: Guilford Press.

Wingblad, B., Andreasen, N., Minthon, L., Floesser, A., Imbert, G., Dmortier, T., et al. (2012). Safety, tolerability, and antibody response of active Aβ immunotherapy with CAD106 in patients with Alzheimer's disease: Randomized, double-blind, placebo-controlled, first-in-human study. *The Lance/Neurology*, 11, 597–604.

Winstock, A. R., Mitcheson, L. R., DeLuca, P., Davey, Z., Corazza, O., and Schifano, F. (2010). Mephedrone, new kid for the chop? *Addiction*, 106, 154–161.

Winstock, A., Mitcheson, L., Ramsey, J., Davies, S., Puchnarewicz, M., and Marsden, J. (2011). Mephedrone: Use, subjective effects and health risks. *Addiction*, 106, 1991–1996.

Winterer, G. and Weinberger, D. R. (2004). Genes, dopamine and cortical signal-to-noise ratio in schizophrenia. *Trends Neurosci.*, 27, 683–690.

Wise, L. E., Thorpe, A. J., and Lichtman, A. H. (2009). Hippocampal CB_1 receptors mediate the memory impairing effects of Δ^9-tetrahydrocannabinol. *Neuropsychopharmacology*, 34, 2072–2080.

Wise, R. A. (1980). The dopamine synapse and the notion of "pleasure centers" in the brain. *Trends Neurosci.*, 3, 91–95.

Wiskerke, J., Pattij, T., Schoffelmeer, A. N. M., and De Vries, T. J. (2008). The role of CB_1 receptors in psychostimulant addiction. *Addict. Biol.*, 13, 225–238.

Wittchen, H.-U., Zhao, S., Kessler, R. C., and Eaton, W. W. (1994). *DSM-III-R* generalized anxiety disorder in the National Comorbidity Survey. *Arch. Gen. Psychiatry*, 51, 355–364.

Wolfe, B. L. and Meyers, R. J. (1999). Cost-effective alcohol treatment: The community reinforcement approach. *Cognitive Behav. Pract.*, 6, 105–109.

Wolff, K. and Winstock, A. R. (2006). Ketamine: From medicine to misuse. *CNS Drugs*, 20, 199–218.

Wolk, D. A., Price, J. C., Saxton, J. A., Snitz, B. E., James, J. A., Lopez, O. L., et al. (2009). Amyloid imaging in mild cognitive impairment subtypes. *Ann. Neurol.*, 65, 557–568.

Wong, C. C. Y., Mill, J., and Fernandes, C. (2011). Drugs and addiction: An introduction to epigenetics. *Addiction*, 106, 480–489.

Wong, D. F., Kuwabara, H., Schretlen, D. J., Bonson, K. R., Zhou, Y., Nandi, A., et al. (2006). Increased occupancy of dopamine receptors in human striatum during cue-elicited cocaine craving. *Neuropsychopharmacology*, 31, 2716–2727.

Wood, D. M., Brailsford, A. D., and Dargan, P. I. (2011). Acute toxicity and withdrawal syndromes related to gamma-hydroxybutyrate (GHB) and its analogues gamma-butyrolactone (GBL) and 1,4-butanediol (1,4-BD). *Drug Test. Analysis*, 3, 417–425.

Wood, D. M., Davies, S., Puchnarewicz, M., Button, J., Archer, R., Ovaska, H., et al. (2010). Recreational use of mephedrone (4-methylmethcathinone, 4-MMC) with associated sympathomimetic toxicity. *J. Med. Toxicol.*, 6, 327–330.

Wood, D. M., Green, S. I., and Dargan, P. I. (2011). Clinical pattern of toxicity associated with the novel synthetic cathinone mephedrone. *Emerg. Med. J.*, 28, 280–282.

Wood, D., Cottrell, A., Baker, S. C., Southgate, J., Harris, M., Fulford, S., et al. (2011). Recreational ketamine: From pleasure to pain. *BJU Int.*, 107, 1881–1884.

Wood, R. I. (2008). Anabolic-androgenic steroid dependence? Insights from animals and humans. *Front. Neuroendocrinol.*, 29, 490–506.

Wood, R. I., Johnson, L. R., Chu, L., Schad, C., and Self, D. W. (2004). Testosterone reinforcement: Intravenous and intracerebroventricular self-administration in male rats and hamsters. *Psychopharmacology*, 171, 298–305.

Woods, J. H., France, C. P., Winger, G., Bertalmio, A. J., and Schwarz-Stevens, K. (1993). Opioid abuse liability assessment in rhesus monkeys. In A. Herz (Ed.), *Opioids II, Volume 104: Handbook of Experimental Pharmacology*, pp. 609–632. New York: Springer-Verlag.

Woods, J. H., Katz, J. L., and Winger, G. (1995). Abuse and therapeutic use of benzodiazepines and benzodiazepine-like drugs. In F. E. Bloom and D. J. Kupfer (Eds.), *Psychopharmacology: The Fourth Generation of Progress*, pp. 1777–1789. New York: Raven Press.

World Anti-Doping Agency. (2011). *2010 Adverse Analytical Findings and Atypical Findings*. Available online at: www.wada-ama.org/Documents/Resources/Testing-Figures/WADA_2010_Laboratory_Statistics_Report.pdf, accessed 8/10/12.

World Health Organization (WHO). (2010). *Persistent Organic Pollutants: Impact on Child Health*, p. 59. Geneva, Switzerland: WHO Document Production Services. Available online at: http://www.who.int/ceh/publications/persistent_organic_pollutant/en/index.html, accessed 11/27/12.

Wrenn, C. C. and Wiley, R. G. (1998). The behavioral functions of the cholinergic basal forebrain: Lessons from 192 IgG-saporin. *Int. J. Dev. Neurosci.*, 16, 595–602.

Wright, J. P., Dietrich, K. N., Ri, M. D., Hornung, R. W., Wessel, S. D., Lanphear, B. P., et al. (2008). Association of prenatal and childhood blood lead concentrations with criminal arrests in early adulthood. *PLoS Med.*, 5(5):e101, 0732–0740.

Wu, T.-C., Tashkin, D. P., Djahed, B., and Rose, J. E. (1988). Pulmonary hazards of smoking marijuana as compared with tobacco. *New Engl. J. Med.*, 318, 347–351.

Wurtman, R. J., Wurtman, J. J., Regan, M. M., McDermott, J. M., Tsay, R. H., and Breu, J. J. (2003). Effects of normal meals rich in carbohydrate or proteins on plasma tryptophan and tyrosine ratios. *Am. J. Clin. Nutr.*, 77, 128–132.

Xi, Z.-X., Peng, X.-Q., Li, X., Song, R., Zhang, H.-Y., Liu, Q.-R., et al. (2011). Brain cannabinoid CB_2 receptors modulate cocaine's actions in mice. *Nat. Neurosci.*, 14, 1160–1166.

Xing, T., Chen, L., Tao, Y., Wang, M., Chen, J., and Ruan, D. Y. (2009). Effects of decabrominated diphenyl ether (PBDE 209) exposure at different developmental periods on synaptic plasticity in the dentate gyrus of adult rats *in vivo*. *Toxicol. Sci.*, 110, 401–410.

Xu, F., Gainetdinov, R. R., Wetsel, W. C., Jones, S. R., Bohn, L. M., Miller, G. W., et al. (2000). Mice lacking the norepinephrine transporter are supersensitive to psychostimulants. *Nat. Neurosci.*, 3, 465–471.

Xu, M., Guo, Y., Vorhees, C. V., and Zhang, J. (2000). Behavioral responses to cocaine and amphetamine administration in mice lacking the dopamine D_1 receptor. *Brain Res.*, 852, 198–207.

Xu, M., Hu, X.-T., Cooper, D. C., Moratalla, R., Graybiel, A. M., White, F. J., et al. (1994). Elimination of cocaine-induced hyperactivity and dopamine-mediated neurophysiological effects in dopamine D_1 receptor mutant mice. *Cell*, 79, 945–955.

Yamamoto, B. K., Moszczynska, A., and Gudelsky, G. A. (2010). Amphetamine toxicities: Classical and emerging mechanisms. *Ann. N. Y. Acad. Sci.*, 1187, 101–121.

Yang, C. R. and Chen, L. (2005). Targeting prefrontal cortical dopamine D_1 and *N*-methyl-D-aspartate receptor interactions in schizophrenia treatment. *Neuroscientist*, 11, 452–470.

Yang, X. W. and Lu, X. H. (2011). Molecular and cellular basis of obsessive-compulsive disorder-like behaviors: Emerging view from mouse models. *Curr. Opin. Neurol.*, 24, 114–118.

Yates, M. L. and Barker, E. L. (2009). Organized trafficking of anandamide and related lipids. *Vit. Horm.*, 81, 25–53.

Yehuda, R., Bierer, L. M., Schmeidler, J., Aferiat, D. H., Breslau, I., and Dolan, S. (2000). Low cortisol and risk for PTSD in adult offspring of holocaust survivors. *Am. J. Psychiatry*, 157, 1252–1259.

Yehuda, R., Marshall, R., and Giller, E. L. (1998). Psychopharmacological treatment of post-traumatic stress disorder. In P. E. Nathan and J. M. Gorman (Eds.), *A Guide to Treatments That Work*, pp. 377–407. New York: Oxford University Press.

Yolton, K., Xu, Y., Strauss, D., Altaye, M., Calafat, A. M., and Khoury, J. (2011). Prenatal exposure to bisphenol A and phthalates and infant neurobehavior. *Neurotox. Teratol.*, 33, 558–566.

Yorgason, J. T., Jones, S. R., and España, R. A. (2011). Low and high affinity dopamine transporter inhibitors block dopamine uptake within 5 sec of intravenous injection. *Neuroscience*, 182, 125–132.

Young, A. M. and Goudie, A. J. (1995). Adaptive processes regulating tolerance to behavioral effects of drugs. In F. E. Bloom and D. J. Kupfer (Eds.), *Psychopharmacology: The Fourth Generation of Progress*, pp. 733–742. New York: Raven Press.

Young, E. A. (1993). Induction of the intermediate lobe POMC system with chronic swim stress and β-adrenergic modulation of this induction. *Neuroendocrinology*, 52, 405–411.

Young, J. G., Eskenazi, B., Gladstone, E. A., Bradman, A., Pedersen, L., Johnson, C., et al. (2005). Association between in utero organophosphate pesticide exposure and abnormal reflexes in neonates. *Neurotoxicology*, 26, 199–209.

Young, J. W., Henry, B. L., and Geyer M. A. (2011). Predictive animal models of mania: Hits, misses and future directions. *Br. J. Pharmacol.*, 164, 1263–1284.

Yu, H., Li, Q., Wang, D., Shi, L., Lu, G., Sun, L., et al. (2011). Mapping the central effects of chronic ketamine administration in an adolescent primate model by functional magnetic resonance imaging (fMRI). *Neurotoxicology*, 33, 70–77.

Yuan, J., Chen, L., Chen, D., Guo, H., Bi, X., Ju, Y., et al. (2008). Elevated serum polybrominated diphenyl ethers and thyroid-stimulating hormone associated with lymphocytic micronuclei in Chinese workers from an E-waste dismantling site. *Environ. Sci. Technol.*, 42, 2195–2200.

Zadina, J. E., Martin-Schild, S., Gerall, A. A., Kastin, A. J., Hackler, L., Ge, L. J., et al. (1999). Endomorphins: Novel endogenous mu-opiate receptor agonists in regions of high mu-opiate receptor density. *Ann. N. Y. Acad. Sci.*, 897, 136–144.

Zajecka, J. (1993). Pharmacology, pharmacokinetics, and safety issues of mood-stabilizing agents. *Psychiatr. Ann.*, 23, 79–85.

Zajecka, J., Tracy, K. A., and Mitchell, S. (1997). Discontinuation symptoms after treatment with serotonin reuptake inhibitors: A literature review, *J. Clin. Psychiatry*, 58, 291–297.

Zanettini, C., Panlilio, L. V., Alicki, M., Goldberg, S. R., Haller, J., and Yasar, S. (2011). Effects of endocannabinoid system modulation on cognitive and emotional behavior. *Front. Behav. Neurosci.*, 5, 57. doi:10.3389/fnbeh.2011.00057

Zeng, C., Armando, I., Luo, Y., Eisner, G. M., Felder, R. A., and Jose, P. A. (2007). Dysregulation of dopamine-dependent mechanisms as a determinant of hypertension: Studies in dopamine receptor knockout mice. *Am. J. Physiol. Heart Circ. Physiol.*, 294: H551–H569.

Zenith International. (2012). Global energy drinks market spurts ahead to $37 billion. Press release, February 14, 2012. Available online at: http://www.zenithinternational.com/articles/1012/Global+energy+drinks+market+spurts+ahead+to+37+billion, accessed 4/13/2012.

Zetzsche, T., Rujescu, D., Hardy, J., and Hampel, H. (2010). Advances and perspectives from genetic research: Development of biological markers in Alzheimer's disease. *Expert Rev. Mol. Diagn.*, 10, 667–690.

Zhang, B., Carroll, J., Trojanowski, J. Q., Yao, Y., Iba, M., Potuzak, J. S., et al. (2012). The microtubule-stabilizing agent, Epothilone D, reduces axonal dysfunction, neurotoxicity, cognitive deficits and Alzheimer-like pathology in an interventional study with aged tau transgenic mice. *Neurobiol. Dis.*, 32, 3601–3611.

Zhang, L., Dong, Y., Doyon, W. M., and Dani, J. A. (2012). Withdrawal from chronic nicotine exposure alters dopamine signaling dynamics in the nucleus accumbens. *Biol. Psychiatry*, 71, 184–191.

Zhang, Y., Thompson, R., Zhang, H., and Xu, H. (2011). APP processing in Alzheimer's disease. *Mol. Brain*, 4, 1–13.

Zhou, Q.-Y. and Palmiter, R. D. (1995). Dopamine-deficient mice are severely hypoactive, adipsic, and aphagic. *Cell*, 83, 1197–1209.

Zhu, J. and Reith, M. E. A. (2008). Role of the dopamine transporter in the action of psychostimulants, nicotine, and other drugs of abuse. *CNS Neurol. Disord. Drug Targets*, 7, 393–409.

Zivin, J. A. (2000) Understanding clinical trials. *Sci. Am.*, 282(4), 69–75.

Zobel, A. W., Nickel, T., Kunzel, H. E., Ackl, N., Sonntag, A., Ising, M., et al. (2000). Effects of the high-affinity corticotropin-releasing hormone receptor 1 antagonist R121919 in major depression: The first 20 patients treated. *J. Psychiatr. Res.*, 34, 171–181.

Zoeller, R. T. and Crofton, K. M. (2005). Mode of action: Developmental thyroid hormone insufficiency—Neurological abnormalities resulting from exposure to propylthiouracil. *Crit. Rev. Toxicol.*, 35, 771–781.

Zou, X., Patterson, T. A., Sadovova, N., Twaddle, N. C., Doerge, D. R., Zhang, X., et al. (2009). Potential neurotoxicity of ketamine in the developing rat brain. *Toxicol. Sci.*, 108, 149–158.

Zubieta, J. K., Smith, Y. R., Bueller, J. A., Xu, Y., Kilbourn, M. R., Jewett, D. M., et al. (2001). Regional μ opioid receptor regulation of sensory and affective dimensions of pain. *Science*, 293, 311–315.

Zvosec, D. L., Smith, S. W., Porrata, T., Strobl, A. Q., and Dyer, J. E. (2011). Case series of 226 γ-hydroxybutyrate-associated deaths: Lethal toxicity and trauma. *Am. J. Emerg. Med.*, 29, 319–332.

Author Index

Subject Index

Page numbers followed by *f* denote entries that are included in a figure; *t*, table; *b*, box. Page numbers followed by n indicate the entry is include in a note.

theophylline
  biological activity of, 29*t*
  CNS stimulation by, 26*b*
  structure of, 29*f*, 393*f*
  tea, 29
therapeutic drug monitoring, 24, 25
therapeutic effects
  definition of, 4
  steady state plasma levels and, 20, 20*f*
therapeutic index (TI), 30–31, 38
thiamine. *see also* vitamin B₁ (thiamine)
  deficiency, 280*b*, 283
Thimerosal, 502*b*–503*b*
thiopental (Pentothal)
  depot binding, 524–525
  lipid solubility of, 19
  solubility of, 534
  structure of, 533*f*
thioridazine (Mellaril), 595*f*, 599
thiosemicarbazide, 217
Thorazine. *see* chlorpromazine (Thorazine)
thresholds, neuron firing, 53
L-threo-dihydroxyphenylserine (DOPS), 153*b*
thyroid gland, 97, 103
thyroid hormones, 481–483
thyroid-stimulating hormone (TSH), 98, 98*f*, 481, 482*f*
thyrotropin-releasing hormone (TRH), 98*f*, 99, 481
thyroxine (T4), 97, 481, 482–483
tiagabine, 218–219
tianeptine, 568, 569*f*
tiapride, 299
tight junctions, 16, 17*f*
tobacco. *see also* smoking
  chewing of, 229
  Columbus and, 373
  susceptibility to addiction by, 244
  treatment of dependence on, 390–392
  withdrawal symptoms, 389*f*
tobacco hookworm, 381n1
tobacco smoke (TS)
  adverse effects of, 393
  components of, 390*f*
  midbrain DA neuron activation, 380*f*
tocopherol (vitamin E), 615
Tofranil. *see* imipramine (Tofranil)
tolcapone (Tasmar), 149, 606
tolerance
  acute, 33
  alcohol, 270–272, 272*f*
  alcohol metabolism and, 282
  antipsychotics and, 602, 607
  behavioral, 33–36, 38
  to caffeine, 395–396, 399
  cannabinoid exposure and, 419–422
  characteristics of, 33*t*
  conditioning and, 330
  description of, 38, 325
  to GHB, 463–464, 463*f*
  hallucinogen, 440, 442
  inhalant-related, 453
  to ketamine, 445, 447
  to marijuana use, 415
  mechanisms of, 33–34
  metabolic, 33, 34, 38
  model of, 329*f*
  morphine-induced hyperthermia, 35*f*
  neuroadaptation and, 256*f*, 329–330
  to nicotine, 377, 381–383, 388
  NMDA receptors and, 332*b*–333*b*
  opioid, 317, 325–327, 336
  pharmacodynamic, 33, 34, 38

phenomenon of, 22
prevention of, 333*t*
psychostimulant exposure and, 356–358
repeated exposure and, 32–36
toluene, 454, 454*f*, 455*f*
topical applications
  advantages, 12*b*
  disadvantages, 12*b*
  drug administration, 9
tourniquets, 317
toxic doses (TD₅₀), 30, 31*f*, 38
toxic metals, 498–506
tracts, CNS, 64
traffic accidents, 275*f*, 283
transcranial magnetic stimulation, 563
transcription
  epigenetic regulation of, 47–49, 48*f*
  function of, 47*f*
transcription factors
  epigenetic influences on, 48
  function of, 47, 47*f*
  hormone function as, 100
transdermal administration
  addiction potential and, 238
  advantages, 12*b*
  benefits of, 9–11
  disadvantages, 12*b*
  inotophoresis and, 10–11
  ultrasound and, 10
transfection, process of, 311
transgenic mice, 136. *see also* animal models
  object recognition tests, 213, 213*f*
  use of, 140
transgenic organisms, 135
translation, function of, 47, 47*f*
translational research, 118–120, 121
transporters, 86
tranylcypromine (Parnate), 149, 539, 555*f*
traumatic brain injury, 123, 215
trazodone, 555*f*
treatment programs, opioid addiction, 331–336
Tremor Control System, 125*f*
tremors, observation of, 110
Trexan. *see* naltrexone (Trexan)
TRH. *see* thyrotropin-releasing hormone (TRH)
triazolam (Halcion), 535*f*
tricyclic antidepressants (TCAs), 515.
  see also antidepressants
  action of, 148
  for anxiety disorders, 539, 540
  LC cell firing and, 516*f*
  mechanisms of action, 564–567, 571
  overdoses, 567
  for Parkinson's disease, 617
  serotonin neurons and, 555*f*
  side effects, 563*t*, 566–567, 571
  structures of, 566*f*
trifluoprazine (Stelazine), 595*f*
trifluopromazine (Psyquil), 595*f*
trihexyphenidyl (Artane), 191
triiodothyronine (T3), 97, 481
Trilifon. *see* perphenazine (Trilifon)
3,4,5-trimethoxyamphetamine (TMA), 437, 438*f*
trimipramine, 566*f*
trinucleotide repeats, 626–627
trk receptors, 92–93, 93*f*
tryptophan
  depletion of, 170*f*, 518
  serotonin synthesis and, 169*f*
  sources of, 168

structure of, 168*f*
tryptophan depletion challenge, 554
tryptophan hydroxylase, 94, 168
TSH. *see* thyroid-stimulating hormone (TSH)
Tsien, Joe, 201
tuberohypophyseal dopamine pathway, 150
D-tubocurarine, 195, 198*t*
twin studies
  major depression, 552
  mood disorder, 546, 546*f*
  of schizophrenia, 589
twins, monozygotic, 48
Tylenol. *see* acetaminophen
tyramine, drug interactions, 22
tyrosine, 144, 145*f*
tyrosine hydroxylase (TH), 368
  catecholamine synthesis and, 144–146, 145*f*
  knockout models, 155*b*
  loss of function mutations in, 152*b*
  reduced activity, 448
tyrosine kinase receptors (trks), 92–93, 93*f*
tyrosine kinases, 93n7
Tysabri. *see* natalizumab (Tysabri)

U
Über Coca (Freud), 340–341
UBQLN1 gene, 622
ulcer medications, 268
ultrasonic vocalizations, 114
ultrasound, skin permeability and, 10
unconditioned stimulus (US), 210
Underground Steroid Handbook (Duchaine), 466
undifferentiated schizophrenia, 577
Uniform Controlled Substances Act, 232
United Nations Environment Programme Governing Council, 484–485
United States Pharmacopeia (USP), 5*b*
up-regulation, description of, 28
Uprima. *see* apomorphine (Uprima)
urine
  acidification of, 24
  alkalination of, 23
  catecholamine metabolites in, 149
  pH, 14*t*, 23
  theophylline and, 29
uterus, contraction of, 99, 103

V
vaccines
  addiction treatment, 336
  for Alzheimer's disease, 626*b*
  against cocaine, 360
  Thimerosal in, 502*b*–503*b*
vagal nerve stimulation, 563
vaginal adenocarcinomas, 480
Vaillant, George, 262
val66met gene (BDNF), 562
validity, types of, 110
Valium. *see* diazepam (Valium)
valproate (Depakote), 27*b*, 570–571
vardenafil (Levitra), 92
varenicline (Chantix), 392, 393
varicosities, 147
vasoactive intestinal peptide (VIP), 138
vasopressin
  function of, 103
  neurotransmission, 80
  synthesis of, 99
vectors, definition of, 11
venoms, black widow spider, 198*t*